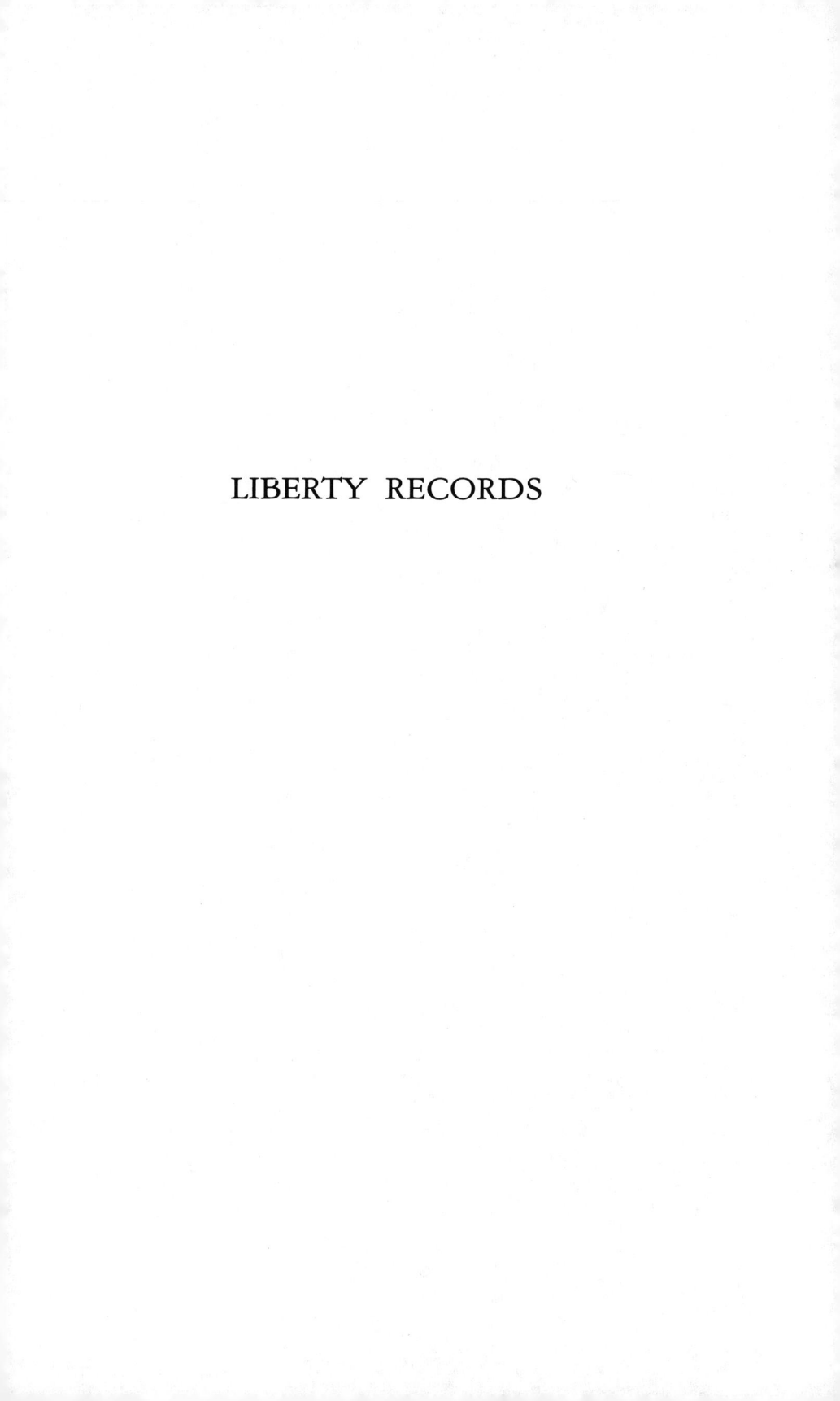

LIBERTY RECORDS

LIBERTY RECORDS

A History of the
Recording Company and
Its Stars, 1955–1971

by
Michael "Doc Rock" Kelly

with a foreword by
SI WARONKER

McFarland & Company, Inc., Publishers
Jefferson, North Carolina, and London

"Doc Rock" is a registered trademark owned by Michael Bryan Kelly.

The Liberty and Liberty family trademarks reproduced herein are now in the ownership of Capitol–EMI Music, Inc., and used by permission.

All references to chart positions herein are based on *Billboard* magazine's "Hot 100" chart surveys, as researched and compiled by Joel Whitburn, and are used by permission. Joel Whitburn has published books listing every entry to hit *Billboard*'s "Hot 100," "Top Pop Albums," "R&B (Black)," "Country," and "Adult Contemporary" charts, plus many more. For more information write to: Record Research, Inc., P.O. Box 200, Menominee, WI 53051.

British Library Cataloguing-in-Publication data are available

Library of Congress Cataloguing-in-Publication Data

Kelly, Michael Bryan.
   Liberty Records : a history of the recording company and its stars, 1955–1971 / Michael Bryan Kelly "Doc Rock."
     p. cm.
   Discography: p.
   ISBN 0-89950-740-9 (lib. bdg. : 40# alk. paper) ∞
   1. Liberty Records.   2. Sound recording industry—United States.
I. Title.
ML3790.K44   1993
338.7'61780266'0973—dc20   92-50307
                                                                                CIP
                                                                                MN

©1993 Michael Bryan Kelly. All rights reserved

Manufactured in the United States of America

McFarland & Company, Inc., Publishers
Box 611, Jefferson, North Carolina 28640

*To Bob Barber/The Morning Mayor,
Mongo Barker, J. Walter Beethoven,
Dick Biondi, Prof. J. Jazmo Bop,
Johnny Canton, Charlie Christian,
Jim Collinson, Johnny Dark,
Dan Diamond, Rick Douglass,
Bob Elliott, Richard Ward Fatherly,
Sara "Rhonda Rock" Garey, Bill Hanson,
Doc Holliday and Belle Star,
Larry James, Phil Jay, Roger Johnson,
Mr. Lee, Louie Louie, Larry Miller,
Larry Neal, Bob Potter, Ricky the "K,"
Rock Robbin, Rockin' Robbin,
Rockin' Robins, Rob Robbin,
Lloyd Thaxton, Charlie Tuna,
Rick Wrigley, Julie Wells,
Lyle "Superjock" Wood—
thanks for all the music!*

Acknowledgments

This book has benefited from the valuable input and support of dozens of people who worked at, for, or in the general vicinity of Liberty Records in the fifties and sixties. Those people included the following:

Lou Adler, Jerry Allison, Tommy Alsup, Don Altfeld, Al Altman, Steve Babb, Bill Berry, Jan Berry, Hal Blaine, Bob Bogel, Jack Bratel, Gretchen Christopher, Gloria Cochran Julson, Dennis Condon, Dimitri Coryton, Bobbie Cowen, Bud Dain, Jackie DeShannon, Al Frazier, Mel Fuhrman, Ron Furmanek, Dave Hoffman, "Bones" Howe, Jeff Hubbard, John Ierardi, Fanita James, Roger Johnson, Ken Kim, Billy J. Kramer, Allan Lavinger, Bob Levinson, Gary Lewis, Julie London, Guy Marriott, Lee Mendel, Artie Mogul, Jimmy O'Neill, DeeDee Phelps, Bob Reisdorff, Ken Revercomb, Carol Robbins, Joe Rosignoro, Stan Ross, Al Schlesinger, Sharon Sheeley, Bob Skaff, Jeff Tamarkin, Mel Taylor, Gary Troxel, Candy Walters, Alan Warner, Lenny Waronker, Dotty Woodward, and Harry Young.

In addition special thanks must be given to those who generously provided additional information or materials: Michael Aldrid, Bob Celli, Snuff Garrett, Bill Hathaway, Frank Kisko, Bob Lucieer, Dean Torrence, and Bobby Vee.

Profound personal thanks must go to my wife, Buzzie G. Kelly, for her support and inspiration, and also for her endless hours of dedicated effort in the editing, proofing, and preparing and indexing the final manuscript. Special thanks also to my dear friends Lauri Klobas and Henry Heffner for the loyal support and invaluable assistance they provided.

And finally the most heartfelt appreciation is extended to Mr. Si Waronker. Without him there would have been no Liberty Records to write about; we would have been deprived of endless hours of recorded entertainment and pleasure; and this book would have been far less complete.

Contents

Acknowledgments vii
Foreword xiii
Preface xv

Part One : Anatomy of a Record Label

1	Rock 'n' Roll Record Labels	3
2	Liberty in the Beginning	7
3	1955 The Liberty Girl, Julie London	13
4	1956 The Little Liberty Girls, Patience and Prudence	19
5	1957 Eddie Cochran, Snuff Garrett, Sharon Sheeley, and Margie Rayburn	23
6	1958 "Witch Doctor" and the Chipmunks	43
7	1959 Martin Denny, Bobby Vee, Dolphin Records, the Fleetwoods, the Frantics, and Little Bill and the Blue Notes	52
8	1960 Johnny Burnette, Buddy Knox, Ernie Freeman, and the Ventures	77
9	1961 Avnet, Gene McDaniels, Timi Yuro, Vic Dana, Troy Shondell, and Dick and DeeDee	101
10	1962 The Crickets, Jan & Dean, the Marketts, the Rivingtons, Danny and Gwen, Walter Brennan, Jackie DeShannon, Willie Nelson, and Vikki Carr	131
11	1963 Ricky Nelson, Fats Domino, and More from Bobby Vee, Jan & Dean, Jackie DeShannon, the Fleetwoods, and the Crickets	164
12	1964 Matt Monro, Billy J. Kramer with the Dakotas, the Searchers, the Beatles, Irma Thomas, Johnny Rivers, the Swinging Blue Jeans, and the Hollies	199

13	1965 Gary Lewis and the Playboys, P. J. Proby, T-Bones, Hal Blaine, O'Jays, Jimmy McCracklin, and Cher	222
14	Liberty Stereo Little LPs, EPs, 78s, and Picture Sleeves	261
15	1966 Bob Lind and Del Shannon	267
16	Liberty Acquisitions, Special Series, and Subsidiaries	282
17	1967 Nitty Gritty Dirt Band, Vikki Carr, Hardtimes, Love Generation, Sunshine Company, Classics IV, and the Fifth Dimension	313
18	1968 Canned Heat and Dave Dee, Dozy, Beaky, Mick, and Tich	326
19	1969 The Fifth Dimension and Also-Rans	332
20	1970 Ike and Tina Turner and Sugarloaf	334
21	1971 Liberty in the End	336

Part Two : Making Liberty Hit Records

22	Music Publishing — Metric Music	341
23	Record Producing	348
24	Recording Music	356
25	Engineering a Hit	363
26	Picturing Music	375
27	Promoting Records	378
28	Publicity	396
29	Selling Records	399
30	Distributing Records	402
31	Merchandising Records	405
32	Radio Airplay	407

Part Three : Four Liberty Superstars

33	Bobby Vee	415
34	The Ventures	442
35	Jackie DeShannon	457
36	Jan & Dean	470

Part Four : The End of Liberty

37	Selling Liberty ... and Selling It and Selling It	*515*
38	Life After Liberty	*522*
39	Overview	*526*
40	Epilogue: Where Did They Go?	*528*

Appendixes

1	#1 Hits	*551*
2	Artists in the Top 200	*553*
3	Liberty, Dolton, Imperial, and Soul City Top Rankings	*554*
4	The Top Liberty, Dolton, and Imperial Hit Makers	*556*
5	The Top Twenty Liberty Family Artists	*558*
6	Percentage of Success	*559*
7	Chronological Hit Lists	*560*
8	Graphs of Hits Per Year	*565*
9	Top 100 Hits by Artists	*568*
10	Top 100 Hits Listed by Month and Year	*589*
11	Singles Discography	*603*
12	Liberty LP and EP Discography	*726*
13	Liberty Family 45 Sleeves and Labels	*750*

Index   *757*

Foreword

Almost forty years ago I started a company called Liberty Records. Due to ill health I left my company less than ten years later, but it stayed in my heart, and I always kept track, albeit from the sidelines, of what happened to it.

A few months ago, I got a call from a man half a continent away. He told me that he had been collecting Liberty records for decades and was now writing a book about Liberty Records. He inquired if I would be interested in talking to him.

Over the next several months, Michael Bryan Kelly (aka "Doc Rock") and I became good friends. I told him of my life and my company and shared my unpublished memoirs with him. He asked me questions that made me think. He told me things he had learned about Liberty from others that at times surprised me and always interested me. And he brought back memories and emotions that I had thought were never to resurface.

Mike has done a tremendous job of researching this book. He has conducted more than sixty interviews with people who were involved with Liberty over the years, and he has been scrupulous not only in getting details but in getting them right. His love for the music shows, and his appreciation of the importance of accurate history is evident in his writing. The product of this love and appreciation is not only a history of Liberty Records, but also a documentation of how the world's favorite music was made in the fifties and sixties.

I read much of his manuscript in progress, and it has been a fascinating experience. I can't wait to reread the published book, and I hope that you find it as irresistibly informative as I have.

Si Waronker
Founder, Liberty Records

Preface

In 1966 I was a college student working part-time at a Dr Pepper bottling plant. Because even then I had a keen interest in rock 'n' roll, conversations with the other young workers often centered on music. At that time the "British invasion" of 1964 was just petering out, Motown was going strong, acid rock was gaining momentum, and all kinds of music were on the radio.

In short this was the post–British era, in which a new artist who recorded while on drugs and had one small hit was considered infinitely more valid and important than singers who had written and recorded a string of hits in the first decade of rock and roll. It would still be a few years until the first rock and roll revival, when the music of the period from 1955 to 1965 would gain respect.

One afternoon the singing duo Dick and Deedee came up in conversation. Dick and Deedee's first hit record, "The Mountain's High," had been a hit on Liberty Records way back in 1961. However, their most recent record, "Be My Baby," had charted on Warner Bros. within the last year.

One coworker mentioned that Dick and Deedee were married. I was skeptical. I seemed to remember reading or hearing someplace that, contrary to common belief, not only were they not married but not even involved. (Nor, as the other misconception went, were they brother and sister.)

When I expressed my doubts, my coworkers didn't believe me. Although I had not bought any lately, I knew that at home I had a few old music-lyric-fan magazines that had cost only fifteen cents each a few years earlier. These magazines had published brief biographies of some of the acts whose lyrics appeared in each issue. There was not much to read—the "articles" were simply regurgitations of standard record company bios. But I thought an old issue might just have something on Dick and Deedee.

With this in mind, I said to my colleague, "Tell you what, I'll look it up."

The instant reaction to my innocent remark was unbridled derision: "Look it up? Where the heck could you look it up? They don't have books about stuff like that—old records that little kids listened to!"

The comments hit me hard. I loved this music; I was not a little kid; and I still played the old records, preferring them in fact to a lot of the newer music on the radio. I went home that night and dug out my old magazines. Dick and Deedee were not in there. And my coworkers were right—there were no books in which I could look for the familial relationship, if any, of Dick and Deedee.

For the next several years, this dearth of documentation about the music and artists of the first golden decade of rock 'n' roll haunted me. Finally, in 1969, two books were published. One, Lillian Roxon's *Rock Encyclopedia,* ignored most pre-

Beatle artists and derided the ones that *were* mentioned. The other, Joel Whitburn's *Record Research*, gave only the chart statistics for hit records. No biographical information was included.

I guess somewhere in the back of my mind, ever since the day the Dick and Deedee controversy arose, part of me knew that I was going to write rock 'n' roll books. Of course now there are many published works on early rock 'n' roll, including my own previously published volume, *The Beatle Myth*. But there is still precious little published information about artists like Dick and Deedee, who were on labels like Liberty Records.

Growing up, I had many favorite songs on the radio. These included "Witch Doctor," "Sittin' in the Balcony," "Tonight You Belong to Me," "National City," "Dreamin'," "Rubber Ball," "Lovey Dovey," "The Big Hurt," "Tower of Strength," "Needles and Pins," "Surf City," and many more. To my amazement, when I found the records on which these songs appeared, they were all on one label—Liberty Records!

Liberty? What is Liberty? Why was it started, by whom, and why the name? How did all those wonderful songs by such great artists get on that label? And why did it stop at the end of the sixties?

Now I know. By the way, what *was* Dick and Deedee's relationship? Sibling, romantic, or musical? Dick was really Dick St. John Gosting, and Deedee (also written "DEE DEE" and "Dee Dee") was Mary Sperling. They were junior high schoolmates, not siblings, lovers, or spouses.

Now you know, too.

Part One

Anatomy of a Record Label

CHAPTER 1

Rock 'n' Roll Record Labels

The heart of fifties and sixties rock 'n' roll was the single. Without those little 45-rpm seven-inch singles with the big hole, the world of music, entertainment, and teenage life would have been very different during the post–1955 period. For the later years of that period, LPs were also considered essential to popular music. In fact, though, LPs have always been very important. The main difference was that before the mid-sixties, there were no album-oriented rock (AOR) stations. Radio stations did play LP cuts in the fifties and early sixties, but none did so to the exclusion of 45s.

In the future, pop music will probably appear on CDs. But after twenty or thirty years, popular music can hardly be called rock 'n' roll anymore. It is hard to reconcile the fifties ponytails on "American Bandstand" with the black lace underwear on MTV music videos.

Because records were so important for so many years, it is no wonder that some rock 'n' roll fans, collectors, and, some say, radio stations, have had favorite record labels. Even if the casual listener didn't pay attention to labels, some radio stations certainly were influenced by them. If a certain label recently had a big hit, another artist's record released soon afterward on the same label was hoped by record companies to benefit from association. The release of Carole King's first single, "It Might as Well Rain Until September," in 1962 was planned for Companion Records but was switched to a sister label, Dimension Records, when Little Eva's "Locomotion," released on Dimension, went to #1.

Being on a certain label did not guarantee that a record would be a hit. But certain labels were known for certain kinds of music, such as country and western, pop, or rhythm and blues (R&B). People might even learn where to look for the kind of music they sought personally or professionally.

Several record labels, for one reason or another, figured importantly in the history of rock 'n' roll. Sun Records is known for discovering Elvis Presley, and the history of the label—and its contractees—is well known. Besides Elvis, Sun Records had Roy Orbison, Johnny Cash, and Carl Perkins.

As well known as the Sun Records story is, it can be debated just how important Sun truly was to the development of rock 'n' roll. While Sun did discover Elvis, Elvis was little more than a regionally popular hillbilly singer while with Sun. Only after he left for RCA did Elvis find major distribution of his songs, Ed Sullivan, and legendary fame. RCA pressed and shipped each new Elvis 45 in quantities of more than one million copies, even before orders were placed, just to assure a million-seller of each Elvis song. Had Elvis stayed on tiny Sun Records, he might have been a briefly popular regional singer instead of a legend. Ed Sullivan would probably not have happened, and advance pressings of a million copies would have been impossible. Without the power and influence of RCA, Elvis could hardly have become the "King of Rock 'n' Roll."

Another of Sun's now-famous artists of the fifties was Roy Orbison. Roy had just one minor hit, "Ooby Dooby" (Roy Orbison, 1956; Matt Lucas, 1963), while he was on Sun. Not until later, when he moved to Monument Records (and later to MGM Records to a lesser extent), did fame and fortune come to Roy Orbison. It was on Monument that Roy had his big hits, including "Only the Lonely" (1960), "Running Scared" (1961), and "Oh, Pretty Woman" (1964). Only then, with those essentially pop arrangements, did Roy Orbison become known to the rock 'n' rolling teenagers of the world.

Johnny Cash had four top-forty hits while he was with Sun. But by far the bulk of his career hits came when he was on Columbia Records. Another famous Sun artist was Carl Perkins. For all his legendary fame, however, Perkins was essentially a one-hit artist, for "Blue Suede Shoes." Later songs, such as "Pointed Toe Shoes" and "Pink Pedal Pushers," were far less successful. Taken together Elvis, Roy, and Carl had just six top-forty records and one top-ten record among them while on the Sun label.

Another well-known Sun artist was Jerry Lee Lewis. Jerry Lee later moved to Smash Records and had a few more hits before moving on to country music, but his rock 'n' roll legacy is based on his handful of Sun hits. Five of his Sun records reached the top forty, and three of them made the top ten, making him by far the biggest star Sun ever had. Yet he is best known today as a country singer.

Supporters of small record labels argue that a small label like Sun developed a few great artists, elevating those labels above the larger ones and their shotgun approach. The latter are said to release many records of questionable quality, hoping for luck to bring in a hit now and then, while the former custom-craft the recordings of a few artists. Did Sun follow the pattern? Other early Sun artists were Rudi Richardson, Smokey Joe, Doctor Ross, Ernie Chaffin, Billy ("The Kid") Emerson, Slim Rhodes, Earl Peterson ("Michigan's Singing Cowboy"), Edwin Bruce, Tracy Perdarvis, the Miller Sisters, Billy Riley, Ray Smith, Vernon Taylor, Bobby Sheridan, Alton and Jimmy, and dozens of others—none of them exactly big names in rock 'n' roll. (Apparently Sun, too, used something of a shotgun approach. It just had a smaller shotgun.)

Sun did play a major role in discovering a few important early artists. It is not known if those artists, or others who would have filled their places in rock 'n' roll history, would have been discovered by someone else, someplace else, if it hadn't been for Sun. Moreover, Sun artists were essentially rockabilly singers, and rockabilly was a fairly minor and short-lived segment of rock 'n' roll, lasting only until about 1959, when Buddy Holly began adding string sections to his records. At any rate Sun's contribution to rock 'n' roll in terms of number and size of hit records was fairly minor.

Another collectible record label about which much is written is Philles Records, founded by and named after Phil Spector and Lester Sill. The label was largely a one-man operation—namely Phil Spector. He produced four basic singing groups:

Bob B. Soxx and the Blue Jeans, the Ronettes, the Crystals, and Darlene Love. These were all-girl groups, and while girl-group music was a wonderful and dynamic component of early rock 'n' roll, it was almost as short-lived as rockabilly. Two nongirl groups on Philles were the Alley Cats and the Righteous Brothers. An impressive lineup, except that Spector engaged in much intermingling of group members. The fantastic voice of one singer, Darlene Love, was in fact the force behind most of the Bob B. Soxx's records, as well as many Crystals hits, and of course Darlene Love's own Philles records. It would be stretching things only slightly to say that Philles had two enduring artists, Darlene Love (recorded as Darlene Love, Bob B. Soxx, and the Crystals) and Ronnie Spector (recorded with two other girls, her sister and her cousin, as the Ronettes).

Philles did have another major artist—the Righteous Brothers. But even they had only four top-forty hits for that label. The only "sound" or type of rock 'n' roll, Phil Spector produced was the girl-group, "Wall of Sound." This is not to take anything away from Spector. Those records were and remain great. But Spector did have just one arrow in his quiver while at Philles: he successfully used the same basic girl-group-recording formula with the Righteous Brothers, with the Ronettes even singing on some Righteous Brothers recordings. When Spector later tried to use the same technique with Ike and Tina Turner, the result was "River Deep, Mountain High" (1966), a bomb that failed to reach the top forty. (Years later, in 1971, Ike and Tina's biggest record ever was "Proud Mary"—on Liberty Records.) Philles lasted only just over three years, with Spector becoming a recluse after the Turners' fiasco.

The point is not to be critical of Phil Spector or Philles. His label produced several of the best girl-group records ever made, and he resurfaced later to work with, among other artists, the Beatles. His record label may be legendary, but it was actually very limited in scope, success, and time, with all the records from the same repetitive formula. Only one of his girl-group records made #1 ("He's a Rebel," 1962), and only one Righteous Brothers recording ("You've Lost That Lovin' Feelin'," 1965) hit the top of the charts.

There is an interesting difference between Philles and Sun Records. When Sun recording stars eventually moved on to other labels, they continued to have hits. When Philles artists went on to other labels (with the exception of the Righteous Brothers), each promptly disappeared.

Why did Sun artists succeed elsewhere? Probably because Sun discovered and developed talent that could later stand on its own in other surroundings. Why did Philles artists not succeed elsewhere? Probably because Philles specialized not in developing artists' talents but in developing hits and production techniques artists could not duplicate elsewhere. When the Crystals tried to rerecord their hits for a TV album thirty years later, their new arranger found he could not dissect the original arrangements by listening to the old records—so busy and heavy-handed, so dense and complex was the production. And of course Darlene Love, who was not a Crystal but often recorded *as* the Crystals, was not around to help out.

Many other record labels besides Sun and Philles are to a greater or lesser degree well known and thought of as important in the history of rock 'n' roll. When they are well known or considered important it is often primarily because they featured one or two well-known artists. Capitol had the Beatles and the Beach Boys; RCA had Elvis; Monument had Roy Orbison.

Of course a lot of other record labels besides Sun, Phillips, Capitol, Monument, and RCA released rock 'n' roll records. A tremendous number of records came from small, independent outfits with just a few artists. Tuff Records, for instance, had a few girl groups like the Jaynettes ("Sally Go 'Round the Roses," 1963), and Riviera Records had the Riverias ("California Sun," 1964).

Some big record labels steered clear of rock 'n' roll for many, many years. Until 1963 Columbia released only adult pop music and was strictly non–rock 'n' roll, evidently considering this new teen music faddish and unprofessional. After that it began to develop rock 'n' roll hits from its adult pop artists. Pop song stylists Steve Lawrence and Eydie Gorme had top-forty hits as solo acts in 1963 on Columbia ("Go Away Little Girl" and "Blame It on the Bossa Nova") and as a duet ("I Just Want to Stay Here and Love You"). Suddenly Columbia saw how much money could be made selling records to teenagers. It was not long before rock 'n' roll records by Dion, the Rip Chords, the Byrds, and even Bob Dylan appeared on Columbia.

In the big-band era of the forties, a few major established labels like RCA, Capitol, Decca, Mercury, Columbia, and MGM accounted for 80 to 90 percent of all of the hits. Later, in the rock 'n' roll era, the major labels considered tiny independents like Tuff and Philles to be hardly worth noting. Yet every record label that ever released even one rock 'n' roll hit record doubtless has an interesting story to tell, whether the label was small or large. (A few of the small labels were Luniverse, Arwin, Coed, Arlen, Enrico, and Sar.)

Between the giant labels founded in the swing era and the tiny independents of the rock 'n' roll era were operations that were neither tiny outfits nor major established companies. One such label, fairly minor compared to the majors, but huge compared to Philles or Tuff, was Liberty Records.

CHAPTER 2

Liberty in the Beginning

Liberty Records was born in 1955, the same year generally if not necessarily accurately regarded as the year rock 'n' roll was born. Like Liberty rock 'n' roll was new and small at the time. No one had any idea of the eventual staying power and scope of either. As important as rock 'n' roll would be to Liberty in later years and, indeed, as important as Liberty would become to rock 'n' roll, Liberty was not originally a rock 'n' roll record label. Not by design!

California-based Liberty Records was the product of the productive personality of Simon Waronker. Waronker was born March 4, 1915, and the story of his life pre–Liberty could fill a fascinating book and make an excellent Hollywood biopic.*

Si came from a poor section of Los Angeles. When he was five his father bought him a tiny violin. His mother made him practice religiously. "All little Jewish boys had to play the violin." His instructor was Theodore Gordohn, who arranged for Si to skip from the third to the fifth grade because of his musical virtuosity.

Si's shrewd and opportunistic father took over his son's career and sold tickets to Si's recitals. Soon, again due to his musical skill, young Si was enrolled in junior high when he was only nine. "Hell! I was no 'boy wonder' — certainly not a 'genius' — only a talented kid who was being pushed by everyone who thought of their own gains." When Si was ten they skipped him another grade and gave him half of each day off to practice his instrument. At eleven, he was in high school. He graduated at thirteen.

He won several scholarships, one taking him to Philadelphia (thirty-five days by ship, the first two vomitous) to study. He got out of having to work on board by entertaining with his violin. "This was my first lesson that music is a great communicator." Unhappy living with greedy relatives, he earned another scholarship, and at the age of fifteen he left Philly for France to study.

Living on thirty dollars a month in 1930s Europe, he learned to dissect music, to be a man (French girls), and about Hitler as only a Jew could. Expelled from school with his fellow students for attending a nude orgy, Si accepted another scholarship in Mondsee, Austria. The local crown prince admired Si's playing, and Si lived well, but the conservatory he was attending closed in 1931, so off to Berlin with another scholarship.

Still living on thirty dollars a month, in 1932 Si "was afraid to go out at night. I saw swastikas painted on nearly every street corner. The words *Verdammte Juden* on store windows. . . . Anyone who did not have blond hair took the chance of being beaten to death." One day he learned that for the past three years his "shrewd"

---

*All quotes in Si Waronker's biographical sketch are from Si himself.

father had been sending him thirty dollars a month, but that his actual scholarship had always been one hundred dollars a month! A minor concern, since "the madmen with swastikas were ... beating people to death with clubs because they were Jews" or just suspected of being Jewish.

After a gang chased Si one night, he determined to leave for Paris, but his father saw to it that he eventually ended up on a boat for Los Angeles instead. His professor back in Berlin was killed just days after Si escaped, and he refused to play his violin for the Nazi crew of the ship.

Si's first job back in LA was playing violin in a strip theater on Main Street for one dollar a day. Seven months later his second job was playing at the Coconut Grove in San Francisco for fifty dollars a week. Next he worked in the musical *Anything Goes* for sixty-five dollars a week with Emil Newman at Fox Studio.

Si played for Chaplin's *Modern Times* and met well-known composer Alfred Newman. "Al was not only my mentor — but I regarded him as my personal god. He taught me more than all my previous teachers. Through him, I met many of the most important people in Hollywood — musicians, authors, composers.... I believe history will recognize him as one of the most influential composers of the twentieth century."

Si worked with Emil and Alfred Newman, playing in the Fox orchestra for three years and being in charge of all of the musicians at 20th Century-Fox from 1939 to 1955. He learned to budget, plan, and execute music. He was married, happily settled. Then....

One day in 1955, Si Waronker's phone rang. Of all people, it was his cousin Herb Newman. Herbie was perpetually broke, but Si didn't have to worry about a touch. Herbie's father — Si's Uncle Max — was always loaded. Herbie had an idea he said he wanted Si's help with. Out of the clear blue, Herbie said to Si, "Let's go into the record business."

Si recalls that he "damned near fainted. Herbie had to be smoking hash to come up with this idiotic idea. I had a good job — made good money but spent it — a good home — a good life — and a lovely wife and two wonderful kids. Why would I want to join the rat race?"

So Si told Herbie no and hung up. It seems that Herbie was one of those guys who didn't take no for an answer. He called Si back again and begged to meet with him to discuss the notion of starting a record company. This was the mid-fifties. The 78 was just being replaced by the 45, and the LP was also coming into its own. Along with that, hi-fi was all the rage; rock 'n' roll was emerging, and with it top-forty radio; and even stereo was being talked about.

Si's curiosity got the best of him. He had never been one to be afraid to take a big, unexpected step. He had traveled the world on a shoestring while still a minor. And music, the stuff record companies exist for, had always been his life. Finally Si relented and agreed to meet that evening.

After dinner Herbie and Uncle Max came by. Si recalls their conversation to this day and quotes it as follows:

> **Herbie:** I work for Decca Records. I want to quit and go on my own.
> **Si:** Why?
> **Herbie:** I know sales and I know we can be a success.
> **Si:** What do you want with me?
> **Herbie:** With your musical background and my sales experience, we can't lose.

Si: How about money? I'm broke!
Uncle Max: Don't worry. How much will it take?
Si: At least twenty-five thousand dollars for starters.
Uncle Max: Do you think maybe a few dollars less?
Herbie: Dad, you promised to back me.
Si: Let's assume I do all the creative work and you worry about sales—who's gonna watch the store?
Herbie: I've got the perfect guy. He works for Decca too.
Si: What does he do?
Herbie: He works in the accounting department and wants out.
Si: I'll let you know. Bye. Say hello to your mother.

After they left, Si asked himself, "What am I thinking about? I've got to be an idiot to get involved." He had to admit, though, that his ego was being tickled.

Si was torn by indecision. He adored his work and thrived on his association with Al and Emil Newman. His position at 20th Century-Fox was important, prestigious, and relatively well paying. Just as important, unlike his relatives, who were evidently unhappy working at Decca, Si truly enjoyed his job and the fun of working with his colleagues.

That was the con argument. The pro argument for Cousin Herbie's scheme was, Suppose they started a record label and were successful? At forty years of age, how many chances would he get to better his lot?

Or maybe he was too old to learn new tricks? "Hell, no!"

At last Si set his reservations aside and told Herbie he would take a chance with it. With one wise proviso: that Si be the one who ran the show.

His relatives agreed. The split would be forty-forty, with 20 percent for the accountant. But what to call the company?

"After many meetings, I began to worry. The suggested names for the company were awful. In the middle of one night, I awakened with a start. I dreamt I was holding the torch on the Statue of Liberty. Liberty—Liberty Records, Inc. Beautiful. I called a meeting of the board and [told them of my idea. One snag was,] I remembered being in New York and seeing the Liberty Music Stores. I sent both of them out to find me a copy of any record with that name but could never find a Liberty record out of the music stores. I thought it was a great name if no one else had ever taken it. I called an attorney friend who called Sacramento and Washington, D.C. The attorney found that the store in New York was out of the recording business, and the name was free. We quickly tied up the name and Liberty Records was on its way.

"The store itself did try to squawk, saying they had used that name for a long time. At times they used to record for their own use. But they never had a commercial license to record nor a license with the union. We won.

"I then called Dale Hennessy, a superb artist who was working in the set-designing department at Fox, and asked him to make a logo that we could trademark. He had it within three hours. A Statue of Liberty of red, white, and blue. My attorney quickly had the logo trademarked, and the company set up as a corporation. I had committed two hundred dollars for legal fees, artwork, and phone calls."

Now that the company had a name and a logo, the next necessity seemed to be somebody to record. Si's "board of directors" was looking for a Liberty Records recording, with no luck. Here they were, in LA, with talent, talent, all around and not a note to record.

The famous Liberty logo, as it appeared on millions of Liberty records.

This was the first of many times to come when Si's extensive connections in the music business would come in handy. He went to see his old friend and mentor, Lionel Newman. Hearing about Liberty Records, he thought that Si was "nuts" to take this path and told him so. After that reaction Si was actually afraid to tell Alfred, but eventually he won Lionel over.

"I finally convinced Lionel to be the artist for the first session. We decided to record four tunes—two vocals and two instrumentals. Lionel was to sing on two sides, using the name Bud Harvey. The titles were 'Again' and 'As If I Didn't Have Enough on My Mind,' written by Lionel. The instrumentals would be 'Captain from Castille,' and 'Street Scene,' written by Alfred. We talked Billy May and Nelson Riddle into doing the arrangements and finally told Alfred—who told me—'If you want to be a schmuck I can be one too. I'll conduct as a gift.'" Lionel Newman had written a tune called "Again," but there were so many successful versions of that song out already that he and Si decided to record some original Newman material at this, the first session Liberty had.

With all this arranged, Si called his Uncle Max, and asked, "Where's the money?"

    Uncle Max: Don't worry. You'll have it.
    Si: We are recording in a week.
    Uncle Max: Sooooo, you'll have it.

"From that point on, I couldn't find Herbie or Uncle Max. All I remember is getting Herbie's copy of our agreement in the mail with no explanation. My mother, who knew nothing about this at the time, called to tell me that Herbie and his other cousin Louis went into the record business together and were recording that night."

What was Si to do? He had no money, but he had made commitments to the orchestra, the arrangers, the copyists, even to Capitol Records for studio rental and the pressing of 1,000 45s at ten cents each.

"I guess somebody up there felt sorry because on the day of the recording I went to see my neighbor, who was an assistant vice president of the California Bank, and told him my tale of woe. His name was Jack Murray. He was a wonderful man who told me that he could only loan on collateral and his limit was two thousand dollars. Strangely enough, that is what I needed. He finally came up with the idea of putting up my furniture as collateral. The bank would have frowned, but I guess they never found out. We recorded as planned." When the records were finally released,

Liberty did not even have an office! Si used a call service for messages. Although his relatives had run out on him, the accountant stuck, so now it was an eighty–twenty proposition. However, the 20 percent partner still went to work at Decca every day.

Unexpectedly Liberty's first two releases were reviewed by both *Cashbox* and *Billboard,* and given rave reviews, of all things, for the quality of the sound! But why shouldn't they, when Newman wrote the songs, Billy May and Nelson Riddle arranged them, Lionel Newman conducted, and Alfred Newman was in the sound booth. With that combination behind the music, how could the sound be anything less than terrific?

Now Si was really in the record business. The one thousand 45s that Capitol pressed for ten cents each were soon sold out to distributors at forty-three cents per, and another nine thousand copies were soon pressed and sold as well. The bank loan was paid off long before Si's furniture was in any real jeopardy, and Liberty was nearly seven hundred dollars in the black. Liberty still had no office and no employees—in fact, not having them was what made the seven hundred dollars come out as profit: no overhead.

Being a record mogul turned out to be pretty nice. Si found himself being wined and dined by music publishers who wanted to get their tunes recorded and released on Liberty.

Composer-singer-musician Bobby Troup, who was at Liberty from nearly the first day, recalls the birth of Liberty:

"Liberty started when Si Waronker was a contractor at 20th Century–Fox. At this time, this was when all the big studios, MGM, 20th Century–Fox, Paramount, Warner Bros. all had staff orchestras. It was a heyday for musicians because they could get a contract for a whole year. Alfred Newman was head of music at 20th. Si thought that it was a great shame that Newman's great scores were not being perpetuated. Si formed Liberty not so much to have a big commercial success as to record the great movie soundtracks of the day."

It is understandable that this point of view developed. Several sources reported that it was Si's movie background that caused him to found Liberty, and that it was orchestral music that he wanted to record.

Simon himself cleared up the misunderstanding. "I couldn't get the soundtracks from movies. In those days, Decca Records was very big at the time, and they were the ones who had a deal with Fox and did soundtracks. Or if a music director at a studio had a contract with a company, then that is where a soundtrack went. I did about three soundtracks in the whole history of the company, one from Universal. Soundtracks were so expensive to make, and they made a small return. So I did not start the company with soundtracks at all in mind. Gosh, I'd have been in real trouble [if I'd done that]. I realized that the only way to make the company work was with singles. Albums were only made after a single had proven itself to be salable."

Si went into business with a distributor named Jack Ames. Si would supply the music, Jack would supply the distribution on a very small scale. The first 45 on Liberty was by Lionel Newman. Liberty 50001 was "Conquest," backed with (b/w) "The Girl Upstairs." The latter was a slow, jazzy, horn- and sax-laden fifties version of big-band music, very evocative of the era and eminently listenable. The former started like an up-tempo TV detective-show theme, then slowed a bit to a rolling rhythm that periodically picked up the original faster tempo as the song developed. The tune was very creatively arranged and conducted and is still interesting to hear today.

The second was "In Time" and "Hands Off" by Bud Harvey, who was actually Lionel Newman again, using a pseudonym to fool the public, or somebody.

The first Liberty LP was LRP 3001, *Mucho Cha Cha Cha by Don Swan and His Orchestra*. Bobby Troup recalls that "later they decided to add some jazz. Jimmy Rowles, the pianist, did an LP called *Rare — But Well Done* as the Jimmy Rowles Trio." After that failed to set the world on fire came *John Duffy at the Mighty Columbia Square Wurlitzer* and *Nightfall* by Harry Sukman at the Steinway concert grand.

The rest is history. Liberty Records signed one top artist after another, making many discoveries and establishing a musical dynasty that has survived to this day. Rock 'n' roll writers seldom mention the subject of money, but, except for a very few artists, everyone in the music business is in it for one thing — the money. Si started Liberty to make money as much as to make music. Popular music is not art, it is not called the "music art." It is called the "music business." And now Si was in business.

And Cousin Herbie? A day before the Liberty deal was to be consummated, Herbie had started his own company with Lou Biddle — Era Records. Era had some early success, notably "Suddenly There's a Valley" in 1955 (#9) and "Wayward Wind" (#1) by Gogie Grant, who had three other Era records that did not make the top forty. The other Era artist of note was Dorsey Burnette, who in 1960 had "Tall Oak Tree" (#23), rock 'n' roll's first ecology record, and "Hey Little One" (#45). Dorsey's brother Johnny would later come to Liberty.

Soon Lou Biddle split from Cousin Herbie's Era Records and started yet another company, Doré (pronounced Dorrie) Records. The main records that company produced were: (1) "To Know Him Is to Love Him" (#1 in 1958) by the Teddybears, who were spearheaded by Phil Spector, later a producer at Si's Liberty; (2) "Baby Talk" (#10, 1959) by Jan & Dean, who were to become huge stars at Si's Liberty in the sixties; (3) "Come Softly to Me" (#45, 1959) by Ronnie Height, a poor cover version of a Liberty #1 record that same year by the Fleetwoods!

In spite — or perhaps because — of all this cross-pollination between rival labels, Si and Herbie never associated again.

CHAPTER 3

1955

The Liberty Girl, Julie London

Si Waronker's first Liberty recording session with Lionel Newman had proved to Si that his dream could work, and he began to develop other ideas for Liberty. His first vocal discovery was not exactly the newest rock 'n' roll sensation.

It happened like this. One of the wine-and-dine–Si Waronker publishers who was especially nice to Si was Eddie McHargue. Eddie worked for a company that was owned by Fox, and had published Liberty's first release. After dinner, Eddie took Si to a little club to hear a musician play. The musician in question was Bobby Troup, a guy who had just become known for composing the popular tune "Route 66."

It was Eddie's idea that Bobby record for Liberty, but Bobby said he couldn't because he had six more months under contract to Bethlehem Records. As an alternative he suggested that Liberty might record his girlfriend, who was singing across the street at Walsh's 88 Club.

The girlfriend was Julie London.

Julie was an actress who had appeared in half a dozen low-budget films in the forties and early fifties, such as *Jungle Girl* in 1944 and *The Fat Man* in 1951. In 1947 she married Jack ("Dragnet") Webb and retired from acting to raise her children. In the fifties and sixties, Julie returned to acting and appeared on TV programs from "Zane Grey" to "Laramie." Finally Julie became well known to baby-boomers as Nurse Dixie McCall on NBC-TV's medical drama "Emergency" in the seventies. Dr. Joe Early on "Emergency" was played by Bobby Troup.

As well known as she eventually became as an actress, Julie Peck, as she was born, was first a singer; she had first sung on radio when she was three. The song bore the unlikely title "Falling in Love Again."

Bobby tells how he first came to be acquainted with Julie. "I met Julie when she came to see me at the Club Golden Celebrity Room. I was stricken. I thought she was wonderful. I thought, God, I'd like to marry her. I knew the girl she was with at her table, so I went over and sat down. I didn't know who she was, but I thanked her for coming to see me. She said, 'I didn't come to see you, I came to see your guitarist.' That night she invited all of us out to her house, the whole group, where she had a marvelous sound system. We listened to records, then all of a sudden she got up and sang 'Little Girl Blue.' I just couldn't believe it! That anyone that pretty could sing, because beautiful women usually don't have that much talent. That started the whole thing.

"She was just wonderful, but I had gone to every music contact I knew, Capitol and all the rest, but no one was interested in Julie. So I told Si, 'Si, Julie is really just a wonderful singer. Not just because I am in love with her, but she really is great.' This was nineteen fifty-five, so Julie was about twenty-eight years old."

But Si knew none of this the fateful night he and Eddie strolled across the street to the 88 Club, a move he will never forget.

"We were lucky to walk in just as the show was starting. The lights were turned off and a spotlight was focused on this girl sitting on a stool dressed in a tight-fitting black long-sleeved turtleneck sweater. Her hair was reddish-brown, her face beautiful, and cleavage that was unbelievable! There were only two musicians with her. A guitar, Barney Kessel, and a bass, Ray Leatherwood. Barney played a two-bar introduction and this girl started to sing 'S Wonderful' [George Gershwin], and then, yes, 'Cry Me a River.'

"The lyrics poured out of her like a hurt bird. The combination of Barney Kessel and Ray Leatherwood with this girl was incredible. If only I could record what I saw and heard. Her name was Julie London. I rushed back to Bobby Troup and begged him to set up a meeting with Julie. He then told me that Julie wouldn't record for anyone. She had one bad experience with a small company and was disenchanted. Furthermore, she and her then husband Jack Webb were just concluding a bitter divorce. I actually pleaded for the chance to at least talk to her. Bobby was impressed with my perseverance and set up a meeting with Julie, Bobby and me.

"We met at Julie's house, and we did get along. She told me that she had no confidence in herself and furthermore, if she did record, it would have to be with a big-band with Pete Rugolo doing the arrangements. She didn't know all I had was now less than seven hundred dollars left. However, I convinced her that we could record with Barney & Ray and after we selected the tunes, we could then add the big-band sound she wanted. She finally agreed. I immediately called Western Recorders on Sunset, hired Tom Neal as engineer and set up a session for the next night which was Julie's night off.

"We started at seven P.M., and at four A.M. the next morning, we quit. We had recorded thirty tunes, including 'Cry Me a River.' I had an acetate dub made of what I considered the best tunes. I wanted thirteen songs because in those days, twelve tunes were the normal album.

"I called Julie and went to her house to let her hear what she had done. She listened once, then turned to me and asked, 'When do we add Pete Rugolo?' I asked her to play the album again. After listening the second time, she said, 'I knew it all along. You have no intention of adding what you promised.'

"We finally compromised. We would release a single of 'Cry Me a River' backed with 'S Wonderful' with just guitar and bass. If I were wrong, the next release would be with Pete Rugolo.

"Now Bobby suggested I talk to Julie's manager, Bob Ginter. I made an appointment with Bob and he agreed to see me the next day. We got along famously from the first day we met. I leveled with him and a mutual admiration set in immediately. We agreed that no contract would be drawn and we would start with a handshake. I had no office. He had room for an extra desk and we kept the call service to start."

After that, things moved fast for Si Waronker and Liberty Records. "I sent ten copies of the record to thirty distributors nationwide. I was still working at Fox, and the record activities were done at night. I still had one hundred dollars left. In a week—my call service fired—the phones were too busy for them to handle. I hired a girl for fifty dollars a week with a guarantee of two weeks' work. (I had my hundred.) Later, after 'Cry Me a River,' Bobbie Dieterly left Cadence Records to work as my female man Friday, my first person I hired who had any background."

"Cry Me a River" was an instant success. Si's biggest problem became filling the orders that were pouring in. "I went to Capitol and showed them legitimate orders for fifty thousand singles and asked for and got credit. Glen Wallichs, president of Capitol, later told me that Capitol was watching me carefully and he had okayed my credit.

'Cry Me a River' was a smash hit and I could taste the smell of success." On the heels of the 45, Julie London's first LP, *Julie Is Her Name,* also began to sell well. "When the disc jockeys got their copies of this album, they almost invariably talked about the cover. I must say, it was certainly provocative. I'll never forget Al Jarvis, a popular disc jockey at the time, saying on the radio, 'Today, I have a surprise. I'm not going to play Julie's record—I'm going to play her album cover.'"

Si tells how he made the cover. "I liked provocative covers. Julie London's was an accident, an amateur photographer, Phil Howard, got that. She was not standing up, but reclining on a couch. The background is clean, we cut out the couch. I cropped it for her cleavage. It hit exactly what I wanted, because there was a certain dirty appeal about it. It was successful, so I guess I was right on it. That was cleavage like you never saw. She was lying on a couch on her back, her hair was there, and we kept on going, moving her a bit until we got exactly what we wanted. We blew that up. The message was there."

The hit 45 and smash LP were a natural one-two punch for Liberty. Julie recalls her debut Liberty single, which became a hit prior to Christmas 1955. "I got 'Cry Me a River' from Arther Hamilton. I had gone to school with Arther and he eventually ended up writing for Jack Webb. He was writing songs for films like *Pete Kelly's Blues.*"

Si was in the control booth during the recording of "Cry Me a River" and remembers that the session went less than smoothly. "In nineteen fifty-five the union scale was ten dollars per hour per man, thirty dollars minimum. You could do six sides in that three hours, and we did it. We'd rehearse it, and then say, 'Let's do takes!' Everybody worked for scale, because there was not the kind of money there is now. [When we needed to edit a song together, we used to make] a copy of the master and started cutting with that. Then, if it worked, we would cut the master tape. 'Cry Me a River' was cut together from parts of about fourteen different takes. Bobby Troup was in the next studio, playing piano, enjoying himself. We recorded the equivalent of three albums in three nights for very little money. Bobby wanted to be the producer, and we always made him the producer."

In October 1958 *Julie Is Her Name*, Vol. 2 was released, and several years later, in 1960, the original LP was reissued. Julie London made money for Si Waronker.

Having a composer for a husband was handy for torch singer Julie London. "Julie did a Christmas song of mine with the Johnny Mann Singers in nineteen fifty-six or fifty-seven called 'I'd Like You for Christmas,'" remembers Bobby Troup. "Nothing happened with it."

In fact Julie London never had another hit single. But she sure sold those LPs with the sexy cover photos.

Julie London's first Liberty LP cover. This is the photo that was taken of her reclining on a couch and which turned on as many radio programmers as her voice did.

With success, Si's life began to get more difficult. Working at Fox all day and working practically all night was taking its toll. Publisher Eddie McHargue called Si again with another artist for Si to consider putting on Liberty. It was an orchestra leader from Miami who wanted to record an album. Don Swan was willing to do all his own arrangements and Robins, Feist & Miller would subsidize the recording costs up to $2,500. There would be no cost to Liberty except pressing and promotion. This sounded OK to the nearly broke Si.

Doing the album, they came up with the idea of *Tea for Two–Cha Cha Cha*. This album was a hit. Everybody got his money back, and Si soon left Fox. Four offices were rented at 1556 N. La Brea, and both Si's 20 percent partner and a telephone were installed on the premises.

With the hiring of a receptionist, Liberty Records was in business. Liberty actually existed.

And although Julie London never had another hit single, Liberty Records was never chintzy with the LP action, and throughout the history of the label, the artists were encouraged to spend studio time (more often than not at the artist's expense) preparing cuts for another LP or single. Julie cut more than thirty Liberty LPs in the next decade. The early LPs had titles like *Make Love to Me* and showed dreamy close-ups of Julie and her long tresses—and her alluring cleavage. Some LP covers, such as *Nice Girls Don't Stay for Breakfast* and *Feeling Good* went so far (and the phrase is used advisedly) as to depict Julie on a bed. There is no doubt that Julie London's voice and visual image were responsible for much of Liberty's early financial success.

Husband Troup: "Julie was a fixture at Liberty Records. She really was Miss Liberty, because before Julie was on it, Liberty Records was nothin'. That first album of hers took them out of the doldrums and put them on a national scale." It made her wealthy as well. But Julie did not get royalties on her record sales. She was on a flat fee for six years. She made about fifty thousand dollars a year, plus any money she made herself in clubs or films. She was never with any other record company, except for some sides she did before Liberty for Bobby Troup. "I had done two albums with Bethlehem, a jazz label, and I did interest Red Clyde, their A&R man, in Julie. She recorded four sides with my group, 'You're Blasé,' 'Motherless Child,' and two others. I'd been pushing her to sing because I thought she was really good. When they sent the songs to New York, they were not that enthusiastic about it, so I had to tell Julie that Bethlehem was not going to pick her up. After she became very well known on Liberty, Bethlehem, having only four sides, released *Bethlehem's Girlfriends* with Chris Conner and Carmen McCrae."

For Julie's second Liberty LP, Si wanted to go on a different bent. So Bobby said, "Let's go from the bass and guitar to a big orchestra. She recorded a thing called *About the Blues*. All the titles were about blue things. In the meantime I wanted her to make a demonstration record for a song I had written called 'Their Hearts Were Full of Spring.' I took my guitarist, Al Caiola, from the club on the Sunset Strip and went to one of her Liberty recording sessions in Hollywood. Si heard her doing my song and said, 'God, that's a great sound with Al. Why don't you stay down here, Al, while we record an album?' So he did, and recorded the album *Oh, Lonely Girl*. That was her third album. The second was *About the Blues*. She did about thirty albums for Liberty. The most appealing cut from each album was released as a single, but none of them really splashed like 'Cry Me a River' had."

Bobby Troup provided a lot of material for Julie's albums: "She did more of my songs than of anybody else. She did about fourteen of my songs. The Four Freshmen did ten, Stan Kenton did eight. I still have three reasonably good standards. I wrote a song when I was in school for a college musical, called *Daddy*. It was the number one song for nineteen fortyone." Then there was the ever-popular "Route 66." The third was a song with Neil Hefti called "Girl Talk." That did quite well.

He also continued to record for Liberty himself. "I did an album called *Words and Music by Bobby Troup*. It was a good group on that album. That was quite a good album. It sold nothing. Then I did another album called *Here's to My Lady* with a picture of Julie, the back of her head, with me giving a toast to her. And that didn't sell. I recorded for Victor, for Capitol, for everybody, and I just didn't do that well. Capitol thought that I was going to be the white Nat King Cole. They thought that I had a really different-sounding voice! And also, my big hit song was introduced by Nat King Cole, 'Route 66' in nineteen forty-six, and it is still going."

Liberty was very advanced, technologically and otherwise. The LPs were recorded in "Spectra-Sonic Sound, the ultimate in Hi-Fi." They employed the new RIAA equalization curve, had a frequency response of 40–15,000 cps, and boasted the first transistorized recording studio in Los Angeles. Also, in Julie London's case, the cover photography was very sexy. If they didn't sell you the record on the basis of superior sound, cover art was always a strong selling point as well. LRP 3009 was even titled *Spectra-Sonic Sounds* by Leo Ornaud & Orchestra.

"Spectra-Sonic Sound" makes Si Waronker laugh today. "I made that up, and thirty-five years later, I still don't know what it means! I was always doing that."

CHAPTER 4

1956
The Little Liberty Girls, Patience and Prudence

Liberty's success came slowly at first, but it did come. Early in 1956, a single called "The Trouble with Harry" was released. This single was a favorite of Si Waronker. Based on the classic Hitchcock movie of the same name, it was a minor hit by artists known only as Alfi and Harry. In reality, Alfi and Harry were just one man, songwriter Ross Bagdasarian. Ross would turn up again and would prove to be a very valuable and tricky guy around Liberty.

Ross Bagdasarian aka David Seville

"Ross Bagdasarian and I were great friends," asserts Si Waronker. "You can put this down and I will back it up in court if I have to. He never had a contract. The reason is that we were very close. When he first came to me by Mark McIntyre, the father of Patience and Prudence. I knew Mark from his being a piano player of a band I conducted in the service. When he got out, he came to see me to get started in the music business, and he introduced me to Ross. Ross was a character all of his own. Completely out of it! He came to me with a recording he had made at Goldstar. Goldstar was a little studio where I think about eighty-five percent of the hit records on the West Coast were made. It was a little recording studio on Santa Monica Boulevard. They worked all night for ten dollars an hour studio time. And they recorded more doggone hits, many of which they never got paid for.

"Ross and Mark and a couple of other musicians—Flash Johnson was one of them—and they did a little simple song. They asked me what I thought. I said to add a little bit here and there, a couple of little things. I asked him what he was going to call it. He said that Armen was his wife's name. I told him that was a great name for the song, which became 'Armen's Theme.' 'But Ross,' I said, 'I don't know if the name Ross Bagdasarian will go good on a record. How about changing it to something more commercial?' So we came up with the name David Seville.

"Ross and I worked together like crazy and fought like cats. I liked unusual songs, like 'The Trouble with Harry.' My whole theory in Liberty Records whether it was rock 'n' roll or that type of music was to have something unusual. If you'll notice most of the recordings had very few people in the band. If we could get away with four men in the band, that was great. Because to me, the fewer the people, the more unusual the record became. And unusual records were more important to me than the usual run-of-the-mill because I figured we had a better chance with something different from the rest of the market."

Patience and Prudence

Liberty had trouble making money at first, and making the pop charts was only a little bit harder. The first top-ten hit single for Liberty came in the summer of 1956. It was unusual, almost a novelty tune. The singers were young sisters Patience and Prudence. Their father, Mark McIntyre, was a songwriter, and he felt his two little girls were not too little to make a new recording of the old standard "Tonight You Belong to Me." With fellow songwriter and Liberty associate Ross Bagdasarian (aka Alfi and Harry), McIntyre took Patience and Prudence, who were obviously minors, to Liberty with a demonstration tape. Shortly a professional "Spectra-Sonic Sound" recording was made and pressed into vinyl. Sure enough, Mr. McIntyre's little girls had a hit. In fact it was Liberty's first two-sided hit, the flip side being "A Smile and a Ribbon." Patience and Prudence's follow-up record, "Gonna Get Along Without Ya Now," also made the top twenty, and inspired several later rock 'n' roll versions (Skeeter Davis, 1964; Tracey Dey, 1964; the Honeys, 1965; Trini Lopez, 1967).

Si Waronker recalls the Patience and Prudence sessions vividly. "Patience and Prudence was a good example of the small group recording. We had three men in the orchestra, bass and guitar and the drum, and added piano on Mark McIntyre, who was the girls' father. We did that to save money. The three extra guys in the band got very little, twenty-five or thirty or fifty dollars. It was great because if the record was a hit, they got a bonus. Everything was fun until people got too rich. But I liked small bands. The simpler it was, the better I liked it."

As soft as a Julie London record was one of Patience and Prudence's follow-up singles. "We Can't Sing Rhythm and Blues (in Spite of Wearing Blue Suede Shoes)" seemed to reflect Liberty's inability to crack the rock 'n' roll market at this early date.

Si Waronker was impressed by Ross Bagdasarian's acumen when he brought Patience and Prudence to Liberty. Bagdasarian was a thirty-seven-year-old songwriter who was looking for an outlet for his songs. Liberty became that outlet in late 1956, when Bagdasarian's composition of "Armen's Theme" became a top-forty hit. ("Armen's Theme" was also a Liberty hit in 1963 as sung by Bobby Vee, under the title "Yesterday and You"—a title by which it is still sometimes known.) It was a swingy jazz number reminiscent of the big bands, a kind of music Ross obviously preferred.

David Seville's next hit was "Gotta Get to Your House" a year later in late 1957. It was an "answer record" to a Columbia Records hit, "Come On-A My House" by Rosemary Clooney (incidentally also written by the busy Bagdasarian*). A real novelty tune, it was another small combo production, just a piano and something

---

* *With his cousin, the novelist William Saroyan.*

Chapter 4 · 1956 21

The sheet music for Patience and Prudence's stand for independence in an affair of the heart.

sounding like a pencil on the back of a chair, which it probably was. Over this bed Ross spoke about the color of his girlfriend's hair, house, and eyes. As the song progressed, if that term can be used, he jumbled the respective colors of each of these objects into his love. At the end of the record, when he arrives at his girl's house, he is disappointed to find that she is not home.

Liberty Records had been in business for less than two years. They had released about forty singles and had gotten on the charts six times, once with Julie London, three times with Patience and Prudence, once with Alfi and Harry (Ross Bagdasarian), and once with David Seville (also Ross Bagdasarian). Quite a mixed bag, and no real rock 'n' roll yet at all—the kind of music for which Liberty would eventually become famous.

CHAPTER 5

1957
Eddie Cochran, Snuff Garrett, Sharon Sheeley, and Margie Rayburn

Si Waronker recalls what the Southern California record business was like in the late 1950s. "There were just a handful of aspiring record companies started or headquartered in Hollywood. Imperial Records—Dot Records—A&M Records was just starting. The men such as Lew Chudd of Imperial, Randy Wood of Dot, and Herb Alpert and Jerry Moss of A&M must be given credit for being true pioneers of the Hollywood music scene. There were countless other labels that attempted to break through. Most of these one-attempt companies had very little chance to succeed because of the financial drains on the business. The major companies, such as Capitol, RCA, Decca, and Columbia, had vast resources to call on. We independents had to work harder—develop new artists—try to build catalogs. This was of prime importance. In the event of a dry spell of no current hits, the catalog had to sustain the overhead. This took a great deal of money. I had very little money."

British Decca

"One day I received a phone call from London, from a representative of British Decca Records, that Sir Edward Lewis would like to meet with me in London the following week. I shook with joy! But I had to put a plan in motion. Ah! Album covers—eye appeal. The success of the Julie London cover proved the point. Murray Garrett and Gene Howard were well-known and very creative photographers. We were all friends. Murray and Gene had a vast catalog of excellent photos. Between Murray and Gene and me, we came up with ten future covers. They also took pictures of Picasso's *Three Musicians* and Degas' *Les Ambassadeurs*.

"Next was the presentation of music. I had Julie, Lionel Newman, Don Swan, and several bits and pieces of projects then in work and then proceeded to make a dub [acetate record] of all I could gather and left for England. British Decca and EMI of London were the two most influential and important worldwide distributors of records at the time. Sir Edward Lewis turned out to be a true British gentleman and a very shrewd businessman and a delightful man to discuss the business with. He was also very helpful with his advice for the future of Liberty.

"After two days of discussions and my presentations of future product, Sir Edward asked me how much money I thought would be needed to continue as I outlined. When I was in Los Angeles preparing for my London trip, I figured seventy-five thousand dollars would be great but I would settle for fifty thousand dollars if necessary. To answer Sir Edward, I quoted the figure of one hundred thousand dollars — hoping to get at least fifty thousand dollars. For their money British Decca would get worldwide distribution of Liberty Records, of course not including the United States or Canada. Sir Edward and I agreed to an advance of one hundred thousand to be paid back out of royalties in a five-year period. I then left and headed back to New York and then to Los Angeles.

"When I arrived back in Los Angeles, I found an agreement and a check for one hundred fifty thousand dollars! There was also a personal note from Sir Edward saying 'Si, we at Decca feel that your company will be a success. However, your ambitious program will need the additional fifty thousand dollars.'

"Now we could go to work. I spent all my time in the studio and spent little time in the office."

Rock 'n' Roll

By 1957 most of Liberty's output had been torch music from the likes of Julie London, instrumentals from the likes of Lionel Newman, and jazz and specialty music from the likes of Bobby Troup and Don Swan.

What about rock 'n' roll? This was the mid-fifties, Elvis was getting big, Chuck Berry was emerging, everything was about to break loose. Why was Si limiting himself to pop music? Why wasn't he into rock 'n' roll? Wasn't the writing on the wall (and the cash in the till) from the teen appeal of Patience and Prudence?

It is commonly believed that Si's orchestral background dictated his intentions for Liberty, and that he probably was dragged kicking and screaming into rock, even then accepting it only when it had strings and things. When Si Waronker started Liberty, did he foresee rock 'n' roll and expect Liberty to have a lot of rock 'n' roll records? Did he even like rock?

"Oh, sure. Rock 'n' roll to me was a combination of blues and the black type of rhythmic sounds we used to hear. Then where I got so excited with the good rock music was, they were pounding a message lyrically at you. Whether you understood it or not, they tried. The Chuck Berrys and the great ones that started it, they tried to make you believe music. Nothing was phony. The feeling that the first people in rock 'n' roll had was natural. It was a helluva lot more natural than it is today. That's the reason the excitement was there.

"I foresaw rock 'n' roll, I liked rock 'n' roll, I wish I could have done more with it. Oh, God, I was trying to get as much as I could. That was the reason we [much later] bought Imperial Records. There was a very good reason why we started with Don Swan and Julie London and not rock. I couldn't get into rock 'n' roll and break through. You see, there were only a couple of companies in those days that were really set up for it. Atlantic Records, Motown [later], these labels had a system where they let their artists go. By that I mean they put their artists in a room and said, 'Go ahead and keep on going until you come up with something that you think is right.' They recorded more stuff than anybody I have ever known.

"Dot Records was not really rock 'n' roll, but they made a little attempt at it. But I don't know more than two or three companies that could break through even with the distributors. The rock distributors were not even the same people. It was almost like a different type of business. The rock business was completely different. Today, for instance, if you wanted to get symphonic music to release, you wouldn't go to just any company. You'd have to buy from Angel or London or one of those companies that are so good at it. Even the sales force was completely different. Even now at Warner's, where my son Lenny is, the sales departments are broken down for different types of music, as well even as for different artists.

"Consequently, trying to break into a new, different kind of music is as difficult as hell. Because they don't believe you. That is why I wasn't doing rock 'n' roll at the first. If I could have gotten a Chuck Berry, I would have started with him instead of Don Swan in two seconds! But why should he go with me?

"The first real rock that I ever got a chance to hear was when I went to Nashville. And I heard this country rock. I said, 'Oh, my God! This is fascinating music!' I loved it! I couldn't . . . I envied . . . the experience of going in there with no music and nothing more than a tune you can hum and coming out with a record was something that I never—I didn't believe! But it used to happen that way!"

Si did not go alone. Also on the trip was Snuff Garrett, who came to Liberty first as a promotion man. Ultimately Snuff's forte turned out to be music, even though he never learned to read a note. His knack showed up on that Nashville trip.

"Snuffy Garrett went there with no tunes, no nothing, and no artists, and [he] came back with six records. And all recorded in a studio where everybody got together and sort of knew where the next guy was going musically, they felt this together, and the first rock was done the same way. These guys would sit in a doggone garage with a cheap tape recorder and keep on going until they got through what they were looking for musically. I wish to God I could have gotten into that. But I wasn't set up for it financially and it was cheaper to record with Julie London and just the bass and guitar anyway.

"When Snuffy asked to go to Nashville, saying that he could get what I wanted for very little money, I said 'Go ahead.' He found ten different acts. He got to know people like the Burnette Brothers and others. He had six different records, three unknown, all good. That whole Nashville sound was excellent. Everything he did got released."

But the Nashville trip came in 1959. In 1957 rock 'n' roll still seemed an elusive butterfly.

Eddie Cochran

Often in life, luck—or at least being in the right place at the right time—makes all the difference. In 1957 Si needed hits, and he wanted rock 'n' roll. The answer to both requirements walked into his office.

"One day that I spent in the office was a lucky one. The receptionist called me and said a boy with a guitar would like to see me. I told her I was busy. Her answer—'He's cute. Please see him.' Finally, after more pestering from her I said 'Okay.'

"Well, a little cute guy with a Texas accent, a cowboy hat, cowboy boots, and a guitar that seemed bigger than the boy himself sauntered in and without saying a word opened his guitar case, took out his guitar, and started to play and sing. After about fifteen minutes, I yelled, 'Hold it. I hear you. What's your name?' He answered 'Eddie Cochran. I'm your next star.'

"I said 'Congratulations. Who is your manager?' He said Jerry Capehart. Jerry took this boy under his wing and devoted all of his time to Eddie." Discovering Oklahoma rocker (well, he was actually born in Albert Lee, Minnesota) Eddie Cochran was the easiest thing Si Waronker ever did, thanks to Eddie's own talent and chutzpah. Almost as easy, and certainly as fortuitous, was getting the first song for Eddie to record, a new song by young songwriter John D. Loudermilk. Si insisted that Eddie record it.

Under the name Johnny Dee, songwriter John D. Loudermilk had just released his own version of "Sittin' in the Balcony," a borderline novelty tune, on Colonial Records.

"They had to hate me for what I did with 'Sittin' in the Balcony,'" apologizes Si belatedly. "I copied that song. I was always very hungry for hits. I guess we all were. A friend of mine, Gibbs, was working for NBC. He heard 'Sittin' in the Balcony' on the air by John D. Loudermilk under the name Johnny Dee. He told me it was getting an awful lot of play and I should hear it. He sent it airmail, and I got it and said 'I'm gonna record that son of a gun!'

"We were honest in most things, but we wanted hits. So we covered each other. I was covered so many times it hurt. Kitty Wells covered a Julie London record. When I say 'covered,' I mean 'copied.' I copied that record. I'll take all the blame on that. If you put them together, you'll hear that everything is identical. Even the ending, the echo, the reverse reverberation, as I call it. I just overdid the reverb, but that's about the only difference.

"We started that record at seven o'clock that night and ended at five o'clock the next morning. I shipped the same day. So the Loudermilk record developed into a cover of Eddie's record! And it's dirty, I know it is, but that is the way the business was in those days. But I admit it. Loudermilk never called; I never even knew him. He was good. As a matter of fact, I think that his record was better than ours with Eddie. Except we shipped faster, and I called every one of the distributors and said, 'Let's lay on this record because we do have competition.'"

Si rushed out Liberty's version by Eddie Cochran. Eddie's really was a direct copy, note for note and lick for lick, of Loudermilk's original, right down to the use of that deep echo chamber. But Loudermilk's was essentially a demo recording, and rather thin-sounding, while Eddie's was a well-produced, Elvis-style rocker with heavy reverb. Loudermilk's original barely made the top forty, while Eddie's record got into the national top twenty. Liberty had beaten the other label and gotten solidly into rock 'n' roll, all in one record.

Si has another story about "Sittin' in the Balcony." "I had an artist named Johnny Olenn that I had signed. He could have been something very, very important. I wanted him to record that tune, but he wouldn't come in from Vegas. So Eddie was the one who was available. He was there. That's how it happened that he recorded 'Sittin' in the Balcony'."

Liberty's success with "Sittin' in the Balcony" was entirely due to Eddie's performing style. He played a hard-rocking guitar and sang in a voice that was reminiscent of a contemporary rocker at Capitol Records, Gene Vincent ("Be-Bop-A-Lula," 1956), or of Elvis on songs like "Jailhouse Rock" or "Money Honey."

Eddie Cochran in a studio break.

Eddie had already had a cameo role in the flick *The Girl Can't Help It*, for which Little Richard did the title tune. In that movie, Eddie performed "Twenty-Flight Rock" in a Carl Perkins style. It was a song about picking up his girlfriend, who lived on the twentieth floor, to go dancing to a jukebox, but her elevator was broken, so he was too tired to rock, and it was expected that Liberty would want to release that first. But when the song "Sittin' in the Balcony" was uncovered, the switch was quickly made. Both songs had a light content delivered in an Elvis/Perkins/Vincent style, a good combination in 1957.

Over the next two years, Eddie Cochran was to have a total of seven hits on Liberty, three in the top forty and one in the top ten. Other Eddie Cochran singles, like his second hit, "Drive-In Show" (1957), which sounded a lot like "Sittin' in the Balcony" and featured Liberty's Johnny Mann Orchestra and Chorus; "Jeannie, Jeannie, Jeannie" (1959); and "Teenage Heaven" (1958–59) also sold well although not well enough to make the national top forty. His only top-ten hit was another borderline novelty tune, "Summertime Blues" (rerecorded and made into a hit again in 1968 by Blue Cheer and yet again in 1970 by the Who). The deep, Amos-'n'-Andy–Kingfisher voice on the record is really just Eddie doing the impression his friends knew well. The flip side of "Summertime Blues," "Love Again," was written by Eddie's girlfriend, Sharon Sheeley.

"Summertime Blues" was Eddie's last major record. By 1959 Eddie Cochran was no longer having hits.

In retrospect Eddie Cochran has been considered a legendary master of rock 'n' roll. In fact in the early 1970s United Artists Records released an Eddie Cochran LP in their Legendary Masters Series, and EMI released a Cochran Legendary Masters CD in 1990. Other entries in the Legendary Masters Series were Fats Domino, Ricky Nelson, and Jan & Dean, three artists who had long strings of hits over many, many years. Eddie Cochran had only two top-twenty hits plus one other top-forty hit over a three-year period, not a very impressive score. He died prematurely in April 1960 in a car crash while on tour in England.

Eddie was very important as a factor in the development of Liberty Records, even in the development of rock 'n' roll as a musical form. A fan of rock 'n' roll has only to listen to any of Eddie's singles, LPs, or compilations to see that he was a master of the music. Every song he cut sounds like it could have been released as the A side of a 45.

So Eddie was a master of rock 'n' roll. Was he also a master who was knocked down in his prime, a major artist who would have had many more hits but just never had time?

A month before his death, his last hit single was released. Ironically titled "Teenage Heaven," it reached only #99 on the top one hundred songs. Even with the publicity attendant on his death, and the ironic title of the song, sales and air play did not pick up after Eddie's death. This is in contrast to Buddy Holly's last record, also ironically titled. "It Doesn't Matter Anymore," written by Paul Anka, was released several weeks before Holly died in a 1959 plane crash. Before the crash the single languished in the radio stations' reject files. After the crash it shot up to a very respectable #13. A year later, however, Cochran's death did nothing for his posthumous sales.

But the question being addressed is, Was Eddie's career stunted by his untimely death? Eddie's last top-ten hit had been back in the fall of 1958; his last top-forty hit in the fall of 1959. Both the total output and the chart success of Eddie Cochran prior to his death indicate that, as great a rocker as he was, he may in reality have been a typical rock 'n' roll flash in the pan—having two or three hits, then fading into relative obscurity. This is not to criticize or denigrate Cochran's music. Many fantastic records have come from one-shot artists, such as "Silhouettes" by the Rays and "Tobacco Road" by the Nashville Teens.

Eddie Cochran was a wonderful rocker who was responsible for several great records. His music has been appreciated by later generations of rock 'n' roll fans and inspired later artists such as the Stray Cats. Whether he would have ever had more Liberty hits had he lived cannot be known. Perhaps in death he achieved a stature neither he nor his music would have attained had he lived to become a has-been. In any event he certainly did a lot in a short time for Liberty in the company's early days.

Using record-chart data to try to divine what would have happened if Eddie had lived may be an objective way to assess his potential. But those who knew Eddie personally and professionally come to a very different conclusion.

Snuff Garrett of the Nashville trip, who was soon to become a young producer at Liberty, would be a major force in shaping Liberty Records, not to mention rock 'n' roll in general over the coming years. He saw much more potential in Eddie Cochran than we as fans ever got to enjoy.

"I did Eddie Cochran's last session. I sent him his airline tickets in London so he could fly home and finish the album. He was killed on the way to the London airport. So I went down to Liberty on Sunday morning to talk to the press and pull together background material.

"His last three songs, that I cut with him, took until six or seven A.M. and he flew to London about nine or ten o'clock. They were 'Cut Across, Shorty,' 'Cherished Memories' written by Sharon Sheeley, his girlfriend. Liberty had just turned Eddie over to me, and that was my first session with him. I am sure I'd have had big hits with him, expanding on his own directions. He was in the middle, just getting going, a helluva guitar player."

We all missed out when Eddie Cochran's recording career ended with his young life.

Sharon Sheeley was in the car with Eddie when he died and was almost killed herself, suffering multiple breaks in her neck and back. With her friend and roommate Jackie DeShannon, a Liberty artist, Sheeley ultimately wrote 352 songs that were recorded. Two of Eddie Cochran's posthumous Liberty 45s were "Sweetie Pie" and "Weekend." On each the flip side was Shari (as she was sometimes known) Sheeley's solo composition, "Lonely." Sharon never got over the loss of Eddie, to whom she was engaged when he died. She later married deejay Jimmy O'Neill, host of TV's "Shindig" program, but only because he loved her so much; it was understood that she still loved Eddie Cochran, even in death.

It is hard to write a book about Liberty without access to Eddie Cochran as a primary source. Were he alive today, an interview with him would be mandatory and would doubtless be very illuminating about his work and the workings of Liberty.

Fortunately, although Eddie is gone, his girlfriend/fiancée, Sharon Sheeley, is not. For the last couple of decades, Sharon has been a self-proclaimed recluse. She has made a point of not doing any interviews, either about herself or, especially, about Eddie. However, she kindly consented to discuss her involvement with the music business, with Liberty, and with Eddie for this book.

"Si Waronker was the founder of Liberty, and he told me this story. Liberty was going under in the early days, nineteen fifty-five, real fast. Al Bennett was a young hustler. He came to Si with a proposition. He paid off all of Si's debts for half interest in the company. Al did it. But Si lost half his company. Soon, Julie London's hit 'Cry Me a River' [1955, #9] saved the company. That was like getting a check in for three hundred dollars and paying one month's rent, but then what?

"Then the next hit was Eddie's 'Sittin' in the Balcony' [1957, #18]. That kept them afloat a little longer. And then came 'The Chipmunk Song' [1958, #1], which pulled Liberty way up.

"I got involved with Liberty because of the crush that I had on Eddie Cochran. I fell in love with him from his picture on a movie poster for *The Girl Can't Help It*. I told my girlfriend that I was in love with this guy, and she said, 'Yeah, you and every other girl in the country.' But I got to meet him and become his girlfriend through a series of events, beginning with writing a hit record.

"I was really in love with Eddie from afar, but I knew that this definitely got his attention. So what I did was to sign with Eddie's manager, Jerry Capehart. And then I got involved with Liberty because Jerry asked me to write some songs for Eddie. And of course Eddie was on Liberty. So I wrote 'Love Again,' which became the B side of 'Summertime Blues.' Also 'Cherished Memories,' and 'Something Else,' which is now a standard. That is how I got involved with Liberty Records. I was not quite eighteen, or perhaps I was eighteen at that time."

"Lonely," the song that was on the flip side of two Eddie Cochran posthumous releases, "Weekend" and "Sweetie Pie," was written by Sharon. "During Eddie's life, 'Lonely' was not on the back of anything, it was just an album cut." Was making "Lonely" a dual flip side a way for Liberty to generate royalty money for Eddie's bereaved girlfriend? Sharon: "They weren't trying to get more money for me. How about for *them*? They had only so many cuts by poor Eddie, and they repackaged them so many times, different album covers, different titles. No, Liberty never did anything to make money for us.

"Finally in nineteen sixty I went under contract with Liberty's Metric Music as a songwriter, with Jackie DeShannon," whom Sharon met through a unique set of circumstances.

"I was in the hospital after Eddie was killed for months and months, with a broken neck, a broken back, a broken heart.... I became a total shut-in. I just stayed in my room; I wouldn't take any phone calls. I wouldn't see any of my friends. Previous to Eddie's death, I had dated this disc jockey, Jimmy O'Neill, who worked at KRLA and later hosted ABC-TV's 'Shindig.' I would date him when I wanted to make Eddie jealous. Now Eddie was gone, I didn't need Jimmy, but Jimmy wouldn't give up. He would call my mother every day and my mom would tell him that I would not take any calls.

"Eddie Cochran was one of the most talented performers ever," testifies Sharon. However, he is little recognized today. Obviously the main reason for his lack of recognition was his early passing. However, Sharon puts forward another reason Eddie has not gotten his due respect: "One of the points that I want to get across in the movie [Sharon is working on a script of Eddie's life story], and I hope your book can also get this across, is that in the 1950s, things went a little differently than they do today. In those days if an artist had a manager, he would routinely take writing credit for the artist's songs, even if he did not write a note of them." Indeed, manager Norman Petty practiced this form of larceny with his star artist, Buddy Holly. When "That'll Be the Day" became the first hit for Buddy in 1957, it was on the Brunswick label and had been produced by Petty. The writing credits on that release read Holly-Allison-Petty. But on the version released a year earlier on Decca, the writing credits were Holly-Allison. Since there was not a bit of difference in the lyrics or melody between the two recordings, there could have been only one reason for the addition of Petty's name on the version he produced. In exchange for his managerial and production services, Norman Petty was given (or took) one-third of the composer royalties.

The writing credits on Eddie Cochran's Liberty hit "Summertime Blues" (and on 1958's "C'mon, Everybody") are Capehart-Cochran. But, as Sharon tells the story: "I know that Capehart did not write anything on 'Summertime Blues' because Eddie wrote 'Summertime Blues' in my apartment. The whole damn thing. But Jerry always had to put his name on every single thing Eddie wrote. So one day I asked him, 'Jerry, if you are such a great songwriter, how come you never wrote another note after Eddie died?'"

In 1968 the Vogues had a top-ten hit with a song credited to Jerry Capehart as sole composer. The song was called "Turn Around, Look at Me" (Reprise Records, 1968, #7). Does this refute Sharon's claim that Capehart did not write any songs on his own? "Eddie wrote 'Turn Around, Look at Me' for me when we first became engaged. I confronted Jerry with that when it was a hit in 1968. It wasn't bad enough that he ripped Eddie off for half of everything while Eddie was alive. He stole that whole song after Eddie was gone.

"Eddie was sold down the river by Jerry Capehart and did not make anything." So Sharon Sheeley got her royalties, but Eddie did not get his. But Liberty had nothing to do with that. Sharon outmaneuvered Liberty, who would have taken advantage of her otherwise, and Eddie was taken advantage of by his own manager.

From Sharon's insider's assessment, Eddie Cochran's career would have revived and sustained, had he lived, by dint of his raw talent. That is certainly quite possible. Over the rock 'n' roll years of the 1950s and 1960s, a number of artists who had early chart success followed by a dry spell came back in a big way a few years later. One example is Little Stevie Wonder, who went almost three years between his first and second top-ten records in 1963 and 1965, and Aretha Franklin, who saw six years pass between her first (1962) and second (1967) top-forty hits.

Although Eddie's part of the Liberty story ended with his death, Sharon's affiliation with Liberty extended beyond her fiancé's life, and her name will turn up again.

Additional insight into the life and death of Eddie Cochran comes from his Liberty "father," Si Waronker. What with his violin background and his experience as a concertmaster at Fox, few think of Si Waronker as someone who helped shape the sound of rock 'n' roll in the early days of the 1950s. It is usually only the younger producers, like the 1960s' Phil Spector, who are regarded as important. In fact Si was around for all the Liberty sessions. Why hasn't his contribution been recognized? "On any Liberty album, you will never see my name, 'Si Waronker.' You might see 'An SW Production' on them — that was me. I never wanted credit for any of the stuff that was made. So I gave others the credit. Bobby Troup was always the producer on Julie's, because they were going together at the time, but I was there.

"Even on the Eddie Cochran records, I was producer. The first record we made was 'Sittin' in the Balcony.' I had everything to do with that recording. 'Summertime Blues' I had less to do with. Jerry Capehart had a great deal to do with it, and I think I put his name down as producer on that one. But I put my name on very few of them. What did I need the credit for? I was president of the company anyway. But I was involved in all of them.

"I did all of the recordings except [for] what Snuffy did about fifty percent of the way along. When he started, I was with him on the first group of recordings he did, then he went on his own. He was not a musician and he still isn't. But he had a great ear and he knew what he wanted to hear so fine, however he did it I couldn't care less. I thought the guy was talented."

While Si thought that Eddie was very talented, he is not sure that Eddie's career would necessarily have continued had he lived.

"Eddie was a kid: He was seventeen years old when I met him. When he died, a few years later, he was still seventeen. He was growing up within a group of young innovators; at that time, rock 'n' roll was something new. If a kid had a tune, that was great. But everybody wanted to become a composer. But I think Eddie's career was more limited than a lot of people would say. He was a part of a group that had a lot to do with the rock music of that time. He did have a delivery that was very unusual. Although it sounded forced to me at the beginning, as time went on, he improved.

"There was one problem he ran into. Sharon Sheeley tried to straighten this problem out with him. Sharon tried to write tunes with him. She had more to do in the writing than he did. He wanted to write his own tunes like every one of them wanted to have their own publishing company. One of the things that hurt Eddie's career more than anything was that he tried to be dependent on what he himself could give to it by his own writing. Sharon wrote some stuff with him and did a good job. But his compositions were almost like copying—there was nothing that original, unfortunately, on the last two or three records.

"We tried desperately hard [to get hit material]. When he went to London on the tour, looking at this kid, he would have been a sensation onstage; he was a cute little guy, good looking, people took to him. But no, I don't know how much farther he would have gone musically if he had not died. If Eddie would have had one more hit, or if he would have lived today, he could have been a big gigantic star like we see today that make so much money. Eddie had that opportunity, if he had just lived another year or two and gotten material. That is all he needed.

"Eddie was one of the sweetest kids I've ever known. He had total run of the offices. He could walk in and out of recording sessions, do anything he wanted—he was like my son.

"What makes me happy is that the Eddie Cochran did see some success. And what makes me terribly unhappy was his untimely death and the way it happened. That was a heartbreaker."

Back to Eddie's first hit, "Sittin' in the Balcony." One advantage it had over John D. Loudermilk's original was the much greater gain (volume) that the Liberty record had. Eddie's record was hot! Besides working with talented youth like Eddie Cochran, and knowing hit material when he heard it, Si was an innovator in the studio. A lot of credit for making hot recordings has gone to producers like Phil Spector with his Wall of Sound girl-group records on Philles Records, and Frank Guida with his noisy Gary "U.S." Bonds waxings on LeGrand Records. Certainly, compared to pop and band recordings of the prerock days, these producers were doing something new. But it was not something new at Liberty. Si was recording "hot" way beyond what the experts and the engineers thought was acceptable in the mid-fifties.

"I had a habit of recording at a high level. I always figured that if we could get more volume on the record itself, the customers could put the record on and it would sound better at a lower level. It was an idea I was playing with. I put the recordings to the limitations of all the volume I could get on the master and hoped that it worked. I was the one that started that. It was a way to get the hiss and the scratches out, make the music loud."

Si may have been an expert at economizing, such as when he recorded Julie London and Patience and Prudence with a small combo instead of a full orchestra, but he also knew when it was worthwhile to spend a little extra. "I tried to press on better material. It used to cost me a penny a record more to use a little more vinyl on the 45s. By using a little more, we were able to get a little more volume, too. That helped. Most of the Liberty records you heard were louder than other labels; maybe not as good, but loud. God, I'd put on as much as the record would take, as much as the [cutting] needle would take before it chattered off the disk!"

Lenny Waronker

When Si started Liberty back in 1955, his son, Lenny, was 14 years old. For the next eight years, Liberty would shape his life as much as it would shape his dad's — and more.

Every college kid needs a summer job. When your dad has his own record company, your summer job problems are over. Lenny's dad made him assistant for promotion to Snuff Garrett. Lenny's first studio assignment from Snuff was working on an Eddie Cochran reissue compilation.

"I was working with Snuff and got to go through Eddie's tapes. It was great. I didn't remix or add instruments. It was just reviewing material and compiling it for release. That was in nineteen sixty-one or sixty-two. I was going to college, and during the summers I was Snuff's gofer. That was great because I got to observe what Snuff was doing. He would take me to New York, Nashville; he taught me about how important pop songs were. My dad thought it would be a good experience. I didn't study music in college, I just took anything to get through. Then, when I graduated from college and was all ready for my career in the music business, Dad quit the business. Not that it mattered, because I still had a job there, but it was ironic."

Si believes that Lenny's work with Snuff Garrett got him in with Warner's. "Because of his work with Snuffy, I suppose they thought he could do A&R. At any rate, that was what they hired Lenny to do at Warner Bros. that started it all. Now he is president of the company."

"I remember the first Liberty session. I remember all the things my dad did to make the business keep going, it was curious. The thing that used to amaze me was how much he got done with so little. Artwork was a big issue."

Si was making a living and supporting his family with music all the time Lenny was growing up. This seemed only natural to Lenny, since his dad had been involved in music his entire life. For himself, not being a trained musician, Lenny never so much as thought about going into music too. "But when my dad started the Liberty company, I saw that it was a thing that I could do. That by getting involved in Liberty, I could be in music and didn't necessarily have to be a musician. In his case he was lucky because he did have a musical background. But he worked hard. I remember getting up and going to school, and he'd be pulling in, getting home from a session.

But it all happened very quickly, and he got caught up in it. It was a dream come true, and he never told us about the bad times, so it was very exciting.

"I think that the mind-set at the beginning was interesting. It was about survival, about a dream. The fight to survive was amazing. I don't know how many times he went out of business. He fought for that. And then having the success, the real success, that was amazing. To see him go through all those phases certainly affected me and the way I thought. He cared. It was not just to make money, he really cared about the quality. What I learned from him was that I never took for granted, ever, a good record or a successful record, either one.

"I don't know what the up side of the record business was in those days. It was a baby business and a neat thing to be doing, but I don't think anybody knew for sure what it would become. It wasn't like you could go in the studio and if you did well, you'd make millions of dollars. Especially on the West Coast, there were record companies, but not many. So the idea of building his assets to sell for millions, that wasn't it. I really feel there was a tremendous amount of pride, instincts about the public, his business sense, having aesthetic concerns, and a lot of his own creative beliefs that went into the company.

"Most record companies were started by people who had a specific musical point of view. I am not sure if Dad had one, but it was sure more than just making money.

"He brought home the music, and then the artwork. He brought home the album covers, and I never understood why he did that; it drove me crazy. But he understood the importance of the whole package. There was an aesthetic concern there. What made the company work was his understanding and concern about things that really counted in music and the way that music was presented."

Next time you buy a CD carrying the Warner Bros. label, think about Si and the standards he set at Liberty in the 1950s.

Billy Ward and His Dominoes

Billy Ward and His Dominoes were musical veterans by the time they came to Liberty. They had been around since the early 1950s and released songs on the Federal, King, Jubilee, and Decca labels. In the summer of 1957, three months after Eddie Cochran's Liberty debut, they appeared on the label and became the first black contributors to the company's success. None of Billy Ward and His Dominoes' previous records had been big hits, in spite of their featuring lead singers who later had solo hits, Clyde McPhatter ("A Lover's Question," 1958) and Jackie Wilson ("Lonely Teardrops," 1958).

Though they were black, the Dominoes' style was very pop oriented, which permitted them greater general success than they might have had otherwise in the largely segregated music scene of the 1950s. Their recordings were very full, almost big-bandish, with dramatic, almost melodramatic vocal deliveries. On Liberty, Billy Ward and His Dominoes had three hits, two on the top forty, including updated classics like Hoagy Carmichael's "Stardust" (Tommy Dorsey, 1940; Artie Shaw, 1941) and "Deep Purple" (Larry Clinton with Bea Wain, 1938).

As usual Si was at the heart of the artists' success. "Talk about luck and Liberty, and people being friends of mine! When Billy Ward's contract was up with Decca, he wanted a Liberty contract. But he wanted not money so much but control of his

Si Waronker, as he appeared in 1961.

product. I said fine and we finally signed him. And I said, 'What do you want to record first?' He said, 'I have an idea of "Stardust."'

"'Stardust'! Holy mackerel—Nat King Cole just came out with 'Stardust'! But Billy Ward said that he had an idea to sing it better than Nat King Cole. I told him, 'That I gotta hear. OK, let's see what you're talking about.' We recorded the darn thing and I'll be damned if it didn't become a hit! But that was again through the publishing company that I was friendly with; they sent Billy Ward to me. I recorded a lot of their tunes. Luck had a great deal to do with it, but also I had good connections and did a lot of hard work.

"Gene Mumford was the lead singer with Billy Ward. I remember him, because he was really the voice of the record, and Billy Ward got the credit for it."

Billy Ward and His Dominoes' last hit, a 1958 Liberty release, was a real curiosity. Before it is discussed, some music-biz background is necessary.

"Cover" Records

A common practice in the early days of rock 'n' roll was for a white artist to record a song that had already been released by a black artist. Sometimes the original black version was on a small record label and produced on a tight budget (tighter even than Si's!) in a back room somewhere, with maybe only one microphone. These records often were not being well distributed and, more important, were not played on radio stations with large white audiences. In order to "cover" the white audience not reached by the black record, a white artist would often use the black original record as a demo, record his or her own version of the song, and perhaps have a hit. Pat Boone recorded sixty hit songs in the 1950s and 1960s, and 10 percent of these were white "cover versions," as they were called. (The term referred to the fact that the white version was recorded to cover a market not covered by the original.) In recent years many remakes of formerly popular songs, even LP cuts and singles recorded many years after the original, are loosely referred to as "cover versions." They are not cover versions in the classic sense, however, since they are not recorded to cover a market not covered by another, current hit version.

In later years, the 1950s cover versions have been regarded as unfair white rip-offs of original black hits. The assumption is that, had the cover version not come out and stolen sales from the original, the original would have been a big hit for the black artist on the small record label. However, this is probably a misconception. The original black versions would, in most cases, never have become hits. Some original versions, for example, "Work with Me, Annie," had blue lyrics. The cleaned-up version by Georgia Gibbs, "Dance with Me, Henry," saved that song from oblivion.

The Gladiolas' original recording of the classic hit song "Little Darlin'" was excellent, probably better than any other version. But it was too poorly recorded (from a commercial, 1950s pop standpoint) and too poorly distributed to ever have become a hit. However, the Diamonds' Mercury Records cover version that everyone remembers today sold in the millions.

The composer royalties the original black artists got from the white cover versions made the blacks far more money than they would have made from sales of their own versions. It was not a question of "which version was better," but rather of "which version was more appealing" to the most record buyers. A Mack truck is "better" than a hatchback; yet a Mack truck may not be suitable for most people.

Fats Domino had some of his early records covered by Pat Boone. The teenagers of the time loved Pat's cover versions. Unrealistic rock fans, writers, and critics of later decades have regarded Pat Boone's covers as uninspired rip-offs. Yet Fats Domino has always regarded Pat's cover versions as blessings from heaven, giving his music exposure he alone could never have achieved.

In the early 1980s Fats Domino spied Pat Boone in the audience at a club where Fats was singing. He invited Pat up on the stage, and with his arm around Boone, praised him. Without Pat's cover versions, he explained, Fats's—and his name— would never have been heard of by the millions who bought Pat's records and, in turn, made Fats a rich man and his compositions even more famous. Fats considered Pat a pioneer largely responsible for the ultimate success of rock 'n' roll as well as for Fats's own success. Then the two of them sang a duet.

How do cover records tie in to the Liberty story? Well, at Liberty, the last Billy Ward and His Dominoes hit turned the tables on the trend of white cover versions, giving Liberty the distinction of releasing the first rock 'n' roll *black* cover version. Jan & Arnie (later Jan & Dean, later to move to Liberty) were a white group on a tiny independent label, Arwin Records. In 1958 they wrote and sang a hit they had written called "Jennie Lee." Jennie Lee was a popular stripper in Los Angeles. She was not, as record company publicity at the time misstated, a popular secretary at Arwin Records!

Billy Ward and His Dominoes on Liberty recorded the black cover version of the white original of "Jennie Lee." Jan & Arnie made the top ten, but Billy Ward missed the top forty entirely. The black cover version on Liberty essentially failed.

Billy Ward and His Dominoes subsequently moved on to ABC–Paramount Records. There, with the Hal Daniels orchestra, they tried to rekindle the flame with records like the mid-1960 release "You're Mine," written by Ward himself, but nothing came of the effort.

Margie Rayburn

The last addition to Liberty's rock 'n' roll roster for 1957 was Margie Rayburn. Margie's husband, Norman Milkin, was (what else?) a songwriter as well as a banjo player with Spike Jones. He had a friend, yet another songwriter, who was a member of the Champs ("Tequila," 1958). This second composer was Dave Burgess, who wrote a song called "I'm Available," which Margie recorded for Liberty. In the last part of 1957, "I'm Available" became a big hit for Margie Rayburn, whose career was managed by her husband. Alas, "I'm Available" was Margie Rayburn's only hit.

"I'm Available" has such a breathy, soft sound that many people write it and Margie off as a one-hit Wonder with no real talent. In reality Margie had sung with Ray Anthony and toured with Gene Autry, as well as done the nightclub circuit and released records on at least two other labels before signing at Liberty. Moreover, she had already had a number of singles on Liberty before "I'm Available" and had even more afterward. Her first was "Take a Gamble on Love" in 1956, and her last was "Maid of Honor" in 1960. In all Margie had three releases before her one hit, and eight after. She was not an excellent singer, but she was listenable, and her hit was beautiful.

Margie's many Liberty singles illustrate an important point in the Liberty story. At Liberty, artists' hit records were often just the tip of their musical iceberg. Many artists had a lot of other, often very good singles besides the ones that became hits. In fact, often an artist's very best material died on the record store racks. Although, according to her friend Si, that was not really true in Margie's case.

"Margie Rayburn was a frustrated singer. She always wanted to record, but I never wanted to record her. What were we doing? A forty-year-old woman. She would sing, but she had nothing unusual, nothing that means anything [No "hook," as Si would call it]. She came in one day with a tune called 'I'm Available.' But here was a woman of forty sounding like a little girl of seventeen or eighteen.

"If you listen carefully, you will hear that there are only three men on that. Well, we weren't going to waste money, but I did add a bass and a drum on 'I'm Available.' It was cute. Something might happen with this one. A lot of her records she would make herself and bring them in and say, 'Hey, how about putting this out?' On 'I'm Available' I said, 'No, no, no. On this one I think we *have* something here.' I knew we had a hit. Because she did not sound like any forty-year-old woman on it."

The flip side of "I'm Available" was a simple song called "If You Were." Written by Ross Bagdasarian, it has lines like "If you were a rose and I were a vase, I'd

Mixing a Liberty hit in the Studio.

hold you." The singing is nothing like the soft, sweet, girl-groupy overdubbing of "I'm Available." Instead, it sounds like something Doris Day would sing. The accompaniment reflects economy: stand-up bass, piano, maybe a guitar, and percussion that sounds like a trash can or phone book being struck with someone's hands. As Si says, "We didn't spend anything on that. On some of these things, we'd have two men or three men, or if we could get away with it, we'd have just one. She did one of Ross's songs to get in good with the inner circle!

"We released the record 'I'm Available' and it got to be a hit. Oh boy! This was almost impossible to live with. In those days, if an artist got a hit, he or she could go on tour. The artist didn't get a great deal of money for touring, but [he or she] made pretty good dough." Margie was a little old, but she had a good figure, and with makeup, at a distance she could pass for a younger woman.

"Margie Rayburn went on her three- or four-month tour, came back, and she knew everything about the music business." Margie had decided she should make an album. "I said, 'Margie, you don't know the music business. You've earned about seventy thousand or eighty thousand dollars on this record here. Keep it, please! Take the dough, put it away, make these little records here. If they are good, we release them. If they are not, we forget about them. You can't afford to do what you say, making an album.'"

Margie persisted. Her Liberty contract read that all the royalties she made went toward her next project. If she made an album, the cost of the album would be deducted from her royalties before she was paid. It was a standard contract. On a 5 percent royalty that earned fifty thousand dollars, if the next recordings took twenty thousand dollars to record and release, then the artist had only thirty thousand dollars coming.

Si said to Margie, "Don't do it. You are a woman, not a kid; you have a husband. You are not just starting a career." Her husband agreed with Si but was afraid to cross his wife, who according to Si said, "No, I want to make an album. I know exactly what the kids want; I have been out there talking with them. I know what they like to hear; they tell me." So Si let her do it, telling her she would be wasting a lot of her own money. Si did not believe in Margie's project: "But if you want it, I'll do anything I can to help."

Well, Margie ignored Si's offer of assistance. She wanted to make her album all alone. She spent seventeen thousand dollars on the LP, titled *Margie*. "We couldn't give it away," regrets Si. "We even tried taking singles off of the album, to see if we could get some play on it. She never had another hit." But she never learned. Instead of getting a big chunk of royalty money, she got very little, because she blew it all on what Si characterized as "junk stuff that couldn't sell."

Sounding like Patti Page or Kay Starr or maybe Doris Day, one of her follow-ups to "I'm Available" was the faster-paced "Oooh, What a Doll." Her double-tracked voice on the flip side, "Smoochin'," sounds much more like "I'm Available", with the "woo-hoo-hoo" trademark of hers from that previous record.

But besides being a hit and going to Margie Rayburn's head, "I'm Available" was important to Liberty for an obscure reason. Margie overdubbed her voice on "I'm Available" to make herself sound like a harmonizing trio. Such vocal overdubbing would become a mainstay of what developed into the "Liberty sound" in later years.

LPs

Originally there were relatively few hits at Liberty, as Margie Rayburn could have testified. But Si kept a steady stream of Liberty LPs pouring out. As he put it, he'd record anything, just to keep the name of the company in front of the distributors, and in an effort to "build catalog" as he called it.

LRP was the prefix for LP catalog numbers. LRP 3012 was *Lonely Girl*, Julie London's second album. Just before that, LRP 3011 was by a young poet named Rod McKuen, *Songs for a Lazy Afternoon*. LRP 3021 was by the Johnny Mann Singers, who would fill the role of background singers for many Liberty stars in later years.

LRP 3002 was cleverly pun-titled, *Jazz for Jean-Agers* by Claude Gordon & Orchestra. Blue jeans were replacing slacks as the pants of choice for teenagers in 1957, much as rock 'n' roll was replacing jazz. Thus the title of the next Liberty album: *Rock 'n' Beach Party*. This title reflected two musical trends that would play a big part in the future of Liberty, rock 'n' roll and California's beaches. The artist, Nino Tempo, was an experienced big-band sax player and future session player for producers like Phil Spector.

With his sister, band vocalist April Stevens, Nino would have a number-one record in 1963, "Deep Purple." Not only that, but in 1991, he would have a top hit

CD instrumental on the charts. But back in 1957 he was breaking fertile musical gound for Si.

LRP 3061 starred the boy who really brought rock 'n' roll to Liberty, Eddie Cochran, who was happily *Singin' to My Baby* in 1957.

Scandal at Liberty

In the fall of 1957, Si's Liberty Records was rocked by scandal. It all started when Randy Wood of Dot Records called Si with an offer to buy Liberty. Could Si's investment really pay off this quickly? Dot itself had just been purchased by Paramount Pictures. The rest of the story is best told in Si's own words.

"Dot Records was immensely successful at that time and was now trying to grow even faster by merging or buying companies that showed promise. Randy Wood wanted Liberty. He convinced me that the combination of Dot and Liberty could be a force in the industry.

"Randy had a fine organization—sales, promotion and certainly honesty. Randy wanted the company, but with no other shareholders. He felt he could handle my minority partners by buying their interests. The price agreed to for Liberty was one million dollars. Randy and I agreed, and Price-Waterhouse was given instructions to audit the books of Liberty and started their work immediately. When Randy and I were in the midst of our negotiations the question of finances was discussed. I knew that our accounts receivable were about one million dollars and our payables were about six hundred thousand. The figures were given to me by the Liberty sales manager and bookkeeper.

"On the morning of December twenty-third, nineteen fifty-seven, Randy called and asked to meet that afternoon. He would have the Price-Waterhouse report, and we could go over it and try to finalize our negotiations. We met at three P.M. in his office. I thought it strange that he was alone. It was now evident that what he was to say was for my ears only.

"Randy started by telling me that Price-Waterhouse [had] made a very thorough investigation and had to do more than what they anticipated because of the complexities they encountered. In their final analysis it was their conclusion that Liberty was bankrupt.

"Oh, no! How could this be possible? After two years of heartbreaking work—bankruptcy? Why? Randy called for the auditors to come in. They showed me." Somebody had been cooking the books at Liberty! "When an order for five hundred records came in, a zero was added. An order for one thousand—an extra zero added, making ten thousand instead of one thousand. The government hadn't been paid some $167,000 in taxes.

"How could I [have been] so stupid not to know this was going on? It is true that I was in the studio almost all of my time and when not there, in my office listening to songs, meeting with artists, publishers, etc. The business part of the operations were left to others. Randy didn't think I had a chance to get out of my mess and suggested that after bankruptcy, I come to work for him at a substantial salary."

Don Blocker, who later was national promotion head for Liberty, explains exactly what happened to Si's company.

"Si Waronker's original partner was Jack Ames, who was sales manager. When

Si had success with Julie London and others and had albums to sell, Jack Ames told Si, 'Well, I'm going on the road.' Jack Ames would go into distributors with the Liberty catalog and say, 'How many do you want of these?' The distributor would say, 'Give me ten of these, fifty of these, twenty-five of these.' Jack Ames was very upset at the quantities. So when he was on the airplane back, he'd just take the ten and add two zeros. All of a sudden, they got an order for one thousand albums. Si Waronker said, 'My God, this is fantastic. They are buying these things!' And that got Liberty into trouble originally. Liberty became so much in debt that we couldn't get records pressed."

Liberty would have been in big trouble at this point, had it not been for the recent hiring of Al Bennett, who would someday become the president of Liberty Records. Don Blocker: "Al Bennett, with his persuasiveness, his Southern charm, and his personality, was able to get records pressed. At times, on the road, I would run out of money. We had no credit cards, and I would be stranded until they sent me money. But we were just a bunch of young guys, and we just went out and we sold records."

But at the time Si did not know if his company could survive this blow or not. "The Christmas and New Year's holidays were miserable. When I confronted my sales manager and the bookkeeper, they naturally denied everything, but I called a few of our distributors, and they verified everything that Randy showed me. I immediately fired the bookkeeper and offered a buy-or-sell agreement to my twenty percent partner [sales manager]. Fifty thousand dollars—he could have first choice. We agreed on one week for him to buy or one week for me, with the agreement that the one who retained possession and retained one hundred percent of the stock would hold the other harmless from all debts. I knew the outcome. The distributors, artists, and creditors would come to my rescue. They did.

"I now owned one hundred percent of almost eight hundred thousand dollars in debt. I immediately went to see Bob Ginter. He had Julie London send me a letter stating that she would never record with or for anyone but me. Ross Bagdasarian, always a great friend, the same letter. Mark McIntyre [the father] of Patience and Prudence, 'Tonight You Belong to Me,' and every other artist on the label all gave me letters of confidence. All I now needed was about sixty thousand dollars. Fifty thousand dollars to my partner, the rest for operating expenses for a month.

"There were a few of our thirty-five distributors who were very close to me, and I didn't hesitate to call them. The deal I offered was to have them advance me ten thousand dollars and for that they could pay thirty-five cents a record instead of forty-five cents until they doubled their money. As for their surplus inventory— please hold them for a couple of months and pay only when their records sold. In three days I didn't get sixty thousand dollars. I got eighty thousand dollars. God bless them: Milt Salstone, Chicago; Bob Hofstadter, St. Louis; Bob Chatton, San Francisco; George Harstone from Los Angeles.

"There were two other problems. We had been pressing records with RCA Victor and owed them one hundred fifty thousand dollars, and Liberty owed the government one hundred eighty thousand dollars for back excise taxes. I met with RCA and offered to clear the debt in eighteen months. They would agree if the government would. This is now January of nineteen fifty-eight. What a year, nineteen fifty-eight. Anyway I called the IRS and asked for a meeting in my office. One of my most unforgettable experiences occurred that day. Here I'm expecting a big, tough guy with no sympathies and in comes this big, tough-looking Southerner. I went into my act, telling him that I had supreme confidence in my ability, showed him the financial books, my letters from the artists, and the pending deal with RCA. Naturally I did not mention the distributors' contributions.

"After about two hours he asked how I intended to pay the IRS. I begged for a six-month extension. He stood up—I almost fainted—put on his hat and started to walk out. When he reached the door, he turned to me and said, 'Not six months—one-year extension.' God bless the IRS. Now I needed hits, big hits, and lots of hits."

And Si was gonna have hits, too, and big ones—although no one could have predicted where they would be coming from.

CHAPTER 6

1958
"Witch Doctor" and the Chipmunks

So far Liberty had made it big with some records, but none of the Liberty hit artists to date had shown much staying power. Since the story of early rock 'n' roll is a saga replete with tales of one-shot artists and flashes-in-the-pan, Liberty's lack of enduring hit makers was understandable and excusable. As stated before, many of the greatest records of rock 'n' roll have come from one-shot artists. Yet it is comforting to fans and record companies alike to have a roster of established, reliable artists who can be counted on for hits year after year.

Between Margie Rayburn at the end of 1957 and the Christmas season of 1958, Liberty had no new successes. And by 1958 Liberty had just one sustaining artist — Julie London. And Julie had no more hit singles after "Cry Me a River," just a series of albums.

Snuff Garrett also recorded Julie. "Si also wanted me to record Julie London after he did some. I did ten or twelve albums with her. We're still business partners, she and her husband Bobby Troup and I, almost forty years later."

Around this time a 16-mm Liberty promotional film of Snuff Garrett with Julie London and others was made, which still exists. A more important event of this era was the hiring of the man who would later become the president of Liberty Records.

Al Bennett

Si heard about a 31-year-old man who had left Dot Records when Dot was sold to Paramount. "This guy was supposed to be a supersalesman, first-rate businessman, and have an unbelievable personality. I made arrangements to meet with him for dinner. I loved his approach. Nothing could faze him. His first question was 'How much are you willing to pay?' My answer was 'Exactly what I get. Nothing!' He started to laugh and then asked, 'When do I get a raise?' My answer: 'When I do.' He then said, 'Okay, buddy, you've got a deal.'

"I then added that if he lasted one month, he would get 10 percent of the stock of Liberty. His name is Al Bennett. Al turned out to be exactly what was needed to bring Liberty to its full potential. He could sell a burnt match. He decided to take a trip to see every distributor to discuss our bulging inventory and to instill goodwill."

Eddie Cochran's first release for 1958 was a rocker called "Jeannie, Jeannie,

Jeannie." Right after that came the most important record in Liberty history, and it came from Ross Bagdasarian.

"Witch Doctor"

In 1958 David Seville went in two directions. One direction didn't really pay off too well. The other ... well, that's another story!

The first direction was in a traditional instrumental style. "Bonjour Tristesse" was a big-band-type jazz number taken from the Otto Preminger Columbia picture of the same name. It was slow-paced, especially compared to the flip side, "Dance from Bonjour Tristesse," which was practically a novelty tune. This record was not a commercial success, nor apparently was it intended to be. When Si heard the titles, he reacted unexpectedly. "Oh, gosh, that was one of our throwaway records! When I say throwaway, there was really no rhyme or reason for the record. That was what started Ross on the gig of 'Armen's Theme,' that type of instrumental."

And the other direction, the other story? Was it a success? Well, it seems that David Seville invested the last two hundred dollars he had in the bank in a tape recorder with the goal of recording some kind of a hit. While toying with his new acquisition, he got the notion to record his voice at slow speed, then play it back at normal speed, and voila, the novelty classic "Witch Doctor" became a #1 single for Liberty. The song was named after a book, *Duel with the Witch Doctor*, or perhaps as Si recalls, a figurine of a witch doctor on Ross's bookshelf.

"The 'Witch Doctor' came from Ross's bookcase, with a figurine of a witch doctor. The next day he told me he was going to write a tune called 'The Witch Doctor.' I told him, 'Come on, Ross — but go ahead and do it.' In the meantime Al Bennett had just joined the company, and he was on that trip to meet with all of the distributors and assure them that we would take back the return records, don't worry, we are not going under, and all of that. Really a goodwill trip. Meantime, we finished the 'Witch Doctor.' Al was in Chicago and I sent him an acetate dub and said, 'This is our next hit. Play this for Howard Miller, will you?' Then I shipped acetates to eight distributors and told them to get on it."

Allan Lavinger, who became Liberty's first director of merchandising, helped get the song out. "I sat there personally typing six acetate labels for the mailing and stuck them on the records. We sold four million in six or eight weeks."

But it took a bit to convince Al Bennett that the record would sell.

"When Al got his copy," recalls Si, "he called me and said, 'God damn it! What are you doing making records like this? We are trying to make a record company out of this mess, and you are coming out with "Ooo-Eee-Ooo-Ah-Ah"?!' I told him, 'You sell the goddamn records, I'll make 'em.'

"After 'Witch Doctor' sold two million, eight hundred thousand, which is the exact count on that one, Al changed his opinion."

Allan Lavinger remembers, "The pressing plants couldn't keep up. I heard Al [Bennett] begging plants to press it all the time, saying he would pay them in twenty days or thirty days or whatever. He needed credit and did not have any."

Fortunately for Si and Liberty, 1958 was the era of the rock 'n' roll novelty tune, with songs like Larry Verne's "Mr. Custer," the Hollywood Argyles' "Alley Oop," and Sheb Wooley's "Purple People Eater" making regular trips to the top of the charts. Plus, to adult musicians' ears, nearly all of rock 'n' roll at the time had lyrics

The original "Witch Doctor" Liberty 45 label.

that were either incomprehensible or indistinguishable. With Liberty's release of "Witch Doctor," the entire country was soon chanting incomprehensible witch-doctor talk, "Ooo-eee-ooo-ahh-ahh, ting, tang, walla-walla bing-bang!" along with Ross/David. This was the first national #1 record for Liberty, and it could not have come at a better time, financially or politically. "The 'Witch Doctor' to me was the most important record we ever made, because that is what saved the company" testifies Si Waronker.

"Ross Bagdasarian was a man I considered to be one of the most talented artists I ever knew. He had an approach that reminded me of Charlie Chaplin [with whom Si had worked at Fox]. He wrote, sang or narrated songs like 'Armen's Theme,' 'The Trouble with Harry,' and 'Witch Doctor,' whose lyrics are most memorable to me. This was Ross with his incredible sense of humor."

One thing about the "Witch Doctor" record: Ross had recorded only one side, but for a single, Liberty needed the flip side. Si offered to "help."

"I had never written a tune but here was my big chance. As a joke Ross said 'Let's write one together.' Hah! The tune was called 'Don't Whistle at Me, Baby.' We had no orchestra, so we had to improvise. Ross hit a phone book that I held. This was to sound like tom-toms." "Don't Whistle at Me, Baby" sounds a little like Capitol Records satirist Stan Freberg, who made fun of rock 'n' roll songs like "Heartbreak Hotel" by Elvis and "The Great Pretender" by the Platters, and [sounded] a bit like Eddie Cochran on a song like "Drive-In Show."

Si: "On the label we titled it 'The Music of David Seville.' This was my first and last songwriting experience and the only time I ever got a penny for writing or publishing. I never started a publishing company. That was one of the reasons the reputation was so good. I never took anything anybody ever wrote and said, 'OK, you can have a contract if we can publish your tunes,' which almost every other company did do. But this time writing the lyrics to me was very funny, and to hold the doggone telephone book was even funnier, because we had no money at all for an orchestra."

The only problem remaining was how to follow up a song like "Witch Doctor."

The Chipmunks

According to some sources, in a few months Seville found the answer while staring out his car window at some Yosemite squirrels scampering about in front of his large auto. He used the same speeded-up recording gimmick that produced the voice of the witch doctor to create Alvin, Simon, and Theodore, the Chipmunks.

In reality, the events leading up to the Chipmunks were much less romantic. Ross wanted to do an original Christmas song but Si had doubts: "Nobody could ever compete with 'White Christmas.' Ross was adamant. He went to a small independent studio and hired three girls to sing the tune, 'We Were Strolling Through the Park' in a slow waltz rhythm and brought it to my office saying, 'Forget the lyrics. This is the idea for my Christmas record.' I thought he was crazy."

Luck was again about to play a part in the Liberty story.

"It so happened that I had an adjustable turntable. He walked over to the turntable and started to play the record again but accidentally set the speed at seventy-eight rpm rather than forty-five. This, of course, speeded up the sound and the three girls sounded like mice. Ross's eyes lit up like a Christmas tree and he said, 'See, smart ass, I told you so.' He grabbed his record, slammed the door, and said, 'I'll see you later.'

"About four days went by, and Ross comes back saying, 'Okay, Boy Wonder, I'll show you.' He closed my door, locked it, and put on his new version.

"Instead of 'I Was Walking Through the Park One Day,' it now was 'Christmas, Christmas Time Is Here.' Lines like 'All I Want Is a Hula Hoop,' etc. All three voices were his, speeded up. And he said, 'Now you get it? Those are my Chipmunks.'"

But his Chipmunks sang for less than a minute, and then Ross's little experiment ended. Running the tape so fast ate up the seconds. Si said, "So what are you going to do with forty-five seconds? How about some dialogue and some identity to the squirrels?"

"Chipmunks, you idiot, not squirrels! But you've got a point. Why don't we name them?"

Si suggested they grab a sandwich. "I then called our studio and said to get a session for seven P.M. The engineer said no, he was working on a sales presentation for Al Bennett, now sales manager and vice president of the company. I told the engineer what to do with the sales presentation, and Ross and I started to work as planned. Suddenly, Ross goes into hysterics and screams, 'I've got their names! You're the smart ass, so one of the Chipmunks will wear glasses and we'll call him Simon. Ha ha! The dummy engineer who didn't want us to record is named Ted [Ted was Theodore Keep, Liberty's recording engineer]. We'll call him Theodore, and the boy genius downstairs will be Alvin.' Al Bennett's full name is Alvin Silas Bennett."

After the three Chipmunks had been christened, Si had one more suggestion. "'Now, how about you, Ross? You're the keeper of these animals. You've got to have

Chapter 6 · 1958

As the Chipmunks originally appeared on their first album cover.

a name.' Ross and I were like two infants laughing." The name they selected for Ross was the pseudonym Ross had already used on "Armen's Theme," David Seville.

Everyone named, there was still the first Chipmunks record to create. "Ross had already done the speeded-up voice with 'Witch Doctor.' It was the three-part harmonies of the Chipmunks that really got him excited, and I said 'Let's go to work.' He asked me, 'What is your idea?' Well, the funniest comedian I know is Señor Wences. He had a head in a box that answered him in a funny voice. I told Ross that was what I had in mind. After an hour and a half of screaming at each other, he said, 'Well, on the record I have to scream at *someone*.' So we came up with the idea of screaming 'Alvin!'

"As it stood, the first recording had just 'Christmas, Christmas Time Is Here,' the chorus, maybe forty-five seconds. I told him we need at least two and a half or two minutes on a record. We can't get away with anything shorter. So we had the introduction, which I recorded forty times, and we cut them together sounding like the middle eight bars of something. In that, with all of the foreplay between David Seville and the Chipmunks, we had to have some reason for them to talk to each other. After that, we ran out of stuff. He just yelled, 'Alvin!' Ross was always out in the studio, and I was always in the booth.

"When we got through, it was five or six in the morning. That was the most exciting part of my life, because we knew we had it. We didn't even take time to press it. We just made dubs — twenty or thirty acetates — and shipped them to distributors. The minute one put it on the air two days later, we knew we had a hit because the first order was one hundred thousand copies. Then they said, 'Back it up with another fifty thousand.' In one day, we sold six hundred thousand records! That was unbelievable in those days."

It may not have replaced "White Christmas," but "The Chipmunk Song" has become a Christmas standard. And Liberty had now become a force in the record business. "The Chipmunks' first record broke all sales figures for a single recording," documents Si. More than six million records sold in less than six weeks. The timing was perfect. We also were lucky to have penetrated the children's market at Christmas with an item that was selling for under a dollar. Even with the cooperation of all the pressing plants that were pressing records on a twenty-four-hour basis, we had problems keeping up with the orders that were pouring in." It made the top forty the following four Decembers and has since become a Yuletide perennial.

"I wonder what the sales figures would be in today's market," says Si. "I also wonder how many bootleg records were sold. I do know that in New York, where the street hawkers are now selling T-shirts, toys, fake watches, etcetera, they were then selling bootleg Chipmunk records. The total of records actually sold will never be known. Ross Bagdasarian and I became closer than ever. January of 1958 the 'Witch Doctor' and December of 1958 the 'Chipmunks.' Now it seemed that all of the catalog began to sell. I guess success breeds success."

The subsequent Liberty LP *Let's All Sing Along with the Chipmunks* was for little kids, with songs like "Yankee Doodle" and "Pop Goes the Weasel." But Bagdasarian knew he had a good thing, and included on the LP songs that would make musical history: "The Chipmunk Song," "Alvin's Harmonica," and "Ragtime Cowboy Joe." "Alvin's Harmonica" made the charts in 1959, 1961, and 1962, and "The Chipmunk Song" did so in those years plus 1960. "Ragtime Cowboy Joe" was top twenty in the summer of 1959.

A later song, "Rudolph the Red-Nosed Reindeer," charted in 1960, 1961, and 1962. Rather impressive. Not even the Beatles or Elvis would hit the charts so many times with so few records.

"The Bird on My Head" was Ross Bagdasarian's immediate follow-up to "Witch Doctor." Barely making it onto the top forty, Ross/Seville again speeded up his voice, this time not for a witch doctor or a chipmunk, but for the part of the bird, sort of a missing link between "Witch Doctor" early in the year and "The Chipmunk song" at the end of 1958.

Snuff Garrett was a great booster of Bagdasarian. "Ross Bagdasarian and I were close friends, we owned wine vineyards together. He was one of the most sensational people that ever walked the earth, the greatest sense of humor you'll ever know. I made one record with him, during the Watts riots, we cut at RCA, 'Eefin' Alvin,' and the riots were going on outside."

"Eefin'" was a breathy gimmick used on a series of novelty records in 1963, basically indescribable in print. On Guyden Records, the Goodlettsville Five released "Eff" and the flip-side Bill Baily rip-off "Baily's Gone Eefin,'" both written by Jerry Kennedy. On Epic Records, the Ardells performed the "Hootenanny" [Glencoves, 1963]-inspired "Eefananny," produced by Jerry Kennedy. And Joe Perkins made the only chart-successful Eef record, "Little Eefin' Annie" (based on "Little Orphan Annie") on Sound-Stage Records, with no apparent Jerry Kennedy involvement. So, Snuff and Ross's "Eefin' Alvin" was in good, if weird, company.

Chapter 6 · 1958

Ross Bagdasarian, aka David Seville.

LPs

Counting the cash from David Seville's "Witch Doctor" and Chipmunks records, Liberty realized that Seville had scored Liberty's only two #1's, both in the same year, and then—Liberty released some more albums. Other LPs at this time were *Spotlight on Bud and Travis; Roaring '20s in Hi-Fi,* an LP by Si's old colleague Lionel Newman; and a *Singin'* '30s LP. *Julie at Home* was Julie London's newest seductive release.

The Johnny Mann group had had no hits yet in 1958. One of their early LPs was a companion record to the instrumental Liberty fight-song LP, *Half Time,* but with vocal versions of college songs. Later Johnny Mann would provide the music for ABC's late-night Joey Bishop TV show, a "Tonight Show" competitor. Johnny Mann would prove his true worth at Liberty later.

The very first Liberty LP had been LRP 3001, Don Swan's *Mucho Cha Cha Cha.* Well, from out of Liberty's recent past came Don Swan, back with LRP 3068, *All This and Cha Cha Cha, Too* and later LRP 3114, *Hot Cha Cha.*

From the 1940s and RCA, Spike Jones came to Liberty. Spike Jones never enjoyed the success at Liberty that marked his earlier associations, but he had fun with rock and roll and songs such as "Spookie, Spookie, Lend Me Your Comb" (a satire on the hit "Kookie, Kookie, Lend Me Your Comb" by TV actor Edd ("Kookie") Byrnes of TV's "77 Sunset Strip" fame), and "Mairzy Doats" on an LP called *60 Years of Music America Hates Best*.

The Chipmunks' next LP was *Sing Again with the Chipmunks*, and Julie London expanded her repertoire when she showed both cleavage *and* legs on the cover of *Around Midnight*.

Hollywood veteran Harry Sukman released an LP, *Command Performance*, a title that would be used again several years later for an unrelated Liberty album release by Jan & Dean.

Also-Rans

Besides the big records that became classic hits, Liberty released many obscure ones each year that are now lost to history.

Diana Lee sang in a totally uninhibited style. She opens her 45 "You Upset Me" with what can only be described as a Rebel yell. The whole song, in fact, is more yelled and screamed than sung, with a tiny guitar-drum combo in the background. Imagine Ellie Mae Clampett after a jug of "Kickapoo Joy Juice" and you get the idea. The flip side, "L-O-V-E Love," sounds like Ellie Mae doing her impression of a cross between Wanda Jackson and Frankie Avalon, with Buddy Holly hiccups thrown in—a real period classic.

Patience and Prudence were back in 1958 with "Witchcraft," an original if undistinguished song in their usual girlish, soft style. The flip side, "Over Here," is about bullfighting.

The Lettermen were at Liberty in 1958, some time before their hit period at Capitol Records. Their style at Liberty was quite unique and unlike their later style. "Hey, Big Brain," is about a guy who answers simple questions like "What is 1 and 1" as if they were tough, to a background borrowed from "Kookie, Kookie, Lend Me Your Comb" as if performed by the Hollywood Argyles. On the other side, "Guiro" consists of humming in harmony, then yelling "Guiro!" The harmonizing foreshadows their later Capitol hits, but just barely. Really odd, except in the context of hits like "Witch Doctor," "The Chipmunk Song," and "Heartbreak Hotel."

Terry Miller sounded like a young Robert Goulet on "Walkin' with the Blues" and "Single and Searchin'," singing far too well for a 1958 kids' song about meeting a girl at a candy store.

Ideas at Liberty

A lot of thought went into most projects at Liberty, from the albums to the record labels. Si Waronker and his staff/friends used to sit for hours and hours and try to think of new ways to merchandise and record. There were two rows of little stars on the top of the album covers, which made it much easier to find Liberty LPs in those tight record racks in the stores. "The stars were made for that. We built our own two-track machines at the end of nineteen fifty-seven when we moved into our first big office, at La Brea, because the studio did not have them and we couldn't afford to buy them! So we built them. All I did was take two recording heads and place them together, hooked up to two different microphone systems. We recorded that way, on one-quarter-inch tape.

"As soon as I got the idea for Liberty Records and got clearance, we used the Statue of Liberty. The first label was one color because we couldn't afford full-color printing. The rainbow was something I added to give it more oomph. But when we were pressing the Chipmunks record, they ran out of colored paper and it was pressed with no Liberty logo at all! As time went by, and we saw what we could do for an extra nickel, we did the rainbow-color version.

"Our first label, I ordered green paper. I told them to keep it on hand: we would be around a long time. Then I found records with a black label! They told me that they had run out of green. First Capitol pressed for us, then RCA. Then a couple of independent pressers. They had to get their paper, and very often it was different. We wanted our own pressing plant, but I had to stop somewhere. A lot of Liberty labels are bootlegs. You can see them because the colors are not reproduced so well. When I was in New York and the Chipmunk record was so big they were hawking them on the corner like knock-off watches, I saw them in black labels and yellow labels. They were bootlegs."

Si came up with other innovations too. "In fact, I was the guy who started the hot wrap on albums. I figured, hey, it costs only two cents an album more, and they will store indefinitely that way. But everybody wondered what the hell I was doing! I'm the guy who started putting the glossy finish on albums for another penny an album. We tried anything to get a reputation of quality, any kind of music. The paper sleeve inside the album cover was another idea we did later, even adding printing on it after a while. It was to protect the record. The cover was decorative. The record stores had the smell of the lamination of the covers."

In the years 1956 through 1959, there were many attempts to come up with successful albums. Si loved jazz and befriended performers who would go to a recording studio such as Gold Star and record material that they would then take around to all the labels. At most companies these jazz musicians couldn't get past the secretary. But Si knew many of them from his Fox years, and since the material was already recorded and cost Si nothing to release, it was an easy way to acquire some nice jazz for the catalog: Abe Most — Jimmy Rowles — Barney Kessell — Hollywood Saxophone Quartet — Red Norvo.

It was not jazz, certainly, which saved Liberty in 1958. It was "Witch Doctor" and "The Chipmunk Song," plus the other hits that got Liberty out of hock: "Summertime Blues" and "C'mon Everybody," written and performed by Eddie Cochran, and Ross Bagdasarian's follow-up to "Witch Doctor," "The Bird on My Head."

As much as Ross Bagdasarian, Al Bennett was responsible for pulling Liberty out of the musical morass in 1958. So, at the year-end Liberty Christmas party, Si burned all of the company's debt paper in a small ceremony.

Then he gave gifts of Liberty stock to the Liberty employees who had worked without paychecks without even complaining. Bobbie Dieterly got 2 percent, Hal Linnick (treasurer) 5 percent. Attorneys Seymour Zucker and Ray Sandler got 5 percent each. And Al Bennett? His share was already 10 percent, and was raised to 25 percent that Christmas. Finally Al was made the new president of Liberty, while Si stayed on as chairman of the board. The New Year was celebrated by all, at a party with Dick Clark, a staunch supporter of Liberty.

CHAPTER 7

1959

Martin Denny, Bobby Vee, Dolphin Records, the Fleetwoods, the Frantics, and Little Bill and the Blue Notes

Around 1959 Liberty began to diversify. Bud and Travis, a country duo, were added to the label. Their hit singles in 1959 on Liberty included "The Ballad of the Alamo" and the semi–rock 'n' roll song "Tell Her No" (not the same song as the Zombies' 1965 record). "Tell Him No" was much bigger as done the same year by Travis and Bob on Sandy Records. Still, it was indicative of a continuing trend at Liberty away from adult pop to the emerging teen-pop sounds.

Eddie Cochran had his least successful chart single, "Teenage Heaven." Sung to the tune of the Kansas State song, "Home on the Range," it talks about staying up all night and living in a house with a swimming pool.

Ross Bagdasarian hit the mark again with "Alvin's Harmonica." Like so many Chipmunk holiday-related records, "Alvin's Harmonica" was played for many years, and indeed is still played today at Christmastime. It not only made the top of the charts in 1959 but charted again in 1961 and 1962.

"Alvin's Harmonica" was yet another fluke, that wonderful luck that seemed to bless Si's Liberty in its first eight years. "Ross wanted to record a Chipmunk tune with Alvin [who was now the star] playing the harmonica. In those days multiple channel recording was in its infancy, so any sounds that we wanted to superimpose had to be done on the master track. We had finished the recording without the harmonica or Ross superimposing the final track. Ross would always put his voice on last.

"I hired Jerry Adler, in my opinion the best available harmonica player in Hollywood, to play on the record. Ross was on the stage with Jerry to cue Jerry when to play. I was in the sound booth. We started our first take. Jerry put on his earphones and we started. Jerry thought this was a rehearsal. The intro started. The Chipmunks were singing, with Alvin insisting that he wanted to play the harmonica. This was the cue Ross gave to Jerry. Jerry froze, and the sounds that came out of his harmonica were hilarious. Ross was gesticulating to keep the tape rolling. I yelled at Ted, the engineer, to keep the tape going and almost died from laughing. Poor Jerry. He thought the take was just a rehearsal. Oh, no. This had to be it. Jerry begged for another chance. Ross hugged Jerry and I promised Jerry a substantial bonus and sent him home. Ross now had a reason to have David scream at Alvin. 'Alvin, Alvin, what are you doing?!' The record was a smash hit."

Liberty merchandising director Allan Lavinger adds that "'Alvin's Harmonica' almost wasn't released. On it David Seville says, 'All right Alvin, make a fool of yourself!' Al Bennett said you can't have a record with the word 'fool' for kids. We all had our jaws hanging down. I guess 'fool' means something else in Arkansas where Al was from. But it did go out and sold about a million and a quarter."

The Chipmunks were odd, to say the least, compared to the other things that were making the charts in the late 1950s. In his own way, Martin Denny, with his sound-effects-laden records, was no less odd. In fact, about the only animals not on Martin Denny records were chipmunks!

Martin Denny

Martin Denny was a pianist who played classical music at age ten amd then later, following college, toured South America with a jazz group. Playing at Don the Beachcomber's in Honolulu, Denny decided to settle in Hawaii. When he signed with Liberty, Denny had a three-man combo. Julius Wechter (who later founded the Baja Marimba band) played marimba and vibes and did the arranging for the group, and Harvey Ragsdale played marimba and bass. That pretty well defines the Denny sound, except for one important detail. That detail was August Colon, "Augie," who played bongos, congas, and contributed a plethora of bird calls. Their sound was esoteric as well as exotic. Augie's—er—talent for making bird and animal noises was so spectacular that he even had his own Liberty LP, *Chant of the Jungle*.

In 1958 Denny's LPs sold respectably well. In 1959 Martin Denny provided Liberty with a hit 45, "Quiet Village." He also had several smaller hits in the same vein. "Quiet Village," composed by bandleader Les Baxter, became a musical classic, turning up as late as 1984 as mood music in the Sylvester Stallone–Dolly Parton feature film *Rhinestone*.

Martin Denny was signed to Liberty by none other than Si Waronker himself. Arnie Mills was one of the Hollywood agents with whom Si was close because of his movie studio days. Mills's biggest client was Liberace. Denny and his group were signed by Arnie when he was in Hawaii, and Arnie brought to Si a dub of a recording Denny had made of "Quiet Village."

Si listened to the dub and liked it. "I told Arnie that everything was great about the recording, but that it was so slow that I was ready to fall asleep. It was so slow it was almost boring. I said I wanted to rerecord it at a faster tempo. We also added many more bird sounds than on the original demo.

"'Quiet Village' was a very big hit. I don't want to say it was a million seller. It was very hard and rare for a record to sell a million in those days. Everyone liked to say they had sold a million, but it was really more like three hundred thousand when anyone claimed a million. But this was a big seller."

Snuff Garrett: "Martin Denny was produced by Si, but I did A&R and picked out songs for him like 'I'm in a Dancin' Mood' that I liked a lot, and I did a hit with him, 'A Taste of Honey,' in nineteen sixty-two."

Si Waronker liked albums with a hook. For example, Martin Denny records featured animal noises, so an entire LP could have songs with noises. "With Julie London, we could do a whole album [like 1958's suggestively titled *Your Number,*

Martin Denny's *Quiet Village* LP cover. We never saw Denny, just the exotic models.

Please] that sounded like that song. I used to like to do thirteen tunes that had the same sound. Every cut had a certain thing that sounded like the thing preceding it. We were selling mood as well as tune. We didn't want to change the sound. I used thirteen cuts for luck.

"Martin Denny had that one record, 'Quiet Village,' that meant a great deal. And that was him. Martin Denny was really a cocktail piano player. He had one guy with him who really had the talent, one guy who did the bird sounds. He left. Then Augie was the one who stayed with Martin. He did some of the bird sounds, and we finally had him do them all. To keep them handy, I made a whole bunch of different bird sounds on a separate tape, in case we needed more and they were out of town. Jimmy Rolls also played piano in the group." Sometimes Martin Denny himself had to be in the control booth. "Denny made a lot of money. But the birds! We put birds in everything, because people wanted to hear birds."

Martin Denny LPs had names like *Exotica* and *Primitiva*. "*Exotica* was a name I made up," says Si. "I never heard that word before. But the dame in the cover photo looked exotic, so I called her 'Exotica' for a Martin Denny album. Sandy Warner was her name, and we used her on every one of the Martin Denny covers because she photographed so beautifully." There were also *Exotica II; Exotica III; Fantastica,* by the Russ Garcia Orchestra; and *Primitiva* by Martin Denny. And the immortal *Hypnotique,* inevitably by Martin Denny. "All of those *ica* endings and *itiva* endings I came up with because I thought I was being cute. And I don't know why, but nobody got wise."

Si Waronker was always coming up with new names. His early Liberty albums had liner notes boasting of extra-good recording quality. "With 'Spectra-Sonic,' I just wanted an identity. You're the only person who ever asked about that. That was a spur-of-the-moment type of thing. We had such a super sound, supposedly, that we charged a dollar more per record sometimes. These were just tricks I pulled to try to get someplace when I was broke."

Rock 'n' roll would sell Liberty's 45s, but the early LPs had been sold by Julie London and Martin Denny, all of them featuring very sexy covers. So Liberty tried some more hot-cover-art albums. Franklin MacCormack had no hit singles, he was a poet from the Bible belt. His album, *The Torch Is Burning*, was subtitled "The Poetic Voice of Franklyn McCormack." How can a voice be poetic? Just more of Si's shenanigans. "We just put that album out to let the record distributors know Liberty was still in business. We had no money, and no artists, so we just did this album. We didn't expect it to sell, and it didn't sell any at all." But the girl on the front was a blond variation on the dark, exotic beauty of Sandy Warner of the Denny LP covers, and her chest development on the cover of *The Torch Is Burning* was even more impressive than Julie London's. And speaking of sexy LP covers, the Sandy on the cover of Martin Denny's *Primitiva LP* was almost — well, instead of the "Exotic Sounds of Martin Denny," it should have been called the *Erotic Sounds of Martin Denny*.

Between recording the torch and mood-music LPs, Liberty found time for *Half Time*, an LP of college recording marching band songs. Liberty then signed the up-and-coming Henry Mancini. The contract apparently wasn't ironclad, however, as in 1959 Mancini went to RCA and the hit TV-theme LP, *Mr. Lucky*. Oops, a good one got away!

An historian or archivist relies on a variety of sources to piece together the story of an organization such as Liberty Records. Recollections of participants are helpful, but they can be hazy, imprecise, and contradictory. Actual records are very valuable. Industry record charts, such as *Billboard*, are beyond value. And then there are the catalogs put together and sent out periodically by the company itself.

What better source could there be than the company's own catalogs. Here the people inside the company — the people in charge and having day-to-day involvement — put down in black and white a permanent accounting of what was released, when, and with a photo of each album cover. Sounds ideal.

Except, looking at Liberty's 1960s catalogs, it appears that Martin Denny had at least four LPs released before the *Quiet Village* LP. *Exotica* is LP number 3034, and *Exotica II* is LP number 3077. *Primitiva* is LP number 3087. *Exotica III* is LP number 3116. Those numbers would seem to indicate that four Denny LPs were released in 1958, the year before "Quiet Village" was a hit.

But the number on 1959s *Quiet Village*, which Si says was the first Denny LP, is 3122! How can that be?

Si: "You've got to forget about the numbers, and I'll tell you why. Here is a company that started, it should be, with album one. And then go consecutively up the ladder. But I did not want it to go two, three, four. So I would go from 1, then add a thousand. So thirty-one hundred could very well have been in reality LP number thirty-one. We screwed the numbers up purposely. That way, everybody thought that we had this big catalog. I don't know why I thought of these crazy things. But none of the numbers make any sense. I thought it was good merchandising. But now I think it is mostly funny."

Funny? It sure drives an historian crazy. "Yes, but I never thought Liberty would last long enough for anyone to care about its history! I will say that as time

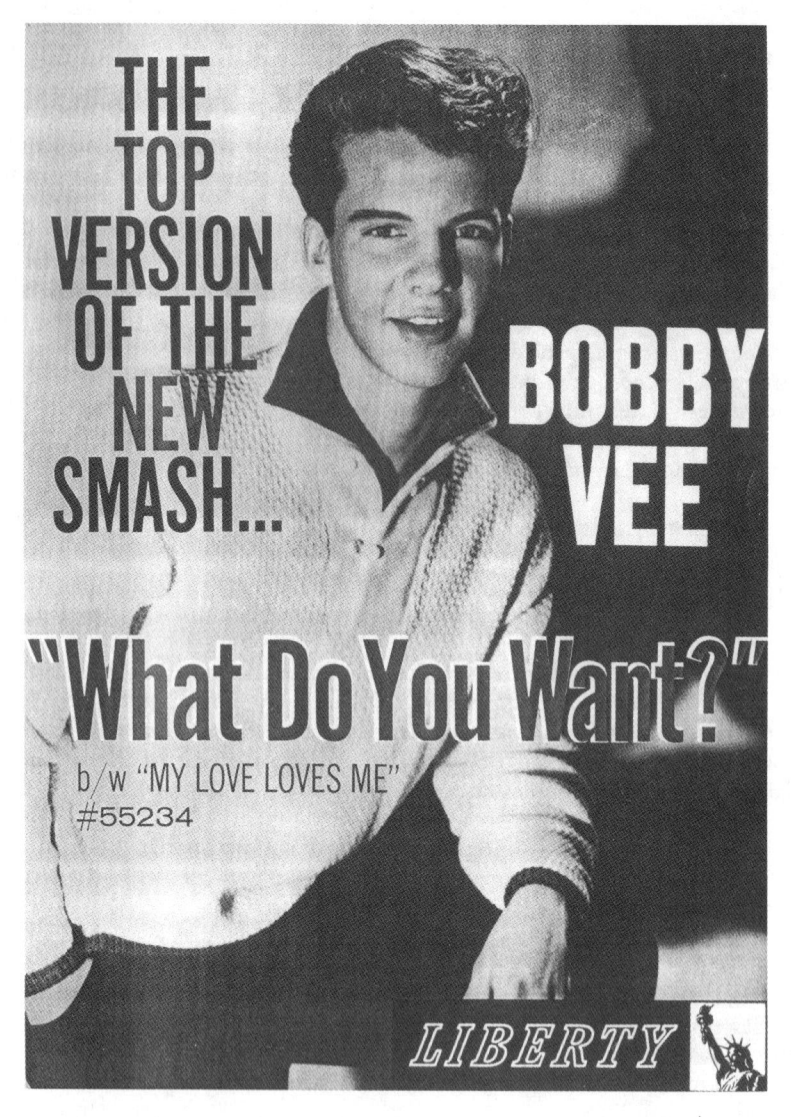

Liberty trade ad for Bobby Vee's first Liberty recording. (*Courtesy Bob Celli.*)

went on and we did build the catalog, then numbers became more meaningful. But originally number thirty-one hundred two could have meant album number thirty-two."

Bobby Vee

More rock 'n' roll loomed near, as Liberty unexpectedly signed the biggest rock 'n' roll act of the label's history. In 1959 a young man (fourteen-year-old boy, actually) from Fargo, North Dakota, filled in for Buddy Holly the day the latter died in the plane crash that also took Ritchie Valens ("La Bamba," 1959) and the Big Bopper ("Chantilly Lace," 1958). This fill-in gig was Bobby's first performance, professional or otherwise, but it launched a career that has lasted into the 1990s.

Legend has it that a Liberty talent scout was at the show the night Bobby Vee filled in for Buddy Holly, saw him, and signed him to Liberty. But Bobby himself tells what the real chronology of events was.

The concert at which Buddy Holly was to have starred was February 9, 1959. No talent scout there. But Bobby and his brother's band, the Shadows, were well received, continued to work locally after that night, and cut "Suzie Baby" for a local label, Soma, three months later. It was a hit, the song became a local #1 record, and many labels contacted Bobby about a national deal.

Amos Heilicher was the regional promotion man for Liberty Records (or perhaps a powerful record distributor in Minneapolis — there is a difference of recollection on this point) who contacted Bobby in June 1959. This contact resulted in a deal to pick up "Suzie Baby" nationally, with an option to pick up Bobby's contract.

That summer, on the strength of the one local hit, "Suzie Baby," Bobby made the decision not to enroll in high school that fall. At sixteen, he had a terrible sick feeling in the pit of his stomach as he worked on his dad's front porch in September, watching all the other kids walking to school. He was afraid that in dropping out he had made the wrong decision, as his school counselor said he had.

Liberty picked up Bobby Vee's contract in December 1959, and in January Bobby flew to California for his first session, at which he cut "What Do You Want?" with Snuff Garrett.

"What Do You Want?" was currently the number one record in England, as performed by newcomer Adam Faith. Faith eventually had two dozen hits in England, and two minor hits in the United States on Amy records in 1965, the biggest being "It's All Right."

Bobby Vee's older brother Bill's garage band was called the Shadows. Bobby Vee had served as the lead singer for the Shadows when they filled in for Buddy Holly, but only because he knew the lyrics to a few songs. Guitar bands did not become popular (except as local entertainers) until the later 1960s. By the time of his death, even Buddy Holly had left his Crickets behind, preferring strings and things as musical accompaniment. So Bobby Vee and the Shadows were offered separate contracts by Liberty. The Shadows faded into the shadows, while Bobby Vee moved permanently into the limelight after a couple of false starts in 1960. That first Liberty record, "What Do You Want?" did chart but was not a top-forty hit nationwide.

Getting back to Liberty's bankable moneymakers, new LP releases at this time included Martin Denny's *Exotic Percussion* as well as Seville's *Around the World with the Chipmunks*. Then, with a Bob Wills and the Texas Playboys LP added to the Bud and Travis product, Liberty almost seemed ready to become a country label. Bobby Vee, in 1959, was the only new Liberty rock 'n' roll success since Margie Rayburn back in 1957, and Bobby had strong country roots.

Liberty released many records by other artists besides the hit makers. A few of the more notable or successful of those will be mentioned for each year to help give a more complete picture of the Liberty story. For instance, Joe London was an obscure Liberty artist who recorded a single titled "It Might Have Been" in November.

Indeed it might have been, but for Joe it wasn't. Equally obscure was Buddy Lee Stuart. His Liberty single was "I Miss Your Kissing." His sound was a pop-soft rock 'n' roll sound, sort of a cross between Jack Jones ("Wives and Lovers," 1963) and the Crew Cuts ("Earth Angel," 1956). Like Joe London, Buddy failed to score a hit with Liberty.

It was almost 1960, and Liberty began to see the writing on the wall—rock 'n' roll was here to stay—the music, if not all the artists! In the fast-paced world of the new sound, Margie Rayburn, Patience and Prudence, Billy Ward, and Eddie Cochran records were already strictly oldies. Liberty did have Bobby Vee, but he could turn out the hits only so fast, and the label needed more than one hit maker.

Dolphin Records

It was time to branch out. Liberty's own record label (the physical paper glued to the records, on which the title was printed) had originally been either red, blue, or green paper with hard-to-read silver printing and a reproduction of the Statue of Liberty at the top. In 1959 the Liberty label color was changed to black, which made the silver printing considerably easier to read. The other big modification was the addition of a rainbow section filling the left side of the label, with the Statue of Liberty now depicted there. This was how the Liberty label would appear, with minor variations, for the rest of the company's history.

In 1959 Liberty acquired subsidiary or sister record label, Dolphin Records. The paper label of the new subsidiary, Dolphin, seemed patterned after the new Liberty design. The paper was light blue, with contrasting dark blue printing. At the top were three modernistic (for the time) dolphins. "Dolphin" was printed down the left side, where a section corresponding to the rainbow section of the Liberty label was closed off. The farther down each letter was printed, the fainter it got, as if the letters were sinking deeper into the ocean. The Dolphin label was distinctive yet clearly showed its relationship to Liberty's label, and it was extremely eye pleasing and easy to read.

The pastel blue of the Dolphin label complemented the ultrasoft sounds of the first Dolphin release, "Come Softly To Me." This song was a groundbreaking rock 'n' roll event. Until this record, the vast majority of rock 'n' roll had been of the hard-driving, bluesy variety, typified by Lloyd Price, Chuck Berry, Bill Haley, the Coasters, Bobby Day, and a host of others. True, there *were* rock 'n' roll ballads, such as "Love Me Tender" (1956) by Elvis, "Sea of Love" (1959) by Phil Phillips, "Stardust" (1957) by Billy Ward and the Dominoes, "All I Have to Do Is Dream" (1958) by the Everly Brothers, and "Raining in My Heart" (1959) by Buddy Holly. But while despite being ballads, these songs were still forcefully delivered. Even the Teddybears' "To Know Him Is to Love Him" (1959), a very mellow record on the pastel blue Dore label, grows to an emotional crescendo here and there. But Dolphin's "Come Softly to Me" opened up new vistas of possibilities for the music.

Bob Reisdorff

Bob Reisdorff was the founder and owner of Dolphin—the Si Waronker of Dolphin, you might say. He started Dolphin (also known as Dolton) before he got

This was the only Dolphin record ever released. The name was changed to Dolton at the insistence of another company named Dolphin.

the Fleetwoods, when he was head of promotion of C&C Distributing, based in Seattle. C&C handled all the independent labels, which was everything except RCA, Capitol, Columbia, Decca—the majors as they were called. C&C had nearly everything else from the Northwest. There were a few smaller distributors who had Dot Records in Oregon or Coral Records in Seattle or some other small local arrangement of that sort.

Bob Reisdorff had ambition. He wanted to be more than a promotional man for a regional distributor. "I thought that if I was going to stay in the music business, I should start my own company. I liked my employer, Lou Lavinthal, very much, along with his partners, Stan Solman and Stan Jaffe. They became my partners. We formed Dolton and started a publishing company together.

"I did this through Si Zucker at Liberty's legal department." Reisdorff knew Zucker through their mutual record connections; there was no true Liberty connection as yet. "Si Zucker was so pure, he wouldn't even drink cocoa because it has some kind of element in it that would make you jumpy or nervous [the 'element' was caffeine]; he certainly would not drink liquor. But he had a very sedentary way of life, and apparently that caught up with him. He died as a young man about nineteen seventy-five or eighty. He was a delightful man, I liked him in every way. He was also a CPA and was always going through the books at Liberty to see if everything was right for the company.... Another man, Hal Linick, was the officer and stockholder in charge of artist royalties at Liberty."

For the previous two or three years, as a record distributor, Bob Reisdorff had been doing nothing but listening to records. "I did not care what the labels told me about the music. I would listen to every record and every flip side, as well as many,

many albums, putting the needle down for the count of twenty. Hundreds and hundreds of records — we had everything, Atlantic, King, Specialty, Imperial, Mercury, MGM, London, Dot, Gone, on and on. About all we did not have was Epic and Coral."

Because of this experience, Reisdorff knew the music business, but even more than that, he knew the Northwest music scene. "Regional hits were important, because that could form a base for a national hit." And he had an ear for hits after years of reviewing records daily and constantly, around sixty singles a week, and album cuts on top of that.

"The most fascinating part of the job was listening to records. If I liked one, I would go with it. I sometimes made a record a Northwest hit by pushing it. I pushed a record by Mantovani that became a hit in the Northwest. Sometimes the label would take a record I had broken regionally and go with it for the rest of the country.

"I would listen to any album that looked like it had promise. We broke the Liberty hit 'Quiet Village,' by Martin Denny. When that became a hit in Seattle, Liberty refused to release the song as a single, so we had to sell people the album. When I got all the DJs playing 'Quiet Village,' we sold a monumental number of albums for our size market. Finally Liberty released it as a single, but they had to cut the LP version down from about four or five minutes to about two and a half to three. They had Augie, who was a real native Hawaiian, doing all of the animal sounds. And Julius Wechter played vibes and later became prominent as an A&R man."

There is an alternate version of how "Quiet Village" got off the Denny LP and became a single hit. It is told by Bob Lavinger, Liberty director of merchandising, who worked at Liberty as long as anyone, from 1958 to 1970.

"Martin Denny's 'Quiet Village' became a hit. It hit first as an R&B record in Detroit. Some black DJ in Detroit played it and it started from there. It was a B-side, too, of something called 'Llama Serenade.'" But what about Bob Reisdorff's story about pushing 'Quiet Village' when it was an album cut in Seattle and asking Liberty to release it on a single? "Well, maybe that is why they threw it on the back of this other thing," Lavinger speculates. "Also, the forty-five cut was cut down from the album version and speeded up a little bit to fit radio and jukebox requirements."

Controversies like who broke "Quiet Village" fade to little significance when compared to other problems Bob Reisdorff had to deal with.

"Organized crime tried paying me when I was a promotion man. They wanted me on their payroll because the Northwest was breaking a lot of records. I went straight to my employer with the fifty dollars in my pocket, and he said, 'Fine, take the money.' Lou was a gem of a guy, and I loved him, but I told him that they already were leaning on me saying that there was more where that came from. I told him it was not necessary. This guy was just in the record business, not the other stuff."

Bob Reisdorff resisted the attempts to influence his musical "taste" and continued to select songs on their merit, ignoring the Mafia attempts at influence.

"I always listened to flip sides, always. As a matter of fact, Andy Williams called me when he made 'Hawaiian Wedding Song' because Archie Blyer at Cadence Records was pushing the other side. There was no doubt in my mind what was the hit side. The minute I got it I went out to key disc jockeys and called other ones and said, 'Listen to this.' Archie called me and asked me if I really believed.... I said, 'Archie, believe me, believe me, it's the right side, and it will be a big one!' It was already big for us.

"It was a month later that Andy Williams called me and thanked me very much."

It was all this concentrated experience listening to every new record that came out that permitted Bob to recognize 'Come Softly' as a potential hit when he first heard the tape.

"After the label was formed, I had waited to hear something come along that I liked, which turned out to be Gretchen Christopher."

The Fleetwoods

"Gretchen had taken a homemade tape to Norm Bobrow, who for a long time was an important disc jockey in the Seattle area. He was not top forty, but was jazz and offbeat things. He was a great talker on the air. He opened the Colony Club on a shoestring and was always on the edge of bankruptcy. He happened to find Pat Suzuki, 'Miss Ponytail,' and Gretchen. I was helping to book talent into the Colony; I knew all the Northwest DJs and some California ones, too, and had connections.

"Norm brought me Gretchen's tape called 'Come Softly,' and we laughed at the title." Eventually, for the record release, the title was changed to "Come Softly to Me" to avoid any unintended double entendre. But until it was released, it was always called "Come Softly." "Norm said that he had told Gretchen to take it to me [Bob Reisdorff], so she did."

From here the story of the discovery of the Fleetwoods is best told by the leader, if the Fleetwoods can be said to have had one, Gretchen Christopher. Gretchen's professional career began when she was still in high school, when she got a job at Norm Bobrow's Colony Club. "I was dancing solo at the Colony," relates Gretchen. "Pat Suzuki was singing there. I had auditioned as a singer, not realizing who Pat Suzuki was, and was sort of patted on the head and told, 'Well, since we have Pat Suzuki, we don't really need a singer.'

"I told them, 'Well, I dance, too.' In fact, I was appearing as a dancer, as well as singing a solo, on television. I asked Norm, who was not only the owner and manager of the club but Pat's manager, to watch my dance performance on TV, which he did. I came over to the club after that, and he said about my dancing, 'You're wonderful. But you don't need that male partner. In fact, he's a detriment rather than an asset.' And apparently he thought that I had a wonderful quality in my face that was similar to the quality that Pat Suzuki had. Not that we looked alike, but a similar quality. Norm called Pat down to meet me, and he was then going to allow me to 'showcase' on spring vacation—which of course is performing without pay. But the Colony was a class club that was getting national attention at the time because Pat Suzuki was about to appear on Broadway in *Flower Drum Song*. When Bing Crosby came to Seattle, he came to the Colony because of the fine reputation that she was getting.

"From there it was a classic story. The following week Norm called me in

Gretchen Christopher, founding member of the Fleetwoods. (*Courtesy Gretchen Christopher.*)

Olympia. Pat Suzuki was ill, and Norm wanted to know if my mother and I could come to Seattle on the Greyhound bus, and then I could do the show in her place. He felt sure that Pat would be well enough to do the second show. So he paid all the expenses for us to come up and stay in a hotel.

"When I did the show, I got rave written reviews. The audience that night responded so warmly that Norm had me do the second show with Pat and then stay and perform the weekend. The written reviews were in the *Seattle Post-Intelligencer,* by Emmett Watson, who is like Herb Caen is to San Francisco. One of my classmates told me, 'You made Emmett Watson!' I said, 'What's Emmett Watson?' She said, 'Only *the* columnist in the *Seattle P-I.*'

"His rave review, unfortunately, caught the eye of the liquor board. I was only eighteen years old at the time, and while you could attend this very nice supper club with your family and drink a Shirley Temple if you were five years old, as a minor you could not perform there unless you were eighteen inches up off the floor on the stage! Of course the band was on the stage. I was the floor show, dancing, with my ballet and jazz background."

The Colony Club connection was opportunity knocking at Gretchen Christopher's door. A less talented, less resourceful, less intelligent—and less prepared—woman might have let that opportunity slip by. But Gretchen had been working for most of her young seventeen-odd years, unconsciously for the most part perhaps, toward the moment that knock would come. The roots of the Fleetwoods reach back to Gretchen's kindergarten-preschool days with fellow Fleetwood-to-be, Barbara Ellis.

"Barbara and I had been playmates when we were about five, and had gone to first and second grades together. I don't remember that we were any great friends then, but we had been as preschoolers.

"I moved out to the country and attended South Bay Grade School until the ninth grade, and attended different schools from Barbara." Then they were reunited when Gretchen attended Washington Junior High School. "Barbara also came to Washington Junior High School. We were both selected as cheerleaders there, so we served as cheerleaders together on Pep Staff. I loved cheerleading because it was the closest thing to dancing that school had to offer. I choreographed a can-can dance for the cheerleaders for the spring concert, and we also did some singing in the spring concert. I think that's where the idea of singing together came from. After that she went to North Thurston High School and I went to Olympia High School.

"Then, in our senior year, she came over to Olympia High, and that was when we got together to sing. We were planning to have a girl group, and we auditioned a couple of other girls." One, by her own characterization, "couldn't carry a tune in a bucket," and the other was too busy with other activities.

"The song that we auditioned them with was 'In the Still of the Night' [Five Satins, 1956]. But they just kept singing louder and louder, and I was telling them, 'Sing softly, softly. Think of the *still* of the night.' When that audition for group members was over and unsuccessful, I stayed. I think I had been playing the piano chords for the auditions. Anyway I used those chords, building on the idea of 'Softly,' and that was how I started writing 'Come Softly to Me.'

"Later, when I was partially finished with it, Barbara joined me. I invited her to harmonize, to sing along with me and the chords I was playing on the piano. And I bounced some of my lyric ideas off her."

That was how Barbara and Gretchen got together, and that was also how the original song "Come Softly" came about. It was a song that seemed complete in itself.

In time, however, "Come Softly" took a back seat to another song that Gretchen liked. "Barbara and I were doing an arrangement of 'Stormy Weather' and thought that it would be nice if there were a blues trumpet behind it. We contacted a combo at our high school, and they brought Gary in. He couldn't play in our key, and we couldn't sing in his. So that was the end of that." But it was the beginning of the Fleetwoods: "Gary asked to walk me downtown after school that night.

"We were standing on the street corner waiting for my mother to pick me up. Gary started humming what he considered in his head to be a jazz trumpet riff. I could hear that it was based on the same chord progression as 'Come Softly,' so I asked him to keep it up but slow it down as I sang 'Come Softly' in counterpoint against it. He had never heard the song; I had just composed it. It was a pretty remarkable incident. I think that I probably had the ability to hear that his humming and my song would fit together because of my classical exposure, Bach and music like that. I didn't think of that myself at the time, but some disc jockey later mentioned that counterpoint goes right back to Bach, and I had danced to some of that. I was raised on classical music as well as jazz and the old standards."

While at the Colony Club, Gretchen met Seattle record promoter Bob Reisdorff. She made the most of this acquaintance. "I took him a home tape recording I had made; he listened to it and said it would sell a million! He was right. 'Come Softly to Me' became the first gold record produced in the Northwest." (The second was the Fleetwoods' "Mr. Blue.")

As it was presented to Bob Reisdorff, "Come Softly to Me" was far from ready for release as a 45. He needed to edit it and seek appropriate musical accompaniment.

Bob Reisdorff: "The song went on for seven or eight minutes on the tape that the Fleetwoods made at home. They did not know any better; they were just enchanted with the whole thing. It was spontaneous. Gary [with his "Do Doobie Do Dum Dum"] was doing a takeoff on the Del Vikings' 'Come Go with Me.' They all had a good natural musical sense of feeling. I was personally enchanted with their a capella tape, with just Gary's keys, which was on the actual record as well." That was the only accompaniment on the original tape — Gary's key ring clinking in time to the song.

"We were also thinking of recording Bonnie Guitar for Dolphin. So I was trying to think of an instrumental background for this tape, never having produced a record in my life. I was a good critic, but this was my first time creating a record myself. Everything was ready to do."

Bob wanted Bonnie Guitar's help producing the record. But he says that Bonnie said no. "'Don't do anything. The reason you love it so much is because you love it as it is.' I told her she was right. She was a very good guitar player, however, and she did put an acoustic guitar on it. Then Bonnie and I took the tape down to LA to Western Studios on Sunset Boulevard, got ourselves a bass player, and added a bass.

"At three o'clock in the morning, after we finished mastering it, I took the tape to Gene Weed at KFWB which was the dominant station at that time. I knew him and others there. They are talk now, but they were a huge top-forty pop station then. He put the acetate on for me at three o'clock in the morning and said they would give me a decision whether they would program it or not."

At this point Reisdorff was sure that all would be smooth sailing for the company and the record from that point on. However, he was in for a rude awakening the very next day.

"I went back the next day, and they said, 'No, Bob.' I said, 'Why?' Their response was, 'Well, it just sits there.' I was surprised. I had total conviction that it was a hit and that everyone else would think so too. I was crushed! How could I be so wrong? But I had a few hundred pressed and took them back to Seattle to all the disc jockeys that I knew so well. They put it on the air and the phones lit up. It was an instant hit, a totally different experience than in LA. That was the beginning of Dolton [Dolphin] Records."

The simple, soothing sound of the Fleetwoods, and their soothing name, did well on Dolphin. It was one of the first major rock 'n' roll hits to be recorded as voices only at first, then to have instruments added.

Designating the song on the label as Dolphin Record No. 1 was apropos. Not only was it Dolphin Records' first release and the Fleetwoods' first record, it quickly became the #1 record in America as well. The Fleetwoods went on to have ten hits and more than a half-dozen LPs up through 1963, a very good run for late-1950s rock 'n' rollers!

When "Come Softly to Me" became #1, it made quite a statement about what kind of music teens wanted. Consider how many 1950s and 1960s artists—including Chuck Berry, Fats Domino, and Bill Haley—never had even one #1 record. Today, most rock critics and writers either ignore the Fleetwoods or disdain their soft-rock sound. Yet American teens in 1959, after absorbing a steady stream of country and rhythm-and-blues-flavored rough, boisterous, aggressive rock 'n' roll, were more than ready for "Come Softly to Me." In terms of the Liberty sound, this music was much more Julie London than Eddie Cochran, and neither of them ever even approached #1.

"Come Softly to Me" was, however, the only #1 Dolphin Records ever had. Technically, "Come Softly to Me" was the *only* record Dolphin ever had. It seems there was this other record company that was already using the name Dolphin.

"I picked 'Dolphin' for the label's name because I had an affection for dolphins. I think *The Boy on the Dolphin* was a film going around at the time, and dolphins have such a fairy-tale kind of quality about them that I loved. It was not deeply thought out or anything—no one sat around for hours thinking about it. But they are lovely creatures, beautiful things.

"The name 'Dolphin' was cleared by the musicians' union; I believe that was the agency that gave those clearances for the name for a new company. But after we had our first hit, we got a letter from one of the major book publishers. It was a very nice letter: 'We envy your success, but we are afraid we are going to have to ask you to change the name.' I decided that I might as well keep the first three letters, so I just changed it from 'Dolphin' to 'Dolton.' Although the word 'Dolton' meant nothing at all. It was absolutely meaningless."

There is every reason to suppose that Bob Reisdorff's explanation of the reason the Dolphin name had to be dropped is accurate. However, Snuff Garrett recalls it slightly differently. "John Dolphin in downtown LA sued so they changed the label's name to Dolton."

In any event Bob Reisdorff did change the name of Dolphin Records. "In order to comply with their request, and our legal position was rather weak although we were not at fault, we changed our name. I suppose we could have gone ahead, but the letter had been written and we could possibly have been in trouble. I don't know whether that was true or not; I wasn't sophisticated enough at that time to know or to make the judgment. But I was advised to change it by the attorney at Liberty, Si Zucker."

He went to Si Zucker for help at this time, because it was Si who had originally

This Dolton (not Dolphin) tune was written by Jackie DeShannon and Sharon Sheeley. "Trouble" was written fort he Kalin Twins on Decca Records.

helped him set up Dolphin. "Si was head of the legal department at Liberty and was also a major stockholder. After much prodding—I had to torture it [how to start a label] out of him but I got it after six or seven months—he gave me the papers to put together the publishing and the record label, told me how to do it."

Interestingly, when Dolphin was rechristened Dolton Records, the blue label representing the ocean stayed, the letters turning lighter blue as they got deeper in the blue "ocean" stayed—even the three swimming dolphins at the top of the label stayed! Only the name was changed to protect the company.

How does a record label—the actual, physical paper label come about? It was easy for Bob Reisdorff.

"When we did Dolton number one, the record of 'Come Softly to Me,' we were under the clock to a certain degree. We had to get labels printed up. We wanted something simple. And we did not want to go through all of that expense of doing a full-color label. So instead of a full-color label, we had the shadings of blue, probably that was a two-color job. For the design I went to a fellow down the street who had a sign up, 'Graphic Artist,' or whatever it was. I went up and said, 'Hi. We have a music company. We're going to put out a record. Can you design a label?' So he did."

Why did Dolton Records start with 1 instead of some long number like other labels, which start with 55044 or 20001? Bob Reisdorff: "When I was in distribution, I would drop in to see Lou Chudd, the head of Imperial, whenever I was in LA. One day I told him that I had come down with a master for my own label. He advised me seriously, 'Don't do it. Don't do it. Don't put it out, it will sour you on the business. Forget it. Don't get into that!' But it was too late. I told him that I'd already told the printer to make the record label for Dolton number one. The label company said, 'Well, we've never done that before! No one starts with number one.' I told him, 'But this is the first record!' 'But, it's never been done!' But I said, 'What does it matter? It is the first record. I want it to read record number one. I'm not going to fool anyone to thinking we're an old company by using a big number."

Later the name change from "Dolphin" to "Dolton" took awhile to accomplish. In the interim "Come Softly to Me" was switched over to Liberty and quickly rereleased as Liberty record number 55188. The "55" stood for 1955, the year Liberty began, and "188" stood for record number 188, although Liberty had not actually released exactly that many 45s. Many numbers were assigned but were not released, and on rare occasions the same record number was used twice for different releases.

How did Liberty come to own Dolton? Through the Liberty attorney who had helped set up Dolphin originally. According to Reisdorff: "I had promised Liberty they could distribute Dolton nationally, because Si Zucker, the Liberty attorney, had helped me create Dolton. So I told them that if anything ever happens, you have distribution." From there it was only a logical next step for Liberty actually to buy Dolton.

Head Fleetwood Gretchen Christopher feels that she had something to say in the deal, as well. Gretchen explains: "My function was to look out for the Fleetwoods, and I was not compensated for that. I don't think it was even acknowledged that I was the leader or anything—at least not by me—though I do remember other artists assuming I was, to my astonishment, and asking if I received 10 percent extra for being leader! No, it never occurred to me. I just felt a sense of responsibility, just as a human being. In retrospect, yes, I was the one who made things happen. Someone else might express a desire, but I would take it seriously, make it a reality. Or someone else might express dissatisfaction, but I would be the one to go to the source, to work things out. I've always been a communicator—in my dancing, my music, my writing. From the beginning, Bob had me handle public relations for the Fleetwoods and appointed me spokesperson for interviews with the media." In the Fleetwoods' much later (1983) agreement, Gretchen is acknowledged as the Fleetwoods' founder and manager.

"During our Liberty days, Bob Reisdorff gave me a first edition of a classic book, which I value for the inscription he wrote: 'To Gretchen, who started the whole thing. Love, Bob.'

"Early on, there was a time when there were offers from other companies to buy the Fleetwoods' contract. But if Dolton had lost the Fleetwoods, then Dolton would have been an empty shell. Bob went with Liberty, which was already distributing Dolton, because they offered to buy the whole Dolton company, which they did. We had no choice in the matter. I felt we were auctioned off the block like slaves; because as artists, we received no part of the compensation from that sale.

"In Hollywood I auditioned and was selected to tour as the solo vocalist with a jazz group. Lou Rawls, who also auditioned, was their second choice. I was very tempted—loved to sing jazz—but decided, in fairness to everyone, I'd not put my solo career before the Fleetwoods. I felt our 'Fleetwooding,' as long as it lasted, was Barb's and Gary's one opportunity in show business. I felt I would have others, since I was committed to the arts and entertainment as my profession; whereas Barb's greatest aspiration had been to be a housewife, and Gary's was to work on cars, maybe have his own garage someday."

Having Dolton become a part of the Liberty family was not all sweetness and light, however Bob Reisdorff always had to look out for his own company. "I was in conflict with Liberty in many ways. Bob Skaff was head of promotion, and it was hard to get him to push and shove for Dolton. I demanded my own promotion man, but did not get him. There was a lot of very hard feeling there. I would describe Liberty as a very badly run company. It was not efficiently run. It was a crony-run company. I was very disappointed when they didn't even have a desk or a telephone for me.

"Al Bennett was a very dynamic man, a salesman type. Not, I don't think, a great business head. And not a musical man at all. But he was a very likable man, and as much as I was in conflict with him, I never disliked him. I would just be angry with him. When Avnet Electronics owned the company briefly, they forbade him to fire me when we had a big blowup.

"A lot of people were calling me, wanting to distribute 'Come Softly to Me.' One of the people we [C&C Distributing] had gone with and were helping a lot came and got the record off me and took it home and covered me. Which I thought was a very nasty, rotten thing to do. Especially when they were smiling in my face and saying how I had helped them with so many other records. This was an East Coast company with a made-up group. Era in LA tried to get the master off of me or at least get distribution, then they covered me when I said no." (By "covered me," Bob means that Era released their own version of "Come Softly to Me" on Doré Records by Ronnie Height, a black singer from Seattle.)

Having your own record and your own record company was, as Lou Chudd had warned, not all peaches and cream: "Randy Wood called from Dot. I knew all these people. They threatened, pressured me, that if I did not let them distribute, then they would cover me. So I stalled like hell to keep them from covering me since I was already committed to Liberty. I needed to get enough pressings out there to be safe. Even then, the Gone Records version, by Richard Barrett and the Chantels, took Chicago before we could get a foothold. We lost fifty percent of the volume. Their version was a fluke, because when any station heard our original, they went to it."

Getting Dolphin Records into the Liberty family was a pet project of Snuff Garrett's, and it was not as easy to accomplish as it may have seemed to Bob Reisdorff on the outside. "Bob Reisdorff, the founder of Dolphin, was a helluva nice guy. We got all these calls at Liberty that his first Dolphin release was a big hit up in Seattle, and we wanted it for Liberty, but Al said, 'Let's promote some of our own records! We can't pick up any more records, we're overloaded now, we can't get any more on the air, to hell with it. Let's work some of these records we've got.' He was right in his own way, but a week later the record was even bigger. So we went back and said this is going to be a monster, if we don't pick it up, someone else will.

"Al could have picked 'Come Softly to Me' up on Liberty, but since he waited, we only got the distribution on the Dolton release, which was a monster. Years later, when he bought Dolton out, it cost him a fortune, when he could have had it on the label for a production deal of some kind in the first place. It was a gigantic mistake from that moment. Actually Liberty copies were pressed during the Dolphin controversy, but it was still a Dolton/Dolphin record. In the 1980s he ran a place called the Broome Street Bar in New York City. Bob is a very nice guy I respect a lot."

Some of the threats to cover "Come Softly to Me" were not idle. Within a short time several competing cover versions of Gretchen, Gary, and Barbara's record were being played around the country. Gretchen recalls that there seemed to have been a leak in the organization someplace, that someone sneaked a tape of the song over to Si Waronker's cousin Herbie's Doré Records for a cover version.

Bob Reisdorff is less sure that any leak got "Come Softly to Me" covered. "Once a record is out, anyone can record a cover version. There is no way you can prevent it. It was out as a regional record in the Northwest first, as most of my records were. If they were not local successes, we did not issue them nationally. Although with the clout the LA people had, they could have gotten a tape of a pressing from the pressing company and copied that.

"Since the Fleetwoods were the composers, any version of the song 'Come Softly to Me' is OK for the song. But we wanted all of the record sales because we felt our version was infinitely superior to all of the others. No one else got that special quality, the blend of those three voices. The wonderful, natural, naive sound. And the Fleetwoods sort of meant it when they sang the way they sang."

Dolton's original version of the song was cut out in some cities, including all-important Philadelphia, home of Dick Clark's "American Bandstand." The Gone people, being East Coast, knew Clark; Bob Reisdorff didn't. How did Bob Reisdorff fight this battle? "I had all of the ABC-TV stations in Washington, the ones in LA and San Francisco, and the governor of Washington send messages to Dick Clark, and they did. The message was not to play the Gone version. We knew there were subterranean deals going on. They were never cash, they were always done like someone got a little bit of publishing interest on some song or some slice of some pie in exchange for carrying the Gone version. It was not something that could be recognized by the IRS as payola.

"But we wanted to avoid giving away anything yet still get our record played. We knew that we had a wonderful song to start a publishing company with. I felt that the only line of defense was a strong offense, with Dick Clark. Finally the Fleetwoods were booked on "Bandstand," and I met Dick Clark. He told me, 'I have never, ever had so much attention on any record.' But I had wanted to make sure we didn't get left out. After all, the Gone people were hot to trot and far more experienced than I in working in those markets. I don't know if we influenced Dick Clark or not, but we tried." The Fleetwoods' appearance on "Bandstand" is featured on Dick Clark's *Best of Bandstand* video tape.

On that "Bandstand" tape, Gary stands in the middle, singing, while the girls start on a high step that they have to negotiate in heels while smiling and singing and looking into the TV camera! One can't watch that tape now without wondering if Gretchen and Barbara might fall. When Gretchen saw that tape, the same thought occurred to her. For the most part, nervousness didn't show that much on the Fleetwoods' faces, although Gary recalls being rather uptight.

"Oh, boy, I was scared on that show! Except those guys who sang 'Get a Job' on that tape—they look even more scared. It wasn't only me. But that was our very first appearance."

And the "big step"? "They were worried about that from the very start. We were on the Ed Sullivan show right after that. It was a lot worse, because on the Ed Sullivan show, you sang live.... On 'Bandstand,' they played the record. So we just sang to ourselves and it was a lot nicer. But on the Ed Sullivan show, they had one microphone that was way up in the air in front of me. And I don't know how they ever heard anybody but me. And the band. They put a loud band in there with us; they had singers behind us, also. It was a large production."

Did Ronnie Height's cover version of "Come Softly to Me" bother the Fleetwoods? Not Gary:

"We were from the Northwest, and at that time I didn't even know what a cover record was. We heard people talking about the cover version, but I didn't know anything about it. When we got to New York on that first promotional tour, and besides his cover, I think there were about three more. We ran into a couple of the groups who were singing, promoting that song. We were going around New York promoting it. It was pretty funny because we saw each other all over town, at all of the radio stations. Pretty soon we all knew each other. And I guess it was laughable. But even then Reisdorff was telling us, 'This is excellent advertisement and you guys are getting all of the benefit because you wrote it.' It certainly wasn't anything to be upset about."

Maybe that is what Bob Reisdorff told Gary, but Gretchen has other feelings, at least about the way Ronnie Height got the song. "I have spoken with him in recent years. From what he says, it sounds like his getting the tune to record was kind of an inside job. Somebody who had access to our recording got it to him to cover, so that they were almost simultaneously released. According to what he says, there was almost a betrayal of trust there."

Be that as it may, Height's cover reached #45 on *Billboard*, as opposed to the Fleetwoods' #1 charting that lasted for four weeks, and Height's did not hit the chart until two weeks after the Fleetwoods' original. Did he hurt the Fleetwoods' sales? Gretchen Christopher: "Oh, the way I figure about that, he was not the only one who covered it. Another guy, Richard somebody, had a version. I mean, it was incredible, because here is a song that we had created and [now others were doing it, too]. But the covers may even have helped. Disc jockeys were getting two or three different versions of this record—you know, 'What is this?' Maybe it brought it more to their attention.

"About three years ago [around 1989], Ronnie Height [who recorded the Doré cover version] contacted me. An agent that I did a show for also knew him and gave him my number. Ronnie phoned me and asked if he could send me a tape of a rerecording he had done of 'Come Softly to Me' that did not yet have the female parts. He wondered, if I liked it, would I be willing to do the female parts on his new recording? I listened, chose not to. He actually wanted to tour as the Fleetwoods in Europe, now. As founder and manager, maintaining the original sound, quality, and image of the Fleetwoods has been an ongoing concern for me, and I told him I certainly would not give permission to anyone to use the Fleetwoods' name unless I were actively involved in the performance."

Certainly everyone knew about "Come Softly to Me" by the Fleetwoods in 1959—cover versions notwithstanding. The newfound power of top-forty radio made sure of that. Gretchen even remembers an incident that was typical of the kind of thing that happened in 1959 that would never happen today: "I'm told that one DJ in Alaska locked himself in the control room and played 'Come Softly to Me' for twenty-four hours straight! I don't know exactly why, but I guess it was just so different and he loved it or something and he got lots of calls for it. But stories like that are fun."

Thanks to Gretchen's guidance and inspiration, the Fleetwoods' sound was unique and could not really be duplicated in the cover artists' versions. "No one knew what to call it. Because it wasn't rock and roll. I guess some disc jockeys even had contests to give a name to the Fleetwoods' sound. What the name ultimately ended up being was 'the Fleetwoods' Sound!' which was kind of nice."

Was Bob Reisdorff surprised that the Fleetwoods' 'soft rock' innovation could be such a huge smash? "The field was much more open then to different sounds. There wasn't just one sound. You could have 'Tammy' by Debbie Reynolds and 'Don't You Know' by Della Reese, and Bill Haley and the Percy Faith Orchestra, and rhythm-and-blues records and the Fleetwoods all together. It was much more diverse then, not dominated by one fad. There were fads, but it did not eliminate everything else, which I liked and thought was very good."

"Dolton was created in order to record us," asserts Gretchen. At least, it was activated to serve that purpose. "We recorded a capella in Seattle and then the tapes were flown to LA by Bob Reisdorff and Bonnie Guitar. Guitar and bass were overdubbed there, on 'Come Softly to Me' and 'Graduation's Here' and the flip sides of those. And they added Si Zentner's trombone on 'Mr. Blue.'

"With 'Outside My Window,' we started coming down to record in LA. We did record 'Tragedy' in LA, it was all live. The musicians were there, we were all in the studio together. It created a special energy.

"There is a song we recorded on the album *Before and After,* which was our tenth or twelfth album, somewhere around there, called "Almost There." The song gets higher and higher, until at the end there is a part that I was singing that went higher and higher in harmony. And I was able to do it even though my voice is low, alto or tenor, but I was able to absolutely soar because there were all of these strings and things behind me, live in the studio. It is a wonderful feeling to have that kind of support for that kind of singing. But of course I usually didn't do that kind of singing."

The Fleetwoods' first songs were a capella originally, with a few instruments dubbed on afterwards. Later they recorded live with musicians. But on a few songs, they added vocals after the fact to instrumental recordings that were prepared by the producer ahead of time. "There were a couple of songs on which we overdubbed our vocals later. They got the tracks down, and then we went in. That was very difficult. Very disconcerting. I'd much rather sing live and have very few instruments—except, as I say, on those incredible high notes. To the Fleetwoods it was very important to do our vocal arrangements first, have the instrumental arranger listen to that, even tape it, and then do the instrumental arrangement around our vocal arrangement. And if they would start duplicating notes we were singing, I'd let them know! 'Please! That's my note!'"

Being Dolton artists, with Bob Reisdorff as their producer instead of Snuff Garrett, the Fleetwoods' sound was quite unlike that of the traditional Liberty sound characteristic of Bobby Vee, Johnny Burnette, Buddy Knox, Gene McDaniels, and the others. But Gretchen Christopher herself also gets credit for the sound of her group. After all, she was the one with the invocation to "Sing softly, softly." In the process, she seems to have invented the soft-rock sound that artists like the Carpenters ("We've Only Just Begun," 1970), Simon and Garfunkel ("Sounds of Silence," 1965), and the Paris Sisters ("I Love How You Love Me," 1961) would later re-create.

For the Fleetwoods' second ground-breaking #1 soft-rock classic, the cover was appropriately colored blue on blue.

True, there were other soft sounds before Gretchen's. But these earlier records were either solo efforts instead of group harmony sounds ("Love Me Tender," Elvis, 1956; "I'm Available," Margie Rayburn, 1957), adult-pop-jazz instead of teen top forty ("Cry Me a River," Julie London, 1955), or they included vocal dynamics that vacillated from soft to relatively loud ("To Know Him Is to Love Him," the TeddyBears, 1958).

As a further testament to the impact of the Fleetwoods, in 1990 Linda Ronstadt asked Gretchen about her new, post–Fleetwood music. "She also said that she had been looking for a recording of the Fleetwoods' arrangement of 'Bye Bye, Blackbird,' and I started to say, 'I think you're out of luck, because it's out of print,' but then I remembered that it was on the new CD. Which surprised me, as I thought, Why have they chosen that one? It seems so out of left field! So I sent Linda the CD."

The Fleetwoods' immediate follow-up to "Come Softly to Me" came out in May, and was appropriately titled "Graduation's Here." The Fleetwoods wrote the song, and it made the top forty. Considering how many really fine rock 'n' roll hits in the 1950s and 1960s came from one-shot artists and artists who had one big hit, one small hit, and then no more hits, the Fleetwoods could have disappeared after their #1 record, plus "Graduation's Here," with no hard feelings.

"Graduation's Here" was another ultrasoft record, but it did not score a big hit. Did this mean that the Fleetwoods' success with "Come Softly to Me" was a fluke? Was the ultrasoft sound itself a fluke, and "Come Softly to Me" more of a novelty record? Did teens really want only strongly performed, rhythm-and-blues-flavored songs with the occasional country-and-western slant, or were they ready for records that owed as much to pop as to black or hillbilly music?

The Fleetwoods' third Dolphin/Dolton record answered that question. It was their original classic "Mr. Blue" (Dolton 5), which quickly became the second #1 hit for the Fleetwoods and established them among the great artists of the late 1950s. Not very many 1950s–1960s artists ever had two national #1 hits, especially two out of three and within a half year of each other!

Another triumph for Si Waronker and Snuff Garrett's emerging Liberty rock and roll, as adapted by Bob Reisdorff. Liberty/Dolton, with its pop savvy, made the Fleetwoods stars. Most record companies would not have touched the soft rock 'n' roll sound of Two Girls and a Guy. (Bob Reisdorff: "The Fleetwoods wanted to call themselves 'Two Girls and a Guy.' I thought it was an awful name. They asked me, 'What should we call ourselves?' I asked them what their phone exchange was. She said, 'Fleetwood.' I said, 'Great, I like that!' The Cadillac Fleetwood was not out yet.")

On the label for "Come Softly to Me" appeared the legend "Vocal with Orch." That is an ironic legend, since the "Orch." was made up of Gary's key ring plus an acoustic guitar and an electric bass dubbed on later. But the Fleetwoods' recordings, including "Mr. Blue," were always done oddly. "Mr. Blue" was recorded in a radio station at 622 Union Street in Seattle. It had a little room used as a recording studio on the second floor. The building was knocked down back in 1962 and is now a parking lot.

Bob Reisdorff: "We did strange things with the Fleetwoods. We would record the Fleetwoods a capella in Seattle, then go down to Los Angeles with the tape and overdub the orchestra for the albums and things. That was unheard of. They thought it was such a freaky thing to do. Everyone else either recorded the singers and the musicians all at once, as the union required, or else they would record the instruments first, then add the voices later. Then they might add more instruments if needed. But some instruments always came first. But not with the Fleetwoods."

Recording that way was "difficult," said Bob Reisdorff. "It was difficult because, for example, on 'Mr Blue" Si Zentner played the trombone. He was playing on key, and the Fleetwoods (already on tape) were off key. But I took it the other way. I knew he was a fine trombonist, so I said, 'Si, excuse me, the trombone is off pitch.' We had to have him listen to the playbacks in the control room. Here he had thought he was going to whip it out, 'Bang!' but it took three times before he understood that they were between the keys, and he had to adjust to them. But everybody had to adjust to the Fleetwoods. Sometimes we could not use piano, if we wanted to, because they had to play between the keys to match the Fleetwoods' vocals, and a piano can't be adjusted like that.

"After a while, we started using Bonnie at the sessions to hold the thing together, sometimes, to keep them consistent. Finally we did record them with some music, but the Fleetwoods were best when they were absolutely private, almost alone. They even asked me to leave the studio once, when they were recording 'Unchained Melody.' They loved doing it, they were doing it with great feeling. They'd done it maybe thirty times and I was wanting something else, and so they asked me to leave. I thought, 'Well, that might work,' and I left and that was the take we used! But you see, that song was absolutely free form, that was almost a capella, they didn't hold to a rhythm pattern at all, you don't have to with that song."

The Frantics

Dolphin/Dolton's second group appeared in the early summer of 1959. They went by the name of the Frantics. The Frantics' three "hits" never made the top forty or, for that matter, even the top eighty! The titles were "Straight Flush," "Fog Cutter," and "Werewolf." And although they were worthy instrumental recordings, absolutely no one but the Frantics' mothers, and the fans of Northwest/Seattle rock and roll, remembers these obscure releases today—nor the names of the group members save Ron Peterson (lead guitar).

"The Frantics had a number of things that got on the national charts," says their producer Bob Reisdorff. "We recorded them only three or four times at the very beginning. Not everything they did went out nationally. They were Seattle artists who played all the high school dances, a routine early rock group, a pretty good garage band, not great. Even then it was rare for an instrumental to make it compared with a vocal. But we could never come up with anything that was big enough. We did better in the Northwest with those than in the rest of the country."

Little Bill and the Blue Notes

Little Bill and the Blue Notes were the next artists to appear on the blue Dolton label in the summer of 1959. Their only hit was "I Love an Angel," and while it was big in the Northwest, it was only #66 on *Billboard*, making them another one-hit artist for the rock 'n' roll history books. "I Love an Angel" had a slow, sax-laden sound that is reminiscent of Ron Holden's top-ten "Love You So" (Donna Records) that came out a year later. Holden's more successful record might well have been influenced by Little Bill's, as Bill was from Tacoma, Washington, while Ron was from Seattle. Little Bill was Bill Engelhart, who had suffered from polio and used crutches. He wrote both his hit and the up-tempo flip side, "Bye Bye Baby." The Blue Notes were Buck England and Tom Morgon.

Bob Reisdorff sighs when he talks about Little Bill. "The Little Bill and the Blue Notes story has been twisted and turned, but it is so simple. 'Come Softly' had already come out and was a hit. Little Bill came to me with 'I Love an Angel.' I liked the song very much, and I sent them to Joe Boles to make a demo for me." Joe Boles, who died in 1962, had a recording studio in his basement in 1959, and used to record local acts. "Joe stepped in and tried to sign them up himself as if he had discovered them. This was a great shame, because Joe was the only one I recorded with at the time. He was an amiable man, very nice, but he tried to get them for himself. He was very unhappy about the whole thing. Because when I stopped him he said, 'You want to keep me out of the whole thing?' I told him, 'Joe, I sent them to you to make a demo for me.' He was very uncomfortable and nervous about the whole thing.

"So I told him I would give him a penny a record just to pull out. I was deeply resentful and I hate this kind of dealing, but it is a way to get things finished and done with. I quickly found another studio and didn't record at Joe's any more. I thought it had been an extremely unethical thing for a very nice man to do. That was the story on Little Bill.

"I never did a follow-up with Little Bill. That all occurred during the transition, and if you can't find the right material, there is no sense recording. That is not a universal opinion. Many people will rush to get another record out right away. I did yield at times to that kind of thing, much to my regret, because being fast was important. But I tried for the most part not to do anything, saying, 'Another month is not going to hurt,' but it's awfully hard to find a hit song; it's really incredibly hard."

Both of Bill's sides were produced by Bonnie Guitar, who at this point was to Dolton what Snuff Garrett was to Liberty. Bonnie was an artist in her own right, with the top-ten "Dark Moon" popular on Dot in 1957, and country hits into the 1980s. Her real name was Bonnie Buchingham. Her friends started calling her Bonnie Guitar in the early 1950s, and the name stuck. At one time Bonnie and Bob Reisdorff appeared on the cover of *Cashbox* magazine together.

Bonnie had two Dolton 45 releases, Dolton #10, "Candy Apple Red" b/w "Come to Me, I Love You," and Dolton #19, which was the same two songs re-released together.

Since they were all on Dolton, and all from the Northwest, Fleetwood Gary Troxel knew all of the main artists on the label. "We knew the Ventures, because they were from the Northwest. We knew the Frantics. Little Bill and the Blue Notes we also knew. And I saw him more recently, when the Fleetwoods were inducted into the Northwest Rock 'n' Roll Hall of Fame.

"Bonnie Guitar was an artist on Dot Records during the 1950s and was one of the four people who wanted to start this record company that turned out to be Dolphin or Dolton.

"Bonnie had the musical ability to help out in the studio. In fact, that is her guitar on 'Come Softly.' We recorded that thing so many times, but I am sure the guitar is hers."

Many of the other artists who recorded for Dolton are not recorded in Bob Reisdorff's memory, such as the Five Whispers or the Echoes. But he remembers the ones who had the hits. "I think all of our first six or seven records were hits or at least made the charts. And I felt deeply humiliated and embarrassed if they didn't. Because I thought that that was the way it should be. I swore that I would never scatter-shoot. Gary Hodges' 'Too Old to Cry' was a good one; I think it was a *Billboard* pick of the week, but it didn't do very much."

Bob Reisdorff may have been good at picking or crafting hits in the early days of Dolton, but no one at parent company Liberty was sure which way the musical winds would be blowing in the next decade. One of their last 45s for the 1950s was "I Got a Bongo" by Jack Costanzo, backed by "Barracuda." "I Got a Bongo" was a mild novelty number along the line of "Short Shorts" by the Royal Teens, but with a lot of bongos and voices. Guys, gals, sexy voices, squeals, low voices, and some Spanish, plus a false ending, all talking about a great thing between boy and girl called "bongo love." Hmmm. The other side was an instrumental with yells (Spanish) and claps, bongos, of course, and a false fade-out that comes back.

"Jack was a very well-known bongo player, almost famous at the time, the best bongo player around," says Si. "We sold quite a lot to the Hispanic audience. I think 'Barracuda' was supposed to be the hit side." There were also Jack Costanzo albums, *Bongo Fever* and *Learn to Play the Bongos*. Cute, but hardly pop-hit material.

Vicki Benét wasn't aiming at teen record buyers when she cut "Love Me" in 1959. A photo of Julie London gets across the idea of her request.

The Little Sisters seemed to be another try at the Patience and Prudence groove. "A Little Star Came Down" is a Christmas song. The flip side, "Are My Ears On Straight?" is sung from the point of view of a toy doll at Christmas who has the ability to talk to her little girl owner. Hmmm again.

Margie Rayburn was still releasing 45s in 1959. "Laddie-O" is a boy she really likes being with, and "Unexpectedly" is about love at first sight. Hylton Shane sang of his true love for "Sandra, My Love," deep in an echo chamber. His mellow singing voice is replaced on the flip side by a hick twang, a cover version of the current hit record by man-and-wife team Gene and Eunice, "Poco Loco" (a little crazy).

Mike Clifford, who would have a hit in 1962 with "Close to Cathy" on United Artists records, sang the standard, "I Don't Know Why" in a pleasing rock tenor. The song would become a hit in a couple of years for Linda Scott on Canadian-American Records. The flip side, "I'm Afraid to Say I Love You," owes a lot musically to "Teenager in Love" Dion.

And so Liberty released many different kinds of songs in the quest for hits.

With the addition of Dolton, though, Liberty had two working labels, and rock 'n' roll was really working for both with a total of three #1 hits in just twelve months. The money was rolling in. It was time to begin signing new artists in earnest.

Liberty had started 1959 as a successful company but with one glaring weakness, described by Si Waronker himself with just two words: "Si Waronker. I tried to be a one-man show with some success and a lot of luck. Both Al Bennett and I agreed that an artist and repertoire department was a must. The first one to become an A&R man was Snuff Garrett. Snuffy—another 'one of a kind'—was twenty-one years old at the time, and his background was truly colorful. At fourteen he became a disc jockey in a little town in Texas and in order to gain fame, he sat on a flagpole and did his broadcasts from there for several days. He was a walking encyclopedia of music and musicians. Even though he had no formal music education, he certainly knew a commercial sound when he heard it. We knew that people liked him because he worked for us as a promotion man for a year, and the disc jockeys were unanimous in their praise. Snuffy was an instant success as an A&R man. He was responsible for bringing artists such as Johnny Burnette and Buddy Knox, as well as arranger Ernie Freeman. In 1959 he had a string of eight consecutive hits."

The glaring weakness was forgotten with that kind of success happening for Liberty.

CHAPTER 8

1960
Johnny Burnette, Buddy Knox, Ernie Freeman, and the Ventures

The period between the very late 1950s and 1964 was without a doubt the most amazing period in the history of popular music—amazing because the records that became mainstream popular hits ranged so incredibly wide in terms of types of music.

Before and after the 1959–1963 period, mainstream popular music would always be dominated by one or two major types of music. Big-band music, adult pop music, pure rock music, disco, rap—each type of music came along in turn and took over. Meanwhile, during the reign of each of these music forms, off to the side, there were always radio stations that played country, jazz, pop.

But during the period 1959–1963, the top-forty stations, aiming at teenagers and generally termed rock-and-roll stations, included on their lists music of every type. And since stations played only records that were bestsellers, that means that the kids were buying records of every musical type. The songs of various flavors that made the top of the charts during the period under discussion included:

Country

"Battle of New Orleans" (Johnny Horton)
"El Paso" (Marty Robbins)
"Big Bad John" (Jimmy Dean)

Pop

"Mack the Knife" (Bobby Darin)
"Go Away Little Girl" (Steve Lawrence)
"Blame It on the Bossa Nova" (Eydie Gorme)

Instrumentals

"The Happy Organ" (Dave ["Baby"] Cortez)
"Last Date" (Floyd Cramer)
"Calcutta" (Lawrence Welk)

Semiclassical

"Exodus" (Ferrante and Teicher)
"Asia Minor" (Kokomo)

"A Summer Place" (Percy Faith Orchestra)

Jazz

"Stranger on the Shore" (Mr. Acker Bilk)
"Midnight in Moscow" (Kenny Ball and His Jazz Men)
"Petite Fleur" (Chris Barber Jazz Band)

Novelty/Comedy

"Mr. Custer" (Larry Verne)
"Alley Oop" (Hollywood Argyles)
"Monster Mash" (Bobby ["Boris"] Pickett)

Folk

"Michael" (The Highwaymen)
"Blowin' in the Wind" (Peter, Paul, and Mary)
"Puff (the Magic Dragon)" (Peter, Paul, and Mary)

There are just three in each category. There were many more, as well as many more categories, including surf music, girl groups, love ballads, R&B/soul, dance, spoken, and the records that combined forms, such as country/instrumentals. Several types might be included on one record. The Tokens' "The Lion Sleeps Tonight" was a #1 hit teen/rock/ballad/African/folk song with a doo-wop refrain and background high soprano performed by opera singer Anita Darien. If MTV had existed in the period 1959–1963, the day's programming would have looked like a vaudeville variety lineup instead of a steady stream of the hard-rock music that it is today.

Liberty was ready to fill the nation's teen appetite for virtually all of these kinds of music. With the addition of the new successes of 1959, Liberty had artists as wide ranging as David Seville and the Chipmunks; country and western recording artist Willie Nelson and cowboy actor Walter Brennan; rockers the Ventures and Eddie Cochran; girl singer Margie Rayburn; R&B stylist Billy Ward; bandleaders Felix Slatkin and Si Zentner; teen pop artists Jan & Dean; and the Joiner, Arkansas, Junior High School Band.

The first new Liberty/Dolton artist to emerge in 1960 had a strange name, to say the least. It was (supposedly) the Joiner, Arkansas, Junior High School Band. The record was a marching-band type number, so the premise sounded reasonable, and it was the band's only hit. Liberty always favored novelty items, and this song, "National City," while a nice instrumental, was clearly not in reality performed by a junior high school band. The gimmick (or hook, as Si might call it) was good, taking advantage of the current vogue of instrumental and novelties in 1960.

Ernie Freeman was one of Liberty's most gifted arrangers, and like Si, he had a sense of humor, which Si fondly recalls. At one of Si and Ernie's recording sessions, they had about a half hour of studio time remaining after the planned material was recorded. Wondering what they might do with the time, Ernie brought out a dance band arrangement of the 1906 march "National Emblem." Ernie himself intended to play the Hammond organ as the soloist on the number. Si couldn't believe what happened when the time for the solo came around. "When bar four came around, Ernie goofed and in the keyboard run that was supposed to cascade down musically, Ernie's fingers got scrambled and what came out was this great band playing. Suddenly the soloist was someplace else.

"After the first take, the musicians were on the floor laughing. I thought this had potential. Ernie, of course, didn't want his name on the record, so it was up to me to find a suitable name for the band and the artist. Al Bennett was now president of Liberty, and I thought it fitting to make him famous, so I named the record 'Alvin Silas Bennett Conducting the Joiner Arkansas Junior High School Band'" (later shortened to the Joiner, Arkansas, Junior High School Band).

The record was an immediate radio smash. Evidently the disc jockeys enjoyed having something different to play on their shows. The record eventually got to #53 nationally, but was considerably more popular in certain regions. Ultimately Ed Sullivan's office called Si to ask about these junior high school kids—he wanted them for his Sunday night show! Imagine middle-aged black musicians being on TV impersonating an Arkansas junior high school band! Si: "I immediately took a much-needed vacation."

The "Band" did several follow-ups, including the soundalike "Arkansas Traveler"

Chapter 8 · 1960

All the music emanated from this building at 6920 Sunset Blvd. in Los Angeles. The previous building was just around the corner at 5667 S. La Brea.

(aka "I Caught Myself a Baby Bumblebee") and "Hot Time in the Old Town." Fun as these are, there wasn't any real need for more of them. A later release, "Hop Scotch," by the Joiner, Arkansas, Junior College Exchange Students Band, complete with bagpipes, ended the cycle.

"National City" had the distinction of being the first Liberty hit to appear on the newly designed label — black with a gold Statue of Liberty and full-color rainbow background. Just before that, Bobby Vee's "What Do You Want?" had charted, wearing the last of the old-style labels.

The label was designed by Garrett and Howard, a design firm that did most of the design work and photography for Liberty. Murray Garrett and Gene Howard did basically everything.

At the end of 1959 Bobby Vee's independently produced "Suzie Baby" had done well. But now it was time to see what could be done with Bobby at Liberty. After "Suzie Baby," Bobby Vee released the Adam Faith #1 British hit "What Do You Want?" Bobby's U.S. version sold poorly, however, and it began to look as if "Suzie Baby" was just another one-shot. But producer Snuff Garrett was not ready to give up, and he chose for Bobby's next song a tune from the musical *Bye Bye Birdie* called "One Last Kiss." Though very good, Bobby Vee's version was only a marginal seller.

This was the second Liberty label. Compare it to the illustration of the "Witch Doctor" 45, p.45.

Then Snuff pulled off a master stroke. He brought to Bobby's attention an old rock 'n' roll song (in 1959, an oldie!) he liked. It was an R&B song, "Devil or Angel" (the Clovers, 1956). Bobby Vee didn't care for the song. In fact, he had never even heard of it. In 1959 (and especially 1956) in Bobby's hometown of Fargo, North Dakota, kids listened to country music, not R&B.

Bobby soon grew to like "Devil or Angel" just fine. Within weeks of the Liberty recording session, it became a top-ten hit for Liberty and made Bobby Vee famous. The LP that went with the 45 was called *Bobby Vee Sings Your Favorites,* more oldies plus current hits, and thus was launched the career of one of the fifteen most consistent hit makers in the history of *Billboard* magazine up to the 1980s. *Your Favorites* included Bobby's recordings (*not* cover versions) of other recent rock 'n' roll hits, including Brenda Lee's "I'm Sorry," Jimmy Clanton's "Just a Dream," and Sam Cooke's "You Send Me."

Bobby also paid tribute to Buddy Holly on this, his first LP, by recording Holly's "Everyday." This recording and the 45 "Devil or Angel" showed that Bobby Vee could sing a variety of songs and make them work for him. But did it firmly plant the seeds of rock and roll in Liberty's musical garden? Now it becomes clear why even artists like Margie Rayburn cranked out so many releases. One could never tell from one release to the next when a hit might or might not crop up, so it was best to stick with something for a while and see if anything developed. As the old saying goes...

If at first you don't succeed... the Statues were the next addition Liberty made to its roster, looking for a big hit. The Statues were from Nashville. Their leader, Jimmy ("Buzz") Cason, was also a songwriter. The trio was rounded out by Richard

Williams and a former Jordanairs bassman who had backed up Elvis, Hugh Jarreet. The Statues recorded "Blue Velvet" (Tony Bennett, 1951) in a style reminiscent of Billy Ward's "Deep Purple." The record was a solid hit but failed to make the top forty, and the group as such was heard from no more.

Buzz later wrote many hits, a few of which were Liberty's "Popsicle" by Jan & Dean and "Sandy" by Jan & Dean admirers Ronny and the Daytonas. Buzz also sang backup for everyone from John Denver to Elvis. Some real talent passed through the door of Liberty over the years.

If at first ... but this time Liberty *had* success, the biggest since Bobby Vee. It was the era of the solo male vocalist in rock 'n' roll, and the newly recruited Johnny Burnette filled the bill nicely. Bobby Vee had developed a country-flavored style based on the Fargo country sound and the Tex-Mex sound of Buddy Holly blended with Snuff Garrett's appreciation of rhythm and blues (remember the Clovers' "Devil or Angel") and Si Waronker's pop background. Johnny Burnette also had country roots. In Memphis he and his brother Dorsey formed the Rock and Roll Trio with friend Paul Burlison. As late as 1985, Rock and Roll Trio music was used in the Patsy Cline movie biography, *Sweet Dreams*. The trio all knew Elvis before Elvis ever made any records, and their influences were similar to his.

The Rock and Roll Trio had played fairs and amateur shows. Their hopes for success were raised when they got a contract in 1956 with Coral Records, the same label that later signed Buddy Holly. However, the trio's sound was not really rock 'n' roll — more a country-with-a-beat sound and certainly not commercial — so they had little success and soon broke up. Dorsey Burnette then signed a solo contract with Era Records, a sister label to Doré. Dorsey had two hits on Era, "Tall Oak Tree" and "Hey Little One," before he became a producer for other record labels.

Both Burnettes were songwriters. In 1958 Dorsey had written "It's Late" and had a single of it on Imperial Records, which did not chart. The next year "It's Late" was a huge hit by Ricky Nelson on the same label.

Johnny Burnette

After the trio broke up, Johnny Burnette was signed by Freedom Records, a small Liberty subsidiary label named on a variation of the Liberty concept. On Freedom, Snuff Garrett recorded three unsuccessful singles with "Johnny Burnett" [*sic*] including 1959's "Kiss Me Baby." Soon Johnny was switched to Liberty, where his country/R&B sound was blended with Liberty's pop element. At first there were more failures, such as the unreleased "Love Kept A-Rollin'," written by Eddie Cochran's old girlfriend, Sharon Sheeley. And thereby hangs a tale.

Before he had his hits, Johnny Burnette and his brother, Dorsey, kept their hand in by working with Ricky Nelson. They sang with him, they played on his records, and they wrote songs for Rick.

"Love Kept A-Rollin'" was a song that Sharon cowrote with Johnny Burnette. He recorded it for Freedom, but it was not on one of his three Freedom 45s and did not see commercial release until a 1985 compilation by Alan Warner, *Let's Have a Party,* on Capitol. I asked Sharon Sheeley how it came to pass that she collaborated with Johnny on this song.

Sharon started writing with Johnny Burnette because he was a good friend of

Johnny Burnette and Dick Clark about the time of "You're Sixteen." *(Courtesy Snuff Garrett.)*

Eddie Cochran's. "Johnny Burnette and his brother Dorsey wrote many songs for Ricky Nelson, but they never got a number one record with him like I had done with 'Poor Little Fool.' So one day Johnny came over to my house. He was drunk, 'All I want to know, little girl, is how did you come to write that song? Let's sit down and write something.' And we did.

"Actually, I had already written three-fourths of a song for Ricky. Now Johnny was over crying and giving me this hard luck story about how he was doing so poorly, he could not even feed his five kids. He felt that if I would help him out just a little bit with a song, he could make it: 'I need to get back in with Rick.' I really felt bad about his plight. My mom was in the kitchen shaking her head no. Eddie had been there all afternoon and had helped me with some chord changes that I could not straighten out. It was my song. But I told Johnny, 'OK, John, the bridge on this song needs to be tuned up. Fix it, and I will give you half credit on the song. Then, next time you're onto a good song, you have to share too. Is that a deal?' John said, 'It's a deal, honey. I'll never forget you for this.'

"We went into Gold Star the next day and cut the demo. Eddie Cochran sang the demo. Talk about proof of who wrote it. But after we cut the demo, Johnny said to me, innocent little sucker, 'Can I take it over to Rick?' And I said, 'Sure, go ahead.' So he ran right over there and told Rick that he had written the whole damn thing. Rick went into the studio with it that night and had a hit called 'Just a Little Too Much' [Imperial, 1959, #9; flip side, 'Sweeter Than You,' also #9]. And it said on the record label that it was written by Johnny Burnette.

"Johnny and his brother Dorsey loved each other more than anything in the world, but they fought ... something terrible over anything. The next day Dorsey came over and told me he was going to break Johnny's neck—he was going to kill him for stealing the song. 'Don't you let him get away with that! Don't you let him get away with that!' Dorsey kept telling me. I assured him that I wasn't going to. I have Stan Ross at Gold Star, I have Eddie Cochran, I have all of the proof in the world. I am going to sue him; he can't get away with this. But later Eddie set me down and said, 'Honey, if Johnny needed the money that badly, let him have it.' I said, incredulously, 'Let him *have* it?' 'Let him have it.' I was eighteen, Eddie was nineteen, and I did it. Then, three weeks later we were walking down the hall at Gold Star, and who is coming toward us but Johnny. Eddie squeezed my hand real hard, like saying, 'Just be a lady.'

"I can't tell you how many times—after Johnny started having his own hits—how many times he tried to give me that money back. How many times he said, 'I'll have it changed. God, it was awful I did that to you, God, that was terrible.' I just told him, 'John, please, it is past.' But every once in a while, when I hear 'Just a Little Too Much' played, it still annoys me, understand? So, to answer you how Johnny and I came to write 'Love Kept A-Rollin', he told me 'You can have all of that song.' We had written three songs before 'Just a Little Too Much,' and he said, 'You can have all of those, all of them. I am taking this one. You cause me trouble, I'm going to break your leg.' You should have heard him." Might Burnette have reacted that strongly? Si's experiences with him were consistent with that image. "Johnny was a rough cat. He would drink a lot. He could get pretty physical when he had too much to drink. I got along fine with him; I had no problem with him."

"'Love Kept A-Rollin'" did not come out until after Johnny was dead. The company needed some information and asked Ms. Sheeley, 'Sharon, are you the sole writer on this song?' I told them, 'No, I wrote it with Johnny Burnette.'"

Johnny had failed to have hits with the trio and with his Freedom releases, but no sooner were strings added to his music than Johnny Burnette began bringing in hits. His first, "Dreamin'," nearly made the national top ten, and his next, "You're 16," did. Why did Johnny Burnette do so much better at Liberty than he had with the trio? The answer, of course, is the Liberty sound.

The Liberty Sound

Rhythm and blues was played for black audiences; country and western was tailored for rural audiences; jazz, classical, opera, and every other kind of music had its place and its audience. And, of course, countless whites loved R&B, and many urban dwellers loved country and western. But if any music was to become *the* pop music in America, it had to attract the vast majority of Americans, who shared three characteristics: (1) time to listen to the radio and records; (2) money to spend on records and on things that were advertised on radio (soda pop, pimple medication, and cars, to name a few); and (3) similar musical tastes. Only one group of Americans met those criteria in 1960: white, city-dwelling, middle-class teenagers. What they liked was what sold and was "popular." (Of course, what they liked was also liked by a great many blacks and rural Americans as well.)

The music people like is determined by what they have heard. The white city-dwelling, middle-class teens of the early rock 'n' roll years had grown up with very little exposure to rhythm and blues, country and western, and other music. Their families had raised them primarily on pop and big-band music or, more recently, Julie London and Martin Denny. The most consistently popular rock 'n' roll music during the first decade of rock and roll was a blend of rhythm and blues, country and western, and pop. In other words, the Liberty sound. Take a rockabilly/country influenced singer (say, Bobby Vee), give him a rhythm and blues beat or song (say, "Devil or Angel"), add a pop arrangement (violins, for instance), and you have hits like "You're 16" by Johnny Burnette and, of course, "Devil or Angel" by Bobby Vee. Perhaps if Eddie Cochran had lived long enough to have recorded in the new Liberty style he would have had more hits after "Summertime Blues."

The End of Eddie

On April 17, 1960, Eddie Cochran was on his way to the airport when his taxi crashed. Eddie was killed, and passenger Sharon Sheeley was severely injured. Fellow rocker Gene Vincent, also in the car, was hurt as well. Eddie was survived by his mother, and his older sister, Gloria Cochran Julson, who recalls Eddie and his music fondly. "When Eddie would do shows nearby where my husband and I lived, we would always go and dance among all the kids! I'm sixty-seven now, and Eddie would be fifty-two. There was a big difference." In spite of the age difference—when his first hits came out, she was already thirty-four, old for a rock 'n' roll fan in the 1950s—Gloria liked rock and roll. Perhaps a wide range of musical interests ran in the family.

"Ed liked all kinds of music. He was into country first, then he went into rock and roll. He could even play classical music on his guitar, if he wanted to, which he would do once in a while by himself. He was self-taught. That is what made it so great. Before he was on Liberty, he had a contact with Echo Records with Hank Cochran as the Cochran Brothers. They had about four records, then Eddie wanted to do rock and roll, but Hank didn't want to, so they split up and Ed went to Liberty."

Would the Liberty sound have helped Eddie, as it had helped Johnny Burnette? "I don't know if Eddie would have gone that way or not. I know that when Snuff put violins on one of Eddie's records, he didn't like it and wanted Snuff to take them off." Did they get into a physical fight about it? Gloria laughs. "No! Because Eddie was in England at the time, and he called Snuff from England and asked him to take the violins off, which he didn't. But they had talked about how when Ed got back over here, that they were going to cut some records together."

Occasional differences with Snuff notwithstanding, Eddie did enjoy being part

Eddie Cochran and Gene Vincent, who shared the cab ride that took Eddie's life.

of the Liberty family. "It was Eddie's manager who got him his contract with Liberty. He was very happy being at Liberty. The only thing I could ever say about Liberty was that they did not give him enough publicity. He had to work like a dirty dog to get everything he got. If Eddie had had someone to give him the publicity and work with him like they should have, he would have beat Elvis Presley all to pieces!

"I think Eddie had more talent [than Elvis], because Eddie could play that guitar like nobody. Presley couldn't. Presley also didn't write songs, and Eddie did write. Eddie had more talent, but it was just that Presley got more publicity. And that is what it takes in that business. He was in the New York Hall of Fame, and in the one in Minneapolis awhile back. And they are giving a great big celebration in Albert Lee, Minnesota, where he was born. He was well liked, but over here [he] just did not get the publicity that he should have. He was a sensation in Europe.

"What I think it was, Liberty really did not have the money to do what they should have done for their artists. He had to work for everything himself." Gloria basically agreed with Liberty promotional ace Bud Dain.

Bud feels that Liberty knew how to make hit records but not how to make stars, be the artist Eddie Cochran or Jackie DeShannon: "I sure do. I have met Jackie. She has been out to our house two or three times. "[The company] that has Eddie's songs now, if they'd had him at the beginning, I think they would have made a star out of him. But Liberty just did not know how to do it."

Liberty head Si Waronker agrees with Gloria and Bud Dain's analysis, to an extent. However, he feels that Liberty did everything it could possibly think of to promote Eddie. "We promoted our artists as much as possible. Why wouldn't we? The more money they made, the more money Liberty made. The bigger star they became, the better it was for the company. What reason would we have for not promoting somebody? The problem was, How do you make someone a star? No one knew then, and no one knows now, today, either. If we had known how, we would have done it. But no one knew how.

"I had plenty of complaints against me. I was a bastard in running the company in many ways. I wanted the company run my way, and my way had to be 'Let's do it now, I can't wait until tomorrow or the day after.' If you talk to people, a lot of them won't like me.

"If you talk to anyone who has an opinion that disagrees with what I tell you, go with them. Let them have their say. If they feel Liberty should have made Eddie a bigger star, let them say it. I don't mind. Go with their point of view."

At the time of his death, Eddie was in a hit slump. Would he have been able to make a comeback, had he lived? Sister Gloria is sure he would have.

"Yes, I think so, I really think so. Because 'Summertime Blues' now is a classic, so I think he would have kept on. Eddie was tired of traveling, though, and he wanted to get into the production end of it. I think he might have done that when he got back from England. He wanted to do the arranging and stuff like that for other artists. He might have done that because he was getting awfully tired of traveling. That's no fun, those one-night stands."

Gloria confirms comments by Sharon Sheeley that Eddie Cochran did not get all the money that was due him from his hits.

"Mother has said many a time that she just wishes that he had been here to have gotten the royalties instead of her. Because he wasn't getting very much at that time. And what he did get, that 'wonderful' manager of his managed to [keep]. He did, he did. Poor Eddie had to do without so that Jerry Capehart could live in Hollywood and be a big shot. [Jerry took writing credit for songs he did not write] and Eddie let him do it. Of course Ed was young. In fact, he had told Mother that when he came back here, he was going to get rid of Jerry. Because Jerry was getting to be more of a liability than an asset." So when Eddie died things were about to change in terms of management and production and career.

Snuff Garrett

Most of the Liberty recording in those days was done at a studio called United Recorders. It is still in business, but all of the old-time staff are long gone. A notebook they used to keep of all the sessions, all the personnel, dates, takes, everything, was misplaced long ago.

The most important person at any recording session, often as important as the artist, in fact, was the producer. This was the person in charge of organizing and running the session. While the artist would get the credit or blame for a record that was a hit or a miss, the producer was responsible for making a record that would sell.

In 1960 no one at Liberty (or any other label, for that matter) knew better what would sell and how to blend the necessary musical elements than Snuff Garrett. Snuff had worked in the record business in one form or another for years before he came to Liberty, and had all the knowledge and contacts necessary to make Liberty hit records.

Snuff Garrett was born in 1938 in Dallas, Texas. At age fourteen, he decided to get into show business in some fashion. His first "position" was with Gene Edwards, a local DJ at KOIF, who later did all the voice narrations on the TV oldie record album ads. After two years at the station, going to school during the day and working odd jobs at the station after school and at night, Snuff began working as a record promoter for distributors, because he had ins with the DJs. One of the men he met doing that was Al Bennett, then vice president of Dot Records.

Snuff: "I was rooming with some of the DJs, and one of them [Bill Jenkins] wanted to go to California to make the big time. So when he was fired at the station, we drove together to LA. Bill is still a newsman at KABC in LA. He got a job right away in Palm Beach, so I stood at the corner of Sunset and Vine and hustled jobs like stuffing records into mailers for little labels like Era to mail to stations. When I applied for a job one day, the secretary turned me away because her boss was away at a meeting with executives of Dot Records. I said, "Is he with Al Bennett?" She said he was, so I left my number for Al to call, the pay phone at Ma Brown's boardinghouse, where I was staying for twenty-eight bucks a week. Al called me three hours later, took me out for a good meal, for a change, and he hired me as a gofer for him at Dot's new California office.

"I didn't have my twenty-eight bucks rent that week, so I'd sleep in Plumber Park, then walk to a gas station to brush my teeth, and take a spit bath in the restroom, and go to look for work. When Al bought a house, his wife Cathy invited me to sleep on their couch, and I cried.

"Soon I was a promotion man again, for Dot and London Records. Then I got homesick and I went back to Texas, to Lubbock, and did DJ and TV work in Wichita Falls and Fort Worth. I ran a club called 'Snuff's Hot Spot.' I got Trini Lopez ["If I Had a Hammer," 1963] his first record deal with King Records. Meanwhile, Al Bennett invested in ownership of Liberty because Si Waronker was in financial trouble. Al became president of Liberty and had 'Witch Doctor' and 'The Chipmunk Song,' and they were off to the races."

So Al and Snuff talked, and Al gave Snuff a job as promotion man for Liberty in 1959 for ninety dollars a week, a three-hundred-dollar cut from his Texas earnings. For six months Snuff tried to talk them into letting him produce records. Finally they let him pick an artist to produce, and he chose someone he had hung around with was recording unsuccessfully for Liberty's subsidiary, Freedom Records. This was Johnny Burnette and his brother, Dorsey. Johnny's previous record was a bad song called "The Preacher and the Bear," so Snuff said, "The first artist I want to do is...." And they said, "Not only the first, but maybe the first and the last." Who could predict how Snuff soon would turn around Johnny Burnette's record career?

Snuff: "First we cut an old Hank Williams song called 'Settin' the Woods on

Fire.' It got on "Bandstand" and got played in Chicago and sold enough to let me cut some more records. I always went to New York and Nashville looking for songs, because I didn't think there were enough good songs in LA. During that year, I started having hits. The first was Johnny Burnette's 'Dreamin',' about the third record I cut with him.

"Then, Amos Heilicher, the Liberty distributor in Minneapolis, sent Al a demo of a kid they thought sounded like Buddy Holly. Al gave it to me, it was called 'Suzie Baby.' I liked it, so I signed Bobby Vee.

"The first song we cut was a cover of a song out of England, 'What Do You Want?' The second was 'One Last Kiss' from *Bye Bye Birdie*. The third was 'Devil or Angel.' So I had 'Dreamin' and 'Devil or Angel,' both top-ten hits; then I cut a song I found in Chicago called 'You're Sixteen, You're Beautiful, You're Mine,' with Johnny Burnette, and with Bobby I did 'Rubber Ball,' which I found in New York.

"My pay went from ninety dollars a week to one twenty-five to two hundred to three hundred to four hundred and five hundred. Then I said, 'I don't want more money; I want a piece of the record; I want my name on the label of the 45s.' [In those days,] they would put the producer's name on the album but not on the single. Al Bennett and I had knock-down drag-outs over that, but I finally got that.

"Early on, the first records I cut, they would put only the initials 'SG' on them; that was what I fought for and got that far."* Why might label credit as a producer be something worth going for? In those days the producer got no royalties, but Snuff finally made a deal with Al for a penny a record. "So I went from five hundred dollars a week to fifty thousand to seventy thousand a year."

After "Dreamin'" (SG) in July 1961, Johnny Burnette's second hit in November was "You're 16" (SG), which was redone (not "covered" in the classical sense) by Ringo Starr in 1973 and went to #1. Johnny Burnette's other three most commercially successful singles, "Little Boy Sad" (SG) the next February, "Big, Big World" in May, and "God, Country, and My Baby" (Producer: Snuff Garrett) in October, slid progressively further from the top of the charts. Other very fine records, like "I've Got a Lot of Things to Do" (Producer: Snuff Garrett) failed to sell at all in spite of having the Liberty sound. By late 1961 Johnny Burnette was another Liberty used-to-be. His popular recording career was much like Eddie Cochran's. And, like Eddie, Johnny died not too long after the hits quit happening. On August 1, 1964, Johnny Burnette drowned in a boating accident.

Garry Miles and Other Also-Rans

Staying with the solo male vocalist formula, the next Liberty starter in 1960 was Garry Miles. Miles was in reality old friend Buzz Cason of the Statues. But as "Garry"

---

* *The Eddie Cochran 1959 Liberty hit "Teenage Heaven" bears no producer credit. His posthumous record "Sweetie Pie" from the fall of 1960 bears the legend "SG." His late 1961 record, "Weekend," carries the proclamation, "Producer: Snuff Garrett." However, Sharon Sheeley, Eddie's fiancee, says that Eddie produced his own records, and that the SG credit was added to reflect the reissue effort, not the creative one. She ought to know. Besides being present for many of Eddie's writing and recording sessions, Sharon's composition "Lonely" was used as the flip side of both of these posthumous and commercially unsuccessful singles.*

he had just one hit, and it made the top twenty, which was something of a miracle. The song was "Look for a Star," and had been featured in the British movie *Circus of Horrors*. Why was it a miracle that this Liberty record was a hit? Well, in addition to cover versions, it was fairly common around 1960 for more than one artist to release the same song at the same time, with both versions aimed at the same white teenage market. (Can one even imagine several alternate versions of "Karma Chameleon" by different artists being hits at the same time in 1984?!) A good example was Doré's Ronnie Height releasing the Fleetwoods' original composition "Come Softly to Me" in 1959.

"Look for a Star" was very popular in 1960, and not just with Liberty record buyers. Besides Garry Miles on Liberty, Garry Mills on Imperial had a top-thirty hit with "Look for a Star." Obviously, given the name he was using, Liberty's Garry Miles/Buzz Cason was ripping off Imperial's Garry Mills's name and song. Meanwhile, back at Doré (Ronnie Height's label), Deane Hawley also made the top thirty with "Look for a Star." And incredibly, pop orchestra leader Billy Vaughn, who had some thirty hits on Dot Records over the years, made the top twenty simultaneously in 1960 with a fourth version of "Look for a Star."

With four versions all so popular at the same time, "Look for a Star" surely set some kind of a record. With that much popularity, had there been just one version, that one undoubtedly would have sold well enough to have reached #1.

In another burst of originality, a singer named Nick Noel released a Liberty 45 that sounded more like Perry Como than Perry Como did. Nick sang very mild "rock and roll" songs in the mold of Como's Capitol hits like "Dungaree Doll" and "Juke Box Baby," and the best thing about "Sugarbeat" was the pun in the title between sugar beets and the sweet rock 'n' roll beat. The flip side, "Jingling Jeans," referred to having some pocket change in denim pockets back in the days when a large cheese pizza cost just seventy-five cents.

Much better was Jackie DeShannon's record "Teach Me." This was the first of two score singles she would record for Liberty. This first brings to mind Brenda Lee, for whom Jackie would later write hits, as sung by Timi Yuro, a singer who was to arrive at Liberty very soon. "Lonely Girl" sounds like a female Bobby Vee. In all it is easy to imagine that there were those who saw potential in Jackie, who in spite of her failure to have a hit this year, was considered to have potential as a female Elvis. We shall see.

Buddy Knox

In December Liberty tried another solo male vocalist with strong rockabilly tendencies. Buddy Knox, the only person born in Happy, Texas, ever to appear on the "Ed Sullivan Show," was best known for his big 1957 hit "Party Doll" (an abbreviated version of which he performed on Ed Sullivan, along with "Hula Love"). "Party Doll," written by Buddy, was also a top-five hit in 1957 by Steve Lawrence on Coral Records, the second biggest seller of Lawrence's career. After eight hits on Roulette Records, Buddy Knox signed with Liberty. For Knox, this was a good move. Roulette had paid him less than $100,000 for a half dozen big hits.

Buddy Knox's first Liberty 45 was "Lovey Dovey." Snuff Garrett took the recording to Randy Wood, the head of Dot Records, which was in the Liberty building,

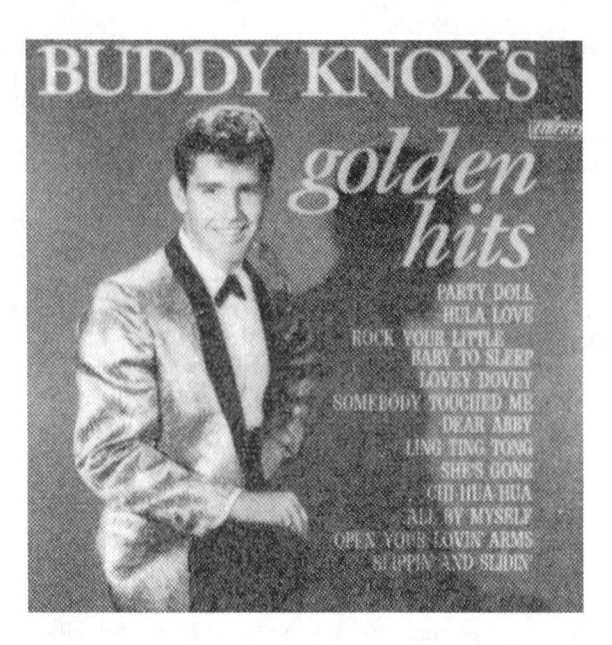

Buddy Knox was not on Liberty as long as other artists, and he rerecorded hits from other labels, such as "Party Doll," for this Liberty compilation.

just to get his opinion on it. The opinion was that it was a sure hit. And it sure was. Buddy Knox had nine single releases while he was at Liberty and one LP, *Golden Hits*.

The most identifiable element in Buddy Knox's "Lovey Dovey" is the phrase "Bop-bop-a-Judy-Boppa." But that phrase did not originate with "Lovey Dovey," or even with Buddy Knox! The phrase originated in a song by Ruth Brown called "Somebody Touched Me," which Buddy recorded for Roulette. Buddy then used it on his last Roulette record, "I Think I'm Gonna Kill Myself" (one can't *imagine* why a song with a catchy title like that did not score...), and his first Liberty record, "Lovey Dovey."

Some of the artists who came to Liberty may have taken some convincing to sign with the label. Buddy Knox, however, was highly motivated to sign up. You might say that Buddy Knox's getting hitched up with Liberty Records was not so much a courtship as a shotgun wedding. Just before his Roulette contract was about to expire, two tough guys came to his New York apartment and used a pistol to try to convince him to "re-up." Instead they convinced him to accept a standing offer from Snuff Garrett to come to California and sign with Liberty, which he did that very night!

Even though he was coming in from New York, Buddy Knox was doubtless seen by Al Bennett as yet another Texan that Snuff was bringing up to work for Liberty, like Johnny Burnette and Ernie Freeman. And like the other Liberty artists, Buddy Knox became the beneficiary of Snuff Garrett's Liberty sound: that mix of country and western, R&B, and pop that became the new rock and roll. And Buddy had nothing but admiration and respect for Snuff's studio prowess. Heck, he revived Buddy's career, and Buddy appreciated the guidance.

Snuff even put the Johnny Mann Singers on Buddy Knox's rockabilly records, as well as Darlene Love and the Blossoms plus drummer Hal Blaine on various of the two dozen sides Buddy cut at Liberty.

When Snuff overdubbed strings on Eddie Cochran's recordings, it was not appreciated by Eddie. How did Buddy Knox feel about strings on his records?

He liked it fine. It got him hits, as it did for other similar singers like Johnny Burnette.

For Liberty, signing Buddy Knox was a gamble, as few rock 'n' rollers ever lasted as long as Buddy already had and still sold consistently, especially moving from one label to another.

The gamble paid off. Buddy Knox's first Liberty hit, "Lovey Dovey," made the top thirty. A previous version by Clyde McPhatter (formerly with Billy Ward and His Dominoes) had missed the top forty in 1959, and later versions by Otis and Carla and Bunny Sigler also failed to make the top forty.

Si Waronker worked little with Buddy, feeling that "Buddy Knox was a nice kid. I had no problem with him."

The payoff for signing Knox to Liberty was short-lived. Buddy composed many of his records, but Snuff Garrett picked "Ling Ting Tong" as the follow-up to "Lovey Dovey." After all, "Lovey Dovey" had the "Bop-bop-a-Judy Boppa" refrain, while "Ling Ting Tong" had the phrase "I some okum boon die-ay, I some okum boon." Same diff!

The song had already been a hit in the mid-1950s for the Charms and the Five Keys. Now it was a final hit for Buddy Knox (and the Blossoms and Hal Blaine) on Liberty.

Roulette was infamous for not paying royalties to artists. At Liberty not only did Buddy get paid, but his sessions were paid for by Liberty and not deducted from his royalties. Buddy Knox had no more hits. He did have several good sides, however. One was 1962's "Chi-Hua-Hua," written in a few minutes right after Buddy's wife's pet Chihuahua dog named Pepe was run over. The last Liberty record that got any action for Buddy Knox was "Hitchhike Back to Georgia" early in 1964. It charted regionally but was not commercial nationally. In spite of his consistently good performances on records, it was the last time Buddy threatened the national charts.

Snuff, Trini, and "Rubber Ball"

Being signed to Liberty was not always so easy as it was for Knox, even if Snuff was in your corner. "A lot of people hung around Liberty," recalls Snuff. "We were 'Action Center'; we ran hard and played hard. Don and Phil Everly were there all the time, Lenny Adler was there all the time, Frank Zappa was always hanging around, Lenny's roommate Randy Newman, Sonny Curtis of the Crickets, who wrote 'I Fought the Law' [Bobby Fuller Four, Mustang Records, 1966] and 'Walk Right Back' [Everly Brothers, Warner Brothers, 1961] and a lot more. I signed a lot of guys like the Crickets and Buddy Knox who had already had success, and I was going to try to do it again with them a second time.

"Then one day this guy who[m] I got to be the new lead singer for the Crickets in Texas, I paid his way to California. I told Al I was going to sign him. Al got mad: 'You can't sign all the friends you have. Drop some of your friends, and you can sign him.' So I went to the Liberty studios and cut some demos that I still have, played them for Al. 'Those are the stupidest things I ever heard. You can't sign him! You got all these other buddies. Make some hits with them, and then you can sign him or anybody you want to.' That was Trini Lopez, so I didn't get to sign him, and he was the biggest thing in the world nine months later" on Reprise Records with "If I Had a Hammer."

With six new successful artists, 1960 had been the best year yet for Liberty, even without Trini Lopez. The Chipmunks were still selling records. Bobby Vee's 1960 hits had included the classic "Rubber Ball." This song was written by singer Gene Pitney, who in a few weeks would have the first of his two dozen hits on Musicor Records, including "Liberty Valance" and "Town Without Pity." However, due to contractual conflicts, Pitney's name could not appear on "Rubber Ball." Instead, he published the song under his mother's maiden name, telling her that if anyone asked her about "Rubber Ball," she should say she wrote it. Nervous that she would be grilled, Gene's mom spent many an hour at the piano, learning "Rubber Ball" backward and forward. It was a great song, appropriately very bouncy, full of the Johnny Mann Singers' girl-group section and strings and things.

Was it worth the trouble to change the composer credit just to get this song onto vinyl? Probably, according to Si.

"Today people have others who write for them, or they are their own composers. But in those days, my God, to find a good tune was so hard. Find me a good tune and I could make a hit with any of five artists! Today it is different." So which was the most important at Liberty when it came to making an individual hit record, the song, the artist, or the producer-arranger? Si has no doubt. "The tune. The tune first. The producer-arranger I would say was second. The artist was third. Because if the tune was worthwhile, then a decent A&R man who knew what he was doing was going for a certain sound. The arranger knew how to get the sound that the producer or the A&R man wanted. You could take any one of any four artists, and if they would take the instructions that were given to them, you'd have a record."

So a good song like "Rubber Ball" could be sung by either Bobby Vee or Buddy Knox or Johnny Burnette with Snuff Garrett producing? "Yes, yes, yes. Anyway, that is my theory. A lot of people might disagree with that. And I would argue, but not a helluva lot. I always said, 'Give me a story line in a book, and many people can write it. After all, songs like 'Star Dust' have been recorded and made a hit many times. Because the tune itself is great. Some of the Elvis Presley tunes or Beatle tunes, the melody was something you never forget. If someone brought me a good tune, I could make a record. It might not be the biggest hit of them all, but I promised if I had the tune I could make something that would be listenable. Anyway, that was my theory. As I say, a lot of people would disagree with me."

Bobby's 1960 LPs included *Bobby Vee* and *Bobby Vee with Strings and Things*, a reference to the Liberty sound.

Ernie Freeman

What was the true genesis of the Liberty sound? Si Waronker's paradoxical penchants for strings and for small combos, his love of rock, and his hot recording techniques all contributed. But Snuff made a big contribution of his own. "When

I was a kid in Texas, a disc jockey, I used to listen to a tape of things I liked that I had made at the station, and there was this kid on Imperial I liked, a trio, how can one guy be a trio in records, and he was a blues piano player I dug a lot, Ernie Freeman, songs like 'Rainy Day' and 'Lost Dreams,' and I played those all the time. When I got into A&R at Liberty, Si asked me who was my arranger going to be, and I thought of Ernie Freeman."

Ernie Freeman was a pianist whose hits as an artist included, over the years, "Percolator (Twist)" under the name Billy Joe and the Checkmates on Doré (Billy Joe was really Louis Bideu) and "Raunchy," a 1957 top-of-the-charts Imperial Records instrumental cover version of composer Bill Justice's huge hit on Phillips Records.

"Since Ernie had made records, I thought he lived in a great big gold house on top of a gigantic hill with limos all around. He was on a record, after all! I'd never met him or set eyes on him, but I loved his stuff. Si's best friend at the time was Felix Slatkin, conductor of the Hollywood Bowl Symphony Orchestra; he and Si played fiddle together. Si was the concertmaster at 20th Century–Fox before he owned Liberty. So when Felix and Si asked me who I wanted as arranger, I went into an elaborate buildup about Ernie without mentioning his name, not sure if we could get him. They thought I was trying to get Henry Mancini or someone big like that. I said Ernie Freeman, and they got hysterical because it was totally unlike the kind of music they did.

"They okayed it. We got Ernie. I told him what I wanted, got him under contract to me, and we went throughout the Liberty years."

Rock 'n' roll, Liberty style, was big money and here to stay at Liberty. The question was, How could Liberty cash in on rock 'n' roll without the risk of auditioning bunches of kids, releasing lots of chancy singles, and then hoping some would become hits? Moreover, Liberty particularly wanted to keep on selling LPs.

There were two solutions to this problem. The first: Let reliable Bob Reisdorff do something on the Dolton label. Liberty often signed artists who had already had some recording experience and success elsewhere, such as Bobby Vee with his local release of "Suzie Baby," Johnny Burnette of the Burnette Trio, Buddy Knox from Roulette, and Billy Ward from several previous labels. By contrast, Dolton developed original artists, foremost among them the Fleetwoods. After their 1959 successes, in 1960 the Fleetwoods scored three times, "Outside My Window," "Runaround," and the sad "The Last One to Know." "Runaround" was a revival of a top-twenty song from 1954 by the Three Chuckles on X Records.

An important ingredient in the mix that makes hit records and hit groups is promotion. And a big part of promotion is touring. Bob Reisdorff regrets that "the Fleetwoods toured very little. They were not really performers, they never were a performing group, it just wasn't there. The sound was there, but not the stage presence. Gretchen, having studied dance, wanted to move on stage, but that would always leave the others standing like posts! So that was almost an impossibility." One wonders how the Fleetwoods got so big, or how much bigger they might have been had they toured more.

Since the Frantics quickly disappeared after their own Dolton debut record in 1959, the Fleetwoods had Dolton as their own private label for awhile. But now, in 1960, the Fleetwoods had to start sharing again.

A Ventures LP cover on which they made sure their faces showed clearly.

The Ventures

The first sharers of Dolton were the Echoes. Their Dolton record, "Born to Be with You," was a regional seller in 1960.

A bit more of a success for Dolton were the Ventures. The Ventures were two construction workers who became musicians almost by accident when they met on the job and discovered a mutual fascination with the guitar. Their first hit, the Dolton single "Walk, Don't Run," was #1 on nearly every top-forty radio station in the country. It was a new version of a song that had previously appeared as a country LP cut and before that a jazz instrumental. Now it was an up-tempo rock-guitar blazer, which would be played and played on stations around the world for more than thirty years.

The Ventures were Bob Reisdorff's other big discovery, besides those two girls and a guy, the Fleetwoods. "I first heard 'Walk, Don't Run' when it was played on KRJ, a very big station. I thought it was great; I loved that record when I heard it. Shortly after that, Josie came to me, sent by C&C distributors whom she had first gone to see." Josie was Josie Wilson, Ventures guitarist Don Wilson's mother. "I told her, 'Josie, you do not need me, honestly. But I will get you the same deal that I have with Liberty Records.' She agreed, and I sent a master down to Liberty. Liberty turned it down flat. I couldn't believe it! I called Al Bennett: 'Al, this thing is a hit, a smash hit. I'm telling you.' He said, 'But we don't like it. How many has it sold?' I had no idea, but I knew it would sell like crazy. Al said, 'If you think so highly of it, why not put it out on Dolton?' That started my involvement with the Ventures.

"Several weeks later I was having dinner with Josie, when she asked me, 'Bob, do you really feel this will be a national hit?' The regional sales had convinced me of that for sure. 'Josie, I'll tell you how much I believe in it. I will give you ten thousand dollars [equal to maybe one hundred thousand dollars today] for half of Blue Horizon.' The embarrassing part was that I had to borrow the money from my mother. But I got my money back and more, even with just that first Ventures record. But I would have not been involved at all with the Ventures and Blue Horizon if Liberty had taken the record when I offered it to them on Josie's behalf.

"So Josie and I owned that company. We had an honor agreement with Liberty which was very good, and I honored it, too. My offices were in the Liberty building, and anyone who came in through the door would be Liberty's. But anyone we got on the outside was Blue Horizon's or Dolton's."

"Walk, Don't Run" had two flip sides. The original one was "Home," the second was "The McCoy." Why the change of flip sides? "The Ventures were horrified by the flip side of 'Walk, Don't Run.' The one I originally put on was a song that they wrote. I explained to them, 'You wrote it! You are going to make a penny a record for this.' Oh, they were outraged for a while. After a while, they calmed down, especially when people started to say to them, 'You know, I like that flip side!' But working with the artists, no matter who they are or where they come from, is probably one of the hardest things about the business. It always is.

"The Ventures were in about their late twenties when they cut 'Walk, Don't Run.' They had been to me before with something that wasn't 'Walk, Don't Run.' They told me in just the last year or so that it really was 'Walk, Don't Run,' but it was unrecognizable from the later version. But they did not bring that one to me in the beginning. But they have had a remarkable record. A lot of the albums were on the charts, the two twist albums, and maybe the mashed potatoes one.

"The Ventures were rank amateurs with very little stage presence or ability at the time. They have developed considerably from those days. Don Wilson was the best performer of the original four. When Mel Taylor became the drummer, he has a lot of drive and force as a person, and he helped a lot on the presence of the group. Bob Bogle couldn't move at all well. He developed better movement as he matured."

While the Ventures' "stage professionalism" may have been less than stellar at times, their music professionalism was never a problem. "The Ventures used to rehearse very conscientiously. We would never go into the studio until every song was very, very well rehearsed. Studio time was terribly expensive. It was, in my view, ridiculous to go into the studio and rehearse. If it took four hours to get an arrangement down, to get it as best as they could, why use the expensive studio for a rehearsal hall? As a producer I would not go in if I did not like the arrangement. Or I would say, 'It's not there yet. You gotta work some more.'"

The follow-up to "Walk, Don't Run" was a similar-sounding record named "Perfidia." This song has been recorded many times as a vocal, by artists from Glenn Miller to the Four Aces. But the Ventures hyped up the tempo and poured out an instrumental rendition well worthy of its top-twenty rating.

The Ventures came at just the right time, when rock 'n' roll instrumentals were beginning a four-year wave of popularity. The Ventures continued to be hugely popular through the 1960s. They had more than a dozen Dolton hit 45s, six in the top forty and three in the top ten. But their real sales power was in LPs.

LPs

Now, Liberty always was big on LPs. With no hits to speak of, Julie London and Martin Denny had already sold millions of LPs for Liberty, as Si Waronker built his catalog. The Ventures performed the same trick for Dolton. By 1980 the Ventures had sold more than ten million LPs—in Japan alone! With the Ventures added to the Dolton stable alongside the Fleetwoods, Liberty's blue-label subsidiary helped the company have a very good year indeed in 1960.

So the Ventures were one thing that helped move Liberty more solidly into the rock 'n' roll field. Liberty's second solution to the "how-to-cash-in-on-rock 'n' roll-fast-and-sell-LPs" problem was to begin a various artists–oldie LP series. Liberty did not yet have a tremendous amount of material to draw on for a series of golden hits compilations, but foreshadowing the success of the TV-oldie LPs of the 1970s, 1980s, and 1990s, Liberty leased masters of old rock 'n' roll hits from other companies. By mixing these leased masters with their own artists' hits, Liberty put together the first three in a series of what was unquestionably the best rock 'n' roll various artist–oldie LP series ever developed. Today these LPs are collectors' items.

Many other labels have had oldie LPs that have sold all right, but no one did as many albums as well as Liberty. Smash Records released an oldie LP, *All-Time Smash Hits,* (pun doubtless intended), but since they stuck with songs from their own label, they had to fill out the LP with things that were not smash Smash singles, like Jerry Lee Lewis's "Hit the Road Jack," which despite its title was not a hit. Roulette Records had a long series of oldie LPs, but the selection of the songs was at times questionable. Many of the Roulette songs were not national hits, there was an overabundance of R&B tunes that were not nationally known, as opposed to national rock 'n' roll artists, and some songs were recycled and turned up on LP after LP in the Roulette series.

None of this for Liberty! The Liberty Golden Hit LPs were filled with big hits. Eventually the Liberty various artists–oldie LPs were numbered *The Original Hits, Volume 1,* and so forth. But in the beginning the LPs had separate titles. For instance, *The Original Hits, Volume 4* was first titled *Memories Are Made of Hits,* a takeoff on the Dean Martin 1955 hit, "Memories Are Made of This." One of the most cleverly named was *The Original Hits, Volume 2,* first titled *The Original Hits Past and Present.* As implied by the name, this LP had oldies on one side and current tunes on the other. Of course, in a few years, the "Past and Present" phrase made no sense, because the current records were soon oldies themselves. And that was why the designation *Original Hits, Vol. 2* was later given Liberty LP 3180.

The cuts on *Past and Present* were divided into two groups on the two sides of

PAST

STRANDED IN THE JUNGLE
THE CADETS

COME SOFTLY TO ME
THE FLEETWOODS

SHORT FAT FANNIE
LARRY WILLIAMS

CITY OF ANGELS
THE HIGHLIGHTS

I'M AVAILABLE
MARGIE RAYBURN

CHERRY PIE
MARVIN & JOHNNY

SUMMERTIME BLUES
EDDIE COCHRAN

PRESENT

YOU'RE SIXTEEN
JOHNNY BURNETTE

PERFIDIA
THE VENTURES

LOVEY DOVEY
BUDDY KNOX

FOREVER
THE LITTLE DIPPERS

SMOKIE PART II
BILL BLACK COMBO

RUBBER BALL
BOBBY VEE

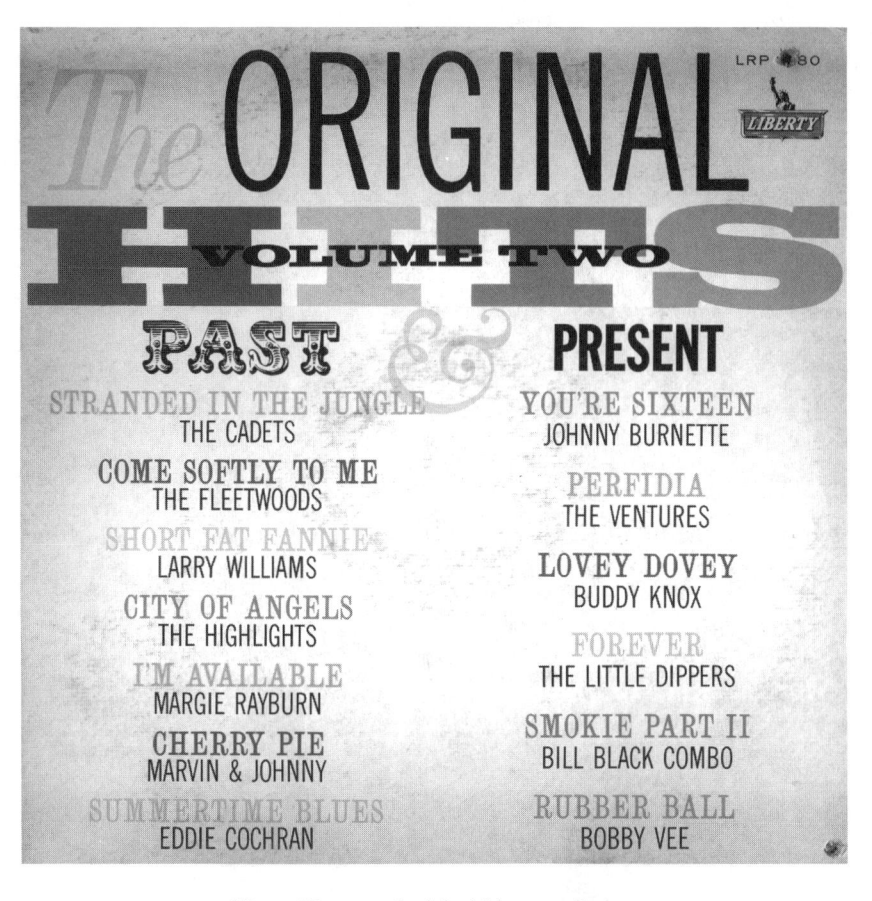

Liberty LP cover of original hits compilation.

the LP. The past side, featuring oldies, was side 1, and the label was printed in an old-timey lettering. The lineup:

Past

"Stranded in the Jungle" (The Cadets)
"Come Softly to Me" (The Fleetwoods)
"Short Fat Fannie" (Larry Williams)
"City of Angels" (The Highlights)
"I'm Available" (Margie Rayburn)
"Summertime Blues" (Eddie Cochran)

Most 1950s and 1960s LPs had six songs per side, but Liberty's *Past and Present* had seven songs on side 1. Two of the seven, the Margie Rayburn and Eddie Cochran songs, were familiar Liberty label hits, while one, by the Fleetwoods, was from Dolton. All seven had been on the top thirty, with three being top-tenners and one having been a #1.

Memories Are Made of HITS

RUBBER BALL
BOBBY VEE
BONGO ROCK
PRESTON EPPS
GONNA GET ALONG WITHOUT YA NOW
PATIENCE & PRUDENCE
ROCKIN' LITTLE ANGEL
RAY SMITH
DEEP PURPLE
BILLY WARD & THE DOMINOES
ALWAYS
SAMMY TURNER

DREAMIN'
JOHNNY BURNETTE
MULE SKINNER BLUES
THE FENDERMEN
SITTIN' IN THE BALCONY
EDDIE COCHRAN
DOWN YONDER
JOHNNY & THE HURRICANES
CORRINE, CORRINA
RAY PETERSON
TRAGEDY
THE FLEETWOODS

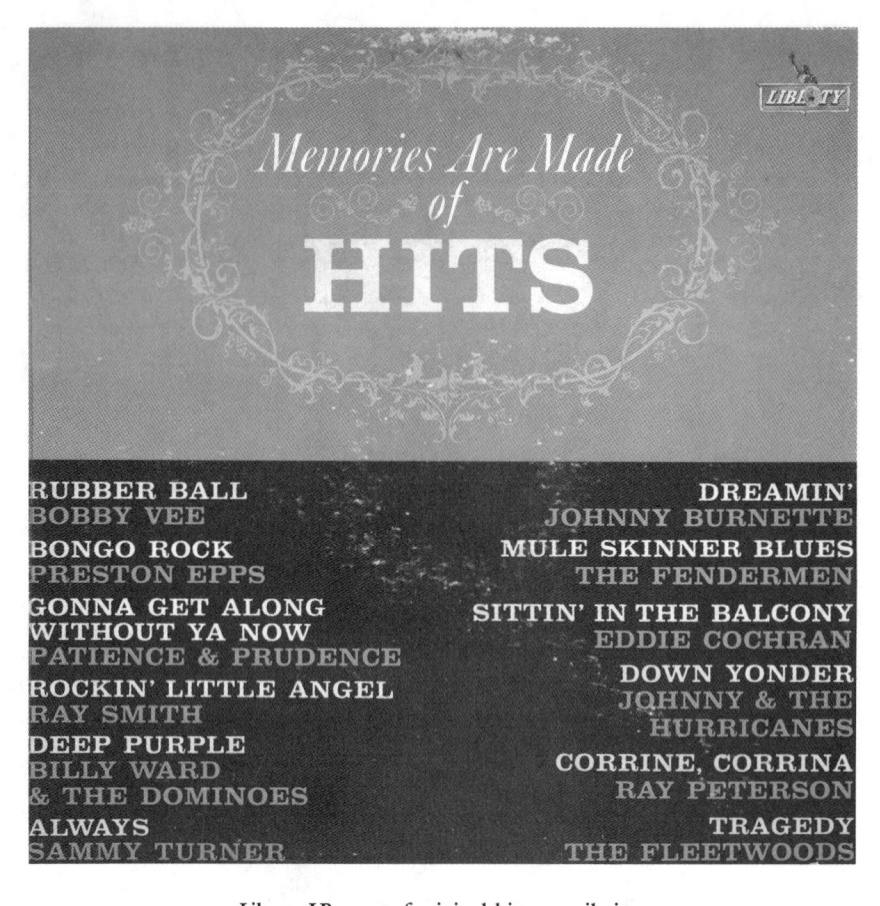

Liberty LP cover of original hits compilation.

On side 2, the present side, the printing was in modernistically plain, bold letters.

Present

"You're Sixteen" (Johnny Burnette)
"Perfidia" (The Ventures)
"Lovey Dovey" (Buddy Knox)
"Forever" (The Little Dippers)
"Smokie Part II" (Bill Black Combo)
"Rubber Ball" (Bobby Vee)

Side 2 had six songs. Three were from Liberty, by Johnny Burnette, Buddy Knox, and Bobby Vee. One, by the Ventures, was from Dolton. Again, all were top-thirty hits. Three were top-ten hits, and all six were current songs from 1960. One song, the Little Dippers' "Forever," was a top-ten hit on the University Record label, which was a small label distributed by Liberty. The Little Dippers were in reality the

Anita Kerr Singers, appearing here in disguise. Their usual label, RCA, had turned down the recording, so Anita sneaked off to Liberty/University for refuge. On RCA the Anita Kerr Singers did break through in 1962, this time calling themselves Anita and th' So-and-Sos. Their RCA girl-group records were "Joey Baby" and "Tell Tale."

Snuff Garrett supervised all the golden greats collections. He picked the songs, supervised the cover designs, named them, and even had the idea for the different label fonts on *Past and Present*. "I always tried to get the best hits for those."

As hard as Snuff worked at Liberty, and as sharp as Al Bennett was, and as wise as Si Waronker could be, much of the early success of Liberty was due to a series of fortunate circumstances. Finding Julie London when Si had actually wanted Bobby Troup; accidentally playing a David Seville recording at the wrong speed; Eddie Cochran's getting in to see Si because a secretary liked him; and getting "Sittin' in the Balcony" sent in by airmail just when Eddie was available — these and many more happenstances were all lucky breaks, cases of being in the right place at the right time. Si admits to being fortunate in many ways, but other factors also he knows helped the label succeed during the first five years.

"There was a lot of luck. There was also something else that was very important at Liberty. Due to the fact that I was connected so long and with so many people at 20th Century-Fox, I was very close to the publishers. The song pluggers, people like Eddie McHargue, brought me anything that was hot. They also sent me people when anyone asked for a recommendation of a record company. There was a bandleader by the name of Don Swan. He came from Florida. No one would record him, but we did. But he paid for the sessions. I had no money. I recorded in the studio with him, then Don gave me the masters. I told him I would release it but that was all I could do; I couldn't pay him, just give him the best shot I could." That was the first album Liberty ever made, *Mucho Cha Cha Cha by Don Swan and His Orchestra*, LRP 3001.

"So a lot of it was luck, but a lot was referrals because people knew that I would not cheat them."

"In 1960 or 1961, we had a big record-company convention in Miami. The newspaper headlines called it 'Booze, Broads, and Bribes.' That's when the government started their investigation of corruption in the record business. Every company that I know had to sign a consent decree that if it they were guilty [of paying payola,] they would do it no more. Liberty was one of the few companies never cited. Even Columbia and Decca and RCA were all cited for payoffs. We never were. Now, I am not saying that we were completely innocent. Nobody was. But let's put it this way — we never got caught doing anything! But those were the things that gave Liberty a good reputation." (A good reputation? Liberty LP 3185 by Hangnail Hennessey and W. Brubeck has a title that gives one pause: *Rides, Rapes, and Rescues*.)

Liberty's success was also in knowing (or figuring out) how to promote records that had potential. "There are many ways of promoting records. The funniest was when we did the Chipmunks. We did an album called *Alvin for President*, when Kennedy was running. Alvin and the Chipmunks were now a household name. So, why not run him for public office? Ross always wrote everything the Chipmunks recorded. The end of the tune had a mob scene chanting 'We want Alvin. We want Alvin!' We called a press conference to introduce the next president and played the song for all to hear. It didn't cost anything, just a few bottles of booze. We even went so far as to print ALVIN FOR PRESIDENT bumper stickers and sent a message to President Kennedy challenging him to a debate. In fact Kennedy sent us a letter saying that he enjoyed the idea. It was promotion. God, we did get a great deal of publicity on it. That was the kind of thing we did. It was fun. Everything was fun from nineteen fifty-five to nineteen sixty. We worked our heads off. I'd start at nine in the morning and go until two the following morning. I enjoyed it."

On the other hand, the long hours took their toll on Si. Nineteen sixty was the year of his first stroke.

"Wall Street was watching the growth of Liberty and was making serious inquiries about taking the company public. We finally made a deal with Crowell-Weedon. They were a very-well-thought-of brokerage house. We now had something to offer. We had purchased the Gene Autry Studios on Sunset Blvd., had over 150 employees, a substantial artist roster and a string of successes that was the envy of most of our competitors.

"Our deal was to capitalize the company with one million shares, sell one hundred fifty thousand shares to the public and keep five hundred thousand shares in the treasury and the balance to the shareholders of record. My majority interest amounted to two hundred thousand shares. The one hundred fifty thousand shares were quickly oversubscribed and the company was handed a check for a million dollars. We now had sufficient cash to really grow. We expanded in every direction. We now had five A&R men, including Phil Spector—offices in New York on West Fifty-seventh Street and offices in Nashville. The time flew and Crowell-Weedon now recommended we have a secondary offering. This would take about three months to accomplish. In the meantime I was having several occurrences that were disturbing Dr. Newman—such as dizziness and lapses of memory."

The doctor told Si's wife, Jeanette, that he was killing himself. He made his doctor and wife keep it a secret, and he did cut back on his smoking. But Si's health would never be the same again, and he was told to take a vacation, which he did.

In Europe.

CHAPTER 9

1961
Avnet, Gene Mcdaniels, Timi Yuro, Vic Dana, Troy Shondell, and Dick and Deedee

According to Liberty president Si Waronker, "Liberty's best profit margin came in nineteen fifty-nine/sixty." They released many records in those years, and a couple of dozen became hits. The increased number of releases did not reduce the percentage that became hits; quality was not sacrificed for quantity. "We didn't waste money in recording when I was in charge. Then, in 1962, when I was fighting the people in the company, our percentage went down. Some of the records could have been hyped better."

Did Si say, "When I was fighting the people in the company"? Who would Si be fighting in his own company, and why?

Avnet Electronics

When Si arrived back in Los Angeles from his European vacation, there was a telephone call from John Marshall of Merrill-Lynch. He had very good news for Si. Avnet, a New York–listed electronics company, wanted to discuss the possibility of a merger with Liberty. This was just the kind of golden opportunity that Si had hoped for.

A meeting was arranged with Bob Avnet, the president, who made a very convincing argument. He was impressed with Liberty's financial statements and inquired as to Si's health. Si said, "Great." After all, he was just back from Europe, and everything was going smoothly for Liberty. It was decided that John Marshall, Al Bennett, and Liberty attorney Ray Sandler would travel to New York and meet with the Avnet board of directors.

A week of intense negotiations resulted in an agreement. Avnet stock was selling for twenty-eight dollars a share. Liberty was selling for thirteen dollars a share. The deal was made that Avnet would exchange two shares of its stock for each three shares of Liberty. As it worked out, Si received one hundred fifty thousand shares of Avnet, a market value of more than four million dollars. In the period 1956 to 1961—four million dollars. And Si was forty-six years old.

Little did Si know that he was soon to lose control of his company, that this merger marked the beginning of the end of Liberty, and that he would be fighting within the ranks of Liberty before the year was out.

Gene McDaniels' *Tower of Strength* LP cover.

Although there were political problems aplenty on the horizon for Liberty, the politics seldom entered the recording studios, and Liberty/Dolton was now in its prime as a rock 'n' roll record label. By 1961 Liberty had enough accumulated hits to ensure that *Original Hits, Vol. 3* was full of Liberty songs by Martin Denny, Bobby Vee, Patience and Prudence, Billy Ward, Johnny Burnette, Gene McDaniels, and the Rollers.

Gene McDaniels? The Rollers? Liberty artists? Who were Gene McDaniels and the Rollers?

Gene McDaniels

Gene McDaniels was the first new Liberty star of 1961. Gene was the son of a Kansas City minister, and Liberty was the first record label he had ever worked for. "Green Door" [Jim Lowe, 1956] and "In Times Like These" were two early Liberty singles Gene recorded. Then success came in a big way for McDaniels with "A

Hundred Pounds of Clay," a top-five hit and the first of eight Liberty chart singles for Gene. The song was unusual, retelling and updating the story of how "He" took one hundred pounds of clay and "created a woman, and a lot of lovin' for a man." The song was popular for four months in the spring and summer of 1961, and established Gene McDaniels as a major rock 'n' roll star.

Parents thought the record was disgusting, if not sacrilegious. Even with the pop-influenced Liberty sound, they felt it poor taste to retell the story of creation in a rock 'n' roll song.

Gene McDaniels's records were produced by Snuff Garrett. "Snuffy" was to many Liberty artists what Sam Phillips was to Sun, what George Martin was to the Beatles, and Phil Spector was to Philles.

Snuff cut a record one day in 1961 and told Al Bennett, "I want a raise." He said, "What do you mean you want a raise? Take whatever you want." So Snuff got two cents a record then. He asked Al when the raise started. Al said, "It's official right now." They signed a little note, and then Snuff played him the little demo he had just made of "A Hundred Pounds of Clay" by Gene McDaniels.

The story of Gene McDaniels at Liberty illustrates the importance of producer Garrett. As Snuff relates, "Gene had been signed by Liberty as a jazz singer, and Si Waronker did albums with him that way. I was in A&R then, and one of the first songs I found was a beautiful song called 'In Times Like These,' which I got on Gene's first album. Si cut that, and it became the title of the album.

"The way I got 'A Hundred Pounds of Clay' was, a New York publisher presented me a whole stack of demos and they were all junk. He said I could skip the bottom one, but I figured I spent so much time on the rest, I'd listen to it. I loved it. I called Si and Al that day from New York and told them I needed a black guy to sing this great song, more rhythm and blues than the demo. They suggested Gene McDaniels, but I felt he was not right for it; he was too good a singer for it. They insisted. They were in the hole about twenty-two thousand dollars on these jazz albums Gene and Si had cut. 'If you cut it with him and it's a hit, we can deduct that money from the royalties.' I had no choice."

"A Hundred Pounds of Clay" reached #3 nationally, and started a string of eight hits for Gene on Liberty.

"My favorite with Gene was Carole [King] and Gerry's [Goffin] 'Point of No Return.' I don't know where Gene is now. I wasn't his favorite person, and he wasn't mine, we didn't hang out, we just recorded."

Recorded hits, that is. "Tower of Strength" and "A Tear" were Gene's other Liberty hits in 1961, to be followed by four more in 1962 and one in 1963.

Snuff guided many of the Liberty artists in selection of material. More importantly, he refined the Liberty sound, which became such an integral part of rock 'n' roll in the early 1960s.

The Liberty Sound — A Closer Look

The Liberty sound — a series of ingredients that were slowly gathered together at Liberty — was important enough to study some more. First, it was an artist, usually but not always a solo male vocalist, like Bobby Vee, Johnny Burnette, Buddy Knox, Garry Miles, or Gene McDaniels. Each of these young men had good "singing voices," with clear tone, on-pitch delivery, and often even vibrato. Most had a strong country or rockabilly flavor, although Gene McDaniels's background was more rhythm and blues and gospel.

Around this male vocalist, Snuff (or sometimes Ross Bagdasarian or Lou Adler) wrapped an orchestra. Remember Johnny Mann's early LPs on Liberty? The Johnny Mann Orchestra and Chorus became the "house band" for Liberty. The Johnny Mann female singers sang the girl-group-style backgrounds for Bobby Vee's "Rubber Ball," to mention just one example. The entire Johnny Mann group sang background on many hit records.

The "orchestra," which at least partly reflected the influence of Si Waronker's movie days, provided timpani, strings, a harp, and woodwinds in addition to electric guitars manned by young rock 'n' rollers such as former members of Buddy Holly's Crickets. Added to all this were the trap sets of Hal Blaine and Earl Palmer. Hal Blaine's drum licks were featured on a great many Liberty hit records (as well as on later records by the Beach Boys, the Mamas and the Papas, and half of the rest of the California hits of the 1960s). In later years Hal had a single under his own name on RCA, "(Dance with the) Surfin' Band" and "The Drummer Plays for Me" (1963), and an LP on Dunhill, *drums! drums! a go go* ([sic], 1965).

Liberty's other house drummer, Earl Palmer, also played drums on many other labels, contributing to the success of best-selling hits by Bobby Vee, Doris Day, Ernie Freeman, Fats Domino, Little Richard, Ricky Nelson, and countless others. Some say that Earl Palmer has been on more hit records than any other performer. Ricky Nelson also benefited from another member of the Liberty family, Johnny Burnette. Johnny and his brother Dorsey wrote and played guitar on several of Ricky's songs, including "Waitin' in School" (1958), and "Just a Little Too Much" and "It's Late" (both 1959).

The Liberty sound was immensely popular in the early and mid-sixties. Some so-called rock 'n' roll "purists" would argue that anything with strings was diluted, imitation rock 'n' roll. In fact, some feel that if all of the performers are not black, the record can't be legitimately called rock and roll. Another less radical and more realistic point of view is that it was only when labels like Liberty added pop elements was the R&B/country-and-western music finally shaped into mainstream rock 'n' roll.

A sound quite similar to the Liberty sound was used by Roy Orbison at Monument Records, Elvis at RCA, Ricky Nelson at Imperial, Gene Pitney at Musicor, Tommy Roe at ABC, Bobby Rydell at Cameo/Parkway, and others. These guys and this sound sold countless millions of records. But the sound was pioneered by the little LA company headed by the boy violin virtuoso, now head of Liberty records, Si Waronker.

Starting sometime in the mid-sixties, the Liberty-type sound began to come under fire as being too professional, too slick, too pop, and too far removed from the original combo rhythm/country blends of Bill Haley, Elvis, and Chuck Berry. These criticisms were unjustified.

The only reason early rock 'n' roll used a combo format was the same reason that early Liberty records used such small bands: financial considerations. The artists and the small labels (like Sun) they were on could not afford to hire orchestras. As soon as the money started coming in, virtually all the combo artists, including

Occasionally Liberty distributed promotional flyers for its LPs. This is one side of a flyer from 1961.

Chuck Berry, Elvis, Buddy Holly, Roy Orbison, and the Beatles began adding horns and even strings to their records.

Roy Orbison confirmed that only budget limitations kept early artists locked into the combo sound, kept them from using violins, timpani and the like. "I couldn't do what I wanted to do," said Orbison about Sun Records. "By the time I left Sun I was wanting to do the material that I eventually wound up singing a couple of years later" (*Goldmine*, February 1, 1985). Elvis made similar statements in his later years, to the effect that the small-combo sound of Sun Records was not what he wanted to be recording. Rather, he wanted to record with violins, like his singing idol, Dean Martin. Elvis recorded "Mystery Train" only because Sam Phillips at Sun played an old 78 and made Elvis copy it. Elvis's roots were Southern/country and pop. Sam Phillips added blues to the mix because it was cheap, requiring only a combo. At RCA big money was available for Elvis's sessions, and Elvis entered the world of rock 'n' roll.

Phil Spector's "Wall of Sound" was based on stringed instruments (other than guitars), as was much of the Beatles' music, including "Yesterday" (1965), "Michelle" (1965), and "Eleanor Rigby" (1966), to name three examples. Rather than being too pop, Liberty was maybe about five years ahead of its time. Most significantly, the Liberty sound brought rock 'n' roll to radio stations and middle-class teenagers who might never have related to pure rhythm and blues, country and western, and other extreme musical forms. As evidence of this, look at how poorly the records of Roy and Elvis fared with their combos at Sun and other labels, and how poorly Johnny Burnette did with his trio, but how successful they were with the Liberty-type sound. In 1961 Johnny's hits were "Little Boy Sad," "Big, Big World," and "God, Country, and My Baby," which was about a serviceman's shipping out to Germany and missing his girl.

The Liberty sound was "reinvented" every few years at other labels anyway. Little Anthony (Gourdine) and the Imperials had one big hit ("Tears on My Pillow," 1958, End Records) and three small follow-ups, all within a year. Then they faded from popularity. In late 1964 they reappeared amid the clutter and clatter of the infamous British Invasion with "I'm on the Outside Looking In" on dcp records [*sic*] and scored more than a dozen other hits through 1974. ("dcp" stood for Don Costa Records, the label of their producer.)

The point? Anthony credits the group's return to popularity with what he called the great, innovative, original notion that Costa dreamed up for them in 1964 — record with more than a band, record with a string orchestra. Wow! What a concept!

Recall that Si Waronker's background was movie musicals. At Liberty he and Snuff added this musical element to the R&B/country and western of the early R&B combos to create popular rock 'n' roll, a synthesis of R&B, country and western, and pop, making it possible for rock 'n' roll to take over the pop market worldwide. He knew what he was doing when he created the Liberty sound, although he did not call it that. He called it rock and roll, with pop mixed in "in order to be understood. If you listen to most Liberty records, you'll find out that the lyrics are understandable. And the other thing, you'll find out that the way we used the reverberation was a little bit different from most people. As you say, the system of recording helps those records."

Along with the Johnny Mann Singers and the strings and everything? "Snuff loved that. Oh, yeah. Let me tell you, Snuff Garrett was the most talented guy I know. He was a little nutty, but who isn't? But he was a kid of twenty when he started, as a promotion man. Then violins were what I always wanted Snuff to add all the time, so he said, 'How about adding the strings yourself?' So I said, 'OK, fine!'

"And on several of his records, at the beginning, we'd walk in there and I'd put the strings in. Because it was easy. In those days, we went from one-track, monaural recording, to what we called stereo, which was nothing more than two channels. Then later to three-track. When we went to three-track, it got to be a cinch. Because we could always use the third track for the string section.

"I had a system with the violins that would feed one track into another. We had three tracks — there was no such thing as twenty-four tracks. So I put the violins on one track. Then I would feed them [electronically], while we were recording the session, from track one to track three, and then back into track two. This added a little bit of a delay. That was the string sound that you are talking about. That was done at United Records with Bill Putnum. He and I came up with this crazy idea: Why not feed it in different tracks at the same time? We made eight violins sound like fifty! That was how you got those string sounds.

"We had to use tricks because we had no money. Money in those days — either you had enough to pay your session with the musicians, or you just didn't record again. That was one reason rock grew so fast. They used so few people, and the guys used to record by themselves in their own garages, pay no studio time, pay no musician time, and in that way, they were able to get an awful lot of product out. Out of fifty recordings, maybe twenty or ten would be great because they had the time to do it. Today you can't afford to do all of that stuff. You go in there, and an album can take over a million bucks to make, to record. I get sick every time I hear of this.

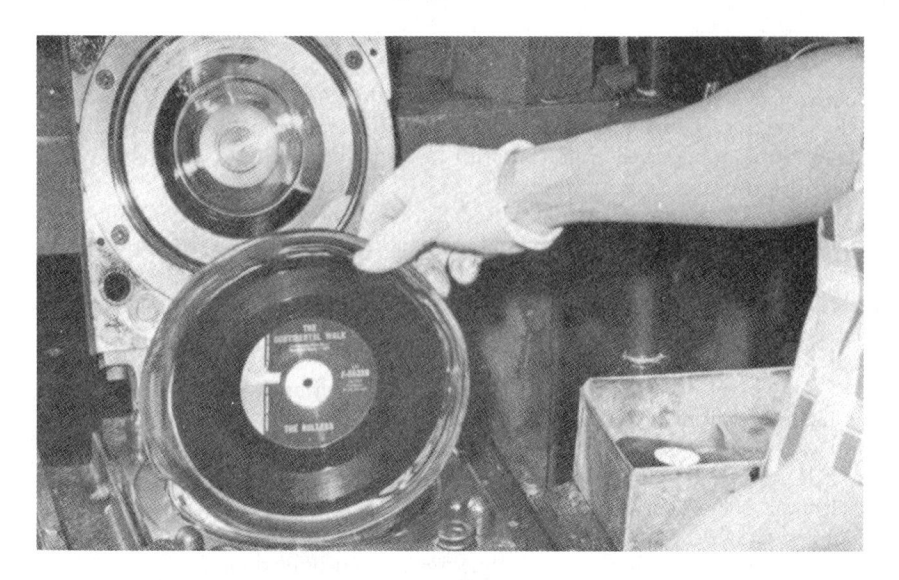

The Rollers' "The Continental Walk" rolls off the pressing machine.

When I hear what some artists pay for an album, I just give up. And the whole business has changed. A whole book could be written about the changes."

Not that Liberty was too inflexible to use the combo style at times. In 1961 the Ventures' combo on Dolton rocked out with hits like "Ram-Bunk-Shush," the label's first hit for 1961, and "Lullaby of the Leaves," "(The Theme from) Silver City," as well as "Blue Moon."

And on Liberty, the Rollers, an R&B combo from San Bernardino, had one hit, "The Continental Walk" (which was not a cover version of the Hank Ballard original—later variations were "Doin' the Continental Walk" by Danny and the Juniors and "Do the New Continental" by the Dovells, both in 1962). The Rollers' song was a Stroll dance record, produced by Snuff Garrett and written by sometime group member Don Covay. The other members were Eddie and Al Wilson, Don Sampson, and Willie Willingham. Covay also wrote "Pony Time," a hit in the same year from Chubby Checker on Parkway Records. Even that record had pop roots, though, being a reworking of "Boogie Woogie" from the pre–rock 'n' roll big-band days.

It is too bad that Liberty did not hang on to Don Covay. But he was a slippery guy. Using his own name, he scored more than a half-dozen hits on five different record labels between 1961 and 1973. One was his own version of "Pony Time" on Arnold Records before Chubby's bigger version, and another was "I Was Checkin' Out, She Was Checkin' In" on Rosemart in 1973.

Timi Yuro

In July 1961, Miss Timi Yuro joined the Liberty family of hitmakers. She was the first new (successful) Liberty female rock 'n' roller since Margie Rayburn back in

1957. Given the full Liberty sound treatment, she would have ten Liberty hits before she was done. Mostly forgotten today, Timi had more hits than the better-remembered Liberty singers Gene McDaniels (eight) and Eddie Cochran (seven). Of all of the Liberty artists signed as of 1961, Bobby Vee and only Bobby Vee (thirty-seven) would ever outsell Timi Yuro with 45-rpm singles! Her current obscurity can only be attributed to musical sexism.

However, as Snuff relates, Liberty let Timi do her own thing. "Timi Yuro really produced herself no matter who sat in the booth. Clyde Otis was her producer, he was our East Coast producer. A year later, he left, so I hired a friend of mine, Phil Spector, and put him as head of the East Coast. He cut Timi from then on. At least I had him do a new dub down on an album she had already cut, a record that I didn't care for the mix."

Timi was from Chicago and was personally signed by Si Waronker's president of Liberty records, Al Bennett. Si felt she had talent. "Timi Yuro was a little tiny girl with a great voice. She was very frustrated, had many emotional problems. She could sing if you had the right tune. She started out in a duo, Timi and Tommy. I recorded one tune with her, then turned her over to a black A&R man from New York we had for a while, Clyde Otis. He had a big hit with her. But she was another artist who couldn't follow through. She was a very troubled girl."

Together Timi and Clyde developed a slightly different sound and slower tempo for Timi's releases. Her first hit, "Hurt," made the top five, and the flip side, "I Apologize," also charted. This record had established her, much as "A Hundred Pounds of Clay" had established Gene McDaniels, who got money for Liberty.

Studio engineer Bones Howe worked the Timi Yuro session, and was impressed by its producer, Clyde Otis. "I was the engineer on 'Hurt.' I remember the black producer who cut it. He took me to dinner the night we cut the record and said, 'Did you ever cut a number one record before?' I said, 'Yes, a couple.' He said, 'Well, you're gonna cut one tonight.' I always remembered that. And he knew. That is what A&R is all about, knowing that a great song and a great artist will make a hit."

Timi's eight other hits included "Smile" and "What's a Matter, Baby?" Her last hit for Liberty was "Gotta Travel On" in 1963. She was often called "Miss Timi Yuro" because her androgynous name and deep singing voice sometimes called her gender into question. She left Liberty for one final, minor hit on Mercury Records in 1965.

Liberty's national head of promotion, Don Blocker, knew Timi. "Si Waronker signed Timi Yuro. He had cut a track with her, but Clyde Otis heard the track and cut 'Hurt' with her. Timi was overmanaged or overinfluenced by her mother. That led to her demise. But Timi's mom had a restaurant, and when Willie Nelson, who was on the label, was flat broke, he'd go over there and she would feed him. That's why, years later, Willie Nelson cut a duet album with Timi Yuro. It may not have been released. But Timi was very Italian and very emotional."

As with most Liberty artists, Timi was permitted to release a number of LPs, more than a half-dozen. The first was *Hurt!!!!!!!!* Later came *Soul,* one called *What's a Matter Baby,* and *The Best of Timi Yuro.*

Bobby Vee continued to prosper in 1961, with two two-sided hits. One was the banned "Stayin' In"/"More than I Can Say." Dick Clark banned "Stayin' In" from "Bandstand" because it was about having a fight over a girl's reputation in the school

HURT!!!!!!!!
And That Reminds Me
I Won't Cry Anymore
A Little Bird Told Me
Just Say I Love Him
You'll Never Know
I Should Care
I'm Confessin'
(That I Love You)
I Apologize
For You
Trying
Cry

Timi Yuro LP cover.

cafeteria. "Stayin' In" was written by John D. ("Sittin' in the Balcony") Loudermilk, who would write many 1960s rock 'n' roll hits for a variety of artists and labels.

Bobby also had "How Many Tears" and "Take Good Care of My Baby," both written by legendary singer-songwriter Carole King. Bobby recorded this second Carole King song because Snuff chose it in preference over two other songs that were presented to him, "Little Sister" and "(Marie's the Name of) His Latest Flame." These two songs then became a two-sided hit for Elvis — perhaps Bobby Vee would have scored yet another two-sided 45 himself, had he chosen to do those songs. But one can hardly criticize his choice: "Take Good Care of My Baby" was Bobby's only #1 hit and the fourth biggest chart record in the history of Liberty/Dolton/Imperial.

The other 1961 record that Bobby got both sides of on the charts was "Run to Him"/"Walking with My Angel." And whereas Bobby lost two songs to Elvis when he did "Take Good Care of My Baby," this time he — let's say — inherited a song that was intended to go to someone else. When a stack of prospective songs for Bobby to consider for recording was picked up, a second stack intended for the Everly Brothers was also picked up by mistake. "Run to Him" was in the Everly stack, and its harmonies do bring the brothers to mind. Bobby recorded the song several different ways, experimenting with different harmony parts until the one they liked was found.

Si Waronker couldn't say enough kind things about Bobby. "Bobby Vee, there was another sweet kid. He is a nice boy. He would do anything, in other words, he was the kind of artist you wanted, any company would have wanted to keep. You asked him to do a certain tune, he would do it. You asked him to do it a certain way, he would do it. And I liked the sounds that came out of him. He deserved all the credit he got. I am glad he does so well still [constantly touring into the 1990s]."

Bobby Vee explains his success with two-sided hit records by picking the best songs and doing the best job with them he possibly could. Si has his explanation for two-sided hits as well.

"When we had four or five tunes recorded [with an artist like Bobby Vee], we took the two that we felt were the best or the most commercial and put them on a single. We would back them and hope that one of the two would take off. We'd make bets on which one we thought would work. I used to lose. Snuffy would win more than I would. And I'll be damned if in a couple of instances, we had two-sided hits! But there was such guesswork. We never usually thought that a flip side would get played. Sometimes if we owed someone a favor, we'd let them publish the song on the flip side to repay them. [They got composer royalties for each copy sold.] But we didn't do it for any other reason."

In the late 1960s a theory became popular that held that in the pre–Beatle early 1960s, rock 'n' roll LPs were unimportant and poorly produced. The claim was that 45s were often carefully crafted with an eye toward scoring a chart hit. Then, when an artist had a successful 45, a shoddy LP would be hastily thrown together. Anyone who bought very many Liberty LPs in the early 1960s would know that this theory was completely false. Sure, in some cases, albums were hastily tossed together to cash in on a hit single. But more often they were something that the company and the artist really cared about. On a Liberty LP, once the lean days of 1955–57 were past, every song usually got the full treatment given to 45 singles. Moreover, many Liberty/Dolton artists, like the Ventures, Julie London, and Martin Denny (whose 1961 album was *Romantica!*), actually sold more LPs than they did 45s, and actually cut more LPs than they had hit 45s. Frequently, as Si explained, which song was to be the single was often not even decided until after several songs, even an entire album, was on tape.

Quality was always job number one at Liberty. While the business was intended to make money, that goal was not pursued at the expense of making honest records—including the flip sides.

Phil Spector used to put two-minute instrumentals on his groups' flip sides, something Si would not tolerate. "You know why he did that. Look who is credited with writing those things. That way he got composer and publishing royalties for the flip sides. I was completely against that sort of thing. I used to fight like hell at Liberty that the artist have nothing to do with publishing. If they had a tune that they did, they really wrote, and was good enough to record, that was fine. But don't go out and find somebody else's tune and think you want to go into publishing. I had no publishing company to make money [out] of others that way with, but Liberty had to have one for tunes people brought in that had no publisher."

The Fleetwoods proved that they still had what it took as singers (and selectors of material) in 1961, when their revival of Thomas Wayne's composition and 1959 hit "Tragedy" took them to the top of the charts yet again. This melancholy love song fit their style perfectly. It had been a hit right when "Come Softly to Me" had come out, and was obviously a favorite of the group. The Fleetwoods' other hit of the year was written by Sharon Sheeley and Jackie DeShannon, "(He's) The Great Imposter," a record that easily made the top forty on the strength of the material and the patented Fleetwoods soft-rock performance.

Gretchen Christopher was a fan of early Liberty star Julie London. Julie's influence manifests itself on a Fleetwoods LP (released for their recording of the Jackie DeShannon–Sharon Sheeley song "(He's) The Great Imposter," the Fleetwoods' ninth hit record). "'Cry Me a River' was one of the songs that I used to sing as a child. I wrote a song that was along those lines. We did it for our fourth album called *Deep in a Dream*. The song was called 'Blues, Go Away.' It was a very smokey, bluesy, torchy kind of song. When I finished it, I said to myself, 'I've written a standard!' It became the first Fleetwoods solo to appear on an album. Actually, Barb and Gary were there, but then their voices were dialed out when the engineer mixed it."

After writing "Come Softly to Me," couldn't the Fleetwoods have written more hits? "They have things in their albums that they wrote," explains Bob Reisdorff. "But I kept urging them to write more, saying, 'Look, you have an opportunity you will never have in your life again! Write, for God's sake! Write!' But it was very hard to get them to do it. That was a pattern that I found throughout my time in the record industry. People worked hard at first, but once they got their hit or got some prominence, they got very lazy. I never had a driven artist, I wish I had had.

"Gary Troxel did write some songs, including 'Poor Little Girl,' which was on the Fleetwoods' *Deep in a Dream* album. His cocomposer was Vic Dana, who was also his substitute when the group toured while Gary was in the Navy."

How did Gary's stand-in become his writing partner? "I was in the Navy in San Diego, and I could come up to Los Angeles on the weekends, which I did almost every weekend. That was when that would have happened."

Gary was on active duty when the auditions for his stand-in were held, so he was not there for the auditions. He was away for about six months. In all, his hitch was in 1961 and 1962, prime Fleetwoods years. "I joined the reserves before the Fleetwoods happened. It came to the point where I had to go."

Vic Dana

Bob Reisdorff was happy to have Vic Dana signed to Dolton as a solo artist even before Gary came back from the Navy. "Vic Dana was extremely professional and committed, but on the other hand at that time he did not write songs. And he didn't know he could. He later wrote some songs that Glen Campbell recorded."

So besides the Ventures and the Fleetwoods, Liberty's Dolton subsidiary label signed another artist who was a great LP seller. Vic Dana first came to Liberty/Dolton as a temporary stand-in for Gary Troxel of the Fleetwoods, who had gone into the Navy. This subbing led to a solo contract, which resulted in thirteen hits,

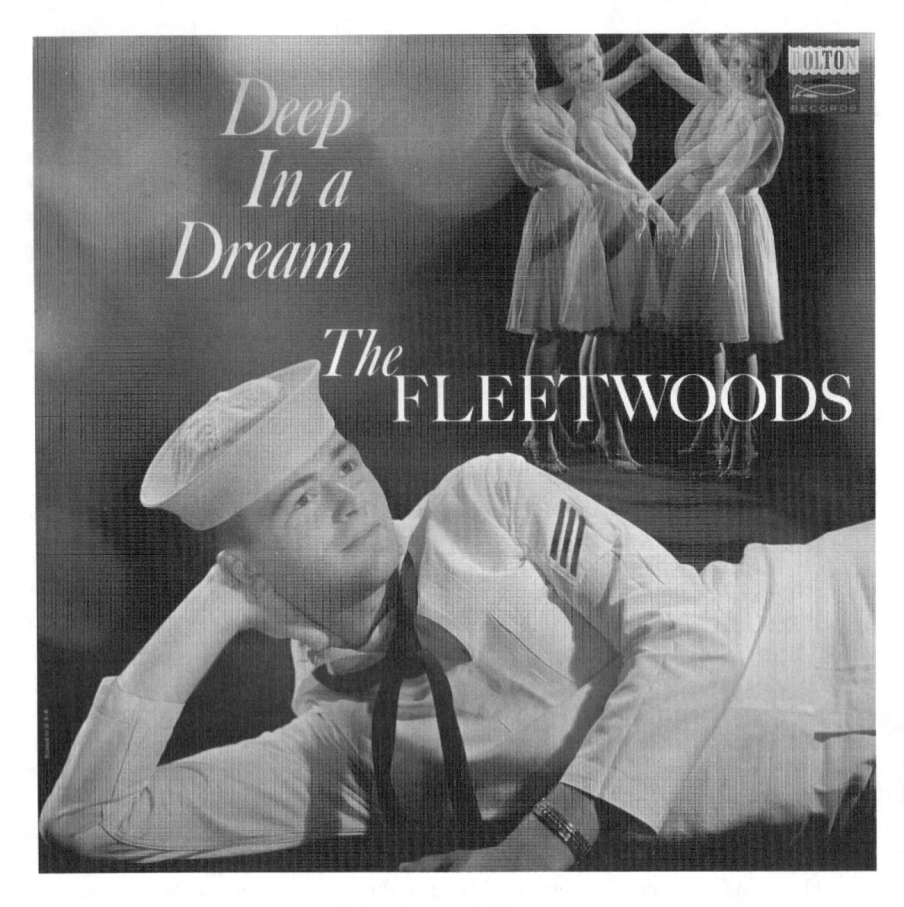

Early Fleetwoods LP cover.

three in the national top forty. One, "Danger," in 1963 made the nineties nationally yet was a rocking top-forty hit in the Midwest!

Bob Reisdorff laments: "I have never had a performing group who became known. I had Vic Dana, who did quite well for a while." The Fleetwoods toured very, very little. Gary was in the Navy and was shy, and the group was primarily a studio unit. But Vic Dana was almost a born performer, as Bob Reisdorff elaborated.

"He had been taught to dance; he had danced with Sammy Davis, Jr., as a kid. Sammy told his mother to take him to Hollywood so he could have a real career. And she did. He was a Firestone tire salesman when he was nineteen. His brother talked him into replacing Gary for that year [Gary spent] in the Navy.

"Vic Dana replaced Gary for performing purposes only. But I got Gary out of the Navy for a year. I had to go on my knees for these naval people and try to get through to them that this is a one-time opportunity for young Gary. If it is thrown away, it is over and gone forever. You cannot take a year off.

"But they said, 'Well, these carpenters who are apprentices, we take them off and they pick up where they left off when they return.' I had to explain that it is not comparable. I would cite these rock 'n' roll groups—who of course these naval people had never heard of—who had a one-shot deal that was not capitalized on with a follow-up. The Penguins with "Earth Angel," the Five Satins with "In the Still of the Night"—you need a follow-up. So we got him out for a year during 'Mr. Blue' and 'Tragedy.' They had their two big hits; then there were the top-twenty hits and top-fifty hits, 'The Great Imposter,' Barbara singing lead on 'Goodnight My Love.'"

Did Vic Dana appear only on stage as a Fleetwood, or did he also appear on Fleetwoods' records? Lead Fleetwood Gretchen: "No, Vic Dana did not do any recordings with the Fleetwoods. We'd said that whoever we signed would get a solo recording contract [with Dolton]. So that is how Vic Dana got his solo recording contract. We discovered him, so to speak. Auditions were set up, Bob put ads in the trades or something like that, and we auditioned many, many people before narrowing it down to several: Vic, and two of the fellows from the Lettermen. Then they [the Lettermen] decided that they wanted to give their group one more try, and they did, and they got their first hit! ["The Way You Look Tonight," 1961.] But that is how Vic got his recording contract."

Dana's first Dolton hit, "Little Altar Boy," has become a Christmas classic. Dana was the only Dolton artist to employ the Liberty sound, and although he could rock on songs like "Danger," he mostly evened out his sound, cutting pop ballads like "Red Roses for a Blue Lady." While Vic Dana released more than a dozen Dolton LPs, he never became a rock 'n' roller in the same league with the other Liberty/Dolton hit makers.

Along with signing hit maker Vic Dana, another change took place at Dolton around the same time. Shortly after Liberty acquired Dolton, it was suggested that the label be redesigned—that the old one (made by a local Seattle artist) be altered. The word *Dolton* had been down the side of the label in a partitioned section, coincidentally like the Liberty label. Now the word was moved to the top of the label and placed inside the body of one of the dolphins. The dolphins themselves were redrawn to permit this. There formerly were three (or on some Dolton records, two) slim dolphins shaded blue. On the new label, there were still two smaller blue dolphins, but the third dolphin was enlarged to contain the word *Dolton*.

Does Bob Reisdorff remember the changes? "I don't know why the changes were made. I am sure I was deeply involved and concerned at the time. I know I was content with the job that the artist did. I liked it at the time."

In the winter of 1962–63, "Liberty wanted us to use their graphics studio [to redo the Dolton label]. I said 'Sure, design something, and we'll look at it.'" This third and final Dolton design was dark blue, although the exact shade varied with different releases. The three new Dolphins were placed on the side of the label again, but were very small, too small to hold the word *Dolton*. That word was placed inside some white ocean waves. As a final flourish, the Liberty rainbow colors were used to color the letters: *D* was orange, *O* was red, *L* was purple, *T* was blue, *O* was green, and *N* was yellow, green, or purple. In fact, the shades of all of the colors were apt to vary.

Bob Reisdorff was easy to please. "The dark blue Dolton label was designed by Studio Five, which Liberty had. We had that label most of the time. It seemed superior to me to the light blue one."

Speaking of labels, would it be an advantage for a new record to be released

GRETCHEN CHRISTOPHER   GARY TROXEL   BARBARA ELLIS
THE FLEETWOODS   DOLTON RECORDING

Above and opposite: Two versions of the Fleetwoods: Vic Dana *(opposite)* was a stand-in for Gary Troxel *(above)* while the latter was in the Navy. Gretchen Christopher is always pictured on the male member's right, Barbara Ellis on his left. *(Courtesy Gretchen Christopher.)*

on a label that had already had another hit? Did the appearance of a song on a label that had already had a #1 record give that new record a better chance with distributors, or was it just the sound of the new record alone that mattered? Bob Reisdorff: "I do think that it mattered with very small companies. When Roulette came out and had the hit 'Party Doll' with Buddy Knox, then came along with Jimmy Bowen and 'I'm Stickin' with You,' that gave the label prestige. The second guy couldn't sing, but I think if a label has one hit, then another hit, I feel people do pick up on it and look for the label somewhat.

"Although for a really good song, I don't think it would matter to anyone what label it was on in a negative sense. I never ran into a negative attitude concerning a label, where they felt they did not want to play a record because is was on RCA, say, or London or End or whatever. Well, something on King Records might get ignored and things on those so-called 'race labels,' because there was a time when they were ignored for years till R&B started to happen. I always thought that it was a great shame, because there were wonderful things done that were not played.

"Cadence [which had the Everly Brothers and the Chordettes] was a label that didn't put out that many records. But they tried to put out something that had value within its own terms. I think they might have been paid attention to for that. When you get a company that just grinds out the records and never has a hit, in that sense a small label might do poorly. Big ones aren't hot enough relative to the number of records they put out.

"With Dolton, we were careful what we put out. We released a lot more records

Chapter 9 · 1961   115

THE FLEETWOODS   DOLTON RECORDING ARTISTS   Personal Management:
GABBE, LUTZ, HELLER & LOEB
ARNOLD MILLS, associate
New York — Hollywood

in Washington than we issued nationally. During the Seattle years, which were only about two, we put out very few records nationally. We continued to release records regionally after we moved to LA, rather then denigrate the name of the label by releasing [nationally] a lot of records that were not hits. If they became big locally, then they could go out nationally."

Troy Shondell

Liberty signed another male singer in 1961, Troy Shondell, from Fort Wayne, Indiana. In Indiana Troy had recorded "This Time" for his own makeshift record label, Gold Crest. When the record became locally popular, Liberty astutely negotiated a deal for national release on Liberty. The song then made the top ten,

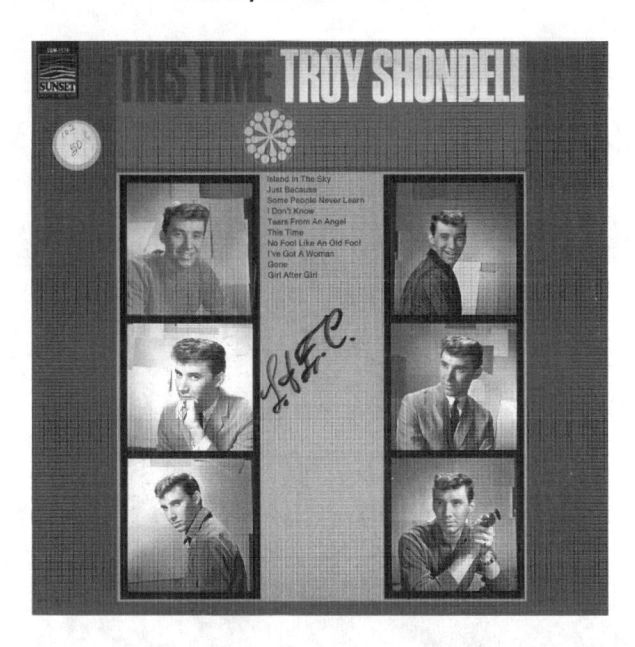

Troy Shondell, whose independently recorded hit "This Time" was released nationally on Liberty.

but two follow-ups sold poorly, and Troy did not stick around for long. Naturally, he did have a few LPs for Liberty. Troy Shondell's sound was sort of a cross between Jimmy Clanton ("Just a Dream," 1959) and Johnny Burnette. "This Time" made the big time, the national top ten, and became a classic slow-dance love ballad about breaking up: "This time I'm really losing you."

Troy's last name, appearing as it did on Liberty records that were released in 1961 and 1962, inspired Tommy James ("Hanky Panky," 1966; "Crimson and Clover," 1968) to name his own group Tommy James and the Shondells!

According to his LP liner notes, written by Bernie Soloman, Troy was a prolific songwriter, penning more than four hundred songs per year, many of them hits, though none of them cited. He did not write any of his own hits, nor did he play the trumpet, which his trumpet-playing father taught him to use after a fashion when he was under four years old! Eventually becoming accomplished on keyboards and tenor sax, Troy is remembered by Snuff Garrett. "Troy Shondell had a record ["This Time"] we picked up as a master. The next record they wanted done in house, so I cut a couple of things with him, and I had Spec cut a couple of things with him. Neither one of us went to glory with anything. We did a record, 'Tears from an Angel' on one side that I cut and 'Island in the Sky' on the flip side, cut by my good friend Phil Spector. I put them both out shootin' at the moon, me on one side and Spec on the other side; we didn't care which side made it as long as we could do something. We picked those as the two best sides of all the ones we each did with Troy."

Well, there is a bit more to the story than that. Both sides of the single did chart, "Tears from an Angel" at #77, and "Island in the Sky" at #92. And there is no way to tell which side was produced by Phil versus Snuff, as both sides of this 45 carry the legend "Producer: Snuff Garrett." A typesetter's error? "Tears from an Angel" did have the distinction of being yet another tune written by Sharon Sheeley and Jackie DeShannon.

In the fall of 1961, the Doré Record connection came up again at Liberty. Back in 1960 the Doré version of "Look for a Star" by Deane Hawley had competed with Liberty's own version by Garry Miles. Now in 1961, Deane Hawley himself was signed by Liberty. The only one of his several Liberty singles to go anywhere was one called "Pocketful of Rainbows," and it was a very small hit by Liberty/Dolton standards.

Dick and Deedee

By way of contrast, Dick St. John was an aspiring songwriter, which meant he fit right in at Liberty in the early 1960s. However, he was not doing too well getting people to record his songs, and in 1961 he became a singer himself, at Liberty. His first single was written by himself with a friend. The song was named "I Want Someone," and the friend was named Mary ("Deedee") Sperling. Actually "I Want Someone" was Mary's composition, and Dick helped her to complete it.

Together, Dick and Deedee recorded "I Want Someone" as a duet on a mono tape recorder. The unique sound of Dick and Deedee came about by accident. As they tried to make a tape and sing along with it and make another tape too, the two recorders never played in perfect synch. The strange echo effect, with Dick singing the high and low parts and Deedee filling in the middle harmonies, blew people away. They took the tape to producer Don Ralke of Liberty. He signed them and became their mentor.

Their record was first released on Lama Records and, after it became a local hit, was moved to Liberty. In fact Dick and Deedee were never really signed to Liberty, but to Don Ralke and the Wilder brothers, who produced them and delivered tapes to Liberty. Not only that, Dick and Deedee were almost placed with Smash or RCA, but Liberty won out.

For the flip side of "I Want Someone," Dick wrote a song called "The Mountain's High." Contrary to the popular legend reported in many sources, Dick was not inspired by a drawing he, an art student, had done. As fate would have it, the kids and DJs turned Dick and Deedee's platter over and the flip side, "The Mountain's High," became the hit side.

Dick and Deedee were an odd couple. Since they were not married or romantically linked, the rumor (unfounded) that they were brother and sister spread. "The Mountain's High" had a very odd sound, which luckily caught on so well that the song ultimately scored in the top ten. Their sound had a rock 'n' roll beat, but very little obvious R&B or country influence.

The follow-up, "Tell Me," made the top forty. "Tell Me" was slower than "The Mountain's High," and must have been planned as a follow-up back when "I Want Someone" was planned as a hit. Either that or Dick still believed in his original composition as a potential A-side hit. You see, "Tell Me" is really "I Want Someone" just slightly rewritten. The way it sounds, it had to have been either a soundalike follow-up, or else the same song rewritten to salvage his earlier composition.

Dick and Deedee's only Liberty LP.

After an LP, *Tell Me the Mountain's High,* Dick and Deedee departed Liberty for a hit or two in the mid-sixties on Warner Bros. Ironically their big hit on WB was "Thou Shalt Not Steal," written not by Dick but by John D. Loudermilk, who earlier had written Eddie Cochran's Liberty hit, "Sittin' in the Balcony" and the A side of Bobby Vee's two-sided Liberty hit, "Stayin' In."

While Don Ralke produced Dick and Deedee, Liberty producer Snuff Garrett branched out and did the cover photography for the Dick and Deedee Liberty LP. Wayne Scrivner of *Dig!* magazine wrote these 1961 liner notes for Dick and Deedee:

> When you buy this album, hold on to it. As time goes by, tastes in music will change. They always do. But the sound of Dick and Deedee will be as refreshing in 1972 as in 1962. And don't think I won't be around in 1972 to say "I told you so." It's a date!

Dick and Deedee's LP is playing as this is being written, and it is as refreshing now (twenty years after 1972) as it was then, with "I Want Someone" and "Moon River" highlighting side 1, and "Unchained Melody" featured on side 2. The sound is just as unique now as it was in 1961. But, in light of the British Invasion, acid rock, folk rock, disco, punk, new wave, heavy metal, and rap, one wonders if Wayne Scrivner of *Dig!* actually does still own, let alone listen to his copy of *Tell Me the Mountain's High!*

Deedee agrees. "Oh, yes, the 1970s were generally disco. I doubt if too many people listened to that album then, or do these days!"

Dick and Deedee's singing roots go back to late childhood. "Dick and I went to school together in junior high; we have known each other literally all of our lives. We lived in a close proximity to each other. In high school we got summer jobs at the same place, C's Candy. I was selling candy, and he was in back breaking down boxes. On break, we'd go out and talk. I was writing lyrics and he was writing music. So we decided to try to put some of them together. That was how we wrote "I Want Someone." That was the song that everybody believed in; they put a lot of money into the session; they hired strings, an orchestra. Everything was live, you didn't have very many tracks and you had to get it right all at once. It was arranged by Don Ralke and a wonderful arranger with tons of musicians. And then they had nothing for the back side! And they wanted to do these two songs together [at one session]. Dick had come up with "The Mountain's High," and we did just a quick throwaway session. They just threw it on the back of this other song that they thought was so great.

"That record was area tested on our manager's own label, not on Liberty, in the San Francisco Bay area. And 'The Mountain's High' was just huge! It became number one very quickly, so they were able to sublet it to Liberty for national release. That was how we got on Liberty in the first place.

"In LA, the minute it was released, there was a radio strike in town. They had pickets out in front of all the radio stations, and they barred any promotion men from entering the building with new product. Just at that time, our record was made a Disc-covery on the two top LA stations."

These Disc-coveries were called a "Pick to Click," a "Pic Hit," a "Wax to Watch," a "Best Bet," or a "Climber" at various stations in the 1950s and 1960s. Such records are projected to become big sellers. Stations featured these songs every hour for one week; then a new song was selected for special attention the next week. "Normally this lasts for just a week, then the station would specify a new Disc-covery and push *it* for a week. The strike went on for weeks and weeks, and the play list was never changed." Dick and Deedee's Liberty 45 was spotlighted for an inordinate amount of time. Meanwhile, it was becoming a hit—kids were buying it—but its status as such was not reflected on the top forty, where it was frozen as a Disc-covery due to the strike.

"When the strike was over and the play list changed, 'The Mountain's High' went from Disc-covery to number one, bam! They said that no record had ever done that up to that day, and I don't think any record has ever done it since!"

"But the popularity of our record was spotty. Liberty wasn't very strong on the East Coast at that time. By the time they started promoting it in the East, the superfast success in LA was already decreasing in the West. So we did not get the national momentum of having a hit everywhere at once, which would have made it even bigger. It eventually did well everywhere, but not all at once."

What was it like for Dick and Deedee to be on Liberty? "We were very young teenagers, and we were suddenly assigned to this label. We actually had very little contact with Liberty in that, once we suddenly had a hit record, we were on the road all the time. In those days, too, there were no television shows promoting everything. All there really was was Ed Sullivan. So we were on the road. We did go back and record other songs, but that again was done by the same procedure with our producers in their studio, not with Liberty. They [Liberty] just leased the recordings. We didn't have the same vantage point as an artist who was signed more directly to Liberty.

"Having my name changed to Deedee was startling! All my life I thought I'd been known by a certain name. I had no say in the change. I was never even told about it until after the fact. Actually Dick came over with the record, and I just stared at it. He said, 'That's your new name.' I said, 'Wait a minute! How come your name stayed the same, and my name changed? My name is Mary. Why couldn't it be "Mick and Mary"? Where'd they come up with this?' I guess they thought it had to be catchy, and there was one of the big disc jockeys in San Francisco, where it had done so well—he later became very influential in the underground radio of the 1970s. His daughter, now also a DJ, was named Dierdre, Deedee for short. Maybe he came up with it, I don't know who came up with it. So that was that, that was what it already said on the label, and that was what it became!"

Sort of. Depending on which 45 or LP one looks at, the name is either "Dee Dee," "DeeDee," or "Deedee." So which is correct? "The correct spelling of the distaff half of the group name is *Deedee*. I lowered the second *D* when I was still singing with Dick and signing autographs. You won't believe this, but it took too long to lift the pen off the paper to start the second capital *D*, so I just wrote a little *d* to keep a continuous flow with the pen. I know that sounds totally ridiculous, but when confronted with signing my name hundreds of times in succession, this was the easiest solution. I've just kept the small *d* ever since."

Did not being signed directly to Liberty mean that Dick and Deedee seldom saw other Liberty stars? "My experiences were usually whatever Dick's were. We were usually together when we walked into the building or whatever. We went to high school with Jan and Dean and Arnie."

Dick and Deedee did shows with people like Ray Peterson and other hot stars, and often used the fledgling Beach Boys for their backup band for local gigs.

But mostly the male-female duo was too busy to socialize. "Liberty sent us on an East Coast promotional tour. In lieu of any other way of promotion, since there was no television, they sent us back east on a 'whirlwind tour' of all the radio stations. This entailed a Liberty promotion man out of New York meeting us and taking us barnstorming. We saw maybe six or ten radio stations a day. And this entailed taking them all out to breakfast, lunch, or dinner! You crammed it all in; we gained about twenty pounds. We were turning into blimps slowly [but] surely after a while. It was in the winter, and we'd never been in snow before, so we weren't getting very much exercise." Deedee jokes, "When we got off the plane, our parents walked right past us!"

Were there any Dick and Deedee fakes like the ones the Fleetwoods encountered when they toured radio stations, or were there any Dick and Deedee cover records like the cover versions of the Fleetwoods' "Come Softly to Me"? Deedee explains that Dick and Deedee were not really copyable. "We had a very, very unique sound. Part of it was done in the studio. We overdubbed different harmonies, four parts to every song; I did the middle two voices. People couldn't really imitate that sound."

Speaking of the Dick and Deedee sound ... that sound got Dick and Deedee into some interesting situations. "We were often taken as a black act because we sounded that way. Once we went up to Sacramento into a jazz-type club, and when we walked in, they said, 'Who are you?' We said, 'You hired us, we're Dick and Deedee.' They said, 'You can't be!' We got through that OK; they seemed to like us well enough."

Deedee was often nervous about live appearances, especially in the early Dick and Deedee stage performances. But when Dick lost his voice, apparently from all those shrieking falsetto parts he screamed out, she got over it. "I had stage fright, and my knees would shake. But what cured that was when Dick completely lost his voice once. It was down the road a bit, after several hits. Even if you called him on the phone, he had a little bell he would ring to let you know he was on the line. He couldn't talk. He had nodules that had grown in his throat. Some artists, maybe Tina Turner, get them and never have the surgery; they get that gravelly sound and that is their trademark. But Dick couldn't speak. We were booked on a tour, and they didn't want to cancel. We said, 'How can we possibly sing? He can't utter a sound!' They said, 'You'll have to lip-synch.' Well, we thought, who's gonna be fooled by that? It's ridiculous! They convinced us to go out there.

"Everyone else on the show was singing live with the band. Then it was our turn, and we'd walk out there as someone would punch a tape recorder and we'd start to mouth these words. I would have to announce that Dick had lost his voice and we appreciated their being here. It forced me to have to give a little speech every night, introduce each song, and carry the whole show. Being forced into that position night after night, I just got used to it and it took away all of my stage fright. There were the times the tape recorder would break down or the tape would stick right in the middle of a song and we'd have our mouths open and stop...."

In the annals of rock 'n' roll, there are countless tales of artists getting cheated out of their royalties. Record companies might give a lower percentage of payment than the industry average. Someone might under report sales. Or a company might move out of town and just never pay up!

There were other ways that an artist would lose out on royalties, ways that cut not only the artist but also the record company out of the profit picture!

"We heard from disc jockeys stories of underground warehouses around the country with bootleg records. In fact, years later someone told us about a record we [Dick and Deedee] had that came out right after 'The Mountain's High' but before 'Tell Me.' It was called 'Goodbye to Love.' It was a complete disaster, it didn't sell three copies. It had a duck call on it, and it was pretty awful! We tried to make it like 'The Mountain's High' to have another hit, but it didn't happen. But, in anticipation of its happening, Liberty pressed many copies and shipped them out.

"Well, the bootleggers got hold of this new record and, thinking it was going to be a big hit like 'The Mountain's High,' pressed up their copies! [When it was not a hit], all the returns came back to Liberty! They said that it was the first time that they had ever gotten more of a record back than they had ever pressed up! They couldn't figure it out, where had they all come from? That just showed you that there was a big bootleg operation going on in addition to what was being reported legally."

After Liberty, Dick and Deedee moved to Warner Bros. "They sent us on a tour to London. They thought that they could break us into the British market by having us go over there and be on television shows and all that. We met Brian Jones of the Rolling Stones, and through him met his record producer, Andrew Oldham. Dick was a true character, a unique individual, and he got this idea into his head, this mind-set that Andrew Oldham was going to record us. He was so convinced of this that he decided not to let Andrew Oldham out of his sight. We'd just met him in this club, and Dick wouldn't let him leave!

"Finally, in desperation, to pacify Dick, he said that he had some old tracks that the Rolling Stones did that they were never going to release. 'If they are in the right key, the Stones did all the music, backups even, you can come by and put your voices on. But I don't have the time to do a whole new session.'

"Dick had him bring the tapes to the hotel that night, and sure enough, they were in the right key. They put this deal together quickly, called Warner Bros., and went into the studio. I was a little nervous, the Rolling Stones were really big in England at the time. I didn't know who would be waiting in the studio for us when we walked in.

"As we walked in, there was a floor mat with little teeny holes. My high heel caught in one of the little holes and I fell flat on my face. I had the wind knocked out of me. At that moment, in come Keith Richards and Brian Jones and Andrew Oldham. I am lying there. We are introduced, 'This is Dick and Deedee,' and here I am sprawled flat out on a mat with the wind knocked out of me! I couldn't even speak, I just went, 'Ummgh.' So I tried to compose myself and pretend this was a normal event. I gathered up everything that had gone flying all over the room, I got up, composed myself, and they just acted like, 'Oh, well, I guess she always does this kind of stuff.'

"We managed to put the vocals on the songs, and one came out as a single on Warner's. We did it a lot on 'Shindig,' and—nothing ever happened. I don't know why. We had a very strange career; we'd have a hit, then we'd have a miss. It was the oddest thing, and even now I can't tell the rhyme or reason for it."

Dick and Deedee were not with Liberty very long. Of their eight hits between 1961 and 1965, only the first two were on Liberty. Before 1962 was gone, Dick and Deedee had left and scored the remainder of their hits for Warner Bros. Records. How and why did Dick and Deedee leave Liberty so soon after arriving? After all, the Liberty artist contracts were usually for three or five years.

Liberty hit composer Sharon Sheeley remembers it well. "Dick St. John was getting screwed by Al Bennett for royalties. He came to me crying. He was so distraught, he was beside himself. He's a very emotional person. And Deedee was saying to me, 'I don't know what to do.'

"I told Dick exactly what to do. I said, 'Dick, don't be so distraught. Just go in there and make a scene. [Liberty President] Al Bennett cannot stand a scene; he just can't. But you have to go in there between five and five-thirty, because that's when they all have their big card game. That's when they shut the doors and open the liquor cabinet.' Al was into straight gin and poker.

"I set it all up in advance. I told Al beforehand, 'You know my friend Dick is not very stable. And he wants out of his contract.' Al retorted, 'Fat chance, Sheeley!' And he laughed.

"I told him, 'Well, Al, it's going to be me or him.'"

"'We'll talk about this tomorrow, darlin'.'"

"I said, 'You promise? Because it *is* him or me!'

"So Dick did it. He faked a heart attack, a nervous breakdown. He fell down on the floor. And Al could not wait to get him out of his office!

"After that I told Al, 'You have two choices. You let them go, or you let me go.' Al said, 'They are outta here!'

"Dick came over to see me then, and he hugged me and said it [had] worked. I told him it would, just because Al Bennett could not stand a scene—that was a big weakness of his."

Deedee will never forget the day Dick had his nervous breakdown as well. "Dick masterminded that. Sharon was our dear friend. She is just a remarkable person, absolutely remarkable. At that time she had a house in Hollywood, and all these people were always there, Phil Everly, Jackie DeShannon, and Dick and I; we all just hung out there. Jackie was on Liberty, and Sharon wrote for Liberty. Well, we found out what was happening. She got her BMI statements, which are written in stone; you just don't fudge with BMI. It is very clear cut how many units sold. She had written something for Bobby Vee or somebody; this person was number one at the exact same time that we were number two, yet our sales were purportedly so much less that it was unrealistic. Our producers, who leased the record to Liberty, went in and found another one hundred thousand sales overnight, like miraculously, right? But still it wasn't half what it should be. It was at that point that we realized that probably something was going on there."

Being at Liberty had been a good deal for Dick and Deedee at first, but now it was going sour. "Our producers told us that they would get us on any label now that we had two hit records. But you have a number of years left on the Liberty contract. Dick said, 'What if we get out of the contract?' The producers said that would be great, but that they had already asked them and they said no. Dick told them, 'We'll do it!'

"I wasn't real sure about this, but I agreed at least to go along with it and keep quiet. Dick was something else, quite a performance! Even in the reception area, he was shaking. Because in the car going over, he said, 'Now we have to get really upset. If we go in pretending, they will know. We have to get really angry.' So Dick started thinking about all the terrible things in his life. He got to where even his hands were shaking before he went in there! I was wondering, 'Is this guy really cheating us? Is this really a good situation?' But I went ahead.

"Inside they kept telling us, 'Mr. Bennett, the president of Liberty, is really busy right now.' Dick started yelling, 'I can't wait! I have to see him now!' He finally stormed down the hall with me in his wake and into his outer office. His personal secretary said, 'You can't go in there!' Dick said, 'Yes I can!' He stormed in and really startled the guy. He was on a conference call.

"He had an alarm button under his desk. If there was really a crisis, he would push this button and about five people would run in, you know?

"The funniest thing of all, I can't believe this, if they put it in a movie people would be on the floor for five minutes laughing. Dick went through this monologue about how his mother had been hospitalized because of stress because he was having this nervous breakdown. And it was all because of record sales. He couldn't stand it any more. Dick's performance, you couldn't believe it! Even I was staring. Then he went to make his final point. But when he went to sit down, he missed the sofa and fell on the floor! And he was trying to keep composed and keep his cool, but everybody else was trying not to burst out laughing because he was so upset, but it was so funny to see someone storm around angrily, then go in a huff to sit down and miss the sofa and land on the floor. It did not hurt anything but his pride and his concern about his performance. Al pushed the buzzer and all the emergency people ran in thinking his life was in danger. In the end they said, 'No problem. You want a release? Be our guest!' They did say that someday we'd come back crawling on our hands and knees. 'Maybe we'll take you back out of the goodness of our hearts,' something like that."

As it turned out, Dick and Deedee's managers already had a deal set with Warner Bros., where Dick and Deedee had more hits than they'd had on Liberty, including the John D. Loudermilk composition "Thou Shalt Not Steal." The title is ironic—Dick and Deedee "stole" "Thou Shalt Not Steal" from a Newbeats (*Bread and Butter,* 1964) album, where it was sung in a very close copy of the Dick and Deedee style.

Dolton Royalties

Was it Dolton founder Bob Reisdorff's experience that Liberty indulged in some, well, say "creative bookkeeping" when it came to artists' royalties? For sure! "It is much to my regret that I did not spot what they were doing quickly enough. Holding back royalties was not uncommon in the industry, and they were by no means the worst of them. Hal Linnick was the head of the accounting department. He just saw dollars and cents, profit and loss, period. He had very few scruples about other people."

Of course, to avoid getting caught short-changing artists on royalties, some creativity and thought were needed. "The way they did it was with the reserves. Say a distributor buys fifty thousand of an item. You give him a reserve of ten thousand that he can send back and get a refund for. The rest he eats if the record does not become a hit and sell well. These reserves would be kept for about a year on the Liberty books as 'sold records.' Then, when they cancelled the reserves, they did not account for, out of the ten thousand granted, whether they got only four thousand back from that distributor or whether they got the full ten thousand back. That is how they made money, when they did not pay royalties on the difference between the amount of the reserves that were returned versus the amount that they claimed were returned." In other words, if four thousand of the ten thousand on reserve were returned, that meant that six thousand were sold and the artist was due royalties on six thousand. But Liberty would claim that all ten thousand were returned and keep the royalty money due the artist. Multiply this times hundreds of distributors nationwide, and it adds up. "I did catch on to that trick, but late.

"Another way they got me was telling me in nineteen fifty-nine at the start of Dolton that the royalty rate was three percent, when it was just going to five percent. I didn't know any different, so the contract with the Fleetwoods was three percent in the beginning. We were so busy going on tour with the Fleetwoods and fighting off those two covers to inquire or to look into it. By the time I did, I found out that I had been ill advised for greed. I really hated that. I did make it up to the Fleetwoods in the sense that by the time 'Mr. Blue' came out, I did get them five percent; Liberty revised the contract."

But Bob Reisdorff never encountered Liberty doing any really big royalty ripoffs. He doubted they ever miscounted sales by three hundred thousand. "I don't think it was that evil. If you say thirty thousand, yes, working the reserve system, because that is where they hid it. But you would get the bulk of it. They were far less sleazy than some of the labels. Even the big ones like RCA and Decca and Capitol would do a little creative bookkeeping, too. I'm not trying to exonerate Liberty, and I'm not trying to say that they weren't worse than the big ones. The big ones, like RCA, sure as hell better not be caught [ripping off royalties] because it would be a huge embarrassment for such a gigantic corporation. But at Liberty it was done in a way that they thought that it could possibly be interpreted their way if a lawsuit came up.

"They were paying us royalties, too, for distribution. Lou Laventhal, my partner, caught it before I did; it was after I had been at Liberty for a while. They sent him a statement, but I did not read mine until I got a call from them. It troubled me to work with people who would do things like that. Because I certainly passed on everything that I got in the proper amounts to everybody. But I was very unhappy about that."

Bob Reisdorff is quick to make it clear that he does not think that Liberty actually cheated him. He just heard rumors that Liberty, like all companies in those days, kept as much of the money that came in for themselves as possible. In negotiating things like royalty rates, Liberty drove a hard bargain and did not give away anything. He heard rumors of outright cheating, though, rumors which Fleetwood Gretchen Christopher confirms.

"I feel certain that we did not get all that was due us. 'Come Softly to Me' was the first gold record produced in the Northwest. The second one was 'Mr. Blue.'" Both were big hits that should have yielded huge royalty checks for the artists and composers. But Gretchen says that most of the money didn't ever reach them. "At the time, I told Ed Silvers that. He was a promotion man for Liberty, and a good friend, and I told him in 1961 or 1962 that I thought that we were being ripped off by Liberty."

It was years before Gretchen's suspicions were confirmed. "Years later, when he was head of Warner Bros. Music, Ed called me and said, 'You were right! Al Bennett was screwing you over! I couldn't believe it when you told me that. 'Cause I loved the guy, and I still love him. We had great fun, telling jokes and playing golf and things. But you were right, they were one of the biggest ripoff artists in the business, Liberty Records.'

"All I knew was that, in one year, we had to our credit four million-sellers, two as recording artists and two as composers. 'Come Softly to Me' and 'Mr. Blue' as artists, and 'Come Softly to Me' and the flip side, 'I Care So Much' as writers. Now, that should represent a lot of money, four million-sellers in one year. I don't know just how much, but I do know that we were never rolling in money."

Is Gretchen bitter about being cheated out of a small fortune? "You know, I don't necessarily wish that things were any different, because I like the person I am. Who knows, maybe if we had had tons of money, life would have been different, and not necessarily as good."

Dick St. John's story started with a homemade tape of his own composition, just as the Fleetwoods' had with Gretchen's homemade tape. That was not an uncommon way for a new artist to surface in the world of pop and rock 'n' roll music.

Suzanne Mullins' sole Liberty 45. Today no one seems to remember this innovative female rocker.

Early in 1961, Liberty released a 45 by an unknown female singer no one today seems to remember, Suzanne.

"You May Never Know" was written by Suzanne Mullins, and produced by J. H. Mullins (her husband, father, brother, sister, or mother?). The recording was credited to "Suzanne with the Band-Aides." This is a garage tape if there ever was one, probably bought and released by Liberty in a bit of talent-scouting. No one recalls the record any longer. The song is so offbeat that it is hard to describe. Suzanne has a jazz-sounding style and voice, except that she also sounds a bit country as she sings of her unrequited love. She sings to her lover that "you may never know" how much she loves him. The band is a rock combo, but with a flute thrown in for good measure. A lot of echo is used, and the pace is fast. The ending of the song is very abrupt, coming after only a minute and fifty seconds and sounding almost but not quite like a mistake. This is one of the best and most unique things Liberty ever put out that never hit, a female rocker who could have changed the face of early 1960s popular music had she hit the charts.

The beautiful flip side is "Unchained but Unforgotten." This is a slower song, still full of echo and Suzanne's haunting voice. The theme is almost unique in the music of the day. She has broken up with her guy; she still loves him; yet she is glad to be broken up. Who hasn't been there at one time or another.

A rather collectable record Liberty issued in the middle of the summer of 1961 was an answer song to a record that was a currently huge country and pop crossover smash for Faron Young on Capitol Records, "Hello Walls." Willie Nelson wrote this classic song, in which a man who has lost his love is lamenting his loss in conversations with the parts of the house they had lived in together, including the walls!

The Liberty answer record, "Hello, Fool," had lyrics written by Jim Coleman to fit Willie Nelson's melody. The story line here is simply that the walls and windows and such of the same house are telling the protagonist of the first record how it was his own fault that he lost his love. The artist of this answer record was a country DJ who never had a pop hit. However, he does have a couple of claims to fame. He was once married to singer Skeeter Davis ("The End of the World," RCA, 1963) and he achieved wide fame as the host of television's "Nashville Now" program on the Nashville Network.

The last new Liberty artist of 1961 was Si Zentner. He was not really new, he had been around for a while but just now had his first hit for Liberty. Si Zentner graduated from trombone player with Jimmy Dorsey, Harry James, and Les Brown to the position of orchestra leader. Famous names he played for prior to signing with Liberty included Dinah Shore, Frank Sinatra, Sid Caesar, Bing Crosby, and Danny Kaye.

In late 1960 a single he cut for Liberty was "The Swingin' Eye," a jazzy piano number that was inspired by the many jazzy TV detectives on the air at that time, such as the TV program "Burke's Law." The flip side was "Armen's There," a nice band version of the 1950s number written by Ross Bagdasarian. That song, like Ross himself, tended to crop up in the Liberty story every few years!

Si Zentner supplied the prominent trombone counter melody for the Fleetwoods' #1 Dolton hit, "Mr. Blue."

Si Zentner's specialty at Liberty was playing current songs with a big-band treatment. He recorded about a dozen Liberty LPs on the strength of just one hit single. His hit: "Up a Lazy River," a remake of a top-twenty hit by Hoagy Carmichael in 1932. Si's revival did not even make the top forty but the song had been a top-twenty hit for Bobby Darin earlier in the same year—that's why Si cut it. Si Zentner released a 1961 LP *Big Band Plays the Big Hits* including "Apache" (Jorgen Ingmann, 1961), "Raindrops" (Dee Clark, 1961), "Wonderland by Night" (Bert Kaempfert, Louis Prima, both 1960), "Save the Last Dance for Me" (Drifters, 1960), and "Will You Love Me Tomorrow" (Shirelles, 1960).

A companion LP by the Johnny Mann Singers was *Ballads of the King*, featuring Presley hits "Are You Lonesome Tonight" (1960), "Love Me Tender" (1956) and "One Night" (1958).

Liberty's LPs for 1961 were a diverse selection. Gene McDaniels' *100 lbs. Pounds of Clay* sold quite well. A seductive cleavage shot of Julie London in a fur graced the cover of *Whatever Julie Wants*, a play on the title of the hit "Whatever Lola Wants" by Dinah Shore and Sarah Vaughan (both in 1955). Julie was also a *Sophisticated Lady* in 1961. Bob Wills did another country LP of his own compositions, while Liberty released two square-dance LPs and *The First Country Collection of Warren Smith*.

Earl Palmer, the drummer who played on Bobby Vee sessions at Liberty, got his own Liberty LP, *Drumsville!* "Dream Lover" (Bobby Darin, 1959), "Hound Dog" (Elvis, 1956), and "'Til I Kissed You" (Everly Brothers, 1959) were among the selections this young black musician pounded out for his Liberty LP. Two of the cuts, "Honky Tonk" (Bill Doggett, 1956) and "New Orleans Medley" were released on a Liberty 45 in 1961. The medley incorporated three Fats Domino hits, "I'm Walkin'," "Blueberry Hill," and "Ain't That a Shame."

Johnny Mann and his singers followed up their Elvis songfest with *Ballad of the*

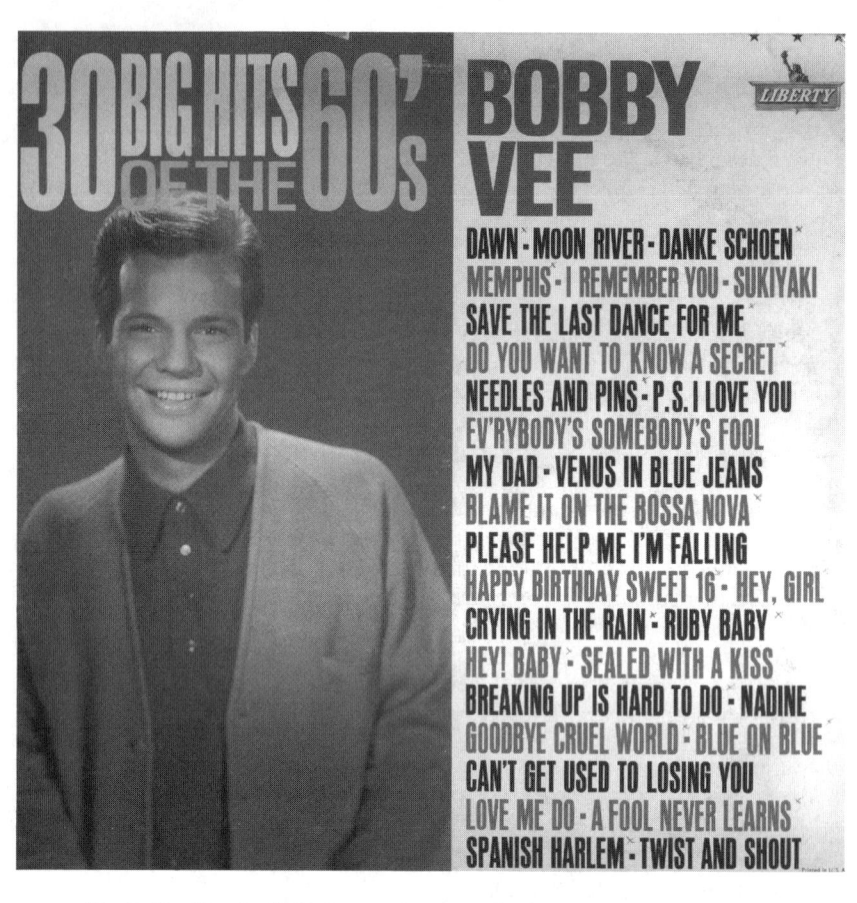

The Bobby Vee-Snuff Garrett touch was applied to *30 Big Hits of the 60's.*

King—Volume 2, this time the King being Frank, not Elvis, with Sinatra songs like "All The Way" (1957), "Young at Heart," and "In the Wee Small Hours of the Morning."

In the early 1960s, the first rock 'n' roll revival began. The new musical form was about five years old, and already people were longing for music from the "good old days" of early rock 'n' roll. Bobby Vee was one, and in June, he released the LP *Bobby Vee Sings Hits of the Rockin' '50s,* including "Do You Wanna Dance" (Bobby Freeman, 1958), "Donna" (Ritchie Valens, 1959), "Summertime Blues" (Eddie Cochran, 1958), and "Earth Angel" (Penguins, Crew Cuts, Gloria Mann, 1955).

Another Liberty LP release for 1961 was Vee's *Take Good Care of My Baby.* The title song, written by Carole King and Gerry Goffin, was the only one of Bobby Vee's thirty-eight Liberty hits to make #1 in the nation. Up until then, only David Seville's cartoonish characters, the Chipmunks and the Witch Doctor, had gotten Liberty to #1, and only the Fleetwoods (twice) had gotten Dolton to #1. A talented artist with a string of hits as long as Bobby Vee's was entitled to at least

One Liberty version of Buddy Holly's band, the Crickets.

one chart topper, and "Take Good Care of My Baby" was just the right song for Bobby Vee.

Another Bobby with a long string of hits, Bobby Vinton, would turn up at Epic records in a year or so. Casual fans of rock 'n' roll would often confuse the two Bobbys, even though Bobby Vinton's style was much softer overall than Vee's. The confusion was added to in 1968 when Bobby Vinton had a top-forty record of "Take Good Care of My Baby."

Johnny Burnette's Hits and Other Favorites was a popular Liberty LP. The Chipmunks released *The Alvin Show* from the soundtrack of their weekly CBS TV series. Martin Denny released a live LP. And, although Eddie Cochran had not had a hit lately, his death in April 1960 prompted a posthumous Eddie Cochran LP, *Never to Be Forgotten*. Selections included his early recording "Twenty Flight Rock," plus "Milk Cow Blues," "Blue Suede Shoes" (Carl Perkins, Elvis, 1956), and "Long Tall Sally" (Little Richard, 1956).

In the also-ran category, Felix Slatkin released a minor selling 45, the theme from "King of Kings." In October 1963 another movie song, "Theme from the Sundowners," was released by Liberty. Recorded by Felix Slatkin, the song was not a top-forty hit. Slatkin died in the second month of 1963 after recording many Liberty LPs.

Jackie DeShannon's name kept turning up in 1961. "I Wish I Could Find a Boy" and "I Won't Turn You Down" were originally delivered and heartfelt. "I Won't Turn You Down" is about a good-looking guy who called a girl who stays home alone because she is not too pretty. She wants to get around, so she won't, like so many other girls have, turn this handsome guy down. Another 1961 also-ran release, "Baby," shows another side of Jackie, very fast-talking and jazzy.

Dick Lory, who would admit on a 1962 single that he himself was no handsome guy, recorded a cover version of Willie Nelson's composition "Hello Walls." Since Willie was at Liberty at the time, this Liberty cover of Faron Young's current Capitol hit version may have actually been recorded independently of the hit version.

Crickets

In December 1961, the Crickets signed up at Liberty. The Crickets, with original lead Buddy Holly, had gained fame at Coral Records in the 1950s. As Buddy had gained fame, the Crickets had broken up shortly before Holly's February 1959 death. Without Buddy, the group had lost a lot of its impact. The remaining Crickets' signing with Liberty was a good move, since Bobby Vee, the "Buddy Holly of the 1960s," was of course at Liberty. If there is disagreement that the Bobby Vee delivery and Liberty-sound violins can be compared with Buddy Holly, the reply is, listen to Buddy's last, 1959 singles, "It Doesn't Matter Any More" and "Raining in My Heart." These sound like they could have been recorded at Liberty by Bobby Vee, which in fact, they later were. It was just a matter of time until Bobby Vee met the Crickets!

CHAPTER 10

1962
The Cricketts, Jan & Dean, the Marketts, the Rivingtons, Danny and Gwen, Walter Brennan, Jackie DeShannon, Willie Nelson, and Vikki Carr

The year 1961 had been a banner year for Liberty. The new Liberty artists, like Gene McDaniels and Timi Yuro, were very successful, and older, established acts, like Bobby Vee and Johnny Burnette, were still doing very well in sales and on the charts.

In 1962 the hits of the established artists continued, but the rate of adding new (successful) artists began to slow somewhat, from six in 1960 and seven in 1961 to only five in 1962.

Bobby Vee scored big for Liberty in 1962 with "Sharing You," squeezed between two more double-sided hits, "Please Don't Ask About Barbara" with "I Can't Say Goodbye to You," and "Punish Her" with "Someday."

Of the four dual-hit sides, two have interesting stories behind them: "Please Don't Ask About Barbara" and "Someday."

On "Barbara" there was a tricky guitar solo. According to legend, the part was so difficult that it took the session guitarist fifty-two takes to get it right.

The Cricketts

Many of Bobby Vee's hits, including "Take Good Care of My Baby" and "I Can't Say Goodbye," were written by well-known singer-songwriter Carole King. However, Bobby's song "Someday" was written for Bobby by songwriter Dick Glasser specifically, on assignment, as a belated follow-up to Buddy Holly's 1958 Crickets song, "That'll Be the Day." Bobby recorded "Someday" with a band who living in his apartment house who knew very well how to play Buddy Holly style. They were Holly's old band, the Crickets. Cricket drummer Jerry Allison told how he happened to get hooked up with Liberty.

"We were friends with Snuff from back when he was a jock in Lubbock [the home of Buddy Holly and the Crickets] and Wichita Falls [Texas]. We moved to LA in about 1960, about the time that Snuff started working with Liberty. He brought us up. The Crickets were on Coral Records at the time. But as soon as that deal

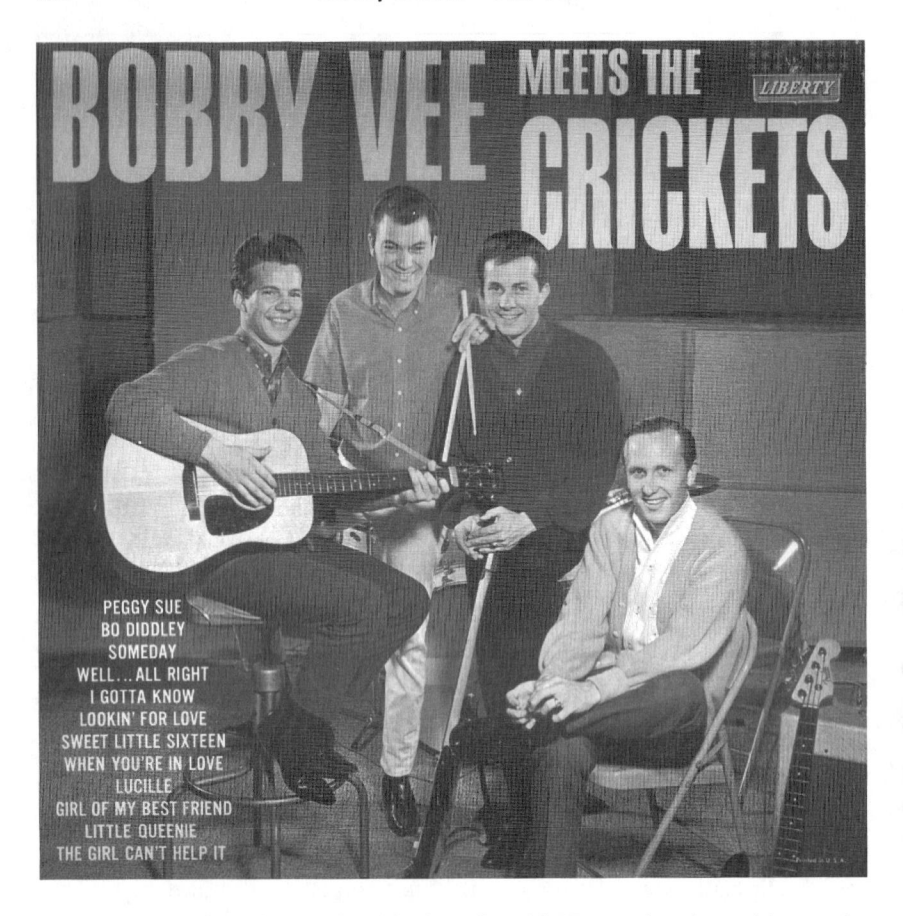

Another version of the Liberty Crickets is pictured on this LP cover, but the musicians on the enclosed record are not the same Crickets.

ended, Snuff signed us to Liberty. Dorsey and Johnny Burnette worked with Ricky Nelson, wrote 'It's Late,' that was in the late 1950s. When we moved up to LA in 1960, we hung out with Dorsey and Johnny a lot. We met them through Snuffy. We had a house up in Hollywood Hills, and we used to handle quite a few beers together. That was back in the 1960s.

"We met Bobby Vee through Snuff. Later, we lived in the same apartment as Bobby, the Ben Venue, and we hung out a lot."

Together Bobby Vee and the Crickets cut an entire Liberty LP, *Bobby Vee Meets the Crickets*. The LP featured many great songs, like "Well . . . All Right," "Peggy Sue" (Buddy Holly, 1957) and a song written by the Crickets, "When You're in Love." The success of this LP led to another similar Liberty collaboration LP, *Bobby Vee Meets the Ventures* from Dolton Records. The two projects were another of Snuff's ideas.

Snuff explained how the projects came about. "That Crickets album was for their upcoming tour of England. Bobby sounded like Buddy Holly, the Crickets'

Chapter 10 · 1962

original singer, and I aimed him that way. *Meets the Ventures* was just an offshoot of that. I didn't think that was good at all. Bob Reisdorff, the head of Dolton, the Ventures' label, and whom I really admired, did that one with me, but the LP just didn't work. If we could have gone back and done it again, we could have done a great album, but as it was done it wasn't right for the Ventures or for Bobby, to my way of thinking."

The *Bobby Vee Meets the Crickets* LP had some odd characteristics, according to Crickets drummer Jerry Allison. Allison had been an original Cricket back in the Holly days, and even helped write Buddy Holly's big hit "Peggy Sue." More than that, Peggy Sue was Allison's girlfriend and later his wife. Originally the song was to be called "Cindy Lou," but in a bid to impress Peggy, Allison got Buddy to change the title.

Allison agrees that it was Snuff's suggestion to cut an LP with Bobby Vee. "It was Snuff's idea the best I remember to do the *Bobby Vee Meets the Crickets* album. We were friends with Bobby so it sounded like a fun thing to do. Tommy Allsup played guitar on it, I remember that, and he'd played on some of the earlier stuff with Buddy and Joe B. and me, back in Clovis, New Mexico. We cut a whole bunch of tunes; I don't know if all of them have been released since or not. I think Bobby released some of them on another album. I thought that was a good rock 'n' roll album."

(Many of the cuts that the Crickets made with Bobby Vee on that project never saw the light of day until an EMI CD, *Bobby Vee Meets the Crickets,* was released in the early 1990s.)

Having the Crickets work with Bobby Vee was something of an innovation at the time. "The Crickets never toured really with other Liberty artists, or backed them up on stage instrumentally," relates Jerry Allison. "We worked with Bobby Vee some, but he had his own band at the time that he usually used.

"We did a 'Bobby Vee Meets the Crickets' tour in England in 1962. I was in the Air Force reserve at the time, and the Cuban missile crisis came up right then, so I didn't get to go on the tour. I think that is the only time the Crickets ever played with Bobby. I really can't remember the tour, because I wasn't there. That was the only Crickets tour I ever missed. The album that was made to go with the tour, *Bobby Vee Meets the Crickets,* did really well in England. You still see a lot of them floating around.

"Funny thing about that album. The group that did the tour was not the one on the album. And we always get asked in interviews, 'Who was on this record and that record,' because in those days, they never listed on the albums who played on them. Take the *Bobby Vee Meets the Crickets* album cover. The picture has Bobby and Joe B. and Jerry Naylor and myself. Jerry Naylor didn't play any instrument on the LP at all! He was just, like, a member of the Crickets; we worked with him at the time. And he was there for the picture. Joe B. was in the trucking business at the time and he happened to be in town; he was a former Cricket, so that looked good; we figured 'Let's get Joe B. for the cover!' He didn't play on the album at all, either!" Shades of the first Ventures LP cover, which featured a set of impostors posing as the Ventures!

On the *Bobby Vee Meets the Crickets* cover, of the three Crickets pictured, only Jerry was on the record, and no one on the cover or on the record went to England on the actual tour! The only time drummer Jerry Allison ever played anything besides drums on Liberty or elsewhere was on this album. He played guitar on the Holly number "Well . . . All Right," because "I just happened to know the licks."

Although the Crickets did not tour with Bobby Vee, they did play on his records once in a while. Jerry Allison put in time as a session drummer at Liberty when many hits were cut by the likes of Johnny Burnette and Bobby Vee. "I guess I played drums on quite a bit of Bobby's stuff, and on most everything Johnny Burnette did. I played drums on 'Dreamin', 'Little Boy Sad,' 'You're 16'—just about all the stuff Snuff cut with him in that period.

"When Buddy Knox was at Liberty, we worked with him quite a bit, but he had his own band as well. We worked with Eddie Cochran a lot. Buddy and Joe B. and I, on our first tour, we went with Eddie Cochran, and we got to be good friends with him. When we went back to LA, we cut that last record with Eddie. I played on 'Three Steps to Heaven' [a tribute to Buddy Holly, Ritchie Valens, and the Big Bopper, who all died in a plane crash in February 1959; versions were released by Eddie Cochran, 1959; Ruby Wright, 1959; Tommy Dee with Carol Kay and the Teen-Aires, 1959]. I also played on the other songs in his last session: 'Cherished Memories' and 'Cut Across Shorty.' Snuff and Si Waronker produced the session."

Being a session musician at Liberty meant that Jerry Allison was privy to a lot of inside happenings at the label. For example, Allison was there when Bobby Vee, on Snuff's advice, passed on those two Elvis songs before they were Elvis songs.

"It was pretty funny. 'Take Good Care of My Baby' was a pretty big record. I didn't play on that session, but I was there, and I was tryin' to get Snuff not to put that out, 'cause I thought it was too much like Adam Wade's record 'Take Good Care of Her.' Snuff said, 'It doesn't matter, it doesn't matter.' But that is pretty funny because I definitely remember Bobby Vee sittin' around playin' 'Little Sister' and 'Marie's the Name' around that Ben Venue apartment, but that was after Elvis had it out. He liked the song, you know. Now that I think about it, it seems like Snuff might have cut 'Roses Are Red' [Bobby Vinton, 1962, #1] with Johnny Burnette. I'm not sure. I remember that demo comin' through there before Bobby Vinton had it out and got number one."

Yes, Snuffy did have Johnny Burnette cut "Roses Are Red." In fact LRP 3255 was titled *Roses Are Red* by Johnny Burnette.

Does Jerry remember anything about fifty-two takes being needed to get the guitar solo on "Please Don't Ask About Barbara" just right?

"I don't know if I was there or not for that session. I remember 'Take Good Care of My Baby' because like I was tellin' Snuff at the time, it was too much like 'Take Good Care of Her' [a top-ten hit by Adam Wade, 1962]. I could have been there, because Snuff and I hung out a lot, and Bobby and I hung out a lot. I don't remember playing drums on that. I do remember playing on Bobby's hit 'Rubber Ball.' I remember the lick [on "Please Don't Ask About Barbara"], but I don't know who played it. Tommy Allsup [of the Crickets] played on a lot of sessions then, and so did Barney Kessel and Howard Roberts, some great players were on the sessions in those days. Looking back at it now, it sounds kind of like a Tommy Allsup lick."

Sounds like a Tommy Allsup lick? How much personal style or input could a musician inject into a song, versus what Snuff said to do or what was written on the page of music? "Actually, a lot. Ernie Freeman did most of the arrangements in those days; he knew all the musicians and their capabilities and all that. I don't think he ever wrote out guitar parts, though. Unless it was some special part, like that little lick on 'Barbara.' Like, for the instrumental solos, he'd just pretty well write, 'Guitar Solo.' Of course, now that I think about it, with all of those big string sessions, there weren't a lot of eight-bar guitar solos! But the guitarist could come up with his own licks and have a lot of freedom."

And percussion session work?

"When I was playin' drums, I would go by the arrangements. Where the breaks came, I would do fills. That was pretty much open to do whatever I liked. If Snuff didn't like it, he wouldn't tell me what to do, he'd just say, 'Do something besides that.'"

What about house drummers, like Earl Palmer and Hal Blaine? "Hal Blaine always had a big bag of tricks, seems like a big box of triangles, tambourines, whistles, and all that stuff. He was always real good; they both were. Liberty often used two drummers in a session, and I worked with both of those guys quite a bit."

Outside the studio, as a Cricket, Jerry Allison has spent many years performing on stage. As a veteran of the live stage performance, his opinion on performers' smiling while performing on stage was solicited. When 1950s or early 1960s artists are performing, they invariably smile. On the Bandstand/Arthur Murray videotape of Buddy Holly and the Crickets, as well as on the Ed Sullivan tape of the Crickets with Buddy Holly, when Jerry Allison plays a driving, complicated drum part, he smiles. Audiences can see all sorts of tricky, difficult guitar parts played in the old films, and the guitarists smile. There is Lesley Gore singing "It's My Party," and during the line "I'll cry if I want to," she smiles. By contrast, on performances from the post–Beatle era, nine times out of ten, the musicians onstage or on TV grimace as if playing that darn instrument was the hardest, most trying, and unpleasant thing they ever did in their lives, even on simple licks. Jerry Allison has noticed that phenomenon.

"Yeah, they act like it is the hardest thing. We still try to smile, but a lot of guys these days act like the lick is making them real mad! Or else like they are mad at the instrument or mad at what the other guy is playing, maybe." But in today's country music, you still see guitarists and drummers playing hard parts with apparent ease, smiling. Old rock and roll seems to have more in common with today's country music than with today's rock music. "The records they play on the country stations, they sure sound just like 1950s rockabilly and rock 'n' roll," says Allison. "Waylon Jennings records always have a good back beat. That was rock and roll to me."

Who is putting on an act, the ones who look happy, or the ones who grimace and look sad?

"Ha! I don't know. Well, if there's a crowd out there and they are enjoying it, then I am always happy when I'm playing, I know that. Sometimes I can't get real happy if there's not a crowd. But I will try to put on an act and play like I'm happy. I think that it is really sad, if those guys who are grimacing, if that is how they really feel when they are playing."

Of course a performer can be too nervous to smile or too happy not to. Jerry remembers being on TV in the 1950s. "Can you imagine being from Texas, then being in New York on the Ed Sullivan show? That is fun. It is definitely fun!" Was it also scary? "It was when we first got there, but when it got to the time where we were doing a lot of TV shows and we'd played those songs a lot, it was not *as* scary.

Gene McDaniels with his producer, Snuff Garrett, at a party at Liberty president Al Bennett's house about "Tower of Strength" time. *(Photographer, William R. Eastabrook; courtesy Snuff Garrett.)*

The fact that it was a live TV show, that made us nervous." And now, today before each show, does Jerry Allison get jitters and nerves? "Yeah, you don't want to make a fool of yourself no matter how old you get. And there is always that doubt as to the audience reaction: what if you play the same old songs and they say, 'Hey, we've heard that enough!'"

More would be heard from the Crickets at Liberty later.

Meanwhile Bobby Vee continued to do well. His biggest Liberty record of 1962 came out in December. "The Night Has a Thousand Eyes" was one of the biggest songs of that winter, making the top five.

Timi Yuro's releases for 1962 included her ode to growing up in love, "The Love of a Boy," which she professed could change a girl into a woman. The Ventures rocked again with the "2,000 Pound Bee." Gene McDaniels hit the top ten with his classic song of failing relationships, "Chip Chip," and he made the top forty with "Point of No Return" and "Spanish Lace," as well as an LP called *Spanish Lace*.

"Chip Chip" was a record that was somewhat hard to make. Snuff Garrett liked the song, but thought that its lyric theme was wrong. Originally it was about soap chips being produced by a man carving an image of his true love from a bar of soap. Snuff had the song reworked. Instead of whittling tangible chips, the chips became the sound of a mansion of love being chipped apart by lying, cheating, and crying.

Even with the song rewritten, Snuff's troubles were not over. He had the Liberty orchestra gathered, he had Gene McDaniels at the mike, he had the Johnny Mann Singers present and accounted for—but he did not have the piece of steel the drummer was supposed to hit to produce the "chip" sounds on. After trying a substitute piece of metal, he called a break in the session while the drummer went to get the proper piece of steel. Was it worth it? The record was a great one, and did make the top ten.

Jan & Dean

In 1962 Doré Records once again made a connection with Liberty Records. Remember the Liberty cover version of Jan & Arnie's "Jennie Lee" by Billy Ward and His Dominoes? Arnie Ginsburg moved out after "Jennie Lee," Dean Torrence moved in, and Jan & Dean moved to Doré in 1959. "Jennie Lee" had been a "bomp" record, a song with a lot of vocal parts that consisted of "bomp bomp bomp bomp." On Doré Records with new partner Dean, Jan Berry again produced national hits including another "bomp" song, "Baby Talk," #1 on many charts in 1959. When Jan & Dean's contract with Doré expired in 1961, they took an audition tape to Liberty but were turned down. They then took their tape to Challenge Records and made the top thirty with an up-tempo, updated, "bomp" version of the old standard "Heart and Soul" (Four Aces, 1952).

With this success fresh in the air, Jan & Dean returned victoriously to the offices of Liberty, and this time they were signed to a five-year pact. During that five years, Jan & Dean scored eighteen hits for Liberty. This chart record made Jan & Dean second only to Bobby Vee for number of hit singles on Liberty! But by the time Jan & Dean hit their stride in the mid–1960s, Bobby Vee had begun to score more top-forty hits but fewer top-ten hits, making Jan & Dean the big new moneymakers for Liberty for a time.

It was the redoubtable Snuff Garrett who got Jan & Dean on Liberty. "I signed Jan & Dean for my friend Lou Adler. Louie and I were good friends, he had Jan & Dean and was with Johnny Thompson, whom I had known when he worked for Coral Records. Johnny and Gene Autry had a label called Challenge Records, which had a big hit right off, 'Tequila' by the Champs. Louie had some masters with Jan & Dean from Challenge, also from Doré Records, a subsidiary of Era

Jan & Dean were photographed wearing so-called "Beatle Boots" on the cover of their first Liberty LP, years before the Beatles' first hit record.

Records. The owner of Era was Si Waronker's cousin. Era had Gogie Grant and Dorsey Burnette.

"One day Dorsey and Johnny were driving me to the airport to go to New York, and Dorsey sat in the back and sang me a song he'd just written. I flipped and wanted it for John on Liberty, but Dorsey cut it while I was gone for Era, and it was a hit, 'Tall Oak Tree.'"

So there were a lot of Challenge/Era/Doré/Liberty connections that Snuff used. "I got some money from Al and gave it to Louie for the Jan & Dean masters from Doré and Challenge and we put out *Jan & Dean's Golden Hits on Liberty*. Then we did a single, I did one side, the only Jan & Dean song I ever did, 'Tennessee.' Louie cut the other side, 'Your Heart Has Changed Its Mind,' a Neil Sedaka song. 'Tennessee' was no step in the right direction. Jan & Dean was Louie's act; I felt like a fish out of water working with Jan & Dean, so Louie worked with them with great success."

Success for Liberty, you bet! In 1965 LA teenage dance-show host Lloyd Thaxton

The Mar-kets were early Liberty surfers.

referred to Liberty as "Jan & Dean's private label." This was an exaggeration, but did serve to spotlight the importance of Jan & Dean at Liberty.

But that was later. Bobby Vee was still Liberty's top hit maker–moneymaker in 1962. Jan & Dean's first record came out in January, but by December the duo had yet to crack the top forty. After a while Liberty must have thought it had been sold a bill of goods when it took on Jan & Dean! Even a "bomp" Christmas song, "Frosty (the Snowman)" and a "Baby Talk" follow-up, "She's Still Talkin' Baby Talk," failed to catch on. The year 1962 was a long, lean one for Jan & Dean.

It was ironic that Jan & Dean came to Liberty after Liberty's Billy Ward had covered Jan & (Arnie) Dean's 1958 hit, "Jennie Lee" for Liberty years before. Now Jan & Dean were themselves on Liberty, still singing in the same "bomp" style of their 1950s and early 1960s hits on their 1962 records "Tennessee" and "A Sunday Kind of Love," but with only regional popularity.

The Marketts

In addition to Jan & Dean, in January appeared the Marketts (sometimes spelled "Mar-kets"), an instrumental group from the LA area. The members were really studio session players, including Tommy Tedesco, Ben Benay, Ray Pohlman,

Bill Pittman, Gene Pello, Tom Hensley, and Richard Hobaica. Many of them appeared on records by everyone from Bobby Vee to Jan & Dean at Liberty.

The Marketts' first single foreshadowed something to come. Perhaps hanging around the LA studio scene so much clued them in to the coming trends. It was titled "The Surfers' Stomp," and at #31 was the first surf record to make the national top forty. The pastime-sport of surfing was getting very popular in Southern California, so perhaps it was inevitable that surf records should begin to be heard. After one more Liberty single, "Balboa Blue," charted at #48, the Marketts moved to Warner Bros. Records, and three more hits, including one very big top-five hit, "Out of Limits." Originally released as "Outer Limits," the name was changed when the then popular TV show "Outer Limits" complained.

The Rivingtons

It was late in the summer of 1962 before Liberty took the new-artist plunge again. This time they signed a group calling itself The Rivingtons. The Rivingtons were the first black group Liberty had worked with successfully since Billy Ward and His Dominoes back in 1957. The Rivingtons were from Florida and, under the name of the Sharps, had provided background noises for Duane Eddy's guitar hit, "Rebel Rouser" in 1958 on Jamie Records. "Noises" might be a good way to describe the sound of the Sharps/Rivingtons, as their sound was sort of a cross between Jan & Dean's and Billy Ward's. Sort of.

The Rivingtons were raucous, while Billy Ward was mellow, except on that cover of "Jennie Lee," which featured a bluesy variation of Jan & Dean–style "bomps." In other words, musically, the Rivingtons resembled a black version of Jan & Dean. The Rivingtons outbomped even Jan & Dean when they sang, but their Liberty "bomp" records "Papa-Oom-Mow-Mow" and "The Bird's the Word" sold as poorly as Jan & Dean's 1962 Liberty "bomp" records, "Tennessee" and "Sunday Kind of Love."

The Rivingtons were discovered by Kim Fowley, who introduced the group to Jack Levy and Adam Ross. Levy and Ross owned Pan-Ar Productions, and when they heard a homemade demo tape of "Papa-Oom-Mow-Mow," they knew they had to have it. The same night they heard the demo, they took the Rivingtons to Radio Recorders studio and recut the song in one take. Originally, Levy and Ross had Capitol Records in mind for "Papa," because they were affiliated with Capitol Records. But Capitol felt it was a little too rough for them. So Jack knew Bob Skaff over at Liberty and took it by there. Immediately Liberty went for it.

Being one of the few black artists on Liberty, the Rivingtons were not sure that their record was getting sufficient promotion, so they went the rounds themselves. In particular, they went to station KGFJ. When they started to play it, it started catching on a little bit. A black disc jockey named Rudy Harvey, who also had an R&B TV show, had them on, and at that point "Papa-Oom-Mow-Mow" really took off. Next the jocks at KFWB got behind the record and made it #1.

On the national chart, the highest "Papa-Oom-Mow-Mow" ever reached was #48. But a national chart ranking of #48 does not mean that the highest it ever got was #48. The number 48 is the average of all the local rankings for that week. A song that ranked at #48, national average, had to have been a top twenty or top ten, or even a #1 song in some parts of the country and some cities.

The #48 ranking is also a reflection of the fact that "Papa" took a while to catch on around the country. It hit the top forty in many regions, but not all at the same time, so its impact was spread out.

When artists like Jan & Dean and Dick and Deedee showed up for their first live shows, venue managers and audiences alike were often surprised to find that these artists were white. From the sound of their records, some people thought that they must be black, and even booked them into black venues and tours. Ironically, the Rivingtons, who really were black, never had that kind of thing happen. In fact, until the audiences saw them in person, few knew that they were black.

There is a lot of talk in the music area about record companies that wanted to downplay the race of their black artists in the 1950s and early 1960s. Sometimes the album covers would feature a drawing, or even a picture of white couples dancing. The 1991 movie *The Five Stairsteps* dramatized just such an incident. And in fact, in 1961, when R&B singer Clarence "Frogman" Henry had crossover hits with "I Don't Know Why (But I Do)" and "You Always Hurt the One You Love," the album released by Argo Records showed a white couple strolling past a park bench on which a white man was crying.

The Rivingtons' photo actually was put on their LP by Liberty. On the back cover, that is. Well, it was 1962.

The Rivingtons wrote their own hit songs. Rocky Wilson came up with the line "Papa-Oom-Mow-Mow," and the rest followed naturally. The group could not afford horns, so many of the background vocals were devised to take the place of horns.

The Rivingtons' music is highly regarded thirty years later. Other singles, like "Kickapoo Joy Juice"—about a concoction containing chili pepper, black-eyed peas, an old shoe, and some airplane glue—and the deliciously raucous soulmate to "Papa-Oom-Mow-Mow," "Mama-Oom-Mow-Mow," are delightful today, even if they were not accepted by the majority of teens of 1962.

"The Bird's the Word" was a unique Liberty record in that it referred to a current dance, the Bird, popularized in such songs as "Do the Bird" (1962) by Dee Dee Sharp and "Birdland" (1962) by Chubby Checker, both on Cameo Records. The Rivingtons' "The Bird's the Word" in turn inspired the Trashmen's much bigger top-five record "Surfin' Bird" (1963). In fact, the Rivingtons sued the Trashmen for song theft, and won. Liberty never got heavily into dance-craze records, neither did they develop many girl groups.

The lack of girl groups was not for lack of trying. Alan Warner is a Briton who worked for EMI in England. He went to United Artists in 1968, and UA became Liberty/UA during his lengthy tenure. After that, he came to EMI in America. He talks about Liberty girl groups: "I compiled an LP in 1985 called *Dream Babies*, with the original 1963 Capitol 45 recording of 'The Shoop Shoop Song' [Betty Everett, 1964], called 'It's in His Kiss' by Merry Clayton. It also has an early [1964 Imperial/Liberty] 45 by Cher, but they put on the wrong recording. Unfortunately they put on the album cut, not the single cut, of Cher's 'Dream Baby.' It's so much better. And the Liberty girl group the Pandoras with 'About My Baby' are on *Dream Babies,* and the wonderful Alder Ray Liberty girl-group record. And Liberty's the Victorians' 1963 'What Makes Little Girls Cry.' Liberty, indeed, was not into the girl-group sound, except, of course, Vikki Carr's 'He's a Rebel,' Snuffy Garrett versus Phil Spector."

There were many tries, besides those Alan Warner describes. In the spring of 1963 for example, the peak of the girl-group era, Liberty released "Slow Motion" by Henrietta and the Hairdooz, a bluesy girl-group sound written and produced by Ed Silvers and arranged by Garry Sherman—most probably an independent production acquired by Liberty for release. The lyrics of "Slow Dancing" advocate dancing slowly, presumably more sexually than the twist for example, and the song changes tempo from slow to fast several times during its two-minute ten-second running time.

The Liberty sound carried Liberty through the early 1960s, a period of fads. It remained to be seen whether Liberty would get involved in the next two big rock 'n' roll trends, surf and drag and the British invasion.

Danny and Gwen

Related to the emerging surf and drag movement was a Liberty novelty 45 by Danny and Gwen. Produced by Snuff Garrett—who else?—in the summer of 1962, it told the story of a boy driving his date to the river to park, and was complete with sound effects. Danny's purported goal in taking Gwen out is to watch the "submarine races," but in fact, necking is his real motive. Gwen plays it coyly at first, acting as if she really believes there will be a submarine race, but by the end of the one minute fifty-five–second saga, she is all set for another trip to the "races" the next evening for another make-out session! Two years later Jan & Dean would record a totally different novelty tune titled "Submarine Races" for their *Ride the Wild Surf* LP. In their opus Jan is trying to ditch Dean so he can be alone with his girl, but Dean, ever the dullard à la Stan Laurel (and ten times dumber than Gwen), thinks there really is going to be a submarine race and can't wait to see it.

Walter Brennan

The final new artist at Liberty in 1962 was veteran character actor Walter Brennan! Brennan specialized in playing grizzled old-timers. He did this easily, since a World War I encounter with mustard gas had altered his features as a young man. Today it is hard for people to realize that Walter Brennan was more popular on the teenage top-forty rock 'n' roll radio stations in 1962 than the Rivingtons were, but compared to only two non–top-forty Liberty hits for the Rivingtons, Walter Brennan had three—two in the top forty, and one entering the top ten! The titles, all in 1962, were "Houdini," "Mama Sang a Song," and his biggest hit, "Old Rivers." A follow-up, "The Kelly Place," did less well.

The style of Brennan's records was in the nature of recitations dealing with Western folklore. Brennan had already used this approach with Dot Records in 1960, where he had a top-thirty hit, "Dutchman's Gold." Now at Liberty, produced by Snuff Garrett and backed up by the Johnny Mann Singers just like Bobby Vee or any other Liberty artist, he gained real popularity with kids.

Around Liberty in those days, there was a catchphrase, "Give Me Liberty or Give Me Dot." Walter Brennan fit right in.

"Old Rivers" was a recitation about a farmer and his mule who dies. Incredibly, this was a composition Snuff Garrett really believed in. But many artists turned

Chapter 10 · 1962   143

CHART AFTER CHART
Add up sale after sale with four big chart action LP's

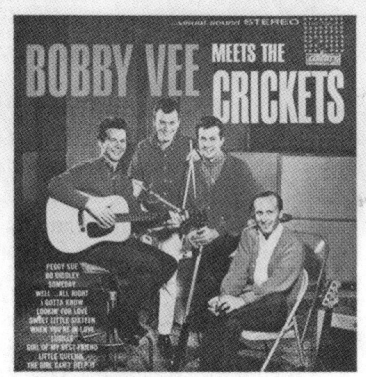

BOBBY VEE MEETS THE CRICKETS   LRP-3228/LST-7228

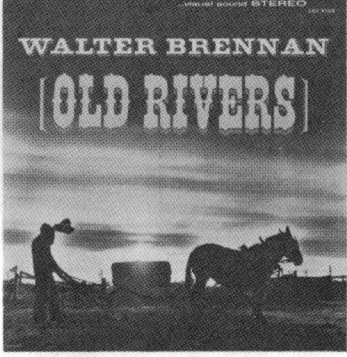

OLD RIVERS   Walter Brennan   LRP-3233/LST-7233

A BOBBY VEE RECORDING SESSION   LRP-3232/LST-7232

MASHED POTATOES AND GRAVY The Ventures   Dolton
BLP-2016/BST-8016

LIBERTY
A SUBSIDIARY OF AVNET ELECTRONICS CORP.

A Liberty trade ad (during the Avnet days) for four Liberty LPs. Interestingly, two are by Bobby Vee, the label's giant.

down the record before Walter Brennan cut it, including Tony Curtis and Johnny Cash. The flip side of Brennan's recording was "The Epic Ride of John H. Glenn," written by Robert Scott, M.D., a friend of Liberty vice president Al Bennett, which Scott thought was to be the A side. Either way, A side or flip side, the composer royalties are the same, so Scott didn't really lose out. He benefited from Snuff's belief in "Old Rivers" and his willingness to buck his boss and choose "Old Rivers" for the hit side.

Snuff still remembers the hassles over "Old Rivers." "Walter Brennan was one I cut. 'Old Rivers' was one of the two favorite records I ever cut. 'The Epic Ride of John H. Glenn' was the other side, written by Al Bennett's doctor. Al told me to cut it, and I said why, and he said don't ask why, just cut it with somebody. Joe Allison had started the Liberty country department, but he went back to Tennessee and I gave it to Tommy Allsup, who then became the head of the Liberty country department, did all the booking for me. Tommy and a guy named Cliff Crawford had a song called 'Old Rivers' they had tried to place all over—Johnny Cash, Tennessee Ernie Ford, Jimmy Dean—no one wanted it. I loved it on the demo version.

"Meanwhile, I needed someone to cut 'Epic Ride' for Al. I called Tony Curtis, whom I had just met at a party and he said yes, but he was leaving for New York. I had Ernie Freeman and everyone there trying to decide who could cut it. Charlie Adams, a friend of Gene Autry's, an old music publisher, said Walter Brennan. I said yes. He called Walter, I talked to him on the phone, we set up a date for the next night with a royalty deal. I met him as he came in the door for the session. Cliff Adams went into the booth with him to show him where to start and stop and so forth. We did a ton of records with Brennan after that."

In my own collection is a Liberty promo record of "The Old Kelly Place."

"'The Old Kelly Place' is my favorite song I ever did with him. I loved it," Snuff asserts.

"Anyway, after we cut 'Old Rivers' Ernie Freeman told me, 'Boss, this is the worst piece of trash you ever came up with; this is awful,' which is what he told me after I cut 'A Hundred Pounds of Clay.' The doctor and his friends sat there while I spent two hours and fifty minutes cutting 'Old Rivers' take after take and the last ten minutes cutting 'The Epic Ride of John Glenn' in two takes. The doctor called Al and complained.

"I took 'Old Rivers' to Chuck Blore, KFWB program director, at nine-thirty A.M. after we cut it. KFWB was the big station. He shrugged. I went home and played it for twenty-four hours. The next morning Al told me his kids and their friends and teachers all said 'Epic Ride' was a smash. I knew it was a turkey and said 'Old Rivers' was a smash, so why don't you hire them and fire all of us who think we know music? I was really upset.

"I called Chuck Blore back and said I wasn't sure it was a hit, I was positive. He said he was glad to hear it because he just left a sales meeting and no one was sure of anything there. So he said release it and I'll make it Record of the Week. It was a hit. And I never went to that doctor."

In later decades people reviewed the early 1960s music with a bias—they looked at the hits and artists of that era through what might be called Beatle-colored glasses. With Beatles music and later rock music as a standard against which to compare other artists, the Rivingtons are generally considered an important group, while

Walter Brennan is not even considered at all. Yet, to the teenagers of 1962, Walter Brennan was far more important, as shown by his greater number of hits and the fact that the Rivingtons never even got onto the national top forty. And don't think that adults might have added significantly to Walter Brennan's popularity. Adults in 1962 did not buy 45s! Those were almost strictly for teenagers, usually thirteen- to seventeen-year-old girls.

Compared to the late 1960s, rock 'n' roll in the period 1959 to 1964 was a very diverse music. White, black, solo, group, vocal, instrumental, fast, slow, serious, novelty, sung, spoken, country, Mexican American, pop, or blues—name it and it was popular in the early 1960s. After the mid–1960s, rock 'n' roll became much more homogeneous, with mostly male vocals, groups, and soul dominating the music.

Incidentally, Walter Brennan was not the first or best-known western actor to be on a Liberty 45. A few months earlier, Brennan crony and costar John Wayne had released "I Have Faith" and "Walk with Him" without success.

Jackie DeShannon

Bones Howe on Jackie DeShannon: "I was the engineer on Jackie DeShannon's first Hollywood session. She was going to be the female Elvis Presley, and she had these tight jeans on and was jumping around the studio like everyone thought Elvis did. I still see her, we are these two middle-aged people now [Bones is fifty-eight]."

The female Elvis? Well, Liberty and Dolton each had some also-rans of interest in 1962, and Jackie was one of Liberty's. Before she came to Liberty, Jackie DeShannon had already made a few recordings for Sand Records and Edison-International Records, and a song called "How Wrong I Was" on Gone Records in 1960, under the name Jacki Dee. Phil Everly of the Everly Brothers has told Sharon Sheeley that he knew Jackie DeShannon in Nashville when she was Jacki Dee. But it was Liberty that saw promise in her work and signed her, releasing her song "The Prince" in April. But the song and the singer failed to catch on at the time. Back in 1961 one of Jackie DeShannon's compositions, "Dum Dum," had gone top five as recorded by Brenda Lee on Decca.

It is unclear exactly when Jackie DeShannon was born. Different sources give her birthday as August 21, 1935, 1944, or 1948. At any rate she was from Hazel, Kentucky, and her southern-country influences were a thread that ran throughout her music.

While still less than ten years old, she sang on the radio, and she recorded for Glenn Records in 1959 under the name "Sherry Lee Meyers." After her family moved to Illinois, she had a country-and-western radio show. At fifteen, she hit the road, singing jazz. She has written or cowritten almost seven hundred songs in her career. In 1966 she married Liberty promotional staffer Bud Dain.

Liberty songwriter Sharon Sheeley well remembers meeting Jackie for the first time. It happened several months after the tragic death of Sharon's fiancé, Liberty star Eddie Cochran, in April 1960. Sharon was devastated by Eddie's death. She had quit seeing her friends, quit songwriting, quit virtually everything. "One night I went out for a little dinner date with Dick Anatieko, who worked at Liberty, just to get out of the house. He [was one of the friends I had then who] would not give up on me. I just went out for a simple little dinner, but when I got home, there was [Los Angeles DJ and later "Shindig" TV host] Jimmy O'Neill and Jackie DeShannon sitting in my living room. I thought to myself, 'What the hell is he doing? What a nerve!' I was in a real grumpy mood. I was only about twenty-one, and everyone was giving me pep talks about how I was too young and too talented to give up. That was all Dick said at dinner, then I come home, and look who is there on the couch. Jimmy and this girl, Jackie, who was overweight at that time, her teeth were less than perfect, at that time she was not at all as pretty as she later became.

"I yelled, 'What are you doing?!' Jimmy said, 'Sharon Kathleen, can't you be nice? You have got to want to write again and to live again. And this girl is the greatest singer I have ever heard.' My answer was to go into the kitchen and have a tantrum. I threw down a plate and broke it. My mother came in, and I chased her out of the house.

"Pretty soon this girl I had never seen before, Jackie, came in the room. With tears in her eyes, she said, 'I didn't mean to upset you.' So then I felt really, really bad because I had hurt her feelings. I told her that I was sorry and that it was nice of her to have come over. She told me that she had just signed with Liberty Records as an artist and they had put her up in a crummy rinky-dinky little rat-infested motel. Jackie said, 'Jimmy was nice enough to invite me over. I loved the song 'Poor Little Fool' that you wrote and I am sorry, I didn't mean to—.'

"I said, 'Oh God, I'm really sorry.' So we all started talking and sitting down and I said, 'Well, if you really want to sing, sing me a song.'

"'What would you like to hear?'

"'Anything that makes you comfortable.'

"She sang 'God Bless the Child' and I fell off the couch. I still get chills today thinking about how incredible her voice was. Just her and her guitar. But my God! Today, we have a lot of white girls who can really belt a song. But she is still one of the best. She and Dusty Springfield. I was so moved by Jackie's voice that it was almost as if Eddie were in that room, with his talent, saying 'Why don't you really listen [to this girl].' Jackie moved into our house the next day and stayed for two years!

"In the next two weeks, we wrote "Dum Dum" (Brenda Lee, Decca, 1961, #4); "Heart in Hand" (Brenda Lee, Decca, 1962, #15); "The Great Imposter" (The Fleetwoods, Dolton, 1961, #30), all on the charts almost at the same time.

They also wrote a song called "Trouble," which was not a hit but was on singles by two artists. The Kalin Twins ("When," 1958, #1, Decca), an Everly Brothers–type act, were the first to do "Trouble." Then the Fleetwoods had "Trouble," although their version was never known to Sharon, even though Gretchen Christopher and Sharon are close friends thirty years later. This was probably due to the fact that the Fleetwoods' 45 did not chart, although neither did the Kalin Twins' version.

It is easy to understand why Sharon has not kept track of every recording of every song she wrote. "I have written or cowritten six hundred fifty songs that have been recorded," states Sharon with justifiable pride.

"Everything we wrote, almost, was recorded. We did the most incredible demos of our songs. We had Leon Russell on piano, Glen Campbell was our guitar player, Billy Preston played the organ, David Gates from Bread was our bass player, and of course we had Hal Blaine on drums. With Jackie singing, we cut demos. The darn records never sounded as good as our demos did!"

How did the songwriting team of Sheeley-DeShannon operate? "Jackie was more into the music, mainly because I don't play an instrument," explains Sharon Sheeley. "But I can hear great chord changes in my head. Jackie loved my great riffs, as she called them, and I would just suggest things for her to try. I would say I did three-fourths of the lyrics. Once in a while Jackie would come up with a great idea, but basically I did all the lyrics." Jackie was very much a singer as well as a songwriter, and recorded many of her own songs, as well as songs she wrote with Sharon.

Speaking of composers doing their own songs, did Sharon Sheeley ever record any records? Not for Liberty. She did record one single in 1964 for British Decca by Jack Goode, who produced "Shindig" on American TV and was a British starmaker. Sharon was a big name in England, and a beautiful young girl. The song was a DeShannon-Sheeley composition called "Homework." To make a long story short, her seven-year contract was torn up by mutual agreement. Sharon characterizes her own singing as making 'Annette Funicello sound like Barbra Streisand.' When Sharon sang, her range was so limited that there were many notes she could not hit. Jackie DeShannon had helped out, singing some of the more difficult sections of the song. Thus the song was part Sharon's little, weak voice, and then Jackie came in on the hard notes. Jackie's "Tina Turner" voice did not exactly blend seamlessly with Sharon's "Annette" voice.

Shortly after this incident, but for unrelated reasons, the songwriting team of Sheeley-DeShannon split up for good.

Jackie's other Liberty-connected relationship, her marriage to Liberty promotion man Bud Dain, had also eventually broken up. "I had been dating Jackie DeShannon since I had been in New York as head of East Coast promotion," Dain relates. "She came out on a promotion trip. That's when she hadn't really had a hit, although Snuffy was producing her. But everybody thought she was a superstar as a songwriter for Brenda Lee, 'Dum Dum' and 'Heart in Hand' and then 'The Great Imposter' with the Fleetwoods.

"Then Jackie went to England. Over there she wrote 'Come and Stay with Me' for Marianne Faithfull, and came back engaged to Jimmy Page! At the time he was a studio musician. She dumped me for Jimmy Page. I wanted to know, 'How can you dump me for this guy? He's a studio guitar player!' She said, 'Yeah, well he is going to be great!' Bud Dain was a vice president, Jimmy Page was just gonna join the Yardbirds and then Led Zeppelin, I mean, who in the hell was he to be messing with a promotion man?! But that was kind of my attitude, so maybe that is why I got Liberty records played.

"Jackie also came back from England with Jack Goode, who in England had a music program on TV called 'Ready, Steady, Go.' When he came here, it was to do a pilot for a similar show with Jackie and Sharon. It was called 'Young America Sings the World,' later named 'Shindig.' That is how Jackie DeShannon turned up on 'Shindig' so often.

"It was the trip to England where Jackie started to meet everybody. They all loved her songwriting. That is why they invited her to be the female vocalist on the 1964 U.S. Beatles tour. She also knew this nut named Georgio Gromelski who had found the Rolling Stones and was their original manager. He also had the Yardbirds at the time.

"Jackie DeShannon had the best eye for talent of anyone I have ever met anywhere at any time and place. She was a gigantic fan of Bob Dylan's when he was at Gurdy's in New York. She came back with a dub on 'Catch the Wind.' She said that the Yardbirds were the greatest band she had ever heard. That's when Eric Clapton and Paul Samwell-Smith, who later produced Cat Stevens, were in the band. And there [were] Jeff Beck and Jimmy Paige. She was friends with Ray Charles and the Raylettes, with Elvis. She had a great eye for talent and was a great talent in her own right . . . was maybe too talented to settle into any one direction. She would fall in love with a new phase of music every six months [and] have the talent in some cases to pull it off and in some cases maybe not quite pull it off because maybe it was not quite right for her.

"She liked Herb Alpert's music and actually mailed out copies of 'The Lonely Bull' single to DJs, because she was a big fan of Herb's.

"She started as a country singer, then started writing rock and roll, then got involved in blues, and that is what would happen to her. There is no telling what Jackie would have done [had she concentrated on one area or style]. Her mom and dad were wonderful, very supportive, very encouraging and behind her all the way. When a new area of music came up that she became enthralled [by], there was no one who could tell her not to do it. She did an album like Linda Ronstadt's Nelson Riddle album, but she did it ten to twelve years earlier!

"But I think that hurt her tremendously, because the market would not accept serious change at that time.

"We were married for seven years, nineteen sixty-six to seventy-one; we had a lot of success together. She is a fabulous person. I think the reason the marriage maybe wasn't successful was because she was on the road six months of the year, and I was on the road the other six months. We did not break up due to lack of respect. I had dinner with her a year ago. We are still friends."

Is it true what Sharon Sheeley said about Jackie, that her demos are better than the records? "Oh, no question about it. No question about it!"

Willie Nelson and Other 1962 Also-Rans

Around the same time that Jackie DeShannon released her debut Liberty single "The Prince," "Half a Man" was released on Liberty by another young singer-songwriter, a man named Willie Nelson. A year before, Faron Young had placed in the top twenty for Capitol Records with Willie's composition "Hello Walls," and Patsy Cline had made the top ten with Nelson's song "Crazy" in 1961 on Decca. With a couple of releases and LPs *And Then I Wrote* and *Here's Willie Nelson,* Willie left Liberty. Too bad these great writers couldn't get Liberty some hits in 1962.

Another fine writing team at Liberty was Herb Alpert and Lou Adler. They began as Jan & Dean's managers and sometime writers in the pre–Liberty days of that duo. In the spring of 1962, Liberty released a song they had produced and had written with George McCurn called "Your Daughter's Hand," which McCurn sang in a way that was very much like Sam Cooke. The A side was in fact a song written by Sam Cooke, "The Time Has Come." This song, which opened with Big Ben chimes, McCurn sang in a low-voiced Brook Benton style, however. The record was

This Liberty LP shows how the early Willie Nelson looked.

released at the same time as Bobby Vee's popular 1962 Liberty hit, "Please Don't Ask About Barbara."

The Spinners were on the verge of a hit career spanning a decade at Motown and Atlantic when they stopped off at Liberty to cut "Dream," a standard done on different labels by Betty Johnson, Dinah Washington, and Etta James in recent years. But Liberty just wasn't the right label for the Spinners.

The Fencemen were probably session musicians gathered to record "Swingin' Gates," an organ-led instrumental which sounds an awful lot like "Green Onions." The latter was a current megahit organ record played by Booker T. and the MG's, who were also session musicians for Stax Records in Memphis. The Liberty record was fun, as was the equally derivative flip side, a semiclassical, mostly piano instrumental "Bach 'n' Roll." This cut was clearly inspired by the hit "Asia Minor," a takeoff on the Grieg Piano Concerto in A-flat minor by Kokomo (pianist Jim Wisner, incognito) of the previous year. "Bach 'n' Roll" even had an ending that was a direct copy from the Kokomo 45 on Felsted Records. Both sides were produced by Dick Glasser, who would soon take over production chores from Bob Reisdorff for the Fleetwoods.

Another also-ran for 1962 was Dick Lory. Dick got the full—and I mean full—Liberty treatment. Snuff Garrett produced. The Johnny Mann Singers sang backup. And much of the instrumentation seemed literally stolen from Martin Denny's Liberty hit instrumental of 1959, "Quiet Village." The song was a Bobby Vee-ish ballad (meant as a compliment, by the way), with a soaring falsetto added for good measure. The singing sounded like a cross between Gene Pitney and Liberty's own Johnny Burnette. The lyrics, by one James Marcus Smith, were about a fellow who was a loser in love and an object of ridicule simply because he was not a "Handsome Guy." But his ace in the hole: he had a handsome heart!

Who was Dick Lory? Almost no one, not even Si Waronker, recalls now. "Dick Lory was not actually his real name. In many instances we had one artist change his name two or three times to see if that would bring some luck. If disc jockeys saw that a guy had had a bomb before, they might not consider a new record with the same name. Dick Lory was probably one of those." Well, close, Si. Dick Lory was in reality Dick Glasser, songwriter and Liberty producer of the Fencemen, whom we just met.

Liberty did something strange with "Handsome Guy." Invariably in 1963 45s had a flip side, even DJ–radio station copies. "Handsome Guy" did not; for some reasons the same song appeared on both sides of the promo copies of this record.

Shirley Collie sang in a country harmony style reminiscent of Skeeter Davis ("The End of the World," RCA, #1, 1962), except Shirley had a better voice. "No Wonder I Sing" seems in fact to have been an answer song to Skeeter's single. It talks about many of the same things, the stars in the sky and wanting to die, but now she has found a darlin', and now, "No Wonder I Sing."

Another Collie 45 carried, "Keeping My Fingers Crossed" and "If I Want Long Enough," which were both traditional country female laments about waiting for a man to return.

This was the year producer Phil Spector started his Philles Record label. However, he got irritated with his partners back east, so when Snuff Garrett offered Spector a position as a producer for Liberty, he readily accepted. He kept the job for half a year, and popular press says that he produced less than a half dozen tracks for Liberty.

One release he did generate in the summer of 1962 was "How Many Nights (How Many Days)" by Bobby Sheen. It was a good if undistinguished also-ran. It is interesting to note that the flip side of the Bobby Sheen 45 was not a Spector production. Spector had little use for nonhit sides, like his throwaway instrumental flip sides. However, Spector must have liked Bobby Sheen. A year later, teamed up with Darlene Love and Fanita James of the Blossoms, Phil would make him the Bobby of an artist dubbed "Bob B. Soxx and the Blue Jeans" on Phil's record label ("Zip-a-Dee-Do-Dah," Philles Records).

Vikki Carr

One of the biggest and longest-running disputes in the annals of early 1960s rock and roll focuses on the song "He's a Rebel," released by Vikki Carr on Liberty in late 1962. And poor Vikki isn't even a rock 'n' roll singer!

A legend promulgated by the popular press is that one day while at Liberty, Spector heard Snuff playing a demo in the Liberty offices. It was a song written by Gene Pitney, who wrote some of his own records ("[I Wanna] Love My Life Away," 1961) and an Imperial hit for Ricky Nelson ("Hello, Mary Lou," 1961), as well as Bobby Vee's 1961 Liberty 45 "Rubber Ball." The demo was called "He's a Rebel." Snuff planned to have a Liberty singer named Vikki Carr do the song. Spector loved "He's a Rebel," made a copy of the demo, then told Snuff that he was going on vacation.

Instead of vacationing, Spector went straight to a recording studio. He'd just had a hit record, "There's No Other (Like My Baby)," (1962) on Philles Records

Snuff's version of "He's a Rebel" was recorded perhaps simultaneously with Phil Spector's. But who knows?

with his girl group, the Crystals. But the Crystals were back east, so he hired Darlene Love and the Blossoms, local studio singers, and quickly cut a cover version of "He's a Rebel" by the pseudo-Crystals and released it on Philles. This cover version became a #1 record in most cities, while Snuff's original by Vikki Carr, recorded the same day with the same session musicians in the same building, became another Liberty also-ran.

Vikki Carr herself told a similar story to magazine writer Jack Dey for DISCoveries' June 1991 issue:

> When Phil Scaff [sic] left Liberty Records, he took certain material with him. And Snuff Garrett who at that time in the early '60s was the golden boy at Liberty Records, he had this song for me and they said this is going to be your first single. So, I was all excited about it; it was going to be really, really great. We finished recording it in Los Angeles and we took a little break. As we were walking out of the studio, we heard "He's A Rebel" coming back at us from across the hall in another studio. Phil Spector had taken that material with him and he never even had the Crystals record it. He got some girls together. He does mention that, yeah, this is supposed to be Vikki Carr's first single. But in Australia they preferred my version to the Crystals' version. (page 30)

As exciting as that story reads, Snuff tells a vastly different version. "Phil Spector did not steal 'He's a Rebel' from me and Vikki Carr. The music publisher, Aaron Schroeder, screwed us both. He gave it to me 'exclusively,' and he did the same for Spec. We cut it on the same night; he used Darlene (Love); I used Vikki Carr. I heard during our session that he was cutting it the same night across town. We used a lot of the same musicians.

"Then, when Darlene's came out under the name the Crystals, 'The Big Bad

Liberty Records covered us.' But it was not true. And Spec, not only that, cut a better record. The only saving grace of my version of 'He's a Rebel' was that it was the first record with Vikki Carr, got her on the label. Spec's was better; I haven't heard Vikki's since we cut it.

"But Spec didn't intentionally go out to cut my throat, and I certainly didn't go out to cut Spec's throat. I don't give a hang what these other books say. As far as I am concerned, we both got screwed by the publisher. That's my version. And I am one of the only two who were there, so who're you gonna believe?"

Well, someone else was there: Vikki Carr.

Basically, Snuff's recollection and Vikki's recollection match. The main difference is: Was the song stolen by Spec, and did he and Snuff feud about it? Snuff is adamant. "Spec did not steal the song from me. Aaron Schroeder, the publisher, gave me an exclusive on it, and he also gave Spec an exclusive on it. Everybody is trying to make a thing out of it all the time. But it wasn't, we just both got taken by the publisher. Vikki's was the big hit in my home, Dallas, KOIF radio, and Australia—places like that. But Spec had the record."

Vikki Carr's record, Liberty 45 #55493, apparently was not her first single. Liberty 45 #55465 was Vikki's "I'll Walk the Rest of the Way" b/w "Beside a Bridge." Not only that, Liberty #55490, "Submarine Races" by Danny and Gwen, was also Vikki Carr. She was Gwen, named after producer Snuff Garrett's oldest daughter, then aged two. (Was it really a good idea for Snuffy to cast his daughter as being on a date with a wolf? At age two, no less!) Danny was in reality Cricket Jerry Naylor.

Vikki's version of "He's a Rebel," credited to "Vikki Carr [and] the Singing Strings of Ernie Freeman," is a fine record. "The Singing Strings" refers to the name concocted for an LP Snuff planned to do with Ernie, his arranger, an idea that was later abandoned. But Vikki's record has all the same basic elements as the better-known Spector version of "He's a Rebel": heavy drums, dualing on the lead voice, instrumental break, and a fade-out full of "no, no, no." That being stated, it should be stressed that these elements are mixed differently. The drums on the Liberty version have a distinct military-marching flavor, tying in to the "Rebel" theme. The break is only half as long. And the fade-out is tamer than Darlene Love's vocals on Phil's. But the main difference is the clarity of the Liberty version. Ernie Freeman's "Singing Strings" are clearly violins. In Spec's "wall of sound" recording, as his technique of stacking tracks has been dubbed, the mix disguises the violins.

Vikki delivers the song with a rock 'n' roll style she never had elsewhere, least of all on the flip side of her 45. She was really a pure pop singer. But besides being a hit in Australia, Vikki Carr's "He's a Rebel" was actually #1 in Dallas, Texas!

When publisher Aaron Schroeder pulled this trick on Snuff, it was the last straw. The previous year Aaron had pulled another stunt, when he brought "Rubber Ball" to Snuff. Bobby Vee recorded the song and had one of his best records ever with it in 1961. It turned out so well that Snuff wanted to meet the songwriter, Anna Orlowski. Snuff thought, "'My God! A secret writer! But who in heck is Anna Orlowski and when can I meet her?' Aaron kept sidestepping me and everything. It was a long, long time before we found out that it was Gene Pitney who wrote 'Rubber Ball.'"

As mentioned earlier, Pitney was a BMI composer. Since he had an advance from ASCAP for "Rubber Ball," he had to go through with the song, but used his mother's maiden name.

Aaron Schroeder got half writer's credit for "Rubber Ball." That could be another case of someone's taking credit for a record that really was written independent of that individual. But since Aaron wrote the Elvis Presley hits "I Got Stung," "I Was the One," "Big Hunk of Love," "Stuck on You," "It's Now or Never," "Anyway You Want Me," and "Good Luck Charm," I guess it is safe to assume that he and Gene Pitney really did collaborate on "Rubber Ball."

In rock historian Alan Betrock's seminal book *Girl Groups – The Story of a Sound* (Delilah, New York, 1982), he repeats the tale of Phil Spector's stealing "He's a Rebel" from Snuff. He states that Phil pretended to go on vacation from Liberty when he really used the time to record "He's a Rebel," and that Snuff was "putting the final touches on his version for Liberty when Spector arrived at Gold Star" (page 35). He further faults Liberty for not promoting Vikki Carr's version well. He says that Liberty president Al Bennett, A&R head Snuff, and promotion head Bob Skaff were in Chicago celebrating the opening of a new branch office. "While they partied, Spector tended to business, and the next week the Crystals' 'He's a Rebel' appeared [on the charts]" (page 36).

A similar account was offered by authors Bob Shannon and John Javna in their impressive rock reference book, *Behind the Hits*. In part they state that Spector was still working for Liberty when he got hold of "He's a Rebel" and "had to get out of his contract with Liberty right away so he could use the song first" (page 108). The authors quote writer Gene Pitney as saying that Spector "said he was ill and moving to Spain, so Liberty finally released him from his production demands."

In July 1991, on reading Betrock's and Shannon-Javna's accounts of the recordings of "He's a Rebel," Snuff Garrett bristled.

"Both of them are full of it. Here is what annoys me about this stuff. Thirty years later, guys who weren't even there write about this stuff. They have no idea what they're talking about.

"Spec may have known [that 'He's a Rebel' was being recorded by both of us]. I sure didn't. But Spec's leaving Liberty had nothing to do with 'He's a Rebel.' It's a great song, but it doesn't have anything to do with reality. That went on weeks and weeks before that and had nothing at all to do with it. Spec was already long gone from Liberty when 'He's a Rebel' came about. What is funny is, when the record came out, Spec cut a far better record than I did. It is just as simple as that. It doesn't take a rocket scientist to figure that out.

"What they [Philles Records] did with the record, Lester Sill's son went on the road that night after they cut it, and went out and yelled that they had been covered by Liberty. He said that their little company had been covered by Liberty. It wasn't true, but it worked. I would have done the same thing. That was the record biz. That was also probably the last time that Spec flew, because he hated to fly."

Did Snuff Garrett and Phil Spector remain post–"Rebel" friends? "I never had a bad word with Spec in my life, or him with me. Hey, I was the one who got him the job at Liberty. Everyone was down on me because Spec was a pain in the neck in the New York office." And why did Spector really leave Liberty? "I have no earthly idea. It was Spec's wish to leave."

Some sources claim that Phil Spector took a position at Liberty only to hide out from his partners at Philles Records and to stall for time in his other business affairs. "Well, that sounds good today, too. But I was head of A&R at Liberty, a small label that had become a major, and I was also producing and had a lot of good results.

So I was in New York in a suite we kept at the Hampshire House and talked to Spec. We had been talking for two or three days, and he wanted to come to Liberty. I thought that would be great. With me on the West Coast and him on the East Coast, I thought we could really lock up some things. I had total respect for Phil Spector. Period. But I had a helluva fight at Liberty when I hired him. It doesn't sound like a lot of money today, but at that time twenty-five thousand plus royalties was a big salary."

Did Spector produce any hits while he was at Liberty? "No, no he didn't. He recorded Bobby Sheen, then took Bobby with him for Bob B. Soxx and the Blue Jeans. But saying Spec had a master plan [to hide out at Liberty and not try to make hits for Liberty] was not true. He would not have signed Bobby Sheen to Liberty if he didn't have intentions of doing things at Liberty.

"I hired Spec in good faith. I picked him out of a lot of good people, but he just didn't fit into the corporate kind of thing. Neither did I, actually. The funniest thing of all was when we were setting up his office, he said, 'I want this room as my office.' Well, that room was a conference room. I said, 'What?' He repeated, 'I want this as my office. And I want that conference table turned around and a front put on it and make it my desk.' I said, 'What?'

"I went to Al Bennett [with this request], and Al went crazy. But [Spector] got it. It was the biggest desk in the history of the entertainment business."

What did Spector do with this huge desk? "He brought a bunch of games in and he would sit there and play games."

"One day I got a call in my office from Al Bennett. There was a woman, a very classy lady who ran the New York office. I can't think of her name. She had called and she was furious . . . livid because Spector told her to water his plants. His office was full of plants he wanted her to water at this time in the morning and this time in the afternoon. She wasn't going to do it.

"I told Al, 'Just have her do it. And even have her oil the leaves. Gimme a break and cut all the bull.' So those things happened, and I tried to give Spec all the avenue to allow him to excel. I was always on Spec's side. To my knowledge Spec's never been against me, ever."

Snuff Garrett has many interesting insights into the Phil Spector persona. "When I was leaving New York once, Spec rode out in my limo with me. When I got off at the airport, he said, 'Do you mind if I stop off and see a couple of people on the way home and tell them it's my limo?' I didn't care, so I told Bruno the driver to take him anyplace he wanted to go, and he owns it, and it is his, and all. So he went out and catted around and had a good time.

"This is my best Phil Spector story. It happened before he ever came to Liberty Records, but I knew him already. Once I was in Wichita Falls, Texas, a hundred forty miles north of Dallas, where my first wife lived. I'd fly up there and see my kids when I was in Dallas. Out driving around in the car with the kids, I heard a brand-new record on the car radio." Snuff was totally blown away by the sound on this new song. Since he used to work at this same radio station in Wichita Falls, he called them up and they told him the artist and the record label and everything about this great new record. "I flew back to Dallas, caught a commercial flight to New York, and the next morning I was in Donny Kirshner's office. He was a big music publisher, Nevins-Kirshner.

"When I walked into Donny's office, Spec was sitting in the corner." This was long before Spector came to work at Liberty. Snuff told Don Kirshner, "I found a smash hit record that I'm trying to buy. It is a smash." Snuff named the record, and Don said that he had heard it a few days earlier, but that one of his staff had heard it with him and didn't think it was a hit. "I don't know who that is," countered Snuff, "but I think he is totally wrong. It's a smash."

In response to Snuff's strongly voiced opinion, Don Kirshner called his person into the room. At that point, things began to get interesting.

Snuff: "Donny said to his man, 'Art, you told me this record wasn't a hit; Snuff said it is a hit.' Art said to Donny, 'It's not a hit.' And I said, 'It is a hit. I'm telling you it is a smash.' In fact, I think it ended up on Smash Records. They beat me to it. Anyway, I said, 'That's a number one record.'

"This guy pulled a wad of money out of his pocket and said, 'Put your money where your mouth is. I'll give you ten-to-one odds.' I said, 'You've got a deal. I'll take a hundred dollars' worth. OK?'

"Spec was sitting over on the floor in the corner. He said, 'Hey, man. I haven't even heard the record, but I'll go with Snuff. Give me a hundred, too.' That is how attuned Spec and I were in those days."

Snuff wasn't able to get the record before he had to make a trip to London, and it did come out on Smash Records in 1962. "When I got back three weeks later, I called Jerry at *Cashbox* magazine—I can't remember his last name. *Cashbox* invented the bullet. Jerry told me, 'Snuff, this is our first record with a bullet; it is #1 with a bullet.'" It was a hit after all.

"So Spec and I both collected on the bet. The guy's name who[m] we bet against was Artie Rip. The record was 'Hey, Baby.' Artie couldn't afford to pay us off. So we had to go to Donny to get paid. Donny had both sides [as publisher] of the next Bobby Vee record. I told Donny, 'Both Spec and I get paid before I release the Bobby Vee record.'

"Spec and I both got a check. I bought a green couch with my thousand dollars. I used to call that my Artie Rip couch.

"That's the best story I know about me and Spec. It was fun. That is how we were. And there was never any dissension between Spec and me, not to my knowledge. I was the first to say he cut a better record on 'He's a Rebel.'"

Was Snuff in Chicago not tending to business with "He's a Rebel" while Spec was on the ball? To that Snuff says, "Hell, sure I was in Chicago, but we had other records to promote besides . . . 'He's a Rebel.' But as soon as I heard Spec's, I told everyone his was a better record.

"But I was shocked when I found out I didn't have an exclusive on that song. I think it was Tommy Tedesco who came over from Spec's session and told me about it. He came in and saw the lead sheet and said, 'Hey, I just cut this with Spec over at Gold Star.' That was the first I knew about it. That did not make me happy at the time, I can tell you that. But I took it that I was screwed by the publisher, not by Spec."

Engineer Bones Howe, who worked around all the LA studios, happened to be at Gold Star the night "He's a Rebel" was being recorded. Bones's account of the evening's events tends to confirm Snuffy's, although Bones was not actually involved in the "He's a Rebel" affair. "I was there, though. I saw them recording the Vikki Carr version in studio B the same night that Phil was mixing the Crystals version in studio E or C. He was mixing down in one studio, and they were cutting Vikki in another. It was a real cover battle." Does that mean that Bones thinks that Spector stole the song from Snuffy? "No, no, no. The story as I understood it was that Phil had the song first. In those days the song was the thing, and there were battles over songs. And publishers would double-deal songs sometimes. Maybe Snuff had it first and then Aaron Schroeder felt that Vikki Carr might not have a hit, so he was buying himself some insurance with Spector. And if so, he was right, wasn't he?"

Schroeder may have been right, but what he did was not right, and Snuff really never forgave the publisher's double-dealing.

"To my knowledge I never recorded another Aaron Schroeder song after that 'He's a Rebel' incident," says Snuff. "When he did that to me that time, that was the end. Well, I did cut one more, years and years later. I saw him in New York, and he gave me a song. So I got him. I told him that I had this hot new star on television and radio, some bull like that. I held on to the song. It was 'This Diamond Ring' that I cut with Gary Lewis."

Although Phil Spector and Snuff never did feud, Spec's stay at Liberty was brief nonetheless. One might say that he didn't really fit in. Si Waronker agrees.

"Phil Spector and Snuffy were great friends. I was never that friendly with Phil. Phil signed with the company. And he wanted to take charge of the New York division—this was after we had become a little more successful. Snuffy had come up with this idea that he wanted to have strings with his rock music. Which I thought was great! The more [strings], the merrier! C'mon! And Snuffy got very hot.

"So when Phil came along a few years later, it was very interesting, because he had one god that he looked at musically . . . and that was Richard Wagner, the great composer! Listen carefully to all of Phil Spector's records, and it was the 'Ride of the Valkyries' in there. And he was the one that filled up the studio with musicians, and I guess he got famous with this approach.

"But Phil was [not] under contract with Liberty for long, just a few months. We could never stay together. He could never see his way to stay with us, nor could we keep him, simply because this guy was too rough to deal with! [Laughs]

"I'll never forget having an office on Fifty-seventh Street, walking in, and finding out that when I had to go to the bathroom I couldn't go! In those days the offices were converted apartments. Phil had the bathtub filled with sand and had growing plants in there. The sink was filled with plants and that, growing something. And then I had just finished a Martin Denny record, full of animal sounds as always. I was playing the damn acetate there in the offices, and I started hearing birds! I thought, 'What the hell are birds doing on this record? I know I put in a bunch of crazy sounds. I used to record all of the Martin Denny records without Martin Denny playing, thank God! So I know that there are not supposed to be so many birds on this record. Somebody screwed up my acetate!' So I turned off the record, and I was ready to commit suicide." But the bird noises kept on after the record had been stopped! Si looked around. "There I saw that Phil had birdcages all around the offices, and he had birds in them! So this was Phil Spector. I just said, 'Well, I give up on him!'"

Be that as it may, thanks perhaps to Spector's competition on "He's a Rebel," Vicki Carr, like Jackie DeShannon, would have to wait a few years to have a big hit. As good as the Liberty/Snuff Garrett sound was, it was no guarantee of a hit. Even without a competing version by a producer like Phil Spector, things could go wrong, as Snuff himself is the first to admit.

"One of the first artists I cut was an Australian star named Johnny O'Keefe. We spent seventeen thousand dollars promoting him, the most we ever spent. We did a nationwide tour. One of those songs we cut was number one four or five times in Australia. It is almost their national anthem, called 'She's My Baby.' In the United States it was a Great National Secret, and it shouldn't have made it here—it wasn't that great a record.

"Liberty didn't want Spec, but I fought my ass off to get Spec on Liberty because I thought that Spec was the most talented person out there. I thought he was a genius. We were good friends and I respected him a lot. He got in, but then everything went wrong. Spec is his own kind of cat; we all are. I have nothing but the greatest respect for Spec, always have. But he was not into being a big corporation team player. Neither was I, but he couldn't handle it at all. Spec and I got along great, it was all the other meetings and things. He just sat there and stared at them and thought they were squirrelly and so did I." Probably no one at Liberty except Snuff liked Spec after the "He's a Rebel" debacle.

Ever since the Chipmunks made Christmas 1958 so merry at Liberty, Christmas singles and albums had been a tradition. In 1962 *Merry Christmas from Bobby Vee* mixed traditional songs like "White Christmas" and "Silent Night" with a great song that Liberty singer/songwriter Dick Glasser contributed, "A Not So Merry Christmas." Released on a 45 for the holidays, "Christmas Vacation" was looked forward to by Bobby Vee not to get a visit from Santa, but as a time to spend more time with his girl.

Christmas with the Chipmunks was a standard, and *'Twas the Night Before Christmas Back Home* by Walter Brennan was suitably sentimental and folksy.

Folk songs were gaining in popularity in 1962. The Sundowners LP *Folk Songs for the Rich* showed a sense of humor about folk music. And for a sideways sense of humor, *The Alligator* by Henry Gibson showcased the unique style of the comic poet years before he gained fame on TV's "Laugh-in."

Meanwhile, as Vikki Carr's record was forgotten, over at Dolton, the Five Whispers were given a tryout, but "Midnight Sun" didn't catch on either.

Dolton newcomer Vic Dana had ended 1961 for Dolton with "Little Altar Boy" and now kicked 1962 off for the label with his only hit of the year, "I Will," which like "Altar" came pleasantly close to the national top forty.

Arranger Hank Levine had been helping out at Dolton, and now he had an idea for an instrumental release of Henry Mancini's catchy instrumental from the film *Hatari*, "Baby Elephant Walk." His recording was released under the name of the Miniature Men, and hit the charts the same week as Lawrence Welk's more commercially successful recording on Dot Records. Bob Reisdorff: "I did a version of the 'Baby Elephant Walk,' with Hank Levine as the Miniature Men. That was a fairly big session. The Miniature Men was his name; that is, it belonged to him."

In fact the strange group name had been created for another Dolton release a few months before, "Miniature Blues." Bob explains how Hank "made the name up, of course. He did some arranging for us with the Fleetwoods and Vic Dana. Ernie Freeman I also used as an arranger. "We tried to get hits within the prevailing patterns. I don't like that kind of thing, but that's what happens. It's like rap or anything else that comes along. You have to deal with it or acknowledge it—I don't know if I would have done rap or not."

Bobby Vee's Liberty Christmas LP was released on Liberty's Sunset subsidiary, minus a few tracks.

Sometimes Reisdorff did stray from prevailing patterns. For example, recording John Wayne. "We recorded John Wayne. He was very professional. That was the first time in my entire career that anyone ever got to the studio before I did. He was standing there waiting. He introduced himself as Duke. 'Hi, I'm Duke Wayne.' Oh, yeah, I hadn't noticed! I mean, he looked and acted exactly the way he does on the screen. I said, 'I'm Bob Reisdorff.' And he said, 'I guess you are my director.'" One supposes that the recording industry equivalent of a movie director is a producer!

Which highlights a big reason for doing records in LA. Being in Southern California meant, for Bob Reisdorff, having access to people and facilities one did not even dream were possible in Seattle!

"People wondered why I left Seattle for LA. I said, 'Who wouldn't! You've got access to the best musicians possible. You not only have one in each category. You probably have at least seven that you can call on. You have backup voices. We used the Blossoms with Darlene Love a lot with the Ventures when we needed backup voices. Most commonly it was the Blossoms. They were doing a tremendous number of sessions. I would be very sad if they did not remember me, because I remember them so well. I loved, loved working with them. Such pros! They were wonderful. Personally I liked them enormously. But they were so quick to pick up and so musical.

"The studios were wonderful. Goldstar and United were the ones I used most. I used RCA occasionally. You could not beat those studios. The engineers were so with it, so on the ball. That made for the excitement and the meaning. I don't know if you could survive in Seattle in those days [without access to such facilities and personnel].

"I wish I could have played guitar so I could say, 'You know what I'd like to hear? Let me show you,' and then play something. But I could never play any instrument. I didn't even know terminology. But on an orchestral session I could walk into the studio and say, 'I don't like it. And I don't like the strings here or the horns here. Why don't we give this to the strings and that to the horns?'" Bob did not understand that sheet music could not be blithely switched from horns to strings. "They would say, 'What?!' And I would say, 'Can't you do it fast?' Sometimes they were so professional they could do it. That part of the business was fun.

"To tell you the truth, it was always such a relief to work with people who had been in the business and knew exactly what to do. There were a couple of times I did sessions with people like Glen Campbell, Billy Strange, Bud Coleman, people like that, when we had to fill in a song on a Ventures album and the Ventures were out of town. I'll tell you, those session guys are so overwhelming musically. They are so quick to pick up on exactly what you want. You could just play the demo or whatever and then the ideas are flying around and twenty minutes later there is a song. They were incredibly fast, dedicated, wonderful people to work with. Those pros were hard to beat. It was not a common practice, but when we did need one more cut, no one ever spotted the difference when we used session musicians."

Another thing that was absent in Seattle, and not all that plentiful in Hollywood in 1962 for that matter either, was black recording artists. Just as Si Waronker was frustrated in his mid-1950s efforts to recruit rock 'n' roll singers ("If I could have gotten a Chuck Berry, I would have started with him in two seconds!"), Bob Reisdorff yearned to have black people on his label. "I certainly liked working with black musicians whenever I could get them, because they brought something into the room that was a little bit different. I didn't record many [black] people because they didn't come to me. Ernie Freeman was, of course, black, a soulful man. But he was kind of burned out; everyone was using him as an arranger. He could do those orchestral sweeps, string sweeps that were very popular at the time."

There was one occasion on which it was a bit sticky for Bob Reisdorff, having access to the wealth of talent that existed in LA. "The *Telstar/Lonely Bull* album was very, very popular, very big, right up there with Herbie Albert's original version. I know Herbie. In fact, I called him to come and play on the Ventures album, because I knew that he was a great trumpet player. I did not know that 'The Lonely Bull' was his recording! So he came down to my office and he said, 'I don't think that my partner'—Jerry Ross, who[m] I knew, 'would like that, Bob.' I asked him, 'Why not. Why would Jerry object? I understand you play the trumpet. That's what I want, that wonderful, big, warm, open trumpet on "The Lonely Bull" on this album.'

"'Well, "The Lonely Bull" is my record.'
"'Herbie! You're kidding. Congratulations! I didn't know!'
"So the record business had its moments. But of course I did get a good open-trumpet guy."

With the addition of Vic Dana, Dolton pretty much completed their hit-artist roster, as the Five Whispers and the Echoes never gained national popularity. Only six acts—the hit-making Ventures and Fleetwoods, plus Vic Dana, the small-timers the Frantics and Little Bill and the Blue Notes, and the made-up group the Miniature Men—comprised the entire Dolton charting catalog.

Speaking of the Ventures and the Fleetwoods, the Ventures made a lot of money for Dolton and Liberty, but it was mostly from their LP sales, which were high worldwide, including in Japan. Their 1962 hit 45s were "Lolita Ya-Ya" from the film *Lolita,* and "The 2,000 Pound Bee (pt. 2)," neither of which made the top forty.

The Fleetwoods' only hit of the year, "Lovers by Night, Strangers by Day," fared better, even making the top forty nationally.

"They Tell Me It's Summer" was the flip side of "Lovers by Night, Strangers by Day." This flip side was written by Randy Newman, who credits the Fleetwoods with giving him his first big break, a national release. Gretchen could almost have gotten cowriter's credit if she'd wanted to. "As with a lot of the songs, in the arranging I came up with almost as many lines in the countermelody, the answers and fills, as what had been written originally. But our less-busy version was released in this case. I liked the sound of that song. It was kind of different.

"Even on songs I helped complete or rewrite in the studio, like Terry Wadsworth's 'Love Alone' [The Fleetwoods' LPs *Softly* and *In a Mellow Mood*), I didn't take any writer's credits. However, Barb's and my writers' credits were sometimes shared with or attributed to Gary ["Graduation's Here" and "Oh, Lord, Let It Be"]."

The Fleetwoods were definitely Dolton artists, not Liberty artists, even though their product was distributed by Liberty and they did have contact with Liberty VIPs like Al Bennett. "Bob Reisdorff once told me that Al Bennett was afraid of me. I asked him, 'Why? Why on earth would anyone be afraid of me?' I guess the reply was something like, 'Because you question things. You read the contracts. The other kids didn't read them, they just signed them.'"

In the process of talking to various Liberty artists, it is clear that many had different experiences at the company. Bobby Vee never felt cheated or slickered. Sharon Sheeley felt she had to fight for everything she deserved.

Even within one recording group, the experiences were very different. The way Gary Troxel of the Fleetwoods related to the Liberty execs was nothing like the way Gretchen Christopher did.

Gary saw things as pretty mellow. "We always got along with Liberty people like Al Bennett. All I can remember [is] they were the big shots, they were always behind the desk. We almost never saw much of them actually. But we did meet them, and when they saw us, they always remembered our names. Gretchen and Bob Reisdorff did the negotiation for us. Bob was not exactly between us, but he was always in there when we were negotiating, and Gretchen was in there doing a lot of the talking.

"Our relations with Liberty were fine. We threw them for, I don't know how much of, a loop. When it came time to renew our contract in nineteen sixty-two, they didn't realize that we had been getting five percent of ninety cents. They thought that they were doing us a favor offering us this in our new contract. We said, 'We are already getting that!' But I thought that everything was fine."

When time came in 1962 to renegotiate their contract with Liberty, Gretchen took an active part and, finding things far less mellow than Gary remembers, fought for the very things that made Gary's life easier. "I met eyeball to eyeball with Al Bennett and his accountant, his lawyer, and his top men and stood my ground, because I had very strong ideas about what was equitable. I wasn't asking for the world, but my own sense of integrity and equity said the certain things should be provided the artist and should not be taken from the artist. The other members of the group were not in on this, although they would reap two-thirds of the benefits.

"Bob Reisdorff later told me that Al Schlesinger [the Fleetwoods' attorney for the renegotiation] said that he 'has a great deal of respect for you because you asked for things that he would never have asked for in the contract.' The way of the business is that the artist just doesn't get those things. Not that they were unreasonable, but he'd just never dreamed that he could have got them. So he didn't bother asking. 'But,' he said, 'you went in and held your ground and asked for what was due and what was equitable and got those things.' He is considered one of the best lawyers in the music business. And we are still friends."

It wasn't just at contract renegotiating time that Gretchen had to make sure that the group's best interests did not get overlooked by Liberty.

"After we were part of Liberty, they tried to get us to sign riders to our contracts. Every once in a while, they would bring a piece of paper to us and ask us to sign. Well, Barbara and Gary would sign. But on one occasion I remember Bob Reisdorff's saying, 'Well, you know, you do not have to sign this.'

"I recall one I did not sign. They wanted to deduct a dollar per album — before our royalties for the album cover! Just a way for them to get more off of our royalties. A dollar per album sold and we received only pennies! Those were some of the sorts of things that they tried to get us to give them, and I guess that is why Bob said they were afraid of me. Or Al was afraid of people who think and who question the fairness of things. Some artists did not do that."

Standing up to Al Bennett seems to have been a female trait at Liberty, or at least a trait that Gretchen shared with Sharon Sheeley.

At the very end of 1962, a collection of Bobby Vee's many hits to date was released, fifteen songs in all, three more than the conventional LP in those days contained. Snuff Garrett masterminded this project as he did so many at Liberty. He called the LP *Bobby Vee's Golden Greats*. Snuff always "wanted to be involved in the cover and everything at Liberty. On *Bobby Vee's Golden Greats*, I used a phrase that I had coined because everyone else said 'Greatest Hits.' I thought that 'Golden Greats' was really a cute phrase, and Bobby was the first one we used that on." Later, there were others, such as *Julie's Golden Greats*.

"When Bobby and I went over and shot the cover photo for *Golden Greats*, I was wearing a white sweater; I took it off and put it on Bobby. I liked being involved in everything."

When an artist like Bobby Vee released multiple albums, the backs of the successive albums carried ads for the artist's previous albums. Originally, the ads included photos of the LP covers. If an artist had produced too many LPs to fit all of

BOBBY VEE'S GOLDEN GREATS

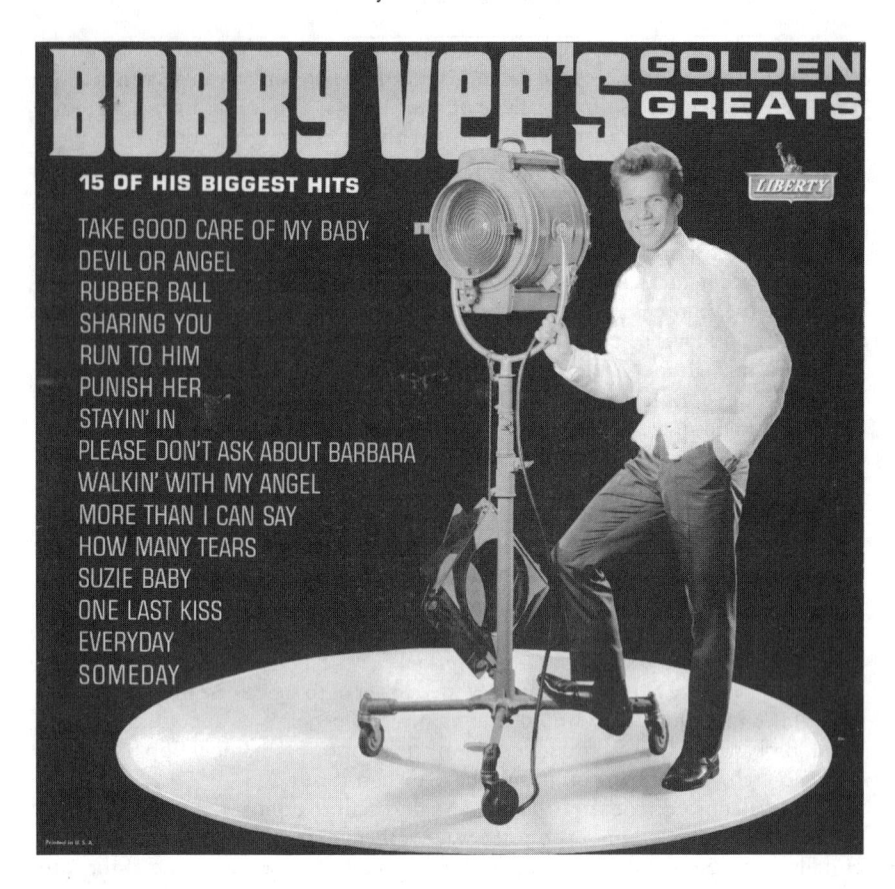

15 OF HIS BIGGEST HITS

TAKE GOOD CARE OF MY BABY
DEVIL OR ANGEL
RUBBER BALL
SHARING YOU
RUN TO HIM
PUNISH HER
STAYIN' IN
PLEASE DON'T ASK ABOUT BARBARA
WALKIN' WITH MY ANGEL
MORE THAN I CAN SAY
HOW MANY TEARS
SUZIE BABY
ONE LAST KISS
EVERYDAY
SOMEDAY

Bobby Vee, wearing his producer Snuff Garrett's sweater, and singing 15 songs instead of the usual dozen.

the illustrations in the allotted space, the photos were deleted from the listings. It was Si's idea to put ads for the other LPs on the back covers: "I wanted one to advertise the other." Also on the backs were fan-club addresses, another of his ideas. "I had all kinds of gimmicks. We put fliers of things to come in the records, the fan clubs; we put a lot of things in there."

Finally, on the album was the address for Liberty, often including Si's invitation for the consumer to "Write for Free Catalog." "Sometimes a record was not selling well, or it was selling well but some cities would not even touch it. Someone would hear it on the air someplace, but they could not find it. So they would write us or call us and order it that way. And usually, we would send it to them for nothing. The other reason we had the address on the albums was, if a record would skip or something, we had a rule in the company, if anything was defective send them a new one, don't make them return the old one."

By the end of 1962 everything looked as rosy as could be for Liberty — but as black as night for Si Waronker. Now that Avnet practically owned Liberty, Si found himself being subjected to what he considered unreasonable demands.

Chapter 10 · 1962

"Avnet wanted me to be in New York every month. I was on the board of directors and also the third largest stockholder. This worked for about three months. The last meeting I attended ended with an argument.

"Lester Avnet, the chairman of the board, was a former violinist with the Los Angeles Philharmonic. He wanted me to record a symphony orchestra. This demand was made at the board meeting. This idea was ludicrous. How could Liberty compete with Columbia or RCA? Capitol got their symphonic catalog from EMI of London. EMI purchased Capitol some years back. I tried to explain my objections, to no avail. One word led to another, and I refused to attend any more board meetings. I suggested sarcastically that Al Bennett take my place on the board—told them to go to hell and stormed out, never to return again."

CHAPTER 11

1963
Ricky Nelson, Fats Domino, and More from Bobby Vee, Jan & Dean, Jackie DeShannon, the Fleetwoods, and the Crickets

By 1963 Liberty was in an odd situation. So far there had been just over two dozen Liberty acts with chart hits of one size or another (excluding Dolton artists and also-rans). In January 1963 only one of those had a current song on the charts. In fact, of all twenty-six, Bobby Vee was one of only three Liberty top-forty artists who would ever have a really big hit again. Timi Yuro was another, with a mild 1963 hit 45, "Make the World Go Away." Bobby's hit was, of course, "The Night Has a Thousand Eyes." And Bobby still had a lot of good music to do with Liberty. "Charms," "Be True to Yourself," "A Letter from Betty," "Never Love a Robin," and "Yesterday and You" would be Bobby Vee's subsequent hit songs in 1963 alone.

"Yesterday and You" is worthy of special note. One of the earliest Liberty singles, back in 1956, had been David Seville's own version of "Yesterday and You" (Seville wrote it as well) under its original title, "Armen's Theme." Liberty trombonist Si Zentner had an instrumental rendition on a Liberty 45 in 1960. There were doubtless assorted LP versions by various artists over the years as well. But Bobby Vee had the only hit version of Ross's ode to his wife, Armen.

By now Si Waronker's involvement with Liberty was definitely minimal. After being there when "Armen's Theme" was being written, and naming it, he never even heard Bobby Vee's version almost ten years later. And as a vocal? "The lyrics had to come later," says Si. "The original 'Armen's Theme' was an instrumental."

As well as Bobby Vee continued to do at Liberty, the company could not survive on just one artist's hits, not even Bobby Vee's. Where were Johnny Burnette and the other five Liberty additions for 1960? Where were Gene McDaniels and the other six new Liberty 1961 artists? And where were the 1962 acquisitions, Walter Brennan, the Rivingtons, and Jan & Dean?

The Rivingtons, Walter Brennan, Gene McDaniels, and Johnny Burnette were no longer scoring major hits. But Jan & Dean . . .

Jan & Dean

As already chronicled, Jan & Dean had a history of hits on Arwin, Doré, and Challenge Records. At Liberty for a year now, however, their numerous releases had yet to crack the national top forty. In 1963 Jan & Dean were making ambitious plans, if not hits. After having three Liberty singles fail to reach the magic circle of the top forty, their stock at Liberty was pretty low. The Liberty motto—When All Else Fails, Cut an LP—saved Jan & Dean. With no national hits to speak of on Liberty, Liberty naturally and audaciously released *Jan & Dean's Golden Hits*!

Their manager, Lou Adler, had acquired the rights to some of their old songs. From Doré Liberty leased Jan & Dean's early songs "Baby Talk" and "We Go Together" for *Golden Greats*. From Challenge Liberty leased 1961's "Heart and Soul." 1958's "Jennie Lee" from Arwin could not be acquired, so Jan & Dean recorded a new version, with Dean singing Arnie's part. The rest of the LP was made up of the 1962 Liberty cuts which had been regionally popular, "Tennessee" (a remake of "Jennie Lee") and "A Sunday Kind of Love" (which had a lot in common with "Heart and Soul"). That left just six songs needed for the even dozen required for an LP, for which new recordings were produced. Freddy Cannon's "Palisades Park" (1962), complete with roller-coaster sound effects, Ritchie Valens's "In a Turkish Town," and two other tunes, "Queen of My Heart" and "Poor Little Puppet" (a 1961 single on Warner's by Cathy Carroll) were chosen.

The two remaining cuts prepared for *Golden Hits* deserve special mention. The original Jan & Dean sound had been developed on the 1958 single, "Jennie Lee," attributed on the label to Jan & Arnie. Arnie Ginsberg was a friend who left the group when Dean Torrence returned from the Army Reserves in 1959. And rumors of Dean's involvement notwithstanding, William Berry, Jan Berry's father, states positively that Dean did not sing on the original "Jennie Lee" hit record.

But the "Jan & Dean Sound" (as their Doré LP had been titled), ever since "Jennie Lee," had quite simply been "bomp-bomp-bomp." The "bomp" sound was subsequently aped by many artists and used on many records. A partial list includes "Blue Moon" (1961) by the Marcels and "Barbara Ann" (1961) by the Regents, as well as almost all of Jan & Dean's recordings on Arwin, Doré, Challenge and Liberty. Composer Barry Mann even had a top-ten record called "Who Put the Bomp (in the Bomp-Bomp-Bomp)" in 1961.

Many black artists, from Frankie Lymon and the Teenagers to countless unrecorded a capella street-corner groups from the 1950s used bomplike nonsense lyrics when they sang years before Jan & Anybody ever put anything on tape. But Jan & Dean (and Arnie) can legitimately lay claim to being the top-forty popularizers of the specific "bomp" refrain.

Jan & Dean knew that they were the ones who had put the bomp in the bomp-bomp-bomp, so they recorded their answer song to Barry Mann's "Who Put the Bomp" hit on their *Golden Hits* LP: "We Put the Bomp!" (Several other artists also recorded variations, such as Frankie Lymon's "I Put the Bomp.")

For the final song on their LP, Jan & Dean decided to do "Barbara Ann," a recent hit by the Regents and itself a direct "bomp" descendent of "Jennie Lee."

Jan sang the low, bomp part as usual on "Barbara Ann." Using Liberty's overdubbing facilities, Jan & Dean provided background harmony parts themselves, while Dean, as usual, provided the falsetto. But, in all of their recordings to date, Dean had never before sung a lead part in his high falsetto. Thus the sound on "Barbara Ann" was unique for Jan & Dean, with the lead vocal done in falsetto. At this same time a new group on Vee Jay Records was coming off three hits with harmony and falsetto leads, "Sherry," "Big Girls Don't Cry," and "Walk Like a

Man." Each of these new Four Seasons records featured the same basic sound as Jan & Dean's sound on "Barbara Ann."

Keying off the new Jan & Dean sound on "Barbara Ann," in mid–March 1963 Jan & Dean unveiled their new Four Seasons–style sound with a song called "Linda" (Ray Noble and Buddy Clark, 1947; Charlie Spivak, 1947). "Linda" was written by Jack Lawrence in the 1940s for a baby named Linda Eastman (who later married Paul McCartney). Jan & Dean's idea of choosing an old song came from the old songs revived with bomps by, for example, both the Marcels on "Blue Moon" (Mel Torme, 1949), "Melancholy Baby" (Tex Beneke/Glenn Miller, 1940), "Heartaches" (Ted Weems, 1947; Harry James, 1947), "Summertime" (Bob Crosby theme), and Jan & Dean's own "Heart and Soul" (Larry Clinton and Bea Wain, 1938; the Four Aces, 1952) and "A Sunday Kind of Love" (Claude Thornhill Orchestra with Fran Warren, 1940s), but this time the bomps were replaced by "Li-Li-Li-Li-Linda," and the lead was in falsetto.

It worked! After more than a year on Liberty without real chart success, Jan & Dean had their first top-forty record. But of all the Liberty artists who eventually had a string of good hits, only Jan & Dean had taken so long to get going.

Jackie DeShannon

The same month as "Linda," a former Liberty also-ran released her first hit record. Jackie DeShannon was a songwriter who eventually wrote more than six hundred songs, many recorded by artists like the Searchers, Bobby Vee, Brenda Lee, Marianne Faithfull, the Byrds, P. J. Proby, the Critters, Peter and Gordon, and others. Liberty had put out a half dozen 45s by Jackie to date.

Happy days for Jackie came in 1963, as she finally made the singles chart — even though her first 1963 single, "Faded Love," stayed on *Billboard*'s top one hundred for only three weeks, stopping at #97. "Faded Love" was the last hit for country singer Patsy Cline, a singer Jackie sometimes sounded like (though not here). It is a great song, but even Patsy's version, out on Decca Records at the same time as Jackie's Liberty cover version, spent only three weeks on the chart, stopping at #96.

Jackie wrote a great many of her own songs, so for her the lack of smashing success must have been doubly disappointing. Her other two 1963 Liberty hits also failed to reach the magic forty. However, both of her 1963 minor hits, "Needles and Pins" and "When You Walk in the Room," were later copied note for note and inflection for inflection by the Searchers and became great British invasion hits! The Searchers even took Jackie's phrasing on the words *"needles and pins-ah"* and made it their own.

Si certainly saw the potential in Jackie. "I thought that Jackie DeShannon was going to be very big. If she had been recording in today's market, she would have been a big artist. She could also write. She went with Eddie Cochran for a while. Then she went with a couple of other artists for a while. She had five or six good records; she had talent. Not all of it was pulled out of her yet, but she was improving all the time. I liked Jackie."

After "Needles and Pins," the next Liberty hits were "Surf City," by Jan & Dean; "A Letter from Betty" b/w "Be True to Yourself," by Bobby Vee; "Make the World Go Away," by Timi Yuro; and "It's a Lonely Town," by Gene McDaniels.

Surf City

"Surf City" was a huge record for Liberty. It was originally written by Brian Wilson of the Beach Boys, who was present for the session and provided the falsetto notes usually attributed to Dean. Brian's title for the partially completed tune was "Two Girls for Every Boy," the opening and closing line of the song. When Jan & Dean completed writing it, they had changed the title to "Surf City." Good thing, too, or it would have been a pretty unpopular oldie once the women's movement took hold. However, a close listen to the lyrics reveals that the situation is not that each boy has two girls; boys just happen to be outnumbered two to one by girls.

When the record was released, it was quickly taken to the top of the charts — all the charts. When "Surf City" was #1 on the pop charts on July 20, 1963, it was also the #3 record on the R&B chart, and the only record by a white act on the R&B top ten at that.

Another thing happened when "Surf City" was released. Many people thought the record was by the Beach Boys. The Beach Boys had just charted with "Surfin' Safari" and "Surfin'" and "Surfin' USA," and to date no one else in the world had recorded surf records like those. Now Jan & Dean had one, partly written and sung by head Beach Boy Brian. One midwest DJ outcued "Surf City" one day by saying, "There's 'Surf City,' by the Beach ... Kids!"

So many people mistook the record for the newest Beach Boys single that Capitol Records, the Beach Boys' label, began getting complaints from record distributors. They wanted to know how come stations had a new Beach Boys single before they did and when they would be getting it. The mistake was an honest one, since Brian Wilson (uncredited) was on the song, and almost thirty years later, Dean admitted to me that he was not at the "Surf City" recording session. Jan cut the biggest hit the duo ever had without him, and had Brian Wilson sing the falsetto parts usually attributed to Dean! (For more on Jan & Dean and "Surf City," see the Jan & Dean interview in part 3.)

Years later Dean sang lead (uncredited) with Brian on the Beach Boys' hit "Barbara Ann," so things equal out.

Si Exits Liberty

At that point Si Waronker stopped going to the office. The founder of Liberty was no longer able to come to work. The stress, tension, and conflict had driven him into ill health. There were conflicts with Al Bennett over musical direction, staffing in promotion and A&R, and royalty policies. On top of that Avnet had taken over Liberty, trying to run it by remote control from the East Coast, and treating it as if it were a factory, not a house of music.

"Liberty was capitalized in public for a million shares. We sold one hundred thousand shares at ten dollars a share. I remained with one hundred fifty-four thousand shares that I never sold. Later when we sold the company to Avnet, we traded even, with their stock worth twenty-two dollars a share.

"I thought I was working in a business that I knew so well, the music business. But with Avnet, suddenly I was working for a company that made steel and

Once upon a time had the No. 1 single in the country. So they made an LP and naturally titled it. All the good people who bought their single then bought their LP, and it too became the No. 1 album in the country. It could only happen in America.

A Liberty trade ad during the Avnet period, as indicated in the lower right hand corner under the Liberty logo.

electronics. And they are telling me what they would like to hear—a symphony orchestra. I told them no go. And the board of directors meetings were rigged ahead of time; everyone said yes, never no."

Si's comments are reminiscent of a comment made by Tommy Allsup: "Hits are not made in meetings; they are made in the studio."

"Another reason I left," continues Si, "was that Al could sell anything, but he knew nothing about music [and still] tried to say what was good. Al Bennett pulled in a whole bunch of people like Don Blocker, Bud Dain, Don Bohanan, Kenny Revercomb, and they were all put in the promotion department, supposedly. I didn't agree with it, with their being hired. But that was beside the point. He was running the sales department, so that was his job. Part of the argument we had at the time was, what the hell did they know about it? That was more of the internal struggle. I was brought up as a musician, musicwise, and some of the other guys knew nothing about music. In many things we had a different perception of what the music should be. I had one idea, the other guys had another.

"It was fun from 1955 until 1961. It was great. After that, even though we were successful, it was a fight. I won for a long time, but when I got sick, I lost my so-called power because I took less interest in it. But I didn't give up. I fought like hell, and I fought too hard and got sick.

"So finally, after another stroke, and after a fight with Avnet (I wouldn't record a symphony orchestra for them), I had recorded the last Martin Denny album. Al played it for the board. They liked it but wanted two more cuts of current tunes on it. 'Current tunes? What the hell for? Don't give me this crap about current tunes. The album is mastered and ready to press, go ahead and do it.' I was home. I didn't even go in in those days. Well, the record came out with two extra tunes recorded by someone else besides me. That was the end of it. 'Between that and recording the symphony orchestra, you guys do it yourself. I'm through.' I still had a contract with four years to go at fifty thousand bucks a year, in those days a very good contract." Although Si "quit the business" around August 1, 1963, he was unable to break his contract until later, in 1964, when he resigned officially.

After eight years the man who had founded Liberty had lost it to outside interests and former friends.

Tracey Dey and Other Also-Rans

Another new artist was signed by Liberty in 1963, another female vocalist, Tracey Dey. For the first time, an artist was recorded without ever meeting Si Waronker. No one but record collectors remembers Tracey Dey today, but she was very active at this time, singing under a variety of names on several record labels.

Unfortunately Tracey's consistently excellent girl-group-sounding records just as consistently failed to become national hits. Her one Liberty success, albeit non-top-forty, was "Teenage Cleopatra" in 1963. Her records were usually produced by Four Seasons alumnus Bob Crew (Four Seasons producer) and Bob Gaudio (Four Seasons keyboardist and songwriter). Besides Liberty, her songs came out on Vee Jay Records and Amy Records. Besides her output on Liberty, through her Four Seasons connections, Tracey Dey also recorded a "Sherry" (Four Seasons, 1962) answer song, "Jerry (I'm Your Sherry)," which was produced and written by the Seasons on the same label as "Sherry," Vee Jay Records. Then, the Four Seasons produced and wrote another Tracey Dey–Four Seasons answer record on Parkway Records. It was an answer song to "Rag Doll," called "Society Girl" by the Rag Dolls (in reality, Tracey)! With all of this and more, it was amazing Tracey never made it big, on Liberty or elsewhere!

Another could-have-been Liberty gambled with in 1963 was Joe Carson. Ex-Cricket Tommy Allsup was the producer for his record, "The Last Song (I'm Ever Gonna Sing)." The song was written by Crickets drummer Jerry Allison and guitarist Sonny Curtis, whose Texas roots showed here. This was a heavily country version of the Liberty sound which did not catch on — except of course on the country charts.

As of 1963, in spite of many tries, when it came to 45s Liberty had become primarily an outlet for Bobby Vee and Jan & Dean. But that would be enough. After the spring 1963 release of "Linda" came the first in a series of big Jan & Dean surf and drag smashes, the classic "Surf City." (Does Si Waronker recall "Surf City"? "Oh, God, yes!") "Surf City" went to #1, giving Liberty its fourth #1 in its eight-year history, and the first since Bobby Vee's "Take Good Care of My Baby" in 1961. To round out the year, Jan & Dean did two — count 'em, two — "Surf City" follow-up singles, "Honolulu Lulu," about a girl surfer, and "Drag City," which is self-explanatory. Both of these were top-ten records. At Liberty Jan & Dean had hit their stride at last.

Since surf music by the likes of Jan & Dean and the Beach Boys was big in America, it only made sense that it might also be popping up over in England. On the heels of Jan & Dean's surfing successes, Liberty issued a surf 45 by the Dakotas, a British instrumental combo headed by Michael Maxwell. "The Cruel Surf" and the flip side were both written by Mike, and while the record made #15 in England, it failed to catch on in the United States. The Dakotas were Manchester's biggest group but never had another national British hit as an instrumental group. The Dakotas' producer was George Martin, who also produced the Beatles and, significantly, a young singer named Bill Kramer. Think about that for awhile.

Andy and the Marglows offered a tasty alternative to record buyers in the fall of 1963. They were a black doo-wop group with a definite 1950s sound on their bomp-and-falsetto-filled remake of "I'll Get By." The song had been a top-ten record for the Ink Spots in 1944 and a #1 hit for Dick Haymes with Harry James the same year. The flip side, called "Superman Lover," featured the bass voice opening with, "Is it a bird? Is it a plane?" No, it was the Superman lover, with power in his fist and power in his kiss. Why, he even danced the mashed potato while flying in the air! What he could not manage to do was climb the charts.

Thanks to Bobby Vee and Jan & Dean, things were not too bad in the accounting department at Liberty in 1963, even though the Liberty hit artist list was getting short. Of course, there was always the other Liberty motto: When All Else Fails, Release Some LPs. Besides the 1962 *Jan & Dean Golden Hits,* there were Buddy Knox's *Golden Hits,* and Gene McDaniels's *Hit After Hit,* featuring all of his hits plus a few others like "Love Me Tender" (Elvis, 1956) and "Tall Oak Tree," Dorsey Burnette's 1960 Era Records hit. Julie London made *Love on the Rocks,* sang Latin in a *Satin Mood,* and presented her *Golden Greats* plus *The End of the World* inspired by the 1963 Skeeter Davis RCA chart-topper. Julie also recorded the LPs *You Don't Have to Be a Baby to Cry* after the Caravells' 1963 record, *Love Letters,*

JAN & DEAN take LINDA SURFIN'

LINDA ● MR. BASS MAN ● SURFIN' SAFARI ● RHYTHM OF THE RAIN ● WALK LIKE A MAN
● THE BEST FRIEND I EVER HAD ● MY FOOLISH HEART ● SURFIN' ● THE GYPSY CRIED ●
● ● WALK RIGHT IN ● ● ● LET'S TURKEY TROT ● ● ● WHEN I LEARN HOW TO CRY ● ●

Jan & Dean take "Linda" surfin'. The Beach Boys sang and played on Jan & Dean's musical beach, appearing unbilled on this LP.

and *The Wonderful World of Julie London*. On the novelty side, *Christmas with the Chipmunks, Volumes 1 and 2* and *The Chipmunk Songbook* held no surprises but kept the legend of Alvin, Simon, and Theodore alive and the cash registers and sleigh bells ringing.

The Liberty *Golden Hits* series added volumes 6, 7, 8 and 9, including more of the best of Liberty and other labels' rock 'n' roll output of the past few years. Timi Yuro's 1963 LPs numbered three, *Make the World Go Away*, plus *What's a Matter Baby* and *The Best of Timi Yuro*. The Si Zentner, Eddie Haywood, and Felix Slatkin orchestras released LPs. Walter Brennan released two LPs during this period, and the *Incredible Nancy Ames* debuted on Liberty LPs.

On the strength of the single "Linda," Jan & Dean recorded their first stereo LP, *Jan & Dean Take Linda Surfin'* (some LP cover edges called the LP *Mr. Bass Man Takes Linda Surfin'* by mistake. The song "Mr. Bass Man," a 1963 Kapp Records hit by Johnny Cymbal, was on the LP, but this hardly explains the mistake). By the time "Linda" had peaked in the top thirty, Jan & Dean knew that their next release would be a surf song. That new group on Capitol Records, the Beach Boys, formed late in 1962, and their first hit, "Surfin'," a "bomp" song, had been based largely on Jan & Dean's 1959 "Baby Talk." Jan & Dean even invited the new group to appear on their *Linda* LP. The five Beach Boys and Jan & Dean formed a super-group on the LP, and together the seven of them cut new versions of the first two Beach Boy surf hits, "Surfin'" and "Surfin' Safari." The rest of the LP was rock 'n' roll songs of early 1963, like the Cascades' "Rhythm of the Rain," Johnny Cymbal's bomp hit, "Mr. Bass Man," and the Four Seasons' falsetto smash, "Walk Like a Man."

Liberty country LPs from this era came from *Here's Willie Nelson*, also Bud and Travis's *Naturally* and *Perspective on Bud and Travis, Bob Wills Sings and Plays,* one called *The Carter Family Album,* and *Tex Williams in Las Vegas.* Martin Denny had three or four more LPs (plus the hit 45 "Taste of Honey"), and the Original Hits series expanded to include *Original Country Hits, Vol. 1* and *Original Country Hits, #2,* as well as the newest and most tune-filled LP in the rock 'n' roll series, *15 Number One Hits — The Original Hits, Vol. 10.*

A movement gaining new converts in pop and rock 'n' roll music in 1963 was folk music. Liberty moved in fast to take advantage of the folk or "hootenanny" trend, with *A Portrait of Nancy — Folk Songs by Nancy Ames,* and the Johnny Mann Singers sang *Golden Folk Hits and Golden Folk Hits, Vol. Two.*

There were many other 1963 Liberty LPs by the likes of Spike Jones, Leon Bibb, and the Martial Solal Trio. Of interest to the rock 'n' roll fans was *Something Old, Something New, Something Blue, Somethin' Else!!!!!!* This LP was by the recent addition to the Liberty family, the Crickets. Being neighbors to Bobby Vee, the "Buddy Holly of the '60s" and a fantastic artist in his own right, helped the Crickets land their Liberty contract. Even though their Liberty singles, like "Please Don't Ever Change," "He's Old Enough to Know Better" and "Little Hollywood Girl" did not really dent the national charts, Liberty naturally had them cut another LP, *The Crickets.* Meanwhile, the first rock 'n' roll revival continued to pick up steam. Bobby Vee's earlier LP, *Hits of the Rockin' '50s,* had sold very well, so with the arrival of the Crickets, Bobby Vee recorded *I Remember Buddy Holly.* This LP was the next best thing to having Buddy Holly back again, and had all of Buddy's hits as well as "Buddy's Song," the great medley of Buddy's songs written for Bobby Vee by Buddy Holly's mother!

Although they never charted in America, the Liberty Crickets were well received in England. They had four top-forty hits between 1962 and 1964 on British Liberty, including one that made the top five in July of 1962, "Don't Ever Change." This song was covered by the Beatles in their audition sessions for Decca before their hit days.

Jerry Allison reflected on those records. "The most successful thing we ever did on Liberty, that Snuff produced, was 'Don't Ever Change.' It went to the top of the British charts in the summer of 1962, something like that.... Glen Campbell and a fellow named Jerry Naylor sang that. Glen played guitar on it." The flip side, "I'm Not a Bad Guy," was written by Jerry Allison himself, who says, "Glen played some hot guitar for us on that, I thought. Jerry Naylor sang that one, and Glen Campbell night have been singing harmony."

Glen Campbell? Jerry Naylor? But what about the Crickets? Exactly who made up the group called the Crickets varied from time to time — a pattern that began back in Buddy Holly's day. "He's Old Enough to Know Better" was written by Jerry

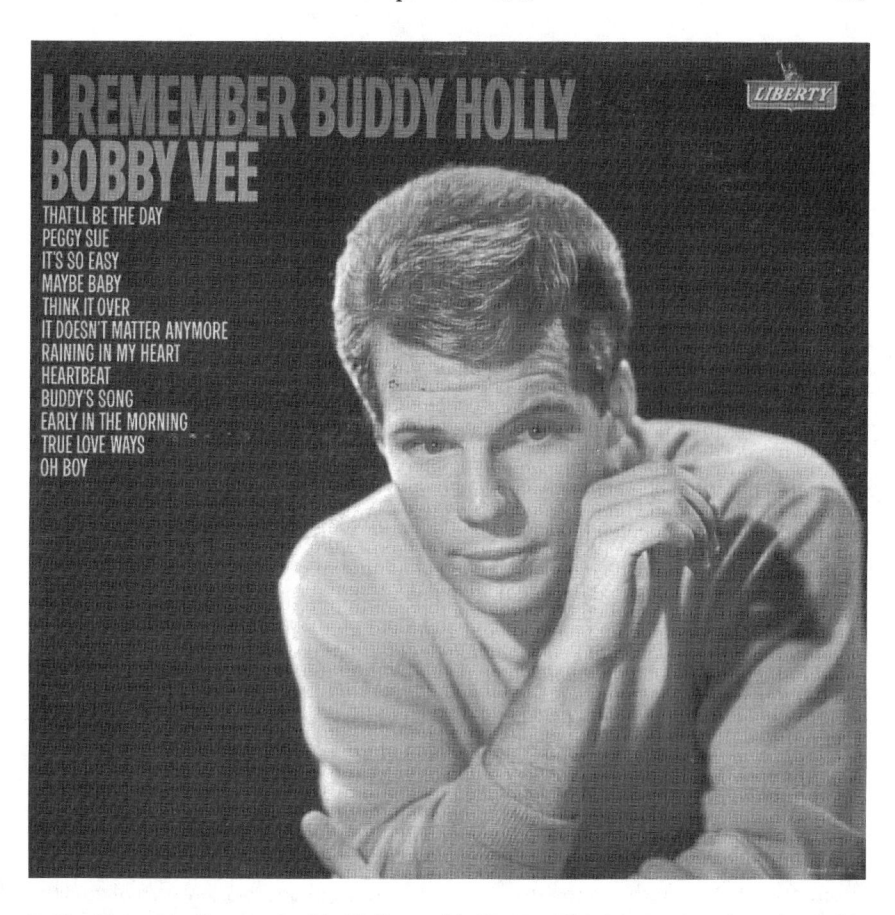

Bobby Vee paid tribute to Buddy Holly on this LP. "Buddy's Song" was written by Buddy Holly's mother.

Allison and sung by Jerry and Cliff Crawford, with Bobby. The other side, "I'm Feelin' Better," was sung by Cliff and Bobby and written by Bobby. Allison: "That record did some good in England, but not a whole lot. We were sort of hung for Crickets at the time, because Sonny Curtis—he'd been a Cricket from the time when Buddy Holly moved to New York—Sonny started playing with us. But Sonny was in the Army at this time, so we went through a bunch of Crickets. Glen Campbell sang on a bunch of stuff."

How did the Crickets cope over the years with the task of replacing Buddy Holly as the lead singer? "Sonny Curtis started playing with us when Buddy moved to New York. Sonny always liked country music better, I believe. That's what he is off doing by himself now. Replacing Buddy has always been a real chore. We had some really lean years where we didn't even work. Like during the British invasion, the only place where we could get work was in Britain." Ironic. Before deciding on the name "Crickets," Buddy and Jerry had toyed with the idea of using the name "Beetles"! And the real Beatles did name themselves after the Crickets, then undercut business in their own country. "There was the period when our old stuff wasn't yet old enough, and it wasn't new enough either. The work is better right now than it has been in thirty years as far as jobs and doing TV things and working in England and audiences' reactions.

"Replacing Buddy has been hard to cope with. We have a fella right now, Gordon Paine, who used to play for Waylon. When we used to open the show for Waylon, Gordon'd come out and sit in with us every night. He sort of grew up liking rock 'n' roll and listening to it. And so that is working out real good. Joe B. Mauldin and Gordon and I go on the road all the time now. It's working real good because he really, like, studied the way Buddy played the licks, like the down licks on the guitar, instead of up and down strumming. He doesn't try to look like Buddy or anything. He tries to sing the songs like they were recorded. It works real good, he has a good feel for 1950s stuff."

I asked Jerry Allison what it meant when a record said "produced by Snuff Garrett." What did he do? Did he make the appointments for the session? Did he tell the artist how to sing it? "Both. Now a lot of people get their name on a record as producer, and they didn't really produce. But Snuff really did. We'd go in there and play the songs for him and he'd say, 'Yeah, let's cut that one, let's cut this one.' Actually, he was the one who found the song 'Don't Ever Change.' He'd been cutting a lot of things by Gerry Goffin and Carole King, and that was by them best as I remember. He'd done their things with Bobby Vee, like 'Take Good Care of My Baby.' He found 'Don't Ever Change' and said 'it'd be good for you guys.' So he set up the studio time and lined up the pickers and then he was sittin' in there and sayin', 'Sing it again!' Snuff picked out material, but it was chosen by mutual agreement. But Snuff sort of had the final say-so. Then later, when Buzz Cason was producing us, Buzz had the say-so. We sort of mutually agreed more with Buzz."

The flip side of "Don't Ever Change" was written by Jerry Allison himself. "I'm Not a Bad Guy" was slightly reminiscent of the Everly Brothers, but very bright and up in attitude. Everything about the record is unusual and works—the piano, the drum and cymbal, the lead guitar, and the vocals are all full of special hooks and twists. Shoulda been a hit. How frustrating it was to be putting out such fine work and not make the charts.

The Crickets' Liberty single "Little Hollywood Girl" was another Goffin-King song. "Seems like, the deal on that one was, they wrote it for Bobby Vee, but he was out of town or something like that, maybe he had just put a record out, something like that. So Snuff said, 'We'll cut it with you guys real quick.'" Would the song have come out much differently by Bobby Vee? "Well, it would have had the same players and producer and everything. Only the singer would have been different."

The Crickets never scored big chart successes while on Liberty. Most artists would love the chance to record for a hit label. For the Crickets getting hits may have been difficult, but getting signed was not a problem. In fact Snuff did not have as much trouble getting the Crickets onto the label as he did with some of his other Texas friends. "We were sort of friends with Al Bennett," explains Jerry Allison. "In fact, I always called Al 'Big Time,' and he called me 'Small Time.' Al probably raised cain anyway. We were probably a perfect example of Snuff getting his friends on Liberty. Snuff also signed Buddy Knox about that time. But Al was always really good to us. I don't know if he ever pressed that many records on us, but we always got along real good."

I was curious if Jerry had any ideas about why his Crickets were so scarce on Liberty. Was the fault not enough company support, poor material choices, production problems, the group not performing up to standards—or is that the secret of making hits (if he knew that, he'd have all hits)? "Well, that's exactly it. You never know. Although it seems like sometimes the record company is at fault—of course, this is the complaint artists always have with record companies — it seemed like they didn't have the product available. We'd go out and play jobs and say, 'Hey, here's our new record,' we'd play it live, but it didn't matter because people couldn't find it to buy it anywhere. Some of those records, I thought for the time, were good. I was real happy with the records, the way they came out, and it seemed that 'Don't Ever Change,' for instance, for it to be number one in England like it was and not do anything in the States, something was wrong at Liberty. So the songs were picked good, they were pretty good records, but somebody fell down in promotion, somewhere, something—it wasn't our fault!

"Buzz Cason produced a song we did called '(They Call My Baby) La Bamba.' Leon Russell arranged it, a variation of Ritchie Valens's record. That almost did some good. It was number one in Boston and big in some other places around the country. It never did zip off like we thought it would. We thought our version was sort of in the surfing field. We do that song on shows now because Ritchie Valens's version is popular again. So we do our old version. That was our last successful—I hate to say 'hit'—our last successful record in England." (It was #21 in 1964 in England.)

Did the lack of hits make Allison bitter? No way! "There were some fun days around Liberty in the early 1960s."

Lack of hits did not deter Liberty from cutting LPs, by the way. The Crickets cut four, with no big hits to justify them. Liberty would record an LP at the drop of a sheaf of sheet music! At Liberty if you had a hit, you did an LP. If you had a flop, you probably got to do two LPs. If you once thought of doing music, you were likely to cut three LPs! As Snuff explains, "There was only one philosophy behind doing so many albums at Liberty, even when an artist had not had a hit 45 in awhile. To Al Bennett, that philosophy was billing."

Jerry Allison fondly recalls the Crickets' Liberty albums. "Four LPs, *Bobby Vee Meets the Crickets, Something Old, Something New, Something Borrowed, Somethin' Else!!!!!!, Presenting the Crickets*, and *California Sun*. That was the one where we cleverly covered the Beatles, in 1963, before they were big here. We did the song 'California Sun' (Joe Jones, 1961; Rivieras, 1963), plus 'Please Please Me,' 'She Loves You,' 'I Want to Hold Your Hand,' 'From Me to You.' I never have seen that album. I don't think I even have a copy of it. I think it is pretty rare. At least it sold well under a million."

Liberty Albums

Why did Liberty record so darn many albums? Until he lost control of the company in 1964, almost everything that happened (or didn't happen) at Liberty was the result of Si Waronker's personality and professionalism. "I believed in albums.

The Wonderful World of Liberty Records

Liberty offered music to the world in the early sixties.

My theory was that there were two kinds of labels, a hit single label and the album label. The album label would look to have a catalog, and I believed in catalogs. So when you had an artist who was on the verge of a hit all the time, never quite making it but on the verge of it, you'd say, 'Why don't we put out an album, and maybe a single will crawl out of that thing.'

"We found out that it did not cost us that much more to make albums. A single cost a dime to press. An album cost twenty-five cents. Covers did not cost very much. Packaging and all, about seventy cents. You pressed only one or two thousand to start with. If it showed any action at all, we'd press ten thousand. We sold the albums for three-something to the distributors. They sold it to the stores for forty percent more, and the stores sold it for four ninety-five or three ninety-five, or from three ninety-five down.

"So the profit on the album was about a dollar to the company. Selling ten thousand would cover the costs and give you catalog. It was a lot better than having a lot of singles lying around. If a single is dead, you might as well throw [it] away. The albums you can always get some money back on, even selling them for twenty-five cents. But you'd never have enough to get hurt in it. [The reliance on album catalog] was a theory that I held deeply, and today it is used all the time. They don't even make single records anymore today. Everyone wants catalog. CDs are out of catalog."

Mono or Stereo?

Something that is forgotten today is that albums used to come in two versions, mono and stereo. And stereo cost a dollar more. Why? "There was no reason for stereo to cost more, no reason at all. Why were CDs twelve ninety-five and now they are seven ninety-five? Just to make money. And they make a fortune on them. I know the cost because I still have connections in the business. The cost of a CD is about three dollars. They sell for eight dollars or more. The next thing will be DAT, and they will be even more expensive, and still for no reason whatsoever.

"I loved stereo. I had a theory that I had two ears, and I love to hear something in both ears. I don't have four ears, so I did not like quadraphonic. I don't like surround sound. It is disturbing to me. At one point, when stereo was really growing, say about 1963, some people would not buy mono any longer. After all, if they had shelled out bucks for new stereo phono gear, why should they settle for mono? Suddenly mono catalog was in danger of going as dead as old 45s did. The solution: Create stereo where none existed before!"

"Simulated stereo," Si called it. "It was a dirty trick, but we had to do it. We had to convert our old stuff to stereo. I'd go into the studio and rerecord a monaural into two-track [bass and treble] then into three-track by feeding each into the third channel, then pulling them back out in any which way we wanted by adding a little more high or middle range on one channel and bass on the other. Many were converted that way. No great trick."

A lot of criticism over the years since the early 1960s has been aimed at pre–Beatle albums. The notion is that lots of time, money, effort, talent, and resources went into the 45 singles, but that the album cuts were nothing but quick fillers. I asked Jerry if the Crickets knew ahead of time what the hits would be. "Naw, they were usually picked after the fact." And how much time was a recording session in those days, the early 1960s? "Sessions were pretty well pinned down to three hours. Everybody was real touchy about it. If you went over a minute or even 30 seconds it went into overtime and you had to pay people overtime and another twenty-five percent, something. I used to know all of that because I contracted the sessions. It was pretty well three hours."

Did that time limit on studio sessions mean the songs were rushed through? Another part of the criticism of pre–Beatle albums was that the material was kitsch, rushed through, not crafted. The Beatles spent weeks on their albums, and in 1966, Brian Wilson spent six months in the studio cutting "Good Vibrations." Were albums cut in three-hour sessions thrown together? Jerry Allison: "We had everything pretty well worked out before we went into the studio, so we could get it all done in three hours. We might cut three or four tunes in a session." In other words the songs in an early 1960s Liberty Crickets album were not hastily thrown together, instead of crafted like a Beatles album or psychedelic song from the later 1960s. The songs were carefully crafted and worked out.

The difference was where the crafting was done. Brian and the Beatles and other later artists used studios for rehearsal halls—expensive ones, at that. But by then it could be afforded, because rock and roll had become big business and there was enough money for big artists to indulge in such extravagances. In the old, pre–Beatle days, just as many hours might be poured into an album. But the rehearsals were done at home, in the basement, onstage, or wherever. Only the "final draft" was done in the studio, with the best or most appropriate cut chosen for the single after the fact.

There were certainly cases in which an artist made one recording that became a hit, and then their record company gave them a tiny budget to come up with an album as fast as possible. But just because only a few hours are spent in the studio to record an album does not mean that many, many additional hours were not spent in rehearsals and development before the sessions.

Although they were not very popular while they were at Liberty, the Crickets still tour thirty-five years later. The touring wasn't hurt by the success of the 1976 movie *The Buddy Holly Story*. "The Buddy Holly movie was based on the book by John Golrosen that was a pretty good book, but the movie I thought was terrible," relates Allison. "But the book that they took it from, the author did a lot of research and got it pretty straight."

A photo of Jerry Allison with Jan & Dean and Gretchen Christopher of the Fleetwoods is [of] an interesting group of people. How did that come about? "That photo was in front of Grauman's Chinese Theater. I just happened to be around when they were doing some Liberty record company publicity stuff, and they said, 'OK, all you people who are on the Liberty labels, let's get up and take pictures.'"

The Crickets did not stay at Liberty very long. Jerry Allison "moved back to Texas in nineteen sixty-one and stayed for about a year. I did all of Snuff's contractin' stuff before I went back to Texas. I should have stayed in LA. Then I did move back to LA, but I never was that crazy about session work. I just never enjoyed it that much.

"The Crickets left Liberty about nineteen sixty-five when I moved back to Texas, and we cut some records in Clovis, New Mexico, for Liberty. We just quit makin' records then, and they quit puttin' them out. I didn't do that much session work, either; that was kind of plannin' ahead too much for me. If I'd have really wanted to, Snuff always used me as much as I wanted to play. But I didn't like playin' with strange bands, and bein' told, 'Play like so-and-so did on such-and-such. I sorta like to play like I like to play. And also, I didn't like to practice that much and keep my chops up. I just went to Texas and started workin' college gigs and like that for a while. That's been a long time ago, hard even to remember all that."

If the Crickets, small potatoes at Liberty, got to do four LPs, then how about bigger artists?

Jan & Dean got to do at least one LP per hit while at Liberty, although Jan & Dean usually tried to score more than one chart song per LP. Their 1963 hit 45s "Linda," "Surf City," and "Drag City" each had their own LPs. *Surf City and Other Swingin' Cities* was a real oddity. Of course, it featured "Surf City" as well as the Jan & Dean (not Brian) top-tenner "Honolulu Lulu." Then the rest of the LP was both pop, country, and rock 'n' roll songs about other cities, like "Kansas City" (Wilbert Harrison, 1959), "Detroit City" (Bobby Bare, 1963), "Manhattan," "I Left My Heart in San Francisco" (Tony Bennett, 1962) and "Tallahassee Lassie" (Freddie Cannon, 1959). Liberty was always big on concept LPs, and most Jan & Dean LPs exuded concept.

Expensive Hot-Rodding

Surf City was full of "City" songs, while *Drag City* was full of car songs and was Jan & Dean's best LP to date. It set a new record for the cost to produce a Liberty album: twenty-six thousand dollars, and Jan & Dean really heard about it. However, the investment was worth it, as *Drag City* was their first Liberty LP to feature all original material and to produce three hit songs, "Drag City" (1963), "Dead Man's Curve" (1964), and "Popsicle" (1966).

Liberty may have felt that twenty-six thousand for one LP was an extravagance, but someone who was there knows how the money was spent—engineer Bones

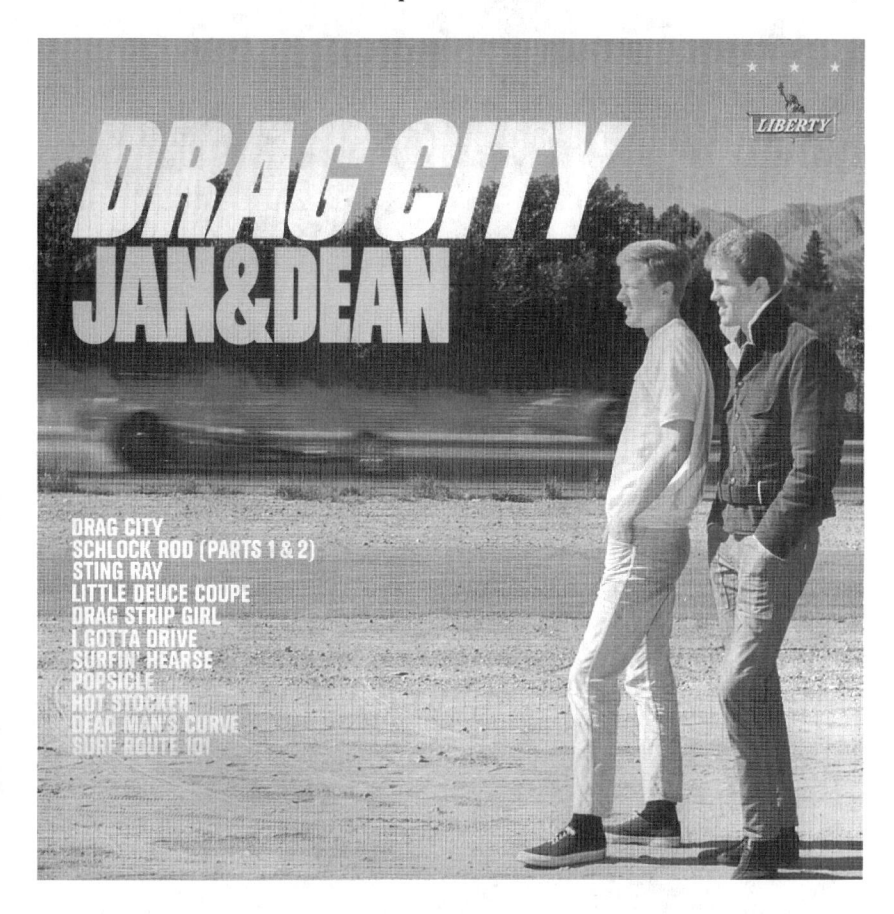

Drag City was the most expensive LP Liberty had ever recorded, and was Jan & Dean's best-selling.

Howe. "Albums were not considered to be important in those days. If you sold two hundred thousand, that was a big deal. There was a rule of thumb that if you had a number one record, you sold two hundred fifty thousand albums. But I always wanted to have more than one hit on an album. Producing the Fifth Dimension, I wanted to have more than one hit on an album. If you had a hit single, next the album came out, and the second single was in the album, the first cut on the B side or some kind of nonsense. I was one of the guys to press for more than one single per album. The *Aquarius* album actually had four hit singles on it and we sold over a million units. But the label was only singles-oriented; they'd be ready to quit after two hundred thousand."

What does Bones have to say about the notion advanced by critics of early rock and roll that 1960s albums were kitsch thrown together to cash in on a carefully crafted hit single? "It's true, but we had a good time doing it. It was really fun in those days. The critics are just jealous because they were not there. We had a good time; I am telling you, we had a really good time." Yet Jan's *Drag City* LP was

Jan & Dean have another smash hit faster than you can say L-i-b-e-r-t-y

JAN & DEAN
#55613
HONOLULU LULU

PRODUCED BY JAN BERRY FOR SCREEN GEMS, INC.

Liberty Records

LIBERTY

A SUBSIDIARY OF AVNET ELECTRONICS CORP

crafted so that every cut was the quality of a single. "Sure. You have a guy like Jan who is really doing innovative things. In those days, he and Brian Wilson were doing innovative things with tracks. When we went in to do 'Drag City,' we knew it was the single. Other records, like 'Honolulu Lulu,' they were marginal records and when you went in you really didn't know. But 'Drag City' was a major production. 'Dead Man's Curve' off that album, no one was really sure about it because there was a little darkness in that records."

Apparently there were albums in the early 1960s, and then there were *albums*!

LPs and Also-Rans for 1963

Dick and Deedee's second and last Liberty hit, "Tell Me," charted in 1962. Until informed by me, Si Waronker had never known the circumstances of Dick St. John's dramatic breaking of his Liberty contract and flight to Warner Bros. records. Si's comment upon hearing about Dick's tantrum act? "God Almighty! I think that's wonderful!" Si was upstairs at Liberty at the time, not on the front line any longer and had no involvement in these kinds of dealings, which he found intolerable. "Now you know the real reason I left in 1963. I wanted no part of it! I couldn't handle it. Al Bennett was hiring A&R people. Even though I was in charge of everything that had to do with the creative end of it, I had no control. I was in the hospital for three weeks. When I came out, we had three new A&R men. I said, 'Where the hell did they come from?' Well, Al Bennett hired them. I said, 'I couldn't care less,' and I gave up. Those were the bad years. Even though my resignation was in 1964, I was in court with them in 1962 and 1963. Trying to get this thing settled up. I had to break my own five-year contract with Al Bennett!"

In 1963 the Chipmunks hit again, this time with the "Alvin Twist" (the song that was featured in a May 1991 Chipmunks TV cartoon).

In 1963, Dolton continued with just three successful, charting artists, the Ventures, the Fleetwoods, and Vic Dana. Of the three, only the Ventures had no chart action in 1963. Well, that is not exactly true. The Ventures always sold a lot of records—albums, that is. Which made them and Bob Reisdorff very happy. "Speaking generally about artists, if they have a hit and some money is coming in, you tell them, 'OK, I will give you an advance of two hundred dollars a week each.' And their response is, 'Oh, my God, that's wonderful!' Then seven, eight weeks later, two hundred dollars is not near[ly] enough to satisfy them. I used to urge them to be cautious about money, because it might never happen again. The exception was the Ventures. Even when they were down in popularity here, they sold so well in the rest of the world, certainly in the Orient."

Dodie Stevens

In 1963 Dodie Stevens moved to Dolton. She had been on Crystalette and Dot, where her biggest hits, respectively, were "(Tan Shoes and) Pink Shoe Laces" in 1959 and an Elvis-answer record, "Yes, I'm Lonesome Tonight" in 1960. Bob Reisdorff

Opposite: Liberty trade ad for the #11 hit, "Honolulu Lulu."

worked with Dodie when she came to Dolton. "Vic Dana and I had a company briefly. Vic acquired Dodie, and we recorded a song based on a big hit. There was a hit that was from a man's point of view completely, and was one of those things that was perfectly suited to do a woman's version of as an answer or a response. It sort of asked for an answer record. The original was a big hit. We got her answer out as quickly as possible, but two weeks earlier it would have had a much better chance. It did something, but I don't remember if it even made the charts. But there was a lot of excitement about it at the time.

"She was good. She was a terrific talent but she was much too sophisticated for the time. She was a beautiful girl. She had already been married once and was about twenty-two or twenty-three. I don't remember the song now." Perhaps it was Dolton 45 #88, "Sailor Boy," in response to the Shirelles hit, "Soldier Boy."

As with all labels, a lot of good records get released that do not become hits. Did Bob Reisdorff and Dolton Records ever regret passing up any songs or artists they could have had? "People were always sending me songs. I turned down some great hits, I've turned down some great artists. I turned down Elton John; he came to me first in nineteen sixty-seven or sixty-eight. I turned down 'The End of the World' (Skeeter Davis, RCA, #1, 1963) for Vic Dana. He wanted to do it. It would work for a man as well as for a woman. But I told him, 'I cannot stand the lyric.' It was stupid of me; it was personal animosity toward the lyrics. 'Don't they know it's the end of the world because I've lost my love.' I want to shake people like that and say, 'Of course, you carry on! It's never the end of the world.'"

In reality the song had been written about the death of the composer's father. More than that, when Skeeter Davis recorded the hit record, she was singing about her late partner in the "Davis Sisters" act, who had died in a car accident. The end of the world was the loss of a loved one to death, not to a rival lover!

Would knowing that have changed Bob Reisdorff's opinion of the song? No doubt. "Everyone thought that it was about the end of a love affair, right? That is the way it seemed to me. I took it with disgust. I was in my late thirties, and I had been up and down in love affairs like the devil. I just had this hatred for this song."

Bob hated other hits as well. "I hate the lyric of 'I Left My Heart in San Francisco,' as well. When I heard 'Where little cable cars climb halfway to the stars,' I wanted to vomit! I just *hated* that lyric. That song was not brought to me, though I might have recorded it in spite of my revulsion. But I would have asked, 'Couldn't you find another line?' Anything else!" Ah, the trials and tribulations of running a record label!

Reisdorff continues, "I kept selling my company. Talk about the artists who were frivolous [with] money! Every time I got some money together, I would say, 'I think I've had enough of this business.' So I sold Dolton with the other owners—the C&C partners and Bonnie Guitar, who got some shares for her participation. Then I was in California for about three years with Liberty, running Blue Horizon. That was the company that owned the Ventures. Josie Wilson and I owned that company. Josie Wilson was Don Wilson's mother; Don was the rhythm guitarist of the Ventures. Josie was extremely instrumental in getting the Ventures successful. I doubt that they would have been brought to anybody's attention if she had not played a role. She was the one who pushed and shoved, difficult for such a shy woman, and she put the whole thing together. Before they were on Dolton, she did it all."

Dolton artist Vic Dana's minor hits for 1963 included the pop-flavored "More" and the now-forgotten Gene McDaniels–style rocker, "Danger." His style varied so much from song to song that sometimes, as Bob Reisdorff commented, "Vic Dana was an artist you could love on one record and not like at all on another. Some of the stuff we did was during the time Bobby Vee and his sound were big favorites. You had to have that kid sound, it seemed, which kind of conflicted with some of the songs we were doing. I like Vic on some songs very, very much. He was very good in nightclubs."

Cover Versions

Both of Vic Dana's 1963 songs, "More" and "Danger," have stories connected with them. Dolton did not do cover versions, unlike Dot, which specialized in them. Bob: "The only cover version we did was having Vic Dana do a vocal version of 'More,' an instrumental hit for Kai Winding. The Dolton 'Baby Elephant Walk' was not a cover of Lawrence Welk or Henry Mancini, the composer. Hank Levine created a 'group' he called the Miniature Men and recorded the song for a single before anyone else." Both versions hit *Billboard* the same week.

"It is easy to lose a record to a cover version. I did a record with Vic that Dean Martin covered. We covered a Western artist on a song. It was already dropping on the Western charts, so we figured it was all right to do a version of it. We did a pop, top-forty version. I asked Liberty, 'Get this out now, please.' I used to do these things myself because I was so distrustful of the efficiency of companies. They let it go over the weekend.

"Dean Martin's people recorded it, and one of the engineers from United Studios called me and said, 'Bob, there is something happening that you should know about. Come down.' When I got there, he took me to these secret stairs so I could see what was happening. It was Dean Martin doing a cover on our cover! They raced it to the plane and distributed the DJ copies very quickly and probably did almost-simultaneous shipping. That is the kind of action on which everything depends. Some key people I called later said that they got Dean Martin's about a day or two before ours, so they had to go with that version. There was nothing I could do. If I'd had the five-day jump, it would have made a world of difference. The versions were very comparable. I wish I could remember the title of the song."

The song was "A Million and One." Dean Martin's hit the national chart on July 23, 1966, and peaked at #41. Vic Dana's showed up a couple of weeks later on August 6 and peaked at #71.

In light of the 1990s use of the term *cover version* to mean any remake, even decades later, of another artist's recording, it is interesting to hear a 1950s and 1960s record producer who recorded cover versions and whose hits were covered by other artists discuss the term and the topic. Bob Reisdorff: "A cover is anytime one record is released and some person hears it wherever, in a studio or in a shop, and decides to make a competing version. If the original has a weak label or weak distribution, the cover can be a major factor." In the 1980s and 1990s, the term *cover version* has been used much more loosely to mean any remake of a song, not just a competing single release. So if a CD album features a Beatles song or a Beach Boys song, it is called a cover version, even though twenty-five years have passed since the original was a hit, and the new version is not even a single.

"That is not a cover version. Only something released at the same time, competing as a hit version, is a cover. Dot Records made a habit of picking up regional hits and covering them. Once a record is released, it is not public domain, but it is accessible to anyone who wants to record it; that's the law. You do not need anyone's permission to record a song. All you have to do is pay the publisher, and maybe get a theoretical license, but you must pay your royalties, at least if the publisher is a big company that will send auditors around to check on you. Harry Fox worked in the 1960s and 1970s for publishers worldwide. He would go and collect the royalties for companies and collect a rather modest amount of money for that service. The cover version can never be something that is done months later, or perhaps even weeks later on an album. That is not a cover, just another version of that song. Using it any other way is wasting a good word."

The story of "Danger"? When asked about that song, Gretchen Christopher recalled that she once helped Vic Dana with a song that may or may not have been "Danger." "On some session where Vic was recording, I sang into his ear. I think he was overdubbing a harmony part, and I think I was singing it into his ear so he would know what to sing!"

Final Fleetwoods

In 1963 Gretchen's Fleetwoods made the top forty one last time with an excellent remake of the old Jessie Belvin (1956) and Ray Peterson (1959) hit, "Goodnight, My Love."

Besides writing many of their album cuts with Gary, Gretchen and Barbara wrote singles, including "Graduation's Here" (1959) and the flip side, "Oh, Lord, Let It Be." Shaping the Fleetwoods sound, Gretchen was the group's unofficial vocal arranger. She did not say, "I am the arranger, here's what to do." She explained, "What I sang pretty much gently dictated what the other members would sing. We were all excellent at harmonizing, and occasionally I'd outline chords and notes I was hearing in my head for them to sing. That is where arrangements like 'Goodnight, My Love' came from.* We did that with a totally different arrangement from what had been out before [Jesse Belvin, 1957; McGuire Sisters, 1957; Ray Peterson, 1959]. And the same thing with 'Tragedy' [Thomas Wayne, 1959]. I didn't realize this during our recording days, but years later it came to me that whenever I sang lead, the backup would sort of fall apart. The background parts just were not very imaginative. There were harmonies, but for the most part there were not the interwoven counterpoint things that I would do, or things like having answer lyrics. 'Unchained Melody' (from our first LP, *Mr. Blue*) is a notable exception. I love what they sing behind me and how they follow my dynamics. We recorded it a cappella in Seattle with studio lights out, and it's all feeling.

"Now, if they were copying another arrangement, it would be different. Like

---

* "Goodnight, My Love" was cowritten by George Motola (and John Marascalco), who died in February 1991. Gretchen sang "Goodnight, My Love" a cappella for George's funeral service on board the boat and "The Lord's Prayer" as his ashes were scattered at sea.

on our thirteenth album, *Buried Treasure,* I sang lead on 'Will You Still Love Me Tomorrow?' [Shirelles, 1961]. Barb and Gary just emulated the original arrangement on that pretty much. And it sounds great. On 'Blues Go Away,' the backgrounds did not contribute as much. Perhaps that song did not lend itself to a three-part arrangement. Anyway, our producer, Bob Reisdorff, and the engineer dialed them out, and it became a solo."

Gretchen's recording of "Blues Go Away" is a haunting tune that sounds good any time of any year, but is perhaps best appreciated when listened to at three o'clock in the morning in the dark, maybe on headphones. But judging from Gretchen's own recollection, it also sounded good in an office environment in 1961. "I remember at Liberty Records, I was in the hallway near Al Bennett's office. From one of the offices in the hall, I heard my song 'Blues, Go Away' being played from *Deep in a Dream,* which had not even been released yet. I could hear people saying, 'Who's that singing?' Everything got kind of hushed, I could hear people coming in from the other room to listen, and somebody saying, 'That's Gretchen Christopher, the Fleetwoods.' But 'Blues Go Away' was totally different from anything that the Fleetwoods were doing as a group, and it was never released as a single or anything. I think that, reflecting on Julie London's 'Cry Me a River,' she might have been a mentor or a model for me way back when for that particular song."

On most of the Fleetwoods' songs, especially the singles, Gary Troxel's male voice is easily heard among Gretchen and Barbara's harmonies. But on their last chart success, "Goodnight, My Love," Gary's voice is not really in evidence. Was he absent from the group or from the session at that time? No, he was there, all right. He just sang background instead of lead.

"My singing lead on all the hits was always a sore point with Gretchen," Gary recalls. "I assumed that since I was the male of two girls, in the group I should sing the lead. So that is why I sang the lead on the two big hits."

"He is on 'Goodnight, My Love,'" agrees Gretchen. "Barb Ellis is singing lead on that one. 'Goodnight, My Love' is the one hit she sang lead on. As usual I did the vocal arrangement, and Gary just followed; whatever I did, he harmonized along with or sang in unison, it sounds like, on one part of the bridge. That's what his replacement discovered when he was learning Gary's parts. So the third voice, that's Gary! Barb has the lead, I answer her, and Gary is harmonizing with what I am singing. I am the lead voice of the countermelody, and he is the third voice.

"On other songs, if Gary sang lead, I would still be the lead of the countermelody, and Barb would do the third part. And if I'm singing lead, who knows who's doing what! In fact, that happened on our thirteenth album. I sang lead on 'Man in a Raincoat,' which Barb loved when it was released. She was no longer singing with us, but she just loved that cut. She said, 'I am so angry with the producer, because if he had released it, it would have been another hit for the Fleetwoods.' That was one of the numbers on that album that was especially strong to do, to promote the album in personal appearances. But Gary said he could not remember what he had sung, and he couldn't pick it out from listening to the record, so I guess there is more truth than joking in the questions like 'Who sang what part?' and 'Was Gary on that song?' Because he could not remember his part, he was resistant to singing that live in the 1980s, when it was released."

One would think that, singing with two females, Gary's lone male voice would be easy to distinguish. "Gary had a fairly high voice, too, and the ability to sing pretty high. And all our voices blended well."

Who *was* the "lead singer" of the Fleetwoods? Well, clearly Gary sang lead on many records, but as Gretchen reminds us, "It is interesting to note that the Fleetwoods' string of hits began and ended with female leads." The first hit, "Come Softly to Me," was originally composer Gretchen Christopher's lead, to which Gary Troxel's voice was added, making it a shared male-female lead.

"Graduation's Here," which Gretchen also cowrote and sang lead on, was the trio's second top-forty hit.

Barbara Ellis sang lead on "Goodnight, My Love," which became the Fleetwoods' ninth top-forty hit, their eleventh and final single on *Billboard*'s Hot 100.

So, while Gary often sang lead, he was by no means either the official or the unofficial lead singer of the Fleetwoods!

"Tragedy" and "Goodnight, My Love" were favorites from Gretchen's high school days. And while she did not always pick the Fleetwoods' material, she did veto some songs. "There were times when there was material that I wouldn't go along with. Not very often, but once in a while there would be something I really felt did not merit being done. I believe that sincerity is what makes it work—you know, the belief in the material."

Even though it was not a huge hit, "Goodnight, My Love" is among Gretchen's favorite Fleetwoods records. "Come Softly to Me" is Gretchen Christopher's personal all-time favorite Fleetwoods hit "because it was the first, and because I basically composed it, and because it was so different from anything else that was going on, so distinctive. And it was a hit all over the world that is still played. If I am doing an interview and they want to know what to play, 'Come Softly to Me' is what I say. But I never tire of 'Tragedy'; I love the vocal arrangement, all of the stuff that Barb and I do in it, and I love the vocal arrangement on 'Goodnight, My Love'—the stuff Gary and I do behind Barb. And it wasn't a hit, but when people used to ask 'What's your favorite Fleetwoods recording,' I used to say 'Blues Go Away.' But that was not the 'typical Fleetwoods sound,' just a real from-the-heart, from-the-soul, solo song that I did. And it was autobiographical."

It was odd that Gary was often considered to be the lead singer, when it was Gretchen who was the extrovert of the group. Gary was so shy that Bob Reisdorff recalls it as a real problem sometimes. "Gary Troxel was shy, very shy, almost inarticulate. Yet I thought he had the quality to be a teenage idol. He was very good looking, but he was so-o-o shy. In Hawaii, they appeared with Dion and the Belmonts. There was almost a riot. A young girl went up on the stage to give Gary a lei, and he wouldn't budge an inch to reach down and pick it up! He was so locked in to the exact performance. He was a very nice person, but so very shy.

"When he was being interviewed on radio, he would answer questions with a facial expression or a shrug of a shoulder. Or just shake his head. One disc jockey commented to him live on the radio, 'You know, shrugs and nods don't go out very well over the air, Gary.' Barbara was a quiet person, too. Gretchen was the only one who had any interest at all in the area of entertainment. Her experience was very modest, performing her Isadora Duncan–type dance of her own invention at the Colony, but relatively, she was experienced."

When Barbara sang lead, as on 'Goodnight, My Love,' Gary was hard to hear, almost like he was not there. Was he? "Oh, yes, absolutely. Barbara had a sweet

Photo of Fleetwoods from back of *Deep in a Dream* LP. Gary Troxel's Navy clothes were authentic; he spent much of the peak years of the Fleetwoods' career in the service.

voice, Gary had a husky little voice that sometimes would be nasal. And you could not change it. You couldn't talk him into altering it because he wouldn't know how. But at other times, he wasn't nasal."

Apparently Gary never felt pressured to change the way he sang, which after all was a very successful and original style. There was not too much for producers to do, according to Gary. "We had already defined the Fleetwoods sound. As far as choosing material, we got to say what we wanted. I don't think we were ever forced to do anything. I have heard people comparing the Carpenters to us, saying that they were 'just a modern version of the Fleetwoods.' I always thought that, just about any song that they sang, we could have done well with also. Different time, different place."

Of course Dolton artists the Ventures and Vic Dana, as well as the Fleetwoods released LPs in 1962 and 1963, among them *Twist with the Ventures, Vic Dana Town and Country,* and the *Fleetwoods' Greatest Hits.*

An interesting LP contribution from Dolton: The Ventures jumped on the surf-craze bandwagon, sort of, with an LP *Beach Party,* which contained not a single surf or drag song!

Speaking of surf and drag, the instrumental group on which the Marketts' only Liberty LP, *The Surfing Scene,* included their two hits, "The Surfer's Stomp" and "Balboa Blue." Other notable tracks were the "Bristol Stomp" (the Dovells, 1962) and the only vocal surf song extant at the time, the Beach Boys' "Surfin'" (1962)!

Changes at Liberty

Si Waronker had founded Liberty Records back in 1955 at the urging of a relative who told Si he would make more money and be happier working for himself. The relative certainly was right. The project had gone well. On a loan of a couple of thousand dollars, millions of Liberty and Dolton records were sold. Si Waronker had never expected rock 'n' roll to exist, let alone to dominate the record label back when he founded it. However, through the Liberty LPs, he kept the pop and adult sound alive, and through both LPs and 45s he made an unmatched contribution to the successful development of rock 'n' roll.

In 1963 Si was ready to retire gracefully. He had made a lot of money on his investment of a mere two thousand dollars. The profit margin increased by a quantum leap when Si now sold Liberty for a cool twelve million dollars.

The sale meant big changes at Liberty, but another, even bigger change took place around the same time. Liberty had begun back in 1955. In 1959 Dolphin/Dolton was added as a subsidiary. In 1963, a third label, Imperial Records, was added to the family.

Alan Warner was a British citizen who, like me in the United States had been collecting Liberty Records since about 1960. Shortly after that Alan entered the record business himself, and he sheds light in Liberty's acquisition of Imperial Records.

"The Liberty logo was so great, and I was such a fan of Snuffy Garrett's and of Ernie Freeman's arrangements when I was in England. It was a major American label at that time, when I was just starting in the business. It was great when, in the course of my work, I finally got to meet some of those people." Alan was with EMI, a major British record company, and then Liberty/UA, from 1961 to 1968.

As Alan explains, the first Liberty record to be released under the Liberty name in England was Bobby Vee's "Run to Him" in June 1962. "It was already a hit through Decca, on their London Records label." In fact Bobby Vee had already made the British charts via London Records several times, with "Rubber Ball," "More Than I Can Say/Stayin' In," "How Many Tears," and "Take Good Care of My Baby" in 1961. But after "Run to Him," the records carried the familiar Liberty logo.

"The most fascinating thing about Liberty," in Alan Warner's opinion, "was that it was a white, West Coast label, which was very much into jazz and easy listening. Then they more or less fell into rock and roll almost by mistake, I think. Initially that was not the thrust of the catalog. It was Julie London, Martin Denny, and the novelties by the Chipmunks and the 'Witch Doctor' record, who were rock 'n' roll but novelty.

"Then Al Bennett came along and Snuffy Garrett, of course, with his stable of people—Johnny Burnette and Bobby Vee and then Gene McDaniels—those two men with their artists really kind of turned the label around.

"As I said, Liberty was very much a white label at the start, but then the product they acquired was a different story. One of Al Bennett's great strengths was in acquiring significant product that fleshed out and balanced the Liberty catalog. Acquiring Imperial and Aladdin and Minit about nineteen sixty-three, and Blue Note, really brought great strength. And of course, Dolton Records." Alan Warner's comments are very telling; he was an insider in the later days who has been into the Liberty tape vaults, and what he says certainly carries a lot of truth. Except that—as Snuff explained the Dolton acquisition—Al kicked and screamed when Snuff wanted to acquire Dolton/Dolphin product and put off the deal so long that it cost Liberty several artists and tons of cash when Liberty later did absorb Dolton.

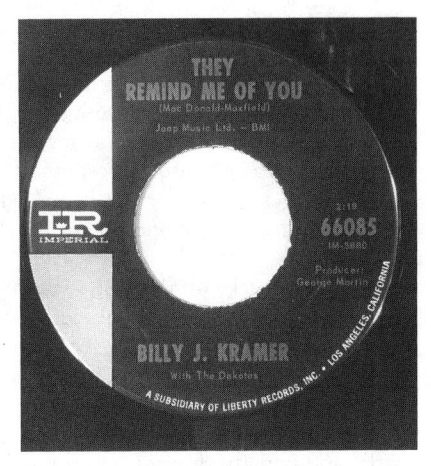

The Imperial label as it appeared before and after the Liberty acquisition. "Just a Little Too Much" was actually written by Sharon Sheeley, not Johnny Burnette.

Imperial Records

When acquired by Liberty, the Imperial Records paper label was redesigned to resemble the Liberty label, with the name and logo moved to the left side. Imperial had been around since the very early 1950s. In its earliest days, it had recorded scores of early R&B groups. The Spiders, for example, were discovered by Imperial Records in the Pelican Club in New Orleans. The Spiders' R&B hits on Imperial included "I Didn't Want to Do It" in 1954. "I'm Slippin' In" and "Sukey, Sukey, Sukey" were two of the other hits the Spiders had on Imperial. Imperial itself had several subsidiary R&B labels. One was Post Records, and among the many Post artists were the Sharp Tones. Their hits included "Made to Love" and "Since I Fell for You" in 1954. The Hawks were another early Imperial group, whose early and mid-fifties hits included "Joe the Grinder" and "It Ain't That Way."

Snuff Garrett: "What Imperial was used for after the purchase, we had so many records to come out, it was harder to get air play and we needed another label. We could have twice as many releases and more promotional people. When Bobby Skaff was running it, it was for imports, the Hollies, things like that. Slim Whitman was still there, so was Fats Domino, but Rick Nelson was gone to Decca in 1963, but I was also gone by the time they bought Imperial."

Fats Domino

In the rock 'n' roll era, Imperial developed an impressive roster of acts prior to the Liberty takeover. Fats Domino, for instance, had recorded some sixty chart songs on Imperial between 1954 and 1964, plus about twenty LPs. Slim Whitman had one hit on Imperial, in 1957, and that one did not make the top ten. Yet his popularity justified an amazing two dozen or so LPs. In 1957, Fats and Slim were joined on Imperial by Ricky Nelson. Rick's first releases were on Verve Records in May 1957, but Verve had failed to get him into an ironclad contract, and Imperial soon lured him away in September the same year.

Ricky Nelson

The signing of Ricky Nelson by Imperial came several years before Imperial joined the Liberty family of record labels. But the acquisition of Rick was a major turning point in Imperial's own history. Up until then virtually all of the Imperial artists had been black. Of the scores of black artists, only Fats Domino had gained widespread (read "white") acceptance (read "sales"). Antoine ("Fats") Domino was doing rock 'n' roll before it was called that. He was discovered by Imperial in a New Orleans club, and he got his nickname from his 1949 Imperial hit "The Fat Man."

But with Ricky on the label, sales picked up. Before it was all over Ricky had thirty-six hit songs on Imperial, with twenty-five in the top forty, fourteen in the top ten, and two #1 records. He recorded relatively few LPs, due perhaps to his time-consuming involvement with Ozzie and Harriet, both his parents and the name of the TV show he costarred in.

Although Ricky Nelson had eight top-five hits for Imperial on the national charts, and perhaps three or four times that many that were #1 on many local radio stations, he had only two national #1 records. One was 1961's "Travelin' Man." The other was "Poor Little Fool" in 1958. Although "Poor Little Fool" predated Liberty's acquisition of Imperial by some five years, there was a Liberty connection in this early record: Sharon Sheeley.

Sharon wrote "Poor Little Fool" when she was sixteen years old. That was the youngest that any woman has ever written a #1 hit record to this day. Writing the song was not too hard for young Miss Sheeley, and getting Ricky Nelson to record it was even easier.

"When I was sixteen," explains Sharon, "Ricky Nelson was seventeen. And girls are always smarter than boys at that age. I know he was gorgeous. I know he was the biggest idol in the country because Elvis had been drafted. But he was still just a seventeen-year-old boy, and that is just how I approached him. I went after the seventeen-year-old boy, not the idol, not the star.

"I told Ricky that a friend of my father's wrote a song that Elvis was recording. That is all I had to tell him. Then he had to have that song. And he believed me. That was the funny part about it. He didn't doubt me for a second. I was so convincing, he thought he was beating Elvis. So he cut it. Then, of course when Lou Chudd of Liberty called me and said I should come and have my dad's friend come and sign these songwriting contracts, I had to tell them that there was no 'friend of my dad's' involved, that I wrote 'Poor Little Fool' myself. And Elvis was not recording it. When they heard that, they almost died, all of them. All, that is, except Ozzie. Ozzie stood back and applauded me.

"But Ricky, he was so horrified, he was so angry. He was furious that 'Poor Little Fool' was already an album cut. Another distinction for that song was that it was the first song ever in the music business to be 'reversed.' Instead of being recorded as a single, it was released as an album cut, then put out on a single. Now they do it that way all the time, put out an album and then pull the singles off of it. But at that time, no one ever pulled a single off of an album.

"So when they wanted to pull 'Poor Little Fool' off the album for a single, Ricky was fighting it tooth and nail. He was furious because it had been written by a girl and that he had been fooled by a girl. That was the attitude then. Phil Everly has told me that he was on a tour bus, flipping through a magazine, and Buddy Holly said, 'God! Listen to this! A girl wrote "Poor Little Fool!" A girl!' He was so flabbergasted.

"And Phil said, 'And I still remember Eddie Cochran saying, "Aw, man, there goes the neighborhood!"' I was the only female out there at all writing rock and roll." And my record went to number one and none of theirs did. Buddy and Eddie went to number eight and number four, but not number one."

Albums

In addition to big sellers like *Surf City* and *Drag City* albums by Jan & Dean, *The Best of Timi Yuro* and Julie London's *Golden Greats* were released. Julie's LP was especially nicely titled, considering that only one song on the LP, "Cry Me a River," was a hit. But then Snuffy invented the term *Golden Greats* to label compilation LPs that may or may not feature *Golden Hits*. Julie had another 1963 LP, named after one of Bob Reisdorff's favorite ditties, "The End of the World."

Bob Wills Sings and Plays, Here's Willie Nelson, Tex Williams in Las Vegas, and *Bud and Travis Naturally* came out of Liberty's unusually active country division. The *Versatile Martin Denny* kept bird-noise music alive, and his *A Taste of Hits* LP unrocked such 1963 radio hits as "Judy's Turn To Cry" (Lesley Gore) and "Que Sera, Sera" (High Keys). A nice LP named after his 1963 hit, *The Night Has a Thousand Eyes,* was turned out by Bobby Vee. On that album, a Jackie DeShannon song appeared called "You Won't Forget Me." The song sounds great by Bobby, as if it were written just for him, but in fact it had been a 45 by Jackie in 1962 and was the title of an Imperial album of hers as well.

Speaking of albums and the song "You Won't Forget Me," Columbia Record Club issued a members-only LP in 1963 called *Headliners '63*. Three Liberty acts were featured on this Columbia album—the Ventures, Julie London, and Bobby Vee. Bobby's tune was "You Won't Forget Me."

The Columbia Record Club sampler albums might seem like small potatoes. After all, the royalties that Liberty and artists made were minimal, totaling perhaps about fifteen thousand dollars according to Si Waronker. However, if the record club made a Liberty album their record of the month, sent to all members unless they specifically requested it not be sent, the rewards could be much higher. Si Waronker explains: "Once we got one of those, we could be assured of sales that could be as high as a million . . . which is an awful lot. That was almost unheard of in those days, when an album that sold two hundred thousand was big, big!"

Back to Imperial LPs, their most interesting albums of 1963 were *Best of the Blues*. Volume 1 was split among Charles Brown, T-Bone Walker, and Jimmy McCracklin, and volume 2 featured Fats Domino, Floyd Dixon, Lightnin' Hopkins, Amos Milburn, and Peppermint Harris.

On Dolton *The Fabulous Ventures* were *On Stage and in Space,* and Vic Dana sang *More About Shangri-La* and *Red Roses for a Blue Lady*.

1963 Also-Rans

Liberty released more than sixty singles in 1963. Some seventeen made *Billboard*'s Hot 100 chart. Not bad. But artists of yore were fading fast. Gene McDaniels's

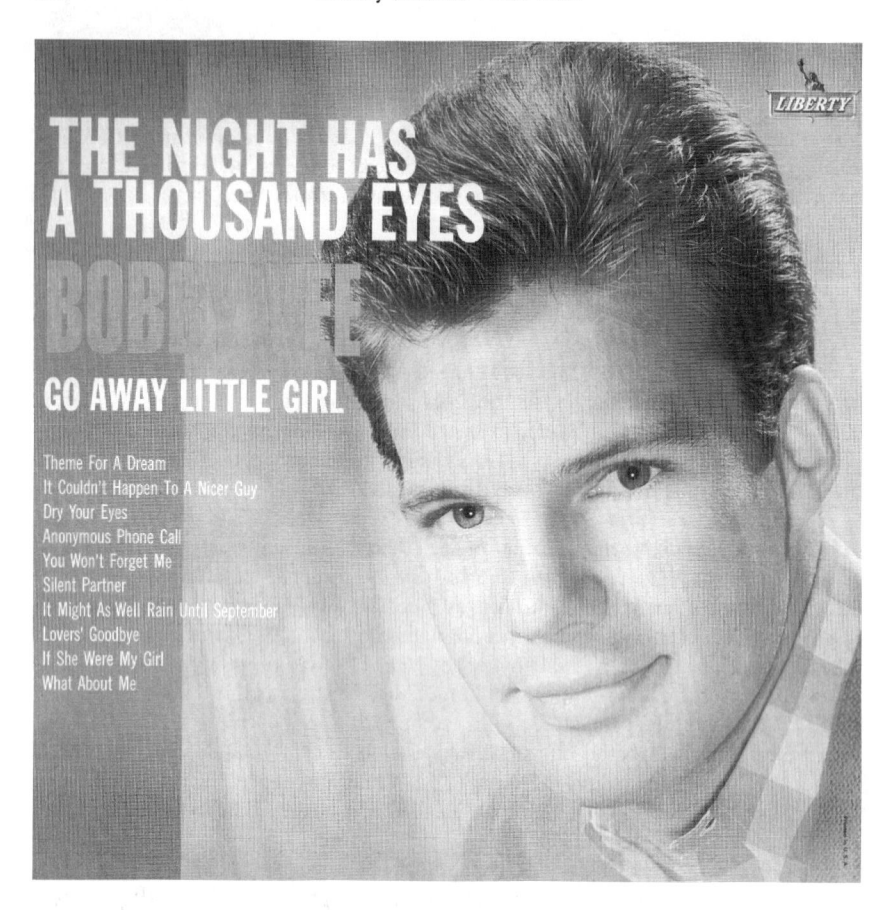

Bobby Vee as he appeared in 1963.

"It's a Lonely Town Without You" was his last hit, topping at #64. Timi Yuro's "Make the World Go Away" did OK at #24, but her last record, "Gotta Travel On," dropped her off the chart at #64.

The Rivingtons' follow up to "Papa-Oom-Mow-Mow," was a wild one called "Mama-Oom-Mow-Mow," which failed to sell. And artists as diverse as Walter Brennan, Dick Lory, Molly Bee, Ernie Freeman, and Vik E. Lee, were among the Liberty also-rans who never got onto the top one hundred at all in 1963.

At Dolton the Fleetwoods looked to be an also-ran in 1963. Their top-forty hit, "Goodnight My Love," was Dolton #75. But Dolton #74 was "Sure Is Lonesome Downtown," a true also-ran. Dolton artists Lenny Bryan and the Wanderers Three were less fortunate and never did score any hits. And the Ventures' "The Ninth Wave" wiped out.

Nick Noble was born in Chicago on June 21, 1936. That made him a tiny bit long in the tooth for the preteen record market in 1963. And he sang in a style almost like Bob Goulet's. Citing his first hit illustrates these two deficiencies, age and teen appeal: "The Bible Tells Me So" on Mercury Records in 1955. After four top-forty tunes for Mercury Records in the mid-fifties, Nick disappeared from the national charts. However, his following in his hometown was solid, and his Liberty release of "Closer to Heaven" in 1963, actually a charming performance not too far off the mark, was a big regional hit in Chi-town.

Another Liberty record that was regionally popular but never made the national one hundred was an R&B turn on the old tune "Shortnin' Bread" by the Blisters. With a sound straight out of the 1950s, it probably never had a chance.

The Rivingtons tried to keep the fire alive with another bird song, a dance called "The Shaky Bird pts 1 & 2." The songs were much like their hits from the previous year, and suffered by comparison.

Liberty never had the great success with girl groups that other labels had. The Four Cal-Quettes illustrate why. In 1963 the Angels on Smash Records had the hard-biting "My Boyfriend's Back," the Chiffons on Laurie drooled over their boyfriend because "He's So Fine," and the Pixies Three, the ultimate shriekers on Mercury Records, threw a wild party at "442 Glenwood Avenue." Then there were the Four Cal-Quettes. On "Movie Magazines," they sounded like Patience and Prudence from the 1950s, singing about looking for a cute boy in the photos. "I Cried" on the flip side was much better in terms of girl-group appeal, but it lacked a good hook.

Although both Slim Whitman and Ricky Nelson made money for Imperial from the time they were signed in 1957, no new major pop artists appeared on Imperial for several years. Imperial did take in some charity cases. The Wailers' "Tall Cool One" was a 1959 hit on Golden Crest Records, but the LP was released on Imperial in 1963.

Farmer Jules was an Imperial also-ran in 1959. His "Love Me Now" sold sporadically.

Besides being white, April Stevens had the distinction of being the first, and for many years the only, female act to be signed by Imperial. In the winter of 1959-60, she hit the charts with "Teach Me, Tiger." The song was a sexy, breathy ballad, worthy of Liberty's Julie London, and inspired by the catchphrase "Hi, Tiger" uttered on a Top Brass TV ad for hair cream. On TV Barbara Feldon, later to play Agent 99 on the Don Adams TV series "Get Smart," made the line famous by whispering it huskily while wriggling on a tigerskin rug. April Stevens's hit was quite popular in many parts of the South and Midwest, but it missed the national top forty. April did have an Imperial LP, *Teach Me, Tiger,* but her real fame came in 1963 on Atco Records, when she sang several hit duets including "Deep Purple" and "Whispering" with her brother, session sax man Nino Tempo.

Ernie Freeman was a noted arranger at Liberty and Imperial during this period, working with such artists as Bobby Vee and Ricky Nelson. He had his own Imperial 45s between 1957 and 1960, including "Raunchy," also a hit for Bill Justice (who composed it). Ernie passed away in 1981. In 1963 he arranged and conducted Vic Dana records for Dolton, including "Close Your Eyes" and "Love Is All We Need." The first of these two was produced by Dolton head Bob Reisdorff. The second was produced by Dick Glasser, who wrote the Holly-soundalike song "Someday" for Bobby Vee and the Crickets.

In the fall of 1961, a minor Imperial hit was scored by a group calling themselves the Three Friends. Their single was "Dedicated to the Songs I Love." It was a clever takeoff on the Shirelles' (1959) and Five Royales' (1961) hit "Dedicated to the One

I Love," and the lyric included titles of and references to uncountable rock 'n' roll songs of the era!

Sandy Nelson

Finally, in late 1961, Imperial found another artist who could sell a lot of records. His name was Sandy Nelson. He had been in the Barons, the original high school band of Jan & Dean (and Arnie), but Sandy left Jan & Dean before they began recording. He had other jobs in those days as well, working for Snuff Garrett. "Sandy Nelson was just a drummer for the Burnette Brothers when they did weekend dance parties along the coast between San Francisco and LA for Lou Stumpo, a DJ. I set these shows up, Johnny on guitar, Dorsey on bass, and this unknown drummer, Sandy. We'd drive up, Johnny and Dorsey paid Sandy so much a night, they split the door with the local management, and my third was a hundred fifty a weekend when I was making ninety at Liberty during the week in nineteen fifty-nine."

Finally on his own at Imperial, Sandy became the country's foremost drummer, and his first record, "Teen Beat," apparently had the teen beat, since the teens sent it into the top five songs in the country. That was on Original Sound Records, but Imperial immediately wooed Sandy Nelson away from Original Sound, much as they had wooed Ricky Nelson (no relation) from Verve four years earlier!

Luckily for Imperial, Sandy had a few more drum hits left in him. A year after "Teen Beat," the Imperial single "Let There Be Drums" reached the top ten, and a two-sided follow-up, "Drums Are My Beat" and "Birth of the Beat," made the top forty. Sandy's next half dozen songs failed to make the top forty, but a little thing like poor singles sales never daunted the enthusiasm of Liberty or Imperial. With only three top-forty hits to his name, Sandy Nelson recorded more than two dozen Imperial LPs! That's some ten LPs for each successful single! Sandy Nelson had fans, but they were fans who bought LPs, not 45s.

Fats, Ricky, and Sandy had hits through the early 1960s. Fats then left Imperial after a decade's association. At his new home, ABC Records, he never had another sizable-selling record.

Sandy Nelson was Imperial's last pre–Liberty success. It wasn't until the fall of 1963 that Imperial got another hot singles artist. The O'Jays were on Imperial before the Liberty takeover, and they were big in R&B, but only a minor pop success. Their only Imperial record to chart before the takeover was 1963's "Lonely Drifter," #93 on *Billboard*.

Of course, 1964 was the year of the "British invasion," when the Beatles and assorted other British groups began having popular records in the United States. A common misconception has it that the popularity of the British groups ended the careers of many established U.S. artists. That is not true. At Liberty and Imperial, Bobby Vee, Jan & Dean, the Ventures, Ricky Nelson, and Sandy Nelson each continued to sell 45s and/or LPs, as had been their habit. Neither Liberty nor Imperial canceled contracts with established artists just because the British were coming. Nor did the established artists fall suddenly from popularity. Dolton had precious few hits after 1964, but Dolton's decline was well under way in 1963, before the British invaded.

SANDY NELSON PLAYS

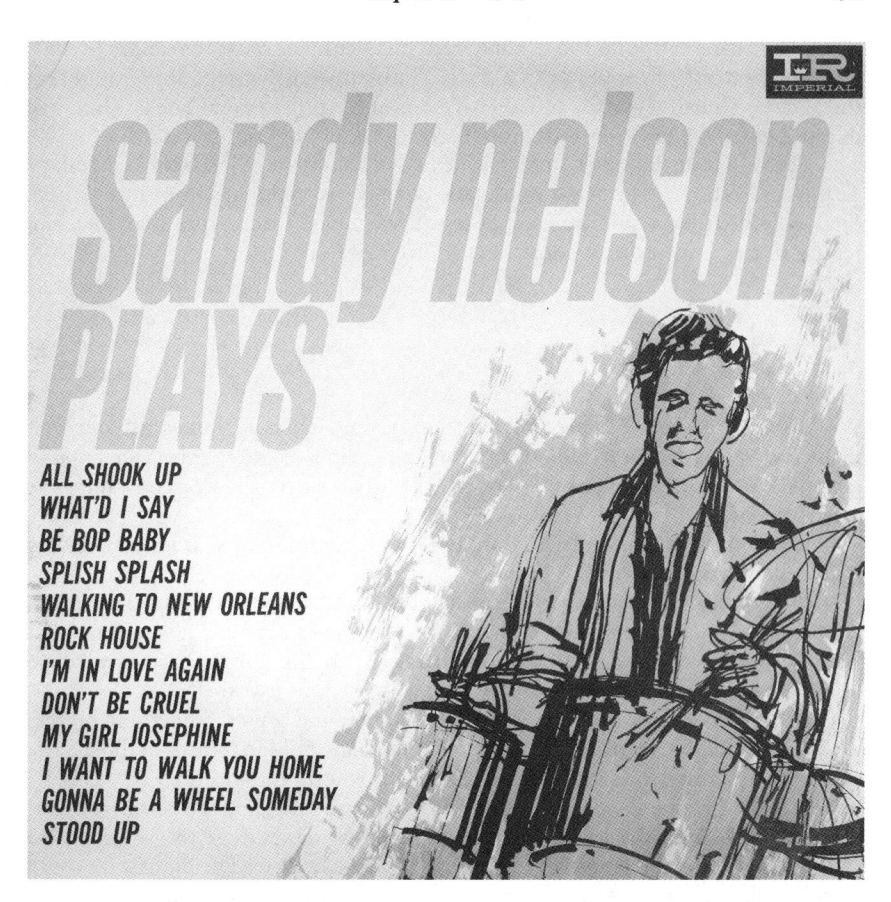

ALL SHOOK UP
WHAT'D I SAY
BE BOP BABY
SPLISH SPLASH
WALKING TO NEW ORLEANS
ROCK HOUSE
I'M IN LOVE AGAIN
DON'T BE CRUEL
MY GIRL JOSEPHINE
I WANT TO WALK YOU HOME
GONNA BE A WHEEL SOMEDAY
STOOD UP

Sandy Nelson was one of the rare drummers to have hit records.

Careful research has revealed that the invasion, instead of hurting established artists, for a time squeezed new American acts out of the contending. Of the two new Liberty hit groups in 1964, both were British, and of the five new Imperial hit artists in 1964, three were British. But even that statistic is misleading. Sure, Imperial signed only two American hit acts in 1964. But two new American rock 'n' roll acts in that one year set a new record for Imperial, so that label didn't actually cut back on new U.S. artists in 1964, but simply added some British artists alongside the Americans.

Imperial under Liberty ownership had just a handful of releases in 1963. There wasn't time for anything else before New Year's. The last two Imperial hit 45s before the acquisition were both by Rick Nelson, "That's All" backed with "I'm in Love Again," and "Old Enough to Love" backed with "If You Can't Rock Me." Neither side of either record made the top forty. Between those two Imperial releases, Ricky's first Decca release came out.

Liberty was somewhat brave taking over Imperial at this point in Imperial's history. While Imperial had a great heritage, of the last fifty-seven releases since

Rick's last charter in June 1963, none were hits. This, in spite of releases by such previously successful people as Rick, Fats Domino, Sandy Nelson, Shirley and Lee, the Majors, Thurston Harris, and Nino Tempo and April Stevens. The last Imperial release before the takeover was "Everybody's Rockin'" by the Delcardos.

The only post-takeover Imperial hit in 1963 was from Rick Nelson, "Today's Teardrops." The new Imperial would release only two more 45s from Ricky's back catalog before they would quit trying to squeeze blood from a turnip and let him release in peace in his new home over at Decca.

What's a Hit?

The term *hit* has been used a lot in these pages. Generally, it means a song that made *Billboard*'s Hot 100. However, it can also mean a record that became popular regionally, "bubbled" under the Hot 100, or sold well yet did not chart for some arcane reason.

What would the gospel according to Liberty, meaning Si Waronker, be when it comes to defining a hit?

"Sometime you would have a record hit the top fifty, and it would sell five thousand singles. Some of it was on the up and up; some of it wasn't. I would say that if a record got very good air play and broke even, anything over that was what we called a 'minor hit.'

"A real hit was anything over one hundred thousand copies. Something big was of course a million records, but there weren't too many million records in those days. Twenty-five to fifty thousand records would get you on the top forty.

"The more money you had available to spend, the better chance you had to get a hit. After a recording was done, it took as much work to get the damn thing played. Promotion was very important. I had a budget. The highest we could spend on any album was fifteen thousand dollars. That was maximum. Anything under that was great. If the record then showed promise and the disc jockeys picked it up, we sent the artist out or did other promotion. Consequently, as you had more money coming in, you could 'make' more hits. When we had no money, we had records that could have been hits but we couldn't promote them properly. That is why small companies can't compete. Where are they going to get the dough to promote? We had hits when we had money to promote records.

"If we hit the record big, we usually got it throughout the country, because we sent a promotion man to every station and gave away records, a form of payoff if you want to call it that.

"There was an awful lot of talk about the situation with the published charts. If we had a record that looked like it might take off, we had to take a full page ad. If not, we got no place. No one would dare to pay payola to a deejay. But sometimes a distributor would get one thousand free 'promotional' copies of a record from a record company. He would give these to a friendly record store, which would sell them. Then the distributor would get that money and give it to the deejay. It was untraceable. I hated it; I didn't want any part of that stuff. But it did happen."

Royalty Skimming

There was something else going on that Si hated even more. And it was going on in his own company. Artists were, more and more, experiencing the kinds of problems getting their royalties that Dick and Deedee had gone through with Al Bennett back in 1961. Si had not known about it then. Now, in 1963, it was too widespread not to be noticed.

However, even the most critical people who complained about getting shorted by Liberty never mentioned Si Waronker's name, even in passing. Si Waronker himself minces no words about artists who complained about not getting their royalties. "They didn't get paid! These are the real reasons I quit. I had five strokes in two years. After the last one, I didn't want to see anyone or anything. I didn't even see Julie. If ever I see Julie again, I will tell her the true story. She is probably bitter now, because I put a blanket over myself and disappeared. I made a break with everybody, and I disappeared. A lot of the people were teed off at me. They didn't know I was under doctors' instructions to stay away from everybody. 'Quit everything or wind up six feet under.' I decided I'd like to stay on earth awhile. I'm still here, and most of them are gone! And I hope to continue on.

"When we started in nineteen fifty-five, to me the artist was the most important thing we had. That was our commodity. They had to get paid. And sometimes it was very difficult to pay them at the very beginning. But as time went on, they got paid. Even with Ross Bagdasarian, we didn't even need a contract. I recorded Julie London without a contract. They got paid because I made damn sure they got paid.

"When Al Bennett came in, in nineteen fifty-eight, we were in trouble financially. By nineteen sixty everybody was rolling and not only getting paid, but getting paid more. And this continued on until we sold out. When we sold to Avnet, they controlled the purse strings and everything else. That was another reason I quit. I didn't want to go to New York every month and sit on the board of directors' meeting as the largest stockholder in the thing. They took about a million and a half of Liberty's cash out of the bank for their coffers, because they had paid out so much money in stock. They paid out two hundred thousand shares of stock that traded hands. Liberty didn't have any money after that to pay their artists or anything else, from the end of nineteen sixty-three up until it busted up in nineteen seventy.

"I couldn't take it. I had five strokes. The pressures were so great that I told Bennett that he could take the company and shove it. That was when all hell broke loose, because there was no money and the company was losing money. Avnet had taken the cash. Avnet made a deal with Bennett and a few of the other guys, who made some stock out of it, that they would buy back the company, and they wanted me to become part of the deal to purchase it. I told them I wouldn't do it. I wouldn't give back the stock. I had their stock and decided to keep it. Later I sold it and came out fine."

Another point of view on these days at Liberty was provided by Bob Reisdorff. "Avnet Electronics bought Liberty from Al Bennett and Si Waronker, who were the two largest stockholders. They paid them about five million. Al and Si made a bundle on the deal. All of the staff was retained intact. There was considerable hostility on the part of Bob Avnet. He later killed himself.

"The problem with Avnet was that they would look at production costs as if

Liberty were a factory. But of course, in the record industry things do not work that way. They would look at Si's costs and be shocked. I myself thought that Si Waronker was spending too much money, money that was not necessary. But of course, I was Dolton and he was head of Liberty A&R. Avnet was very unhappy with the big productions that Si was doing with Felix Slatkin, whose son is now the famous [Leonard] Slatkin conductor. They wanted Si out, and I think he did leave, in 1962."

All this politics in the company could have hurt the music. But as Bob tells it, "I don't think there was any stress that's felt in the various departments. I certainly did not feel it. Of course, I was their golden boy, because with Dolton I had a volume of four and a half million. The twist was on, and the Ventures' twist albums sold like hotcakes. They were enormously successful. Avnet liked me a lot, I looked very good. In addition, I was such a conscientious person when it came to spending a lot of money with little anticipation of results. So I would be very conscious of studio costs and musician costs, everything related to the production of a product.

"I did not run a full session. I ran a half session. Then, if I decided that something needed strings, I did something that the unions did not allow, but then they did not know everything. I'd overdub a string section but save the bucks by seeing how it came out without the strings first."

Si Waronker picks up the dreaded story of Avnet. "Bennett bought back the company from Avnet in sixty-four or sixty-five and he sold it again to TransAmerica. From that period, sixty-four to sixty-eight, nobody got paid. Liberty's reputation was horrendous. I couldn't take it. Thank God I got out of it. That was the real reason I just quit. And Ross got his catalog instead of money, which was a gold mine for his kids, everything he wrote or recorded. But a lot of them had to fight like hell and stand in line to get [even] part payment on their royalties. It was pretty awful. I heard more about it after I left than I wanted to hear. That was why when I quit I made that the end of it and saw nobody. I did not talk to a soul in that company as long as it lasted. Artists did not get paid. Or they got underpaid. The holdback on reserves [was] much too much."

Al Bennett went from 10 percent ownership at the start to 25 percent in 1959, to 50 percent when Liberty was sold to Avnet, to 100 percent when it was bought back. "He was the complete boss, but his reputation on paying was not very good. Al lived very well, but the artists did not see their money. And that was the time when so many good records came out. And unfortunately many of the artists never saw the money. But the ones that started with us, in 1955 to 1960, they all got paid. Honesty to me was something that did not exist in the record business, but I tried like hell to be honest. But I could not swear for anybody else. But it is true that the nonpayment or underpayment went on."

With all of this strife going on in the offices, in the studios, it was the beat that went on — without Si Waronker.

And without Bob Reisdorff, although his leaving was an anticlimax after the Avnet strife. But Liberty had been taking over Dolton progressively for some time. At the very end of 1963, Bob Reisdorff sold out completely and quit the business, at least temporarily. All he retained was a publishing company. Dick Glasser, who had headed Metric Music, Liberty's music publishing arm, took over the Dolton Division. He did quite well. For example, the first Vic Dana song he produced, "Red Roses for a Blue Lady," was the biggest disk Dana ever cut, his only one ever to make the top ten.

CHAPTER 12

1964
Matt Monro, Billy J. Kramer with the Dakotas, the Searchers, the Beatles, Irma Thomas, Johnny Rivers, the Swinging Blue Jeans, and the Hollies

This was the year that the Beatles came to America, soon to be followed by a great many other British record stars.

Where was Liberty during the British invasion? They had five hits by Bobby Vee and seven by Jan & Dean. But where were the British songs?

Liberty jumped on the British bandwagon by getting the British group the Searchers in the spring of 1964 — sort of. Snuff Garrett was no fool. Liberty Records had a lot of hits in England with the likes of Gene McDaniels, Jan & Dean, and Bobby Vee. Remember, the first song that Snuff recorded with Bobby after his independently recorded debut single, "Suzie Baby," was a cover version of a British #1 by Matt Monro.

Matt Monro

Now Liberty signed Matt Monro, who'd already had ten hits in England. Monro was a bad choice. All the successful British invasion acts had consisted of four or five guys, like the Beatles, the Searchers, the Dave Clark Five, ad infinitum. True, there had been a few duos, à la Peter and Gordon. Liberty took a chance on British solo superstar Matt Monro. True, he was a major British star. "Walk Away," his only Liberty hit, made the top forty here but was top five in England. True, he had more than a dozen British hit singles. Matt Monro's version of "Yesterday" made the top ten in England, while the Beatles themselves did not even have a hit with "Yesterday" over there.

But Matt Monro was neither a group nor a mop-top, and finicky American teens were not looking for accented male balladeers in 1964. So Matt Monro had only one top-forty U.S. hit on Liberty. To show there were no hard feelings, Matt did get to do six Liberty LPs, including one called *Yesterday,* so for Liberty, Matt Monro was not a total loss.

Matt Monro was a big star in England, where his version (not the Beatles') of "Yesterday" was a top-ten hit.

Billy J. Kramer with the Dakotas

But what about Liberty combos? How about Billy J. Kramer with the Dakotas? The Dakotas had one hit in the United States, "The Cruel Surf," in 1963 before they teamed up with Billy. The team then had six hits in England starting in 1963 and pretty much the same songs were hits in the United States in 1964, *after* the Beatles hit the States. But actually Billy J. Kramer with the Dakotas were signed to Liberty in 1963. Their next three records, all 1964 U.S. hits, were originally released on Liberty Records in the pre-Beatle days of 1963: "Do You Want to Know a Secret," "Bad to Me," and "I'll Keep You Satisfied."

Then, in 1964, two, "Bad to Me" paired with "Do You Want to Know a Secret" were released briefly on one 45. Then the songs were switched to Imperial Records, which Liberty had recently acquired. Incidentally, Liberty also had Beatles music by the spring of 1963.

Starting in March, Billy J. had six British invasion hits, including "Bad to Me" (written by John Lennon and Paul McCartney) and "Little Children," a two-sided hit single with both sides on the top ten. "From a Window" (also Lennon-McCartney) was another top ten. "I'll Keep You Satisfied" (again a Lennon-McCartney composition) made the top forty, as did "From a Window" (more Lennon-McCartney) along with the nonhit flip-side, "I'll Be on My Way."

In England Billy J. Kramer and the Dakotas had of course begun as separate entities, sharing the same producer, George Martin. Martin had the idea of combining the two artists. Then, since he also produced the Beatles, he arranged for John and Paul to give Billy J. Kramer with (not "and") the Dakotas several songs. Even

Liberty made sure that record buyers knew that Billy J. Kramer's songs were Beatle compositions.

the Beatles' 1964 American hit "Do You Want to Know a Secret" was originally a 1963 British hit for Billy J. Overall, four Billy J. records out of six made the top forty. But, in a few short months, the group was American history.

The Searchers

Not enough? Well, in December 1963, still before the Beatles hit the U.S. charts, Liberty released another act soon to take part in the British invasion. Liberty got the American rights to one single, "Sugar and Spice," which had been the Searchers' second British hit a year earlier. However, it did not chart in America at that time.

Liberty rereleased "Sugar and Spice" in the U.S. after the Searchers already had two Kapp Records singles on the U.S. charts. That time it made it to #44. The trouble was, in spite of huge popularity in England, the Searchers were not one of the more popular British acts in America. Of thirteen U.S. Searchers "hits," only seven made the top forty and only one made the top ten. Liberty's one Searchers record was not among those fortunate few.

The Beatles

A fact that has never been widely known is that the Beatles actually came to America (on records) in 1963, not 1964. Several Beatles records that were hits in the United States in 1964 were originally released in America in 1963, but without the huge promotional push that Capitol Records put on in the winter of 1963-64, the records all failed, including "From Me to You" and "Please Please Me." In fact, "She Loves You" was featured on Dick Clark's "American Bandstand" Rate-A-Record in 1963 and fared incredibly poorly.

A fact that is even less well known is that the Beatles were actually signed to Liberty in 1963, before they were signed to Capitol and had their 1964 invasion hits. But the deal went sour, in spite of Snuff Garrett's best efforts. "The British invasion was a major influence on everything. I had some of my biggest hits at that time, too, the string with Gary Lewis and the Playboys. I tried to get the Beatles. I spent a day and a night with them when I was in England with Al Bennett, the president of Liberty. It was John's birthday and they were playing at the London Palladium. Dick James, whom I'd known, their publisher, said that the Beatles knew me because I knew Buddy Holly real well. I went over and met them backstage. They said, 'Oh, we luv your Bubby Vee records' in their Liverpool accents.' But they really liked my Gene McDaniels stuff the best, 'A Hundred Pounds of Clay' and 'Tower of Strength.' All of those were covered in England, but they liked the American originals. The only song of Gene's to make the British charts was 'Tower of Strength,' but apparently he made quite an impression on the British record public anyway."

"Gene McDaniels is, I think, vastly underrated," says British record executive Alan Warner. "He became an important writer later. 'Feel Like Makin' Love,' which was #1 by Roberta Flack [1974, and was also a hit for Bob James, 1974] was written by Gene. He became Eugene McDaniels and continued recording. He is just a very fine artist; there was a very fine package out on him in the late 1980s, with retrospective liner notes." Snuff Garrett's production work with Bobby Vee impressed the Beatles as much as his work with Gene McDaniels. "The Beatles all said they loved 'Shaving You'—that's what they called Bobby Vee's hit, 'Sharing You.'"

At their first recording session, the Beatles even recorded their version of Bobby Vee's #1 hit, "Take Good Care of My Baby." If only that had been on the *Meet the Beatles* album in the United States, Bobby Vee's career, by no means over at that time, could have benefited nonetheless from the kind of shot in the arm that Beatle versions of "Rock and Roll Music," "Match Box," and "Kansas City/Hey Hey Hey" gave to the sagging careers of the likes of Chuck Berry, Carl Perkins and Little Richard.

After his meeting with the Beatles in 1963, Snuff was excited to say the least. "I got in at five A.M., came into the hotel bedroom, and started jumping up and down on the bed, woke up Al Bennett, and I said, 'I have found it, these guys are really big here and they are gonna destroy America.' Al said, 'What the hell are you talking about?'

"I said, 'I made a deal with Brian Epstein for the Beatles. They don't want any advance, but we have to give them fifty thousand in promotion money.'

"Al said I was crazy, he wouldn't give fifty thousand to anybody.

"I kept at him all day, and we finally went to see the managing director of EMI, L.G. Wood. Capitol had already turned down the Beatles twice, so I pitched for the Beatles and Al backed me up. We all three flew back to the United States together.

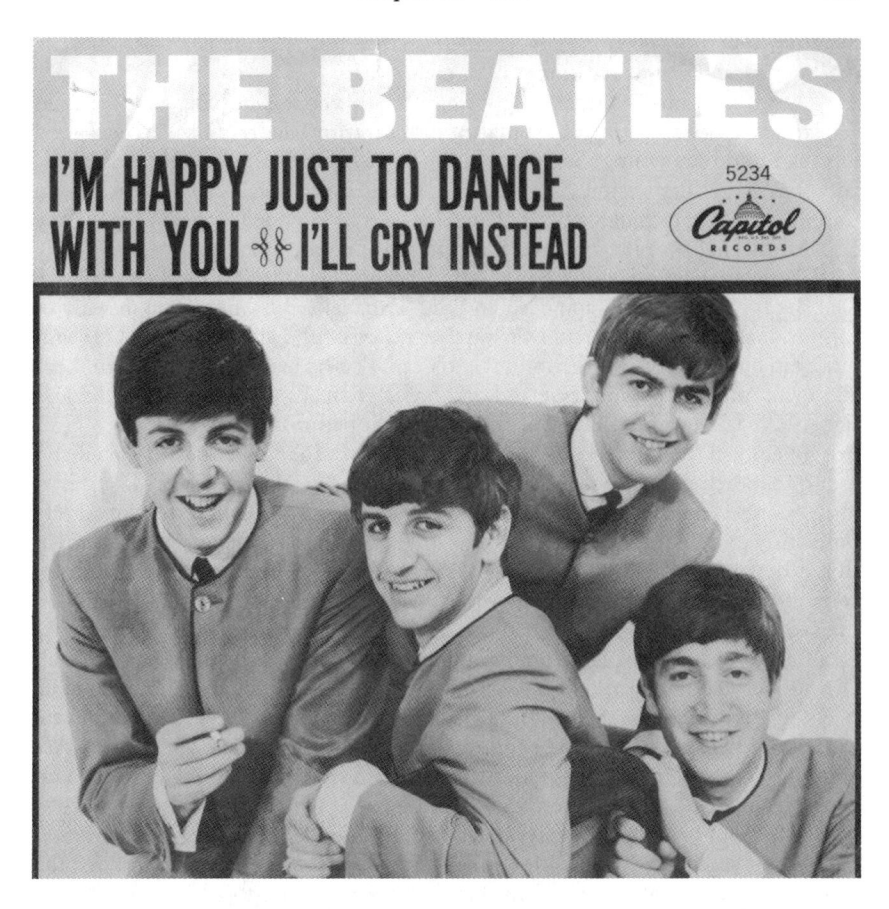

The Beatles themselves were almost licensed to Liberty in America.

I was sure they would be huge, but Al was worried because their Swan and Vee Jay releases had flopped in the United States in 1963.

"So L.G. was going over to see Allen Livingston, the head of Capitol, for a third time, and if they turned him down, Liberty could have the Beatles. Well, Capitol turned them down again, so L.G. told them, 'You will take the Beatles and you will make the Beatles, or we will change people here.' So to save their jobs, Capitol execs, who did not like the Beatles or their music in the least and tried to resist them at every turn, finally and reluctantly, figuratively kicking and screaming, launched the biggest promotion in the history of the record business. But to hear them talk about it, it was all their idea to have the Beatles, when in fact they did not even want the Beatles.

"But Liberty missed the Beatles. I would see them throughout the years, and they were always nice, always good guys."

Liberty head of national singles sales Lee Mendel was there when the Beatles were considered for Liberty at a staff meeting. "We all became very deeply involved in thinking up products. Snuffy came back from England one day, walked into a meeting, and said, 'There is a group called the Beatles. They are fantastic. They are the biggest thing; they are going to be enormous.'

"Mike Sloman was a small, slight Englishman who was working with Decca in England and he somehow got Al to sign him up with Liberty. Mike, having got a job, had to do something. So he got in touch with some of his people in England and started getting samples of product coming over. Because, for some reason Capitol completely ignored its parent company, we ended up picking up the Hollies, picking up Billy J. Kramer; we picked up Matt Monro.

"Separately we were offered the one Searchers record, and I signed up Dave Dee, Dozy, Beaky, Mick, and Tich and did 'Zabadak.' But Mike came in with all this product from England, and we were very successful. Later, when the EMI contracts ran out, Liberty lost them all back to Capitol, who had originally turned them all down. Mike returned to England and had a company called Festival U.K. and signed Olivia Newton-John." But the Beatles slipped from Liberty's grasp.

Imagine if the Beatles could have been at Liberty and recorded with the Liberty sound that they so cherished on Bobby Vee and Gene McDaniels records like "Sharing You" and "A Hundred Pounds of Clay." Rock 'n' roll would have developed very differently in the 1960s, 1970s, 1980s and 1990s, had that happened. Well, perhaps that is dreaming a bit. After all, the Beatles, signed to Capitol, never actually recorded *for* Capitol; their recordings were just leased to Capitol. But imagine the influence the Beatles might have had on Liberty artists.

Given the pressure placed on Capitol by its parent company in England, it isn't any wonder that the Beatles were so big in America. In addition to their undeniable talent, the jobs of all the top people at Capitol were on the line. That could motivate extra effort here and there, one supposes, and explain why records like "She Loves You" and "From Me to You," which were released in the United States in 1963 on Swan Records and Vee Jay Records and flopped, made it when reissued in 1964 following Capitol's unprecedented Beatles promotion avalanche.

Si sure regretted missing out on the Beatles contract. "We could have had the Beatles. In fact, before we sold to Avnet, we were trying to get Frank Sinatra's Reprise company, including forty percent of the company, to buy him. Warner's won by offering him a film contract. But on the Beatles, when Snuffy went to London, Al Bennett snuffed [so to speak] that deal out. It took a great deal of money, and the Beatles' manager was a very difficult guy to deal with. It was more than anybody would handle. Snuff was friendly with the Beatles and got very close to getting them. I think that Liberty Records would still be in existence today if that deal could have been made. Because everybody then would have loved everybody else, and we would have been going." Capitol had an option on the Beatles that they could exercise. Why did they hesitate?

"At Capitol there were two A&R men who were fighting to give the Beatles anything they wanted. Glenn Wallack and the rest of them weren't too happy with it. Capitol did not have too much of rock and roll. That company was built with Johnny Mercer as the musical boss. He wanted what he wanted, and Glen Wallack would go along with it. When they were sold is when they started to move. Before then they wanted the pretty music, Sinatra, and they were very successful. They were the first California independents."

Could Liberty have beaten out Capitol if it had struck while the iron was hot, even with the Capitol option? Al Bennett was a supersalesman, after all. "I think

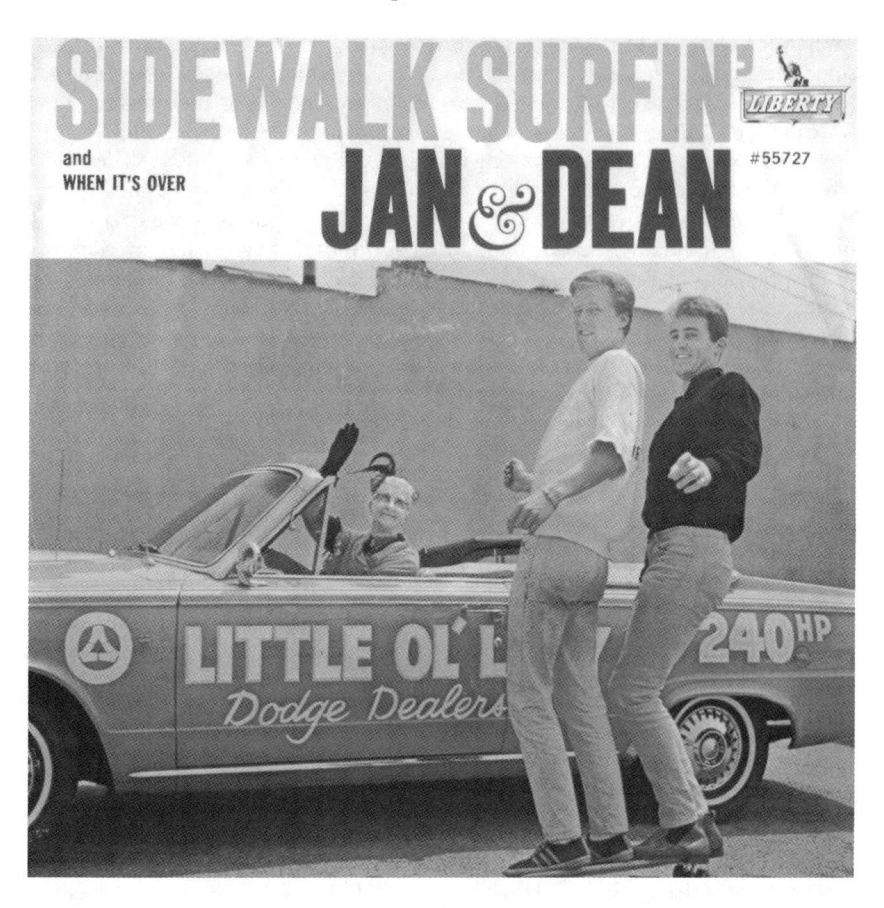

Jan & Dean going tandem down the street, showing off for Kathryn Miner, the "Little Old Lady (from Pasadena)."

if Bennett had used his southern charm and personality, gone and worked at it, given them a piece of the action, yes, he had a very good chance. Snuffy was right, he was close to them, he was liked by everybody. Liberty could have had the Beatles."

Americans Like Jan & Dean

But a brush with the Beatles and hits by Billy J. and the Searchers notwithstanding, the mainstays at Liberty were still American artists like Jan & Dean, who were at their peak in 1964, with hits like "Drag City" (a chart carryover from 1963); "Dead Man's Curve" and "New Girl in School" (a two-sided hit); "The Little Old Lady (from Pasadena)"; "Ride the Wild Surf" and "The Anaheim, Azusa, and Cucamonga Sewing Circle, Book Review and Timing Association" (another two-sided hit) and "Sidewalk Surfin.'" In Oklahoma, the flip side of "Sidewalk Surfin',"

"When It's Over," also made the top forty, making Jan & Dean's tally three two-sided hits and two one-sided hits in one year. Three of those eight sides featured sound effects, such as car engines ("Drag City"), screeching tires and breaking glass ("Dead Man's Curve"), and a skateboard on a sidewalk ("Sidewalk Surfin'").

There was no music more exciting than Jan & Dean records in 1964. The sound effects, the fast tempo, and the tight harmonies all made for terrific music. One thing that made Jan & Dean records so energetic was that Jan used two trap sets for his sessions. Originally, he had tried having ace drummer Hal Blaine overdub his drums, playing the same licks twice, synchronized on tape. Not satisfied with the results, he had Earl Palmer come to the sessions as well as Hal. Together they rehearsed until they were playing their drums in perfect synch. This pioneering effort on the part of Jan is just one of the things that set Jan & Dean records apart from other similar records of the era.

What no one knew at the time was that Jan & Dean was not a duo, but actually a "supergroup," made up of hit artists, session singers, songwriters and session musicians. Jan, as leader of the group, was on all but a handful of LP cuts. Dean, as second banana, was on somewhat fewer cuts, and in fact his voice was missing from many of their hits, thanks to Jan's studio mixing techniques. Some of the Liberty hits Dean's voice is not on include "Surf City," "Little Old Lady (from Pasadena)," "Sidewalk Surfin'," "You Really Know How to Hurt a Guy," and "I Found a Girl."

Anyone who listens to the session outtakes (available at one time on bootleg albums) of "Little Old Lady" and compares them to the 45 can hear that the falsetto voice and parts are entirely different. Dean was there for the sessions but mixed down on the final track, along with some trumpet parts. It is also clear that Dean is on a great many—the vast majority of—singles and album tracks. To Jan & Dean fans, singles like "Surf City" have always been of relatively minor importance and interest; it has been the LPs that have entertained and interested fans.

Dean was clearly on "Submarine Races," "Schlock Rod," "Drag City," "Batman," "The Restless Surfer," "Linda," "Heart and Soul," "Ride the Wild Surf," "Baby Talk," "Frosty," and "Popsicle," to name but a very few Liberty 45s and LP cuts.

But Jan's girlfriend (and at one time a replacement for Michelle in the Mamas and Papas), Jill Gibson, did the high notes on "Easy as 1,2,3." Brian Wilson and Phil Sloan did them on "Surf City." Phil did them on "I Found a Girl" and apparently on "Sidewalk Surfin'" and "Little Old Lady." Neither Jan nor Dean is on "Move Out, Little Mustang." Tony Muchello was part of a singing group called the Matadors. The Matadors sang background on Jan & Dean's LP *Surf City*. Tony sang lead with Jan on the "Surf City" hit single.

Unlike most acts, Jan & Dean had not been signed directly to Liberty. "Jan & Dean were not brought in by us," explains Si Waronker. "They were really part of Lou Adler. He really had control of them. We had everything to do with releasing the records and saying what we liked and didn't like, but Lou controlled them. I've gotta give him complete credit for that, even though Jan & Dean worked for our company. I give Lou Adler a great deal of credit, because he knew what he was doing. Jan & Dean never did sign with Liberty. If I remember correctly, it was Lou who signed with Liberty, and he had those guys under contract. But I could be mistaken. There were so many of them at one time. I used to be upstairs in my office then, at the very end, and so much of the business was run by Al Bennett."

In light of the success of Jan & Dean's dragster sound, Liberty felt compelled to try to develop other hit sounds. For instance, the T-Bones were a group of studio musicians headed by Joe Saraceno and including Dan Hamilton, Joe Frank, and Tommy Reynolds. "Rail Vette" was an instrumental that opened and closed with drag race sounds and overall sounded suspiciously similar to an instrumental Jan & Dean *Dead Man's Curve* album cut called "Barons, West LA" (Jan & Dean's high school alma mater). Given its pedigree, it may be thought surprising that "Rail Vette" did not win acclaim. The writer was jazz musician Dave Pell; the producer was hit maker Perry Botkin, Jr. And Dan, Joe, and Tommy would score a string of winners in the early 1970s on Dunhill Records as Hamilton, Joe Frank, and Reynolds ("Don't Pull Your Love"). But that is how the record biz goes.

LPs and Also-Rans

Another interesting release from mid-1964 was Billy Daniels doing the Johnny Mercer tune "That Old Black Magic," which had already been a hit for Freddie Slack, for Glenn Miller (both in 1943), Sammy Davis, Jr. (1955), Louis Prima & Keely Smith (1958), and Bobby Rydell (1961). Was it time for another version? Apparently not, in spite of a dynamic, moody, bluesy rendition, for it was only an also-ran.

More on target, maybe, for the teen market was a 45 by Mike Harris, who wrote both sides. The B side, "Come Along with Me," sounded like Buddy Holly, hiccups and all, singing with Ritchie Valens's band playing fast and Latin on a number that sounded like Valens's tune "Come On, Let's Go"—plus a Del Shannon organ and some bongo drums! Good enough, and totally unlike the other side of the record.

The A side was a minimasterpiece entitled "We Never Knew." It opens with the phrase "With this ring," repeated three times by a female chorus. Next Mike begins to sing, sounding like Vic Dana or Brian Hyland with a background that is a lot like Terry Stafford's recent hit "Suspicion" (Crusader Records). It seems he is an orphan of eighteen, with a girlfriend of seventeen who is also an orphan. As they are getting married, and we hear a suggestion of the wedding march to prove it—a man yells, "Stop the wedding!" He is the singer's long-lost father, and the singer and his fiancée are brother and sister! Suddenly the pace of the song slows, and Mike sings, "She's gone," three times to a final suggestion of the wedding march. Pretty heady stuff for teen top-forty radio in 1964! No wonder it hasn't been heard of since.

A nod to Beatlemania came in the form of "I Want to Kiss Ringo Goodbye," a novelty by a woman using the "nom de record" Penny Valentine. The gist of the record is that Penny has had designs on Ringo for some time, but now he has gone off and gotten married, and she didn't even get to kiss the drumming mop-top good-bye.

Liberty's 1964 LPs were far too numerous to enumerate. The artists included, of course, Julie London, Martin Denny, Nancy Ames, Felix Slatkin, Walter Brennan, Spike Jones, Matt Monro, and the Johnny Mann Singers. Jan & Dean did well in 1964 with hit 45s and LPs with titles like *Dead Man's Curve/New Girl in School*, and *Ride the Wild Surf*. There was even *The Little Old Lady from Pasadena*.

Sensing a fad or two in all of this, Liberty released LPs that covered all bets.

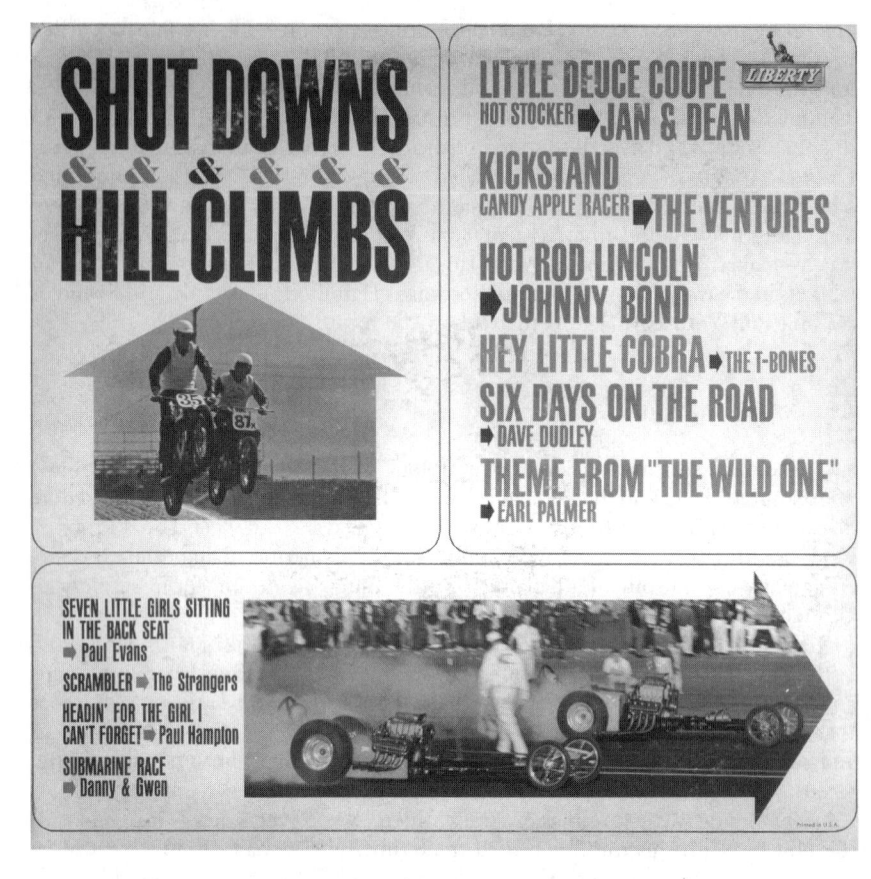

After Jan & Dean made millions for Liberty with their car songs, the company began a series of car releases featuring more obscure recordings. Note the inclusion of Danny and Gwen. Gwen was Vikki Carr.

In fact, every LP released between Jan & Dean's *Dead Man's Curve*, LRP 361, and their *Ride the Wild Surf*, LRP 368, carried Jan & Dean-ish themes. First was LRP 362, *Sounds of the Big Drags* (actual competition). LRP 363 combined cars and beaches, *Boss Drag at the Beach* (with the T-Bones). LRP 364 got even closer to the water, with the Hornets performing *Big Drag Boats*. On LRP 365, *Liverpool, Dragsters, Cycles, and Surfing!* were featured new versions of everything from "Can't Buy Me Love" (Beatles, 1964) and "Twist and Shout" (Isley Brothers, 1962; Beatles, 1964) to "Three Window Coupe" (Rip Chords, 1964) and "Malibu Wipeout." Then there were *Shut Downs and Hill Climbs*, LRP 365, and *Mustang* by the Zip Codes, LRP 367. None of these sold nearly as well as the Jan & Dean originals. The point that the company seemed to miss was that budgets, like the sinfully huge one spent on *Drag City*, and talent, like Jan Berry had, were what made Jan & Dean records sell, not just the fun fads of the day. It took more than cover photos of cars and beaches and a few sound effects with the music to sell more than a few copies of an album.

Country LPs by the likes of Joe Carson were issued. The Crickets did another LP. The Original Hits, both the rock 'n' roll and country series, continued. Bobby Vee was on tour in England before the Beatles came to the United States, so he released *The New Sound from England* ahead of any other invasion devotees, with the blessings of his friends and admirers the Beatles. The Beatles had recorded Bobby's biggest hit, "Take Good Care of My Baby" (1961), at their first recording session back in 1961.

The way that British radio, record companies, producers, and artists viewed American rock 'n' roll in those days was very curious. Alan Warner grew up in England with three versions of the music — American originals, British cover versions, and BBC renditions. "Liberty had the same problem getting air play in England that the other companies had. The BBC was pop or light music, very little rock 'n' roll. They had only MOR music. That's what frightens me about new-age music, I guess. Anyway, they had watered-down versions of everything, cover versions recorded by BBC artists. The BBC is governed by the government-run post office. They can broadcast only during the hours under which they have a license from the government. They still cannot broadcast 24 hours a day. They are allowed only so many hours per day of recorded versus live music; the musicians' unions are very strong."

By limiting the amount of recorded music that is played, they make more jobs for themselves. Here in America, all radio stations in the early days kept singers, piano players, bands, and even orchestras on hand at almost all times to play jingles and IDs that have been done on tape since the 1950s.

Alan Warner reveals: "The BBC had ways to get around this limitation. One, they could play sound tracks, which were not considered recordings since they were recorded for another medium, movies. The other thing that they [could] do, and still do to some extent, is to employ their own orchestras and singers." Thus, again by limiting records, the union kept more musicians employed.

"In those days, you had the dance bands, the BBC Symphony Orchestra [or] the BBC Light Orchestra, playing 'wonderful,' watered-down versions of pop tunes of the day. Something would come along like 'Singin' the Blues' by Guy Mitchell. And a local [British] artist like Tommy Steele would release a British record of it. And then the BBC would employ their people to do cover versions of that."

The BBC had another barrier to outside talent. "Anyone who performed on the radio had to pass a BBC audition. Even if they had a #1 record, like Cliff Richard, they had to pass a BBC audition before they could perform on the air, even if they had sold a million records."

Americans have mixed feelings about cover records. When Pat Boone covered a Fats Domino record, it sold like crazy but was criticized by reviewers. When the Beatles covered Little Richard and Chuck Berry and Carl Perkins and everyone else, American teens loved it and there were no critics. How did British teenagers feel about all of the British cover versions of American rock 'n' roll songs?

"Radio Luxembourg [a "pirate," non–BBC station] had sponsored shows which played the original American versions," recounts Warner, "but they were leaning heavily on the British artists, who were out there working and on television. Until the Beatles changed things and told everybody [in England] about Motown and all that, there was so little knowledge of American records and artists, it was very difficult to find out what the original versions were. In fact, in the introduction to my book *Who Sang What in Rock and Roll,* I quote that. One of my favorite records when I was in school was 'Just Walkin' in the Rain' by Johnny Ray. Now, there is an American record which is a cover, which we heard in Britain. It was not until many years later that I learned that that was a cover. There was no way that you would know that at the time. It was sold as the big record. I guess we just took it for granted that British artists did American songs.

"There was, for example, a British girl, Carole Deene, who covered three successive Sue Thompson records ["Sad Movies," 1961; "Norman," 1962; "James, Hold the Ladder Steady," 1962]. Isn't that amazing? Everything Sue Thompson came along with, this other girl covered! Sue didn't have a chance. Then pirate radio came along, and it all changed. The originals got played. Until then there was no competition; the BBC had a monopoly. And British producers would have someone in America send them American hit singles, and the British producer would copy them with a British artist."

In the United States, in 1964, being British was almost a guarantee of a contract, if not of a release. Yet Americans were still in possession of more than 90 percent of the positions on the American music charts, and Imperial's first successful artist for the British-invasion year 1964 was American Irma Thomas in March. When Liberty absorbed Imperial, it not only redesigned the paper label, but it also changed the record-numbering system.

Previous Imperial 45s had had label numbers starting with one numeral: 5. Liberty had always started its record numbers with two 5s, in honor of the year in which the label was born. In other words, the Searchers' Liberty 45 was numbered 55689, but (back in 1963) the first O'Jays release under the old Imperial numbering system had been 5967. That 5967 looked too much like a Liberty record number and might cause confusion during inventory, ordering, cataloging, and so forth. So a new Imperial numbering system was created. It was patterned after the Liberty 55 but designed to be easily distinguished. The choice? Double 6s. Thus, Irma Thomas's first Imperial song, "Wish Someone Would Care," was numbered 66013.

Irma would have four chart songs in her career, all on Imperial, and this was her first and biggest, making the top twenty. Thomas should have been a big star.

One of the most successful compositions that the Sharon Sheeley–Jackie DeShannon team ever yielded was an up-tempo masterpiece on the flip side of Irma's "Wish Someone Would Care" 45. It was called "Breakaway." How could the flip side of a mild top-forty hit have been so successful? As Sharon explained the history of "Breakaway": "Tracey Ullman had a number one in Europe with that song, and it was the second largest record by anyone except by the Beatles. It was unbelievable. It sold millions of records."

I loved "Breakaway" from the first time I laid ears on Irma Thomas's version. I could not believe that it had not been a hit. It was only years later that I noticed the composer credits were Jackie and Sharon. Having acquired Tracey's version on an LP of hers, I still prefer Irma's version, and Sharon agrees: "Irma Thomas does it the best." Except I suppose for Jackie's demo version, which I hope to hear before I die.

Irma Thomas

In the old Imperial tradition, Irma was discovered singing in a New Orleans club. Born in Ponchatoula, Louisiana, in 1941, she sang in church and school while

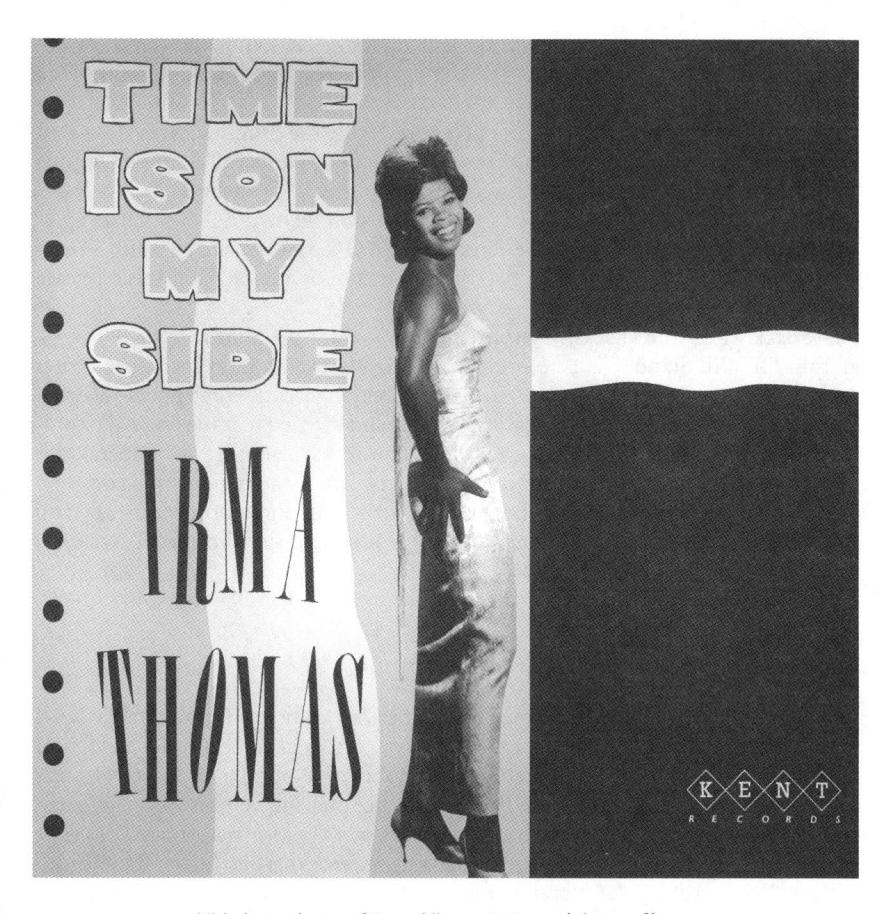

This is a reissue of Irma Thomas's Imperial recordings.

growing up. After cutting a few sides for the Bandy label, she got a job as a waitress in a club that featured live bands. One night she sang with one of the bands, and that performance led to a contract with Ron Records.

Several years of touring and recording found her at Joe Banashak's Minit Records. Early in 1963, Lou Chudd, owner of Imperial Records, bought Minit. Later that year Liberty bought Imperial, and thus Irma Thomas found herself in the Liberty fold. Irma was recorded quite a bit by Imperial but managed only four hits, and only one of them made the top forty. In the best Liberty tradition, she recorded several LPs.

Irma Thomas's best-known song is "Time Is on My Side," though like "Breakaway," its fame is not due to Irma's version but only because it was rerecorded by the Rolling Stones. Irma Thomas always resented the huge popularity of the Stones' version, which became their first top-ten hit. She had put everything into her version, only to see the Stones, who according to her were these British kids who couldn't sing at all, steal her arrangement exactly and score hugely. In later decades she refused even to do the song when requested by her fans, so deep was her disgust.

Irma's second Imperial hit was the last by Ricky Nelson on this label, "Congratulations." By now Rick had started hitting on Decca, and his old Imperial work had become moot.

The swan song of Imperial's other Nelson, Sandy the drummer, was also heard in 1964. His ninth and final hit was a new version of his original 1959 hit on Original Sounds Records, "Teen Beat." Anachronistically titled "Teen Beat '65," it was a percussion throwback that sounded great in the middle of the 1960s. Charting at #41, it also inspired "Let There Be Drums '66" in 1965, a remake of Sandy's similarly titled 1961 Imperial hit. The 1961 version made #7; the 1965/66 version made #120.

Speaking of throwbacks, a surprise hit of 1964 was the Showmen's ode to rock 'n' roll, "It Will Stand." This recording had already been a mild hit in the winter of 1961-62 on the Minit label. Now, in 1964, Imperial, recently come under the wing of Liberty records, in turn, bought Minit Records and decided that the original recording of "It Will Stand" had stood up well enough to have another go. Imperial was right, and the song did make the national charts, if not the national top forty.

For the year that makes the Imperial hit-artist tally three British acts, the two Nelsons as holdovers from before the Liberty acquisition, the Showmen's rerelease, and label newcomer Irma Thomas.

Johnny Rivers

Besides Irma Thomas, the other 1964 American addition to the Imperial label was Johnny Rivers, aka John Ramistella. In Rivers, Imperial via Lou Adler had found an artist with the hit-making potential of a Bobby Vee or a Jan & Dean. His first hit, in May, was "Memphis," and his version became the version for many fans, especially those who had never heard Chuck Berry's mid-fifties original. Johnny Rivers began his string of hits by specializing in redoing old hits: "Maybelline" (Chuck Berry, 1955), "Mountain of Love" (Harold Dorman, 1960), "Midnight Special" (Paul Evans, 1960), and "Cupid" (Sam Cooke, 1961).

But Johnny Rivers had begun his career cutting demos of his own compositions for consideration by other artists. His early recordings were sung in whatever style suited the session. He sang like Elvis on "That's Rock and Roll," like Eddie Cochran on "You're the One," like Ricky Nelson on "Everyday," like Roy Orbison on "Darling, Talk to Me," like Buddy Holly on "Customary Thing," and like Johnny Burnette on "Answer Me, My Love."

Johnny Rivers's first duties at Imperial had involved production work. In 1963, before the Liberty takeover, he produced a girl-group record for Imperial by Misty and the Do-Drops. "Come Shake Hands with a Fool" was written not by Rivers but by Billy Page, and was a catchy if undistinguished girl-group record. The flip side, "Answer Me, My Love," a song Rivers himself had cut earlier, was also quite good, and showed that Johnny Rivers knew rock 'n' roll. It also meant that he was destined to fall under the shadow of the Liberty logo when the takeover came to pass.

Taking into account his years of composing, demo work, titles like "That's Rock and Roll," and producing, it was no wonder that at Imperial Rivers was soon recording hits of both oldies ("Memphis," Chuck Berry, 1955, Johnny Rivers, 1964; "Mountain of Love," Harold Dorman, 1960, Johnny Rivers, 1964) and original compositions for release on Imperial. Before he was done, Johnny Rivers had scored with nearly two dozen Imperial hits, thirteen in the top forty, seven in the top ten, and one, "Poor Side of Town," in 1966, at #1. This was Imperial's third #1. (The other two were Ricky Nelson's "Travelin' Man" and flip "Hello Mary Lou" [written by Gene Pitney] in 1961, and Ricky's "Poor Little Fool" in 1958.) It is mildly interesting that two of Imperial's three #1 hits had the word *poor* in their titles. Imperial would never have another #1 hit, but Johnny did create for the Liberty family his own Soul City record label.

On Soul City the 5th Dimension had eleven hits, making the top forty twelve times, the top ten four times, and #1 twice, with "Aquarius/Let the Sun Shine In" and "Wedding Bell Blues" (both in 1969). Bones Howe, who served as engineer on Jan & Dean Liberty sessions, acted as producer on the 5th Dimension hits. The Soul City label looked just like the Liberty and Imperial labels, except that the left side of the label was gold, and where the Statue of Liberty was located on Liberty's label, Soul City pictured a soulful singer.

Interestingly some artists, for example, Bobby Vee, had nothing but good relations with the Liberty staff. Others, such as Jan & Dean, had good relations for a time but certainly had no intentions of renewing when their contracts expired. Dick and Deedee got out of their contract after only two hits. The 5th Dimension, says Alan Warner, had problems, recounted by Fred Bronson in the *Billboard Book of #1 Hits*. Bronson said that "the Fifth Dimension had trouble at Liberty, that Al Bennett did not want one of their big hits released. There was apparently much discomfort between the people involved. But most of the people I've known who have been pro–the Liberty team of management, were close to Al. Timi Yuro, who[m] I have known, was very pro–Liberty. She moved to Las Vegas later. I think Jackie DeShannon also had a good relationship with Liberty."

Aside from the fact that he established Soul City and catalyzed the success of the 5th Dimension, perhaps the most amazing thing musically about Johnny Rivers was that, when he had hits with remakes of oldies, and he had nearly a dozen, he sang them all in his own distinctive style. What makes this amazing is how well he emulated other artists, chameleonlike, in his prehit and demo days.

But to return to Imperial's 1964 new acquisitions, the other three were British. Alan Warner explains generally how that came about. "Since Bobby Vee was on tour in England in nineteen sixty-three when the Beatles were big in England but not yet known in America, I was aware of the Liberty British EMI deal for various British acts. Although Liberty did not get the Beatles, they did sign various other acts to Liberty and the associated labels, the Hollies on Imperial, Billy J. Kramer with the Dakotas, artists like that."

Although British artists were on Liberty in the United States, calling them Liberty acts can be stretching things a bit. As Billy J. Kramer explained, "My records were on Polydor; that is the company I was on in England. I didn't even know they were being released in the United States on Liberty and Imperial. I felt good about it when I found out, because I had always liked Liberty artists like Bobby Vee." Does that mean that Billy J. Kramer never so much as set foot in the California Liberty offices? "I think I dropped by the building and met them briefly once, on my way to Australia."

Johnny Rivers became a big star with his Liberty/Imperial remakes of fifties rock 'n' roll songs.

The Swinging Blue Jeans

The Swinging Blue Jeans debuted in March with "Hippy Hippy Shake." The Blue Jeans were among the wilder British rave-up artists, and the song was a well-received, note-for-note copy of the original recording by Chan Romero, who wrote the song in 1959 in LA. The Blue Jeans had two more Imperial hits, but only the first one of the three made the top forty. In a few months the rock 'n' roll winds had blown the Swinging Blue Jeans off America's musical clothesline.

The Hollies

The third of Imperial's British artists, the Hollies, came out in May, the same month Imperial brought out Johnny Rivers' first record. And like Johnny Rivers, the Hollies proved more durable than the rest of Imperial's 1964 recruits.

The Swinging Blue Jeans, like Johnny Rivers, made their name reviving old fifties hits.

Most of the artists who eventually became big successes on Liberty, Dolton or Imperial, started off well with a nice big hit on the first try. A notable exception had been Jan & Dean. It had taken that duo more than a year of trying before one of their Liberty singles caught on nationally, and then they scored success after musical success.

The Hollies were also slow starters. Their first Imperial record was a remake of Doris Troy's "Just One Look" (1963). American kids were not impressed, and "Just One Look" was on the U.S. national chart for only one week. More than a year later the Hollies finally managed just barely to squeak onto the top forty with "Look Through Any Window." Their next, "I Can't Let Go," missed completely, and the Imperial execs must have begun to feel that with the Hollies, when compared to Billy J. and the Blue Jeans, they had signed the wrong British invasion group to the label.

Finally, in 1966, the Hollies began making hits. "Bus Stop," "Stop, Stop, Stop," "On a Carousel" and "Carrie Ann" were all top-ten hits in 1966 and 1967. At that point Imperial was so confident about the Hollies that "Just One Look" was

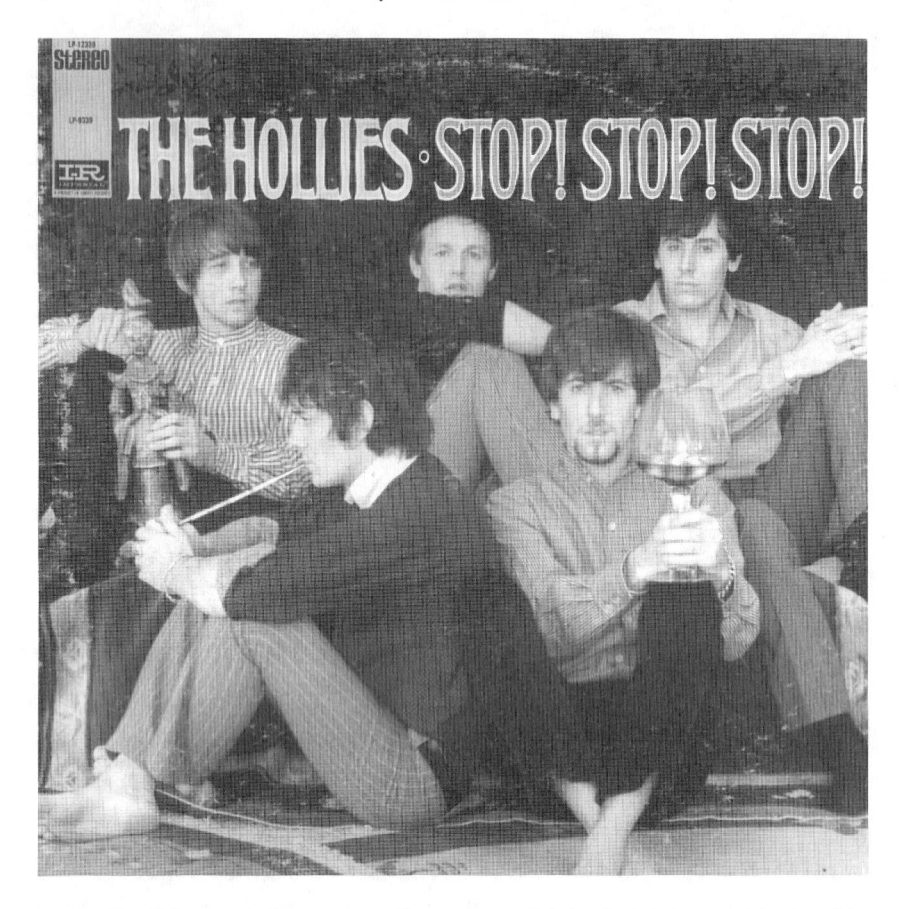

The Hollies did not actually record for Liberty or Imperial, but had their material released in the United States on Imperial.

issued again. By now there were very few kids left who remembered either Doris Troy's original version or the Hollies' earlier flop. Even so, "Just One Look" by the Hollies missed the top forty the second time around and also seemingly jinxed them, as 1966 saw the end of their run of U.S. hits and of their contract with Imperial.

The Hollies' remaining singles, from 1967 to 1975, failed to catch on, and with the exception of "He Ain't Heavy, He's My Brother," all failed to make the top forty. For Liberty/Imperial, as well as for the American rock 'n' roll scene in general, the British invasion was largely just a memory by 1967. Nevertheless, hits that never made the top forty still made a lot of kids happy and still made lots of money. And, if you were a Liberty/Imperial artist, even smallish hits called for releasing lots of LPs!

More LPs and Also-Rans

The Hollies' first LP was called *Here I Go Again,* after a turn by the same name that was a top-five hit in England but just an LP title in the United States. In all, the

Hollies had six Imperial LPs, including *The Hollies Greatest Hits*. Billy J. Kramer with the Dakotas had three LPs. The Swinging Blue Jeans had one. Irma Thomas had two LPs. Her *Wish Someone Would Care* LP included "Time Is on My Side."

Also influenced by the British were the Crickets. In England the Crickets had three top-forty hits in 1963–64. The Beatles covered the Crickets' UK hit, "Don't Ever Change," although the Beatles' version was never released. Paul McCartney says that the first twenty songs he and John Lennon wrote were "Buddy Holly songs." But when Holly's band, the Crickets, released a creditable 45 of "From Me to You" and "Please Please Me" in the United States in 1964, it was totally ignored.

Jackie DeShannon, who spent time in England, sang "It's Love, Baby," which sounded like British femme rocker Lulu—Jackie always sounded like somebody. The flip side was also British-influenced: "He's Got the Whole World in His Hands," a #1 hit by Laurie London in Britain in 1958 on Capitol Records, done in a gospel style by Jackie.

Johnny Rivers went on to record about ten LPs for Imperial. Several of these LPs were recorded live at the Whiskey A-Go Go, a club where Rivers' popularity first emerged. In fact, most of his early 45s were recorded live at the Whiskey.

All of the Liberty labels released many, many records that are unknown today except to hard-core collectors. To discuss these would not only be time consuming but impossible. These missing links are records which were by unknown artists, by known artists, and by artists which fit neither category. All these records had in common was that they did not become hits.

As illustrations, three Imperial singles from late 1964 come to mind. One was "Move Out, Little Mustang" by the Rally-Packs. This song was written by Brian Wilson of the Beach Boys and by Los Angeles DJ Roger Christian, who cowrote many hits for Jan & Dean on Liberty. The Imperial "group," the Rally-Packs, did not actually exist. "Move Out, Little Mustang" had appeared on Jan & Dean's 1964 Liberty LP *The Little Old Lady from Pasadena*. However, even though it appeared on their LP, "Move Out, Little Mustang" was not sung by Jan & Dean. The voices on both the LP and the identical 45 were those of P. F. Sloan and Steve Barri. That was not a big deal. Sloan and Barri not only sang backup on many Jan & Dean 45s and LPs, and of course Phil Sloan occasionally sang the falsetto parts usually ascribed to Dean Torrence.

Engineer Bones Howe worked with Sloan and Barri many times. He knew who sang what. "The Fantastic Baggies LP sessions were where I met Sloan and Barri. Phil Sloan was the high voice on almost all the records of that era, including certain Jan & Dean records."

Another late 1964 Imperial 45 was "It Was I" (Skip and Flip, 1959), again Sloan and Barri but using the name the Fantastic Baggies. Sloan and Barri wrote many Liberty songs for Jan & Dean as well as Imperial songs for Johnny Rivers, including "Secret Agent Man." Plus, Sloan and Barri, using the Fantastic Baggies name, had an Imperial LP of their own called *Tell 'Em I'm Surfin'*, which has become a real collector's item and was reissued in the 1980s. That LP had two more Jan & Dean LP songs, written by Sloan and Barri and rerecorded by them for their *Baggies* LP.

A few weeks after "Move Out, Little Mustang" was released, Imperial released "It's as Easy as 1, 2, 3." This song was sung and written by Jill Gibson, the girlfriend of Jan Berry of Jan & Dean. The song had originally been a duet by Jill and Jan on

The friends of Jan & Dean on Liberty. The Fantastic Baggies (Phil Sloan and Steve Barri) sang on Jan & Dean records; Jill Gibson was Jan's girlfriend and was once in the Mamas and Papas; the Rally-Packs were really the Fantastic Baggies, and this cut, on which neither Jan *nor* Dean sings, was nonetheless featured on Jan & Dean's *Little Old Lady* LP.

a Jan & Dean Liberty LP. This version was a rerecording by Jill. Jill wrote the song with Don Altfeld, Jan & Dean's fan club secretary, who later became a doctor. Jan produced the record. Amazing how much trivia could be involved in the story of a nonhit at Liberty!

Last, an Imperial also-ran missing link. Scott Simon released an Imperial 45 in October 1964. The song was "Move It, Baby," but the song did not move on the charts.

As can be seen from just these three obscure Imperial 45s, the full story of the Liberty family of labels is a strange, interesting, and complex one indeed.

The Fleetwoods had bade farewell to the charts in 1963 with "Goodnight, My Love"—their final eight releases, all on Dolton, failed to click nationally. So 1964 was the first year since the beginning of Dolton that the Fleetwoods did not chart. However, they continued to record and release records.

Gretchen Christopher remembers the Fleetwoods' 1964 Dolton records like it was yesterday. "'Before and After (Losing You)' is a song that was released as a single but wasn't a hit. That was the only one that I was sure *would* be a hit!" Any why not? It was arranged by Ernie Freeman, produced by Dick Glasser, and written by Van McCoy. With a lineage like that, plus the patented Fleetwoods delivery, Gretchen was entirely justified in expecting "Before and After" to become a hit.

"I think Dick Glasser was the producer who wanted to do 'Mr. Sandman'" (Chordettes, 1954), which had come out a few weeks before "Before and After." "Dick had kind of an arrangement in mind for it. Not that he dictated the whole arrangement, but he did have a concept in mind. I think there is an organ in it—it makes me think of a roller rink: 'Everybody skate!' But that was his idea." Besides the organ, the record has what sounds like two hundred violins. What the arrangement is missing is the vocal steps of the original, which would have been perfect for the Fleetwoods' voices.

"'Non l'ete per armati' was a song given to us to record by Liberty. It meant 'This Is My Prayer,' and it came from the San Remo Song Festival, where it was the winner. It was given to the Fleetwoods for the first American, English-language recording. It was very pretty, but nothing really happened with it." "This Is My Prayer" was placed on the flip side of "Mr. Sandman," a nice but inferior tune.

The Fleetwoods hated this record, which was on the newly redesigned Dolton label.

"Liberty Records wanted us to do 'Ska Light, Ska Bright,' because it was the latest craze from England. They thought it was going to take off here, and they wanted us to lead the way. The ska did not make it in the United States, but our record was totally silly!"

Gary Troxel didn't like "Ska Light, Ska Bright" any more than Gretchen did. "I don't have much to say about 'Ska Light, Ska Bright.'" That record makes Gary laugh today. "Liberty wanted to jump on the ska bandwagon, and we didn't make it." He laughs some more. "They wanted us to do something ska, so we did that."

Actually, "Ska Light, Ska Bright" is a pretty good record. Seldom did the powers that be at Liberty Dolton force any bad tunes on the Fleetwoods, although Gary does recall at least a few. "Some of the songs that I did not like that we recorded were on the very last album. It's too bad, it was released anyway."

Gretchen remembers another unusual Fleetwoods song. "Barbara wrote and cut one that was kind of a surfing parody called 'Surfer's Playmate.' She sang it, and Bob asked Gary and me to do a backup that was totally un–Fleetwoods! So we got just as wild as we could be, just screaming on parts of it; it was fun to do, so I put that on our thirteenth album, *Buried Treasure*."

Vic Dana, perhaps the least likely Dolton artist to endure, viewed from a rock 'n' roll fan's point of view, had a top-thirty record, "Shangri-La," and also had two small hits, "Love Is All We Need" and "Garden in the Rain."

The biggest Dolton hit of the year was by the Ventures, and it was both their only hit of the year and the third biggest record they would ever have. Of all things, it was an update of their first hit in 1959, "Walk, Don't Run." The new recording was dubbed "Walk, Don't Run '64," and was rendered in a surf-sound after the fashion of the Chanteys' instrumental smash "Pipeline" on Dot Records. In the ensuing years, having two different records share the same name, artist, and label has caused some confusion. In fact, even on the Liberty LP *Golden Greats* by the Ventures, "Walk, Don't Run '64" is misidentified on the cover and the label as "Walk, Don't Run" (original version)!

Exit Bob Reisdorff

In 1964 the Dolton artists were having to get along without Bob Reisdorff for the first time in their careers. Reisdorff sold out Dolton completely at the very end of 1963 and quit the music business except for retaining a publishing company. But, like an old firehorse, when the bell rang, he found himself back in harness heading where the action was. "I went back into the business in 1964, this time to work for Liberty. Al Bennett asked me to open up a company for them in London, which I did, which was a nightmare. Liberty had not done it before. They were doing it simultaneously in Germany with Sigfried Loch, but Sigfried was German and had been in the business there and knew everyone.

"They sent me over three months early, but I had been a fool enough to not have thought it over in advance. I had to get a building, I had to staff it, I had to learn British law regarding the record business. I committed myself to a year and a half and stayed there for that time. After I left, the Britisher Alan Warner came along; I believe he was with United Artists when Liberty sold out to UA, which in turn was owned by TransAmerica. We ultimately worked for them."

Little did Bob know that a British acquaintance of Alan Warner's, Michael Aldred, was working in the record business at that time, loved Liberty's records, and would have dropped everything he was doing to have Bob's position.

Exit Alvin, Simon and Theodore

Besides Dolton's doing without Bob Reisdorff, the year 1964 was also the first full calendar year that Liberty had been Si-less. Si Waronker had quit "going to work" in the summer of 1963, and in 1964 he finally got out of his contract. In business, of course, contracts are of great importance. Not having a contract could be good, if you wanted your liberty and freedom back as Si did, or it could be bad, if you wanted to get paid, like David Seville, creator of the Chipmunks.

Si Waronker: "Here is the sad part of the Chipmunks. When I quit Liberty, I wanted no part of anybody, except Ross Bagdasarian [aka David Seville]. Ross and I remained great friends. He was still at Liberty, but Liberty was going through hell at this time. They had sold the company to Avnet and lost a million bucks the first year. Ross had no contract, just our handshake. The way I had always paid him was simple. If he did not sell any records, he got nothing. The first twenty-five thousand copies he sold of a record, he got three or four cents a record. That went up to a dime if he sold a million. From two million he got twelve percent.

"Well, when I left, the company was not being run right. Avnet had sold it back after a year, and Ross wanted his royalties, but he had no contract, and Liberty had no money! I called Al Bennett and said, 'Al, you gotta pay this guy because he's gonna cause you trouble. Why don't you make a deal, give him back all of his catalog and whatever money you can afford to pay.' I did all of the negotiating for

Ross and for Al and got him his catalog and all the rights for all his songs, 'Armen's Theme,' "Witch Doctor,' 'Chipmunks,' everything. Ross also got all the rights to the Chipmunk trademarks, in lieu of the back royalties owed him. That is how Ross's family got the stuff that allowed them to continue on with the Chipmunks on records, tapes, CDs, TV, and videos. Now they use girls' voices for the Chipmunks instead of men, and it doesn't sound nearly as good."

In May 1991, the Chipmunks TV program had a story in which the 1990s Chipmunks were confronted by the 1950s Chipmunks who had traveled forward in time via a time machine. To see which group was better, the 1950s and 1990s Chipmunks staged a battle of the bands, singing "The Alvin Twist." The competition was a tie, but the 1950s group decided to go back to their own time after all. Their reasoning was, if they were not in the past to blaze the musical trail, then the 1990s Chipmunks would not even exist!

As the 1950s Alvin was getting into the time machine to leave, the 1990s Alvin handed him a harmonica, saying "Believe me, you'll need it!" This inside reference to the Chipmunks' record "Alvin's Harmonica" would be lost on today's cartoon audience of grade-schoolers. It must be aimed at middle-aged baby-boomer parents or is just an inside joke for the Bagdasarian family. (This gag overlooks the fact that the "Alvin Twist" came after "Alvin's Harmonica" in the 1950s, by the way.)

By the end of 1964, Si was long gone, Ross Bagdasarian was gone, and the Beatles had been lost. But the company had survived the Avnet debacle, and one of the biggest acts in the label's history was about to be discovered.

CHAPTER 13

1965
Gary Lewis and the Playboys, P. J. Proby, T-Bones, Hal Blaine, O'Jays, Jimmy McCracklin, and Cher

The panic of the British-invasion days was over by 1965. What had looked like an unending tidal wave of British bands had turned out to be merely a 10 percent solution of mostly short-lived rock 'n' rollers with British accents. Even at the peak of the British invasion, the U.S. top one hundred was still 90 percent American hit records.

Was Liberty hurt by the British acts? Well, the number of songs they had on the charts was up by about 10 percent in 1964 over the preceding year. And Jan & Dean, Liberty's biggest-selling act at the time, had more than twice as many hits in 1964 as they had had in 1963. Overall the invasion did not seem to have hurt them. Dean explained it like this:

"We were happy about the British invasion! Luckily we were right in the middle of it. If we had been just starting, it might have blasted us out of the water. If we had been just on the tail end of it and starting to have career problems of our own, our career would have gone into the toilet that much quicker. But we were at the strongest point of our career, so they towed the rest of us along with them.

"All of a sudden, rock 'n' roll was considered important by the establishment for the first time. The record companies said, 'This is multi-million-dollar stuff! Hey, the records *can* sound better. Listen to those records! Hey, production quality is important. Oh, gosh!' So, they went out and bought eight-track recorders and sixteen-track recorders for the first time. They bought filters. They bought everything."

Liberty added four new successes to their list of artists in 1965, and none was British born or bred. That is, as compared to two new artists back in 1964, both of whom were British, but neither of whom scored more than one Liberty hit single.

Gary Lewis and the Playboys

In January 1965, one of the new Liberty American artists was one who would ultimately become the fourth most successful hit-single artist in the history of Liberty records. Gary Lewis and the Playboys, like Bobby Vee six years before, were

Chapter 13 · 1965

GARY LEWIS AND THE PLAYBOYS
EVERYBODY LOVES A CLOWN
& TIME STANDS STILL #55818

Few people recall that Gary was originally the Playboys' drummer, not a singer, and that the band featured a cordovox—an amplified accordion requiring no pumping.

a discovery of Snuff Garrett. Snuff found Gary Lewis's band playing at Disneyland. Snuff supposedly did not even know that Gary Lewis's father was comedian Jerry Lewis, but that was not true. At any rate Snuff saw and heard something he liked, perhaps, in fact, a new Bobby Vee, even though Gary's voice was not half as strong as Bobby's. At the time Snuff happened to have a good song he felt would be perfect for Gary. The song: "This Diamond Ring."

Snuff's instincts were still good. Coming out in January, "This Diamond Ring" had a hit golden ring to it and quickly became gold. Produced by Snuff, arranged by Leon Russell, and written in part by Al Kooper, "This Diamond Ring" went to #1, making it the fifth and final #1 hit in the history of the Liberty label. It did so well that Leon and Snuff released an answer record on Liberty, "(Gary, Please Don't Sell) My Diamond Ring" by Wendy Hill, that sounded so much like the original that—well, it is nice to have the answer song done by the same crew that did the original.

One note about this cut. The stereo version (available on the classic EMI 1985

Death, Glory and Retribution
15 ROCK RARITIES INCLUDING DEATH DISCS, PROTEST SONGS AND ANSWER RECORDS

THE BEACH BOYS
GLEN CAMPBELL
THE ISLEY BROTHERS
JAN AND DEAN
JOHNNY BURNETTE
JODY REYNOLDS
BLOOD ROCK
BOB GIBSON
JODY MILLER
JEANNE BLACK
WEIRD AL JANKOVIC
SAMMY LYNN
WENDY HILL
GERALDINE STEVENS

Alan Warner compiled a number of LPs containing Liberty artists' classics. This one is from 1985 and includes Wendy Hill's "(Gary, Please Don't Sell) My Diamond Ring" answer record to Gary Lewis's first hit.

compilation LP *Death, Glory, and Retribution)* is quite different, primarily missing Wendy's singalong vocal overdubbing. In addition, some instruments are missing, and the instrumental break in the middle of the song is very fuzzy. Stereo was still a musical stepchild in the mid–1960s.

Gary Lewis and the Playboys were just right for the times. Gary Lewis was, in essence, a new Bobby Vee/Johnny Burnette/Buddy Knox/Eddie Cochran/Gene McDaniels/Troy Shondell. But, pretty much disdaining the Liberty sound and featuring as he did his own band, the Playboys, Gary *looked* like the newly popularized bands, the Beatles/Searchers/Hollies/Kingsmen/Spoonful/—three guitars and a drummer. In 1965 alone, Gary Lewis and the Playboys had five records in the national top five: "This Diamond Ring," "Count Me In," "Save Your Heart for Me," "Everybody Loves a Clown," and "She's Just My Style."

They made the top ten with each of their first seven records, and the top forty with all but three of their fifteen hits. That was a success rate unequaled by anyone in the history of Liberty, Dolton, Imperial, or any of the other Liberty Records subsidiaries! Jan & Dean had more hits. Bobby Vee had more two-sided hits. But Gary Lewis and the Playboys had the hottest streak in the label's history.

To whom did Gary Lewis owe his success? Snuff Garrett's ace production touch deserved much of the credit, and perhaps even more credit was owed to the arranger of the Lewis sessions, none other than Leon Russell.

It was Snuff who really guided Gary Lewis's entire musical career, even though by that time Snuff had left Liberty and was working as an independent producer. "I stayed at Liberty seven years, then went into business for myself. When I left, I cut my first record and brought it back to Liberty, my old home. Al turned it down, so did everybody in town. Then Bob Skaff, Liberty promotion head, went to bat for me. The record: 'This Diamond Ring.'

"I had offered that song to Bobby Vee, but he turned it down. He denies it. He says I didn't. What did I need, a brass band in front of it? I won't argue, but it was in my desk and I was in trouble with Bobby. We needed a hit.

"The band wasn't Gary Lewis and the Playboys, it was the Playboys. Jerry [Lewis] was one of my idols as a kid, and our offices were next door; I'd hang around his sets when I was in LA. Lou Brown, his piano player since the Dean Martin days, is a funny man. He told me to see the Playboys at Disneyland, but I turned him down. A few weeks later he took me to see them rehearse at Paramount. Gary Lewis was the drummer, another Playboy sang, but when I heard them, I knew that with Gary as the singer, "This Diamond Ring" would be a hit. If Gary could sing. And if I could get some television coverage through Jerry.

"So I cut 'This Diamond Ring' with the Playboys, and I got the money for the session from Gary's mother, Patti, twenty-five hundred. Gary was the singer, but I used Ron Hicklin as his backup singer to help the sound; Gary then used him a lot to sing along with Gary. I dubbed them all together. The original singer in the Playboys was a nice kid.

"The record came out on Liberty, so I called Murray the K, whom I knew, and asked him to play the record. He said he wanted Gary to be on his rock 'n' roll show.

"I said, 'He'll do the show for free, just play the record!' Murray the K played the record, and that was the only record I ever did that broke in New York, twenty-five thousand copies.

"Jerry Lewis had been on Ed Sullivan's first show with Dean. In two weeks he was due to be on Ed Sullivan again, so I said he should get Gary on. He called Ed right then and set it up.

"Gary asked me to go along, and when we got there they were rehearsing, and I almost had a heart attack. I sat Jerry down. 'Jerry, the Playboys are not together enough, they're not rehearsed enough, and Gary is not attuned enough to singing yet.' But everything on Ed Sullivan was live, nothing prerecorded or lip-synched. I told Jerry, 'If Gary doesn't lip-synch that, it's gonna be awful.' So Jerry set it up with Ed to have Gary lip-synch the record, told him that was the way it was going to be, and that was the first if not the only time anyone ever lip-synched on Ed Sullivan.

"There would have been no way to get the record sound on stage; all of the little tricks they had done in the studio. Not only with the voice over dubs, but with the track. Speeded up piano, tricks with the tymps, all of that. So the record sold one

This is the team that made "This Diamond Ring" possible: arranger Leon Russell, Patti Lewis (Gary's mom), Gary Lewis, and producer Snuff Garrett. *(Courtesy Snuff Garrett.)*

million and four hundred thousand, and we had a lot of hits with Gary. I was really on a roll at that time."

Lee Mendel saw Gary Lewis's rise to fame, and saw his dad help him up the ladder of success, starting with the Ed Sullivan show. "Gary's father rehearsed Gary Lewis for five or seven days, because he had never worked in public before."

Though at times it seemed that the Playboys were almost nonexistent, there really were Playboys. One of the later Playboys was Carl Radle, the bass player, who died of an OD. He was from Oklahoma and became a very hot rock bass player. But to look at the 45 labels, it would appear that the Playboys were strictly an afterthought. On "This Diamond Ring," the words "and the Playboys" were nearly the same size as Gary Lewis' name. But, on the top-ten follow-up, "Count Me In," the Playboys' billing was in a typeface about half the size of Gary's own name. On each succeeding hit record label, the words "and the Playboys" got smaller and smaller. On the fourth hit, "Everybody Loves a Clown," the Playboys' name was as small as the composer credits! In fact, the change in print size was just a happenstance.

As Gary recalls, there was no significance to it at all. "I noticed it. Nothing was going on. The Playboys played on all of the basic tracks. Snuff would call in session musicians to do overdubbing, but yeah, the Playboys did the basic tracks on all the hits. They were definitely on the records. Leon may have mixed it *down* a little bit, but they were on them. Good people were called in to do overdubs, like Hal Blaine on percussion, Tommy Tedesco would do guitar things, real good people. Ron Hicklin sang harmony with me on everything. He was great. Sloan and Barri sang background on some album things."

Gary Lewis himself recalls the 1960s very fondly and vividly, and recounts the same series of events, from the discovery at Disneyland, to the printing of the band's name on the Liberty labels. For one thing, he cleared up once and for all whether the band really was discovered at Disneyland or, as some sources say, on TV's "Shindig." "No, it was Disneyland. We got the job being one of the house bands there for the whole summer. We had to go in and audition with a bunch of other bands and we got the job for three months.

"We played at a place called the Space Bar in Tomorrowland. That is where Snuff Garrett first saw us. He said, 'Come on by Liberty Records and let me play a bunch of these demos for you that people have submitted to us, and I'll talk to your parents about signing papers and everything.' I was still a minor and couldn't sign anything. That was how it started right there." Sounds like Snuff found a way to meet Jerry Lewis.

Originally Gary Lewis was the drummer of the Playboys, not a singer. Had he any aspirations to be a singer? "No! Not at all! I was going to a theater arts college in Pasadena, California, the Pasadena Playhouse. I was doing dramatic things; classes consisted of rehearsing to do plays. You were graded on how you did your play. It was all things like *Othello* and *Oedipus Rex,* and I was bored. I didn't care for any of that stuff at all."

What, besides a distaste for the classics, changed his life from the theater to rock 'n' roll? "When the Beatles came out, that made up my mind for me exactly what I wanted to do. Because I really didn't have any idea. I wanted to go into show business, but I really didn't know what field. I *knew* I didn't want to try to be a *comedian*! You know [being Jerry Lewis's son], that would have just been disaster from the word *go*. So the Beatles came out, and that made up my mind for me.

"I got my drums out of Beacon storage, put together a band of classmates..., and we just started rehearsing. That was January nineteen sixty-four, and we rehearsed all the way up until summertime, to where we thought we could get a job at Disneyland.

"The very first time we did 'This Diamond Ring' on the Ed Sullivan show—that was the most remarkable experience of my whole life! First, it was the Ed Sullivan show. Then, my dad was booked on that same show also. And then, here we were doing this [brand new] tune. I didn't know if it was going to be a hit or not. We loved the song, and we were so excited to be doing the Ed Sullivan show. My dad was telling me that entertainers worked ten and twenty years to be able to get on the Ed Sullivan show. And here I was, the very first record, on the Ed Sullivan show."

Was Gary nervous? "Oh, jeeze! Yes, I was *so* nervous! And you know, they would do dress rehearsals and actually have an audience. And when Ed introduced us, he said, 'And now, ladies and gentlemen, Jerry Lewis's son's combo!'

"I thought, What! What are you talking about? What about the Playboys? What about Gary's own identity? What about the records they hope people will buy under that name? Imagine going to record stores and asking for the record by Jerry Lewis's son's combo!"

Gary had to go to Ed after the break and correct him. "I wish I had a tape of that incident."

"After that 'This Diamond Ring' went so great [as a hit] that Ed had us on four more times on the four tunes that followed it. That is the most remarkable experience for me, doing Ed Sullivan five times with the first five records."

What about Gary Lewis and the Playboys on "American Bandstand"? "That is one of the shows that I never did in my entire career. 'American Bandstand,' never on that show. That is very interesting. We must have been very busy or something!" People always talk about how everybody in rock 'n' roll was on "Bandstand" except the big two, Ricky Nelson and Elvis Presley. To that list we can add Gary Lewis. "I know we didn't do it."

Gary did do other shows that Dick Clark hosted, such as the Sands Hotel in Vegas main room with Del Shannon and the Mamas and Papas in a 1988 oldies show. But during that show, all of a sudden the music stopped in the middle of Gary's singing. "I turned as if to say to the band, 'What the hell are you doin'?' And here is my dad, walking out on stage." He was playing nearby, and came on stage and hugged and kissed Gary, driving the crowd wild. Was Gary's dad proud of him? "Oh, yeah. He always said, 'I don't care what you do with your life as long as you give it one hundred percent and love it with all your heart.' He never encouraged or discouraged me to do anything. And I am really glad of that; there was no pressure to be anything."

"This Diamond Ring" has two flip sides. Why? "The first flip side was 'Hard to Find,'" explains Gary Lewis, "a song written by a jazz bass player named Leroy Vinegar. We just liked it. We had been doing it for a long time, we had it down, and it took hardly any kind of studio time. I think we did it in one or two takes. Liberty really liked that kind of session. Snuff went along with it because it took almost no time at all. We already had it down. So that was the B side.

"Then, halfway through 'This Diamond Ring's success, Snuff said, 'You know, 'Diamond Ring' is selling an awful lot. Do you think that we should have something on the B side that we have the writer's rights on?' So we went in and just cut that—piece of crap—that was on there. 'Tijuana Wedding!'" "Tijuana Wedding" is a nondescript instrumental with a big break in the middle, where an echo-laden Hispanic voice speaks in Spanish for a very long time. Who does the Spanish on that record? "You know, I have no idea. I wonder if it was listed in the musicians' book that way: 'Spanish-speaking person.' I don't have any idea who did that, but that was the reason. Snuff said, 'This Diamond Ring' is sellin' an awful lot.'"

What does Gary Lewis have to say about the case of Bobby Vee's turning down or not turning down "This Diamond Ring"? "You know, Bobby swears to me that never happened. But that is exactly what Snuff Garrett told me. He said, 'Now this is a great song. Listen to this, this is a great tune. I don't know why Bobby doesn't want to do this one.'

"It's weird, I remember it as plain as day! But when I have played with Bobby, he has told me that it just is not true. He says he would have done that song in a minute!"

It may be weird, but it's not half as weird as the flip side of Gary Lewis's 1965 hit, "Everybody Loves a Clown." This song, "Time Stands Still," which Gary and Leon wrote, starts out innocently enough. But two-thirds of the way through this two-minute record, Gary begins "singing" like his comedian dad, Jerry Lewis. Not in the singing voice Jerry used in his 1950s hit "Rock-a-Bye Your Baby," but in this

Gary Lewis and his producer, the legendary Snuff Garrett.

comedic, nasal, wobbly voice! From that point on the record is a riot! Many fans, including myself, truly enjoy the song.

Can Gary Lewis fathom anyone's really liking "Time Stands Still?"

"Oh, now, come on! We actually cut that song as a birthday present for my dad one year! And it wasn't supposed to be on anything! It was a joke, a gag present for my dad on his birthday. Then, boom! Here it is on the flip side of 'Everybody Loves a Clown.' And here it is on *Golden Greats*! I'm not really unhappy about it, because I have writer's rights on that. So that's OK. But when people *request* that, I cringe—'No!'" But who better to do an impression of Jerry Lewis than his son? After all, who has not been mistaken for his dad at one time or another? "It did work. I will admit that."

Jan & Dean

Jan & Dean's hit-single output fell by about 50 percent in 1965 compared to 1964. Not that four hits is slouching around. First they came out with "(Here They Come) From All Over the World" (the theme from the *TAMI Show*). The *TAMI Show* was a videotaped "movie" shot live at the Santa Monica Civic Auditorium and

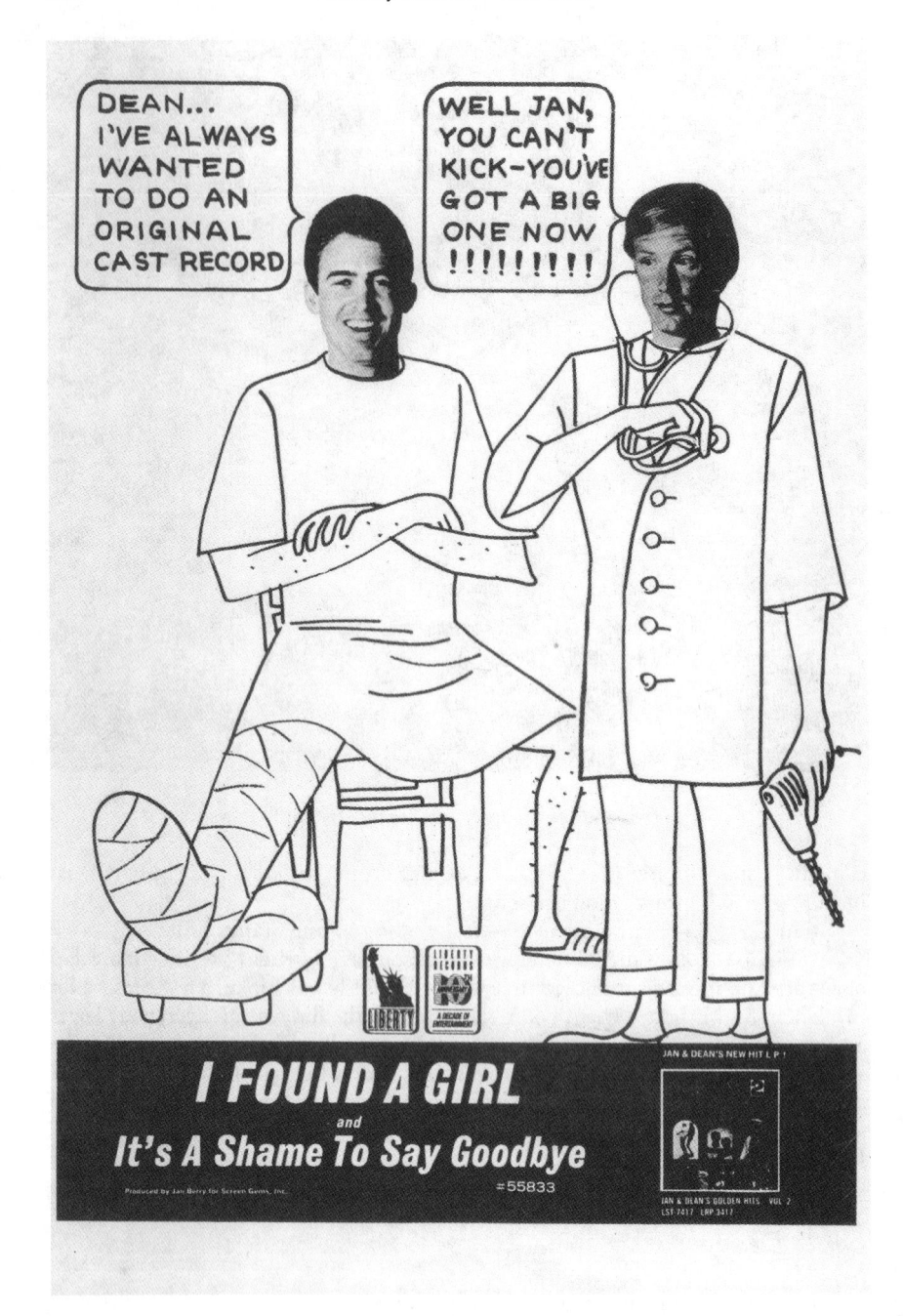

Above: This Jan & Dean trade ad correctly showed Jan in a cast but incorrectly portrayed Dean as the medico. Jan was the medical student; Dean was a commercial design student. *Opposite:* Jan & Dean illustrated this 45 by visiting the Hollywood Wax Museum.

JAN & DEAN
#55792 *LIBERTY*

YOU REALLY KNOW HOW TO HURT A GUY

JAN & DEAN
#55792 *LIBERTY*

YOU REALLY KNOW HOW TO HURT A GUY

Photographs taken at Tussaud's Hollywood Wax Museum Hollywood, California

shown in movie houses around the world. Almost every important act (it seemed) was on the bill: Lesley Gore, Billy J. Kramer with the Dakotas, Marvin Gaye, the Barbarians, the Beach Boys, James Brown, the Supremes, Smokey Robinson and the Miracles, Gerry and the Pacemakers, the Blossoms, Chuck Berry, and as hosts-performers, Jan & Dean, who also sang the title music. All these artists were represented in Jan & Dean's hit 45 "From All Over the World."

When that record was released, it marked the end of Jan & Dean's surf hits like "Surf City" and sound-effects-laden drag songs like "Dead Man's Curve" and the beginning of their shift to more prosaic topics. Well, almost. The flip side of the *TAMI* theme 45 was called "Freeway Flyer," all about traffic cops who have quotas on the number of speeders they cite each day. The record ends, however, with a police siren and a car crash, presumably the cop totaling his pursuit vehicle. Although this side of the 45 was not a national hit, it did make many local charts across the country.

Liberty national LP sales manager Lee Mendel saw Jan & Dean around Liberty. "Jan used to do silly things, like walking into doors, as a joke. He was just a big good-natured guy who had a good time, lived a good life, and drove a Corvette."

Yeah, Jan & Dean were fun-loving and unpredictable. For years, they had done novelty tunes and up-tempo records. Now, next up for Jan & Dean was a change of pace for them, a slow, lovesick song, "You Really Know How to Hurt a Guy." Were Jan & Dean going soft? Well, not exactly. Dean refused to sing on it and went down the hall to sing lead with Brian Wilson on the Beach Boys' version of "Barbara Ann." And the picture sleeve for "You Really Know How to Hurt a Guy" had a picture, a different one on each side, of people being tortured. "You Really Know How to Hurt a Guy"—get it? Well, the pictures were taken in a wax museum and done for laughs.

Dean did not laugh when "Barbara Ann" became a #1 hit. He had been promised a gold record, which he did not get. And he had been forbidden by Liberty to sing on Beach Boys records, so when on the long, LP version of "Barbara Ann," one of the boys said, "Thanks, Dean," Dean experienced some nervous moments. He had been warned about appearing on other labels' records by some of the suits at Liberty.

Some twenty-six years later, Si Waronker pooh-poohs Dean's worries. "I don't think that anybody would have cared. We were pretty easygoing when it came to that kind of stuff." That is pretty easy for Si to say—he wasn't even in the company anymore by 1965!

The next Jan & Dean hit of the year was written by the Sloan-Barri team, as the *TAMI Show* theme had been. Called "I Found a Girl," it was a catchy top-forty tune, with Dean again abstaining and Phil Sloan singing the falsetto parts usually taken by Dean.

Jan was in medical school at this time, which is the only possible explanation for his writing about what he did for their next "hit." "A Beginning from an End" was about a woman dying in childbirth while her husband waits in the hospital corridor. The record is eerily effective, but hardly top-forty teen material in the middle of the mop-topped British invasion! Released around Christmas 1965, the single only reached #109 on the *Billboard* charts. Jan learned a lesson from the poor sales of this record and turned over an old leaf the next year, releasing much lighter material.

Chapter 13 · 1965   233

JAN & DEAN '66
A BEGINNING FROM AN END
& FOLK CITY   #55849

...a big new single for a big new year!

Released by trade demand from their current hit LP "FOLK 'N ROLL" · LST-7431/LRP-3431

More things are happening at Liberty

Produced by Jan Berry for Screen Gems, Inc.

This was one of the few sixties singles, if not the only one, to deal with dying during childbirth.

An interesting side note is that the trade ads for "A Beginning from an End" stated that it was released from their current Liberty LP, *Folk 'n' Roll,* by public demand. The entire LP was uncharateristic for Jan & Dean. As indicated by the title, it was full of folky tunes, Dylan's "It Ain't Me, Babe," a recent hit by Jan & Dean's friends, the Turtles (White Whale Records); the Beatles' "Yesterday"; and Pete Seeger's "Turn! Turn! Turn!" currently a hit by the Byrds. At three minutes, twenty-nine seconds, the latter song was one of the longest cuts Jan ever produced. The folk influence was probably from Phil Sloan of the Sloan and Barri team, who had been writing and singing for Jan & Dean for some time. Phil had just changed his name

This is the Jan & Dean album the duo was working on when Jan had his wreck; it was mutated and released against Dean's wishes.

to "P. F. Sloan" and begun to release folk songs on Lou Adler's Dunhill Records, and he contributed three of the compositions for this album.

The album cover of *Filet of Soul* shows Jan's left leg in a cast. Earlier in the year Jan & Dean had been filming scenes for the feature film *Jan & Dean Go Wild*, when two trains they were using for a scene collided. Dean had been on the train flatcar with the camera crew for earlier takes but had gotten off for the final take. Jan didn't get off and nearly died in the collision that followed. The entire location crew was injured, so Jan had to take care of himself. Luckily he remained conscious and using his medical training, was able to pinch off an exposed artery in his own leg that was spurting blood. Then, continuing to hold the artery, he walked to a highway and hitchhiked to a hospital.

No movie career for Jan & Dean.

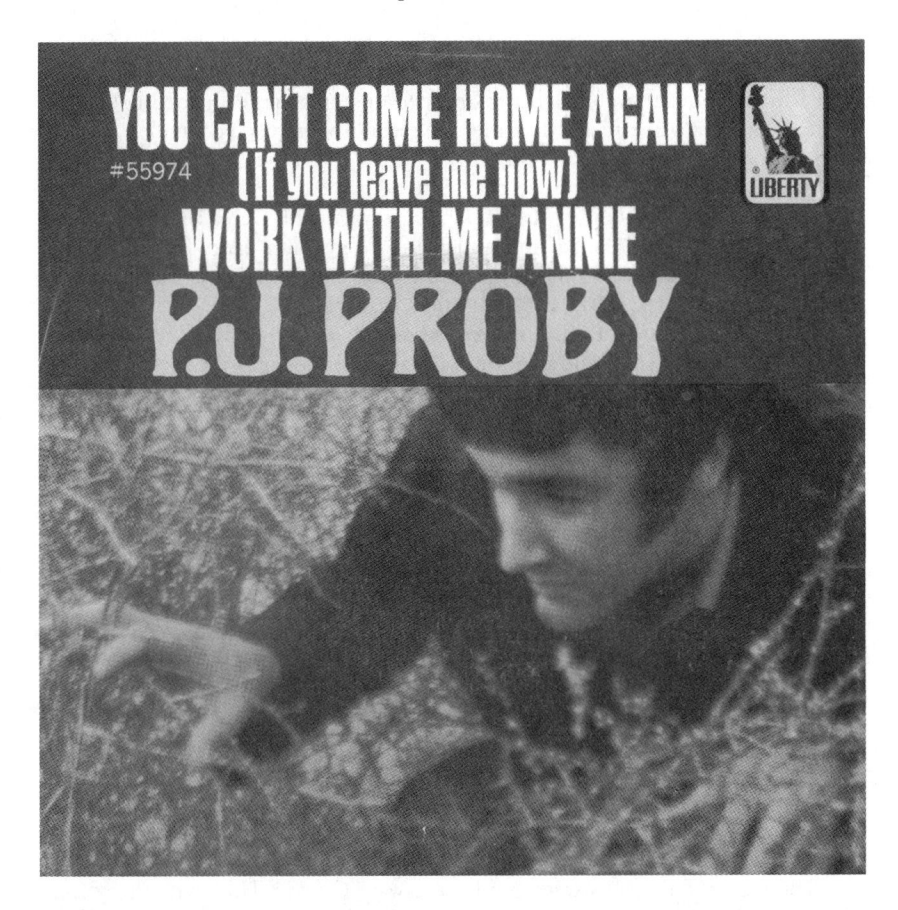

Texan P. J. Proby had so many more Liberty hits in England than in the United States that he moved to England permanently.

P. J. Proby

P. J. Proby was the next of the new Liberty artists to appear in 1965. Proby was thought by many to be British, but he wasn't. And there is no way to tell what P. J. stood for, since his name was James Marcus Smith. However, he did spend time recording in California under the pseudonym Jet Powers, so perhaps.... Anyway, this Texan managed to become a semiregular on ABC-TV's 1964–66 weekly rock 'n' roll showcase, "Shindig" ("Shindig" had no true regulars, just a host and artists who turned up either once, twice, or semiregularly). Being on "Shindig" didn't help Proby to score any U.S. hits, but it did get him an airline ticket to England, courtesy of "Shindig"'s producer.

In England Proby's success hinged mostly on his Elvis imitation, which he was quite capable of doing—one of his pastimes while in California had been cutting demonstration records for Elvis. Proby started off on Decca Records, but after two top-ten discs, he switched somewhat involuntarily to Liberty. There followed a string of nine top-forty British hits, making him something of a superstar in England.

Why the move from one label to another? It seems that P. J. tried to split his loyalty—between a British and an American record company. Lee Mendel, who ran Liberty's International Division, caught the scam. "P. J. Proby signed with Liberty, then went to England and decided that since he had left the continent, it was OK to abrogate his Liberty contract. In England he signed with Decca UK and had two enormous hits. Then we sued him and Decca to get him back. He was uncontrollable, and he blew an enormously promising career. Martin Davis ran Liberty UK after Bob Reisdorff left. He was P. J. Proby's manager."

It was ironic that while the United States was so mesmerized by the British groups, an American male solo artist captured the attention of British youth. Proby's style was very wild, and on one occasion while onstage, he accidentally ripped his pants, which he wore skin tight. The reaction to the pants splitting was great—much like the U.S. reaction to Elvis's swivel hips or the Beatles' mop-tops. Thereafter P. J. Proby's pants seemed to split with predictable regularity while he was performing onstage! P. J. had just two U.S. records on Liberty show chart action. The second and most successful, "Niki Hokey," made the top thirty in 1967. In spite of not having any real U.S. hits to speak of, with that many British recordings, Liberty did manage to squeeze out a P. J. Proby LP or two—or four!

P. J.'s first Liberty U.S. single, "Somewhere" (from *West Side Story*) had been in February 1965. His poor showing was hardly noticed by Liberty's accounting department, since Gary Lewis was filling the coffers so well by himself.

In September Liberty signed up a new American band, the Gants. The Gants had an exciting rock 'n' roll band sound and hit the charts that month with "Road Runner" (Bo Diddley, 1960). The record was very powerful and fit into both the British band and American surf and drag trends. Unfortunately it failed to make the top forty. It was up to Jan & Dean and Gary Lewis, with assistance from Bobby Vee, to keep Liberty's light shining in 1965.

The Gants' follow-ups were good. One was "Crackin' Up," written by Elias McDaniel (aka Bo Diddley), who had written "Road Runner." Another was a hard-rock version of Johnny Burnette's old Liberty standard, "Little Boy Sad" (1961). Neither record made the top one hundred. The Gants' four LPs included *Road Runner, Gants Galore,* and *Gants Again* and featured oldies like "Stormy Weather," newies like "Gloria," and British sounds like "Yesterday."

T-Bones

Liberty's last new hit artist for 1965 was the band called the T-Bones, who had recorded "Rail Vette" and other hot-rod tunes a year earlier. A popular TV commercial of 1965 was an Alka-Seltzer ad that featured a series of shots of stomachs, ranging from a bodybuilder's to a businessman's. On the ad's soundtrack there was a catchy guitar instrumental. The current Alka-Seltzer slogan was "No Matter What Shape Your Stomach's In," so the T-Bones single was called "No Matter What Shape," the same instrumental as heard in the ad. The record made the top five, which was a lot better than P. J. Proby or the Gants had done. The T-Bones' follow-up, "Sittin' and Chirpin'," flopped.

The T-Bones had only four LPs, *No Matter What Shape,* then *Sittin' and Chirpin',* also *Doin' the Jerk* and, last, *Everyone's Gone to the Moon (and Other Trips).*

Also-Rans

Liberty had several also-rans of note in 1965. There was Wendy Hill's cute Liberty 45 "(Gary, Please Don't Sell) My Diamond Ring," which failed to catch on. She also recorded "Donna, Leave My Guy Alone," a British-flavored single in a nasal voice totally unlike her singing on "My Diamond Ring."

Sometime later, in 1966, a group called the Bobby Fuller 4 had a big hit with "I Fought the Law" and also had "Love's Made a Fool of You" (both old Crickets' LP cuts) on Mustang Records. But in August 1965, Bobby Fuller, another Buddy Holly soundalike, released "Let Her Dance" on Liberty, without success.

Totally feminine was Carole Shelyne, a young actress and singer, sort of, who turned up in a variety of movies and TV shows in the mid-sixties. She was easily identifiable by her trademark blond hair and large, horn-rimmed glasses. Her record: "Boys Do Make Passes at Girls Who Wear Glasses" b/w "The Girl with the Horn-Rimmed Glasses." While she and her songs had a certain amount of charm, and her gimmick was good, her voice seemed shallow and had little appeal.

The venerable Chipmunks raised their tiny heads again in 1965. The British Herman's Hermits had recorded for a British LP an album cut titled "I'm Henry the VIII, I Am." The song was a heavily [Cockney] accented, novelty filler. The leader, Herman (aka Peter Noone), could not even remember any of the verses except the first one, which he repeated, saying, "second verse, same as the first." The song was not released as a 45 in England. But it was a huge U.S. hit, and within weeks after it appeared on the U.S. MGM label, Ross Bagdasarian was back in the studio with his alter egos Simon, Theodore, and Alvin, plus David Seville. The magic must have been gone, although an accompanying LP, *Chipmunks a Go-Go,* did appear, naturally.

In the final weeks of 1965, Ken Dodd with Geoff Lowe and his Orchestra released "Tears (for Souvenirs)," and the Deep Six tried with "Rising Sun," but neither had any hits.

An interesting record that did not spark any interest when it arrived the first week of December 1965 was "Dick Tracy," produced and arranged by the team of Snuff Garrett and Leon Russell. The song was a sparsely arranged hillbilly-flavored ditty about the comic strip cop Dick Tracy and his sidekick, Pat, and his sweetie, Tess. The artist was J. J. Cale. Snuff remembers that "J. J. Cale had the song 'After Midnight' in 1972 on Shelter Records, that was originally on Liberty."

"Japanese Sandman," an odd record, sounded vaguely Oriental and sung in falsetto by Johnny Hunter in a way that Tiny Tim would later. Johnny sang the flip side in a style resembling Frankie Laine's, "If the Things in My Room Could Talk." It seems the bureau and the floor and the bed have seen him sadly tossing and turning, distressed over losing his love. It was almost a derivative of "Hello Walls."

A British Liberty also-ran was by the Sounds, Incorporated, a sax-led instrumental combo that had two hits in England in 1964. "In the Hall of the Mountain King" was played for rock with an ever-increasing pace as the tune developed. "Time for You" on the other side was a ho-hum guitar number.

LIBERTY ENTERTAINMENT IS FOR EVERYONE!

Judging from this mid-sixties graphic, Liberty either sold Frisbees or they sold records.

LPs

Catching up on a few of Liberty's other LPs of the time, Liberty commemorated the 1964 death of Johnny Burnette (last hit in 1961), and perhaps cashed in on the attendant publicity, with *The Johnny Burnette Story*. David Seville had the *Chipmunks Sing the Beatles*. Bobby Vee went *Live on Tour* and sang medleys of *30 Big Hits of the '60s*. This last LP was very interesting, and was another idea of Snuff's (who else?).

"*Thirty Big Hits of the 1960s* was my idea. Anything I worked on was basically my idea, because I worked really hard and all the time." Bobby was in a slump hit-wise, so the concept album of a medley of other people's hits was a master stroke. Thirty hits, male, female, fast, slow, ballads, and rockers were selected, arranged, and strung together in medleys of five songs each. The medleys worked amazingly well, due in equal parts to Bobby's voice and talent, Snuff's production, and Ernie Freeman's arrangements. Sticking five disparate songs together seamlessly is no easy task. For example, the first medley on side one consisted of Andy Williams's "A Fool Never Learns" (1964), the Beatles' "Do You Want to Know a Secret" (1963–64), James Darren's "Goodbye, Cruel World" (1962), Eydie Gorme's "Blame It on the Bossa Nova" (1963), and the Four Seasons' "Dawn" (1964). Probably no other singer since rock 'n' roll began, other than Bobby Vee, could carry off a trick like that and make all the songs sound like his own!

The Standells had a hit on Tower Records with "Dirty Water." Prior to this hit, the LP-mad moguls at Liberty had gotten the Standells for a fine LP, *In Person at P. J.'s*, with great live versions of "Louie, Louie" (Kingsmen, 1963), "Ooh Poo Pah Doo" (Jessie Hill, 1960) and "You Can't Do That" (Beatles, 1964). Listening to this LP today takes one back to the day of the 1960s when every local high school had a band that played at weekend dances.

Bud and Travis, Martin Denny, Si Zentner, Spike Jones, Matt Monro, Vikki Carr, Nancy Ames, and, of course, Julie London each had two or three or more Liberty LPs in 1965. Besides *Folk 'n Roll,* Jan & Dean had *Command Performance — Live in Person* with live versions of Beach Boys, Everly Brothers, Beatles, and Jan & Dean songs, including songs Jan & Dean performed in the *TAMI Show* movie in 1965.

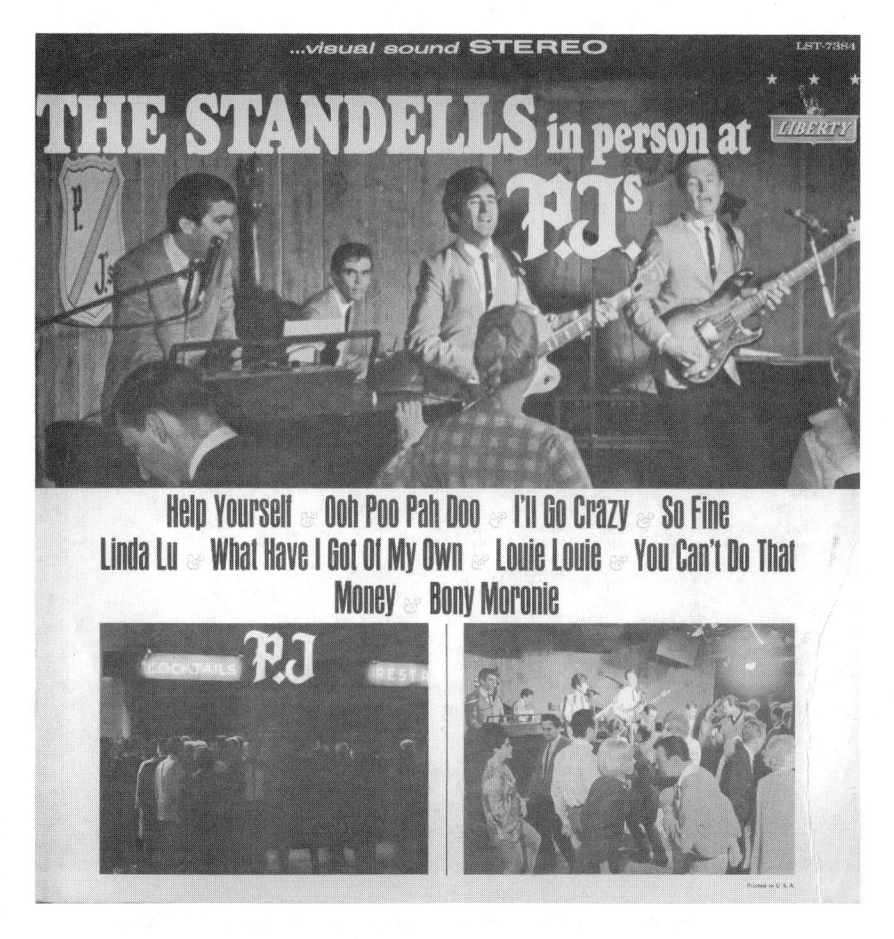

If anyone wants to know what it sounded like to dance to a live band in the sixties, the Standells' Liberty album is just the ticket.

Jan Berry had been paying close attention for years to Si Waronker's Liberty orchestra approach to rock 'n' roll. In 1965 Jan personally arranged, conducted, and cut twelve of Jan & Dean's biggest hits with a full orchestra for *Jan & Dean's Pop Symphony No. 1*. Jan was studying both medicine and music at college, and he did an excellent job of emulating Beethoven, Mozart and others on this LP; selections were actually played on the air by classical radio stations around the country. To sell even more LPs, *Jan & Dean's Golden Hits Volume 2* was issued. Unlike their original Liberty LP, *Golden Hits,* this one actually included hits! Twelve Jan & Dean hits, including one #1, five top-ten, and five top-forty chart songs.

The Liberty orchestra was used by Jan & Dean regularly, and not just for *Pop Symphony*. Jan & Dean's singles like "Dead Man's Curve" and "Sidewalk Surfin'" used a French horn and a harp, and tracks on LPs such as *The Little Old Lady (from Pasadena)* spotlighted instruments like the oboe, bassoon, harp, harpsichord, and other instruments that — not usually associated with rock 'n' roll — were, in fact, used

If anyone wants to know exactly what it sounded like to attend a Jan & Dean concert in the sixties, the *Command Performance* Liberty album is as close as you can get to it.

on many, many hits. The Liberty orchestra, as hand picked in modified form by Jan Berry, included many well-known session men and jazz musicians. Besides Earl Palmer and Hal Blaine on drums, there were Emil Richards, percussion; Bill Pitman, bass guitar; Tommy Tedesco, rhythm guitar; Gene Cipriano, woodwinds; James Getzoff and Sid Sharp, violins; Tony Terran and Cappy Lewis, trumpets; Bill Hinshaw and Vince DeRosa, French horns, and others.

At Liberty even the session musicians got to make LPs! Earl Palmer's drums LP has already been mentioned. Trumpeter Tony Terran had his own LP on Imperial, *The Song's Been Sung*, full of rock 'n' roll hits like "Volare" (Dean Martin and Domenico Modugno, 1958; Bobby Rydell, 1960), "Jambalaya" (Brenda Lee, 1956), and "The Lion Sleeps Tonight" (Tokens, 1962). Guitarist Tommy Tedesco had three Imperial LPs, including *The Guitars of Tom Tedesco*.

One of the things that made Jan & Dean records so exciting was the fact that the world's greatest rock 'n' roll session drummer played on all of Jan and Dean's records. His name was Hal Blaine.

JAN & DEAN GOLDEN HITS VOLUME 2

LINDA · SURF CITY · HONOLULU LULU · DRAG CITY · DEAD MAN'S CURVE
THE NEW GIRL IN SCHOOL · THE LITTLE OLD LADY FROM PASADENA · THE ANAHEIM, AZUSA
AND CUCAMONGA SEWING CIRCLE, BOOK REVIEW AND TIMING ASSOCIATION · RIDE THE WILD SURF
SIDEWALK SURFIN' · FROM ALL OVER THE WORLD · YOU REALLY KNOW HOW TO HURT A GUY

How many artists in the mid-sixties had scored enough hits to fill an entire album? Dean wrote the liner notes, which show his personal style of humor.

Hal Blaine

In 1991 Hal Blaine came out with a great book called *The Wrecking Crew*. The book chronicles the personal life of the author and also tells many stories about artists including Jan & Dean and the Beach Boys. The title of this autobiography refers to the group of session musicians who played background on innumerable hit records including a great many Liberty records, in the 1960s. These young musicians were called the Wrecking Crew by the older musicians, who did not understand the new music, the new ways of playing, or the new ways of recording.

The Wrecking Crew, as featured on countless Liberty records, included electric bass—Carol Kaye, Ray Pohlman; string bass—Lyle Ritz, Jimmy Bond; guitars—Tommy Tedesco, Barney Kessel, Howard Roberts, Glen Campbell, Bill Pitman; piano—Larry Knechtel, Al Delory, Michael Melvoin, Don Randi, and Leon Russell.

"I got involved with Liberty through Jan & Dean in the very early 1960s, right

Famed session drummer Hal Blaine had a special set he used for Jan & Dean concerts. *(Courtesy Lloyd Hicks.)*

after their first Liberty record, when Lou Adler got them their deal. I believe I was on 'Linda.'

"The Wrecking Crew was such a big part of Liberty Records. We did so many of their records, the whole Liberty stable. I was never contracted to them; I was just that busy drummer that got so lucky in LA. And that all seemed to start with Jan & Dean. Before Jan I was working with Johnny Rivers and a bunch of people at Liberty, or Imperial."

It has been said that Hal Blaine stipulated to producers that he get a gold record if a session he worked on produced a million seller. "There was no stipulation. I just used to tell the producers, in a nice way, 'Gosh, if this is a hit record, I'd sure love a gold record!' and they'd always say, 'OK, you got it, man!' knowing we'd all bust our butts to make it a hit record! Of the three hundred sixty-five songs I did that were top-fifty records, about a hundred and four or a hundred and five came through gold. There were forty-one number ones, two hundred and some top-forties. There were over three thousand that were top one hundred. It was quite a career to me!"

In *The Wrecking Crew* Hal listed all of the top-ten hits he played on. Top-ten Liberty family records included:

1963
"Surf City" (Jan & Dean, Liberty)
"Drag City" (Jan & Dean, Liberty)
"The Night Has 1,000 Eyes" (Bobby Vee, Liberty)

1964
"Dead Man's Curve" (Jan & Dean, Liberty)
"Little Old Lady (from Pasadena)" (Jan & Dean, Liberty)
"Mountain of Love" (Johnny Rivers, Imperial)
"Out of Limits" (Marketts, Liberty)

1965
"This Diamond Ring" (Gary Lewis and the Playboys, Liberty)
"Count Me In" (Gary Lewis and the Playboys, Liberty)
"Everybody Loves a Clown" (Gary Lewis and the Playboys, Liberty)
"Red Roses for a Blue Lady" (Vic Dana, Dolton)
"Save Your Heart for Me" (Gary Lewis and the Playboys, Liberty)
"Seventh Son" (Johnny Rivers, Imperial)

1966
"Elusive Butterfly" (Bob Lind, World Pacific)
"No Matter What Shape" (T-Bones, Liberty)
"Poor Side of Town" (Johnny Rivers, Imperial)
"She's Just My Style" (Gary Lewis and the Playboys, Liberty)
"Sure Gonna Miss Her" (Gary Lewis and the Playboys, Liberty)

1967
"Baby, I Need Your Lovin'" (Johnny Rivers, Imperial)
"Come Back When You Grow Up" (Bobby Vee, Liberty)
"Tracks of My Tears" (Johnny Rivers, Imperial)
"Up, Up and Away" (5th Dimension, Soul City)

1969
"Aquarius/Let the Sun Shine In" (5th Dimension, Soul City)
"Wedding Bell Blues" (5th Dimension, Soul City)

This impressive list is only top-ten hits on Liberty. There were many, many others that were top forty or top one hundred, plus hundreds of album cuts by Liberty artists including Gene McDaniels, Timi Yuro, the Johnny Mann Singers, Jackie DeShannon, Johnny Burnette, Dick and Deedee, the Rivingtons, the Ventures, and many more. Outside of Liberty, Hal Blaine was the drummer for the Baja Marimba Band and the original drummer on the Tijuana Brass records.

"'You Really Know How to Hurt a Guy' by Jan & Dean was a song I played on." There was a lot of "You've Lost That Lovin' Feelin'" drums on that record!

"I never worked on the Chipmunks or Martin Denny. I did work with Kathy Rich and World Pacific Records with Bud Dain.

"One of the owners of Liberty lived up the street from me," recalls Hal Blaine. "There was a very tragic story; he was divorced. He had a young daughter, around ten, he took her oddly enough to Palm Springs one weekend, and they went horseback riding. The poor child fell off a horse, hit her head, and died. One of the real tragedies in our neighborhood.

"Jan & Dean, I did all of their records. They always had two drummers side by side, Earl Palmer and myself. Earl Palmer today is the secretary/treasurer of Union number forty-seven in LA. Those were the only records that I ever worked with two

These pictures show Jan conducting the orchestra for Jan & Dean's *Pop Symphony* album.

drummers except for later on, occasionally. And very late, the John Lennon album with Jim Keltner; we did dual drums."

On a Jan & Dean record, Hal would play a different little fill or bit at the end of each line of the song. It made the records very striking. "Yes, well we always wrote those things out. Purposely. Then Earl and I would match them. I had a lot of freedom with everyone I worked with. I would usually write those parts out, then Earl would write out identically what I wrote and then we would play them in unison, exactly one drum to another. And that is why they came out so good!"

"Drag City" sounds like one of the songs with dual drums, because the record comes across so powerfully. "Definitely, definitely. They'd put one drum right and the other left in the mix, and then both down the middle."

Did Hal have names for those little fills? "No, not really. We just wrote them. A lot of people did not know that we were schooled musicians. I could write out anything so anyone could play it. A lot of planning went into those sessions."

Much of the Wrecking Crew was used on Jan & Dean's *Pop Symphony* LP, as it had been on many of the original hits. "*Pop Symphony* was great fun." The drums bridged the gap between rock 'n' roll and classical sound.

"In the winter of 1990-1991, Jan & Dean had kind of a reunion down at the Golden Bull down near Huntington Beach. I went down and played a whole set with them. And then they got me up for the finale. It was really fun. It was really super. I was really close to Jan & Dean; I traveled with them and used to hang with them an awful lot. They were just terrific kids. Jan calls every once in a while, we talk, the best he can.

"I was Snuff Garrett's drummer. I did Gary Lewis and the Playboys; I worked on his father's things, so it was like a family thing. And I did Bobby Vee, Johnny Burnette, Dick and Deedee, the Rivingtons, the Ventures. I know that I did every record Gary Lewis ever did. Ron Hicklin did the vocal arrangements and sang background. I don't think anyone ever knew that, or even knows it today.

"Ron Hicklin was one of the great studio singers. He could sing higher than anybody. And he could match anybody's voice. For years, whenever we'd go into a Beach Boys session, I mean a soundalike, Orange Crush or some product where they wanted a Beach Boys sound, they always hired Ron Hicklin. Ron, and Tom and John Baylor, the Baylor Brothers, very big producers in LA today, they could match anything vocally. It was beautiful.

"I was Phil Spector's drummer. I was on everything Phil Spector ever did." Hal Blaine always brought a box of goodies to recording sessions—bells, clackers, castanets, maracas, noisemakers of every type. He might end up using these on a session. Or at other times, studio groupies might be allowed by a producer like Phil Spector to "play" one of these noisemakers on a session. For example, long before Cher became a famous Liberty/Imperial artist, she made noises with Hal's toys on Phil Spector sessions.

Did Hal know a hit when he was playing it? "A lot of times you'd be thinking, Is this record even worth cutting? Then, next thing you know, it is top ten. And everybody is happy about it, of course!"

"Orchestra Conducted by Hal Blaine." That was the legend on the Jan & Dean live *Command Performance* LP. Jan & Dean rerecorded the vocals for this LP in the studio, blending them with the crowd noises from the actual concert. "With Jan & Dean, a lot of times when they did overdubs, I'd conduct the overdubs. The orchestra would come in and overdub their horns and strings. They were usually written by George Allison Tipton, a very fine writer, who does all of those soaps and other shows. He'd be in the booth, to get the proper sound mix, and then they'd let me conduct, because I knew the arrangement. Also I'd go on the road occasionally with Jan & Dean. I was very close to the guys. I had some Jan & Dean drums prepared for those shows."

Besides his session work on Liberty, Hal had his own releases on RCA, such as "The Drummer Plays for Me," a 45 on RCA by Hal Blaine and the Young Cougars. "When RCA first signed me, Lee Hazelwood was producing, and we made a lot of surf records, hot-rod records, that was the 'theme of the day.' It was the same Wrecking Crew on those records—Glen Campbell playing guitar, Leon Russell on piano, Billy Strange. The 'Young Cougars' was just a made-up name. The female voices were the Blossoms, the same gals who did everybody's work. They did all the Phil Spector work, you know: They were the Crystals and the Ronettes and they were everybody. They definitely sang on a lot of Liberty records. Grace has died; I don't know where Fanita James is; Darlene Love has done movies."

Hal also had an LP on the Dunhill label. "*Drums A Go-Go,* my LP on Dunhill Records, was a fun project."

How did a typical Jan & Dean session go? "Jan & Dean would do a basic track, then they would overdub whatever they wanted. It made a difference for the union. You had to identify it as a 'tracking session.' And then for that everyone got an extra ten dollars. It was not a great deal of money, and it did not last very long. The reason that came in was that often [before multi-track recording was an option], a producer would call a session, and then had to give twenty-four hours' notice if they wanted to cancel the session. But sometimes the cancel call would come only an hour before the session, and they would say it was because the singer was ill or on the road or the plane didn't make it or something. Then all the session musicians were out that work. Maybe some had been holding that slot open for two weeks or even a month. Then, later, when they could track, they didn't need a singer present; they could do tracks. That was a way we could get around their canceling a session at the last minute.

"By the same token, what would happen was the guys would make tracks, and if the singer did not like the song, they would give the track to some other singer. Liberty or some of the other record companies would actually use the track on somebody else! If the record didn't make it, they'd give it to another artist and come out with it again, make a couple of changes, you know, put some strings on or some horns, make it sound a little different, and another singer might do it as another song entirely. Using the same tracks. So that was when they decided to disallow tracking, because it got out of hand. They said if someone wanted to track, they had to pay a penalty, an extra ten dollars a man. The union had an anonymous hot line. If you did a session and the singer was not there, then you reported it to the union. Then if they did not pay the tracking bonus, the union would jump on them and see that they did. It was pretty silly, it lasted for a year or maybe less than a year. Then they canceled the whole thing.

"I overdubbed an album, *Hear the Beatles Tell All,* for Vee Jay Records, of Beatles interviews."

Back in the early 1960s, few people knew or cared who session musicians, let alone drummers, were. Would the name *Hal Blaine* be better known today, if this were his heyday? "We were sort of the forefathers of kids knowing session players' names. Producers started putting our names on albums. They found it was valuable to put our names on those things. Producers like Bones Howe started insisting that we be given credit. Also background singers, he would see that they had credit. They never got credit before."

The names *Bones* and *Lanky* were listed (along with, at times, Wally Heider, Chuck Britz, and Joe and Henry) as the engineers on Liberty LPs, including Jan & Dean's. "Bones Howe was a graduate electrical engineer. Lanky was the head engineer on the thing, and Bones was kind of the assistant engineer. Didn't take Bones long to become a producer.

"The Routers ["Sting Ray" on Warner's Records] was Joe Saraceno producing. It was session people; I was on those records. We also did the Liberty record 'No Matter What Shape Your Stomach's In' by T-Bones with him. And the Marketts on Liberty, 'Outer Limits.'" Dime stores used to sell "hit 45s," cheap copies of big hit records. "We used to do those; that was some of our basic training. It was possible for the same people to be on the real record and the copy. I just did them in the early days."

Obviously Hal Blaine has no respect for drum machines. But how about today's new, young, live rock drummers? "The kid drummers today don't know what dynamics mean. They just play as hard as they can."

Other Snuff Garrett Productions

About the same time that Jan was producing Hal Blaine and the Wrecking Crew on the *Pop Symphony* project, Snuff Garrett produced *The Roy Orbison Songbook*. Arranged and conducted by Nick De Caro, this LP had instrumental renditions of twelve of Orbison's biggest records, from his first, "Only the Lonely" (1959), to his #1 smash, "Oh, Pretty Woman" (1964). While *Pop Symphony* was, at the risk of being redundant, symphonic with a Hal Blaine beat, *The Roy Orbison Songbook* was more rock 'n' roll as played by a full orchestra. Both "worked."

Snuff always had big music in his head, no matter what might turn out on the recordings. "The Roy Orbison song album was fun. I also did a Liberty album, *Tommy Garrett's Fifty Guitars*. I always wanted to hear a lot of guitars play like an orchestra, so when I got success, I got to do albums and we started the label called the Liberty Premiere series, and the first album was this wild idea that I had, fifty live guitar players. I was very proud of it, but I thought that 'Snuffy Garrett' didn't have enough class to it, so I called myself Tommy Garrett. Just this morning I was in a meeting with a guy who showed me the *Fifty Guitars* album and said how he'd had it for years and years and how it was one of his and his wife's favorites, and was I maybe related to Tommy Garrett. He freaked out when I told him that was me. About the last thing I did at Liberty was the *Roy Orbison Songbook*. Before that I did *Ballads of the King* with Johnny Mann, Elvis songs, the Sinatra songs, *Ballads of the King, Vol. 2*."

Liberty 1965 LP oddities included the soundtrack of Hollywood's *Genghis Khan*, and an LP by an unknown group, the *Big Beats Live! At the Off Broadway*. Plus, probably as a side effect of so many people at Liberty's having Texan roots, *Mr. President, Speeches of President Lyndon B. Johnson* came out in 1965.

Dolton in 1964

At Dolton there were no new artists in 1965. But veteran Vic Dana had four chart songs, including the top-ten hit "Red Roses for a Blue Lady" and another called "Crystal Chandelier." Vic also had an LP for each of his hits in 1965.

Lee Mendell recalls how Vic might have done even better in 1965, had he opened the door when opportunity knocked one day that year.

"Vic Dana was asked to do a theme for a movie but he didn't have time to do it. So they gave it to Tom Jones. It was 'What's New, Pussycat,' Tom Jones's first big hit. Vic never had a hit that big." Instead, he released "Bring a Little Sunshine," a #66 record.

The Ventures' sole hit was a rocker called "Diamond Head," but they still had a half dozen LPs in 1965, including one called *Play Guitar with the Ventures*. This last LP was the first in a series Dolton called the "Guitar Phonic Series." Eventually there were seven LPs in the series. Each one taught some element of playing the guitar, each folded open with illustrations, and each featured popular instrumentals, such as (volume 1) "Walk, Don't Run" (Ventures, 1960); (volume 2) "Wipe Out" (Surfaris, 1963, 1966); and (volume 3) "No Matter What Shape" (T-Bones, 1965). The songs in volume 3 were those most requested by owners of volumes 1 and 2. Volume 4 taught bass guitar with "La Bamba" (Ritchie Valens, 1959) and other songs. Volume 5 was *Play Country Guitar with Jimmy Bryant,* and volume 6 was *Play Guitar with Chet Atkins.* Chet had inspired the Ventures to cut their first Dolton hit, "Walk, Don't Run." Volume 7 featured the Ventures again, doing "Louie, Louie" (Kingsmen, 1963) and others.

The original Dolton hit makers, the Fleetwoods, had an oddly noteworthy release in 1965. It was a rerelease of their 1959 song "Come Softly to Me" on Dolton 307. The original release was Dolphin no. 1. Around the same time, a stereo version of the song began popping up on stereo LPs.

In fact, all of the post-fifties, stereo releases of the original 1959 "Come Softly to Me" feature bongo drums which were not on the original hit recording. When Gretchen Christopher was asked about these versions, she answered, "As I understand it, they lost or misplaced the original master tape of 'Come Softly to Me.' So they have had to use a second version with bongo drums since then. To me, they sound very different. The minute you put them on, I can tell the difference." Nicely, when Dick Clark released a "Best of Bandstand" videotape with new vocal tracks in the 1980s, he used the original, nonbongo version. Gretchen: "I am glad they used that version. I don't know if someone has since found the original master tape or if they are using a copy. But the CD 'The Best of the Fleetwoods' (Rhino Records, courtesy of Capitol Records) released in nineteen ninety has the original master, so perhaps they have located it."

That all sounds OK. But when I asked Gary Troxel, lead singer on "Come Softly to Me," about it, he said, "I remember when we rerecorded 'Come Softly to Me' [with drums] in the 1960s for a new Dolton release."

Does Bob Reisdorff recall the bongo drum version? No, he has never heard it, and he comments, "They didn't sound too good, I bet. I don't know how they happened to mix up those masters. That was probably a version we thought we had discarded."

Well, the answer is, there are two drum versions of "Come Softly to Me." The first version is the original track with a bongo drum added. As Bob Reisdorff surmised, when instrumentation was added to the Two Girls and a Guy a capella tape in 1959, someone must have tried bongos along with the bass and guitar. That version turns up on stereo albums. But there is also a second version that, as Gretchen said, sounds different from the first instant and, as Gary said, was recorded in the 1960s.

It seems that in 1965, Liberty producer Dick Glasser rounded up the old trio for a new rendition of their first record, "Come Softly to Me." Arranged by Jack Nitzsche, it is a fine updating of the original. It was probably not necessary, but as it had been six years since the first version, relatively few record buyers (young teenagers) were even aware of the original or remembered whom it was by and just exactly what it sounded like.

This promotional copy of the 1965 rerecording of the Fleetwoods' first hit arrived at a radio station on June 9, 1965.

Released in June 1965, as Dolton No. 307, on the new version the vocals were altered slightly, the instrumentation altered more radically. Gary's keys are replaced by a percussion instrument (box? tom-tom? tambourine?) playing the same rhythm, accompanied by a stand-up bass playing the part that was essayed on electric bass in 1959. Instead of starting with Gary's trademark "dum-dums," the bass and percussion start out. The only other instrument is a trumpet (Gary's old instrument of choice) which joins in later.

The vocals are very close to the original, with a slight alteration of rhythm or feeling here and there.

To music historians, this version can present a headache!

Imperial was very active with new artists in 1965. They had to be—of their 1964 American and British additions, only Johnny Rivers was currently having hits. "Midnight Special" was a remake of a 1960 song Paul Evans had made the top twenty with on Guaranteed Records. Evans was a talented songwriter ("When," the Kalin Twins; "Roses Are Red," Bobby Vinton), but "Midnight Special" was a traditional folk song about a railroad train. Johnny's version became the theme for an NBC-TV rock music series, and was a two-sided hit, backed as it was with his commercial remake of Sam Cooke's "Cupid." Johnny Rivers's forte was remakes. His other two hits of the year were "Where Have All the Flowers Gone" (Kingston Trio, 1962) and "Under Your Spell Again," previously released by Lloyd Price ("Stagger Lee," 1958).

Other than Johnny Rivers's success, hitwise, Imperial's older artists, Irma Thomas, the Swinging Blue Jeans, and Billy J. Kramer with the Dakotas, had all faded. And the Hollies had yet to catch on. And, of course, Imperial old-timers like Ricky Nelson were also finally showing some signs of running out of steam, as Ricky had had his thirty-fifth of fifty-three hits in 1965.

Liberty reissued Imperial oldies on a special gold-colored label in its Golden series.

Georgie Fame

New talent was needed. Perhaps because the British acts of 1964 had pretty much been flashes in the old pan, Imperial tried only one Britisher in 1965. Georgie Fame (real name Clive Powel) was quite big in England. He would end up with twelve big hits there, including three #1s. When Imperial picked up his American contract in February 1965, Georgie had just had his first U.K. #1 hit, "Yeh, Yeh." His jazzy, accented delivery of "Yeh, Yeh," a phrase associated with the Beatles, made the song seem to be the epitome of the novel British music. In fact the song had already been a minor U.S. hit in 1963 under the name "Yeh-Yeh!" as the follow up by Mongo Santamaria to the big record "Watermelon Man."

Contrary to popular belief, being British was not enough to guarantee hits in the United States in the mid-sixties. On Imperial "Yeh, Yeh" made it only halfway up the U.S. top forty, and Georgie Fame's other two records, "In the Meantime" and "Get Away" (#1 in England) never even cracked the American top fifty!

Normally a Liberty/Dolton/Imperial artist who had three even medium hits, and who had a ton of recorded material backlogged in England, would have a whole list of LPs released. Apparently Imperial felt burned by the British invasion's failure to deliver the big hits. At any rate, Georgie Fame had just two Imperial LPs, *Yeh, Yeh* and *Get Away*.

It was not unusual for one of the Liberty labels to pick up an artist who had already recorded for another label. Buddy Knox, for example, came from Roulette, and Jan & Dean from Challenge, Doré, and Arwin. In a switcheroo, several years after Georgie Fame left Imperial, he came back for a one-shot top-ten hit, "Bonnie and Clyde," but on Epic Records.

O'Jays

In like fashion the O'Jays were a group who established themselves on Imperial in 1965, then went on to other labels. The O'Jays had formed in the 1950s in Ohio as the Triumphs, and recorded on King Records in 1961 under the name the Mascots. A Cleveland radio announcer named Eddie O'Jay dubbed them the O'Jays, and in 1965 they finally hit the upper reaches of the pop charts with an Imperial release "Lonely Drifter" just before the Liberty takeover. Now, two years later, "Lipstick Traces (on a Cigarette)" did much better, charting at #48, and the group appeared promising. But with their next record, "I've Cried My Last Tear" and the next year's "Stand in for Love" in 1966, the O'Jays were back in the nineties and soon left for Bell Records, Neptune Records, Phil. Int. Records, and eventually TSOP Records, where they had 23 hits including the #1 in 1973, "Love Train." One that got away.

Jimmy McCracklin

An artist who came to Imperial from other labels in 1965 was Jimmy McCracklin. McCracklin was an R&B vocalist, pianist, and harmonica player who was a boxer before he recorded unsuccessfully for Globe Records in 1946, and successfully on Checker ("The Walk," 1958) and Art-Tone Records ("Just Got to Know," 1961). Moving to Imperial, he released a number of 45s, first charting in 1965 with "Every Night, Every Day," and scoring with two quick follow-ups. However, none of these records did better than the nineties on the top one hundred.

Jackie DeShannon

In 1965 something unusual happened involving Jackie DeShannon, who had released Liberty singles in 1963 ("Faded Love" and "Needles and Pins") and 1964 ("When You Walk in the Room"). She had not recorded any big hits, but her forte was really song writing. Her compositions had been hits for Marianne Faithfull ("Come and Stay with Me," 1964), the Searchers ("When You Walk in the Room," 1964) and Brenda Lee ("Dum Dum," 1963), to name three. Jackie also released the expected Liberty LPs.

In May 1965 when Jackie switched from Liberty to the sister label, Imperial, things began to happen for her. Jackie benefited from the fact that Liberty and its subsidiaries never discouraged their artists from getting into the studio and recording as much as they wanted to. Certainly you can't have hits unless you record, and who knows which song may be the right one? Besides, Liberty/Dolton/Imperial had always made money selling LPs by artists who did not do so well on singles.

So, at Imperial, Jackie DeShannon recorded and recorded and recorded. Between 1961 and 1964, Liberty had released sixteen 45s by Jackie DeShannon. In the next six years, she issued 22 more on Imperial. Her extra advantage may have been her marriage to Bud Dain, sales and promotion director for Liberty's World Pacific Records subsidiary.

On the singles front, the switch to Imperial seemed to work for Jackie DeShannon. Her first Imperial 45, "What the World Needs Now Is Love," was her first

This is how Jackie DeShannon appeared, in silhouette, when she had one of her biggest hits, "What the World Needs Now Is Love."

record as a performer (as opposed to a songwriter) to make the top ten! It was featured on her LP *this is Jackie De Shannon* [sic], which pictured her frolicking in the ocean wearing a dress. It was great to have a hit, even if it was written by record producers Hal David and Burt Bacharach instead of by Jackie herself. The song was recorded live, with no overdubs or retakes. It appealed to her especially strongly because of the visual images the lyrics bring up, such as mountains, hillsides, and fields. Jackie was able to visualize these scenes much like scenes in a movie—and Jackie was a great movie fan.

It was no accident that Jackie got that little tune to record. Don Blocker of the promotion department can attest to that.

"Bob Skaff talked Burt Bacharach into giving him 'What the World Needs Now Is Love" for Jackie DeShannon. He wasn't about to give up that song to a relative unknown. I remember when we signed her. She called me from Chicago and said, 'Mr. Blocker, can you send me one hundred dollars so I can get out there?' Al Bennett said to me, 'What? One hundred dollars? What are you doing, Goddammit!' I wasn't involved in signing her, but we had to get her out."

Jackie's run of subsequent hits paid back that one hundred dollars many times over, although her hit list was spotty. She did work with David and Bacharach material several times afterward. She did have seven Imperial hits through 1969, and three were top forty. "Put a Little Love in Your Heart" was the biggest hit of her career, making the top five in 1969. Jackie wrote it, which must have been truly gratifying. Of her ten Liberty and Imperial chart songs, she wrote all but three. The fact that her composition of "Put a Little Love in Your Heart" has become something of a classic is a source of justifiable pride for a woman who, like Sharon Sheeley, wrote so many hits for other artists.

Jackie seemed to be the victim of sexism. Normally, if an artist wrote his own hits, the fact would be ballyhooed as extra evidence of how great he was. But Jackie never got credit for her songwriting. Even on her own LPs, the composing credits were almost never listed on the outside of the LPs. Fans had to study the fine print on the record labels themselves to find out that Jackie wrote about 50 percent of all of the songs she ever recorded.

In the 1970s, Jackie recorded for Atlantic, Amherst, Columbia, and Capitol Records, with minor hits on the first two. But she is best remembered for her Imperial Records hits.

As mentioned, Jackie had only ten hits on Liberty/Imperial. But she, like the other Liberty/Imperial/Dolton artists, recorded many, many more songs which were released on singles, but failed to catch on. Running a record company and releasing records are a sort of Russian roulette. There is no way to tell which records will make it and which ones will not. For every successful popular record, many equally good records may be released that fail to catch on. For example, examine Jackie's full Liberty/Imperial output of singles (her ten hits are marked with asterisks):

Liberty

1960
"Teach Me"
1961
"Think About You"
"Wish I Could Find a Boy"
"Baby"
1962
"The Prince"
"Just Like in the Movies"
"You Won't Forget Me"
1963
"Faded Love" *
"Needles and Pins" *
"Little Yellow Roses"
1964
"When You Walk in the Room" *
"Should I Cry"
"Oh, Boy!"
"Hold Your Heart High"
"He's Got the Whole World in His Hands"

Imperial

1965
"What the World Needs Now Is Love" *
"A Lifetime of Loneliness" *
"Come and Get Me" *
1966
"Will You Love Me Tomorrow"
"Windows and Doors"
"I Can Make It with You" *
1967
"Come On Down"
"The Wishing Doll"
"Changin' My Mind"
"I Keep Wanting You"
1968
"Nobody's Home to Go Home To"
"I Didn't Want to Have to Do It"
"The Weight" *
"Effervescent Blue"
1969
"Laurel Canyon"
"What Is This"
"Put a Little Love in Your Heart" *

"Love Will Find a Way" *
"Do You Know How Christmas Trees
Are Grown?"

1970
"Brighton Hill"

"You Keep Me Hangin' On/Hurt So
Bad"

Liberty

"It's So Nice"

Recording all of her 45s and LPs could not have been cheap. Studio time, musicians, even blank reels of recording tape cost money. Compared to, say Bobby Vee, Jackie was not bringing in the kind of hits and sales that would justify so much time and money invested in sessions and vinyl releases. Did Jackie have to pay for these sessions? Doubtful, given that her friend was Sharon Sheeley.

Songwriters DeShannon and Sheeley

Recall how Dick St. John tantrummed his way out of his Liberty contract due to nonpayment of royalties? Dick St. John's tale of woe with regard to nonreceipt of royalties is far from unique. In the world of rock 'n' roll, the stories of artists' getting cheated out of their performer and composer royalties are legion. Dion ("Runaround Sue") apparently got shafted by Laurie Records, as did the Chiffons ("He's So Fine"). And Del Shannon ("Runaway") was said to be still waiting for his 1961 money from Big Top Records when he committed suicide in 1990. Buddy Knox ("Party Doll") was short-changed by Roulette Records, and although he had no complaints about Liberty, Liberty was evidently one of the companies that cut some sharp deals and some corners in that area. Liberty superstar Bobby Vee reports that he never had any trouble getting his royalties, although he did have to pay the expenses for the recording sessions and publicity for his hits. Is the artist being rooked when charges for recording sessions are deducted from royalties?

Sharon Sheeley seems to have had a better head for business than Bobby, which benefited both herself and Jackie. "Jackie and I always called Bobby Vee 'Bobby Wheee!' because he was so cute and naive. Look, after he had gotten eight number one hits, he still owed Liberty money, according to the company's accounts. But that never happened to Jackie because of that one lucky day when Jimmy O'Neill brought her to my house. I had a great, great head for contracts, something that was taught to me by Ricky's dad Ozzie Nelson when I was a kid. Jackie had just signed with Liberty as an artist, but they had not signed her as a writer. When we went in together to sign as writers, I told Al Bennett, then the head of Liberty, that this was how it was going to be.

"'One. You have exactly ninety days to get a song we have written recorded in commercial form, meaning it has to be an actual record being released. Not recorded, not a demo, but a release. Otherwise the ownership of the song reverts to us as songwriters to do with as we please.

"'Two. We have unlimited demo expense. In other words, if I want to call the entire Philharmonic Orchestra in on a demo session, I can do it. We, Jackie and I, do not pay any demo expenses.'

"That contract was the talk of the industry. Carole King called us and said, 'How'd you get that contract?'

"Well, after I negotiated that contract, Al Bennett had tremendous respect for me. He challenged me one time on a contract. He called in all of his top guns to work on me. I told him, 'Al, you can sit here and argue all you want to. But every minute that little thing goes around on your clock, every minute that goes by is gonna cost you another fifty dollars. So you make up your mind. And he sat there for five minutes; it cost him six hundred dollars. At the time everybody was getting cheated, three hundred dollars a month. Jackie and I were getting fifteen hundred dollars a month. Simply because Al Bennett let that clock go too many times. And when he tried to get out of it, I said, 'Fine, Al, then you are not getting any of these songs. Don't sit here and say, "I am your 'father' and I know what is best for you," because I am not buying that bull, this is what we want. This is what we deserve, and this is what we are going to get. Or there are other people out there who would be thrilled to have us.'

"That was the biggest bluff I ever pulled since I had conned Ricky into recording 'Poor Little Fool' by saying Elvis was doing the song.

"But we did not let Al Bennett down. He got every penny back; we wrote him hit after hit after hit. They recouped it all. Even then, they were only allowed to recoup for a year. Say they advanced us fifty thousand. If they did not recoup that fifty thousand that year, it was washed; they could not carry it over to what we were doing the next year. Our songwriting contract went year to year, period, twelve months at a time. Everyone else was signed for five or seven years. But we got to renegotiate every year. And every time it got harder and tougher.

"So very few artists knew about business. The Beatles and the Rolling Stones hit about the same time. Mick Jagger was making ten times what the Beatles were making. The Beatles were so desperate to be rock 'n' roll stars that they signed for three cents a record, and there were four members in the group. Jagger signed for nine cents because he had gone to business college and he knew what he was doing. At first a person will sign anything to get a deal. Years later it wears thin, being a star and not getting anything.

"I loved Al Bennett. He was very good to me, as long as I stood up for myself. He was always very good to me. If I wanted something special, he would give it to me. He would say 'You're a good girl' and he would gamble on me as a songwriter."

Mel Carter

In June 1965 Imperial acquired Mel Carter. Mel had already had one hit, "When a Boy Falls in Love," written by and released on Sam Cooke's record label, Derby Records, back in 1963. His turning up on Imperial two years later was quite a surprise for fans. Mel Carter's initial Imperial success was with "Hold Me, Thrill Me, Kiss Me," a top-tenner. In the next twelve months, he had a total of six Imperial hits, three in the top forty. He also had LPs with titles to match his singles, and one LP called *Easy Listening*. And a wild manager, according to Lee Mendell. "Mel Carter had a manager named Zelda Sands. She used to tear through the corridors, yelling, screaming. She prized Mel."

Of the three new arrivals at Imperial so far in 1965, only Jackie DeShannon would show staying power. In July another woman was added to the label, and like Jackie and Mel, she had experience already. Her name? Cher Bono.

Cher

Sonny and Cher had been around for a long time, but no one knew it. Sonny had been a session man for Phil Spector at Philles Records, and under names like Caesar and Cleo, Sonny and Cher together had tried to score on other labels before. In fact, under the name "Cherilyn," Cher had released an Imperial single in 1964 called "Dream Baby," "written and produced by Sonny." In July 1965 they had their first successes together, notably "I Got You Babe" on Atco.

Sonny branched out in August to have a top-ten record of his own, "Laugh at Me," and a minor follow-up. Sonny's solo records were on Atco, like Sonny and Cher's. Someone at Imperial was on the ball, however, and got Cher's solo contract, so that Cher appeared with Sonny on Atco but by herself on Imperial!

Guess who that someone was? Snuffy strikes again! "A girl who used to come around and ask me where I got my cowboy boots and my Indian moccasins was a girl named Cher. I knew her long before they had hits. When my wife Yolanda and I bought a house, Sonny and Cher lived next door. They were not doing well at all, so we decided I would cut her. I had the song written for her, 'Gypsies, Tramps and Thieves.' Bob Stone did that, then I had a lot of hits with her.

"Talk about mixed emotions. I'm sitting here looking at a pretty picture of her I've had for years, from that era. She wrote on it, 'Snuff, you bastard, what are we gonna do with you, Love, Cher.' It's called mixed emotions. We got along great but she didn't like the records I made with her. But I didn't make them for her, I made them to sell to people."

But that is getting ahead of the story. "All I Really Want to Do" by Cher came out the same month as "I Got You Babe" by Sonny and Cher and made the top twenty the summer of 1965. Her two top-ten Imperial releases were "Bang Bang" (1966) and "You Better Sit Down, Kids" (1967). Her "flops" included "Behind the Door" (1966) and "Hey Joe" (1967). In all she had seven Imperial hits, ending in 1967, five on the top forty.

Cher's Imperial LPs numbered only three. She may have been too busy with Sonny over at Atco to spend much time recording for Imperial. But her selection of songs showed a broad interest, from girl groups ("Our Day Will Come," Ruby and the Romantics, 1963) to jazz ("The Girl from Ipanema," Stan Getz and Astrud Gilberto, 1964) to folk ("Like a Rolling Stone," Bob Dylan, 1965).

Other Imperial artists having LPs at this time were Jimmy McCracklin, Johnny Rivers, Slim Whitman, and Sandy Nelson. Yes, Sandy was still pounding the skins at Imperial, even though his last hit had been "Teen Beat '65," a non-top-forty single in 1964.

An Imperial also-ran worthy of note was Jimmy McCracklin. He had several LPs already to his name, but "Arkansas Pt. 1" was his first single to garner any measure of success. Subsequently, he switched from Imperial to another Liberty subsidiary, Minit Records, for two more also-rans.

Some more Liberty LPs from 1965 included Gary Lewis's LPs *This Diamond Ring,* including tracks like "The Night Has a Thousand Eyes" (Bobby Vee, 1964). Released in the summer of 1965 was Gary's second LP, *A Session with Gary Lewis and the Playboys.* Snuff produced it, Jan & Dean's engineer, Bones Howe, mixed it, and Leon Russell arranged the songs, including "Travelin' Man" (Ricky Nelson,

"Golden Greats" was a term Snuff Garrett coined for use when "Greatest Hits" didn't quite fit.

Imperial, 1961), "Runaway" (Del Shannon, 1961), and "Little Miss Go-Go," a surf and drag song that sounds more like Jan & Dean than Gary Lewis and of course boasts the Fantastic Baggies instead of the Playboys on backup vocals! Besides the top-five hit "Count Me In," this all-star LP included Gary's third top-five hit in a row, "Save Your Heart for Me" (Brian Hyland, 1963).

In the oddity department, besides being a flip side to "Count Me In," "Little Miss Go-Go" appeared on a weird Liberty 45 available only by mail. By sending in a cereal box top, fans could acquire a black-and-silver label 45 with "This Diamond Ring" plus "Little Miss Go-Go" on side two, but a wacky Gary Lewis/Leon Russell composition, "Doin' the Flake" on side one. The "Flake" referred, of course, to cereal. Snuff did the production chores, and the record number was unique, 65-227-1 for side one and 65-227-2 for side two. The way the record came about was rather odd.

"I got a call from Post cereals," explains Snuff Garrett, "and we made a deal. They wanted three masters and a new song, so we wrote 'Doin' the Flake,' which came out pretty flaky. Lou Brown, Jerry's piano player, and I and Leon Russell wrote that and 'Little Miss Go-Go' that was on the first album. I put Gary's name on all of those songs as writer, but he never wrote a word; it was always Leon and me (as Tommy Lesslie)."

The background singers on "Little Miss Go-Go" sounded like the Fantastic Baggies, Sloan and Barri, but according to Snuff Garrett, "it was Al Capps and Ron Hicklin."

Gary Lewis recalls that it was Sloan and Barri on "Little Miss Go-Go." Gary: "It was! I am sure of it. Because I remember asking, 'Who is that?' Al Capps was the bass voice on 'She's Just My Style.' He can't sing that high! Al Capps sang [sings basso profundo] 'Don't you know that she's....' I guess it has been too long for Snuff to remember." Well, after all, to Snuff it was one of many, many sessions with many, many artists and tunes. To Gary Lewis it was one of a relatively few, important sessions. "But I am sure it was Sloan and Barri. I knew Al Capps because he was singing background, he and Ron Hicklin, from the very first song we ever did. So I knew Al Capps, and I remember when Sloan and Barri came in, I said, 'Who are these guys?' And Leon Russell told me. I believe they did only that one tune. There may have been one other one."

Gary Lewis agrees that the song should have been a single. "It was on our greatest hits green album, and we do it on stage, too, because it is a good tune. We sang it in your hometown, Lawrence, Kansas, last year when we played Liberty Hall."

Gary's Producer, Snuffy

Snuff and Gary may disagree today on who sang on what, but in the 1960s, they worked in complete harmony. "Snuff knew exactly when to put records out. 'Save Your Heart for Me' was a ballad; it was about getting out of school, going out somewhere, finding a new romance. We had it all cut in January of that year. Snuff told me, 'We gotta save this one, we gotta keep it in the can, because it's gotta come out when school gets out.' I think that added to the sales of it. Isn't it amazing that that record runs less than two minutes, a minute and fifty-six seconds, something like that! You know, when I am doing it on stage, it does seem really short! But the DJs, they liked them short."

Was the Brian Hyland 1963 version of "Save Your Heart for Me" the inspiration for the Gary Lewis version? No. "The way Snuffy put it to me, he said, 'There are these great writers, Geld and Udell, who have written a lot of good stuff. Listen to this one.' It was a demo.

"At the time I did not know that Brian Hyland had done it [as a flip side]. I just listened to the demo and said, 'Yeah, that is pretty, that is nice.' Snuff always had demos for me to listen to first. He didn't just pick it, have the charts made up, and go into the studio and say 'This is the tune.' I was always totally prepared for what the tune was going to be. I wonder if the demo I heard was the same demo that Brian had originally listened to?"

Snuff was doubtless one of the two or three main forces behind the success of Liberty Records. His ability to spot and develop talent, his knack as an arranger, and his solid business sense were an invaluable asset to Liberty. But what was he really like? There are probably as many opinions as there are people who have known him. Buddy Knox and Bobby Vee loved him. But Sharon Sheeley relates that she and Eddie were not so greatly impressed by Snuff.

"Snuff Garrett was a workaholic." I asked her about the huge influence he had on the Liberty sound that so many artists like Bobby Vee and Johnny Burnette boasted on their records. "He did that only after Eddie died. It always annoyed me so much when I picked up an album and it said, 'Produced by Snuff Garrett.' Snuff Garrett never produced an Eddie Cochran record or album, ever. What he did was to go in and remix things after Eddie died. Before Eddie died Snuff Garrett almost got himself killed by doing that. Eddie had done a great Ray Charles song, 'Hallelujah, I Love Her So,' then went on the road. While he was gone Snuff Garrett went in and overdubbed some violins. Those things are so obvious on there, they come screeching in over Eddie's track. It's so obviously overdubbed, and not only that, but it is right over Eddie's guitar solo, which he played so brilliantly. That is why I love the British Eddie Cochran albums. Over there they took all of the overdubbing off of Eddie. You can hear the way he really cut it. Well, when Eddie came off the road and heard those violins, Eddie was so mad, he threw Snuff Garrett from wall to wall; I thought he was gonna kill him.

"Phil Everly still talks about how brilliant Eddie Cochran was. He tells how, when they all went on the road, every act would have their band get on the bus. And there would be Eddie and Giro, that was his bass player. That was Eddie's band. Eddie used to say, 'I can use any house drummer wherever we go, because the drummer is totally insignificant in what I do.' It was true. It's Eddie Cochran's guitar with that bass. The bass was the bottom of his records. That's his brilliance. I just wish you knew how brilliant Eddie really was. He was probably the most brilliant rock 'n' roller. Definitely he was, of his time. But that day he wanted to kill Snuff Garrett. Because Eddie Cochran did not have violins on any of his records. It was pure rock 'n' roll.

"Snuff and Eddie had just a horrible fight. This was just two weeks before Eddie went to England, and he never returned. After that was when Snuff Garrett just started taking over. I never liked Snuff Garrett. He was just too money conscious, and he never cared about people at all.

"To illustrate why I do not like Snuff Garrett, Jackie and I wrote a song called 'Blue Ribbon,' about going down to a store called Tiffany's and buying this thing. Anyway, Snuff cut this song with Gene McDaniels. Everyone, including Al Bennett, called me and said that this was the greatest record they had ever heard. 'Wait till you hear it.' Jackie and I did go in and sat down to hear it, and it was an absolute killer, the best work Gene had ever done. Snuff was all high, saying that this was going to be a number-one hit. Then he sat down to talk with us. 'You know, girls, on this one, it is going to have to say, "Sheeley, DeShannon, T. Garrett."' Snuff's real first name was Tommy.

"I just said, 'Snuff, never.'"

"'Then I won't release it.'

"I called his bluff and said, 'Then don't.' But Jackie said, 'Wait a minute, I have a say-so in this.' I told her, 'The only way you have a say-so in this, Jackie, if you are so panicky that he is not going to release it, is if you make a deal to give Snuff a share of your share of the song. But I will resent having his name on it. He did not create the song.'

"Al came back: 'I'll can it, Bitch!'
"I said, 'Then you can it!' And Jackie said, 'That's right, you can it!'
"Jackie was like that. She is sweet and adorable, but she is no brain surgeon. But Snuff did can it; he killed that record. He killed Gene McDaniels; he killed everyone else around him.

"Out in the car Jackie was screaming and yelling, 'He's right! It's a number-one hit. We should do it.' I said 'No! A third of something is not better than nothing. Nothing is better than selling out to this man. And we just can't do it, because if we let them, they will just continue to do it.' Of course, he continued to do it, anyway."

Away from the politics of Liberty, in 1965 Matt Monro and P. J. Proby each did a couple of LPs, and another gigantically popular British singer, Tommy Steele, surfaced with a Liberty LP. In England Tommy Steele had more than a dozen hit singles with original songs and familiar American tunes like "Singing the Blues" (Guy Mitchell, Marty Robbins, 1956) and "Tallahassee Lassie" (Freddy Cannon, 1959). As a British-invasion artist, Tommy did nothing for Liberty, except for his LP *Everything's Coming Up Broadway*. Vikki Carr, Johnny Mann, and other Liberty standards also released 1965 LPs.

Vic Dana and the Ventures accounted for Dolton's LP output for the year. Imperial released Hollies, Jackie DeShannon, Sandy Nelson, and Johnny Rivers LPs, plus Slim Whitman's *15th Anniversary Album*.

CHAPTER 14

Liberty Stereo Little LPs, EPs, 78s, and Picture Sleeves

Albums and 45s were not the only kinds of records that Liberty released. There were also seven-inch records that were not singles.

Little LPs

Very hard to document are the Liberty Stereo Little LPs. These were seven-inch discs that had a small hole and played at 33⅓ rpm. Not available to the general public, they were made for use on jukeboxes. They could have anywhere from one to three songs per side. The songs were taken from Liberty conventional twelve-inch LPs. In fact the Little LPs had the same title and often the same record number as the full-size LPs. To tell them apart, there was a second number in parentheses under the LP number.

Here is a small sampling of some typical Little LPs:

Sophisticated Lady was number SE-66. Released in the fall of 1961, it included the title tune, written by Duke Ellington, "Bewitched" by Rodgers and Hart, and Cole Porter's "Another Old Fashioned, Please."

In 1962 Martin Denny had Little LP number SE-82, called *A Taste of Honey*, named after his last Liberty hit single just that summer. The six cuts included Liberty alumnus Bobby Troup's "Route 66," "Stranger on the Shore" (Acker Bilk, 1962, #1, Atco Records), and Dave Brubeck's "Take Five."

Neither the Julie London nor the Martin Denny Little LP had any hits on it. By contrast *The Best of Timi Yuro* was nearly all hits: "Hurt," "Smile," "Insult to Injury," "The Love of a Boy," and "I Apologize." Numbered SE-93, it included only one nonhit single, "Just Say I Love Him."

Little LP SE-96 was on the Dolton label. *The Ventures Play Telstar/The Lonely Bull* was a typical Ventures outing, with six of their reliable recordings of other people's hits.

Years after his last hit single, "A Taste of Honey," Martin Denny was still selling lots of Liberty albums. His *20 Golden Hawaiian Hits* had only six hits in the Little LP version, SE-144.

But talk about giving a low cut count! Liberty ace trombonist Si Zentner had a seven-inch, small-hole, stereo disc with only one cut per side in 1963. Numbered S-4, it was another jukebox oddity, untitled, with cuts taken from his *More* LP.

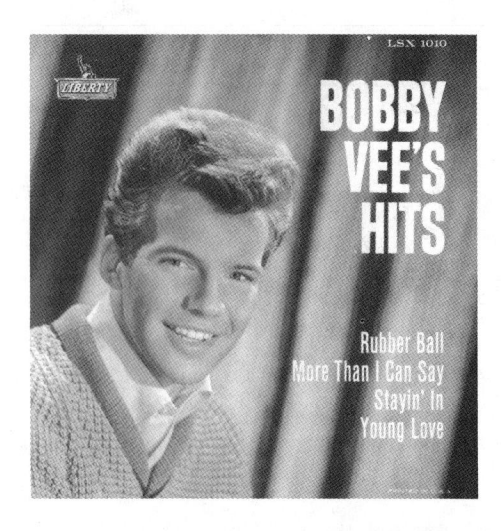

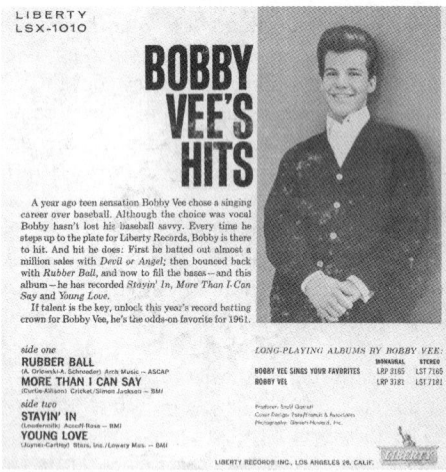

A middle ground between the two songs on a single and the twelve songs on an LP were the four songs on an EP. Three of these cuts were hits for Bobby Vee.

"More" was the theme from the movie *Mondo Cane* and was popular both instrumentally by Kai Winding on Verve Records and vocally on Dolton by Vic Dana in 1963. The cuts were both oldies that were being revived in 1963. Side one was "Till Then," (the Classics, Musicnote) which was a World War II hit by the Mills Brothers, and "Birdland" (Chubby Checker, Parkway), which was composed and first recorded by Huey "Piano" Smith and the Clowns.

It would be great to be able to document all the Liberty 33⅓ seven-inchers. But if anyone kept track of the releases, the information was lost during the many

Chapter 14 · Liberty Stereo Little LPs, EPs, 78s, and Picture Sleeves   263

Top: This Ventures Dolton EP had six songs, half an LP. *Middle:* Martin Denny's EP was released several years later. Labeled a Stereo Little LP, it was meant mostly for jukebox use. *Bottom:* Julie London's EP had a much larger Liberty logo than usually used.

times the company and its tapes and files have changed hands. It is, after all, called "popular music," and new young executives of new parent companies could hardly be bothered with saving documentation of odd little discs that were never even offered for sale to the general public.

45 and 33⅓ EPs

For about every five hundred or so 45 single records that were released nationally by all of the record companies in existence in the 1950s and 1960s, maybe one EP was released. An EP was a 45 rpm seven-inch record that looked like a single. The difference was in the number of songs included. Instead of two songs, one on each side, there could be a total of three, four, five, or six songs per record. Occasionally an EP would play at 33⅓, but most ran at 45.

RCA Records released a great many EPs by Elvis Presley. Many Elvis fans, being rather artist-centric, tell how, when they were little record buyers, they thought "EP" stood for "Elvis Presley." In reality it stood for "Extended Play."

Liberty had a series of EPs that began at the very beginning of the label in late 1955, evidently before the first Elvis EP at RCA. Carrying the prefix "LSX" and numbered in the one thousands, the first was LSX-1001, "Cry Me a River," by Julie London. An EP was a price compromise between a 45 and an album. A typical retail price breakdown might go like this: "Cry Me a River" 45, $0.98 for two songs; *Cry Me a River* EP, $1.49 for four songs; and *Cry Me a River* LP, $3.98 for twelve songs (LP titled *Julie Is Her Name*).

Each EP was packed in a cardboard jacket just like an LP cover. The front was colored and the back was black and white with liner notes, track listings, and notes about Liberty LPs by the artist.

The EPs were aimed primarily at the teen market. After Julie London's *Cry Me a River* EP, there came *I'm Available* by Margie Rayburn, *Witch Doctor* by David Seville, and others by Gene McDaniels, Johnny Burnette, the Chipmunks, and Bobby Vee. *Bobby Vee's Hits*, LSX-1010, came out in 1961. It had three chart songs, "Rubber Ball," "More Than I Can Say," "Stayin' In," all from the LP *Bobby Vee*, and "Young Love" from *Bobby Vee Sings Your Favorites*.

In those days, the battle was going on between 78s and 45s. Although they are extremely rare today, Liberty did press some 78s. Julie London's singles were pressed on both 45s and 78s from 1955 to 1957. And apparently there were some singles that played at 33⅓ rpm.

Si Waronker himself "did not want to press 78s, because I hated it. And yet some of them could have been great. The 78s were starting to go out when we first started. So we would press about four 45s and one 78, if that. Then it became an issue of pressing a 45 versus an LP, the 33.

"Then I wanted to have 33 singles. I tried that. It wouldn't work, but I wanted a 33 single because I thought the quality could be better. I even came out with a translucent vinyl, sort of red and orange, to see if I could drum up something, but it didn't work.

"We tried EPs, but it was a no-win situation as far as I was concerned. You needed four tunes to make it work. The difference in price between a 45 and an LP and an EP made it so it would never take off. The promotional staff used to argue

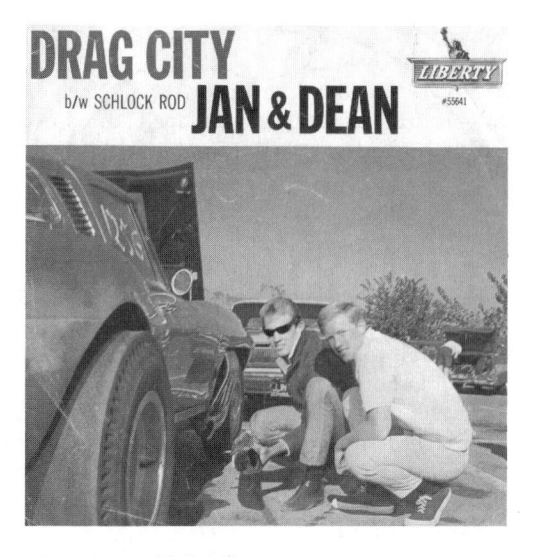

Jan & Dean were mighty cool at the drags. Their Liberty 45 sleeves often had a reverse different from the front.

for EPs, but I told them they were just for promotion. Then if the people wanted them, we would release them. But there would have to be a demand for them. Other companies tried them, but I felt they were wasting their time. And the stereo EPs were more or less a racket. You could charge twice as much as for a 45, but it cost practically the same to press and package."

Liberty released only about sixteen EPs, then retired the series in 1961 after only a little over five years. Apparently it just wasn't worth it for Si and Liberty, although Elvis made it work at RCA.

33⅓ Singles

In the 1961 *Liberty Annual Report to Stockholders*, reference is made to the introduction of 33⅓ rpm singles, which it was hoped "could provide even greater stimulus" to Liberty's record sales. However, no 33 singles are known to exist.

Picture Sleeves

One of the nicest things about buying 45s in the 1950s and 1960s was getting picture sleeves. Unlike LP and EP covers, which were cardboard and colored only on one side, 45 singles had full-color, glossy paper covers. However, the same picture was usually reproduced on both sides.

Si was an advocate of the picture sleeve. "I liked picture sleeves. It got some identity on the shelves. The only thing that cost money was the artwork. If an artist didn't photo well, we used a photo of a girl or a classic painting. But I thought packaging was a very important thing. Unfortunately cassettes and CDs have very little room for artwork."

Usually picture sleeves were reserved for hit artists. An unproved artist got a regular Liberty generic sleeve, whereas artists with a proven track record, like Jan & Dean or Bobby Vee, got the benefit of picture sleeves.

An interesting characteristic about picture sleeves: They were reversible, like the 45s they protected. That is to say, both sides of almost all picture sleeves carried the title of both sides of the record. However, one side of the sleeve carried the A-side title first in large print, and the B-side title second, in smaller print. The flip side of the sleeve carried the B-side title first and the A-side second.

Why the difference? If the A-side became a hit, as planned by Liberty, then the stores could rack the 45s with the hit side of the sleeve showing. But if the B-side became the unexpected hit, then the records could be flipped over and racked with that title showing. Most companies listed the titles on sleeves in this manner. Most used the notation "b/w" between the two titles, meaning one was "backed with" the other. Liberty used that notation occasionally, but more often they just used the conjunction *and* or just an ampersand.

Liberty sometimes did something different with a picture sleeve. For instance, some Jan & Dean sleeves had different flip sides. This may have been ads for Liberty LPs by Jan & Dean, such as on the "Sidewalk Surfin'" picture sleeve; lyrics to the hit, as on the "Ride the Wild Surf" picture sleeve; or a different photo of Jan & Dean, as on "You Really Know How to Hurt a Guy" picture sleeve.

This last sleeve is worth special mention. In almost every case of picture-sleeve photography, the photo is fairly generic. That is, the photo could go with just about any songs by that artist. But for "You Really Know How to Hurt a Guy," a special Jan & Dean photo session was conducted at a wax museum, depicting Jan & Dean in scenes of torture—"Hurt a Guy" being the operative phrase.

The best thing about picture sleeves: They were free. In a store there could be a dozen copies of a given hit record. Some of the copies were in picture sleeves, and others were in generic Liberty sleeves. Both cost the same.

Confronted with that choice, which would you choose to buy?

CHAPTER 15

1966
Bob Lind and Del Shannon

The year 1966 was the third consecutive one in which Imperial outperformed its adoptive parent Liberty on the national charts. In fact, every year from the Imperial takeover until the end of Liberty, Imperial would exceed Liberty's success.

In 1966 Imperial's black crooner Mel Carter would complete his hit career with no less than four chart records, including "Love Is All We Need," which had been a hit in 1958 for Tommy Edwards and in 1964 for Dolton's Vic Dana, and the top-forty "Band of Gold."

The Hollies continued one of the hottest runs of the British invasion, with the major hits "Bus Stop" and "Stop Stop Stop," and "I Can't Let Go" as well.

Early in the year, Johnny Rivers recorded "Secret Agent Man," a song about a spy named John Drake—the main character in the popular British TV series "Secret Agent." This theme song was written by Phil Sloan and Steve Barri, singers on, and composers of, many Jan & Dean recordings. Under the name the Fantastic Baggies, Phil and Steve even had their own 45s and an LP on Imperial. The television program "Secret Agent" had a nonrock instrumental theme in its original British release, and the American TV executives wanted a new rock vocal song for the U.S. showings. Sloan and Barri later commented that they had no idea at the time that the song would become a hit instead of just an obscure TV theme, and that if they had known, they'd have worked harder on it!

Johnny Rivers's other records of 1966 were also big Imperial hits: "I Washed My Hands in Muddy Water" and the ballad "Poor Side of Town."

Cher Bono was still going very strong, and seemingly leaving rock 'n' roll in her past, as she made a loud impact with "Bang Bang" and the movie song "Alfie," and a small noise with "Behind the Door." Imperial's other female vocalist, Jackie DeShannon, continued her relentless assault on the charts, with "Come and Get Me" and "I Can Make It with You," which ranked #83 and #68, respectively, on *Billboard*'s Top 100.

Both Georgie Fame and the O'Jays had their last Imperial hits, "Get Away" and "Stand-In for Love," although each artist would be seen again on other labels.

Over at Liberty, label heavy-hitter Bobby Vee was in a slump in 1966, and his only chart hit for the year was the very nice but promptly forgotten "Look at Me, Girl." Keeping his name alive was another great medley album, *30 Big Hits of the '60s, Volume Two*. Snuff had conceived of the idea for Bobby's first medley LP and produced volume 1, but he had left Liberty by this time, so Dave Pell was chosen as coproducer with Dallas Smith. Instead of medleys of five songs each as in volume 1 this time each cut contained only two songs. Typical of the wide range of tunes were the first medley, "A Hundred Pounds of Clay" (Gene McDaniels, 1961)/"Elusive Butterfly" (Bob Lind, 1966), and cut seven, "Pony Time" (Chubby Checker, 1961)/"You Can Have Her" (Roy Hamilton, 1961). Imperial Mel Carter's recent hit "Love Is All We Need" was also included. Dallas and Bobby would work together again.

The inclusion of the song "Elusive Butterfly" on Bobby's medley LP was interesting. This Bob Lind tune was a huge early 1966 hit that appeared on World Pacific Records, which was a new subsidiary of Liberty Records.

Bob Lind

A Liberty distributor discovered Bob Lind, relates Lee Mendell. "We had a distributor in Denver named Bill Davis, who found Bob Lind and really liked what he did. Bill brought Bob Lind over to the office and had him sit in Al's office playing 'Elusive Butterfly.' Everyone liked it and felt it was kind of Dylan-ish and kind of flower-power, mid-late 1960s. It was great, but he was a one-hit artist. One record and off he went."

The numbering system for World Pacific followed the pattern that had been begun when Liberty started out with 55001 and that had been continued when the acquired Imperial numbering system began with 66000. "Elusive Butterfly" was numbered 77808. The follow-up later in the year was 77822. Both follow-ups charted out of the top-forty range, with "Remember the Rain" (#64) doing very slightly better than "Truly Julie's Blues (I'll Be There)" (#65).

Just a couple of the old-line Liberty/Dolton/Imperial artists were still having hits in 1966. Gary Lewis and the Playboys, who were not that old yet, kept up their steady stream of successes with "Green Grass," "Sure Gonna Miss Her," "My Heart's Symphony," "Paint Me a Picture," and "Where Will the Words Come From," all scoring #21 or better on *Billboard*. Gary's song "Green Grass" was actually banned on some radio stations—in those days, "grass" commonly referred to marijuana in many people's minds, although nothing was further from Gary's mind when he released the record.

Looking back, the long-term influence of marijuana on American youth was not as pervasive as most adults had feared it would be. Also looking back, the influence of the Beatles and the British invasion of the mid-sixties on American rock 'n' roll was not as large as has commonly been thought. This was documented at length in my previous book, *The Beatle Myth*. Contrary to popular belief, American artists were not hurt by the British invasion. At their peak the British records "dominated" only about 10 percent of the American charts, and they caused the end of no big American rock 'n' rollers' careers.

Gary Lewis agrees. Did Gary Lewis never once find being an American rock 'n' roller in the mid-sixties a handicap? "No, not at all. I never did see how the Beatles or the British invasion could hurt any artist. I mean, if you have the good material, and you have the right people working with you, and you have everything it takes to make a hit record, then you're gonna have that hit record. Just because people are liking the British acts, does that mean that they are not going to go out and buy a great tune that they like just if it is by an American person?

GARY LEWIS & THE PLAYBOYS
SURE GONNA MISS HER
AND I DON'T WANNA SAY GOODNIGHT
#55865

Another top-ten hit for Gary Lewis and the Playboys was "Sure Gonna Miss Her."

"I was never threatened by the British invasion at all, ever! I loved the Beatles, and I never looked at it like I was in competition with them. Or I never looked at it like, 'Oh, damn, they got another hit! That means I am going to have more trouble getting on the charts!' I never said any of that stuff. Never. Not today, not at all, never, nothing like that, ever."

How did the Playboys do on the Beatles' home turf, in England? "We went nowhere. Absolutely nowhere. I couldn't get *arrested* over there! It's true. I went over there when 'Everybody Loves a Clown' came out, I did all the local TV shows, went all over the country there, just nothing. Absolutely nothing. And then come to find out in nineteen eighty-two, 'Count Me In' and 'My Heart's Symphony' were hits over there. I don't get it."

Gary's delayed chartings overseas are interesting, since Liberty's Jan & Dean also had late chartings overseas. They made the top ten in the Netherlands in 1981 with "Surf City" and "Dead Man's Curve." Also, "My Heart's Symphony" was #36 in 1975 in England. Something must have happened over there around the turn of the decade. "Maybe so. I don't know how big the hits were, but on royalty statements

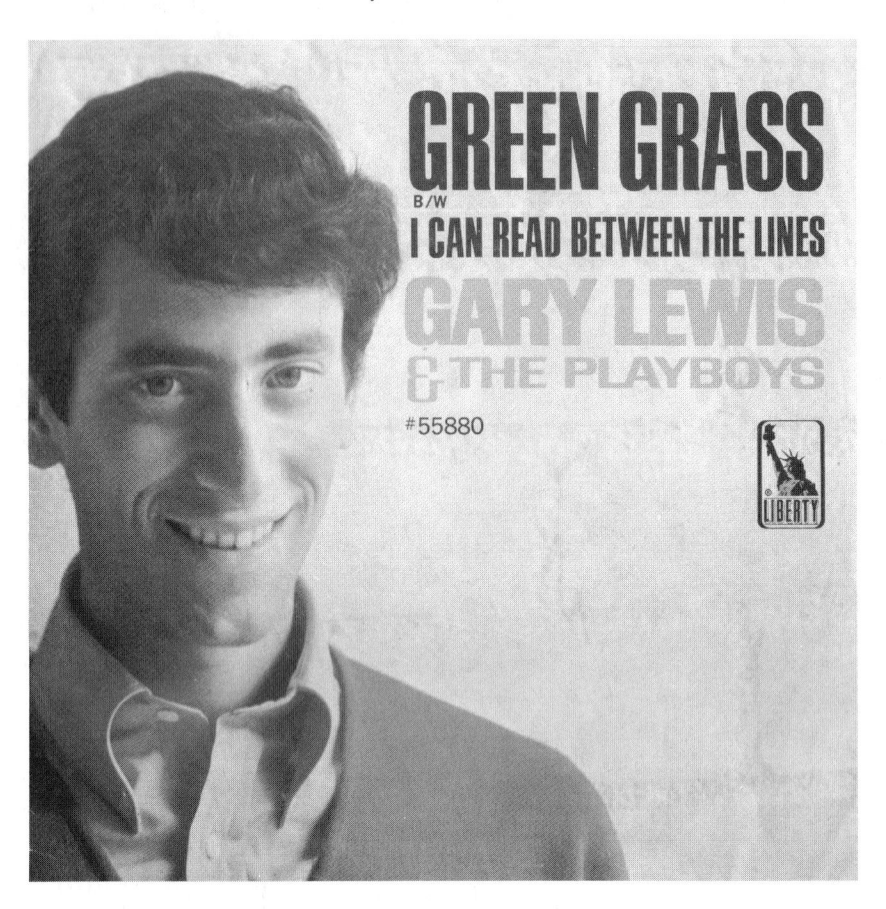

Some stations wouldn't play Gary Lewis's "Green Grass," thinking it was a song about smoking pot!

that I still get, it says 'Sweden, Holland, Germany, Finland.' I don't know. It took an awful long time to get those two songs played in England!"

It seems ironic that Gary Lewis was so lacking in popularity overseas. After all, Gary's dad, Jerry Lewis, is hugely popular as a comedic actor in France. Didn't Gary Lewis ever sell any records in France? "I have never seen 'France' on any royalty statement. I definitely would have heard about it. France and England were really hard."

Popularity has always been a hard nut to crack. No one knows why a certain artist, or a certain record, is a hit or not. But certainly being on a successful, good-size, well-known record label with a good track record and a good staff doesn't hurt. How did Gary Lewis feel about being on Liberty, not a tiny label but also not one of the big, established labels? Might he have wished he had been on a larger label, such as Capitol? Or was he happy with Liberty and the work conditions there?

"I didn't even think about that. When we signed with Liberty, I thought it was a big company! I didn't know anything. And it didn't really matter, because I was getting my chance to do music. I was also kind of glad I was a minor. I couldn't sign anything myself, do any business, make any mistakes.

"We recorded down the street at Western Recorders and United Recorders. They were almost right next door to each other, and that is where everybody recorded. They did not really have studios at Liberty. It was a tiny little building. Now the royalty statements all come from Capitol, which owns Liberty. I don't actually have a signed contract with Capitol, but they are the one releasing all the CDs and tapes.

"At the time I didn't realize it, but it was such a great thing to have Leon Russell arrange my songs. Boy! He really put it all together. He did all the musicians, wrote out all of the charts. He was so instrumental in creating the sound. Snuffy had the ability to pick the hits, and he knew when to put them out, and Leon had the ability to put them all together really well."

Gary Lewis does not have an ego. He realizes that it takes many elements to make a hit record and to have a successful record career—a song, a singer, an arranger, a producer, many elements.

Liberty founder Si Waronker always maintained that the tune was the most important element in making a hit record, much more important than the performer. Between that performer and the tune, Si placed the producer. Give the right song to the right producer, and any artist could have a hit.

Which does Gary Lewis think is the most important, the tune, the producer, or the artist? "I think it is the producer first, I really do. 'Cause Snuffy—without Snuffy—who knows if anyone would have thought that 'This Diamond Ring' was a good tune? He was the one who really believed in it, and every single other tune he picked for me. I mean, he never made a mistake. He never made a mistake. So I think he was the most important, as far as my career." It is true that, before Snuff place the magic touch on him, Johnny Burnette, for example, had no hits. But with Snuff's support, he became huge. "Right. And Gene McDaniels after that, and Buddy Knox and Bobby Vee and myself. Yeah, he had a pretty good string going. Snuff was very important.

"It was a great trio, of [him], Leon, and myself. I liked it. We all worked really well together, too. You know, Snuff said to me, 'Gary, you've got to trust me. You've got to believe in me. Don't argue with me. If you don't like what I am picking for you to put out, just be quiet. Just trust me.' So I said, OK, we'll see how that goes." It went pretty well. Gary Lewis and the Playboys' first five records were top-four hits; the next five were top-thirty. "After the first four or five, I said, 'Well, jeez, he's right! I'll keep my mouth shut! Boy, it just kept going, you know?

"Snuff could have run Liberty Records. He was raised by Al Bennett in Lubbock, Texas. And when I came to Liberty, Al Bennett was the president of Liberty."

Al Bennett, as president of Liberty, may have been the big boss. But apparently Al was open to other people's ideas, even when those ideas were in conflict with his own. Gary Lewis recalls a disagreement Al had with Snuff.

"I recall a time when Al Bennett called me and Snuff into his office and said, 'I want to put the *Diamond Ring* album on the racks in K Mart.' Snuffy hit the ceiling! He said, 'Absolutely not! There is no way you are going to do that and sell these albums for two dollars. No! Absolutely not!' And that was the end of that. I mean, Al Bennett, he listened to Snuff, it was as if Snuff was the boss."

Many people, including some artists, experienced conflict with Al Bennett, particularly when it came to money. Gary Lewis was one of those people who found Al fair and honest.

"There was never a problem with me and Al Bennett. I kind of lost contact with the business end of Liberty when I went into the Army in 1967. I went into the Army, but I was still under contract."

Being in the Army was a problem for many rock 'n' rollers in the 1950s and 1960s. Elvis of RCA Records, of course, was drafted. Dion and the Belmonts of Laurie Records had to split up when the draft board called up the Belmonts. Dean Torrence had to spend six months in the reserves in his pre–Liberty days, right when Jan & Dean were about to start having hits, and so the first few hits were released by Jan & Arnie. And Gary Troxel of the Fleetwoods on Dolton had to split his early Fleetwoods days between being a Fleetwood and being in the service. Luckily, the careers of Elvis, Dion and the Belmonts, Jan & Dean, and the Fleetwoods survived the experience, although in some cases, the post-service success was not as great as that of the pre-service days.

Gary Lewis was drafted in the middle of his hit career at Liberty. He felt this affected his career in a negative way.

"I would get away on leave time and come down and record some things. Like 'Sealed with a Kiss' and 'Listen to the Rhythm of the Falling Rain' while I was in the Army. They were in the can to be released. But I was not able to go around and promote them or anything like that. They still went top forty, I don't remember exactly how high they went. They were medium hits. If I had not been in the Army and could have toured with them they might have done a little better. I definitely think that touring and promotion helped make hits. I still do."

Jan & Dean in 1966

Given that touring is important to making records into hits, it is no wonder that Jan & Dean, who were more bona fide old-timers that Gary Lewis, had no big hits after 1966. Jan was in a major automobile accident on April 19, 1966, that ended their touring for more than ten years. Yet they did have "Batman" (at #66, a small hit, the last before Jan's car accident), "Fiddle Around" (at #93, a tiny hit recorded in 1962 and resurrected because Jan was in a coma and was not able to record) and "Popsicle" (#21, recorded in 1963 for their *Drag City* LP and resurrected for the same reason as "Fiddle Around"). Dean hated "Fiddle Around," but he liked "Popsicle." In fact, he chose it for rerelease as a single in 1966.

"Batman" should have scored higher on the charts. Based on the then-top-rated TV program about the Caped Crusader, and with one of Jan's most elaborate productions in two years, it was a very exciting record. However, it *was* a novelty tune, and the days of novelty records were pretty much past (with notable exceptions, such as "They're Coming to Take Me Away, Ha-Ha" by Napoleon XIV, Warner Brothers Records, 1966, #3). Perhaps the record suffered from a lack of sufficient promotion by Liberty's "dynamic duo." Both were full-time graduate students, they were involved in the production of their own TV series slated for NBC in the fall, and they were starting their own record label. And during the song's chart run, Jan had his accident.

Coupled with the "Batman" single was the Jan & Dean *Batman* album. It featured only three songs, the title hit and two comic-book tunes, "Robin, the Boy Wonder" and "The Joker Is Wild." Also included was an instrumental of the TV "Batman" theme, and a singalong in the style of the recent Beach Boys hit, "Barbara Ann," on which Dean shared lead with Brian. This song, "Flight of the Batmobile," is a fun cut. Many errors are made in the lyrics, and one wonders if it was to be recut later, had Jan not had his accident. It sounds like a party record, rather like the recent hits by Johnny Rivers recorded at the Whiskey à Go-Go. Perhaps that is why, at the end of the cut, Dean says, "Where's Johnny Rivers?"

The other eight tracks are comedy sketches spinning the legend of Captain Jan and Dean, the Boy Blunder, crime-fighting alter egos of Jan & Dean. They drive an atomic-powered woodie (instead of a Batmobile), received their secret crime-fighting powers and abilities from their mentor, the little old lady from Pasadena, and they change into their secret identities by singing the title line from "The Little Old Lady (from Pasadena)."

The cuts are full of puns, and even the tracks comprising the sketches have titles like "A Stench in Time" and "A Hank of Hair and a Banana Peel."

This LP had to be cut twice. The first version, never released except as a bootleg, had Jan & Dean impersonating Batman and Robin. This project was nixed by the Liberty legal department, justifiably fearful of a copyright infringement suit.

Batman has no pictures of Jan & Dean. Had Jan not crashed, undoubtedly some comic photo session would have been undertaken, with Jan & Dean wearing hilarious superhero-type uniforms. One more Jan & Dean LP was planned in 1966. In fact, all the instrumental tracks were in the can, and Jan & Dean were about to begin cutting the vocals. Then the crash.

Del Shannon

The family's new-artist list was just as short. Liberty signed only Del Shannon, who had already had over a dozen hits on Big Top, BerLee (his own label), and Amy. On Liberty he released a new 1967 version of "Runaway" (Del Shannon, 1961). Slow and string-laden, it did not sell, and his only hit at Liberty—which could be described as a minor success at best—was a remake of Toni Fisher's Signet Records hit "The Big Hurt," from 1959. It was #94 on *Billboard*.

Other Shannon singles included a 45 of which he wrote both sides, the slow "Never Thought I Could" and the fast "Show Me." Leon Russell arranged, and Leon and Snuff coproduced, but to no good result. Another 45 had "She Was Mine," which Del again wrote, on the back and the Stones' number "Under My Thumb" for the front. Del produced the sessions, and arranger George Tipton did the scoring. Yet the songs were lackluster. Del's trademark falsetto was nowhere to be heard, nor were the driving vocals and the shrieking Musitron keyboard. Perhaps he was trying to update his sound; his version of "Thumb" was better than most.

Also-Rans

The 1966 also-rans make a better story. On Liberty the Johnny Mann Singers had been backing up Bobby Vee, Gene McDaniels, and others for years. Their own

Above and opposite: Both the single and the LP of "Batman" got full-page trade ads.

Chapter 15 · 1966

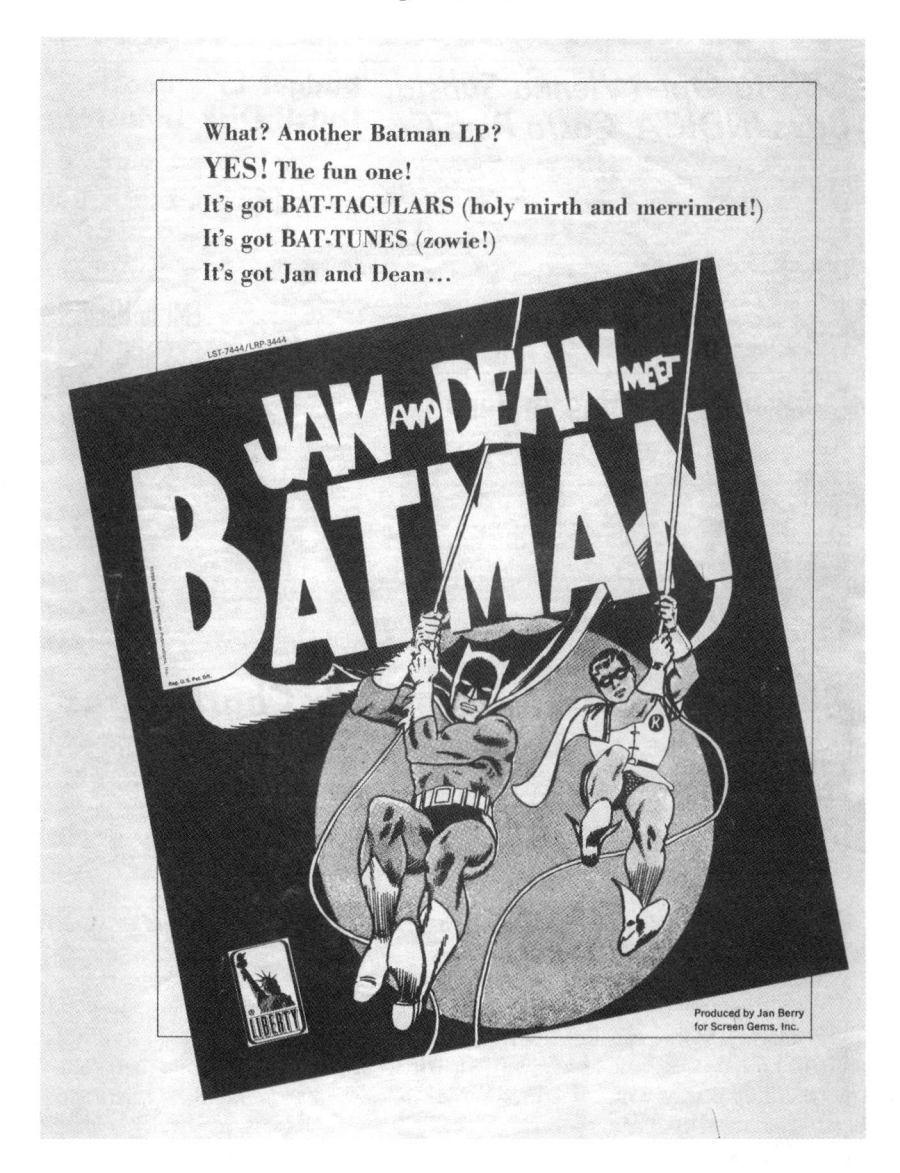

> What? Another Batman LP?
> YES! The fun one!
> It's got BAT-TACULARS (holy mirth and merriment!)
> It's got BAT-TUNES (zowie!)
> It's got Jan and Dean...

LPs had sold very well. Now they had one single that came close to making it, inspired by a hit by another Liberty act. Liberty's T-Bones followed up their hit "No Matter What Shape" Alka-Seltzer ad music from the previous year with an instrumental called "Sippin' and Chippin'." Taking a cue from the T-Bones' Alka-Seltzer tune, the Johnny Mann Singers reeled off "The Cinnamint Shuffle," a song and dance featured on TV commercials for Cinnamint gum. The real name of the tune was "The Mexican Shuffle," but the gum chewers did not bite.

More Latin sounds issued from the persona of one Ruben Rodriguez and his Guadalajara Kings. Latin instrumentals as recorded by former session trumpeter

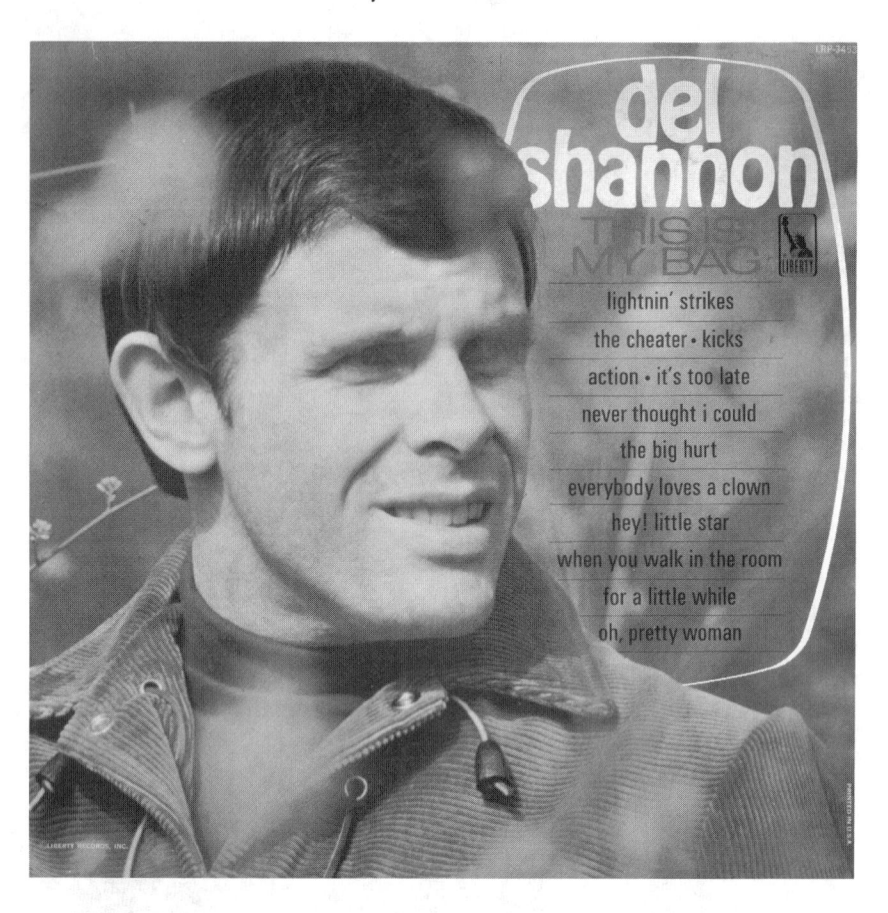

Del Shannon passed on the tune "Action," which became a hit for Freddie Cannon on Warner Bros. Records, but he did do it on this Liberty LP.

Herb Alpert (formerly Jan & Dean's comanager) had been riding the singles and album charts for four years for Alpert's own A&M Records. Hot on the heels of this string of hot tamales came Ruben with his Alpert soundalike, "I Remember You." The recording was very nice, featured some violins, and sounded like a mixture of Alpert's recent hits—"Tijuana Taxi," "Spanish Flea," and "Casino Royale"—which it probably was. The flip side was the standard "Granada." It started out sounding like Alpert's first trumpet hit in 1962, "The Lonely Bull."

In case anyone doubts the connection between Ruben and Alpert, both of Ruben's sides were featured on a Liberty LP, *Tequila & Cream*. That title is significant. In 1965 Alpert released an LP titled *Whipped Cream (& Other Delights)* that not only made #1 on the LP charts, but stayed on the charts for 185 weeks. Ruben and Liberty should have been a tenth as popular!

A really fine girl group, the Pandoras, yielded "About My Baby (I Could Write a Book)" in 1966. A little late for girl groups, this song features lots of overdubbing, a Darlene Love–type fade-out vocal, and tells how each chapter would tell more of the great story of her guy. What would the purpose of such a book be? So other girls would know what to look for in a guy. The Pandoras straddled the fence, girl-group-wise.

On the back was "New Day," sung in a late-1960s flower-power style sans overdubbing, and talking about pure happiness, not about being hung up on a guy. A real gem, every bit as good in its own way as the A side.

Imperial had an also-ran in 1966 that was in a vein similar to the Johnny Mann Singers. Slim Whitman was a VIP at Imperial, with well over two dozen LPs to his credit. His last single to do anything had been in 1957. Now, in 1966, "I Remember You" (Jimmy Dorsey, 1942; Frank Ifield, 1963) pretty nearly got him back on the hit charts—but not quite.

Imperial released an odd single in the summer of 1966. The name on the label, the California Suns, was inspired by the hit single "California Sun" (Rivieras, 1964; Joe Jones, 1961). The song was called the "Masked Grandma" and was an answer song to "The Little Old Lady (from Pasadena)," Liberty's Jan & Dean hit from two years earlier. "Masked Grandma" was about a "Little Old Lady just a little bit meaner than the Little Old Lady from Pasadena." It was written by Carol Conners (who wrote the Rip Chords' 1964 top-five hit, "Hey Little Cobra") and LA DJ Roger Christian (who cowrote Jan & Dean's "Little Old Lady" hit). Further, it was produced by Marshall Leib (who had been a member of the Teddybears of Doré Records' 1958 "To Know Him Is to Love Him" fame and a pair of 1959 Imperial 45 flops). In spite of this splendid pedigree, if all the copies of "Masked Grandma" that sold were laid edge to edge, they probably wouldn't have reached from the meat counter to the checkout.

LPs

Imperial in 1966 released Georgie Fame's LP *Get Away*. More LPs were from Johnny Rivers, Jackie DeShannon, and Sandy Nelson, among others. The Ventures' LPs included *Running Strong* and *Wild Things*.

Liberty is best known for rock 'n' roll records. But it is truly amazing how broad their range of releases really was. The twenty-five Liberty albums between LRP 3430 and LRP 3455 break down as follows: one album by a Baptist church choir; a movie soundtrack by Bobby Vee and Jackie DeShannon; two albums by the venerable Martin Denny; a non–Chipmunks Ross Bagdasarian album; a Julie London album, *The Pair Extraordinaire*; an organ album; a trombone album; two Johnny Mann albums; *Her Majesty's Royal Marines, Vol. 2*; a Del Shannon album; a Bobby Vee album; two albums each by Gary Lewis and the Playboys and the Gants; and *Yesterday*, by Matt Monro (his version of the Lennon-McCartney tune was #8—in England). We must not forget Ruben Rodriguez and the Guadalajara Kings, and there were three albums by Jan & Dean.

Untimely End of Jan & Dean

On a somber note, as previously stated, Jan Berry of Jan & Dean suffered a severe brain injury in a car accident in 1966. Jan & Dean were to star in their own

278   Liberty Records • Part One

LIBERTY: THE FIRST FAMILY OF RECORDED ENTERTAINMENT

LIBERTY RECORDS
IMPERIAL RECORDS
MINIT RECORDS
WORLD PACIFIC RECORDS
PACIFIC JAZZ RECORDS
SOUL CITY RECORDS
BLUE NOTE RECORDS
SUNSET RECORDS
LIBERTY STEREO-TAPE

Liberty Records, Inc., through its many labels, brings the finest in recorded entertainment into your home. Great stars performing the greatest of the new hits and the best of the old. In Liberty's family there is entertainment for everyone.

Liberty Records had something for the entire family in the late sixties.

NBC-TV series in the fall, and had been filming their own feature movie, but Jan's accident ended that—and ended their hits at Liberty. Jan & Dean's five-year contract with Liberty was up, and the duo was forming their own label, J&D Records, when the car wreck occurred.

Liberty did rerelease some old Jan & Dean LP cuts as singles. One, from *Drag City*, "Popsicle," made the national charts. "Popsicle," also known as "Popsicle Truck," was a bomp song. It had been written back in 1962 by Buzz Cason ("Look for a Star" on Liberty in 1960 under the name of Garry Miles, and "Blue Velvet" as a member of the 1960 Liberty group the Statues.) Other Jan & Dean records that were released from the vaults by Liberty after Jan's accident and that became regional sellers were "School Days" (Chuck Berry, 1958) and the previously mentioned "Fiddle Around."

A great deal of mystery and misinformation has cropped up surrounding Jan's accident. There has long been a legend that Jan was having a temper tantrum concerning the draft. The Vietnam draft was in full operation in 1966. Jan had a medical school deferment, which kept him safe from the draft. But the draft in particular and the military in general have a long history of wreaking havoc with rock 'n' rollers' careers. Supposedly the Army announced that it was going to draft Jan, and he responded by driving off in a huge fit and totaling his Sting Ray. In fact, this version of the events has been immortalized in the 1978 CBS-TV biopic, *Deadman's Curve*.

In reality there may have been a draft board slipup, but Jan's attorney was capable of straightening out any such minor snafu. Jan himself cannot tell much about the accident—he was nearly killed and subsequently spent weeks in a coma. However, Jan's father, Bill Berry, recalls the known facts clearly.

"Jan was on the brink of a career in movies, TV, and recordings. On April sixth, nineteen sixty-six, he left his home on Park Lane Circle in Bel Air, drove to the West Gate on Sunset Boulevard, and went past the UCLA athletic fields; then he passed 'Deadman's Curve' and turned right on Whittier Drive in Beverly Hills on his way to a luncheon meeting with Bud Dain at the Beverly Hilton. Jan wanted Bud to be the manager of his soon-to-be J&D Record Company. Whittier Drive is a narrow street, and a gardener's truck was illegally parked on a curve on the west side with the tailgate down, making it impossible to pass without going into the oncoming traffic lane.

"Since there were no witnesses, the most plausible deduction from the evidence of marks on the pavement and curb indicated that Jan swerved to the right to avoid a head-on collision, hit the curb, and veered into the truck.

JAN & DEAN · GOLDEN HITS
VOLUME THREE

EVE OF DESTRUCTION · DETROIT CITY · LOUIE, LOUIE · MEMPHIS · BATMAN
YESTERDAY · EVERYBODY LOVES A CLOWN · 1-2-3 · DO WAH DIDDY DIDDY
LITTLE DEUCE COUPE · HANG ON SLOOPY (MY GIRL SLOOPY) · WALK RIGHT IN

Volume Two had twelve hits. Volume Three, released by Liberty without Jan & Dean's participation after Jan's car accident, had only one hit, "Batman," which was only #66 in spite of its creative excellence and camp approach.

"Hearing the crash, a neighbor called an ambulance. Paramedics and police cut loose the seat belts to extricate him and took him to UCLA hospital. A wheel was on a neighbor's lawn, which raised the possibility that it could have been responsible for the accident.

"About one week before the accident while driving on Sunset in the same area, a knock-off wheel came off [of Jan's car], but he was able to control the car to the side of the road.

"The accident, as portrayed in the movie *Deadman's Curve,* was far from the truth. It was created simply to make the movie more dramatic. There was no communication between the writer or the director with Jan or his family about what was in the script."

Something that the movie did accurately portray, apparently, was Jan's casual and carefree style of driving his Sting Ray, going by engineer Bones Howe's personal experiences with Jan's driving. "I rode in that Sting Ray. I rode home with Jan a few times. It was scary driving with him."

Since Jan was in the hospital, neither he nor Dean, but the art director's daughter, appeared on their last Liberty LP cover.

After the day of the accident, there were no more newly recorded Jan & Dean records. However, this did not stop Liberty from releasing Jan & Dean material. Besides "Popsicle" and the unauthorized 45s "Fiddle Around" and "School Days," Liberty released three Jan & Dean LPs after Jan's accident.

The first postaccident LP was called *Filet of Soul*. This album made #127 on the *Billboard* charts. Not bad, considering it was a mishmash of outtakes, half-finished live concert recordings, and a version of "Dead Man's Curve" that was ironically minus the sound effects of a car crash. This LP featured the Beatles' "Norwegian Wood," which Dean hated, but was so hastily thrown together that the mono version of the LP had a different recording of that song than was on the 45. (For more on this LP, see the interviews with Jan & Dean.)

The second postwreck LP was called *Golden Hits, Volume Three*. Now, Jan & Dean's original *Golden Hits* in 1961 had five hits. *Volume Two* in 1965 had twelve hits. But *Volume Three* didn't have any, save "Batman," which had been unappreciated by the public and topped at #66.

The third postwreck LP was *Popsicle*. Since the song "Popsicle" was only supposed to be the flip side of "Norwegian Wood," Liberty neglected to include it on Volume Three and had to rush out the *Popsicle* LP, which was simply a compilation of old Jan & Dean album cuts. Since Jan was in a coma, photos to adorn these LPs were hard to come by. *Popsicle* just had a little girl eating a banana Popsicle. The other two albums shared nine old 1965 pictures of Jan & Dean, with Jan using the crutch that was a legacy of his train injury that year.

Jan's wreck really was the end of Jan & Dean, at least for the next decade.

The End of Dolton

Another sad event in 1966 was the passing of Dolton Records. Vic Dana had two late Dolton hits, "I Love You Drops" (a top-thirty charter) and "A Million and One." After two more releases, he moved to Liberty for a pair of final hits.

The Ventures had one last Dolton hit on the way out, a #54 instrumental hit of "Secret Agent Man." This was the same song that Johnny Rivers had on Imperial the same year — except that the Ventures record beat Rivers' #3 hit out of the chute by a month. After that record the Ventures had five more Dolton releases that did not chart; then they moved over to Liberty. The last Dolton release was Dolton 327, "Theme from the Wild Angels" b/w "Kickstand," by the Ventures.

The End of the Fleetwoods

The Ventures' Dolton labelmates, the Fleetwoods, had not had a chart record in three years. So in 1966 they called it quits. Actually, as Gretchen Christopher explains, the Fleetwoods' career ended in a series of events over the years. "We retired from recording in February of 1966 after seven years," recalls Gretchen.

When asked why he called it quits, Gary Troxel says, "Well, the contract ran out. I don't know if I would have left the group. I just kind of thought that we more or less went our own way. When you don't have a contract, there is not much for the group to do. We did a show here and there after that. When someone wanted us to sing, we usually did."

The Fleetwoods' last Dolton 45 was 317, "For Lovin' Me," which came out in early 1966. Gretchen: "Liberty wanted to sign us again, pick up our option, but they didn't want to pay us any guarantee. And so we just decided, 'Forget it,' that we'd retire. We were disappointed with their business practices and with the different A&R people we were working with, especially the last couple we had worked with. It certainly was not like working with Bob. Recording with Liberty was not bringing us as much happiness as it previously had."

And the touring Fleetwoods? "Actually, while Gary was in the Navy and we brought in Vic to replace Gary for touring, we cut back pretty much. Tours were just turned down at that point, after the first couple of years when Gary was in the Navy. I continued to do promotion, interviews, even for the armed services, that were broadcast overseas and continued to do performances on my own as 'Gretchen Christopher of the Fleetwoods.' So I kept the name going. And I have always done radio interviews and things, continuing to promote the group and the music and keep the name alive."

CHAPTER 16

Liberty Acquisitions, Special Series, and Subsidiaries

The execs at Liberty were never content just to sit back and take care of business at Liberty. They were always on the lookout for other hot properties that they could acquire and develop. More than that, people who hoped to have hits or needed help would sometimes come to Liberty for a boost.

Liberty president Al Bennett was a real wheeler-dealer, and very ambitious. He had aspirations far beyond those of a little rock 'n' roll record company. Bud Dain knows what kind of plans Al had for Liberty. "Al Bennett read a book called 'My Years at General Motors' by the head of General Motors, and he fell in love with the division concept. So we divisionalized. There was Liberty/Imperial/Minit Division, and the World Pacific/Pacific Jazz Division, and the Blue Note Division. It worked real well, because each guy had his own promotion department and each guy had his own A&R department. They competed with each other but worked under the same roof. Blue Note was always in New York, as was UA."

Then there was always the takeover method of expansion. Bud Dain remembers that "little labels in LA would find out they could not handle the national distribution and make a deal with Liberty or someone else." And presto, Liberty would have a new division.

Between splitting forces, repackaging, gobbling up smaller fish, and reissuing, Liberty always had something going, even if, in a rare moment, they did not have several records in the nation's top forty.

Various Artists Compilations

One small example of this penchant for getting material outside the Liberty building occurred on the Liberty Original Hit collection LPs. Snuff Garrett looked far and wide, high and low, for masters to lease from other companies to include on these LPs. He left no stone unturned. For instance, Ernie Freeman, a friend of Snuff's and an arranger at Liberty, had a big hit with the instrumental "Raunchy" in 1957. Given that he later came to Liberty, that he was a friend of Snuff's, and that Liberty now owned the Imperial catalog, it would have made sense if Snuff had included Freeman's version of "Raunchy" on a greatest hits LP. But he didn't.

Chapter 16 · Liberty Acquisitions, Special Series, and Subsidiaries   283

15 NUMBER 1 HITS
THE ORIGINAL HITS – VOL. 10

- SURF CITY ★ Jan & Dean
- TAKE GOOD CARE OF MY BABY ★ Bobby Vee
- BLUEBERRY HILL ★ Fats Domino
- TEQUILA ★ The Champs
- COME SOFTLY TO ME ★ The Fleetwoods
- PARTY DOLL ★ Buddy Knox
- ALLEY OOP ★ The Hollywood Argyles
- WITCH DOCTOR ★ David Seville
- WALK – DON'T RUN ★ The Ventures
- MOTHER-IN-LAW ★ Ernie K-Doe
- TOSSIN' AND TURNIN' ★ Bobby Lewis
- FLYING SAUCER (Parts 1 & 2) ★ Buchanan & Goodman
- RAUNCHY ★ Bill Justis
- MULE SKINNER BLUES ★ The Fendermen
- DO YOU WANT TO DANCE? ★ Bobby Freeman

LRP-3344

How many other companies released oldies LPs with fifteen #1 hits?

Actually, it had been back in the early days of Liberty Records when a series of Liberty Golden Hits LPs was started. Called the *Original Hits*, this series included volumes 1 through 11. Volume 10 was also titled *15 Number One Hits*. With fifteen songs instead of the standard twelve, and all of them #1 hits, this LP was a real rock 'n' roll bonanza! The #1 hit designation was loosely defined, but the lineup was impressive:

"Surf City" (Jan & Dean, Liberty)
"Blueberry Hill" (Fats Domino, Imperial)
"Tequila" (The Champs, Challenge)
"Come Softly to Me" (The Fleetwoods, Dolton)
"Take Good Care of My Baby" (Bobby Vee, Liberty)
"Mother-in-Law" (Ernie K-Doe, Minit)
"The Flying Saucer 1 & 2" (Buchannan and Goodman, Luniverse)

"Raunchy" (Bill Justice, Phillips)
"Tossin' & Turnin'" (Bobby Lewis, Beltone)
"Party Doll" (Buddy Knox, Liberty)
"Witch Doctor" (David Seville, Liberty)
"Mule Skinner Blues" (Fendermen, Soma)
"Alley Oop" (Hollywood Argyles, Lute)
"Do You Wanna Dance" (Bobby Freeman, Josie)
"Walk, Don't Run" (Ventures, Dolton)

original golden greats vol.3

Walk-Don't Run **THE VENTURES**	Teen Beat **SANDY NELSON**	Red River Rock **JOHNNY & THE HURRICANES**
Sleep Walk **SANTO & JOHNNY**	Topsy-Part II **COZY COLE**	Hearts Of Stone **BILL BLACK COMBO**
Tuff **ACE CANNON**	Bongo Rock **PRESTON EPPS**	Walkin' With Mr. Lee **LEE ALLEN**
Smokie-Part II **BILL BLACK COMBO**	So Rare **JIMMY DORSEY**	Tequila **THE CHAMPS**

This is the third cover design for the Liberty oldies series.

The list is all the more impressive when all of the Liberty/Dolton/Imperial/Minit Records hits are taken into account! "Party Doll" had originally been a hit on Roulette, but after Buddy Knox moved to Liberty, he recut the song quite well. Putting Bill Justice's "Raunchy" on the LP was magnanimous.

Freeman's recording was a cover of the original recording by "Raunchy" Bill Justice on Phillips Records. In fact Bill Justice composed the catchy instrumental. The two versions were equally huge, top-five hits in 1957. But even though Liberty owned Freeman's cover, Snuff placed Justice's original on *Liberty Original Hits, Vol. 10*.

With the success of the *Original Hits* series, Liberty initiated other various artists series. *Original Golden Greats* was a direct descendant of *Original Hits* but added some new touches. For instance, *Original Golden Greats, Vol. 3* was all instrumentals. On Imperial, a series *Best of the Blues* was released, and three LPs were released in a *New Orleans* series, in honor of the town in which so many Imperial artists were discovered. Pacific Jazz released a *This Is the Blues* series. Liberty also produced the *Original Country Hits* series and *Original Rhythm and Blues Hits* series.

Chapter 16 · Liberty Acquisitions, Special Series, and Subsidiaries   285

This Imperial Legendary Masters LP didn't feature any hits, but the cuts were classics nonetheless.

Finally, there were one-shot compilation LPs like *Gems of Jazz* on Blue Note, *Shut Downs and Hill Climbs* on Liberty and *Solid Gold Hits* on Imperial.

Also on Imperial was a set of albums called the *Legendary Masters* series. These albums drew on the old, early 1950s, original Imperial master tapes, as well as the master tapes of Aladdin, Caddy, Combo, Crown, Dig, Dootone, Flair, Flip, Hollywood, Kicks, Lucky, Modern, Music City, Rhythm, RPM, Showtime, and Vita record companies. The *Legendary Masters* albums folded open, with extensive documentation inside, including titles of other released and unreleased recordings not even on the LP but recorded by the featured artists. The cuts included both local R&B hits and misses of old-time groups as well as many previously unreleased songs. Volume 1 was *Rhythm and Blues, the End of an Era*. It featured artists like the Shaweez, the Spiders, and the Jivers. Volume 2 was *Rural Blues*, and volume 3 was *Urban Blues, Volume 1*. These LPs are invaluable collectors' items today.

Catalog Acquisitions

When Liberty gobbled up Imperial in 1962, the deal did not end with the Imperial catalog and imprint. Imperial had its own subsidiaries, which Liberty acquired in the deal. Liberty had begun as a white-artists label, not by choice but by local demographics. A half dozen years later, Liberty was still mostly white, with a few exceptions such as Gene McDaniels and Billy Ward. Dolton, too, was white. As Dolton founder Bob Reisdorff explained, no black artists ever approached him up in Seattle. The only black artist Dolton ever carried was the Five Pearls.

By contrast Imperial was well-known for its black roster, from Fats Domino to Ernie Freeman. But compared to the other, smaller independent labels Liberty acquired, Imperial was hardly R&B at all.

Aladdin, Post, Philo, and R&B were among the small, mostly West Coast R&B labels that Liberty absorbed.

Subsidiaries and Special Series

The thrust of Liberty was mainstream rock 'n' roll/pop/top-forty music. Imperial and Dolton were maintained in pretty much the same vein. But the Liberty offices also dabbled, sometimes rather heavily, in other kinds of music. Rather than clutter their pop hit catalog with artists and songs that would mean nothing to the teen record market, Liberty established several subsidiaries, some of which have already been mentioned in passing, or in the cases of Dolton and Imperial, in some detail.

Dolton

Dolton was a Seattle label that was formed in 1958 by Bob Reisdorff. Its first release was the Fleetwoods' "Come Softly to Me" in 1959, which was a number-one million seller. For that one release only, the label was called Dolphin. The only other artists on Dolton who gained any prominence were the Ventures and Vic Dana. The ironic thing about that was that Vic Dana was signed to a solo contract only because he was hired to fill in for Gary Troxel of the Fleetwoods while he was in the Navy. That little contractual affiliation certainly worked out OK for Dolton and Liberty over the years! Liberty acquired Dolton in 1960.

Si Waronker liked Bob Reisdorff and Dolton records. And why not? It made Liberty money with little or no work. "Bob Reisdorff tried as hard as any man I've ever known to make what he considered hits. And he was damn successful at doing it. In Seattle he could not get final polish on a record, or distribution. So he moved to LA. When Bob brought in a record, after we bought his company, everything he bought, I liked it. Because he tried very hard. And when he didn't know something, he asked questions. I have nothing but good things to say about him. And I add that he was a gentleman."

After 1966 Dolton LPs were referred to as the "Liberty 2000 Series." Once Bob Reisdorff had sold out and left, the distinction between the two labels was mostly on paper.

Freedom

What an apt name for an offspring of the Liberty label! Freedom was a small label that released records in the rockabilly vein. One artist on Freedom was Texan

The second of Johnny Burnette's three Freedom releases. His name was spelled correctly on this one.

Jewel Akens. Jewel was named by his mother—she'd expected a daughter! As part of a group called the Four Dots, he appeared on one Freedom single with help from Jerry Capehart, Eddie Cochran's manager. Eddie is thought to have played guitar on Jewel's record. Interestingly, Jewel Akens's big hit of 1965, "The Birds and the Bees," was on Era Records. That is the label founded by Si Waronker's relatives with the scratch originally earmarked as Liberty's seed money.

Freedom was also the label on which Johnny Burnette appeared as Johnny Burnett (without the final *e*), singing "Kiss Me Baby" and "Sweet Baby Doll," before he signed with Liberty proper.

Freedom Records, although much less well known than Dolton, was actually Si Waronker's first Liberty subsidiary. "'Freedom' came when we needed a second label." He started it largely for practical reasons. *"Billboard* would list only so many records by one label at a time. The distributors would take only so many records out of one company. So we had to have a secondary label, and we called it 'Freedom.' Freedom had few releases; it was only for when we had an overabundance of releases. We decided that if we had eight records on Liberty, we would put one or two on Freedom. That way our promotion people could go out there with not too many on one label."

Why was Johnny Burnette put on Freedom? "Because no one thought that anything was going to happen with Johnny! He was almost like a throwaway. Then suddenly he sold some records." Yeah, suddenly, under the production genius of Snuffy!

Imperial

Imperial was a very old label that had been in the forefront of R&B recording for many years. Most of the artists on Imperial before the Liberty acquisition were black. Si says, "We bought Imperial because finally we would have something that had a catalog, and especially more black and rock 'n' roll artists. The people that were out, like our promotion and sales people and Al Bennett, well, this is difficult, but they were all Deep Southerners. It was not a matter of not wanting black artists. It was a matter of not being able to draw them. We had Billy Ward and Gene McDaniels and one A&R man for awhile who was black. So we needed a black label.

"Basically Imperial had black artists, and it was a good deal, although it did not turn out to be as good a deal as we expected. We paid the guy a million bucks for the company. But the guy had more records out there in the stores that we had to take back than it was worth." And Ricky Nelson and Fats Domino were leaving because "Lou Chudd, Imperial's founder, didn't want any more part of the business. He wanted out. He had made his money, and he was not well. He wanted out as quickly as he could get out. But the catalog made Liberty damn near into a major company.

"Lou deserved credit for being one of the few men who did not overpress. He would stop at one or two million, whatever he thought was needed, and stop. He did not want to take them back. If a record flopped, a distributor could keep the leftovers. Then when the next record came out that was a hit, the distributor would take the new records and pay the company with the old leftover records. It was a hard business."

After the acquisition Imperial's character changed. Most of the hits were by white instead of black artists. Fats Domino had been on the label since the 1940s. He left the label about the time of the acquisition, and although a number of Domino singles were released after that, none became hits.

Ken Revercomb, who had previously been in the promotion department at Liberty, was put in nominal charge of Imperial Division: "We were a unique company in that we were all very young men in what was then an old man's business. After a couple of years in promotion and sales, I became the general manager of Imperial Records when Liberty purchased it.

"Al Bennett's General Motors Division structure was a problem. Liberty's gross was not big enough to support branches. I myself was very antibranch." In fact, after Liberty bought it Imperial continued with its independent distribution instead of using the Liberty branch system. "Needless to say, that caused some friction. As the branch system needed additional volume, they started to suck Imperial records into it.

"Imperial occupied the original Liberty building on La Brea, while the company

Fans of Pet Clark's hit "Downtown" could mistakenly buy this cunningly titled Imperial album of her older recordings.

bought the building on Sunset. Although it was just a few blocks, it might just as well have been in New York. I ran it just that way, independently." Well, *independently* might be a word that is a bit too strong. Ken Revercomb may have been the boss in his building, but as Si Waronker put it, "Any and every deal that was made after I left in 1963 was made by Al Bennett. No one else made any deals, and Al ran everything. Good or bad, Al was responsible for everything that was signed or released.

"When Liberty bought Imperial from Lou Chudd, it was [in bad shape]. The only acts we inherited were Slim Whitman and Sandy Nelson, and Sandy had cut his foot off in a motorcycle accident. I had a drummer with no foot! Jeannie Sealey was the Imperial secretary. She's now a country singer. We were two against the world. There was friction, people in the company who were not too thrilled with my being head of Imperial Records. But I felt that Imperial was the place I could make my niche, and I got lucky.

"One of the first things I brought out was an album. Since we didn't have any artists or anything, but Petula Clark on Warner Bros. had 'Downtown.' I found out we had enough masters to bring out an LP, and we called it *Uptown*. And we did a Fats Domino LP of old masters called *Here We Go Again*. We did that kind of thing until we could get going. But one of the first acts we signed was Johnny Rivers, then the Hollies, Billy J. Kramer, and Mel Carter. The child, Imperial, outgrew the parent, Liberty.

"Capitol had the first right of refusal on all the British artists, but they passed on them, and so I got them for free. No money. They'd just ship over all the masters, and I'd release what I wanted to. It was haphazard.

"Doin' the FLake" was recorded by Gary Lewis for a Kellogg's boxtop offer when Johnny Rivers' "Whiskey à Go-Go" background disqualified him.

"Almost everything we released was a hit for awhile. We had Irma Thomas. Allan Touisant sent her out. She was so ugly that we didn't dare put her picture on the cover. So we put a kitchen light bulb on there and called it *Take a Look*. But she could sure sing.

"We recorded Johnny Rivers live at the Whiskey à Go-Go for the grand total of eighteen hundred dollars including the artwork and sold almost a million albums. He came from Nashville and played a guitar; he was not too good at that. He came out here on the run; he was trying to get away from Audrey Williams and got a gig at the Whiskey à Go-Go. Lou Adler picked him up and brought him in, and we signed him. It wasn't that big a deal.

"Kellogg's wanted a premium for a cereal box top deal. They approached us and we said, 'Fine, we'll use Johnny Rivers, he's the biggest thing we've got.' We were all set and ready to go until they realized his biggest credential was *Live at the Whiskey à Go-Go*. They turned the deal down because of the connection of whiskey and American breakfast cereal. So we did Gary Lewis and the Playboys instead. It was a big success. We did maybe seven hundred thousand copies. But you could have put the National Anthem on there and it wouldn't have made any difference. On the cereal box, it was gonna do a half million anyway.

"Ricky Nelson left Imperial when I came in. Ozzie came in and that was the year of the first million-dollar contract. I couldn't live with that at all. The whole company wasn't worth a million dollars.

"One of the coups was getting Cher Bono. Sonny was a promotion man around town. He brought in the master of 'I Got You, Babe' and wanted twenty-five thousand for it, which again was too much money. Everybody liked it, but Sonny and Cher had been around as Caesar and Cleo and they were kind of commonplace around town. After a lot of soul searching, Imperial did not take the master and they went to Atlantic. But Imperial did do one thing at the time that was interesting. They had signed Sonny and Cher, but not as individuals. So Imperial signed Cher.

"But Imperial was mine, and I am really kind of proud of that. When I left, it was under a hail of bullets. They were getting the calf ready to take to market, and although I was an executive in the company, I didn't know about it. They wanted to dissolve Imperial, put everything under the Liberty label. They felt it looked better from a goodwill point of view. I took great exception to that. That was too much for me, so I left. Later UA did the same thing to Liberty.

"I was long gone by then; I left in 1967. I had a deal with Randy Wood at Dot for my own label, but Randy had sold to Paramount, and Paramount, unbeknownst to me, had fired Randy Wood. So there I was without a gig. I eventually ended up at Dot, and it was the biggest mistake I ever made. I just languished there for two years; then I went on to form my own production company.

"But I was in love with Imperial, although I did not make a helluva lot of money."

The reason that Ken Revercomb did not make a "helluva lot of money" for his time heading up Imperial was that once it was bought by Liberty, Imperial was no longer in reality a record label in its own right. Imperial did not record any acts or conduct recording sessions. Instead Imperial became a second arm of Liberty. In other words, Liberty and Imperial did not compete; Imperial was sort of Liberty's side door.

To a large extent Imperial eventually became an outlet for the "Liberty overflow" rather than a black label. Again, as with Freedom, there was a feeling that having too many new records on one label was a detriment. That is, if a label rep was making the rounds of record distributors or radio stations pushing new product, having too many different records to brag about in the few minutes that are available can be awkward. But long-established Imperial, with its lengthy history of big hits, was a much more credible outlet for material than little hitless Freedom had been.

Particularly, Imperial was used for the mid-sixties British-invasion material to which Liberty acquired the rights: the Hollies, Georgie Fame, and Billy J. Kramer with the Dakotas, even in cases when a British artist like Billy J. had originally been on Liberty in 1963 and early 1964.

In addition old Imperial material from before the buyout was repackaged and reissued as LPs and oldie 45s. Even the Imperial singles and albums of new material by American Cher Bono were not true Imperial material — Sonny produced those sessions independently and delivered the masters to Liberty/Imperial. That's why Sonny's voice can be heard on some recordings, even though Sonny and Cher were signed to Atco Records.

The Imperial purchase was very worthwhile. The label cost only $1 million, with a proviso that the cost of any records that had been released prior to the purchase that were returned by distributors after the purchase would be deducted from the million. That eventually totaled more than three hundred thousand returned units.

Liberty Jazz Series

In 1956 Si started the Liberty Jazz series. Numbered as a 6000 series with the prefix LJH, this brief series ran for only thirteen titles, or perhaps fewer. The numbering began with LJH 6001, *Jazz in Hollywood,* and ended with LJH 6013, *Buddy Childers Quartet.* However, since Si liked to skip numbers to keep people from knowing for sure how prolific the company was, one cannot be sure that a full thirteen LPs were actually issued.

Si Waronker was always a jazz enthusiast. "Yeah, we had a lot of jazz. The jazz series was when Howard Rumsey and the Lighthouse All Stars played in a place on Redondo Beach. The Lighthouse All Stars were people like Bud Shank. They would come there and jam. Meanwhile we would record as much as we could. He really ran that part as a Howard Rumsey series."

"There were an awful lot of jazz things that I wanted. I wanted desperately to have a jazz label, or at least jazz as a part of the label. But the only real jazz we could get was the saxophone quartet, which was not really jazz but more like a string quartet but with great saxophone players. I can't say that we were too successful with our jazz label."

Liberty Stereo Releases

In the period 1960–61, Liberty began to promote stereo. In fact, several stereo albums were issued in a series that was created expressly for the purpose of promoting stereo. LST was the prefix indicating stereo on Liberty albums. LST 100 and 101 were *Liberty Proudly Presents Stereo* and *This Is Stereo,* by various artists. There were three other albums. One, that even Si does not recall, was curiously titled *Terror Tales by "The Old Sea Hag."*

LST 100 is like a Liberty time capsule. "Liberty Records proudly presents, STEREO, Visual Sound. Close your eyes, and you will see!" Reads like another of Si's gimmicks, like Spectra-Sonic and Exotica. "Visual Sound Stereo" was the phrase used on all Liberty stereo albums for the better part of a decade.

After that proud announcement by one Jimmy Wallington, a series of hi-fi/stereo performances are dished up for the listener of LST 100, including a sound tour of the Liberty Studios. The first is a marching band. The engineer Ted Keep, after whom the Chipmunk Theodore was named, is introduced. Ted supposedly then cues up a series of special stereo tapes: jets taking off at the International Congress of Flight at Las Vegas; a Ping-Pong match between Ted and Jim; Spencer Hagen's group playing "Bubble Bath"; and the Chipmunks racing through the halls of Liberty. Julie London talks and sings; Martin Denny's Exotic Sounds presents "Stranger In Paradise," full of the usual bird noises; Don Swan, who recorded the very first Liberty LP, plays "I Love Paris in the Springtime."

We also visit a supposed A&R meeting in the Liberty conference room, where the song "Caravan" is reviewed. Most interesting is the assertion on this LP that Liberty Visual Sound Stereo presents not just the sound in the middle, but also sound left, right, back, front, and even up and down! C'mon, Si! Even quadraphonic sound didn't go up and down!

LST was the stereo prefix in general. The 100 series was devoted to special releases. Ninety-nine percent of Liberty stereo albums had the LST 7000 series numbers, and they were simply stereo versions of the regular LRP 3000 series albums.

Classical Album Series

Si's background was in serious music, dating back to his early childhood experiences with the violin. Therefore it can come as no surprise that Liberty — meaning

Si—took a flyer with a Liberty Classical series. The numbering system began with SWL 15001, *The Comedians* (Kabalevsky), and ran for only a half dozen or so titles.

"We tried to do a classical series," muses Si, "but it never really happened. I wanted to buy Westminster when it looked like it might become available. But it would have taken so much money, and to do it right, you would have to set up a whole different distribution system. You'd need someone to run it who knew what they were doing.

"I finally decided that, someday, if we could buy an existing company with the people to go with it, then I would do it. We got a few things, but I can't say we had classical music."

Liberty Premier Series

Jazz. Classical. It almost seems as if Bobby Troup's opinion, that Si started Liberty as an outlet for the kind of serious, quality music he encountered at Fox, but which never lived beyond the films it was featured in, had a kernel of truth. Si asserts that Liberty was never intended to serve that function, but his son, Lenny, now president of Warner Bros. Records, takes the middle ground between Bobby Troup's position and his dad's.

"This is just my opinion, based on something that my dad gave to me that had to do with what Bobby Troup said. It had to do with important music, or music that he felt had value. Look at the things he worked on: the Fleix Slatkin recordings, which were really important to him. I shouldn't speak for him, but I know it was important.

"Liberty had serious music that was done in a way that could be easily accepted by people who weren't familiar with serious music. So I think that Bobby Troup may have had some sense of some of what my dad was trying to do when he was thinking about it. There was a side of it that had to do with art, and a side that had to do with commerce. But even the commerce side was interesting.

"Dad told me something that I will never forget. He told me that if you go into the studio, look at the charts, study them, know what is going on, figure out what makes sense to do. Then you really look at the charts and see what *isn't* there. Those are the ones you go after. That is indelible in my mind. It went right to my brain. I think I was fifteen or sixteen; I don't remember where or when he said it, but it was great and it stuck.

"The David Seville stuff fit that category, Julie London fit that, Martin Denny fit that, the Slatkin stuff fit that, 'Witch Doctor,' none of that had anything to do with what the current trends were.

"I think that, early on, he had more success with those things that were different than with the things he did when he was trying to have commercial success. It was always a little off the wall. He understood that.

"I sat in on an A&R meeting that was very aggravating for him but very interesting for me. It was with Snuff and a guy named Clyde Otis, who came from Brook Benton at Mercury. My dad had hired him away from Mercury, and he worked with Timi Yuro.

"Clyde was making a kind of record, a certain kind of record. And he never varied from that. The same arranger, the same sound, the same engineer, the same studio, the same way. And Snuff, to some extent, was trapped in that too, because he was successful. So my dad had an A&R meeting, which was about the dangers of getting caught up in that. But those guys couldn't figure it out. Why mess around with something that is working? But his feeling was that it was not messing around with something that was working—it was experimenting and trying something else. Don't do away with it; develop it.

"Dad understood the need for that, because he had been around tremendously talented and in some cases innovative people who had to think that way to have created what they did. Whether it was Alfred Newman, Bernard Hermann, or Charles Chaplin. The sum total of all that exposure effected the way he saw things, taking chances. Even if you weren't a visionary, at least give it a shot. That kind of thing was his strength; he had vision and has always had vision. When those people finally didn't listen to him, it hurt. That was one reason he left. Only a few people knew where he was coming from.

"As rock 'n' roll became a real phenomenon, my dad knew it was important. He knew everything from classical music to the popular music of his youth and movie scores. He knew how that all fit together in an interesting way. There was a musical point of view. It wasn't specific, but it was there.

"In terms of what Bobby Troup said, about my dad's wanting to preserve good music, there was something there, because I sure picked up on it. It made a tremendous impression on me, more than anything else. The idea of meshing serious music and commercial music was, I think, something that he was interested in."

Rock 'n' roll is usually thought of as a blend of country music and R&B, and there were a few records that fit that category, especially early on. But the bulk of rock 'n' roll, even Bill Haley, was actually a fusion of country, blues, and pop. And in Si's case, perhaps a bit of classical influence as well. Putting violins on Bobby Vee and Johnny Burnette records was brilliant and directly related to Si's musical training and background. "Oh, sure," agrees Lenny. "Snuff spent six months with Si before Snuffy produced, watching my dad work with Felix and the string sections. That was something that happened."

So, besides the short-lived Classical series, there were all those violins, and the Liberty Premier series.

If the original concept behind Liberty had been to record, preserve, and disseminate the semiclassical movie scores that Hollywood turned out but were lost after a movie closed, the Liberty Premier series would almost seem to fulfill that alleged original concept of Liberty, at least to a certain extent. Si's son, Lenny, who was a young teenager when his dad founded Liberty, sees that as a possibility.

The Liberty Premier series—some three dozen LPs, were released—contained "beautiful music" as opposed to rock 'n' roll. Felix Slatkin was the star of about a third of the Premier LPs. Movie themes, Broadway tunes, big-band ballads, and other nonrock pieces were given lush, orchestral arrangements and performances by "the Fantastic Strings of Felix Slatkin."

Almost one-half of the Premier series LPs were the offspring of Snuff Garrett, he the producer of the rock 'n' roll hit Liberty 45s. "The 50 Guitars of Tommy Garrett" were heard doing country songs, Hawaiian songs, Brazilian songs, Latin songs, Broadway songs, you name it and the fifty guitars of Tommy Garrett did a Premier LP of it.

The remaining LPs in the series were by Liberty trombonist Si Zentner, "50 Velvet Brass," and other similar aggregations.

The logo for the Liberty Premier series LPs.

Si had always known that for Liberty to succeed he needed hit pop singles. Yet he still had a fondness for the music he grew up with at Fox. "The Premier series was where we started to use big orchestras. Felix Slatkin came from Fox and was a concertmaster. A first-class conductor. The Premier series was where the big sound came in."

Si always wanted a hook, as he called it, a raison d'être for anything he did. "The hook was that it was premier, special. Why was it special? Basically it wasn't, except that it was pressed on the best vinyl. We played tricks with echo chambers."

There were always unforeseen events in the record biz. A big one happened with the Premier series. "The second to the last album I did, Felix was to come record on a Tuesday morning, and on Monday night he dropped dead at a very young age. But we recorded Tuesday morning anyway. It was one of the best albums we ever did. All the artists would not take any money for the session. They wanted all of the money to go for Felix's wife and kids. What else could we do? That was one of several albums with an artist's name who had very little to do with it, or was not even there."

Liberty Special Series

There was only one LP in the Liberty Special series. It was by country-folk singers Bud and Travis, *In Concert*. In fact, it was the live, "in concert" hook that justified this series for Si Waronker.

"I was a little nuts. I had a Spectra-Sonic series, a Premier series, and a Special series. Since the Bud and Travis album was recorded live, we called it a 'Special Series' record. Everything had to have a little bit of a hook. I thought it was a good way of selling records."

Minit Records

Only a dozen or so LPs were released on the Minit label. One was by Ernie K-Do, to commemorate his Minit 45 hit records "Mother-in-Law," "Te-Ta-Te-Ta-Ta,"

The Minit Records logo.

and three subsequent charting follow-up songs. Jimmy Holiday, Aaron Neville, the O'Jays, and Jimmy McCracklin rounded out the roster of blues artists that recorded on Minit.

Pacific Jazz Records and World Pacific Records

Pacific Jazz was another whole story. Here an entirely different brand of music was produced.

The artists were people like Zoot Sims; Bud Shank; the Jazz Crusaders; Wes, Buddy, and Monk Montgomery; and Gerry Mulligan. The selections were titles like "& Come 11," "Good Groove," "Tempo de Blues," and "2 Degrees East, 3 Degrees West."

Si said that he "wanted a jazz label because I was always hot about jazz. We just bought it. We bought Howard Rumsey. There were a lot of good jazz artists on the little Howard Rumsey label. We must have had twelve or fifteen releases that he recorded for us."

On the World Pacific label, things got really esoteric. There were about ten sitar LPs by Ravi Shankar. There were albums of Japanese music by Kimio Eto. And Bud Shank, who also appeared on Pacific Jazz Records, turned up on the World Pacific 1400 series.

But there was also a World Pacific 1800 series, on which almost anything could turn up. Some examples: *The King and I* from the musical, *Endless Summer* from the movie, *A Spoonful of Jazz* by Bud Shank (turning up yet again), *Blew Mind* by the Hardtimes, and LPs with rock guitar, twelve-string guitar, folk songs, jazz albums, Brazilian music, big-band music, and orchestral music. The De-Fenders were a Ventures-type group that played Fender guitars. The Kentucky Colonels, the Stoneman Family, and Tut Taylor were three of the country artists on WP 1800. The WP 1800 series also featured a few hit artists. Bob Lind's LP *Don't Be Concerned* featured his big World Pacific label hit, "Elusive Butterfly," and his *Photographs of*

Chapter 16 · Liberty Acquisitions, Special Series, and Subsidiaries

The World Pacific/Pacific Jazz logo.

Feeling had twelve original songs. An American group that was often taken for a British-invasion group, the Hardtimes, was signed to WP 1800. Their hit, "Fortune Teller," was featured on their LP *Blew Mind*. WP 1800's most interesting LP was *A Spoonful of Jazz*, Bud Shank doing jazz versions of all of the hits of the Lovin' Spoonful!

World Pacific was another part of Si's desire to have catalog. "That was another one bought to add to the catalog. I felt that the more catalog you had, the more substance you had. In case you hit a dry spell, at least you could repackage. That would pay off today on CDs."

The emphasis at World Pacific was probably on LPs, not 45s, as it was with the Premier series. But Bud Shank, who had at least a dozen World Pacific LPs (as well as half a dozen LPs on Pacific Jazz), also had a hit 45 on the Pacific Jazz label. The song was the Lennon-McCartney composition "Michelle," in early 1966. The Hardtimes' 45 "Fortune Teller" also made a chart appearance.

The biggest pop seller on 45s from World Pacific was Bob Lind. Besides his two WP LPs, he got three songs on the national charts, including the top-five hit "Elusive Butterfly."

Dotty Woodward was one of the main forces behind Liberty's jazz labels. Dotty is the widow of Liberty art director Woody Woodward. Unfortunately Woody died around 1985 of a brain aneurism. His illness was very unexpected, and he was in a coma for three months before he died. Both worked for Pacific Jazz Records, making Dotty one of the few women to work at Liberty outside of secretarial staff and singers.

"When Woody and I were married, he was managing Rare Records on Hollywood Boulevard, and I was managing Pfier Nichol's record department. We both worked for Ray Avery. I was also working for the disc jockeys at KFWB radio.

"Dick Bock started Pacific Jazz in the summer of 1952. I went to work for him about six months later. Dick used to work for Albert Marks at Discovery. Dick recorded Gerry Mulligan and Chet Baker and their very well-known group at The Hague. Roy Hart was a drummer who owned 'Drum City' with Ramo Velli, and put up some money, so Roy and Dick and a man named Phil Terrifsky started Pacific Jazz. It grew and grew and grew, and eventually Liberty bought Pacific Jazz."

How was Dotty recruited by Pacific Jazz? "Dick Bock just came in one day in February nineteen fifty-three and said, 'Dotty, I need a secretary, are you available?' And I said, 'OK!' It was just the two of us; our office was in the middle of Drum City. Dick and I did it, I was his girl Friday, and I did everything from promotion to the books and publishing.

"Woody joined Pacific Jazz in nineteen fifty-five. It was a very small label, with Gerry Mulligan, Chet Baker, Chico Hamilton, Harry 'Sweets' Edison, Bud Shank, and Laurindo Almeida. Soon, we took on a bookkeeper, formed a corporation with Dick as president and Woody as vice president. In nineteen ninety a big concert called 'A Salute to Pacific Jazz Records' was held in LA at the Wadsworth Theater. The only three people who are left from Pacific Jazz were introduced: myself, photographer Bill Claxton, and Roy Hart, who had been a partner at one point."

Si says he bought jazz because he liked jazz. Dotty expresses it a bit differently. She says that Liberty bought World Pacific "because it was a good product. We were a hot item with a very good catalog and a lot of good music that we published. It was a good investment for Liberty. We also had a wonderful studio on Third and Robertson in West LA. Neil Diamond owns it now. It was part of the deal and Liberty kept it. They negotiated separately for Woody as an art director; only Dick Bock went with the deal. Woody wrote a book in the late 1950s called *Jazz Americana*. It is out of print and goes for thousands of dollars today."

Dotty takes justifiable pride in the accomplishments of Pacific Jazz. "We recorded the Maharishi in the beginning before the Beatles discovered him. We recorded stuff way before it happened, like the two-thousand-year-old man with Mel Brooks and Carl Reiner, on our own. We recorded stuff that was ahead of its time and became big later.

"A funny story. The Maharishi decided that this certain lady should marry Dick Bock. She was the one who decided Dick should get rid of the record company. So when Al Bennett proposed the situation, it worked out real well. Because Liberty paid very close attention to the market, which I didn't. That was their thing. So apparently it was all predestined!

"There were very few women in the record business at that time. Dottie Vance from Victor and I were the only ones doing promotion in those days. I went to every record date; I am a major jazz fan, and most women were not, even the wives. I knew the musicians because we were all poor and young."

The name of Bock's label was changed from Pacific Jazz to World Pacific because of a conflict with another company's name in the late 1950s.

"Dick was made head of World Pacific Division of Liberty, as it was called by then. Dick was president and Woody was vice president of World Pacific. Woody went to work for Liberty as art director when they bought jazz in about 1965, and later for United Artists when they bought Liberty. He left there in 1970 and freelanced from then on. But from 1965 to 1970 Woody was at Liberty. Studio Five did the art for Liberty before Woody came. They were awful. They just did very sedate covers. Woody used a lot of photographers, Ken Kim as well as Dean Torrence of Jan & Dean. In fact, I think he did the photography on the Nitty Gritty Dirt Band album; I'm not positive."

One of the most oddly memorable of the many Jan & Dean album covers was the one for their *Popsicle* album. This was a strange album, a pastiche of old LP tracks rushed out by Liberty after Jan & Dean had left the label and Jan had his crash. The LP was intended to cash in on the 1966 chart success of their 1963 LP cut "Popsicle," released belatedly on a 45. (For the details on the release of the 45 "Popsicle," see the interview with Dean Torrence.) The album cover was memorable because it did not show Jan & Dean at all, but an extreme closeup of a very cute little girl eating a popsicle!

"My daughter Carole was on the cover of *Popsicle* in nineteen sixty-six. It is a good picture. We did it over at North Hollywood Park, and she must have eaten twenty popsicles. Her name on that cover was 'Carole Diane.' She was about nine years old then."

Speaking of the 1980s, Dotty relates how "Dean had not seen her for many years, and Carole is quite attractive. Once when she was a teenager, she walked in, and Dean, who hadn't seen her for many years, said, 'Popsicle has really grown up!' Quite a change from a little kid to something else!

"In the mid-1980s, Carole was used on the cover of an album by a singer named Julie Kelly, from the waist down, for the album *We're on Our Way*. It is quite a change from a little girl to quite a voluptuous figure! They didn't want to put a photo of Julie on the cover for some unknown reason. Woody had my daughter do it," sort of a body double for Julie. "But Julie is gorgeous, and is a very dear friend of mine. She sounded both black and white, and they did not want to just say, 'Hey, Julie's white,' and she is, so they just used Carole." This is an interesting switch on the old practice of using white models on the covers of albums by black singers back in the late 1950s and early 1960s.

"I think Woody put the first black artist on a Liberty cover. It was a trumpet player. It was a big hassle and Woody went out on a limb to do it. Liberty was most opposed to it! It was a big fight because they didn't want to put any blacks on the cover. But they did."

Woody's name was on the back of hundreds of Liberty family album covers. "He had three Grammy nominations for covers. The Fifth Dimension's *Up, Up and Away*, a Nitty Gritty Dirt Band cover, and the Jazz Crusaders' *Talk That Talk*."

How did the Woodwards' and Pacific Jazz Liberty's days end? It came when Liberty was bought in the late 1960s. Liberty and UA fought; UA won out. In the regime change, Dave Stuart, a "terrible person," as Dotty termed him, fired everyone at Liberty, including Woody. "A lot of Pacific Jazz stuff was released on Blue Note records after that."

An interesting sidelight: According to Dotty, Woody redesigned the Liberty labels. "Woody designed the labels as a free-lance person with Cathy Keep."

Soul City

Johnny Rivers had a record label under the Liberty wing, which was primarily (if not exclusively) an outlet for the Fifth Dimension. They had a string of six or more Soul City LPs before moving on to Bell Records. The Fifth Dimension was hot! With a dozen hit 45s on Soul City, including two number ones and four top-ten hits, they were in the running for the "most successful artist" title at Liberty.

Their Soul City hit list reads like a diary of popular music in the late 1960s.

"Go Where You Wanna Go"
"Another Day, Another Heartache"
"Up, Up, and Away"
"Paper Cup"
"Carpet Man"
"Stoned Soul Picnic"
"Sweet Blindness"

"California Soul"
"Aquarius/Let the Sun Shine In"
"Workin' on a Groovy Thing"
"Wedding Bell Blues"
"Blowing Away"
"The Girls' Song"

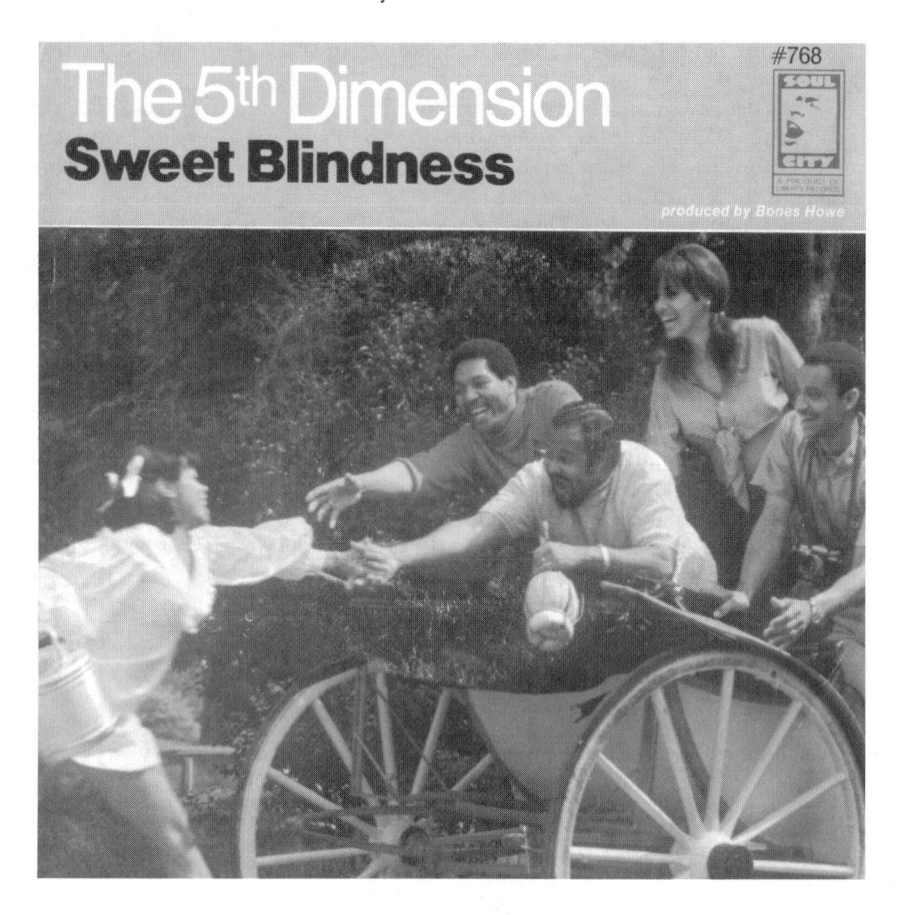

This "Sweet Blindness" sleeve carries the Soul City logo.

aura Records

On the 45s, the silver print on a blue label sometimes read "aura RECORDS A Division of LIBERTY RECORDS INC. Los Angeles, California." Other 45s read "a subsidiary of world-pacific records [sic]." Aura was a very small label, with only a handful of jazzy, pop-flavored, R&B artists. Sonny Knight did the first aura LP, followed by the Delegates. The Delegates were a jazz trio made up of leader Billy Larking on organ, Mel Brown on drums, and Henry Swarn on guitar (usually bass).

It is a rarity to find an aura 45 today. Aura #403 was "I Just Called to Say Hello," a slow blues number by Sonny Knight bearing the "world-pacific" legend on the label. "Pigmy Part 1 and 2" was an instrumental by the Delegates, aura #4505. The new numbering system apparently reflected new ownership by Liberty, as stated on the label.

"Aura. I don't remember that label," muses Si. "That could very well have been one of those cases where an artist came in who already had a label of their own with records out. We just took over the distribution of it."

Chapter 16 · *Liberty Acquisitions, Special Series, and Subsidiaries* 301

Aura was another Liberty subsidiary label.

Blue Note

A relatively large Liberty subsidiary was the jazz label Blue Note. Here there were several hundred LPs by the likes of Cannonball Adderly, Herbie Hancock, Art Blakely, and Jimmy Smith. An entire book could be written about this one division of Liberty Records that Si acquired.

"Blue Note. That was another small West Coast company—most we bought were—and this one had something in jazz. I always thought that jazz and rock and roll had something to do with one another. And I loved jazz, I always did. We wanted to have some jazz labels. We tried to buy more of them, but some just couldn't be acquired."

Bob Levinson, who did PR for Liberty, was familiar with Blue Note. "Blue Note began with two German brothers in New York. Anytime a blues or a jazz artist would come to New York to perform, these two brothers would get them into the studio and get them on tape. It is a great archive."

Sunset Records

Sunset Records was strictly an LP outlet. Any artist who had ever appeared on Liberty (such as the Standells, Gene McDaniels, and Timi Yuro), Dolton (such as Vic Dana and the Ventures), or Imperial (including Ricky Nelson and Sandy Nelson) could turn up on a Sunset album.

Sunset albums had the appearance of legitimacy. That is, they were not greatest hits compilations; they featured nice cover art, usually featuring a large, full-face photo of the artist, and liner notes.

But all the songs on Sunset albums were songs that had already been released on other LPs. And if there were any hits at all, they were seldom very-well-known big hits. The songs on a Sunset album could have wide diversity. Tunes selected for

The Sunset budget-label logo.

a single LP could be from 1960, 1963, and 1966, with almost every year in between represented as well, each in a style distinctive to the times (twist, surf, ballad, and so on).

On the one hand this miscellany could be a disappointment to a buyer who was a fan of the artist's current sound and style and expected more of the same when he or she bought a Sunset LP. Also, a fan who already had all of the artist's LPs would be getting nothing but reruns on a Sunset record. On the other hand, a Sunset album could bring one a new (actually old) perspective on an artist and provide a sampling of past material without having to invest in a lot of old, perhaps hard-to-locate records. Finally, if a fan had worn out the old albums, here was a chance to get new, clean, stereo recordings of old favorites.

But basically Sunset was a way for economy-minded Si Waronker to make money without new production costs. "Sunset was a repackaging gimmick. We made those as cheaply as we would, cheaper vinyl. It was a way of getting rid of master inventory. Another thing. When these distributors who would buy these records for forty-five cents or fifty cents, it didn't cost you any more than that to press it, and you were getting rid of things. It kept the money flowing in."

The Sunset logo, placed where the Statue of Liberty would appear on a Liberty label, was a modernistic sketch of a setting sun superimposed with wavy lines representing, one supposes, clouds. The background strip down the left side was light blue (to represent the sky?) instead of rainbow. Rainbow colors were used, however, on the wavy/cloud lines.

Years later, after UA had taken over Liberty, UA in London revived the Sunset label for all sorts of records, including old Liberty-family artists (P. J. Proby, Slim Whitman, Jackie DeShannon, Vikki Carr, Eddie Cochran), greatest hits packages (*The Very Best of Jan & Dean*), reissues of old U.S. albums (*Johnny Rivers Live at the Whiskey à Go-Go)*, and things by artists that were unrelated to Liberty originally (Shirley Bassey, *Band of the Life Guards*, and Ferrante and Teicher). They even released an old Liberty Premier series album, *España*, by the 50 Guitars of Tommy Garrett (our old friend Snuff).

The name "Sunset" was chosen to represent something near the end, a finish to something brighter—like a hit-record career.

Liberty "All-Time Hit" Single Records

Remember, Si always wanted catalog, meaning LPs. He felt, apparently correctly, that LPs could sell for years. Singles, while great moneymakers, star makers, and LP come-ons, had a very short shelf life. After a few weeks they were old and you could not even give them away, let alone sell them.

Except—as Liberty "All-Time Hit" singles! The hook here was two hits on one 45. No pesky flip side to deal with. Selling for the same as a regular 45, these records had the same Liberty label, except that all printing and illustrations were in silver on black. The record numbers started with 54000 instead of 55000 as Liberty had, or 66000 as Imperial had.

Every important hit Liberty ever had could be found on an "All-Time Hit" 45. Everything from "Cry Me a River" to "The Little Old Lady (from Pasadena)." Dolton hits by the Fleetwoods, the Ventures, and Vic Dana were also offered, as were hits from Demon Records.

The hook Si had planned for the "All-Time Hit" series was colored wax. "I wanted to press them in gold vinyl, but we couldn't get it. That was another gimmick. Everything I had anything to do with had to have a gimmick."

"Distributed by Liberty Records Sales Corp."

There were several record labels Liberty did not actually own but did distribute. A small label might have some good talent signed up and might make some good records. It might even get popular locally. But a small label might be totally unable to get its product distributed nationally.

However, if a small label could hook up with Liberty and get Liberty, for a cut of the profits, to distribute its records—well, then all its problems would be solved.

According to Si, having a small label distributed by somebody else could also have tax advantages. "Madonna has her own label, Sire, which is distributed by Warner Bros. It gives the artist a better tax write-off. A lot of little labels that may have had only one record on them were done that way.

Demon Records

In 1958 Demon Records was "Distributed by Liberty Sales Corp.," as stated on the label. Also on the hot pink Demon label was a likeness of the devil, two pitchforks, and the slogan "The Highest in Fi—."

Don Blocker, head of national promotion for Liberty, remembers how Al Bennett acquired Demon for Liberty: "We distributed a very successful small label, Demon Records. 'Western Movies' by the Olympics was one of my all-time favorite rock 'n' roll records." How did Liberty get involved with Demon? "Very simply, they were in adjoining offices with Liberty Records. We had started to gain a reputation as a hot singles indie label. Plus, Al Bennett was a great charmer.

The Demon Records label was carried by Liberty.

Demon was not sure of its distribution or what to do with its records. One of the owners, Joe Greene, a black guy, interestingly enough, wrote an old standard, 'Across the Alley from the Alamo.' Al convinced them that Liberty could do a better job for them. Therefore, we acquired distribution of Demon Records."

The Demon hits were "Western Movies" (#8, 1958) and "Dance with the Teacher" (#71) by the Olympics, an R&B group formed at a California high school in 1954 as the Challengers. They changed their name to the Olympics to capitalize on the Olympic Games which were taking place at the time.

The Olympics were joined on Demon by two songs by a Yuma rockabilly singer named Jody Reynolds, "Endless Sleep" (#5) and "Fire of Love" (#66). All these records were from 1958.

"Western Movies" was about a girlfriend who loved to watch cowboy movies to the exclusion of all else. "Endless Sleep" was one of the best death/tragedy hits of the late 1950s. It was all about a couple that argues; then the girl runs off. The boy tracks her to the shore, where he finds her among the breakers and saves her from an "Endless Sleep."

"Demon was a thing we started that goes way back," reports Si. "We released them as part of the company, but they were made by somebody else. In other words, they came to us with the master and the label at the same time, which is very common today. They had already released it and it was doing nothing, so instead of putting it on Liberty, we just picked it up on their label and used our so-called know-how."

University Records

"'University' was another distribution deal. The record was already released and we took over the distribution," says Si. "It was not a subsidiary." But it was a Little

The University Records label was carried by Liberty.

Rock, Arkansas, label that had at least one hit, "Forever" by the Little Dippers, which made #9 in 1960. "Forever" was a song that came out about the same time by country singer Billy Walker on Columbia Records, by Pete Drake and his Talking Steel Guitar on Smash in 1964, and Mercy on Warner's in 1969.

The Little Dippers were in reality the Anita Kerr Singers, session singers who were on hundreds of recordings and charted with "Joey Baby" (#94, 1962) on RCA themselves under the name Anita and the So 'n' Sos. The follow-up to "Forever," "I Wonder, I Wonder, I Wonder," which was also on University, did not chart.

Robbee

Another distribution deal was the one with Robbee Records. Robbee was located in the now-demolished Carlton Hotel in Pittsburgh, a long way from the LA headquarters of Liberty. Robbee was named after the son of label owner Lennie Martin, and the symbol was the mysterious Robbee bird.

Their most successful record was "Ronnie" by Marcy Jo, which was #81 on *Billboard* (and #64 on *Cashbox*) in 1961. Lou Christie ("The Gypsy Cried," 1963, Roulette Records; "Lightning Strikes," 1965, MGM Records) can be heard singing background on "Ronnie."

Marcy Jo, whose last name was Sockel and whose show biz name was sometimes spelled Marcy Joe, had another Robbee single on which Lou Christie sang, which got a lot of airplay in the Midwest, "Since Gary Went in the Navy." The title is ironic, since another label associated with Liberty, Dolton Records, had a Gary who had in fact gone into the Navy. However, Fleetwood Gary Troxel's military stint just a few months earlier was unrelated to Marcy's record. Marcy Jo, by the way, moved on to Swan Records, where none of her four releases on that label charted.

Lou Christie's own group, Lugee and the Lions, released "The Jury" b/w

The Robbee Records label was carried by Liberty.

"Little Did I Know" on Robbee, which was later reissued on World and AMM Records.

In spite of Lou Christie's connections with the label, when Robbee releases carried the legend "Produced by Lennie & Lou," it referred to Lennie Martin and Lou Guarino, not to Lou Christie. Only a few Robbee releases, including "Ronnie" and "Since Gary Went in the Navy," carry the legend "Distributed by Liberty Record Sales Corp."

Marcy Jo's records were in the girl-group mold. Another Robbee act, the La Rells, released Robbee 109, "Everybody Knew," before moving to good ol' Liberty Records for #55430, "Sneaky Alligator."

In-House Pressings

Perhaps this is not the right term for these special pressings, but Liberty, being a record company, occasionally arranged in-house pressings that were never intended for retail sale—or sale of any kind, for that matter. There is absolutely no way to determine how many of these in-house pressings there were, the quantities pressed, or what the "titles" were. After all, no written records have been kept of what Liberty pressed and sent to the record stores for official sale. So why should there be any written records of these special, in-house pressings that were not a part of any conventional series or line?

Three examples of in-house pressings are known, however. One is demonstration LPs. A demonstration LP was a record album that contained sample cuts from a variety of Liberty LPs by different artists and were intended to provide people at stations, distributors, and stores around the country with musical hors d'oeuvres that

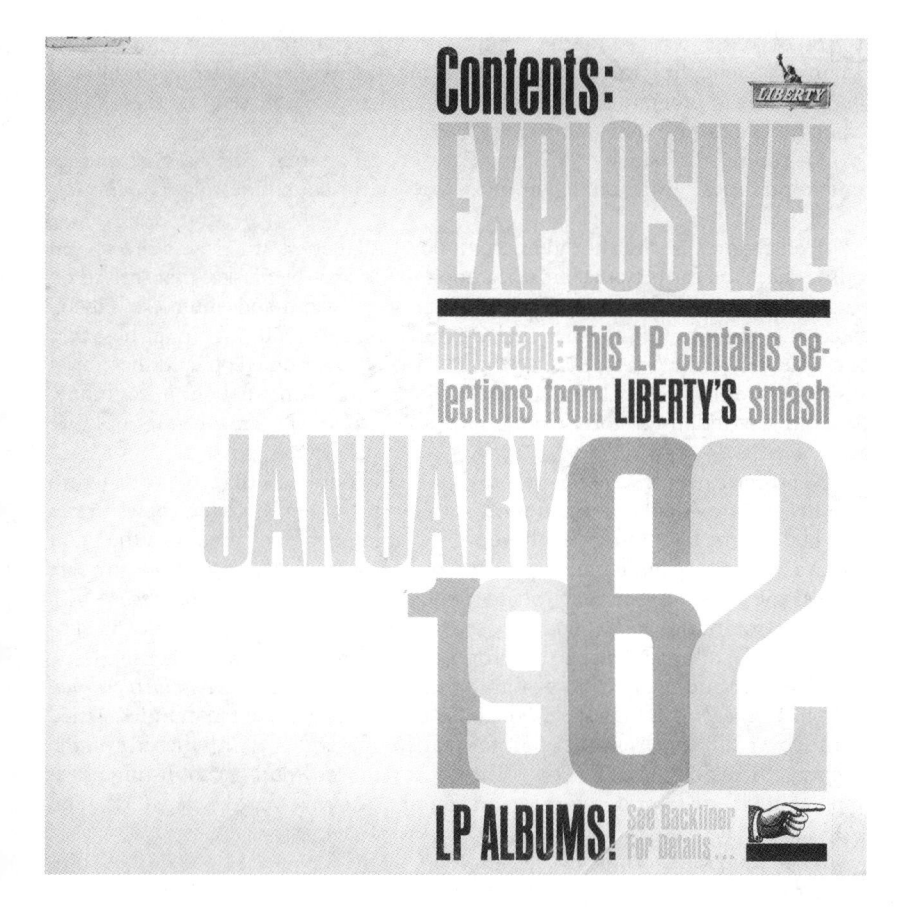

Chapter 16 · Liberty Acquisitions, Special Series, and Subsidiaries 307

There were only a few in this series of demonstration sampler albums.

might tempt them to play, buy, and stock the Liberty records represented by the demonstration record.

One such promotional record, MM 412, is titled *Demonstration Record: January 1962 Album Releases*. The front cover reads, in large red, pink, black, and gray letters, "Contents: EXPLOSIVE! Important: This LP contains selections from LIBERTY'S smash JANUARY 1962 LP ALBUMS! See Backliner For Details." The backliner has four paragraphs by National Promotion Director Bob Skaff extolling the virtues of this "greatest show on wax." The back cover says, "Audition Record Not for Sale," and the inside label reads, "Salesmen's Demonstration Record."

There are selections from twelve Liberty LPs, each of which is pictured. The holder, presumably a DJ or station program director, can use an enclosed order form to order any of the albums for one dollar each, compared to the usual price of four dollars in a record store or three dollars at a discount store. Artists featured include Gene McDaniels, Timi Yuro, Eddie Cochran, the Blue Grass Gentlemen, Johnny Burnette, and the Jimmy Dorsey Orchestra. None of the songs is a chart hit recording, although most are well-known songs.

Si, of course, was behind the demo LP deal. "We only did two or three of those albums. We thought it would be a good way to promote things, offering the albums for one dollar to program directors, but we found out we were sending them to the wrong people. So we quit doing them."

Of course, the January 1962 sampler is one in a series, albeit a brief one, of similar pressings. By contrast the next type of in-house pressing is definitely one-of-a-kind.

Don Blocker, national head of promotion for Liberty until 1964, was involved in this one. Don came from a radio tradition in Omaha, Nebraska, that thrived on promotional tricks and gimmicks. In that tradition of fun and gimmicks, Liberty prepared a gag project for a national DJ convention in 1960. Liberty published a newsletter called the *Liberty Record* which Norm Winter worked on, and the project was an outgrowth of that. It was just a little joke, but no one thought it was funny. "We did a satire on top-forty radio," relates Don Blocker. "How wrong could we be!

"Top-forty people were so insecure, but we did not know that. We cut a record with Bob Arbogast, a humorist around town, and gave ten thousand copies free to everybody at the convention. Well, top-forty radio people resented it to the point that we got letters from stations written on toilet paper, saying, 'You guys are thieves, you stab us in the back, what are you doing, you can wipe that record with this.' That sort of thing. We took a big setback with that. We never released it commercially." Thank goodness! So much for that category of in-house pressing!

The third and final category of in-house pressings was the *Liberty First Annual Stockholders Report*. This was a 33⅓ Compact EP lasting about ten minutes. Titled on the cover "Liberty Annual Report for year ending Jan. 1, 1961," the title on the label was "The Sounds of Liberty." There was no record number to distinguish it from other Liberty records, but the matrix numbers on the two sides were LAR-1 and LAR-2.

The record sales income for the year 1960, by the way, was $5,658,739.89, plus another $176,926.20 from song-publishing royalties and $16,733.28 from "other income." This made Liberty ninth, after just five years of operation, in a field of fifteen hundred record companies in the United States.

Produced by Studio Five and directed by Felix Slatkin, the "report" starts out with lush orchestrations and introductory comments by David Seville. Side 1 is dominated by David and Julie London, with excerpts from their respective oldie hits, as well as other music of the 1950s like Patience and Prudence and Felix Slatkin to appeal to stockholders. Side 2 finally brings up younger sounds, although the term rock 'n' roll, anathema to oldsters in those days, is never mentioned. With excerpts from hits by Bobby Vee, Johnny Burnette, and Gene McDaniels, the idea is put across that teenagers have money to spend on Liberty records. The acquisition of Dolton is highlighted, and Fleetwoods and Ventures music is played. Si Waronker even addresses the stockholders.

Finally, to convince the stockholders that the company has what it takes to appeal to youngsters, the ages of the VIPs are cited: Al Bennett, thirty-four; Hal Linick, twenty-nine; and Snuff Garrett, a mere twenty-two!

This EP may or may not have served to satisfy the stockholders in the winter of 1961. But with the photos and text that appear on the cover that accompanies the record, this EP serves today as a satisfactory time capsule of Liberty in the early 1960s.

Liberty Enters Tape Cartridge Field STORY ON PAGE 2

The LIBERTY Record

VOLUME 4, NUMBER 1 — PHOTO QUARTERLY — APRIL, 1966

SUNSET RECORDS DEBUTS WITH 20 RELEASES

Liberty's New Division Features Top Talent

LOS ANGELES—Under the guidance of its general manager, Edward Barsky, Sunset Records, a division of Liberty Records, Inc., has debuted into the economy field with 20 powerful LP releases featuring top recording stars selected from the parent company's artist roster.

Barsky, former independent distributor and, prior to joining Liberty, head of Metro Records, MGM's budget line, has spent several months researching the industry and feels strongly about the label's initial release.

In addition to coordinating closely with the firm's district managers throughout the nation, Barsky is going a step further for maximum saturation. He is now "on the road" personally visiting all distributors and rack jobbers. Sunset's first release features such sterling names as Julie London, The Ventures, Gerry Mulligan, Ricky Nelson, Fats Domino, Si Zentner, Henry Mancini and Martin Denny among a host of other big-name performers. Liberty firmly believes the added exposure accorded the artists, most of whom are still on Liberty rosters, can only benefit the current catalog. "The majority of economy album buyers pick-up this product in a supermarket or chain store" said Barsky, "therefore a budget customer who buys and likes a Ventures LP, automatically steps up to the parent label next time around." Barsky also pointed up a few of Sunset's superior qualities. "The record is pressed on pure vinyl and the jackets are four color."

Sunset maintains a dual distribution set-up via the sales of its product direct to independent distributors and direct to rack jobbers. Pricing is the same on Monaural and Stereo versions.

The label is now planning fifteen more releases for June and a series of new instrumental albums by The Sunset Strings, highlighting the current releases of the day.

Herewith is the entire product schedule for the first release:

"The Country Heart of Walter Brennan" (SUM-1100/SUS-5100)
"This Is Petula Clark" (SUM-1101/SUS-5101)
Martin Denny — "Paradise Moods" (SUM-1102/SUS-5102)
"Fats Domino!" (SUM-1103/SUS-5103)
"Julie London" (SUM-1104/SUS-5104)
Henry Mancini — "Sounds And Voices" (SUM-1105/SUS-5105)
Felix Slatkin — "Love Strings" (SUM-1106/SUS-5106)
"Timi Yuro" (SUM-1107/SUS-5107)
Bob Wills & Tommy Duncan — "Together!" (SUM-1108/SUS-5108)
"Versatile Nancy Ames" (SUM-1109/SUS-5109)
Si Zentner — "Big Band Brilliance" (SUM-1110/SUS-5110)
"Bobby Vee" (SUM-1111/SUS-5111)
Slim Whitman — "Unchain Your Heart" (SUM-1112/SUS-5112)
"Her Nibs Miss Georgia Gibbs" (SUM-1113/SUS-5113)
Sandy Nelson — "Walkin' Beat" (SUM-1114/SUS-5114)
"Floating Voices Of The Johnny Mann Singers" (SUM-1115/SUS-5115)
The Ventures — "Runnin' Strong" (SUM-1116/SUS-5116)
Gerry Mulligan — "Concert Days" (SUM-1117/SUS-5117)
"Ricky Nelson" (SUM-1118/SUS-5118)
T-Bones — "Shapin' Things Up" (SUM-1119/SUS-5119)

Ed Barsky, General Manager, Sunset Records, displays a few albums from the label's first release.

BULK MAILING
U. S. POSTAGE
PAID
Permit No. 25267
Los Angeles, Calif.

SUNSET
A PRODUCT OF LIBERTY RECORDS

The Liberty Record was a quarterly newsletter produced by Liberty to promote their artists, the latest releases, and to announce new products. Issues were on newsprint, ran 16 pages measuring 11½ x 15 inches. Norman Winters, who has since gone on to do publicity for Michael Jackson-related projects, was the force behind *The Liberty Record*. This copy is courtesy of Lee Mendell.

The first year that Liberty went public, the annual report to the stockholders was made on vinyl! *(Courtesy Bob Lucieen.)*

Summary

On the surface, Liberty and its first subsidiary, Dolton Records, give the impression that this Southern California record company cared about nothing except white rock 'n' roll and novelty tunes. That may have been the way it looked when the company started and made most of its singles sales, but artists of color and music of various ethnic backgrounds—folk music, jazz, music of India, and soul music—were a major part of the Liberty family.

Lee Mendell, who served in such Liberty executive positions as national singles sales manager, national LP sales manager, and manager of the international division, explains some of the rationale behind the diversification of Liberty.

"The General Motors concept of divisions that Al Bennett subscribed to was to have more companies so you could have more than one Bobby Vee–type singer on different labels. At one time we had 'Up, Up, and Away' on Soul City by the Fifth Dimension, on Liberty by the Johnny Mann Singers, and on Imperial by the Sunshine Company, all competing as different parts of the same company. Each division had its own head, its own promotion, its own A&R. The Fifth Dimension was a smash in America, Johnny Mann was a hit in England, and the Sunshine Company died. So it worked.

"Within World Pacific, there were also more labels. There was aura, which was kind of an R&B label; there was World Pacific Jazz; and there was Soul City, which was Johnny Rivers's label. So Liberty ended up with three straight-ahead pop labels. Then Imperial had a country division, and Liberty had a country division. As there is a finite amount of airplay, which is the locomotive to sell music, it was easier if we had different promotion teams for different companies. The only central services we had were things like accounting and manufacturing, and LRDC, Liberty Records Distributing Corporation. Other than that, each company had its own staff.

"Another division was the recording arm of the International Division. They had a recording budget for tunes that might never be released in the U.S.A. One of the artists that this division recorded was the Ventures. The international division also made music videos, one of the first to do that. We needed them to promote artists in those days. We had a budget to make six a year. We sent them to England for "Top of the Pops" on the air and to Germany for the "Beat Club." Domestic didn't care about them and wouldn't fund them, so we did it in international.

"Still another division was the budget Sunset label, which I named, by the way. The name referred to the end of the day, and that is what you do with budget records, you mark them down. We also created some things on Sunset. We had the Sunset Music Machine, and Dave Pell recorded things.

"Liberty also had a rack jobbing division, and a mass merchandising division as well, called Musical Aisle, which even operated retail record stores in Louisiana."

Lee Mendell made a success of Liberty's tape division. "Liberty was enormously successful as a company that brought new and vibrant and interesting and—as it turned out to be—eclectic talent. In those days if an artist were looking around for a label, where would they go, what label would have the greatest appeal, panache, style, élan, whatever it was? Liberty was certainly amongst them. When I started the tape division, because of the catalog and what we did, we were the number three company in the tape area. But we had absolutely no right to be there, because Liberty was only the eighth largest record label."

"Diversity" certainly was Liberty's middle name and doubtless a key to its success. Even without taking into account the subsidiary labels, Liberty had big hits with artists as important as the pop songstress Vikki Carr, (former) teen rocker Bobby Vee, the bands Canned Heat and the Nitty Gritty Dirt Band, and the instrumental combo the Ventures, all within the span of a year's time. This was the same time Imperial had Johnny Rivers's updated rockabilly sound and Soul City had the smooth soul sounds of the Fifth Dimension.

Says Lee Mendell, "A great deal of it had to do with Al Bennett. I never recall his saying, 'We are not going to have that kind of artist on our label.' We had Nancy Ames, the T-Bones, Jimmy McCracklin, Irma Thomas, the Cascades."

Was Si's campaign of buying up small West Coast labels an attempt to take over California? "No." There were just a lot of small companies around, struggling, who were open to a bailout—musical safety in numbers. To them Liberty was a giant, although it was not big when compared to the old labels.

Si remembers how easy it was to initiate a label back then. "To start a company today would be impossible. To start a company in those days wasn't as hard. It was difficult because you were fighting Decca, Columbia, RCA, and Capitol. Those were the four major companies that you're fighting. Each one had a major catalog. With small companies you are only as good as your current hit.

"But, say, Capitol, my God, they had so many good things that even if they didn't have a hit on the charts, they had enough stuff on the LP charts that the business was OK. They were so far ahead when we started in 1955, my goodness! Besides, Capitol was bought by British EMI; Decca was bought by British Decca. That was why Liberty did not go into classical music. These other companies had everything recorded already. The only way a small company could ever get bigger—and as a publicly owned company we had to show growth—the only way to do it was by accumulating small companies that could barely make it. Combined like that we had a catalog of several hundred instead of just a few.

"I tried to buy Crescendo Records, but could never get it." And Si also tried to buy Reprise, but was outbid by Warner's.

Did acquired companies keep their autonomy? "No. Whenever you let them stay autonomous, the company went to hell. As soon as they got their money, they said 'Why work?' Howard Rumsey had some autonomy, but no one else did except just to wind up their affairs.

"The exception was Bob Reisdorff. He had full autonomy with Dolton, and he deserved it. He was ambitious and wanted something good. These other guys wanted out."

Between divisions, subsidiaries, special series, and distribution deals, Liberty indeed became a diverse force to be contended with in the 1960s music world.

CHAPTER 17

1967
Nitty Gritty Dirt Band, Vikki Carr, Hardtimes, Love Generation, Sunshine Company, Classics IV, and the Fifth Dimension

In 1967 Liberty signed four artists who had hits, but none made the label any real money. The first new Liberty hit maker was alto saxophonist Mike Sharpe. In January he had his only success, "Spooky," an instrumental he wrote. It did not make the top ten, but it is a title a reader would do well to keep in mind.

Nitty Gritty Dirt Band

In April the second new Liberty artist, the Nitty Gritty Dirt Band, had spotty success. Their first record, "Buy for Me the Rain," was not top forty. Their next successful record was in 1971, "Mr. Bojangles," and it became their only top-forty record for ten years. They had no more Liberty singles, but did have minor hit records later on United Artists when Liberty folded. When a new Liberty was subsequently created, they had one more minor entry, "Fire in the Sky" in 1981, for a total of nearly a dozen Liberty and UA chart records over fifteen years. Their appeal was country/folk/rock, which meant it was limited; only three of their songs made the top forty. They did sell a lot of albums, though.

Don Blocker recalls how the band came to Liberty. "Bill McCuen was a sort of an odd fellow we brought in. He played some odd music for me, and I said, 'I'm gonna sign this act. I like this stuff. I don't know why, but I like it. I'll go up and get the papers, but what are you going to call the group?' He said, 'the Nitty Gritty Dirt Band.' I told him that was a terrible name. 'You're going to have to change that name, but we can work on that later.' Somehow it never got changed."

Vikki Carr Returns

Next up for 1967 on Liberty was someone who became somewhat less popular than the Dirt Band, Vikki Carr. Vikki had been around for some time. In 1962 she had competed against the Crystals' "He's a Rebel" for Liberty with no national success at all. In September 1967 "It Must Be Him" placed her on the charts at last, in the top five at that, and led to a string of six records through 1969, seldom making

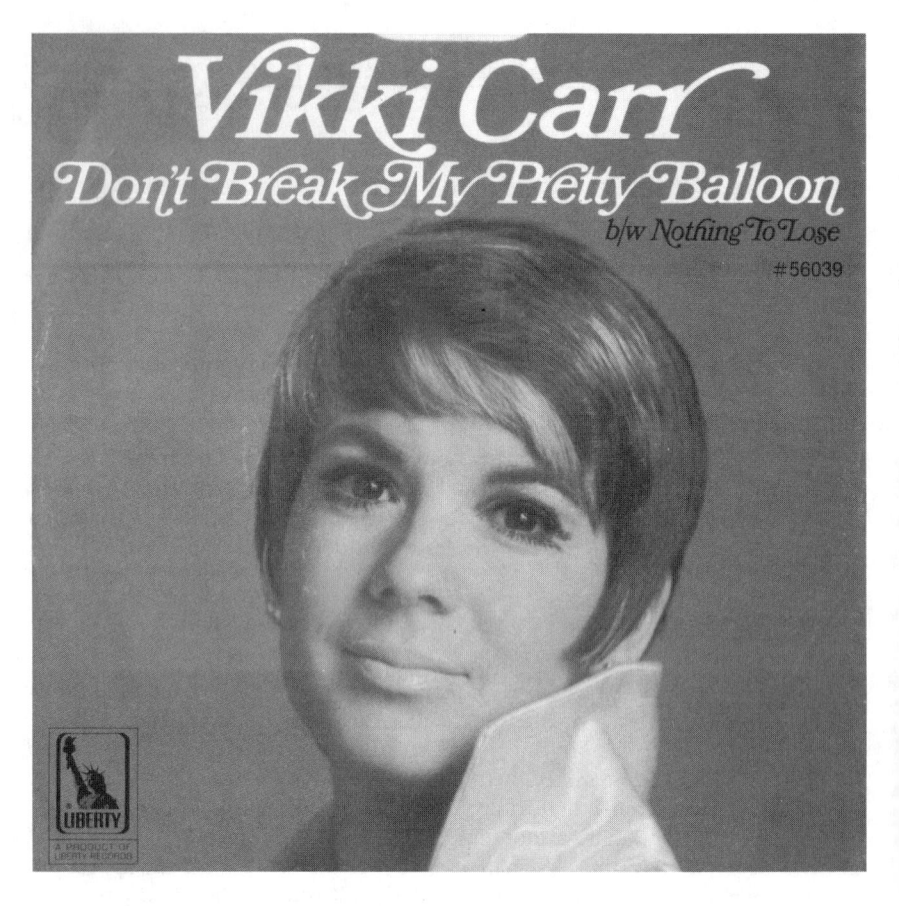

Vikki Carr was the most successful sixties nonrock singer at Liberty.

the top forty. Her appeal was pop, which limited her singles' popularity as much as the Nitty Gritty Dirt Band's was limited by their country/folk/rock style.

When Vikki Carr appeared on NBC-TV's "Tonight Show" in 1967, she commented how long she had waited for her first hit. Johnny Carson was astonished that she had never had a hit, as she was fairly well known as a pop nightclub entertainer. Vikki did not mention two things on that program: first, that not only had her first few releases (on Liberty) flopped, but that her first Liberty hit, "It Must Be Him," was originally released in 1966, then reissued in 1967, at which time it did become a big hit. She also failed to mention the "Submarine Races" record she made for Liberty years before under the name Danny and Gwen.

Victor Lundberg

The last 1967 Liberty newcomer up on the block was yet another one-shot artist, Victor Lundberg. Lundberg was a Michigander who had worked in radio, owned his own ad agency, and was a veteran of the Army Psychological Warfare Department in World War II. In the 1967 era of anti–Vietnam War protests and hippiedom, Lundberg's patriotism plus his background in both entertainment and brainwashing inspired him to record a mawkish recitation called "An Open Letter to My Teenage Son." It was a top-ten record but was on the charts for only a very few weeks. An answer song, "A Letter to Dad," was recited by Every Father's Teenage Son and reached #93 on Buddah Records (not to be confused with Every Mother's Son on MGM, "Come on Down to My Boat," 1967). The two records were highly topical, with references to long hair, sandals, and the Vietnam War. Today both records are curious, dated artifacts.

Even in 1967 Lundberg's record was considered, well, an oddity. "Oh, I hated that record," laments Lee Mendell. "We were at a record company convention in Palm Springs, sitting by the pool, when Jack Bratel, the sales manager, called the office to see how things were going, and said, 'a hundred thousand? One hundred thousand?!' Then he came over and said to all of us, 'We just got orders for a hundred thousand on the Lundberg.'

"So you go into the great debate, which is, 'What is a good record?' Is that the record that is number one? The answer probably is yes. If it is number one and sells five million copies, it's a good record. I would never take the Lundberg home and play it myself! That's a fair comment."

Also-Rans

Among the Liberty also-rans for 1967, the Deep Six, who had come up for air with "Rising Sun" in 1965, resurfaced with "Image of a Girl." The song had been a hit in 1960 for the Safaris. The Deep Six version was sung in the patented style of the Association, who had been making the top of the charts for Valiant Records with songs like "Windy," "Cherish," and "Along Comes Mary" for the last year. And while the record-buying public continued to support the Association for some time to come, they had no affection at all for the Deep Six, who quickly sank from view and out of earshot.

A group called the Raik's Progress yielded "Why Did You Rob Us, Tank?" and "The Sewer Rat Love Chant," featuring psychedelic garage-band guitars and lyrics that make no sense at all and certainly have nothing to do with the titles on the record. The Raik's Progress sound more like "I Had Too Much to Dream Last Night" by the Electric Prunes for comfort.

Liberty was grabbing at straws by the late 1960s. The heyday of Liberty when artists like Johnny Burnette, Jan & Dean, and Bobby Vee had hit after hit, and new sounds were pioneered by Si, Snuff, and Bob Reisdorff, were a distant memory. Now it seemed that a lot of energy was being spent copying other labels' artists' sounds.

An interesting Imperial also-ran was "Mumph" by Ludwig & the Klassics. Apparently some session musicians under the direction of Buddy Prima, "Mumph" is an instrumental adaptation of classical music, with some studio talk allowed in. The flip side was the standard "My Heart Reminds Me" (aka "And That Reminds Me") that Della Reese, Kay Starr, and the Four Seasons also recorded for their labels, with considerably more success.

GARY LEWIS & THE PLAYBOYS
#55949
THE LOSER
(With A Broken Heart)
B/W **ICE MELTS IN THE SUN***

"The Loser (with a Broken Heart)" was #43 in the spring of 1967.

J. J. Light

"J. J. Light was an artist who had one hit called 'Heya' in 1967," reports Lee Mendel of Liberty's international division. "He was of Indian background, and he had this hit and was totally unable to cope with success. We sent him over to England, and he couldn't get off the plane. It may have been the first time he was ever on a plane. Our man with the British company, who is a very good friend, still often talks [twenty-three years later] about trying to get J. J. Light off the plane to do promotion. Unfortunately they took him off the plane into a nursing home."

A very hot duo from 1965 to 1973 was Sonny and Cher. In 1967 their seventh top-forty hit was "The Beat Goes On," a top-tenner that seemed to be an anthem for a generation. In the summer of 1967, "Tommy Reynolds the T-Bones" was the artist name as printed on the Liberty 45 label of an instrumental version of "The Beat Goes On." Tommy had been an original member of the T-Bones, and would later be the "Reynolds" of Hamilton, Joe Frank & Reynolds at Dunhill Records. Apparently by now he had taken over the group. What did he do with it?

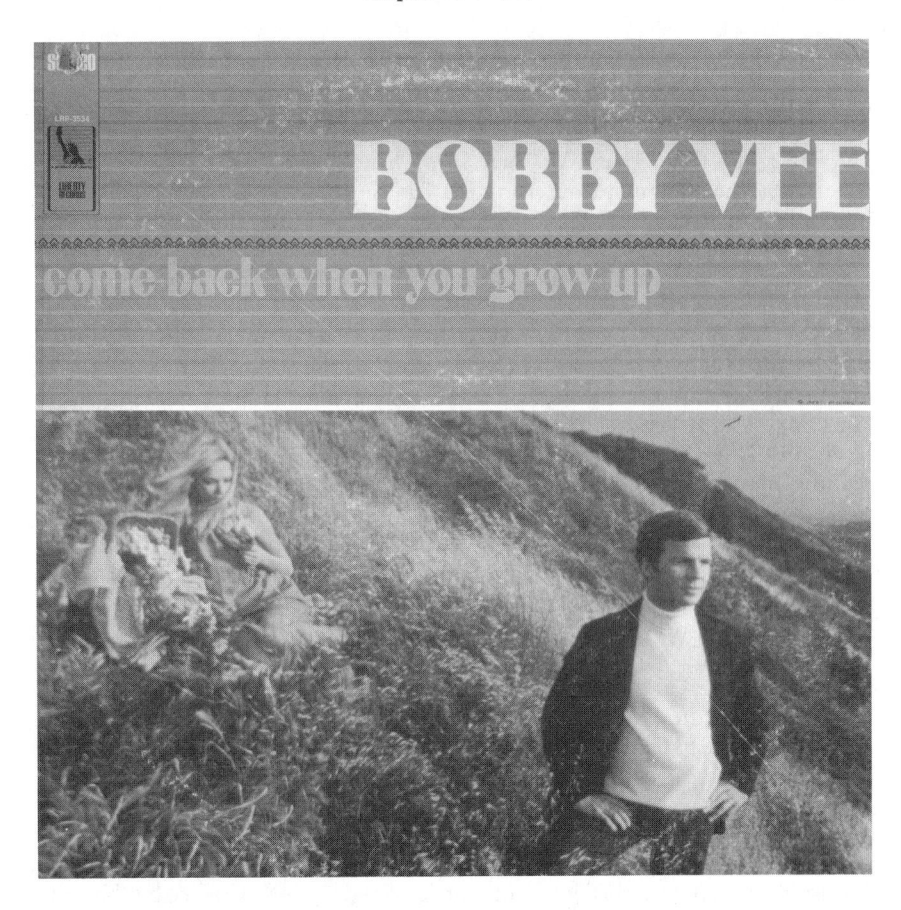

Bobby Vee had his biggest hit almost ten years after his first hit.

For the last several years, the Ramsey Lewis Trio, first on Argo and then on Cadet Records, had been making the charts with mostly slow, always jazzy, instrumental remakes of hits like Dobie Gray's "The In Crowd," the McCoys' "Hang On Sloopy," and the Beatles' "A Hard Day's Night." Tommy Reynolds's version of "The Beat Goes On" sounded more like a Ramsey Lewis record than some of Ramsey Lewis's own.

Bobby Vee Returns

The very next Liberty release, an original song by an old Liberty standby, could not have come at a better time. "Come Back When You Grow Up" was a mild, small-combo ballad by Bobby Vee. The story was of a boy in love with, or at least the object of love of, a younger girl who needs to get a few more years under her belt before the boy can get that close to her. "Come Back When You Grow Up" reached #1 on most charts, and was the biggest-selling record of Bobby's entire illustrious career. Yet it was "only" #3 on *Billboard*'s Hot 100. Why?

The record was a sleeper and a slow waker-upper. It had to be released a couple of times and jump-started into hitdom. When it was first released in midyear, it was assigned Liberty Record number 55964, with an unusual but highly appealing flip side called "Swahili Serenade." Then it was immediately reissued as 55964 again, but with a new flip, "That's All There Is to That."

In fact, there was more to it than that. The song did not become a big hit. But, into the summer, Liberty began to sell copies here and there around the country. Apparently most of the scattered sales were in smaller towns, the kinds of places that can't make a record a hit like New York or Los Angeles could.

In response to these sales, Liberty reissued "Come Back When You Grow Up" as 55982. The flip side was "That's All There Is to That" on some copies. But other copies carried yet *another* tune, "Growing Pains," on the back! This time the record finally took off and ultimately reached #3. However, it sold more copies than any other single Bobby Vee ever had on Liberty (or elsewhere, for that matter), including his #1 hit "Take Good Care of My Baby." The only reason it did not reach #1 was that the sales were spread out over so many weeks that the punch was too diffused to be registered conventionally.

And the three different flip sides? None appeared on the LP *Come Back When You Grow Up!* One, "Growing Pains," was on a previous Bobby Vee Liberty LP, *Look at Me, Girl.* (This record, and Bobby Vee's career in general, are discussed at length in the Bobby Vee interview later in this book.)

Almost immediately after that success, another old Liberty hand, Ross Bagdasarian, released a 45 in October of 1967 under his own name (as opposed to David Seville or the Chipmunks monikers). "Red Wine" and "The Walking Birds of Carnaby" were Italian-sounding instrumentals of Ross's own composition. A word of explanation: *bird* was British slang for a girl, and "Carnaby" was a fashionable London street "birds" were wont to stroll along.

Dolton added no new artists in 1967. Ventures releases included the 45 "Theme from the Wild Angels," written by Mike Curb. The Dolton LP label was renamed "Liberty 2000 Series" at this time, not quite ending Dolton's existence but blurring its identity. The 45 label was redesigned. The anachronistic Dolphins were gone, and the overall look came closer than ever to the Liberty look. The main part of the label was black, with a blue strip (Dolton had always been blue) down the left side much like the rainbow strip on Liberty. A new Dolton logo was used, an orange LP disc coming out of a black LP cover, with the legend, "Dolton—A Product of Liberty Records," underneath.

Similar labels were used for other Liberty subsidiaries, World Pacific Records and Soul City. World Pacific used a two-tone blue strip with an abstract globe symbol for a logo, while Soul City had a yellow strip with a male singer's face pictured in abstract.

Hardtimes

There is a common belief among music critics that an inferior recording artist—any artist, in fact—who gets a television showcase will be able to get hit records merely by virtue of the publicity. Ricky Nelson, who got to lip-synch his records at the end of many (but by no means all) of the episodes of the TV series "The

Chapter 17 · 1967 319

Kittyhawk Graphics, the design firm owned by Dean Torrence (Jan & Dean), designed the Sunshine Company's LP cover.

Adventures of Ozzie and Harriet," is the most-often-cited example. However, many of Ricky's hit records made the charts before they were ever sung on TV, and many of the songs he sang on TV never made the charts.

Dick Clark was reputed to be able to make performers, good ones and bad ones, into stars by featuring them on his television programs. That may have been true in some cases, but it was not true in all instances. At the end of 1966, the Liberty subsidiary World Pacific Records released "Fortune Teller" by a San Diego group called the Hardtimes. In spite of getting regular exposure on Dick Clark's weekday afternoon music showcase "Where the Action Is," "Fortune Teller" was the only Hardtimes single to chart, and it peaked at #97 on the national top 100.

Love Generation

Imperial added three new artists, starting in June with a relevant, current group, the Love Generation. They had two hits, "Groovy Summertime" and "Montage from How Sweet It Is," but neither turned out to be top-forty material.

Sunshine Company

In July the Sunshine Company appeared on Imperial. Their sound was a return to the "bomp" sound, updated, of course, on great songs like "On a Beautiful Day"—a national also-ran, but a big top-forty record in the Midwest. The cover of their LP of the same name was designed by the design firm of Liberty veteran (and graphics artist) Dean Torrence. Besides three also-rans, the Sunshine Company had three hits, "Back on the Street Again," which made the top forty; one called "Happy"; and "Look, Here Comes the Sun." "Back on the Street Again" was their biggest record, only #32 nationally, a real shame, since these were fine harmony records. This Southern California pop quintet was very fine, and lead singer Mary Nance had a voice that should have propelled them into the realm of similar groups such as the Mamas and Papas and Spanky and Our Gang. But it was not to be.

Classics IV

Finally, for its last new 1967 act, Imperial introduced a more successful group, the Classics IV, featuring Dennis Yost. The group had sent demo tapes from Florida to several companies including Liberty/Imperial. Their first Imperial hit was the Mike Sharpe Liberty single from earlier in the year, "Spooky," the big difference being that the Classics IV version was a vocal instead of an instrumental and made the top five, lyrics courtesy of producer Bud Buie and a friend of his. The Classics IV had eight Imperial chart recordings in all, including two more top-five songs, "Stormy" (1968) and "Traces" (1969).

Johnny Rivers, Cher, the Hollies

However, the real successes for the year 1967 were from Imperial's tried-and-true hit makers, Johnny Rivers, Cher, and the Hollies. Rivers started the year off with a hit remake of the Four Tops' 1964 hit, "Baby, I Need Your Lovin'." Next he remade the Miracles' "Tracks of My Tears," again successfully. Whenever it began to seem that Johnny Rivers only did revivals of older hits, he came up with an original smash like his hit at the end of 1967, "Summer Rain." This was the first year that all of Johnny's hits were ballads instead of rockers. And all three made the top fifteen.

Cher had a small hit in the fall of 1967 with a remake of the Leaves' 1966 top-forty hit, "Hey Joe," but she barely cracked the charts. Then, at the end of the year, she proved that she still had what it took as her last Imperial hit, "You Better Sit Down, Kids," made the top ten. Sonny and Cher had always been an oddity, with their unisex clothes and hair, and their soundalike singing styles. "You Better Sit Down, Kids" was a curiosity. It was sung from a divorced father's point of view, telling them to be good because their mom is gonna need their help a whole lot more than she did before. It was written by Sonny, as were "Bang Bang" and many other of Cher's hits. Besides being Cher's final Imperial hit, "You Better Sit Down, Kids" was produced by Sonny, as he had all of her seven solo hits, all on Imperial. Ironically, her next label (of many) was Kapp Records, where her producer would be Liberty alumnus Snuff Garrett.

Johnny Rivers was still riding the charts by updating oldies, here a Miracles tune.

The Hollies also left Imperial in 1967. It was almost as if everyone sensed a sinking ship in their future, as well they might. A pair of top-forty hits titled "On a Carousel" and "Pay You Back with Interest" sounded very British as usual. Then it was off to Epic Records for a dozen more hits. After the Hollies had fled Imperial and scored big with "Carrie-Anne" on Epic, Imperial took a fling by rereleasing the Hollies' very first U.S. record, a remake of Doris Troy's 1963 hit "Just One Look." It did better the second time around, reaching the forties instead of the nineties on the top one hundred.

Jackie DeShannon

Jackie DeShannon, she of the ever-changing look and style, released "Wishing Doll," a wistful tune about beautiful dresses wished for Jackie herself by the doll. The song was from a United Artists film entitled *Hawaii*, and Jackie went on a nationwide tour of radio stations to promote the song. Yet the song could be called

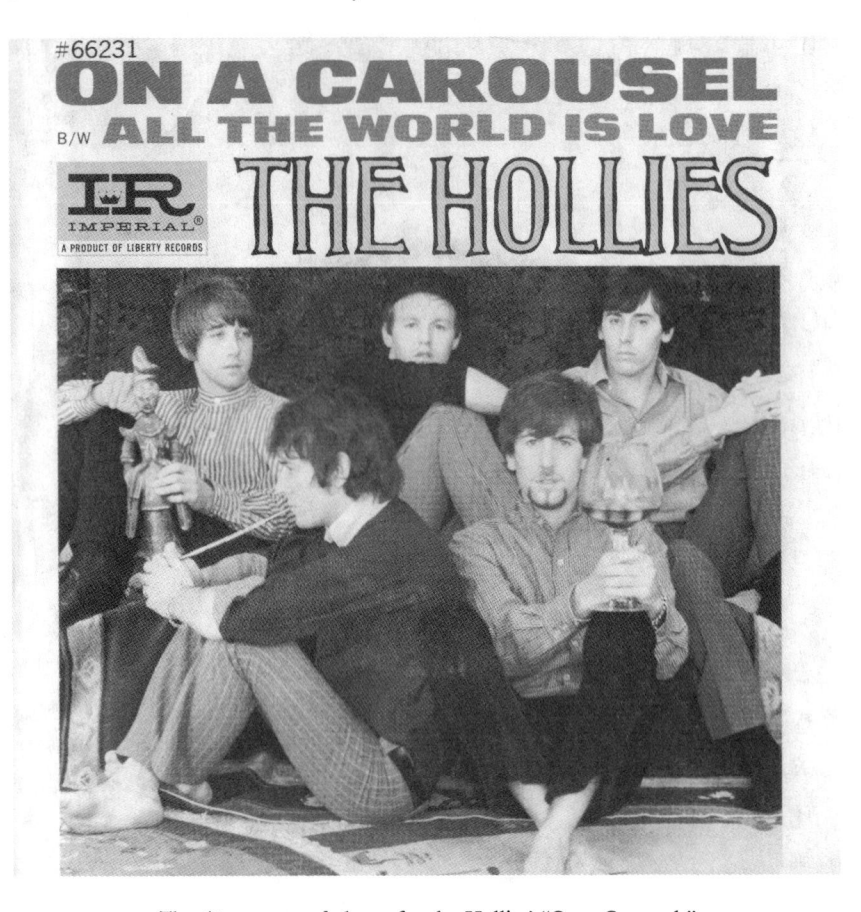

The 45-rpm record sleeve for the Hollies' "On a Carousel."

a hit only by the generosity of Jackie's fans. It was featured on an LP fittingly titled *New Image*. (Fittingly because Jackie's image was in a constant state of flux).

LPs

The latest Imperial LPs were *The Love Generation* and *Symphony for Soul* by the Total Eclipse, and LPs by Sandy Nelson, Jackie DeShannon, Johnny Rivers, and Slim Whitman, to name an expected few.

On the Liberty label proper, LP releases of the year were from Del Shannon, Bobby Vee, Red Skelton, Si Zentner, Johnny Mann, Martin Denny (*Exotica Today* and, of all things, *Exotica Classica,* whatever that meant), Julie London, and so on. Julie London was twelve years older than when she debuted on Liberty as resident torch singer and moneymaker extraordinaire. But she was still up to her old tricks. Her 1967 LP was titled *Nice girls don't stay for breakfast* [sic], and showed the familiar cleavage, this time peeking over the top of a trench coat she has seemingly worn to bed!

Chapter 17 · 1967 323

This cover was for the LP that contained the Mickey Mouse Club TV theme song.

The title tune, by spouse Bobby Troup, is representative of the cuts on the LP, written by such musical luminaries as Oscar Hammerstein II, George and Ira Gershwin, Richard Rodgers, and Jimmy Dodd.

Jimmy Dodd?

Yes, the leader of the TV Mousketeers was a prolific songwriter. He wrote most of the songs performed on "The Mickey Mouse Club." And the final cut on side two of *Nice girls don't stay for breakfast* is none other than the seemingly terribly out-of-place "Mickey Mouse March," sung by sultry Julie quite unlike the version Annette Funicello used to croon. Julie explains the appearance of this odd sister on the LP.

"I was backstage in Australia, and I was rehearsing for a show at a nightclub. I had my little girl, Kelly, who was just a couple of years old at the time, with me. She got antsy, so I started to sing the song 'Mickey Mouse' to settle her down or just get her attention. The guitarist started playing it behind me, and we ended up doing the song in the show that night. And it went over well." (Kelly seemed to survive the experience, getting married in 1991. And the song got onto a Liberty LP.)

Speaking of old-time Liberty LP stars, Johnny Mann's singing group had been

This Fifth Dimension LP, produced by Bones Howe, carried the legend "The 5th and Mr. Bones" inside.

heard on countless Liberty releases over the years. He also released LPs on Liberty. Then in 1967 the Johnny Mann Singers made the singles charts for the very first — and last — time. In June the Singers' version of the Fifth Dimension's "Up, Up and Away" (a hit on Liberty's Soul City subsidiary) came in at #91 on *Billboard*. What's more, it hung on for three whole weeks. Way to go, Johnny Mann!

In all seriousness Johnny Mann was talented and a great asset to Liberty. He also played "Doc Severinson"-type bandleader to Joey Bishop's "Johnny Carson" when Bishop had a latenight talk show on ABC opposite NBC's "Tonight Show."

Si Waronker met Johnny Mann through Si Zentner, and the two men became very good friends after they met in the early days of Liberty. "Johnny did a couple of dates as leader of vocal groups around town. We became friends, and he asked to do records as a vocal group. We tried one and became very good friends. He sold enough copies to pay his way. So I signed him, and the Johnny Mann Singers backed a lot of Liberty artists. He had a good music background and came through for me."

Fifth Dimension

From out of nowhere came the group whose hits have already been referred to, the Fifth Dimension. They were Liberty artists, in that they were on Johnny Rivers's label, Soul City. The members were Marilyn McCoo, Florence LaRue, Billy Davis, Jr., Lamont McLemore, and Ron Townson.

Their meeting was an atypical encounter. Marilyn was being crowned Miss Bronze California by Florence, and the scene was being photographed by Lamont. Chatting later, they discovered that they all liked R&B music, and more important, could all sing.

Marilyn and Lamont formed a group called the Hi-Fi's [sic] with two other members, but they broke up and the other two later formed the Friends of Distinction. With Billy, Florence, and Ron, Marilyn and Lamont formed a new group and called themselves the Versatiles only a year before their name change to the Fifth Dimension and success at Liberty/Soul City.

And what success they had! While Liberty as a company seemed to be losing it and perhaps (with hindsight) even winding down, the Fifth Dimension came on like gangbusters. After a false start in 1966 with "I'll Be Loving You Forever," "Go Where You Wanna Go" in January 1967 made the top twenty comfortably. "Another Day, Another Heartache" did less well, missing the top forty. Both were produced by Johnny Rivers, as was their third, "Up, Up, and Away," their immortal top-ten classic that won five Grammys—Best Performance by a Vocal Group, Song of the Year, Best Contemporary Single, Best Contemporary Group Performance, and Record of the Year.

The Fifth Dimension had four hits in 1967 (the fourth was "Paper Cup"), and a total of a baker's dozen hits on Soul City between 1967 and 1970. With that success Johnny Rivers became a very important young man indeed at Liberty.

CHAPTER 18

1968
Canned Heat; Dave Dee, Dozy, Beaky, Mick, and Tich

A lot of music had passed under the Liberty bridge by 1968. Liberty Records was thirteen years old and under new management; Dolton was nine; Imperial was twenty years old. The heyday of the company was past. Liberty had only eight hits from four artists. Liberty had not had fewer hits than that in any year since 1958.

In spite of the general doldrums, music was still coming from the Classics IV on Imperial, two in 1968: "Soul Train" and the bestseller "Stormy." Also Gary Lewis and the Playboys had Liberty hits like "Jill" in 1967 and a top-twenty in 1968 with "Sealed with a Kiss" (Brian Hyland, 1962), Gary's second hit with a song originally recorded by Brian Hyland. Bobby Vee scored a surprise when he had the biggest-selling record of his entire career in 1967, "Come Back When You Grow Up," and had other successes in 1967 and 1968, such as "Beautiful People" (Kenny O'Dell, 1967), "Maybe Just Today," and a hit medley, "My Girl/Hey Girl" (Temptations, 1964; Freddie Scott, 1963). All of these successes, including the R&B medley, were produced by Dallas Smith, coproducer of Bobby's 1966 *30 Big Hits of the '60s, Volume Two*, LP. And Vikki Carr had a record on which each side scratched the top one hundred.

Del Shannon was still in there swinging. He and Brian Hyland ("Sealed with a Kiss," 1962) wrote "You Don't Love Me" for the flip side of Del's remake of a classic oldie. The oldie was "Raindrops" (Dee Clark, 1961), and on the plus side, it featured rain and thunder sound effects like the original. On the negative side, the take lacked any spark or trace of falsetto, even in the fadeout, which on the original version did feature falsetto. It just was not working for Del Shannon.

Nor was Johnny Rivers any longer doing so well. His 1968 hits "Look to Your Soul" and "Right Relations" were small potatoes compared to the previous year's smash "Summer Rain." And the Sunshine Company, whose future had been so bright last year, concluded their hit run with "Look, Here Comes the Sun."

Though Johnny was off his mark as hit-making artist, his Liberty subsidiary label Soul City was doing fine, thanks to the Fifth Dimension. "Sweet Blindness" was lucky #13 at its national peak, "Carpet Man" made the top thirty, and "Stoned Soul Picnic" was #3 on *Billboard* and #1 on most station playlists.

The success of "Stoned Soul Picnic" was a surprise to some people at Liberty. According to Lee Mendell, "Al Bennett predicted 'That will never sell. That will

Del Shannon never had a hit on Liberty, but not for want of trying.

never *ever* sell!' Four months later we gave him a large, one- or two-foot-tall Tin Ear Award, a silver tin ear award, because it had sold a million."

Perhaps the most welcome success of the year was perennial Jackie DeShannon's hit version of the Band's "The Weight." The song was written by Band member Robbie Robertson, and was the first of eight hits the Band would have on Capitol Records. In spite of this advantage, Jackie's version hit the charts a week before the Band's own recording and outperformed it in both position and longevity.

At the end of 1968, another old artist appeared out of the blue at Liberty. The Mermaids had made a big splash in 1964 with "Popsicles and Icicles," a traditional girl-group record, for the tiny Chattahoochie Record label. Now they broke into the future with a song from the pen of Steve Winwood, late of the Spencer Davis Group, later to have hits of his own, 1971–86. "Paper Sun" was practically psychedelic as produced by Kim Fowley. The title of the flip side, "Song Through Perception," speaks for itself to anyone who was young in 1968. All in all a fine record and a fine flop.

Canned Heat

The new music of the 1960s finally came together for Liberty with one new group in 1968, Canned Heat. The members of Canned Heat came from all over, from New York to California to Mexico City. The personnel lineup changed considerably over the few years the group had hits. One member of Canned Heat died of a drug overdose, a fate typical of late-1960s rockers. Canned Heat had four Liberty chart singles, including two in the top twenty, "Going Up the Country" and "On the Road Again." By their fourth hit, they had slid well off the top forty, showing the poor staying power typical of the entire rock 'n' roll era. Dean Torrence of

Can you find Dean's portrait on the back of this Canned Heat Liberty LP designed by Dean Torrence?

Liberty's Jan & Dean designed some of the Canned Heat LP covers, including *Best of Canned Heat*.

Lee Mendell, as head of the Liberty international division, worked hard on behalf of Canned Heat. "I created the first international campaign for an artist, which was Canned Heat. We created graphics and artwork and set up a tour called 'On the Road Again' with a train and all the graphics but with different languages in each country. It was the first time in my knowledge that we had an international campaign."

Dave Dee, Dozy, Beaky, Mick, and Tich

Imperial added one new popular artist in 1968. Dave Dee, Dozy, Beaky, Mick, and Tich — if ever a group deserved to have hits, it was these guys. Their music was

It took an effort to remember the name of this Imperial group.

fresh and original. Unfortunately "Zabadak" was their only record to sell, and it missed the top forty. The follow-up was of epic proportions, an indescribable, dramatic, throbbing ode called "The Legend of Zanadu." Their LP, *Time to Take Off*, is a must for the late 1960s collector.

Also-Rans

"Zabadack" was released in January. In December Imperial had an also-ran duo, both in artist and title. The song was a medley of "By the Time I Get to Phoenix/I Say a Little Prayer" (Glen Campbell and Dionne Warwick, both originally recorded in 1967). The artists were Big Dee Erwin ("Swinging on a Star," 1963) and Mamie Galore.

Liberty, too, had 1968 also-rans, like Tony Scotti, who released two Liberty singles, one a further updating of the classic "Devil or Angel" (the Clovers, 1956; Bobby Vee, 1960). Nothing came of this version or of Tony Scotti.

COMPLETE CATALOG OF LONG PLAY ALBUMS 1967/1968

LIBERTY RECORDS
IMPERIAL RECORDS
MINIT RECORDS
WORLD PACIFIC RECORDS
PACIFIC JAZZ RECORDS
BLUE NOTE RECORDS

A PRODUCT OF LIBERTY

The Liberty catalog, as it appeared in the winter of 1967-68, including all the subsidiaries. This catalog listed only LPs and "All-Time Hit" singles, not regular 45 pressings.

LPs

Julie London, the original "Liberty Girl," who made the company a success back in 1955, was still creating catalog for Si Waronker's former company in 1968. Around Thanksgiving, she ranked #125 on *Billboard*'s chart with "Yummy, Yummy, Yummy (I've Got Love in My Tummy)," with an accompanying album by the same name. The tune had been a top-five rock hit in the spring for the Ohio Express (Buddah Records). The sounds of the Ohio Express were considered "Bubble Gum Music," aimed at preteens and not taken seriously by most critics. But often Bubble Gum songs were considered borderline suggestive, with titles like "Chewy, Chewy, Chewy" and "Down at Lulu's," both top-forty hits by the Ohio Express, and "Jam Up and Jelly Tight" by Tommy Roe. Hence sex-siren Julie London's version, unpopular with everyone including her husband:

"Julie knew all the people at Liberty, but that was about it. She did not associate with them a lot. Snuff Garrett did later become Julie's producer. I produced her first six or seven albums. But she knew what she wanted to do, she could handle songs. He had her do 'Yummy, Yummy, Yummy.' It was a terrible title, a terrible song. She was embarrassed by it. Don't ever listen to it. It is terrible."

LRP 3537 was by Rod McKuen, whose first Liberty LP had come out back in the 1950s. And LRP 3538 was *World Famous* by Barney Peters. That marked the end of the LRP series of albums.

LRP-3 had been the LP prefix for Liberty album catalog numbers from the beginning. Back in the early days of Julie London and Martin Denny's *Exotica* some Liberty albums were released in stereo. When they were, the catalog number stayed the same, except for the prefix, which became LST-7. Thus, the *Burke's Law* original TV soundtrack album came out in a mono version, LRP 3374, and a stereo version, LST 7374. This went on for most of the 1960s.

Finally, in the era of Canned Heat and the Nitty Gritty Dirt Band, the LRP mono releases were dropped. From then on, Liberty albums were released in stereo only.

Almost. For a few months, a small quantity of mono LPs was still released for use as promotional copies for radio stations. For some reason, these mono promos were not marked promo, and instead of the white label normally used for promo releases, the labels were the standard black Liberty labels.

But for all practical purposes, just as the 1950s had been a strictly mono world, the late 1960s were all stereo.

CHAPTER 19

1969
The Fifth Dimension and Also-Rans

As the 1960s came to a close, the Liberty Records family was slowly undergoing a metamorphosis. Dolton closed down completely in 1969, and its only active artists, Vic Dana and the Ventures, moved over to Liberty. Vic would have to wait a year to chart a Liberty single, but the Ventures made it big on Liberty in June. From the popular TV show of the same name, the Ventures scored big with "Hawaii 5-0." It made the top five and was the second biggest hit the Ventures ever had, second only to their first hit, "Walk, Don't Run," back in 1960. The late Johnny Burnette's brother and former member of the Rock and Roll Trio, Dorsey Burnette, turned up on Liberty in January 1969 for one minor success, "The Greatest Love."

A rare novelty tune came out in 1969, and it wasn't on Liberty. But the cover version was. The original was on Ariel Records, apparently the only record ever released on that label. It was called "Mah-Na-Mah-Na," and was taken from the "Sweden Heaven and Hell" soundtrack, as well as being featured on the Benny Hill TV show soundtrack. The original artist was called Piero Umiliani.

Liberty's version of "Mah-Na-Mah-Na" was by Liberty veteran Dave Pell, who in 1963 had released a Liberty LP, *Jazz Voices in Video*. It is such a close copy that it is hard to tell the difference, except that Pell didn't make the charts, while Umiliani made #55.

Three Liberty veterans did better. Vikki Carr appeared on the charts with "With Pen in Hand," and another song, "Eternity." Bobby Vee sang what could have been the theme song for Liberty at this point near its conclusion: "Let's Call It a Day Girl." And Gary Lewis revived the Cascades' 1964 Valiant Records hit, "Rhythm of the Rain," for a moderate hit. Without the rain and thunder sound effects of the original, it sounded a bit stark, but that was only to the ears of old-timers. The kids of 1969 loved it, and apparently still do, according to Gary Lewis.

"I still hear my version and the Cascades' version of 'Rhythm of the Rain' on the radio a lot. It's great. I was watching MTV a little while ago and they were interviewing some heavy metal band and they were saying, 'Boy, it's really hard to get played nowadays because of all these oldies stations!' And I said, 'Yeah! Great! Glad to hear it!' There are a lot of neat oldies stations that tell me all the time, 'If you do something new, send it to us and we will play it.' I ask them if they can do that on an oldies format. They say, 'Sure we can do that because you are an oldies name. Even if it's something new, we'll play it.'"

Imperial had no new hit artists in 1969, but Johnny Winter, albino brother of Edgar Winter ("Frankenstein," 1973), had an also-ran with "Rollin' an' Tumblin'."

Later Johnny would go to Columbia, again with little commercial success. Jerry Wallace ("Primrose Lane," 1959, Challenge Records) crooned two innocuous country ballads, "Son" and "Temptation (Make Me Go Home)." But nothing was shaking.

Amid Imperial's lackluster performance as a whole in 1969, Jackie DeShannon landed the biggest hit of her career at the close of the decade: her triumphant and well-deserved classic, "Put a Little Love in Your Heart." Snuff Garrett had little to do with Imperial, since its acquisition came around the time he went independent. But he knew Lou Chudd, who was the owner of Imperial, and says: "The biggest hit ever on Imperial was 'Put a Little Love in Your Heart,' Jackie DeShannon's song," which Jackie both wrote and sang. It just went to show that talent will win out given time. Yet Jackie's follow-up, "Love Will Find a Way," which she also wrote, scarcely made top forty. What an enigma Jackie was.

Perhaps the only other Imperial artists who could be said to have done respectably in 1969 were the Classics IV, whose "Traces" and "Everyday With You, Girl" were solid records, even if "Change of Heart" and "Midnight" were only middling successes.

Johnny Rivers still did good work, but his time seemed to have passed. "These Are Not My People," "Muddy River," and "One Woman" charted but were hardly destined to appear on any Various Artists' Greatest Hits compilations in the future.

On Johnny's Liberty subsidiary label, Soul City, the Fifth Dimension were the powerhouse of the Liberty family. Besides the hits "Workin' on a Groovy Thing" and "California Soul," they scored two #1s in 1969, the first being "Aquarius/Let the Sun Shine In."

"Aquarius" almost didn't get recorded by the group. The group heard the song when they all saw *Hair* on Broadway — it is the opening number of that rock musical. They asked their producer, Bones Howe, about it, but he was against it. After all, he said, several artists had already recorded it, and none of them hit.

Then someone suggested combining "Aquarius" with another *Hair* number, "Let the Sun Shine In." Bones cut the track in October 1968, and the group, appearing in Las Vegas, added their vocals two months later. It sold three million copies and won two Grammys including Record of the Year.

The other 1969 Fifth Dimension #1 was "Wedding Bell Blues." Liberty promotion man Bud Dain knew part of the secret of success for at least a couple of the Fifth Dimensions hits.

"Laura Nyro's 'Stone Soul Picnic' was #1 in LA and New York only. 'Wedding Bell Blues' was #1 in LA and Cleveland. So when the Fifth Dimension recorded them, they knew it was a number one tune." Too bad there were not more coverable tunes like those around to help Liberty in its final days.

CHAPTER 20

1970
Ike and Tina Turner and Sugarloaf

In 1970, less than two years after Dolton had folded, Imperial closed down. The Classics IV had one last hit, "The Funniest Thing," and then followed the Ventures and Vic Dana over to Liberty for a minor hit with "Where Did All the Good Times Go" (as anyone at Imperial might well ask) before moving to MGM South for a final two hits.

Jackie DeShannon had her own two final small Imperial showings with "Brighton Hill," which she wrote, and the medley "You Keep Me Hangin' On/Hurt So Bad," which she borrowed from the Supremes and Little Anthony. Then Jackie, who had started on Liberty in 1963 and then slid over to Imperial in 1964, returned to the Liberty fold for one charting, "It's So Nice."

Johnny Rivers held on to the last, with "Into the Mystic" and "Fire and Rain." This last record, which only got to the nineties on the Hot 100, was the last Imperial 45 released. Johnny then went to United Artists, which bought Imperial, and continued reviving oldies. In 1972 he got the fifth biggest of his thirty-odd hits, "Rockin' Pneumonia—Boogie Woogie Flu," originally by Huey "Piano" Smith and the Clowns on Ace Records in the 1950s.

Ike and Tina Turner

The new artists at Liberty were Ike and Tina Turner and Sugarloaf, a Denver band. The legendary man-and-wife team were unable to deliver hits throughout the 1960s, and they moved from one label to another like gypsies. The list is long: Kent, Sue, Philles, Minit (a Liberty label), and Blue Thumb, to name some. Their first Liberty record to sell was "I've Been Loving You Too Long" in November 1970. "I Want to Take You Higher" took them higher, into the top forty in August.

Sugarloaf

Sugarloaf was a rock quartet who came to Liberty almost too late for it to matter. "Green-Eyed Lady" was their first Liberty release and took them to the top of the charts in short order. The follow-up, "Tongue in Cheek," was #51 in 1971 and their last on the Liberty label, which was replaced by the United Artists label for the next and final Sugarloaf release.

Lee Mendell: "Sugarloaf was in the days when Mike Stewart became involved and decided that 'Liberty' was not a good name for a record label, that the Liberty image was not good on the street. Which was something that I was never able to understand. But since he was president.... A promotion man named Dennis Gammon was deeply involved in breaking 'Green-Eyed Lady.' He also broke 'Come Back When You Grow Up' in North Carolina. He found it and nurtured it and grew it and spread it, which is what a promotion man is supposed to do. If it wasn't platinum, it was certainly gold."

Also-Rans

One of the last of Liberty's also-rans: A group known only as Cornerstone, in March, had "Holly Go Softly," with no success. Another was Dana Valery, who sang a revival of Gene McDaniels's 1962 #21 Liberty hit, "Point of No Return." The other side of her disc was "Put Your Hand in the Hand," which would come out a few months later by the Canadian group Ocean on Kama Sutra Records, and reach #2!

There were, of course, lots of other also-rans at this point. The dearth of hits at Liberty was not for want of trying. Liberty released some eighty-two singles in 1970. With six songs charting, that is a "success" rate of only 7 percent, half the label's overall rate during its full lifetime. Someone had lost the touch.

CHAPTER 21

1971
Liberty in the End

By 1971 Liberty was gone. The name was just being used for a few last releases. The fourth-from-last release was #56215. A real also-ran, it was "Remember Mary" by Sweet Marie, a male band that sounded like, well, like Sugarloaf.

In March 1971, Ike and Tina Turner's "Proud Mary" was #56216, and it catapulted the Turners into the top five for the first time. Perhaps Liberty did have relatively few hits in 1970 and 1971, but between Sugarloaf and Ike and Tina, the ones they did have were pips!

"Proud Mary" (Creedence Clearwater Revival, 1969) by Ike and Tina was the third-from-last release on Liberty, and final top-forty hit for Liberty Records. What a swan song! It made the top five, and became the biggest of the Turners' twenty-plus chart singles ever! In May 1971, Ike and Tina's follow up to "Proud Mary," "Ooh-Poo-Pah-Doo" (Jessie Hill, 1960), was issued on United Artists, which had absorbed Liberty Records.

The second-from-last, #56217, was an unsuccessful record (in terms of chart success, that is) by Canned Heat, "Woolly Bully" (Sam the Sham, 1965, MGM Records). Then they followed everyone else who was left to United Artists for a final hit, "Rockin' with the King" in 1972.

The last Liberty album was LST-7656, *Open the Door*, by the Humblebums. Just which door it was, or what a humblebum might have been, is anyone's guess. The group never had any hits or even any 45s, as far as research indicates.

Last of all from Liberty was record #56218. That was a long count from the original release in 1955, 55001 by Lionel Newman. Newcomer artist Sugarloaf did the honors with their "Tongue in Cheek." Fittingly, if less than satisfyingly, their song topped out at #55 — 1955 had been the year Liberty had begun. Then they, too, moved to UA, for one hit before winding up their career with two records on the Claridge label in 1975.

Si Waronker, thankfully, was not around to see the end of Liberty. The first fans knew of the end of Liberty was sale bins stuffed with old Liberty LPs. On a business trip in Portageville, Missouri (population seventeen hundred), I saw a sign in a hardware store window advertising an LP closeout, "2 for $1."

It was intriguing. What kind of LPs would be in a closeout sale at fifty cents each in a hardware store in downtown P'ville? The answer awaited inside, where there were four boxes stuffed full of Liberty and Dolton 1960s LPs, sealed, both mono and stereo. Jan & Dean, the Fleetwoods, the Ventures, Gary Lewis and the Playboys, Gene McDaniels, Timi Yuro — you name it, they were there. Gaps in my collection were filled; old, worn copies were replaced; alternate LP jackets were acquired; and stereo copies of LPs originally bought in mono were picked up. There was quite a bit of extra carry-on for the weekend return flight back home!

Two decades later, Si Waronker was able to explain why those closeout records were on sale there in a hardware store in a small town in the country.

"The ending of Liberty, unfortunately, was not the most pleasant ending of all time. In 1969, I had left the country, traveling in my boat worldwide. Two years later, Liberty was sold to TransAmerica, who combined it with United Artists, which they owned as well. Liberty was not doing well because of management. Al Bennett was very capable in many respects, but he did a few things that they did not enjoy. So TransAmerica decided to get rid of him and put in a guy named Stewart to run the company.

"Meanwhile, Liberty was going downhill, downhill, you barely heard of them. Then they combined the Liberty catalog into United Artists'. UA was then sold to a European company, who decided to take the whole UA and dump it, and the name Liberty, at the same time. Everybody who was part of it went on their own 'merry' way. Snuffy left before that. But the company went to pieces, and it was a pity to see it happen. Liberty went from being Liberty to being United Artists to being EMI.

"Way back, I had made a deal with Sir Edward Lewis of British Decca. I had promised him Liberty would stay with him for all time. But when I left, Al Bennett broke the contract with Ted Lewis, which was a heartbreak—because there was one of the nicest guys who ever lived. But Al wanted to go with EMI, then go on to have his own distribution in Europe, which was deadly—you can't do it unless you are big enough. As soon as EMI got their hands on any part of that Liberty/UA catalog, they just dumped it.

"What happened to Liberty's stock was that the schlock operators got the stock. Schlock operators are certain people who go to the manufacturers and buy all of their cutouts and returns and give them just ten cents on the dollar. If you are desperate enough, you take the money. At the very end, that was what they were doing.

"EMI got rid of all the catalog to the schlock operators. Then the records were sent to little towns on the outskirts of cities, and to places like Hong Kong, where they were sold for twenty cents apiece. The new owners would then turn around and give them away when you bought ten gallons of gas, or sell them at fifty cents or whatever apiece. That's how 'Liberty' [at the end] got rid of all their stuff. The poor artists got screwed because they never got paid their royalties on those records, nor did the publishers. It was a terrible thing. It never happened when I was there, thank God!"

A bonanza for fans; a sad and ignominious end for Liberty.

Part Two

Making Liberty Hit Records

When kids (or in the case of Julie London records, adults!) turned on the radio and heard great Liberty hits like "Rubber Ball," "Chip Chip," or "Everybody Loves a Clown," and hopefully went out to buy a copy, most probably they just grooved on the music. If their thoughts went behind that to imagining how the songs came about, they might picture their favorite artist standing behind a microphone wearing headphones and singing into a tape recorder. But that was about it.

In reality there is a whole lot more to the making of a hit record. Before a song can be bought in a store, it obviously has to be composed. But there is another step. A composed song can't be recorded until after it has been published. (Well, it *can* be recorded before it has been published, but it normally is not, unless perhaps, for example, it is written on the spot by the performer.)

After a song is written and published, another step usually occurs before it is recorded. Someone has to bring that published song to the attention of one or more appropriate artists. That is the job for what is traditionally called an "A&R man." "A&R" stands for "artists and repertoire," and "man" stands for "person."

The next step is for a producer to set up a session. This will involve booking a studio, seeing that the artist learns the song, and arranging for the musicians and studio singers. Often this is done via a contractor, such as a studio musician who knows other musicians and calls them to get them to the session, much as a building contractor arranges for plumbers and electricians to help build a house.

Within the session the goal is to make a recording that can become a record. In the studio an engineer is necessary and critical to the process of capturing the music with microphones and storing it on recording tape.

Along with the music session, a photography session is typically set up. Picture sleeves, album covers, and advertising call for recent photos of the artist.

Probably the most important phase of making a hit record (as opposed to just recording and releasing another song no one ever hears or buys) is promotion. Every record has to be promoted, so people know that it exists.

Related to record promotion is artist publicity. Publicity is important to getting the product or at least the source of the product known.

Meanwhile, back at the record company, the sales staff has to be doing the physical act of selling the product that has been produced, promoted, and publicized.

An extension of sales involves distribution, getting the record out to all the various markets.

Sales and distribution can be helped by merchandising, making the product attractive.

And finally the song has to be played on the radio. Radio airplay is directly related to promotion and is absolutely necessary to have a hit record.

Publishing, production and A&R, session musicians, engineers, photography, promotion, publicity, sales, distribution, merchandising, radio play — these are the behind-the-scenes elements that bridge the space between recording and buying records, which are the only two steps normally thought about by the consumer.

Each of these steps was covered by someone at Liberty Records. A great many people were involved in each of these steps. And job responsibilities at Liberty were not always cut and dried. For example, the first Liberty staffer we will meet is Dick Glasser. He is introduced as a music publisher. However, he also wrote songs, sang records that were released on Liberty, produced for Liberty's Dolton subsidiary, performed A&R chores, and more.

Here are the stories of a representative sample of the people who were responsible for making Liberty hit records.

CHAPTER 22

Music Publishing — Metric Music

Liberty Records owned a music publishing company they called Metric Music. And although Liberty also owned Cornerstone Song Publishing Company (part of Dolton), ASA Music Company, and Simon-Jackson, Inc., plus a part interest in Exotica Publishing Company and Liberty Songs, Inc., Metric was Liberty's primary publishing arm.

In spite of this impressive list of publishing companies, Si Waronker never wanted to get into music publishing. "We had Metric Music more as a convenience for an artist. If someone wrote a song and wanted to record it, but it wasn't published yet, Metric could publish it."

Dick Glasser

Dick Glasser was the first person at Liberty to take Metric past Si's notion of a "convenience for artists" and began to make Metric a dynamic arm of the Liberty family.

"Al Bennett was best man at my wedding," tells Dick Glasser to show how important Liberty was in his life. "I worked at Liberty for four and a half years, starting in 1960, when I had just moved out from Ohio. I started as a songwriter and decided to move here to establish myself in the music business as a professional. Snuffy Garrett introduced me to Al Bennett and Si Waronker."

Dick knew Snuff from Texas, when Snuff was a DJ and Dick had sung on some demo records for him while still in Cleveland. In one memorable radio stunt Dick recalls, Snuff sat atop a flagpole for about thirty days. When Snuff got Dick hired at Liberty, it was Dick's first professional job.

"When I came to Liberty, the label did not have an active publishing operation per se. It was basically a nonactive operation. They were just throwing things in there as they came. So I took on the chore of managing Metric Music and basically from scratch. The first writer I signed was Jackie DeShannon. We were quite successful in the first year with her and Sharon Sheeley. In that same period I signed Randy Newman, giving him his first assignment as a writer. We had many other writers who had success but are not recognizable names today.

"After I had been at Liberty for a few years, Bob Reisdorff decided that he wanted some kind of a change. Liberty decided to take his label Dolton over and

341

The Ventures, rolling around on the floor, made sure their faces showed. On later LPs they often relied on female models alone.

worked out a deal with Bob. He and I had developed a friendship and close rapport, and he recommended me to take over the Dolton subsidiary. The first record that I produced on Dolton was 'Red Roses for a Blue Lady,' by Vic Dana. We had a string of hits after that. I produced 'Walk, Don't Run, '64' with the Ventures, a remake of their old hit."

Al Bennett didn't like the new version. "When he heard it, bless his heart, he said [in a loud, LBJ-style Texas accent] 'Well, Dick, sounds good. But I think it's a little early. I don't think it'll sell.' About three weeks later Bob Skaff came in and said that San Jose picked the record and it was top-ten in three weeks."

What did Al say about the hit? "Well, he always had a way around it. He didn't deny it. But he always had a way of saying, 'Well, I told you that you could put it out, but I didn't know if it was gonna sell.' He had a way with words and a lot of charm and charisma."

"Walk, Don't Run '64," was in essence an updating of the Ventures' 1959 Dolton debut hit. It made #8, becoming one of the Ventures' biggest. The next year, encouraged by that success, Glasser produced a 1965 remake of the Fleetwoods' 1959 Dolton debut song, "Come Softly to Me." This one was not a chart success. However, Dick's years at Liberty were, overall, a personal success.

"Liberty was a close-knit family. Al Bennett, Si Waronker, everyone shared in the enthusiasm and success of that company over a period of three or four years. I became very close with Al Bennett. It was an important part of my life, a growing period, and an education in the industry. It was the starting point in my career, and I went on to be the head of Warner's A&R department in mid-sixty-four. That was a great opportunity, but I hated to leave Liberty when I had grown up with the Skaffs and Al Bennett and the rest. It was a close-knit operation.

"Al Bennett, in my mind, is one of the key figures of all time as far as executives is concerned. He had a way about doing business, about the way he treated his employees and his fellow workers. He had tremendous sincerity, and everything about the man was genuine. You will probably find people in the industry who would disagree, but from my point of view, he was one of the best, and he set some good examples and strong guidelines for those who grew up with him. It has been carried on in the industry, believe me."

Besides running Metric, Dick Glasser did record some songs, notably a 45 called "Handsome Guy." Don't look for Dick Glasser's name on the label, however. He used the pseudonym "Dick Lory" for that release. "Snuffy cut 'Handsome Guy.' It became number one in Australia, as a matter of fact. They tried to get me to come over and tour with the record, but I was absolutely tied down with my obligations with Metric." Dick Lory giving competition to Johnny O'Keefe, the Boomerang Kid, on his home turf? Glasser laughs at the suggestion. "Well, I suppose you could say that! At the same time, I was a writer, and Johnny was in town on a tour. We struck up a relationship and he took some of my compositions back with him, one of which was 'Take My Hand.' That became #1 for Johnny in Australia. So I guess you could say I was competitive in Australia."

Why did Dick Glasser use the Lory name in particular? "I really don't have an answer for that. It just kind of rang a bell at the time. People were throwing names around, and I had been a recording artist at CBS in the early days as Dick Glasser, with some success. We decided not to use that name, and Lory had a little more color so we changed it. The whole record was a carryover from my younger days when I wanted to be a singer. Snuffy would occasionally come across a song and say I should record it. 'Handsome Guy' was one of those. Unfortunately, we never got lucky in the United States. But that one did make it over there.

"We didn't follow through with an album or anything, but it makes a nice conversation piece. It was interesting, and I got to meet a lot of people through that record on the telephone." These connections assisted Dick Glasser when he negotiated foreign deals for Liberty's publishing, including an exchange program. "As an example of the exchange program, the Lennon-McCartney composition 'Do You Want to Know a Secret' was published by Northern in England, but by Metric in the U.S."

Jackie DeShannon and Sharon Sheeley were important to Metric as composers and as demo artists. Metric had the publishing on Jackie's 45s "Needles and Pins" and "When You Walk in the Room." "That went back to the demo days of Metric. We went in taking considerable time making demos and trying to match them up with certain artists. They would absolutely copy our demos note for note, because they were almost masters. In the case of Jackie's demo of 'Needles and Pins,' it turned out so well that we decided to release it as a record." Jackie's "demo" made #83 in the spring of 1963. And then it was recorded by the Searchers in England, thus serving as a demo after all. The same goes for Jackie's "When You Walk in the Room," which the Searchers also copied note for note from Jackie.

Jackie DeShannon and Sharon Sheeley also did well with demos for Brenda Lee. "Owen Bradley, who was producing Brenda at the time, used to call and say, 'We have Brenda coming up on a session next week. We need this and that and the other thing, and I am sure that you will probably have something note for note how you want Brenda to do it.' It got to that point after we had several hits, and Jackie could sound exactly like Brenda Lee."

It was nice to have a #1 record in Australia. But it was not a major factor for Liberty. A big hit in the United States could sell anywhere from five hundred thousand to a million or more copies. A #1 hit in Australia might sell thirty thousand to fifty thousand copies, not a big deal for Liberty. "But it makes a nice starting point for a lot of acts. The European and foreign markets can often be instrumental for breaking things domestically. It's like coming in the back door."

The Liberty/Dick Glasser/Australia connection has another twist. In 1962 Vikki Carr's version of "He's a Rebel" was a big hit in Australia. Then, years later, after Dick Glasser left Warner's, he produced Vikki Carr for CBS.

Combining publishing with A&R and producing, Dick Glasser cut the demo with Cliff Crawford of "Old Rivers," because he was one of the writers. Eventually this song was a big hit with Walter Brennan on Liberty. "But the number one priority at hand right then was to make a demo of 'The Epic Ride of John Glenn' for Al Bennett. When this project came up, I said, 'Hey, how about doing "Old Rivers" on the B side of this thing? But we had no artist to do it. Then Snuffy got involved to nail down someone to narrate. Tex Ritter, Tony Curtis, John Wayne, it went on and on.

"A guy I had been associated with years before, Charlie Adams, was a dear friend of Gene Autry. We were trying to think of a way to get to Walter Brennan. I called Charlie, who put me in touch with Gene Autry, who put me in touch with Walter Brennan. I went to Desilu, where Brennan was filming, and played him both demos. He got into the lyrics of 'Old Rivers'; I played it again. He said, 'I like that Glenn, but I really like this 'Old Rivers'! He started to narrate it right there, and I got goose bumps like you can't believe.

"I didn't produce Walter Brennan's hit, but I did sign him to the label, and they did copy our demo to the T." "Old Rivers" was #5 in 1962.

"I worked with Gene McDaniels vocally. I can't say I taught him how to sing by any means. But I was very in tune with Snuffy, and the phrasing for songs like 'Chip Chip' and things that Snuffy had chosen for Gene. Gene was into jazz, so to get him into a commercial bag was something of a chore. But it worked."

Yeah, I'd say it worked. "Tower of Strength," "Chip Chip," and "A Hundred Pounds of Clay" testify to that!

Al Altman

Al Altman now works in radio and TV. But he worked with Metric Music from 1964 to 1966. Al Altman started in programming and air work in Massachusetts.

Then he went to work for Mutual Distributors in Boston. Al recalls, "We did extremely well for Liberty records; we broke a lot of their records for the New England area during their strong years, when they had songs like 'The Mountain's High,' 'Tower of Strength,' all the Bobby Vee things. Bobby would come to town, and we would go do the record hops."

At one point Liberty offered Al Altman the opportunity to work for Liberty, either by going to California and being a promotion man, as he already had been in Boston; by going to New York and working in sales; or a third choice, which he took, by going into publishing in New York. "Ed Silvers was just leaving the job, so I came in and ran the New York office from Labor Day, 1964, working for Metric Music.

"Phil Skaff was the big man running Liberty, with Al Bennett as the real boss. Phil hired me."

Metric Music worked with a number of songwriters, including the previously mentioned Randy Newman, Sharon Sheeley, and Jackie DeShannon. Bob Stone, who wrote "Gypsies, Tramps, and Thieves" after he left Metric, was signed by Al in New York. Metric also had Bob Lind with "Elusive Butterfly."

A real strength of Liberty was the Travis catalog, which Liberty/Metric obtained when it bought Imperial Records. That acquisition brought a vast array of music, including most of the Fats Domino tunes and a lot of R&B and rock tunes that did well in the 1950s and early 1960s.

"When I left Liberty/Metric, I went to Screen Gems. There I did the *Hundred and One Hits* album, and also when I worked for Chapell, I did the *Chapell Story,* which was two hundred twenty-two songs on two records. Those were samplings of the music." Each song was excerpted for twenty to thirty seconds, providing samples to attract new versions by new artists of songs the company owned. "I tried to do that with the Travis catalog. I felt that if I did that at Liberty, it would have done extremely well. But they just didn't seem to have the money to develop their catalog as much as they could have. They were very much record people, and publishing is a whole separate area that needs real time devoted to it. It doesn't happen on its own."

How exactly does song publishing work? "It is almost like having a baby, from conception on. First you need the song. But even before that, sometimes you have to put the writers together. Somebody walks in with a lyric or a melody that is strong, and you team those people up. Conception. The song is in its rawest form. In fact a song can come in in any form whatsoever. A lot of times it was just somebody playing a piano, or a guitar, and we'd listen to it. If I liked it, we'd set up a session at a studio and do a demo. In 1964 it would be mono, a rhythm track, and if the writer could sing a little, we'd have him sing to save money.

"After that a good publisher takes that song and tries to marry it to people who are recording. Then you need to find the right producer and the right record situation." That marriage might include Bobby Vinton with his producer Bob Morgan on Epic Records, or Bobby Vee with his producer Snuff Garrett on Liberty.

"Once the song is recorded, the publisher and writer make money from the performance of the music and the mechanical sales, the actual record sales. Publishers share in that also. And sheet music. And foreign rights. Plus jingles and commercials. It is a big, big-penny business, but those pennies can add up to hundreds to thousands to millions. Royalties are much greater now. In those days it was two cents a record."

Royalties are, of course, the money writers and performers get when their music is bought and sold, or even just performed. Every time a local garage band plays hit songs at a corner bar or a high school dance, they are supposed to pay royalties to the publisher and writer. Of course they almost never do. It is sort of like collecting sales tax at a garage sale.

In addition, every time any radio station plays a record, the publisher is supposed to get paid, along with the artist and the composer. Except no one keeps track of the records played at every little station in Kansas or, for that matter, California. But this does not mean that writers are getting cheated, exactly. As Al Altman explains, "[Estimates of the number of] performances of the music [are] based on monitoring and sampling of radio stations, and that is fed into a computer. Then a formula is used to figure out how much the writer and the publisher [are] going to make. Of course, the writer and the publisher make equal money from performance and from mechanical sales. The publisher and writer make money from the performance of the music, from the sheet music, from the foreign rights, and from the sale of records both domestic and foreign.

"In publishing a song, it goes through several phases. First it is written. Then the song is demoed [a demonstration recording is made]. The song is then shown to various producers, artists, etc. After that, hopefully, someone picks the song and says that they are going to record it. If they go in to do a session, usually they will do a session of three or four songs, hypothetically. If I am one of those three or four songs, I still have to wait and see if it turns out to be the A side or the B side. In other words, it is a slow process when you publish a song. It may not become the single." In other words, in music publishing the whole process from writing to having a hit is very slow. Perhaps nine months after it is started, there is hope it will be coming out and be a hit record, but there is never any guarantee. The process takes a lot of patience, and Al notes, "A lot of people don't have that patience."

Metric songs were recorded on many labels, on RCA, Columbia, Decca, all labels. There is no telling where a song might go, once it is published. "Once a song has been recorded, and released, then anyone can do their rendition of that song, as a record release, or as a live performance, as long as they do not change the lyrics or the basic content of that song. When it is released, that gives people the freedom. Otherwise they have to get a license for their record to be released."

Of course, commercials are another matter altogether. To use a song to sell or promote a product, or as a part of a jingle, whether the lyrics are changed or not, requires prior clearance from a publisher. "And you have to pay for the rights to use a song," Altman explains. "For example, if you want to use the song 'Groovin',' you have to pay for those rights. Otherwise you can't use that song.

"That is a capsule summary of what the publishing business is all about.

"The problem with publishing is the lack of immediate feedback. With a record, you get it out and sometimes can get immediate reaction. Very soon you know if you have a hit record or not. Especially in the early days with Liberty Records. Back then radio stations and disc jockeys were more free to take chances, play a record twenty times, and do things—especially before the first payola scandal hit. That really did change the business a lot. It made it into a meeting business. People suddenly became afraid to make judgments on their own. So they had meetings, and if they all agreed they liked it or did not like it, they felt safe.

"Each week, I got calls from the various record companies that I represented, like Liberty Records, United Artists Records, Cadence Records, Imperial Records, et cetera. They would call me to ask, 'How did such-and-such record do?'"

At one point, as a joke, Al Altman sent these companies a list, telling them in jest that when they called, instead of having to discuss each record, he would just give them a number from his list. The list had forty humorous reasons explaining, supposedly, why a record was not being played.

"I had my own top-forty list. It was called the top-forty reasons stations gave for not playing a record. Number forty was 'It actually is on the air.' The rest of them were various typical reasons it was not on the air: 'Too fast,' 'Too slow,' 'Too much surf,' various reasons."

Al laughs about it now, as he did then, but no one he sent the list to got the joke at the time. "Well, they all thought the list was a terrible idea! It was just a joke. But they all disliked the idea."

Today, it is universal that record companies have publishing companies. In the Liberty days, if a record company had a publishing company, it was, as already said, more a convenience for the artists than anything else. "The New York office provided a place for Bud Dain and Jackie DeShannon and people to come into when they traveled to perform or promote. They had an office to stop by. It was a good meeting place, a place where they could drop their hats, make their phone calls, and do their business." Al Altman has many fond memories of working for Liberty/Metric. But eventually he moved on. "Another job came along which afforded me different opportunities, so I took it, and that was why I moved on to Screen Gems.

"Liberty was a company of young, aggressive, very together, and forward-looking people. It was a good fraternity of people and a good many of them not only remained in the music business but have continued to be successful. That doesn't happen with a lot of companies.

"Liberty Records was a great company, and it was what the music business was all about in the 1960s. It really was. We owned the charts. At one point, when I was in local distribution in Massachusetts, we had nine of the top-ten tunes. My boss told me, if I got ten out of ten, he'd give me a raise. I said, 'Thanks.'"

Al is still in the music business and now works for SESAC, a music-licensing organization like BMI and ASCAP.

CHAPTER 23

Record Producing

As John Wayne once said to Dolton founder Bob Reisdorff, a record producer is something akin to a movie director. He (or she) tells everyone what to do, and the final product is that person's vision of what the whole thing is supposed to come out like.

Lou Adler

"Liberty was the beginning of the West Coast record scene," Lou Adler believes. It sure started things for Lou. As he outgrew Liberty, he founded Dunhill Records, whose most notable artists were the Mamas and the Papas and the Grass Roots. Prior to that, in his Liberty days, Lou found an artist who would be huge on the Liberty subsidiary Imperial Records—an artist who would then develop his own Liberty subsidiary, Soul City Records, and record the Fifth Dimension.

"I uncovered Johnny Rivers playing at Gazzari's on La Cienega Boulevard near Beverly." Lou Adler was just out for an evening's entertainment. "I went to see Don Rickles, I think, a few doors down from Gazzari's. I did not know Gazzari's, and I'd just heard of Johnny Rivers once or twice through the Everly Brothers, who[m] I was producing at the time. The line for Rickles was long enough to take some time out. I noticed this club that people were drifting in and out of, so we went in to see what was going on. I went in, and what was going on was, Rivers was onstage with a bass player and a drummer dressed in a suit and tie. He was playing rock and roll, mostly Southern, a lot of Chuck Berry, John Lee Hooker. It was an adult audience, at least eighteen but mostly twenty-one and over. They were dancing like they were at a hop! To see that kind of dancing going on in a club was very unusual for the West Coast at that time.

"Rivers spotted me and told me that he was going to record an album at Gazzari's, live, and would I produce it? I said yes, if I could have first option on it as a record company after it was finished."

Producing Johnny Rivers was pretty easy. His live show was perfect for recording as it happened. Even so it was recorded twice. "We cut the tapes. Then Rivers left Gazzari's, the Whiskey à Go-Go opened, and we then recut the album live, basically the same songs, at the Whiskey a few nights after it opened. That's how the album came to be."

Why did Johnny Rivers end up on Imperial instead of the parent company, Liberty? "It is vague in my mind. I've heard him say recently that he wanted it because it was a smaller label. We liked it because Ricky Nelson was on it and a couple of other people who sort of had that countrified rock and roll. Rivers had a lot of Southern in him. I think Imperial suited him a little better at the time.

"Rivers was the first artist that I signed to Dunhill Productions, which later became Dunhill Records."

Jan & Dean, big Liberty stars for many years, were actually signed not to Liberty but to Lou Adler. Lou in turn had a production deal with Liberty Records. It is sometimes said that Jan signed with Liberty more or less solo and brought Dean along. But Lou confirms that Jan & Dean were signed as a duo with Liberty through Lou. Jan had made some records on his own around the same time the duo appeared on Liberty. One was called "Tomorrow's Teardrops" on Ripple Records, in which producer Lou Adler was closely involved. "Ripple was my label, and we had other labels that were released locally but did not have national distribution.

"Before Liberty Jan & Dean were produced by Herb Alpert and myself for Doré Records. Right before 'Heart and Soul,' Herb and I broke up." That record was on Challenge Records, a year pre–Liberty, and was a national hit for Jan & Dean. After Challenge, Lou Adler and Herb Alpert went their separate ways. "Herb and I divvied up. I took Jan & Dean, and 'Heart and Soul' was the first record I produced on them on my own."

Legend has it that Jan & Dean had wanted to be on Liberty previously, but were unable to strike a deal until they had the strength of the "Heart and Soul" hit record to work from. "Nope," says Lou Adler. Well, then, how about the legend that when Lou and Herb split up, Lou got Jan & Dean, and Herb got the money that he used to set up A&M Records? "Nope. There wasn't much money. Actually what he got was the tape recorder that he recorded 'The Lonely Bull' on." That record became the first Tijuana Brass hit.

Once Jan & Dean arrived at Liberty, Jan began to take over the production role for Jan & Dean records from Lou Adler. "It was a twofold situation. Jan was growing into being a producer. At the same time, I was signed to Screen Gems, Nevins-Kirshner. So I was not allowed to put my name on their records as a producer. But Jan was becoming the producer at that point. My hands-on involvement continued all through those records, but we pretty much did the records in the same way."

Although neither Jan & Dean nor Lou Adler carried the title of "promotion," both worked in that area at Liberty. Any artist or producer would always want more promotion than the label was willing or able to provide. Jan's father, especially, felt Liberty did not promote Jan & Dean records sufficiently, but Lou holds that these feelings are misapprehensions.

"I think that Jan & Dean promoted their records anyway [regardless of Liberty's degree of promotion]. Jan & Dean had a sort of a grass-roots approach, as did I, being local from Los Angeles, University High School kids. For years, Jan had had himself listed as 'K-JAN Radio' so that he would receive free records as a radio station. So he just reversed the process and he did do a lot of that [kind of promotion].

"But it wasn't so much that Liberty didn't promote them. I think that Jan's dad, Bill Berry, had a negative outlook about all record companies. But we were fighting a lot of trends with Jan & Dean. Surf records, later on for example, had not really taken hold; that was not a national situation. Jan & Dean actually helped break it before the Beach Boys did. The Beach Boys' first couple of records were local also. It was just a case of having to prove a particular sound to the record company. I felt

Jan Berry (Jan & Dean) and longtime friend, producer, and composer Lou Adler.

that Liberty was OK. They were people who enjoyed the record business and they were friends. I think that they tried hard. I never found that much fault in them."

Jan & Dean were different from the artists who had been at Liberty up to that time. They wrote and produced their own records, and they did not act like junior adults, dressing up in suits like Bobby Vee and Johnny Burnette. Except on rare occasions very early on, they did not wear suits and ties, but T-shirts and cutoffs. "Jan & Dean were a West Coast version of Fabian and Avalon. I was like, I hate the word, but a promoter. I liked the package. We did the whole thing with the way they dressed and how we approached fan clubs and everything. It was much more teen-fan oriented than anything that Liberty had. Snuff's approach with the artists he had was more formal, the material and so forth. It was almost bordering on adult. We went for Avalon's and Fabian's audience." Of course, Avalon and Fabian did not write their own songs, produce their own sessions, and did not graduate from college and attend graduate school!

As far as the area of "production" went, Lou Adler took the title *producer* seriously. "Jan & Dean and Johnny Rivers were a Dunhill production until I went to Nevins-Kirshner, which was eventually bought by Screen Gems–Columbia. Then Jan & Dean were probably managed out of the Dunhill office. I became less involved over time, as Jan became more involved, where he could take over all of the different procedures of producing the record. He grew from a guy playing piano to orchestrating everything, then starting to produce and starting to mix. Gradually he became a producer, which allowed me to step aside yet keep in there enough to have input into what kinds of records they made and give him production advice. But Jan was pretty much running the recording sessions eventually. I was about six years older than Jan and Dean."

The "Dead Man's Curve" 45 sleeve featured a dramatic painting on one side, and bookmarks on the other side (see page 479).

Lou was frustrated by Jan Berry's train accident, which broke his leg, and his car accident, which pretty much broke his skull. "We had a couple of false starts that were unfortunate. Jan & Dean could have gone in a lot of different directions [movies, TV, record company]. Especially because of the fact that they looked so great. I am sure that they would have entered other areas besides recording, and that new activity could have become their forte. But every time we started something in another area, something happened. It was almost as if something stopped it every time. But everyone who is close to Jan knows that he is self-destructive. Who knows how much that interacts with fate."

Jan was the driving force of the duo. Today Dean has taken over that role, as Jan's disabilities, a legacy of the car accident, have left him unable to resume the leader role. But even before the accident, Dean was more important to Jan & Dean than many gave him credit for.

"Dean was a sidekick, but he was very valuable. Dean was more valuable than Jan ever gave him credit for. I think at one point that Jan even bought his name!"

A West Coast recording artist who was close to Jan & Dean once said, "It could have been Jan & Anybody." True? Well, Lou Adler offered a few thoughts. "From a record standpoint, if someone else were able to duplicate some of the things that Dean did, I am sure that they could have. Maybe not as fresh or as good. But there were people around that group, in and around the surf records, that were doing a lot of the things that Dean was doing. But no one in the music/entertainment field looked like Jan & Dean on stage.

"When we first happened on the scene, most everyone was Italian and short, coming out of Philadelphia. Then these two guys busted out into those hops. The first time we went to Philadelphia, eyes popped open, like, 'Where are they from?!' Six-foot, blond-haired guys in sweaters that matched and white shoes. I mean, it was a crazy moment."

The effect of Jan & Dean in the Midwest was also striking. Middle America could relate better to middle-class, suburban garage kids in casual clothes than to the Eastern, working-class, urban club crooners. "It was strange. Kansas was one of those places where we started getting letters with pictures of people with woodies and surf boards. And we said, 'Where is the ocean?'

"Jan & Dean even projected a much more unusual and accessible image than the Beach Boys did. There was something about these two guys that people grabbed onto. The way of life that they were [singing] about I think got across well with these two guys. They had a lot of charisma. In the Midwest, in Chicago, in Texas, they were very big."

Lou Adler started with Jan & Dean, but as Herb Alpert went on to other activities, notably A&M Records, Lou went on to other things as well.

"When I went to work for Aldon Music and Nevins-Kirshner, I became the person who worked with Snuffy on all of those Carole King, Bobby Vee records, Gene McDaniels things. I brought those songs out because I represented that publisher. I was basically a song-plugger. I would go to New York and tell the writers, Carole King, Barry Mann, and the rest, what follow-ups were possible. Kirshner had access to the ones in the East, and I had access to the ones in the West. I would tell them what records were becoming hits that I had a shot at placing the follow-up with Snuffy or some other A&R man or producer. I could direct them so that they would write the songs and cut the demos for the follow-ups.

"I mean, Carole King's demos sounded like Bobby Vee records! 'Run to Him' is a good example, also 'Take Good Care of My Baby.' When she was 'doing' Bobby Vee, it was great. We spent a lot of money on demos in order to make them sound great. Then a lot of our arrangements were lifted for the hit recordings. The demo pretty much laid out what the next record would be and what it would sound like."

Carole King's demo of Bobby Vee's record "I Can't Say Goodbye," the charted flip side to 1963's "Please Don't Ask About Barbara," is a tremendous recording in its own right. These demos were so good that they created a problem for Lou Adler. "I could never get Carole King demos back. It's true! I'd give out demos [to record A&R people and producers and artists to listen to], and they would keep the demos. Whether they used them or not, they'd keep them for themselves!"

The style of Carole King's demos for Bobby Vee and other Liberty artists endured beyond Liberty and King's demo work. "When I went in to cut *Tapestry* with her, that was the sound I went after. A simple sound to try to recreate what she had been doing with the piano way up front.

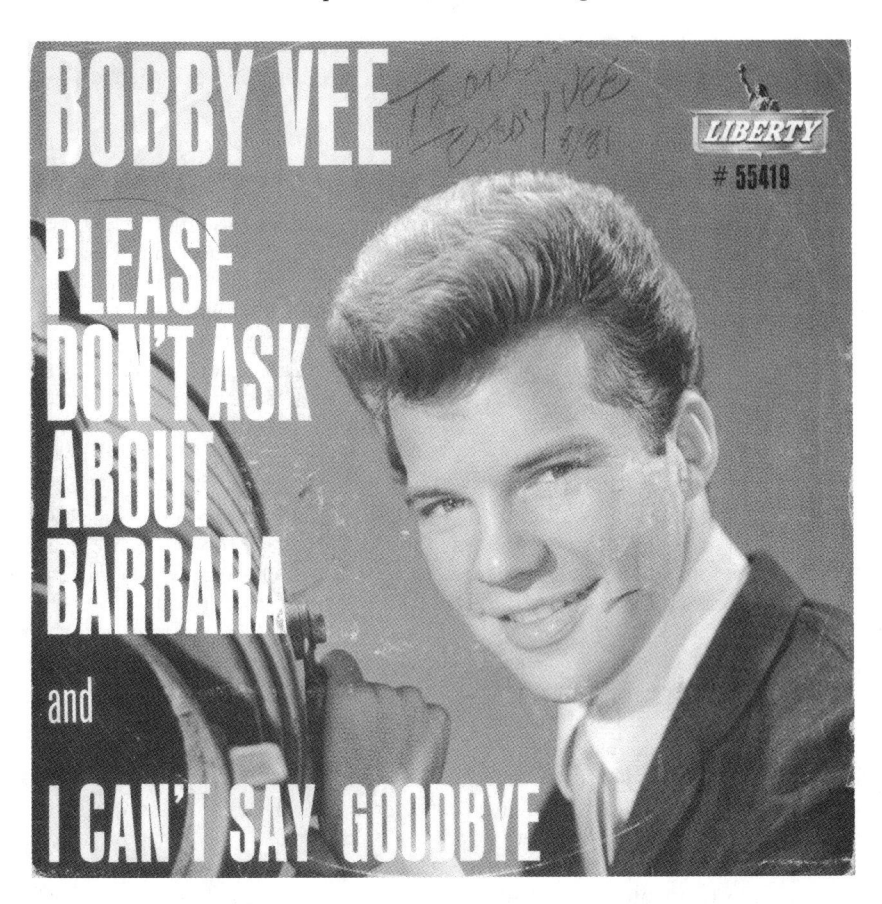

One of Bobby Vee's eight two-sided hits. "Please Don't Ask About Barbara" had a tricky guitar line.

"Jackie DeShannon was also close to it. The music business in Los Angeles and Hollywood at that time was very close-knit. It was all around Vine Street and up to La Brea. Sharon Sheeley, Sonny Curtis, Roger Miller, the Everly Brothers, and more were all in one group, and it wasn't very big. So there was a lot of good exchange of ideas and a lot of great fun. The camaraderie was such that everyone wanted everyone else to make it."

If Carole King's demos were so great, then why not release them like Jackie DeShannon's demo of "Needles and Pins"? In fact, Carole King's 1962 Dimension hit "It Might as Well Rain Until December" was a Bobby Vee demo. And it went beyond that. Releasing demos was not that unusual. "We had a label called Dimension. A lot of our demos came out on Dimension. If no one would do a song we felt strongly about, we'd put the demo out. Like the Bobby Vee single that Carole King had a hit with. 'Locomotion' by Little Eva was written for Dee Dee Sharp. All of the Cookies' records ["Chains," Don't Say Nothin' Bad About My Baby"] were originally written for Philadelphia artists. Any time no one would do it, we'd put it out."

Thus the roles of writer, artist, producer, publisher, demo maker, and A&R were combined and overlapped again and again at Liberty and elsewhere.

Ted Glasser

Ted Glasser came into producing at Liberty through the back door, so to speak. Not that this was an unusual way to do it. Liberty's premier producer, Snuff Garrett, started as a DJ, then a record store stock boy, then as a Liberty promotion staffer. It was only when he got a chance to produce that Snuff came into his own. Still, he didn't plan to be a producer. And neither did Ted Glasser.

Perhaps the name Glasser sounds a bit familiar? Dick Glasser started at Liberty by setting up Metric Music for Al Bennett. Four or five years later, he left for Warner's. One day, Dick was in Nashville for sessions when he called his brother Teddy Glasser at home in Ohio.

"He asked me if I had any songs," Teddy tells it today. "'Oh, yeah, I've got some.' So I met him in Nashville, then drove back to California with him. That was nineteen sixty-five." Teddy never returned to Ohio. He went to work at MCA as a publisher for four years, where he signed the writer for "Born to Be Wild." His success at MCA caused Liberty execs Bud Dain and Bob Skaff to offer him a job as staff producer at Liberty in 1968.

The first act Teddy Glasser signed at Liberty was the Frost Brothers, Thomas and Richard: "We had only one record that hit the charts." It was called "She's Got Love," and was released on Imperial, charting at #83 in the fall of 1969. Two later records, including one that was the third-to-last ever released on the Imperial label, failed to chart at all. What happened to the group?

A guy named John who managed the group the Frost Brothers worked at Liberty as head of promotion but got fired. He was the one who had brought the Frosts to Teddy's attention. It was an awkward situation once he was fired, just half cooperation on the job. "Things fell apart and Liberty decided to drop the group," explains Teddy.

"The second record I cut was a chart record with a new group I signed for the label, so Bud Dain gave me raise after raise. I also got Vic Dana on the charts, where he had not been for years. We had a record with him called 'Red, Red Wine,' written by Neil Diamond, that was number seven in Chicago and sold over a hundred ten thousand records in Chicago alone. Then, after I got Vic cookin' again, his contract came up and Columbia signed him." By this time, UA had bought Liberty, and the UA executives fired Teddy, not seen as very valuable now that he had lost his hit artist, Vic Dana, to Columbia Records.

"Red, Red Wine" could have been a bigger hit, but it was released by Liberty after Columbia had signed the singer, so Liberty was not willing to promote the disc since they didn't even have him anymore! It still went to #72 in 1970.

Sandy Nelson was a (former) star of Imperial Records, with seven Imperial hits prior to the Liberty buyout. The last time he had made the charts for Imperial was in 1966, when "Drums A-Go-Go" limped to #124. Teddy Glasser brought Sandy's career out of a long slump in 1964. "I did two or three albums with Sandy, and got him in the nineties on *Billboard,* I think it was with 'Manhattan Spiritual.' [Actually it was #119, but who's counting?] He started to get some momentum internationally. That was through Lee Mendell and Jack Bratel [Liberty execs who worked the international market]. They even had me produce one [album] just for the international division with him.

"Liberty was innovative as hell, and [they were] risk takers. Al Bennett was very easygoing and easy to work for. He'd let you have your head and go for it. He never, never came to a session or meeting or anything and said, 'Why are you guys doing this, why aren't you doing that?' He never did that. He gave us a free hand. 'I'll close the door and let you guys create.' He never got in the middle of anything, which was really nice. Al was one of the best to work for. I loved him."

It appears that Al was better liked by his staff than by such artists as Gretchen Christopher, Sharon Sheeley, and Dick St. John.

CHAPTER 24

Recording Music

A lot of artists have already been presented in these pages, and there are more to come. But artists were just one part of the process of turning songs into hit records. For every hit artist, there were several background voices that added to the sound of a record, and a whole group of session musicians who made the recording session happen. As representatives of the myriad singers and players who contributed to Liberty records, one background singer and one guitarist are featured.

Fanita James of the Blossoms

The premier session singers of the LA music scene of the early to mid-1960s were the Blossoms. With lead singer Darlene Love, the Blossoms sang background on records by nearly everyone, including Duane Eddy, Elvis Presley, Jan & Dean, the Crystals, and who knows who else.

The Blossoms sang on so many Liberty records, including those produced by Snuff Garrett, that they might as well have been signed to the label. However, the main difference between being a background singer and being a signed artist is payment. Artists got royalties based on the sale of a record. Session singers got a flat hourly fee for showing up for a session.

The Blossoms became known to the public when they sang weekly on the TV program "Shindig." Besides backing up all of the stars on this weekly rock 'n' roll TV program, they sang songs themselves. They can also be seen backing up Marvin Gaye in the 1965 rock movie *The TAMI Show*.

Fanita James was an original member of the Blossoms, who could sing in many styles—black, white, soul, pop, country, you name it.

"I was at Liberty Records almost as much as I was at home, but it is hard to remember any details at all."

One of the best places to see Fanita and the Blossoms today is on the videotape *Girl Groups, the Story of a Sound*, which was put out without the Blossoms' knowledge a few years back. They perform a song that was a hit by the Velvettes, "Needle in a Haystack," in a clip from "Shindig." "You know, I didn't know anything about that tape until a Tom Jones fan bought ... and gave it to me. Then I finally got some [performance royalties] for that tape."

The Blossoms' videotape version of "Needle in a Haystack" is arguably better than the Velvettes' hit record on VIP Records, a Motown label.

While a lot of her Liberty work is lost in the forgotten past, Fanita does know that she sang on Jan & Dean records. "We did a lot of things with Jan & Dean and

Lou Adler. I am sure we were the voices on 'Let's Turkey Trot' [Jan & Dean's Liberty *Linda* LP]. We did so many things with them. It's hard to remember specific songs and sessions. I feel so stupid [for not keeping track of things I did]. I had no idea that this thing was going to become so monumental. I wish I'd kept a journal. How stupid! It's like when we worked with Elvis Presley. The man gave us so many little gifts with his name on [them], and I don't have one of them. Isn't that sad?"

Another Liberty act for whom the Blossoms sang backup was Jackie DeShannon. "Jackie DeShannon was the cause of our being on 'Shindig.' We were doing a session for her at Liberty. Jack Goode, the producer of 'Shindig,' came to the session. The minute he heard us, he said, 'OK, that's it, I want those girls!' Isn't that funny? Thanks to Jackie DeShannon. Jackie brought in Leon Russell, David Gates. We didn't do Jackie's big hits, but we did early ones of hers. I think we were on 'Needles and Pins.' What a good songwriter she was."

Since Fanita was a singer on the Crystals' version of "He's a Rebel," perhaps she can shed some light on the controversy of whether Phil stole that song from Snuff (as most people claim) and used the Blossoms instead of the Crystals in order to steal a march on Spec, or whether Spec thought he had a valid exclusive on the song as did Snuff.

"The only thing I ever heard about 'He's a Rebel' was that Phil Spector was mad at the Crystals. It was his song, but he was angry with the Crystals about something, so he refused to fly them out from New York. He just got us to do it here. I always thought Phil had the song as an exclusive. I never knew any different. I think I would have heard some kind of scuttlebutt.

"The follow-up to 'He's a Rebel' was supposed to be 'It's My Party.' Darlene sang lead; it was to be released under the Blossoms' name. We learned it and we were doing it slow—we would drag it. But Phil never put it out! Then here comes Lesley [Gore] and, boy, was that a big record! Isn't that something?"

On the subject of clearing up Blossoms mysteries, did the Blossoms sing, as some say, the background on Lou Adler's wife's, Shelley Fabares's, #1 record on Colpix, "Johnny Angel"? "I don't think so; I don't remember that. But did you know we did 'The Shoop Shoop Song' by Betty Everett [on VJ]? She sang the lead, we did the background. When we heard that on a movie, I said, 'My goodness! Why are they bringing all these songs back?' It was just Darlene and I."

With all the hit songs the Blossoms contributed so much to, including the ones sang that were released by the Crystals, Fanita could have become rich, had she been paid as an artist instead of a background session voice.

Does Fanita regret never making the big time as a star—millions of dollars in royalties? "No! We were just so happy doing what we were doing. We worked as long as our throats held out. We weren't like the musicians. They could just blow. We had to sing. We worked seven days a week. They'd call and get us out of bed. It's a wonder my marriage lasted twenty-six years. My husband would fuss.

"Lou Adler was good at that. He would call us at one in the morning after he'd laid the tracks out. Then we'd come out, and they would not be ready for us, so we'd go fall asleep on the floor. Those were the days when it was the real stuff. There was no jive; it was wonderful. And we made money. We made lots of money for those days. We were cheated out of a lot, too. But to be handed a check for three thousand dollars, my God, that was a lot of money back in those days. For singing! I love it! It's my life!"

Tommy Allsup

Tommy Allsup is known as T by his friends. He is best known as a sometime Cricket—a member of the group that Buddy Holly formed in Texas in the 1950s. But he was better known in the 1960s in LA as a session musician and contractor who did a lot of work for Liberty Records—and of course, his overlapping function was as a producer, besides heading the Liberty country-and-western division and writing songs in his spare moments.

"I worked with the Crickets after Buddy got killed for a while, but I was not a member of the Crickets at the time they were with Liberty. However, I did record with them at Liberty.

"I was not actually a Cricket, but I played guitar on all of the stuff they did at Liberty. I played on *Bobby Vee Meets the Crickets*. I was in the recording version of the Crickets of that album.

"I was house producer for Liberty. I was producing all of their country-and-western material during those years. We had Willie Nelson, we did all of his first albums. We had a country artist named Joe Carson who had country hits on Liberty. An artist named Warren Smith. Tex Williams. And Bob Wills and the Texas Playboys. Walter Brennan. We had a very good country roster for that time.

"Slim Whitman became a part of Liberty when they bought up the old Imperial catalog. I did an album with him just before I left Liberty. Snuffy and I left about the same time, at the end of 1964. I was there from the early 1960s through 1964. Walter Brennan was the one who hit the country charts and the top forty, too. Willie Nelson did some of his best things at Liberty. We had a great country-and-western department. Joe Allison actually started it in 1960; then he left in 1961 and I took it over.

"When Avnet took over, they didn't like country and western and started phasing it out. Snuff and I left about summertime in 1964 and were going to start a production company. I moved to Texas and built a studio. He stayed out there and became a millionaire!

"Avnet destroyed everything at Liberty. Liberty could not get it back together after that. Some stockholders got greedy, [saw] a chance to sell it and buy it back, but it never did happen after it came back. I hated it, you needed to work there or have an appointment to get in.

"The first thing they did was they sent an economist down to ask me how much money we were making off the country-and-western department. We weren't making any money. But it exploited the label, people heard about Liberty Records, and we were breaking even. But the big money was coming from the rock 'n' roll end of it. But only Decca made money at country and western."

Sounds as if Avnet was trying to run Liberty like a business instead of a record label—like an assembly line, cost and production? "That's it, that's exactly right! You don't cut hits in meetings. You do it in the studio. You gotta get away from restrictions. You can't do nothin' when you're restricted.

"Si left while I was there, but I was contractor on a lot of his production. Al Bennett was the real brain child behind Liberty Records, you know." Did Tommy experience the trait that the Fleetwoods and Dick and Deedee and some others encountered, where Al Bennett tried to keep the money in the company instead of paying the artists? "Well, I don't know that there were that many artists that had royalties coming at that time. It can go either way there. I think he was a pretty fair guy. I mean, I always got my production royalties, and I never heard anything. There were a couple of artists that were griping, you know, but Liberty had spent a lot of money on them. I'm not defending Liberty, but when you do publicity and you run ads, you do five sessions, you can tie up a lot of money in a short time.

"Bobby Vee probably had a lot of royalties coming, but not that many artists back then got into the royalty situation. By the time royalty time came around, they had recorded two or three albums, and they'd eaten up all of their profits. So if anyone was hollerin', it would be that type of act. I would have to defend Al Bennett. Probably there has never been a more honest guy in the record business. He was sharp, but he had a lot of great ideas for sellin' records. He sure made the label a success when he first came. And before that, he made Dot a success. He was a sharp guy. But you gotta pay bills. When you have a huge building with a hundred employees, so it takes a lot of money to operate. He kept that thing afloat.

"Liberty was a label that in the early 1960s could beat any major label on a hit. Put 'em out one on one, and Liberty could beat RCA or Columbia or anybody, at that time, for getting airplay and sales. I am talking about the pop field.

"We were weak in the country area. Because the promotion people at Liberty were all geared to top-forty. When we used the country stuff back then, there were a few independent promotion men around the country that artists would hire, and the label would hire them to work certain records. So there was not really a country promotion staff at Liberty at that time. It was that way with all of the labels. There were just country promotion men who promoted country music in general. But really all you had to do back then was just mail it out to the radio stations. There were not that many acts. If it was a good record, you got played.

"There were not too many country crossovers [country songs that hit the pop charts big] in those days. Johnny Horton, 'The Battle of New Orleans,' 'Wolverton Mountain' — there were a few exceptions but not that many."

Now, Tommy Allsup the producer is also Tommy Allsup songwriter and Tommy Allsup session guitarist. "I played guitar on the Ventures' *Twist* album. Jerry Allison [drummer for the Crickets] and I made up two songs on the session. We went in and knocked out that album in a couple of days. The Ventures were broke up at the time. Bob Bogle and two of the guys were there, but the lead guitar and drummer were gone, so Jerry and I played with them. Half Crickets, half Ventures. We made some bucks off of those songs over the years. Especially the foreign royalties were very good on it. We just got the session money the first time though, no royalties. We got songwriter royalties for those two songs. That was a bonus. Bob Reisdorff was a nice guy. Since we kind of helped him out of a tight spot and filled in for those guys who were gone, he [rewarded] us by letting us put in a couple of original songs on the album." Those songs were "Guitar Twist" and "Opus Twist." "I've never heard that album. I haven't run across it in years. I'd like to hear it."

"Bluer Than Blue" was a Ventures song that charted really high that me and Dick Glasser wrote. I play guitar on that. It was about the same time that the twist thing happened. It was one of the few times that the Ventures recorded with strings, I think. It lent itself to that melody.

"The Fleetwoods, I played on their stuff with Reisdorff, and Vic Dana. I guess I worked with most of their artists. I was doing most of the contracting for Liberty and I'd set up the sessions.

"Hal Blaine had been on the road with Patti Page. Dick Glasser used Hal for some demo sessions for Metric Music. I know for a fact that was the first time he ever did session work. He might have recorded with Patti Page or someone before that, but he did not do session work. I don't know if he thanked Dick or not, but Dick sort of started him out. We also started Leon Russell out. I used to have Glen Campbell show up at my sessions when I couldn't do them. I was there just a little while before he was.

"I did guitar for Jan & Dean, Timi Yuro, Johnny Burnette, Gene McDaniels. I did almost everyone who was on the label. Except ones where they picked up the masters recorded someplace else, like the Rivingtons. But me and Jerry Allison were on the biggest part of them. Earl Palmer was the drummer. If Earl wasn't there, then Jerry was. We did Bobby Vee sessions, too.

"I was doing Jan & Dean sessions when Lou Adler could hardly pay for them. He was just barely making enough money to do the sessions. They'd had a couple of pretty good records on Doré Records, but Lou was just barely getting by on Liberty with them. Liberty had a little studio where Lou worked. And he had some other studios where he had extended his credit. Then he got a job with Aldon Music, with Don Kirshner, and then he made history in music. They had all those rock 'n' roll hits [on Dunhill—the Mamas and Papas, the Grass Roots] before they sold out to Columbia. But Liberty gave Lou money to produce sessions and got him going."

Maybe Tommy Allsup didn't consider himself a total Cricket, but he put in his session time with Buddy Holly. "With Buddy Holly, I was on 'Heartbeat,' 'Reminiscing,' 'Love's Made a Fool of You,' 'It's So Easy'—I did quite a few. It would have been nice if Buddy could have been on Liberty. But they weren't cookin' when Buddy was alive."

Liberty *was* cookin' when Eddie Cochran was alive. After his death, Tommy laid some new licks on Eddie's old tracks. "Lenny Waronker's first recording job was taking a bunch of old Eddie Cochran tracks, just Eddie playing guitar, and Jerry Allison and I went in and overdubbed the rhythm on them. That was Lenny's first project in the record business. It was an album on Liberty. Lenny was about sixteen or eighteen at the time."

Another memorable session Tommy worked on was the infamous "Please Don't Ask About Barbara" session, about which legend has it that the session guitarist had so much trouble getting the guitar part that it took fifty-two takes. Jerry Allison thought that Tommy was playing that part. He was right. "That was the only hard part on the guitar that I ever ran across. The songwriter wrote that song in C. I learned that lick in C—you have to have open strings to play that lick. But it was too low for Bobby Vee, so he did it in E-flat, which was up a third. To play open in E-flat, you have to put a capo up there. I wasn't used to playing with a capo, so I had to relearn that thing. Ernie Freeman had written a whole arrangement around that thing, around that guitar lick. I got kind of confused, but now I know. That was the only problem I ever had getting hung up on a record. The capo was all foreign to me."

"No, we never did fifty-two takes on nothin' with Bobby. But I'll tell you, with Norman Petty we did [a lot of takes] when we [were] doing Buddy Holly's stuff. And not particularly on Buddy's stuff. I've done fifty-some takes on one song. With Bobby Vee we probably did nine or ten maybe. They've blown that out of proportion. Others have asked me about that: 'Did you get hung up on that song?' Yes,

I sure did! But Bobby Vee never did fifty-two takes on a whole album, really. He was always pretty fast. Seven or eight takes sometimes."

In modern recording sessions, seldom are all the parts of a record recorded at once. More likely guitars, singers, drums, lead vocals, and other elements of a recording are laid down in different sessions on different tracks using at least a twenty-four-track recorder. Recording studios are often used as rehearsal halls, and a part is only added to the tape when it is perfected. That is why it might take days or weeks to record one song.

In 1960 there were only two tracks, sometimes three, and everything was done at the same time in one session. Rehearsals were completed prior to coming to the studio. Thus, a song might be recorded in just a few minutes, perhaps an hour or two at the most. But this relatively brief elapsed time for a song should not be confused with lack of quality or caring. It merely represents coming to a session prepared, the creative process completed and the final performance ready to go, live.

"We did everything live, with strings and vocals and everything. That was why [having trouble with that guitar part] was frustrating. Today we just go in later and punch it in. Then we had only three tracks. The voice was in the middle, and you split the band on the two outer tracks. That was it. Sometimes you could overdub if you could isolate the vocal, but it was kind of unheard of back then. You could do it, but it was mostly live. It's great recording everything live. They are trying to get back to it here in Nashville, but no one knows how to do it, how to record like that now. The engineers have learned how to do drum tracks alone, then add a bass, add a guitar, and there are not [m]any good engineers around who can mix a live session. There's still a few.

"It is nice to cut live. I worked with Si Waronker on sessions with thirty violins. Those Ricky Moreno albums had fifty people in the studio. You need a good engineer who can mix that stuff together. That is why it all sounded so good and felt so good."

How could it help but sound good when so many professionals came together for a common purpose? Here, a picker from Texas who cut his teeth with the likes of Buddy Holly got to do sessions with a full complement of session people. "You felt like you were working with the Hollywood Bowl Symphony, with ten or eleven strings. Most of that stuff with Vee, we had eight violins, two violas, and two cellos. I don't know why that number, but that is what they used."

As a session contractor as well as musician, Tommy Allsup would get the call telling how many of each instrument was needed for a given session. "Eight-two and two, that's what Arnette always told me to call." Actually, that was a carryover from Si Waronker's studio days, when the film orchestra always had that many under strings contract. There would be four violins playing one line, four playing the second line, two violas playing the third line, and two cellos playing the fourth line of music. The effect was like a string quartet. Sixteen-six and six was the biggest orchestra Si ever used.

As a session musician, Tommy Allsup rubbed elbows with more than just other session players. There were also the stars. Like Bobby Vee, and Buddy Knox.

"Buddy Knox—we started together, that was my first session on Liberty. The night we cut 'Lovey Dovey.' Buddy Knox was as flabbergasted as I was! Buddy got a hit first thing. I got all the session work I wanted after that. I was working in a little ol' joint out there, you know, in south LA." Playing in the "little ol' joint" was not much money and not much fun, sort of a musical dead end. Then, Liberty came along.

"Sessions, then contracting, then the country-and-western division at Liberty." Liberty was good to Tommy Allsup. "Tex Williams is dead, Joe Carson is dead. Bob Wills is dead. But the music of Liberty lives on."

CHAPTER 25

Engineering a Hit

A lot of creative energy goes into making hit records. Writing, producing, and performing on records are more art than science.

By contrast, there is a nuts-and-bolts aspect to the recording of music—the engineering of a session. Someone has to see that the sounds that reach the microphones get into the control booth and onto recording tape in good shape. Obviously, a button pusher and knob twister is a more tangible, less creative part of the process of making hits than writing songs and singing lyrics. Or is it?

Stan Ross

"I became an engineer out of high school in Hollywood. They needed someone at a studio as a part-time worker. I got that job, worked for somebody for four years. Then I decided, 'why shouldn't I have my own studio?' So in nineteen fifty my partner Dave Gold and I opened up Gold Star Studios. That lasted for thirty-four years.

"It was a wonderful relationship. We had a hundred fifty gold products, and we were thrilled."

Today Stan Ross is "independently inactive." He vacations and plans his work around his vacations. However, he does a lot of Latin albums for Mexico and South America, which he likes because it is a live orchestra. "I work now by using my ear and giving my input." He's not really working any more, but he remembers vividly the glory days of Liberty and Gold Star Studios.

"Ted Keep was the engineer who worked for Liberty. But we at Gold Star did do a lot of Liberty records. I did all the Eddie Cochran sessions that came out prior to his contract with Liberty. Most of Eddie Cochran's records were glorified demos. Especially after he passed away. They went back into the archives and took out all of the demos he had done for American Music. So a lot of the records released by Liberty were actually records made at Gold Star but released by Liberty. Most of the albums were recorded at Liberty Records."

Sharon Sheeley complains that Snuff Garrett's name appears on Eddie Cochran records that she says Snuff did not actually produce. "Things were repackaged, and if Snuff did that work after Eddie died, he would be producer for that repackaging. Jerry Capehart was there for all of Eddie's sessions while Eddie was alive. But the production was done group-style, you know. There was no individual in charge who said, 'That's wonderful, let's print it.' It was a combination of, if Eddie liked it, and Jerry liked it, and the musicians liked it, then we said, 'That's fine, let's go on.' They'd ask me, 'Any problem with you as an engineer?' I'd say, 'No, no problem here, sounds good to me. Let's keep it and go on from here.' That was how it went.

"Later, I recorded Cher for Imperial when Liberty owned it."

What were the duties of an engineer, besides saying that a song sounded good to him and got onto the tape with no problems? "The main thing was to come up with the sound, with the proper balance. It was a little more difficult than it is today because it was mono. We didn't go stereo. Most of the stuff we did was strictly monaural, which meant that what you heard was what you got. That was how you cut records. You recorded it as it was played, and then you listened to it. But you couldn't change anything. If you didn't like something, you did the whole thing over again.

"Today, it is impossible to record that way. There are twenty-four tracks, and everybody is recorded separately. You listen to it, and if somebody says they want more voice, you say, 'Sure, no problem,' and you bring the voices up that are already on the tape, or you add new voices to the existing recording.

"For an engineer it was a little more difficult in the mono days. Because the people in the session judged the engineer on what they heard on playback, when you gave them what you thought it should be." In other words, the engineer mixed the relative volume of everything and added echo, and that final combination might or might not be the way the artist or producer wanted it to sound. "A lot of things like the reverb echo and things, I put them on just to have fun. The mix and the echo [were] the engineer's decision, not the producer's. All the reverb goes on the master original recording. No one really cared in those days. If it sounded OK to everybody, they'd say, 'Leave it, sounds good!' If they didn't like it, they'd have to go back and make another take. You didn't have the option of hearing it with or without reverb. The reverb was on it, so I might listen to it and say, 'Hey, it wound good with reverb. Elvis is using it, so why not you?'

"We recorded in the back studio at Gold Star. That studio didn't have an echo chamber, so we used tape reverb. It sure sounded fine."

Several Liberty people have talked about how sessions were short, but that did not mean that only a small amount of effort went into the sessions. Rehearsal time outside the studio also contributed to a good recording. Now Stan Ross explains how even many hours spent in the studio to produce a certain recording would appear on the books to be just a brief session. The real session was called a "fun session." Later a second session was scheduled for the musicians' union, but the recording from that short session was not used.

"A lot of times, records were cut a second time just to satisfy the musicians' union and make it all legal. Demos were not union dates, they were fun dates. Everyone would have fun; it was strictly ten hours to sing out new tunes."

Today, decades later, a new, young engineer who was not born when the artists were recording their hits might get the task of compiling a CD rerelease of songs by an artist. How would that engineer know which take to put on the CD? The one with a lot of reverb or the one with a little? Or maybe the union stereo session instead of the original "fun" session. "That's right, and some of them have done it over again. We did all of Phil Spector's sessions here at Gold Star, including the Righteous Brothers. On those later sessions, we recorded sometimes on four-track. For the CDs, they remaster them. One track had rhythm, voices on another track, background singers were on one, and the horns and strings were on one track. We cut 'Unchained

Melody,' but when I heard the CD, I heard the new violin track that was put on it for the CD. They transferred our four-track to a multitrack, then added some more strings. Because now you hear a bigger string line than we originally had on the record. Many times, a lot of changes take place for the product.

"A lot of the things we did for Liberty Records, like the Patience and Prudence 'Tonight You Belong to Me' demo. Liberty was in a good position at that time to pick up demos. There were only about two or three labels, Liberty, Dot, Challenge, and Era/Doré, labels that were able to pick up independent masters from people who just did demos, and put them out. And they had a lot of luck with them! My God, they had smash hit records. Liberty had 'Tonight You Belong to Me,' and Margie Rayburn with 'I'm Available,' both our demos. 'Chanson d'Amour' by Art and Dotty Todd was a demo Era put out. Challenge had 'Tequila' by the Champs, which was a demo that formed a whole new generation of performers. And Liberty was one of the companies that was smart enough to pick up these demos, instead of rerecording them with an established artist like RCA or Capitol would do.

"People like Si at Liberty and Herb Newman, may he rest in peace, over at Era, and at Doré, Lou Biddel, Randy Wood at Dot, they heard these demos and said, 'Why don't they just come over?' So they would sign up the act that cut the demo and rerecord the tune.

"You had Liberty, Dot, Challenge, Era, and Doré. Those were the big five of Hollywood. All the songwriters who had some concept for doing records would go there. It was wonderful! They could go around to five different companies and maybe they would get a bite. It made making demos a very popular thing, which I felt was wonderful. It was fun, it was relaxed, no one was uptight. They'd go in the studio, maybe just go for the one tune, they'd give the guys [musicians] maybe twenty dollars apiece and they'd be happy, in for an hour then out, and it makes demos that sometimes sounded like the real thing. They were flipped out!

"Another example is 'To Know Him Is to Love Him.' I cut that demo with Phil Spector's Teddybears, and the demo actually came out on Doré Records. But it wasn't cut for Doré. It was cut because Phil Spector came in to do a demo just to see what it sounded like. Doré liked it and they put it out.

"Later, when he was a big producer, Phil Spector recorded at Gold Star. Spector was a booth man. He'd go out in the studio to sit at the piano and show them what he was doing. But he wouldn't stay out there very long. He would have the arranger, Jack Nitzsche or Gene Paige, come out to his house and he'd sit at the piano and show him what he wanted. Once they were in the studio, Phil would never sit with the musicians out there and show them on the piano what he wanted. He let the arranger show them. He was a booth man.

"Liberty made a wonderful use of demos. We didn't record for Liberty, we had no contract with Liberty, but we'd record things that they would put out. We did a lot of things with Mark McIntyre and Ross Bagdasarian; 'Armen's Theme' — we experimented with that. We at Gold Star also gave him his Chipmunk effect; we experimented on that. And 'Witch Doctor,' a big, big seller for Liberty. These are all things that were experimentation. When it came time to cut it, he had to do it over at Liberty, so he worked at Liberty studios on La Brea, and that is where they cut 'Witch Doctor' and 'The Chipmunk Song.' But the original concept of 'Armen's Theme,' the one-finger piano thing, we did at our studio."

Stan Ross tells an interesting story of the first use of "phasing effect" on a hit record. Phasing is when two recordings of one song are played exactly together, then as one goes a bit faster than the other, a strange sound effect is produced. The record was not released on Liberty, but the story is important enough to include anyway.

"We did 'The Big Hurt' with Toni Fisher. In those days, the pressing plants had their own labels. Allied Records, a big pressing plant in Hollywood in the 1950s and 1960s, had Signet Records. They put out 'The Big Hurt.' I was the engineer on that, the first record to use phasing. It was an accident. It was a binaural recording, and Bill Shankle, the producer who also wrote the song, didn't believe in two-track. He wanted mono and that was it. If he heard the voice, it was good. If he did not hear the voice, it wasn't good. It was all live at one time, orchestra, singing, everything. I gave him a take that I liked but I thought the voice was too shallow on. He liked it and took it home, then decided I was right. I offered another take, but he liked that one, said it was exciting. I said, 'It's only exciting because the voice is low.' He said no.

"So we put two versions of the same take together, synced them, and played them together. The speeds didn't match exactly, and as they passed, they phased. We learned to control the beast and used it. It often happened by accident before that, and everyone always canned it and started over. But we used it this time. We talked him in to using it; he was reluctant but said 'Yep, use it.' He's dead now, but I give him a lot of credit for being brave enough to use it."

How much involvement did artists and producers have in the booth, the engineer's control room? "Today artists and producers know a lot more about recording than they did then. Then they didn't care; they'd just walk in the studio and they wanted it to be ready and sound the way they wanted. Today, artists and producers are pretty much on top of the electronics of recording, because there is so much available. They are more knowledgeable.

"Most of the time, they left me alone in the booth and I did what I felt was good for them. But they'd hear it back and say, 'Gee, the voice sure is buried there.' And I'd say, 'Wait till you hear it on a small speaker.'"

By a small speaker, Stan Ross means a speaker other than the huge, hi-fi speakers in the recording studio. Many studios in the early 1960s used a small speaker to check the final mix. At RCA, a small speaker without an enclosure was in the studio to play the final mix through, to simulate the kind of sound kids might get through a pocket-size transistor radio. At Dot, Randy Wood had a wire that ran out of the studio to his car radio speaker. At Motown a small speaker was on the desk of an office worker. Through that speaker, prospective releases could be heard and evaluated, and decisions about recordings and mixes could be made. Stan Ross at Gold Star could show a producer that what sounds good on the big speaker might not sound so good on a small speaker, and vice versa. This is one reason some oldie aficionados don't believe the songs should be released on CDs today — the songs were usually never meant, or mixed, to be played on hi-fi systems.

"When they did hear it played on a small speaker, they would say, 'You are right, you are right.' But even on the small speaker we had, the transmission was missing. And radio transmission is very important. Radio transmission is wonderful. There is something about AM radio that is magic.

"I used to do my Sonny and Cher masters, then give a dub to a West Coast disc jockey named Don Steel. He would play the acetate dub at three the next day, and I would listen to it on the radio in my car, to see how I did, what to add to it. This was before I mastered it. Maybe I'd hear it and say, 'OK, the voice is fine, I just need to add a little top overall.' That was it. I'd go back to the mastering room and add maybe 2dB at 3k [increase the three-thousand-cycle sound by two decibels], and maybe some at 10kc [kilocycles] or whatever, and master it that way, and that was the way the record came out, and it sounded great that way."

Now the strange fans who prefer to listen to an oldie on an AM radio 45 to hearing it on a brand-new CD are vindicated! In the 1960s, some records were made to be heard on mono AM radio, not stereo digital sound. "Radio transmission tells you the truth," asserts Stan Ross. "There is a dynamics of air transmission that is fantastic."

Gold Star tried to duplicate this radio effect in the studio, so they would not have to wait for Don Steel to play a dub on the air. But it never worked. "We had three-tube oscillators to transmit over so we could hear it outside on our car radios. It was OK, but it wasn't the real thing. It wasn't the same as hearing it on a real, ten-thousand-watt radio station like KHJ or something. That transmission sound was fantastic. Radio play is the best sound. A CD has better fidelity because it has been made very carefully. But the recording itself was not made as carefully."

This is strange. One would expect a fan or maybe an artist to feel that way about music. But an engineer should value high technical quality over any considerations about how a record sounds on AM radio. "It's an old story. Do you go for the technical, or do you go for the feel? Records in the 1950s and 1960s were done by emotions. They were impact records. You couldn't 'create' a feel, it was either in the groove or it was not in the groove. I've heard records that were sensational even though they had a terrible mix. But they were so good, who cared? Troy Shondell's 'This Time' may have been a bad recording, but the feel was so great that you didn't care about the recording. I'm an engineer, but I've got to say to hell with it. It doesn't matter; the mix doesn't matter. The important thing is what's in that groove. That's my feeling. I think that a lot of records have been 'manufactured,' and you just can't do that to music. Take Michael Jackson and Madonna. They are great artists, but I'd sure like to hear them with big brass and some strings behind them; they'd sound even better. The old arrangers like on Bobby Vee and Johnny Burnette just aren't around any more. That was the Liberty days.

"Liberty was very lucky to be where it was at the time that it was. The West Coast was becoming the hub of the music scene and there were many talented people around. It was a wonderful period."

After a few years, Gold Star did less material that Liberty put out. "Later, Liberty opened their own studio and we did less and less of it. They had the songwriters come there to do their demos, and that was the end of it. We didn't see them any more, in terms of Liberty releasing our recordings."

Bones Howe

Bones Howe was born in Minneapolis and grew up in Sarasota, Florida. His interest in music began at a very young age. His parents had an old wind-up Victrola, and as soon as he was able to wind it and put records on it, he began playing records. In the late 1940s, Bones became interested in jazz, and by 1949 he was playing jazz drums, and while he was still in high school, he was playing gigs in clubs.

The first thing that comes to mind when considering Bones is how he got his nickname. It was given to him when he was in line at orientation for the ninth grade in junior high. A new acquaintance, Bill Baker, was in line with him and gave Dayton Burr Howe his nickname, Bones. Bones already had a nickname, Mr. Jones, that his dad called him, but Bill told him that he looked more like "Mr. Bones" than "Mr. Jones," and the name stuck.

Bones attended Georgia Tech after high school, and by his second year he was playing jazz six nights a week. In what he calls the "Shake, Rattle, and Roll" days, he toured with a black R&B band. One summer tour in 1955, he was the only white member of a band that played the Atlanta Civic Auditorium with an all-black review. The only other white person was Roy Hamilton's ("Unchained Melody," Epic Records) accompanist. This was a fairly unusual situation in the South in those days.

Bones met a lot of jazz musicians who came through Atlanta on road bands— Mel Lewis, Shelley Mann, Max Bennett, lots of different men. Many of them encouraged Bones to come out to LA after he sat in on their jam sessions. At the time Bones was studying electronics and communications, and they told him that there was no one in the record business making records who knew anything about music. So after graduation in May 1956, Bones packed his drum kit in his car and, with two hundred dollars in his pocket, headed for Los Angeles.

His first job in LA was working at Radio Recorders studio on Santa Monica Blvd. as an apprentice. A year later he began mixing sessions, and by the fall of 1957 he was fast becoming "the" jazz engineer on the West Coast. He was kept busy by Dave Pell, Red Clyde, Shorty Rogers, and other musician-producers, and by 1960 he was doing most of the jazz sessions in LA. This included "lots of work" for Dick Bock of Pacific Jazz, which ultimately became a part of Liberty Records.

One thing he did was to make stereo jazz recordings for himself, when all the record companies wanted was mono. Those tapes, made starting in 1957, were set aside and languished for thirty years in his garage until he brought them out and made "a lot of money" from them.

"During all the fifty-six and fifty-seven sessions with Elvis, we did two tracks with him, one track with his voice and the other with everything else on it. I had a bunch of those tapes, which were thrown away. I saved them, and they came out on one of the essential Elvis packages, one that I wrote the liner notes for. I was tape op (operator) for Elvis in fifty-six and fifty-seven, and I was coproducer of the sixty-eight comeback special with Steve Bender."

In 1961 an engineer named Bill Putnum moved to LA from Chicago and started United Recording. Bones remembers how this "put a pretty heavy assault on the engineering people in LA. I had managed to stay put at Radio Recorders when the new Capitol and new RCA studios were established and people came hiring around LA. But in 1961, I went to work for Bill and Tony Perry at United. They subsequently bought Western, and that became the famous United Western Studios.

"Chuck Britz was an engineer who was one of the owners of Western Recorders, which was a little dumpy place at six thousand Sunset. United was a shiny new place at sixty-five hundred Sunset a half block away. Chuck remained at Western when it was bought and merged with United. Western was like Gold Star, a great-sounding, funky kind of studio. Bill Putnum was a smart man who knew what you had to do to stay ahead and attract artists. If you can't build it, you buy it. When Bill told me he was going to buy it, I told him, 'Oh, that dump?' But he refurbished it, and Western Studio Number Three became the hot studio in town.

"Another engineer was Wally Heider, who owned Wally Heider Recording. He came out of the big-band era in Sheridan, Oregon. He was a lawyer who had a portable recording outfit, and he would go out on weekends. His wife wouldn't see him from Friday morning, when he left for his office, to Monday night. He would fly to New Jersey or wherever Woody Herman or Les Brown or someone was playing and he would tape them. I was making lots of big-band records in the studio, and we would trade tapes all the time. He worked as a mixer at United, but he went off and started his little studio doing voice recordings and mix-downs until finally he had four studios there. He died a couple of years ago, but was a great guy, a legendary figure. He was smart; he gave away free sessions to get people in there. He duplicated Studio Three at Western, and Heider Three became the hot studio, literally a better room. I did all my work there from 1968 on.

"During my time at Radio Recorders, I used to run into Herbie Alpert and Lou Adler all the time. They were hanging around Bumps Blackwell and Keen Records at the time, and they ended up producing some records in that period." Later, Herb and Lou told Bones that he was recommended to them as an engineer for their records by Radio Records management, but that Lou had avoided working with him because he was a jazz engineer. But his nonjazz credits as an engineer in fact included the pre–Liberty Imperial LP by Ricky Nelson, *Rick Is 21*.

Bones worked at United and Western for a year and a half with Al Schmidt and Eddie Bracket, whom he had met at Radio Recorders. Eddie Bracket was the engineer on all of Snuff Garrett's recordings, including Gene McDaniels, for Liberty. Jim Economides was another engineer, actually a second engineer at that time, who started as a "studio set-up guy and didn't become a mixer until much later. But Eddie was doing all the Liberty sessions in 1961.

"I did an Everly Brothers session, 'Don't Ask Me to Be Friends,' with Lou for Warner Brothers," says Bones. "That was a Carole King song, and Louie was working with her publisher, Nevins-Kirshner Music, called Screen Gems at the time. It was the first time Louie and I had worked together since Radio Recorders. Lou took a dub home and was so impressed with the sound that he called me afterward and raved about the perfect mix I'd done. It was around then that Jan started calling me to work on Jan & Dean sessions. Bill Putnam had me doing Sinatra sessions at the same time, and I did jazz-oriented things that came through the door." Bones's workdays went from one in the afternoon until four in the morning.

That was in the fall of 1962. Right after that Bones left to become an independent engineer. Eddie Bracket, Al Schmidt, and Bones were the three busiest guys in town and thought that they could have their own company. They would simply bill independently for any sessions they engineered, charging the equivalent of what a sideman or session musician would make. This was not much money, but it would be more than they made as studio engineers. But before their plan could be put into effect, Eddie was hired away by Snuff to be the Liberty engineer, and Al went to work for the A&R department of RCA.

In November Bones quit United and Western to become the first independent engineer in LA and more than doubled his income the first year. Several years later

Bones says, "I [was what I] would call reasonably hot. Then the one guy I thought would never call me, because he thought I was a jazz engineer, was Lou Adler. Louie and I worked almost constantly together after that. I did all the Johnny Rivers records with him, and the first three Mamas and Papas albums."

That was the connection with Jan & Dean. Lou had been Jan & Dean's original producer and still worked with Jan at every Jan & Dean session. "I worked on all their records. Lank started 'Surf City' and I finished it. I did the entire *Surf City* album and I mixed the single. I did everything from that point on, except Lank did a couple of sessions. He worked on every album someplace, there was so much work on those things, and Jan would come in to record at every hour of the day and night. I was doing other people, so Lank and I pretty much pitched the Jan sessions back and forth like a football.

"One of Jan's projects was the big orchestral one, *Pop Symphony*. Lou had an idea that there could be a rhythm section called the Bel Air Bandits. He tried it several times with various people, including me. Later other sections existed, and it would have been the Los Angeles equivalent of the Atlanta Rhythm Section. Lou never got it together, but it was a great name — 'Bel Air Bandits' — so the name ended up being used for Jan & Dean's football team and later their touring backup band. But it was going to be a backup session band called the Bel Air Bandits. We made an instrumental recording once, never released. Chuck Britz was the engineer for that."

Jan & Dean albums carry the legend "Engineers: 'Bones' Howe and 'Lanky' Linstrot," or later, just simply "Bones and Lanky." This always conjures up the image of two incredibly thin guys fooling around with wires and microphones. Lanky *was* an incredibly tall young man, real name Harold, and was in fact slender in his younger days. "Dave Pell once recorded an instrumental called 'Lanky Bones.' We got made fun of a lot. Lanky went on to become an engineer at the Liberty studios, and Eddie was the Liberty house mixer until Snuff left."

Bones wrote a song called "Sting Ray," which appeared on the Jan & Dean Liberty LP, *Drag City*. Bones wrote the song for an LP by the Routers, a studio group produced by Joe Saraceno. "The first Routers [who were on Warner Bros. Records] record was 'Let's Go,' which was meant to be the flip side of a record that was a big production. We recorded it in the last fifteen minutes of a session, with the string players clapping their hands. 'Sting Ray' was used for the follow-up.

"The inspiration for 'Sting Ray' was my high school days. The boys who had graduated one year came back the next year to raid on all the senior girls. They were all working and had cars, so they'd drive by on the highway next to the school all day and honk. Each guy had his own distinctive honk, and the girls in class would hear a horn and say, 'There's George!'

"It just happened that State Farm Insurance had been recording their commercial in the studio and had left a car horn they used in their commercials. So I devised a melody around the horn. It was just an idea, but ended up on the single and the Jan & Dean cut. I made some money off it. After the fact they did another record, 'A-Ooga,' where someone copped my idea.

"After that, I became Joe Saraceno's engineer. We did 'Out of Limits' with the Marketts, originally called 'Outer Limits.' But the TV show made us change it. I was also paid informally as coproducer on that, but I did not get label credit. I rearranged the song that was brought in, and that was when I realized that I had potential as a

"Lanky" and Jan Berry.

producer. I had an idea, and Joe, who was a real wheeler-dealer, said, 'OK, Bones, if you can fix it, you get half a point on the record."

Again it seems that all the roles, that of songwriter, producer, engineer, drummer, were frequently commingled in the LA music scene. "This happened a lot. We all worked on things together." This created some problems, though. "I got into a very embarrassing situation with Phil Spector. In front of a lot of people, Phil said, 'You really produced the Mamas and Papas. Now it can be told.' But I didn't produce them. Louie was the producer; he called me and John into the room. That is what a producer does: He didn't have to actually tell everyone what to play. Some producers do, some don't. Lou always had great ideas about background vocals. We all made our contributions but it was always understood that Lou was the producer. I felt sorry for Lou when John started to take over during the second Mamas and Papas album, because Lou taught everyone how to do it. Lou was my mentor, for sure. I still quote him whenever I can.

"Johnny Rivers, a Liberty/Imperial artist, discovered a group called the Versatiles and he renamed them the Fifth Dimension [for his Liberty subsidiary label, Soul City]. John always was a mystical guy. He had this idea that they could be the black Mamas and Papas. Lou was producing both the Mamas and Papas and Johnny, so he was around the sessions. The first Mamas and Papas record was going to be 'Go Where You Wanna Go,' but all of a sudden everyone decided that 'California Dreamin'' was a better record.

"So 'Go Where You Wanna Go' was put on the back burner. In typical recordbiz fashion of those days, Johnny decided to cover that with the Fifth Dimension. He called me and said, 'Look, I want you to get for me everyone who played on that session, because I want to duplicate that record.' So that was what we did. We went in and duplicated the record with the Fifth Dimension. That was the launch of that group. In those days they did not put engineers' names on records. But on the *Up, Up, and Away* album with that song, you'll see my picture on the back."

Bones was overextending himself in those days. He was the original drummer with the Sloan-Barri period of the Grass Roots, "Where Were You When I Needed You," up until Steve Barri produced the Grass Roots by himself. "I wasn't a member of the Grass Roots, but the demo of that song couldn't be duplicated, so they just used the demo with new voices laid over it." Bones played drums on P. F. Sloan's two LPs for Dunhill. And he was playing on all the Sloan-Barri demos, which included many songs released by Jan & Dean. He was engineering the Mamas and the Papas for Lou, all the Gary Lewis and the Playboys records for Snuff, miscellaneous engineering around town, and he was producing the Turtles for White Whale Records. He seemed to be meeting himself coming and going.

"I got up to the point of picking keys and working on the arrangement of 'Happy Together' when I got fired because I was not spending enough time with the Turtles. This was a lesson to me. I had to figure out what I was going to do. What I wanted to do most was produce, so I stopped everything at Christmas of 1966.

"When people called me to engineer, I told them that I was not available to engineer but I was available to produce. The Association [Valiant Records] called me to engineer, and I said no, but that I could produce them. I became the producer of the Association, and 'Windy' and 'Never My Love' [#1 and #2, 1967] came out of that relationship. But on January 1 of 1967, I had nothing to do!"

That was when Johnny Rivers, who was producing the Fifth Dimension, called on Bones as an engineer to complete the Fifth Dimension's *Up, Up, and Away* album by Jimmy Webb, which he had previously begun. Bones consented to do it. Then, when Johnny Rivers and Jimmy Webb had a fight, the Fifth Dimension refused to work with Johnny any more.

"By that time I had had two number-one records with the Association, so Johnny called me up, 'You have to produce the Fifth, you're the perfect guy.' That relationship lasted for seven years, 'Aquarius,' 'Stoned Soul Picnic,' 'Wedding Bell Blues,' and more."

The credit on those albums was "Production and Sound by Bones Howe," an unusual way to assign credit. "That was a credit that I devised because I felt that I was doing something that no one else was doing. I was engineering, producing, choosing songs, arranging, doing everything in the production area, and also going in the studio and cutting the songs. Those records were a very large part of the entire billing for Liberty/Imperial/Soul City.

"A whole bunch of us came out of these same sets of sessions. And I have to tell you, it is not now like it was in the old days. I am not one of those people who sits around and talks about the good old days, but as someone who continues to produce and to work full-time in the business, there was an openness then that is gone now.

"Lou and I used to go to Terry Melcher's sessions when he was producing the Byrds and I was producing the Turtles and engineering for Lou, who was producing Johnny Rivers. That sort of thing would absolutely never happen today. People are so secretive about what they do. So protective. In those days Dean would sing on the Beach Boys' 'Barbara Ann,' Brian and Tony sang on 'Surf City,' I sang on 'The

Little Old Lady,' those things happened. I sang a lot of falsetto parts, between Phil Sloan and [me] we sang most of the falsetto parts. As a singer Dean is a wonderful graphics artist—a real-l-l-ly talented . . . artist."

The stereo and mono versions of Jan & Dean's Liberty albums were always different. For example, the stereo "Sidewalk Surfin'" was missing the skateboard sound effects, and other songs had variations in length of fade-outs, sound effects, and vocal parts. As the engineer for the Jan & Dean sessions, Bones shed light on the source of these differences.

"The mono and stereo versions were mixed completely separately. First of all, the only thing that anybody cared about at the record company was the mono release. That was the record. And the stereo was always whatever you wanted it to be. We recorded on three tracks, not twenty-four tracks; maybe we had four tracks near the end of that period. By the time we were finished, all the instruments ended up on one track, the vocals on another, and the background vocals on the third. And there were no time codes to allow us to hook up two machines together. So oftentimes, to finish what Jan wanted, there were additional overdubs done while we were mixing down." These would not be on the master tapes, just on the final recording.

"Jan would try any kind of crazy thing he would think of. We'd run the tape slow and speed it back up to get the voices in tune with the music; you wouldn't believe the things we tried." And the tracks that were speeded up? "Jan would listen to a tape over and over again, then say it wasn't exciting enough and speed the tape up. As an engineer you grow up doing these things; then when you become a producer you decide if you want to do them yourself."

The new 1990s reissue by EMI of Jan & Dean's Liberty hits has all remixed versions of the original Liberty recordings. The lead vocals on, for example, "Surf City," were originally all on one track. But now they are spread across the mix from left to right. How could they do this if the original tapes had them all together? "They did some digital or electronic tomfoolery. The original stereo albums on Liberty are exactly how they really were." That means instruments in the middle, backup vocals in one speaker, and the lead vocals in the other speaker.

Three tracks placed limitations on artists, producers, and engineers. Sometimes they would already have filled up all three tracks, but they still had parts they wanted to add to the recording. "Another reason stereo and mono would be different—in order to open up a track so we could put new things to it, we would combine tracks. We could copy from one three-track machine to another and combine two or three tracks into one track. By the time we got finished putting two layers of lead vocals on, plus two layers of background vocals, the track would begin to get mushy. Jan would call the entire rhythm section back in the studio for another session and overdub the entire rhythm section over the track again. So in some cases, not only is the vocal double, but the rhythm section is double.

"That sound was so exciting that after that, Jan would use two drummers, two bass guitars, two everything. Studio Three at Western was always full, jammed with people. This was probably after 'Drag City,' the 'Three Window Coupe' period."

Phil Spector is the producer who has a reputation for overdubs, bringing session people back to add parts, doubling vocals and jamming the studio. Did Jan copy Phil, or was he just running out of tracks and solving generation loss problems? "Yeah, that sort of thing. But everyone listened to everybody and was influenced by everyone."

And how were sound effects like car crashes and skateboards placed in the recordings? "What we did most of the time was we spun the sound effect in over the mono and then cut that to another mono machine and then cut that in at the end. We got the sound effects off of old radio station sound-effects records with a red, white, and blue label. They were pressed on what was called flex, not real vinyl, and the sound was very gritty. We equalized the heck out of it to clean up the sound.

"The 'Dead Man's Curve' crash was a whole project in itself. Jan wanted it to go on and on, so we extended the original effect. We even added a bumper falling off!"

"'This Diamond Ring' was the first time I worked with Snuff," says engineer Bones Howe. "Snuffy took the song to Bobby Vee when he was as cold as yesterday's apples, and Bobby Vee turned it down. Then Gary Lewis, who had this silly little band with an accordion in it, cut the song and had a number-one record." What about Bobby's denial? "All I know is that Snuff said to me that Bobby Vee didn't want to cut it. You don't know if you aren't in the room." Jerry Allison says that Bobby did turn it down. "Jerry was Snuff's walkin' around guy. He would know better than anybody."

"One thing for sure. For most of the records made in the 1950s and the 1960s, the artist was dragged kicking and screaming into the studio to cut the songs. It was a producer's medium, no doubt about it. As a producer I was the only person who knew what the finished record was going to sound like, in my head. The group just came through the studio and put their voices on. And that was a big responsibility, because after you have one or two hits, the expectation is that every record you make will be number one. It was a burden, but it was the fun of doing it.

"Albums were not considered to be important in those days. If you sold two hundred thousand, that was a big deal. There was a rule of thumb that if you had a number-one record, you sold two hundred fifty thousand albums. But I always wanted to have more than one hit on an album. Producing the Fifth Dimension, I wanted to have more than one hit on an album. If you had a hit single, next the album came out and the second single was in the album, the first cut on the B side or some kind of nonsense. I was one of the guys to press for more than one single per album. The *Aquarius* album actually had four hit singles on it and we sold over a million units. But the label was only singles oriented; they'd be ready to quit after two hundred thousand."

Si felt that albums were desirable because they built catalog, whereas singles were dead after they had been a hit, little pieces of plastic you couldn't give away. "Until you get to nineteen ninety-one and you get to *Goldmine,* a record-collecting magazine that lists over one hundred thousand original 45s for sale and auction each issue. The thing about it is, nobody knew what we were doing [that they were making records that would be collector's items thirty years later], least of all us. And thank God. Because we would not have been able to do it, had we known."

CHAPTER 26

Picturing Music

With a CD the cover art of a "record" is not as much of an inducement to purchase as with an album. After all, the cover is only about four inches across. But in the days of Liberty there were seven-inch 45 singles, which often had full-color picture sleeves, and twelve-inch 33 ⅓ LPs, which always had a large front and back cover to be filled up with pictures and text.

"Up until the time that I left Liberty in 1963, I designed about ninety percent of the covers Liberty had," explains Si Waronker. Another name worth mentioning (although there were many others who did photography and design at Liberty) is Dick Hendler. Dick redesigned the logo and did the majority of the design and packaging at Liberty.

But photography was a more critical element to everyday releases at Liberty, and that was done by others, such as Ken Kim.

Ken Kim

The person most responsible for filling the space on LP covers (except for the liner-note writer, who provided text) was the photographer who provided the pictures. Now living in Nashville, former photographer Ken Kim is of Korean descent, but he is a California native, born in Anaheim in 1925. Three decades later he pioneered the field of LP photography and cover art at Warner Brothers Records.

"I was art director for Warner Brothers Records from about nineteen fifty-nine to the mid-sixties. That was fun to see, because I got to see something start from virtually nothing. Warner's just wanted to get into the record business, and they really did it! Woody Woodward [art director at Liberty Records] and I were very good friends. When I left Warner Brothers Records, he was the first one who started to give me work as a freelance. We worked together for five or six years, the early to mid-1960s.

"Back in those days, all of us who were art directors took pictures on the side, as it were, to kind of expand our vistas. I finally got so interested that I gave up a lot of my art direction and design to get into photography a little more. But the names I remember—I did a lot of covers for the Tommy Garrett Fifty Guitars album series by Snuffy Garrett.

"I also remember Jan & Dean. I did a few sessions on them. In fact, Dean and I became kind of close friends after Jan had his accident. Dean actually went into the business as an album cover designer; his company was called Kittyhawk

Graphics. Dean lived down the street from me, under the Hollywood sign, in Humphrey Bogart's old house."

Dean Torrence was always interested in art, both as a postgraduate art student, and as a recording artist. But he found a lot of resistance at Liberty in the 1960s to letting the recording artist have any input into the artwork and design of LP covers. They just wanted to slap on a photo of the artist and the list of songs and that was it, whereas he wanted to do a concept, a whole coherent package. Later, at Kittyhawk, Dean did many complex LP covers for various artists.

Ken Kim was around in the days when the artist always lost to the company when it came to cover-art decisions. "The recording artists finally prevailed, of course, but in those days, the early days, the recording artist did not go anywhere near the art department — other than to show up for a photo session. There wasn't anything [sinister] to it; it was just the way things were done. And that is when I was an art director. And [without recording artists' involvement] life was much easier in those days [laughs]!

"That is not to say that we did not get good covers. In fact, when Warner's started, there were no stars on the label, so concept covers were the thing. That was where I came in, and it was really fun as a designer. The artists we had, their pictures were very seldom used. Artists like Warner Barker. Later names like Allan Sherman and Bill Cosby and Bob Newhart were on Warner's and we used their pictures." So it seems that, in the album art director game, the concept album came first, with art in the form of drawings. Later the era of covers consisting mostly of photos and portraits came in. Dean probably wanted to combine the two.

Much of the early cover photography for Liberty was done by something called Studio Five, which was sort of a competitor to Ken Kim. "Studio Five was a graphics studio with a photo department. They did quite a few for Liberty but were not a part of Liberty. Liberty had a minimal art department, with an art director and maybe one or two graphic artists who would do production work on some of the inhouse material, merchandising ads and such. But for the most part album covers were done on the outside by freelancers like myself. In a lot of cases, they bought just the photography and then did the graphics in-house. Having been an art director, Woody let me do my own covers and follow through with the graphics. That made me a lot happier because I had better control over both ends of it.

"I remember shooting Bobby Vee and going outdoors with him. At that time I was not doing studio work. Working in LA like that, locations shots were pretty common because the weather let you shoot most of the year outside. I remember shooting him in a park around some flowers for a love album. I also did some Bud Shank covers."

Many Liberty 45s had picture sleeves, but many more did not. Why, and how was it decided who got picture sleeves and who did not? "We did picture sleeves, but the decision was strictly money motivated. If they felt that the name was big enough or the single was strong enough, had potential, or if the producer prevailed and had got his way, we did a sleeve. Or if the artist's last single was number two on *Billboard*, then it went without saying."

Certain artists had 45 sleeves that tended to be of a certain type. For example, Bobby Vee's picture sleeves were just that, sleeves with pictures of Bobby. By contrast Jan & Dean's sleeves tended to have pictures of cars, of Dean skateboarding, things like that. "I would assume that Woody's thinking there was that Jan & Dean were creative in their way at the time, and the fans expected a creative look to their product. Bobby Vee was different. The whole merchandising outlook in those days was different. If it was a ballad, or a pretty song, you just showed something pretty on the cover. The buying public was used to that at the time. If they saw a flower, they knew you were going to give them a ballad."

Talking to the artists of Liberty, most of them saved few if any of their own records. Almost no one kept photos. Might an art director be more likely to save things? "Oddly enough, I don't have any of my old covers. You know, you go along thinking that it is never going to end. Then, when it has ended, you look back and wonder where everything is."

One of the more negative aspects of album cover art in the 1950s and early 1960s was the practice of sometimes putting photos of white people on the covers of LPs by black artists, or of just putting on no picture at all. The practice was not universal by any means, but it did occur—though not at Liberty.

"At Liberty that kind of thing never happened to me. Later I worked at Motown, when the Supremes were established, and they always used photos of black artists. Lou Chudd founded Imperial, a label with many black artists, which became part of Liberty. I did some work for them. Lou was quite a story. He used to walk around with money bulging from his pockets, and when he ran across a potential artist, he'd pull out some money and sign them. That was how he conducted his business. Anytime a supplier finished a job, he paid them immediately. It was some sort of fetish with him. He probably felt it got him better service. As far as I was concerned, it did. And they were always on the cover. In fact, if I didn't have a photo of them, I painted a portrait of them. So there was no taboo there, of course. You know, I never ran into that. Maybe I led a sheltered life."

Far from experiencing prejudice, in fact, Ken, who was a member of a minority himself, encountered the opposite attitude. After he was hired as an art director, several other Koreans were also hired in southern LA. He was once told by Capitol that they were trying to get the whole art department oriental because the work was better and the work habits were unmatchable. Ken Kim is proud of this. "I felt I had spearheaded something."

Ken has long since left the rock 'n' roll cover photography business behind. "I started as an artist and an art director and a designer. When I got out here to Nashville, I kept my photography going for a while. But it was very physical. Then I started something I always wanted to do, which was paint. I am an easel painter and I do editorial illustrations for the Baptist Sunday School Board books and tracts and a few album covers. Nashville is the Bible belt. I want to develop an art style and become a fine artist."

CHAPTER 27

Promoting Records

Of all the unknown, little-publicized areas of the record business, record promotion is probably the most important. The best record in the world may never sell a copy or get played once on the radio if it is not promoted properly. And by the same token, some simply awful recordings can sell quite well and get massive airplay if the promotion is handled properly.

Properly? The payola scandals of the very early 1960s were an example of highly effective promotion, but it certainly was not considered "proper" by certain segments of society—notably those who did not like rock 'n' roll.

Liberty's promotion department was possibly one of the most effective in the entire record business. A founder and shaper of the Liberty promotion department was Don Blocker.

Don Blocker

Don Blocker came to California from Omaha, Nebraska, in 1956, with aspirations to be an actor. The excitement of the music business satisfied whatever creative desires he had, although he did start on the bottom rung of the proverbial ladder.

"I got a job at the Music City store in Hollywood. One day I walked into the stockroom and saw this skinny kid with great big bug eyes with a tie and suit on, and I asked him, 'What are you doing?'

"He said, 'I'm stackin' records.'

"'What have you got a suit on for?'

"'Well, it's my first day, and I didn't know what to wear.'

"'What's your name?'

"'Snuff Garrett.' We subsequently became friends, and he introduced me to Al Bennett.

"Al and Randy Wood were in the process of moving Dot Records to California about this time. Some time later Al told Don that he was going to go over to Liberty Records. Don told him, 'Al, they're busted, they're eight hundred thousand dollars in debt.' But Al told him that he felt he could pull Liberty out of its troubles. As Don pulled away in his car, he heard a record on the radio: 'Ooo, eee, ooo-ah-ah, ting, tang, walla-walla bing-bang.'"

Don recalls, "Al Bennett had a hit even before he got over to Liberty!"

In the end Don Blocker followed Al Bennett to Liberty, and Don ran the national promotion for Liberty Records up to 1964. During that time the promotion biz went through a lot of changes.

"When I started in the record business in nineteen fifty-six, radio stations were still being charged for singles, in some cases, and certainly for albums. One of the successful things that Dot Records, which had a strong tie-in with Liberty, did was sending out free singles to radio stations around the country. At no charge. And sometimes they sent albums. When I was with the distributor, and a little bit at Liberty, we still had a list of radio stations that subscribed to our label—for fifty dollars a year, they'd get our albums. It was not long after that when no one charged anymore. It was part of promotion to send albums and singles out."

One of the early big hits of Liberty was a record that Don Blocker had intimate knowledge of but little fondness for.

"I went up to Seattle when Bob Reisdorff was a local promotion man for C&C Distributors. Bob wanted me to hear a record, just an acetate, not a commercial pressing, that went, 'Dum dum, dum-do-dee dum. . . .' I said, 'Bob, can you turn it up a little bit?' He played it some more. I said, 'Bob, what is that?' 'Some local kids.'

"Frankly, I didn't like the record. But he was our promotion man up there and I wanted to stay in good with him. So I brought it down, and everybody flipped over it, and Liberty bought the master." Good move, Liberty, as the song was "Come Softly to Me," which was a #1, million-seller. Lucky Don Blocker didn't let his personal taste get in the way of his professional responsibilities!

After "Come Softly" was such a big hit, "Al Bennett encouraged Bob Reisdorff to move down and work out of the Liberty office in LA. Then Bob had the Fleetwoods and a few other acts he fooled around with." All Bob Residorff's artists were on Dolton, which became a subsidiary of Liberty. After the Fleetwoods, Dolton got hold of another hot act, and Don Blocker was there again. This time his musical taste and business sense were in harmony—but Al Bennett's were not. Thus this new act missed being on Liberty in 1960.

"I went to Seattle again. In those days, there were always local hits breaking out all over, in Seattle, Atlanta, Oklahoma City, Kansas City, wherever. John Stone, a DJ and music director at KJR, told me, 'I've got an instrumental up there that everyone is playing the heck out of. Man, the phone calls are tremendous. It's called 'Walk, Don't Run,' by a local group.

"I heard the song and said, 'That's a hit.' I took it back to Al Bennett and said, 'Al, we gotta call them and we have to get this record right now.' Al said, 'I don't like it; it's not a hit.' 'But, Al—' But Al said, 'It's not a hit record. It's just a hype.'

"One week later the record was huge. But I had already had to tell the Ventures that we were going to pass on it because we didn't think it was a hit. So now, a week later, we called them back and said we wanted the record. The Ventures said, 'Oh, no. You didn't want it a week ago. You're not going to get it now.'

"Al called Bob Reisdorff down. 'Bob, you know those Ventures? You know that group and their mom up there, Josie Wilson. I want you to get that record.' Well, Bob said he couldn't after it had been passed up a week ago. Al said, 'I want you to go up there and get that record for us.'

"Bob Reisdorff did a very wise thing. He said, 'Al, I'll go get it. But it's gonna be on Dolton, not Liberty.' Al started cursing. Bob just said, 'Al, I ain't gonna do it then.' So the Ventures really should have been on Liberty Records. Waiting cost Liberty Records, in royalties and a buyout from Bob Reisdorff of Dolton Records, about a million bucks. Just because he waited a week."

The caption reads: The Ventures were huge international stars, as indicated by this Dolton LP cover.

The Ventures were very big in Japan, although their nonmusical activities hurt them there for a while. "They had made a lot of money in Japan, but they got kicked out of there because their drummer was caught smoking grass, many, many years ago. That hurt them for many years; it was disastrous for them. It took them many years to get back." But they still tour there regularly in the 1990s.

At one time, as head of promotion, Don Blocker was actually the boss of Liberty ace producer Snuff Garrett. Before becoming a producer and an A&R man, Snuff served as a promotion man, with considerably less success than he would later achieve in production. But it was Don who was responsible for getting Snuff, who became the most important creative force there ever was at Liberty, into the Liberty fold.

"Snuff Garrett, as an A&R person, held Liberty together. Al Bennett had a knack for hiring the right person for the right job. But Snuffy was sort of Al Bennett's stepson for a while." When Snuff had returned to Texas from LA when he was still only fifteen or sixteen, he probably didn't have any plans to return. But two years later, promotion head Don Blocker told Al Bennett, "'We need a local promotion man. Let's call Snuffy and get him back out here.'"

"Al was against it, and said, 'No, I'm not going to hire that kid. He's too much trouble; he went home and I had plans for him.' But eventually he said 'OK, call the kid.' I called Snuffy while he was on the air. While he was on the air, he went in and told his boss he was quitting. We sent him a hundred dollars to drive out here.

"Snuffy was our local promotion man out here for a while until one time he and Al got together and Snuff started cuttin' records. The rest was history." As Ken Revercomb, the next Liberty promotion man we'll meet, put it, "Al Bennett kind of raised Snuffy back in Texas. But when he brought Snuff to Liberty, he was worthless, he was awful as a promotion man and everything else." Finally, almost in desperation, they said to Snuff, "Here, try producing." And thus the careers of Bobby Vee, Johnny Burnette, Gary Lewis, and other Liberty stars became possible.

Don Blocker almost got into another area of Liberty besides promotion — artist management.

"Originally Snuff Garrett and I were going to manage Bobby Vee. But Al Bennett wouldn't let us because he felt it was a conflict of interest. So we went out and found a manager. Bobby Vee had one in Minneapolis, but we maneuvered him away from that manager because we thought that he couldn't do Bobby any good. We got him the same manager who had Vikki Carr."

When looking over the Liberty history, one might wonder, Why did Bobby Vee sustain so long at Liberty? Other artists, such as Gene McDaniels or Johnny Burnette, who had as much talent as Bobby Vee, had some hits but did not sustain. Don had an idea. "What we found out was that in the case of perhaps a Johnny Burnette, and certainly in the case of a Gene McDaniels, they weren't as manageable as was Bobby Vee. I think that helped Bobby along in his career.

"In those days, as a producer and an A&R man, Snuffy had you under his thumb. He was very commanding. If you could not work with Snuff, then you weren't going to have too many hits. Johnny Burnette and Dorsey Burnette were real tough boys from Memphis. There were constantly antagonistic. They actually accosted me outside of Liberty Records one time, and they were going to beat me up. They accused me [as head of promotion] of not working on Johnny's record. They tried to intimidate me. That's the type of guys they were. They were nice enough, but they were a little crazy. Especially Dorsey Burnette. He didn't have both oars in the water, and he was a drinkin' fool. Not that we all weren't."

Maybe now we know why Johnny Burnette did not have a longer record career. Threatening to beat up the head of promotion of your record company is not exactly the way to win friends and influence people who have control of your career. Next time the promotion man has a record of a certain artist in a stack he has to promote, he's going to recall the treatment he got from that artist and his memory of that might just possibly color his choice of records to promote.

"Those were the days of hip-pocket business in the record business. Liberty Records generally speaking gained a reputation of covering other records. It was accepted then. But that hurt Liberty I think in the long run. Covering became a no-no by the 1970s, and that hurt them.

"Bill Stewart put on the second [and last] annual DJ convention in Miami, Florida. For some reason Omaha was important. Todd Stores started top-forty format there; it was not in Dallas. And it was really a top thirty. Todd's family owned a brewery and were fairly wealthy. Todd was a heavy drinker, and they didn't want him around, so they bought him a daytime radio station that was doing very poorly. Only network radio did well in those days, so he decided he was going to play records on his station; I believe it was KOWH.

"Well, driving around to bars all of the time, Todd Stores noticed that on the jukeboxes, people played only certain records over and over again. So he resolved to program his radio station like that. He originally did it on a daytime station with a play list of just thirty records. I was a kid living in Omaha from nineteen forty-six–nineteen fifty, and I heard that top thirty.

"In Omaha in those days, they had every gimmicky promotion. Once the station actually caught common houseflies and painted them red, blue, and gold and turned them lose. If a listener found a gold one, you got one hundred dollars. You literally could not buy a fly swatter in town, and people would drive down the street swatting flies! In those days those things were unheard of. They did the first treasure hunt. And it pulled ratings."

It was at this convention that Liberty distributed a satire of top-forty radio on a special record, free to all the top-forty radio people attending the convention. The Liberty people expected that these radio folk would be up for a big joke at their own expense. As Don Blocker found out, radio folk may like a good joke, but not one at their own expense, and Liberty "took a big setback with that."

The convention record wasn't the only time that Liberty got negative feedback with a seemingly innocuous release. Don Blocker knew Liberty star Gene McDaniels from those days in Omaha, and how his first hit, "A Hundred Pounds of Clay," generated a lot of flak.

"Gene McDaniels was from Omaha and sang jazz. Snuffy worked with Carole King and Gerry Goffin and Don Kirshner and Lou Adler. That is how Snuff got his songs. He really knew how to work writers and publishers to get songs.

"We got a lot of negative mail on 'A Hundred Pounds of Clay' saying that it was a sacrilegious tune. How dare we release it, et cetera.

"Gene McDaniels was a very confused gentleman. He was never happy being black. His first wife, from Omaha, was black. But he always went with white girls after that. The Omaha ghetto he was from bred some unhappy people.

"Bob Skaff convinced Al Bennett to spend six thousand dollars to buy the *Whiskey à Go-Go* album from Lou Adler. That is all that was paid for that album. Al Bennett screamed and yelled, 'six thousand bucks, you guys gotta be crazy!'" Of course, that LP was one of the best-sellers of all times and launched a career that included two dozen Johnny Rivers hits for Liberty/Imperial and spawned the Soul City record label.

Today hundreds of thousands of dollars are spent on album projects as a matter of routine. But in the 1960s, that was just not done. Not on newcomers, unknowns like Johnny Rivers, and not on veterans, established hit makers with million-sellers under their belt, like Jan & Dean.

"Liberty spent, on Jan & Dean's second or third or fourth album, the unheard-of amount of twenty-six thousand dollars. It was probably *Drag City*. The effect was like the earth was caving in at Liberty Records, because they spent twenty-six thousand dollars."

There was good reason for limiting spending budgets. From time to time Liberty spent a lot of money promoting records that stiffed in a major way. For example, there was a big singing star in Australia named Johnny O'Keefe. Long before the British invasion, Liberty had ideas about bringing Australian music to America.

"We took Johnny O'Keefe on the road and I said, 'Let's call him the Boomerang Kid.' Johnny O'Keefe was eccentric, crazy, a drunkard, smoked grass—he was one of the wildest men I have ever known. We finally got him to New Orleans. We spent seventeen thousand dollars to promote Johnny O'Keefe and thought that we were going to the poorhouse.

"We had some terrible records.... We did 'God, Country, and My Baby' with Johnny Burnette. I'll never forget it. Johnny Burnette was managed by a DJ, Earl McDaniels, in LA."

Liberty also had some successful records, of course. Just a few. A few hundred. In 1962 Don Blocker felt that Liberty needed something for pianist Martin Denny, who hadn't had a hit since 1959, although his Liberty albums sold well enough. "Is there something we can cover instrumentally?' Tommy LaPuma said, 'Don, there's a jazz thing out there called "Taste of Honey." It's kind of jazzy, but they're playing it out there.' So we went and got the record and covered it. Eddie Kano had the original."

Martin Denny's 45 got to #50 and was in turn covered by the Victor Feldman Quartet, whose Infinity Records single reached #62. "Martin Denny had a big album with it. But quite frankly, on that album and on all the albums after that, Martin did not play keyboard because he was not good enough. We used a guy named Bob Florence, Vikki Carr's conductor, on keyboards. Martin Denny did play on 'Quiet Village' in nineteen fifty-nine.

"Liberty was never a big album seller. If you sold fifty thousand copies, that was great. Selling one hundred thousand was completely unheard of. But the *Taste of Honey* album was the biggest seller during my years.

"The Ventures were an exception to the LP rule. All the Ventures albums sold one hundred thousand initially, whether they had a hit or not. Local bands bought all their albums and learned from them; they always wanted to hear what the Ventures were doing next. When I was head of A&R at Liberty, one day a guy called from Santa Barbara. He said he had an idea for the Ventures and wanted to come in and talk. He came in, and I asked him what he did. 'I sell appliances, refrigerators. But I have a phonetic system for teaching the guitar.' The phonetic system never worked, but I didn't care. We came out with a series called *Play Guitar with the Ventures*. They were very successful. We sold a lot."

"Louie, Louie" was written in the 1950s by R&B artist Richard Berry, who had an uncommercial but great 45 on it. "Liberty had the original rock version of 'Louie, Louie.' It was on Etiquette Records, by the Wailers. I bought the master because it was selling in the Northwest. But I couldn't convince anyone to go out and work it, especially Bob Skaff, who was head of promotion at that time. He said, 'It's a white group but they sound R&B. I can't promote that.' He wouldn't work it, and he didn't work it.

"Then the Kingsmen came along with an identical version. Our version was first, and I got it released on Imperial but could not convince anyone that it was a hit."

"Louie, Louie" was just one record that Liberty missed out on and Don Blocker regrets just a bit. Red Foley had a truck-driving record called "Giddyup, Go" that Don Blocker liked. Lorne Greene of "Bonanza" had a current #1 hit with "Ringo."

So Don Blocker had an idea to cut a less country version of "Giddyup, Go" with Dan Blocker, who played Hoss on "Bonanza." Don Blocker feels that Liberty would have had a hit with it. "The reason we didn't was that they wanted five thousand dollars, and I couldn't convince Al Bennett to let us spend the money."

Don Blocker takes pride in certain things he did at Liberty. "But I blew a lot of things. I was the guy who passed up 'Wipe Out.' A gal brought it in and told me, 'Don, this is a big hit in Fresno; you gotta take it.' But I didn't believe she was right. So it went to Dot."

Don Blocker's good days at Liberty ended when Avnet bought the company. "John Avnet was a complete alcoholic and a psycho. He eventually committed suicide and jumped off a building right on Sunset Boulevard. But it had no connection to Liberty. John Avnet was screwed up from being in the war, not a dummy, but screwed up.

"Avnet bought Liberty for ten million dollars, and about a year and a half later, Al Bennett bought it back for three million. In those days, the record business was exciting, but buyers did not know how to evaluate a record company. They didn't know that one hundred thousand old Bobby Vee albums that were listed as assets had no value whatsoever; they were a liability. But in those days the naïveté of companies wanting to buy record companies got them in an awful lot of trouble." Companies like Avnet thought that record inventory was like electronics inventory, but it wasn't. Electronic parts have a far longer shelf life and usefulness than pop records did.

"I got burned on the Avnet deal, but most of the guys did. We were given stock options, plus I bought additional stock when the stock was up to eleven or sixteen dollars, I don't recall the figure. When our Liberty options came up, the stock had taken a nosedive. We were complete believers in Liberty and Al Bennett and what we were doing, and we were very naïve about the stock market. I had also bought Avnet stock, and I really got burned on that. It wasn't a lot of money, but it was for me then. But Al Bennett was nobody's friend. I didn't go to his funeral. Al Bennett would con his own mother. That's the kind of guy he was. A lot of guys remained friends with him, but I didn't. Al Bennett was a great user."

Al Bennett—apparently either you loved him or you hated him.

Don Blocker knew Al from the day Al decided to move from Dot to Liberty. Liberty promotion man Ken Revercomb came along not much later.

Ken Revercomb

"Al Bennett hired me in the Chipmunk days through his association with Randy Wood and Dot Records and brought me to California from Cleveland. Liberty was absolutely bankrupt just a few months earlier, when they talked Al Bennett into joining the place. Randy had sold Dot to Paramount, leaving Al out of a job. Al was working with Heartstone as a distributor. When Liberty approached him, Al had a hundred sixty thousand severance, if you will, from Dot Records. One choice Al had was to join Liberty and finance it with one hundred thousand. Some people advised Al to just start his own label and don't inherit the headache. But he joined Liberty and they released 'Witch Doctor,' which provided money for the Chipmunks. After that we kind of dazzled everybody with our footwork."

As a promotion man for Liberty, Ken was not in California that much. He was not head of national promotion like Don Blocker. Ken "chased transmitters," meaning he would drive around the countryside looking for the towers with blinking red lights indicating stations to push records at.

"In the early days, I mean, when you went out to call on distributors, you'd throw your hat in first and see if it came sailing back out. It was a love affair, and we all had a lot of fun. We had more fun than [we] made money. The company made money, though. Our biggest year we made twenty million, something like that, which was a lot of money back then.

"One day we were out chasin' transmitters, and we saw this thing with blinking red lights. It said, 'WIGS.' We looked in our book, and that radio station wasn't listed. So we went in and said, 'Look, we'd like to talk to your program director, please.' He said, 'Well, man, we got no program director.' 'Well, then, let me talk to your station manager.' He said, 'What the hell are you talking about? We sell hairpieces and wigs.' That red light in back was on the water tower. 'WIGS' was their logo!

"We used to pull a lot of capers. I'd go out and find maybe thirty-five or thirty high school girls gettin' out of school and give them each some records, then tell them to go into a one-stop and ask for a certain record. Of course, the store didn't have it. But I knew that; we'd just released it. Then I'd stop by and call on the one-stop and say, 'Boy, I've got a record here that is just hotter than hell,' and he'd say, "Yeah, I just got twenty-five calls for that thing!' Creative selling.

"We made a silk purse out of a sow's ear. And while there was a lot of payola at the time, to the best of my knowledge none of us ever did that. But one thing we did do, we got a lot of people jobs. For example, we traveled extensively, millions of miles. Say I knew an up-and-coming disc jockey in Mobile, Alabama, who we thought was good. And say there was a big station in Kansas City that was looking for a jock. They respected our opinion; we'd recommend this guy, they'd get a tape and hire him. We didn't recommend anybody who wasn't deserving, and it worked out pretty well. Then it goes without saying that, if we got a man his job someplace, when it came to airplay, and it was a jump ball between two records, why, generally we'd get the break.

"On the other hand, Liberty had so many hits back then that we always got a listen-to. They were afraid not to listen to our records. We got the benefit of a lot of doubt, and we were good enough or lucky enough to get good material. That was pretty much how it worked."

Si Waronker already told the story of how the song "National City" was recorded by Ernie Freeman and released as by the Joiner, Arkansas, Junior High School Band. Ken Revercomb provides additional insight into this great, strange Liberty record from 1960.

"Snuffy was doing a Bobby Vee session, I am pretty sure. After a break some musicians were playing 'When the monkey wrapped his tail around the flagpole.' We threw the key open and recorded it. As a joke, we released it. It was Ernie Freeman. We released it as 'National City,' and Al Bennett's home town was Joiner, Arkansas.

"I was on the road doing promotion then and went into Tampa, Florida. Everyone called wanting this marching band. I went into a Tampa station and visited a DJ named Bob Waters, who picked his own music. He was absolutely falling apart [laughing]. He said, 'You gotta hear this tape. It is the greatest interview and I can't play it on the air. It's about your record, 'National City.'

"Bob Waters proceeded to play a tape of a phone call he had made to what was obviously an old rural box phone. A country, older man's voice said, 'Ah, he—hello, Joiner, Arkansas, High School.'

"My man introduced himself. 'I'm Bob Waters, WTAM in Tampa. I'd like to talk to you about your Joiner High School Marching Band.'

"It was quiet for a moment. The principal reflected, then he said, 'Walters....'

"'No, no, no, Waters.'

"'Oh, ah, oh, Waters? We've got a pretty fair football team. And a good basketball team. But, man, we got no fuckin' band!'"

Don Blocker introduced the Australian singer Johnny O'Keefe character earlier in this chapter. As it turns out, Ken Revercomb was also involved in that debacle. Johnny O'Keefe actually had two ill-fated Liberty 45s in 1959: "Own True Self" and "It's Too Late." But here—well, let Ken tell it his own way:

"Johnny O'Keefe was bigger than Elvis—in Australia. We signed him to Liberty before Imperial was bought. I was the only one in the company who traveled to every distributor we had. In those days we just chased transmitters. I picked Johnny O'Keefe up in Miami and set up a boomerang contest. We had a publicity photo of a guy obviously from Australia with a rack of boomerangs. Why not?

"Well, I had thirty playground boomerang champions and a big promotion through WPIX in New Orleans. The idea was, beat the boomerang champion and win one hundred dollars. The first kid stepped up, and Johnny indicated his rack of boomerangs and said [Australian accent], 'I say, would you have one of mine?' The kid said, 'Aw, no, I'll just throw this cherry stick.'

"Well, he threw it to Mississippi, I mean it got out there and looked like it was an inch long. It came whirlin' back; he sidestepped it and caught it. I thought, 'Oh my God, we are in trouble. Even if my guy throws it out of sight, how're we gonna judge it?' And this is the first one!

"So Johnny threw his, it went thirteen feet, and it fell down. To make a long story short, there were twenty-three who beat him. So I sent Al Bennett a wire: 'CHAMP DETHRONED. SEND $2300.' Al wired back: 'WHAT CHAMP? WHAT $2300?' Needless to say, that ended the contest and everything was cancelled. And I don't think we ever sold even two thousand three hundred records in the whole United States. That was one of the secret files at Liberty that was about a foot thick that they didn't want anyone to know about because we blew twenty–twenty-five thousand traveling him around the country. All he did was buy Chinese food and overcoats to give away as samples. And we peaked in New Orleans with the boomerangs."

Sometimes Liberty lost, and sometimes it won. By all accounts Liberty was never the same after the fabled Avnet deal. But if Liberty lost prowess in that deal, Al Bennett gained, according to Ken Revercomb. "Al Bennett was very good at selling the company back then. We bought Commodore and Post, the publishing companies, and Imperial. When he sold to Avnet, he basically sold 80 percent of the company and bought it back 100 percent. In the meantime all the long-term debt had been eliminated. And that was how we just went onward and upward. We were the Kiddie Corps of the time with a lot of luck and a lot of love and a lot of talent, too."

Al was good with the company, but Ken was no slacker in the promotion department. He could sell things no one else could—like old surplus records that no one wanted.

When a record company gets a surplus of old 45s or LPs that it cannot sell, either because they never were hits or they had outlived their popularity, they "cut" those records out of the catalog and sell them at two or three for a dollar retail per LP or five or ten cents per 45. The term "cut-out" can also refer to the holes that are cut out of the record label or the record jacket, either with a drill or a hot-metal rod. Or the end of an LP cover might be clipped. This way no one can mistake them for current product and try to make unauthorized sales.

Ken Revercomb recalls cut-outs. "I was in charge of getting rid of all the old surplus product. Nonhits. As a matter of fact, I made a career of selling cut-outs. All through the glory years at Liberty/Imperial, I gave I don't know how many gold records out. But I never got one until I got rid of eleven million records and they gave me a platinum one for sales in excess of eleven million!" Getting rid of eleven million records without making noise, especially nonhits, is not easy. If it gets around that there are so many dud records coming out, it hurts the company's goodwill. So Ken Revercomb would devise schemes to get rid of records through nonmusic outlets.

"I went to a used car lot in Tucson. Why Tucson? If I failed, I didn't want anyone to know about it. And if I were successful, I also didn't want anyone to know about it." Ken made a deal with Harry's Used Cars. For one hundred dollars, Ken would put a thousand dollars' worth of nonhit cut-outs in each car. After all, there wasn't one car on the lot Harry wouldn't discount one hundred dollars. "You gamble the ad, and I'll gamble the records. We advertised a thousand dollars' worth of music with each car purchase for Harry's blowout sale over Labor Day." The thousand dollars was actually eighty dollars at cut-out prices, so Ken would make twenty on each car.

Was it a success? "Three days later we had emptied his lot. It was like a Hitchcock movie; there was nothing but a few candy wrappers and light bulbs in the place. I said, 'Jeez, Harry, we did it! We gotta get more cars!' Harry said, 'The hell with you! I been trying to get outta here for four years.' So I went to Wichita, et cetera. I mean I got rid of a ton of records like that! It was that kind of thing that I did."

As it turned out, there was one thing that was a lot better than cut-outs that Ken tried like the dickens to sell, but try as he might, he never could manage to succeed. "I probably worked harder on Willie Nelson than on any other act that we had. I had him for five years and couldn't give him away. Do you believe that?"

Jimmy Holliday was a guy down on his luck when Liberty gave him work and turned him over to Ken Revercomb. To make him feel important and give him some authority, Ken told him about a new studio they had built upstairs. 'Jimmy, there are only two keys to this studio. You've got one, and I've got one. I don't want anyone up there if one of the two of us isn't up there.'

"The next day we heard all this commotion and noise up there. 'What was that?' Well, the Ventures had gone up there to rehearse, and Jimmy didn't know the Ventures from anybody. He threw the bass drum and everything else down the fire escape! He told them, 'There isn't supposed to be anyone up here unless Mr. Ken knows about it.'" Just another day at Liberty Records!

"One day, a fella had an epileptic fit on the walk in front of Liberty. We had an open-door policy, but this was a bit much. So we called down to the La Brea Clinic to get help for this guy sitting there rattlin' in front of the front door. It didn't look good for business anyway. All of a sudden a girl calls me to say the doctor has arrived. I went out and here is this fellow in a blue blazer with a crest over the pocket who introduced himself, 'Good afternoon, I am Dr. Royal Payne.' Did central casting send this guy over? Sure enough, it was his real name."

Of course, a stranger having an epileptic seizure had nothing to do with the record business. And Jimmy Holliday throwing the Ventures' drums down the stairs had only a little more to do with it. But these are the kinds of things one remembers thirty years later when one has lived and breathed a vocation that becomes nearly an avocation as well. And Ken Revercomb remembers those things well.

"I think that Liberty, more than anything else, was a feeling. I don't think there has been anything like it since."

In 1962 Ken graduated from the promotion department to be the first Liberty head of the Imperial Records division.

Bud Dain

Bud Dain was one of several fraternity brothers of Liberty national promotion head Don Blocker. "I went back to Omaha and told these guys, 'You gotta come to California, I'll give you jobs; I'll put you to work with the company.' One of the guys was Bud Dain, and I put him to work. Bud worked at Liberty. Bob Fead was another who came; he later became head of national sales for A&M records for several years and is now head of Famous Music Publishing.

"Liberty was my life. I lived it eighteen hours a day. It started in the mail room of Liberty Records in nineteen sixty. Snuff Garrett was the local promotion man at the time. I was in Omaha, Nebraska, at the time. Going to college, senior year. Don Blocker was from Omaha, back visiting for Christmas. 'You want to come to California and be the Southern California promotion director for Liberty Records?' Dain said, 'Sure! What's that?'"

Don told Bud not to worry about it; he'd explain it to him. Later he sent Bud a couple of Bobby Vee records from California, "What Do You Want" and "One Last Kiss." This was before Bobby's first Liberty hit, "Devil or Angel." Bud was a jazz fan, but he went to LA anyway for a job paying eighty-five dollars a week. Doesn't sound like much, except that inflation since equals a factor of almost ten, and eight hundred fifty dollars a week sounds a lot better.

"I started in the mail room for two weeks. Then I started doing promotion. They took me around to radio stations." But Bud was still into jazz. In fact, his brother had a little jazz band. So one day his first month on the job, Bud left the mail room and ventured upstairs to the offices, where he had met everybody by that time.

"Snuffy was sitting upstairs, Snuffy weighed about ninety pounds then. I mean, he was the skinniest guy. He wore these continental clothes, whereas I was coming out of an Ivy League tradition. He was sitting with Johnny Burnette, who[m] I'd just met and who had just hit with 'Dreamin'.' Johnny had on, I'll never forget it, a red shirt, red socks, black half boots, and black mohair skintight slacks. I said, 'Gee, I don't want to bother you guys, but I have this jazz tape I want you to hear.' Johnny

Bud Dain was sales and promotion manager for Liberty subsidiary World Pacific Records when he was photographed with his wife, Liberty/Imperial artist Jackie DeShannon. *(Photo by Sue Cameron.)*

yelled, 'We don't want to hear any fucking jazz!' I thought, 'Whoa, who are these guys?'

"But Johnny Burnette was the greatest guy in the world. He and Dorsey became very close friends of mine, and I loved him. But it was a little bit of culture shock for me!"

So Bud Dain went into local promotion for a while; then he moved to New York to run the New York office of Liberty. "When Snuffy came in and signed Phil Spector, Phil went in and stole the dub of 'He's a Rebel' that had been sent to Snuffy for Vikki Carr. Snuffy was in the studio mixing 'He's a Rebel,' and he heard Phil Spector down the hall mastering the Crystals' record, which destroyed us. I think we had the number one record in Dallas with Vikki or something like that; we won in one market."

Whoops! yet another version of the "Legend of 'He's a Rebel!'" Oh, well.

Next, Bud Dain returned to California and became vice president in charge of promotion for Liberty on a national basis. "Then Al Bennett started buying up companies. One was World Pacific. He bought it for, I think sixty grand, some ridiculous figure, from Dick Bock, because Dick just couldn't handle the distribution problems. I was made general manager of World Pacific. I did that for two years. We had Bob Lind; we did an incredible job. Dick Bock and I came up with 'Michelle' by Bud Shank ... some albums with Chet Baker that did fantastically."

Not every promotion man at Liberty could dream up boomerang contests and selling cars stuffed full of cut-out records. So what did a promotion man like Bud Dain do at Liberty?

"My job at that time was to get records played. But there had just been a payola bust in the late 1950s. So when I got into the business, there was literally no payola. There was no payola in the traditional sense. There was great promotion of great product. I just went around and made friends with the program directors, the music directors, the disc jockeys of all the top-forty stations. I went everywhere, every size market. I'd go to Omaha and Kansas City; I went to Billings, Montana; Charlotte — wherever I could go to get my records played. I could not get to them that often; there were only so many hours in the day. But at one time, I was at home for only two weeks out of ten months. At that time Liberty had five records in the top ten: 'Hurt,' by Timi Yuro; 'Take Good Care of My Baby,' by Bobby Vee; 'This Time,' by Troy Shondell; 'The Mountain's High,' by Dick and Deedee; and 'Tragedy,' by the Fleetwoods. And 'Tower of Strength,' by Gene McDaniels. And eight more in the top twenty. And it was because we lived on the road. I wore out an air-travel charge card; it would not print; the letters were worn down."

A life on the road may have been wearing, on the staff as well as on the charge cards. But it was absolutely necessary if Liberty was to have all those top-twenty records. "The only way people in America buy records is from hearing them on the radio. In other countries that is not true. In Japan, for instance, there is only an hour or two of commercial radio a day. So in Japan, they have fifty or seventy-five fan magazines. The kids get involved that way, plus hearing some records on Armed Forces Radio, and some on the government radio. But mostly they do it by reading about the groups and the success of their records, and then buy them that way."

The story of the British Jan & Dean fan who had never heard the second half of "Dead Man's Curve" until he bought the record, due to the fact that the BBC only played rock 'n' roll a few hours a week and cut records short so as to fit more selections into the allotted air time, did not surprise Bud Dain. "Yes, there was a little on the BBC. Then there was the pirate station [Radio Luxembourg] out on ships; they would play records. And there were TV shows like "Boy Meets Girl" and "Ready, Steady, Go." And the kids there bought fan magazines. The artists used to buy the old blues records. Jimmy Paige, McCartney, any of the British rock 'n' roll legends, they were all giant black–country blues fans. Guys like Elmo James and Robert Johnson and T-Bone Walker. Then they moved up to Little Richard and Presley and those people. That is what they cut their teeth on.

"But they did not hear music on the radio. In the U.S., you had five thousand radio stations with one thousand playing rock 'n' roll. I grew up in Omaha with Todd Stores and KOWH, which was the first top-forty radio station in the world. So I as a promotion man went to all of the radio stations and saw all of the disc jockeys, and I'd take my singles, the real commodity of the time, and play them for the music director. If nothing was happening with the record, I'd try to get him excited about it. A lot of times I'd just ask them for a favor, 'Play my record.' And a lot of times they did, because they were playing seventy to eighty records at the time.

"In LA, it was KFWB and KRLA. And Jimmy O'Neill, the host of "Shindig," was there. He hosted a show for me recently in Las Vegas. I knew all the DJs; Sam

Riddle, who owns "Star Search," was my roommate; I knew Gene Weed, who now owns the "Country Music Awards" show. Jimmy O'Neill, all the jocks were all my friends; they all became my closest friends. I was in the right place at the right time. I was twenty-two, I fell in love with LA, and all the guys were my age. Snuffy was becoming a hot record producer; the first record I ever worked was 'Dreamin' by Johnny Burnette.

"Everything was clicking. We were a little tiny record company, and Snuffy was hot; I was hot as a promotion man. Everything Snuffy produced was a hit. Plus there were the Dolton successes. I took the Ventures' 'Walk, Don't Run' to KRLA. They put it on the air, and within twenty-four hours, people were lined up around the block to buy the record. Everything we touched was a hit. It was Snuffy and a great promotion staff. We had the best promotion staff; we could get anything played. We were famous for it. Bob Skaff was a killer in promotion. Eddie Silvers in Miami was one of our promotion guys. He became chairman of the board of Warner Brothers music. Tommy Lapuma was our man in Cleveland and LA. and is now a great record producer for George Benson and Barbra Streisand.

"That was the secret to Liberty Records. It was a merchandising, marketing, promotion company with one record producer, Snuffy, plus Bob Reisdorff who contributed immensely to the company. And Dick Glasser, who ran the publishing company and produced Vic Dana, later the Fleetwoods and others. And even the producers were promotion men. Snuffy would go to the radio stations; so would Glasser.

"We also took artists to the radio stations. That's how the label was built."

It sounds like everything was coming up roses at Liberty. But there must have been at least one failing at Liberty, one weak link that kept the label from being even more successful than it was.

"The failing of Liberty? To be honest, we never had—and I want to phrase this very carefully, I don't want to say we did not have great artists—we never had extremely creative artists. With the exception of Snuffy, Reisdorff, and to some extent Dick, we never had the great creative producers. That hurt some of our very talented artists. We were so heavy into merchandising that we marketed our way to success rather than [built artists].

"What really hurt Liberty Records in my opinion was Snuffy left, Dick left, Reisdorff retired, and we were left with a bunch of guys who could market records but weren't the incredible creative people that were coming out of England and out of New York that A&M was developing and Warner Brothers was developing, Lenny Waronker and Richard Perry, guys like that.

"In all respect to Al Bennett, who was an incredible marketing man, he had a company full of marketing and promotion men, and that was what hurt us. Al would rather negotiate a deal than sign a great act and pay them the right money." Like the Beatles. "He went to London, and Jerry Moss was over there, giving honest, fair deals. Not that he was dishonest. But the others would offer good creative deals, while Al would just try to charm his way in, but those days were over. We had Brian Epstein ready to sign, which would have led us into all the other acts. But Al did not do it. Not that Capitol was too smart either; they were forced into that.

"Liberty was probably the best little rock 'n' roll record company of its day. But when the new rock 'n' roll talents emerged out of San Francisco and England, Liberty was caught short. They didn't have the people who could go and hang out with Bill

Graham. So Al did it! Al went to Europe. He wouldn't let any of the young guys go. I used to beg him. But he wouldn't let us. He went over there and tried to sweet-talk everybody into deals, and it didn't work."

"Find me a good tune and I could make a hit with any of five artists!" That was what Liberty founder Si Waronker said when asked what was the most important aspect in making a hit record. The tune was the most important thing. Getting a good producer was second, and the artist came last. Did Bud Dain agree with this?

"I totally disagree. I will give you two answers. If you are talking about a pure hit record, there is absolutely no question in my mind that the song is the most important factor, number one. The producer is number two. The artist is number three. But—that will get you a hit record and nothing else. In my opinion the record company should be run so that the artist is number one. And the producer number two. And then they will find a hit song. The hit song always will, as a hit 'script,' be the part of the puzzle that makes the artist a monster. But what Liberty and a lot of companies did was go for the hit song, and the hell with the artist."

Like Phil Spector, who had hit records as a producer, with great tunes, but no one knew who was in the Crystals, who the lead singer was? "Exactly. That is hit manufacturing. Phil Spector was the star. At Liberty, Snuffy was the star. But at A&M and CBS and Warner Brothers, the *artist* was the star. As they should be."

When I was growing up, my favorite records always tuned out to be on Liberty. No wonder I latched onto a label, Liberty, rather than onto certain stars. Snuffy was the star! "Snuffy had the best ear for a song of anybody bar none. The man has a great ear for hit songs. But the man was the star. And that is why he always had problems with his artists later. Cher and Vikki and Bobby and anyone else he worked with.

"That is not a put-down. He was a wonderful star. I love him; I was his partner for four years; he's crazy. I care about him a lot and respect him a lot. But if I were running a record company today, I would take my lead from Jerry Wexler, Clive Davis, Jerry Moss, Moe Austin, Jack Capp, David Geffen, Berry Gordy, those are the killer geniuses of the music business because they always made the artist number one. Then they knew they would find the hit song. That way, when they had a hit with Janis Joplin or Cat Stevens or Barbra Streisand or Joe Cocker, then the artist had longevity on their own without their having to keep coming up with hit songs and the artist living or dying by having the hit song. They created stars.

"Liberty never knew how to develop a star. Not Eddie Cochran. They never knew how to develop Jackie DeShannon. And I was part of it. I knew what a hit song was and how to get it played. But I did not know how to develop an artist. I did develop Canned Heat, but Liberty always held you back from developing artists like that. I went to New York to try to sign Johnny Winter, and Al Bennett would not give me the money.

"When I was head of Liberty A&R we signed Ike and Tina and the Classics IV. But take Johnny Rivers. Johnny went through wars with Al Bennett that would dwarf World War II to develop his career. Johnny was a creative guy, he had a lot of success, but he did it in spite of Liberty Records. And it took everything he had to fight Al Bennett, to let him be his own man, and to let him create the albums he wanted to create. Al Bennett would have had him doing everyone else's hits and an album called *Johnny Rivers Sings the Top Ten.*

"Johnny Rivers was his own motivator; that is what Liberty needed more of, and that is what the record business became."

Sometimes Liberty did get artists who were, as it were, stars. An example was Jan & Dean. They were known by name (it probably helped being called "Jan & Dean"!) and were due to have their own movie, record company, and TV show when Jan had the near-fatal accident that ended his career. But then, they were not directly under Liberty but were signed to Lou Adler. And remember, Lou promoted a package and an image, not just a record. Maybe that made the difference.

Bud Dain had a close relationship with Jan & Dean.

"I was supposed to start a record label with Jan Berry. He wanted me to run it. We were going to have dinner at Dan Tana's on Melrose the night that he had his accident. He never made the meeting, but I was going to leave Liberty and start a label with him and Dean.

"At Liberty we did 'Surf City' and 'Dead Man's Curve' and all the stuff with Brian Wilson. I remember meeting Jan & Dean and their manager Lou Adler in Philadelphia. They did a hop for WFIL and DJ Humble Harve. We did hops at drive-in theaters from the roof of the concession stands. That was how we'd do favors for the jocks so they would play the records. We'd send artists on tours to do hops all over the country. Free. Artists made nothing in those days. But it was a way for them to get exposure and then make money."

Many a famous name passed through the Liberty family. Working there for years, as did Bud Dain, led to many interesting encounters.

"Snuff told me that the most talented person he ever worked with in his entire life, the most brilliant arranger, was Leon Russell." Leon was a large part of the Gary Lewis and the Playboys sound, and was on many sessions with acts like Jan & Dean as well. As a graphic artist, Dean got involved with Canned Heat, designing the LP covers for Liberty. Bud Dain signed Canned Heat.

"I walked into a little club called the Ash Grove. Canned Heat was in there doing country blues on a Friday night. I saw one set and signed them on the spot. I signed the Nitty Gritty Dirt Band who brought me the Allman Brothers, only they were called the Hourglass then. Bill McCune, who managed Steve Martin, discovered them in St. Louis and brought them to me. I signed them; failed with the first album. Duane left because he was a minor and went to Memphis. Then Gregg came to my office one day and asked for a release. I said, 'I won't give you a release; I think you are too talented. He said, 'You gotta give me a release. I want to go be with my brother. It's not right for me to be out here.' I said, 'You got it.'

"I ran into him twelve years later in the studio with Cher. I didn't think he would remember me. He walked up to me and said, 'I'll never forget what you did for me. Because you gave me the chance to go when you could have locked me up out here.' I said, 'Well, that made it all worthwhile.'"

Liberty Records covered the musical spectrum, from Julie London to Jan & Dean to Canned Heat to Willie Nelson. And Bud Dain promoted them all.

"Joe Allison started the country music division of Liberty. One of the first records was 'Old Rivers,' but it went pop with Walter Brennan. Then they signed Willie Nelson and Hank Cochran. Willie Nelson's first album was on Liberty's Imperial label. 'Touch Me' and 'Half a Man' were songs on that album. But Liberty, being on the West Coast, had a lot of trouble competing with the Nashville companies. Liberty had a couple of country hits but they weren't of any real importance.

Willie Nelson had what I would consider major turntable hits on Liberty. It really kind of opened the doors for him. And Hank Cochran. Then Joe Allison and Scottie Turner came in and operated the division. But, no, they were not really competitive. In those days, it was all CBS, RCA, Capitol, Decca, and it was real tough to get into the country business. Of course, a country hit sold only twenty thousand copies, so who cares. You had to have ten or fifteen hits at any given time to make a country division worthwhile. RCA could have twenty records on the charts.

"I did country promotion, but we never devoted ourselves to it. I was too occupied with the pop. To do justice to the country records and the radio stations would be a full-time job, and we really didn't have the time. We just weren't competitive."

As hard as Bud Dain, Ken Revercomb, Don Blocker, and the rest of the Liberty promotional staff worked, many artists, such as Jan & Dean (or at least Jan's dad), who did much of their own promotion, and Johnny Burnette, who almost beat up Don Blocker over the issue, felt they were not worked on as hard as they could have been. The Rivingtons, who had only two top-100 hits on Liberty, felt that, being black, they were particularly poorly promoted by Liberty. Liberty didn't know the black DJs and didn't understand black music.

Would Liberty promotion agree that Liberty could not properly promote a black artist? "I think that was a fair assessment. I think that the black labels like Atlantic and Atco and Motown and Chess and Checker pretty much controlled the black radio, much as other labels controlled the country radio. We had our reputation like that in pop radio. When a white label like Liberty tried to promote a black act, they'd send white promotion men around to black stations. Honestly, I never felt unwelcome at the black stations. But the Atlantic guy was there every day, and Bud Dain was there once a month when he had one or two black records. So I would say that was pretty much on target.

"We did try to develop a black music division. We did that by buying Minit Records, which was part of the Imperial buy. And we hired some black promotion guys who went around and spent all of their time at the black radio stations. It sounds segregated, and it was in the sense that, in those days, there was more pure black radio and pure country radio, pure top forty and pure MOR. But it was not segregated in the sense of any kind of prejudice. When I went to the black stations, they were very gracious. But I wasn't there often enough. Meanwhile, Randy Wood, the black guy running VJ Records [not the Randy Wood at Dot Records], he was a very bright, talented record man, so he went to the white stations, and there was no problem. It was segregated in the sense of music, but not in the sense of whether the person was black or white."

When "Surf City" was #1 on *Billboard*'s pop chart, it was #3 on the R&B chart. "That was pure accident, not promotion. That record was just so popular and so good and right in the pocket that everyone liked it. Jackie DeShannnon and Brenda Lee used to get played on the black stations because the jocks didn't know they were not black. The first time I took Jackie to a black station, the guy said, 'Wait a second! You're not Jackie DeShannon! Jackie DeShannon's black!'"

A black group called the Showmen hit in 1961 with a record called "It Will Stand," on Minit Records. After Liberty acquired the Minit catalog as part of Imperial, "It Will Stand" was reissued on Imperial. How come?

"It Will Stand" had not been a real big hit the first time it was out, number sixty-one. But a couple of stations started playing it, and it became a much bigger sales record than it was a chart record. It seemed to go from market to market. It was never a hit in all cities at the same time. It was an incredible record. It hit in some cities three months after it hit in others. As Bud Dain said, "It was an incredible record! It just restarted by itself. We didn't push it out a second time. Someone just started playing it in Charlotte or Atlanta, and we just rereleased it."

CHAPTER 28

Publicity

Promotion is how records are pushed, how airplay is yielded. Publicity is often confused with promotion or perhaps thought to be functions of the same people. In fact, publicity is entirely different. Promotion is getting people—DJs and record buyers included—exposed to a record. Publicity is getting the artist known to the public. Perhaps if Liberty had had as strong a publicity department as it had a promotion department, it would have had more stars to go along with all its hit records.

In actual fact, Liberty had no publicity department at all but hired outsiders to serve that function.

Bobbie Cowen

Bobbie Cowen was one of the PR people that Liberty contracted with in the 1960s. Bobbie and her associate were pioneers in the field.

"I had one of the first PR offices that specialized in pop music. I think there was one lady in New York named Connie Dee and there was Beverly Noga with me in my office. Her mother Helen had a nightclub in San Francisco called the Black Hawk. June 1965. Sonny and Cher were among our first clients. Bev and I were also in record promotion.

"Rock and roll was still new enough that there were few outlets for publicity, at least compared to the various publications that were available for publicizing television and movie actors. We were writing the book [on publicity] at the time. We would find these high school kids that the magazines were hiring to write about rock and roll, this new phenomenon. Touring was just starting. So we would phone all over the country to break our artists. At the same time, we were doing Southern California record promotion.

"There was a kind of a rivalry we had going over one record with CBS. It was the Byrds' 'All I Really Want to Do' versus Cher's version on Liberty/Imperial.

"We got an awful lot of airplay and kept running into those Liberty promotion guys at the radio stations. Because Sonny and Cher were breaking so hot here in LA, we were able to get an awful lot of play. I'm not sure eventually who won that battle, but the Byrds went on to become the Byrds."

And, of course, Cher eventually went on to become Cher. As far as who won, the Byrds' version on "All I Really Want to Do" topped the national chart at #40, lasting for ten weeks in the summer of 1965. Cher's version climbed up to #15 and stayed on the charts two weeks longer.

"We did a lot of hanging out with the Liberty people, because there was a bar across the street from Liberty Records called the La Brea Inn, and all those guys used to go there after work and hang out with the disc jockeys who also used to hang out there. But we didn't really have any other clients [apart] from Liberty."

Bob Levinson

Bob Levinson's PR company, Levinson Associates, was hired by Lee Mendell to handle Liberty's public relations for two years when Lee was vice president. Before that Liberty had its own publicist on staff.

In its capacity as publicist, Levinson's company represented Liberty corporately and represented all the artists and the product. This was not advertising, which is paid for. Publicity is what Bob Levinson calls "free space. If you look at a copy of *People* magazine and see albums being reviewed, it didn't just happen magically. Somebody made that product available to the magazine and to the reviewers, and someone was influential in making them pick those albums as opposed to somebody else's. This is a short course in what publicity is. It is dressing up the company and the artists, it is throwing parties, it is dealing with those people who are important to the company and will give it a better image in the industry and the community and sell more product. During that period we were involved in everything that Liberty and its subsidiaries were doing. It was quite a big job. That is why we had a full-time staff member on [the] premises at Liberty at all times."

Most companies had an employee at that time who handled requests that came to the company. Levinson's company was in the forefront of independent promotion, and subsequently became the largest music PR firm in the world. "Later promotion became the single most important factor in getting records played."

Rock 'n' roll was still small time. "Music was evolving out of mainstream pop and R&B. The magazines relating to music were more general interest magazines than music magazines. *Life* and *Look* were one and two in giving artists visibility. There were trade publications, *Billboard* and *Cashbox* and *Record World*, and the tip sheets. You needed to let people know the product was there as opposed to the competition. Mac Davis was a regional promotion man for Liberty in those days."

"It was an all-inclusive kind of job. The biggest magazine was *Sixteen*. The whole concept was to get into those pages on a regular basis and establish a regular following for the music. In terms of television, you had very little that you could utilize. There [were] 'American Bandstand' and 'Where the Action Is.' There [were] 'Shindig,' 'Hullabaloo,' and 'Boss City,' a local show."

Did a magazine like *Tiger Beat* or *Sixteen* carry only those acts that were popular, or did they carry acts simply because the publicists saw to it that there was coverage? "The magazines made those artists popular. If you could strike a deal with an editor to have an artist featured month in and month out, then that artist was going to be popular, because you were establishing a relationship between that artist and very impressionable young readers."

Does that rather broad statement, that an artist who was featured in the mags *was* going to be popular, mean that a publicist could make a no-talent into a star?

"For the record, I handled most all of the major teen idols over the next ten or fifteen years, not just Liberty. Ultimately, it has to be in the grooves from a music standpoint. If it isn't there musically, then it's not going to happen for any sustained period of time. You can create interest and you can create focus. But no publicity ultimately means anything if you really don't have something great to work with. You can only take it so far, then the material has to stand on its own. It all starts with the song."

Payola, so endemic to the music business in the 1950s, never came into play in the publicity area. There was no need to pay magazine editors as radio station music directors had been paid. "For all the impact publicity has, ultimately nothing beats air play. Whoever paid what to whom, that was another part of the business, that was promotion. In publicity, if you had a good relationship with an editor, you were going to get coverage. If you wanted to get something beyond good coverage, you strike a deal.

"Going back to the teen field, if you strike a deal with *Sixteen*, you would make a deal with that magazine so it would have exclusive access to your artist or to a certain type of coverage for that artist. What that meant was that every month in that magazine, your artist would be featured, your artist would develop a following through that magazine. If you were lucky enough to make a deal with the number one magazine in that field, then you were off and running. On the other hand, if the magazine was not interested for some reason, then it was all uphill.

Why would a magazine agree to feature a particular artist? If it was not getting paid to do the features, then what did a magazine have to gain from such a deal?

"The magazine's gain was not made by a payment for the coverage. What the magazine did was put itself in a position to build an act, then make a lot of money through the sales of the magazine. That was the quid pro quo in that area. It wasn't very sophisticated, it was straight trade out. You want and we want and we serve a mutual purpose.

"Liberty was very well established at the point that I got involved, but it certainly wasn't established in rock and roll. There wasn't much rock and roll to be established in. The Hot 100 in *Billboard* was really the pop charts, and the artists who were selling were artists like Johnny Mathis."

CHAPTER 29

Selling Records

An obviously critical part of running a record company is selling records. But, unlike the recording of records, the selling of records—selling nationally, not over the retail counter—is an area of mystery of which the average record fan may be completely unaware. As always, there is overlap between sales and other areas.

Jack Bratel

Jack Bratel was the Liberty national sales manager from 1963 to 1975. He started in Cleveland as a promotion man in 1957, then ran a distributing company, then ran a Liberty branch. Soon he became Midwest regional sales manager. That was when he came to LA for the 1965 Liberty Christmas party and stayed.

His job as national sales manager involved selling and marketing product to the Liberty-owned regional branch operations and independent distributors, their sales forces, and their promotion men. As a former promotion man he knew the importance of radio stations, knew people at radio stations, so often called them directly as well. But it was not just a job to Jack Bratel.

"I enjoyed it. It was so much fun, enjoyable, and challenging, it was more a way of life than a job. Hours were long. We were out on the West Coast; the East Coast had a three-hour jump, so we would start at seven or eight in the morning, get on the phone. I would talk record product and promotions to the managers and promotion men as well as retail stores and radio stations. We did anything that needed to be done. We'd pack up records and mail them out any time there was something hot that had to get out there. We'd drop everything and stuff records into envelopes. And that was the fun part.

"Liberty Records was a very amazing company. There was a very close camaraderie at Liberty. For a lot of guys I knew, Liberty was the company they wanted to work for because they were promotion minded, aggressive; the company was full of really nice guys. I liked all of the people in the company. There was a lot of competition, but there wasn't much backstabbing or political stuff going on by comparison to what I knew went on in other companies. Al Bennett's divisions fostered competition, yet we were all in the same company. We fought to the death, but it was like a game; you'd never hurt them; after the record was over, you'd be good friends.

"When I visited Dallas, the Liberty people before me had done so well that Dallas loved Liberty and loved me. I could do no wrong!

"It was unique. For the last three or four years, I have been talking about having a Liberty reunion. When Al Bennett passed away a few years ago, the people who showed up at his funeral were the Liberty family. Well, not the entire Liberty family." Just the ones Al had not alienated. As Jack tells, Al could be one's best friend.

"The man had so much charisma, it was incredible. We'd be on the phones in the morning doing business, and he'd come walking through the building on a sunny summer morning. He was already back from playing golf, all sharp and tan, golf outfit on. He'd stop and ask each of us how we were doing and what was going on. He was a dynamic human being and was involved in everything. You wanted to break down doors for him.

"We had the best-run, most promotion-minded, swingin' company there was. I hired Eli Byrd, Joe Simone, [and] Tommy Lapuma when we opened the Cleveland branch. These guys had never been in the record business before. They weren't with the company a month when we had the Liberty Christmas party. The company flew us all out to California. Those guys couldn't believe it. And I mean to tell you, it was a spectacular Christmas party. It was in a big hotel. All the Liberty artists performed."

Mel Fuhrman

"I opened up the first branch in New York in 1962 and was the East Coast sales manager for years. Then I went out to LA and opened up some labels for Liberty, such as the budget label Sunset Records. Then I came back east when we bought Blue Note and ran that. I was also national sales manager for a time. Liberty was a wonderful company. I worked for Liberty for seven years, and even now, thirty years later, most of my friends are still from the Liberty days.

"Al Bennett and I were very close, and Liberty was a very close-knit company. I was also close to Vikki Carr and Vic Dana and the Ventures, that whole crew. I was the one who broke 'This Diamond Ring' here in New York.

"Jerry Lewis, Gary's dad, called me up and said, 'I'm in New York, and I want you to come up to my suite and talk to me.' I came up to the Regency Hotel; it was late morning, and his wife Patti answered the door. Jerry Lewis was sitting like a king in this suite in a bathrobe having breakfast. He was kind of austere, and he said, 'This is my kid, and I want you to take care of him. I want this record done da-da-da-da....' His wife admonished him, 'He's a record man, he knows what to do, let him do his job.' I said, 'Yeah, Jerry, we'll break this record; I know where to take him.'

"I took Gary Lewis to radio stations and ran around with him. I was never overly fond of Gary. He was kind of like a snotty rich kid. But we did break the record.

"Vikki Carr was wonderful to work with. I loved Vikki Carr. She appeared at Basin Street East and we made a party for her there. We always made parties for the visiting West Coast artists. I had a lot of fun with Julie London. She used to cuss like a sailor. I remember there was a priest in the record business, Father O'Conner, and after her act at the Americana Hotel, Julie came over to my table and sat down. Me, her, and Father O'Conner. She said [expletives deleted], and I said, 'Oh, my God!' But he was like a record business kind of priest, so he was cool.

"Al Bennett was a wonderful guy. Once he came back from England to my office in New York, and he brings in a picture of these four guys with bangs and long hair. He said, 'I saw these guys in England. What do you think?' He hadn't played the record. I said, 'With those looks, they ain't gonna get anywhere.' It was, of course, the Beatles. We laughed about them. Maybe the hair was one reason we passed on the Beatles.

"I made the first party ever for Graham Nash when he came over as part of the Hollies on Imperial. It was at Basin Street East. It was his first trip to New York, and he was all bug-eyed. He was ecstatic—he couldn't believe he was at parties in New York.

"I broke Lenny Waronker in as a promotion man when he was a kid sent to New York with Al Bennett's late son and Tommy Lapuma. Tommy is now a big producer at Warner Brothers. He had one short leg and he used to stamp the hit side of all the promo copies of Liberty 45s with a rubber stamp of a club foot."

Lee Mendell

Lee Mendell came to the West Coast for another company. Bud Dain, who was then Liberty's regional promotion manager, hired him as regional sales manager in about 1962. Lee covered the ten western states except Hawaii. "My job was to make sure the stock was out there, presell the releases, go see the sales staff, visit the dealers, make sure stock was in the stores if any act was playing locally, visit any act that was playing locally, take inventory, visit the rack jobbers—in short, make sure the product was out there."

Mendell had this job for a year and a half. Next he went into national LP sales as Bob Feed (now president of A&M Famous Music) took over national singles sales marketing.

One of the deals that Lee Mendell made for Liberty was to distribute Fantasy Records (Creedence Clearwater Revival) outside the United States. At this point Mendell ran the Liberty international division. "We licensed Fantasy worldwide except in France and Germany. He also kept the Liberty name and logo going after UA abolished it. In Japan there were distribution licensees for Liberty. Liberty international was maybe thirty or thirty-five percent of the company. We had companies in England, France, Germany, and Canada. We licensed to other countries."

Sometimes the international division was the tail that wagged the dog at Liberty. "'It Must Be Him' was one of the first instances of an American record breaking in the UK and then force-feeding itself back into the United States. It was a big hit in England before it was a hit here, as was Vikki.

"The credit for the success of Liberty goes to Al Bennett. I have a very high regard and a very warm spot for Al Bennett. I found him to be charismatic, animalistic, magnetic, and bright and intelligent. He allowed people within the company to grow and to make their own decisions. He was unique and forward-thinking."

CHAPTER 30

Distributing Records

Record distributors did just what their name implied—they distributed the records. They would get hundreds or thousands of copies of a particular record, then get those copies to the stores and even to the radio stations. They did not get the records for free. However, if they overbought, they could return the extras to the record company for a refund or for credit. In a rare case the distributor might get records for free. That is, they might get paid in records. For example, when the New Orleans distributor put up the money for the Johnny O'Keefe Boomerang Contest and lost it when Johnny was beaten by all comers, Liberty was giving that distributor free records for a mighty long time.

John Ierardi

John Ierardi was the Boston distributor for Liberty Records in the 1960s. He had originally worked in the record department at Jordan Marsh and went to work as a distributor after college. "Liberty was one of the labels that was carried by Mutual Distributors. When UA bought them, they had a distribution branch of their own called Liberty/UA. I became assistant branch manager for Liberty/UA, then ran the stereo tape division for Liberty/UA during the time of Canned Heat and Nitty Gritty Dirt Band."

But other records sold as well. "One of the records that I was playing a lot in a lot of the department store record departments in Boston was called *A Bunch of Banjos on Broadway*. It was Spike Jones's banjo player playing "Hello Dolly" and "Mame." They were selling it so fast just by playing it in the stores that I was doing very very well with it in that area. It was turning people on, and they were buying a hundred copies at a time."

After that Ierardi was in and out of Liberty/UA at Mike Stewart's whim. He worked in stereo tape, then production; then he worked in the International Department under Lee Mendell. "When Jerry Thomas let Mendell go, then the whole department went, so I became an independent distribution sales rep, much more lucrative.

"I think that a big problem Liberty had during that era was that they would have a good artist like Vikki Carr that they'd do an album with. They would put a couple of good songs on it, then the rest of the stuff you never even heard of. It looked like somebody's uncle wrote them and you'd stuck them on this album, a real mishmash of stuff. It looked like they picked a lot of things that looked like potential singles, but no one ever heard of them. There were no standards, like Julie

London used to have on her albums, just songs. Very unsalable product was there. As the end of the 1960s got nearer, the material got weaker and weaker.

"Putting out albums by people like Jan & Dean . . . when they had hit singles, fine. But when they didn't, just putting out albums one after another just didn't sell. Until they had a Golden Greats, which would sell. But when I was a distributor in Boston, Liberty had hit after hit. 'Take Good Care of My Baby,' 'The Mountain's High,' 'It Must Be Him,' all those things one after another. It was going great. They had a great potential as singles, but somehow when they put the albums out, the albums never sold as well as the singles did unless they had a Golden Greats album. Their strength was in singles and the ability to make hits. I never saw the strength in their albums.

"The only albums that had staying power were the ones that had hits on them. They did not have staying power on, like, Mantovani, where every album sold. If there are a bunch of albums by Bobby Vee with no hits on them, they won't sell. People will finally buy the Golden Greats album."

Dean Torrence of Jan & Dean has said that he preferred having at least two hits on an album instead of just one. Would that have helped sales in John Ierardi's opinion? "Well, it didn't work that way. It was better to do repackaging, taking the best songs and recognizable songs off several albums and putting them on one new album. People will buy that instead of something with just one or even two hits on it."

What about hard-core fans who will buy everything a favorite artist puts out, regardless of the number of hits on the album? "Pop music does not sustain hard-core fans here in the U.S. like they have in Britain. Two years down the line, if you haven't had a hit you might as well forget it."

Apparently selling singles was one thing, but at only about ninety-seven cents a pop retail for 45s, a distributor would rather sell LPs. The proliferation of album-oriented rock following the 1960s, and the replacement in record stores of single records with cassette and CD albums, must be a welcome development for distributors everywhere.

Al Altman

At Liberty Al Altman was the head of Metric Music, Liberty's publishing company. But before that he worked at Mutual Distributors in Boston, where he brought out new hits by the likes of Dick and Deedee, Gene McDaniels, and Bobby Vee. Some days a distributor worked almost exactly like a promotion person.

"There was a way that I sometimes promoted new records at radio stations. When I'd get a lot of records in, I'd have maybe seven or eight or ten new releases. I'd drop eight of them in the wastebasket. The radio station people would say, 'What are you doing? Don't throw them away!' I would say, 'Well, these two here are the only two I wanted you to play.' That was one way that I would get them to concentrate on the ones that I wanted them to play. The ironic thing was that by throwing them in the basket, I usually got them to listen to everything that I gave them. And of course, if they didn't use them on the air, they could use them for giveaways at a record hop or whatever.

"There was a song called 'The Kiss' by Jackie DeShannon around nineteen sixty-three. It became fairly popular in the Boston area. To mark my records when I would promote them, I used to write on them 'Zoom,' 'Boom,' 'Smash,' 'Bang,' and all kinds of crazy things to mark the A side for the stations so people would know what was going on. For 'The Kiss,' I had someone in the office French-kiss all the records so that there were lipstick marks all around the 45 hole of the record. We bought her a tube of lipstick and that was what she did. It was kind of interesting."

Then Al Altman took those specially kissed 45s to the radio stations, where the gag was very well received. "I had one guy at one of the stations, Arnie 'Woo Woo' Ginsburg, who broke a lot of our records." Arnie quickly saw the humor in marking the record with a kiss instead of an *X*, and responded to the joke with a humorous comeback of his own. "Arnie said to me jokingly, 'How can I give this record away? There could be germs on this!' That was the kind of ends I went to, in fun, in order to promote records. It made it interesting."

Oftentimes record collectors will find radio station promotional copies of old 45s that were marked in various ways by the promotion men or by the radio station music directors. Many records carry a stamp of the station's call letters, the designation "Plug Side," or the date the record was received. Those dates are interesting verification of exactly when a record came out, although that was not the real reason they were marked and dated. "A lot of times they would do that to prove that they did get the record. A record might take months after it was released before it would actually break. They would have to dig back in their files. Somebody would say, 'Hey, how come I didn't have this record?' You like to be able to say, 'Yes, you did have the record. We gave it to you four months ago but it is just now breaking.' A lot of records initially broke regionally, like Dick and Deedee's record.

"Sometimes the promotional man would date the record; more often than not the radio station would date it when they received it so that they would have their own record of when they got it. If they had it for a couple of months and nothing happened, it would either go into a pile of records to be given away at record hops, or it would be thrown away. That was the primary way that a station had to know how long it had been since they'd received the song in their record library. Keeping track was really the only way that a station could keep their library from overflowing with songs that didn't ever make it."

CHAPTER 31

Merchandising Records

Merchandising at Liberty was where it all came together. Everything that had come so far was meshed into a product people could buy.

Allan Lavinger

Allan Lavinger came to Liberty on July 4, 1958, and stayed until 1970. He was hired by Al Bennett, who must have really turned on the charm. "I took a cut in pay to come to Liberty, so I was not sure it was a good idea. I was just married, had just bought a house. But it panned out. 'Summertime Blues' was a hit at that time; the Chipmunks came out that fall.

"When I came in, it's like any new thing, I just did everything, I put catalogs together, I did, like, merchandising. I needed a title, so I asked what they were going to call me. So they said, why don't you call yourself 'merchandising director, director of merchandising,' in those words. So that's what I was most of the time. For awhile I did A&R coordination, which is merely the impossible task of trying to get the A&R people to turn in the information in time for us to set type and get the jackets made. Those A&R people were impossible.

"I did packaging. I had the production department under me, the people who did the actual orderings. I used to produce the coverings and packaging. By producing, I mean working with all the people, gathering the information, working with the photographers, the art directors, the designer, the printers, the color separators, all of that sort of thing to get it out.

"I used to write liner notes when they needed just hack stuff to get an album out. They would also hire DJs to write liner notes. That was a legal way to give payola, pay them more than you would normally pay to have them write liner notes.

"At one point Al Bennett was smitten with the General Motors concept of record companies, divisions, like Chevrolet and Buick and Pontiac and all that. So he set up Liberty with Imperial and World Pacific and Blue Note and stereo tape division, and Sunset as a budget line.

"Bobby Vee, Vikki Carr, and Martin Denny had the same manager, Arnie Mills. One day Arnie played a trick on Al Bennett. He made a mock-up of a *Life* magazine cover. He used a photo he took of Bobby Vee looking up, with the Capitol Tower in the background. He ran into Al's office and said, 'Al, look! We got Bobby Vee a *Life* cover all lined up! Here's a mock-up of the cover.' Al almost had apoplexy because of the Capitol building being in the background, another record company entirely. Arnie mumbled something about its being the only photo they had and needing to use it. Al just about came unglued until Arnie finally admitted it was a joke. For years that mock-up was on Al Bennett's coffee table.

"Once we had so many good records out that everyone except the secretaries was sent out to do promotion. They gave me the easiest run, since I was not an experienced promotion person, just to Oakland and Portland and Seattle and Denver. The company had so much money early on, nineteen sixty, they gave every executive and middle management executive a bonus. I'm sure they did it for their own tax reasons. I got a five grand bonus, a lot of money back then. My wife and I planned to go to Hawaii with it, but we never went. We got a divorce instead!"

It's clear that many people liked Al Bennett but that many others didn't. Allan Lavinger explains the discrepancy. "Al Bennett was good to me, so I liked him. He was not good to most people. He was a sharpie. Pulling every trick in the book, holding back royalties, holding back reserves, and all that other stuff.

"I worked at Liberty from nineteen fifty-eight until UA cleaned house in nineteen seventy. What happened was, there was a great deal of animosity between UA and Liberty. Mike Stewart personally fired me along with all the others; he was a big wheel and a big, obese guy. Al was head of the board of directors, but there were a lot of things that they did not like. One day they had a board meeting in Carmel. The story I got, they asked Al to step out in the corridor for a couple of minutes, and they voted him out while he was out of the room. Then they took over and fired the whole team, including me.

"Al Bennett formed Cream Records. Then, after that folded, he bought into Carol Shelby's mag wheel company. I spent twelve years with Al in that company."

CHAPTER 32

Radio Airplay

Once a song has been written, published, hooked up with an artist, packaged, promoted, publicized, distributed, and merchandised, there is only one remaining thing that can be done. It needs to get played on the radio. That defines success for a record label.

Sure, the public needs to buy the record. But that is beyond the control of the company. If everyone has done his or her job, and if the record is any good (whatever that means), then if it is played on the air, the public will buy it. It if is not played, no one will know it ever existed.

In spite of the efforts of the Liberty promotion staff to travel around the countryside chasing transmitters, it was really the work they did in LA, New York City, and a few other key markets that made or broke hits. Few records were picked by a DJ in Topeka, Kansas, to become a national hit. But the DJs in Leavenworth did pay close attention to what was being played in the big cities on the coasts when developing their own stations' play lists.

There were two kinds of DJs when it came to Liberty Records. There were the few, huge, highly paid influential DJs in LA or New York who had listeners numbering in the hundreds of thousands. And there were the other 90 percent of DJs, who worked for little more than minimum wage and whose listeners numbered in the thousands or even hundreds.

One of the latter-type DJs was Bob Barber, known in the fifties and sixties as the Morning Mayor of Topeka, the capital city of the state of Kansas.

One top DJ who helped make hits was Jimmy O'Neill. Jimmy is best known nationally for hosting the TV program "Shindig" in the mid-sixties. But he had already been a top LA DJ for half a decade before the national opportunity came along.

Bob Barber

Bob Barber came to K-TOP (Kay-Top) radio in Topeka from Baltimore and station WITH. Before Barber came to Topeka, K-TOP (*TOP* stands for Topeka) was a Mutual network station, except for a morning program on which the owner of the station sang a live show. The owner's name was Axton, and in the mid-fifties his sons came along and convinced him that rock 'n' roll was the coming thing and that K-TOP should become a rock station.

"Charlie Christian [radio name], the oldest son, was a music student and a very good musician. He was with the Second Field Army marching band in Baltimore as an arranger. He would monitor the stations up and down the East Coast. WITH was a powerhouse in rock 'n' roll. K-TOP wanted to do that in Topeka.

"Charlie Christian liked what I was doing on the air and asked me to come out here. I was trying to support a family in Baltimore and not doing very well, so the story he told me sounded good. Of course, he gave me a story that I swallowed hook, line, and sinker." Charlie Christian and the other son, Dave Axton, were both DJs on K-TOP.

"I couldn't believe what I got into when I came out here in 1957. K-TOP was a little cement-block building that was one story high. We had one big room, and all the salespeople and the copy people and the john were in that one room.

"I walked into this cement-block building and thought, what am I doing here? You had to wade through rosebushes to get in the one doorway. My first radio job in Cumberland, Maryland, was better than this! But we had a lot of fun, and I got to enjoy it. Later they added on a barracks for offices from Forbes Air Force Base when it closed down.

"KTOP was top dog here for eight years with rock 'n' roll. Then [a competing rock 'n' roll station] KEWI [KeeWee] came on with more power. And they had no qualms about letting their signal spill over." KTOP was fourteen ninety, KEWI was fourteen forty, so spilling over meant running very close together on the AM dial. "KEWI used to monitor KTOP. If, for example, I announced that next up was a certain Elvis song, they would rush that record on before I could get it played. With their expanded signal, anybody trying to get Elvis Presley would tune the dial to where it came in best, and wind up on KEWI."

Was a DJ like Bob Barber able to be influential, to pick a song for a hit and push it and create a hit? For that matter, did promotion men from places like Liberty come around and try to influence them? Not really.

"We were so led by the nose, that unless an artist was local from Kansas or Oklahoma or even Topeka, we had very little control over it. We were not hit makers, we were followers. We followed *Billboard* and that sort of thing. Records came out in such quantities, we just played established hits."

Well, then, did an artist's being on a certain label make a song more attractive to a K-TOP DJ? Was the fact that records by Bobby Vee and Johnny Burnette were big hits on Liberty mean that a record by a new act like Dick and Deedee got a closer look or a better reception because it, too, was on Liberty?

"I don't remember that specifically. You would know that a Beatles record or an RCA record would have the push behind it to eventually become popular in Topeka, and we wanted to be the first to play it. But I don't think we were influenced much by labels. I don't remember anything specifically."

In the very early 1960s, K-TOP had a pick album each week. Cuts were played from the album all day long for that entire week. How were the pick albums chosen? "Some of them were just plain obvious; some of them were arbitrary. You didn't have a reason to push one album more than another, unless you had a favorite artist you were pushing or they had a single going. Stores would sell albums because a hit single was on it. And maybe the hit single was available in limited number and the album in a greater number. So you went to get the single and got the album, a bait-and-switch thing."

The pick album on K-TOP for the week of June 3, 1963, was *Bobby Vee Meets the Ventures*. Was featuring that LP a deal with a record store or a distributor?

Wouldn't Liberty have been happy to have the big, top-forty station in town feature their LP for a full week? "The pick was arbitrary, or someone we liked." If not as a response to a promo man's efforts, then why was Bobby Vee picked? "Well, Bobby Vee was a very big name in this town. He had a fan club here. He did very well in this town saleswise. He was very well liked here. But there is a sad story [with Bobby Vee] here.

"Bill McCall and Johnny Dark [other K-TOP DJs] and I brought him to Topeka, to Meadow Acres Ballroom, at great expense. We had to borrow the up-front money. I remember to the penny, the three of us borrowed seven hundred dollars to pay him the up-front money. But we lost our ass. The worst part of that was, we didn't make enough at the gate to cover the second seven hundred. But the turnout was pretty good.... We promoted the heck out of it. We had free use of air time, and man, did we use it! But we did not make the second seven hundred, and I had to make it good all on my own. These guys had talked me into it, although I can't put the blame on them because I was enthusiastic, but they didn't have any money and then they'd left town or something.

"We still hear from Bobby. He has done some shows here in town, and has been back on K-TOP with interviews here recently. He has fond memories of Topeka. After all, he got paid!"

Jimmy O'Neill

Jimmy O'Neill started in the music business in Enid, Oklahoma, as a local DJ. He had moved to WKY radio in Oklahoma City in 1957, when he was seventeen. After climbing the radio ladder some more, Jimmy was discovered in Pittsburgh at WTAE by Jack Kent Cooke and hired for the new KRLA in Los Angeles, a new rock station, formerly a country music outlet.

Jimmy was very popular, and soon had his own local TV show on Channel 13, "Teenage Nightclub." He became the top LA DJ when he was just nineteen years old, and was also associated with Pandora's Box nightclub by the time he was twenty-one. He was the host of ABC-TV's "Shindig" from 1964 to 1966. In spite of its countrified name, "Shindig" was a rock 'n' roll program. At one point ABC had considered making it a country music program, but when those plans were abandoned, the name was retained.

Jimmy O'Neill gained national fame through "Shindig," but his fame in LA was much more lasting.

"My association with Liberty was really through Sharon Sheeley, who[m] I was married to and dating in a period from nineteen fifty-nine to nineteen sixty-six. Bud Dain, fresh from Omaha, walked into the studios at KRLA in late nineteen fifty-nine and introduced himself as the local promotion man from Liberty Records. I liked him on sight and we became good friends.

"I already knew Liberty from my pre–LA days—Alvin, Simon, and Theodore, by Ross Bagdasarian; Eddie Cochran. So I remember when I was still pretty new in town, one of the first people they introduced me to was Ross Bagdasarian. They told me about all the tricks they used in the studio to make the Chipmunk hits. I was absolutely starstruck, to tell you the truth. I was a lot more starstruck with Liberty Records, to be quite frank, than I was with the majors like RCA and Capitol. All

Jimmy O'Neill as he looked in early 1991, spinning the oldies on his old station, KRLA (1110 AM) in LA.

of a sudden Liberty had become the hot label that made all these hits, and then I was meeting these people and they were red hot.

"Bud Dain took me down to some dive in Long Beach to see Jackie DeShannon before she released her first song. I was absolutely astounded by her talent. Bud later married Jackie DeShannon. I introduced Jackie to Sharon, and they wrote several hit records together.

"I used to hang out at Liberty now and then, and I got acquainted with many of the people there. I had so many personal friends there, I saw Liberty from several different perspectives: the professional viewpoint, the friendship viewpoint, and even more personal through my girlfriend—later, wife—Sharon, who was under contract to Liberty's Metric Music.

"I remember to this day—every time I hear something in the news about the Cuban Missile Crisis—I remember being in Al Bennett's office when somebody came running in and said, 'President Kennedy's gone on television. We're on the verge of war with Russia! Because they've got missiles in Cuba!'

"Al had this giant TV screen behind a curtain. He pushed a button on his desk and the curtain opened; he pushed another button and the TV came on. This was nineteen sixty-two, and I thought, 'Whoa, this is some office we've got here!'

"A dozen of us, Snuffy, executives I was visiting, we all watched President

Kennedy's speech in Al Bennett's office. So I have lots of not just fine memories but freeze-frame historical moments that I experienced in the building on Sunset Boulevard that used to be Liberty.

"Liberty had no competition [when it came to promotion]. They were the most aggressive record promoters in the LA record business on the West Coast in that era. That was the first thing that impressed me about them: Gol, these guys never give up! And they are so nice about it. I mean, they can be pushy without being offensive.

"So I remember being very impressed that they had such an efficient and professional and likable bunch of executives over there. I'm sure they worked very hard at becoming my best friend, and I fell for it lock, stock, and barrel. They were great at it, and they were very likable guys and they became my best buddies. Bud Dain began inviting me out to bum around, go to a movie, go to a party, bum around, do this, do that, and he paid all the bills, so I was having a great time. We were double-dating.

"I didn't feel like I was being bribed by these people who were wining and dining me all the time. I really thought they really liked me and I really enjoyed their company. I felt like we were really best buddies. They were just great at that. They really had a sharp promotion department.

"And of course, during that era, Snuff Garrett was so hot, everything he touched in the studio turned to gold. They made it a point for me to meet Snuff Garrett and Bobby Vee and Jackie DeShannon and all their artists, so I remember thinking, 'I really feel like a part of the Liberty family, even though I'm not.' I don't know how many disc jockeys they did that on. But it sure worked with me. I loved those people, their stars, their producers, their promotion people, from Al Bennett and Si Waronker on down. So I felt like a part of the Liberty family, and that was how they operated.

"The fact is, it was easy to feel comfortable in that situation, because they were making genuine good product. It was kind of fun to be the first person in the world to play Bobby Vee's brand-new record or something like that, you know? I felt like a part of history. So I was just eating it up, and naturally they were too."

How does Jimmy O'Neill respond to the complaints by Jan & Dean, Eddie Cochran's sister, and the Rivingtons that Liberty did not promote their records well enough? "As a disc jockey, I think they were topnotch in the promotion. My response to that question is that artists never think they are getting enough. They always want more. But I know that Bud used to say to me, 'Jimmy, I've got a dozen new releases. This is "the One."' And I used to think, 'Aw, too bad about the other eleven guys!' They had to do a little shotgunning. If they were going to get into the top ten, they had to test here and test there to see which one or two they were going to put the full force of the company behind.

"Liberty always had more worthy product than they could promote 100 percent. Unless they are number one no star is ever completely happy. Especially when they are prebeing the company's number one point of focus. I remember when Jan & Dean were just starting out here in Southern California, before they were on Liberty, they were a local hit here in Los Angeles. [When Liberty picked them up], I am sure they were bitter about not being snapped up as the number-one push. But there came a time when [Eddie Cochran, Jan & Dean, and the Rivingtons] for a moment at least, each was the top priority at Liberty Records.

"I remember when they first brought me the Rivingtons' 'Papa-Oom-Mow-Mow.' I remember when they first brought me Jan & Dean right after they'd signed them, and Jackie DeShannon. But it is interesting those artists should make that comment, because I remember with every one of those artists, the full force of the company coming down on me. Maybe it just didn't happen soon enough for them!

"Bud would call me: 'Jimmy! This is so hot, Al wants to talk to you.' I'd be sitting in Al Bennett's office, and he'd be personally hyping this record! Maybe these artists weren't aware of activities like that.

"But when you are hot like Liberty was, how can he come off sincere when he tells you he has twelve number-one records? Especially when they know that we are only going to add three songs total to the play list for the week! And we gotta deal with *all* the record companies. So that is what they are up against."

Besides the promotion by Liberty, what did it mean to the likes of Jimmy O'Neill when a new record showed up wearing the Liberty logo? Was the fact that a song was on a Liberty record mean that it was likely to be worth taking seriously?

"Once you have seen a dynamite hit on a certain record label, especially if it was a record you personally loved, you do notice that label when it comes across your desk, and you are much more inclined to listen with a keen ear to a label that has [been] established in your mind as both a successful label and a label that makes records that you like and would enjoy playing on your show. Sure, absolutely.

"For me, the end of Liberty Records, the end of the party, was when they went public and a lot of executives got burned. It wasn't fun anymore. Everyone thought that they were going to get rich, the stock did zoom for a while, then it began to go down. The feelings and the ambience in the building changed."

The more things change, however, the more they stay the same. Today Jimmy O'Neill is back at his old radio station, KRLA, playing the best oldies on the air.

Part Three

Four Liberty Superstars

Liberty had many recording artists who sold a great many records and who were extremely important to the company (and to popular music) in their day. Julie London made the company in the mid-fifties. David Seville saved the company in the late fifties. Eddie Cochran brought rock 'n' roll to the company. As important as these and other artists were in their day to Liberty, they were merely the first three of many artists who played a major role in the history of Liberty and the development of American popular music.

But certain artists had a special place in the Liberty family, and who also hold a special place in the annals of 1950s and 1960s popular music. One of those is Bobby Vee. Coming to Liberty in the late 1950s, Bobby became the first great Liberty superstar and one of the most respected and talented of the "teen idols," a true male mainstay of popular music in the U.S.

At almost the same time, the Ventures came to Liberty via Dolton Records. The Ventures are the most successful instrumental group in the world and have influenced millions of guitarists, both famous and unknown, in the past thirty years. No one at Liberty sold more LPs than the Ventures.

In the early 1960s, the first female superstar since Julie London came to Liberty Records. Jackie DeShannon had been recording for years but without any national success. A regional hit in the Midwest brought her to the attention of Liberty, and she has been a force to contend with in the music world ever since.

And also in the early 1960s, Jan & Dean came to Liberty. Unlike the other Liberty superstars, Jan & Dean came with a proven track record of hits at other labels. Also unlike Bobby Vee and the Ventures, Jan & Dean, once at Liberty, got off to a very slow start. Their early Liberty records charted very poorly, if at all. But over the years, they grew to a level equaled by very few at Liberty or elsewhere, and influenced artists from the Beach Boys to Herman's Hermits, both groups of which were big Jan & Dean fans.

Bobby Vee, the Ventures, Jackie DeShannon, and Jan & Dean, interviewed in depth, have made comments that provide great insight into their careers, the Liberty company, and rock 'n' roll of the 1950s and 1960s.

CHAPTER 33

Bobby Vee

By far the most prolific hit maker in the history of Liberty Records was Bobby Vee. As documented in my previous book, *The Beatle Myth,* in the wake of the subsequent popularity of the British groups, of soul/Motown, of acid rock, and other 1960s music, Bobby Vee and his contemporaries have been largely forgotten by the music business and by rock historians, if not by their fans. However, Bobby Vee and his peers—Tommy Roe, Bobby Rydell, Ricky Nelson, Paul Anka, Bobby Vinton, Frankie Avalon, Neil Sedaka, Dion, and others—were the superstars of their day, the male mainstays of the golden decade of rock 'n' roll.

However, the average 1960s British artist had just fourteen hits in America, compared to thirty-seven for the male mainstays of rock 'n' roll.

Bobby Vee, all by himself, had more hits than Billy J. Kramer with the Dakotas and the Swinging Blue Jeans and Wayne Fontana and the Mindbenders and Freddy and the Dreamers and the Zombies and the Nashville Teens and the Honeycombs and Manfred Mann and the Manfred Mann Earth Band, combined! You can add to that impressive invasion hit list the longer list of hits of Gerry and the Pacemakers, or the Dave Clark Five, or Chad and Jeremy, or Peter and Gordon, or even the Animals, or the entire hit list of the Kinks, and you still won't have a combined list of hits equal to the hit list of just one of the more popular of the male mainstays, like Ricky Nelson or Paul Anka!

Bobby Vee (born Robert Thomas Velline) was one of the earliest and most successful of the rock 'n' roll teen idol–male mainstays. His career began by unfortunate happenstance. Bobby's older brother, Bill, had some friends who got together and jammed on guitars and drums in a nieghbor's basement. Bobby, at fifteen, was too young to join in. In February 1959, however, they were all excited about the rock 'n' roll show "The Biggest Show of Stars for 1959" coming to their town, Fargo, North Dakota. The show included Ritchie Valens, the Big Bopper, and Buddy Holly. Tragically, as dramatized in the movies *The Buddy Holly Story* and *La Bamba,* on the way to the show on February 3, 1959, a plane crash took the lives of three of the show's headliners, stars Ritchie Valens ("Donna," "La Bamba," 1959), the Big Bopper ("Chantilly Lace," 1958), and Buddy Holly ("Peggy Sue," "That'll Be the Day," 1957).

The plane was a private charter hired by these artists to allow them to get to the next city of the tour early enough to do their laundry. Dion Di Mucci, also on the tour, had wanted to take the charter, but the tour manager wouldn't allow him to go, as he had promised Dion's mother to take good care of Dion.

The remaining acts in the show included Dion and the Belmonts, Frankie Sardo, and the new Crickets. Today any one of those remaining acts (except perhaps

415

Bobby Vee in the 1959, pre–Liberty, "Suzie Baby" days, when he was getting calls from various labels. *(Photo by Gail Messerschmidt; courtesy Bobby Vee.)*

Sardo) would be considered able to carry a show solo. But in 1959 each act would play for only a quarter hour or so, then leave the stage. Without Valens, the biggest current star on the bill, and the Bopper and Holly, the show was considered too short to go on. Soon Frankie Avalon ("Dede Dinah," 1958; "Venus," 1959), newcomer Fabian ("I'm a Man," 1959), and Jimmy Clanton ("Just a Dream," 1958) were to be added to fill the void, plus Paul Anka ("Diana," 1957; "You Are My Destiny," 1958) after Frankie fell ill.

The Shadows. Bobby Vee is in front; his brother Bill is behind him.

But the substitutions took time to arrange. Meanwhile there was a show to do that night, and the "Biggest Show" had been severely shrunk by the tragedy.

In a last-minute attempt to salvage the evening, an appeal was sent out by the local rock 'n' roll station KFGO (most towns had only one station that played the kids' music) for local talent to fill in.

Bill Velline's "group" volunteered. They went downtown and bought matching ties (for twenty-five cents a man) and sweaters and made up a group name backstage on the spot, the Shadows. By then Bobby had been added to their lineup, since he was the only one in the neighborhood who wanted to sing or who knew any lyrics. The group had never played for an audience before, in fact had only formed two weeks earlier. But Bobby's singing style on "Bye Bye Love" and "Long Tall Sally" resembled that of his recently deceased idol, Buddy Holly, and they were warmly received by the audience. On the strength of this one show, the Shadows began playing for dances around the area.

Their local popularity as a party dance band led after a few months to a deal with a local record label, Soma Records. "Suzie Baby" was the resulting release, written by Bobby Vee, performed by "Bobby Vee and the Shadows with vocal by Bobby Vee."

"Suzie Baby" was a moody ballad, an excellent debut, somewhat reminiscent of Buddy Holly on "Well, All Right" and of Holly soundalike Robin Luke on "Susie Darlin'" (1959). The use of the name Sue, as in "Peggy Sue" and "Susie Darlin'," was probably no coincidence. The regional popularity of "Suzie Baby" was great enough to get the attention of Snuff Garrett at Liberty Records out in California. Soon Liberty's 45 release of the song was making Bobby famous.

As for the Shadows. Well, bands were not "in" at the time. Even Buddy Holly had disbanded his original Crickets and adopted an orchestra sound. So Liberty did not retain the Shadows. Bobby tried his hand at producing the Shadows, creating the Vee Record Company of Moorehead, Minnesota. "What'll I Do" was Vee #001, written by Bill Velline and performed by "Bill Velline with the Shadows." But it didn't happen for them.

Bobby Vee talked to me about his career in a series of telephone and backstage conversations between August 1981, and August 1990, in Sauk Rapids, Minnesota; Topeka, Kansas; and Kansas City, Missouri.

> **Doc Rock:** Bobby, when someone who does not know about your involvement in rock 'n' roll asks you what you do for a living, what do you tell them?
>
> **Bobby Vee:** I generally say, "I'm in the music business," which I guess I have been in one way or another for the last thirty years. During the 1960s, I was primarily a recording artist, although I would do many tours. I worked a lot on the road in the early 1960s, and the later 1960s, not so much. Through the 1970s, I guess I really learned to work in front of an audience and it is a totally different environment and experience from being in the studio.
>
> **Doc Rock:** I've seen you in concert eight times between nineteen sixty-three and nineteen ninety-one, and your showmanship is excellent. Your voice is 100 percent, you respect your material and your audience, and you deliver truly exciting entertainment for your fans.
>
> **Bobby Vee:** Thanks.
>
> **Doc Rock:** We all know that selling records makes money. As far as being "in the music business," which generated the most income for you, your Liberty records or your tours?
>
> **Bobby Vee:** There is a lot of money to be made in the record business, but an awful lot of it is turned back into producing new product, the next hit 45 or the next LP. The majority of the money that was made came from being out on the road. You can do as much of that as you want to do, generally. On the other hand, a hit record, a million-selling record, if it pays the artists 7 percent or 8 percent would generate sixty-seventy thousand....
>
> **Doc Rock:** That's not too bad, several years' salary for most people!
>
> **Bobby Vee:** That's not too bad, but there are a lot of expenses that go along with that.
>
> **Doc Rock:** Were the tours made possible by having the Liberty hit records, or did the tour make the hits happen?

A publicity photo of Bobby Vee *(center)* with Liberty executives. (Back row: Don Blocker, Al Bennett; front row: Arnold Mills, Bobby Vee, Johnny Thompson.)

Bobby Vee: It seems to happen all sorts of different ways. When I first started out, we worked the area without a record.
Doc Rock: The Shadows in Minnesota?
Bobby Vee: Yes, then eventually we were lucky enough to come up with a hit, and that enabled us to go and appear in a lot more places. But there are bands that are together for six, seven, eight years and are able to make a reasonable income, enough to keep the band together, then come up with a hit record that takes them just that much higher. There does not seem to be any set format for how it develops.
Doc Rock: Do the royalties on a record run out after a given length of time? When they reissue "Rubber Ball" again on a CD thirty years after it was a hit on Liberty, do you get money again? Or is it like TV shows, where the residuals run out?
Bobby Vee: No, the royalties continue. And a hit record, especially now when there is so much interest by collectors in original rock 'n' roll, there are a lot of reissues that will sell consistently but in small quantities.
Doc Rock: Do those sales accrue toward the status of million-seller for a record that did not quite sell a million when it was first a hit? Do reissues on either 45s or LPs or CDs count, or is it just the original Liberty 45 that is counted?
Bobby Vee: The certification of a million-seller can come at any point. As soon as a record company can document and prove that they sold a million records.
Doc Rock: So is the certification on the song, or on the individual record?
Bobby Vee: No, it is on the individual record.
Doc Rock: So inclusion of a hit on a various artists LP won't count?
Bobby Vee: No, it is on the original product only.
Doc Rock: Did you know the other Liberty acts very well, like Gene McDaniels or Dick and Deedee?

Above and opposite: Bobby Vee records were released on every Liberty label variation.

Bobby Vee: It was quite a small label, there weren't that many acts there, so we were fairly close and occasionally our schedules would come together and we would be in the studio at the same time.

Doc Rock: So you did not use independent studios—Liberty had its own studios?

Bobby Vee: Yes, Liberty had its own studios, and we also used some of the studios that were available in Hollywood. I cut most of my records at United Studios in Hollywood. And then of course, people like Johnny Burnette were having hits at Liberty at the same time that I was in the early 1960s and we did a few tours together.

Doc Rock: On Colpix Records there was a *Teenage Triangle* LP that featured three Colpix artists, James Darren, Paul Peterson, and Shelley Fabares. This LP, and a follow-up, *More Teenage Triangle,* [are] very collectable today. It would have been great if Liberty had done a teenage-triangle-type LP with, say, Troy Shondell or Johnny Burnette, and Bobby Vee and perhaps Timi Yuro....

Bobby Vee: There was an LP that was put out, a similar type of concept.

Doc Rock: Really? I will look for it. [Note: I found it!]

Bobby Vee: Yes, I have a copy of it. It had three of my songs, plus three each from the Fleetwoods, Johnny Burnette, and the Ventures! It was called *Teensville.*

Doc Rock: Did Liberty direct your career, outside of the records? That is, did they tell you how to dress or walk or talk or anything?

Bobby Vee: No. It was the record business, just making records. Cranking out the hits.

Doc Rock: Back to the hits—tell me about your Liberty sessions. When recording your next hit, did you record various versions of a song and then pick out one "take" to release? And, did you record many songs, then get surprised by which one Liberty decided to release as a single? Just how did the recording sessions and song selections go?

Bobby Vee: Generally speaking, in the United States anyway, the product was all well thought-out and the people involved with the product, Snuff Garrett and I, did have the final say on what was released. In Europe they would sometimes pull something, some song that they felt was right for their market and release it, and I would have no way of knowing. I still don't know, I've never kept up on it that closely. But I know there is product, singles and LPs that were released, different combinations of songs than we put out in the U.S. Occasionally I come across one of them and get a surprise!

Doc Rock: When your original Liberty contract expired, did the company make a good offer and did you renew?

Bobby Vee: Yes, I signed with them in nineteen fifty-nine, early nineteen-sixty I guess, and I was with that label for the majority of eighteen years.

Snuff Garrett and Bobby Vee in the studio. *(Courtesy Snuff Garrett.)*

Doc Rock: Wow! How long was the term of the original contract?
Bobby Vee: The original contract was for five years.
Doc Rock: OK, that is what I'm leading up to. Another Liberty act, Jan & Dean, had a five-year deal, and when it came up for renewal, Liberty offered the exact same package they had offered them before. Of course, Jan & Dean were a much bigger attraction by that time and were not too happy with the same old deal. Did Liberty do better by you, make you a better offer at renewal time when your five years [were] up?
Bobby Vee: I felt we had a fairly good deal when I came in, because Liberty was buying not just me but also "Suzie Baby," a record that was already a hit. We were, in fact, negotiating with six or seven different labels, and chose Liberty not just because they offered the most money, but because we felt it was a *good* label.
Doc Rock: So when it came to records or money, you got along well with Liberty?

Bobby Vee: Yes, my working relationship with the label was always good. When I came back, I always got a better shake than I had before.

Doc Rock: I know that when Jan & Dean came to Liberty originally, they were turned down, so Jan & Dean went with Challenge Records, then later got signed to Liberty. So, maybe their deal was more or less on Liberty's terms when it finally happened?

Bobby Vee: I don't know what kind of a deal that they had. Generally at that time, artists were getting from 3 percent to about 6 percent.

Doc Rock: OK, if the artist's percentage was small, then did Liberty put out all of the expense of producing the songs?

Bobby Vee: No! Those expenses did come out of the royalties. You'll hear artists complaining about having million-selling records and still not making any money off their record royalties. That's because they are paying back costs to the label for things that the label fronted initially: studio time, musician fees, publicity, all kinds of overhead.

Doc Rock: But you got paid all right?

Bobby Vee: But I think I am just about to get back into a royalty position with them now. When I left I was a hundred thirty-four thousand dollars in the hole. Because toward the end of my contract, I was getting a guarantee against royalties and the albums that didn't sell worked against that. So I have been paying that off out of my royalties all these years. Just think of the money the record company makes. I got 6 percent, they get maybe thirty cents per record probably. They make a lot of money off that stuff.

Doc Rock: That money provides security.

Bobby Vee: Well, Gary Troxel, the lead singer of the Fleetwoods, never trusted the business and didn't tour after a while. He kept his job in a Seattle grocery store as a manager or something, and they replaced him on the road.

Doc Rock: Over the years, your vocal quality changed. Was that on purpose, as a result of training, or sort of changing with the times? Your vibrato, for example, changed from a short, shallow vibrato to a longer, deeper one. I like both.

Bobby Vee: The only voice training I ever had was to teach me how to use my voice without hurting myself. Working with singers is tough. You want them to be who they are but use their voice so they don't blow themselves out but can be themselves. You can hear me sort of growing up on vinyl. There were records that I wish I hadn't made, or records that I made for the wrong reason. For the most part, I have always had a sense for doing things I liked and paying attention to my own sense of how it sounded and felt and knowing when it was right. Snuffy was always good about that. He let me do my own vocals. He would make suggestions and that kind of thing, but he never tried to sing the song for me, which a lot of times happens with a producer and can be a big mistake.

Doc Rock: [Jokingly] Is it true that you knew Jackie DeShannon personally?

Bobby Vee: Ha! Yes, I have known her for many years. She's an old friend.

Doc Rock: She wrote two of your songs, "Hark! Is That a Cannon I Hear!" and "You Won't Forget Me," and was at Liberty, so I figured you knew her. Plus, I have the soundtrack LP from the movie you starred in with her, *C'mon, Let's Live a Little*.

Bobby Vee: Oh, sure.

Doc Rock: How come is it that, in the old days, Hollywood rock 'n' roll in movies was never authentic, was never the same as real, popular rock 'n' roll on the radio? More recently, movies like *Batman* are full of authentic music, and every other film has a soundtrack full of 1960s oldies. But in the 1960s the music in films was usually kitsch, even when done by great artists.

Bobby Vee: Yes, I know, it was a terrible situation.

Doc Rock: Yeah, who picked the songs you two did in that movie? Where were the hits? Jackie's "(Don't Take Me) For Granted" is pretty good, sort of a Phil Spector type of tune, and your "Over and Over" was a nice country song, but by and large the music is not typical Jackie DeShannon or Bobby Vee; it is typical Hollywood imitation.

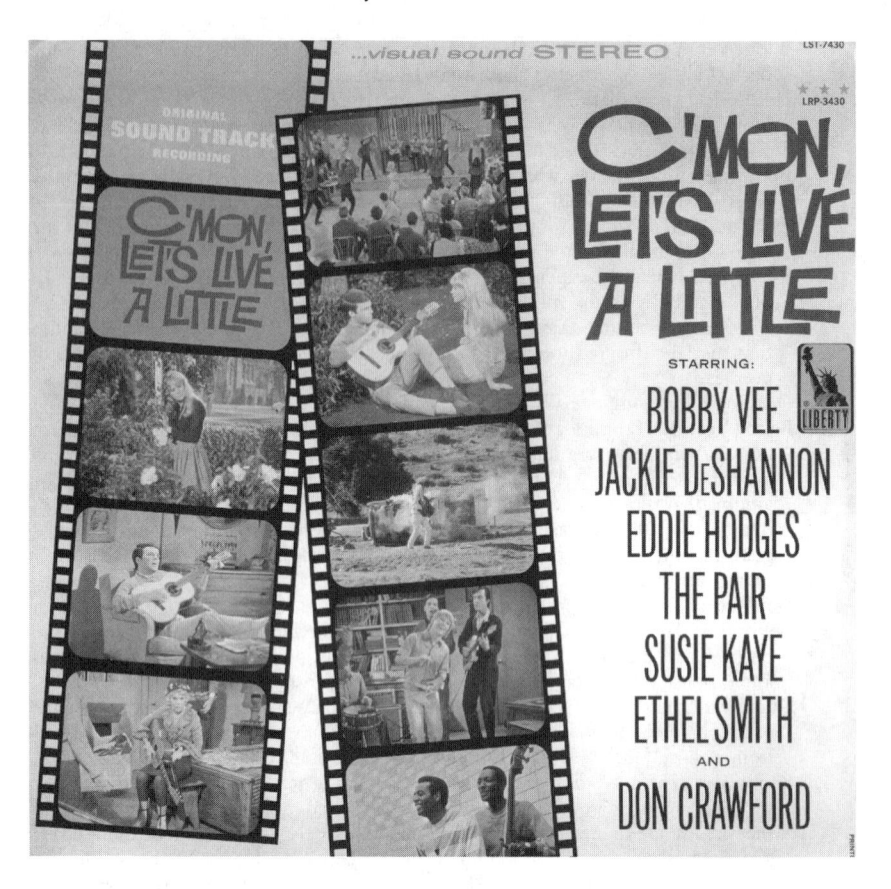

Bobby Vee and Jackie DeShannon starred in the film *C'mon, Let's Live a Little*, and Liberty released this soundtrack LP.

> Bobby Vee: And you are right, that's not the case anymore. What happens now is—well, in the old days, it was a case of people not in the record business trying to be! They may be good at making movies, but they are not necessarily tuned in to the contemporary top-forty market.
> Doc Rock: Who was your usual producer, Snuff Garrett?
> Bobby Vee: Yes, Snuffy produced most of my things.
> Doc Rock: What happened to him on the movie then? Did the movie people just push him aside and take over?
> Bobby Vee: Yeah! He was not really even considered for it.
> Doc Rock: That was crazy!
> Bobby Vee: Yes, it was crazy. Especially in view of the fact that in later years Snuffy made a lot of money for the movie market through LPs, the Clint Eastwood things, and the Burt Reynolds things he does for movies, *Every Which Way But Loose* and those soundtracks. What he does is he puts material together and artists together and goes into the studio as if he is cutting hit songs with hit artists. And of course the end product is a sensational LP!
> Doc Rock: That's great. But I had high hopes when I bought the *C'mon, Let's Live a Little* LP, but was frankly disappointed. It turned out not to be what I was expecting!

Bobby Vee: Yes, it is very unfortunate. And there were very talented people involved in it; Leon Russell did a fair amount of the arranging and played keyboard on the whole LP, Glen Campbell was playing guitar, and so forth, so some of the top studio people were in on it. But if you're sitting there with a song that doesn't make sense, that has no appeal...

Doc Rock: So you were aware of what was going on at the time—you realized that the music was not the greatest?

Bobby Vee: Yes, we knew that most of the material was weak, but there was no option. You did your best. There were a couple of good songs in there, though.

Doc Rock: Speaking of good songs, the flip sides of your records were about the best of any artist I ever heard, usually every bit as good as the A sides. How did you happen to have so many good B sides, and how come you didn't have more two-sided hits?

Bobby Vee: I'll tell you, I was probably lucky to have had as many as I did. [Bobby Vee had eight two-sided hits on Liberty.] It was surprising, but it was a different approach to the record business. When we went in and recorded, we always tried to come out with two strong pieces of material. A lot of labels, including Liberty, did that. But eventually what happened was that, I think the industry got to the point that they didn't want to, well, it diminishes your sales when your air play is split, if one station is playing one side and the other station is playing the other side. That really does diminish the impact that the record will make. So, because of that, labels started putting out promotional copies with one song on both sides of the record. That practice also eliminated music directors' having to look at the records and say, "Which side do they want me to play? I haven't got time to be sitting here listening to both sides of all of these records." So I think it was probably by mutual agreement that they quit allowing two-sided hits by releasing one-sided records to radio stations.

Doc Rock: I'm glad 45s in the stores still had flip sides even after that.

Bobby Vee: You're the guy that used to walk up to the jukebox and play the B side, right?

Doc Rock: Yeah, right!

Bobby Vee: I used to do the same thing! I was the king of the B sides! I loved to do that. I already knew what the A side sounded like because I heard it on the radio. But lemme see what is on the B side! Maybe that was why it was so important to me to have a good B side, I guess.

Doc Rock: You mentioned Snuffy. When I was a kid buying Liberty records, I always saw that on the label and wondered just what the heck a "Snuff Garrett" might be!

Bobby Vee: He was the big producer at Liberty. He was one of the first to command royalties on the records he produced, as well as to get credit, his name on the label. When Snuff came to Liberty, they basically had Julie London, the Chipmunks, and Eddie Cochran, and that was about it. After that, Snuffy brought in so many others.

Doc Rock: Like Bobby Vee and Johnny Burnette.

Bobby Vee: The first session I did was a split session with Johnny Burnette. We each had an hour and a half to do a record. He did the first hour and a half, and he recorded "Cincinnati Fireball" and "Dreamin'." It was a killer in the studio. See, I'm sitting there, how old was I, sixteen or seventeen, listening to this song. Incredible string section and everything. It was amazing. Then I went in and cut a cover record of a hit in England, "What Do You Want," which was really great, a nice production. But it scared the heck out of me, trying to follow Johnny Burnette's session. It was pretty intimidating, really. My record came out first and got to number ninety-three. Then Burnette's came out. Bam! It's a hit. That is when Snuffy went in and said, "It's time to renegotiate." Which Liberty gladly did.

Doc Rock: In the studio, did you record live with the orchestra, or did Snuff Garrett record the instrumental track first and then have you dub in the vocals later?

Bobby Vee: All of the recording I did was done live, especially through the early 1960s. It changed a bit later as the technology sort of unfolded and more tracks became

**DEFINITELY NOT A MAYBE...
DEFINITELY A HIT!!!**
MAYBE JUST TODAY
56014
BOBBY VEE
PRODUCED BY DALLAS SMITH

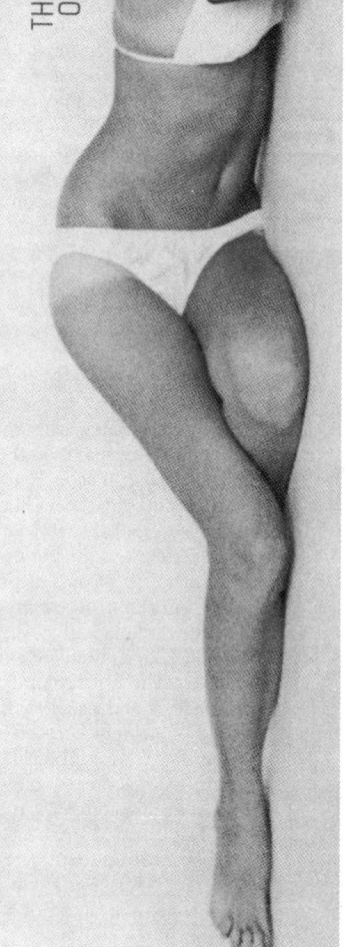

LIBERTY
A PRODUCT OF LIBERTY RECORDS

THE LIBERTY BELLE GIVES YOU THE HOTTEST OF THE HOT!

available, and people really got into overdubbing parts and that kind of thing. But all of the early songs were done live in the studio.

Doc Rock: That must have been very exciting, recording live with the orchestra, instead of just sitting alone with headphones.

Bobby Vee: Yes, it is. It's exciting having that many people involved in the same ... mission, I guess you'd call it. A lot of effort, a lot of work went into it. It was particularly demanding of the engineer, to mix everything that was coming in. And of course, the arranger had to have all of his "dots" in the right places. But you're right, it was exciting, a wonderful way to record. Much later I went down to Nashville to do some recording with a friend of mine, Roger Cook, a songwriter and producer, and he suggested that we go in and do the session live. It was really fun! I enjoyed approaching music from that standpoint again.

Doc Rock: Of course, there is a lot more chance that someone will goof up that way and ruin a take, isn't there? I have tens of thousands of 1950s and 1960s singles now. The *first* one I ever bought was your nineteen sixty-two hit "Please Don't Ask About Barbara." I have heard that it took like fifty-two takes to get the guitar part right on that one in nineteen sixty-two, and you had to sing the song fifty-two times straight! Although Tommy Allsup, who was the guitarist on that session, has told me that it did not take fifty-two takes.

Bobby Vee: Yeah, well it wasn't quite that many takes, but it might as well have been! It was in an awkward key for the guitarist to play, and we sat for that for—I don't know—it probably took us two hours to get the one song. This was at a time when you were given about forty-five minutes to do each song!

Doc Rock: Did you feel that what you were recording was your own sound, or was it created by producers? It has been often said that Elvis was better at Sun, that his personal style was diluted at RCA, or that Roy Orbison did better stuff at Sun than at Monument, or even that the early Buddy Holly stuff with his own Crickets was better than later in New York with the orchestra.

Bobby Vee: Yeah.

Doc Rock: But yet, in interviews, Roy Orbison said that he and Elvis did not like their early material, that Sam Phillips at Sun played old, thick 78s and made the Sun acts imitate the style that was on these records, when they really wanted to do the kind of songs with violins and so forth which they later got to do after they left Sun. The small-combo sound at Sun was the result of financial constraints. They couldn't afford a full orchestra and a big production. Likewise, Buddy Holly's brother has said that the last songs, "It Doesn't Matter Any More" and "Raining in My Heart," with strings and things, were considered by Buddy to be his greatest records, his "new sound." So, I guess I'm asking if you preferred the "Suzie Baby" sound of the Shadows and it was the producer who changed your style, or if you were still into the music as much personally when you recorded with the orchestra?

Bobby Vee: No, I enjoyed the orchestra, and I also enjoyed going in and recording small with just a rhythm section. And I've been able to do that throughout my career. "Come Back When You Grow Up," which was my biggest hit, came out in the late '60s, and that was done with only about four or five or maybe six pieces on the record.

Doc Rock: Really! I was sure glad to hear that song on the radio. That came at a time in top-forty when I needed a record like that to listen to.

Bobby Vee: Well, thank you! Yeah, that was a real sleeper. It came out in the early part of 1967 and there were so many different things happening in music in San Francisco and so forth, the record just snuck in. It didn't make the charts until July, and it took the entire year to make the top of the national charts.

Doc Rock: My opinion was that the DJs did not want to play it because it didn't sound like what they believed records should sound like at that time. It wasn't acid rock

Opposite: A trade ad, featuring "The Liberty Belle," for Bobby Vee's new single.

The first two songs listed on the cover of *A Bobby Vee Recording Session* were Bobby Vee hits, plus the Carole King song "I Can't Say Goodbye."

or Motown or British or whatever. But the people loved it and bought it. They had to buy it, actually, because the DJs were not playing it and if they wanted to hear it, they had to buy it!

Bobby Vee: I think you're right! That probably helped.

Doc Rock: Hal Blaine was a big session drummer on the West Coast. Was he your drummer?

Bobby Vee: Yes, Hal Blaine did play on a lot of my things, probably starting in about the mid-sixties. Prior to that, we used Earl Palmer. Earl is still a studio musician out in Los Angeles. He also played on all of Little Richard's material out in New Orleans, at the Cosmos Factory down there, the Cosmos Studio.

Doc Rock: Probably few people knew your music shared roots with Little Richard!

Bobby Vee: Jerry Allison of the Crickets played on some songs. There is no mistaking Jerry Allison's drumming. He has the little fills that he does, and it is his signature.

Doc Rock: The Angels were a girl group who had hits like "'Til" and "My Boyfriend's Back." They were also session background singers for artists like Dean Martin, Lou Christie, even Sinatra, I've heard. Did you ever use the Angels?

Bobby Vee: No, we never used them.

Bobby Vee in the studio. *(Courtesy Bob Celli.)*

Doc Rock: I really liked the girl-group backgrounds on your records, on songs like "Rubber Ball" and "Charms."

Bobby Vee: Those were part of the Johnny Mann Singers, who recorded for Liberty, too.

Doc Rock: Did you have a preference for male or female backings, or did you like having a combination?

Bobby Vee: We usually used a combination, whatever seemed right for the individual piece of material. But I also did a lot of harmony parts myself. I enjoyed doing that.

In fact, I think I would have had just as much fun as a background singer as I did have as the lead singer.

Doc Rock: What were the influences, besides Buddy Holly, on your music? Elvis used to say that Frank Sinatra and Dean Martin, surprisingly, were people he admired and imitated. Carl Perkins was on TV and stated that Elvis, Johnny Cash, and Orbison were his personal models. Chuck Berry wanted to sing like Nat King Cole, as did Ray Charles originally. Jan & Dean have said that the Monotones ["Book of Love," 1958] and Chuck Berry and the Diamonds ["She Say," 1959] were their big influences, which all is surprising. Although the Monotones did sound like early Jan & Dean.

Bobby Vee: Yeah.

Doc Rock: What kinds of things were you listening to and, if not imitating, were at least influences on your music?

Bobby Vee: My roots go back to country music. People like Hank Snow and Hank Williams.

Doc Rock: I've heard you joke on stage about being "Hank Vee!" It was from the "Hanks" that you got the almost-rockabilly sound of your early recordings?

Bobby Vee: And of course I was in my early teens when rock 'n' roll was first coming on in the mid-1950s and late-1950s. So I was in on the early days of Elvis. Returning to what you were talking about before, about Sun Records, to me, the early Sun records were the most exciting Presley records. I think that happens frequently in the careers of artists. Before they have a self-image of who they are and what they sound like, they unaffectedly go in and just let their emotions fly. The early records by the Everly Brothers and Jerry Lee Lewis and Buddy Holly were the best.

Doc Rock: I see your point. But Elvis was doing what Sam Phillips told him to do—it wasn't totally unaffected!

Bobby Vee: But to me, when it comes to style and changes, Buddy Holly was kind of an exception 'cause I don't think that he ever did anything that wasn't loaded with "spirit." I think that he was an exception in that area.

Doc Rock: I agree! Buddy Holly is one of the very few artists that you can play any song off of any LP or whatever, and the song seems to work.

Bobby Vee: True!

Doc Rock: And there are not too many artists like that. I think you certainly are one of them.

Bobby Vee: Well, thank you.

Doc Rock: The only popular artists, for instance, that I can put on any LP of theirs and listen to it all the way through without getting bugged and getting up and turning it off or skipping cuts are Buddy Holly, Jackie DeShannon, Elvis Presley, Jan & Dean, Lou Christie, and definitely Bobby Vee.

Bobby Vee: I appreciate that. That is nice company!

Doc Rock: Speaking of your LPs, my favorite Bobby Vee Liberty LPs are, of course, *Golden Greats*, and *Thirty Big Hits of the 1960s, Volume One*, plus *Recording Session*. Did you have any of your own LPs that you particularly liked, that you still listen to?

Bobby Vee: I think the albums that were particular favorites of mine, I liked my second LP, *Strings and Things*, and I liked *Bobby Vee Meets the Crickets* because I think that had a lot of nostalgia for me, and it was a fun LP to do. I had an LP out in the late 1960s, *Gates, Grilles, and Railings*, that again was an LP that I really enjoyed making and a lot of talented people worked on it. The *Nothing Like a Sunny Day* LP was good, it was a nice place, a nice time in my life, and I enjoyed that whole project, working on the whole thing. The *Come Back When You Grow Up* LP, I thought that was nice, too. There was some good material on that.

Doc Rock: Back to Buddy Holly, I think the first Buddy Holly song you recorded was "Raining in My Heart" on your fifth LP. Except for "Love Made a Fool of You." Did Buddy Holly ever record that?

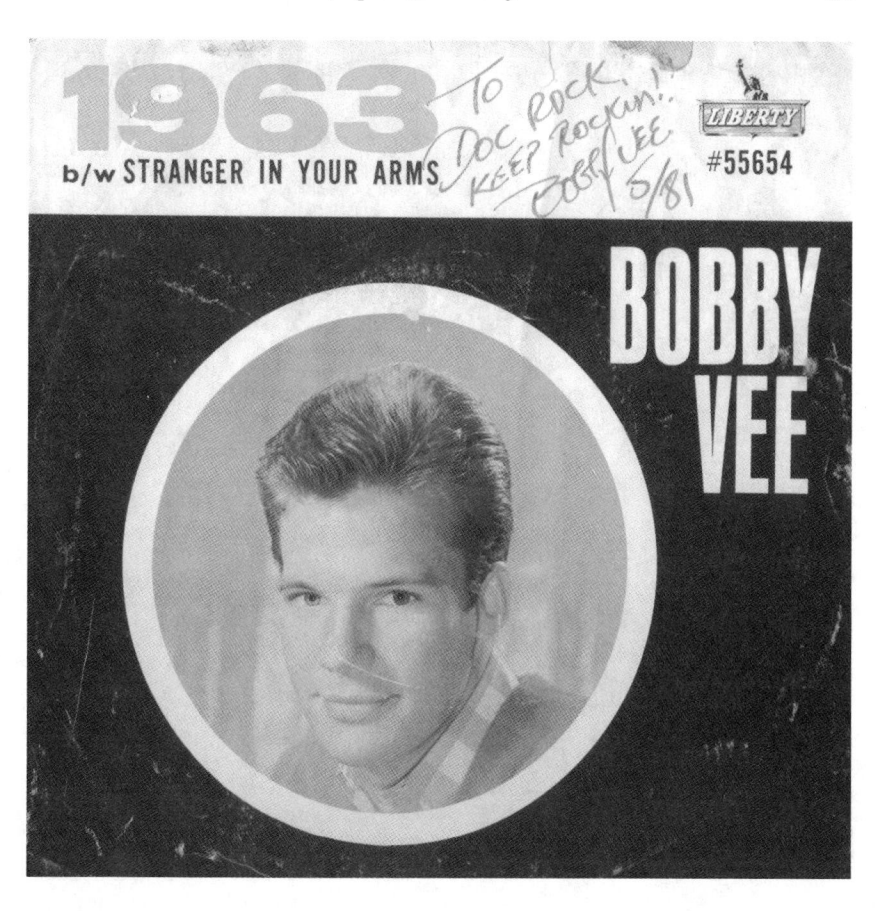

The picture sleeve for "1963" and the hit "Stranger in Your Arms," which charted at #83 in early 1964. This was a vocal version of "Armen's Theme," and was listed under that title on the LP *Bobby Vee's Golden Greats, Vol. 2*.

Bobby Vee: Yes, he did that as a demo.
Doc Rock: That was on your third LP.
Bobby Vee: His recording was not released until quite a few years after his death. The song was presented to me along with a couple of other songs that he had done and hadn't released and I recorded that, I think it was on my third LP. It was released in England as a single and was a top-twenty hit over there.
Doc Rock: So what was the first Holly song you recorded?
Bobby Vee: Actually, I think the first Buddy Holly song that I did was "Everyday."
Doc Rock: Sure, the flip side of "Rubber Ball" and on the *Strings and Things* LP.
Bobby Vee: It was also the first song on the *Teensville* LP we talked about. It was about that time that I was forming a relationship I guess with the Crickets, Buddy's old band, because they were living in Los Angeles at that time. Jerry Allison, the drummer, was already playing on some of my hits. He played on "Rubber Ball" and some of the early things. They were living in the same apartment building I was living in, and we used to hang out a lot together. Plus, we had a lot of musical interests in common. It was because of all of that that the theme of *Bobby Vee Meets the Crickets*

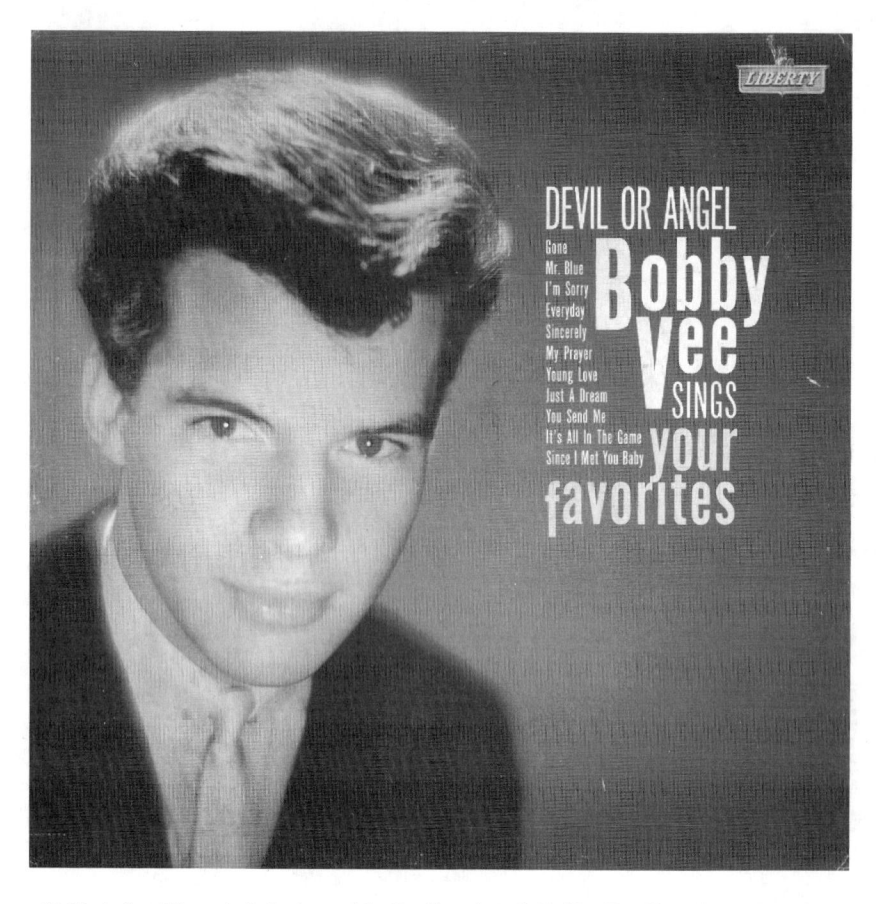

[Album cover: DEVIL OR ANGEL — Bobby Vee Sings Your Favorites (Liberty). Songs listed: Gone, Mr. Blue, I'm Sorry, Everyday, Sincerely, My Prayer, Young Love, Just A Dream, You Send Me, It's All In The Game, Since I Met You Baby.]

Bobby's first LP carried the long title *Devil or Angel: Bobby Vee Sings Your Favorites*.

developed. That was a concept album and acted as a vehicle for the Crickets to get back into records. It was a fun project. It was one that I look back on with a lot of fond memories. And, it sold pretty well [#2 in England]!

Doc Rock: The first LP by anyone that I ever bought was *Bobby Vee's Golden Greats*. On that was your song "Someday," which wasn't a single but stood out for me as a favorite, the guitar playing and so on. I really enjoyed it, and then later I found out it was from *Bobby Vee Meets the Crickets*.

Bobby Vee: "Someday" was specifically written as a sequel to Buddy Holly's "That'll Be the Day." Dick Glasser, a friend of mine, wrote the song.

Doc Rock: He also wrote "Bashful Bob."

Bobby Vee: Well, we just told him to write an answer song to "That'll Be the Day" and "Someday" was what he came up with.

Doc Rock: Very interesting! Another song that was not a single, not an A side, was the song "1963." I think it was the flip side of "Stranger in Your Arms" in early 1964.

Bobby Vee: Yeah, boy, that's really an obscure one! I don't think anyone has mentioned that song to me since nineteen sixty-three!

Doc Rock: Gosh, I sing that in the shower almost every morning! I really liked it, but then to me nineteen sixty-three was the best year of all for rock 'n' roll. What year, musically, do you look back on fondly?

Bobby Vee: Gee, I don't know. I've not really thought about that.

Doc Rock: For me the British invasion was very exciting in nineteen sixty-four. Yet, while I loved that music, it squeezed out some American music I also loved. I mean, if the radio stations' play lists have just forty songs, and you add 10 percent British records, then 10 percent of the American records have got to go! And it was no reflection on their music, it was criticized, yet it was still good as ever, but there was just no room on the play list! That was when I became a record collector!

Bobby Vee: Yes, that was a frustrating time for some American artists. I suppose we were just getting back what we had been dishing out. The charts had been dominated by American artists, and many American artists had been having hits for years like myself, in England.

Doc Rock: Speaking of England, I read an interview back in nineteen sixty-four that you gave. I have always wondered the real story behind it. You had the single "I'll Make You Mine" and "She's Sorry"—

Bobby Vee: Right.

Doc Rock: —which I liked an awful lot, and the interview said that George Harrison had listened to the record and said he liked it and approved.

Bobby Vee: Right.

Doc Rock: That was true?

Bobby Vee: Yes, that was true as a matter of fact. The LP for those songs, *The New Sound from England,* I looked at it as a project. I had been over in England touring. I had already had about ten hits over there; "Take Good Care of My Baby" had been number one there as it was in America, and "The Night Has a Thousand Eyes" was at that time in the top five in England. The Beatles had just had their first British hits but were still unknown in America. I saw that there was this tremendous energy thing in England and it all stemmed from the Beatles. This four-piece, rock 'n' roll sound again, like the Shadows, that was exciting to me. I guess it also reminded me namewise of the Crickets and a little bit stylewise of the rockin' fifties rock 'n' roll, the stuff that wasn't so polished, that still had some rawness to it. I always enjoyed that about the 1950s, some of the stuff was so raw, like early country music. So it appeared to me and to my producer, Snuffy, who was over there with me, that this was gonna be something to contend with, something that was going to be a major force. As a result I put out what was probably the first tribute album to the English invasion, then got swept up in it. And the LP was called *The New Sound from England.* There were only a couple of Beatle songs at that time that were popular. The Beatles' things had been released, but the first time around they didn't mean much. The stations didn't play them. And so then we did a couple of those ["She Loves You," "From Me to You"] on the LP, and then I wrote the rest of the songs.

Doc Rock: You know, it was interesting that you did Beatles songs on your LP. So very many of the first invasion records were originally American hits, and the British invasion groups' LPs were chock-full of old American rock 'n' roll songs. And as you say, it was all based on the sound of American rock 'n' roll.

Bobby Vee: That was true. But when I returned to England to tour again, the press was just disastrous! They all thought that I was trying to jump on the bandwagon with those songs; they hated me for it!

Doc Rock: Unfair! Why was it OK for them to do American music and American songs, then not OK for you to do some English stuff?

Bobby Vee: Well, it was just ironic. I was sitting in my hotel room one night and I got a call from my manager, and he said, "You gotta come over. There's a party here. EMI [or one of the major companies] is throwing a little party, and the Beatles are here." So I went over.

Doc Rock: Talked you into it, did he!

BOBBY VEE SINGS THE NEW SOUND FROM ENGLAND!

...visual sound STEREO LST-7352

SHE LOVES YOU • SUSPICION • SHE'S SORRY • FROM ME TO YOU • I'LL MAKE YOU MINE
I'LL STRING ALONG WITH YOU • DON'T YOU BELIEVE THEM • GINGER • ANY OTHER GIRL
BROWN-EYED HANDSOME MAN • YOU CAN'T LIE TO A LIAR • TAKE A WALK, JOHNNY

Although the Beatles were Bobby Vee fans, sang many American songs, and approved of this project, American and British fans alike rejected this LP.

Bobby Vee: Yeah! He didn't have to twist my arm! Even at that time, even though they weren't big in the States, they were in England. I went and I met all the guys and they all had nice things to say about the new record; they felt it was a compliment to them. And then they talked about some of my old songs. It was very enjoyable. I once got a bootleg tape of the Beatles doing "Take Good Care of My Baby." It was evidently a song they had recorded back around that time and didn't have a vehicle for it, didn't have a record company or whatever. But it is surfacing now. [The Beatles' version of "Take Good Care of My Baby" is available on a cassette tape from LM Records, *The Beatles 1961,* LSMC 3061, released under license from Ultra Sound Co., Inc., New York, and an LP, *20 Hits of the Beatles,* P20 623 from Phoenix Records, 45 East Milton Avenue, Rahway, NJ 07065.]

Doc Rock: When the British invasion happened in the U.S., the music scene changed somewhat. To some extent certain American artists' music suffered a loss of popularity. Do you feel that the kids buying records decided that the British sound was more to their liking? Or do you think, like I do, that the radio listeners merely grew older, quit buying records, and then there was simply a new batch of kids who came along and accepted the British as their music, just like their older brothers and sisters had accepted as their own Bill Haley, Elvis, Buddy Holly, Bobby Vee, Chubby Checker, the Beach Boys, and the Shirelles, each in their turn? Did taste change, did kids say, "We don't want to hear our old favorites' stuff anymore," or did the audience change and new kids say, "This is our music, we don't need the older artists?" A new audience, not a change in taste of the old audience? A new audience which would have gotten into some other, new artists of their own had not the British arrived, but the British just happened to arrive at that time for that group of youngsters?

Bobby Vee: I think that there is a turnover of audiences, a new, younger generation that comes up. Further, it is entirely possible for recording artists to become parodies of themselves. They have a certain sound, and it sells, and all of a sudden everything just kind of sounds the same. People get bored with it or whatever; they look for something new, something more stimulating. Then there is a new audience that comes along, and something else is exciting for them, electronics or whatever, and—

Doc Rock: And the other stuff sounds old to them, out of fashion like last year's clothes?

Bobby Vee: I do believe that. But I don't think any less of "Peggy Sue" today, just because it is old—

Doc Rock: No, no, no!

Bobby Vee: —and I don't think any less of "Wake Up Little Suzie" or "Bye Bye Love."

Doc Rock: Like a Rembrandt painting in a museum. If it was good before, it is still good today even if they are not painting that way anymore today.

Bobby Vee: Yes, right.

Doc Rock: And a song that was good then is still good today, even though they are not singing that way today.

Bobby Vee: I believe that is true. About nineteen eighty I had an album that was a collection of my old songs released in Great Britain, the *Singles Album,* and to my amazement it went to number four in the national charts and it was a gold album! I think the people who bought that album were probably people who bought those songs the first time around, or wanted to have bought them, or whatever. Bought them and lost them and bought them again now, or something like that. Or maybe it reminded them of a space and time in their life that was meaningful to them. It is hard to understand.

Doc Rock: But mostly it was the same age group who originally bought your records; they just got older along with you.

Bobby Vee: And again, there has been a lot of focus lately on the records of the 1950s and the 1960s. There are a lot of young people who collect now, too. The late 1950s and early 1960s took, I believe, a lot of unfair lumps [from] writers caught up in the English movement of the mid–1960s. I think part of it also had to do with turning away from anything established in all areas of society [during the Vietnam era].

Doc Rock: Imagine, Bobby Vee, establishment! Adult stations had their own music in those days!

Bobby Vee: I'm sure that listening to your radio show there are a lot of young people that like that sound and there are a lot of young groups that are getting back into rockabilly. The 1960s sound seems to be coming around again. We seem to be borrowing different things from ourselves.

Doc Rock: The audience at your show the other night [was] certainly . . . of the pre–Beatles age group.

Bobby Vee: Sure was!

Doc Rock: And that holds up the theory that people didn't change their minds about your music, they just got a little bit older and didn't listen to top-forty radio or buy singles anymore.

Bobby Vee: That's right.

Doc Rock: We were speaking of bootlegs awhile ago. Have there been any Bobby Vee bootleg LPs?

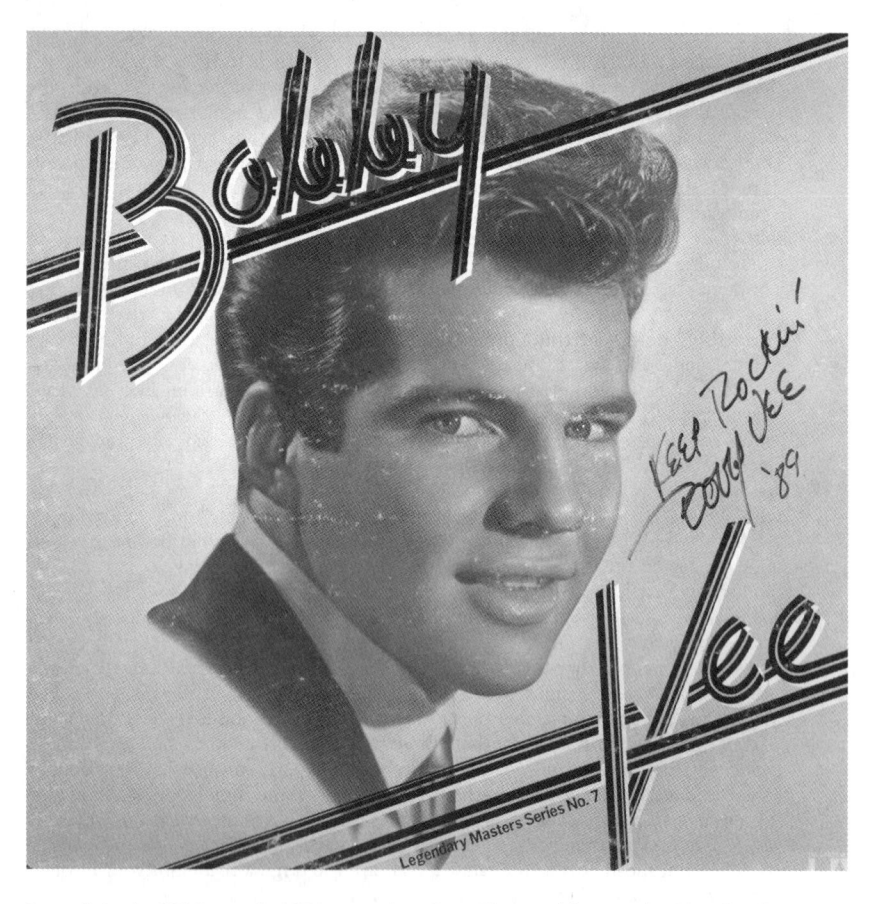

Seventh in the UA Legendary Masters series of two LP sets with extensive historical liner notes inside was *Bobby Vee*. This LP was never released, and only a very few, rare test-pressings exist, including the one pictured here.

> **Bobby Vee:** I've seen a couple. My first record, "Suzie Baby" on Soma Records, I've got a copy of that bootleg, and a couple of the things that I did with a small label in the late 1970s. For some reason I think they were bootlegged when the record was out. Because the song was getting airplay, and it was a small company, they probably weren't able to protect themselves like the majors.
> **Doc Rock:** So it was more like pirating than bootlegging?
> **Bobby Vee:** Yes, pirating.
> **Doc Rock:** After Liberty became a part of United Artists, you did a new version of "Take Good Care of My Baby" under your real name, Robert Thomas Velline. It was a slow-ballad version. At first it sounded odd to me, but now I really enjoy it. How did that come about?
> **Bobby Vee:** I had been doing that version of "Take Good Care of My Baby" for maybe a year or so live, and my producer felt that it would fit into the concept of an LP I was doing. He really talked me into putting it on there; I didn't want to do it. He persuaded me that it was a nice version and that we should give it a shot. That eventually came off the LP as the single. It wasn't worked very hard, and I don't know

if it would have done any better than it did if it had been worked. But it wasn't worked very hard by the label, and I was going through some changes at that time and really didn't have much interest in forcing the issue, I guess.

Doc Rock: That was about the time that Paul Anka and Neil Sedaka were both sort of making a comeback in a slowed-down style, and it fit right in with those records, I felt. You mentioned that "Love Made a Fool of You" was presented to you to record. Were there ever any songs which were presented to you but you passed up, which then went on to be hits by another artist? Or, were there songs you wanted to do but your management wouldn't go along with? For instance, Brenda Lee carried around the sheet music to "I'm Sorry" for months before they let her cut it, and then it was a huge hit, her first number one.

Bobby Vee: Oh, yes, it was big.

Doc Rock: And Sammy Davis, Jr., did not want to record "Candy Man," his big hit, but his children talked him into recording it!

Bobby Vee: Is that right?

Doc Rock: Did you have any situations like those?

Bobby Vee: Let me think ... well, "Devil or Angel," my first Liberty hit after "Suzie Baby," I was not particularly fond of. I wasn't even aware of the song as having been a hit by the Clovers before, I was listening to country music back then. But it was a favorite of my producer's, Snuffy Garrett. He said to me, "Gee, I'm amazed you've never heard this song before!" He said, "Let's do it, and if it doesn't work, we won't use it." It must have worked, because it started off my Liberty hits. From then on, I would give Snuffy the benefit of the doubt. He had a golden ear and still does. There were times when I felt that it was right to do something, and he would go along with me. Then there were times ... I remember being presented with songs that eventually came out by Elvis Presley. Both sides were presented to me. One was "His Latest Flame" and the flip side, "Little Sister." Both songs were presented to me, and I really liked them. I wanted to do them. But Snuffy didn't like them and said, "Naw, let's not waste the time." We didn't do them, and of course Presley came out with them, both top-five hits! Instead we recorded Carole King's "Take Good Care of My Baby."

Doc Rock: Which was number one, so I guess you did OK, huh? I heard that Snuff Garrett offered you "This Diamond Ring," which was Gary Lewis's first hit, a number-one hit, but you turned it down. Is that story correct?

Bobby Vee: Snuffy loves to tell that story, but actually that wasn't the way it went.

Doc Rock: OK, let's hear the real story!

Bobby Vee: The song was around, but it was never presented to me. Snuffy really liked the song, but I never had a chance to turn it down. I think I probably would have recorded it if it had been offered, because I did like the song. Anyway, Snuff had struck up this relationship with the Lewises at that point, and Gary wanted to get into the record business, so he took Gary in and cut it with him. And it was a big hit for him.

Doc Rock: So the publicity at the time, that Snuffy discovered Gary Lewis singing with the Playboys at Disneyland and signed him without knowing he was Jerry's son, that was just some publicist's pipe dream!

Since you were there recording in the 1950s, when I was just listening to the radio, perhaps you can help me. I have been researching the question of records that have a fade-out ending. The records of the 1940s and 1950s generally ended cold, but the records of the 1960s almost all have fade-out endings. Do you have any idea what was the first record, or first hit record, to have a fade-out?

Bobby Vee: Gee, you know, that's a good question, an excellent trivia question! I really don't know. It's a great question.

Doc Rock: It was probably a studio artist rather than a live artist. Live artists, ones who did live shows first, then recorded their most popular songs later, were used to ending songs solidly. A studio artist created songs in the studio and could just let a song fade out at the end. Except of course that Buddy Holly was primarily a studio artist, and he didn't perform his hits live before he recorded them, yet his songs did end cold.

Bobby Vee: I really don't know, I had never thought about that. The Buddy Holly endings were always . . . he had a particular style for ending his songs. He ended them very abruptly. But, I don't know, that would be a good thing to think about.

Doc Rock: On your songs, the first hit you had which faded was probably "Rubber Ball." "Suzie Baby" had a hard ending, so did "Devil or Angel" and "Since I Met You, Baby." The earliest song I can find that you could call rock 'n' roll and that had a fade-out at the end is Hank Ballard and the Midnighters' "Work with Me, Annie," which was in nineteen fifty-four. Of course, that song wasn't popular. And the cover version, which was a hit, "Dance with Me Henry," by Georgia Gibbs, didn't fade out! The oldest hit with a fade-out that I have found so far was the Five Satins' "In the Still of the Night" from the fall of 1956. Or maybe the Cadets' "Stranded in the Jungle" from the summer of 1956.

Bobby Vee: That could be right!

Doc Rock: Back to your music, but on another level. Did you have much involvement in the packaging of your material? Dean Torrence of Liberty's Jan & Dean designed the cover, did the artwork on your *Do What You Gotta Do* album.

Bobby Vee: That's right.

Doc Rock: Were you as an artist ever involved with that end, or was that totally separate?

Bobby Vee: No, I didn't make those decisions. I think that cover was probably because Dean was a part of the Liberty family. He was given the benefit of a number of albums that came out. He was a very talented guy in that area as well. He came up with some nice packages for me.

Doc Rock: Returning to the music, you did the song "One Last Kiss." That song was originally done as a joke, a parody in the show *Bye Bye, Birdie,* wasn't it?

Bobby Vee: That's right.

Doc Rock: What happened that you wanted to record it straight? I like it a lot, don't misunderstand me, I liked it before I knew it was from *Bye Bye, Birdie.*

Bobby Vee: That, again, was Snuffy's idea. The first few records I did after "Suzie Baby" were songs that Snuff had some personal stake in—that he liked or felt would be a hit. He called me when he heard that song. To him that was a hit song! He called me at home and said, "Jeez, I got this incredible song, and it is in this Broadway musical, and I think it's gonna be a hit! Come on out here and record it," and I did. I flew out and I recorded the song and ended up using a song I had cut in Minneapolis for the B side, overdubbing strings on the track. We kind of rushed the thing out. It wasn't a big hit. It got a fair amount of airplay, but we were not fast enough! There were also a couple of other versions of it, so, again, diminishing returns once stations started playing all these different versions—people get confused.

Doc Rock: You had some additional lyrics on that song that were not on the original. It went, "Oh-oh, oh-oh, oh-oh," where you said, "Darling, it isn't right, why must we say goodnight, don't make me go like this." Were those lyrics on the original but just not used in the show, or were they written for you?

Bobby Vee: I really don't remember, it was probably just some ad-libbing.

Doc Rock: The fans were originally girls, the record buyers; your fans were mostly girls, don't you think?

Bobby Vee: Ah, yes, definitely.

Doc Rock: But now it seems like most people who collect or who have a big interest in the older records are males.

Bobby Vee: Yes, almost across the board.

Doc Rock: So why do you suppose the original appeal was to girls, but now the girls don't care about it and the guys are going after it, after the fact?

Chapter 33 · Bobby Vee

Bobby's hairstyle is in transition on this cover designed by Dean Torrence.

Bobby Vee: It's interesting, I really don't know. I don't know why that is, but invariably the collectors today are men.
Doc Rock: When you are up at your cabin by the lake with your family like now, at home, what music do you listen to?
Bobby Vee: Actually, I'll tell you, if I have my way, I'll go for days without listening to anything! Just listening to the sounds of silence and the lake and the wind. But musically I really hop and skip around a lot. I've got a pretty sizable record collection, and my kids are at an age where they are buying a lot of records, so they are adding to it. I find myself listening to a lot of things they listen to and enjoying it a lot.
Doc Rock: As far as your music today, when you do shows, do you ever do some of the more obscure songs, like "Bobby Tomorrow" [an English hit but an American flip side] or "1963"?
Bobby Vee: Well, from time to time I will throw in something; just by myself I'll do "Anonymous Phone Call."
Doc Rock: Oh, boy, I love that one, written by Hal David and Burt Bacharach.
Bobby Vee: You know, one of those crazy songs. I have been thinking about developing a spot that could be ever changing. I could do a song for three or four months and keep rotating it. There are a lot of the fringe kinds of things that we will get

requests for, and it is a real compliment. I always appreciate it; I wish that I could do more of those things, sort of off the cuff. But I think that what I will do is develop a spot that I can do with just my guitar, or maybe one or two songs of the more obscure hits that we can throw in—"Anonymous Phone Call," "A Letter from Betty," "Be True to Yourself," that was a bigger hit, but you know, one of those things.

Doc Rock: I always liked the "story" songs, like "The Night Has a Thousand Eyes," a big one, but I always enjoyed the songs that sort of had a story line to them.

Bobby Vee: Yes, right. I do as well.

Doc Rock: But when you do an obscure song, I guess that there is always the chance that everyone but the hard-core fans will go out for a Coke and the show will lose momentum.

Bobby Vee: Right.

Doc Rock: It has been fantastic talking with you. I want to thank you for your time. I've been wanting to ask you these questions for about twenty years.

Bobby Vee: All right. Listen, I enjoyed talking to you down there when I was there last. It is always fun to talk to people who have some stake in it. I know that you have a good collection of your own, and I am sure that the people enjoy your sharing your information with them and sharing your collection with them. I think that is a real treat.

Doc Rock: Today, the treat was mine, interviewing Bobby Vee.

Today, the treat is still out there for everybody, because Bobby Vee is still touring, occasionally recording, and he is singing better than ever. His stage presence, already excellent, continues to improve every year. His three sons have formed a band called the Vees, and they do a variety of kinds of music. The four of them occasionally write songs together.

Bobby Vee Discography

SOMA
(Bobby Vee/Shadows)
1110 Suzie Baby
      Flyin' High

LIBERTY
1959 55208 Suzie Baby (w/Shadows)
            Flyin' High (w/Shadows)
     55234 What Do You Want?
            My Love Loves Me
1960 55251 One Last Kiss
            Laurie
     55270 Devil or Angel
            Since I Met You Baby
     55287 Rubber Ball
            Everyday
1961 55296 Stayin' In
            More Than I Can Say
     55325 How Many Tears
            Baby Face
     55354 Take Good Care of My
            Baby
            Bashful Bob

     55388 Run to Him
            Walkin' with My Angel
1962 55419 Please Don't Ask About
            Barbara
            I Can't Say Goodbye
     55451 Sharing You
            In My Baby's Eyes
     55479 Punish Her (w/Crickets)
            Someday (When I'm
            Gone from You)
            (w/Crickets)
     55517 Christmas Vacation
            A Not So Very Merry
            Christmas
     55521 The Night Has a Thousand Eyes
            Anonymous Phone Call
1963 55530 Charms
            Bobby Tomorrow
     55581 Be True to Yourself
            A Letter from Betty
     55636 Yesterday and You
            (Armen's Theme)

Chapter 33 · Bobby Vee

		Never Love a Robin
	55654	Stranger in Your Arms
1963		
1964	55670	I'll Make You Mine (w/Eligibles)
		She's Sorry (w/Eligibles)
	55700	Hickory, Dick and Doc
		I Wish You Were Mine Again
	55726	Where Is She
		How to Make a Farewell
	55751	Pretend You Don't See Her/(There'll Come a Day When) Every Little Bit Hurts
1965	55761	Cross My Heart
		This Is the End
	55790	You Won't Forgive Me
		Keep on Trying
	55828	Run Like the Devil
		Take a Look Around Me
	55843	The Story of My Life
		High Coin
	55854	Gone
		A Girl I Used to Know
1966	55877	Save a Love
		Look at Me Girl
	55877	Save a Love
		Butterfly (alternate flip)
	55921	Here Today
		Before You Go
1967	55964	Come Back When You Grow Up (w/Strangers)
		Swahili Serenade
	55964	Come Back When You Grow Up (w/Strangers)
		That's All in the Past (alternate flip)
	56009	Beautiful People (w/Strangers)
		I May Be Gone (w/Strangers)
1968	56014	Maybe Just Today (w/Strangers)
		You're a Big Girl Now (w/Strangers)

	56033	My Girl—Hey Girl (medley)
		Just Keep It Up (And See What Happens)
	56057	Do What You Gotta Do
		Thank You
	56080	I'm into Lookin' for Someone to Love Me
		Thank You
1969	56096	Jenny Came to Me
		Santa Cruz
	56124	Let's Call It a Day, Girl
		I'm Gonna Make It Up to You
	56149	Electric Trains and You
		In and Out of Love
1970	56178	No Obligations
		Woman in My Life
	56208	Sweet Sweetheart
		Rock 'n' Roll Music and You

SHADY BROOK

013	I'm Lovin' You
	Sayin' Goodbye
026	You're Never Gonna Find Someone Like Me (Long and Short Versions)
030	It's Good to Be Here
	If I Needed You

UNITED ARTISTS

50755	Signs
	Something to Say
50875	Electric Trains and You
	Sweet Sweetheart
XW199	Take Good Care of My Baby/Every Opportunity (Both by Robert Thomas Velline)
XW1142	Well All Right
	Something Has Come Between Us

COGNITO

010	Tremble On
	Always Be Each Other's Best Friend

CHAPTER 34

The Ventures

Dolton Records was a small company. The only artists who come to the minds of most collectors when they hear the name *Dolton* are the Fleetwoods and the Ventures. On the face of it, the Fleetwoods may seem the bigger of the two. After all, the Fleetwoods had two #1 hits in 1959, the first year of their career. No other Liberty/Dolton/Imperial artist—not Ricky Nelson, not Jan & Dean, not Gary Lewis, not Fats Domino—had more than one national #1 hit (although many had several songs that went #1 regionally). However, while the Fleetwoods did have two #1 hits and a very long hit-singles career (four years) compared to many artists of 1959, they had only about a dozen hits all told.

On the other hand, there were Dolton's other stars, the Ventures. Without a doubt the Ventures were and still are the most successful instrumental artists in rock 'n' roll, and rock, history. They are the Beatles or the Rolling Stones of instrumental rock 'n' roll. True, they had relatively few hits compared to those other superstars, "only" fourteen national hits. But in a world full of rock 'n' roll one-shot artists, their hit-single career lasted a long time—nine years. They are touring even today.

And Ventures LPs? Well, they have recorded more than eighty (count 'em, eighty) LPs in the United States, more than 150 LPs worldwide! They kept the same lineup of four members for more than twenty-five years! Their other claims to fame include six gold LPs: *Walk, Don't Run* (1960); *Telstar and the Lonely Bull* (1963); *Golden Greats* (1967); *Hawaii Five-0* (1969); *10th Anniversary Album* (1970); and *Pops in Japan* (1970); three gold singles: "Walk, Don't Run" (1960); "Walk, Don't Run '64" (1964); and "Hawaii Five-0" (1969); and one gold eight-track tape: *Golden Best 20* (1970, Japan).

From 1960 through 1966 the Ventures sold more than one million LPs each year. In 1963 they were voted one of the top-five artists in the world! They have sold over 10 million LPs in the tiny country of Japan, alone!

The Ventures were formed by Bob Bogle (originally lead guitar, later bass) and Don Wilson (rhythm guitar). They immediately added Nokie Edwards (lead) and Mel Taylor (drums). Bob Bogle told the history of the group in a telephone interview from California in October 1983 and backstage at a Ventures performance in Parsons, Kansas, on November 12, 1983.

Doc Rock: I've heard a couple of stories about how you guys got your first song, "Walk, Don't Run." Was this an LP cut by somebody else originally?
Bob Bogle: "Walk, Don't Run" was written by Johnny Smith, a very well-known jazz guitarist. He was a real good friend of Chet Atkins. So Chet Atkins put "Walk, Don't Run" in one of his LPs, called *Hi-Fi in Focus*. That was back in the 1950s. When I first started learning guitar, Chet Atkins was one of my big influences. So "Walk,

Don't Run" was on one of my favorite Atkins LPs. As a matter of fact, we did a couple of songs later from Chet's LP. Our third release, "Lullabye of the Leaves," was also from that same LP.

Doc Rock: So Chet Atkins, country artist and rock 'n' roll producer for the Everlys and other, RCA artists, was an influence on you. Did you play these things just for your own enjoyment?

Bob Bogle: Don Wilson and I started learning to play the guitar together about a year before we started recording. We were playing some shows, and "Walk, Don't Run" was one of the songs we had in our repertoire. Everyone liked that song so much, they kept requesting it. So we finally decided to just record it and see what would happen, it had always gotten such a good response. We got the recording released on Dolton Records through Liberty's distribution. And we had an instant hit all over the world!

Doc Rock: I have heard two "Birth of the Ventures" stories. One is that "Walk, Don't Run" was a homemade recording, another that it was recorded professionally in a studio. Which is true?

Bob Bogle: Well, they're both almost right! We went in with a home recording to the president of Dolton Records, who was Bob Reisdorff. He was based in Seattle, he had the Fleetwoods already. They were very famous, very popular, they had already had a couple of big, big hits. He listened to our material on our home recording. He said that "I don't think that you have what I need here."

Doc Rock: You're kidding?

Bob Bogle: No, true! So we went in a studio by ourselves, just Don and me, and we had Nokie Edwards on bass, and went in and rerecorded "Walk, Don't Run." It was a professional studio, but in those days it was a guy's basement, a two-track Ampex reel-to-reel, that type of equipment.

Doc Rock: Only one microphone, probably?

Bob Bogle: Yes! That was about the best you could do in those days, especially in that area of the country. We recorded it, then we had three hundred copies made at our own expense.

Doc Rock: Now *those* original pressings must be pretty rare collectors' items!

Bob Bogle: We hand-carried those records around to radio stations in the local area. The DJs really liked it, and they started playing it on their shows. Soon Bob Reisdorff heard it on the radio, and right away he called us!

Doc Rock: Good thing he had your name and number still handy!

Bob Bogle: Ha! Well, this version was much different than the first version he had heard, of course. He called us up, and he said, "Jeez, you got a hit record there! Come on in and let's see if we can work out a distribution deal!" We went in immediately and got it released on Dolton through Liberty's distribution channels throughout the United States; and through Liberty's leases, released in foreign countries. And "Walk, Don't Run" was just an instant, worldwide hit.

Doc Rock: I can remember the first time I heard it, and I loved it from that moment on. I must say that I never quite understood that title, "Walk, Don't Run." It was a fast-tempo song, I always felt it could have been called "Run, Don't Walk!" Is it true you named it after the signs they have up at swimming pools?

Bob Bogle: We didn't name it. But we asked the writer about that later on. Within about a year we met Johnny Smith, and I've met him quite a few times since.

Doc Rock: He got good composer royalties from your hit.

Bob Bogle: He lives in Colorado Springs, Colorado. I saw him last about three or four months ago. We were through there on tour and he came down to the club; we had a real nice visit. But I asked him where he got that title. He said it was an instrumental with no lyrics or title, he was in New York down in the subway system, and he would see all of these signs, "Walk, Don't Run," in the subway! And so he thought, "That would be a pretty catchy title for a tune!" And, you have to realize that the way that he recorded it originally was much different from our version. It was pure

444   Liberty Records • Part Three

HAWAII FIVE-O
THE VENTURES
HAWAII FIVE-O · AQUARIUS/LET THE SUNSHINE IN · DIZZY
SPOOKY/TRACES/STORMY · LOVIN' THINGS
GAMES PEOPLE PLAY · I CAN HEAR MUSIC · THE LETTER
GALVESTON · THEME FROM "A SUMMER PLACE"

The Ventures' second biggest hit is sold by a native of the 50th state.

jazz, and slow. We converted it to rock 'n' roll and stepped up the tempo and all. But the way he did it, it was more like a walk!

Doc Rock: That is interesting! The Fleetwoods, the other big Dolton artist you mentioned, got their group name off of a telephone exchange, Fleetwood 5-2413 or whatever.

Bob Bogle: Right.

Doc Rock: So, where did the name the Ventures come from?

Bob Bogle: We first started out by calling ourselves the Versatones! When we first started out, Don and I were working in construction. We thought that we were pretty versatile—we could lay bricks and play music, too!

Doc Rock: Did you know each other first as guitarists or as bricklayers?

Bob Bogle: Bricklayers. As I say, we learned to play guitar together, because we were always working on the same jobs together. For some reason, we kept on winding up together in small towns, going out on contracts, with nothing to do after work. So, we bought a couple of guitars in a pawnshop and just started learning how to play them, just to pass the time, for our own personal enjoyment. After a few months, we had a pretty good repertoire worked up, maybe twenty songs or so, and we just started drawing audiences when we were practicing. We'd find an empty ballroom

The Ventures. *(Courtesy Joe Rosignoro.)*

in a hotel we were staying in, anyplace we could practice in these small towns, because we couldn't make that much noise in our rooms!

Doc Rock: "Noise," right!

Bob Bogle: Soon, we started playing concerts in the different towns around, laying bricks by day and playing in clubs three or four nights a week. Just the two of us. No bass, no drums.

Doc Rock: And little, tiny amplifiers probably!

Bob Bogle: We had one small amp we'd both plug into. But it was OK, and people really liked it. The name "Ventures" came because we were starting off on a new venture, musicians instead of bricklayers.

Doc Rock: I'll bet! They must have all been surprised later when you became stars, and they could say they "knew you when." That is, if they conected the Versatones with the Ventures!

Now, the first hit was "Walk, Don't Run." But, what about "Walk, Don't Run, '64." How did you happen to record that, and were you surprised that it, too, was such a big hit?

Bob Bogle: We were a presurf guitar instrumental group. The term wasn't even used

446   Liberty Records • Part Three

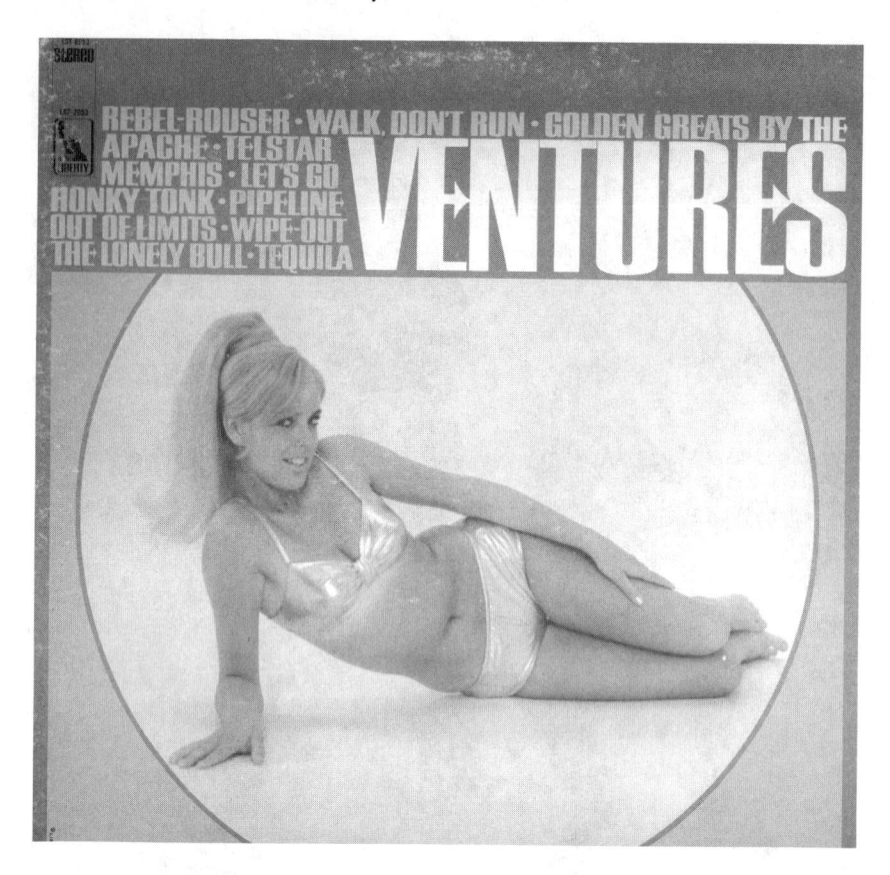

Apparently fans liked these girls better than the boys on the covers. Although the cover lists "Walk, Don't Run," the title of their original hit in 1960, this record actually features their 1964 top-ten updated version, "Walk, Don't Run '64."

> when we first started. But besides the surf vocalists, Jan & Dean, the Beach Boys, there were all the surf instrumental artists, Dick Dale, the Surfaris, the Chanteys. By nineteen sixty-three, the term *surfing music* got popular and we did two surfing LPs.
>
> **Doc Rock:** So, just like Jan & Dean, who were around with hits for five years before they did their first surf song and became classified as surfers, you guys became classified as a surf group several years after you actually started out!
>
> **Bob Bogle:** Yes, because we did "Wipeout" (Surfaris, 1963) and "Pipeline" (Chanteys, 1963) on those LPs. Then, I don't know who, but someone suggested that we re-record "Walk, Don't Run," surfing-style! When you hear it, it sounds like a "Pipeline" type of styling.
>
> **Doc Rock:** Yes, it does.
>
> **Bob Bogle:** So, we just decided to redo it and change the title.
>
> **Doc Rock:** More composer royalties for Johnny Smith! No wonder he likes to see you! Your album *Golden Greats* on Liberty includes "Walk, Don't Run '64," but they did not bill it as such on the jacket. They left off the designation, "'64."
>
> **Bob Bogle:** Really, is that so!
>
> **Doc Rock:** Yes, which is kind of interesting!

Bob Bogle: I never noticed that before!

Doc Rock: Well, that LP also has your version of "Pipeline" on it, and it sounds more like the Chanteys' version than the Chanteys' does! I have even been fooled myself when playing it on the radio! But I notice that on other LP cuts that you do which were originally hits by other artists, your version often varies considerably from the hit. Was there any special reason one way or the other on that?

Bob Bogle: No, I would say that we generally try to stick pretty close to the original version. Early in our career, we got started with a format that worked for us. We would take current vocal hits and do them instrumentally.

Doc Rock: Like Ricky Nelson's "Lonesome Town."

Bob Bogle: Yes. We'd take songs that were just coming up on the charts, pick out about six of those that were still coming up, and put out an LP with six of those and six originals that we could write. This is what activated our publishing company. Right at the time that LP came out, those six songs would be in the top ten!

Doc Rock: Very clever! That was similar to how Dick Clark would put together his road shows full of stars. He would look to see whose new record was starting to climb the charts, new artists with no bookings as yet. Then he would sign up these newcomers first, before anyone else, and get them pretty cheaply since they were totally new and not yet stars, had no experience in such things. Then, when the tour hit the stage, their songs would be at their peak of popularity, and the tour would be a big success!

Bob Bogle: Same thing!

Doc Rock: I was going to ask you how you accounted for selling so many LPs when as far as hit 45s went, you had relativly few—not in an absolute sense, but where most artists would have only one LP for every one or two or even three hit 45s, you would turn it around and have one hit 45 and three LPs!

Bob Bogle: Yes, that's right! We were releasing six LPs a year. We've had a total of more than eighty-five albums released in the United States.

Doc Rock: That is impressive!

Bob Bogle: Worldwide, more than a hundred fifty LPs. Because we recorded a lot of special LPs for Japan. I think what was most responsible for our volume as far as unit sales in LPs was musicians. When we do concerts, probably over half of our audience is always musicians! We always have people who come up to us and say, "I learned how to play from your albums and have been following your career." These are always musicians that we are talking to when we do our concerts. I think they always waited for our LP to come out and, like I say, the hit records that we were doing instrumental versions of gave us a lot of title strength. It got to where all these budding guitarists would buy our new LP because it was always right into what was happening today. They would pick up guitar licks from us on those songs.

Doc Rock: So that is where the *Guitar Phonics* series of instructional albums stemmed from.

Bob Bogle: Correct.

Doc Rock: I often get requests for "No Matter What Shape" by the Ventures or "Wipe Out" or "Pipeline" by the Ventures. "Green Onions" by the Ventures. And, of course, these were not Ventures songs, they were by the T-Bones, Booker T., and others.

Bob Bogle: Originally.

Doc Rock: But there is a good chance that these people have been listening to these songs on a Ventures LP for ten or twenty years!

Bob Bogle: And in a lot of cases, our LPs actually outsold the originals 45s.

Doc Rock: There goes the theory that pre–Beatle LPs were junk, that the cuts were just fillers, that the rock 'n' roll LP did not sell well!

Bob Bogle: As far as a lot of people are concerned, those LP cuts *are* our music! We, too, always get lots and lots of requests for "Wipe Out," "Pipeline," "Telstar," and those things.

BOBBY VEE MEETS THE VENTURES

LIBERTY

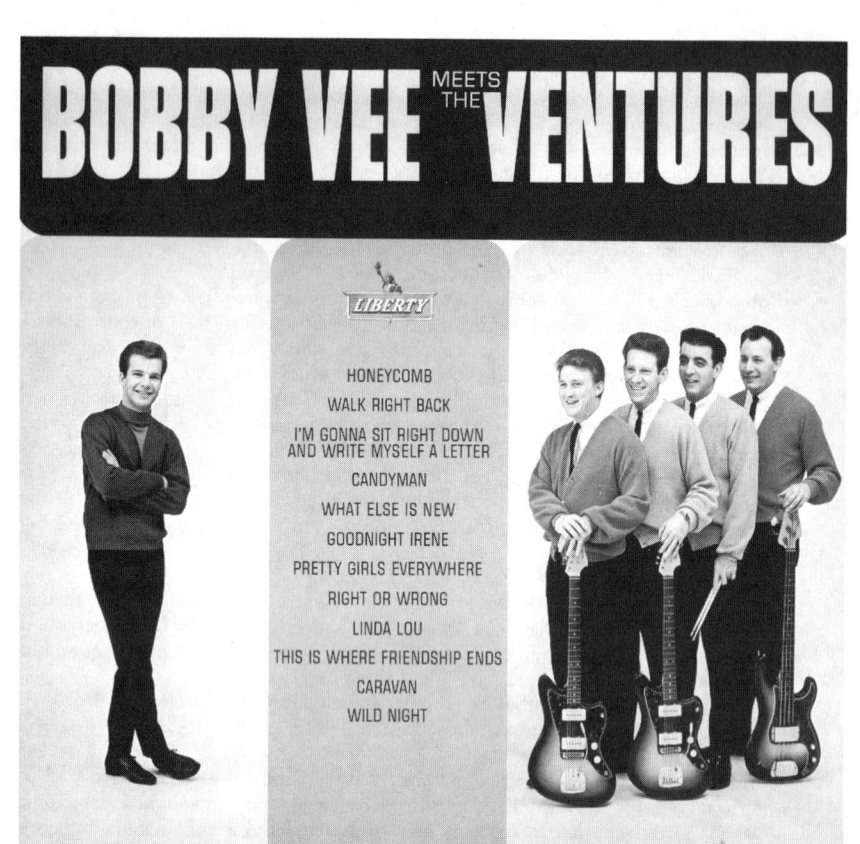

HONEYCOMB
WALK RIGHT BACK
I'M GONNA SIT RIGHT DOWN AND WRITE MYSELF A LETTER
CANDYMAN
WHAT ELSE IS NEW
GOODNIGHT IRENE
PRETTY GIRLS EVERYWHERE
RIGHT OR WRONG
LINDA LOU
THIS IS WHERE FRIENDSHIP ENDS
CARAVAN
WILD NIGHT

Inspired by the success of *Bobby Vee Meets the Crickets,* Bobby also met the Ventures in 1963. Actually they toured together as early as 1960.

Doc Rock: "Ram-Bunk-Shush" was your third or fourth record. It was a slow number.
Bob Bogle: It was more of a shuffle.
Doc Rock: After "Perfidia" and "Walk, Don't Run," wasn't that sort of a risky move?
Bob Bogle: I can't remember now why we decided to record it, we just thought it was a catchy tune. I don't think that we were too concerned with the change in the tempo. The dance the Shuffle was really happening in those days, "Honky Tonk" [Bill Dogett, 1961], and goin' to "Kansas City" [Wilbert Harrison, 1959], and that type of thing. So it was a pretty popular beat back in those days.
Doc Rock: I'm a big Bobby Vee fan. You did an LP on Liberty, *Bobby Vee Meets the Ventures.*
Bob Bogle: Right.
Doc Rock: That has always been a real favorite of mine. How did that come about?
Bob Bogle: Bobby was with Liberty, and we were on Dolton. At the time we went with Dolton, Bob Reisdorff was in the process of selling Dolton to Liberty. We all moved to Los Angeles together, as a matter of fact, because they retained Bob Reisdorff as president of the Dolton division of Liberty Records. So, we were immediately thrown into contact with all of the Liberty artists, Gene McDaniels, Johnny Burnette, Bobby Vee.

Doc Rock: Liberty was a good label, wasn't it?

Bob Bogle: It really was, they were very hot in those days, in the early 1960s.

Doc Rock: People often fail to realize that. They think of Sun or Philles or something, they don't realize that Liberty was quite an important rock 'n' roll record label!

Bob Bogle: That's right, and it was. And we started doing a lot of tours with these Liberty people, especially with Bobby.

Doc Rock: Did you back him up, or did you just do your own set of hits?

Bob Bogle: We backed him up! They'd send us off on tour together. We'd come out and do an hour, then they'd come out and do an hour with us playing the music.

Doc Rock: What years would those be, about?

Bob Bogle: Well, that would have been starting in 1960. And all through the early to mid-1960s. And you know, Bobby Vee was only sixteen years old, with all of those hits. So when we started traveling a lot with him, we would keep him with us so we could kind of look after him!

Doc Rock: Ha!

Bob Bogle: I don't know how he'd feel, hearing me say that! I kind of felt protective, because we'd traveled a lot in construction, but he was very, very young. We had him on a lot of tours together and it worked.

Doc Rock: So that touring together inspired the LP?

Bob Bogle: His producer was Snuff Garrett, and ours was Bob Reisdorff. They got together and said, "Why don't we do an LP with these guys, they work together so much." So, we went in and did that LP, and it worked out really good for us.

Doc Rock: The first song on that early-1960s LP was "Goodnight, Irene," and it sounds just like "Psychotic Reaction," of all things, the Count Five hit from nineteen sixty-six! Someone should get sued for the arrangement on that one!

Bob Bogle: You don't say! Anyway, Bobby was also a real close friend; we just thought the world of him, very close.

Doc Rock: He is still a very fine singer, and very nice. I talked with him just recently and saw him perform. He doesn't need a special microphone or any gimmicks or anything! He can just plain sing!

Bob Bogle: That is true. He is a very good entertainer, and a terrific guy, too.

Doc Rock: Another big Liberty artist was Jan & Dean.

Bob Bogle: Right!

Doc Rock: Did you have any contact with them? I know that you had an LP, *Supergroup,* that Dean Torrence did the cover artwork for.

Bob Bogle: Yes, we have done a few shows with them. As a matter of fact, a few years ago, we alternated with them at Disneyland in LA. We did three shows each, we did a half hour, and then they did a half hour.

Doc Rock: Wow, that would have been great to hear!

Bob Bogle: Oh, it was a great evening! It was on the Space Mountain stage, which is the largest stage, and you can get about fifteen hundred people in there, I'd guess. But with what they got inside there, plus all of the people crowded around, there were about three thousand people in the area. It was all that the area could handle. So, it was a great time for both of us!

Doc Rock: Instrumentals are always hard to learn the titles of. People hear a song, and don't know what it is called. And, when you do know the title, it is often a mystery, like "Walk, Don't Run," what it means or where it came from. Do you have people coming up to you, asking for requests with strange titles, or not having any idea at all what the titles are to some of your songs?

Bob Bogle: Yeah, a lot of times we'd write these songs. Now, we had to come up with so much material, it was almost like a factory! Today one LP by an artist might be pushed for months and months. We were turning out these LPs and songs, we'd work on the melodies, the chords, and the arrangements in rehearsals. And we just wouldn't have titles for them! We'd do an LP, we'd be working on what we called "Original number one," "Original number two," and "Original number three," and

Another Dean Torrence cover, this one on Sunset for the Ventures.

so on. The producers and everyone would say, "We gotta have titles for these songs!" So, we'd answer, "We're workin' on it, we're thinkin'!" What we did was get help from people, suggestions from people like the secretaries around Liberty. They would help us name songs. I don't even know where half of those titles came from! Someone would suggest a title and someone else would say, "Yeah, that kinda fits," and we'd say "Yeah, sure, fine, whatever, put it down!"

Doc Rock: So, when the LP came out, you'd look to see what the songs were on it!

Bob Bogle: It was good music, we cared about it, but we were not too self-important; an instrumental is an instrumental. And we were touring so much, we had no idea what LP was coming out with which songs on it.

Doc Rock: That's wild!

Bob Bogle: For example, one interesting story came in connection with our very first LP, entitled *Walk, Don't Run,* after the single. The success of that, all of that happened so fast. The single hit so fast, Dolton didn't even have any picures on us. We rushed into the studio and recorded the LP when we saw the single was hitting, and then immediately they had us booked for live appearances. We went out on a promotional tour. So, when they got ready to put the artwork on the LP cover, they discovered that they didn't have even one picture of us!

Chapter 34 · The Ventures 451

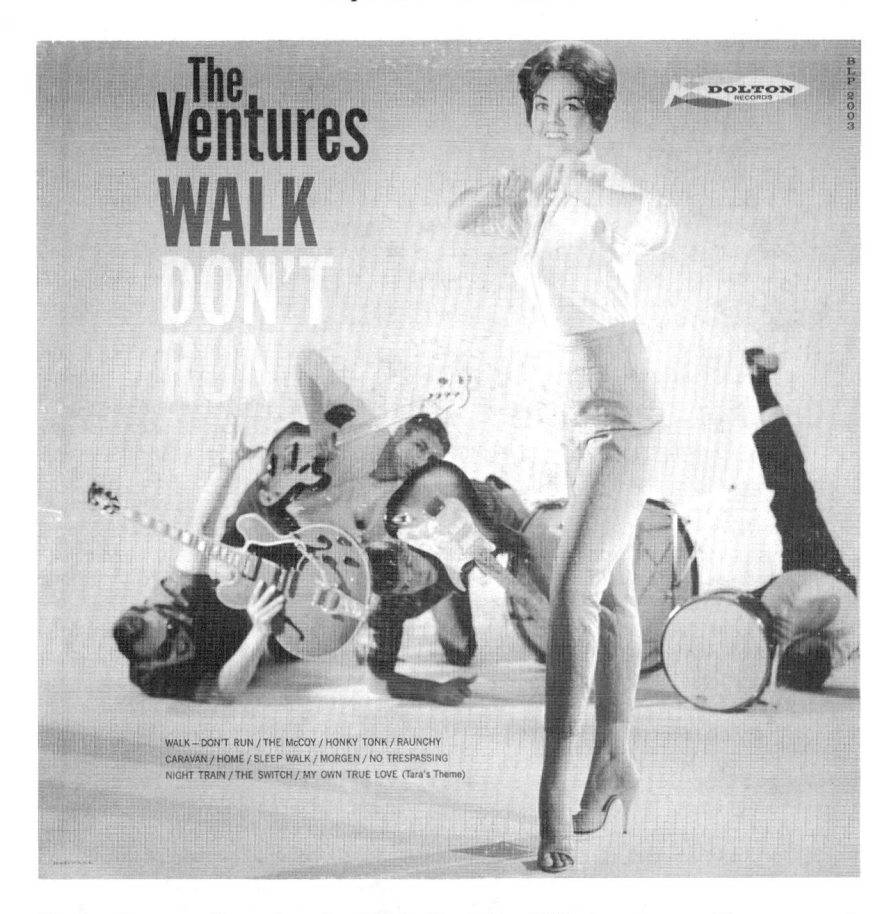

The first Ventures album, featuring "Walk, Don't Run." The four guys on this cover weren't even the Ventures! This shot was re-created four years later by the real Ventures on their *Walk, Don't Run '64* cover, shown in chapter 22.

Doc Rock: And you were gone, out of town!
Bob Bogle: Yep! So, they got the stock boys from the mailing room downstairs at Liberty Records, and they put sunglasses on them, had them lying on the floor, holding guitars in front of their face, and it wasn't really us!
Doc Rock: Ha! That is a story. Think of some big, new artist of recent times, Hammer or Vanilla Ice! That kind of thing just couldn't happen today!
Bob Bogle: It was a funny story! People would come up and say, "Whatever happened to such and such guitar that you had on that cover? I went out and got one just like it to sound like you." And I'd say, "Well, that wasn't mine, and I never did see that instrument, so I don't know what happened to it!"
Doc Rock: That first tour—how did that compare with bricklaying?
Bob Bogle: Oh! It was simply—we were in a wonderland for awhile. We were just so amazed by the whole thing, we were delirious! The very first professional show we did after the record started hitting was Dick Clark's national Saturday-night TV show.
Doc Rock: Had to wear suits back in those days on that show, didn't you! I don't think

Dick enforced a dress code in the 1980s, do you? Although your image was a lot preferable, I feel.

Bob Bogle: That's right. And he flew us out to New York, and we taped the show and then left and came back and went on tour. The first tour we ever went out on was with Jimmy Clanton. He had had just a string of hits, he was like a superstar to us....

Doc Rock: "Just a Dream," "Go, Jimmy, Go," "A Letter to an Angel."

Bob Bogle: We were just in awe of this guy, and there we were, backing him! It was like a Cinderella story. We just couldn't grasp what was going on.

Doc Rock: A great many artists including Bobby Vee, the Fleetwoods, and Jan & Dean as well have been rerecording their old hits lately for K-Tel and for other companies. Have you done any of that yet?

Bob Bogle: Not exactly. We did do a greatest hits album, and we test-marketed it in Portland, Oregon. The test did very well. It was a private enterprise, we did it ourselves on our own label. And while the test went very well, we never did go national with it because it takes such a tremendous amount of money, investment, to get something out all over, nationwide. We approached K-Tel with our idea, and they wanted to do something with it. But we couldn't agree on a price, and nothing came of it.

Doc Rock: Are you still getting royalties on the old songs? On TV series, as you know, as years pass and reruns are shown, the actors get less and less until finally they get no money at all from reruns. But do you still get royalties from reissues and so on?

Bob Bogle: Yes, we do, they still send us statements all the time. We still get quite a bit of volume, especially worldwide. And, we are still recording. In the States, on our own label and through an independent distributor, but in foreign countries we're still making leasing deals for the material. We are still actively recording. As a matter of fact, we did an LP for NASA's twenty-fifth anniversary of space flight. They asked us if, being an instrumental group, if we'd do a commemorative LP. They are not allowed to exploit themselves commercially, you know. But other people can. And naturally they appreciate and benefit from all of the notoriety they can get; the more people are interested in space, the more it helps them. So we did this commemorative LP, it's all space tunes in there, it was called *NASA'S Twenty-fifth Anniversary Album*. It was a great honor to be asked to do it.

Doc Rock: Interesting, NASA wants you, but you aren't good enough for K-Tel!

Bob Bogle: In fact, NASA sent us all kinds of tapes and video clips and pictures and even audio tapes of the controllers talking to the astronauts. On one of the songs we used some of those voices, it is very interesting.

Doc Rock: "Hawaii Five-0." That song came rather late in the game for you, singleswise, in nineteen sixty-nine. That came as quite a surprise. I was of course still playing Ventures' records personally, but to hear them again on the top ten was quite surprising!

Bob Bogle: Yes, well, Mel had a next-door neighbor who was involved in that show, and he was the one who wrote the theme song. He was Mort Stevenson. So he asked us to do it, but they wanted it orchestrated. We went into the studio and recorded it with just the original four pieces on the basic track. Then we brought in the strings and horns and put them in on top of us. It was a little different sound for us, but we're there on the basic track. We perform that song onstage, of course without the orchestra; we do it with the basic four pieces.

Doc Rock: It was a nicely done job. Many people even think that your single was also the actual TV sound track! It came out wonderfully.

Bob Bogle: Like I say, it was orchestrated; there were about thirty pieces on that, so it had a big sound.

Doc Rock: As you very well are aware of, most hit records are vocals. Many DJs would use the few instrumentals that did get popular as spacers, to end up the hour, to fit right into the news.

Bob Bogle: Yes.

Chapter 34 · The Ventures

For over twenty years, the VENTURES have been the best-selling rock-pop instrumental group in the world. Their unique instrumental guitar sound has spanned over two decades and two generations. The Ventures have recorded eighty albums in the U.S. and one-hundred-fifty worldwide, selling in excess of sixty-five million copies.

The Ventures
EXCLUSIVE REPRESENTATION

SPOTLITE ENTERPRISES LIMITED

221 West 57th Street, 9th Floor
New York, N.Y. 10019
(212) 586-6750
TELEX 640552 SPOTLITE NYK

8400 Sunset Boulevard
Sunset Towers West, Suite 2E
Los Angeles, CA 90069
(213) 654-5063

The Ventures in the sixties and the eighties.

Doc Rock: I have even noticed that, unlike vocals, many of the old instrumental hits did not even list the timing of the song on the label, evidently so that the DJs cannot back-cue the records and use them to fill out the last sixty-five seconds or whatever of the hour.

Bob Bogle: Right.

Doc Rock: And on top of that, the DJs would often talk over these instrumentals, as well, finishing off their hour or their shift, promoting the next hour or the upcoming show or whatever. As an artist of instrumental hits, did this bother you, to have them talk over your records and cut them short?

Bob Bogle: No, no, I didn't mind. I was happy that they were using them. A lot of DJs told us that they used our singles for "news kickers." Sometimes they'd use only half of a record, but you know, it is like the old saying in show business, "Say anything you want to about me, but just spell my name right!" In other words, any publicity is good publicity.

Doc Rock: Great! As far as vocals go and as opposed to instrumentals, it is quite limiting to have no vocals. You cannot use catchy lyrics, or any kind of a vocal hook or gimmick on the record.

Bob Bogle: Sure, that is true.

Doc Rock: Just how do you find alternate ways to make the umpteenth guitar instrumental attractive and interesting?

Bob Bogle: Well, it is really tough! You are missing an entire dimension, or even two dimensions, the personality of a lead singer, and the message of the lyrics. It is really tough. That is why the ratio of hit vocalists to instrumentalists has such a wide discrepancy. Probably less than 2 percent of the hit records were instrumentals. They were practically all vocals, and it is sure tough to get an instrumental hit. We had about seventeen singles on the charts altogether, but a lot of those were not considered "hits." They might have made it to number sixty or something like that, which means that maybe they sold one hundred thousand copies. That is not really enough sales to qualify as a hit record on a single. But we had less than a half dozen million-sellers, as far as singles are concerned. It is very tough to come up with instrumental songs, and really tough when you have to compete with vocalists.

Doc Rock: Well, you have certainly done it successfully!

Bob Bogle: Thank you. I think we draw an entirely different type of audience, too. That part of it, I like. We don't get the radicals, or the little teenie-boppers who are crazy about the singers. We get the musicians, and we always have a real nice, respectable audience wherever we go now.

Doc Rock: Speaking of that sort of thing, what did you think of the San Francisco, acid-rock-guitar kind of thing, the mid–late 1960s. Loud, nonmelodious guitar instrumentals, high audiences.

Bob Bogle: Yes, well, I never could really get into that. Most of our stuff is of the more melodious type.

Doc Rock: Although Glenn Miller would have disagreed with you!

Bob Bogle: Even though we were a top-forty group, we stayed away from that because of everything that it represented. The kids start getting into drugs and everything like that, you know. We've always tried to maintain a clean image, a clean, family show.

Doc Rock: More the Bobby Vee/Jimmy Clanton–type image!

Bob Bogle: Right! The family can come and see us and bring their kids, and no one is offended.

Doc Rock: That is wonderful. Since you were so prolific in terms of recording and selling LPs, did Liberty/Dolton encourage you to get in the studio a lot and record?

Bob Bogle: Oh, yes, it was very nice and friendly. Liberty was a family operation, and everyone was very friendly. We could come in, hang around, drop into people's offices, record whenever we wanted to. Until the late 1960s. When Liberty was sold, everything changed. We came one day, and there were guards at the front doors! We tried to walk in, and they stopped us! We'd been going there for ten years, we were big artists, and all of a sudden we couldn't even get in the building! They didn't care who we were, they wanted to know who we were coming to see. Who we had an appointment with! We told them we were just coming to hang out, to drop in and see some people, but they wouldn't even let us in. They didn't know us, we didn't know them. It was all very different from then on, and not as nice.

Doc Rock: That is too bad. One last question, going back to the early days. Your early publicity indicated that the Ventures were a duo, but later there seems to be four of you. Actually, there always were four pieces, weren't there? A drummer and three guitars. What was the deal?

Bob Bogle: From the beginning, Don and I were the Ventures. But from the start on records, we had the other two, Nokie and Mel. I started off doing lead, then I switched to bass early on, and Nokie took over lead. We used them on all of the early records, but it was . . . contractually, it was a while before they became full-fledged Ventures.

Doc Rock: Well, we are glad that they did. The Ventures will always be one of the greatest names in rock 'n' roll, and your music has been an integral part of our lives, for our entire lives. Thanks!

Bob Bogle: Well, thank you for saying so, and I'll see you at the show.

The shows that the Ventures do today are every bit as exciting as the ones they did in 1959, and probably even more so. They have decades of music to play, and decades of experience as to just how to play it for maximum effect and enjoyment!

Ventures Discography

BLUE HORIZON

100	Cookies and Coke	
	Real McCoy	
101	Walk – Don't Run	
	Home	
6052	Night Run (Marksmen)	
	Scratch (Marksmen)	
6054	The Twomp (Don Wilson)	
	Heart on My Sleeve (Don Wilson)	

DOLTON

1960	25	Walk – Don't Run
		The McCoy
	25	Walk – Don't Run
		Home (alternate flip)
	28	Perfidia
		No Trespassing
1961	32	Ram-Bunk-Shush
		Lonely Heart
	41	Ginchy
		Lullaby of the Leaves
	44	Silver City
		Bluer Than Blue
	47	Blue Moon
		Lady of Spain
1962	50	Yellow Jacket
		Genesis
	55	Instant Mashed
		My Bonnie Lies
	60	Lucille
		Lolita Ya-Ya
	67	The 2000 Pound Bee – Part I
		The 2000 Pound Bee – Part II
1963	68	El Cumbanchero
		Skip to M' Limbo
	78	Damaged Goods
		The Ninth Wave
	85	The Chase
		The Savage
1964	91	Walkin' with Pluto
		Journey to the Stars
	94	Fugitive
		Scratchin'
	96	Walk – Don't Run '64
		The Cruel Sea
	300	Slaughter on Tenth Avenue
		Rap City
1965	303	Diamond Head
		Lonely Girl
	306	The Swingin' Creeper
		Pedal Pusher
	308	Ten Seconds to Heaven
		Bird Rockers
	311	Gemini
		La Bamba
	312	Sleigh Ride
		Snow Flakes
1966	316	Secret Agent Man
		007-11
	320	Blue Star
		Comin' Home, Baby
	321	Arabesque
		Ginza Lights
	323	Green Hornet Theme
		Fuzzy and Wild
	325	Wild Thing
		Penetration

LIBERTY

	327	Theme from "The Wild Angels" Kickstand
1967	55967	Strawberry Fields Forever Endless Dream
	55977	Theme from "Endless Summer" Strawberry Fields Forever
	56007	On the Road Mirrors and Shadows
1968	56019	Flights of Fantasy Vibrations
	56044	Medley: Walk–Don't Run—Land of 1,000 Dances/Too Young to Know My Mind?
	56068	Hawaii Five-O Soul Breeze
1969	56115	Theme from "A Summer Place" A Summer Love
1970	56153	Swan Lake Expo Seven-0
	56169	The Mercenary The Wanderer
	56189	Storefront Lawyers Kern County Line

UNITED ARTISTS

50800	Indian Sun Squaw Man
50851	Theme from "Shaft" Tight Fit
50872	Cherries Jubilee Joy
50903	Peter and the Wolf Beethoven's Sonata in C# Minor
50925	Honky Tonk Honky Tonk Part II
50989	Ram-Bunk-Shush Last Night
XW207	Last Tango in Paris Prima Vera
XW277	Little People Skylab (Passport to the Future)
XW333	Also Sprach Zarathustra The Cisco Kid
XW369	The Young and the Restless Elise (from "Fur Elise")
XW392	Main Theme from "The Young and the Restless" Elise (from "Fur Elise")
XW578	Theme "Airport 1975" The Man with the Golden Gun
XW687	Superstar Revue Part 1 Superstar Revue Part 2
XW784	Moonlight Serenade Part 1 Moonlight Serenade Part 2
XW942	Theme from "Charlie's Angels" Theme from "Starsky & Hutch"
XW1100	Walk–Don't Run '77 Amanda's Theme (Haunting Memories)
XW1161	Wipe Out Nadia's Theme

TRIDEX

501	Surfin & Spyin' Rumble at Newport

WARNER BROTHERS
(Mel Taylor)

5675	Bullseye (w/Magics) Watermelon Man
5690	I've Got My Love to Keep Me Warm Young Man Old Man
5839	Bang Bang Rhythm Spanish Armada

RENDEZVOUS
(Mel Taylor)

1871	Drumstick Big Bad Pogo

DRUMBOY

107	Apache Ram Charger

CHAPTER 35

Jackie DeShannon

Jackie DeShannon was a radio singer when she was not yet a teenager. Today she is a cult star, an active performer in the 1990s, and head of her own music and production company.

Jackie DeShannon was brought to Liberty in much the same way that Bobby Vee had been a couple of years earlier. Each was noticed when a record on another label started to get some regional action, and Liberty came in to grab them up.

"I had a record that was breaking locally around Chicago, in the Midwest. Al Bennett came into town, and I met him through the distributor that was distributing my record. I liked him a lot. In fact, a couple of other companies were also bidding for the record and to sign me. I flew out [to California] to meet the other people and to meet Al as well. Then, when I came back to Illinois, I talked to my parents and decided that I would sign with Al." Notice that Jackie said she signed with Al, not with Liberty. That goes to illustrate just how very important Al Bennett really was to Liberty.

Jackie DeShannon's credits as a songwriter are at least as impressive as her credits as a recording artist. "I was signed as a songwriter to Metric [Liberty's music-publishing arm] at the same time I was signed as a performer. You see, I had written the song that I had recorded that was breaking and got into the top five at the time. So I was signed as a songwriter and an artist."

As with virtually everyone else who was ever signed to Liberty, Jackie DeShannon thought that being at Liberty was great fun, and that it was a good place to be in the music business.

"Liberty was a forerunner—they just had their own sound, a very interesting something or other in the mix." And of course, the Liberty people were all great, too. Some people called it the Kiddie Corps because everyone was so young. Snuff Garrett, for example, was barely twenty when he started producing his hits with Bobby Vee and Johnny Burnette. Jackie was aware of this youthful ambience around Liberty. "I'll never forget one of the funny comments someone made when I first came to the label. Hollywood High was across the street, and the comment around town was, you didn't know when the kids at Hollywood High got out versus when the executives at Liberty Records got out. This was because everyone at Liberty was very young and very aggressive, and they would eat, sleep, and breathe the records. It was very much a family affair.

"I was a big fan of Al Bennett's. We disagreed many times, but I think Al was one of the great, great record people. Outside of his charisma and charm, I thought he had a great knowledge of the record industry."

According to Jackie, Al was largely responsible for the great atmosphere around

457

Liberty. "Al was very . . . well, he had a pretty good open-door policy. You'd just walk down the hall at Liberty, and it was like a club. There were many, many artists roaming around the halls, and we would stop by and visit one another at various recording sessions. It was a very interesting place to grow up. It was lots of fun." Besides the artists, DJs such as Jimmy O'Neill of KRLA hung out at Liberty. "I like Jimmy very much, and I think he was certainly well received at Liberty."

Liberty was pioneering in those days, and Jackie fit in well with that pioneering spirit. "There was an energy at that time, a real, real energy, because everything was brand new. There was no one to copy. But the thing about being original is that you pay the price, you carve it out. I don't think you really know what's right or wrong, you just go till it feels right. You know only to listen to yourself and your instincts. Unfortunately, I should've listened a lot more as the years went on."

One of Jackie's first albums at Liberty was an LP of folk songs. It was not easy for her to sell Liberty, meaning Al Bennett, on the idea of doing a concept album like that. It was more common to simply assemble a bunch of unrelated songs together on one LP. As a result of this policy, from her LPs, Jackie seems like a woman looking for an image. Examining her LP covers is like looking at a whole gamut of different women. On the Liberty LP *Jackie DeShannon,* she looks like a sultry nightclub singer with hair-sprayed coiffure, but the songs are Bob Dylan and Peter, Paul, and Mary. On Imperial's *Are You Ready for This?* she looks like a hip British chick. On *To Be Free,* she is standing in a field, her hair is long and loose, and she is wearing a long dress and carrying an armful of flowers. On *Laurel Canyon,* she's wearing bell-bottoms, standing on dilapidated wooden steps with her hand on the railing. *For You* has her close up with a "That Girl" haircut, a scrubbed face, and a big smile. *You Won't Forget Me* features a country bouffant look. And so forth. Jackie longed for a hit and an image. One of her Imperial LPs was even called *New Image*!

These sudden shifts in style and lack of coherence were no fault of Jackie's. She was not floundering around or being a flighty female. She did not pick the nightclub portrait for the folkie LP. What Jackie was was a fan of other artists and a songwriter, tailoring songs for many different singers. As such, she had a body of work on tape that the powers-that-were at Liberty sometimes dipped into at will.

"At that time, the emphasis was in putting singles out. That folk album was done as an album. I went in to make that particular album. I don't think that was my first Liberty album. I don't really recall, because they would put together singles to make an album." Jackie wasn't even around when the album was actually released. "At that time I had to go on tour with the Beatles.

"Getting an album out as a concept was not [the way]. You made the singles. Al Bennett felt you should have a number of singles and then fill it out around those tracks. At that time it was hard to get across the album concept, so it was a bit of a struggle when I wanted to record an album. When I came back from New York, when I'd first heard Bob Dylan at Town Hall in New York, I wanted to do an entire album of all his material. It was very hard to get that concept across to Al because Dylan was virtually unknown. So the album that came out was sort of a watered-down version

Opposite: Seven faces of Jackie DeShannon. She seldom got to choose or approve the pictures used. Album covers that she liked were *Are You Ready for This, Laurel Canyon,* and *New Image,* shown here.

JACKIE
DE SHANNON

are you ready for this?
JACKIE
DE SHANNON

Jackie DeShannon

laurel canyon
jackie
de shannon
"The Weight"
STEREO

FOR YOU/JACKIE DE SHANNON

JACKIE
De
SHANNON
you
won't
forget
me
IMPERIAL

new
image

of what I had originally wanted to do." "Watered-down" is right! Only three Dylan songs on side 1 appeared in the final album. But that is how it was done in those days.

Listening to a Jackie DeShannon album was always interesting. From cut to cut, not to mention from album to album, her sound really did change from country to nightclub to Motown to British sounding. For instance, *Are You Ready for This?* is an album that defies concept. And Jackie explains it by revealing that the cuts on that album "are all single dates. That's not an album. Those are individual, single sessions by individual, different producers. And that's fine, and that sometimes works. It's really okay now. It wasn't okay then. [Laughs] But it happens to be okay now. Now I could probably sit down and listen to that album and comment, 'So?' Because that's acceptable now. That's how I look at it now. Now it is not confusing. Now you just accept it as part of a body of work. But when you put it against a body of work early, it can be confusing."

Jackie's version of "Will You Love Me Tomorrow" on the LP *Are You Ready for This?* sounds like Diana Ross. Why?

"I could have gone on a little quirk there. I was in the mood to do something and probably didn't take it very seriously. I sometimes have a funny sense of humor, and I might go in and do a session or a single date or something and have it put on one of those albums, and it's inconsistent and it kind of throws the listener off. Those things were done in single sessions, maybe three songs were recorded at once. Then they'll decide they want an album product. Or maybe they need to make a quota or want to release things by a certain number of artists by fall or whatever. That may have been [the case with "Will You Love Me Tomorrow"], and that came out and they put a cover on it. Again no concept album, no forethought: 'Let's just slap it on.'

"You don't know who's doing it. The A&R person? Who's put it together? I might have been on the road. So that may explain some of the confusion from time to time. You might go in and do a session and decide a song didn't even come out the way you want and you didn't want it released. You'll notice there are distinct periods, and you'll go, 'My God, is the woman insane?'

"I always like to pioneer but not to that extent! You can only take that so far. But that's basically what happened. And once in a while it would happen to a degree where it's really confusing; even for people who know my work intimately, it can be a bit confusing. I might have gone in and tried something and decided that it should be one single but it certainly didn't dictate a way of life or my style."

Another "style" that Jackie sometimes recorded in was a country style, and at times she sounded just like Brenda Lee, who shared a low, husky vocal quality and for whom Jackie wrote many tunes.

"Brenda Lee was very hot at the time, a great talent, a great singer. It was a pleasure to have Brenda do a song. But those weren't concept albums. You went in with a group of songs that you picked that were not necessarily demoed previously or that you wrote. Only later on would we be able to do those kinds of 'concept' albums. I wanted to do that originally and was never allowed to. So they put out twelve recordings. Some of the songs on an album were demos, some were records; I had no control over that. So it was very confusing. Luckily I made decent demos. [Laughs] My recording career has been, needless to say, very unique."

The Searchers recorded British cover versions of two of Jackie DeShannon's early

Liberty recordings. "Needles and Pins" was written by Jack Nitzsche and Sonny Bono, arranged by Nitzsche, and produced by Dick Glasser. It was Jackie's second U.S. chart hit and the Searchers' first. They copied Jackie's record completely, from the jangling guitars that became known as part of the British-invasion sound, to the pronunciation of "needles and pins-ah."

Jon Sebastian of the Lovin' Spoonful was host of a 1980s A&E TV series "The Golden Age of Rock and Roll." In one program he introduced a 1964 clip of Jackie singing "When You Walk in the Room," another song covered by the Searchers. In his introduction Sebastian said that Jackie wrote the song, gave it to the Searchers, and then later recorded it herself. Not true. Jackie recorded it first. In fact, her Liberty version was on *Billboard* in January 1964, while the Searchers' versions didn't chart until October of that year.

"I wrote the song, I recorded it, and the Searchers covered it. They were very keen on covering Jackie DeShannon records. They told me on many occasions they were big fans, and they did copy my songs, my phrasing; it was amazing, they copied everything, every nuance."

Jackie DeShannon was so popular with the Beatles that she was selected to be one of the acts that toured the United States with them in 1964. I went to the concert the Beatles put on in Kansas City, Missouri, in 1964 — but more to see the Fab Jackie than the Fab Four. But the Beatlemaniacs were so noisy that it was next to impossible to tell what songs either Jackie or the Beatles were performing. Jackie remembers that tour, and the noisy crowds, well.

"No one could hear anything. I think that I went on that tour with an entirely different attitude than most of my colleagues, because I knew what I was in for. I was really thrilled to be a part of it. It never bothered me. In my show I tried to make it as up-tempo as I could so that people would have a good time. I didn't expect nor did I want them to feel they had to sit there or try to sit there while I was doing something. We were all there to see the Beatles — I was there to see the Beatles.

"I'm really happy I did the first American tour. I had a really good time. I really enjoyed it, and it didn't bother me at all. I would do 'Shout' and all kinds of up-tempo things. I just enjoyed the experience, and I went there for the experience. I didn't have any grand feelings like I was in a concert hall in Lincoln Center where you should be able to hear a pin drop, because people did come to see the Beatles. I used to say to the others from time to time, 'You know, I don't think they came here — eighty thousand of them — just to see us,' because they would complain, but that's just what was happening.

"I think it was a very unique time, because you had four people to focus on. With Elvis you liked him or you didn't. Up until that time there had really been just the single people who would command that kind of fame. For the first time, if you didn't like George, you could like Ringo. If you didn't like Ringo, you could like John or Paul. It was really very unique in that sense, and I think the marketing campaign, which we're all so accustomed to today, was really ... besides Presley or a very select few."

That marketing included cardboard displays in record shops of John, Paul, George, and Ringo, with their heads held up on springs so that they appeared happily animated.

"I will never forget going into a record store and seeing four bobbing heads. I mean, I'd never seen anything like that, not even Colonel Parker for Elvis. So you had the massive talent, which they were, and you had the ad campaign or the marketing campaign that matched it, and I think that was brand new to rock and roll. So I was really very aware of that in my mind, so for me it was interesting from many points of view."

As a spin-off of the tour, Jackie released a Liberty album, *Breakin' It Up on the Beatles Tour!* Well, it wasn't actually Jackie who released that LP. Liberty did that LP in a rather independent fashion, and again, Jackie had no control over the project. To the best of her knowledge, Jackie doesn't even know when the songs were recorde, whether anyone came out and actually recorded live or not, or what the songs were. It was a long, long time ago, and she wrote songs, recorded demos, and even singles every day back then.

"I don't remember [what ended up on that album]. There may be something available—maybe some other artist had the show taped. I don't know. There may be tapes around; I don't have them. Basically Liberty did a very rush job on that album. The picture was taken at some Liberty party and was blown up to God knows where and it was probably one of the worst covers any artist has ever had. It was horrendous. I was very unhappy. But they did it; I didn't know anything about it. It was out and I didn't know anything about it. Where they got the songs even to put on it, I don't even know.

"Probably some of them are actually demos, because I would demo every week. I would write all week and I would go in on a Friday and record. That's what I did—all day long. It was interesting. You learned to get those songs out and get them out on time because there were artists waiting for them. In those days the singer-songwriter was not as we know it today, and [as a writer] you went to the top five and went for it. If there was an artist that you connected with, you went for it."

Jackie's demos, by all inside accounts, were excellent records in their own right. Most were said to be far better, even, than the actual releases by the stars, such as the Searchers, who subsequently made them hits. "Basically, the demos that I did [were good because] I had some really good people. I always thought the demo recordings were really good. I think one of the things that makes a writer's demo pretty unique, at least the ones we were doing, was that we were doing it primarily with a very, very good rhythm section, and the rhythm section later on became very famous. Plus at that time I was in and out of the studio, and I would grab someone I would go to see at clubs or who was around, and some of those people were pretty fancy names. So they really weren't demos [in the sense of being poorly done].

"They were demos in the fact that we did one in a half hour. If we spent more than forty minutes on it, that was too long! Forget it. We did them very fast. I sang the vocals live and would have the engineer, whoever happened to be there, mix it. The only part I didn't like about singing the demos was that I didn't get a chance to get in and work on the arrangement closely. I had to make the arrangements and do all that before, and sell tickets at the door! [Laughs] So I had to put it all together as well."

A songwriter has a vision in her head when she writes a song. That vision is how she hopes that the song will come out when it is recorded. But the gap between vision and reality can be a wide one.

"You'll write a song, and very rarely, in my experience, has the record measured up to the expectation I had in my mind. You can probably ask any writer and they'll say the same thing. The record may be very, very good, but it's just not how you hear it." And of course that also happens when an artist other than the composer herself cuts the tune. "It's happened too with other artists, where a song would be done and I would never in a million years hear it that way. I've heard 'When You Walk in the Room' done by some very neat people. They were great records, but I would have never done it that way.

"I love those times and the spirit. I have had some disappointing times, looking back. But you have to realize those things were done in a split second. We'd do as many as four in an afternoon. They were like rehearsal tapes. Unless it was a drastic error, we kept going. So they were very quick vocals. If I took three takes, it was a luxury. The object was to record without running up a huge demo bill."

A lot of Jackie's songs were recorded by British artists. Why? "Because they had the publishing thing going across to England. Many of my demos were heard there, and I've had a lot of people who say they met me first from my demos. As I said, I'd make these demos every week. I would just churn them out. They would send them to their publisher in London. People would come strolling through there and they would be so knocked out by my demos that they would play them for every writer who walked through the door. A lot of those writers became very famous."

Even in the United States, Jackie's demos were in great demand. "The demos belonged to the publishing company to go and try to get records. People would keep them, and we wouldn't get them back. It was amazing."

The high quality of Jackie's demos is probably why it is sometimes said that certain Jackie DeShannon singles, such as "Needles and Pins" or "When You Walk in The Room," were really demos that were released after no one else chose the song to record. This was only rarely done. While a demo might show up on one of Jackie's LPs, her singles were always recorded as singles. "I would do my weekly run [of demos], and they would pick out what they thought might be a good single for me. Some demos were legally issued, but some of them there are double versions because there would be a demo and then my producer, Dick [Glasser] would say, 'We're going to do a single,' then they would be recut, but always copying the demo. I would go in and I would produce the demo, and then they would go in and copy the demo, basically. They might add strings or make a bigger production, but the initial feeling of the song—I always laid it down." Jackie DeShannon's singles of "Needles and Pins" and "When You Walk in the Room" were not her demo recordings.

In 1967 Jackie starred in a movie with Bobby Vee, *C'mon Let's Live a Little*. Bobby Vee's character is a hillbilly who comes to a college where urbanite Jackie's father is president. The movie features songs by Jackie and Bobby, available on a Liberty sound-track LP. Those songs from the movie were written by Don Crawford, and are not typical Vee or DeShannon songs.

Jackie feels that if someone missed seeing that movie, they "did not miss much. They probably aren't [like normal Bobby Vee and Jackie songs]. That project was probably not a good career move on my part. It's not one of your greater productions. I don't even remember recording the songs on that album."

Now the confusion of Jackie's sound and look changing so much from release to release becomes more understandable. Between her many demo projects and the cavalier way Liberty released her recordings, plus the fact that her demos might be tailored for a certain artist, her professional body of work became a puzzle that Liberty arranged in a way Jackie would not necessarily have done herself.

"It's so funny, because as I look at things today and what the various women go through [on an MTV video], another outfit every line of the song and a new image on every record. Today it's versatile. When I did it, it was considered having no direction. Again this is a price you pay for pioneering. When you're an original and you cut out the trail, this is what happens. I think as one looks back at the things I've done, I did then what everyone takes for granted for now.

"Hopping in the Concorde is nothing, but when it was first done it was a big deal. And I was the first to do it, so it was a big deal. I feel very much way ahead of my time. I think it's definitely caught up. Everybody understands that concept quite well now, but when I did it, it just flattened people—they couldn't believe it. But I would come up with these things, some of them I was able to push forward and some of them I was not.

"I would like to have done many more things and many more ideas that I had, a lot I can't recall. But there was a constant, I always had to really fight for progress. And as I would win more battles, we would see better album covers and if I would be able to get a bit of control here. Because I had absolutely nothing to say about the color wheel—I would take a great picture, and they would run it through the color wheel twice, and the colors would be wrong, and it wouldn't matter. It would come out anyway, because they wouldn't spend the money to get it corrected. Maybe they didn't know what the correct color was. But you wouldn't see those things built into artists' contracts today; they have a lot of control. And I had zip. None. As rock and roll became big business, they paid attention."

In 1968 Jackie released the first single of the song "The Weight." And her version reached #55 on *Billboard,* meaning it was a top-forty hit in most of the country. The Band's own version came out shortly afterward and reached #63. How did Jackie happen to get the first single on that famous tune?

"The Band album had come out, and people were familiar with the album. Charlie and Brian called me up, they were producing for Imperial at the time, and they felt that my gospel-y voice and my feeling for that kind of material, they thought I would have a smash. My first question obviously was, 'Isn't this going to be a single with the Band?' 'Oh, no, that's not going to happen.' It was my understanding that it had been checked through various sources that they had no intention of putting it out as a single. Obviously, what would I be recording it for if they were? I loved their version, and I thought it was great. I wasn't going to go cover theirs.

"I did record it. And the record started to really break. Then I guess Capitol looked around and said, 'What are we doing?' I don't know what they said. They decided they were going to go with it. And at that time I think they thought maybe I wouldn't get R&B play, as they called it in those days, so Atlantic or their group put Aretha Franklin on it, so there were three out at the same time. I would go into a radio station to promote mine and come out and find the Capitol guy there. It was really funny.

"But we sold a lot of records, and it's been told to me, it's my impression, that we had the most sales at the time. I don't know where it is now, but we certainly in various markets had number one. But the airplay was split so much—the Band had their cities, Aretha had hers, and I had mine. It's one of the records I like the best. That was rather unique because Barry White and myself and everyone else were singing that song around one microphone, which I thought was pretty unique. It was a great, great experience making that record."

This photo of Jackie DeShannon was taken in the fall of 1967 at a taping of the Woody Woodbury show. The guys are a group called the Yellow Balloon, formed to record a cover version of Jan & Dean's 1967 post-Liberty Columbia Records hit, "Yellow Balloon." Left to right: Don Braucht, Alex Valdez (lead), Jackie DeShannon, Frosty Green, and Paul Cannella. *(Courtesy Alex Valdez.)*

Since Jackie was a prolific and fine songwriter, it was a surprise when her first really huge hit was a song by Hal David and Burt Bacharach, "What the World Needs Now Is Love." How did she get that song?

"The company arranged that Burt and Hal would produce a single session. They played me the song, and it was just a natural thing, it wasn't a big deal, it's just that's what happened. They played me 'What the World Needs Now Is Love' and obviously it had been turned down by lots of people. They didn't give me something hot. I don't think they wrote anything for me. They're so prolific I'm sure they just reached in their trunk and picked it out. At least Hal claims they reached in their trunk.

"I loved them so much, and it was a great thrill for me. I didn't think anything about it, but again people thought it was changing a direction. I mean, they certainly don't hang that on anyone now. God forbid that someone's album is like their last album. It's still hard for me to realize that it's okay, that everyone really understands that now, they expect you to be versatile and they expect you to do all this. But I had a real hard time, so I still have some old war wounds. But I thought nothing of it. Hey, it's a great song, let's do it. Let's go. And that's what we did.

I'm not going to write every great song that ever was, and I don't look at it like that with a chance to work with Bacharach and David. Hey, let's go. That's what they do. I did it and I loved it."

Jackie may not be able to write every great song that there ever was, but she sure wrote a lot of great ones, including "Come and Stay with Me" for Marianne Faithfull, which Jackie herself also recorded.

"My version was recorded after Marianne Faithfull. I wrote it in London, and I wrote it thinking in the back of my head of someone like Marianne because I had gone to England to play songs. That song was written right there, and Marianne was staying in the same hotel I was staying in and happened to be recording at that time. I remember I had phoned Al [Bennett] and said, 'I think I've just written a big song, Al.' He said, 'I certainly hope so. I sent you there, you'd better be.' [Laughs]

"I said, 'Marianne is here, and I think the song's perfect for her.' He said, 'Well, get her to do it. Get her to do it.' So I said, 'Do you think I should just keep it or—' 'Get her to do it! Let's go!' I liked her very much, so that was not a problem for me. And she really liked the song and did a great record, a great record. I don't know that I would have made that kind of record—in fact, I didn't make that kind of record."

Jackie released a great many albums on Liberty and Imperial, especially considering that only three of her twenty-four hits actually made the top forty nationally. It brings to mind the phenomenon of Julie London, who had only one hit single but dozens of LPs. Was it the fact that the albums sold well that Jackie had so many released, that she was one of the first album artists of the rock era?

"It's really hard to say. I can't comment because I really wasn't paying attention to the business side. I was happy to record and write."

Occasionally a Buddy Holly song would turn up on a Jackie DeShannon album, sometimes with a British slant. No matter how she interpreted Buddy's tunes, these were always pleasant surprises.

"I was one of the first females to take on Buddy Holly material. I mean, who would do that? I would. Buddy is one of my all-time top three artists. It's so difficult to put your finger on it, but when Buddy Holly made a record, you stopped [and listened]. He was one of the first rock and roll persons to use strings on a record. I was ready to stomp on him. How could you do that? I mean, 'Peggy Sue,' all these great things. But after I'd listened a few times, I said, 'Of course, it would be Buddy Holly who would put it in perfectly and put his stamp on it.'

"But, for Buddy Holly to use strings—I can't say he was the first person—but for me it was my first memory, I'd never heard it done before. It was unbelievable. But he didn't sell out when he did it, his vocal didn't change, he was just as pure as he always was. He was just something in the stratosphere. I can't talk about anyone the way I talk about Buddy Holly. It's impossible."

Jackie DeShannon's look and her musical style are not the only things that change from record to record. The spelling of her name also changes. It was actually "deShannon" originally, but she had to forget that, because it was always incorrectly reproduced. The *d* would be capitalized, or perhaps a space would be incorrectly inserted between the *e* and the *S*.

"The labels that were sent back, things that were written in interviews, people just were not caring enough. So finally, I just sort of gave in and said, 'Well, how about we just make it DeShannon?'" Even then there were problems. "They would continually put the space there; it's not supposed to be."

Now, the official way to write Jackie's last name, which she takes to be basically Irish for "of Shannon," is "DeShannon."

"I think I was very fortunate to come up with a sense of innocence in that when you're breaking ground you really don't know what's on the other side, so every day was a surprise, every day was something different. And you do pay a price for that. But it's such a rush when you do something that hasn't been done before or you're making history or you're setting a precedent. It's just an incredible feeling, and it makes me feel good that someone has the sensitivity like you do that makes it all worthwhile.

"If I can do an interview like this once in a great while it makes me feel like it was worth it.* Interviewers don't have to be die-hard fans, Michael, but so many times they just don't have any knowledge of anything and I just plough through, and I get frustrated. I get very frustrated just thinking about doing interviews, before I even talk to anyone, because I know they don't have the knowledge. I just don't have the patience to educate them. So this is really a great thrill for me to be talking to you."

The thrill was mine.

Jackie DeShannon Discography

RENDEZVOUS
(Sharon Lee)

| 401 | No Deposit, No Return / Kissing Game |

SAGE
(Jackie DeShannon)

| 290 | Just Another Lie / Cajun Blues |

FRATERNITY
(Jackie DeShannon)

| 836 | Just Another Lie / Cajun Blues |

DOT
(Jackie DeShannon)

| 15928 | Just Another Lie / Cajun Blues |
| 15980 | Trouble / Lies |

PJ
(Jackie DeShannon)

| 101 | Trouble / Lies |

SAND
(Jackie Dee)

| 330 | Trouble / Lies |

GONE
(Jackie Dee)

| 5008 | I'll Be True / How Wrong Was I |

EDISON INTERNATIONAL

| 416 | So Warm / I Wanna Go Home |
| 418 | Put My Baby Down / The Foolish One |

LIBERTY

55148	Buddy (Jackie Dee) / Strolypso Dance
55288	Teach Me / Lonely Girl
55342	Think About You / Heaven Is Being with You
55358	Wish I Could Find a Boy / I Won't Turn You Down

* Jackie DeShannon spoke from her Hollywood home October 15, 1991.

	55387	Baby (When Ya Kiss Me) Ain't That Love	66132	A Lifetime of Loneliness Don't Turn Your Back on Me
	55425	The Prince I'll Drown in My Own Tears	1966 66171	Come and Get Me Splendor in the Grass
	55484	Just Like in the Movies Guess Who	66194	Will You Love Me Tomorrow (Cancelled) Are You Ready for This?
	55497	You Won't Forget Me I Don't Think So Much of Myself	66196	Windows and Doors (Cancelled) So Long Johnny
	55526	Faded Love Dancing Silhouettes	66202	I Can Make It with You To Be Myself
	55563	Needles and Pins Did He Call Today, Mama?	1967 66224	Come on Down (from the Top of That Hill)
	55602	Little Yellow Roses Oh Sweet Chariot		Find Me Love
	55602	Little Yellow Roses 500 Miles (alternate flip)	66236	The Wishing Doll Where Does the Sun Go?
	55645	Till You Say You're Mine When You Walk in the Room	66251	Changin' My Mind It's All in the Game
	55673	Should I Cry (Cancelled) I'm Gonna Be Strong	1968 66281	I Keep Wanting You Me About You
	55678	Oh Boy I'm Looking for Someone to Love	66301	Nobody's Home to Go Home To Nicole
	55705	Hold Your Head High She Don't Understand Him Like I Do	66312	I Didn't Want to Have to Do It Splendor in the Grass
	55730	He's Got the Whole World in His Hands It's Love Baby	66313	The Weight Effervescent Blue
	55735	When You Walk in the Room Over You	66313	The Weight (Cancelled) Splendor in the Grass (alternate flip)
	55787	What the World Needs Now Is Love (Cancelled) A Lifetime of Loneliness	66342 1969 66370	Laurel Canyon Holly Would What Is This? Trust Me
	56187	It's So Nice Mediterranean Sky	66385	Put a Little Love in Your Heart Always Together
	MGM		66419	Love Will Find a Way Completely
	13349	Love and Learn I'm Glad It's You	66430	Do You Know How Christmas Trees Are Grown?
	IMPERIAL			1 Christmas
1965	66110	What the World Needs Now Is Love Remember the Boy	1970 66438	Brighton Hill You Can Come to Me
	SP-23	What the World Needs Now Is Love Remember the Boy	66452	Medley: You Keep Me Hangin' On/Hurt So Bad/What Was Your Day Like?

AMHERST

725	Don't the Flame Burn Out	2919	I Wanna Roo You
			Sweet Sixteen
	I Don't Think I Can Wait		Speak Out to Me
728	To Love Somebody	2924	Chains on My Soul
	Just to Feel This Love from You		Peaceful in My Soul
		2994	(If You Never Have a Big Hit Record) You're Still Gonna Be My Star/Your Baby Is a Lady
733	You're the Only Dancer		
	Tonight You're Doin' It Right		
737	Things We Said Today	3041	Jimmie, Just Sing Me One More Song
	Way Above the Angels		You've Changed

CAPITOL

COLUMBIA

3130	Keep Me Warm	10221	Let the Sailors Dance
	Salinas		Boat to Sail
3185	Stone Cold Soul	10340	Fire in the City
	West Virginia Mine		All Night Desire

ATLANTIC

RCA

2871	Vanilla Olay	11902	I Don't Need You Anymore
	Only Love Can Break Your Heart		Find Love
2895	Paradise		

CHAPTER 36

Jan & Dean

Of the top dozen best-selling singles artists on Liberty and its main subsidiary labels—Dolton, Imperial, and Soul City—Jan & Dean are unique. Only they had previously had top-forty hits on three other record labels unrelated to Liberty before signing with Liberty. In all Jan & Dean had more than two dozen hits. On Liberty alone they had eighteen national hits and several other, regional hits. Today Jan & Dean are remembered for their surf and drag hits, "Surf City," "Drag City," and "Honolulu Lulu," all three in 1963; and "The Little Old Lady (from Pasadena)" and "Dead Man's Curve," both 1964. All those songs were top-ten hits. Their other well-known surfing songs included "Ride the Wild Surf," from the movie of the same name, and "Sidewalk Surfin'."

Funny thing, though. There were a lot of surf and drag artists, the Hondells, Ronny and the Daytonas, the Rip Chords, the Beach Boys, the Stick Shifts, the Surfaris, and others. The thing they had in common: Each of those artists, as indicated by their names, was created as a surf and drag artist. Jan & Dean, second only to the Beach Boys in number of surf hits, were different. Their name was not based even distantly on surfing or cars. Why? Because, alone among the surf and drag groups (there were no solo surf singers), Jan & Dean were not originally surf singers. Among the surfer artists, only Jan & Dean had a career in rock 'n' roll before the surf boom of 1963–64. They had big top-ten hits like "Baby Talk" in 1959 and "Jennie Lee" in 1958. Moreover, unlike the other surf artists, Jan & Dean were the only surf and drag artists (other than the Beach Boys) who outlived the surf era. They had top-forty hits like "You Really Know How to Hurt a Guy" and "I Found a Girl" in 1965. In fact, their career ended not because of a loss of popularity but due to personal tragedy.

Another distinction for Jan & Dean was their nonmusical activities. While other popular rock 'n' roll groups were into drugs, transcendental meditation, or other less-than-productive sidelines, Jan & Dean attended college all through their rock 'n' roll days, with Dean getting a graduate degree in commercial design and Jan nearly completing a medical degree.

Jan & Dean would have had more hits, and Jan would have become the first rock 'n' roll doctor, had not Jan suffered severe injuries, including partial paralysis and brain damage, in a car accident in 1966. Even after the wreck, they had several regionally popular records.

Other Liberty artists had been struck down before—Eddie Cochran in 1960 and Johnny Burnette in 1964. The difference here is that, while Cochran and Burnette were not current hit makers when their accidents happened, Jan & Dean were hotter than ever. But let's start the story in 1958.

Jan Berry and Dean Torrence met on the football team while attending Hollywood High. The school mascot was the Barons, so when Jan and Dean and a few other friends (like Sandy ["Teen Beat"] Nelson and Arnie Ginsburg) found out how neat it sounded singing in the locker room (the echo, you know) they formed an impromptu group, the Barons. Jan was into rock 'n' roll already as an avid radio fan. He even printed up some stationery for KJAN radio, a station that did not really exist except as a tape recorder, which he used to play DJ and provide music for school parties. His cohorts in this included Dean Orm Torrence (aka KDOT) and Don Altfeld. Jan and Don met when Don was writing a rock 'n' roll column for a national teen magazine, as well as for the high school newspaper.

Featured in Don's high school column was his personal "pick hit of the week." But he was puzzled by the way the name of the pick hit seemed to change each week between the time he submitted his copy to the paper and the time the paper hit the school corridors.

One day Don went down to the school print shop to look into this matter. There he ran into a boy with printer's ink all over his hands and face. It was Jan. Young Jan Berry was so into music that he had been resetting the news type to reflect his own choice of hit of the week. The two became fast and lifelong friends. Don wrote or cowrote at least thirty songs that Jan & Dean eventually recorded ("Dead Man's Curve," for one), as well as songs for other artists such as Johnny Crawford and Shelley Fabares.

Years later, Don would appear on the Jan & Dean *Batman* LP, and his brother Horace would write liner notes for the *Dead Man's Curve* LP. Don went to medical school with Jan and became an M.D. Favorite songs of Jan and Dean in those days were records like the Monotones' "Book of Love," Duane Eddy's "Movin' and Groovin'," Wee Willie Wain's "Travelin' Mood," the Teen Queens' "I Miss You," Bill Bodaford and the Rockets' "Tear Drops," the Avons' "Bonnie" and "Baby," the Clairemonts' "Angel of Romance," the Lovers' "Let's Elope," the Junior Misses' "Never Never," Sugar Pie and Pee Wee's "Let's Get Together," and the Moonglows' "Soda Pop," "Sincerely," and "I Knew from the Start."

The first Jan & Dean hit was "Jennie Lee" by Jan and . . . Arnie?

Doc Rock: Just who was Arnie?
Dean: Arnie was a high school friend of ours. We all sang on several tapes of "Jennie Lee," calling ourselves the Barons after our high school mascot. Then I had to go into the Army reserves. While I was there "Jennie Lee" came out. It was a huge hit, number one in most cities. But since I was in uniform and unavailable, the Barons became Jan & Arnie.
Doc Rock: Did Arnie leave voluntarily when you came out of the Army?
Dean: Well, he had no choice. I was bigger than he was! No, as matter of fact, he left first.
Doc Rock: So, did you approach Jan?
Dean: No, Jan approached me. One day, casually, at a football game, we were playing football. It had been a long time since he'd been into music, and I didn't want to ever bring up music again, because I was, well, hurt, because Jan had really cut me out on "Jennie Lee." After this football game, he said, "Hey. Wanna come up and do some music, Dean?" I asked him, "What about Arnie?" "Screw Arnie," he said. Well, Arnie was gone. Arnie was surfing; he was really into surfing. So I rejoined Jan. But Arnie and I went through college together. Arnie is really bright, a bright guy, a good designer. He went to the University of Moscow on a scholarship, to Russia for a year.

Jan and Arnie, pre-Dean, rehearsing with Jack Benny for a TV appearance. *(Courtesy Bill Berry.)*

Doc Rock: He is not the DJ Arnie ("Woo Woo") Ginsburg, like is claimed on a Cruisin' LP liner notes, is he?
Dean: No.
Doc Rock: I didn't think so.
Dean: Tsk, tsk! You should have written and told them! He went to college with me for five years.
Doc Rock: Five years! All during the hits. That reminds me of Pete Best, who got kicked out of the Beatles. He always tried to get back at them, make some money. How did Arnie react to Jan & Dean's success?
Dean: He was really a nice kid, he kind of regretted it in a way and kind of didn't. He really knew that it wasn't going to be, to happen, with him.
Doc Rock: So what was the first thing you and Jan did, after Arnie?
Dean: We spent several months working on a song called "Baby Talk." It was as big a hit as "Jennie Lee."
Doc Rock: I just got another copy of "Jennie Lee" the other day, but it was not the Arwin record by Jan & Arnie; it was a Liberty record by Billy Ward and His Dominoes! A black group covering a white record?!

JAN & DEAN

LOU ADLER
PERSONAL REPRESENTATIVE

Jan & Dean, looking quite white while sounding somewhat black.

Dean: Well, they figured it was the other way around. They thought that we were stealing the black sound. So therefore it was OK for the black artist to cover the white artist's song.
Doc Rock: Their version did not make the top forty.
Dean: No.
Doc Rock: I always find it curious, it was OK for a black to redo a white hit, and OK for a British invasion artist to redo an American hit, but whenever a white American redid a black American's song or a British song or sound, they were criticized!
Dean: Well, one of the first shows we ever did, we showed up where we were supposed to meet everybody, and they were surprised to find out that we were white guys and that we just sounded black on records! We'd heard some of them, and we knew they were black, but we didn't know all the other acts were black! We were the only white guys in the tour! The money was good, the card games were fun, so we did it.
Doc Rock: This was when?

Dean: About nineteen sixty. I don't really remember what songs we had at that time. I know we had "Baby Talk" and a few of those. And in those days that stuff sounded black, I guess. So they booked us, just on the basis of these records, figuring we must be a black group.

Doc Rock: That must have been some tour!

Dean: The first night of the tour, we still had no idea that nobody in the audience knew we weren't black. So we were introduced, and we were standing offstage with guys like Bobby Day ["Rockin' Robin" and "Over and Over," 1958], Little Willie John ["Fever," 1956, and "Sleep," 1960] and the backup band for everyone, the Little Richard Band. All very heavy groups, but all very black!

Doc Rock: What happened?

Dean: They introduced us, and the crowd went crazy! Just crazy! Until we walked out onstage. Then it went suddenly silent. They were shocked!

Doc Rock: And so were you?

Dean: And so were we! 'Cause we thought they would keep screaming. We thought they knew we were white, but that they were still screaming for us in spite of it. But it became obvious when we came out that they were screaming for the record they'd heard and thought a black group was singing it. And it was really surprising to them when the two whitest people they'd ever seen walked out!

Doc Rock: Blond, blue eyes!

Dean: Blond, blue eyes.

Doc Rock: Did you lip-synch to a record, or was it live?

Dean: No, we did it live with the Little Richard Band, which was a damn good band. And they really helped us out. They got the people enthused again, because the initial response to our color was—quite noticeable! Then, about halfway through the first song, they started to get over the shock. By the time we finished the second or third song, they were into it again with us. But that initial gasp was, well, kind of funny.

Doc Rock: Kind of.

Dean: The first time, it was a shock. Then we decided it was something we could play for, each show! "Oh, just wait till they see us!" So at each show we would have the lights way down when we were introduced. Then we would go out there and start singing, and they would all be going crazy!

Doc Rock: And the lights would come up while you were singing?

Dean: Yes, and did it really surprise them! That was a very weird tour. We couldn't stay in the same hotels as they could. And we played mostly the South, which made it all very strange. They'd usually have to sneak us into their rooms; most of the time we did that because it was much harder to sneak all of them into our rooms! Very weird, like eating. We'd all eat together, but we got absolutely terrible service. Nobody would wait on our tables. Well, that's show biz!

Doc Rock: Skipping to 1964, when I first heard "Dead Man's Curve" on the radio, I was in my friend's car, and we flipped! Such a great record to have on the car radio!

Dean: Glad you liked it!

Doc Rock: I liked it so much, I went out and bought the *Drag City* LP because "Dead Man's Curve" was on it! Much to my surprise, the version of "Dead Man's Curve" on that LP was not the hit version. I played it for a friend who even thought it was a Beach Boys version! Even now, decades later, you hear that wrong version played on oldies stations.

Dean: That was the first "Dead Man's Curve" and the only "Dead Man's Curve" we had, which was the first version, that came out on *Drag City*.

Doc Rock: And the mono version of that LP had a much longer version of "Dead Man's Curve" than the stereo version.

Dean: Really?

Doc Rock: Yes, the mono version had a much longer fade-out on the *Drag City* LP.

Dean: Hummm, I wonder why?

Aspiring teen idols Jan & Dean in a publicity photo from about the time they signed with Liberty.

Doc Rock: I soon discovered that I had to buy both the mono and stereo versions of all of your Liberty LPs, because many of the songs would have different sound effects, totally different takes of a song, even longer or shorter fade-outs.

Dean: You know, I'm very glad to hear you say that. Fade-outs are very important to me.

Doc Rock: Like the long one on the United Artists' version of "Sidewalk Surfin'" you did in the early 1970s, and the marvelously long fade-out on the Legendary Masked Surfers' single you did of "Gonna Hustle You."

Dean: Well, I just got a Drifters LP, and it is so disappointing because they faded all of the songs early! Ben E. King did some of the most ... neatest vocal things he

Jan & Dean would have been the stars of the movie *Ride the Wild Surf* had not a friend of Dean's kidnapped Frank Sinatra, Jr., and stashed the ransom in Dean's bathroom!

ever did were on the ends. And they cut off all of them! I knew every note and where it went, and when it faded on the singles. All of a sudden you get an LP, and none of it is there!
Doc Rock: If it has a longer fade, that is OK—
Dean: Oh, yes!
Doc Rock: —but if it is shorter than the single, that is no good!
Dean: Right! Exactly!
Doc Rock: There is a crazy beginning and ending on the LP version of "She's My Summer Girl," the flip side of "Surf City." Totally unlike the single.
Dean: Was "She's My Summer Girl" on an LP?
Doc Rock: Yes, a couple, *Ride the Wild Surf,* for one.
Dean: Figures. They put everything on the albums. Boy, get those albums out there. I don't remember those things particularly. I do remember the "Dead Man's Curve" though, and that used to bother me after we cut the good one, the hit one. The first one, we planned it that way, we knew that that version was going on the *Drag City* LP.
Doc Rock: The version with the odd melody and the line "French tail lights" instead of "six tail lights," no background vocals, and no sound effects at all?

Dean: Yes, the first one was planned that way. We knew just how we were going to revise it, but we didn't have time to redo it.

Doc Rock: Why not?

Dean: Well, "Drag City" was a big hit, and they said, "Market studies show that you gotta have the LP out there at a certain particular minute," this is what Liberty is insisting to us. That is when you are going to capture all of your sales, so the marketing people didn't really care what material you put on the LP, as long as you [got] it out there.

Doc Rock: I see. Unlike today, when a group may have months to craft an LP.

Dean: So they wanted it and wanted it, and bugged us and bugged us, so we just didn't have time. We did keep saying, "But we want to redo the next single, which is going to be 'Dead Man's Curve.'" But they could not care less what the next single is. All they are interested in is the current one. As far as they are concerned, you'll never have another one! At least, that is the way they play it.

Doc Rock: Nice of them!

Dean: Yeah. So they said, "No, you can't redo the silly song, we just want the LP!" So we said, "OK, you can have the LP," but we only did it because they finally beat us down. I guess we more or less gave in finally. We told them, "OK, here it is, but we are going to redo the single of 'Dead Man's Curve.'"

Doc Rock: That explains the different versions.

Dean: Yes, we rerecorded "Dead Man's Curve" with extra voices, changed some of the lyrics, revised the melody line, added the car noises, and I think we made it a better recording all the way around. And then that version came out on another LP right after that, the one about the girl in school.

Doc Rock: You mean *Dead Man's Curve.*

Dean: Oh, that was called *Dead Man's Curve/New Girl in School.*

Doc Rock: Except on some copies, it is switched around, with "New Girl" listed first. And on that version, the cover photo is pink and black instead of full color.

Dean: Yes, the pink one was a quick version they got out. We tried to complain to Liberty about it, but that was really before the artist ever got any control over the cover art, which took many years to get. Then, when Liberty did have time, they put the color picture on, not because we wanted it, not because of artistic reasons—'cause they thought that it would sell more. Their market study showed that a color cover would sell 8.3 percent, or whatever, more copies than a black-and-white one.

Doc Rock: So the black-and-white one was first?

Dean: Yes, that was the quick one.

Doc Rock: But why does it list "New Girl in School" first?

Dean: Well, "Drag City" was a top-ten record, so get that LP out there with "Drag City" on it! Jan and I liked to always put out an LP with two hits on it instead of only one like most artists did. These people at Liberty said, "You already have 'Drag City' on there, so save 'Dead Man's Curve' and don't put it on that LP, save it for the next one!" But we told them that we wanted "Dead Man's Curve" on Drag City because it is relevant to that LP. We don't want to do another LP; we just finished this one. They gave in on that one, except didn't let us recut it. They didn't even know if it would be a hit anyway. If they'd known it was going to be a hit, they would never have put it on. They don't want you to be able to get the new song you just heard on the radio on an LP that is already out. They want to sell you another LP.

Doc Rock: That was what happened to me; I ended up buying both.

Dean: Thanks! So, *Drag City* came out, sells what it is going to sell. Then, the "Dead Man's Curve" single comes out, and it was a two-sided hit! They'd never had many two-sided hits before at Liberty! No one had counted on the flip side, "New Girl in School." So, since we had already used "Dead Man's Curve" on the other LP, they said, "'New Girl in School, 'New Girl in School!' A new title! Now we can put out a new LP called *New Girl in School* and people who have *Drag City* with 'Dead Man's

The two versions of the *Dead Man's Curve* LP cover. The original listed "The New Girl in School" first.

Curve' on it will be attracted to buy the new LP because it has a new hit in the title!" Our answer was that "Dead Man's Curve" was a hit, too. So, they added that to the title, but to management, it was a *New Girl in School* LP. They figured it was a residual thing, that most people would not even know that "Dead Man's Curve" was on the flip side.

Doc Rock: But wasn't "Dead Man's Curve" bigger?

Dean: Yes, but they felt that since "New Girl in School" was a top-twenty hit, it would sell one hundred fifty thousand LPs, which is a lotta LPs.

More than 90 percent of all 45 sleeves in the fifties and sixties had the same photo on both sides, but Liberty often put something else on the back. This is the back of the "Dead Man's Curve" sleeve, featuring "The New Girl in School," which was possibly the only bookmark pictures sleeve ever made. The other side is shown on page 351.

> **Doc Rock:** Of course, the original title of "New Girl in School," before it was censored by Liberty, was "Gonna Hustle You." Why was that changed?
>
> **Dean:** Liberty thought the word *hustle* was too suggestive, offensive, and so we changed the line "When summer comes, gonna hustle you," to "New girl in school."
>
> **Doc Rock:** Didn't you tell Liberty that with the original title, it would have sold even better?
>
> **Dean:** Yes, see we pointed that out and Liberty said, "You're wrong. The original words would sell less because no DJ would ever play it!" They felt that line was suggestive! A short time later, the Rolling Stones sang "(I Can't Get No) Satisfaction," a number-one song the DJs did play!
>
> **Doc Rock:** Now for the sixty-four-thousand-dollar question. Ever since I bought my *Dead Man's Curve* LP, for over twenty-five years, I have been trying to decipher the background words to the second verse of "DMC." I have tried to read your lips on stage. But I cannot figure it out? What are those words?
>
> **Dean:** You know, the Carpenters did that song, whatever that album was, *Now and*

> **JUST TUNED MY CAR NOW SHE REALLY PEELS,
> A-LOOKIN' REAL TUFF WITH CHROME-REVERSED WHEELS;
> MY BLUE CORAL WAX-JOB SURE LOOKS PRETTY,
> GONNA GET MY CHICK AND MAKE IT OUT TO DRAG CITY.**

JAN & DEAN'S "DRAG CITY"
A souped-up fast selling single and a brand new rod hot album

LIBERTY RECORDS

The Liberty trade ad for the "Drag City" 45 and LP.

Then, and they, too, heard that part. And so Richard got my number and called me up and wanted to know what that part was. And I was surprised he had heard it, because it was pretty subtle.

Doc Rock: Yes.
Dean: That was one of Brian Wilson's favorite parts, too, on our records.
Doc Rock: So, are you gonna tell me what it was?

Dean: That's ... "Slippin' and-a slidin', driftin' and broad slidin'./Slippin' and-a slidin', driftin' and broad slidin'."

Doc Rock: Well, no wonder I couldn't get it! Who wrote that?

Dean: Me. [Jokes] That's why it was turned down as the A Side.

Doc Rock: Finally, I can sing along with the darn thing! A lot of times, I preferred your mono LPs to the stereo ones, because in stereo, the hits didn't sound like the original singles, even when they were exactly the same. But with some of your hits, like "Sidewalk Surfin'," every time it is on a stereo LP, it is an alternate take from the hit version. How come there is a difference between the stereo and mono albums that are supposedly the same? I mean, in stereo, songs like "Sidewalk Surfin'" and "Little Old Lady (from Pasadena)" are never the same version as the mono releases.

Dean: Probably an engineer's mistake most of the time.

Doc Rock: On your *Legendary Masters Anthology* album, you did put on the monaural version of "Sidewalk Surfin'."

Dean: OK, that's the one I liked the best. As a matter of fact, I like monaural. Whenever I can I use monaural. Because I feel that one of the most important things about a fun, exciting rock 'n' roll record is the levels of everything. In other words it is vital that the mixture of the different components that you have in a song [is] blended just right.

Doc Rock: When it is in mono, you mix it, the artist—

Dean: Yeah, exactly.

Doc Rock: —and when it's in stereo, the kid at home messes with the mix.

Dean: And I don't think the kid at home should be mixing your song.

Doc Rock: And when an AM radio station plays a stereo record of something like "Surf City," it always seems like their equipment is out of whack and either the lead or else the background is almost totally inaudible.

Dean: And even if it is feeding both sides the same, when you change a stereo record to mono like that, the lead part or whatever is in the middle comes out much more loudly than it is on a real mono mix of the song.

Doc Rock: Besides "Sidewalk Surfin'" and "The Little Old Lady (from Pasadena)," "The Anaheim, Azusa and Cucamonga Sewing Circle, Book Review, and Timing Association," even "Drag City" sounds better in mono.

Dean: I think I picked all of those out in mono on the *Legendary Masters Anthology* album; I used mono whenever I could. And the management always fights me, because they feel that everyone is ... "into stereo." I think stereo is fine for records with sweetening, like strings and extra horns and stuff like that.

Doc Rock: *Pop Symphony,* the LP you did of orchestral versions of your hits?

Dean: Sure. That's nice, because there are enough components that you can get the feel of an orchestra around you, and that can be very interesting. But as far as a straight rock and roll record, you just don't give a darn about "where the orchestra is." It's just all together, all mishmashed, coming at you, that is the exciting part, not having it taken apart and killed. Yeah, you're right. Those stereo mistakes were from the engineer, but sometimes any stereo is a mistake.

Doc Rock: I always play my mono LPs. To me the stereo is just sort of a novelty on most songs. But if you play the mono versions of those songs against the stereo versions, even when it is the exact same recording, the mono has an impact that cannot be matched by the stereo versions.

Dean: Yes.

Doc Rock: Back to the area we were talking about, the albums *Drag City* and *Dead Man's Curve/New Girl in School.* Did you tend to have trouble with the executives at Liberty? Is that why you had troubles with the car LPs? Were the LPs you fought for your most popular LPs? In fact, we all know "Surf City" was your biggest single hit. But, which of your LPs did the best on the LP charts?

Dean: Well, there were ups and downs. Liberty might be asleep one month, we could have a number-one hit record like "Surf City" and do barely any business selling LPs.

In 1971 UA had bought Liberty, and they resurrected the "Legendary Masters" name (see chapter 16) for a series of double LPs featuring Fats Domino, Eddie Cochran, Ricky Nelson, and Jan & Dean. Dean designed this cover, depicting the life and times of Jan & Dean from the fifties through Kittyhawk Graphics, Dean's design firm.

>Now, that is not our fault. You cannot sit there and decide, creatively, this or that is why an LP didn't sell. You can't gauge an artist's career by looking at the relative popularity of their LPs. That is bull; that is not relevant. ELO [the Electric Light Orchestra] used to complain about that. They would be in the top ten, and half of the LPs would be returned by the distributors, unsold. Meanwhile, their friends who were also on the top ten but were on other record labels were selling over twice as many LPs. That was the company's (United Artists Records) fault, not ELO's fault, creatively or artistically.

Doc Rock: That is a totally new perspective for me.

Dean: That is why the LP charts were crazy; they often as not would reflect trends in a record company as much as anything. Liberty would be in good shape at one point in time, then they would go into a down cycle for a couple of months. Say they fired one or two key people, in a midstream management upheaval! Just when you have a record coming out! That record is not going to do well, no matter who or what is on it in terms of musical quality.

Doc Rock: That seems unprofessional.

Dean: Another thing, you could miss out if you had a record come out during a convention of people in the record-company business, because they all lose it! They were in Hawaii for two weeks, they'd lose track of the record. Then, when they came back, they felt lazy, all of their enthusiasm is gone, and the group suffered. That's the way it was; it's a dumb business. For all of the millions and billions of dollars these people can make, it was run very shoddily, by people who are not creative or just don't care.

Doc Rock: You're speaking of the old days. How is it now?

Dean: Well, better. They have learned to care, because the record business has had some slow times. EMI has bought Liberty, Capitol, and United Artists. For the first time, the same company has our old stuff and the Beach Boys'. Yet our reissues will not get the media push, the publicity that the Beach Boys' got, because they no longer have the money to spend that they used to have. So our compilations unfortunately do not get the attention the Beach Boys' did.

Doc Rock: When *All Summer Long* came out, old Beach Boy tracks, and sold so well, wasn't that just the innate worth of the Beach Boys' music?

Dean: When the label spends two hundred fifty thousand on television ads—

Doc Rock: I did see a ton of ads for that LP.

Dean: —a quarter of a million dollars, strong, early 1970s dollars, just on television. K-Tel is one company that knew this, but it is expensive. Now, major record companies do not like to put big bucks into TV ads. Know why?

Doc Rock: Tell me!

Dean: Because if they do it for one act, then they are gonna have to do it for every other act. K-Tel could do it, because they had one project that came out every couple of months. They spent the money, but they don't have any acts signed to the label. All they do is lease the master tapes or make new ones. This way, no acts can complain. On Capitol, Glen Campbell would complain, "I have a new LP coming out. I just saw a commercial for the Beach Boys, and you won't do one for me!" So if they do it for Glen, then Linda Ronstadt wants one—the fighting never ends. With fifty groups on a label, you open a can of worms if you start that whole thing. They have told me as much.

Doc Rock: It seems like a shame that one act can't get the ads, just because they deserve it.

Dean: You got the picture. I have often suggested that they do it by levels. The artist could attain these varying levels by sales and by longevity at the label. Being at each successive level would justify or authorize a certain amount of money spent in whatever medium. That way when an artist complains, it can be shown why he doesn't get what another act might get. Yet he knows that he can earn his way to the higher levels by working at it. You get a number-one hit, they push your LP, especially if you've been around a few years. That takes it out of the area of whim, or of who has the pushiest manager.

Doc Rock: The way it is now, the squeaky wheel gets the oil?

Dean: Whenever a label person said, "I hate so-and-so's manager," that meant that the manager was pushing for something, but I also noticed that his artist always got a lot. A good manager with a different approach, not pushy, wouldn't make it. The company moves only when it is kicked.

Doc Rock: This obviously relates to your selection of a label in the 1980s, and your work with Mike Love of the Beach Boys and the records you have released on Hitbound Records and with Radio Shack.

Dean: Sure! Who wants a label that you have to kick? Or one that won't distribute? People don't realize that our record "Baby Talk" [1959] was a national number one; the charts don't reflect that. Yet the song was number one when it was released in LA. Then, by the time that popularity had passed, say about three months, Doré Records finally got it distributed; it physically reached the rest of the country, the

Jan & Dean in the "early days," autographed in 1981.

records did. But by then those key West Coast markets were lost, and [even] if a record is number one everyplace, but not simultaneously, it never makes national number one.

Doc Rock: Is that what happened with your excellent remake of "Sidewalk Surfin'" on UA in nineteen seventy-three?

Dean: A good example. It was released in California and made number one or number three in San Diego. UA was owned by Transamerica, who gave them their operating

Chapter 36 · Jan & Dean 485

Jan & Dean are wearing each other's clothing for this gag photo, inspired by a scene from a 1936 Laurel and Hardy film, *Thicker Than Water*. J & D were big L & H fans.

money. One month Transamerica pulls in the purse strings and says you're not getting as much money this month, UA, because Transamerica in general is not doing well right now. So the record company has no budget that month, and an act with a new record does not get distributed, a new record is just cut off. All of this has no bearing on the quality of records, so chart position is irrelevant overall to the whole area of intrinsic worth of music.

Doc Rock: In other words, when someone reviews an artist's career, critiques their work, they should just review the body of material, not the relative popularity? Like, Van Gogh's paintings are not evaluated by how much he sold them for, but by how well he painted them?

Dean: You got it. This record was a hit in San Diego, but didn't get distributed to the rest of the country. So, while the other songs that were in San Diego's top five were also in the top five nationally, my record was not even seen or heard outside of the city!

Doc Rock: This explains the comment you made on the liner notes of the double LP set of your hits, all in mono by the way, called *Gotta Take That One Last Ride*.

Dean: "This quazi-moto [*sic*] monaural recording is compatible with both your standard quadraphonic or tetrahedral systems. Reviewers: No negative reviews please! These recordings are for fun and dancing only and are not for the purpose of competing musically or artistically with any other recording artist's recordings. Warning: It is expressly forbidden to suck or smoke this recording in any manner or form. If accidentally swallowed, take two hot dogs and a cold shower with a friend."

Doc Rock: Have you tried to seek out a good label for new releases?

Dean: I haven't had to try. I run a probing offense. If they make a down-and-out, I'll take it. We have had many companies showing an interest, but why get involved with a label that does not have it financially or creatively? If they want to guarantee promotion and distribution and all the rest, OK. Otherwise, why go to all the trouble?

Doc Rock: At the time of Jan's accident, which put him in a coma and gave him severe brain damage, what was happening with Jan & Dean?

Dean: We had fairly recently emceed the movie *The TAMI Show*. That was a rock 'n' roll show we hosted and sang in, that also had the Beach Boys, Billy J. Kramer, the Rolling Stones, Lesley Gore, the Supremes—every one who was big.

Doc Rock: And then there was the movie *Ride the Wild Surf*.

Dean: We were going to star in that, it was our movie, until a friend of mine actually kidnapped Frank Sinatra, Jr., and then left the ransom money at my house! After the publicity about that, the film company replaced Jan and me with Fabian and Tab Hunter. We had turned down offers to be in the Beach Party movies, waiting for a good one of our own.

Doc Rock: Your next movie was called *Jan & Dean Go-Go Wild*.

Dean: Yes, but it had problems, too. On the very first week of filming, there was a train wreck, Jan's leg was badly broken, and the film was shelved.

Doc Rock: So, did you give up on the idea of being movie stars?

Dean: Yes! Instead, we decided to become TV stars!

Doc Rock: You mean the NBC-TV series "The Jan and Dean Show," in nineteen sixty-six? I saw that listed in *TV Guide* in 1966, but it never came on.

Dean: Luckily I have a copy of the pilot episode! I have the film, but that was the only episode ever produced.

Doc Rock: "The Monkees" TV show came on that fall. Did the Monkees take over your show like Tab Hunter and Fabian took over *Ride the Wild Surf*?

Dean: No, we were doing our pilots at the same time. And we both had spies on each other's sets! Nesmith was in here just an hour ago. We've become pretty close, so I know what they were thinking, and they knew what we were thinking! We had spies on their set, and they had spies on our set, to see what we were doing, so we all knew what was going on! We would have opposed each other for at least the first year. Which would have been fun, because we were all kinda friends, and we would have interrelated our two series. Matter of fact, we even had an idea of switching them. Because it would have been seen as a rivalry by the fans, just like the Beach Boys were seen that way, when in fact we were friends and sang on each other's sessions. Yet everyone felt they had to be for Jan & Dean or for the Beach Boys. When it came to Jan & Dean or the Monkees on TV, you would have to make a choice, since we'd've been on at the same time. People would have had to decide which was better

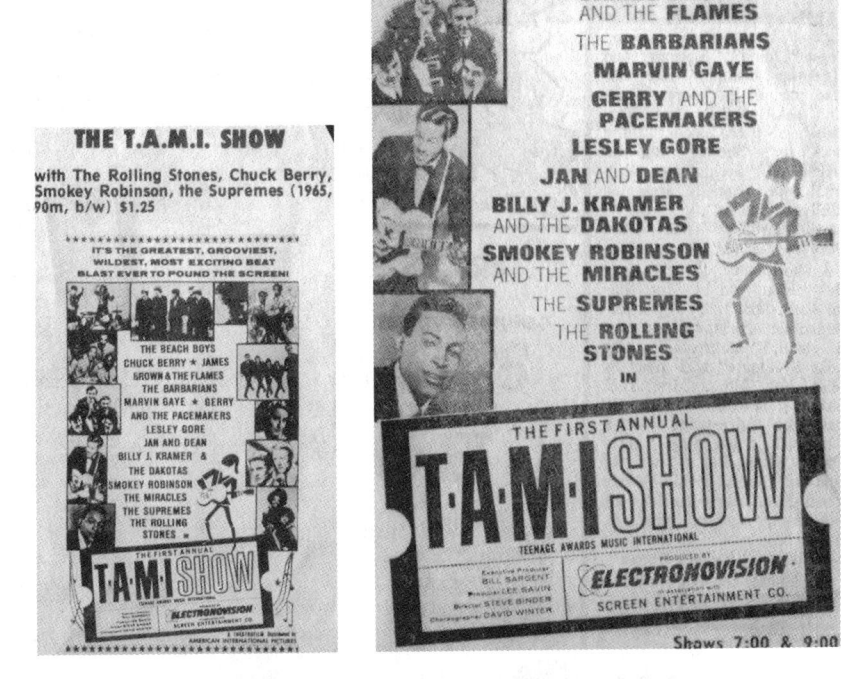

Three newspaper ads for *The TAMI Show*, starring Jan & Dean.

and which was no good. So, to fight that, we planned a switch! On our station they would be on *our* show! And then, on their channel, we would be on *their* show! *Actually doing their show for them!* We'd worked out some really fantastic things to keep it all really interesting, to not pin ourselves down so that people got tired in a year or so. Because we realized in the very beginning that even the pilot was, in a way, *boring!* By the time we finished the pilot, we were bored. We were actually hoping it wouldn't even sell! If anybody ever realized—managers, people who were working on the show—that the two stars of the show were sitting up in their rooms on location, saying "Man, if this thing sells, we're screwed," they all would have been blown away! Everybody else was counting on it. It meant money, success....

Doc Rock: Why didn't you want it? A TV show skyrocketed the Monkees' career, and they were newcomers. If your TV show had gotten on, with the foundation of almost ten years of your hits, why, who knows how many more hits you would have had?! The Monkees had a lot of number-one hits!

Dean: Ahhh, you'd skyrocket for a second or two! See, we had been pacing ourselves for over eight years. Making it able to last for eight years. When we made the pilot, Jan was in the last semesters of medical school and I was in graduate school. Now, the Monkees, they were lucky; they stayed on TV for two or three years, three seasons. They were pretty successful. But soon they burned themselves out, and they were gone from TV and records.

Doc Rock: And all the bucks you'd have made?

Dean: Do you want to be a flash in the pan for two or three years and make that kind of money and pay that kind of taxes on it? Or do you want to spread it out, because we were ending up with a lot more than if we were just flashes.

Doc Rock: Music was changing at the time of your pilot and Jan's accident. What were you doing?

Dean: I guess the Liberty *Filet of Soul* LP was the last thing we ever did. And yet that was what our main breakoff with Liberty was all about. Our contract was coming up; it had been five years, and we were holding that LP over their head. Now, the original *Filet of Soul* LP was years later released as side four, heavily edited down, of the UA *Legendary Masters Jan & Dean Anthology Album*. That is the original, basically.

Doc Rock: With the tape of the live show speeded up over "Dead Man's Curve," and just a few songs amid all of the comedy stuff?

Dean: That was how the original LP was made. We didn't want to have "Dead Man's Curve" on yet another LP, [not] the whole song anyway. So we said, "Let's make it different."

Doc Rock: The voices stood out much more on that version of "Dead Man's Curve" than on the earlier live *Command Performance* LP.

Dean: But in a concert you cannot hear the voices that well, so that was the feel we were looking for, on the live *Command Performance* LP, like you were in the audience. *Filet of Soul* was approximately the same thing, but it was relating to the other area we were into, which was comedy.

Doc Rock: Many of your hits, like "Sidewalk Surfin'" and "Little Old Lady" were largely comedy or satire.

Dean: Yes, that is basically what it was all about, but this was taking it a step further. On *Command Performance,* you got only the one-liners between songs; the real joking was edited out. Here we wanted to get into some of the stuff we really did, which was a lot more involved than one-liners.

Doc Rock: Your 1960s shows were hilarious. I'm told by people who saw you that they were rolling in the aisles!

Dean: Of course. We knew that. We were aware of that. Everyone heard your records; hopefully they were being played. We chose not to give them just the same songs. After four or five years, you just don't want to do that anymore. You go out and you entertain; you give them more, entertaining them and yourselves, too. That way you don't get bored doing the same old songs, and it stays spontaneous.

Chapter 36 · Jan & Dean

Liberty trade ad for the LP *Command Performance* and the single from the album, "(Here They Come) From All Over the World (Theme from *The TAMI Show*)." Actually the 45 was not the same recording of the song as appeared on the LP.

> **Doc Rock:** You say the *Filet of Soul* LP released in nineteen sixty-six, and side four of *Anthology* in the 1970s are the same concert?
> **Dean:** Yes.
> **Doc Rock:** But why are two LPs from the same concert so radically different?
> **Dean:** That's the whole point. We left Liberty over that LP. They put it out; they did it. They waited until we were off the label, and then they did what they wanted to do. See, at that time, everyone had a soul LP. The Beatles had *Rubber Soul*, the

Righteous Brothers had *Blue-Eyed Soul,* so we created a satire of everybody else's LP. Because "Rubber Soul" means—
Doc Rock: The Beatles said it was open to anyone's interpretation, didn't they?
Dean: Exactly, and it was abstract, kinda pretty. Then the Righteous Brothers, *Blue-Eyed Soul,* that was kinda nice, because you really did have blue-eyed soul. That was a little bit more relevant. Then James Brown came out with *Soulful Soul;* soon everybody had some kind of "soul." So we said, "If the Beatles have *Rubber Soul,* and the Righteous Brothers have *Blue-Eyed Soul,* and James Brown has *Soulful Soul,* then we must have, ha! *Filet of Soul*! I mean, it's obvious! Our soul wasn't really in just the music. Rather it was in the presentation of the music; it was in the overall satire and the dryness, and we promoted that, over time.
Doc Rock: Not everyone could tell that "Dead Man's Curve" had been a satire on songs like "I Get Around" and "Drag City," or that "Honolulu Lulu" was a satire on "Surfer Girl," or even that "Sidewalk Surfin'" and "Little Old Lady" were satires on surf and drag music in general?
Dean: With each record, I think, we got a little more obvious with the humor. Finally we wanted to give them an LP that they can really see how obvious it had become, and see how well they would pick up on it.
Doc Rock: Laying it all out.
Dean: Right. But the original *Filet of Soul* had only three songs on it. The rest was talk. Introducing people in the audience we knew. Mistakes. People falling off the stage. Comedy. Introducing individually the entire band. We took that to Liberty. We had spent a lot of our time and money on it. They said, *"Three Songs!"* Before they even heard it, they looked at the cover and vetoed it. "You guys are crazy!"
Doc Rock: What about "Light My Fire" or "Inna-Gadda-Da-Vida," just a few years later? A whole LP side with just *one* song?
Dean: OK, we were avant-garde. Being too early is as bad as being too late! We told Liberty, "But that's it. C'mon, listen to it! Listen to it and you will understand." So picture it; here are all these guys in their seersucker suits, thin ties, management guys. What did they know? All they were interested in, as I told you before, was sales, sales, *sales*!! "Gotta get the LP out there!"
Doc Rock: With lots of songs.
Dean: There wasn't a new Jan & Dean LP out then, so we said why not do something off the wall? Well, that was wrong; that was the wrong theory, they told us at Liberty. "This is the time that you should do something heavy, something *serious*. Not screwing around. Boy, I mean, you haven't had a hit since last summer, and now you are really taking a chance putting out this silly thing! It sounds like you're not serious at all."
Doc Rock: But the serious stuff, the protest songs and drug music, didn't last very long.
Dean: Exactly. This LP was getting back to what we were doing before our one serious LP, *Folk 'n' Roll*—
Doc Rock: —which had the original version of "Where Were You When I Needed You" before the Grass Roots did it, and "Eve of Destruction," which was written by your background group Sloan and Barri—
Dean: —but they didn't look at it that way. They almost had Jan convinced that sooner or later we would make it with serious records. But we were still loose, having a lot of fun with music, not getting frustrated. Until they started confronting us about having only three songs on an LP. There was a big battle, with people throwing people up against walls and swearing at one another. Finally, we said to each other that we would please them because we do want the LP to come out and Liberty just won't release it. We went back and put on three more songs, feeling we just could not compromise the project any more than that by putting any more songs on it. We even felt that this was too many, we had six songs on it. "OK, here it is!"
Doc Rock: Their reaction this time?
Dean: "That's still against all music-biz rules! You guys are nuts! We are not going

to put out this LP!" Then we left on tour. We called back from someplace in Alabama to see what the status of the LP was. They said they were going to have someone remix it into a decent LP. They wanted this guy, Dave Pell ["Ma-Nah-Ma-Nah," 1969], to redo the LP. Jan told them from Alabama, "If Dave Pell touches that thing, I'll break his neck, and I'm not kiddin'!" And they knew he wasn't kidding, so they said that was tough, and they would not release it at all! Jan said, "OK," and hung up on them.

Doc Rock: But the LP did come out; I bought it!

Dean: That was the last communication we ever had with Liberty. We came off the tour, and the next day Jan had his accident. After that they said, "Hey, there's no roadblocks! Jan is out of commission. Hey, there's an accident, his name's on the news; hey, let's get that LP out there!" So they jammed that LP out fast.

Doc Rock: But, it was disappointing.

Dean: It was a terrible LP! Which is a shame. You spend eight years trying to build something, and then in one month they can destroy you. If they want to. Six years later, I had a chance to put it out almost the way it was meant to be, side four, *Anthology* LP. I once went on a local radio show and played the entire *Filet of Soul* tape. Since nobody ever heard it. This was the whole thing. Which is really somewhat boring, but it is so far out, so abstract, it's kind of neat.

Doc Rock: "Ahead of its time."

Dean: Still is, these many years later! [Jokes] Maybe Dave Pell was right!

Doc Rock: The underground FM station in Kansas City played the whole side four version of that thing on the air, straight through, several times!

Dean: Really?

Doc Rock: Yes, and you know, a station like that would normally never touch Jan & Dean!

Dean: Yeah. I think some people realized that we really weren't serious when we did funny things. That we were really thinking more deeply than people gave us credit for at the time. At the time, they overreacted, saying we were not deep at all! Then, five years later, they started listening. Harry Nilsson was the same way! We were very, very good friends, but he said, "Man, I hated *Filet of Soul*. I really hated it. But, now that I know you, I think you were not quite saying what I thought you were saying!" So I played it for him, and he loved it! That was absolutely his favorite! He'd play that for everybody who came up to his house!

Doc Rock: Did you design the cover?

Dean: Yes, I did, but it makes no sense, because the huge "Ah-Choo" on the back cover relates to stuff [coughing noises, belching] they edited out! Even the title, *Filet of Soul*, doesn't relate to anything. They blew it all the way around. It's too bad to see a concept go right into the gutter. The LP didn't do well. Then they said, "Let's put out a single! Let's put out a single, quick! While everyone's still talking about him! He's in a coma! That's great! He could be in a coma for a year! We could keep milking it!"

Doc Rock: What was the single?

Dean: "Norwegian Wood."

Doc Rock: That was a weird case. Normally, if the stereo and mono versions of a Jan & Dean Liberty song are different, the mono LP version matches the single. But on that one the stereo LP version of "Norwegian Wood" is the same as the 45, while the mono LP version is a totally different tape!

Dean: We never intended to release that song at all. I didn't want that to be a single. So I said, "At least let me pick out the B side." "OK, keep the kid happy. His partner's in a coma, it'll be good therapy for him, pat him on the back." They said, "What do you want on it?" I said "I always liked 'Popsicle.'"

Doc Rock: From the *Drag City* LP in 1963—

Dean: Yes, but I told them it had to be remixed. "There is no time to remix!" "Let me remix" or I'm going to start to cry and all of this. So they let me do it. I brought out a lot more voices than there were on the original. On the original the track was predominant. I was really into the vocal parts, they were great, so I remixed it. In the middle, the "Uh-uh-uh-uh" part, it had always bothered me in that it was the same intensity. So I faded that, kind of like you're running out of air and it sets up the instrumental break, leads up to it.

Doc Rock: The banjo.

Dean: Right. Well, it is a guitar. Glen Campbell played it just like the banjo. He's so good! So, the single came out with "Norwegian Wood" marked as the A side. All I wanted was the opportunity to have "Popsicle" out on the other side. I would do the follow-up work.

Doc Rock: The DJ who played it on KOMA in Oklahoma City said that you sent a note out with the record saying to play "Popsicle," so he did!

Dean: Yes. Liberty sent out the usual spotty mailing to stations. Then I mailed out copies of the record using an extensive list to all the radio stations, with "Popsicle" marked and with a note as you said. Every day for a week. I even used pretty rank language, I said, "'Norwegian Wood' sucks! Don't play it, it's terrible!"

Doc Rock: Now I see why he didn't read the note on the air!

Dean: Right! I flatly said that the record sucks, it's terrible! I think they kinda dug that in a way, that I was putting down my own record.

Doc Rock: I never once heard "Norwegian Wood" on the radio.

Dean: Good! So, the day after their mailing, I went to their mail room, used their packages and stamps and everything. All I had to do was write the note. The next day I mailed to all the same people again! The next note said, "Here is another copy just in case someone ripped off the other copy I sent, but whatever you do, don't play 'Norwegian Wood!' If you want to play either side, please listen to 'Popsicle' and play that. I think it's better!" Third day, I did another mailing, same people. Fourth day, I did another mailing, same people, same record. Fifth day, I did another mailing, same people, but I left out the record! It was empty! That was a way to use humor to emphasize my point, and to say "Thanks for playing the record. It has been selling so well, we have no records left to send to you!"

Doc Rock: Another song released after the wreck, as a follow up of sorts to "Popsicle," was called "Fiddle Around." I assumed that was an old cut that Liberty dredged up to cash in on the publicity of Jan's accident. Obviously, with him in a coma, and you off the label, there was no new material available, and "Fiddle Around" had similarities to "Popsicle."

Dean: You're right. It was cut pretty early on Liberty. That song interrelated to a minor single we had out in nineteen sixty-two on Liberty, "Tennessee."

Doc Rock: Which was a spin-off of "Jennie Lee!"

Dean: "Tennessee" was produced by a guy named Snuff Garrett, and so was this "Fiddle Around," about the same time. We never liked "Fiddle Around," so we never let them release it. But they did release "Tennessee." Yeah, I hated "Fiddle Around." I thought that was pretty bad. Jan had an uncle who used to sing it a lot at home — "Whoa, Whoa, whoa, fiddle around!"

Doc Rock: I also ran across "School Days" on a single in Washington, D.C., in nineteen sixty-six, off that nineteen sixty-four *Dead Man's Curve/New Girl in School* LP.

Dean: I never knew about that one. Boy! I wonder how many singles they put out that I never knew about! I never knew "School Days" came out on a single! What was on the other side?

Doc Rock: "New Girl in School."

Dean: Ha!

Doc Rock: It was a top-forty hit there, in D.C., December nineteen sixty-six. No *Billboard* listing.

Dean: Yes, there was a whole rash of singles there when Jan was in the hospital. Liberty flooded the market, because they knew we didn't have anything. They knew their stuff would be the only stuff out there. Exploiters! Meanwhile, I was cutting Karen

Carpenter in the same garage I cut the *Save for a Rainy Day* LP. Richard Carpenter played on "Like a Summer Rain." Do you have that?
Doc Rock: Yes, on J&D Records, your own label after you left Liberty.
Dean: I used that label for demos that got me the deal with Columbia for the hit single "Yellow Balloon" in 1966. I cut that without Jan, he was not well enough.
Doc Rock: I know you like spontaneity. A song that sounds spontaneous was "Schlock Rod," on the flip side of the "Drag City" 45. What a wild recording! Where did that come from?
Dean: "Schlock Rod" was written on a flight to Hawaii — after a bunch of free drinks!
Doc Rock: First time I heard it was when I played it on a jukebox. Everyone in the place looked at me funny.
Dean: That was a very bizarre song.
Doc Rock: I love it.
Dean: I like it, too.
Doc Rock: You even put it on *Gotta Take That One Last Ride,* in original mono.
Dean: Well, that was because I had writer's credit! [Jokes] Had to get something I wrote on there.
Doc Rock: I once made a big chart of all the Jan & Dean songs and composers — you didn't write much, did you?
Dean: Well . . . I didn't get credit for my stuff. I wrote as much of "Surf City" as Jan did, but you'll notice I didn't get any credit.
Doc Rock: But did you sing on it?
Dean: Well, no.
Doc Rock: Good. That falsetto never did sound right to me.
Dean: I didn't sing on it, to tell the truth. Brian [Wilson of the Beach Boys] and I both sang falsetto, and swapped parts on different records.
Doc Rock: Was "Schlock Rod" a one-take affair, a spontaneous session, the kind you like?
Dean: Ha! A couple of takes! Yes, that is exactly what I like. The preparation wasn't that spontaneous, but the recording was. And, it was considered by the label, and to a certain extent by Jan, a throwaway, something that didn't make that much difference. So, "Let's just go ahead, let's do it quick." And we had fun with it. Psychologically, if he treated it as something that wasn't that important, then it came out sometimes a lot better to my taste.
Doc Rock: I really liked it, I think it is very good.
Dean: Yeah, I do, too. I think that after he heard the way it came out, he placed that same value on it, that it was valuable, even though it was quick and we didn't spend a lot of time on it. Sometimes you feel that you have to spend time on stuff, and if you don't, then it is hard to rationalize in your mind that it is still OK, that there is something good about it. But he liked it.
Doc Rock: But Jan preferred to do overdub after overdub?
Dean: Well, yes, he was really a perfectionist.
Doc Rock: Although when you did "Vegetables" by yourself for UA, there were what, fifty-two overdubs?
Dean: But that's different. That does not mean we did it over again fifty-two times. I used up, there were fifty-two overdubs, fifty-two different voicing parts on there, doing different things. I'm not talking about that.
Dock Rock: Was it all you, or were there other people on there too?
Dean: Oh, there were a lot of people on there. But, each voice may have been done on one take, so it is still spontaneous. I'm talking about takes. Sometime you do something so long, like a lead vocal, you do it over and over and over and over again, because of one little note here, one little note there, and then you sacrifice the feel you had for it at the beginning, the enthusiasm that you had for the song. There is a certain point of no return, a point where you reach the place where it is stale, you get tired of it, you just want to finish it and go home. Up to that point, it is

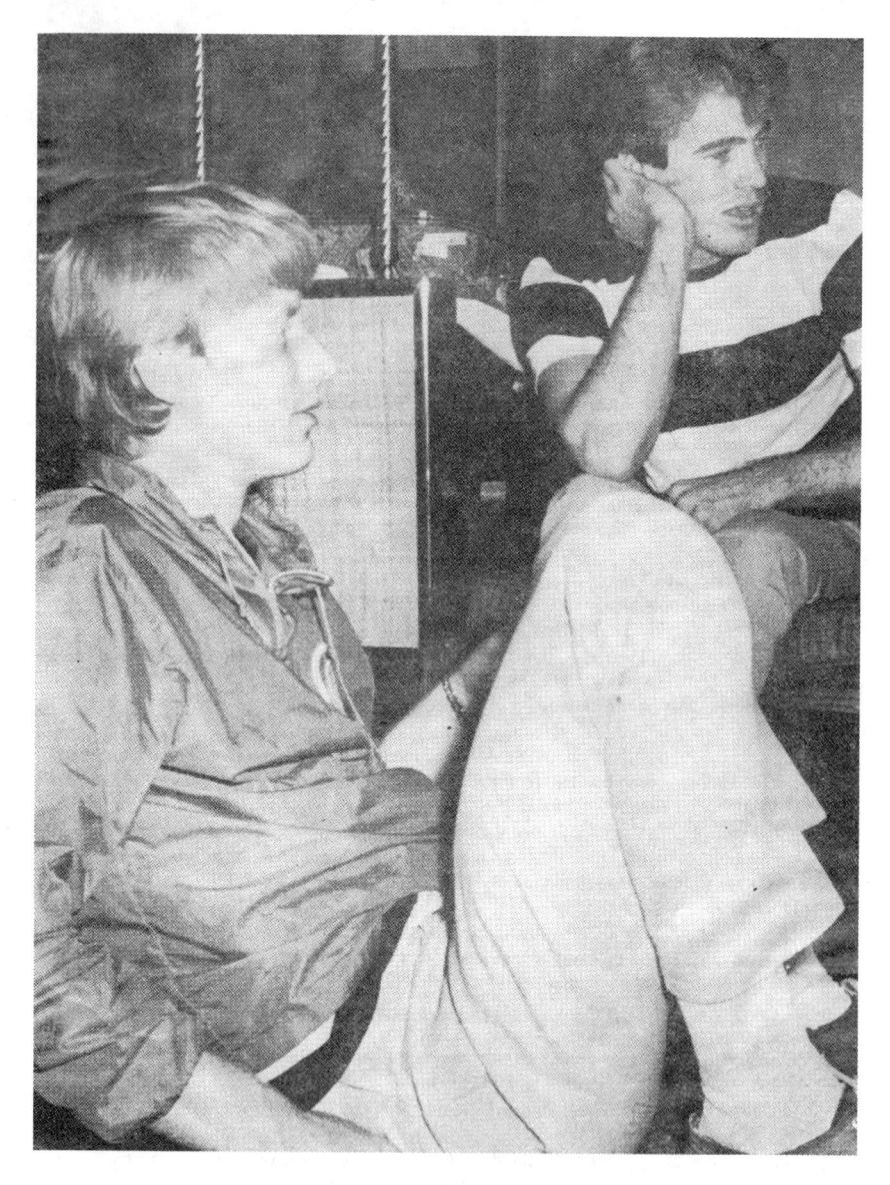

Jan & Dean in 1965.

OK, but sometimes we reached that point and kept going. And, then, the music sounded contrived—or, maybe it just sounded contrived to us! I don't know.

Doc Rock: An interesting part of the *Anthology* album was the documentation, where you gave the information on how many vocal overdubs were made on each hit as well as who sang lead, the kind of recorder used to tape the hit, the studio you used, all of that. The *Anthology* album, coming several years after the wreck, was a great reward for being loyal and continuing to search the record bins for Jan & Dean stuff.

The extensive liner notes answered a lot of questions that had been in my mind for a long time.

Dean: Pretty perceptive of me to know those questions were being asked! Ha! Yeah, I felt it was good, I was really happy putting that out. I felt it kind of finalized my involvement in an era. It was nice to compile it, put it all together, my favorite stuff. And to be able to throw on the most important things, editorially, really that was more of an editorial package than anything else. That's the way I set it up! I put songs on there that had a story to them. Usually it's the other way around. You put songs on an LP that have value as songs, and then if there happens to be anything to say about it, you say it. This was set up differently, and it ended up having a lot of hits on it because there is more to say about hits than there is about stiffs. I tried to say something about the stiffs, like, "You Really Know How to Hurt a Guy" [1965, top-thirty hit], without putting the track on the album. Because I didn't have room for every song, anyway.

Doc Rock: The Turtles' "She'd Rather Be with Me" [1967], that sounds a lot like Jan & Dean, especially the ending. Coincidence?

Dean: No. I was on that. They picked up a lot of stuff from us, musically. The modified bomps, the orchestration, the harmony. I was involved designing many of their LP covers and 45 sleeves. So I was around and sang on pretty many of those records.

Doc Rock: Do you know which ones?

Dean: Eh . . . "She's My Girl."

Doc Rock: How about their *Battle of the Bands* LP, did you sing on any of those?

Dean: Yes, a couple, I don't remember what they were.

Doc Rock: One was "Surfer Dan." That would be a likely candidate.

Dean: No, I didn't sing on that one, of all cuts! I don't remember which ones. What would happen is, I would go down and be talking to them, and they'd say, "Oh, we need some voices." And I'd do a part, not even knowing what song it was! But they had some really fine songs. "Elenore," I nearly got for myself! They hated it when they recorded it. I said I knew it was a hit record. But they had gotten another song that they liked better, from Harry Nilsson, "The Story of Rock 'n' Roll." They said, "Boy, this thing is really a hit! This Nilsson song!" I said, "It's a piece of junk! 'Elenore' is the hit!" Every other day I'd see them, and say, "Well, are you going to release 'Elenore'?" I'd already designed the trade ad for them, and they hadn't even told me they were going to release it! I told them that, and they said, "That's the only reason you want us to release it, you want to get paid for that trade ad!" So I said, "OK, if you don't like it, give it to me!" Because they wrote it, and they would have gotten some publishing money out of it.

Doc Rock: I have a tape of your unreleased version. You recorded it the same way.

Dean: Exactly the same way! I talked them into giving me the track, and I just put on a lead voice or whatever. Split it with them, or something.

Doc Rock: A Supergroup single!

Dean: So they put out "The Story of Rock 'n' Roll," and it stiffed! They followed it right up with "Elenore," and it was number one!

Doc Rock: You mentioned the *Folk 'n' Roll* LP. That had "Eve of Destruction," which was exactly like Barry McGuire's number-one single, the same track, but with Jan's voice on lead. Obviously a song he liked, not your type of song, serious, not spontaneous. But, there was a high falsetto voice on that, the same voice on the hit 45 and your LP. Was that you or Phil Sloan of the Fantastic Baggies?

Dean: That wasn't me. Probably Phil.

Doc Rock: Whenever you weren't available, Jan brought Phil up from the background singers into your lead part?

Dean: Yeah, Phil got my style down pretty good! 'Cause sometimes I was down in the next studio with the Beach Boys . . . doing Brian's lead!

Doc Rock: You're joking about being on Beach Boys records, doing Brian's parts. Who sang on your songs that was famous, and what other artists' records did you sing on? I know the Beach Boys were on your *Linda* LP.
Dean: Yes, the Beach Boys sang on our versions of two of their hits on *Linda*, "Surfin'" and "Surfin' Safari."
Doc Rock: Which were spin-offs, musically, of your first hit, of "Baby Talk!"
Dean: Yeah.
Doc Rock: And they were on your version of "Little Deuce Coupe" on *Drag City*.
Dean: Yes! Brian Wilson learned a lot from Jan about studio techniques when they sang with us, things Brian really excelled at later.
Doc Rock: After the Beach Boys sang on your records, what Beach Boy records did you sing on?
Dean: "Barbara Ann," "I Get Around."
Doc Rock: "Vegetables," the recording you did fifty-two parts on, was originally a song by the Beach Boys from their *Smile* LP. All the time the Beach Boys are associated with Jan & Dean. From nineteen sixty-three to the present, people always confuse your records. On the Beach Boys' "Endless Summer" TV show in nineteen eighty-nine, they discussed Jan & Dean.
Dean: Yeah? What'd they say?
Doc Rock: They told about a nineteen sixty-four show in Hawaii that included Peter and Gordon and Jan & Dean. It seems that Peter and Gordon, coming from cold, foggy England, got terrific sunburns and were lobster red on stage. Then Jan was wrapped up totally like a mummy, and Mike Love was so taken with the image that he took pictures which he still has. Lastly, they said you and Jan chased the Boys with fire extinguishers. Does any of this ring a bell?
Dean: A great moment!
Doc Rock: I thought you probably wrote about it in your diary.
Dean: I didn't have to! We were playing at the naval station, Pearl Harbor probably, Pearl Harbor, a great place! We had been screwing around all day, we were just in one of those moods. We arrived there and we were planning to attack them on stage with CO_2 fire extinguishers. Being a naval station they had plenty of CO_2 for engine fires and such. So we had those. The Beach Boys knew we were probably going to do something, so up onstage with them they had cans of shaving cream. They had sent somebody to the PX to get fifteen or twenty cans of aerosol shaving cream, and they had these stashed.
Doc Rock: That wasn't mentioned on the show.
Dean: They may have forgotten about that. Anyway, someone ratted on them and told us they had shaving cream, and that they were going to be waiting for us. So since we were all in the same dressing rooms, we took their street clothes and put them on over our clothes. Mike's beautiful leather jacket, some of Dennis's real nice silk Hawaiian shirts—we wore all their clothes. We said, "Now if they blast us, it's their own stuff!" And I knew they'd start blasting, then stop when they saw what they were doing. But I wanted to see whether or not they would do it anyway. And, yes, they did it anyway. Actually, I don't think they were smart enough to know it was their clothes right away. So the CO_2 was going, the shaving cream was flying, and the music stopped completely. There was just a huge cloud onstage, and there were all these sailors in the audience, wondering, What the hell is going on? They couldn't see a dang thing. There was just shaving cream coming out of a cloud. When it cleared, they continued, but they were all covered with stuff. We went back to the dressing room, took off their clothes and hung them back where they were, but now they [were] dripping this shaving cream, and we just left. It was great, a lot of fun. It's a real story. Brian's wife Marilyn says she shot the whole thing on eight millimeter and still has it.
Doc Rock: You and Jan went to school together. How about the Beach Boys, did you go to school with them?

Dean: They didn't even go to school [college].

Doc Rock: They didn't even surf, except maybe Dennis. They say the Beach Boys wrote their surfing songs in class.

Dean: Jan did that too. But he did the songs in med school. [Jokes] The Beach Boys probably wrote their songs in wood shop! No, we, Jan & Dean and the Beach Boys, kid each other.

Doc Rock: I have an import LP that tells how Jan attended design school, and Dean was a doctor who had the wreck.

Dean: Well, that's close.

Doc Rock: Often reference books seem to mix up which was Jan and which was Dean! Back to Hawaii—Do you know why Jan was wrapped up like a mummy?

Dean: Jan used to carry his doctor's bag around, he must have gotten carried away with some bandages. We used to wrap him up and put a cigar in his mouth, and he'd smoke it!

Doc Rock: Your fans thought you might name your daughter [born in 1989] after some rock 'n' roll record, such as your own hit, "Linda," or the song "Barbara Ann" you did on an LP in 1961, later a Beach Boy hit you sang lead on for them. But the name you chose, Katie, is really a very nice name. My daughters are named Marlena after the Four Seasons' record and Corinna after Ray Peterson's.

Dean: I got beat up over that one. There was a big fight.

Doc Rock: Over "Corinna, Corinna?" How?

Dean: Back in the Arnie days, I was at Fort Ord, and they lined up all the guys that were going to Korea.

Doc Rock: A fight?

Dean: Well, once we all graduated from infantry school, we were sent to different places. Since I was in for just six months, I stayed at Fort Ord. Some went to the South. But some were going to go to Korea. These were the dregs, the goofy guys, they were all looney tunes anyhow, and they were all PO'd because they were all going to Korea. So I walked by singing, to the tune of "Corinna, Corinna," "Korea, Korea!" As I went over to the restroom, the head, they came up there and walloped me. I said, "Hey, it's just a joke you guys." They didn't think it was funny. [Sings] "Korea, Korea, where you been so long!"

Doc Rock: A good old World War I song.

Dean: No. Really, that old?

Doc Rock: Other people were on your records, beside[s] the Beach Boys. Glen Campbell was on your *Surf City* LP.

Dean: He was on all of it, just about. He didn't sing on any, I don't think.

Doc Rock: Didn't he yell "One more time!" on one song?

Dean: I'm trying to remember . . . no! That was Hal Blaine.

Doc Rock: Your drummer.

Dean: Glen never says anything. He's quiet.

Doc Rock: As you know, I am a record collector. Your older records took me years to find, but once I found something really rare from the 1950s in a ten-cent bin at a discount store, three copies! It was the song "Gas Money."

Dean: Did you buy all three?

Doc Rock: Certainly! Why, do you need copies of some of the old records?

Dean: No, no, no! I was just curious; that's what I would do! If I'm looking for something, when you have been searching, you are so hungry for it, when you finally find it, you take 'em all!

Doc Rock: Right!

Dean: Then, you wonder later why you have so many.

Doc Rock: OK, here is something I have long been curious about. On a live LP, how do you—when I hear you're live on your Liberty LP in concert, and the vocals are overdubbed with more than one voice, which part was done first, and which was done second? And how?

Dean: There is no way of telling. Most of the time—well, we only did one, or was it two live LPs?

Doc Rock: I am speaking of the live *Command Performance* LP, your only live one.

Dean: None of that was live.

Doc Rock: None of that was live?!

Dean: Except the band. And the crowd reaction. All of the voices were done afterwards. So on the double-tracked part, none was the original; both were later. The reason that we did that, not only because of the quality, but the engineer just had too much to do. If you cut out that problem, the lead parts which were probably his main problem if he was recording it all together, he was able to mix the band, and he was able to get the crowd reaction a lot better. So you just waited until you went back into the studio, then put the voices back on.

Doc Rock: So that is why some of the talk between songs is partly cut off, really echoey and distant. The house mike was on the PA, picked up by a mike on the band. Then, when the engineer cut in Jan's mike, the voice got loud and clear.

Dean: Right.

Doc Rock: I see the point. On the *Filet of Soul* as put out by Liberty, there are some cuts that only Jan's mike is on. Your part is barely discernible, the engineer could not balance that live, and Liberty did not have you available to come in and dub it back on.

Dean: Yes.

Doc Rock: When you do shows in the 1990s, how are the fans?

Dean: Great! We have all ages. It's fun to meet everyone, especially the IDCOS.

Doc Rock: IDCOS?

Dean: Sure, the IDCOS. "*Is D*ean *C*oming *O*ut to *s*ign autographs?" Jan signs more autographs than I do.

Doc Rock: Have you ever seen this book, *The Miles Chart Display of Popular Music*? It has a line graph for each record ever on *Billboard* up to nineteen seventy, showing its chart popularity over time. They have supplements for the years after nineteen sixty-nine, but I only care about the graphs of the 1950s and 1960s stuff. I mean, once Jan had his wreck, the music died for me.

Dean: Yeah, and *our* graph went *bzzzzz* [gestures a nosedive].

Doc Rock: Look at this seven-inch, small-hole, 45 picture disc of "Little Deuce Coupe" and "Surf City." I paid seven dollars for this. Have you ever seen it?

Dean: Seven dollars? You got gypped! [Takes the record and handles it by the edges.]

Doc Rock: I am going to make a clock out of it.

Dean: Yeah, yeah, it would make a good clock! But make the hands go backwards! [All laugh.] I was over at Keenan Wynn's house. He had a clock on his wall that said "We never have a drink before five," and all the hours had fives!

Doc Rock: Did you guys—you have one or two instrumentals on some LPs—did you play any of the instruments?

Dean: Yes, we did, but I don't remember, nothing too heavy. None of the lead stuff. Sometimes we'd play paper triangle. I was really big with the pillow! I used to play pillow on a lot of stuff!

Doc Rock: The pillow!?

Dean: It's a good sound! It goes "thwock!"

Doc Rock: Moving to more recent times, when the nineteen eighty-nine *Batman* movie came out, I was surprised your nineteen sixty-six *Batman* LP was not reissued.

Dean: Actually, I liked the *Batman* album; I thought it was funny.

Doc Rock: I love it. Why wasn't it reissued, because with the hit movie, it'd be a natural?

Dean: I wrote the folks, the chairman of the board at Capitol who now own the Liberty stuff—this was seven months ago—reminding them that they had a *Batman* album.

Doc Rock: And the great single, it would sound like a Beach Boy thing to most people, and they are popular.

Dean: Yeah! I mean, even just by mistake they would have sold a couple of hundred thousand copies. Capitol didn't even consider it.
Doc Rock: It's their loss. They'd have made thousands off it.
Dean: I don't think they wanted to. They only like to make billions of dollars. You know, it's no longer just a couple of hundred thousand.
Doc Rock: That's what the individual executive's percentage has to be?
Dean: Exactly.
Doc Rock: Kind of like back in nineteen seventy-three when you recut "Sidewalk Surfin'" and it hit big in San Diego, but UA wouldn't ship it out?
Dean: "No one is interested in skateboards," they always say. I saw some in a five-oh-one Jeans commercial just last night. "What do you think that is, guys?" "I don't know . . . what?" They don't see; they don't hear; I don't know what they are doing. Maybe they are doing drugs.
Doc Rock: Reminds me of the Legendary Masked Surfers 45 "Summer Means Fun" that you recorded for UA, putting new vocals on old Jan & Dean Liberty LP instrumental tracks. The store copies of the new 45s were not the remixed version, even the DJ copy you sent out was the old LP cut, not the remix! Only a copy I got at a station had the remix. They sent out the wrong mix 90 percent of the pressings!
Dean: Only someone *smart* would send out the right version. No consistency. No organization or planning. But even the Batman thing really irritated me. The chairman of the board is a good friend, he didn't even write me a note back. When he was out of work, wanted to write a book, I let him come over to my house and I gave him a couple of hours of my time. The considerate thing to do would have been to write back saying, "Thanks, but no thanks."
Doc Rock: Speaking of dumb things, because radio stations are dumping their turntables for CD players, and because young DJs don't know any better, oldies are turning up on the radio for the first time that are "K-Tel" type remakes. You did some rerecordings of the Jan & Dean hits, without Jan, some years ago. Of course you get royalties no matter which version they play, don't you?
Dean: K-Tel filed bankruptcy, too! They want to pay me like a penny on the dollar. They did give me some stock. I just don't care anymore. I'll just keep buying real estate; then someday I'll buy them all and dump them in the ocean!
Doc Rock: I had a chance to see your last show in nineteen sixty-six, when your "Batman" single was on the charts. It was in Kansas City. But the next weekend you were going to be in my home town, Lawrence, Kansas, with the sixteen-piece band and Mary Wells as the other act. So I didn't go to Kansas City, forty miles away. Then, in the interim, Jan had his accident, and you never played Lawrence or anywhere else again. I'll regret missing that last chance as long as I live.
Dean: That's really strange . . . it's really strange, when I look at it . . . if I'd only known that was the last night . . . I'd have never believed it.

Actually, there have been many Jan & Dean shows since the wreck. Currently Jan & Dean are making more per year doing live shows than they ever made in the 1960s. In the late 1980s, Jan & Dean became the first American rock 'n' roll group to tour China.

Jan & Dean's popularity, stifled by Jan's wreck, was revived in nineteen seventy-eight when CBS-TV aired a reasonably accurate but somewhat severe biography of Jan & Dean called *Deadman's Curve*. This movie was very popular on the network, and the popularity has continued in subsequent syndication. (It is available on home video.) Soon the publicity from this film resulted in Jan & Dean's touring with the Beach Boys. Then they did their own shows once again. They had a syndicated TV special, and appeared on everything from the "Today" show to "Dinah Shore" to the "Midnight Special" to Dick Clark retrospectives.

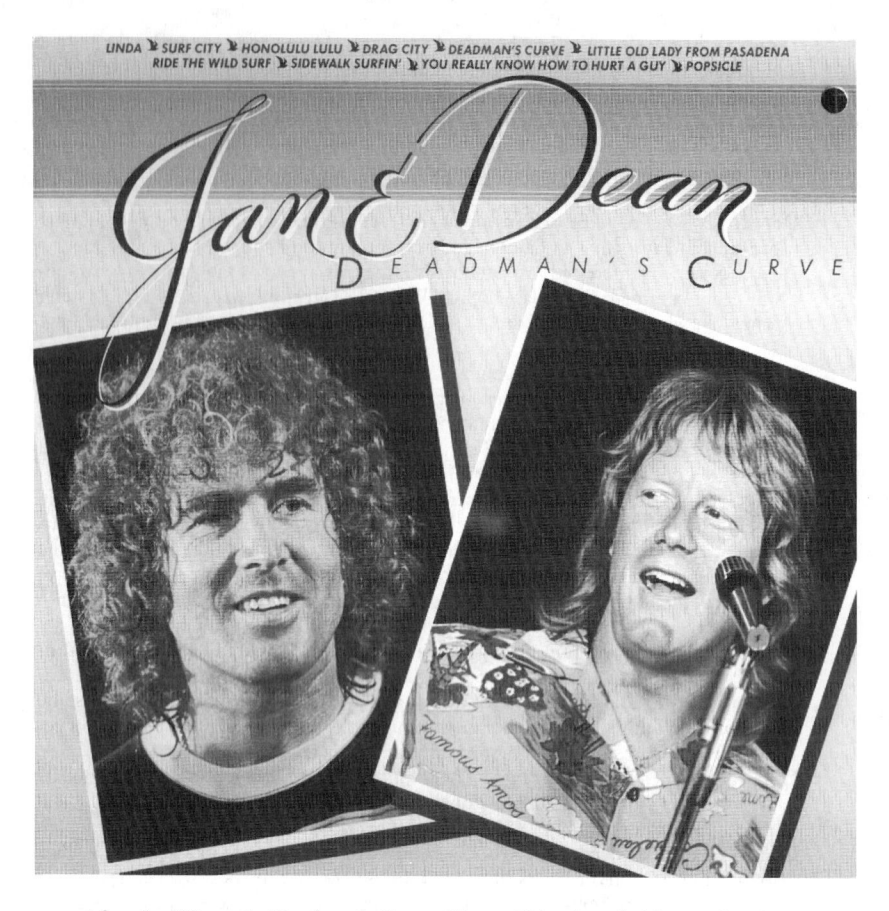

After the TV movie *Deadman's Curve*, Liberty/UA released this soundtrack LP.

Jan organized the Aloha Band and toured solo. Together, he and Dean toured with Papa Doo Ron Ron, named after their song "New Girl in School," and a band named after their 1965 football team, the Bel Air Bandits. Dean continued to appear with the Beach Boys. Then, he and Mike Love of the Boys formed "Mike and Dean," making live appearances, as well as records available through mail order and in Radio Shack stores.

In the late 1960s and the 1970s, Dean operated a commercial design firm, designing primarily album covers. He won a Grammy for his album cover *Pollution*.

Both Jan and Dean have continued to record, solo, as a duo, and in Dean's case, with Mike Love. The records have been released on United Artists, J&D Records, Magic Lamp Records, K-Tel, Excelsior Records, Gusto Records, A&M Records, Hitbound Records, and Ode Records. There have also been about a dozen illegal or quasilegal bootleg LPs, EPs, and singles released. These records have contained previously unreleased material, unknown songs as well as alternate takes, rehearsals, and foul-ups, bleeps, and blunders.

JAN BERRY AND THE ALOHA BAND

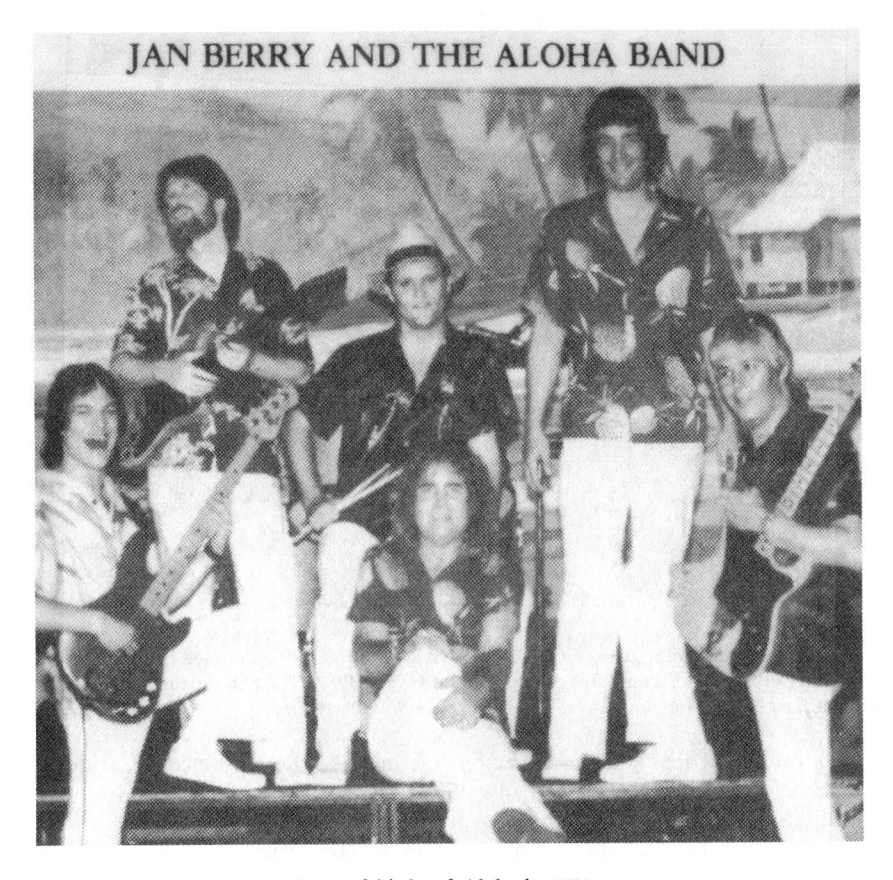

Jan and his band Aloha in 1979.

In the mid-eighties, *The TAMI Show* rock 'n' roll concert movie, which Jan & Dean hosted and appeared in, was released on home video in a highly edited form. Also Jan & Dean released a videotape, *Surfing Beach Party,* consisting of newly taped videos of their hits, and a clip of "Surf City" from their unreleased, 1966 TV pilot. Dean got married for the first time in 1983, and he and his wife Susan had a daughter, Katie, in 1989. Jan was married on August 31, 1991, in Las Vegas following a performance. Jan & Dean are alive and well and living in Hollywood.

Jan's accident has made him very hard to interview for the last twenty-five years. Often his memory of events of the 1960s is hazy or even nonexistent. But on rare occasions, his powers of recall are on a par with his musical prowess. Jan's memory is sometimes open to him, other times closed. It is not a matter of the veracity of the memories, but of their accessibility. His condition has improved with time. And, of course, he has always maintained his intelligence and primary brain power. His main problem has been aphasia—getting the thoughts in his head to come out of his mouth. People often mistake the characteristics of aphasia for retardation or simple-mindedness. Nothing could be more incorrect, as witnessed for example by

Dean, myself, and Mike Love of the Beach Boys. Mike and Dean performed their hits at the opening of Oceans of Fun water park in Kansas City in 1982. The park features rides called "Surf City" and "Honolulu Lulu," both Jan & Dean Liberty hits.

the great productions Jan has released on Ode and A&M Records since the accident, such as "Totally Wild" or "Sing Sang a Song," complex, mature, interesting, and musically sophisticated productions all.

Although he still suffers from the brain damage incurred in his accident in 1966, Jan recalls a lot about the old days.

>   Doc Rock: Do you remember much about the days at Liberty Records?
>   Jan Berry: Oh, yeah, before my accident and after my accident.
>   Doc Rock: Great! Do you remember Dick St. John of Dick and Deedee? I talked to him last week.
>   Jan Berry: So did I. We were on a plane going from the East Coast to the West Coast. On this flight I wrote a song with Sandy, his wife.
>   Doc Rock: Since nineteen seventy, Sandy has been "Deedee," because the original Deedee, Mary Sperling, retired.
>   Jan Berry: We wrote a song called "She's Dancing, Dancing," on the flight. The recording is not completed yet, it is just in rough form, but it was a fun concept.
>   Doc Rock: Well, Dick told me that when he was on his first Liberty tour, that you were on Challenge with "Heart and Soul."
>   Jan Berry: Oh, yeah, that is right, I remember.
>   Doc Rock: Dick said that you were obsessed with getting on Liberty, that you were always asking him, "Dick, who do you know at Liberty, how can I get there? I've got to get Jan & Dean on Liberty."
>   Jan Berry: Ha! Yes, I guess so. That was so long ago. The highlights I remember, but not the details. I do remember talking to Dick and Deedee about Liberty.
>   Doc Rock: Do you remember the president of Liberty Records, Al Bennett?
>   Jan Berry: He was like the leader of the pack. I went into his office to see him after

Chapter 36 · Jan & Dean

JAN BERRY
A & M Recording Artist

W J B INC.
1111 LINDA FLORA DR. 476-6677
LOS ANGELES, CA 90049

Jan Berry's press photo in 1978.

we got big hits. I wanted to renegotiate our Liberty contract to a higher level. At these times there was conflict between Al Bennett and myself. But it worked out.

Doc Rock: Do you remember how you finally got on Liberty?

Jan Berry: I don't really remember. We knew people in the business who worked at Liberty and with their help, it just happened. United and Western Studios, renamed these days, but I had to sign with a record company to record there.

Doc Rock: Is that right?

Jan Berry: It was a good studio, and a good thing, a good arrangement for me. I was able to produce the songs to my satisfaction. Dean was not always present.
Doc Rock: When?
Jan Berry: On "Surf City" and many of those songs, he wasn't even present.
Doc Rock: Dean has said he was not on "Surf City." He was on the album cuts? [Dean is obviously on a lot of songs, especially on a lot of the album cuts.]
Jan Berry: Well, the label still says Jan & Dean, so it doesn't make any difference, but I was still able to produce the records when he was not available. That was a long time ago.
Doc Rock: Dean has always been very frank about that. He said years ago how he was not on "I Found a Girl," about how Phil Sloan was able to impersonate him, and just last summer about how he was not on "Surf City." Do you remember the producer at Liberty Records, Snuff Garrett?
Jan Berry: Yeah, we did "Tennessee" with Snuff, just that one song. We did the performance "live" at United Studios at Beechwood and Sunset. Dean was there; we recorded everything—the vocals, the rhythm track—everything during the sessions at once. It was done on two tracks at the time.
Doc Rock: And Dean was there for that one, of course.
Jan Berry: Yes, sure.
Doc Rock: Do you recall the flip side of that record?
Jan Berry: No.
Doc Rock: It was called "Your Heart Has Changed Its Mind."
Jan Berry: Oh, yeah, right!
Doc Rock: The sound on that is a lot different, produced by Lou Adler.
Jan Berry: That was a ballad.
Doc Rock: Back to "Surf City," if not Dean, then who was on that record with you?
Jan Berry: I don't mean to make a big deal of it, about Dean. Before the accident I was the leader of the pack of Jan & Dean. After the accident I had a long period of rehabilitation, and Dean became the new leader. Then he controlled everything, and so it has come full circle. My day then, now his. He was probably jealous then, and after the accident, then I became jealous! Now the whole jealousy thing is completely finished.
Doc Rock: It all equaled out, eh?
Jan Berry: And we still survived. Not in the studio, but on the road. There is still a lot of road work, more than ever so far on the road. We've been all across the nation and in Canada, and we just did two weeks in the Caribbean. We did several performances, and the rest of the time we just relaxed!
Doc Rock: Last summer I saw you in Newton, Kansas.
Jan Berry: Yes, I saw you backstage.
Doc Rock: You did a very good show.
Jan Berry: Yes, our vocal now is better than ever, the vocals with the wireless microphone [are] perfect, sensitive, super now with no feedback, loud, it is all I need. Now when we go on the road we are happy! Or unconscious, I don't know what it is! [Laughs]
Doc Rock: If Dean was not on every record, he was always a big asset on stage, with comedy and personal appearances, right?
Jan Berry: Yeah, yeah! We always had good rapport. I remember one thing at the Hollywood Bowl, with the Mamas and Papas, we were to sing and then we missed Hollywood Bowl. I was driving to the backstage, and we made it too late. We didn't get on. A week later I had the accident. Strange, huh?
Doc Rock: The last show you did on the road, the weekend before the accident, you were in Kansas City an hour from here, and I could have seen you. But I didn't go because you were coming to my town, Lawrence, the following weekend. But you had the accident between the two dates, so I missed your last show and my only chance to see you.

Chapter 36 · Jan & Dean

Jan Berry: Was it on the news?

Doc Rock: Yes, the newspaper and the news.

Jan Berry: Oh, God, strange world, you missed it! I'll tell you one thing, I am alive, and we'll be there sooner or later!

Doc Rock: I saw you the first time in nineteen seventy-eight with your solo band the Alohas. I met you and showed you my 78 of "Jennie Lee."

Jan Berry: That was a good record. It was before Dean and I got together. He went into the Army, and while in San Francisco he had a transistor and he heard us [heard Jan & Arnie's record "Jennie Lee" on the radio], and he had all of his friends listen to it, and the disc jockey finished the song and he said, "Yes, and it's Jan Berry," and Dean yells, "Oh!" [Laughs.] Finally, when Dean got out, we hooked up.

Doc Rock: Was Dean not on "Jennie Lee"? Was that just Jan and Arnie?

Jan Berry: Yeah.

Doc Rock: But was Dean in the rehearsals, the practice sessions for "Jennie Lee"?

Jan Berry: No. He wasn't on it, [didn't record with me] until the next year.

Doc Rock: When you were at Liberty Records, Snuff didn't work with you very much. You produced your own records, didn't you?

Jan Berry: Right. "Tennessee" was produced by Snuff Garrett, and I think one of the other songs, and that was it. We kept on going with my producing later on.

Doc Rock: And that was a change for the good, because you did better records. That is when the hits came.

Jan Berry: Yeah, right.

Doc Rock: "Linda" was the first Jan & Dean record I bought; I liked it a lot.

Jan Berry: Good. I liked it, too.

Doc Rock: The surfing songs after that were wonderful. Did Brian Wilson sing on much of those, maybe the falsetto parts?

Jan Berry: No. On "Surf City," Brian Wilson sings on the vocal, me and Tony Minichello, who has passed away. On "Little Old Lady" Dean wasn't anywhere around here. Brian Wilson helped with the song on that one. One other track, "Dead Man's Curve," Brian Wilson, I think he wasn't singing the vocals though. The other thing, he did, "Surf City" and "Little Old Lady (from Pasadena)" just the background. Not the lead, just the vocals.

Doc Rock: I never heard of Tony before.

Jan Berry: Yeah, he passed away about four years ago, I guess.

Doc Rock: Where did you know him from?

Jan Berry: He was a third voice on background. He did a lot of other songs, harmony. He was a good musician and sang on the vocals.

Doc Rock: Oh, three voices! You mean "Tony, Vic, and Manuel," the Matadors.

Jan Berry: Yes! That's it, that's the group, that's the name! The background voices! To sing background harmony against my lead.

Doc Rock: What about Phil Sloan and Steve Barri?

Jan Berry: Yeah, we were up there recording together many times. Phil Sloan with the falsetto. "Surf City," "Little Old Lady," the falsettos.

Doc Rock: "Sidewalk Surfin'," he did that one, too?

Jan Berry: Right. Yep.

Doc Rock: What has been going on lately?

Jan Berry: For a year and a half now, I've worked on the studio. I paid everything. Oh, boy! That's a lot of money. [Joking] That's why I'm broke. The record's done, so we've printed it and sent it to a music lawyer. I expect to have it on a label soon. That's good anyway if I get signed, that's gonna be interesting! It's called "Second Wave." If you can get that.

Doc Rock: That is a great title. I can't wait to hear it. Thanks for talking. I know you have another appointment to get to.

Jan Berry: OK. Hey, thanks a lot, and keep on truckin'!

Jan & Dean in the studio. Dean is on the drums. *(Photo by Chuck Boyd.)*

Should fans be shocked that Dean's voice cannot be heard on every hit song labeled "Jan & Dean"? Does this mean that Dean wasn't really—well, Dean? Not at all. Dean has always been open about not having appeared on certain Liberty hit records attributed to Jan & Dean, including "I Found a Girl" and "You Really Know How to Hurt a Guy."

Dean is clearly heard on the overwhelming majority of Jan & Dean songs, including, to name just a few, "Submarine Races," "Schlock Rod," "Drag City," "Batman," "The Restless Surfer" (which, by the way, Jan is not on), "Linda," "Heart and

Soul," "Ride the Wild Surf," "Dead Man's Curve," "Clementine," "Baby Talk," "Frosty," and "Popsicle."

But Jill Gibson did do the high notes on "Easy as 1,2,3." Brian Wilson was on "Surf City." Phil Sloan did falsetto on "I Found a Girl" and apparently on "Sidewalk Surfin'" and "Little Old Lady." Neither Jan *nor* Dean is on one track called "Move Out, Little Mustang," a cut on the Jan & Dean album *The Little Old Lady (from Pasadena)*! All the vocals on that song are by "background singers" Sloan and Barri.

None of this is to say that Dean was not involved with the creative process involved in creating "Jan & Dean" records. For example, he contributed to the rewrite of Brian Wilson's song "Two Girls for Every Boy," which became known as "Surf City" by Jan & Dean, although he got no label credit for his contribution.

Perhaps the best way to illustrate how Dean's involvement on a given release can be difficult to pin down is to compare two versions of "The Little Old Lady (from Pasadena)." There is the Liberty hit version, which has been released and rereleased many times since 1964 on 45s, LPs, reel tapes, eight-track tapes, cassette tapes, and CDs. But there is another version of "The Little Old Lady (from Pasadena)" by Jan & Dean to be heard—in fact, three versions. In the 1970s a bootleg LP titled *Jan & Dean Studio Out Takes, Vol. 2* was released by ajw [*sic*] records. On this LP three 1964 rehearsal tapes of "The Little Old Lady (from Pasadena)," called "The Little Old Lady," "Lady from Pasadena," and "Pasadena Girls," appear. All three versions feature exactly the same instrumental track and background vocals as on the hit 45 version. However, the lead and falsetto vocals are not the same as on the Liberty hit.

The bootleg version called "Lady from Pasadena," for example, features Jan on lead, singing lyrics and a melody that are noticeably different from what he sang on the hit version. A voice that is obviously Dean's can also be heard, singing a falsetto part that is a noticeably different melody from the falsetto part on the hit version. So Dean was there and did sing on "The Little Old Lady (from Pasedena)." The catch is, while the voice doing new lead lyrics and melody on the hit is still Jan's, the voice doing a new falsetto melody on the hit is not Dean Torrence's.

In other words Dean sang on "The Little Old Lady (from Pasadena)" with Jan. But in the final mix, when Jan's rehearsal lead was redone by Jan and his old lead was taken out of the mix, Dean's rehearsal falsetto part was also redone, not by Dean, but by Phil Sloan, and Dean's old one taken out of the mix. So Dean was on the song, but he cannot be heard on the final record. It is sort of a case of the music studio equivalent of having one's part being left on the cutting-room floor. Jan was in the studio day and night, whenever his med school studies allowed him a few minutes' free time. Sometimes when Jan would be there with various musicians and background singers, he would need a voice to complete a track, but Dean would happen not to be present. So someone else might pinch-hit on a part.

What is one to make of the fact that Dean cannot be heard to warble on every J&D cut, or that Tony, Brian, Jill, Phil, and others not only sang backgrounds (like the Fantastic Baggies on the *Little Old Lady* LP and the Matadors on the *Surf City and Other Swingin' Cities* LP) but also dualed leads, did harmonies, and sang falsetto parts?

As a musical act "Jan & Dean" were not two guys. They never pretended to play all the instruments and sing all the harmony. "Jan & Dean" was a group. Jan was the leader of the pack, as he puts it, the driving force, the overachiever/extrovert

Publicity photo of Jan & Dean, circa 1981.

who wrote songs and dissected lab specimens on airliners on the way to weekend gigs while in med school. The group called Jan & Dean included, at various times and places, Jan, Arnie, Dean, Brian, Lou Adler, Glen Campbell, Phil Sloan, Steve Barri, Jill Gibson, Hal Blaine, Earl Palmer, Bones Howe, Billy Strange (guitar), Roger Christian, Tommy Tedesco (guitar), Tony Terran (French horn), George Tipton, Snuff Garrett, Johnny Crawford, and others.

Not every Beatle was on every Beatles record, nor were the performers on Beatles records limited to the Fab Four themselves. Brian Wilson worked on Beach Boys albums while the band was on tour, surprising them with what he had done using other bands and voices while they were gone. And Buddy Holly's Crickets did not sing on Buddy Holly records. Two groups, the Pics and the Roses, did the vocals on Buddy's hits of the 1950s. But the Crickets were still the Crickets!

In his 1990 autobiographical book *The Wrecking Crew*, session drummer and Jan & Dean friend Hal Blaine describes how he and a group of professional musicians known as the Wrecking Crew played on records by supposedly self-contained groups from Paul Revere and the Raiders and the Beach Boys to the Grass Roots and Gary Lewis and the Playboys.

The Jan/"Jan & Dean"/Dean situation perhaps most closely parallels the Phil Spector situation. The records Spector did are now known as "Phil Spector" records. The "Phil Spector Group" consisted of Darlene Love, the Crystals, Ronnie, Bobby Sheen, Nino Tempo, Cher, Jeff and Ellie, Jack Nitzsche, the Ronettes, Barry and

Cynthia, the Righteous Brothers (the Ronettes did some of the high voices on their records), Ike and Tina, the Blossoms, Sonny Bono, and a half dozen regular musicians. With these people and others, in various combinations and under a variety of names, Phil put out records. His "main" visible partner changed over time, from Lester Sills, to Darlene, to Ronnie, to the Righteous Brothers, and so on. Through it all Phil produced, wrote, arranged, ran the business end, and had hits.

Jan was like a West Coast Spector. The only difference was that he almost always called the artist "Jan & Dean," he performed himself more than Phil did, and he stuck with one "main" visible partner longer. And he did live shows, invariably with that partner. Then, in his "spare time," Jan attended medical school, while Dean attended graduate school in commercial design. In fact, Dean received a Grammy award for his LP cover for the group Pollution. That ranks him as probably the only rock 'n' roller to have a decade of hits, two college degrees, and a Grammy for an album cover under his belt!

Imagine what music we might have heard had Jan & Dean done music full-time, like Spec and Brian, instead of splitting their time between school and work.

While it is a surprise to learn that Dean did not perform on every recording bearing the group name "Jan & Dean," it really isn't earthshaking. Dean was there, even if Jan as arranger and producer and even engineer sometimes didn't use Dean to full advantage.

Jan performed a wonderful service to record fans worldwide, and Dean's contribution of support, friendship, business partnership, camaraderie, friend in need, comedy, and stage presence contributed immeasurably to the success, appeal, and longevity of the act — certainly more than any other single person did.

Dean recognizes Jan's contribution. Dean feels that as a writer, producer, arranger, businessman, and artist, Jan deserves recognition for the genius he showed and the accomplishments he achieved. That is why Dean has suggested that Jan be nominated for the Rock and Roll Hall of Fame. For his part, Jan says not a bad word against Dean.

Jan — as Dean said, you deserve the Hall of Fame!

And, to quote the Beach Boys at the end of Capitol Records' "Barbara Ann" — on which Dean did sing — "Thanks, Dean." Thanks for making the duo work. Without you Jan would not have had the opportunity to play fast and loose with those sessions he produced for Liberty release under the name "Jan & Dean."*

Jan & Dean Discography

DOT

(Jan & Arnie)

1958 16116   Gas Money
Gotta Getta Date

1962 EP1097   Jennie Lee
Gas Money
Gotta Get a Date
The Beat That Can't Be Beat

---

* *The Jan & Dean story was told in a series of interviews, beginning in Dean Torrence's Kittyhawk Graphics commercial design office in June 1973, as well as many telephone conversations, and continuing backstage at various live performances in Wichita, Kansas; Newton, Kansas; and Kansas City, Missouri, up to August 1991.*

ARWIN
(Jan & Arnie)

108	Jennie Lee	
	Gotta Get a Date	
MM108	(78 rpm)	
	Jennie Lee (Jan & Arnie)	
	Gotta Get a Date	
111	Gas Money	
	Bonnie Lou	
113	The Beat That Can't Be Beat	
	I Love Linda	

DORÉ

1959	522	Baby Talk (Jan & Arnie)
		Jeannette Get Your Hair Done (Jan & Arnie)
	522	Baby Talk
		Jeannette, Get Your Hair Done (alt. spelling)
	531	There's a Girl
		My Heart Sings
1960	539	Clementine
		You're on My Mind
	548	White Tennis Sneakers
		Cindy
	555	We Go Together
		Rosie Lane
	555	We Go Together
		Rosilane (alt. spelling)
	576	Gee
		Such a Good Night for Dreaming
1961	583	Judy's an Angel
		Baggy Pants
	610	Julie
		Don't Fly Away

CHALLENGE

9111	Heart and Soul	
	Those Words	
9111	Heart and Soul	
	Midsummer Night's Dream (alt. flip)	
9120	Wanted, One Girl	
	Something a Little Bit Different	

LIBERTY

1961	55397	A Sunday Kind of Love
		Poor Little Puppet
1962	55454	Tennessee
		Your Heart Has Changed Its Mind
	55496	Who Put the Bomp
		My Favorite Dream
	55522	She's Still Talking Baby Talk
		Frosty (the Snow Man)
1963	55531	Linda
		When I Learn How to Cry
	55580	Surf City
		She's My Summer Girl
	55613	Honolulu Lulu
		Someday (You'll Go Walking By)
	55641	Drag City
		Schlock Rod (Part 1)
1964	55672	Dead Man's Curve
		The New Girl in School
	55704	The Little Old Lady (from Pasadena)
		My Mighty G.T.O.
	55724	The Anaheim, Azusa, & Cucamonga Sewing Circle, Book Review and Timing Association
		Ride the Wild Surf
	55727	Sidewalk Surfin'
		When It's Over
1965	55766	Freeway Flyer
		(Here They Come) From All Over the World
	55792	You Really Know How to Hurt a Guy
		It's as Easy as 1,2,3
	55816	It's a Shame to Say Goodbye
		(Cancelled) The Submarine Races
	55833	I Found a Girl
		It's a Shame to Say Goodbye
	55845	The Universal Coward (Jan Berry)
		I Can't Wait to Love You (Jan Berry)
	55849	A Beginning from an End
		Folk City
1966	55856	Norwegian Wood
		I Can't Wait to Love You
	55860	Batman
		Bucket "T"
	55886	Popsicle
		Norwegian Wood
	55905	A Surfer's Dream
		Fiddle Around
	55923	The New Girl in School
		School Day

IMPERIAL
(Rally Packs)
66036   Move Out Little Mustang
Bucket Seats

BR'ER BRID
(Our Gang)
001   Summertime Summertime
Theme from Leo's Garage

CANTERBURY
(Yellow Balloon feat. Don Grady)
508   Yellow Balloon (featuring Dean Torrence)
Noollab Wolley
513   Good Feelin' Time
I've Got a Feeling for Love

WARNER BROS.
7151   Love and Hate
Only a Boy
7219   I Know My Mind
Laurel and Hardy
7240   In the Still of the Night
Girl, You're Blowing My Mind

WHITE WHALE
(Laughing Gravy)
261   Vegetables
Snowflakes on Laughing Gravy's Whiskers

J&D
10   Hawaii
Tijuana
11   Fan Tan
Love & Hate
401   California Lullabye
Summertime Summertime
402   Louisiana Man
Like a Summer Rain
1987   1   Oh What a Beautiful Morning!
Wa Ichi Nichi Shiow

COLUMBIA
44036   Yellow Balloon
Taste of Rain

UNITED ARTISTS
50859   Jenny Lee
Vegetables
50958   Gonna Hustle You/Summertime Summertime (Both by the Legendary Masked Surfers)
XW270   Gonna Hustle You (Legendary Masked Surfers)
Summer Means Fun (Legendary Masked Surfers)
XW670   Sidewalk Surfin'
Gonna Hustle You
1973   XW092   Dead Man's Curve (same flip)

MAGIC LAMP
401   California Lullabye
Summertime

ODE
66023   Mother Earth (Jan Berry)
Blue Moon Shuffle (Jan Berry)
66034   Don't You Just Know It (Jan)
Blue Moon Shuffle (Jan)
66050   Blow Up Music (1 Jan 1)
Tinsel Town (1 Jan 1)
66111   Fun City
Totally Wild
66120   Sing Sang a Song (Jan Berry)
Sing Sang a Song (sing along version)

A&M
(Jan Berry)
1957   Little Queenie
That's the Way It Is
2020   Skateboard Surfin' U.S.A. (Sidewalk Surfin' with Me)/How, How I Love Her

RIPPLE
(Jan Berry)
6101   Tomorrow's Teardrops
My Midsummer Night's Dream

EQUINOX/ RCA VICTOR
(Papa Doo Ron Ron)
10404   Be True to Your School
Disney Girls

WORLD
(Papa Doo Ron Ron)

2721 Sunshine Music

HITBOUND
(Dean Torrence/ Mike Love)

101 Da Doo Ron Ron
Baby Talk

ERA

1962 5010 Baby Talk

Jeannette Get Your Hair Done

BUDWEISER

1983 JRC8246 Budweiser Fight Song 'Be True to Your Bud'
Instrumental version (Mike Love & Dean Torrence)

ARTISTIC

1965 227 Midsummer Night's Dream (EP with 7 other songs by other artists)

Part Four

The End of Liberty

CHAPTER 37

Selling Liberty ... and Selling It and Selling It

Clearly Al Bennett was largely responsible for the success of Liberty Records. But on the climb to the top of any ladder, sometimes the fingers of the other people on the same ladder get stepped on. Credit goes to Al for his accomplishments, and artists like Bobby Vee, Gary Troxel, and Buddy Knox, and others such as the Glasser brothers and Tommy Allsup, have nothing but good things to say about Al Bennett. On the other hand, Don Blocker, Sharon Sheeley, and Si Waronker saw another side of Al—for example, Sharon Sheeley, who recalls what a good—shall we say, "businessman" Al Bennett was.

"At the time of Eddie's death, Don Blocker had risen from head of promotion for Liberty to vice president," reflects Sheeley. "When Al Bennett sold out all of the Liberty stock, he cut Don Blocker's throat. Al Bennett was a very clever man. He was always very kind and fair to me. But I am telling you, this man would cheat his mother if he had a chance."

Si Waronker confirms Sharon's statements about Don Blocker. "Don Blocker was brought in with Al Bennett as head of promotion. Then when things were changing all around, he left to own his own production company and manage his own artist, I don't know who he was, someone obscure. He was very close to Al Bennett, but the ending of all of these guys was not as pleasant as you'd like. Everything was chipped away, and Don was one of the guys that lost out because of the way things were run."

Sharon Sheeley explains how the deal was engineered and how it went wrong. "A record company can press up thousands of copies of records that are never going to sell and put them into the warehouses. Then, if you think you are going to have a major hit, you ship all of these records out to record stores, and you hope that all of these records are going to sell. But if after a month or two they do not sell, then all of the record stores ship all of those records back to the record company and say, 'We took these records on consignment, but they didn't sell, so you get them back.' But until they have been returned, they are considered to have been sold.

"Now the record company is stuck with all of these records, which costs them money. Since these businessmen looking to buy Liberty were not in the record business and did now know the ropes, what Al Bennett did was allocate all of these thousands of records that had already been returned once! So, on his books they were sold, and the company looked to be in really excellent shape. As a result Al Bennett was able to sell it for a huge amount for that time. It was an unprecedented sale.

Variety had a headline, 'Liberty Sets High Record.' Al got millions for Liberty Records that time.

"He tells Don Blocker of Liberty, 'Hey, this is the best thing for all of us, we are going to make a killing.' So Don Blocker took his life savings and bought Liberty stock, which was supposed to get very valuable after the buyout. But it was just another incredible swindle, and Don Blocker lost everything he had. And Don is such a dear, sweet man. After being vice president of Liberty with a home in Bel Air.

"Well, after this deal had been closed, all of these allocated records started to come back in from the record stores. It was such a bad development.

"Al Bennett said, 'I thought you guys knew about allocation; you guys should have known. I feel so bad about this. Tell you what—I will buy Liberty back.' And he did. I told you, he would cheat his own grandmother.

"Al could also not stand to be outsmarted or outmaneuvered. Al Bennett could outmaneuver Jerry Capehart [Eddie Cochran's manager, who according to Sharon took Eddie's royalties] the same as I could. But Al could not outthink me, so he really did not try. So Al would call in Bob Skaff and his other staff to outthink me. And they would just all look at Al and say, 'Nope, forget it.' So Al would laugh his big laugh and say, 'Well, you can't blame a man for trying, can ya,' darlin'?'"

The Avnet sale was in the 1962–63 era. Si Waronker lost the will to stay at Liberty at that juncture. "When I owned the company, I had forty-six percent of the stock. I had given Al Bennett twenty-five percent of the stock; five percent went to Hal Linneck, five percent went to the attorney; and a couple of points here and there went to different employees.

"Avnet was an electronics company. Through Merrill-Lynch, I was approached to see if I wanted to merge the company. Liberty was already on the stock exchange. I had a hundred fifty thousand shares of stock, Al had about sixty-five thousand, and the rest proportionally, all unissued stock. This was in nineteen sixty-two, after my strokes. We were ready to come out with a secondary offering, in which we would sell one million shares of stock. There were only a hundred thousand shares outstanding to the public at the time. The stock I owned was unissued stock.

"At the time we agreed to make the deal with Avnet, the plan was to make the deal secretive to avoid insider trading. So they sent both Al and me to Miami Beach together, where there was a convention so we could hide out until the lawyers had drawn up the papers. We used this for a chance to have a vacation.

"In the meantime Al, being the goddamned fool he was in these things, called his girlfriend in Los Angeles, who in turn talked to Don Blocker. Don was a vice president, but everyone was being made a vice president, so that title didn't mean anything. She told Don that this deal was pending.

"Don Blocker went out and bought all this stock in Liberty Records as soon as he heard about the pending deal. Right away, we saw Liberty Records stock shoot up from eight to twelve dollars a share in one day.

"I started to scream, 'Who in the hell let this out of the bag?! It couldn't be the Avnet people, it's got to be somebody in our company. And Al, you are the only one who knows about it. The only person I spoke to was my wife. I didn't even call the office.

"Al said, 'Don Blocker swore that he wouldn't say anything to anybody.' I told him, 'Al, you can get your ass in a jam and mine, too. I'm not taking any responsibility for this.'

"As soon as the deal was announced that we would sell Liberty, Avnet stock, which was selling at twenty-seven, dropped immediately to twenty-two dollars. And Liberty went up to twenty-two dollars, because it was a one-for-one share exchange.

"The cost of Liberty to Avnet Electronics was twelve million dollars. That was what we sold the company for. Of which I received for my stock, four point seven million. I traded my Liberty stock for Avnet stock, and then sold it all because I didn't want to have anything to do with anybody.

"The first year, because of a lot of shenanigans—and I left because I was not happy with things—we got into fights because they wanted me to record things I did not want to record. And Al and I also got into a hassle about the way the company was being run. So I quit—and they lost a million dollars the first year. It was not lost on bad records. It was lost on bad business. No decent merchandise was coming out, and Al was spending dough so it was flowing out of that place like it was made of I-don't-know-what. And I quit. I couldn't take it.

"They sued me, and I sued back; we settled, and I was out of the picture.

"Then Avnet started to lose money like crazy. By the beginning of the second year, they were well into debt. Avnet called their attorneys who set up the deal and said that they would like to sell the company back. I wasn't talking to anyone. But Al came to me and asked if I would be interested in buying back the company. I said no!"

Al kept at Si and offered to make him the majority stockholder again. Si said he would do it on condition that he could appoint five of the nine members of the board of directors. Al could have the other four. "Al never agreed to that. So I left for good and never so much as went back to the building.

"Al bought the company back. Instead of twelve million dollars, Liberty gave back all the stock and notes to Avnet amounting to something less than eight million. So Avnet lost four million on the deal.

"Al then started to run the company from nineteen sixty-four to nineteen seventy.

"In nineteen sixty-eight, Transamerica came into the picture. The broker who put the deal together called me on my boat and said that Transamerica paid, in stock, about thirty-eight million for Liberty. That lasted about a year.

"I know it was nineteen sixty-eight because Snuff had quit and was out of the company. He came to me with Ed Silvers and wanted to start a record company and a publishing company called Amigo.

"In nineteen seventy Transamerica merged Liberty with United Artists, which it also owned. Their man took over and fouled everything up. Al Bennett lost everything, and when he died, he was penniless."

Bud Dain confirms Si's account and adds a few details.

"Transamerica bought Liberty when Al Bennett sold them a bill of goods. They were told by several people, including Snuff Garrett, that they were overpaying for it. He told Jack Beckett and Ed Scarf, who was president of Transamerica. But they didn't believe him. They bought Liberty Records because UA was a failure, a miserable record company. They had a great publishing company, Unart. But they had a lousy record company. They bought Liberty to beef up their music division, and they bought it for its catalog and its executive staff.

"When they bought Liberty, Liberty took over. All the UA guys were demoted. But Transamerica had paid thirty-eight million dollars for what was really a twelve- or fourteen-million-dollar record company. So after about six months when they saw that we were never going to make the projections that had been set [by Al Bennett and Liberty], that was when they fired Al Bennett and all his staff. But I think Al made seventeen million the day they sold the company. He was a great salesman, [with] great charm.

"Then they fired all the Liberty people and put all the previously demoted UA people back in. Eventually, when they discovered that they did not know how to run a record company, they sold everything. They even sold Metric Music and Travis Music. They should have held that forever. I had gone to A&M, so I had a wonderful time. And when Jerry Moss later sold A&M for five hundred million bucks, he didn't sell the publishing company. Now, that is smart.

"The final downfall of Liberty Records came when we sold to Transamerica. They just took it apart. Avnet did not hurt us too much because they gave us the money we needed. Al just did not know what to do with the money, to be honest. He went out and opened branches; we used to have wars about it. I wanted to go out and get great artists, and everything else would take care of itself. But Al was a marketing man, and that was what he really knew. When he sold to Transamerica it was over."

Lee Mendell: "Al Bennett said to me in the mid–1970s, 'One of the biggest mistakes I ever made was selling to Transamerica.'" Mendell feels that Transamerica was a fine company that simply did not understand the entertainment business, from Liberty to United Artists films. "I was on the Transamerica Marketing Group Committee, and on the Transamerica International Committee. I didn't leave until 1975 or 1976. The first or second meeting I went to, Jack Beckett, the chairman of the board, asked me for a kind of a profile of how a record was made. I told him what happened and how you did it. And I ended up by saying, 'And maybe you spend a hundred thousand or fifty thousand on promotion and tours.' He asked me, 'And what is the return on that?' And I said, 'Well, you either lose two, three, or four thousand dollars, or you maybe make a million.'

"Well, for a financial company, that was difficult for them to understand. For them you invest one hundred thousand dollars at six and three-fourths percent, and you get a hundred six thousand seven fifty back. But records [are] a creative industry. There are no structures that say, 'You take Snuffy Garrett, you take a song by so-and-so, you go into the studio, you use this arranger, and you have a hit.' That just is not true. Seven hits out of a hundred records is pretty good. It was difficult for Transamerica to understand how you could invest money and not know what your return was going to be. I suspect some of the companies Liberty bought went through the same trauma.

"The Avnet deal was fortunate and unfortunate, because when Al bought Liberty back, the company did even better. The Transamerica deal did not work out well because it was a case of apples and oranges. They just did not understand the business. Which is a pity, because with their funding, Liberty could have developed into one of the big three or four labels around today. There is no question about it."

Liberty Record Mogull

The Liberty story does not quite end with the Transamerica takeover. On paper Liberty still existed after that, and even still exists today, in a sense.

Si Waronker, although he had long left the company and no longer had anything to do with it, did watch from the sidelines as his company was manhandled and mishandled over the years. Si's opinion is that the end of Liberty "all happened overnight. Once they fired Al Bennett and threw him out, that meant that the company was also finished. It petered out after that because they had nobody to run it. Mike Stewart had run Liberty on the East Coast while Al Bennett was running it on the West Coast. Once Al was out, Mike was in charge of all of it. Liberty became sort of a hot potato until they could get rid of it. Liberty fell apart in the board room of Transamerica when they fired Al. Then they had nothing more than debt and a lot of people left unpaid. I've never talked about that, because I wasn't there."

When Transamerica purchased Liberty in 1968, a man named Beckett was the chairman of the board, and he was the one who fired Al Bennett because Al was spending far too much money, with very little return in terms of record sales.

The company, as owned by Transamerica, became Liberty/UA, and then eventually the name *Liberty* was, for all practical purposes, phased out.

One day in the spring of 1978, Beckett was having breakfast at the Beverly Hilton Hotel when he saw Artie Mogull, who was president of UA at the time. He told Artie that he had to get rid of UA and the Liberty catalog. By this time Liberty as a label and a company was long gone. It was all UA, and Liberty was not on the scene at all.

Artie asked Beckett for ninety days to raise the cash. Beckett agreed. Mogull, who had been president of UA since 1976, answered to the Transamerica board in San Francisco. In fact, Transamerica kept an officer in the UA building, formerly Liberty Records, at 6920 Sunset Boulevard. The UA label at this time had War, ELO, Jerry Rafferty, the Dirt Band, Crystal Gayle, the *Rocky* sound track, and Kenny Rogers.

Artie Mogull did not have the $30 million needed to buy Liberty and UA. Therefore, he sought backing from EMI, a huge British music conglomerate that already owned Capitol (which Artie had worked for) and many other record companies. EMI agreed as long as there was a second operating officer in charge. This was Jerry Rubinstein, formerly of ABC Records.

Mogull and Rubinstein ran United Artists, sometimes referred to as Liberty/UA, until February 1979. Some Liberty material was released during this time. For example, an album called *The Best of Willie Nelson* was issued, consisting of old Liberty material including "Funny How Time Slips Away" and "Hello, Walls." Paired with the TV movie of their careers, a Jan & Dean LP called *Deadman's Curve* [*sic*] was released, consisting of ten of their biggest 1960s Liberty hits.

These albums carried a disclaimer: "Manufactured by United Artists, a division of Liberty/United Records Inc., Los Angeles, California 90028. United Artists Records is a trading name used under exclusive license from United Artists Corporation by M & R Music Corporation, an independent company not affiliated with United Artists Corporation, United Artists Music Co., Inc., or Transamerica Corporation." Of course, M & R Music was Mogull and Rubinstein.

M & R was not successful, and after a few months they borrowed another ten million from EMI for operating capital. This money was to be paid back in installments, as M & R gained success. However, this infusion of capital did not solve their problems, and in February 1979, EMI took Liberty/UA off their hands for $33 million by either exercising an option to buy Liberty/UA or by foreclosing on the thirty million backing—depending on who is telling the story.

The $33 million amount was decided upon because Mogull and Rubinstein had a clause in their original contract that, if the deal fell apart, they would retain and split $3 million between them.

EMI has totally owned Liberty from then on. EMI came out OK in the entire deal, even though Liberty/UA was a shambles by 1979, simply because one of the last acts Liberty/UA got was Kenny Rogers. The first year of EMI ownership, Kenny Rogers records earned $80 million for EMI. So EMI came out smelling like a rose. Liberty/UA had that one artist who made all the money they needed.

Artie Mogull went on in the music business. He was with SBK—one of the most successful new independent labels in the world—which had Vanilla Ice, Smokey Robinson, and Wilson Phillips. SBK (Swid, Bandier, and Koppelman) had started as a publishing company that bought all the old EMI publishing, including Liberty's Metric company. Artie Mogull, when he was head of UA, gave Bandier and Koppelman their own label, called Manhattan Records. Artie Mogull was a consultant to SBK, who may have brought Wilson Phillips to the label. When SBK sold the publishing to EMI, EMI funded SBK Records. Finally EMI bought out the partners and now owns SBK.

During this time the Liberty name was just used for some reissues, mostly in England.

After SBK, Artie Mogull was with the Ventura Entertainment Group. He now runs JRS Records with money put up by Steven Swid, a wealthy entrepreneur. Reports are that JRS has gone through $4 million in its first three months of operation.

In the 1990s, EMI is releasing old Liberty and Imperial material on a new series of Legendary Masters CDs, once again using the old Liberty trademarks and logos. And, there is a new Liberty logo, as well!

Liberty Post Script

The Liberty name seems almost timeless in American popular music. Back in 1942, the founders of Capitol originally planned to call their company Liberty, not Capitol!

After Liberty had been dead during the 1970s, Capitol re-activated the Liberty name for a country label featuring mainly Kenny Rogers. This use of the Liberty name ended in 1984.

Then, in 1992, the Liberty name arose once again. Today, of course, EMI owns the catalogs and names of both Capitol Records and Liberty Records. On January 23, EMI announced that their Capitol Nashville label was being renamed Liberty. Under the direction of Jimmy Bowen ("I'm Stickin' with You," Roulette, 1957), the new Liberty will not be simply a country division of Capitol Records. Although its first big artist will be the immensely popular country singer Garth Brooks, the label

The new Liberty '90s logo.

will feature all sorts of alternative and minority music, with the first release planned by the group Zulu Spear.

Initial press reports of the new Liberty stated that the label had been founded by Al Bennett. Si Waronker's son and grand son, both in the record industry, saw this, quickly informed Si, and corrections were run in the trade press.

The new label will carry a variation of the old Statue of Liberty logo.

Around the same time, EMI's CEO, Jim Fifield announced a new royalty policy for EMI's artists, including the Liberty family. Under old contracts from the '50s and '60s, many artists have been getting far smaller royalty payments than those currently granted in the recording industry. In order to do justice to the pre-seventies artists whose material is currently being reissued by EMI, all old artists' share is being raised to 10 percent.

CHAPTER 38

Life After Liberty

United Artists Records, which bought out Liberty, had a rock 'n' roll legacy behind it. From their film interests, they had released the Beatles' *A Hard Day's Night* LP. Their rock 'n' roll artists had included Jay and the Americans ("She Cried," 1962, "Cara Mia," 1965), Marve Johnson ("You've Got What It Takes," 1959), and many others.

United Artists kept the Liberty artists' music available. First they opened the warehouses and poured thousands and thousands of Liberty, Imperial, and Dolton LPs into the two-for-a-dollar cutout bins. Then UA began reissuing old Liberty material. A budget-priced *Best of* ... series featured the Fleetwoods, Gene McDaniels, Jan & Dean, Jackie DeShannon, Cher, Johnny Rivers, and many other artists, including various artists LPs to replace the old *Liberty Original Hits* and *Golden Greats* series.

Also, a new *Legendary Masters* series, similar to the one Imperial had many years before, was launched. The first four albums, each containing two LPs, featured artwork designed by Dean Torrence and spotlighted Fats Domino, Ricky Nelson, Jan & Dean, and Eddie Cochran. Subsequently other artists, notably Bobby Vee, were added to the series. The *Legendary Masters* albums were luxurious, a fan's dream, a collector's treasure. Each two-LP set featured full documentation and illustrations. For instance, Bobby Vee's included a centerfold with life-size, full-color reproductions of as many of the actual 45 rpm singles as could be squeezed into the pages! Jan & Dean's, called the *Jan & Dean Anthology Album,* included a chart of all of their hits, where and on what equipment each song was recorded, how many copies each single sold, how well each song did on the national charts, even what year and make of cars Jan and Dean were driving, and their girlfriends' names at the time each song was recorded! A 45 single was released along with the *Anthology Album,* featuring the first Jan & Dean song from 1958 on one side ("Jennie Lee"), and the newest on the flip, from 1968 ("Vegetables").

These LPs had twelve by twelve-inch multipage booklets inside, documenting in text and photos the artist's career. Cover art was unparalleled. The music included all the hits of the selected artist and lesser-known cuts as well. In Eddie Cochran's case, many nonhits were included, since his career was so brief and his big popularity came after his death. Foreshadowing the bootleg LPs of the 1970s and 1980s, UA even added some alternate versions of some of Eddie's songs! Bobby Vee's *Legendary Masters Album,* which included some rare and unreleased material as well as all of his hits, is the rarest. After a few hundred test pressings were made, the album project was canceled, and the samples were shunted to the cutout bins.

The *Legendary Masters* series aside, the old Liberty/Dolton/Imperial material was constantly reissued. As late as 1978, when Jan & Dean's story was told in the CBS-TV movie, *Deadman's Curve*, UA issued a new *Deadman's Curve* LP.

Then, in the early 1980s, UA was taken over by EMI, which had also absorbed Capitol. Alan Warner was around during those transactions, which had their roots back in the late 1960s. "Another American label I was looking after for EMI was United Artists. In England there was then a trend away from major American labels being licensed to British labels, and a trend toward major American labels establishing their own independent operations in London. Warner/Reprise broke away from Pye, Atlantic broke away from London, and United Artists in 1968 set up their own independent operation and asked me to join them, which I did.

"UA was then bought by Transamerica, and Transamerica soon after bought Liberty as well. So the two catalogs came together worldwide, and it became Liberty/UA in America as well as abroad. In America, of course, Liberty was a West Coast operation, and UA was an East Coast operation, so initially they kept Liberty/UA as two companies on both coasts, with Al Bennett operating Liberty/UA on the West Coast, and Mike Stewart, who had been running UA, operating Liberty/UA on the East Coast. Eventually, everything was consolidated and run out of California."

The reissues just keep on coming, however. EMI reissued Liberty/Imperial/Dolton/Minit hits on a series of various artists LPs titled *History of Rock 'n' Roll Volume....* Volume 3 featured only Liberty family artists: from Liberty, Timi Yuro, Bobby Vee, Jan & Dean, Classics IV, Canned Heat, and Gary Lewis and the Playboys; from Imperial, Cher; and from Dolton, the Ventures and the Fleetwoods. In the late 1970s EMI temporarily reactivated the Liberty name and logo. They even reissued some old Liberty LPs, including Jan & Dean's *Little Old Lady (from Pasadena)*, and Johnny Burnette's *Hits and Other Favorites*. The new Liberty is also dipping into the Dolton and Imperial vaults, reissuing, for instance, the Fleetwoods' LP *Greatest Hits*, the Fantastic Baggies' *Tell 'em I'm Surfin'*, and Rick Nelson's *Souvenirs*. New compilations include Eddie Cochran's *Great Hits* and the Fleetwoods' *Buried Treasure*, the latter full of previously unissued tracks. The reissues are complete with the original cover art but missing a song or two. It is nice that the Liberty name was used once again, but the company was not the same one, and the original Liberty Records, like original rock 'n' roll, is a thing of the past.

Alan Warner was very active in reissues in the 1980s. He packaged the Slim Whitman collection for TV sales. Slim had cut nearly three dozen Imperial albums in the 1950s and 1960s. Alan also put together an album of Bobby Vee's Liberty hit recordings, which was sold on British television. That album made the top five on the British LP chart in 1981.

"Around 1986 I did a retrospective series of albums for EMI which zeroed in on the individual labels. There was a Liberty album (called *More Hits, More Often*), a UA album, a Minit album, a Sue Records album, an Aladdin album, and an Imperial album." This is a delightful set of retrospective studies of the respective Liberty-family labels.

A second set of five LPs came out a few months later. A Liberty/UA album in that is also a delight. The cover is framed in a purple marble design that is continued on the back, with a large front-cover photo of Jan & Dean superimposed over a photo of Bobby Vee, each distorted in perspective. Bearing the Liberty and United Artists logos, this album is completely annotated. The cuts are a spectrum of Liberty/UA semirarities:

Side 1 — All United Artists

"She Cried" — Jay and the Americans, 1962, featuring their original lead singer, Jay Traynor

"Not Just Tomorrow, But Always" — Bertell Dache, 1961, written by Carole King, who also sang background, as an answer record to "Will You Love Me Tomorrow," which she also wrote

"Before I Loved You" — Johnny Maestro, 1962, former lead singer of the Crests ("16 Candles," 1958), later lead singer of the Brooklyn Bridge ("The Worst That Could Happen," 1968)

"I Don't Know Why (I Just Do)" — The Belmonts ("Tell Me Why," 1961; formerly with Dion, "Teenager in Love," 1959)

"Don't Just Stand There" — Patty Duke, actress, 1965

"Close to Cathy" — Mike Clifford, 1962

"Sunday and Me" — Jay and the Americans, 1965, featuring their second lead singer Jay (David) Black

Side 2 — All Liberty

"This Diamond Ring" — Gary Lewis and the Playboys, 1965
"Run to Him" — Bobby Vee, 1961
"Mr. Blue" — The Fleetwoods, 1959 (Dolton Records)
"Tonight You Belong to Me" — Patience and Prudence, 1956
"Save Your Heart for Me" — Gary Lewis and the Playboys, 1965
"Dreamin'" — Johnny Burnette, 1960
"Linda" — Jan & Dean, 1963

The credit on the album was "Album conceived, compiled, and documented by Alan Warner."

The liner notes for this LP, while quite comprehensive and generally factual, do contain one error. That error is in reference to the song by Bertell Dache. However, the error is eminently understandable, for every reference book on rock 'n' roll that mentions Dache's recording includes the same error. The liner notes state that Dache was really Tony Orlando, who has indeed made many recordings, both as Tony Orlando ("Bless You," 1961) and as Dawn ("Knock Three Times," 1971).

Alan Warner himself corrects the error he and all the reference books have made. "[They're] all wrong. Jerry Goffin said no, Bertell Dache was not Tony Orlando. There really is a guy named Bertell Dache. Tony was there, but all the other books, including me, were wrong."

Alan Warner further explains that "Ron Furmanek has done some excellent packages of old Liberty material for EMI on CD. The person who does his liner notes says that Liberty was originally run by Si Waronker and Al Bennett, which it wasn't. Al Bennett did not come till later — not much later. But Al was not there at the beginning. It was Si and Jack Ames who were the cofounders. Al was a shining light there for many years later, but he was not there at the beginning."

In the mid-1980s, Alan Warner's EMI American Treasury Legendary Masters series brought new batches of old material, divided up by labels (such as Liberty and Imperial), topics (such as *Death, Glory, and Retribution*), styles (such as surf and girl groups), and artists (such as Jan & Dean). In addition, by 1990, the Legendary Masters title was used again in a series of CD releases of remixed, annotated anthologies compiled by Ron Furmanek and Steve Kolanjian. Each CD contained some two dozen cuts, including bonus (unreleased, odd, or radio commercial) tracks. Artists covered included Gary Lewis and the Playboys, Shirley and Lee, Ricky Nelson, Jay and the Americans, Eddie Cochran, Jan & Dean, and fittingly, Bobby Vee.

Alan Warner was not with Liberty in what he calls its "heyday," as the likes of Bobby Vee were, but he did know Al Bennett in the later years and the writers and artists at Liberty. As he says, "The Liberty label is being used again in the 1980s and 1990s, but it is not really the same company."

CHAPTER 39

Overview

Liberty Records' contribution to the evolution of rock 'n' roll cannot be overemphasized. Liberty hit (no pun) every significant trend of the rock 'n' roll era:

Female singers: Julie London, Margie Rayburn, Jackie DeShannon, Vikki Carr, Nancy Ames, Tracey Dey, Timi Yuro, Cher
Teen idols: Bobby Vee, Ricky Nelson, Troy Shondell, Gene McDaniels
Rockers: Eddie Cochran, Del Shannon, Johnny Rivers
Novelty: David Seville, Chipmunks
Country: Walter Brennan, Slim Whitman, Willie Nelson
Rockabilly: Johnny Burnette, Buddy Knox, Dorsey Burnette
Girl groups: Patience and Prudence, Fleetwoods
Instrumentals: Joiner, Arkansas, Junior High School Band, Sandy Nelson, Ventures, T-Bones
Dance craze: Marketts
Oldies: Liberty Golden Hits LP Series
R&B group sounds: Billy Ward and His Dominoes, the Rivingtons, Ike and Tina Turner
Pop: Johnny Mann, Vic Dana, Felix Slatkin, Martin Denny
Rock 'n' roll: Dick and Deedee, the Crickets, Gary Lewis and the Playboys
Bands: Gants, Nitty Gritty Dirt Band
Surf and drag: Jan & Dean, Fantastic Baggies
British invasion: Hollies, Billy J. Kramer with the Dakotas, Swinging Blue Jeans, Searchers, Matt Monro, Tommy Steele, Georgie Fame
Psychedelic rock: Canned Heat
Hippy/Folk: the Love Generation, the Sunshine Company

All in all, quite an impressive roster. And it does not even include Imperial artists before the Liberty takeover; one-shot artists, lesser lights, and also-rans, like Danny and Gwen, Gary Miles, and the Rollers; or the artists like Ernie K-Doe, Bob Lind, or others who had hits on Minit Records, World Pacific Records, Blue Note Records, and the other Liberty subsidiaries.

Speaking of lesser lights—a lot of people were on Liberty Records but no one knew it. Some were future stars still awaiting their big break. Some were former stars hoping to regain lost popularity. A few were celebrities—or relatives of celebrities—in other fields, such as acting, who perhaps had hopes of making a hit on a Liberty 45. And some were successful on Liberty, but with other kinds of music besides pop and rock, such as country and western or jazz. Some of them were, by year:

1955
Lionel Newman
Hi-Fis
Ken Curtis
Rod McKuen

1956
Frank Gorshin
Henry Mancini

1957
Robert Wagner
Lincoln Chase

1958
Al Casey
The Slades
Bobby Troup
Lettermen
Playthings
Willie Nelson

1959
Mike Clifford
Danny Davis
Gogie Grant

1960
Warren Smith
Spike Jones

1962
Billy Strange
Ralph Emery
John Wayne
Molly Bee
Bob Wills
Roosevelt Grier
Van McCoy
Hank Cochran
Eddie Heywood
Gary Paxton
Ed Townsend

1963
Tex Williams
Nancy Ames
Les Brown, Jr.
Tracey Dey

1964
Marlene Dietrich
Tommy Quickly
Billy Daniels

1965
Tommy Sands
Bobby Fuller 4
Cascades
J. J. Cale

1966
Del Shannon
The Pair
Mickey Rooney, Jr.
Burt Bacharach

1967
Kiki Dee
Mel Torme

1968
Jerry Wallace
Gregg Allman

1969
Mermaids
Dorsey Burnette
Dick Clark
Dee Clark
Eternity's Children

1970
Ike Turner
Bobby Womack

In that list, we see potential that could have changed the sound of music in America, just as much as the scores of artists who not only did not have big hits on Liberty but never gained fame elsewhere, either.

Si Waronker took the best talent in artists, session people, arrangers, writers, and producers, let their creativity flow, injected just the needed pop influence to solidify the rock 'n' roll genre sound, and presto! Liberty Records kept America rocking and rolling to the Liberty sound for the first fifteen years of rock 'n' roll!

Thanks, Si! Your $2,000 investment was sure worth it!

CHAPTER 40

Epilogue: Where Did They Go?

Julie London (b. 9-26-26) and Bobby Troup—Bobby is seventy-two and retired. "Anyway," as he says, "my music has gone out. I don't write anymore because my kind of music isn't being recorded. And Julie is certainly retired, too. The last professional recording she did was 'My Funny Valentine' for the Burt Reynolds picture *Sharkey's Machine,* one of Burt Reynolds's favorite songs. Snuff produced that." The happy couple is living in Encino, California.

Alfi and Harry/Ross Bagdasarian/David Seville/Chipmunks (b. 1-27-19, d. 1-16-72)—Ross, who turned the Chipmunks into TV stars and appeared in films including *Rear Window,* died in 1972. His son has kept recording as the Chipmunks doing disco, punk, and so on.

Eddie Cochran (b. 10-3-38, d. 4-17-60)—Eddie became a rock legend. Sharon Sheeley, once his fiancée, has kept his name alive and is working toward the production of a film about his life, or more correctly her life with him. His sister Gloria Cochran Julson, now elderly, keeps his memory alive, while his nephew Bobby Cochran keeps his music alive. June 21-23, Bobby attended the Eddie Cochran Weekend in Eddie's hometown of Albert Lee, Minnesota. At that celebration, Bobby hooked up with Eddie's former band, and he reports that "there seems to [be] some interest in us doing the soundtrack for a movie about Eddie."

Billy Ward and His Dominoes—After a few more releases on Liberty, and contracts with ABC-Paramount in 1960, Ro-Zan Records in 1962, and King Records, the group retired.

Patience and Prudence—Presumably grew up and led normal lives. Everyone seems to have lost track of them.

Ernie Freeman (b. 8-6-22, d. 5-16-81)—After his work with Snuff Garrett at Liberty, Ernie worked widely as a composer, arranger, conductor, even pianist. His colleagues included the likes of Frank Sinatra and Dean Martin, as well as Connie Francis. Died of a heart attack in Los Angeles.

Margie Rayburn—Retired in Los Angeles.

Martin Denny (b. 4-10-21)—Lives in Hawaii, plays piano for a living.

Little Bill and the Blue Notes—After their one hit on Dolton ("I Love an Angel"), the group had a contract briefly with Camelot Records. Bill Engelhart continues to live in the Seattle area. He was inducted into the Northwest Hall of Fame. In 1988 the group re-formed to play a revival show in Seattle with the Fleetwoods and the Ventures.

Chapter 40 · Epilogue: Where Did They Go?   529

This is a 1981 reissue of Eddie Cochran's recordings.

Frantics—After leaving Dolton, they recorded for Bolo Records in 1962 and for Seafair Records in 1964.

Bobby Vee (b. 4-30-43)—Married with three sons and a daughter, tours United States and overseas every year to SRO crowds, alone or with Freddy Cannon, Gary Lewis, Lou Christie, and others. Owns artist promotional firm. Recut his hits for K-Tel.* Records new material occasionally. Sons have a band called the Vees.

---

* *K-TEL is a record company specializing in TV offers, records and tapes sold by mail order through TV commercials, as well as in stores. Many of its LPs are compilations of original hits by various original artists. When K-TEL wishes to release the original hit recordings of songs, it must obtain permission and pay royalties to the record labels on which the songs were originally released. In order to avoid this hassle and expense, K-TEL has contacted many artists and paid them to re-record their original hits for K-TEL release. Some of these re-recordings are very faithful to the originals, being almost indistinguishable from them. Others of these re-recordings vary greatly from the originals, either because of inability of K-TEL to duplicate the original arrangements; because the singers have lost their voices; because the artists have updated their styles; or because of turnover in a group's personnel since the song was a hit.*

Bobby Vee on tour in the 1980s.

They are very eclectic and do many kinds of music, including "That's All Right, Mama" and "Who Do You Love." Father and sons also write songs together.

The last time Bobby Vee signed with Liberty was in 1978, after it had become United Artists. "I was down in Nashville recording, and the head of the company was changed. He brought in his crew and they started dropping artists. The ink was still drying on the contact; Alan Warner had signed me to the label; and I am in this studio recording as they cut their roster down from four hundred acts to something like a hundred fifty. The writing was on the wall. I was excited about the song, 'So Much Love,' but I knew nothing was going to happen because they were in a totally different thing."

Bobby Vee with my wife, Buzzie, after a show in Kansas City, Missouri, August 1990.

Johnny Burnette (b. 3-25-34, d. 8-1-64)—Johnny died in a boating accident.

Dorsey Burnette (b. 12-28-32, d. 8-19-79)—Dorsey went on to become a country-and-western singer at Capitol Records and a producer at Roulette and Reprise Records.

Buddy Knox (b. 7-20-33)—Buddy was still making music as late as 1964, when he released a British invasion–influenced record "Jo-Ann" (not the same song as the Playmates' 1958 hit) on his own label, Ruff Records. Legend has it that a Midwestern band, the Blue Things, played on "Jo-Ann." While they did record some tracks for Buddy around that time, they were not on "Jo-Ann."

Buddy has recut his hits for K-TEL. He used to own two nightclubs, but he sold them in 1990. He still performs, records, produces, and publishes music. His personal record collection runs into the tens of thousands. Buddy Knox has resided in Canada for many years.

Willie Nelson (b. 4-30-33)—All the success he never had at Liberty, Willie Nelson has had everyplace ever since. Besides many hits on RCA and Columbia, his songwriting is legendary and he has appeared in movies and TV shows aplenty.

Crickets—Still touring thirty years later. In April 1989 the Crickets (Jerry Allison, Joe B. Mauldin, and Gordon Paine) recorded a medley of Buddy Holly songs with Bobby Vee in Minnesota. Says Jerry Allison, "We're still running up and down the road singing 'That'll Be the Day.' The group nowadays is Gordon Paine, Joe B. Mauldin, and myself. Our last record was produced by Paul McCartney, called 'T-Shirt' on CBS Records. We play Europe quite a bit, we just did a month in England, a week in Ireland, and two weeks in Sweden."

How long can the Crickets keep going? "It looks like people can keep on playing rock 'n' roll forever."

Fats Domino (b. 2-26-28)—Fats left Imperial just before Liberty took over, but the loss was minimal. After fifty-nine hits in seven years on Imperial, on ABC-Paramount, Fats had six hits charting successively at #59, #35, #63, #86, #99, and #99. One 45 on Reprise in 1968 kissed the charts at #100. Those failures and even-less-successful contracts at Reprise and elsewhere have done nothing to dim the luster of Fats Domino's legend, and his place in the history of rock 'n' roll is secure as he continues to tour and sell countless reissues of his original Imperial hits.

Gene McDaniels (b. 3-12-35)—Still performs.

Sharon Sheeley—Became a self-proclaimed recluse, apparently because of how often writers distorted her words and her story. Her family was, and continues to be, important to her. "My mom always supported me; she never criticized rock 'n' roll. She told me, 'Good for you. If I wasn't so old, I'd go after Elvis myself!' My half-brother was Robert Woods, whose career *Dead Poets Society* was based on. My brother-in-law is Larry Collins, who wrote 'Delta Dawn' (Tanya Tucker, Columbia, #72, 1972; Helen Reddy, Capitol, 1973, #1) and 'You're the Reason God Made Oklahoma.' Snuff got the publishing on 'Oklahoma.' Then he turned around and put his name on the record like he used to do."

In 1991 a movie was being made of the life of Sharon Sheeley, called *Summertime Blues*, after the 1958 Liberty hit by Eddie Cochran. The screenplay was by Jack Epps, the writer of *Top Gun, Turner and Hooch, Dick Tracy, Secret of My Success*, and was told from the female point of view. With Sharon's involvement from the start, the movie will be much more accurate than *The Buddy Holly Story* or *La Bamba*, the Ritchie Valens biopic, both of which took enormous liberties with the truth of those late rock 'n' roll stars' lives. In fact, in the interests of accuracy, Sharon resumed speaking to Jerry Capehart after fifteen years, but only because she wanted this film to be "absolutely right," and Capehart was involved in Eddie's career. "It won't be like *La Bamba*, which was total fantasy, a beautiful film, but total fantasy," Sharon correctly asserts. "Ritchie's manager cheated Ritchie so badly that his mother has had to take in laundry to live for the last thirty years."

Timi Yuro (b. 8-4-40)—Timi is retired. In 1980 she lost her voice and underwent several throat operations. She recut her hits for K-Tel. Reports are that she is now suffering from severe throat cancer.

Troy Shondell (b. 5-14-44)—Troy now lives in Nashville.

Bobby Sheen—Bob left Liberty with producer Phil Spector, who renamed him Bob B. Soxx. At Philles, he had three hits as Bob B. Soxx and the Blue Jeans

Chapter 40 · Epilogue: Where Did They Go?

Dean Torrence and the author backstage, August 2, 1991, after a show in front of twenty thousand screaming fans in Kansas City, Missouri.

(Darlene Love and the Blossoms were the Blue Jeans), including the top-ten "Zip-a-Dee Doo-Dah," in 1963.

Jan (b. 4-3-41) & Dean (b. 3-10-40)—Jan & Dean are still touring together and, separately. They have made many new recordings, had a TV-movie biography in late 1970s, and recut their hits for K-Tel. One K-Tel cut became a top-five hit in Holland in 1980. They made a home-video tape of surf and drag hits in 1984. Dean formed a Grammy-winning design company. They were the first U.S. rock group to tour Red China, in 1988.

Dean and his bride Susan recently had their first child, Katie. Jan married Canadian Gertie Filip on the eve of his 50th birthday, 1991. The wedding took place on stage at the Star Dust Hotel in Las Vegas in the middle of a concert.

Jan Berry backstage in Kansas City.

Rivingtons—The group recut their hits for K-Tel. The Rivingtons still tour, especially fairs and conventions with white audiences. Their songs still show up in places like the movies *E.T.* and *Back to the Beach,* which featured the song "Surfer Bird."

Marketts—After the group's two Liberty hits, they charted three times for Warner Bros. Records. They subsequently recorded for many labels, including Doré, Mercury, Liberty's World Pacific, and Uni, without chart success. In 1976, as the New Marketts, they tried again on Farr, Seminole, and Calliope. Many members were veteran session musicians and continued in that work all along.

Walter Brennan (b. 1894; d. 9-21-74)—Continued to act in Hollywood movies.

Jackie DeShannon (b. 8-21-44)—Jackie is still singin' and writin'. She wrote "Bette Davis Eyes" for Kim Carnes in 1981. She moved on to Atlantic, Amherst, and Capitol, with a few minor hits on the first two.

Today Ms. DeShannon is CEO of a film and music production corporation called Raider Music and Film. The *Hollywood Reporter* recently carried a four-color promo piece for a new picture called *Becoming Colette,* a Danny Houston film. Jackie did the title track for that production. Jackie lives in Hollywood, is married and has a thirteen-year-old son named Noah.

Tracey Dey—Retired.

Bonnie Guitar (b. 3-25-33)—Bonnie Guitar was a part-owner of Dolton—Bob Reisdorff was, as he said, always selling his compnay!—but, says Bob, "She knew almost nothing about the business of things. She was in the creative end of things for about a year with Dolton. She is in the Northwest Hall of Fame," is married, and still lives in Washington State.

Searchers—The group still actively tours, with some new members.

Matt Monro (d. 2-7-85)—Matt was a major British star. He died of liver cancer at age fifty-four.

Gary Lewis (b. 7-31-46)—Jerry's famous son tried hard rock, then began to tour with a new set of Playboys. Recut his hits for K-Tel.

What is Gary Lewis doing today? Is he a restaurateur or selling real estate? No, he is still doing Gary Lewis! "We are doing shows everywhere. It'd be easier to say where we have not been. I've been in music ever since I started except for the two years in the Army. The only time we have had an off time was the 1970s. The music of the 1960s was just not accepted in the 1970s. Even though we weren't accepted in the 1970s, we still played the smaller clubs. There were still a lot of diehards who loved the 1960s. We just could not get the big venues or the big money. But we still continued to play. From the Bahamas to Alaska to Hawaii. And not just the big cities, but also the little small cities, even cow towns. I like playing the smaller places, because the people are so much more appreciative that you decided to come there to their smaller town. It's great.

"Then the boom, the 1980s happened, the resurgence of the 1960s for whatever reason, and in the 1980s we started doing a hundred to a hundred twenty-five dates a year. It's been that way ever since.

"I was struggling with a decision at one point. 'Gee, should I update everything?' I just did not know what to do. Come to find out that the people are the most happy when you do it the way they remember it. Faithfully. That is one of the biggest things for me onstage. I tell the guys that I want to duplicate this tune just like it is on the record. And keep it just like that. And that is what we've been doing all this time. And I am very happy with the way it sounds.

"I love the way the 1960s were, I really enjoyed the sound of the music, and that is how I want to play it. We do our hits, and I do Freddie Cannon's 'Palisades Park,' Del Shannon's 'Runaway,' Otis Redding's 'Can't Turn You Loose,' and we do a six-tune Beatle medley of some of our favorite tunes. I think that's about it, because most of the stuff is mine. Because we had eight big hits and fifteen hit records all together. We do the major eight. Then we do things off the *Golden Greats* album, 'Without a Word of Warning,' 'Tina (I Held You in My Arms),' 'Little Miss Go Go,' so it is pretty much ours; I'd say two-thirds of the set is my stuff. And then the people that influenced me that I liked before I got into it. Freddie Cannon, Del Shannon, Beatles. I was a fan. I would do a Bobby Vee tune except that there is just too much going on. Horns, strings—I would not be able to recreate it the right way. We do have a keyboard with all the programming you could possibly need. My tunes were a little simpler than Bobby's, I think, because there was not as much stuff happening. That is enough to make everything sound authentic of ours."

So Gary likes touring in the 1990s? "It's great, having a second chance to do it right. We were kids. Make the money, spend the money!" He certainly does not consider himself a has-been simply because his hits are thirty years old. A Sinatra or a Dean Martin is not considered a has-been, simply because he is no longer at the top of the pop charts. "That's exactly right. I don't believe that 1960s music is just a phase or a fad or anything. It is good music, good rock 'n' roll music that is gonna be around forever! I even hear my tunes on Muzak at the supermarket! Which is a wonderful feeling—'Gee, some of my tunes are turning into standards! OK! I love it!'"

If Gary Lewis had not gotten his break with Liberty, what would he be doing today? "I'd probably be acting in legitimate theater. That is what I was going to school for, drama. And maybe I would have been happy, I don't know. But I am certainly happy about all this."

O'Jays—The O'Jays were one of the most successful artists to have ever been on Imperial. Unfortunately for Liberty, all their success came after they left Imperial in 1966. The average top chart position for their four Imperial hits was #83. But beginning on Bell Records, and then on Neptune, Philadelphia Int'l. Records, and T.S.O.P., they had more than two dozen hits, including five in the top ten and a #1 hit in 1972, "Love Train." Originally a quintet, with lineup changes (Bill Isles quit; Walt Williams died; and Bobby Massey retired and became the group's musical consultant), they have continued to perform as a trio. When the name *Liberty* was revived in 1980, the O'Jays were signed, but no releases ever charted.

Bob Lind (b. 11-25-44)—After his promising start at Liberty, his recording career fizzled. Leaving Liberty's World Pacific, Verve/Folkways and Capitol gave him a chance, but it never happened again, and Lind retired from recording.

Irma Thomas (b. 2-18-41)—The Soul Queen of New Orleans recorded for a variety of labels after Imperial. But although she never scored big hits, her live career flourishes. She is very popular in Louisiana and performs at clubs as well as in front of crowds of loyal fans at the annual Jazzfest.

T-Bones—This was never a real group, just a studio concoction of producer Joe Saraceno. However, three of the session players, Dan Hamilton, Joe Frank Carollo and Tommy Reynolds, formed the band Hamilton, Joe Frank & Reynolds. Recording for Lou Adler's Dunhill Records and later Playboy Records, they had several hits including the #1 "Fallin' in Love" in 1975.

Jimmy McCracklin (b. 8-13-21)—This former boxer recorded for over a dozen labels in his long career. After his last chart song, Imperial's "My Answer" in 1966, peaked at #92, he had more releases on Imperial, as well as Minit and Liberty itself. Ultimately, he retired from recording.

P. J. Proby (b. 11-6-38)—James Marcus Smith of Houston retired to England, the country of his greatest popularity.

Del Shannon (b. 12-30-39, d. 2-8-90)—Del had a comeback hit in 1982, "Sea of Love," produced by Tom Petty. Divorced, he remarried, lived in LA, and performed on tour constantly. He, too, recut his hits for K-Tel. He recorded a spirited revival of his hit "Runaway," with altered lyrics, for the theme for the mid–1980s TV series "Crime Story." Del Shannon committed suicide on February 8, 1990.

Nitty Gritty Dirt Band—Broke up.

Canned Heat—Changed members and continued recording. Vocalist Bob ("the Bear") Hite died of a drug-related heart attack (4-6-81).

Ventures—Original founder Bob Bogle (b. 1-16-37) and other members reunited in 1984 after fourteen years of retirement, went on tour, and began recording again. They are still touring and spending up to three months a year playing Japan, their country of greatest popularity.

Fleetwoods—Gretchen Christopher (b. 2-19-40), Barbara Ellis (b. 2-20-40), and Gary Troxel (b. 11-28-39)—Gary returned to Washington State, while the women settled in California.

About seven years after the beginning of Dolton, Bob Reisdorff did try to resurrect the Fleetwoods. "But it was always a job to get all of their needs together in one place and fulfill them. They were scattered at that time."

Yet the Fleetwoods live on in the annals of rock history, as well as in the form of a viable performing act. They appeared in a movie in 1978—sort of. Anyway, their music did. Ed Silvers in a phone conversation asked Gretchen, "'Were you on the set of a movie recently?' I think he said it was *American Hot Wax*, it might have had a different working title. But anyway he said that several people said that they swore they saw me on the set. And they said that the other two Fleetwoods were being portrayed by an actor and an actress, but they thought that I was playing myself!

"When I saw the opening shot, I thought it really did look like me, from the side. But in the close-up it didn't. And the fact is that we didn't have ponytails. That is a typical 1950s thing, but we had very short haircuts, which we grew out into French twists.

"I got a call from a New York producer in nineteen seventy-one asking us to headline four shows in New York. The three of us did that. And we did five engagements over the next two years, the Los Angeles Forum and the Oakland Coliseum, Miami Beach Convention Center, and twice at the New York Academy of Music, all between June of 1971 and June of 1973. That was the last time the three original Fleetwoods sang together.

"About nineteen sixty-four we recorded 'Man in a Raincoat,' which was never released. Twenty years later, in nineteen eighty-two, my kids found my acetate of it and thought it could be a hit if it were released today. Of course, they did not realize that you have to promote it. But I called Liberty Records anyway and asked if they had any plans to release it, and if they did not, if they could release it back to me.

"They did not have any plans, but the head of A&R for the Greenline series, Kathy Keep, told me, 'You can bet that if there is something releasable, Capitol will want to release it themselves rather than have anybody else release it.' After that, she went into the archives and found that song; in fact, she found twenty-seven unreleased masters." She read Gretchen the titles of the songs, saying that they wanted to release a whole new Fleetwoods album. The only four songs Gretchen recognized by title were "Climb Every Mountain," "Imagination," "Will You Love Me Tomorrow" (Shirelles, 1961), and "Man in a Raincoat," on which she sang lead.

Ultimately the label narrowed the selection down to sixteen or seventeen songs, from which Gretchen picked what she felt was "the best mix possible of varied leads and contrasting and complimentary styles and moods of songs. I'd poll everybody from the newsboy, who was thirteen or fourteen years old, to my dad, who was eighty-two years old." The album, *Buried Treasure*, was released on her dad's eighty-third birthday, March 11, 1983.

"It was in nineteen eighty-two that I put the group together again and facilitated the release of that 13th album. Though Barb had retired in the '70s in California, when I put the group back together in early 1982, I asked her first because I had a call for the Fleetwoods to headline with Fabian and Freddie Cannon

Gretchen Christopher received two encores and a standing ovation for her concert "The Best of the Fleetwoods," celebrating the release of the CD by the same name. *(Courtesy Gretchen Christopher.)*

and Gary Puckett at the Southern Cal Expo at Del Mar." Barbara declined to rejoin the Fleetwoods but agreed to Gretchen's being paid to manage, saying, "You're the one who'll be doing all the work." So a new singer was hired. "With Barb's blessing, I trained a replacement for her. I became the official manager of the group by contract among the three of us. I never worked so hard in my life. It *was* my life: writing, coreographing, expanding our performance repertoire to various lengths, including a well-paced, one-hour, twenty-song show, complete with dialogue and costume changes. I designed a logo, letterhead, business cards, wrote a bio and releases, put together a promo pack, and arranged for bookings, transportation, everything necessary to present a class act worthy of the best venues. We performed from Madison Square Garden to the Tropicana in Las Vegas.

"I was completing whirlwind negotiations with Rhino Records, who wanted us to fly in and record a Fleetwoods Christmas album immediately, in conjunction with a proposed appearance in Hollywood. Then Gary officially resigned from the Fleetwoods, giving his notice in writing, November nineteen eighty-three. He left me with 'the sole authority to bind the original and replacement Fleetwoods by contract for an performance commitment as manager deems appropriate to carry out the business of the Fleetwoods.'

"Now, I've put the Fleetwoods back together with two new people, and they sound wonderful. I get goose pimples when we sing the arrangement I'd been hearing in my head for my new song, '(Christmas Is Anytime) Christmas Is You.' We just did a television show and are represented for bookings by the Dick Clark Agency, in Burbank.

"One of the things I cherish most, and for which I'm humbly grateful, is the feeling that, through my music, I've become a citizen of the world. No matter what country people are from, they seem to recognize 'Come Softly to Me.' As recently as nineteen eighty-eight, I promoted the group in England and did a solo concert over there. After singing in Mexico and Finland, I did a peace tour of Leningrad and Moscow, in nineteen eighty-five, when the Soviet Union was still very closed, and I personally distributed *The Fleetwoods Greatest Hits,* as gifts of peace, behind the Iron Curtain. One of my new songs, 'What Time Is It?' which I sang there, seemed to crystalize the spirit of the journey. It's a soft but a very powerful song, judging from the response it's had [total silence followed by a standing ovation]. I believe it could be as far reaching as 'Come Softly to Me' — and with an even more meaningful message."

In 1990 a new CD of the Fleetwoods' best material was released on Rhino. When the CD was released, Gretchen Christopher did a concert, "Gretchen Christopher/The Best of the Fleetwoods," which received two encores and a standing ovation. She performed alone, without Barbara or Gary, although there was one other voice in counterpoint and another voice occasionally. "But the third voice was negligible." A lot of the show she did solo. "I sang lead on all of the hits. Plus I introduced one of my new songs, which I promised I would do. It is an up-tempo number with an instrumental break that I danced to, and the audience loved it. They burst into applause, which amazed me, when I was through with the dance, and then there was terrific applause after that number. It was one of the biggest responses of the evening." It is nice that fans appreciate her new material as well as her oldies.

Gretchen has also continued writing. Linda Ronstadt has asked, even begged, her for some of her new material to consider for Aaron Neville. "That was an honor and a thrill, but also, I am saving that material for myself! I still feel I have unfinished business as a solo artist, which is how I began. But who knows, maybe I will let my songs go to other artists. As people keep saying, 'The important thing is that the music be heard and the thoughts be shared.'"

Vic Dana (b. 8-26-42) — Vic is retired.

Swinging Blue Jeans — The group recut their hits for K-Tel.

Hollies—The British rock band moved to Epic Records where they had one hit, broke up, reformed, at one time included a former member of the Swinging Blue Jeans, had an LP and minor 1982 hit, "Stop in the Name of Love" (Supremes, 1965); the Hollies do oldie shows.

Billy J. Kramer (b. 8-19-43) with the Dakotas—The group broke up. Billy still performs. He is married and lives in the New York area.

Johnny Rivers (b. 11-7-42)—Johnny still records and tours, doing authentic versions of all his hits. He is personally disappointed when he goes to see an act from the 1950s or 1960s and they do not do all their own hits, but instead do new material or someone else's hits. Therefore he does a lot of his own hits in his live shows.

Fifth Dimension—After the Fifth Dimension left Soul City, Bell Records was a good home to them. There they scored some of their biggest hits: "One Less Bell to Answer," #2, 1970, and "(Last Night) I Didn't Get to Sleep at All," #8, 1972—a total of fifteen hits in all. The group almost broke up in 1976, and founding members Marilyn McCoo and Billy Davis, Jr., who married in 1969, continued as a duo in 1976. They were replaced in the group by Danny Beard and Marjorie Barnes.

On ABC Records, after a slow start at #91, McCoo and Davis hit #1 with "You Don't Have to Be a Star (in My Show)." Two more hits and the magic was gone. The Fifth Dimension re-formed in the 1980s and tours.

Vikki Carr (b. 7-19-41)—Ms. Carr moved on to Columbia Records in 1971.

Georgie Fame (b. 6-26-43)—Brit Clive Powell formed the new Blue Flames and recorded and toured. He ended up recording nonrock music and working as a DJ in America.

Mel Carter (b. 4-22-43)—Mel lives and recorded on the West Coast. He has appeared as an actor in several TV dramatic series.

Classics IV—Dennis Yost formed a new Classics IV and recorded in the 1970s. He lives in Dade City, Florida, with his wife, and still tours.

Dick and Deedee—Dick St. John and Mary "Deedee" Sperling broke up in the late 1960s. But they can still be seen from time to time—sort of. Today, Deedee seems very outgoing, self-assured, and self-confident. In the old days she appeared less assertive, almost demure. Is she different now than she was back then?

"If I ever got too close to the microphone, I'd feel this big hand tugging on my dress from behind, I'd jerk away from the microphone! Looking back with hindsight, Dick really felt that—well—I feel he was really using 'Dick and Deedee' as a catalyst for a solo career. This is no secret; it is OK. He felt that he really was the talent and sort of the one that made it all work, and it could really have been anybody [with him], that was his attitude. Who we are now is different from who we were then. In his shadow at the time, I think I probably was very quiet. I observed a lot and wrote a lot. I was always writing and keeping notes about everything.

"We haven't spoken in awhile. He wanted to do shows again, and we were going to do them together. Then, suddenly I heard on the radio that Dick and Deedee were performing in this place in Santa Ana. I was stunned! I called up Dick and I said, 'Listen, there is a bogus group for the first time! We should go check them out and see who they are!' He said, 'Oh, couldn't be. They must have the wrong name or something.' But he acted real funny about it. So as fate would have it, a friend of mine thought that I was going to be performing and went to that show. It turned out that it was Dick and Sandy, his wife. My friend got a flyer from it.

"Dick and Sandy did a Greek Theater show and Dick told me, 'I am going to do this show whether you like it or not. I'll pay you a quarter of the money.' He did send me a quarter of that first show money, but from then on nothing. They have just been performing whenever they can. It's OK; I have resolved it for myself to keep my own peace, which is what is important to me. I don't want to get embroiled in any hostilities; I don't need that in my life at this point. It's OK; it is low-scale; it does not happen too often.

"I do want to do a book myself someday. I have tons and tons of stories. My whole goal would be to make people laugh, because there is not enough of that in the world! The craziest things happened to Deedee!"

On the syndicated radio oldies service called "Kool Gold," on August 4, 1991, a DJ named C. J. Brown provided an update on Dick and Deedee when introducing "The Mountain's High": "Back when they recorded this song, they were just good friends. I had a chance to talk to them a couple of months back—they are now married!"

Apparently Dick St. John now blurs the distinction between the original Deedee (Mary), and the new Deedee (Sandy).

Cher (b. 5-20-46)—Cherilyn broke up with Sonny (b. 2-16-35), had two hit TV series (one with and one without Sonny), starred in the movies, *Silkwood* and *Mask*, about a handicapped boy, and received an Oscar for *Moonstruck*. She still acts and continues to do music videos well into the 1990s.

Why has Cher been so successful in her post–Imperial years? Engineer Bones Howe, who himself has done quite well since the 1960s, looks back at the recording sessions of those days and considers carefully the personalities involved. "I always say, there were a few people who were paying attention while all this was going on. Cher was paying attention, because she was smart and is still around. Michelle Phillips was paying attention. While John and Denny and Mama Cass [were] having a good time, Michelle was paying attention. She is very successful. Michie was a little mouse at the time, but she and Cher were paying attention."

Bones Howe—After his career as an engineer and then a very successful record producer with the Fifth Dimension, Bones moved into the picture business, ultimately becoming executive vice president of music at Columbia Pictures—the head of the music department.

But making music is in Bones's blood. At age fifty-eight, he is feeling the urge to move on again. "I am leaving next year and going back to producing tunes. Acoustic music is coming back, and people call me to come produce. Movie music is a hard job. I know how a movie is made now, but there is no enjoyment in it. 'Never My Love' by the Association is my favorite record."

Ricky Nelson (b. 5-8-40, d. 12-31-85)—Ricky moved on to Decca Records for more hits. He later disdained his old hits, was booed for not singing them at a show, and as a result he wrote a song about the experience, the hit "Garden Party" in 1972. Later still he resumed touring, again doing his faithful versions of his Imperial hits. He did a show for TV syndication and home video with Fats Domino in 1985, including a duet of "I'm Walkin'," Fats's 1957 hit that Ricky successfully covered for

Cher is among the artists featured on this 1985 compilation by Alan Warner.

his own first hit. Ricky died New Year's Eve that year with his band in the crash of his private plane on the way to a show.

Tina Turner (b. 11-26-38) — Annie Mae Bullock broke up with Ike, who allegedly had abused her for years. In 1985 Tina made a major solo comeback with giant hit videos and records.

Snuff Garrett — Continued to produce hit records. Hobby: old cowboy movies. He recorded Roy Rogers doing an endearing novelty tune, "Hoppy, Gene, and Me," and opened his own home videotape sales company. Snuff collects Western art. He sold his music holdings after he had a stroke and reportedly made millions in the deals.

Reflecting on the Liberty days, Snuff said, "It was all fun in those days. We all went in basically the same studios and did our own thing. I lived in studio B at United most of my young life; I didn't even go to bed until I was thirty-four! I just played in there and cut records. After the Beatles the sound changed, so I did 'This Diamond Ring' totally differently. Ernie Freeman went on to work with Jimmy Bowen at Reprise and cut Sinatra and Dean Martin."

Chapter 40 · Epilogue: Where Did They Go? 543

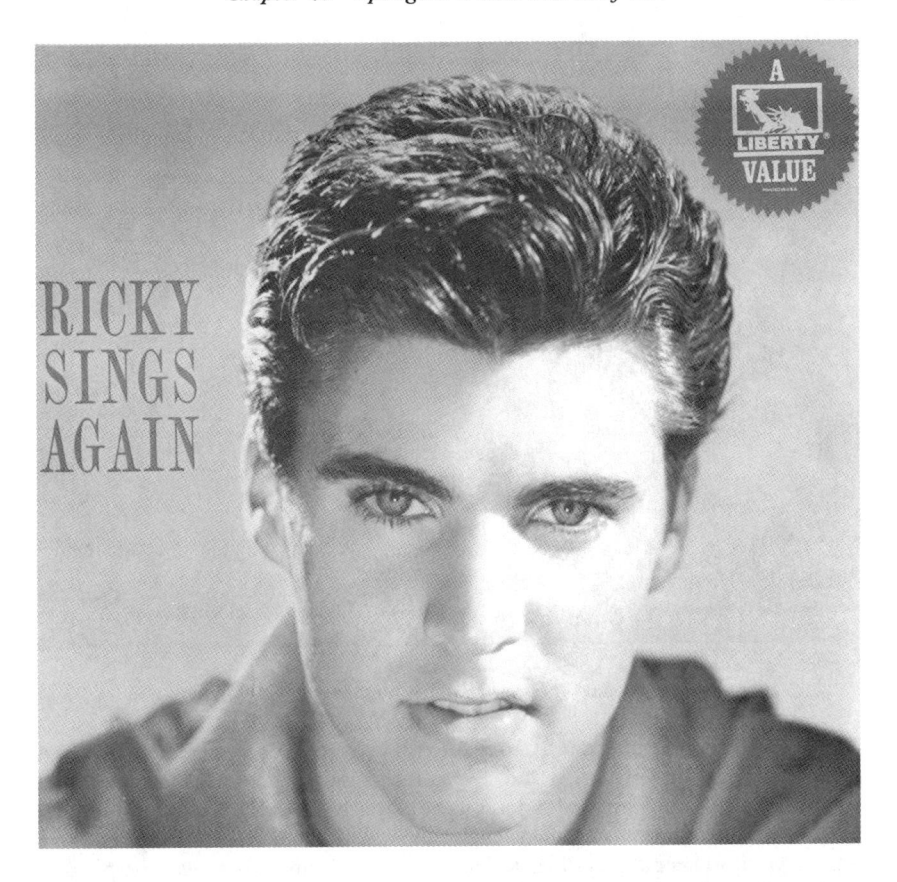

RICKY SINGS AGAIN

The 1980s also saw the resurrection of the Liberty name and the redesign of the Liberty logo, as old material was reissued with original artwork and special Liberty stickers.

Si Waronker always got along with Snuffy very well. He feels that Snuffy would not have left Liberty had Si still been there. "Snuffy went into partnership with Ed Silvers, and when they sold Amigo, a studio, a publishing firm, and a record company, they sold it all to Warner's. Snuffy did some work for Warner's, but wanted to work for himself. He was very independent."

Bob Reisdorff — A half year after he quit Dolton and completed his Liberty work in England, Bob Reisdorff went into the restaurant business with his brother in Soho. Now Bob reports that he is "writing and getting my home in order, taking care of things, things that I had neglected."

Much of the record business has to do with nostalgia. Certainly a book about a record company that has been out of business for decades deals with history — with interest and affection for the past. How does Bob Reisdorff feel about the music business now? "A lot of my records no longer ring any bells with me. I only have one out of ten of my records. I don't even have my gold record awards. I was going to throw them out when I moved. The friend who was helping me pack and move said, 'I'd like to have them.' So I let him take them.

Snuff Garrett today. *(Photo by Lissa Wales; courtesy Snuff Garrett.)*

"I sent the publishing awards to a collector in Seattle, Bruce Heather. He asked me if I wanted them anymore. I said, 'What for? It is not what I am doing anymore. It is not related to my life now. I don't want a bunch of old things that I did in the past on my walls. I wouldn't hang them on the walls if I had them anyway!' So there was no point in keeping all of that. The only thing I cared about was the pictures of the artists I worked with, casual shots in the studio. But I have lost a lot of that stuff including a big Dolton scrapbook. I should have kept more of the records. But it is all right.

"I pull out a record and listen to it about once every six months and listen to one or two cuts or three or an album from one of the groups and from some of them that never made it.

"In New York, on the radio I hear 'Come Softly to Me' a lot, and I hear 'Mr. Blue' quite a bit, 'Walk, Don't Run' occasionally, which I did not produce, but which was on my label, and that is about it. 'Little Altar Boy' by Vic Dana is heard around Christmastime. That was the best record I made with him. It was a beauty, but it was not a big hit."

There is a rock 'n' roll hall of fame in the Northwest that is little known outside that region. It recognizes regional talent that is overlooked by national organizations. Bob Reisdorff's accomplishments are worthy of inclusion in this regional organization, but he feels it won't happen. "The Northwest Area Music Association won't nominate me for their Hall of Fame. It may be because one day, a few years back, someone called me and asked a lot of questions. When he wanted to go into depth on one detail of the record business there, I asked him why he was bothering.

"Then the word got out that if I got the award, that I wouldn't fly back to get it. And that may be true. I'm not sure I would. And it doesn't matter one way or another. It is so regional, I don't know. But I do deserve it, because I was there, I was the first one, that's where I got into the record business and was in sales first and then promotion. Then my label started other people starting other labels.

"Snuffy had a massive stroke when he was in his forties. Bud Dain was with Liberty for a while; he had a big heart attack about nineteen eighty. They were young when they had these things happen to them. That is another reason to get out of the music business. There was more stress in it, and a sense of unreality, jive, glibness. It is in the nature of disc jockeys to be what they are, which is quite egomaniacal, many of them but not all. I am a very pragmatic, plain, I hope sensible sort of person. I don't like that hype, I don't like that at all. I struggled to gain a sense of reality every day of my life. It is a hard world to dwell in. Some of those people are quite smart, sharp minded and smart witted. You can't keep up with their language, and the quick joke, and all of that.

"The music business was all such hype. That world—I am not sorry not to be in it."

Lou Adler—Lou founded his own label, Dunhill Records, and developed the Grass Roots and the Mamas and the Papas. The Grass Roots were formed by the Fantastic Baggies, Liberty singers group Jan & Dean's background group. The Mamas and the Papas added a folk element to the old Liberty sound. For instance, "I Saw Her Again" could easily have been sung by Gene McDaniels. Adler sold Dunhill Records for millions to ABC Records. In 1982 he directed a Canadian film, *Ladies and Gentlemen: The Fabulous Stains,* about a punk-girl-group rock trio striving for success.

Al Bennett—Bob Reisdorff reported that "both of Al Bennett's sons were killed, and his daughter was crippled from birth. She had three marriages by the time Al died. His sons were very lackluster, unlike Al, who had a great personality and great projection. Al was at Cream Records after Liberty was sold. After Cream folded he went into selling tires or wheels or something totally alien and boring after the record business. His older son tried to measure up to Al's success and dealt drugs and was shot. His younger son, in his twenties, had cancer. Al and his father both died of cancer, as well. This son ran his car into a post at high speed and killed himself. That family had a lot of tragedy and sadness.

"Before Liberty Al had been sales manager at Dot Records. That is where he got the capital to buy into Liberty, when Randy Woods sold Dot for five million, a very large sum at the time, around nineteen sixty. Randy still ran Dot after that, though. He mostly did covers of black songs."

Al Bennett died circa 1989. Perhaps a fitting epitaph would be words offered by Bobby Troup: "Al Bennett was the mastermind of Liberty. He got a huge building in Hollywood on Sunset Boulevard and worldwide distribution of Liberty Records. Si was a very hard worker. But Al made a giant out of them."

Si Waronker (b. 3-4-15)—The founder of Liberty Records did quite well when he sold the company in 1964, with cash and stock equaling four million dollars. For his health, Si bought a boat, closed the door on Liberty forever, and traveled the oceans in 1964. He traveled around the world in 1967. His first wife Jeanette died suddenly of hepatitis. After her death he bought a seventy-six-foot yacht at age fifty-three and sailed the oceans again. He was introduced to his second wife, Miriam, on his boat by "Al Bennett, of all people." He married Miriam in 1969, built or bought houses, condos, motels, and apartment buildings. From 1969 to 1978 they moved eleven times, and today live together happily in Beverly Hills.

In 1978 Si was talked into recording a new artist in London, bankrolled by Capitol to the tune of a $25,000 advance. He was overwhelmed by twenty-four-track, piecemeal recording, instead of recording live with an orchestra. After recording nine tracks (piano, drum, and so on) of one tune in four hours, with no singer yet present, he decided that today "the studio engineer is the conductor.... We used to do three complete tunes in three hours.... My comeback was a dismal failure. I hated every minute of our London experience. My music days were over."

Si is seventy-seven, still married to Miriam, and his son Lenny is president of Warner Bros. Records.

Si Waronker did not know about EMI's new campaign of releasing Liberty material in the 1990s on CD. When told about the series, he exclaimed, "No kidding! I'd like to get my hands on those releases. That's great! You'd think that the tapes would have gone to pot by now. It's great, that makes me feel good, that at least the so-called legend won't die!"

Today absolutely no one has anything bad to say about Si. The comments made by ace Liberty producer Snuff Garrett are representative:

"Si is great; he's a bear. He taught me everything. He taught me all the basics and more. He was great. I couldn't have been in a better place. I was lucky. I was a young guy and didn't know one note of music. I still don't and don't care. It was a business and I was in it."

It was a business, and at times a dirty one at that. It was fun, but there were great stresses that almost killed Si. Knowing what he knows now, if he could do it again, would he? Or would he have stayed with his first vocation, the violin?

"No, once I closed the violin case when I was twenty-six years old, I vowed never to look at it again. And I never have. As for Liberty, as bad and as interesting as it was, I would do it again. Because it was a challenge.

"You see, even after I quit and went fishing all the time, I would never quit until I had landed the marlin that I was looking for. I am a persistent little guy. I am too old for all that now, and it was a challenge at every point. But if I could go back, I would do it all again."

And what if? What if Si's health had not gone bad on him and he could have stayed in the business? "Let's put it this way. If I didn't have the strokes, I don't think we would have sold to Avnet. I think we would have gone ahead with our secondary issue and have gotten enough money to be able to do all of the things that I wanted to do, including buying up as many companies as possible. And growing, but at a much slower pace and with more control, the same control that we tried to have when I was really working hard, trying to build up a real A&R staff and build from within also.

"In other words, I wanted to become a major company. But the minute that I started to get sick and saw that I was losing control, my mind gradually told me to get out while I was able to. But had my health allowed, I probably would have stayed at Liberty until I had to retire.

"Eventually Al and I would have had a showdown, but we would have been able to straighten it out. We would have divided responsibilities. His end would have been making the deals, while I would be in charge of the creative end. That was how we had started. But it didn't end that way, unfortunately.

"I had not gone into Liberty to make a killing. But I started by borrowing two thousand dollars, and I came out with four big ones in stock. That was four million in nineteen sixty-three dollars, more like forty million today. I converted most of it, gave most of it away to family, and the rest of it I kept, enough to live very well. I am still living on it, and I have enough to keep on going till the end of me.

"And I am sure that, had I stayed alive in the business, then I am sure that Liberty would still be alive today, even if I saw no money out of it. Because I wanted that company."

In a very real sense, Si, Liberty *is* still alive today. For it is virtually impossible to listen to any oldies or classic rock radio station for an hour without hearing at least one immortal Eddie Cochran, David Seville, Bobby Vee, Jan & Dean, Gary Lewis, Hollies, Jackie DeShannon, Classics IV, or other timeless, Fabulous Fifties or Sensational Sixties, Liberty recording!

Appendixes

APPENDIX 1

#1 Hits

The titles and artists of every Liberty, Dolton, Imperial, and Soul City release that charted at #1 on the *Billboard* Top 100 are listed. The choice of listing the #1 hits is somewhat arbitrary. All records that made the top five on *Billboard* probably enjoyed roughly equal popularity. Further, sometimes a record like "Walk, Don't Run" by the Ventures peaked at #2 only because a big song by Elvis or someone else was holding down the #1 spot at the time. In addition, apparently the *Billboard* charts were not based strictly on sales, but also on opinions and preferences of record clerks, disc jockeys, and others, as well as by publicity and promotion of certain songs and artists. Still, relative rankings and records that were charted as #1 hits are considered important and do generally reflect relative commercial success.

A list of all the Liberty, Dolton, Imperial, and Soul City #1 hits is presented here. Rankings reflect the number of weeks each was at #1. Ties are broken by the number of weeks spent on the top 100.

Liberty, Dolton, Imperial, and Soul City #1 Hits

1. Aquarius/Let the Sun Shine In (5th Dimension, Soul City)
2. Come Softly to Me (Fleetwoods, Dolton)
3. Chipmunk Song (David Seville, Liberty)
4. Witch Doctor (David Seville, Liberty)
5. Take Good Care of My Baby (Bobby Vee, Liberty)
6. This Diamond Ring (Gary Lewis, Liberty)
7. Poor Side of Town (Johnny Rivers, Imperial)

Following is a list of the same #1 hits just presented. However, this time they are segregated by label and listed with the dates each entered the top 100 chart, as well as the number of weeks the song stayed at #1 and the number of weeks the song stayed on the top 100.

Liberty #1 Hits

Date Record Entered Chart	Weeks at #1	Weeks on Chart	Title	Artist
4-58	3	19	Witch Doctor	David Seville
12-58	4	13 (plus 15 weeks in later years)	Chipmunk Song	David Seville
8-61	3	15	Take Good Care of My Baby	Bobby Vee

6-69	3	15	Wedding Bell Blues	5th Dimension
6-63	2	13	Surf City	Jan & Dean
1-65	2	12	This Diamond Ring	Gary Lewis and the Playboys

Dolton #1 Hits

Date Record Entered Chart	Weeks at #1	Weeks on Chart	Title	Artist
3-59	4	16	Come Softly to Me	Fleetwoods
9-59	1	20	Mr. Blue	Fleetwoods

Imperial #1 Hits

Date Record Entered Chart	Weeks at #1	Weeks on Chart	Title	Artist
9-66	1	22	Poor Side of Town	Johnny Rivers

Soul City #1 Hits

Date Record Entered Chart	Weeks at #1	Weeks on Chart	Title	Artist
3-69	6	17	Aquarius/Let the Sun Shine In	5th Dimension
6-69	3	15	Wedding Bell Blues	5th Dimension

APPENDIX 2

Artists in Top 200

The titles and artists of the releases on the Liberty family of labels that made the *Billboard* All-Time Top 200 artists (1955–1986) and their rankings in the *Billboard* Top 200 are listed. The list is limited to the artists who had the majority of their hits on Liberty labels. This excludes, for example the O'Jays, who ranked #138 but who had most of their hits on non–Liberty labels.

- 58 5th Dimension
- 81 Bobby Vee
- 99 Jan & Dean
- 126 Hollies
- 158 Gary Lewis and the Playboys

APPENDIX 3

Liberty, Dolton, Imperial, and Soul City Top Rankings

Artists are ranked according to their records that charted on *Billboard*'s Top 100. Each charted song earns points based on the highest chart position it reached; #1 yields 100 points, #2 yields 99 points, #3 yields 97 points, and so forth. Total weeks charted are also added, and the total number of weeks each artist held the #1 spot. The first four lists are segregated by label, listing every artist who earned 300 points or more.

Liberty

Rank	Artist	Points
1	Bobby Vee	1920
2	Gary Lewis/Playboys	1364
3	Chipmunks/Seville	1327
4	Jan & Dean	1266
5	Gene McDaniels	610
6	Timi Yuro	552
7	Johnny Burnette	443
8	Eddie Cochran	364
9	Canned Heat	318
10	Vikki Carr	307

Dolton

Rank	Artist	Points
1	Fleetwoods	837
2	Ventures	830
3	Vic Dana	719

Imperial

Rank	Artist	Points
1	Johnny Rivers	1612
2	Hollies	628
3	Classics IV	592
4	Jackie DeShannon	513
5	Cher	481
6	Billy J. Kramer	471
7	Mel Carter	395

Appendix 3

Soul City

Rank	Artist	Points
1	5th Dimension	1211

All Labels

Rank	Artist	Points
1	Bobby Vee	1920
2	Johnny Rivers	1612
3	Gary Lewis/Playboys	1364
4	Chipmunks/Seville	1327
5	Jan & Dean	1266
6	5th Dimension	1211
7	Fleetwoods	837
8	Ventures	830
9	Vic Dana	719
10	Hollies	628
11	Gene McDaniels	610
12	Classics IV	592
13	Jackie DeShannon	513

Note: This last list commingles the artists of all four labels.

APPENDIX 4

The Top Liberty, Dolton, and Imperial Hit Makers

The following are lists for Liberty, Dolton, and Imperial of all the artists who charted at least one record in the top 10. They are ranked by the overall number of top 100 hits they charted.

Liberty Top Ten Artists

Rank	Artist	# of Hits	
1	Bobby Vee	36	
2	Jan & Dean	21	
3	David Seville	13	(21 with rechartings of rereleases)
4	Gary Lewis and the Playboys	9	
5	Johnny Burnette	7	
6	Eddie Cochran	7	
7	Gene McDaniels	6	
8	Timi Yuro	6	
9	Vikki Carr	6	
10	Five-way tie Patience and Prudence Billy Ward and His Dominoes Walter Brennan Martin Denny Jackie DeShannon	3	

Dolton Top Ten Artists

Rank	Artist	# of Hits
1	Vic Dana	14
2	Ventures	10
3	Fleetwoods	10

Imperial Top Ten Artists

Rank	Artist	# of Hits
1	Johnny Rivers	21
2	Jackie DeShannon	10

3	Classics IV	8
4	Hollies	7
5	Cher	6
6	Mel Carter	6
7	Billy J. Kramer with the Dakotas	5
8	Irma Thomas	4

APPENDIX 5

The Top Twenty Liberty Family Artists

These are the top 20 artists on Liberty, Dolton, and Imperial commingled. They are ranked by the number of charted songs on the top 100. Ties broken by number of top-ten hits, number-one hits, hits on other labels, and the like.

1. Bobby Vee (Liberty)
2. Johnny Rivers (Imperial)
3. Jan & Dean (Liberty)
4. David Seville (Liberty)
5. Vic Dana (Dolton)
6. Ventures (Dolton)
7. Jackie DeShannon (Liberty/Imperial)
8. Gary Lewis and the Playboys (Liberty)
9. Fleetwoods (Dolton)
10. Classics IV (Imperial)
11. Hollies (Imperial)
12. Johnny Burnette (Imperial)
13. Eddie Cochran (Liberty)
14. Gene McDaniels (Liberty)
15. Cher (Imperial)
16. Mel Carter (Imperial)
17. Timi Yuro (Liberty)
18. Vikki Carr (Liberty)
19. Billy J. Kramer with the Dakotas (Imperial)
20. Irma Thomas (Imperial)

APPENDIX 6

Percentage of Success

The percentage of releases by each label—Liberty, Dolton, and Imperial—that were charted on the *Billboard* Top 100. Interestingly, the fewer number of releases a label issued, the greater the percentage of charted records it scored.

Label	Total # of Releases	# of Top 100 Hits	All Releases That Hit Top 100
Liberty	1,218 releases	194 chart hits	16% charted hits
Dolton	127 releases	39 chart hits	31% charted hits
Imperial	452 releases	95 chart hits	21% charted hits

APPENDIX 7

Chronological Hit Lists

The following is a chronological list for each record label—Liberty, Dolton, and Imperial—of the top 100 hits on the label. The Dolton list includes the record label number.

Liberty

1955
"Cry Me a River"—Julie London

1956
"Tonight You Belong to Me"—Patience and Prudence
"Gonna Get Along Without You Now"—Patience and Prudence
"The Money Tree"*—Patience and Prudence
"Armen's Theme"—David Seville

1957
"Sittin' in the Balcony"—Eddie Cochran
"Star Dust"—Billy Ward
"Gotta Get to Your House"—David Seville
"Drive-In Show"—Eddie Cochran
"Deep Purple"—Billy Ward
"I'm Available"—Margie Rayburn

1958
"Jeannie, Jeannie, Jeannie"—Eddie Cochran
"Witch Doctor"—David Seville††
"Jennie Lee"—Billy Ward
"The Bird on My Head"—David Seville
"Summertime Blues"—Eddie Cochran
"Little Brass Band"—David Seville
"Quiet Village"—Martin Denny
"C'mon, Everybody"—Eddie Cochran
"The Chipmunk Song"—David Seville
(also in 1959, 1960, 1961, and 1962)

1959
"Teenage Heaven"—Eddie Cochran
"Alvin's Harmonica"—David Seville (also in 1961 and 1962)
"Come Softly to Me"†—Fleetwoods
"Judy"—David Seville
"Ragtime Cowboy Joe"—David Seville
"Martinique"—Martin Denny
"Somethin' Else"—Eddie Cochran
"Suzie Baby"—Bobby Vee

1960
"Alvin's Orchestra"—David Seville
"National City"—Joiner, Arkansas, Junior High School Band
"Blue Velvet"—The Statues
"One Last Kiss"—Bobby Vee
"Dreamin'"—Johnny Burnette
"Look for a Star"—Gary Miles
"Devil or Angel"—Bobby Vee
"Since I Met You, Baby"—Bobby Vee
"Alvin for President"—David Seville
"You're Sixteen"—Johnny Burnette
"Ballad of the Alamo"—Bud and Travis
"Rubber Ball"—Bobby Vee
"Lovey Dovey"—Buddy Knox
"Rudolph, the Red-Nosed Reindeer"—David Seville (also in 1961 and 1962)

1961
"Stayin' In"—Bobby Vee
"More Than I Can Say"*—Bobby Vee
"Little Boy Sad"—Johnny Burnette
"Ling-Ting-Tong"—Buddy Knox

560

"A Hundred Pounds of Clay"—Gene McDaniels
"Big, Big World"—Johnny Burnette
"Continental Walk"—Rollers
"How Many Tears"—Bobby Vee
"Baby Face"*—Bobby Vee
"Hurt"—Timi Yuro
"I Apologize"*—Timi Yuro
"A Tear"—Gene McDaniels
"Girls"—Johnny Burnette
"The Mountain's High"—Dick and Deedee
"This Time"—Troy Shondell
"Take Good Care of My Baby"—Bobby Vee
"Tower of Strength"—Gene McDaniels
"Up a Lazy River"—Si Zentner
"Smile"—Timi Yuro
"God, Country, and My Baby"—Johnny Burnette
"Run to Him"—Bobby Vee
"Walkin' with My Angel"*—Bobby Vee

1962

"A Sunday Kind of Love"—Jan & Dean
"Tears from an Angel"—Troy Shondell
"Surfer's Stomp"—Marketts
"Chip Chip"—Gene McDaniels
"Tell Me"—Dick and Deedee
"Please Don't Ask About Barbara"—Bobby Vee
"I Just Can't Say Goodbye"*—Bobby Vee
"The Alvin Twist"—David Seville
"Papa-Oom-Mow-Mow"—Rivingtons
"Old Rivers"—Walter Brennan
"Balboa Blue"—Marketts
"Sharing You"—Bobby Vee
"Tennessee"—Jan & Dean
"What's A-Matter Baby"—Timi Yuro
"Taste of Honey"—Martin Denny
"Houdini"—Walter Brennan
"Punish Her"—Bobby Vee
"Point of No Return"—Gene McDaniels
"Mama Sang a Song"—Walter Brennan
"Spanish Lace"—Gene McDaniels
"The Love of a Boy"—Timi Yuro
"The Night Has a Thousand Eyes"—Bobby Vee

1963

"Charms"—Bobby Vee
"Faded Love"—Jackie DeShannon
"Linda"—Jan & Dean
"Closer to Heaven"—Nick Nobel
"Insult to Injury"—Timi Yuro
"The Bird's the Word"—Rivingtons
"Needles and Pins"—Jackie DeShannon
"Surf City"—Jan & Dean
"The Cruel Surf"—Dakotas
"Be True to Yourself"—Bobby Vee
"Honolulu Lulu"—Jan & Dean
"Yesterday and You"—Bobby Vee
"Drag City"—Jan & Dean
"When You Walk in the Room"—Jackie DeShannon

1964

"Stranger in Your Arms"—Bobby Vee
"I'll Make You Mine"—Bobby Vee
"Dead Man's Curve"—Jan & Dean
"New Girl in School"*—Jan & Dean
"Sugar and Spice"—Searchers
"Hickory, Dick and Doc"—Bobby Vee
"Little Old Lady (from Pasadena)"—Jan & Dean
"Ride the Wild Surf"—Jan & Dean
"The Anaheim, Azusa, and Cucamonga Sewing Circle, Book Review, and Timing Association"*—Jan & Dean
"Sidewalk Surfin'"—Jan & Dean
"When It's Over"—Jan & Dean
"Every Little Bit Hurts"—Bobby Vee
"Pretend You Don't See Her"*—Bobby Vee

1965

"From All Over the World"—Jan & Dean
"Freeway Flyer"*—Jan & Dean
"Cross My Heart"—Bobby Vee
"This Diamond Ring"—Gary Lewis and the Playboys
"Somewhere"—P. J. Proby
"Count Me In"—Gary Lewis and the Playboys
"Keep on Trying"—Bobby Vee
"You Really Know How to Hurt a Guy"—Jan & Dean
"Save Your Heart for Me"—Gary Lewis and the Playboys
"Everybody Loves a Clown"—Gary Lewis and the Playboys
"Road Runner"—The Gants
"I Found a Girl"—Jan & Dean
"No Matter What Shape"—T-Bones
"She's Just My Style"—Gary Lewis and the Playboys
"A Beginning from an End"—Jan & Dean

1966

"Batman" — Jan & Dean
"Sure Gonna Miss Her" — Gary Lewis and the Playboys
"The Big Hurt" — Del Shannon
"Sippin' and Chippin'" — T-Bones
"Look at Me, Girl" — Bobby Vee
"Green Grass" — Gary Lewis and the Playboys
"Popsicle" — Jan & Dean
"My Heart's Symphony" — Gary Lewis and the Playboys
"Fiddle Around" — Jan & Dean
"Paint Me a Picture" — Gary Lewis and the Playboys
"Where Will the Words Come From" — Gary Lewis and the Playboys
"School Days" — Jan & Dean

1967

"Spooky" — Mike Sharpe
"Niki Hokey" — P. J. Proby
"The Loser" — Gary Lewis and the Playboys
"Buy for Me the Rain" — Nitty Gritty Dirt Band
"Come Back When You Grow Up" — Bobby Vee
"Girls I Love" — Gary Lewis and the Playboys
"Jill" — Gary Lewis and the Playboys
"It Must Be Him" — Vikki Carr
"An Open Letter to a Teenage Son" — Victor Lundberg
"The Lesson" — Vikki Carr

1968

"Maybe Just Today" — Bobby Vee
"She'll Be There" — Vikki Carr
"Your Heart Is Free Just Like the Wind"* — Vikki Carr
"Hey Girl/My Girl" — Bobby Vee
"Sealed with a Kiss" — Gary Lewis and the Playboys
"On the Road Again" — Canned Heat
"Do What You Gotta Do" — Bobby Vee
"I'm Lookin' for Someone to Love" — Bobby Vee

1969

"Hawaii Five-O" — The Ventures
"Going Up Country" — Canned Heat
"The Greatest Love" — Dorsey Burnette
"With Pen in Hand" — Vikki Carr

"Rhythm of the Rain" — Gary Lewis and the Playboys
"Let's Call It a Day, Girl" — Bobby Vee
"Eternity" — Vikki Carr

1970

"I Want to Take You Higher" — Ike and Tina Turner
"It's So Nice" — Jackie DeShannon
"Green-Eyed Lady" — Sugarloaf
"Mr. Bojangles" — Nitty Gritty Dirt Band
"Where Did All the Good Times Go" — Classics IV
"It's So Nice" — Jackie DeShannon
"Sweet Sweetheart" — Bobby Vee

1971

"Proud Mary" — Ike and Tina Turner
"Tongue in Cheek" — Sugarloaf

---

*Flip side of the title immediately preceding.
†Originally released on Dolton Records, actually a Dolton hit.
††David Seville or Ross Bagdasarian or the Chipmunks.

Dolton

1959

1 "Come Softly to Me" — Fleetwoods
2 "Straight Flush" — Frantics
3 "Graduation's Here" — Fleetwoods
4 "I Love an Angel" — Little Bill and the Blue Notes
5 "Mr. Blue" — Fleetwoods
  "You Mean Everything to Me" — Fleetwoods
6 "Fog Cutter" — Frantics
13 "Werewolf" — Frantics
14 "Outside My Window" — Fleetwoods

1960

22 "Runaround" — Fleetwoods
25 "Walk, Don't Run" — Ventures
27 "The Last One to Know" — Fleetwoods
28 "Perfidia" — Ventures

1961

32 "Ram-Bunk-Shush" — Ventures
40 "Tragedy" — Fleetwoods

41 "Lullaby of the Leaves" — Ventures
44 "Silver City" — Ventures
45 "The Great Imposter" — Fleetwoods
47 "Blue Moon" — Ventures
48 "Little Altar Boy" — Vic Dana

1962

51 "I Will" — Vic Dana
57 "Baby Elephant Walk" — Miniature Men
60 "Lolita Ya-Ya" — Ventures
62 "Lovers by Night, Strangers by Day" — Fleetwoods
67 "2,000 Pound Bee (Pt. 2)" — Ventures

1963

73 "Danger" — Vic Dana
75 "Goodnight My Love" — Fleetwoods
81 "More" — Vic Dana

1964

92 "Shangri-La" — Vic Dana
95 "Love Is All We Need" — Vic Dana
96 "Walk, Don't Run '64" — Ventures
99 "Garden in the Rain" — Vic Dana

1965

303 "Diamond Head" — Ventures
304 "Red Roses for a Blue Lady" — Vic Dana
305 "Bring a Little Sunshine" — Vic Dana
309 "Moonlight and Roses" — Vic Dana
313 "Crystal Chandelier" — Vic Dana

1966

316 "Secret Agent Man" — Ventures
319 "I Love You Drops" — Vic Dana
322 "A Million and One" — Vic Dana

Imperial

1963

"Today's Teardrops" — Rick Nelson

1964

"Wish Someone Would Care" — Irma Thomas
"Congratulations" — Rick Nelson
"Hippy Hippy Shake" — Swinging Blue Jeans
"Just One Look" — Hollies

"Bad to Me" — Billy J. Kramer with the Dakotas
"Little Children" — Billy J. Kramer with the Dakotas
"Good Golly, Miss Molly" — Swinging Blue Jeans
"Memphis" — Johnny Rivers
"It Will Stand" — The Showmen
"Anyone Who Knows What Love Is" — Irma Thomas
"I'll Keep You Satisfied" — Billy J. Kramer with the Dakotas
"From a Window" — Billy J. Kramer with the Dakotas
"Maybelline" — Johnny Rivers
"Teen Beat '65" — Sandy Nelson
"Times Have Changed" — Irma Thomas
"Mountain of Love" — Johnny Rivers
"He's My Guy" — Irma Thomas

1965

"Yeh Yeh" — Georgie Fame
"Midnight Special" — Johnny Rivers
"Cupid"* — Johnny Rivers
"Every Night, Every Day" — Jimmy McCracklin
"Lipstick Traces" — O'Jays
"In the Meantime" — Georgie Fame
"What the World Needs Now Is Love" — Jackie DeShannon
"Seventh Son" — Johnny Rivers
"Hold Me, Thrill Me, Kiss Me" — Mel Carter
"All I Really Wanna Do" — Cher
"Trains & Boats & Planes" — Billy J. Kramer with the Dakotas
"I've Cried My Last Tear" — O'Jays
"Think" — Jimmy McCracklin
"Lifetime of Loneliness" — Jackie DeShannon
"Where Have All the Flowers Gone" — Johnny Rivers
"Look Through Any Window" — Hollies
"My Heart Sings" — Mel Carter
"Under Your Spell Again" — Johnny Rivers
"My Answer" — Jimmy McCracklin

1966

"Love Is All We Need" — Mel Carter
"I Can't Let Go" — Hollies
"Secret Agent Man" — Johnny Rivers
"Bang Bang" — Cher
"Band of Gold" — Mel Carter
"Come and Get Me" — Jackie DeShannon

"I Washed My Hands in Muddy Water" — Johnny Rivers
"You, You, You" — Mel Carter
"Bus Stop" — Hollies
"Get Away" — Georgie Fame
"Alfie" — Cher
"Stand in for Love" — O'Jays
"I Can Make It with You" — Jackie DeShannon
"Poor Side of Town" — Johnny Rivers
"Take Good Care of Her" — Mel Carter
"Stop, Stop, Stop" — Hollies
"Behind the Door" — Cher

1967

"Baby, I Need Your Lovin'" — Johnny Rivers
"On a Carousel" — Hollies
"Wishing Doll" — Jackie DeShannon
"Pay You Back with Interest" — Hollies
"Tracks of My Tears" — Johnny Rivers
"Groovy Summertime" — Love Generation
"Hey Joe" — Cher
"Happy" — Sunshine Company
"Just One Look" — Hollies
"Spooky" — Classics IV
"Back on the Street Again" — Sunshine Company
"You Better Sit Down, Kids" — Cher
"Summer Rain" — Johnny Rivers

1968

"Zabadak" — Dave Dee, Dozy, Beaky, Mick, and Tich

"Look, Here Comes the Sun" — Sunshine Company
"Look to Your Soul" — Johnny Rivers
"Soul Train" — Classics IV
"Montage from 'How Sweet It Is'" — Sunshine Company
"The Weight" — Jackie DeShannon
"Stormy" — Classics IV
"Right Relations" — Johnny Rivers

1969

"Traces" — Classics IV
"These Are Not My People" — Johnny Rivers
"Everyday with You, Girl" — Classics IV
"Put a Little Love in Your Heart" — Jackie DeShannon
"Muddy River" — Johnny Rivers
"Change of Heart" — Classics IV
"One Woman" — Johnny Rivers
"Love Will Find a Way" — Jackie DeShannon
"Midnight" — Classics IV

1970

"Brighton Hill" — Jackie DeShannon
"The Funniest Thing" — Classics IV
"Into the Mystic" — Johnny Rivers
"You Keep Me Hangin' On/Hurt So Bad" — Jackie DeShannon
"Fire and Rain" — Johnny Rivers

APPENDIX 8

Graphs of Hits per Year

Three graphs are presented of the 45 singles that were released and that charted on *Billboard*'s Top 100 chart per year from 1955 to 1971 by Liberty, Dolton, and Imperial.

These graphs are for comparison purposes only. That is, they should not be seen as indicative of any competition or rivalry between the labels. Al Bennett made all the decisions for Liberty and Imperial, and Dolton was a far smaller company that Liberty supported 100 percent and profited from.

Liberty / Dolton / Imperial Releases per Year

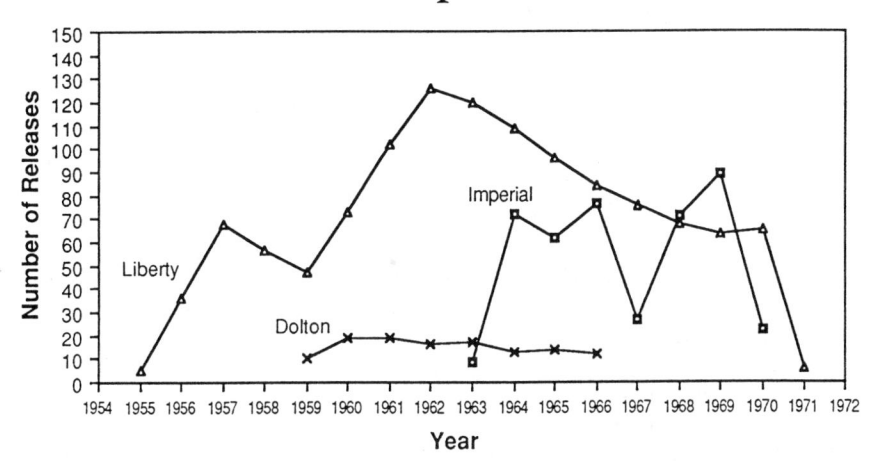

Graph 1 shows the number of 45s released each year. Liberty released its greatest number of singles in the early years, peaking in the early sixties, after which the number of releases declined slowly until 1970 and then dropped to nearly zero in 1971. It is significant that when Si Waronker retired and left Liberty, the number of releases dropped perceptibly.

Dolton released a far smaller number of singles than Liberty, beginning with the label's inception in 1959 and ending with its demise in 1966. However, the number of releases per year remained stable during the label's lifetime.

565

Imperial was purchased in 1963, so the number of "Liberty" Imperial releases for that year is very low. In 1964, the first full year of Liberty ownership, Liberty issued almost as many Imperial releases as on Liberty. Sometimes in the subsequent years even more singles were released on Imperial than on Liberty. However, they were all still "Liberty" records. It is worth noting that Liberty carried mostly original material, while Imperial carried mostly masters that were leased from independent producers or from England.

Both Liberty and Imperial continued to release a far greater number of singles per year than did Dolton.

Liberty / Dolton / Imperial Hits per Year

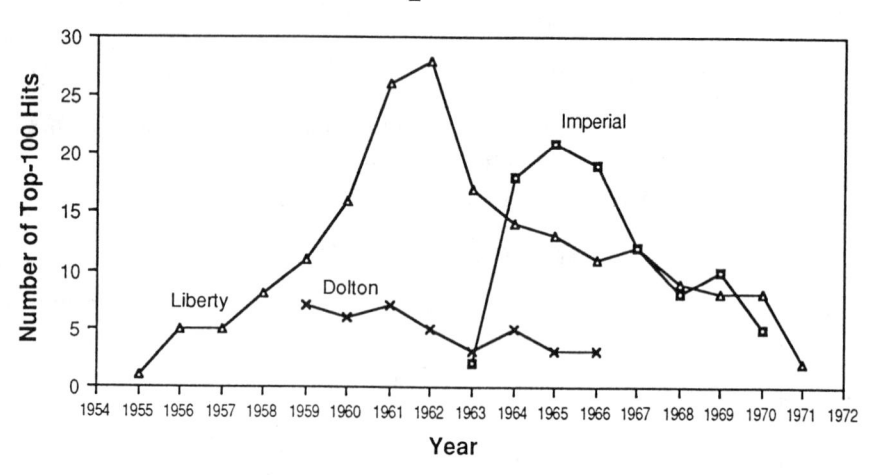

Graph 2 shows the number of hits (records that placed on *Billboard*'s Hot 100) per year for each label. Liberty charted an increasing number of singles each year into the early sixties. Then, as the sixties progressed (and concurrent with the Avnet takeover and Si Waronker's departure from Liberty), the number of hits per year decreased until the label's end in 1971.

Dolton began with a relatively high number of chart songs per year in 1959 and continued to chart a fair number per year from then on.

Imperial took off like gangbusters in its first few years of Liberty ownership and then began a rapid decline, matching that in the number of hits per year for Liberty.

Graph 3 (on next page) is a product of graphs 1 and 2. Graph 3 shows the percentage of all singles released by each label per year that charted. Generally, the greater the number of records released in any given year by any given label, the lower the percentage of singles that charted. (Conversely, the smaller the number of singles released in any given year by any label, the greater the percentage that charted.)

In particular, each label began and ended with a very small *number* of releases. Each label also began with a high *percentage* of releases, and every label but Dolton also *ended* with a high percentage of releases. Apparently, the fewer releases, the better they were; only singles of the highest quality made the cut. Or, perhaps when there were fewer singles, they got more attention from the promotion department.

Liberty / Dolton / Imperial Record Hits

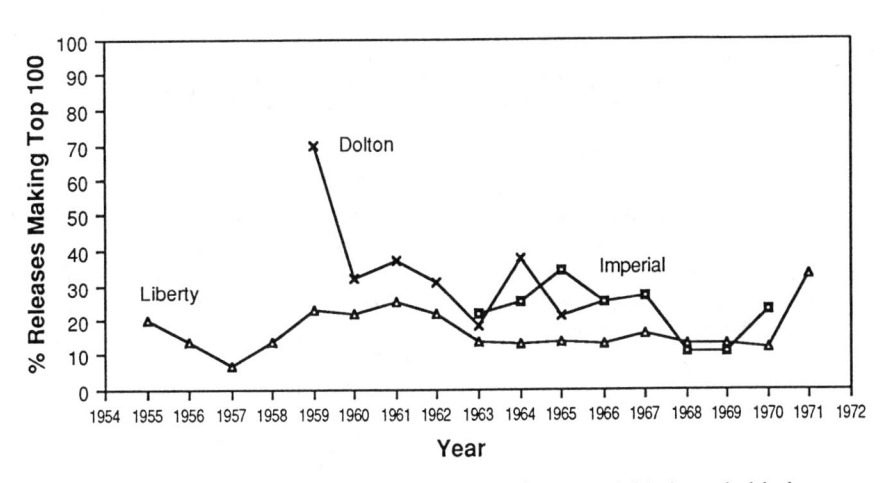

Dolton has the highest initial percentage of success. This is probably because Bob Reisdorff had an act with a hot recording (Fleetwoods, "Come Softly to Me") and created Dolton to release the single, thus starting out hot. By comparison, Si Waronker started Liberty and then looked for a hot property (such as Julie London), thus starting out cool. Imperial was already in mid-stride when it was taken over.

In addition, when Imperial leased masters—for example, from Great Britain—the tunes were often already-proven hits, and there was less risk in releasing them.

It is particularly noteworthy that Liberty scored a smaller percentage of hits as soon as Si Waronker left the helm in 1963.

APPENDIX 9

Top 100 Hits by Artist

A list is presented of every single to make *Billboard*'s Top 100 chart, segregated by label: Liberty, Dolton, Imperial, Minit, Blue Note, aura [*sic*], Pacific Jazz, and World Pacific. The list is presented alphabetically by artist within labels.

Recording codes used in this information (found in column appearing after Artist & Record Title) are: *I = Instrumental; N = Novelty recording; C = Comedy record; S = Spoken word recording; F = Foreign language recording; X = Christmas recording; R = Reissue of a previously charted single.*

Liberty

Date Charted	Peak Position	Weeks Charted	Artist & Record Title		1992 Mint Prices	Label & Number
			Alfi and Harry			
1/28/56	44	6	The Trouble with Harry	[N]	$10	Liberty 55008
			inspired by the film of the same title			
			Brennan, Walter LP			
4/7/62	5	11	Old Rivers	[S]	$5	Liberty 55436
8/4/62	100	1	Houdini	[S]	$5	Liberty 55477
10/20/62	38	8	Mama Sang a Song	[S]	$5	Liberty 55508
			above 3 with the Johnny Mann Singers			
			Bud and Travis LP			
10/17/60	64	9	Ballad of the Alamo		$6	Liberty 55284
			from the movie *The Alamo*			
			Burnette, Dorsey C&W/BUB			
1/25/69	67	6	The Greatest Love		$5	Liberty 56087
			Burnette, Johnny BUB			
7/25/60	11	15	Dreamin'		$10	Liberty 55258
10/31/60	8	15	You're Sixteen		$10	Liberty 55285
2/6/61	17	9	Little Boy Sad		$10	Liberty 55298
5/1/61	58	7	Big Big World		$10	Liberty 55318
10/16/61	18	9	God, Country and My Baby		$10	Liberty 55379
			Canned Heat BUB/LP			
8/10/68	16	11	On the Road Again		$4	Liberty 56038
12/7/68	11	11	Going Up the Country		$4	Liberty 56077
3/15/69	67	5	Time Was		$4	Liberty 56097
10/10/70	26	11	Let's Work Together		$4	Liberty 56151
			Carr, Vikki AC/BUB/LP			
9/2/67	3	15	It Must Be Him		$5	Liberty 55986
12/23/67	34	8	The Lesson		$5	Liberty 56012

Appendix 9 569

Date Charted	Peak Position	Weeks Charted	Artist & Record Title		1992 Mint Prices	Label & Number
3/23/68	99	3	She'll Be There/			
3/30/68	91	5	Your Heart Is Free Just Like the Wind		$4	Liberty 56026
5/3/69	35	13	With Pen in Hand		$4	Liberty 56092
10/4/69	79	4	Eternity		$4	Liberty 56132
			Chipmunks, The BUB/LP			
12/1/58	1 (4)	13	The Chipmunk Song	[X-N]	$8	Liberty 55168
			David Seville and the Chipmunks			
2/16/59	3	12	Alvin's Harmonica	[N]	$8	Liberty 55179
7/6/59	16	9	Ragtime Cowboy Joe	[N]	$8	Liberty 55200
			#1 hit for Bob Roberts in 1912			
2/22/60	33	5	Alvin's Orchestra	[N]	$8	Liberty 55233
9/5/60	95	2	Alvin for President	[N]	$8	Liberty 55277
12/19/60	21	2	Rudolph, the Red-Nosed Reindeer	[X-N]	$6	Liberty 55289
3/3/62	40	8	The Alvin Twist	[N]	$7	Liberty 55424
			Christmas Reissues			
12/14/59	41	5	The Chipmunk Song	[X-R]	$6	Liberty 55250
12/12/60	45	3	The Chipmunk Song	[X-R]	$6	Liberty 55250
12/18/61	39	3	The Chipmunk Song	[X-R]	$6	Liberty 55250
12/8/62	40	4	The Chipmunk Song	[X-R]	$6	Liberty 55250
12/25/61	73	2	Alvin's Harmonica	[X-R]	$6	Liberty 55250
12/22/62	87	1	Alvin's Harmonica	[X-R]	$6	Liberty 55250
12/18/61	47	3	Rudolph, the Red-Nosed Reindeer	[X-R]	$6	Liberty 55289
12/15/62	77	3	Rudolph, the Red-Nosed Reindeer	[X-R]	$6	Liberty 55289
			Classics IV BUB/AC/LP			
10/24/70	69	8	Where Did All the Good Times Go		$4	Liberty 56200
			Cochran, Eddie BUB			
3/23/57	18	13	Sittin' in the Balcony		$20	Liberty 55056
			Top 100 #18/Jockey #18/Juke Box #20/Best Seller #22			
9/16/57	82	6	Drive-In Show		$20	Liberty 55087
3/10/58	94	1	Jeannie, Jeannie, Jeannie		$25	Liberty 55123

Appendix 9

Date Charted	Peak Position	Weeks Charted	Artist & Record Title	1992 Mint Prices	Label & Number
8/4/58	8	16	Summertime Blues Hot 100 #8/Best Seller #13	$20	Liberty 55144
11/24/58	35	12	C'mon Everybody	$20	Liberty 55166
3/16/59	99	1	Teenage Heaven	$20	Liberty 55177
8/31/59	58	9	Somethin' Else songwriter Sharon Sheeley injured in Cochran's fatal car crash	$20	Liberty 55203
			Dana, Vic AC/BUB/LP		
1/10/70	47	12	If I Never Knew Your Name	$4	Liberty 56150
5/16/70	72	6	Red Red Wine above 2 written by Neil Diamond	$4	Liberty 56163
			Dayton R&B		
7/24/82	58	7	Hot Fun in the Summertime	$3	Liberty 1468
			Denny, Martin BUB/LP		
4/13/59	4	16	Quiet Village [I] written by Les Baxter	$8	Liberty 55162
7/20/59	88	2	Martinique [I]	$6	Liberty 55199
10/26/59	28	8	The Enchanted Sea [I] The Exotic Sounds of Martin Denny	$6	Liberty 55212
7/14/62	50	15	A Taste of Honey [I]	$5	Liberty 55470
			DeShannon, Jackie BUB/AC/LP		
2/23/63	97	2	Faded Love	$12	Liberty 55526
5/18/63	84	4	Needles and Pins	$12	Liberty 55563
1/25/64	99	1	When You Walk in the Room	$12	Liberty 55645
8/8/70	84	7	It's So Nice	$6	Liberty 56187
			Dey, Tracey BUB		
9/14/63	75	5	Teenage Cleopatra	$12	Liberty 55604
			Dick and Deedee BUB		
7/31/61	2(2)	15	The Mountain's High first released on Lama 7778 in 1961	$8	Liberty 55350

Date Charted	Peak Position	Weeks Charted	Artist & Record Title	1992 Mint Prices	Label & Number
3/17/62	22	14	**Tell Me** first released on Lama 7783 in 1961	$8	Liberty 55412
9/19/70	77	11	**Fantasy** BUB/LP Stoned Cowboy [I]	$4	Liberty 56190
9/25/65	46	12	**Gants, The** Road Runner	$7	Liberty 55829
10/2/61	93	1	**Hawley, Deane** Pocketful of Rainbows	$6	Liberty 55359
1/20/62	95	1	**Jan & Dean** BUB/LP A Sunday Kind of Love #15 hit for Jo Stafford in 1947	$10	Liberty 55397
5/26/62	69	7	Tennessee	$8	Liberty 55454
2/23/63	28	13	Linda #1 hit for Ray Noble with Buddy Clark in 1947	$7	Liberty 55531
6/15/63	1(2)	13	Surf City Brian Wilson (Beach Boys) helped on words & vocals for this tune	$6	Liberty 55580
9/7/63	11	10	Honolulu Lulu	$6	Liberty 55613
12/7/63	10	11	Drag City	$6	Liberty 55641
3/7/64	8	14	Dead Man's Curve/		
3/21/64	37	8	The New Girl in School	$6	Liberty 55672
6/27/64	3	11	The Little Old Lady (from Pasadena)	$6	Liberty 55704
9/19/64	16	8	Ride the Wild Surf/ from the film of the same title		
10/3/64	77	3	The Anaheim, Azusa & Cucamonga Sewing Circle, Book Review and Timing Association	$6	Liberty 55724
10/31/64	25	8	Sidewalk Surfin'	$6	Liberty 55727
3/13/65	56	5	(Here They Come) From All Over the World from the teen-rock concert film (The TAMI Show)	$6	Liberty 55766
5/22/65	27	9	You Really Know How to Hurt a Guy	$6	Liberty 55792
10/16/65	30	7	I Found a Girl	$6	Liberty 55833

Appendix 9

Date Charted	Peak Position	Weeks Charted	Artist & Record Title	1992 Mint Prices	Label & Number
2/12/66	66	5	Batman [N]	$7	Liberty 55860
6/4/66	21	9	Popsicle	$6	Liberty 55886
9/3/66	93	4	Fiddle Around	$7	Liberty 55905
			Joiner, Arkansas, Junior High School Band		
5/16/60	53	8	National City [I] adapted from the 1906 march "National Emblem"	$6	Liberty 55244
			Knox, Buddy BUB/C&W		
12/19/60	25	9	Lovey Dovey	$7	Liberty 55290
3/6/61	65	7	Ling-Ting-Tong	$7	Liberty 55305
			Lewis, Gary, and the Playboys BUB/LP		
1/16/65	1(2)	12	This Diamond Ring	$5	Liberty 55756
4/3/65	2(2)	11	Count Me In	$5	Liberty 55778
7/3/65	2(1)	11	Save Your Heart for Me	$5	Liberty 55809
9/25/65	4	11	Everybody Loves a Clown	$5	Liberty 55818
12/11/65	3	12	She's Just My Style	$5	Liberty 55846
3/5/66	9	9	Sure Gonna Miss Her	$5	Liberty 55865
5/14/66	8	8	Green Grass	$5	Liberty 55880
7/30/66	13	7	My Heart's Symphony	$5	Liberty 55898
10/8/66	15	8	(You Don't Have to) Paint Me a Picture	$5	Liberty 55914
12/17/66	21	9	Where Will the Words Come From	$5	Liberty 55933
3/11/67	43	6	The Loser (with a Broken Heart)	$5	Liberty 55949
5/13/67	39	6	Girls in Love	$5	Liberty 55971
8/12/67	52	7	Jill	$5	Liberty 55985
6/22/68	19	14	Sealed with a Kiss	$5	Liberty 56037
4/5/69	63	12	Rhythm of the Rain	$5	Liberty 56093
			London, Julie BUB/LP		
11/12/55	9	20	Cry Me a River	$8	Liberty 55006
			Jockey #9/Top 100 #13/Juke Box #14/Best Seller #23		
			Lundberg, Victor		
11/11/67	10	6	An Open Letter to My Teenage Son [S]	$5	Liberty 55996

Date Charted	Peak Position	Weeks Charted	Artist & Record Title	1992 Mint Prices	Label & Number
			McDaniels, Gene		
3/20/61	3	15	A Hundred Pounds of Clay	$6	Liberty 55308
7/3/61	31	8	A Tear	$6	Liberty 55344
10/2/61	5	13	Tower of Strength	$6	Liberty 55371
1/20/62	10	11	Chip Chip	$6	Liberty 55405
4/21/62	99	1	Funny	$6	Liberty 55444
8/4/62	21	10	Point of No Return	$5	Liberty 55480
11/10/62	31	9	Spanish Lace	$5	Liberty 55510
			with the Johnny Mann Singers on all of above		
8/10/63	64	7	It's a Lonely Town (Lonely without You)	$6	Liberty 55597
			Mann, Johnny, Singers AC/BUB/LP		
6/24/67	91	3	Up-Up and Away	$5	Liberty 55972
			Marketts, The AC/LP		
1/13/62	31	9	Surfer's Stomp [I]	$8	Liberty 55401
			first released on Union 504 in 1961		
			Miles, Garry		
6/20/60	16	13	Look for a Star	$7	Liberty 55261
			from the film *Circus of Horrors*		
			Monro, Matt BUB/AC/LP		
11/28/64	23	9	Walk Away	$5	Liberty 55745
			Nitty Gritty Dirt Band C&W/BUB/LP		
4/8/67	45	7	Buy for Me the Rain	$5	Liberty 55948
11/21/70	9	19	Mr. Bojangles	$4	Liberty 56197
			prologue: Uncle Charlie and His Dog Teddy		
10/3/81	76	4	Fire in the Sky	$3	Liberty 1429
			Patience & Prudence		
8/4/56	4	25	Tonight You Belong to Me	$10	Liberty 55022
			Best Seller #4/Juke Box #5/Top 100 #6		

Appendix 9

Date Charted	Peak Position	Weeks Charted	Artist & Record Title	1992 Mint Prices	Label & Number
12/1/56	11	16	Gonna Get Along Without Ya Now/ Jockey #11/Best Seller #12/Top 100 #12/Juke Box #16	$10	Liberty 55040
12/8/56	73	9	The Money Tree all of above with their father Mark McIntyre's orchestra		
7/11/81	26	13	**Patton, Robbie** Don't Give It Up LP	$3	Liberty 1420
2/13/65	91	2	**Proby, P. J.** BUB Somewhere from the Broadway musical "West Side Story"	$5	Liberty 55757
1/28/67	23	10	Niki Hoeky	$4	Liberty 55936
10/28/57	9	19	**Rayburn, Margie** I'm Available Jockey #9/Best Seller #15/Top 100 #16	$8	Liberty 55102
8/18/62	48	8	**Rivingtons, The** BUB Papa-Oom-Mow-Mow	$8	Liberty 55427
3/30/63	52	7	The Bird's the Word	$8	Liberty 55553
4/10/61	80	3	**Rollers, The** The Continental Walk	$8	Liberty 55320
5/2/64	44	8	**Searchers, The** LP Sugar and Spice first released on Liberty 55646 in 1963	$8	Liberty 55689
12/15/56	42	8	**Seville, David** Armen's Theme [I] named for Seville's wife, Armen	$8	Liberty 55041
9/9/57	77	4	Gotta Get to Your House [N]	$8	Liberty 55079
4/14/58	1(3)	19	Witch Doctor [N] Top 100 #1(3)/Best Seller #1(2)/Jockey #2	$8	Liberty 55132
7/7/58	34	5	The Bird on My Head [N] Best Seller #34/Top 100 #36	$8	Liberty 55140

Date Charted	Peak Position	Weeks Charted	Artist & Record Title	1992 Mint Prices	Label & Number
8/25/58	78	2	Little Brass Band		
5/18/59	86	1	Judy [I-S]	$7	Liberty 55153
				$7	Liberty 55193
5/7/66	94	2	**Shannon, Del** BUB/C&W/LP		
			The Big Hurt	$6	Liberty 55866
1/28/67	57	7	**Sharpe, Mike**		
			Spooky [I]	$5	Liberty 55922
9/18/61	6	13	**Shondell, Troy** C&W/BUB		
			This Time	$6	Liberty 55353
			first released on Gaye 2010 (as Troy Shundell) and then on Goldcrest 161 in 1961		
12/25/61	77	6	Tears from an Angel/		
1/13/62	92	1	Island in the Sky	$6	Liberty 55398
10/3/60	70	8	**Slatkin, Felix** BUB/LP		
			Theme from the Sundowners [I]	$7	Liberty 55282
			from the film *The Sundowners*		
8/8/60	84	3	**Statues, The**		
			Blue Velvet	$13	Liberty 55245
8/15/70	3	17	**Sugarloaf** BUB/LP		
			Green-Eyed Lady	$4	Liberty 56183
3/6/71	55	8	Tongue in Cheek	$4	Liberty 56218
12/11/65	3	13	**T-Bones, The** LP		
			No Matter What Shape (Your Stomach's In) [I]	$5	Liberty 55836
			tune is from an Alka Seltzer jingle		
3/26/66	62	5	Sippin' 'n' Chippin' [I]	$5	Liberty 55867
			from the Nabisco Sip 'n' Chip jingle		
5/23/70	34	18	**Turner, Ike & Tina** BUB/R&B/LP		
			I Want to Take You Higher	$4	Liberty 56177
1/30/71	4	13	**Ike & Tina Turner & the Ikettes**		
			Proud Mary	$4	Liberty 56216

Appendix 9

Date Charted	Peak Position	Weeks Charted	Artist & Record Title	1992 Mint Prices	Label & Number
			Vee, Bobby BUB/AC/LP		
8/31/59	77	4	Suzie Baby	$15	Liberty 55208
			Bobby Vee and the Shadows first released on Soma 1110 in 1959		
4/4/60	93	2	What Do You Want?	$10	Liberty 55234
8/1/60	6	19	Devil or Angel/		
9/12/60	81	1	Since I Met You Baby	$6	Liberty 55270
11/28/60	6	14	Rubber Ball	$6	Liberty 55287
			co-written by Gene Pitney		
2/13/61	33	7	Stayin' In		
2/27/61	61	5	More Than I Can Say	$6	Liberty 55296
5/29/61	63	4	How Many Tears	$6	Liberty 55325
8/7/61	1(3)	15	Take Good Care of My Baby	$5	Liberty 55354
11/13/61	2(1)	15	Run to Him/		
11/27/61	53	9	Walkin' with My Angel	$5	Liberty 55388
2/24/62	15	11	Please Don't Ask About Barbara/		
2/24/62	92	1	I Can't Say Goodbye	$5	Liberty 55419
5/19/62	15	10	Sharing You	$5	Liberty 55451
9/1/62	20	8	Punish Her/		
9/22/62	99	2	Someday (When I'm Gone from You)	$6	Liberty 55479
			Bobby Vee and the Crickets		
12/8/62	3	14	The Night Has a Thousand Eyes	$5	Liberty 55521
3/30/63	13	10	Charms	$5	Liberty 55530
6/22/63	34	7	Be True to Yourself/		
6/29/63	85	2	A Letter from Betty		
11/9/63	55	7	Yesterday and You (Armen's Theme)/	$5	Liberty 55581
12/28/63	99	1	Never Love a Robin		
1/25/64	83	3	Stranger in Your Arms	$5	Liberty 55636
2/22/64	52	8	I'll Make You Mine	$5	Liberty 55654
			Bobby Vee with the Eligibles	$5	Liberty 55670

Date Charted	Peak Position	Weeks Charted	Artist & Record Title	1992 Mint Prices	Label & Number
5/30/64	63	8	Hickory, Dick and Doc	$5	Liberty 55700
12/12/64	84	5	(There'll Come a Day When) Ev'ry Little Bit Hurts/		
12/5/64	97	1	Pretend You Don't See Her	$5	Liberty 55751
2/6/65	99	1	Cross My Heart	$5	Liberty 55761
5/8/65	85	5	Keep on Trying	$5	Liberty 55790
7/9/66	52	8	Look at Me Girl	$5	Liberty 55877
7/22/67	3	16	Come Back When You Grow Up	$5	Liberty 55964
11/18/67	37	7	Beautiful People	$5	Liberty 56009
2/10/68	46	6	Maybe Just Today	$5	Liberty 56014
			Bobby Vee and the Strangers		
4/20/68	35	9	My Girl/Hey Girl	$5	Liberty 56033
8/31/68	83	4	Do What You Gotta Do	$5	Liberty 56057
12/28/68	98	3	I'm into Lookin' for Someone to Love Me	$5	Liberty 56080
8/2/69	92	2	Let's Call It a Day Girl	$5	Liberty 56124
11/21/70	88	3	Sweet Sweetheart	$5	Liberty 56208
			Ventures, The BUB/AC/LP		
3/8/69	4	14	Hawaii Five-O [I]	$5	Liberty 56068
			from the TV series of the same title		
6/28/69	83	5	Theme from "A Summer Place" [I]	$5	Liberty 56115
			Ward, Billy, and His Dominoes R&B		
6/17/57	12	24	Star Dust	$8	Liberty 55071
			Jockey #12/Top 100 #13/Best Seller #14—there have been 19 charted versions of this Hoagy Carmichael tune		
9/30/57	20	12	Deep Purple	$8	Liberty 55099
			Best Seller #20/Top 100 #22—3 versions of this tune hit the top 10 in 1939		
6/2/58	55	5	Jennie Lee	$8	Liberty 55136
			Yuro, Timi BUB/AC/LP		
7/24/61	4	12	Hurt/		

Date Charted	Peak Position	Weeks Charted	Artist & Record Title	1992 Mint Prices	Label & Number
10/9/61	72	3	I Apologize #3 hit for Bing Crosby in 1931	$5	Liberty 55343
11/6/61	42	6	Smile/ #10 hit for Nat King Cole in 1954		
12/4/61	93	2	She Really Loves You	$5	Liberty 55375
2/3/62	66	5	Let Me Call You Sweetheart #1 hit for the Peerless Quartet in 1911	$5	Liberty 55410
7/14/62	12	11	What's a Matter Baby (Is It Huring You)	$5	Liberty 55469
12/1/62	44	8	The Love of a Boy	$5	Liberty 55519
3/30/63	81	1	Insult to Injury	$5	Liberty 55552
7/20/63	24	11	Make the World Go Away	$5	Liberty 55587
10/12/63	64	7	Gotta Travel On	$5	Liberty 55634
			Zentner, Si LP		
11/13/61	43	9	Up a Lazy River [I] #19 hit for Hoagy Carmichael in 1932	$6	Liberty 55374

Dolton

Date Charted	Peak Position	Weeks Charted	Artist & Record Title	1992 Mint Prices	Label & Number
			Dana, Vic AC/BUB/LP [X]		
11/27/61	45	8	Little Altar Boy	$5	Dolton 48
3/31/62	47	9	I Will	$5	Dolton 51
5/25/63	96	2	Danger	$5	Dolton 73
8/10/63	42	11	More	$5	Dolton 81
3/28/64	27	10	Shangri-La	$5	Dolton 92
7/11/64	53	7	Love Is All We Need	$5	Dolton 95
10/17/64	97	3	Garden in the Rain	$5	Dolton 99
2/6/65	10	12	Red Roses for a Blue Lady	$5	Dolton 304
5/22/65	66	6	Bring a Little Sunshine (to My Heart)	$5	Dolton 305
8/7/65	51	9	Moonlight and Roses (Bring Mem'ries of You sung by Roy Rogers in the 1943 film *Song of Texas*	$5	Dolton 309
12/4/65	51	7	Crystal Chandelier	$5	Dolton 313

Date Charted	Peak Position	Weeks Charted	Artist & Record Title	1992 Mint Prices	Label & Number
5/7/66	30	8	I Love You Drops	$5	Dolton 319
8/6/66	71	3	A Million and One	$5	Dolton 322
			Fleetwoods, The BUB/LP		
3/9/59	1(4)	16	Come Softly to Me	$10	Dolphin 1
			also released on Liberty 55188 in 1959		
5/18/59	39	8	Graduation's Here	$7	Dolton 3
9/7/59	1(1)	20	Mr. Blue/		
10/26/59	84	2	You Mean Everything to Me	$7	Dolton 5
2/15/60	28	9	Outside My Window	$7	Dolton 15
5/23/60	23	13	Runaround	$7	Dolton 22
10/17/60	96	1	The Last One to Know	$7	Dolton 27
4/17/61	10	12	Tragedy	$6	Dolton 40
9/11/61	30	8	(He's) The Great Imposter	$6	Dolton 45
10/13/62	36	10	Lovers by Night, Strangers by Day	$6	Dolton 62
6/1/63	32	11	Goodnight My Love	$6	Dolton 75
			Frantics, The		
5/25/59	91	3	Straight Flush [I]	$8	Dolton 2
9/14/59	93	1	Fog Cutter [I]	$8	Dolton 6
2/29/60	83	2	Werewolf [I]	$8	Dolton 16
			Guitar, Bonnie C&W		
12/14/59	97	2	Candy Apple Red	$8	Dolton 10
			Little Bill and the Bluenotes		
6/22/59	66	6	I Love an Angel	$8	Dolton 4
			produced by Bonnie Guitar		
			Miniature Men, The		
6/9/62	87	4	Baby Elephant's Walk [I]	$7	Dolton 57
			from the film *Hatari!*		
			Ventures, The BUB/AC/LP		
7/18/60	2(1)	18	Walk—Don't Run [I]	$8	Dolton 25
			first released on Blue Horizon 101 in 1959		

Date Charted	Peak Position	Weeks Charted	Artist & Record Title		1992 Mint Prices	Label & Number
10/31/60	15	13	Perfidia 5 versions hit the top 15 in 1941	[I]	$8	Dolton 28
1/23/61	29	9	Ram-Bunk-Shush	[I]	$8	Dolton 32
4/24/61	69	5	Lullaby of the Leaves #1 hit for George Olsen in 1932	[I]	$8	Dolton 41
8/28/61	83	3	(Theme from) Silver City orchestral backing by Hank Levine	[I]	$7	Dolton 44
10/23/61	54	6	Blue Moon 3 versions hit the top 10 in 1935	[I]	$7	Dolton 47
8/4/62	61	7	Lolita Ya-Ya theme from the film *Lolita*	[I]	$7	Dolton 60
12/29/62	91	4	The 2,000 Pound Bee (Part 2)	[I]	$7	Dolton 67
7/11/64	8	11	Walk — Don't Run '64 new version of their 1960 hit	[I-R]	$6	Dolton 96
10/24/64	35	7	Slaughter on Tenth Avenue written by Richard Rodgers in 1936	[I]	$6	Dolton 300
1/30/65	70	3	Diamond Head	[I]	$6	Dolton 303
2/26/66	54	7	Secret Agent Man from the CBS-TV series *Secret Agent*	[I]	$6	Dolton 316

Imperial

Date Charted	Peak Position	Weeks Charted	Artist & Record Title		1992 Mint Prices	Label & Number
11/16/63	74	6	**Alaimo, Steve** BUB Gotta Lotta Love		$5	Imperial 66003
12/3/66	69	6	**Baby Ray** There's Something On Your Mind	[N]	$5	Imperial 66216
6/26/65	8	15	**Carter, Mel** AC/BUB/LP Hold Me, Thrill Me, Kiss Me		$5	Imperial 66113
10/30/65	38	7	(All of a Sudden) My Heart Sings		$5	Imperial 66138
1/22/66	50	8	Love Is All We Need		$5	Imperial 66148
4/9/66	32	8	Band of Gold		$5	Imperial 66165

Date Charted	Peak Position	Weeks Charted	Artist & Record Title	1992 Mint Prices	Label & Number
7/16/66	49	7	You You You	$5	Imperial 66183
10/1/66	78	5	Take Good Care of Her	$5	Imperial 66208
			Cher BUB/C&W/LP		
7/3/65	15	12	All I Really Want to Do	$5	Imperial 66114
10/16/65	25	7	Where Do You Go	$5	Imperial 66136
3/12/66	2(1)	11	Bang Bang (My Baby Shot Me Down)	$5	Imperial 66160
7/30/66	32	6	Alfie	$5	Imperial 66192
			from the film of the same title		
11/26/66	97	1	Behind the Door	$5	Imperial 66217
9/9/67	94	2	Hey Joe	$5	Imperial 66252
10/28/67	9	13	You Better Sit Down Kids	$5	Imperial 66261
			all of above produced by Sonny Bono		
			Classics IV BUB/AC/LP		
12/23/67	3	15	Spooky	$5	Imperial 66259
5/4/68	90	3	Soul Train	$5	Imperial 66293
			Classics IV Featuring Dennis Yost		
10/26/68	5	15	Stormy	$5	Imperial 66328
2/8/69	2(1)	12	Traces	$5	Imperial 66352
5/3/69	19	11	Everyday with You Girl	$5	Imperial 66378
			Dennis Yost and the Classics IV		
8/2/69	49	7	Change of Heart	$5	Imperial 66393
11/15/69	58	8	Midnight	$5	Imperial 66424
3/28/70	59	5	The Funniest Thing	$5	Imperial 66439
			Dee, Dave; Dozy, Beaky, Mick and Tich BUB/LP		
1/6/68	52	6	Zabadak	[F] $5	Imperial 66270
			DeShannon, Jackie BUB/AC/LP		
5/22/65	7	13	What the World Needs Now Is Love	$6	Imperial 66110
10/2/65	66	6	A Lifetime of Loneliness	$6	Imperial 66132
5/28/66	83	3	Come and Get Me	$6	Imperial 66171
			above 3 written and produced by Burt Bacharach and Hal David		

Appendix 9

Date Charted	Peak Position	Weeks Charted	Artist & Record Title	1992 Mint Prices	Label & Number
9/10/66	68	6	I Can Make It with You	$6	Imperial 66202
8/24/68	55	8	The Weight	$6	Imperial 66313
6/28/69	4	14	Put a Little Love in Your Heart	$6	Imperial 66385
11/1/69	40	8	Love Will Find a Way	$6	Imperial 66419
3/7/70	82	4	Brighton Hill	$6	Imperial 66438
5/30/70	96	1	You Keep Me Hangin' On/Hurt So Bad	$6	Imperial 66452
			Fame, Georgie LP		
2/13/65	21	8	Yeh, Yeh	$5	Imperial 66086
5/1/65	97	2	In the Meantime	$6	Imperial 66104
8/20/66	70	7	Get Away	$6	Imperial 66189
			all of above with The Blue Flames		
			Frost, Thomas & Richard		
10/25/69	83	4	She's Got Love	$6	Imperial 66405
			Haywood, Leon R&B/BUB/LP		
11/20/65	92	3	She's with Her Other Love	$5	Imperial 66123
			Hollies, The BUB/LP		
5/16/64	98	1	Just One Look	$12	Imperial 66026
11/20/65	32	12	Look Through Any Window	$8	Imperial 66134
3/19/66	42	10	I Can't Let Go	$5	Imperial 66158
7/23/66	5	14	Bus Stop	$5	Imperial 66186
10/29/66	7	10	Stop Stop Stop	$5	Imperial 66214
3/18/67	11	14	On a Carousel	$5	Imperial 66231
6/3/67	28	7	Pay You Back with Interest	$5	Imperial 66240
9/30/67	44	7	Just One Look [R]	$5	Imperial 66258
			Kramer, Billy J., with the Dakotas LP		
4/18/64	7	15	Little Children/	$6	Imperial 66027
5/30/64	9	10	Bad to Me		
			first released on Liberty 55626 and then Liberty 55667		
7/25/64	30	7	I'll Keep You Satisfied	$6	Imperial 66048
			first released on Liberty 55643 in 1964		

Date Charted	Peak Position	Weeks Charted	Artist & Record Title	1992 Mint Prices	Label & Number
8/22/64	23	10	From a Window above 3 written by John Lennon and Paul McCartney	$6	Imperial 66051
2/6/65	67	5	It's Gotta Last Forever	$6	Imperial 66085
6/26/65	47	7	Trains and Boats and Planes	$6	Imperial 66115
			Love Generation, The		
6/24/67	74	7	Groovy Summertime	$5	Imperial 66243
8/3/68	86	3	Montage from How Sweet It Is (I Know That You Know) from the James Garner/Debbie Reynolds film *How Sweet It Is*	$5	Imperial 66310
			McCracklin, Jimmy R&B/BUB		
4/10/65	91	1	Every Night, Every Day	$6	Imperial 66094
10/23/65	95	2	Think	$6	Imperial 66129
1/29/66	92	1	My Answer	$6	Imperial 66147
			Nelson, Ricky BUB/AC/C&W/LP		
3/2/63	48	6	That's All/	$9	Imperial 5910
2/23/63	67	6	I'm in Love Again		
4/20/63	100	1	If You Can't Rock Me/	$8	Imperial 5935
5/4/63	94	3	Old Enough to Love	$8	Imperial 66004
11/30/63	54	9	Today's Teardrops	$7	Imperial 66017
3/14/64	63	5	Congratulations		
			Nelson, Sandy BUB/LP		
9/19/64	44	10	Teen Beat '65 [1-R] live version of 1959 hit	$6	Imperial 66060
			O'Jays, The R&B/BUB/LP		
9/14/63	93	3	Lonely Drifter	$7	Imperial 5976
5/8/65	48	7	Lipstick Traces (On a Cigarette)	$6	Imperial 66102
8/7/65	94	2	I've Cried My Last Tear	$6	Imperial 66121
10/22/66	95	3	Stand in for Love	$6	Imperial 66197
			Rivers, Johnny BUB/C&W/LP		
5/30/64	2(2)	12	Memphis	$5	Imperial 66032

Appendix 9 585

Date Charted	Peak Position	Weeks Charted	Artist & Record Title	1992 Mint Prices	Label & Number
8/15/64	12	9	Maybelline Memphis and Maybelline written by Chuck Berry	$5	Imperial 66056
10/31/64	9	11	Mountain of Love	$5	Imperial 66075
2/6/65	20	8	Midnight Special/	$5	Imperial 66087
2/20/65	76	4	Cupid	$5	Imperial 66112
6/5/65	7	11	Seventh Son written by blues great Willie Dixon	$5	Imperial 66133
10/2/65	26	9	Where Have All the Flowers Gone	$5	Imperial 66133
12/18/65	35	8	Under Your Spell Again	$5	Imperial 66144
3/19/66	3	11	Secret Agent Man from the TV series of the same title	$5	Imperial 66159
6/11/66	19	8	(I Washed My Hands in) Muddy Water	$5	Imperial 66175
9/17/66	1(1)	15	Poor Side of Town	$5	Imperial 66205
2/4/67	3	11	Baby I Need Your Lovin'	$5	Imperial 66227
6/3/67	10	9	The Tracks of My Tears	$5	Imperial 66244
11/18/67	14	10	Summer Rain	$5	Imperial 66267
4/6/68	49	7	Look to Your Soul	$5	Imperial 66286
11/23/68	61	3	Right Relations	$5	Imperial 66335
2/22/69	55	6	These Are Not My People	$5	Imperial 66360
6/28/69	41	11	Muddy River	$5	Imperial 66386
10/25/69	89	4	One Woman	$5	Imperial 66418
5/9/70	51	8	Into the Mystic written by Van Morrison	$5	Imperial 66448
9/5/70	94	2	Fire and Rain	$5	Imperial 66453
2/5/77	96	4	Ashes and Sand	$4	Soul City 007
7/4/64	80	3	**Showmen, The** BUB [R] It Will Stand	$7	Imperial 66033
			Sunshine Company, The BUB/AC/LP		
7/15/67	50	10	Happy	$5	Imperial 66247
10/21/67	36	7	Back on the Street Again	$5	Imperial 66260

Date Charted	Peak Position	Weeks Charted	Artist & Record Title	1992 Mint Prices	Label & Number
2/10/68	56	5	Look, Here Comes the Sun	$5	Imperial 66280
			Swinging Blue Jeans, The BUB/LP		
3/7/64	24	8	Hippy Hippy Shake	$8	Imperial 66021
5/9/64	43	7	Good Golly Miss Molly	$6	Imperial 66030
8/1/64	97	2	You're No Good	$7	Imperial 66049
			Thomas, Irma R&B/BUB/LP		
3/28/64	17	12	Wish Someone Would Care	$5	Imperial 66013
7/4/64	52	6	Anyone Who Knows What Love Is (Will Understand)	$5	Imperial 66041
11/7/64	98	2	Times Have Changed	$5	Imperial 66069
12/19/64	63	8	He's My Guy	$5	Imperial 66080

Soul City

Date Charted	Peak Position	Weeks Charted	Artist & Record Title	1992 Mint Prices	Label & Number
			5th Dimension, The R&B/BUB/AC/LP		
1/14/67	16	10	Go Where You Wanna Go	$5	Soul City 753
4/29/67	45	6	Another Day, Another Heartache	$5	Soul City 755
6/3/67	7	12	Up-Up and Away	$5	Soul City 756
			above 3 produced by Johnny Rivers (Soul City is his own label)		
11/4/67	34	7	Paper Cup	$5	Soul City 760
2/3/68	29	9	Carpet Man	$5	Soul City 762
6/1/68	3	16	Stoned Soul Picnic	$5	Soul City 766
9/28/68	13	10	Sweet Blindness	$5	Soul City 768
12/21/68	25	9	California Soul	$5	Soul City 770
3/8/69	1(6)	17	Aquarius/Let the Sunshine In from the Broadway rock musical *Hair*	$5	Soul City 772
7/19/69	20	10	Workin' on a Groovy Thing written by Neil Sedaka	$5	Soul City 776
9/27/69	1(3)	15	Wedding Bell Blues	$5	Soul City 779
1/3/70	21	9	Blowing Away	$5	Soul City 780
4/4/70	43	8	The Girls' Song	$4	Soul City 781

Appendix 9

Date Charted	Peak Position	Weeks Charted	Artist & Record Title	1992 Mint Prices	Label & Number
			Wilson, Al R&B/BUB/LP		
8/17/68	27	10	The Snake	$5	Soul City 767
1/18/69	75	4	Poor Side of Town	$5	Soul City 771
8/23/69	67	7	Lodi	$5	Soul City 775
			above 3 produced by Johnny Rivers (owned Soul City Records)		
			Minit		
			Holiday, Jimmy BUB/R&B		
9/3/66	98	1	Baby I Love You	$6	Minit 32002
			Turner, Ike & Tina BUB/R&B/LP		
5/10/69	98	2	I'm Gonna Do All I Can (to Do Right by My Man)	$5	Minit 32060
3/7/70	57	8	Come Together	$4	Minit 32087
			Womack, Bobby R&B/BUB/LP		
8/17/68	52	13	Fly Me to the Moon	$5	Minit 32048
12/7/68	43	9	California Dreamin'	$5	Minit 32055
12/13/69	93	2	How I Miss You Baby	$5	Minit 32081
4/25/70	90	4	More Than I Can Stand	$5	Minit 32093
			Young Hearts R&B/BUB		
11/16/68	94	3	I've Got Love for My Baby	$5	Minit 32049
			Blue Note		
			Donaldson, Lou LP		
11/4/67	93	4	Alligator Bogaloo [I]	$5	Blue Note 1934
			McDuff, Brother Jack BUB/R&B/LP		
12/27/69	95	2	Theme from Electric Surfboard [I]	$5	Blue Note 1953
			Morgan, Lee LP		
12/19/64	81	4	The Sidewinder, Part 1 [I]	$5	Blue Note 1911
			Smith, Jimmy BUB/LP		
3/3/62	69	8	Midnight Special, Part 1 [I]	$6	Blue Note 1819
3/9/63	63	6	Back at the Chicken Shack, Part 1 [I]	$6	Blue Note 1877

Date Charted	Peak Position	Weeks Charted	Artist & Record Title		1992 Mint Prices	Label & Number
			aura			
			Knight, Sonny			
10/10/64	71	9	If You Want This Love		$5	aura 403
2/6/65	100	1	Love Me as Though There Were No Tomorrow		$5	aura 4505
			Pacific Jazz			
4/2/66	95	1	**Crusaders, The** R&B/BUB/AC/LP Uptight (Everything's Alright)	[I]	$5	Pacific Jazz 88125
10/1/66	99	2	**Holmes, Richard "Groove"** BUB/LP Secret Love	[I]	$5	Pacific Jazz 88130
			World Pacific			
5/16/70	62	8	**Fortunes, The** LP That Same Old Feeling		$4	World Pacific 77937
12/31/66	97	2	**Hardtimes, The** Fortune Teller		$6	World Pacific 77851
			Lind, Bob BUB/LP			
1/22/66	5	13	Elusive Butterfly		$5	World Pacific 77808
4/23/66	64	5	Remember the Rain/			
5/7/66	65	5	Truly Julie's Blues (I'll Be There)		$5	World Pacific 77822
7/25/70	56	9	**Robinson, Freddy** LP Black Fox	[I]	$4	World Pacific 88155
4/5/69	70	6	**Sarstedt, Peter** BUB Where Do You Go To (My Lovely)		$5	World Pacific 77911
1/22/66	65	6	**Shank, Bud** LP Michelle	[I]	$5	World Pacific 77814

APPENDIX 10

Top 100 Hits Listed by Month and Year

The following list is presented of every single to make *Billboard*'s Top 100 chart, segregated by label: Liberty, Dolton, Imperial, Minit, Soul City, and Pacific Jazz/World Pacific.

Liberty

Label #	Month/Year	Artist	Record Title
55006	11/55	London, Julie	Cry Me a River
55008	1/56	Alfi and Harry	The Trouble with Harry
55022	8/56	Patience & Prudence	Tonight You Belong to Me
55040	12/56	Patience & Prudence	Gonna Get Along Without Ya Now
55041	12/56	Patience & Prudence	The Money Tree
55056	3/57	Seville, David	Armen's Theme
55071	6/57	Cochran, Eddie	Sittin' in the Balcony
55079	9/57	Ward, Billy, and His Dominoes	Star Dust
55087	9/57	Seville, David	Gotta Get to Your House
55099	9/57	Cochran, Eddie	Drive-in Show
55102	10/57	Ward, Billy, and His Dominoes	Deep Purple
55123	3/58	Rayburn, Margie	I'm Available
55132	4/58	Cochran, Eddie	Jeannie Jeannie Jeannie
55136	6/58	Seville, David	Witch Doctor
55140	7/58	Ward, Billy, and His Dominoes	Jennie Lee
55144	8/58	Seville, David	The Bird on My Head
55153	8/58	Cochran, Eddie	Summertime Blues
55162	4/59	Seville, David	Little Brass Band
55166	11/58	Denny, Martin	Quiet Village
55168	12/58	Cochran, Eddie	C'mon Everybody
55177	3/59	Chipmunks, The	The Chipmunk Song
55179	2/59	Cochran, Eddie	Teenage Heaven
55193	5/59	Chipmunks, The	Alvin's Harmonica
55199	7/59	Seville, David	Judy
55200	7/59	Denny, Martin	Martinique
55203	8/59	Chipmunks, The	Ragtime Cowboy Joe
55208	8/59	Cochran, Eddie	Somethin' Else
55212	10/59	Vee, Bobby	Suzie Baby
55233	2/60	Denny, Martin	The Enchanted Sea
55234	4/60	Chipmunks, The	Alvin's Orchestra
		Vee, Bobby	What Do You Want?

Appendix 10

Label #	Month/Year	Artist	Record Title
55244	5/60	Joiner, Arkansas, Junior High School Band	National City
55245	8/60	Statues, The	Blue Velvet
55250	12/61	Chipmunks, The	Alvin's Harmonica
55250	12/59	Chipmunks, The	The Chipmunk Song
55250	12/61	Chipmunks, The	The Chipmunk Song
55258	7/60	Burnette, Johnny	Dreamin'
55261	6/60	Miles, Garry	Look for a Star
55270	8/60	Vee, Bobby	Devil or Angel
55270	9/60	Vee, Bobby	Since I Met You Baby
55277	9/60	Chipmunks, The	Alvin for President
55282	10/60	Slatkin, Felix	Theme from the Sundowners
55284	10/60	Bud and Travis	Ballad of the Alamo
55285	10/60	Burnette, Johnny	You're Sixteen
55287	11/60	Vee, Bobby	Rubber Ball
55289	12/60	Chipmunks, The	Rudolph the Red Nosed Reindeer
55289	12/61	Chipmunks, The	Rudolph the Red Nosed Reindeer
55290	12/61	Knox, Buddy	Lovey Dovey
55296	2/61	Vee, Bobby	More Than I Can Say
55296	2/61	Vee, Bobby	Stayin' In
55298	2/61	Burnette, Johnny	Little Boy Sad
55305	3/61	Knox, Buddy	Ling-Ting-Tong
55308	3/61	McDaniels, Gene	A Hundred Pounds of Clay
55318	5/61	Burnette, Johnny	Big Big World
55320	4/61	Rollers, The	The Continental Walk
55325	5/61	Vee, Bobby	How Many Tears
55343	7/61	Yuro, Timi	Hurt
55343	10/61	Yuro, Timi	I Apologize
55344	7/61	McDaniels, Gene	A Tear
55350	7/61	Dick and Deedee	The Mountain's High
55353	9/61	Shondell, Troy	This Time
55354	8/61	Vee, Bobby	Take Good Care of My Baby
55359	10/61	Hawley, Deane	Pocketful of Rainbows
55371	10/61	McDaniels, Gene	Tower of Strength

Label #	Month/Year	Artist	Record Title
55374	11/61	Zentner, Si	Up a Lazy River
55375	12/61	Yuro, Timi	She Really Loves You
55375	11/61	Yuro, Timi	Smile
55379	10/61	Burnette, Johnny	God, Country and My Baby
55388	11/61	Vee, Bobby	Run to Him
55388	11/61	Vee, Bobby	Walkin' with My Angel
55397	1/62	Jan & Dean	A Sunday Kind of Love
55398	1/62	Shondell, Troy	Island in the Sky
55398	12/61	Shondell, Troy	Tears from an Angel
55401	1/62	Marketts, The	Surfer's Stomp
55405	1/62	McDaniels, Gene	Chip Chip
55410	2/62	Yuro, Timi	Let Me Call You Sweetheart
55412	3/62	Dick and Deedee	Tell Me
55419	2/62	Vee, Bobby	I Can't Say Goodbye
55419	2/62	Vee, Bobby	Please Don't Ask About Barbara
55424	3/62	Chipmunks, The	The Alvin Twist
55427	8/62	Rivingtons, The	Papa-Oom-Mow-Mow
55436	4/62	Brennan, Walter	Old Rivers
55443	4/62	Marketts, The	Balboa Blue
55444	4/62	McDaniels, Gene	Funny
55451	5/62	Vee, Bobby	Sharing You
55454	5/62	Jan & Dean	Tennessee
55469	7/62	Yuro, Timi	What's a Matter Baby (Is It Hurting You)
55470	7/62	Denny, Martin	A Taste of Honey
55477	8/62	Brennan, Walter	Houdini
55479	9/62	Vee, Bobby	Punish Her
55479	9/62	Vee, Bobby	Someday (When I'm Gone from You)
55480	8/62	McDaniels, Gene	Point of No Return
55508	10/62	Brennan, Walter	Mama Sang a Song
55510	11/62	McDaniels, Gene	Spanish Lace
55519	12/62	Yuro, Timi	The Love of a Boy
55521	12/62	Vee, Bobby	The Night Has a Thousand Eyes

Appendix 10 593

Label #	Month/Year	Artist	Record Title
55526	2/63	DeShannon, Jackie	Faded Love
55530	3/63	Vee, Bobby	Charms
55531	2/63	Jan & Dean	Linda
55552	3/63	Yuro, Timi	Insult to Injury
55553	3/63	Rivingtons, The	The Bird's the Word
55563	5/63	DeShannon, Jackie	Needles and Pins
55580	6/63	Jan & Dean	Surf City
55581	6/63	Vee, Bobby	A Letter from Betty
55581	6/63	Vee, Bobby	Be True to Yourself
55587	7/63	Yuro, Timi	Make the World Go Away
55597	8/63	McDaniels, Gene	It's a Lonely Town (Lonely Without You)
55604	9/63	Dey, Tracey	Teenage Cleopatra
55613	9/63	Jan & Dean	Honolulu Lulu
55634	10/63	Yuro, Timi	Gotta Travel On
55636	12/63	Vee, Bobby	Never Love a Robin
55636	11/63	Vee, Bobby	Yesterday and You (Armen's Theme)
55641	12/63	Jan & Dean	Drag City
55645	1/64	DeShannon, Jackie	When You Walk in the Room
55654	1/64	Vee, Bobby	Stranger in Your Arms
55670	2/64	Vee, Bobby	I'll Make You Mine
55672	3/64	Jan & Dean	Dead Man's Curve
55672	3/64	Jan & Dean	The New Girl in School
55689	5/64	Searchers, The	Sugar and Spice
55700	5/64	Vee, Bobby	Hickory, Dick and Doc
55704	6/64	Jan & Dean	The Little Old Lady (from Pasadena)
55724	9/64	Jan & Dean	Ride the Wild Surf
55724	10/64	Jan & Dean	The Anaheim, Azusa & Cucamonga Sewing Circle, Book Review and Timing Association
55727	10/64	Jan & Dean	Sidewalk Surfin'
55745	11/64	Monro, Matt	Walk Away

Label #	Month/Year	Artist	Record Title
55751	12/64	Vee, Bobby	(There'll Come a Day When) Ev'ry Little Bit Hurts
55751	12/64	Vee, Bobby	Pretend You Don't See Her
55756	1/65	Lewis, Gary, and the Playboys	This Diamond Ring
55757	2/65	Proby, P. J.	Somewhere
55761	2/65	Vee, Bobby	Cross My Heart
55766	3/65	Jan & Dean	(Here They Come) From All Over the World
55778	4/65	Lewis, Gary, and the Playboys	Count Me In
55790	5/65	Vee, Bobby	Keep On Trying
55792	5/65	Jan & Dean	You Really Know How to Hurt a Guy
55809	7/65	Lewis, Gary, and the Playboys	Save Your Heart for Me
55818	9/65	Lewis, Gary, and the Playboys	Everybody Loves a Clown
55829	9/65	Gants, The	Road Runner
55833	10/65	Jan & Dean	I Found a Girl
55836	12/65	T-Bones, The	No Matter What Shape (Your Stomach's In)
55846	12/65	Lewis, Gary, and the Playboys	She's Just My Style
55860	2/66	Jan & Dean	Batman
55865	3/66	Lewis, Gary, and the Playboys	Sure Gonna Miss Her
55866	5/66	Shannon, Del	The Big Hurt
55867	3/66	T-Bones, The	Sippin' 'n' Chippin'
55877	7/66	Vee, Bobby	Look at Me Girl
55880	5/66	Lewis, Gary, and the Playboys	Green Grass
55886	6/66	Jan & Dean	Popsicle
55898	7/66	Lewis, Gary, and the Playboys	My Heart's Symphony
55905	9/66	Jan & Dean	Fiddle Around
55914	10/66	Lewis, Gary, and the Playboys	(You Don't Have to) Paint Me a Picture
55922	1/67	Sharpe, Mike	Spooky
55933	12/66	Lewis, Gary, and the Playboys	Where Will the Words Come From
55936	1/67	Proby, P. J.	Niki Hoeky
55948	4/67	Nitty Gritty Dirt Band	Buy for Me the Rain
55949	3/67	Lewis, Gary, and the Playboys	The Loser (with a Broken Heart)

Appendix 10

Label #	Month/Year	Artist	Record Title
55964	7/67	Vee, Bobby	Come Back When You Grow Up
55971	5/67	Lewis, Gary, and the Playboys	Girls in Love
55972	6/67	Mann, Johnny, Singers	Up-Up and Away
55985	8/67	Lewis, Gary, and the Playboys	Jill
55986	9/67	Carr, Vikki	It Must Be Him
55996	11/67	Lundberg, Victor	An Open Letter to My Teenage Son
56009	11/67	Vee, Bobby	Beautiful People
56012	12/67	Carr, Vikki	The Lesson
56014	2/68	Vee, Bobby	Maybe Just Today
56026	3/68	Carr, Vikki	She'll Be There
56033	3/68	Vee, Bobby	Your Heart Is Free Just Like the Wind
56037	4/68	Lewis, Gary, and the Playboys	My Girl/Hey Girl
56038	6/68	Canned Heat	Sealed with a Kiss
56057	8/68	Vee, Bobby	On the Road Again
56068	8/68	Ventures, The	Do What You Gotta Do
56077	3/69	Canned Heat	Hawaii Five-O
56080	12/68	Vee, Bobby	Going Up the Country
	12/68		I'm into Lookin' for Someone to Love Me
56087	1/69	Burnette, Dorsey	The Greatest Love
56092	5/69	Carr, Vikki	With Pen in Hand
56093	4/69	Lewis, Gary, and the Playboys	Rhythm of the Rain
56097	3/69	Canned Heat	Time Was
56115	6/69	Ventures, The	Theme from "A Summer Place"
56124	8/69	Vee, Bobby	Let's Call It a Day Girl
56132	10/69	Carr, Vikki	Eternity
56150	1/70	Dana, Vic	If I Never Knew Your Name
56151	10/70	Canned Heat	Let's Work Together
56163	5/70	Dana, Vic	Red Red Wine
56177	5/70	Turner, Ike & Tina	I Want to Take You Higher
56183	8/70	Sugarloaf	Green-Eyed Lady
56187	8/70	DeShannon, Jackie	It's So Nice
56190	9/70	Fantasy	Stoned Cowboy

Label #	Month/Year	Artist	Record Title
56197	11/70	Nitty Gritty Dirt Band	Mr. Bojangles
56200	10/70	Classics IV	Where Did All the Good Times Go
56208	11/70	Vee, Bobby	Sweet Sweetheart
56216	1/71	Turner, Ike & Tina	Proud Mary
56218	3/71	Sugarloaf	Tongue in Cheek

Imperial

Label #	Month/Year	Artist	Record Title
66003	11/63	Alaimo, Steve	Gotta Lotta Love
66004	11/63	Nelson, Ricky	Today's Teardrops
66013	3/64	Thomas, Irma	Wish Someone Would Care
66017	3/64	Nelson, Ricky	Congratulations
66021	3/64	Swinging Blue Jeans, The	Hippy Hippy Shake
66026	5/64	Hollies, The	Just One Look
66027	5/64	Kramer, Billy J., with the Dakotas	Bad to Me
66027	4/64	Kramer, Billy J., with the Dakotas	Little Children
66030	5/64	Swinging Blue Jeans, The	Good Golly Miss Molly
66032	5/64	Rivers, Johnny	Memphis
66033	7/64	Showmen, The	It Will Stand
66041	7/64	Thomas, Irma	Anyone Who Knows What Love Is (Will Understand)
66048	7/64	Kramer, Billy J., with the Dakotas	I'll Keep You Satisfied
66049	8/64	Swinging Blue Jeans, The	You're No Good
66051	8/64	Kramer, Billy J., with the Dakotas	From a Window
66056	8/64	Rivers, Johnny	Maybelline
66060	9/64	Nelson, Sandy	Teen Beat '65
66069	11/64	Thomas, Irma	Times Have Changed
66075	10/64	Rivers, Johnny	Mountain of Love
66080	12/64	Thomas, Irma	He's My Guy
66085	2/65	Kramer, Billy J., with the Dakotas	It's Gotta Last Forever
66086	2/65	Fame, Georgie	Yeh, Yeh

Appendix 10 597

Label #	Month/Year	Artist	Record Title
66087	2/65	Rivers, Johnny	Cupid
66087	2/65	Rivers, Johnny	Midnight Special
66094	4/65	McCracklin, Jimmy	Every Night, Every Day
66102	5/65	O'Jays, The	Lipstick Traces (on a Cigarette)
66104	5/65	Fame, Georgie	In the Meantime
66110	5/65	DeShannon, Jackie	What the World Needs Now Is Love
66112	6/65	Rivers, Johnny	Seventh Son
66113	6/65	Carter, Mel	Hold Me, Thrill Me, Kiss Me
66114	7/65	Cher	All I Really Want to Do
66115	6/65	Kramer, Billy J., with the Dakotas	Trains and Boats and Planes
66121	8/65	O'Jays, The	I've Cried My Last Tear
66123	11/65	Haywood, Leon	She's with Her Other Love
66129	10/65	McCracklin, Jimmy	Think
66132	10/65	DeShannon, Jackie	A Lifetime of Loneliness
66133	10/65	Rivers, Johnny	Where Have All the Flowers Gone
66134	11/65	Hollies, The	Look Through Any Window
66136	10/65	Cher	Where Do You Go
66138	10/65	Carter, Mel	(All of a Sudden) My Heart Sings
66144	12/65	Rivers, Johnny	Under Your Spell Again
66147	1/66	McCracklin, Jimmy	My Answer
66148	1/66	Carter, Mel	Love Is All We Need
66158	3/66	Hollies, The	I Can't Let Go
66159	3/66	Rivers, Johnny	Secret Agent Man
66160	3/66	Cher	Bang Bang (My Baby Shot Me Down)
66165	4/66	Carter, Mel	Band of Gold
66171	5/66	DeShannon, Jackie	Come and Get Me
66175	6/66	Rivers, Johnny	(I Washed My Hands in) Muddy Water
66183	7/66	Carter, Mel	You You You
66186	7/66	Hollies, The	Bus Stop
66189	8/66	Fame, Georgie	Get Away
66192	7/66	Cher	Alfie
66197	10/66	O'Jays, The	Stand in for Love

Label #	Month/Year	Artist	Record Title
66202	9/66	DeShannon, Jackie	I Can Make It with You
66205	9/66	Rivers, Johnny	Poor Side of Town
66208	10/66	Carter, Mel	Take Good Care of Her
66214	10/66	Hollies, The	Stop Stop Stop
66216	12/66	Baby Ray	There's Something on Your Mind
66217	11/66	Cher	Behind the Door
66227	2/67	Rivers, Johnny	Baby I Need Your Lovin'
66231	3/67	Hollies, The	On a Carousel
66240	6/67	Hollies, The	Pay You Back with Interest
66243	6/67	Love Generation, The	Groovy Summertime
66244	6/67	Rivers, Johnny	The Tracks of My Tears
66247	7/67	Sunshine Company, The	Happy
66252	9/67	Cher	Hey Joe
66258	9/67	Hollies, The	Just One Look
66259	12/67	Classics IV	Spooky
66260	10/67	Sunshine Company, The	Back on the Street Again
66261	10/67	Cher	You Better Sit Down Kids
66267	11/67	Rivers, Johnny	Summer Rain
66270	1/68	Dee, Dave; Dozy, Beaky, Mick and Tich	Zabadak
66280	2/68	Sunshine Company, The	Look, Here Comes the Sun
66286	4/68	Rivers, Johnny	Look to Your Soul
66293	5/68	Classics IV	Soul Train
66310	8/68	Love Generation, The	Montage from How Sweet It Is (I Know That You Know)
66313	8/68	DeShannon, Jackie	The Weight
66328	10/68	Classics IV	Stormy
66335	11/68	Rivers, Johnny	Right Relations
66352	2/69	Classics IV	Traces
66360	2/69	Rivers, Johnny	These Are Not My People
66378	5/69	Classics IV	Everyday with You Girl
66385	6/69	DeShannon, Jackie	Put a Little Love in Your Heart
66386	6/69	Rivers, Johnny	Muddy River

Appendix 10

66393	8/69	Classics IV	Change of Heart
66405	10/69	Frost, Thomas & Richard	She's Got Love
66418	10/69	Rivers, Johnny	One Woman
66419	11/69	DeShannon, Jackie	Love Will Find a Way
66424	11/69	Classics IV	Midnight
66438	3/70	DeShannon, Jackie	Brighton Hill
66439	3/70	Classics IV	The Funniest Thing
66448	5/70	Rivers, Johnny	Into the Mystic
66452	5/70	DeShannon, Jackie	You Keep Me Hangin' On/Hurt So Bad
66453	9/70	Rivers, Johnny	Fire and Rain

Minit

Label #	Month/Year	Artist	Record Title
32002	9/66	Holiday, Jimmy	Baby I Love You
32048	8/68	Womack, Bobby	Fly Me to the Moon
32049	11/68	Young Hearts	I've Got Love for My Baby
32055	12/68	Womack, Bobby	California Dreamin'
32060	5/69	Turner, Ike & Tina	I'm Gonna Do All I Can (to Do Right by My Man)
32081	12/69	Womack, Bobby	How I Miss You Baby
32087	3/70	Turner, Ike & Tina	Come Together
32093	4/70	Womack, Bobby	More Than I Can Stand
607	3/60	Hill, Jessie	Ooh Poo Pah Doo—Part II
611	7/60	Hill, Jessie	Whip It on Me
623	3/61	K-Doe, Ernie	Mother-in-Law
627	6/61	K-Doe, Ernie	Te-Ta-Te-Ta-Ta
632	11/61	Showmen, The	It Will Stand
634	11/61	K-Doe, Ernie	A Certain Girl
634	11/61	K-Doe, Ernie	I Cried My Last Tear
641	2/62	K-Doe, Ernie	Popeye Joe
644	5/62	Spellman, Benny	Lipstick Traces (on a Cigarette)

Soul City

Label #	Month/Year	Artist	Record Title
007	2/77	Rivers, Johnny	Ashes and Sand
753	1/67	5th Dimension, The	Go Where You Wanna Go
755	4/67	5th Dimension, The	Another Day, Another Heartache
756	6/67	5th Dimension, The	Up-Up and Away
760	11/67	5th Dimension, The	Paper Cup
762	2/68	5th Dimension, The	Carpet Man
766	6/68	5th Dimension, The	Stoned Soul Picnic
767	8/68	Wilson, Al	The Snake
768	9/68	5th Dimension, The	Sweet Blindness
770	12/68	5th Dimension, The	California Soul
771	1/69	Wilson, Al	Poor Side of Town
772	3/69	5th Dimension, The	Aquarius/Let the Sunshine In
775	8/69	Wilson, Al	Lodi
776	7/69	5th Dimension, The	Workin' on a Groovy Thing
779	9/69	5th Dimension, The	Wedding Bell Blues
780	1/70	5th Dimension, The	Blowing Away
781	4/70	5th Dimension, The	The Girls' Song

Pacific Jazz/World Pacific

Label #	Label #	Month/Year	Artist	Record Title
Pacific Jazz	88125	4/66	Crusaders, The	Uptight (Everything's Alright)
Pacific Jazz	88130	10/66	Holmes, Richard "Groove"	Secret Love
Pacific Jazz	88155	7/70	Robinson, Freddy	Black Fox
World Pacific	77808	1/66	Lind, Bob	Elusive Butterfly
World Pacific	77814	1/66	Shank, Bud	Michelle
World Pacific	77822	4/66	Lind, Bob	Remember the Rain
World Pacific	77822	5/66	Lind, Bob	Truly Julie's Blues (I'll Be There)
World Pacific	77851	12/66	Hardtimes, The	Fortune Teller
World Pacific	77911	4/69	Sarstedt, Peter	Where Do You Go To (My Lovely)
World Pacific	77937	5/70	Fortunes, The	That Same Old Feeling

Appendix 10

aura

Label #	Month/Year	Artist	Record Title
403	10/64	Knight, Sonny	If You Want This Love
4505	2/65	Knight, Sonny	Love Me as Though There Were No Tomorrow

Blue Note

Label #	Month/Year	Artist	Record Title
1819	3/62	Smith, Jimmy	Midnight Special, Part 1
1877	3/63	Smith, Jimmy	Back at the Chicken Shack, Part 1
1911	12/64	Morgan, Lee	The Sidewinder, Part 1
1934	11/67	Donaldson, Lou	Alligator Bogaloo
1953	12/69	McDuff, Brother Jack	Theme from Electric Surfboard

Dolphin

Label #	Month/Year	Artist	Record Title
1	3/59	Fleetwoods, The	Come Softly to Me

Dolton

Label #	Month/Year	Artist	Record Title
3	5/59	Fleetwoods, The	Graduation's Here
5	9/59	Fleetwoods, The	Mr. Blue
5	10/59	Fleetwoods, The	You Mean Everything to Me
15	2/60	Fleetwoods, The	Outside My Window
22	5/60	Fleetwoods, The	Runaround
25	7/60	Ventures, The	Walk – Don't Run
28	10/60	Ventures, The	Perfidia
32	1/61	Ventures, The	Ram-Bunk-Shush

Label #	Month/Year	Artist	Record Title
40	4/61	Fleetwoods, The	Tragedy
45	9/61	Fleetwoods, The	(He's) The Great Impostor
62	10/62	Fleetwoods, The	Lovers by Night, Strangers by Day
75	6/63	Fleetwoods, The	Goodnight My Love
92	3/64	Dana, Vic	Shangri-La
96	7/64	Ventures, The	Walk – Don't Run '64
10	12/59	Guitar, Bonnie	Candy Apple Red
16	2/60	Frantics, The	Werewolf
2	5/59	Frantics, The	Straight Flush
27	10/60	Fleetwoods, The	The Last One to Know
300	10/64	Ventures, The	Slaughter on Tenth Avenue
303	1/65	Ventures, The	Diamond Head
304	2/65	Dana, Vic	Red Roses for a Blue Lady
305	5/65	Dana, Vic	Bring a Little Sunshine (to My Heart)
309	8/65	Dana, Vic	Moonlight and Roses (Bring Mem'ries of You)
313	12/65	Dana, Vic	Crystal Chandelier
316	2/66	Ventures, The	Secret Agent Man
319	5/66	Dana, Vic	I Love You Drops
322	8/66	Dana, Vic	A Million and One
4	6/59	Little Bill and The Bluenotes	I Love an Angel
41	4/61	Ventures, The	Lullaby of the Leaves
44	8/61	Ventures, The	(Theme from) Silver City
47	10/61	Ventures, The	Blue Moon
48	11/61	Dana, Vic	Little Altar Boy
51	3/62	Dana, Vic	I Will
57	6/62	Miniature Men, The	Baby Elephant Walk
6	9/59	Frantics, The	Fog Cutter
60	8/62	Ventures, The	Lolita Ya-Ya
67	12/62	Ventures, The	The 2,000 Pound Bee (Part 2)
73	5/63	Dana, Vic	Danger
81	8/63	Dana, Vic	More
95	7/64	Dana, Vic	Love Is All We Need
99	10/64	Dana, Vic	Garden in the Rain

APPENDIX 11

Singles Discography

A 45-rpm discography is presented for the following Liberty labels: Liberty, Dolton, Imperial, Freedom, Soul City, Pacific Jazz/World Pacific, Demon, University, Robbee, Minit, aura, and Blue Note. Reissue discographies are then presented for Liberty and Imperial.

Liberty

Label #	Artist	Record Title
55001	Lionel Newman	The Girl Upstairs / Conquest
55002	Bud Harvey	In Time / Hands Off
55003	Mary Meade	French Flamingo / Voulez Vous
55004	Lionel Newman Orchestra	Adios Argentina / More Than Wonderful
55005	Bill Shirley	Sometime / Devil's Keeping Busy
55006	Julie London	Cry Me a River / S'Wonderful
55007	Johnny Tyler	Heads Up / One Way Street
55008	Alfi & Harry	The Trouble with Harry / Little Beauty
55009	Julie London	Baby, Baby, All the Time / Shadow Woman

1955
1956

Label #	Artist	Record Title
55010	Artie Wayne	How Do I Love You / Che Si Dice (Wha-Da-Ya-Say)
55011	Hi-Fi's	Bridey Murphy Was Her Name / Easter Lilies
55012	Rock Murphy	Begin the Beguine / Shortnin' Bread Boogie
55013	Ross Bagdasarian	The Bold and the Brave / See a Teardrop Fall
55014	Ken Curtis	Wedding Day / Cottonwood
55015	Holly Twins	It's Easy / Take Me Back

Label #	Artist	Record Title
55016	Alfi & Harry	Persian on Excursion / Word Game Song
55017	Hi-Fi's	Within My Heart / Lonesome Road
55018	Nellie Lutcher	Blue Skies / You Made Me Love You
55019	Rod McKuen	Rock Island Line / Head Like a Rock
55020	Denise Lor	Hurt Me / That's the Way I Feel
55021	Artie Wayne	Angel / Golden Earrings
55022	Patience & Prudence	Tonight You Belong to Me / A Smile & a Ribbon
55023	Hi-Fi's	Somebody's Gotta Lose / Lonesome Road
55024	Russ Arno	Believe in Love / You'll Never Know
55025	Julie London	Lonely Girl / September in the Rain
55026	Denise Lor	With Every Breath I Take / Claim to Fame
55027	Nellie Lutcher	All of a Sudden / Have You Ever Been Lonely
55028	Jimmy Braislin	My Old Hammer / Maverick
55029	Russ Arno	How Deep Is the Ocean / Everyday of My Life
55030	Steve Rowland	Flat Wheel Train / How Many Miles
55031	Duke Mitchell	Be Mine Tonight / It's Too Soon to Know
55032	Julie London	Now Baby Now / Tall Boy
55033	Robie Lester	With You Where You Are / Listen to the Wind
55034	Rod McKuen	Happy Is a Boy Named Me / Repeat After Me
55035	Abbey Lincoln	I Didn't Say Yes (I Didn't Say No) / A Lonesome Cup of Coffee
55036	Happy Pierre	My Man / Eleanor
55037	Hi-Fi's	Dodie / The Last Wagon
55038	Meg Myles	Thirteen Men / Language of Love
55039	Pete King Orchestra	Sixth Finger Tune / Follow the Leader
55040	Patience & Prudence	Gonna Get Along Without You Now / The Money Tree
55041	David Seville	Armen's Theme / Carousel in Rome

Appendix 11

Label #	Artist	Record Title
55042	Dominic Frontiere	Uno Mas
		Jett Rink
55043	Margie Rayburn	Take a Gamble on Love
		Every Minute of the Day
55044	Frank Gorshin	The True Story of Jesse James
		Poor Jesse
55045	Henry Mancini	(Main Theme from) Four Girls in Town
		Cha Cha Cha for Gia
55046	Jones Boys	Anastasia
		All This Is Home
55047	Denise Lor	This Much I Know
		If I See My Love
55048	Holly Twins	I Want Elvis for Christmas
		The Tender Age

1956
1957

Label #	Artist	Record Title
55049	Rita Montgomery/Choralen	I Believe in Santa Claus
		Many, Many Christmases Ago
55050	George Hale/	Pray for Peace
	Johnny Mann Singers	Say Yes to Life
55051	Donna Fuller	Dusky January
		I'm Gettin' Sentimental Over You
55052	Julie London	The Meaning of the Blues
		Boy on a Dolphin
55053	Johnny Olenn	Candy Kisses
		My Idea of Love
55054	Mark McIntyre	Portrait of a Woman
		Viva Los Amantes
55055	David Seville	The Donkey and the Schoolboy
		The Gift
55056	Eddie Cochran	Sittin' in the Balcony
		Dark Lonely Street
55057	Buddy Whistler	If a Dream Could Make You Mine
		'Til Me Hat Floats
55058	Patience & Prudence	We Can't Sing Rhythm & Blues
		Dreamer's Bay
55059	Margie Rayburn	Walking Around in a Dream
		Teenage Heart Throb
55060	Henry Mancini	Hot Rod
		Big Band Rock & Roll
55061	Scott Davis	The World Is Mine
		I'm Thankful
55062	Jones Boys	The Little Hut
		Cherry Red
55063	Dick Kallman	Young and in Love
		I Cry to the Moon
55064	Joe Allegro	I Found a Dream
		Once in a Moment Rare
55065	Gloria March	Other Side of the Moon
		In a Small Forgotten Town

Appendixes

Label #	Artist	Record Title
55066	Alfi & Harry	Safari / Closing Time
55067	Harold Spina	Femmes Fatale / Carnival in Capri
55068	Chris Warfield	You Won't Forget Me / Three Dollar Orchid
55069	Robert Wagner	So Young / Almost 18
55070	Eddie Cochran	Mean When I'm Mad / One Kiss
55071	Billy Ward/Dominoes	Star Dust / Lucinda
55072	Margie Rayburn	Dreamy Eyes / Freight Train
55073	Ria Renay	Every Night / Stone in the Wind
55074	Lincoln Chase	You're Driving Me Crazy / Johnny Dlingeringding
55075	Pete King	An Affair to Remember / So Beats My Heart
55076	Julie London	It Had to Be You / Dark
55077	Four Grads	From This Moment On / You Make Me Feel So Young
55078	Buddy Whistler	Dear Mom and Dad / Keep Goin'
55079	David Seville	Gotta Get to Your House / Camel Rock
55080	Lincoln Chase	Naturally I'm Yours / Save the Last Dance for Me
55081	Myrna Fox	Go, Go, If You're Going to Go / You Can't Have Love
55082	Russ Arno	Got a Feelin' / Baby Come Home
55083	Robie Lester	Whispering Guitar / My Love and I
55084	Patience & Prudence	You Tattletale / Very Nice in Bali Bali
55085	Buddy Lee Stuart	I Can't Forget Last Night / I Miss Your Kissing
55086	Duke Mitchell	Crazy Heart / Careless Years
55087	Eddie Cochran	Drive-in Show / Am I Blue
55088	Margie Rayburn	Mississippi Moon / The Get Acquainted Waltz
55089	Martin Denny	Hong Kong Blues / Ah Me Furi
55090	Joyce Taylor	How Will I Know / Dear Diary
55091	Dick Kallman	7 Wonders of the World / My Heart's Desire

Appendix 11

Label #	Artist	Record Title
55092	Jeff Chandler	Half of My Heart / Hold Me
55093	Jones Boys	Out of My Dreams / Good Night
55094	Ricky Page	Wee Willie / I'm Old Enough Now
55095	Spencer-Hagen Orchestra	Tailspin / Bubble Bath
55096	Cornell Gunter	If We Should Meet Again / Neighborhood Dance
55097	Jana Lund	Johnny the Dreamer / Wishing Well
55098	Rick Marlow	Baby Come Home / Pretty Baby
55099	Billy Ward/Dominoes	Deep Purple / Do It Again
55100	Vicki Benet	After My Laughter Came Tears / Always in My Heart
55101	Anne Henry	My Kinda Guy / Facts
55102	Margie Rayburn	I'm Available / If You Were
55103	The Raves	Don't Bug Me Baby / If I Knew the Way
55104	Lee Ross	Big Man / Lies
55105	David Seville	Pretty Dark Eyes / Cecelia
55106	Jimmy Merritt	Have You Wondered Why / Heart Stealin' Darlin'
55107	Patience & Prudence	Over Here / Witchcraft
55108	Julie London	Saddle the Wind / I'd Like You for Christmas
55109	Vic Schoen	Marion / I Don't Wanna Roam
55110	Tony Mitchell	I Get Along Without You Very Well / Tell Me, Tell Me
55111	Billy Ward/Dominoes	My Proudest Possession / Someone Greater Than I
55112	Eddie Cochran	Twenty Flight Rock / Cradle Baby
55113	David Seville	Bagdad Express / Starlight Starbright
55114	Robert Wagner (Not Released)	About That Girl / Honeysuckle Rose
55115	Kathy Nelson	Santa Dear / Gimmie a Little Kiss Will Yuh
55116	The Doodlers	Sugar Plum / Smokey Pokey
55117	Al Casey	Willa Mae / She Gotta Shake

Label #	Artist	Record Title
55118	The Slades	Baby / You Mean Everything to Me

1957
1958

Label #	Artist	Record Title
55119	The Imperials	The Glory of Love / C'mon Tiger (Gimme a Growl)
55120	Margie Rayburn	Ooh What a Doll / Smoochin'
55121	Bobby Troup	Tangerine / Do Re Mi
55122	Emmy Noble	I Done Done / Little Willie
55123	Eddie Cochran	Jeanie, Jeanie, Jeanie / Pocketful of Hearts
55124	David Seville	Bonjour Tristesse / Dance from Bonjour Tristesse
55125	Patience & Prudence	Heavenly Angel / Little Wheel
55126	Billy Ward/Dominoes	Solitude / You Grow Sweeter as the Years Go By
55127	Lee Ross	Honey Bun (Sit Down on My Knee) / Candy Lips
55128	Sabres	Lulu / Your Face
55129	Bill & Doree Post	Homing Pigeon / Haw Jack, Gee Jules
55130	Margie Rayburn	Saving My Kisses / Boy-Girl
	(Not Released)	
55131	Julie London	Tell Me You're Home / The Freshmen
55132	David Seville	Witch Doctor / Don't Whistle at Me Baby
55133	Page Sisters	Dream Boy / If They Only Knew
55134	Margie Rayburn	I Would / Alright, but I Won't Be Easy
55135	Ray Johnson	Dizzy, Baby, Dizzy / Can't Stop Loving You
55136	Billy Ward/Dominoes	Jennie Lee / Music, Maestro, Please
55137	Barry Martin	Hello Love / When You're Smiling
55138	Eddie Cochran	Pretty Girl / Theresa
55139	Julie London	Voice in the Mirror / It's Easy
55140	David Seville	The Bird on My Head / Hey There Moon
55141	Lettermen	Hey, Big Brain / Guiro

Appendix 11

Label #	Artist	Record Title
55142	Andy Caldwell	Tell Me / She's So Fine
55143	Released as 55151	
55144	Eddie Cochran	Summertime Blues / Love Again
55145	Dick Banks	Dirty Dog / Too Late
55146	Terry Miller	Walkin' the Blues / Single 'n' Searchin'
55147	Playthings	Lipstick / Sittin'
55148	Jackie Dee	Buddy / Strolypso Dance
55149	John Anderson	Flamenco / Whistle Stop
55150	Leo Quica	Caliente / Oh Leola
55151	Tabby Calvin	Big Deal / Lost My Head
55152	John Leslie	Summer Rain / Guilty
55153	David Seville	Little Brass Band / Take Five
55154	Patience & Prudence	All I Do Is Dream of You / Your Careless Love
55155	Willie Nelson	Susie / No Dough
55156	Diane Lee	You Upset Me / L-O-V-E Love
55157	Julie London	Blue Moon / Man of the West
55158	Duke Mitchell	When I Grow Too Old to Dream / Be Mine Tonight
55159	Margie Rayburn	And He Told Me a Lie / To Each His Own
55160	Ned & Gary	I Bust My Seams / Lovin'
55161	Sandy Richards	They / How Long
55162	Martin Denny	Quiet Village / Llama Serenade
55163	David Seville	The Mountain / Mr. Grape
55164	Galen Denny	Gonna Build a Rocket / What Ya Gonna Do
55165	Davy Douglas	Party Crashin' / Rebel
55166	Eddie Cochran	C'mon Everybody / Don't Ever Let Me Go
55167	The Plaids	Hungry for Your Love / Chit-Chat
55168	David Seville/The Chipmunks	The Chipmunk Song / Almost Good

Label #   *Artist*   *Record Title*

Label #	Artist	Record Title
55169	Patience & Prudence	Golly Oh Gee
		Tom Thumb's Tune
55170	Jack & Jill	Young Marriage
		Dear Hearts and Gentle People
55171	Not Assigned	
55172	Not Assigned	
55173	Bee Bee Twins	Night Before Christmas
		Yuletide Tango

1958
1959

Label #	Artist	Record Title
55174	Margie Rayburn	Wait
		Make Me Queen Again
55175	Julie London	My Strange Affair
		Come On-a My House
55176	Jay Johnston	Early Autumn
		Spilled Milk
55177	Eddie Cochran	Teenage Heaven
		I Remember
55178	Wally Lewis	Every Day
		That's the Way It Goes
55179	David Seville/The Chipmunks	Alvin's Harmonica
		Mediocre
55180	Bobby Lonero	The Girl That I Marry
		Little Bit
55181	Billy Ward/Dominoes	Please Don't Say No
		Behave, Hula Girl
55182	Julie London	Something I Dreamed Last Night
		Must Be Catchin'
55183	Margie Rayburn	A Boy & a Girl
		Tell Him No
55184	Henry Mancini	POW
		Cha Cha for Gia
55185	Pam De Orian	Joey
		Pak-La-Va
55186	Vicki Benet	Heartstring Melody
		Love Me
55187	John Leslie	Devil with a Halo
		You Touch My Hand
55188	Fleetwoods	Come Softly to Me
		I Care So Much
55189	John Buzon Trio	Side Saddle
		Lizette
55190	Jack Grayson	Go Ahead On
		Just a Boy
55191	Spike Jones	The Late Late Late Movies Parts 1 and 2
55192	Steve & Donna Steve Venet	All the Better to Love You Ever Since the World Began
55193	Ross Bagdasarian	Judy
		Maria from Madrid

Label #	Artist	Record Title
55194	Jack Costanzo	Barracuda
		I Got a Bongo
55195	Margie Rayburn	Laddie-O
		Unexpectedly
55196	Wally Lewis	Sally Green
		Arms of Jo-Ann
55197	Arbogast & Ross	Chaos Part 1
		Chaos Part 2
55198	Invitations	Sweet Someone
		Invitation
55199	Martin Denny	Martinique
		Sake Rock
55200	David Seville	Ragtime Cowboy Joe
	The Chipmunks	Flip Side
55201	Ray Vernon	Pretty Blue Eyes
		My Sugar Plum
55202	Bud & Travis	Truly Do
		Bonsoir Dame
55203	Eddie Cochran	Somethin' Else
		Boll Weevil Song
55204	Si Zentner	Sock Hop
		Two Guitars
55205	John Leslie	That's the Story of My Life
		Only Forever
55206	Hylton Shane	Sandra My Love
		Poco Loco
55207	Mike Clifford	Should I
	Patience & Prudence	Whisper Whisper
55208	Bobby Vee/Shadows	Suzie Baby
		Flyin' High
55209	Joe London	Lonesome Whistle
		It Might Have Been
55210	Harry Sukman	Bess, You Is My Woman
		Crimson Kimono
55211	Wally Lewis	Lover Boy
		My Baby
55212	Martin Denny	The Enchanted Sea
		Stranger in Paradise
55213	Danny Davis	Beauty & the Beast
		Glory Bugle
55214	Gogi Grant	If and When
		I'll Never Smile Again
55215	George Garabedian Players	Art's Tune
		Artistry in Rhythm
55216	Julie London	Comin' Through the Rye
		Makin' Whoopee
55217	Eddie Cochran	Hallelujah I Love Her So
		Little Angel
55218	Dick D'Agostin/Swingers	I Let You Go
		It's You
55219	Mike Clifford	I Don't Know Why
		I'm Afraid to Say I Love You

Label #	Artist	Record Title
55220	Little Sisters	Are My Ears on Straight
		Little Star Came Down
55221	Bud & Travis	Poor Boy
		Jenny on a Horse
55222	Johnny Burnette	Settin' the Woods on Fire
		Kentucky Waltz
55223	Johnny O'Keefe	Own True Self
		She's My Baby
55224	Felix Slatkin	Hora Staccato
	(Not Released)	Original
55225	Ruth Christie	Let Me Love You
		My Mother's Eyes
55226	Charlie Baker	Star of Wonder
		You Crack Me Up
55227	Julie London	Cry Me a River
		It's a Blue World
55228	Johnny O'Keefe	She's My Baby
		It's Too Late
55229	Gogi Grant	Goin' Home
		All God's Children Got Shoes
55230	Martin Denny	Beyond the Reef
		Forever
55231	Gene McDaniels	In Times Like These
		Once Before
55232	Felix Slatkin	The Happy Hobo
		Turkish Bath
55233	David Seville/The Chipmunks	Alvin's Orchestra
		Copyright: 1960
55234	Bobby Vee	What Do You Want
		My Love Loves Me
55235	Bud & Travis	Cloudy Summer Afternoon
		E Labas
55236	Martin Denny	Frankie & Johnny
		Banana Choo Choo
55237	Bob Orbison	Sarah Lee
		Florecita
55238	Margie Rayburn	Magic Words
		Sentimental Journey
55239	Ross Bagdasarian	Lotta Bull
55240	Si Zentner Orchestra	The Swinging Eye
		Armen's Theme
55241	Gene Mumford	When Day Is Done
		I'm Getting Sentimental Over You
55242	Eddie Cochran	Cut Across Shorty
		Three Steps to Heaven
55243	Johnny Burnette	Don't Do It
		Patrick Henry
55244	Joiner, Arkansas, Junior High School Band	National City
		Big Ben
55245	The Statues	Blue Velvet
		Keep the Hall Light Burning
55246	David Seville/The Chipmunks	Sing a Goofy Song
		Coming 'Round the Mountain

Label #	Artist	Record Title
55247	Gee Nee Sterling	If You've Got the Money I've Got the Time
		Mama Don't Tell Me
55248	Warren Smith	I Don't Believe I'll Fall in Love Today
		Cave In
55249	Johnny Mann Singers	Sweet Georgia Brown
		Varsity Drag
55250	David Seville The Chipmunks	The Chipmunk Song Alvin's Harmonica

1959
1960

Label #	Artist	Record Title
55251	Bobby Vee	One Last Kiss
		Laurie
55252	Gogi Grant	I Never Meant to Fall in Love
		Stay Here with Me
55253	Spike Jones	Ah-1, Ah-2, Ah-Sunset Strip Parts 1 and 2
55254	Dick Noel	Jinglin' Jeans
		Sugar Beat
55255	Milky Ways	My Love
		Teenage Island
55256	Little Hymie	Hoochy Coo
		The Clock Rock
55257	Jack C. Smith	Honeysuckle Rose
		There'll Never Be
55258	Johnny Burnette	Dreamin'
		Cincinnati Fireball
55259	Bud & Travis	Come to the Dance
		Carmen Carmelia
55260	Tommy Duncan/Bob Wills	Heart to Heart Talk
		What's the Matter with the Mill
55261	Garry Miles	Look for a Star
		Afraid of Love
55262	Johnny O'Keefe	Take My Hand
		Don't You Know, Little Baby
55263	Cliff Gleaves	Long Black Hearse
		You and Your Kind
55264	Bob Wills/Tommy Duncan	Goodbye Liza Jane
		Image of Me
55265	Gene McDaniels	Green Door
		Facts of Life
55266	Le Garde Twins	Babysitter
		Where Can the Lovelight Be
55267	Ray Sanders	A World So Full of Love
		Little Bitty Tear
55268	Shirley Collie	My Charlie
		Didn't Work Out Did It
55269	Julie London	Time for Lovers
		In the Wee Small Hours of the Morning
55270	Bobby Vee	Devil or Angel
		Since I Met You Baby

Label #	Artist	Record Title
55271	Frankie & Johnny	Do You Love Me
		My First Love
55272	David Seville	Swanee River
		Witch Doctor
55273	Margie Rayburn	I Miss You Already
		Maid of Honor
55274	Gene Mumford	I Gotta Have My Baby Back
		Brazil
55275	Ross Bagdasarian	Lazy Lovers
		One Finger Waltz
55276	Joiner, Arkansas, Junior High School Band	Arkansas Traveler
		Hot Time in the Old Town
55277	David Seville/The Chipmunks	Alvin for President
		Sack Time
55278	Eddie Cochran	Lonely
		Sweetie Pie
55279	Garry Miles/The Statues	Wishing Well
		Dream Girl
55280	Floyd Tillman	It Just Tears Me Up
		The Song of Music
55281	Ben Sherwin	Have a Good Time
		Johnny Goofed
55282	Felix Slatkin	Theme from the Sundowners
		Gayther's Gone
55283	Martin Denny	Volcano
		Sugar Train
55284	Bud & Travis	Ballad of the Alamo
		The Green Leaves of Summer
55285	Johnny Burnette	You're Sixteen
		I Beg Your Pardon
55286	Gogi Grant	Two Lovers by the Sea
		In a Sentimental Mood
55287	Bobby Vee	Rubber Ball
		Everyday
55288	Jackie DeShannon	Lonely Girl
		Teach Me
55289	David Seville/The Chipmunks	Rudolph the Red-Nosed Reindeer
		Spain
55290	Buddy Knox	Lovey Dovey
		I Got You
55291	Shirley Collie	I'd Rather Hear Lies
		Sad Singin' and Slow Ridin'
55292	The Statues	White Christmas
		Jeannie with the Light Brown Hair
55293	Dick Lory	My Last Date
		Broken Hearted

1960
1961

Label #	Artist	Record Title
55294	Court Jesters	I'm Just a Country Boy
		Long Black Veil
55295	Vikings	Cliff Dwellers
		Choo Choo

Appendix 11

Label #	Artist	Record Title
55296	Bobby Vee	Stayin' In / More Than I Can Say
55297	Robin Dale	Incident at Shilo / Cry, Cry, Cry
55298	Johnny Burnette	Little Boy Sad / (I Go) Down to the River
55299	Felix Slatkin	It's Not Forever / My Own True Love
55300	Julie London	Evenin' / Send for Me
55301	Martin Denny	Volcano / My Tane (My Man)
55302	Warren Smith	Odds & Ends (Bits & Pieces) / A Whole Lot of Nothin'
55303	The Rollers	Bonneville / Got My Eye on You
55304	Ray Sanders	Lonelyville / I Haven't Gone Far Enough Yet
55305	Buddy Knox	Ling Ting Tong / The Kisses
55306	Dick Lory	Pain Is Here / You
55307	Billy Strange	Sadness Done Come / Where Your Arms Used to Be
55308	Gene McDaniels	A Hundred Pounds of Clay / Take a Chance on Love
55309	Julie London	Every Chance I Get / Sanctuary
55310	Doye O'Dell	Run, Thief, Run / Two Sides to Every Story
55311	Bob Wills/Tommy Duncan	After All / It May Be Too Late
55312	Scott Engel	Anything Will Do / Mr. Jones
55313	Suzanne and the Band-Aide	Unchained but Not Forgotten / You May Never Know
55314	David Seville	Freddy, Freddy / Oh Judge, Your Honor, Dear Sir, Sweetheart
55315	Sweetpea Johnson	Crawdad Scene / How Come My Dog Don't Growl at You
55316	Gogi Grant	Adrift on a Star / That One Kiss
55317	Spike Jones	Keystone Kapers / Silents Please
55318	Johnny Burnette	Big Big World / Ballad of the One Eyed Jacks
55319	Dick Lory	Hello Walls / City of Love
55320	The Rollers	The Continental Walk / I Want You So
55321	Andy/Live Wires	Maggie / You've Done It Again

Label #	Artist	Record Title
55322	Cornbread & Jerry	Lil' Ole Me
		Loco Moto
55323	Floyd Tillman	Whatever You Do
		The Record Goes 'Round
55324	Shirley Collie	Dime a Dozen
		Oh Yes, Darling
55325	Bobby Vee	How Many Tears
		Baby Face
55326	Felix Slatkin	Streets of Laredo
55327	Johnny Mann	East of the Sun
55328	Martin Denny	Scimitar
		My First Romance
55329	Felix Slatkin	Theme from "The Pleasure of Your Company"
		Street Scene
55330	Walter Vaughn	Sally Pearl
		Down on My Knees
55331	Bobby Vee	How Many Tears
		Bashful Bob
55332	Gents	Jumpin' the Line
		Why Do I Love Her
55333	Jack Costanzo	Route 66 Theme
		Baked City Theme
55334	Clyde Otis	In Old Madrid
		Poinciani
55335	Untouchables	You're on Top
		Lovely Dee
55336	Warren Smith	Call of the Wild
		Old Lonesome Feeling
55337	Julie London	My Darling, My Darling
		My Love, My Love
55338	Len Wyatt	This I Promise You
		With All My Heart
55339	Spinners	Till the End of Time
		Dream
55340	Gina Boyer	Promise Me Anything
		Say It from Your Heart
55341	Joiner, Arkansas, State College Band	Highland Rock
		Hop-Scotch
55342	Jackie DeShannon	Think About You
		Heaven Is Being with You
55343	Timi Yuro	Hurt
		I Apologize
55344	Gene McDaniels	A Tear
		She's Come Back
55345	Johnny Burnette	Girls
		I've Got a Lot of Things to Do
55346	Jimmy Meng	True and Faithful
		Don't Be Blue
55347	Doye O'Dell	Dreamboat, Still Afloat
		Lights in the Streets
55348	Ray Sanders	Walk Slow
		Two Hearts Are Broken

Appendix 11

Label #	Artist	Record Title
55349	Johnny Oliver	Mail Man, Where's My Check? You've Got to Reap What You Sow
55350	Dick & Deedee	The Mountain's High I Want Someone
55351	Dave Edwards	Sweet Sue Searching
55352	Ralph Emery	Hello Fool It's Not a Lot
55353	Troy Shondell	This Time Girl After Girl
55354	Bobby Vee	Take Good Care of My Baby Bashful Bob
55355	Johhny Mann Singers	Don't Love Me
55356	Earl Palmer	Honky Tonk New Orleans Medley
55357	Rollers	Bounce Teenager's Waltz
55358	Jackie DeShannon	Wish I Could Find a Boy I Won't Turn You Down
55359	Deane Hawley	Pocketful of Rainbows That Dream Could Never Be
55360	Jay Miller	Everything Will Be Alright Straight as an Arrow
55361	Warren Smith/Shirley Collie	Why Baby Why Why I'm Walking
55362	Billy Srange	Long Steel Road Soft Chains of Love
55363	The Statues	The Commandments of Love Love at First Sight
55364	Clyde Otis	High on a Cloud You Stepped Out of a Dream
55365	Betty O'Brien	Love, Oh! Love She'll Be Gone
55366	Buddy Knox	All by Myself Three Eyed Man
55367	P. J. Proby	Try to Forget Her There Stands the One
55368	Chord Spinners	Call Me Love Is a Many Splendored Thing
55369	Len Wyatt	I'll Never Question Your Love My Secret Emotion
55370	Wally Lewis	Streets of Berlin Walking in the Footsteps of a Fool
55371	Gene McDaniels	Tower of Strength The Secret
55372	Felix Slatkin	King of Kings Mandolin
55373	Ray Sanders	Don't Tell Nell When Love Forgets to Die
55374	Si Zentner	Shufflin' Blues Up a Lazy River

Label #	Artist	Record Title
55375	Timi Yuro	Smile
		She Really Loves You
55376	Dora Dee/Lora Lee	He Takes Good Care of Your Baby
		Daddy (Give Me Some Money Please)
55377	Johnny Burnette	Honestly I Do
		Fools Like Me
55378	Bob Wills/Tommy Duncan	Siesta
		I'm Crying My Heart Out
55379	Johnny Burnette	God, Country and My Baby
		Honestly I Do
55380	Dick St. John	Gonna Stick by You
		Sha-Ta
55381	Clyde Otis	Love Theme from "El Cid"
		May Your Blessings Be Many (Your Troubles Be Few)
55382	Dick & Deedee	Goodbye to Love
		Swing Low
55383	Ralph Emery	Legend of Sleepy Hollow
		I'll Take Good Care of Your Baby
55384	Martin Denny	Fandango
		Bonsoir Dame
55385	June Carter	The Heel
		If I Ever See Him Again
55386	Willie Nelson	Mr. Record Man
		Part Where I Cry
55387	Jackie DeShannon	Baby (When You Kiss Me)
		Ain't That Love
55388	Bobby Vee	Run to Him
		Walkin' with My Angel
55389	Eddie Cochran	Weekend
		Lonely
55390	Gina Boyer	Jim
		Written in Tears
55391	Shirley Collie	If I Live Long Enough
		Keeping My Fingers Crossed
55392	Crickets	I'm Feeling Better
		He's Old Enough to Know Better
55393	Raiders	Dardanella
		What Time Is It
55394	Obrey Wilson	Whipping Boy
		That's Where Lonesome Lives
55395	Billy Frazier	Let Me Walk You Home
		Wandering Wind
55396	Eddie Heywood	Dream of Olwen
		Good Earth
55397	Jan & Dean	A Sunday Kind of Love
		Poor Little Puppet
55398	Troy Shondell	Tears from an Angel
		Island in the Sky
55399	John Wayne	I Have Faith
		Walk with Him
55400	Timi Yuro/Johnnie Ray	I Believe
		A Mother's Love

Appendix 11 619

Label #	Artist	Record Title

1961
1962

55401	Mar-Kets	Surfer's Stomp
		Start
55402	Hank Cochran	Lonely Little Mansion
		Has Anybody Seen Me Lately
55403	Willie Nelson/Shirley Collie	Willingly
	Willie Nelson	Chain of Love
55404	Johnnie Ray	Lover's Question
		Nothing Goes Up Without Coming Down
55405	Gene McDaniels	Chip Chip
		Another Tear Falls
55406	Ray Sanders	Punish Me Tomorrow
		You're Welcome Anytime
55407	Gary Paxton	It's So Funny I Could Cry
		Teen Age Crush
55408	Si Zentner Orchestra	Hollywood Twist
		Nice 'n' Easy
55409	Warren Smith	Five Minutes of the Latest Blues
		Bad News Gets Around
55410	Timi Yuro	Let Me Call You Sweetheart
		Satan Never Sleeps
55411	Buddy Knox	Chi-Hua-Hua
		Open
55412	Dick & Deedee	Tell Me
		Will You Always Love Me
55413	Roosevelt Grier	Struttin' 'n' Twistin'
		Let the Cool Wind Blow
55414	Billy Strange	Life of Pretend
		I'm Still Trying
55415	Dick Lory	Handsome Guy
		Pain Is Here
55416	Johnny Burnette	Clown Shoes
		The Way I Am
55417	Billy Frazier	Let Me Walk You Home
		Give Us Back the Twist
55418	George McCurn	Your Daughter's Hand
		The Time Has Come
55419	Bobby Vee	Please Don't Ask About Barbara
		I Can't Say Goodbye
55420	Si Zentner	The Goulash (Shufflin' Blues)
		One Sided Promo
55421	Billy Barnes	Until
		To Prove My Love
55422	Jewel Brown	Ain't Givin' Up Nothing (If I Can't Get Somethin' from You)
		Looking Back
55423	Untouchables	Papa
		Medicine Man
55424	David Seville/The Chipmunks	The Alvin Twist
		I Wish I Could Speak French

620   Appendixes

Label #	Artist	Record Title
55425	Jackie DeShannon	The Prince
		I'll Drown in My Own Tears
55425	Jackie DeShannon	The Prince
		That's What Boys Are Made Of
55426	Martin Denny	Paradise Cove
		Secu Secu
55427	Rivingtons	Papa-Oom-Mow-Mow
		Deep Water
55428	Scott Engel	Anything Will Do
		Forever More
55429	Ralph Emery	Tough Top Cat
		Two Minutes to Live
55430	The La Bells	I Guess I'll Never Stop Loving You
		Sneaky Alligator
55431	Johnnie Ray	Cry
		Scotch & Soda
55432	Timi Yuro	I Know (I Love You)
		Count Everything
55433	Little Eddie	Look No More
	Johnny Mann Singers	Mine All Mine
55434	Betty O'Brien	Why Me
		Money Honey
55435	Kathy Kay	One Boy One Girl
		I'll Stop Being Jealous
55436	Walter Brennan	Old Rivers
	Johnny Mann Singers	The Epic Ride of John H. Glenn
55437	Si Zentner Orchestra	Mississippi Mud
	Johnny Mann Singers	Chattanooga Choo Choo
55438	Molly Bee	Just for the Record
		Lyin' Again
55439	Willie Nelson	Touch Me
		Where My House Lives
55440	June Carter	Mama Teach Me
		Money
55441	Crickets	Don't Ever Change
		I'm Not a Bad Boy
55442	Nick Noble	The Twelfth Dark Hour
		My Heart Came Running Back to You
55443	Marketts	Balboa Blue
		Stampede
55444	Gene McDaniels	Funny
		Chapel of Tears
55445	Troy Shondell	Just Because
		Na-No-No
55446	Deane Hawley	Queen of the Angels
		You Conquered Me
55447	Gina Boyer	I Don't Hurt Anymore
		Twilight Time
55448	Johnny Burnette	The Fool of the Year
		The Poorest Boy in Town
55449	Matt Monro	Softly as I Leave You
		Is There Anything I Can Do

Appendix 11

Label #	Artist	Record Title
55450	Bob Wills/Tommy Duncan	Oklahoma Gals
		Tomorrow I'll Cry
55451	Bobby Vee	Sharing You
		In My Baby's Eyes
55452	Chipmunks	America the Beautiful
		My Wild Irish Rose
55453	Roosevelt Grier	Your Has Been
		Mail Must Go Thru
55454	Jan & Dean	Tennessee
		Your Heart Has Changed Its Mind
55455	Gary Dean	The Right Kind of Love
		Old Standby
55456	Jay Miller	Big Daddy, You Gotta Go
		Providing
55457	Van McCoy	Follow Your Heart
		Lonely
55458	Jewel Brown	I Must Be Dreaming
		If You Have No Real Objection
55459	Bobby Sheen	How Many Nights—How Many Days
		How Can We Ever
55460	Shamrocks	Green Hills
		Lonely Island
55461	Hank Cochran	Sally Was a Good Old Girl
		The Picture Behind the Picture
55462	Ross Bagdasarian	Armen's Theme
		Russian Roulette
55463	Johnny Oliver	As Long as Time Goes On
		Love Is Best of All
55464	Jim Rust	Rusty's Theme
		The Whip
55465	Vikki Carr	I'll Walk the Rest of the Way
		Beside a Bridge
55466	Johnny Mann Singers	Summersong
		Mr. & Mrs. Millionaire
55467	Johnny Olenn	Candy Kisses
		Sally Let Your Bangs Hang Down
55468	Willie Nelson/Shirley Collie	You Dream About Me
	Willie Nelson	Is This My Destiny
55469	Timi Yuro	What's a Matter Baby
		Thirteenth Hour
55470	Martin Denny	A Taste of Honey
		Brighter Side
55471	Pat Carter	Lover Doll
		Sweet Young Girl
55472	Shirley Collie	No Wonder I Sing
		We're Going Back Together
55473	Buddy Knox	She's Gone
		There's Only Me
55474	Eddie Heywood	Land of Dreams
		Tango Americano
55475	Warren Smith	Book of Broken Hearts
		160 Pounds of Hurt

Label #	Artist	Record Title
55476	Si Zentner Orchestra	Boogie Woogie Maxine
		Shadrack
55477	Walter Brennan	The Old Kelly Place
		Houdini
55478	Dick & Deedee	All I Want
		Life's Just a Play
55479	Bobby Vee	Punish Her
		Someday
55480	Gene McDaniels	Point of No Return
		Warmer Than a Whisper
55481	Strangers	Toy Soldier
		Loco
55482	Johnny Southern	In the Middle of a Lonely, Lonely Night
		I Will Get By
55483	Obrey Wilson	Hey There Mountain
		Say It Again
55484	Jackie DeShannon	Just Like in the Movies
		Guess Who
55485	Gary Paxton	Alley Oop Was a Two Dab Man
		Stop Twistin' Baby
55486	Ray Sanders	If I Can Slip Away
		See One Broken Heart
55487	Felix Slatkin Orchestra	Theme from "My Geisha"
		Theme Searching for a Picture
55488	Nick Noble	Hello Out There
		We Could
55489	Johnny Burnette	Damn the Defiant
		Lonesome Waters
55490	Danny & Swen	Submarine Race
		Deep Dreams
55491	Emmett Lord	Women
		Turn Him Down
55492	Crickets	I Believe in You
		Parisian Girl
55493	Vikki Carr	He's a Rebel
		Be My Love
55494	Willie Nelson	Wake Me When It's Over
		There's Gonna Be Love in My House
55495	Crickets	Little Hollywood Girl
		Parisian Girl
55496	Jan & Dean	Who Put the Bomp
		My Favorite Dream
55497	Jackie DeShannon	You Won't Forget Me
		I Don't Think So Much of Myself
55498	Hank Cochran	I'd Fight the World
		Lucy, Let Your Lovelight Shine
55499	Si Zentner	Desafinado
		Elephant's Tango
55500	Gordon Terry	For Old Times Sake
		Wild Honey
55501	Carter Family	Fourteen Carat Nothing
		Get Up Early in the Morning

Label #	Artist	Record Title
55502	Dean Jones	The Proud Don't Cry
		What Did I Do with My New Tattoo
55503	Buddy Knox	Dear Abby
		Three Way Love Affair
55504	June Carter	Overalls & Dungarees
		Waving from the Hill
55505	P. J. Proby	Other Side of Town
		Watch Me Walk Away
55506	Mar-Kets	Stomping Room Only
		Canadian Sunset
55507	Dick Banks	Just Like You
		Be Faithful to Me
55508	Walter Brennan	Mama Sang a Song
		Who Will Take Gramma
55509	Fencemen	Bach 'n' Roll
		Swingin' Gates
55510	Gene McDaniels	Spanish Lace
		Somebody's Waiting
55511	Morgan Condello	Combo Night River
		Ali Baba
55512	Julie London	Desafinado
		Where Did the Gentleman Go
55513	Rivingtons	My Reward
		Kickapoo Joy Juice
55514	Martin Denny	Cast Your Fate to the Wind
		Pay Off
55515	Ernie Freeman	Half as Much
		I'm Sorry for You My Friend
55516	Ed Townsend	Tell Her
		Down Home
55516	Ed Townsend	Tell Her
		Hard Way to Go
55517	Bobby Vee	Christmas Vacation
		A Not So Merry Christmas
55518	Walter Brennan	White Christmas
		Henry Had a Merry Christmas
55519	Timi Yuro	The Love of a Boy
		I Ain't Gonna Cry No More
55520	Hank Cochran	I Remember
		Private John Q
55521	Bobby Vee	The Night Has a Thousand Eyes
		Anonymous Phone Call
55522	Jan & Dean	She's Still Talking Baby Talk
		Frosty the Snowman
55523	Felix Slatkin	Orange Blossom Special
		Maiden's Prayer
55524	Ralph Emery	Christmas Can't Be Far Away
		Christmas Dinner
55525	Johnny Mann Singers	Cotton Fields
		Shenandoah
55526	Jackie DeShannon	Faded Love
		Dancing Silhouettes

Appendixes

Label #	Artist	Record Title
55527	Quotations	Listen My Children and You Shall Hear / Speak Softly & Carry a Big Horn
55528	Rivingtons	Mama-Oom-Mow-Mow / Waiting

1962
1963

Label #	Artist	Record Title
55529	Dick Lory	I Got Over You / Welcome Home Again
55530	Bobby Vee	Charms / Bobby Tomorrow
55531	Jan & Dean	Linda / When I Learn How to Cry
55532	Willie Nelson	Half a Man / The Last Letter
55533	Gordon Terry	I Wish I'd Said That / In a Moment
55534	Nick Noble	Closer to Heaven / Legend in My Time
55535	Fencemen	Sour Grapes / Sunday Stranger
55536	Martin Denny	Blue Carousel / Anniversary Song
55537	Tex Williams	Where the Sad People Are / Five Foot Deep in Teardrops
55538	Si Zentner	Waltz in Jazz Time / A La Mode
55539	Eddie Heywood	Harlem Blues / Sidewalks of New York
55540	Crickets	Teardrops Fall Like Rain / My Little Girl
55541	Gene McDaniels	The Puzzle / Cry Baby Cry
55542	Ed Townsend	That's What I Get for Loving You / There's No End
55543	Molly Bee	All My Love, All My Life / She's New to You
55544	Chipmunks	Old MacDonald Cha Cha Cha / Alvin's All Star Chipmunk Band
55545	Henrietta/Hairdooz	Slow Motion / You Got a Lot to Learn
55546	Ralph Emery	Poor Boy / Touch of the Master's Hand
55547	Joe Carson	Shoot the Buffalo / Three Little Words Too Late
55548	Nancy Ames	Bonsoir Cher / Cu Cu Ru Cu Cu Paloma
55549	Four Cal-Quettes	I Cried / Movie Magazines
55550	Strangers	Card Shark / Mindreader
55551	Timi Yuro (Not Released)	Insult to Injury / Talkin' About Hurt

Appendix 11

Label #	Artist	Record Title
55552	Timi Yuro	Insult to Injury
		Just About the Time
55553	Rivingtons	The Bird's the Word
		I'm Losing My Grip
55554	Kay Arnold	The Gypsy & the Tea Leaves
		We're Not Living in a House (What a Shame)
55555	Never Released	
55556	Nick Cardell	Arlene
		How Can I Help It
55557	Ross Bagdasarian	Cecelia
		Gotta Get to Your House
55558	Gordon Terry	Most of All
		We've Got a Lot in Common
55559	Vikke Lee	"A" You're Adorable
		Hollywood Stroll
55560	Billy & Cliff	Louisiana Sand
		Don't Look Now
55561	Martin Denny	Quiet Village Bossa Nova
		Strawberry Tree
55562	Gene Davis	Take a Good Look
		Won't Come in While He's There
55563	Jackie DeShannon	Needles and Pins
		Did He Call Today, Mama?
55564	Vikki Carr	Rose & the Butterfly
		From 9 to 5
55565	Hollycats	For the Whole Wide World to See
		You Can't Hurt Me Anymore
55566	Eddie/Showmen	Toes on the Nose
		Border Town
55567	Peter James	My Hands Are Tied
		After You
55568	Ray Sanders	Rich Living Woman
		It's Not Funny
55569	Molly Bee	I Was Only Kidding
		He's My True Love
55570	Andy/Marglows	Just One Look
		Sympathy
55571	Martin Denny	More (Theme from "Mondo Cane")
		O Barquinho (Little Boat)
55572	Henrietta/Hairdooz	It Might as Well Be Me
		Penn Station
55573	Matt Monro	The Girl I Love
		Leave Me Now
55574	Victorians	What Makes Little Girls Cry
		Climb Every Mountain
55575	Eddie Heywood	Good Life
		Canadian Sunset Bossa Nova
55576	Nick Noble	Gee Little Girl
		A Rose and a Star
55577	Blisters	Shortnin' Bread
		Cookie Rockin' in Her Stockings

Label #	Artist	Record Title
55578	Joe Carson	I Gotta Get Drunk (and Shore Do Dread It)
		Who Will Buy My Memories
55579	Michael Barry	Cleopatra Rag
		Foot Stompin' Rag
55580	Jan & Dean	Surf City
		She's My Summer Girl
55581	Bobby Vee	Be True to Yourself
		A Letter from Betty
55582	Robert Florence	Anthony & Cleopatra Theme
		Paul's Theme
55583	Tex Williams	Risin' High
		Go into the Mountains
55584	Gary Paxton	Spooky Movies Part 1
		Spooky Movies Part 2
55585	Rivingtons	The Shaky Bird Part 1
		The Shaky Bird Part 2
55586	Billy J. Kramer/Dakotas	Do You Want to Know a Secret
		I'll Be on My Way
55587	Timi Yuro	Make the World Go Away
		Look Down
55588	P. J. Proby	So Do I
		I Can't Take It Like You Can
55589	Johnny Southern	Love of My Life
		Thank You
55590	John Veith	When Johnny Comes Marching Home
		Allee Blue
55591	Willie Nelson	Feed It a Memory
		Take My Word
55592	Buddy Knox/Rhythm Orchids	Shadaroom
		Tomorrow Is a Comin'
55593	Bill Brock/Clansmen	Hard Times
		If You're Afraid to Tell Him I Will
55594	Bob Wills	Blues in "A"
		Rosetta
55595	Ila Van	It Must Be Love
		What's the Matter Baby
55596	Garry Miles/Buzzettes	Candy
		Do the Bug
55597	Gene McDaniels	It's a Lonely Town
		False Friends
55598	Nancy Ames	An Elizabethan Ballad Pt. 1
		An Elizabethan Ballad Pt.2
55599	Billy Gray/Western Oldies	I'll Never Live Long Enough
		I Left My Heart in San Francisco
55600	Dick Lory	Crazy Arms
		There's Going to Be a Fight
55601	Les Brown	Wait a Little Longer
		Sweet Dreamer
55602	Jackie DeShannon	Little Yellow Roses
		Oh Sweet Chariot
55602	Jackie DeShannon	Little Yellow Roses
		500 Miles

Appendix 11 627

Label #	Artist	Record Title
55603	Crickets	April Avenue
		Don't Say You Love Me
55604	Tracey Dey	Teenage Cleopatra
		Who's That
55605	Julie London	I'm Coming Back to You
		When Snowflakes Fall in the Summer
55606	Henrietta	I Love Him
		We'll Work It Out
55607	Eddie Heywood	St. Louis Blues
		Begin the Beguine
55608	Eddie/Showmen	Squad Car
		Scratch
55609	Si Zentner	Broken Date
		Fink
55610	Rivingtons	Cherry
		Little Sally Walker
55611	Hal Waters	Poor Ann
		Poor Man Livin' in a Rich Man's World
55612	Bud & Travis	Tomorrow Is a Long Time
		Haiti
55613	Jan & Dean	Honolulu Lulu
		Someday (You'll Go Walking By)
55614	Joe Carson	Helpless
		Last Song
55615	Warren Smith	That's Why I Sing in a Honky Tonk
		Big City Ways
55616	Vikke Lee	Gee Whiz
		I Hear Those Wedding Bells
55617	Walter Brennan	Keep a Movin' Old Man
		Waiting for a Train
55618	Dakotas	Cruel Surf
		The Millionaire
55619	Ross Bagdasarian	Lucy, Lucy
		Scalliwags & Sinners
55620	Vikki Carr	San Francisco
		Irma La Douce
55620	Vikki Carr	San Francisco
		Look Again
55621	Reggie Boyd	Cotton Picker
		Drummer Man
55622	Martin Denny	Theme from the VIP's
		Cousin Ray
55623	Andy/Marglows	Superman Lover
		I'll Get By
55624	Pygmies	Don't Monkey with Tarzan
		Other Side
55625	Artie Wayne	Where Does a Rock & Roll Singer Go?
		I Hurt That Girl
55626	Billy J. Kramer/Dakotas	Sad to Me
		I Call Your Name
55627	Peter James	Feelings
		Wind Me Up & Let Me Go

628 Appendixes

Label #	Artist	Record Title
55628	Dynamics	Chapel on a Hill
		Conquistador
55629	Martin Denny	Something Latin
		Once Is Enough
55630	Gordon Terry	Sitting Just One Car from You
		Almost Gone
55631	Molly Bee	Some Tears Fall Dry
		Johnny Liar
55632	Chipmunks	Eefin' Alvin
	Ross Bagdasarian	Flip Side
55633	Jerry Lewis	Kids
		Witchcraft
55634	Timi Yuro	Gotta Travel On
		Down in the Valley
55635	Chipmunks	The Night Before Christmas
		Wonderful Day
55636	Bobby Vee	Yesterday and You
		Never Love a Robin
55637	Gene McDaniels	Anyone Else
		Old Country
55638	Willie Nelson	You Took My Happy Away
		How Long Is Forever
55639	Carl Edwards	Brighter Side
		Son, Son, Listen Here Son
55640	Vikki Carr	Right Kind of Woman
		Poor Butterfly Stay
55641	Jan & Dan	Drag City
		Schlock Rod (Part 1)
55642	Bobby Griggs	Farewell Party
		Get a Little Hurt
55643	Billy J. Kramer	I'll Keep You Satisfied
		I Know
55644	Hank Cochran	Go on Home
		Tootsie's Orchid Lounge
55645	Jackie DeShannon	When You Walk in the Room
		'Til You Say You're Mine
55646	Searchers	Saints & Searchers
		Sugar & Spice
55647	Blisters	Rich in My Pocket Poor in My Heart
		Friendly Loans
55648	Si Zentner	Classes De Cha Cha
		James Bond Theme
55649	Spike Jones	Green Green
		The Ballad of Jed Clampett
55650	Buddy Knox	Thanks a Lot
		Hitchhike Back to Georgia
55651	Not Used	
55652	Tex Williams	Late Movies
		Long John
55653	Johnny Mann	African Noel
	Children Choir	Children Board That Train
55654	Bobby Vee	Stranger in Your Arms
		1963

Label #	Artist	Record Title
55655	Martin Denny	Everything Beautiful Happens / Sugar Cane

1963
1964

Label #	Artist	Record Title
55656	Victorians	You're Invited to a Party / The Monkey Stroll
55657	Jerry Berryhill	I Remember Love / Love on the Run
55658	Gene Davis	I'll Tell Her Tomorrow / I'm in the Book
55659	Eddie/Showmen	Movin' / Mr. Rebel
55660	Crickets	Lonely Avenue / You Can't Be In-Between
55661	Willie Nelson	There'll Be No Teardrops Tonight / Am I Blue
55662	Bill Brock	Grandpa's Tambourine / I've Taken All I Can
55663	Leon Bibb	Adieu Madras / Little Boxes
55664	Joe Carson	Double Life / Fort Worth Jail
55665	Timi Yuro	Call Me / Permanently Lonely
55666	Julie London	I Want to Find Out for Myself / Guilty Heart
55667	Billy J. Kramer/Dakotas	Bad to Me / Do You Want to Know a Secret
55668	Crickets	Please, Please Me / From Me to You
55669	Orville Woods	Wicked Women / Darlin'
55670	Bobby Vee	I'll Make You Mine / She's Sorry
55671	Rivingtons	Wee Jee Walk / Fairy Tales
55672	Jan & Dean	Dead Man's Curve / New Girl in School
55673	Jackie DeShannon	Should I Cry / I'm Gonna Be Strong
55674	Hollies	Now's the Time / Stay
55675	Si Zentner Orchestra	I'm Getting Sentimental Over You / Sentimental Journey
55676	Walter Raim	Sticks / Turned Down Theme
55677	T-Bones	Draggin' / Rail-Vette
55678	Jackie DeShannon	Oh Boy / I'm Looking for Someone to Love
55679	Bed Bugs	Yeah Yeah / Lucy Lucy

Label #	Artist	Record Title
55680	Standells	Peppermint Beatles / The Shake
55681	Bud & Travis	Maria Cristina / Sabras Que Te Quiero
55682	Matt Monro	From Russia with Love / Here and Now
55683	Si Zentner	James Bond Theme / From Russia with Love
55684	Spike Jones	Dominique / Sweet and Lovely
55685	Garry Miles	What Kind of Girl Are You / What's New
55686	The 4-Ter	Sweet Sixteen / Basin Street North
55687	Billy J. Kramer/Dakotas (Released on Imperial)	Little Children / They Remind Me of You
55688	Hornets	Motorcycle U.S.A. / On the Track
55689	Searchers	Sugar and Spice / Saints and Searchers
55690	Marlene Dietrich	Where Have All the Flowers Gone English & German
55691	Molly Bee	Our Secret / He Doesn't Want You
55692	Furys	Baby You Can Bet Your Boots / The Man Who Has Everything
55693	Victorians	Oh What a Night for Love / Happy Birthday Blue
55694	Buddy Knox	Good Lovin' / All Time Loser
55695	Eddie/Showmen	Far Away Places / Lanky Bones
55696	Crickets	(They Call Her) La Bamba / All Over You
55697	Willie Nelson	River Boy / Opportunity to Cry
55698	Tex Williams	Pickin' White Gold / Mr. All Alone
55699	Warren Smith	Blue Smoke / Judge & Jury
55700	Bobby Vee	Hickory, Dick and Doc / I Wish You Were Mine Again
55701	Timi Yuro	A Legend in My Time / Should I Ever Love Again
55702	Julie London	Girl (Boy) from Ipanema / My Lover Is a Stranger
55703	Zip Codes	Fancy Filly from Detroit City / Run, Little Mustang
55704	Jan & Dean	The Little Old Lady (from Pasadena) / My Mighty G. T. O.
55705	Jackie DeShannon	Hold Your Head High / She Don't Understand Him Like I Do

Label #	Artist	Record Title
55706	Frank Virtuoso	Dream World
		Move On
55707	Dick Lory	I Will
		I Catch Myself Crying
55708	De Caro Brothers	Candy Coated Lies
		My Heart Stood Still
55709	Sounds, Inc.	Detroit
		The Spartans
55710	Sonny Curtis	Bo Diddley Bach
		I Pledge My Love to You
55711	Tex Williams	Empty Letter
		Closer, Closer, Closer
55712	Billy Gray	Last Call for Alcohol
		Late Last Night
55713	Bud & Travis	How Long, How Long Blues
		Gimmie Some
55714	Garry Miles	Here Goes a Fool
		Ecstasy
55715	Alder Ray	'Cause I Love Him
		A Little Love (Will Go a Long Way)
55716	Billy Daniels	That Old Black Magic
		Woe, Woe, Woe
55717	Martin Denny	Angelito
		Latin Village
55718	Spike Jones	I'm in the Mood for Love
		Paradise
55719	Furys	Dream
		If I Didn't Have a Dime
55720	Eddie/Showmen	We Are the Young
		Young and Lonely
55721	Elio Gallo	Angelito Di Anzio
		Carnival
55722	Standells	I'll Go Crazy
		Help Yourself
55723	Gene McDaniels	In Times Like These
		Make Me a Present of You
55724	Jan & Dean	Ride the Wild Surf
		The Anaheim, Azusa & Cucamonsa Sewing Circle, Book Review and Timing Association
55725	Matt Monro	I Love You Too
		Softly as I Leave You
55726	Bobby Vee	Where Is She
		How to Make a Farewell
55727	Jan & Dean	Sidewalk Surfin'
		When It's Over
55728	Victorians	If I Loved You
		Monkey Stroll
55729	Sounds, Inc.	Rinky Dink
		Spanish Harlem
55730	Jackie DeShannon	He's Got the Whole World in His Hands
		It's Love Baby

Label #	Artist	Record Title
55731	Tommy Garrett	Stranger from Durango / Juarez
55732	Tommy Quickly	It's as Simple as That / You Might as Well Forget Him
55733	Ken Dodd	All of My Life / Happiness
55734	Chipmunks	All My Lovin' / Do You Want to Know a Secret
55735	Jackie DeShannon	When You Walk in the Room / Over You
55736	Vikki Carr	Forget You / Her Little Heart Went to Loveland
55737	Nancy Ames	Malaguena Salerosa / Cu Cu Ru Cu Cu Paloma
55738	Garry Miles	How Are Things in Paradise / Please Take the Time
55739	Bob Summers	After Dark / Mule Train
55740	Kenny Lynch	That's What Little Girls Are Made For / What Am I to You
55741	Naturals	I Should Have Known Better / Didn't I
55742	Crickets	I Think I've Caught the Blues / We Gotta Get Together
55743	Standells	So Fine / Linda Lou
55744	Mike Harris	We Never Knew / Come Along with Me
55745	Matt Monro	Walk Away / April Fool
55746	Sunset Strings	Oh, Pretty Woman / Running Scared
55747	Timi Yuro	I'm Movin' On Part 1 / I'm Movin' On Part 2
55748	Pair Extraordinaire	Patience Baby / Fight for Your Girl
55749	Rosalind Madison	Teasin' and Cheatin' Again / One More
55750	Blackwells	Show Me Around / The Old Coast Road
55751	Bobby Vee	Ev'ry Little Bit Hurts / Pretend You Don't See Her
55752	Gene McDaniels	Emily / Forgotten Man
55753	Tommy Quickly	The Wild Side of Life / Forget the Other Guy
55754	Martin Denny	Hawaii Tattoo / White Silver Sands
55755	Fabulous Echoes	Please Leave Her to Me / Quit Messin' Around
55756	Gary Lewis/Playboys	This Diamond Ring / Hard to Find

Appendix 11

Label #	Artist	Record Title
55756	Gary Lewis/Playboys	This Diamond Ring / Tijuana Wedding
55757	P. J. Proby	Somewhere / Just Like Him
55758	Naturals	It Was You / Look at Me Now
55759	Julie London	We Proved Them Wrong / You're Free to Go

1964
1965

Label #	Artist	Record Title
55760	Tex Williams	Smokey Hollow / Between Today and Tomorrow
55761	Bobby Vee	Cross My Heart / This Is the End
55762	Nancy Ames	Let Tonight Linger On / It Scares Me
55763	Matt Monro	For Mama / Going Places
55764	Bud & Travis	I Talk to the Trees / Moment in the Sun
55765	Not Used	
55766	Jan & Dean	(Here They Come) From All Over the World / Freeway Flyer
55767	Crickets	Everybody's Got a Little Problem / Now Hear This
55768	Spike Jones Orchestra	Hey, Good Lookin' / Jambalaya
55769	Fabulous Echoes	Keep Your Love Strong / I Never Knew
55770	Jose Gonzalez-Gonzalez	Poncho Claus / Tacos for Two
55771	Wendy Hill	Donna, Leave My Guy Alone / (Gary, Please Don't Sell) My Diamond Ring
55772	Pete King Chorale	Circus World / Fall of Love
55773	Chipmunks	Do-Re-Mi / Supercalifragilisticexpialidocious
55774	Penny Valentine	I Want to Kiss Ringo Goodbye / Show Me the Way to Love You
55775	Adamo	Another Love Affair / Dolce Paola
55776	Eddie Fontaine	Blue Roses / Way Down Home
55777	P. J. Proby	I Apologize / Rocking Pneumonia
55778	Gary Lewis/Playboys	Count Me In / Little Miss Go Go
55779	Dick Peabody	Captain Mike / Young Sarge
55780	Wilbert Wade	Come Here, Girl / You Can't Fool Me

Appendixes

Label #	Artist	Record Title
55781	Vern McEntire	Seven Million People / Summer Song
55782	Johnny Hunter	If the Things in My Room Could Talk / Japanese Springtime
55783	Vikki Carr	Should I Follow / Don't Talk to Me (Spanish)
55784	Cordials	Oh, How I Love Her / You Can't Believe in Love
55785	Vikki Carr	There Goes My Heart / Color of Love
55786	Matt Monro	Without You / Start Living
55787	Jackie DeShannon (Not Released)	What the World Needs Now Is Love / A Life Time of Loneliness
55788	Spike Jones Orchestra	Star Jenka / Let's Kiss, Kiss, Kiss
55789	Sounds, Inc.	In the Hall of the Mountain King / Time for You
55790	Bobby Vee	Keep on Trying / You Won't Forget Me
55791	P. J. Proby	Stagger Lee / Mission Bell
55792	Jan & Dean	You Really Know How to Hurt a Guy / It's as Easy as 1-2-3
55793	Fogcutters	Cry, Cry, Cry / You Say
55794	Carole Shelyne	Boys Make Passes at Girls with Glasses / Girl with the Horn-Rimmed Glasses
55795	Rosalind Madison	Neighborhood Girl / No Other Love
55796	Synanon Promotions	Zanke / Main Street
55797	50 Guitars	Corcovado / La Violettra
55798	Soundtrack	Synanon: Hope / Synanon: Mainstream
55799	Johnny Mann Singers	The Voice of Freedom / Try to Remember
55800	Josie Taylor	I'll Love You for Awhile / Tra La La
55801	Fabulous Echoes	Candy / Cry I Do
55802	Rojay Gotee	Thunder 'n' Lightnin' / Miss Jantje
55803	Bud & Travis	Cold Summer / Girl Sittin' Up in a Tree
55804	Vikkie Carr	Theme from "Peyton Place" / Unforgettable
55805	Gene McDaniels	A Miracle / Walk with a Winner
55806	P. J. Proby	That Means a Lot / Let the Water Run Down

Appendix 11

Label #	Artist	Record Title
55807	Tommy Sands	Love's Funny / One Rose Today, One Rose Tomorrow
55808	Earl Dean Smith	Odds & Ends (Bits & Pieces) / Sleep & Dream
55809	Gary Lewis/Playboys	Save Your Heart for Me / Without a Word of Warning
55810	Ross Bagdasarian	La Noche / Naval Maneuver
55811	Kenny Lynch	For Lovin' You Baby / I'll Stay by You
55812	Bobby Fuller 4	Let Her Dance / Another Sad & Lonely Night
55813	Accents	I Really Love You / What Do You Want to Do (Little Darlin')
55814	T-Bones	That's Where It's At / Pearlin'
55815	Jamie Carter	Boy with the Way / Memory of Your Voice
55816	Jan & Dean (Not Released)	It's a Shame to Say Goodbye / The Submarine Races
55817	Clay Hammond	No One Else Will Do / We Gotta Get Married
55818	Gary Lewis/Playboys	Everybody Loves a Clown / Time Stands Still
55819	Martin Denny	Hawaiian Village / Aloha Oe
55820	The Pair (Not Released)	Get Up off It Baby / The Submarine Races
55821	Two People	City Life / Funny Kind of Feeling
55822	Cascades	She'll Love Again / I Bet You Won't Stay
55823	Eddie Fontaine	I Need You / It Can Happen to You
55824	Rosalind Madison	Inconceivable / When Your Old Love Is Your New Love
55825	Jerry Berry Hill	Midnight in the Afternoon / Lemon Pie
55826	Vern McEntire	Give Me Enough Love / The Good with the Bad
55827	Arlin Harmon/Big Beats	Out of the Picture / Work Song
55828	Bobby Vee	Run with the Devil / Take a Look Around Me
55829	The Gants	Road Runner / My Baby Don't Care
55830	Julie London	Girl Talk / Won't Somebody Please Belong to Me
55831	Jerry Berry Hill (Not Released)	Lemon Pie / Midnight in the Afternoon
55832	Chipmunks	I'm Henry VIII, I Am / What's New Pussycat

Appendixes

Label #	Artist	Record Title
55833	Jan & Dean	I Found a Girl / It's a Shame to Say Goodbye
55834	Gene McDaniels	Hang On / Will It Last Forever
55835	Ken Dodd	Tears (for Souvenirs) / You and I
55836	T-Bones	No Matter What Shape (Your Stomach's In) / Feelin' Fine
55837	Ross Bagdasarian	Come On-a-My House / Gotta Get to Your House
55838	Deep Six	Rising Sun / Strolling Blues
55839	Vikki Carr	I Only Have Eyes for You / None but the Lonely Heart
55840	J. J. Cale	It's a Go-Go Place / Dick Tracy
55841	Two People	Knock on Wood / Two of Us
55842	Tommy Sands	The Statue / Little Rosita
55843	Bobby Vee	The Story of My Life / High Coin
55844	Sounds, Inc.	On the Brink / I Am Comin' Thru
55845	Jan Berry	I Can't Wait to Love You / The Universal Coward
55846	Gary Lewis/Playboys	She's Just My Style / I Won't Make That Mistake Again
55847	Matt Monro	Yesterday / Just Yesterday
55848	First Baptist Church of Van Nuys, CA	Amen / America the Beautiful
55849	Jan & Dean	Folk City / A Beginning from an End
55850	P. J. Proby	Good Things Are Coming My Way / Maria
55851	Martin Denny	Call Me / La Paloma
55852	Forerunners	Long Way Down / Magic of a Girl
55853	The Gants	Smoke Rings / Little Boy Sad
55854	Bobby Vee	A Girl I Used to Know / Gone

1965
1966

Label #	Artist	Record Title
55855	Carolyn Daye	Every Now & Then / I Love You a Thousand Ways
55856	Jan & Dean	Norwegian Wood / I Can't Wait to Love You
55857	Vikki Carr	Santiago / The Silencers

Appendix 11

Label #	Artist	Record Title
55858	Deep Six	I Wanna Shout
		Things We Say
55859	Ken Dodd	My Thanks to You
		The River
55860	Jan & Dean	Batman
		Bucket "T"
55861	Betty Turner	Be Careful Girl
		Stand By & Cry
55862	Don Lee Wilson	No Matter What Shape
		Angel
55863	Matt Monro	'Til Then My Love
		Beyond the Hill
55864	Tommy Sands	Waitin' in Your Welfare Line
	(Not Released)	Don't Do It Darlin'
55865	Gary Lewis/Playboys	Sure Gonna Miss Her
		I Don't Wanna Say Goodnight
55866	Del Shannon	The Big Hurt
		I Got It Bad
55867	T-Bones	Sippin' & Chippin'
		Moment of Softness
55868	Tommy Garrett/	Our Man Flint
	50 Guitars	Tender Moments
55869	Vikki Carr	Heartaches
		True Love's a Blessing
55870	Two People	Uphill Climb to the Bottom
		Me and My Shadow
55871	Johnny Mann Singers	Rovin' Gambler
		Cinnamint Shuffle
55872	Don Lee Wilson	Don't Avoid Me
		Angel
55873	Sumpin' Else	Baby You're Wrong
		I Can't Get Through to You
55874	Trombones Unlimited	The Phoenix Love Theme
		Daydream
55875	P. J. Proby	My Prayer
		Wicked Woman
55876	The Young	Now You've Got Yourself a Baby
	(Not Released)	When Will You Be Mine
55877	Bobby Vee	Save a Love
		Look at Me Girl
55877	Bobby Vee	Save a Love
		Butterfly
55878	Guadalajara Kings	Cu-Cu-Ru-Cu-Cu
		Love Theme from "The Sandpiper"
55879	Johnny Christopher	Back in Love with You
		Railroad Tracks
55880	Gary Lewis/Playboys	Green Grass
		I Can Read Between the Lines
55881	J. J. Cale	Outside Lookin' In
		In Our Time
55882	Deep Six	When Morning Breaks
		Counting

Label #	Artist	Record Title
55883	Carolyn Daye	Why Don't You Believe Me
		A Woman Needs Her Man
55884	The Gants	Dr. Feelgood
		Crackin' Up
55885	T-Bones	Underwater
		Wherever You Look Wherever You Go
55886	Jan & Dean	Popsicle
		Norwegian Wood
55887	Clockwork Orange	After Tonight
		Ready Steady
55888	Tommy Garrett/ 50 Guitars	Spanish Lights
		La Cucaracha
55889	Del Shannon	For a Little While
		Hey Little Star
55890	Don Lee Wilson	Don't Avoid Me
		Sally
55891	Eddy Harrison	Danny Fernandez
		One Common Heart
55892	Jerry Tawney	Run to the Door
		Funny Man
55893	Ken Dodd	Thank You for Being You
		Promises
55894	Del Shannon	Show Me
		Never Thought I Could
55895	Johnny Angel	Biggest Part of Me
		Summertime Blues
55896	Two People	Love Isn't Tears Only
		We Don't Do That Anymore
55897	Vikki Carr	My Heart Reminds Me Part 1
		My Heart Reminds Me Part 2
55898	Gary Lewis/Playboys	My Heart's Symphony
		Tina
55899	Billy Maxted	Siren's Song
		Street of Dreams
55900	Sumpin' Else	You're Bad
		Here Goes the Hurt
55901	Deep Six	Why Say Goodbye
		What Would You Wish from the Golden Fish
55902	Gilbert Becaud	Gracias a Dios
		Sand & Sea
55903	The Gants	I Want Your Lovin'
		Spoonful of Sugar
55904	Del Shannon	Under My Thumb
		She Was Mine
55905	Jan & Dean	Fiddle Around
		Surfer's Dream
55906	T-Bones	Fare Thee Well
		Let's Go Get Stoned
55907	Guadalajara Kings	Ciao, Ciao, Bambina
		Confusion por Su Amor
55908	Trombones Unlimited	You're Gonna Hear from Me
		Modesty

Appendix 11

Label #	Artist	Record Title
55909	Carolyn Daye	Until It's Time for You to Go
		A Long Way to Be Happy
55910	The Pair	Girl, I Think I Love You
		Run for Your Life
55911	Julie London	Bill Bailey (Won't You Please Come Home)
		Nice Girls Don't Stay for Breakfast
55912	Mickey Rooney, Jr.	The Choice Is Yours
		I'll Be There
55913	Not Assigned	
55914	Gary Lewis/Playboys	(You Don't Have to) Paint Me a Picture
		Looking for the Stars
55915	P. J. Proby	If I Ruled the World
		I Can't Make It Alone
55916	Two People	I Really Don't Want to Know
		You're Gonna Hurt Me
55917	Vikki Carr	It Must Be Him
		So Nice
55918	Guadalajara Kings	Granada
		I Remember You
55919	Chosen Few	Last Man Alive
		Synthetic Man
55920	Frank Roma	Night
		Now & Forever
55921	Bobby Vee	Before You Go
		Here Today
55922	Mike Sharpe	Break Through
		Spooky
55923	Jan & Dean	New Girl in School
		School Days
55924	Big Hugh Baby	Ice Water
		The Make Out Man
55925	T-Bones	Balboa Blues
		Walkin' My Cat Named Dog
55926	Deep Six	Image of a Girl
		C'mon Baby
55927	Gilbert Becaud	Mes Hommes À Moi
		Mon Amour
55928	Martin Denny	Hawaii
		Tiny Bubbles
55929	Not Assigned	
55930	Raik's Progress	Why Did You Rob Us, Tank?
		Sewer Rat Love Chant
55931	J. J. Cale	After Midnight
		Slow Motion
55932	Gary Lewis (Not Released)	Ice Melts in the Sun
		Down on the Sloop John B
55933	Gary Lewis/Playboys	Where Will the Words Come From
		May the Best Man Win
55934	Burt Bachrach Cond.	Juanita's Place
		Nikki
55935	Unbelievable Uglies	Get Straight
		Sorry

Appendixes

Label #	Artist	Record Title
55936	P. J. Proby	Niki Hoeky
		Good Things Are Coming My Way
55937	Vikki Carr	Now I Know the Feeling
		Until Today
55938	Johnny Mann Singers	Joyful Noise
		Whither Thou Goest

1966
1967

Label #	Artist	Record Title
55939	Del Shannon	She
		What Makes You Run
55940	The Gants	Greener Days
		I Wonder
55941	Si Zentner	Warning Shot
		Mona Lisa
55942	Teddy Lee/Tom Cats	I Really Need Your Love
		Monkey with a Worried Mind
55943	Malcolm Hayes	Hurry Sundown
		It's Not Easy
55944	Embers	Evelyn
		And Now I'm Blue
55945	T. J./Formations	So Glad
		Time to Myself
55946	Don Lee Wilson	Kiss Tomorrow Goodbye
		Sally
55947	Edan Benn	Land of Counterpane
		Little Boy's Prayer
55948	Nitty Gritty Dirt Band	Buy for Me the Rain
		Candy Man
55949	Gary Lewis/Playboys	The Loser
		Ice Melts in the Sun
55950	Vic Dana	Fraulein
		A Little Bit Later on down the Line
55951	T-Bones	Proper Thing to Do
		Tee Hee Hee (My Life Seems Different Now)
55952	Nelson Riddle	Thoroughly Modern Millie
		See the Cheetah
55953	Mark James	Bimbo Knows
		I Can't Let You Go
55954	Pandoras	New Day
		About My Baby
55955	Si Zentner	Dear John
		Haven't Been to Church
55956	Gilbert Becaud	What Now My Love
		The Girls of Summer
55957	Jerry Wallace	Dispossessed
		Runaway Bay
55958	Tony Scotti	One More Mountain
		With All My Heart
55959	Big Hugh Baby	All American Girl
		Eloise
55960	Mike Sharpe	Slootchy
		Crying Time

Appendix 11

Label #	Artist	Record Title
55961	Del Shannon	Led Along
		I Can't Be True
55962	Chosen Few	Asian Chrome
		Earth Above, Sky Below
55963	Tommy Reynolds	The Beat Goes On
		Bonesville
55964	Bobby Vee	Come Back When You Grow Up
		Swahili Serenade
55964	Bobby Vee	Come Back When You Grow Up
		That's All There Is to That
55965	Gants	Drifter's Sunrise
		Just a Good Show
55966	Julie London	Mickey Mouse March
		Baby Won't You Please
55967	Ventures	Strawberry Fields Forever
		Endless Dream
55968	Humane Society	Knock, Knock
		Tiptoe Through the Tulips with Me
55969	Tommy Garrett/ 50 Guitars	Courtin'
		Theme for Someone in Love
55970	Mel Carter	Edelweiss
		For Once in My Life
55971	Gary Lewis/Playboys	Girls in Love
		Let's Be More Than Friends
55972	Johnny Mann Singers	Up-Up and Away
		Joey Is the Name
55973	Tim Conway	Do You Fly Much?
		Race Car Driver
55974	P. J. Proby	Work with Me Annie
		You Can't Come Home Again (If You Leave Me Now)
55975	Roy Smith	It Happens to the Best of Us
		Very Strong on You
55976	Vikki Carr	Fly Away
		Sunshine
55977	Ventures	Strawberry Fields Forever
		Theme from "Endless Summer"
55978	Johnny Mann Singers	Up-Up and Away
		Joey Is the Name
55979	Canned Heat	Rollin' and Tumblin'
		Bullfrog Blues
55980	Trombones Unlimited	Holiday for Trombones
		Night in Israel
55981	Good Feelins	End of a Love
		I'm Captured
55982	Bobby Vee	Come Back When You Grow Up
		Growing Pains
55982	Bobby Vee	Come Back When You Grow Up
		That's All There Is to That
55982	Nitty Gritty Dirt Band	Truly Right
		Teddy Bear's Picnic
55983	Jhamels	Baby, Baby, Baby
		A Road to Nowhere

Label #	Artist	Record Title
55984	Hyle King Movement	Flower Smile / Forever 'n' Ever
55985	Gary Lewis/Playboys	Jill / New in Town
55986	Vikki Carr	It Must Be Him / That's All
55987	Mel Carter	Enter Laughing / Star Dust
55988	Mike Sharpe	Spook-a-Loo / Surgassy
55989	P. J. Proby	Butterfly High / Just Holding On
55990	Billy Maxted	Satin Doll / Shiny Stockings
55991	Don Lee Wilson	Behind These Stained Glass Windows / Hey There Sunshine
55992	Unrelated Segments	It's Gonna Rain / Where You Gonna Go
55993	Del Shannon	He Cheated / Runaway
55994	Kiki Dee	Stop and Think / I
55995	Vulcanes	Let's Go Baby / Walkin' to Memphis
55996	Victor Lundberg	An Open Letter to My Teenage Son / My Buddy Carl
55997	Idle Race	Here We Go 'Round the Lemon Tree / My Father's Son
55998	Vic Dana	A Lifetime Lovin' You / Guess Who, You
55999	Pandoras	Don't Bother / Games
56000	Mel Carter	Be My Love / Look into My Love
56001	Jerry Wallace	This One's on the House / A New Sun Risin'
56002	Hour Glass	Heartbeat / Nothing but Tears
56003	Barney Peters	Dublin in the Green / How Did I Pick a Lemon
56004	Ross Bagdasarian	Walking Birds of Carnaby / Red Wine
56005	Canned Heat	Evil Woman / The World Is a Jug
56006	Tony Scotti	Come Live with Me / (Theme from) The Valley of the Dolls
56007	Ventures	On the Road / Mirrors and Shadows
56008	Gilbert Becaud	C'est La Rose / Forever
56009	Bobby Vee	Beautiful People / I May Be Gone

Appendix 11 643

Label #	Artist	Record Title
56010	Johnny Mann Singers	Don't Look Back
		Instant Happy
56011	Gary Lewis/Playboys	Has She Got the Nicest Eyes
		Happiness

1967
1968

Label #	Artist	Record Title
56012	Vikki Carr	The Lesson
		One More Mountain
56013	Four Gents	He Got Soul
		Wick's Delight
56014	Bobby Vee	Maybe Just Today
		You're a Big Girl Now
56015	Mel Carter	Excuse Me
		The Other Woman
56016	Higher Elevation	Thoughts of Lila
		Here Comes Sunshine
56017	Christopher Robin	Elegant Swan
		Nature Takin' Its Course
56018	Del Shannon	Thinkin' It Over
		Runnin' on Back
56019	Ventures	Flights of Fantasy
		Vibrations
56020	T.I.M.E.	Make It Right
		Take Me Along
56021	Mike Sharpe	Sleeper
		Mississippi Delta
56022	Mel Torme	Brother Can You Spare a Dime
		Day in the Life of Bonnie & Clyde
56023	Vic Dana	Glory of Love
		Let the Good Times In
56024	Lost Souls	Artificial Rose
		Sad Little Girl
56025	Heads	Are You Lonely for Me, Baby You
56026	Vikki Carr	Your Heart Is Free Just Like the Wind
		She'll Be There
56027	Jerry Wallace	The Closest I Ever Came
	(Not Released)	That's What Fools Are For
56028	Jerry Wallace	Another Time, Another Place, Another World
		That's What Fools Are For
56029	Hour Glass	I Still Want Your Love
		Power of Love
56030	Kiki Dee	I'm Going Out
		Patterns
56031	P. J. Proby	I Apologize
		It's Your Day Today
56032	Bloop Group	Gotta Have You
		Oh Why
56033	Bobby Vee	Medley: My Girl—Hey Girl
		Just Keep It Up
56034	The Gruve	Said I Wasn't Gonna Tell Nobody
		You're Gonna Love Me

Appendixes

Label #	Artist	Record Title
56035	Higher Elevation	Country Club Affair / Summer Skies
56036	Del Shannon	Gemini / Magical Musical Box
56037	Gary Lewis/Playboys	Sealed with a Kiss / Sara Jane
56038	Canned Heat	On the Road Again / Boogie Music
56039	Vikki Carr	Don't Break My Pretty Balloon / Nothing to Lose
56040	Tony Scotti	I Just Haven't Got What It Takes / Rose
56041	Bruce & Dutch	I Remember Dillinger / Song of Bruce & Dutch
56042	Producers	Anything Can Happen / Love Is a Groovy Feeling
56043	Ross Bagdasarian (Not Released)	Yallah / Navel Maneuver
56044	Ventures	Too Young to Know My Mind / Walk, Don't Run—Land of 1000 Dances
56045	Gary Lewis/Playboys	Pretty Thing / Sealed with a Kiss
56046	Tommy Garrett/ 50 Guitars	Hang 'em High / Spanish Pearls
56047	Four Freshmen	Cherish/Windy / Come Fly with Me/Up Up & Away
56048	Ross Bagdasarian	When I Look in Your Eyes / Sands of Time
56049	Timi Yuro	Something Bad on My Mind / Wrong
56050	Vic Dana	Didn't We / Then
56051	P. J. Proby	Turn Her Away / What's Wrong with My World
56052	Unrelated Segments	Cry, Cry, Cry / It's Not Fair
56053	Greg Allman/Hour Glass	Changing of the Guard / D-I-V-O-R-C-E
56054	Nitty Gritty Dirt Band	Collegiana / These Days
56055	Mike Sharpe	Charmer / Funky Serenade
56056	Brendetta Davis	I Can't Make It Without Him / Until You Were Gone
56057	Bobby Vee	Do What You Gotta Do / Thank You
56058	Nadia Christen	Take It Easy / Take Me Back
56059	Jerry Wallace	Sweet Child of Sunshine / Our House on Paper
56060	T.I.M.E.	Tripping into Sunshine / What Would Life Be Without You

Label #	Artist	Record Title
56061	Timi Yuro	Interlude
		I Must Have Been Out of My Head
56062	Vikki Carr	Happy Together
		Dissatisfied Man
56063	Tommy Allbert	Idle Mind
		I'm Living on Dreams
56064	Idle Race	The End of the Road
		The Morning Sunshine
56065	Greg Allman/Hour Glass	She's My Woman
		Going Nowhere
56066	Mel Torme	Didn't We
		Five-Four
56067	Suzanne Doucet	Cry My Heart
		Swan Song
56068	Ventures	Hawaii Five-O
		Soul Breeze
56069	Murmaids	Paper Sun
		Song Through Perception
56070	Del Shannon	You Don't Love Me
		Raindrops
56071	Vic Dana	Roses Are Red
		Little Arrows
56072	Hour Glass	Now Is the Time
		She Is My Woman
56073	Shannons	Born Too Late
		Mister Sunshine
56074	Julie London	Come to Me Slowly
		Yummy, Yummy, Yummy
56075	Gary Lewis/Playboys	C. C. Rider
		Main Street
56076	Paul Massey	Butterfly Lake
	(Not Released)	Lemonade Hollow
56077	Canned Heat	Going up the Country
		One King Favor
56078	Murmaids	Paper Sun
		Song Through Perception
56079	Canned Heat/Chipmunks	The Chipmunk Song
		Christmas Blues
56080	Bobby Vee	Someone to Love Me
		Thank You
56081	Mike Sharpe	Bobby's Tune
		Windy Hill
56082	Paul Nero	Light My Fire
		The Windmills of Your Mind
56083	Johnny Mann Singers	If I Only Had Time
		Snow

1968
1969

56084	Spice Racq	Is It Useless
		Would You Be There
56085	Julie London	Louie Louie
		Hushabye Mountain

Label #	Artist	Record Title
56086	Tony Scotti	Nana
		There, I've Said It Again
56087	Dorsey Burnette	The Greatest Love
		Thin Little Simple Little Plain Little Girl
56088	The Jackals	Everywhere She Goes
		Linda Come Lately
56089	Kiki Dee	Now the Flowers Cry
		On a Magic Carpet Ride
56090	Not Released	
56091	Greg Allman/Hour Glass	I've Been Trying
		Silently
56092	Vikki Carr	With Pen in Hand
		Can't Take My Eyes off You
56093	Gary Lewis/Playboys	Mister Memory
		Rhythm of the Rain
56093	Gary Lewis/Playboys	Mister Memory
		Every Day I Have to Cry Some
56094	Higher Elevation	Odyssey
		Highway 101
56095	Jerry Wallace	Son
		Temptation
56096	Bobby Vee	Jenny Come to Me
		Santa Cruz
56097	Canned Heat	Time Was
		Low Down
56098	Vic Dana	Where Has All the Love Gone
		You Are My Destiny
56099	Four Freshmen	It's a Blue World
		By the Time I Get to Phoenix/My Special Angel
56100	The Shannons	Little White Lies
		Are You Sincere
56101	Tony Scotti	Devil or Angel
		Thing Called Love
56102	Tamela Webb/George	Hold On, I'm Comin'
		Peter O'Toole
56103	Mike Sharpe	Spooky
		With a Little Help from My Friends
56104	Cancelled	
56105	Jerry Wallace	Soon We'll Be There
		Venus
56106	Vikki Carr	With Pen in Hand
56107	Johnny Mann Singers	Little Sister
		Carolina on My Mind
56108	Paul Masse	High on a Hill
		Motels & Stations
56109	Vic Dana	Loneliness (Is Messin' Up My Mind)
		Look of Leavin'
56110	Cornerstone	When You Wake Me Girl
		Moving Day
56111	J. J. Light	Heya
		On the Road Now
56112	Julie London	Too Much of a Man
	(Not Released)	Sittin' Pretty

Appendix 11

Label #	Artist	Record Title
56113	Sammy Shore	Cigarette Smoking
56114	Ben Peters	San Francisco Is a Lonely Town
		You're the Happy Song I Sing
56115	Ventures	Theme from *A Summer Place*
		A Summer Love
56116		
56117	Gene Latter	I Love You
		Sign on the Dotted Line
56118	Tony Scotti	I Miss You So
		Those Lazy, Hazy, Crazy Days of Summer
56119	Patti McCaroon	Love Theme from *Romeo & Juliet*
		Shades (of Blue)
56120	McKenna Mendelson Mainline	Better Watch Out
		She's Alright
56121	Gary Lewis	Hayride
		Gary's Groove
56122		
56123		
56124	Bobby Vee	Let's Call It a Day Girl
		I'm Gonna Make It Up to You
56125	American Eagles	Nashville Sun
		Me & Bobby McGee
56126	Martin Denny	Midnight Cowboy
		Quiet Village
56127	Canned Heat	Sic 'em Pigs
		Poor Man
56128	Bro. Sammy Shore	Cigaret Smoking
		Men's Fashions
56129	50 Guitars of Tommy Garrett	Flamenco Funk
		Mexican Standoff
56130	Jerry Wallace	Swiss Cottage Place
		With Aging
56131		
56132	Vikki Carr	Eternity
		I Will Wait for Love
56133	Dave Pell Singers	Mah-Na', Mah-Na'
		Oh, Calcutta
56134	Nitty Gritty Dirt Band	Some of Shelley's Blues
		Yukon Railroad
56135	Dusty Soul	Dusty Soul
		Big Bad City
56136	Dale Robertson	He's Still with Me
		Too Busy Being Me
56137	Vic Dana	Aren't We the Lucky Ones
		I Tried to Love You Today
56138		
56139	Ben Peters	For My Woman's Love
		It's Time for Me to Go
56140	Canned Heat	Change My Ways
		Get off My Back
56141	Velvet Crest	Gotta Make You Mine
		Lookin' Through the Eyes of Love

Label #	Artist	Record Title
56142	Henry Shed	Mama's Hungry Eyes
		Mrs. Robinson
56143	Willie Nelson	I Hope So
		Right or Wrong
56144	Gary Lewis/Playboys	I Saw Elvis Presley Last Night
		Something Is Wrong
56145	Dick Clark	The Day the Children Died
		Wasting of Wesley Joe Grim
56146	Blue Magic	Can I Say I Love You
		One, Two, Three
56147	Jerry Wallace	Glory of My Girl
		Honey Eyed Girl
56148	Cornerstone	Holly Go Softly
		Love, Nothing More
56149	Bobby Vee	Electric Trains and You
		In and Out of Love
56150	Vic Dana	If I Never Knew Your Name
		Sad Day Song

1969

1970

Label #	Artist	Record Title
56151	Canned Heat	Let's Work Together
		I'm Her Man
56152	Dee Clark	24 Hours of Loneliness
		Where Did All the Good Times Go
56153	Ventures	Swan Lake
		Expo '70
56154	Henry Shed	Groove into It
		Let It Be
56155	Jerry Wallace	Even the Bad Times Are Good
		For All We Know
56156	Dana Valery	Clinging Vine
		Get in Line Girl
56157	Noah's Ark	Purple Heart
		Stormy
56158	Gary Lewis/Playboys	Great Balls of Fire
		I'm on the Right Road Now
56159	Nitty Gritty Dirt Band	Cure
		Rave On
56160	Fantasy	Understand
		Stoned Cowboy
56161	Fantasy	Understand
		Stoned Cowboy
56162	Eternity's Children	Alone Again
		From You Unto Us
56163	Vic Dana	Red Red Wine
		Another Dream Shot Down
56164	Frankie Karl	Don't Sleep Too Long
		Put a Little Love in Your Heart
56165	Ross Bagdasarian	I Treasure Thee
56166	Showmen	It Will Stand
		Country Fool
56167		

Appendix 11

Label #	Artist	Record Title
56168	Katja Ebstein	No More Love for Me / Without Love
56169	Ventures	The Mercenary / The Wanderer
56170		
56171	Vivian Stanshall	Labis-Dental Fricative / Paper-Round
56172	Candymen	Happy Tonight / Papers
56173	Vince Hill	Alouette Alouette / Little Bluebird
56174	Ben Peters	Can't Get Over You / Downtown U.S.A.
56175		
56176	John Buck Wilkin	Boy of the Country / Apartment 21
56177	Ike & Tina Turner	I Want to Take You Higher / Contact High
56178	Bobby Vee	No Obligations / Woman in My Life
56179	Cornerstone	It's Gotta Be Real / Without Her, Father Paul
56180	Canned Heat	Going up the Country / Future Blues
56181	Lee Montgomery	Hello L. A. Bye Bye Birmingham / Season of the Witch
56182	Dennis Yost/ Classics IV	God Knows I Loved Her / We Miss You
56183	Sugarloaf	Green Eyed Lady / West of Tomorrow
56184	Albert Collins	Coon 'n' Collards / Do What You Want to Do
56185	Vikki Carr	Make It Rain / Singing My Song
56186	Bobby Womack	Don't Look Back / I'm Gonna Forget About You
56187	Jackie DeShannon	It's So Nice / Mediterranean Sky
56188	Buddy Rich	Keep the Customer Satisfied Parts 1 and 2
56189	Ventures	Storefront Lawyers (Theme) / Kern County Line
56190	Fantasy	Understand / Stoned Cowboy
56191	Richard Thomas/Frost	Where Did Yesterday Go / Open Up Your Heart
56192	Jades	All's Quiet on West 23rd / Love of a Woman
56193		
56194	Ike Turner	Love Is a Game / Takin' Back My Name
56195	December's Children	You're My Girl / Dirty City

Appendixes

Label #	Artist	Record Title
56196	Amon Duul II	Archangel's Thunderbird / Soda Shop Rock
56197	Nitty Gritty Dirt Band	Mr. Bojangles / Spanish Fandango
56198	Jimmy McCracklin	Believe Me / I Never Thought
56199	Slim Whitman	Shutters & Boards / I Pretend
56200	Dennis Yost/Classics IV	Where Did All the Good Times Go / Ain't It the Truth
56201	Andrae/Disciples	Christian People / Too Close
56202	Ray Saunders	Blame It on Rosie / Waikiki Sand
56203	Starbuck	It's Raining / Paint Me a Song
56204	Hughes Corporation	Goodfootin' / We're Keeping Our Business Together
56205	Groundhogs	Ship on the Ocean / Soldier
56206	Bobby Womack	Something / Everybody's Talkin'
56207	Ike & Tina Turner	The Way You Love Me / Workin' Together
56208	Bobby Vee	Sweet Sweetheart / Rock & Roll Music and You
56209	Dana Valery	Point of No Return / Put Your Hand in the Hand
56210	Harry Sukman	Bess You Is My Woman / Crimson Kimono
56211		
56212	Kentucky Express	Girl from the Country / Memphis, Tennessee
56213		
56214	Freddy Robinson	Carmalita / Stone Stallion
56215	Sweet Marie	Remember Mary / Don't You Understand
56216	Ike & Tina Turner	Proud Mary / Mosquito's Tweeter
56217	Canned Heat	My Time Ain't Long / Wooly Bully
56218	Sugarloaf	Woman / Tongue in Cheek

Dolton

Label #	Artist	Record Title

1959

| 1 | Fleetwoods | Come Softly to Me / I Care So Much |

Label #	Artist	Record Title
2	Frantics	Straight Flush
		Young Blues
3	Fleetwoods	Graduation Blues
		Oh Lord Let It Be Me
4	Little Bill/Bluenotes	I Love an Angel
		Bye Bye Baby
5	Fleetwoods	Mr. Blue
		You Mean Everything to Me
6	Frantics	Fog Cutter
		Black Sapphire
7	Gary Hodge	Not for Love or Money
		Too Old to Cry
8	Playboys	Party Ice
		Icy Fingers
9	Jerry Davis	Prove Our Love Is True
10	Bonnie Guitar	Candy Apple Red
		Come to Me, I Love You
11		
12	Jerry David	Prove Our Love Is True
		My Very Best to You
13	Frantics	Checkerboard
		Werewolf
14	Russ & Russanne Elmore	Big Words
		What Does Santa Claus Want for Christmas

1959

1960

15	Fleetwoods	Outside My Window
		Magic Star
16	Frantics	Werewolf
		No Werewolf
17	Jeff Tabor	I'm Lonesome
		Here's Where a Broken Heart Lives
18	Echoes	Born to Be with You
		My Guiding Light
19	Bonnie Guitar	Come to Me I Love You (Akaka Falls)
		Candy Apple Red
20		
21		
22	Fleetwoods	Runaround
		Truly Do
23		
24	Frantics	The Whip
		Delilah
25	Ventures	Walk—Don't Run
		Home
25	Ventures	Walk—Don't Run
		The McCoy
26	Four Pearls	Look at Me
		It's Almost Tomorrow
27	Fleetwoods	The Last One to Know
		Dormilona

Label #	Artist	Record Title
28	Ventures	Perfidia
		No Trespassing
29	Igor & Manias	Big Green
		Gung Ho

1960
―――
1961

Label #	Artist	Record Title
30	Fleetwoods	Confidential
		I Love You So
31	Frantics	Yankee Doodlin'
		One Minute of Flamenco
32	Ventures	Ram-Bunk-Shush
		Lonely Heart
33	Frantics	San Antonio Rose
		Trees
34	Vic Dana	The Girl of My Dreams
		Someone New
35	Peggi Griffith	Lovely Girl
		You're in My Dreams to Stay
36	Chuck Roberts	That's How It's Gonna Be
		Wo Wo Baby
37		
38	Brady & Grady Sneed	Little Bitty Heart
		Leaving It All Up to You
39		
40	Fleetwoods	Tragedy
		Little Miss Sad One
41	Ventures	Lullaby of the Leaves
		Ginchy
42	Vic Dana	Golden Boy
		The Story Behind My Tears
43	Grady & Grady	Blue Bird
		The Saddest Girl in Town
44	Ventures	(Theme from) Silver City
		Bluer Than Blue
45	Fleetwoods	(He's) The Great Imposter
		Poor Little Girl
46	Teddy Ross	Water Boy
		Ain't That Love
47	Ventures	Blue Moon
		Lady of Spain

1961
―――
1962

Label #	Artist	Record Title
48	Vic Dana	Little Altar Boy
		Hello Roommate
49	Fleetwoods	Billy Old Buddy
		Trouble
50	Ventures	Yellow Jacket
		Genesis
51	Vic Dana	I Will
		Proud

Appendix 11

Label #	Artist	Record Title
52	Miniature Men	Miniature Blues
		Soupy's Theme
53	Johnny Victor	Come to Me Johnny
		The Tears You Never Cried
54		
55	Ventures	Instant Mashed
		My Bonnie Lies
56	Hank Levine	Theme from Dr. Kildare
		National Velvet
57	Miniature Men	Baby Elephant Walk
		Bool-Ya-Base
58	Vic Dana	To Love and Be Loved
		Time Can Change
59	Wanderers Three	Cry I Do
		Toro
60	Ventures	Lolita Ya Ya
		Lucille
61	Five Whispers	Midnight Sun
		Moon in the Afternoon
62	Fleetwoods	Lovers by Night, Strangers by Day
		They Tell Me It's Summer
63	Hank Levine	Theme from Hong Kong
		Portrait of a Blonde
64	Vic Dana	I Wanna Be There
		A Very Good Year for Girls
64	Vic Dana	Looking for Me
		A Very Good Year for Girls
65		
66	Wanderers Three	Turn Around
		Glory Road

1962
1963

67	Ventures	The 2000 Pound Bee Part 1
		The 2000 Pound Bee Part 2
68	Ventures	El Cumbanchero
		Skip to M'Limbo
69	Five Whispers	Awake or Asleep
		Especially for You
70	Moonstones	Love Call
		My True Love
71	Hank Levine	Moon on My Pillow
		Anything, Anywhere
72	Three Wishes	Guiding Light
		It's All Said & Done
73	Vic Dana	Danger
		Heart, Hand and Teardrop
74	Fleetwoods	You Should Have Been There
		Sure Is Lonesome Downtown
75	Fleetwoods	Goodnight My Love
		Jimmy Beware
76	Lenny Bryan	Merry-Go-Round
		Somethin' Wild

Label #	Artist	Record Title
77		
78	Ventures	The Ninth Wave / Damaged Goods
79	Hank Levine	Swingin' Village / Tenga Tonga
80	Judd Hamilton	Dream / Your Only Boy
81	Vic Dana	More / That's Why I'm Sorry
82	Wanderers Three	Wanderin' / Hi-De-Ink-Tum
83	Dodie Stevens	I Wore Out Our Record / You Don't Have to Prove a Thing to Me
84	Christopher Montgomery	Giants of Bombora / My Paradise
85	Ventures	The Savage / The Chase
86	Fleetwoods	Baby Bye-O / What'll I Do

1963
1964

Label #	Artist	Record Title
87	Vic Dana	The Prisoners Song / Voice in the Wind
88	Dodie Stevens	Does Goodnight Mean Goodbye / Sailor Boy
89	Vic Dana	So Wide the World / Close Your Eyes
90	Five Whispers	Can't Face the Crowd / Sleep Walker
91	Ventures	Journey to the Stars / Walkin' with Pluto
92	Vic Dana	Shangri-La / Warm and Tender
93	Fleetwoods	Ruby Red Baby Blue / Lonesome Town
94	Ventures	Fugitive / Scratchin'
95	Vic Dana	Love Is All We Need / I Need You Now
96	Ventures	Walk—Don't Run '64 / The Cruel Sea
97	Fleetwoods	Ten Times Blue / Ska Light Ska Bright
98	Fleetwoods	Mr. Sandman / This Is My Prayer
99	Vic Dana	Garden in the Rain / Stairway to the Stars
300	Ventures	Slaughter on 10th Avenue / Rap City
301	Vic Dana	Frenchy / It Was Night

Label #	Artist	Record Title
302	Fleetwoods	Before and After (Losing You) / Lonely Is as Lonely Does
303	Ventures	Diamond Head / Lonely Girl
304	Vic Dana	Red Roses for a Blue Lady / Blue Ribbons
305	Vic Dana	Bring a Little Sunshine / That's All
306	Ventures	The Swingin' Creeper / Pedal Pusher
307	Fleetwoods	Come Softly to Me / I'm Not Jimmy
308	Ventures	Ten Seconds to Heaven / Bird Rockers
309	Vic Dana	Moonlight and Roses / What'll I Do
310	Fleetwoods	Rainbow / Just as I Need You
311	Ventures	Gemini / La Bamba
312	Ventures	Sleigh Ride / Snow Flakes
313	Vic Dana	Crystal Chandelier / What Now My Love
314	Gail Dacorsi	I've Lost in Life / Touch of Yesterday
315	Fleetwoods	For Lovin' Me / This Is Where I See Her

1964

1965

Label #	Artist	Record Title
316	Ventures	Secret Agent Man / 00-711
317	Vic Dana	Hello Roommate / Lovely Kravezit
318		
319	Vic Dana	I Love You Drops / Sunny Skies
320	Ventures	Blue Star / Comin' Home Baby
321	Ventures	Arabesque / Ginza Lights
322	Vic Dana	A Million and One / My Baby Wouldn't Leave Me
323	Ventures	Green Hornet Theme / Fuzzy and Wild
324	Vic Dana	Love Me with All Your Heart / Distant Drums
325	Ventures	Penetration / Wild Thing
326	Vic Dana	Grown Up Games / So What's New

Label #	Artist	Record Title
327	Ventures	Theme from the Wild Angels / Kickstand

Imperial

1963

66000	Shirley & Lee	Never Let Me Go / Somebody Put a Jukebox in the Study Hall
66001	Ho-Dads	Honky / Legends
66002	Slim Whitman	Gortnamona / Maria Elena
66003	Steve Alaimo	Gotta Lotta Love / Happy Pappy
66004	Rick Nelson	Thank You Darlin' / Today's Teardrops
66005	Fats Domino	Goin' Home / I Can't Give You Anything but Love
66006	Lou Courtney	Come on Home / Man with the Cigar
66007	The O'Jays	Stand Tall / Storm Is Over
66008	Joyce Paul	Don't Send Flowers / I'll Give You Me (If You'll Give Me You)
66009	The Majors	I'll Be There / Ooh Wee Baby
66010	Jimmy McCracklin	I Did Wrong / Someone

1963/1964

66011	H. B. Barnum	Backstage / Rented Tuxedo
66012	Slim Whitman	Only You and You Alone / Tell Me Pretty Words
66013	Irma Thomas	Break-a-Way / Wish Someone Would Care
66014	Powder Puffs	(You Can't Take) My Boyfriend's Woody Woody Wagon
66015	Imperialites	Have Love, Will Travel / Let's Get One
66016	Fats Domino	When I Was Young / Your Cheatin' Heart
66017	Ricky Nelson	Congratulations / One Minute to One
66018	Four Buddies	I Want to Be the Boy You Love / Just Enough of Your Love
66019	Sandy Nelson	Drum Shack / Kitty's Theme
66020	Velvetones	Glory of Love / I Found My Love

Appendix 11 657

Label #	Artist	Record Title
66021	Swinging Blue Jeans	Hippy Hippy Shake
		Now I Must Go
66022	Rudy Ray Moore	Baby, That's Why I'm Your Fool
		Four O'Clock in the Morning
66023	Ho-Dads	After Dark
		Space Race
66024	Joyce Paul	Lasting Love
		Painted Smile
66025	The O'Jays	I'll Never Stop Loving You
		My Dearest Beloved
66026	Hollies	Just One Look
		Keep Off That Friend of Mine
66027	Billy J. Kramer/Dakotas	Bad to Me
		Little Children
66028	Wailers	Tall Cool One
	(Not Released)	Frenzy
66029	Pandoras	All About Jim
		Hey Ah
66030	Swinging Blue Jeans	Good Golly Miss Molly
		Shaking Feeling
66031	Bo Rhambo	Blue Mist
		Diane
66032	Johnny Rivers	It Wouldn't Happen to Me
		Memphis
66033	Showmen	Country Fool
		It Will Stand
66034	Sandy Nelson	Castle Rock
		You Don't Say
66035	Jimmy McCracklin	Just Like It is
		Let's Do It All
66036	Rally-Packs	Bucket Seats
		Move Out Little Mustang
66037	The O'Jays	Lovely Dee
		You're on Top
66038	Don Lee Wilson	T'ain't Funny
		What'd I Say Part 1
66039	Ricky Nelson	Everybody but Me
		Lucky Star
66040	Slim Whitman	I'll Hold You in My Heart
		No Other Arms, No Other Lips
66041	Irma Thomas	Anyone Who Knows What Love Is (Will Understand)
		Time Is on My Side
66042	Ross McManus	I'm the Greatest
		Patsy Girl
66043	Lou Courtney	Little Old Love Maker
		Professional Lover
66044	Hollies	Here I Go Again
		Lucille
66045	Wailers	Mashi
		On the Rocks
66046	H. B. Barnum	Ska Drums
		Skakiaan (Skokiaan)

Label #	Artist	Record Title
66047	Fantastic Baggies	Surfer Boy's Dream / Tell 'em I'm Surfin'
66048	Billy J. Kramer/Dakotas	I Know / I'll Keep You Satisfied
66049	Swinging Blue Jeans	Shake, Rattle & Roll / You're No Good
66050	Joyce Paul	Edge of a Heartbreak / Walk Away
66051	Billy J. Kramer/Dakotas	From a Window / I'll Be on My Way
66052	Mel Carter	Deed I Do / What's on Your Mind
66053	Prediktors	Sails & the Sea / Summer Holiday
66054	Misfits	Lost Love / This Little Piggy (I'm a Hog for You)
66055	Lovers	Darling It's Wonderful / I Want to Be Loved
66056	Johnny Rivers	Maybelline / Walk Myself on Home
66057	Barons	Silence / I Just Go Wild Inside
66058	Viceroys	Death of an Angel / Earth Angel
66059	Swinging Blue Jeans	Promise You'll Tell Her / Tutti Fruitti
66060	Sandy Nelson	Kitty's Theme / Teen Beat '65
66061	Fender IV	Mar Gaya / You Better Tell Me Now
66062	Jim Christiansen	Destiny / Sylvie
66063	H. B. Barnum	Calypso Blues / Three Room Flat
66064	Don Lee Wilson	Angel / Tell Laura I Love Her
66065	Bob Moline	Forbidden / If I Were an Artist
66066	Simon Scott	Move It Baby / What Kind of a Woman
66067	Jimmy McCracklin	Believe in Me / Set Six
66068	Jill Gibson	It's as Easy as 1, 2, 3 / Jilly's Flip Side
66069	Irma Thomas	Moments to Remember / Times Have Changed
66070	Hollies	Come on Back / We're Through
66071	Showmen	Somebody Help Me / Country Fool
66072	Fantastic Baggies	Anywhere the Girls Are / Debbie Be True

Appendix 11

Label #	Artist	Record Title
66073	Johnny Shane	Girl Like You / Summer Love
66074	H. B. Barnum	Eternal Love / So What
66075	Johnny Rivers	Moody River / Mountain of Love
66076	The O'Jays	Girl Machine / Oh How You Hurt Me
66077	Slim Whitman	Love Song of the Waterfall / Virginia
66078	Mel Carter	I'll Never Be Free / Richest Man Alive
66079	P. J. Proby	Just Call, I'll Be There / Rocking Pneumonia
66080	Irma Thomas	He's My Guy / (I Want a) True, True Love
66081	Cherilyn	Dream Baby / Stan Quetzal
66082	Fenways	Walk / Whip & Jerk

1964
1965

Label #	Artist	Record Title
66083	Mike Patterson/Fugitives	Cookin' Beans / Jerky
66084	P. J. Proby (Not Released)	Somewhere / Just Like Him
66085	Billy J. Kramer	It's Gotta Last Forever / They Remind Me of You
66086	Georgie Fame	Preach & Teach / Yeh, Yeh
66087	Johnny Rivers	Cupid / Midnight Special
66088	Kenny Lynch	My Own Two Feet / So Much to Love You For
66089	Simon Scott	Midnight / My Baby's Got Soul
66090	Swinging Blue Jeans	It Isn't There / One of These Days
66091	Don Lee Wilson	Angel / Feel So Fine
66092	Fantastic Baggies	Alone on the Beach / It Was I
66093	Sandy Nelson	Chop Chop / Reach for a Star
66094	Jimmy McCracklin	Can't Raise Me / Every Night, Every Day
66095	Irma Thomas	Some Things You Never Get Used To / You Don't Miss a Good Thing
66096	Paul Murray	I Wish You Everything / Is It Me
66097	Jimmy Hann/Dynamics	Busybody / Moonlight in Vermont

Label #	Artist	Record Title
66098	Fender IV	Everybody Up / Malibu Run
66099	Hollies	Nobody / Yes I Will
66100	Johnny Union/Pickets	Do the Freddy Dance / Honey Train
66101	Mel Carter	High Noon / I Just Can't Imagine
66102	The O'Jays	Lipstick Traces / Think It Over, Baby
66103	Slim Whitman	Mansion on the Hill / Reminiscing
66104	Georgie Fame	In the Meantime / Let the Sunshine In
66105	Richie Moreland	Bells in My Heart / Mailman Blues
66106	Irma Thomas	Nobody Wants to Hear Nobody's Troubles / I'm Gonna Cry Till My Tears Run Dry
66107	Sandy Nelson	Land of 1000 Dances / Let There Be Drums
66108	Jimmy Griffin	These Are the Times / Walking to New Orleans
66109	Clydie King	If You Were a Man / Thrill Is Gone
66110	Jackie DeShannon	I Remember the Boy / What the World Needs Now Is Love
66111	Dynamic Explosions	Like Your Love / Work with Me Annie
66112	Johnny Rivers	Seventh Son / Un-Square Dance
66113	Mel Carter	Hold Me, Thrill Me, Kiss Me / Sweet Little Girl
66114	Cher	All I Really Want to Do / I'm Gonna Love You
66115	Billy J. Kramer	Trains & Boats & Planes / I'll Be on My Way
66116	Jimmy McCracklin	Arkansas Part 1 / Arkansas Part 2
66117	Law Firm	Girl from Liverpool / Love Is Bad
66118	Mike Patterson	Don't You Just Know It / Righteous Theme
66119	Hollies	I'm Alive / You Know He Did
66120	Irma Thomas	Hurts All Gone / It's Starting to Get Me Now
66121	The O'Jays	I've Cried My Last Tear / Whip It on Me Baby
66122	Clara Wood	Old & Grey / You're After My Guy
66123	Leon Hayward	Pain in My Heart / She's with Her Other Love

Appendix 11

Label #	Artist	Record Title
66124	Buckingham IV	Endless Sleep
		Your Lovin' Is Really Tough
66125	Georgie Fame	Blue Monday
		Like We Used to Be
66126	Richie Moreland	I Forgot to Remember to Forget
		When the New Wears Off
66127	Sandy Nelson	Casbah
		Drums a Go-Go
66128	Joel Christie	It's All Right Now
		See That Girl
66129	Jimmy McCracklin	Steppin' Up in Class
		Think
66130	Slim Whitman	La Golondrina
		More Than Yesterday
66131	The O'Jays	Let It All Come Out
		You're the One (You're the Only One)
66132	Jackie DeShannon	Lifetime of Loneliness
		Don't Turn Your Back on Me
66133	Johnny Rivers	Love Me While You Can
		Where Have All the Flowers Gone
66134	Hollies	Look Through Any Window
		So Lonely
66135	Billy J. Kramer/Dakotas	Irresistible You
		Twilight Time
66136	Cher	See See Blues
		Where Do You Go
66137	Irma Thomas	Take a Look
		What Are You Trying to Do
66138	Mel Carter	My Heart Sings
		When I Hold the Hand of the One I Love
66139	Clydie King	Missin' My Baby
		My Love Grows Deeper
66140	Law Firm	I Love You More
		Time
66141	Tom Tedesco	La Montana
		Sweet September
66142	Joel Christie	Angels in the Sky
		Lead Me On
66143	Billy J. Kramer/Dakotas	I'll Be Doggone
		Neon City
66144	Johnny Rivers	Long Time Man
		Under Your Spell Again
66145	The O'Jays	I'll Never Let You Go
		It Won't Hurt
66146	Sandy Nelson	Lover's Concerto
		Treat Her Right
66147	Jimmy McCracklin	Beulah
		My Answer
66148	Mel Carter	I Wish I Didn't Love You So
		Love Is All We Need
66149	Leon Haywood	1-2-3
		Soul-On

Label #	Artist	Record Title
66150	A. C. Jones	Hole in Your Soul Part 1
66151	Sue Raney	Hole in Your Soul Part 2 Before the Rain Now Is the Hour
66152	Jimmy Griffin	Hard Row to Hoe He Will Break Your Heart

1965

1966

Label #	Artist	Record Title
66153	Slim Whitman	Straight from Heaven Twelfth of Never
66154	Swinging Blue Jeans	Don't Make Me Over What Can I Do Today
66155	Jimmy Bryant	Model 400 Buckboard Blow Your Hat in the Creek
66156	Frank Pourcel	What's New Pussycat?
66157	Irresistables	As Sweet as You Can Be Why Did My Baby Turn Bad
66158	Hollies	I Can't Let Go I've Got a Way of My Own
66159	Johnny Rivers	Secret Agent Man You Dig
66160	Cher	Bang Bang (My Baby Shot Me Down) Needles & Pins
66160	Cher	Bang Bang (My Baby Shot Me Down) Our Day Will Come
66161	Buddy Cagle	Honky Tonk College Tonight I'm Coming Home
66162	O'Jays	I'll Never Forget You Pretty Words
66163	Ludwig/Klassics	I Forgot Mumph
66163	Ludwig/Klassics	My Heart Reminds Me Mumph
66164	Frank Pourcel Orchestra	Beautiful Obsession Mister Lonely
66165	Mel Carter	Band of Gold Detour
66166	Jimmy Boyd	I Would Never Do That Lazy Me
66167	Frank Roberts	Western Union Words & Music
66168	Jimmy McCracklin	Come on Home (Back Where You Belong) Something That Belongs to Me
66169	Eddie Seay	Do What's Right Soul Good Thing
66170	Satisfactions	Bring It All Down Daddy, You Just Gotta Let Him In
66171	Jackie DeShannon	Come & Get Me Splendor in the Grass
66172	Clydie King	He Always Comes Back to Me Soft & Gentle Ways

Appendix 11

Label #	Artist	Record Title
66173	Johnny Carver	One Way or the Other
		Think About Her All the Time
66174	Tommy Sands	As Long as I'm Travelin'
		It's the Only One I've Got
66175	Johnny Rivers	I Washed My Hands in Muddy Water
		Roogalator
66176	Jimmy Bryant	Julie's Gone
		Lonesome
66177	The O'Jays	It's a Blowin' Wind
		No Time for You
66178	Irma Thomas	It's a Man-Woman's World Parts 1 and 2
66179	California Suns	Little Bit of Heaven
		Masked Grandma
66180	Jimmy McCracklin	Just Let Me Cry
		These Boots Are Made for Walkin'
66181	Slim Whitman	Travelin' Man
		I Remember You
66182	Sam E. Solo	Love Is Not a Game
		Tears Keep Falling
66183	Mel Carter	If You Lose Her
		You, You, You
66184	Sue Raney	Little Things Mean a Lot
		Who's Afraid
66185	June Jackson	Fifty Per Cent Won't Do
		It's What's up Front That Counts
66186	Hollies	Bus Stop
		Don't Run & Hide
66187	Buddy Cagle	Be Nice to Everybody
		Too Many Mountains
66187	Buddy Cagle	Be Nice to Everybody
		The Wild Side of Life
66188	Frank Roberts	All in My mind
		Raining in My Heart
66189	Georgie Fame	El Bandido
		Get Away
66190	Joe Sanchez	Our Love Baby Is Running Down
		Unlucky Me
66191	Glen Garrison	Green to Blue
		You Can't Win 'em All
66192	Cher	Alfie
		She's No Better Than Me
66193	Sandy Nelson	The Charge
		Rock It to 'em J. B.
66194	Jackie DeShannon	Will You Love Me Tomorrow
		Are You Ready for This
66195	Tony Terran	Don't Answer Me
		Dominique
66196	Jackie DeShannon	So Long Johnny
		Windows & Doors
66197	The O'Jays	Friday Night
		Stand in for Love

Label #	Artist	Record Title
66198	Joel Christie	It's All Right Now / Since I Found You
66199	Bobby Mason	People Say / Laura
66200	The O'Jays	Lonely Drifter / That's Enough
66201	Twilighters	Road to Fortune / Shake a Tail Feather
66202	Jackie DeShannon	To Be Myself / I Can Make It with You
66203	George Semper	Shortnin' Bread / Collard Greens
66204	Vulcanes	Green Light / You Always Hurt the One You Love
66205	Johnny Rivers	Man Can Cry / Poor Side of Town
66206	Jimmy Boyd	She Chased Me / Will I Cry
66207	Jimmy McCracklin	It's Got to Be Love / Sorry
66208	Mel Carter	Tar & Cement / Take Good Care of Her
66209	Sandy Nelson	Let's Go Trippin' / Pipeline
66210	Billy J. Kramer	Take My Hand / You Make Me Feel Like Someone
66211	Sue Raney	Smile / Any Old Time of Day
66212	Slim Whitman	Jerry / One Dream
66213	Johnny Carver	Fool's Names, Fool's Faces / What If It Happened to You
66214	Hollies	It's You / Stop Stop Stop
66215	Glen Garrison	Where Do I Go from Here / Strong & Handsome, Sweet & Simple Side
66216	Baby Ray	House on Soul Hill / There's Something on Your Mind
66217	Cher	Behind the Door / Magic in the Air
66218	Buddy Cagle	Apologize / Help's on the Way
66219	Orville & Ivy	Tabasco Road / Shinbone
66220	Georgie Fame/Blue Flames	Last Night / Sitting in the Park
66221	Frank Pourcel Orchestra	While I Love / Any Old Time of the Day
66222	Sue Raney	There Goes My Everything / Try to See It My Way
66223	Cher	Dream Baby / Mama (When My Dollies Have Babies)

Appendix 11

Label #	Artist	Record Title
1966		
1967		
66224	Jackie DeShannon	Come on Down / Find Me Love
66225	Swinging Blue Jeans	Now the Summer's Gone / Rumors, Gossip, Words Untrue
66226	Slim Whitman	What's the World a-Comin' To / You Bring Out the Best in Me
66227	Johnny Rivers	Baby I Need Your Lovin' / Gettin' Ready for Tomorrow
66228	Mel Carter	As Time Goes By / Look to the Rainbow
66229	Tommy Sands	Candy Store Prophet / Second Star to the Left
66230	Glen Garrison	Listen, They're Playing My Song / My New Creation
66231	Hollies	All the World Is Love / On a Carousel
66232	Baby Ray	Elvira / Just Because
66233	Jimmy Boyd	I Would Never Do That / So Young & So Fine
66234	John Carver	I Gotta Go Home / You Are That Something
66235	Jimmy Bryant	Lazy Guitar / Tabasco Road
66236	Jackie DeShannon	Where Does the Sun Go / Wishing Doll
66237	Frank Roberts	Alone & Forsaken / Long Long Way to Georgia
66238	Twilighters	I Still Love You / Meat Ball
66239	Larry Butler	Lonesome / Sandy
66240	Hollies	Pay You Back with Interest / Whatcha Gonna Do 'Bout It
66241	Sunshine Company (Not Released)	Up Up and Away / Blue May
66242	Jimmy Clanton	Absence of Lisa / C'mon Jim
66243	Love Generation	Groovy Summertime / Playin' on the Strings of the Wind
66244	Johnny Rivers	Rewind Medley / Tracks of My Tears
66245	Buddy Cagle	Camptown Girl / Long Time Traveling
66246	Sandy Nelson	The Drums Go On / Lawdy Miss Clawdy
66247	Sunshine Company	Blue May / Happy
66248	Slim Whitman	I'm a Fool / North Wind

Appendixes

Label #	Artist	Record Title
66249	Orville & Ivy	Please Pass the Biscuits / Slow Poke
66250	Ray Chafin	Good Time Girl / Life Is a Winner
66251	Jackie DeShannon	Changin' My Mind / It's All in the Game
66252	Cher	Hey Joe / Our Day Will Come
66253	Sandy Nelson	Peter Gunn / You Got Me Hummin'
66254	Love Generation	Meet Me at the Love In / She Touched Me
66255	Swinging Blue Jeans	Something's Coming Along / Tremblin'
66256	Baby Ray	Your Sweet Love / Yours Until Tomorrow
66257	Glen Garrison	Goodbye Swingers / Hello Mama
66258	Hollies	Just One Look / Running Through the Night
66259	Classics IV	Poor People / Spooky
66260	Sunshine Company	Back on the Street Again / I Just Want to Be Your Friend
66261	Cher	Elusive Butterfly / You Better Sit Down Kids
66261	Cher	Mama / You Better Sit Down Kids
66262	Slim Whitman	Broken Wings / Keeper of the Key
66263	Buddy Cagle	Cincinnati Stranger / Waikiki Sand
66264	Rivendell Singers (Not Released)	Sweet September / Rivendell
66265	Sue Raney	A Banda / Wait Until Dark
66266	Equipe 84	Twenty-Ninth of September / Auschwitz
66267	Johnny Rivers	Summer Rain / Memory of the Coming Good
66268	Johnny Carver	What If It Happened to You / Your Lily White Hands

1967
1968

Label #	Artist	Record Title
66269	Santo & Johnny	See You in September / Live for Life
66270	Dave Dee & Dozy, Beaky, Mick & Tich	Sun Goes Down / Zabadak
66271	Hollies	If I Need Someone / I'll Be True to You (Yes I Will)
66272	Dick Clair	Open Letter to Dad / Tell That Joke

Appendix 11

Label #	Artist	Record Title
66273	Joey Martin	Joey's Letter
		Joey's Prayer
66274	Jimmy Clanton	Calico Junction
		I'll Be Loving You
66275	Love Generation	Maman (Mama)
		W. C. Fields
66276	Not Released	
66277	Larry Butler	Break My Mind
		Funny, Familiar, Forgotten Feelings
66278	Sunshine Company	It's Sunday
	(Not Released)	Reflections on an Angel
66279	Glen Garrison	Your Side of Me
		If I Lived Here (I'd Be Home Now)
66280	Sunshine Company	Look Here Comes the Sun
		It's Sunday
66281	Jackie DeShannon	I Keep Wanting You
		Me About You
66282	Cher	Click Song Number One
		But I Can't Love You More
66283	Slim Whitman	Rainbows Are Back in Style
		How Could I Not Love You
66284	Sandy Nelson	Alligator Boogaloo
		Midnight Magic
66285	Moon	Mothers & Fathers
		Someday Girl
66286	Johnny Rivers	Look to Your Soul
		Something's Strange
66287	Dave Dee & Dozy, Beaky, Mick & Tich	Legend of Zanadu
		Please
66288	Rex Allen, Jr.	World I Live In
		Before I Change My Mind (I'm Going Home)
66289	Love Generation	Love & Sunshine
		Magic Land
66290	Frank Pourcel	Aranjuez
		Importance of the Rose
66291	Roger Sovine	Culman, Alabam
		Savannah Georgia Vagrant
66292	Santo & Johnny	It Must Be Him
		Sleep Walk '68
66293	Classics IV	Strange Changes
		Soul Train
66294	Penny DeHaven	Big City Men
		Old Faithful
66295	Dee Irwin	I Only Get This Feeling
		Wrong Direction
66296	Larry Butler	Lady Madonna
		Honey
66297	Johnny Carver	Feelin' Kinda Sunday in My Thinkin'
		I Still Didn't Have the Sense to Go
66298	Sunshine Company	Let's Get Together
		Sunday Brought the Rain

Label #	Artist	Record Title
66299	Georgie Fame	Last Night
		Funny How Time Slips Away
66300	Glen Garrison	I'll Be Your Baby Tonight
		You Know I Love You
66301	Jackie DeShannon	Nobody's Home to Go Home To
		Nicole
66302	Frank Pourcel	La, La, La
		Congratulations
66303	Frank Pourcel	If I Only Had Time
	(Not Released)	Se Chaque Soir Meurt Une Rose
66304	Classics IV	Mama's & Papa's
		Waves
66305	Danny Wagner/	I Lost a True Love
	Kindred Soul	My Buddy
66306	Mamie P. Galore	This Time Tomorrow
		Tonight's the Night
66307	Cher	Song Called Children
		Take Me for a Little While
66308	Sunshine Company	Darcy Farrow
		On a Beautiful Day
66309	Dave Dee, Dozy,	Breakout
	Beaky, Mick & Tich	Mrs. Thursday
66310	Love Generation	Consciousness Expansion
		Montage from "How Sweet It Is"
66311	Slim Whitman	Happy Street
		My Heart Is in the Roses
66312	Jackie DeShannon	Splendor in the Grass
		Didn't Want to Have to Do It
66313	Jackie DeShannon	Effervescent Blue
		The Weight
66313	Jackie DeShannon	Effervescent Blue
		Splendor in the Grass
66314	Johnny Rivers	Everybody's Talkin'
	(Not Released)	The Way We Live
66315	Penny DeHaven/	Kid Games & Nursery Rhymes
	Buddy Cagle	So Sad
66316	Johnny Carver	Does She Still Get Her Way
		Leaving Again
66317	New Generation	She's a Soldier Boy
		Smokey Blue's Away
66318	Elysian Field	King of Man
		Alone on Your Doorstep
66319	Not Issued	
66320	Dee Irwin	I Can't Stand the Pain
		My Hope to Die Girl
66321	Penny DeHaven	I Am the Woman
		Loving You Again
66322	Roger Sovine	Home Town Blues
		River Girl
66323	Odyssey	Everything Will Be Alright
		Parts 1 and 2
66324	Sunshine Company	Love Poem
		Willie Jean

Appendix 11

Label #	Artist	Record Title
66325	Dave Dee, Dozy, Beaky, Mick & Tich	Break Out Mrs. Thursday
66326	Kim Fowley	Born to Be Wild Space Odyssey
66327	Danny Wagner/Kindred Soul	Harlem Shuffle When Johnny Comes Marching Home
66328	Classics IV	Stormy Ladies Man
66328	Classics IV	Stormy 24 Hours of Loneliness
66329	Girls from Petticoat Junction	If You Only Could Be Me I'm So Glad That You Found Me
66330	The Moon	Faces John Automaton
66331	Buddy Cagle	I'll Get Over You I've Wondered Where She's Been
66332	Gil Bernal	The Man Tower of Strength
66333	Glen Garrison	She Still Thinks I Care That Lucky Old Sun
66334	Dee Irwin/Mamie Galore	All I Want for Christmas Is Your Love By the Time I Get to Phoenix
66335	Johnny Rivers	Better Life Right Relations
66336	Love Generation	Catching Up on Fun Let the Good Time In
66337	Slim Whitman	Heaven Says Hello Livin' on Lovin'
66338	Quotations	Havin' a Good Time Can I Have Someone
66339	Dave Dee, Dozy, Beaky, Mick & Tich	Wreck of the Antoinette Margarita Lidman
66340	Sue Raney	Early Morning Blues & Greens Knowing When to Leave
66341	Johnny Carver	Hold Me Tight My Heart's Been Marching
66342	Jackie DeShannon	Holly Would Laurel Canyon

1968

1969

Label #	Artist	Record Title
66343	Doug Brooks	As Time Goes On I Take Pride in What I Am
66344	Roger Sovine	Love Took My Heart A Railroad Trestle in California
66345	Bonzo Dog Doo Dah Band	Canyons of Your Mind I'm the Urban Spaceman
66346	Girls from Petticoat Junction	Thirty Days Hath September Wheeling, West Virginia
66347	California Smog	Blow in My Ear & I'll Follow You Anywhere Circles
66348	Bobby & I	Catching the Time in Your Hand Love Is for the Sharing

Appendixes

Label #	Artist	Record Title
66349	Kim Fowley	Bubble Gum / Wildfire
66350	Sandy Nelson	Lion in Winter / Rebirth of the Beat
66351	Albert Collins	Ain't Got Time / Got a Good Thing Goin'
66352	Classics IV	Mary, Mary Row Your Boat / Traces
66353	The Spice	What About the Music / In Love
66354	Houston Fearless	Race with the Devil / Someone Else's Blues
	(Not Released)	
66355	Bobby Angelle	I Used to Be Happy / No Other Love Could Be
66356	Wichita Falls	Going to Ohio / Ornamental Sideshow
66357	Buddy Cagle	As If I Needed to Be Reminded / Daddy Please
66358	Slim Whitman	My Happiness / Promises
66359	Dee Irwin/Mamie Galore	Day Tripper / I Didn't Wanna Do It, But I Did
66360	Johnny Rivers	These Are Not My People / Going Back to Big Sur
66361	Johnny Carver	Sweet Wine / With Every Heartbeat
66362	Lance Le Gault	Billie / Louisiana Swamp
	(Not Released)	
66363	Jimmy & Vella	Knights in White Satin / Well
66364	Bobby Blue	Ride with Me Baby / So Alive with Love
66365	Billy Mize	Make It Rain / You Done Me Wrong
66366	Ray Sanders	Beer Drinking Music / Gotta Find a Way
66367	Penny DeHaven	You're Never Gonna See My Face Again / I'm Going Home
66368	Quotations	Can I Have Someone (for Once) / Havin' a Good Time (with My Baby)
66369	Mike Rubini	Ballade of Polly Maggoo / Jade Bird
66370	Jackie DeShannon	Trust Me / What Is This
66371	Billy Watkins	Echoes / Somebody's Love
66372	Wichita Falls	Ginger Blue / Lovely Love
66373	Bonzo Dog Doo Dah Band	Mr. Apollo / Ready Made
66374	Clem Curtis	Caravan / Marie Take a Chance

Appendix 11

Label #	Artist	Record Title
66375	Sandy Nelson	Manhattan Spiritual / The Stripper
66376	Johnny Winger	Forty-Four / Rollin' & Tumblin'
66377	Vicki Vote	Angel Baby / Look for a Star
66378	Classics IV	Everyday with You Girl / Sentimental Lady
66379	Ross Bagdasarian	Jone-Cone-Phone / Spanish Pizza
66380	Packers	Packin' It In / You Got It
66381	Cheryl Miles	Could This Be True / Woman Has Taken Her Place
66382	The Symbols	I Will Still Be There / Wrong Girl
66383	Jades	Gotta Find Somebody to Love / Wheel of Fortune
66384	Slim Whitman	Flower of Love / Irresistible
66385	Jackie DeShannon	Always Be Together / Put a Little Love in Your Heart
66386	Johnny Rivers	Muddy Rivers / Resurrection
66387	Elysian Field	Strange Changes / 24 Hours of Loneliness
66388	Penny DeHaven	Mama Lou / That's Just the Way I Am
66389	Johnny Carver	Mother-in-Law / That's Your Hang Up
66390	Eggy	Hooky / You're Still Mine
66391	Albert Collins	Do the Sissy / Turnin' On
66392	Bobby Blue	Jambalaya (On the Bayou) / Moonlight Bay/By the Light of the Silvery Moon
66393	Classics IV/Dennis Yost	Change of Heart / Rainy Day
66394	Fantasy	I Got the Fever / Painted Horse
66395	Jimmie & Vella	Free Yourself / Love Is Colour Blind
66396	Sam Russell	Footprints in the Sand / Whole Lotta Livin'
66397	New Dawn	Melody Fair / Sometimes in the Morning
66398	Roger Sovine	Little Bitty Nitty Gritty Dirt Town / Son
66399	Sunshine Company	Only Thing That Matters / Bolaro
66400	Wigwam	Helsinki / True Confession

Label #	Artist	Record Title
66401	Glen Garrison	Goodnight Irene / Change Me
66402	Sandy Nelson	Leap Frog / Let There Be Drums & Brass
66403	Billy Mize	Absence of You / While I'm Thinkin' About It
66404	We the People	Earthrise / Moonstep
66405	Thomas & Richard Frost	She's Got Love / Word Is Love
66406	David Bryant	My Dashiki / The Underdog
66407	Buddy Cagle	Guitar Player (Ballad of James Burton) / Mud Is to Jump In
66408	Ray Sanders	Lucille / Three Tears (for the Sad, Hurt & Blue)
66409	U. K. Baby	Heartbreaker / Michael Blues
66410	Sidney Elliott	If Music Be the Food of Love / Who Dat Girl
66411	Slim Whitman	Love Song of the Waterfall / When You Were 16
66412	Albert Collins	And Then It Started Raining / Conversation for Collins
66413	Mamie Galore	Beautiful Inside / You Wore Your Lie So Well
66414	Ross Bagdasarian	You've Got Me on a Merry-Go-Round / You Better Open Your Eyes
66415	The Moon	Not to Know / Pirate
66416	Tribulations	Mama's Love / You Gave Me Up for Promises
66417	Scott Turner	Sister Beth (and I) / Our House on Paper
66418	Johnny Rivers	Ode to John Lee / One Woman
66419	Jackie DeShannon	I Let Go Completely / Love Will Find a Way
66420	Dee Irwin	Ain't No Way / Cherish
66421	Penny DeHaven	Down in the Boondocks / When the Sun Sets in Jackson
66422	Snappers	Call Me Back to Denver / Mirror Man
66423	Johnny Carver	Take Sadie Out to the Country / Willie & the Hand Jive
66424	Classics IV/Dennis Yost	The Comic / Midnight
66425	Jades	Don't Give What's Mine Away / L-O-V-E I Love You
66426	Thomas & Richard Frost	With Me My Love / Gotta Find a New Place to Find

Appendix 11 673

Label #	Artist	Record Title
66427	Billy Mize	Closest I Ever Came
		Mama, the Sparrow & the Tree
66428	Wrinkle	Beatiful Lady
		Mother
66429	Combination Two	Combination of the Two
		I'm a Man
66430	Jackie DeShannon	Do You Know How Christmas Trees Are Grown
		1 Christmas

1969

1970

Label #	Artist	Record Title
66431	(Not Released)	
66432	Travis Bell	Welfare Cadillac
66433	Ray Sanders	Holly Wood
		So Softly & Tenderly
66434	Jimmy & Vella Cameron	Why
		We Sing
66435	Bobby Blue	Sincere Replies
		You'll Want Diamonds
66436	Bobby & I	On Rose Walk
		Be Young, Be Foolish, Be Happy
66437	Penny DeHaven	I Feel Fine
		Stop & Go
66438	Jackie DeShannon	Brighton Hill
		You Can Come to Me
66439	Dennis Yost/Classics IV	Funniest Thing
		Nobody Loves You But Me
66440	London Fogg	Easy Mover
		Trippin'
66441	Slim Whitman	Come Take My Hand
		Tomorrow Never Comes
66442	Johnny Carver	Gonna Come in Like a Lion
		Harvey Harrington IV
66443	Sam Russell	Escape from Sad Times
		If You Don't Know Where You're Goin'
66444	Black Rabbit	For a Little of Her Sunshine
		Free
66445	Ross Bagdasarian	
	(Not Released)	
66446	Royston Thomas	Mommy Said
		She's There
66447	Billy Mize	If It Were the Last Song
		I Learned to Walk
66448	Johnny Rivers	Into the Mystic
		Jesus Is a Soul Man
66449	Roger Sovine	Star
		That Was Once Upon a Time
66450	Wrinkles	It's a Good Day
		Queen Bee
66451	Thomas & Richard Frost	Fairy Tale Affair
		Hello Stranger
66452	Jackie DeShannon	You Keep Me Hangin' On — Hurt So Bad
		What Was Your Day Like

Label #	Artist	Record Title
66453	Johnny Rivers	Apple Tree
		Fire & Rain

Freedom

1958

44001	Johnny Burnett (*sic*)	Kiss Me
		I'm Restless
44002	Four Dots/Jeff Stone	It's Heaven
		My Baby
44003	Wilson Sisters	Each Time You Leave
		That's Me Without You
44004	Bill Lawrence	Hey Baby
		Caribbean

1958
1959

44005	Four Dots	Pleading for Your Love
		Don't Wake Up the Kids
44006	Alpacs/Willie Walker	Three Hundred and Sixty-Five
		Money Mad
44007	Jimmie Maddin	I'm Studying You
		I Just Can't Say Goodbye
44008	Jerry Wright	One Blade of Grass
		Yes Sir, That's My Baby
44009	Sherman Scott	Let's Be Friends
		What It Means to Have a Friend
44010	Upperclassmen	Cryin' Towel
		Cha Cha with the Zombies
44011	Johnny Burnette	Gumbo
		Me and the Bear
44012	Don Gordon	When the Sun
		How Come You Don't Love Me
44013	Four Troys	In the Moonlight
		Suddenly You Want to Dance
44014	Johnny Ellis	Balboa Bop
		Cinderella Doll
44015	Sonny Warner	Riff Runner
		San Antonio Rose
44016	Terri & Jane	Lonesome Lover
		Oh Baby Oh
44017	Johnny Burnette	Sweet Baby Doll
		I'll Never Love Again
44018	Jay Johnston	Living Doll
		Walk a Dog
44019	Barry Martin	Minnie the Moocher
		The Willies
44020	Larry O'Keefe	Ain't a That Somethin'
		Lover's Dream
44021	Dee Dee Douty	Bily Billy
		Give Your Love to Me

Label #	Artist	Record Title
44022	Anna/John T. Webster	Gotta Make Love to You A Million Teardrops
44023	Joe & Juna	Starry Eyes Teenage Heart

1959
1960

44024	Jeff Monroe	River Song Just for a Little While
44025	Smiley Wilson	Long as Little Birds Fly Running Bear

Soul City

1966

750	Rose Brooks	I'm Moanin They're Coming to Take Me Away, Ha Ha
751		
752	Fifth Dimension	Train, Keep on Moving I'll Be Loving You Forever

1966
1967

753	Fifth Dimension	Go Where You Wanna Go Too Poor to Die
754	Willie Hutch	Can't Fight the Power How Come Baby, You Don't Love Me
755	Fifth Dimension	Another Day, Another Heartache Rosecrans Blvd.
756	Fifth Dimension	Up, Up, and Away Which Way to Nowhere
757		
758	Strawberry Children	Love Years Coming One Stands Here
759	Al Wilson	When You Love, You're Loved Too Who Could Be Lovin' You
760	Fifth Dimension	Paper Cup Poor Side of Town
761	Al Wilson	Do What You Gotta Do Now I Know What Love Is

1967
1968

762	Fifth Dimension	Carpet Man Magic Garden
763	James Hendricks	I Think of You Sunshine Showers
764		
765	Fourth Way	Far Side of Your Moon Pink Cloud
766	Fifth Dimension	Stoned Soul Picnic Sailboat Song

676 Appendixes

Label #	Artist	Record Title
767	Al Wilson	The Snake
		Getting Ready for Tomorrow
768	Fifth Dimension	Sweet Blindness
		Bobby's Blues
769		
770	Fifth Dimension	California Soul
		It'll Never Be the Same
771	Al Wilson	The Dolphins
		Poor Side of Town

1968
1969

Label #	Artist	Record Title
772	Fifth Dimension	Aquarius/Let the Sunshine In
		Don'tcha Hear Me Callin' to Ya
773	Al Wilson	I Stand Accused
		Shake Me, Wake Me
774	Hank Schifter	How or When
		Long John
775	Al Wilson	Lodi
		By the Time I Get to Phoenix
776	Fifth Dimension	Workin' on a Groovy Thing
		Broken Wing Bird
777		
778		
779	Fifth Dimension	Wedding Bell Blues
		Lovin' Stew

1969
1970

Label #	Artist	Record Title
780	Fifth Dimension	Blowing Away
		Skinny Man
781	Fifth Dimension	Girl's Song
		It'll Never Be the Same Again

1977

Label #	Artist	Record Title
007	Johnny Rivers	Ashes 'n' Sand
		Outside Help
008	Johnny Rivers	Swayin to the Music (Slow Dancing)
		Outside Help

Pacific Jazz/World Pacific

Label #	Artist	Record Title
300		
301	Wes Montgomery	Quartet Fingerpickin'
		Summertime
302	Billy Higgins	Me & My Lover
		Up in Teddy's New Flat
303	Jackie Davis/Harold Land	Red Shirt
		Blowin' the Blues
304	Paul Bryant/Amy Curtis	Searchin'
		Goin' Down, Git Me a Woman

Label #	Artist	Record Title
305	Rune Overman Trio	Funky Festival
		Old Spice
306	Les McCann	C Jam Blues
		The Shout

1961

Label #	Artist	Record Title
307		
308		
309	Les McCann	Truth
310	Les McCann	Girl from Casper
311	Les McCann	Fish This Week
		Vacushna
312	Julian "Cannonball" Adderley/Gil Evans	Manteca
		St. Louis Blues
313	Gerry Mulligan Quartet	Bernie's Tune
		Five Brothers
314	Teddy Edwards/ Les McCann	Beve's Comjumulations
		Love Is Here to Stay
315	Paul Bryant	Churchin'
		They Can't Take That Away from Me
316	Bobby Hutcherson/ Amy Curtis	Oatmeal
		One More Hammock Please
317	Les McCann	Big Jim
		I Am in Love
318	Les McCann	Gone Up & Get That Church Parts 1 and 2
319	Frank Butler/Amy Curtis	Gone Into It
		Groovin' Blue
320	Bud Shank	The Awakening
		New Groove
321	Richard Holmes/Les McCann/Ben Webster	Harmonica Boogie Shuffle
		Them That's Got
322	Larry "Wild" Wrice	Husky
		Sanctifism
323		
324		
325	Bobby Montez	Guajira Josephina
		Tremendo Cha Cha
326	Carmell Jones/ Harold Land	Blues March
		I'm Gonna Go Fishing
327	Jimmy Witherspoon	Ain't Nobody's Business
		Times Have Changed
328	Bobby Montez	Manana Pachanga
		Bailar Pachanga
329	Les McCann	I Cried for You
		Sweet Georgia Brown
330	Gene Ammons/Richard "Groove" Holmes	Groovin' with Jug
		Morris the Minor
331		
332	Ben Di Tosti	Let's Get Together
		Theme from "Carnival"
333	Gerald Wilson	Blues for Yna Yna
		You Better Believe It

Label #	Artist	Record Title
334	Modesto's Charanga Kings	Quiet Village Cha Cha
		Ven, Vida Mia, a Bailar

1962

335	Les McCann	Next Spring
		Wonder Why
336	Modesto Charanga Kings	Ja Ja Ja
		Pachanga Malanga
337	Ron Jefferson	Little One
		Love Lifted Me
338	Kenny Dorham/	No Two People
	Jackie McLean	Us
339	Richie Kamuca/	Keester Parade
	Cy Touff	What Am I Here For
340	Jazz Crusaders	Sinnin' Sam
		Tonight
341	Les McCann	Little ¾ for God & Co
		Twist Cha Cha
342	Jazz Crusaders	Young Rabbits
343		
344		
345	Olgerita	La Conceccion
		Pa Pa Pachanga
346	Gerald Wilson	Brass Bag
		Canadian Sunset
347	Richard Holmes/	Comin' Through the Apple
	Les McCann	Somethin' Special

1962
1963

348	Carmell Jones	Business Meetin'
		Stella by Starlight
349	Tricky Lofton/	Angel Eyes
	Carmell Jones	Celery Stalks at Midnight
350	Les McCann	Shampoo
		Kathleen's Theme
351		
352	Night Hawks	Bunny Ride
		Sweetie Lester
353		
354		
355		
356		
357		
358		
359		
360		
361		
362		
363		
364	Clare Fischer/	Joao
	Bud Shank	Misty

Label #	Artist	Record Title
365	Gerald Wilson Orchestra	Milestone
		Teri
366	Earl Auderza	All the Things You Are Part 1
		All the Things You Are Part 2
367	Joe Pass	Days of Wine & Roses
		Forward Pass
368	Clifford Scott	Crosstalk
		Samba de Bamba
369		
370	Bud Shank/	Brasamba
	Claire Fischer	Little Boat
371	Jazz Crusaders	No Name Samba
		Tough Talk
372		
373		
374	David Allen	Swing for Joey
		Where You At
375	Toots Thielmans	I'll Be Around
		Pentecostal Feeling
376	Nancy Claire	Baby Blues
		I'm Burning My Diary
377	Marilyn Burroughs	Brightest Smile
		I Will Love You
378	Clifford Scott	I Will Follow Him
		Tweedley Dee
379	Amy Curtis	Native Land Part 1
		Native Land Part 2

World Pacific

380		
381		
382	De-Fenders	(Dance to the) Yakety Sax
		Wild One
383		
384		
385	Charles Kynard	Here Now
		Where It's At
386	Furys	Anything for You
		Cat 'n' Mouse
387	Les McCann	Gospel Truth
		Send It on Down to Me
388	Jazz Crusaders	Boopie
		Turkish Black
389	Les McCann	Bye & Bye
		Get That Soul
390	Marilyn Burroughs	For Your Sweet Love
		Stained Glass Windows
391	Folkswingers	Black Mountain Rag
		This Train
392		
393		
394		
395		

Label #	Artist	Record Title
396	Folkswingers	12 String Special
397		Amor a Todos
398	Sonny Stitt	My Mother's Eyes
		Summer Special

1963

1964

Label #	Artist	Record Title
399		
400		
401	Jazz Crusaders	Heat Wave
		On Broadway
402	Jesse Paul	Johnny Let Me Go
		My First Lonely Night
403	Sonny Knight	I Just Called to Say Hello
		If You Want This Love
404	Les McCann	Back at the Chicken Shack
		Sack o' Woe
405	Sandells	Out Front
		Scrambler
406	Les McCann	Bluesette
		Spanish Castles
407		
408	Long Gone Miles	Long Gone
		No Money, No Honey
409	Clifford Scott	Beach Bunny
		Lavender Sax
410	Bud Shank/Folkswingers	Don't Think Twice
		Freight Train
411	Les McCann	Big City
		Route 66
412	Jazz Crusaders	I Remember Tomorrow
		Long John
413	Stoneman Family	Groundhog
		Take Me Home
414	Jesse Paul	Corners of the Room
		Popcorn & Candy
415	Sandells	6-Pak
		Endless Summer
416		
417	Ann Callison	Only You Can Tell Me
		My Baby's Gone
418	Les McCann	It Had Better Be Tonight
		Que Rico

1964

Label #	Artist	Record Title
419	David Parker	Coffee Pot
		Greek's Tale
420		
421	Sandells	All Over Again
		Always
422	Les McCann	McCanna
		Basuto Baby

Appendix 11

Label #	Artist	Record Title
423		
424		
425		
426		
427		
428	Monty Alexander	John Brown's Body
		Little Children of Peru
429		
430		
431		
432		
433		
434	Gerald Wilson	Could Be
		In the Limelight
800		
801	Bud & Travis	Raspberries Strawberries
		Mexican Wedding Song
802	Don Ralke	Maverick
		Travelin' West
803	Swingers	Love Makes the World Go
		Jackie
804	Gloria Smythe	Gee Baby Ain't I Good to You
		I'll Be Over After a While
805	Annie Ross	Some People
		Let Me Entertain You
806	Don Sargent	Gypsy Boots
		St. James Infirmary
807		
808	Bob Lind	Elusive Butterfly
		Cheryl's Goin' Home
809	Starlings	That's Me
		All I Want
810	Rainbeaus	Maybe It's Wrong
		That's All I'm Asking
811	Darlene Woods	All I Want
		That's Me

1959
1960

812		
813	Stan Rose	Once Again
		Please Don't Tease
814	Jimmy Witherspoon	Ain't Nobody's Business
		There's Good Rockin' Tonight
815	Gamblers	LSD-25
		Moon Dawg
816		
817	Don Randi	Our Last Dance
		Oh Yeah
818	Titans	Blues for Dee
		Lonesome Mood
819	Jon Hendricks	A Good Get-Together
		Everything Started in the House of the Lord

Label #	Artist	Record Title
820	Les McCann	Little Girl from Casper
		They Can't Take That Away from Me
821	Rudy Ray Moore	Easy Easy Baby
		Miss Wonderful
822	Gloria Smythe	Billy
		When You're Smiling
823	Les McCann	Fish This Week
		Vacushna

1960
1961

4501	Sandells	School's Out
		Wild as the Sea
4502	Barbara Wilson	Make Me Happy
		On the Other Hand
4503		
4504	The Delegates	Pigmy Part 1
		Pigmy Part 2

(see aura)

1965

77800	Jazz Crusaders	The Thing
		Tough Talk
77801	Dizzy Gillespie	Sandpiper
		Be's That Way
77802	Gerald Wilson	Limelight
		It Could Be
77803	Mr. 12 String Guitar	Subterranean Homesick Blues
		All I Really Want to Do
77804	Monty Alexander	Spunky
		Rattlesnake

1965
1966

77805	Billy Larkin	Little Jr. Detroit
		Transfusion
77806	Jazz Crusaders	Aqua Dulce
		Soul Bourgeoise
77807	Delegates/Clifford Scott	Little Mama
		Little Jr. Detroit
77808	Bob Lind	Cheryl's Goin' Home
		Elusive Butterfly
77809	Gypsy Trips	Rock 'n' Roll Gypsies
		Ain't It Hard
77810	Jon-Jon Lewis	I'm a Nut
		World Full of Sadness
77811	Sonny Knight	If I May
		Need Your Love So Bad
77812	Hank Diamond	Soul Sauce (Wachi Wara)
		Everything Is Where It Belongs

Label #	Artist	Record Title
77813	Ravi Shankar	Song from the Hills
		Dhun
77814	Bud Shank	Michelle
		I Will Wait for You/Outem a Note
77815	Chet Baker/	Flowers on the Wall
	Mariachi Brass	Tequila
77816	Hard Times	There'll Be a Time
		You're Bound to Cry
77817	Larry Knechtel/	I Hear a Symphony
	Carmel Strings	Lover's Concerto
77818	Gil Fuller	A Patch of Blue
		Sweets for My Sweet
77819	Rhythm Folk	He Was a Friend of Mine
		Your Land and Mine
77820	Kiki Dee	I Dig You Baby
		Small Town
77821	Bud Shank	You Didn't Have to Be So Nice
		Sounds of Silence
77822	Bob Lind	Remember the Rain
		Truly Julie's Blues (I'll Be There)
77823	Mariachi Brass	Bang Bang
		Happiness Is
77824	Bud Shank	California Dreamin'
		Woman
77825	Sunday Servants	I'm Puttin' You On
		Who Do You Love
77826	Hard Times	Come to Your Window
		That's All I'll Do
77827	Joe Pass	Moment to Moment
		Sign of the Times
77828	Tony Scotti	Exit Loneliness, Enter Love
		You Took the Happiness (Out of My Head)
77829	The B.M.O.C.	I'll Remember
		Bring Back the Time
77830	Bob Lind	I Just Let It Take Me
		We've Never Spoken
77831	Folkswingers	Norwegian Wood
		Raga Rock
77832	Sonny Knight	If I Ruled the World
		Angel Love
77833	Gil Garfield	Come on Sunshine
		Mama's Little Baby
77834	Brimstones	Cold Hearted Woman
		I'm in Misery
77835	Gosdin Bros.	Love at First Sight
		To Ramona
77836	Jon Jon Lewis	Sure Lookin' Good
		Shame on You
77837	Ken Jensen	Watch What Happens
		On the Trail
77838	Vince Donofrio	Weather Is Better
		I Won't Be There

Label #	Artist	Record Title
77839	Bob Lind	San Francisco Woman
		Baby Take Me Home
77840	Sandals	Theme from Endless Summer
		6-Pac
77841	Sensations	Look at My Baby
	(Not Released)	What a Wonderful Feeling
77842	Bud Shank	Summer Samba (So Nice)
		Monday, Monday
77843	Tony Scotti	Like Someone in Love
		I Remember You
77844	Billy Larkin/Delegates	Hold On! I'm a Comin'
		Dirty Water
77845	Joe Pass	Play with Fire
		Satisfaction
77846	(Not Issued)	
77847	Raga/Talas	My Group and Me
		For Old Times Sake
77848	Chet Baker/	When You're Smiling
	Mariachi Brass	Sunny
77849	Joe Torres	Sunny
	(Not Released)	Get Out of My Way
77850	Gil & Johnny	I Will Wait for You
		I'll Coat Your Mind with Honey
77851	Hard Times	Fortune Teller
		Good By
77852	Sandals	Tell Us Dylan
		Why Should I Cry
77853	Mariachi Brass	Colonel Bogey March
		La Bamba
77854	Roger Kellaway	Cabaret
		We'll Meet Again
77855	Tony Scotti	Primrose Lane
		After Dark
77856	Roger Tillison	The Price Is High
		Nobody's Lover
77857	Chet Baker	A Man & a Woman
		All
77858	Sonny Knight	The Quiet Man
	(Not Released)	I Can't Let You Go
77859	Bud Shank	Love Theme from "Is Paris Burning"
		Summer Wind
77860	Electric Tomorrow	Sugar Cube
		The Electric Tomorrow
77861	Walter Wanderley	Jet Samba (Samba Do Aviao)
		Sad Samba (Samba Triste)

1966
1967

77862	Rainey Day Friends	Away to Some Other World
		Don't You Feel Rained On?
77863	Mariachi Brass	The Dating Game
		In the Mood

Appendix 11

Label #	Artist	Record Title
77864	Hard Times	Sad, Sad Sunshine / They Said No
77865	Bob Lind	Good Time Special / Just My Love
77866	Eugene Church	U Maaka Hanna / Dollar Bill
77867	Sandals	Cloudy / House of Painted Glass
77868	Gil & Johnny	Alice / Mama's Little Baby
77869	Jack Carroll	More and More / Reflections
77870	Rainey Day Friends	Thru My Painted Window / Not Like Before
77871	Ravi Shankar	Pather Panchali / Gat Kirwani
77872	Vince Donofrio	The Daisy / The Kazoo Symbol
77873	Hard Times	Colours / Blew Mind
77874	Marketts	Sun Power / Sunshine Girl
77875	Johnny Tame	Sand in My Shoes / Steak and Cake
77876	Meditations	Transcendental Meditation / Beautiful Experience
77877	Joyride	The Crystal Ship / Coming Soon
77878	Jack Carroll	Without Your Love / There Will Always Be Tomorrow

1967

1968

Label #	Artist	Record Title
77879	Bob Lind	Goodbye Neon Lies / We May Have Touched
77880	Maharishi Mahesh Yogi	Maharishi Speaks Pt. 1 / Maharishi Speaks Pt. 2
77881	Shirley & Johnny	And I Don't Want Your Love / There Go the Heartaches
77883	Joyride	Pleasure Machine / Coming Soon
77884	New Phoenix	Give to Me Your Love / Thanks
77885	Bud Shank	I Am the Walrus / Sounds of Silence
77886	Bristol Boxkite	If You Love Me / Colors of Love
77887	December's Children	Backwards and Forwards / Kissin' Time
77888	Joyride	Land of Rypap Papyr / His Blues
77889	Skunks	I Recommend Her / I Need No One

Label #	Artist	Record Title
77890	Cathy Rich	Darkest Before Dawn
		Wishyouawish
77891	Russ David	Macarthur Park Part 1
		Macarthur Park Part 2
77892	Terry Ber	Hey That's No Way to Say Goodbye
		Come on Over to My House
77893	Bud Shank	There's Got to Be a Better Way (Theme from Bandolero)
		Tour d'Amour
77894	Lee Raymond	Ever on My Mind
		Would You Like
77895	December's Children	Lovin' Things
		Extraordinary Man
77896	Zone 26	When the World Turns Cold
	(Not Released)	We Chose to Walk
77897	Kevin Shane	Come Morning Time
	(Not Released)	I'm Gonna Change
77898	Ravi Shankar	Charly Theme
		Love Montage
77899	Marketts	California Summer (People Moving West)
		Groovin' Time
77900	Allan Reuss	Zorba
		La Mirada
77901	Zone 26	When the World Turns Cold
	(Not Released)	I Chose to Walk
77902	Harper & Rowe	Here Comes Yesterday Again
		Wake Me When It's Over
77903	Gerald Wilson	Light My Fire
		California Soul
77904	Mary Jane Hooper	That's How Strong Love Is
		I Feel a Hurt

1968

1969

Label #	Artist	Record Title
77905	J. P. Rags	Wonderful World of Children
		Something to Think About
77906	Peter Sarstedt	I Am a Cathedral
		Blagged
77907	Kevin Shane	Come Morning Time
		I'm Gonna Change
77908	Searchers	Umbrella Man
		Over the Weekend
77909	Sandals	Ski Bum
		Winter Spell
77910	December's Children	I've Been Hurt
		Good Time Boy
77911	Peter Sarstedt	Where Do You Go to My Lovely
		Morning Mountain
77912	Elf Stone	Beat the Clock
		Louisiana Teardrops
77913	Cathy Rich	Paper Tiger
		Wild Thing

Appendix 11

Label #	Artist	Record Title
77914	David Tennyson	Emily
		Waterfall
77915	J. P. Rags	If It's Tuesday, This Must Be Belgium
		The Bells of St. Barbara
77916	Sy Coleman	Playboy After Dark
	(Not Released)	
77917	Harper & Rowe	Picture Me High
		Where Is She
77918	Country Mile	Tonight I Will Be Staying Here with You
		I (Who Have Nothing)
77919	Peter Sarstedt	Frozen Orange Juice
		Aretuza Loser
77920	Soul Cadets	Hey Little Girl
		My House of Stone
77921	Craig Hundley	Lazy Day
		Traces
77922	The Carnival	Son of a Preacher Man
		Walk on By
77923	Satya Sai Baba	Satya Nam
		Govinda Kirshna Jai
77924	Jimmy Scruggs	You Don't Care for Me Anymore
		Lean on Me
77925	Cannery Row	Stand by Me
		Sweet Water
77926	Houstons	Solar Light
		Sea of Tranquility
77927	Geraldine Stevens	Billy I've Got to Go to Town
		It's Not Their Heartache It's Mine
77928	Baker St. Philharmonic	Love at First Sight
		Tycho
77929	Craig Hundley	This Time
		Aurelia's Theme
77930	Geraldine Stevens	I've Got to Have More
		You Ain't Going Nowhere
77931	California Earthquake	What a Beautiful Feeling
		The First Day
77932	The Carnival	Laia Ladaia
		Calito De Carnival

1969
1970

Label #	Artist	Record Title
77933	Peter Sarstedt	Step into the Battlefield
		I Thought It Was
77934	Geraldine Stevens	You Ain't Goin' Nowhere
		Love Is Gonna Get You
77935	Craig Hundley	One Tin Soldier
		South American Getaway
77936	Cannery Row	Oh Suzanna
		Don't Pass Away
77937	The Fortunes	Lifetime of Love
		That Same Old Feeling

Appendixes

Label #	Artist	Record Title

1970

Label #	Artist	Record Title
88120	Delegates	Pigmy Part 1
		The Peeper
88121		
88122		
88123		
88124	Gil Fuller	Sweets for My Sweet
		Theme from "A Patch of Blue"
88125		
88126		
88127	Victor Feldman	Do the Jake
		Have a Heart
88128	Ken Jensen Quartet	Captain Jack
		Alan Rock
88129	Zimbo Trio	Reza
		Garota De Ipanema (Girl from Ipanema)
88130	Richard "Groove" Holmes	Secret Love
		Hallelujah I Love Her So
88131	Bud Shank	Sidewinder
		Time for Love
88132	Gerald Wilson	Golden Sword
		La Mentira
88133	Les McCann	The Shout
		Spanish Onions
88134	Chico Hamilton	Satin Doll
		Siete Cuatro
88135	Zimbo Trio	Lost My Love
		She Swings While She Walks

1966
1967

Label #	Artist	Record Title
88136	Buddy Rich Orchestra	Uptight
		Sister Sadie
88137	Richard "Groove" Holmes	It Might as Well Be Spring
		This Here
88138	Don Ellis	Concerto for Trumpet
		33 222 1 222
88139	Buddy Rich Big Band	Norwegian Wood
		Monitor Theme
88140	Buddy Rich Big Band	The Beat Goes On
		Mexicali Rose
88141	Don Ellis	Barnum's Revenge
		Thetis
88142		

1967
1968

Label #	Artist	Record Title
88143	Johnny Lytle	Gonna Get That Boat Part 1
		Gonna Get That Boat Part 2
88144	Jazz Crusaders	Eleanor Rigby
		Ooga Boogaloo

Label #	Artist	Record Title
88145	Buddy Rich Big Band	Big Mama Cass
		Mercy Mercy Mercy
88146	Jazz Crusaders	Hey Jude
		Love and Peace
88147	Richard "Groove" Holmes	Madison Time
		The Odd Couple
88148	Gerald Wilson	California Soul
		Light My Fire

1968

1969

88149	Richard "Groove" Holmes	I Can't Stop Dancing
		Listen Here
88150		
88151	Bobby Bryant	Good Morning Starshine
		Be-In
88152	Freddy Robinson	Before Six
		Coming Atlantis
88153	Jazz Crusaders	Get Back
		Willie and Laura Mae Jones
88154	Wilbert Longmire	Galveston
		Scarborough Fair—Canticle
88155	Freddy Robinson	Black Fox
		Oogum Googum Song

1969

1970

88156	Bud Shank	Let It Be
		Something

Pacific Jazz

601	Gerry Mulligan	Lullabye of the Leaves
		Bernie's Tune

1952

1953

602	Gerry Mulligan Quartet	Frenesi
		Nights at the Turntable
603	Harry Babison Quartet	How About You
		Sanders Meanders
604	Gerry Mulligan Quartet	Makin' Whoopee
		Motel
605	Chet Baker Quartet	Lamp Is Low
		Maid in Mexico
606	Gerry Mulligan Quartet	Walkin' Shoes
		Soft Shoe
607	Gerry Mulligan Quartet	Aren't You Glad You're You
		Freeway
608	Lee Konitz	I Can't Believe That You're in Love with Me
		Sextet
609	Lee Konitz	Lover Man
		Lady Be Good

Label #	Artist	Record Title
610	Chet Baker Quartet	Imagination
		Rush Job
611	Gerry Mulligan Quartet	Cherry
		Carson City Stage
612	Harry Edison Quartet	September in the Rain
		Pennies from Heaven
613	Harry Edison Quartet	These Foolish Things
		Indiana
614	Gerry Mulligan Quartet	I Fall in Love Too Easily
		Winter Wonderland
615	Chet Baker Quartet	The Thrill Is Gone
		Happy Little Sunbeam

1953
1954

616	Gerry Mulligan Quartet	Darn That Dream
		Five Brothers
617	Chico Hamilton	Broadway
		Nuttye
618	Chet Baker Quartet	Goddby-Dandy Line

1954
1955

619	Chet Baker Quartet	Look for a Silver Lining
		I Get Along without You
620	Laurindo Almeida Quartet	Speak Low
		Stairway to the Stars
621	Gordon-Montrose Quartet	Two Can Play
		What a Difference
622	Johnny Holiday	Julie Is Her Name
		She Doesn't Laugh Like You
623		
624	Chet Baker Quartet	Tommy Hawk
		I'm Glad There Is You
625	Al Haig Trio	The Moon Is Yellow
		Yardbird Suite
626		
627	Clifford Brown Ensemble	Gone with the Wind
		Tiny Capers
628	Chico Hamilton	Blue Sands
		The Morning After
629	Steve White Quartet	My New Jet Plane
		Swing Easy
630		
631	Chico Hamilton Quintet	The Squimp
		Mr. Jo Jones
632		
633		
634		
635		
636	Chet Baker Orchestra	Tenderly
		Too Close for Comfort
637		

Label #	Artist	Record Title
638		
639	Chet Baker	Love Nest
		Lush Life
640	Gary Crosby	Please Send Me Someone to Love
		There's No You
641	Chet Baker	Jimmy's Theme
		Let Me Be Loved
642	Bob Brookmeyer Quintet	Santa Claus Blues
		Sweet Like This
643	Mastersounds	Shall We Dance
		Getting to Know You
644	Gerry Mulligan/Lee Konitz/Chet Baker	Almost Like Being in Love
		Lover Man

World Pacific

645	Jack Lidstrom Stompers	Lazy River
		Ole Miss
646		
647		
648	Pat Healy	Don't Ever Leave Me
		Easy Come
649	Freddie Campbell	Sea Waves
		A Foggy Day
650	Gerry Mulligan/Chet Baker Quartet	Jersey Bounce
		Put Your Dreams Away
651	Wes Montgomery Quartet	Fingerpickin'
		New Jet Plane
652	S. Petterstein	History of Jazz
		Origin of Jazz Terms
653	Bud Shank	Penny Whistle Blues
		Steve Allen Theme
654	David Allen	Can't Help It
		Impossible
655	Mastersounds	Gesticulate & Thymes Have I
		Stranger in Paradise

Demon

1501	Little Bobby Bell/Angels	Came, Saw, Conquered
		Whole Wide World
1502	Bystanders	Yellow Mellow Hardtop
		Power of a Prayer
1503	Buddy Long	You Called Me
		Walkin' an' Talkin' to Myself
1504	Chick Carlton	Honey I've Got to Go
		You Enchanted Me
1505	Doc Moody	By April You'll Be Mine
		Crazy Wonderful
1506	Paula Morgan	Only a Fool
		Someone to Love Me
1507	Jody Reynolds	Endless Sleep
		Tight
1508	Olympics	Western Movies
		Oh Well

Label #	Artist	Record Title
1509	Jody Reynolds	Fire of Love
		Daisy Mae
1510	Ronnie Goode	Rocking Bug
		Crazy Bait
1511	Jody Reynolds	Closin' In
		Elope with Me
1512	Olympics	Dance with the Teacher
		Everybody Needs Love

1958
1959

1513	Bill & Mark	Down Deep
		Just So You Love Me
1514	Olympics	Your Love
		Chicken
1515	Jody Reynolds	Beulah Lee
		Golden Idol
1516	Terrifics	I Don't Care How You Do It
		Bump Ti Dee Ump Bump
1517	Buddy Long	It's Nothing to Me
		Just a Friend
1518	Milt Patrick	A Fountain of Love
		You Are My Inspiration
1519	Jody Reynolds	The Storm
		Please Remember
1520	Barons	Gravel Gert
		The Fight
1521	Willie Hines	Gettin' Married
		Young Boy

1959
1960

1522	Gloria Grey	Hold Me, Thrill Me, Kiss Me
		My Honey
1523	Jody Reynolds	Whipping Post
		I Wanna Be with You Tonight
1524	Jody Reynolds	Stone Cold
		The Raven Hair
1525	Ronny Goode	Hokus Pokus
		Totem Pole

University

201	Jimmy Joiner	Even So
		Nero
202		
203		
204		
205		
206	Eddie Hill	Daddy, You Know What
		Monkey Business
207		

Label #	Artist	Record Title
208	Buddy Killem	I'm Comin' After You
		Whatcha Gonna Do Tomorrow
209	Buddy Killen	I'm Comin' After You
		Whatcha Gonna Do Tomorrow

1959

1960

210	Little Dippers	Forever
		Two by Four
211	Little Dippers	Forever
		Two by Four
601		
602		
603	Little Dippers	Tonight
		Be Sincere
604		
605	Freddie North	How to Cry
		OK, So What
606	Carnations	Leap Year
		A Wing and a Prayer
607	Wally Hester	Also, Likewise (and Not Forgetting)
		As the Wild River Rises
608	Little Dippers	Lonely
		I Wonder, I Wonder, I Wonder

Robbee

101	Darrell Glenn	Hoo Doo the Voo Doo
102		
103	Holidays	Miss You
		Pretend
104	Jimmy Massi	If I Had You
		Blue Prelude
105	Rosemary	The Kiss Cha Cha
		Them There Eyes
106	4 Seasons	Nancy's Trampoline
		Mirage
107	Holidays	Then I'll Be Tired of You
		Lonely Summer

1960

1961

108	Benny Benak	Beat 'em Bucks
		The Charge of the Buccaneers
109	La-Rells	Everybody Knew
		Please Be Fair
110	Marcy Joe	Ronnie
		My First Mistake
111	Elroy Face	Bells, Bells
		Cross Your Heart (with Love)
112	Lugee/Lions	The Jury
		Little Did I Know
113	Jimmy Massi	Moon Rock
		The One You Love

Label #	Artist	Record Title
114	La-Rells	I Just Can't Understand / Public Transportation
115	Marcy Joe	Since Gary Went into the Navy / What I Did This Summer
116	Honorable Fats Wilson	Quit Eatin' / Over Again
117	Marcy Joe	Jumpin Jack / Take a Word
118	Lennie Martin	La Femme / Shoes

Minit

601	Matthew Jacobs	Bad Luck & Trouble / Early Morning
602	Boogie Jake	Early Morning Blues / Bad Luck & Trouble
603	Nolan Pitts	What Is Life / Middle of the Night
604	Ernie K-Doe	Make You Love Me / There's a Will There's a Way

1959
1960

605	Doyle Templet	Betty Jane / Is It Really Love
606	Benny Spellman	Life Is Too Short / Ammerette
607	Jessie Hill	Ooh Poo Pah Doo Parts 1 and 2
608	Matthew Jacobs	Chance for Your Love / Loaded Down
609	Allen & Allen Tiddle Win	Heavenly Baby / Tiddle Winks
610	Del Royals	Who Will Be the One / She's Gone
611	Jessie Hill	Whip It on Me / I Need Your Love
612	Aaron Neville	Every Day / Over You
613	Benny Spellman	Darling No Matter Where / I Didn't Know
614	Ernie K-Doe	Taint It the Truth / Hello My Lover
615	Allen Orange	Forever / Just a Little Love
616	Jessie Hill	Scoop Scoobie Doobie / Highland Blues
617	Lee Diamond	Please Don't Leave / It Won't Be Me
618	Aaron Neville	Show Me the Way / Get Out of My Life

Appendix 11

Label #	Artist	Record Title

1960
―――
1961

619	Roy Montrell	The Montrell Mudd
620	Del Royals	Close to You / Got You on My Mind
621	Awood Magic	It's Better to Dream / Pretty Pretty Waitress
622	Jessie Hill	Oh My Oh My / I Got Mine
623	Ernie K-Doe	Mother in Law / Wanted—$10,000 Reward
624	Aaron Neville	Don't Cry / Reality
625	Irma Thomas	Cry On / Girl Needs Boy
626	Five Knights	Let Me In / Times Are Getting Harder
627	Ernie K-Doe	Te Ta Te Ta Ta / Real Man
628	Jessie Hill	My Love / Oogsey Moo
629	Diamond Joe	Moanin' & Screamin' Parts 1 and 2
630	Allen Orange	True Love Never Dies / When You're Lonely
631	Aaron Neville	Let's Live / I Found Another Love
632	The Showmen	It Will Stand / Country Fool
633	Irma Thomas	It's Too Soon to Know / That's All I Ask
634	Ernie K-Doe	A Certain Girl / I Cried My Last Tear
635	Lee Diamond	I Need Money / Let Me Know
636	Tommy Taylor/ Five Knights	I Want Somebody / Polly Want a Cracker
637	Del Royals	Always Naggin' / I Fell in Love with You
638	Jessie Hill	It's My Fault / Sweet Jelly Roll

1961
―――
1962

639	Aaron Neville	How Many Times / I'm Waitin' at the Station
640	Allen Orange	Miss Nosey / The Letter
641	Ernie K-Doe	Popeye Joe / Come on Home

Label #	Artist	Record Title
642	Irma Thomas	Gone
		Done Got Over It
643	The Showmen	Fate Planned It This Way
		The Wrong Girl
644	Benny Spellman	Lipstick Traces
		Fortune Teller
645	Ernie K-Doe	Hey Hey Hey
		Love You the Best
646	Jessie Hill	Can't Get Enough of That Ooh Pah Doo
		Pot's on a Strike
647	Showmen	Com'n Home
		I Love You, Can't You See
648	Eskew Reeder	I Waited Too Long
		Green Door
649	Diamond Joe	Help Yourself
		Play Fair
650	Aaron Neville	Humdinger
		Sweet Little Mama
651	Ernie K-Doe	Beating Like a Tom Tom
		I Got to Find Somebody
652	Benny Spellman	Every Now & Then
		I'm in Love
653	Irma Thomas	It's Raining
		I Did My Part
654	Showmen	The Owl Sees You
		True Fine Mama
655	Calvin Lee	Valley of Tears
		I'll Be Home (Wait & See)
656	Ernie K-Doe	Get Out of My House
		Loving You

1962

1963

Label #	Artist	Record Title
657	Aaron Neville	How Could I Help But Love You
		Wrong Number
658	Eskew Reeder	We Had Love
		Never Again
659	Benny Spellman	Stickin' Whicha' Baby
		You Got to Get It
660	Irma Thomas	Somebody Told Me
		Two Winters Long
661	Ernie K-Doe	Be Sweet
		Easier Said Than Done
662	Showmen	39-21-46
		Swish Fish
663	Calvin Lee	You
		Daddy's Going Home
664	Benny Spellman	Ammerette
		Talk About Love
665	Ernie K-Doe	I'm the Boss
		Pennies Worth o' Happiness
666	Irma Thomas	Ruler of My Heart
		Hitting on Nothing

Appendix 11

Label #	Artist	Record Title
1963		
1966		
32000	Homer Banks	A Lot of Love / Fighting to Win
32001	The Players	I Wanna Be Free / He'll Be Back
32002	Jimmy Holiday	Baby I Love You / You Don't Go Away
32003	Johnny Sayles	Anything for You / Deep Down in My Heart
32004	Fathers & Sons	Soul in the Bowl Parts 1 and 2
32005	Alder Ray	I Need You Baby / My Heart Is in Danger
32006	Diplomats	Don't Bug Me / Honest to Goodness
32007	The Showmen	39-21-46 / Swish Fish
32008	Homer Banks	Do You Know What / 60 Minutes of Your Love
32009	Themes	Bent Out of Shape / No Explanation Needed
32010	The Groovers	I'm a Bashful Guy / Just Go for Me
32011	Jimmy Holiday	I'm Gonna Move to the City / Turning Point
32012	The Players	Why Did I Lie / I'm Glad I Waited
32013	Shawn Robinson	Find Love Right Now / My Dear Heart
1966		
1967		
32014	Jimmy Holiday	In the Eyes of My Girl / Give Me Your Love
32015	The O'Jays	Hold On / Working on Your Case
32016	Jimmy Holiday	Give Me Your Love / Everybody Needs Help
32017	Jimmy Lewis	The Girls from Texas / Let Me Know
32018	Jimmy McCracklin	Let the Door Hit You / This Thing
32019	The Players	There's Got to Be a Way / That's the Way (to Tend to Business)
32020	Homer Banks	Hooked by Love / Lady of Stone
32021	Jimmy Holiday/ Clydie King	Ready, Willing & Able / We Got a Good Thing Goin'
32022	Jimmy McCracklin	Dog Part 1 / Dog Part 2

Appendixes

Label #	Artist	Record Title
32023	Jimmy Holiday	We Forgot About Love
		I'm Gonna Help Hurry My Brothers Home
32024	Bobby Womack	Baby, I Can't Stand It
		Trust Me
32025	Clydie King	Good for Cryin' Over You Days
		Mistakes of Yesterday
32026	Gene Dozier/Brotherhood	Hunk of Funk
		One for Bess
32027	Trensations	Saucy
		Soulin' & Rollin'
32028	Jimmy Holiday	Beauty of a Girl in Love
		Everything Is Love
32029	The Players	I'm So Alone
		Get Right
32030	Bobby Womack	Somebody Special
		Broadway Walk
32031	Gene Dozier/Brotherhood	I Wanna Testify
		Mustang Sally
32032	Clydie King	I'll Never Stop Loving You
		Shing-a-Ling
32033	Jimmy McCracklin	How You Like Your Love
		Get Together

1967

1968

Label #	Artist	Record Title
32034	Vernon Green & Medallions	Look at Me, Look at Me
		Am I Ever Gonna See My Baby Again
32035	Montague	This Is Soul
		I Too Am an American
32036	Homer Banks	Foolish Hearts Break First
		Round the Clock Lover Man
32037	Bobby Womack	What Is This
		What You Gonna Do (When Your Love Is Gone)
32038	Jimmy Lewis	Turn Your Damper Down
		Where Is My Baby
32039	Young Hearts	Get Yourself Together
		Oh, I'll Never Be the Same
32040	Jimmy Holiday	Spread Your Love
		We Got a Good Thing Goin'
32041	Gene Dozier/Brotherhood	Funky Broadway
		Soul Stroll
32042	Ernie K. Doe	Real Man
		Te Ta Te Ta Ta
32043	Pacesetters	I'm Gonna Make It
		What About Me, Baby
32044	Jimmy McCracklin	Pretty Little Sweet Thing
		A & I
32045	Mirettes	Help Wanted
		Play Fair
32046	Gloria Jones	I Know
		What You Want
32047	Turn-a-Rounds	Can't Take No More
		I Need Your Lovin'

Appendix 11

Label #	Artist	Record Title
32048	Bobby Womack	Fly Me to the Moon / Take Me
32049	Young Hearts	Takin' Care of Business / I've Got Love for My Baby
32050	Popular Five	Little Bitty Pretty One / I'm a Love Maker
32051	Gloria Jones	When He Touches Me / Look What You Started
32052	Jimmy McCracklin	Love, Love, Love / Married Life
32053	Jimmy Holiday	I Don't Want to Hear It / I'm Gonna Use What I Got

1968
1969

Label #	Artist	Record Title
32054	Clydie King	Love Now, Pay Later / One Part, Two Part
32055	Bobby Womack	Baby, You Oughta Think It Over / California Dreaming
32056	Homer Banks	(Who You Gonna Run to) Me or Your Mama / I Know You Know I Know
32057	Young Hearts	Sweet Soul Shakin' / Girls
32058	Jimmy Holiday	Baby Boy's in Love with You / If You've Got the Money, I've Got the Time
32059	Bobby Womack	I Left My Heart in San Francisco / Love, the Time Is Now
32060	Ike & Tina Turner	I'm Gonna Do All I Can (to Do Right by My Man) / You've Got Too Many Ties That Bind
32061	Popular Five	Baby I Got It / I Don't Want to Be Without Her
32062	The Untowner	She's Mine / Down the Pike
32063	John Lily/Family	All I Want / Your Love Is Getting to Me
32064	Jimmy McCracklin	Drown in My Own Tears / What's Going On
32065	Love Chain	I Love You Baby / Love Chain
32066	Young Hearts	Misty / Count Down (Here I Come)
32067	Persuasions	Party in the Woods / It's Better to Have Loved or Lost
32068	Ike & Tina Turner	I Wish It Would Rain / With a Little Help from My Friends
32069	Lea Roberts	When Something Is Wrong with My Baby / Prove It
32070	Magic Sam	I'll Pay You Back / Sam's Funk
32071	Bobby Womack	It's Gonna Rain / Thank You
32072	Heron Hitson	Yes You Did / Better to Have Loved

Appendixes

Label #	Artist	Record Title
32073	Gene Taylor	Don't Go Away
32074	Charmaines	You Got My Nose Wide Open / Smile
32075		Keep on Searchin'
32076	Eddie Forehand	Cry Me a River / City of Blues
32077	Ike & Tina Turner	I Wanna Jump / Treating Us Funky
32078	Mighty Gospel Giants	I Can't Stop Serving the Lord / What Have I Done Wrong
32079	Jimmy Holiday	Yesterday Died / Would You Like to Love Me
32080	Little Junior Parker	Worried Life Blues / Let the Good Times Roll
32081	Bobby Womack	How I Miss You Baby / Tried & Convicted
32082	Tina Britt	Hawg for You / My Lover's Prayer
32083	Carolyn Basely	River's Invitation / I Love You

1969
1970

Label #	Artist	Record Title
32084	Young Hearts	Young Hearts Get Lonely Too / Little Togetherness
32085	Jimmy Burns	I Tried / Did It Ever Cross Your Mind
32086	Jimmy McCracklin	I Had to Get with It / You Ain't Nothin' But a Devil
32087	Ike & Tina Turner	Come Together / Honky Tonk Women
32088	Cold Square	Just to See Your Face / Soul Power
32089	Robert Patterson Singers	It Must Have Been the Son / Temptation
32090	Blue Busters	Love Is the Answer / Speak Your Mind
32091		
32092	Jimmy McCracklin	Stick to My Mind / I Just Live by the Rules
32093	Bobby Womack	More Than I Can Stand / Arkansas State Prison
32094	Lorenzo's Soul	Treatment Keep an Eye / Lorenzo's Soul Treatment
32095	Lee Roberts	Stay with Me / Love on My Mind
32096	Heron Hitson	Show Me Some Sign / She's a Bad Girl
32097	Jimmy Holiday	Man Ain't Nothin' Without a Woman / I'm in Love with You

Label #	Artist	Record Title
		aura
4500		
4501	Sandells	School's Out
		Wild as the Sea
4502	Barbara Wilson	Make Me Happy
		On the Other Hand
4503		
4504	The Delegates	Pigmy Part 1
		Pigmy Part 2
4505	Sonny Knight	Fool Like Me
		Love Me (as Though There Were No Tomorrow)
4506		
4507		
4508	Sonny Knight	Rose Mary
4509	La La Wilson Band	Flea Pot
4510	The Delegates	The Peeper
		Hainty
4511	Ray Daniels/ Rick/Ravens	Geraldine
		Soul Train
390		
391		
392		
393	Lewis Sisters	Shooby-Dooby
394		
395	Furies	Cover Girl
		Where My Money Goes
396		
397		
398		
399		
400	Teddy Reynolds/ La La Wilson	I'm a Devil
		My Life Allover
401		
402	Sonny Knight	Called to Say Hello
		If You Want This Love
403	Sonny Knight	I Just Called to Say Hello
		If You Want This Love
404		
405		
406		
407		
408		
409	6 Stars	Beach Bunnies

Blue Note

1952

501	Hegginbotham	Weary Land Blues
		Daybreak Blues
502	Sidney Bechet	Saturday Night Blues
		Steady Rider

Label #	Artist	Record Title
503	Teddy Bunn	King Porter
		Bachelors Blues
504	Teddy Bunn	Guitarin High
		Blue Without Words
505	Art Hodes/Chicagoans	Maple Leaf Rag
		Yellow Dog Blues
506	Art Hodes/Chicagoans	She's Crying for Me
		Slow 'em Down Blues
507	Art Hodes/Chicagoans	Doctor Jazz
		Shoe Shiner's Drag
508	Art Hodes/Chicagoans	Change Made
		Clark & Randolph
509	"Pigmeat" Markham	See See Rider
		You've Been a Good Old Wagon
510	Ike Quebec	Hard Rock
		If I Had You
511	Edmond Hali	It's Been So Long
		I Can't Believe
512	Art Hodes Trio	Blues 'n' Booze
		Eccentric
513	John Hardee	Tired
		Blue Skies
514	John Hardee	Hardy's Party
		Idaho
515	Ike Quebec	Topsy
		Cup Mute Clayton
516	Ike Quebec	Dolores
		Sweethearts on Parade
517	Sidney Bechet	Quincy St. Stomp
		Weary Way Blues
518	Baby Dodds	Winin' Bay Blues
		Careless Love
519	Baby Dodds	High Society
		Feelin' at Ease
520	John Hardee	What Is This Thing Called Love
		Nervous from the Service
521	John Hardee	Sweet and Lovely
		River Edge Rock
522	Sammy Benskin	Cherry
		The World's Waiting for the Sunrise
523		
524	Tiny Grimes	Flying Home Part 1
		Flying Home Part 2
525	Tiny Grimes	C Jam Blues
		Tiny's Boogie Woogie
526	Art Hodes/Back Room Boys	Low Down Blues
		Back Room Boys
527	Art Hodes/Back Room Boys	Jug Head Boogie
		M. K. Blues
528	Art Hodes/Blue Five	Gut Bucket Blues
		Nobody's Sweetheart
529		
530		

Appendix 11

Label #	Artist	Record Title
531	Sidney Bechet	Save It Pretty Mama / Darktown Strutters Ball
532	Sidney Bechet	Shine / Memphis Blues
533	Sidney Bechet	St. James Infirmary / Way Down in New Orleans
534	Babs' 3 Bips/A Bob	Oop-Pop-A Da / Stomping at the Savoy
535	Babs' 3 Bips/A Bob	Lop-Pow / Pay Dem Dues
536	Babs' 3 Bips/A Bob	Dob Bla Bli / Weird Lullaby
537	Babs' 3 Bips/A Bob	Running Around / Babs' Dream
538	Ike Quebec	Someone to Watch Over Me / Zig Billion
539	Ike Quebec	The Masquerade Is Over / Basically Blue
540	Tadd Dameron	The Squirrel / Our Delight
541	Tadd Dameron	Dameronia / The Chase
542	Thelonious Monk	Thelenious / Suburban Eyes
543	Thelonious Monk	Round About Midnight / Well You Needn't
544	Ike Quebec	Blue Harlem Part 1 / Blue Harlem Part 2
545	Art Blakey's Messengers	Musa's Vision / The Thin Man
546	Art Blakey's Messengers	Bop Alley / Groove Street
547	Thelonious Monk	Evonce / Off Minor
548	Thelonious Monk	In Walked Bud / Epistrophy
549	Thelonious Monk	Ruby My Dear / Evidence
550	Art Hodes/Kaminsky/Centobie	Wolverine Bluer / Bujie
551	Art Hodes/Kaminsky/Centobie	Mr. Jelly Lord / I Never Knew
552	Art Hodes/Kaminsky/Centobie	Willie the Weeper / Chicago Gal
553	James Moody	Tropicana / Fuller Bop Man
554	James Moody	Cuba / Moodamorphisis
555	James Moody	Tin Tin Deo / Oh Henry
556	James Moody	Workshop / Moods All Frantic

Label #	Artist	Record Title
557	Harold McGee	Double Talk Part 1
558	Harold McGee	Double Talk Part 2 The Skunk
559	Tadd Dameron	Boperation Lady Bird
560	Sidney Bechet	Jahbero Jazz Band Ball Tin Roof Blues
1563	Kenny Burrel	This Time's the Dream Delilah
1564	Tadd Dameron	Symphonette I Mean You
1565	Thelonious Monk	Monk's Mood Who Knows
1566	The Budd Powell Trio	Orinology You Go to My Head
1567	The Budd Powell Trio	Wail Bouncin' with Bud
1568	The Budd Powell Trio	52nd Street Theme Infidels
1569	James Moody	Prince Albert Part 1 Prince Albert Part 2
1570	James Moody	Maximum Just Moody
1571	Max Roach	Tomorrow Part 1 Tomorrow Part 2
1572	Harold McGee	I'll Remember April Fuguetta
1573	Harold McGee	Donnellon Square Fluid Drive
1574	Harold McGee	Lo Flame Meciendo
1575	Thelonious Monk	April in Paris Nice Work
1576	The Bud Powell Trio	A Night in Tunisia Over the Rainbow
1577	The Budd Powell Trio	Un Poco Loco It Could Happen to You
1578	Wynton Kelly	Where or When Born to Be Blue
1579	Wynton Kelly	Cherokee Moonglow
1580	Wynton Kelly	Summertime Crazy He Calls Me
1581	Wynton Kelly	Goodbye Blue Moon
1582		
1583		
1584		
1585	James Moody	Autumn Leaves Shaded Blond
1586	James Moody	September Serenade So Very Pretty

Appendix 11

Label #	Artist	Record Title
1587	James Moody	Jackie My Little Cat / Bedelia
1588	James Moody	Singing for You / Loving You
1589	Thelonious Monk	Four in One / Straight No Chases
1590	Thelonious Monk	Criss Cross / Eronel
1591	Milt Jackson	Willow Weep for Me / Ask Me Now
1592	Milt Jackson Quintet	Tahiti / What's New
1593	Milt Jackson Quintet	Bag's Groove / Lillie
1594	Milt Jackson Quintet	Don't Get Around Much / On the Scene
1595	Miles Davis	Dear Old Stockholm / Wouldn't You
1596	Miles Davis	Chance It / Yesterdays
1597	Miles Davis	Donna / The Squirrel 2nd Master
1598	Lou Donaldson	Roccus / Cheek to Cheek
1599	Lou Donaldson	Lou's Blues / Things We Did Last Summer
1600	Vic Dickinson	Lion's Den / Tenderly
1601	Vic Dickinson	In a Mellow Tone / Gettin' Sentimental
1602	Thelonious Monk	Skippy / Let's Cool One
1603	Thelonious Monk	Carolina Moon / Hornin' In
1604		
1605	Swinging Swedes	Pick Yourself Up / Summertime
1606	Melle Sextet	The Gears / Four Moons
1607	Melle Sextet	Mars / Sunset Concerto
1608	Horace Silver	Safari / Thou Swell
1609	Lou Donaldson	Best Things in Life / Sweet Juice
1610	Lou Donaldson	If I Love Again / Down Home
1611	Cool Britons	Birdland Bounce / Leapin' in London
1612	Cool Britons	Cherokee / Tea for Me
1613	Gillespie Jazz Ensemble	Sweet Lorraine / Lady Bird

Label #	Artist	Record Title
1614	Gillespie Jazz Ensemble	Hurry Home
		Afio Paris
1615	Gillespie Jazz Ensemble	Say Eh
		Everything Happens
1616	Gillespie Jazz Ensemble	She's Funny That Way
		Wrap Your Troubles
1617	Gillespie Jazz Ensemble	CCL Blues
		Somebody Loves
1618	Miles Davis	Enigma
		Tempus Fugit
1619	Miles Davis	Ray's Idea
		I Waited for You
1620	Miles Davis	Kelo
		C.T.A.
1621	Jay Jay Johnson Sextette	Capri
		Turnpike
1622	Clifford Brown/ Lou Donaldson	You Go to My Head
		Brownie Speak
1623	Lou Donaldson	Cookin'
		Bellarosa
1624	Lou Donaldson	Dedah
		Carving the Rock
1625	Horace Silver	Opus De Funk
		Day in Day Out
1626	Art Blakey/Sabu	Message from Kenya
		Nothing but the Soul
1627	Urbie Green Septet	Dansero
		Skylark
1628	The Bud Powell Trio	I Want to Be Happy
		Glass Enclosure
1629	The Bud Powell Trio	Sure Thing
		Collard Greens & Black-Eyed Peas
1630	Horace Silver	The Preacher
		Doodlin
1631	Horace Silver	Room 608
		Creepin' In
1632	Jay Jay Johnson	Pennies from Heaven
		Groovin'
1633	Miles Davis	Donna
		Well You Needn't
1634	Charlie Christian/ Edmund Hall	Profoundly Blue
	Ike Quebec	Blue Harlem
1635	Jimmy Smith	High and Mighty
		You Get Cha
1636	Jimmy Smith	The Preacher
		Midnight Sun
1637	Jimmy Smith	Tenderly
		Joy
1638	Babs Gonzales	'Round Midnight
		You Need Connections
1639	Johnny Griffin	Mildew
		Chicago Calling

Appendix 11

Label #	Artist	Record Title
1640	Johnny Griffin	Nice & Easy
		Boy Next Door
1641	Jimmy Smith	The Champ Part 1
		The Champ Part 2
1642	Jimmy Smith	Bubbis
		Bayou
1643	Jimmy Smith	Judo Mambo
		Autumn Leaves
1644	Jimmy Smith	Fiddlin' the Minors
		Willow Weep
1645	Milt Jackson	What's New
		You Go to My Head
1646	Milt Jackson	Lillie
		Willow Weep for Me
1647	Clifford Brown	Brownie Speaks
		You Go to My Head
1648	Clifford Brown	Hymn of the Orient
		Easy Living
1649	Miles Davis	Lazy Susan
		Tempus Fugit
1650	Miles Davis	The Leap
		Weirdo
1651	Jay Jay Johnson	Jay
		Old Devil Moon
1652	Jimmy Smith	I Cover the Waterfront
		I Can't Give You Anything
1653	Kenny Burrell	Delilah
		The Dream's on Me
1654	Horace Silver Quintet	Enchantment
		Camouflage
1655	Horace Silver Quintet	Senor Blues
		Cool Eyes
1656	Art Blakey/ Clifford Brown	Quicksilver
		Once in a While
1657	Art Blakey/ Clifford Brown	Wee-Dot
		If I Had You
1658	Julius Walkins	Linda Delia
		I Have Known
1659	Thad Jones	April in Paris
		If Someone Had Told Me
1660	Jimmy Smith	New Preacher Part 1
		New Preacher Part 2
1661	Lee Morgan	Gaza Strip
		Reggie of Chester
1662	Lou Donaldson	Caravan
		Old Folks
1663	Lou Donaldson	L. D. Blues
		That Good Old Feeling
1664	Thelonious Monk	'Round Midnight
		In Walked Bud
1665	Jimmy Smith	Where or When Part 1
		Where or When Part 2

Label #	Artist	Record Title
1666	Jimmy Smith	Love Is a Many Splendored Thing Parts 1 and 2
1667	Jimmy Smith	How High the Moon Summertime
1668	Jimmy Smith	Plum Nellie I'm Getting Sentimental
1669	Sonny Rollins	Decision Part 1 Decision Part 2
1670	Sonny Rollins	Plain Jane Part 1 Plain Jane Part 2
1671	Hank Mobley	Lower Stratosphere Reunion
1672	Horace Silver Quintet	Home Cookin' The Back Beat
1673	Horace Silver Quintet	Soulsville No Smokin'
1674	Kenny Burrell	D. B. Blues K. B. Blues
1675	Hank Mobley	Runk in Deep Freeze End of the Affair
1676	Jimmy Smith	All Day Long Part 1 All Day Long Part 2
1677	Jimmy Smith	Funk's Oats Part 1 Funk's Oats Part 2
1678	Art Blakey	Now's the Time Part 1 Now's the Time Part 2
1679	Art Blakey	Ya Ya Meet Me Tonight Dorothy
1680	Lou Donaldson	Peck Time
1681	Lou Donaldson	Herman's Mambo Grits and Gravy
1682	Jimmy Smith	Penthouse Serenade I Can't Get Started
1683	Jimmy Smith	East of the Sun The Very Thought of You
1684	Hank Mobley	Bass on Balls Stetlawise
1685	Jimmy Smith	Blue Moon Part 1 Blue Moon Part 2
1686	Jimmy Smith	There'll Never Be Another You Jitterbug Waltz
1687	Sonny Rollins	You Stepped Out of a Dream Why Don't Eye
1688	Hank Mobley	Easy to Love Time After Time
1689	Curtis Fuller	Algonquin Pickup
1690	Curtis Fuller	Hugore Oscalypso
1691	John Coltrane	Blue Train Part 1 Blue Train Part 2

Appendix 11

Label #	Artist	Record Title
1692	Lee Morgan	A Night in Tunisia Part 1
		A Night in Tunisia Part 2
1693	Art Blakey	Soft Wind Part 1
		Soft Wind Part 2
1694	Number Not Used	
1695	Jazz Messengers	Avila and Tequila Part 1
		Avila and Tequila Part 2
1696	Art Blakey	Abdullah's Delight
		Elephant Walk
1697	Sonny Clark	Sonny's Crib Part 1
		Sonny's Crib Part 2
1698	Sonny Rollins	Sonny Moon for Two Part 1
		Sonny Moon for Two Part 2
1699	Cliff Jordan	Soul-Lo Blues Part 1
		Soul-Lo Blues Part 2
1700	Louis Smith	Brill's Blues Part 1
		Brill's Blues Part 2
1701	Louis Smith	Tribute to Brownie
		Stardust
1702	Curtis Fuller	Quantrale
		Two Quarters of a Mile
1703	Jimmy Smith	After Hours Part 1
		After Hours Part 2
1704	Jimmy Smith	Just Friends
		Lover Man
1705	Horace Silver Quintet	Safare
		The Outlaw
1706	Bennie Green	I Love You
		You're Mine You
1707	Bennie Green	Just Friends
		Melba's Mood
1708	Bennie Green	Soul Stirrin'
		That's All
1709	Bennie Green	We Wanna Cook
		Lullabye of the Doomed
1710	Bill Henderson	Senor Blues
		Tippin'
1711	Jimmy Smith	Swingin' Shepherd Blues
		Cha Cha J.
1712	The Budd Powell Trio	Buster Rides Again
		Dry Soul
1713	Lou Donaldson	Sputnik Part 1
		Sputnik Part 2
1714	Sonny Clark	Cool Struttin' Part 1
		Cool Struttin' Part 2
1715	Louis Smith	Smithville Part 1
		Smithville Part 2
1716	Kenny Burrell	Yes Baby Part 1
		Yes Baby Part 2
1717	Kenny Burrell	Rock Salt Part 1
		Rock Salt Part 2
1718	John Coltrane	Moment's Notice Part 1
		Moment's Notice Part 2

Label #	Artist	Record Title
1719	John Coltrane	Speak Low
		Softly as in a Morning Sunrise
1720	Lou Donaldson	The Masquerade Is Over
		Blue Walk
1721	Lou Donaldson	Play Ray
		Autumn Nocturne
1722	Three Sounds	Tenderly
		Willow Weep
1723	Three Sounds	Both Sides
		Mo-Ge
1724	Three Sounds	It's Nice
		Angel Eyes
1725	Three Sounds	O Sole Mio
		Bluebells
1726	Three Sounds	Time After Time
		Goin' Home
1727	Bill Henderson/ Jimmy Smith Trio	Ain't No Use
		Angel Eyes
1728	Bill Henderson/ Jimmy Smith Trio	Ain't That Love
		Willow Weep for Me
1729	Sonny Clark	I Can't Give You Anything but Love
		The Breeze and I
1730	Sonny Clark	I'm Just a Lucky So and So
		Ain't No Use
1731	Sonny Clark	Gee Baby
		Black Velvet
1732	Bennie Green	Bye Bye Blackbird
		On the Street Where You Live
1733	Bennie Green	Encore
		Ain't Nothin' but the Blues
1734	Bennie Green	Can't We Be Friends
		Minor Revelation
1735	Art Blakey	Moanin' Part 1
		Moanin' Part 2
1736	Art Blakey	Along Came Betty
		Blues March
1737	Cannonball Adderley's Five Stars	Autumn Leaves Part 1
		Autumn Leaves Part 2
1738	Julian "Cannonball" Adderley	Somethin' Else Part 1
		Somethin' Else Part 2
1739	Julian "Cannonball" Adderley	One for Daddy-O Part 1
		One for Daddy-O Part 2
1740	Horace Silver Quintet	Finger Poppin'
		Come on Home
1741	Horace Silver Quintet	Cookin' at the Continental
		Juicy Lucy
1742	Horace Silver Quintet	Mellow D
		Swingin' the Samba
1743	Three Sounds	Besame Mucho
		Jinne Lou
1744	Three Sounds	I Could Write a Book
		Nothing Ever Changes My Love for You

Appendix 11

Label #	Artist	Record Title
1745	Leon Eason	I'm in the Mood for Love / Lazy River
1746	Leon Eason	Song of the Islands / Because of You
1747	Leon Eason	That's My Home / I'm Just a Gigolo
1748	Ike Quebec	Blue Monday / Dear John
1749	Ike Quebec	The Buzzard Lope / Blue Friday
1750	Horace Silver Quintet	Break City / Sister Sadie
1751	Horace Silver	Blowin' the Blues Away / The Baghdad Blues
1752	Lou Donaldson	Nearness of You / Mack the Knife
1753	Lou Donaldson	Be My Love / Lou's Blues
1754	Duke Pearson	Black Coffee / Gate City
1755	Duke Pearson	Like Someone in Love / Taboo
1756	Three Sounds	Tracy's Blue / Don't Blame Me
1757	Three Sounds	Down the Track / Robbin's Nest
1758	Three Sounds	St. Thomas / That's All
1759	Dizzy Reece	The Rake / The Rebound
1760	Jackie McLean	116th and Lennox / What's New
1761	Sonny Red	Blues Ville / Stay as Sweet as You Are
1762	Freddie Redd	Alone Too Long / Blues in the Pocket
1763	Donald Byrd	Here Am I Part 1 / Here Am I Part 2
1764	Donald Byrd	Amen / Fuego
1765	Jimmy Smith	Makin Whoopie / What's New
1766	Jimmy Smith	When Johnny Comes Marching Home / Mack the Knife
1767	Jimmy Smith	Alfredo / I Got a Woman
1768	Jimmy Smith	Come on Baby / See See Rider
1769	Kenny Burrell / Jimmy Smith	Motorin' Along / Since I Fell for You
1770	Horace Parlan	C Jam Blues / Up in Cynthia's Room

Appendixes

Label #	Artist	Record Title
1771	Horace Parlan	Bags Groove
		There Is No Greater Joy
1772	Lou Donaldson	Blue Moon
		Smooth Groove
1773	Lou Donaldson	Goose Grease
		The Truth
1774	Lou Donaldson	Politely
		Blues for J. P.
1775	Art Blakey/	Chess Players Part 1
	Jazz Messengers	Chess Players Part 2
1776	Jackie McLean	Greasy Part 1
		Greasy Part 2
1777	Dizzy Reece	Blue Streak
		Ghost of a Chance
1778	Horace Parlan	Borderline
		Wadin'
1779	Freddie Hubbard	One Mint Julep
		Gypsy Blues
1780	Stanley Turrentine	Look Out
		Journey into Melody
1781	Stanley Turrentine	Little Cheri
		Minor Chant
1782	Tina Brooks	Good Old Soul Part 1
		Good Old Soul Part 2
1783	Tina Brooks	True Blue
	(Not Issued)	Theme for Doris
1784	Horace Silver Quintet	Strollin'
		Nica's Dream
1785	Horace Silver Quintet	Where Are You?
		Me and My Baby
1786	Art Blakey/	Hipsippy Blues Part 1
	Jazz Messengers	Hipsippy Blues Part 2
1787	Art Blakey	Close Your Eyes Part 1
		Close Your Eyes Part 2
1788	Art Blakey/	Chicken an' Dumplins
	Jazz Messengers	Hi-Fly
1789	Art Blakey/	Paper Moon
	Jazz Messengers	Lester's Left Town
1790	Art Blakey/	Dat Dere Part 1
	Jazz Messengers	Dat Dere Part 2
1791	Three Sounds	Li'l Darlin'
		Loose Walk
1792	Three Sounds	I'm Beginning to See the Light
		Tammy's Breeze
1793	Three Sounds	Love for Sale
		On Green Dolphin Street
1794	Three Sounds	Things Ain't What They Used to Be Parts 1 and 2
1795	Art Blakey/	So Tired
	Jazz Messengers	Yama
1796	Art Blakey/	Night in Tunisia Part 1
	Jazz Messengers	Night in Tunisia Part 2

Appendix 11

Label #	Artist	Record Title
1797	Hank Mobley	Dig Dis / Remember
1798	Donald Byrd	Gate City / Little Boy Blue
1799	Donald Byrd	Bo-Blue / Ghana
1800	Art Taylor	Cookoo & Fungi / Epistrophy
1801	Duke Jordan	Starbrite / Flight to Jordan
1802	Ike Quebec	I've Got the World on a String / What a Difference a Day Made
1803	Ike Quebec	If I Could Be with You / Me 'n' Mabe
1804	Ike Quebec	Everything Happens to Me / Mardi Gras
1805	Ike Quebec	For All We Know / Ill Wind
1806	Lou Donaldson	Hog Maw / Day Dreams
1807	Lou Donaldson	Here 'Tis Part 1 / Here 'Tis Part 2
1808	Lou Donaldson	Watusi Jump Part 1 / Watusi Jump Part 2
1809	Freddie Hubbard	Changing Scene / I Wished I Knew
1810	Freddie Hubbard	Cry Me Not / Osie Mae
1811	Grant Green	Miss Ann's Tempo / Ain't Nobody's Business If I Do
1812	Grant Green	Wee Bit o' Green Part 1 / Wee Bit o' Green Part 2
1813	Stanley Turrentine	Blue Riff / Gee Baby Ain't I Good to You
1814	Little Miss Scott / Stanley Turrentine	Baia / Wee Hour Theme
1815	Baby Face Willette	Somethin' Strange / Swingin' at Sugar Ray's
1816	Baby Face Willette	Goin' Down Part 1 / Goin' Down Part 2
1817	Horace Silver	Filthy McNasty Part 1 / Filthy McNasty Part 2
1818	Horace Silver	Doin' the Thing Part 1 / Doin' the Thing Part 2
1819	Jimmy Smith	Midnight Special Part 1 / Midnight Special Part 2
1820	Jimmy Smith	Jumpin' the Blues / One o'Clock Blues
1821	Art Blakey / Jazz Messengers	What Now Part 1 / What Now Part 2
1822	Leo Parker	Blue Leo / Let Me Tell You 'Bout It

Label #	Artist	Record Title
1823	Leo Parker	Low Brown
		Parker's Pals
1824	Three Sounds	When I Fall in Love
		Parker's Pad
1825	Three Sounds	Here We Come
		Our Love Is Here to Stay
1826	Three Sounds	Now's the Time
		Just Squeeze Me
1827	Three Sounds	Summertime
		Broadway
1828	Dexter Gordon	Soul Sister Part 1
		Soul Sister Part 2
1829	Dexter Gordon	Ernie's Tune
		Modal Mood
1830	Lou Donaldson	Gravy Train Part 1
		Gravy Train Part 2
1831	Lou Donaldson	Polka Dot's and Moonbeams
		South of the Border
1832	Lou Donaldson	Glory of Love
		Avalon
1833	Leo Parker	The Lion's Roar
		Bad Girl
1834	Leo Parker	Rollin' with Leo
		Talkin' the Blues
1835	Horace Parlan	On the Spur of the Moment
		Ray C'Blue
1836	Ike Quebec	Acquitted
		Just One More Chance
1837	Ike Quebec	Heavy Soul
		The Man I Love
1838	Ike Quebec	Brother, Can You Spare a Dime
		Nature Boy
1839	Ike Quebec	Que's Dilemma
		I Want a Little Girl
1840	Ike Quebec	All of Me
		Intermezzo
1841	Ike Quebec	All the Way
	(Not Released)	But Not for Me
1842	Fred Jackson	Dippin' in the Bag
		Hootin' 'n' Tootin'
1843	Fred Jackson	Easin' on Down
		Preach Brother
1844	Fred Jackson	Southern Exposure Part 1
		Southern Exposure Part 2
1845	Stanley Turrentine	Smile, Stacy Part 1
		Smile, Stacy Part 2
1846	Stanley Turrentine	Soft Pedal Blues Part 1
		Soft Pedal Blues Part 2
1847	Stanley Turrentine	Pia
		Dorene, Don't Cry
1848	Stanley Turrentine	We'll See You'll After While, Ya Heh Parts 1 and 2

Appendix 11

Label #	Artist	Record Title
1849	Art Blakey/Afro-Drum Ensemble	Ife l'Ayo / Obirin African
1850	Art Blakey/Jazz Messengers	Contemplation / Backstage Sally
1851	Jimmy Smith	Everybody Loves My Baby / Ain't She Sweet
1852	Jimmy Smith	Honeysuckle Rose / Lulu's Back in Town
1853	Donald Byrd	Hush / 6 M's
1854	Donald Byrd	Jorgie's Part 1 / Jorgie's Part 2
1855	Three Sounds	You Are My Sunshine / Nothin' but the Blues
1856	Three Sounds	Sermonette / Dap's Groove
1857	Dodo Greene	I Won't Cry Anymore / My Hour of Need
1858	Dodo Greene	Trouble in Mind / Let There Be Love
1859	Dodo Greene	Little Things Mean a Lot / You Are My Sunshine
1860	Dodo Greene	Lonesome Road / There Must Be a Way
1861	Dodo Greene	I'll Never Stop Lovin' You / Down by the Riverside
1862	Herbie Hancock	Three Bags Full / Watermelon Man
1863	Herbie Hancock	Alone and I / Driftin'
1864	Don Wilkerson	Camp Meetin' / Homesick Blues
1865	Don Wilkerson	Jeanie-Weanie / Dem Tambourines
1866	Ike Quebec	Lover Man / A Light Reprieve
1867	Ike Quebec	Easy Don't Hurt / It Might as Well Be Spring
1868	Lou Donaldson	Funky Mama Part 1 / Funky Mama Part 2
1869	Lou Donaldson	That's All Part 1 / That's All Part 2
1870	Grant Green	Mambo Inn / Besame Mucho
1871	Horace Silver	Tokyo Blues Part 1 / Tokyo Blues Part 2
1872	Horace Silver	Sayonora Blues Part 1 / Sayonora Blues Part 2
1873	Horace Silver	Too Much Sake Part 1 / Too Much Sake Part 2
1874	Ike Quebec	Lloro Tu Despedida / Loie

Label #	Artist	Record Title
1875	Ike Quebec	Shu Shu Liebestraum
1876	Ike Quebec	Blue Samba Part 1 Blue Samba Part 2
1877	Jimmy Smith	Back at the Chicken Shack Parts 1 and 2
1878	Jimmy Smith	Minor Chant Part 1 Minor Chant Part 2
1879	Jimmy Smith	Sermon Part 1 Sermon Part 2
1880	Freddie Roach	De Bug Lion Down
1881	Charlie Rouse	Back to the Tropics Velhos Tempos
1882	Charlie Rouse	Aconteceu In Martinique
1883	Charlie Rouse	Un Dia Part 1 Un Dia Part 2
1884	Kenny Burrell	Good Life Loie
1885	Kenny Burrell	Chittlins Con Carne Part 1 Chittlins Con Carne Part 2
1886	Kenny Burrell	Wavy Gravy Part 1 Wavy Gravy Part 2
1887	Herbie Hancock	Blind Man Part 1 Blind Man Part 2
1888	John Patton	Silver Meter Part 1 Silver Meter Part 2
1889	"Big" John Patton	Along Came John I'll Never Bee Free
1890	Freddie Roach	Googa Mooga I Know
1891	Freddie Roach	Blues in the Front Moe Greens Please
1892	Freddie Roach	Nada Bossa Party Time
1893	Stanley Turrentine	Trouble #2 Part 1 Trouble #2 Part 2
1894	Stanley Turrentine	Major's Minor Never Let Me Go
1895	Lou Donaldson	Space Man Twist Part 1 Space Man Twist Part 2
1896	Lou Donaldson (Not Released)	Good Gracious
1897	Harold Vick	Our Miss Brooks Vicksville
1898	Three Sounds	The Nearness of You One for Renee
1899	Solomon Ilori	Yaba E Part 1 Yaba E Part 2
1900	Solomon Ilori	Follow Me to Africa Jojolo

Appendix 11

Label #	Artist	Record Title
1901	Joe Henderson	Blue Bossa
		Record Me (Remember Me)
1902	Horace Silver Quintet	Let's Get to the Nitty Gritty
		Silver's Serenade
1903	Horace Silver	Dragon Lady
		Sweet Sweetie Dee
1904	Jimmy Smith	When My Dreamboat Comes Home Parts 1 and 2
1905	Jimmy Smith	Can Heat
		Matilda, Matilda
1906	Jimmy Smith	Pork Chop Part 1
		Pork Chop Part 2
1907	Donald Byrd	Cristo Redentor
		Elijah
1908	Freddie Hubbard	Blue Frenzy
		Mirrors
1909	Jimmy Smith	Prayer Meeting Part 1
		Prayer Meeting Part 2
1910	Jimmy Smith	Red Top Part 1
		Red Top Part 2
1911	Lee Morgan	The Sidewinder Part 1
		The Sidewinder Part 2
1912	Horace Silver	Song for My Father Part 1
		Song for My Father Part 2
1913	Horace Silver	Que Pasa Part 1
		Que Pasa Part 2
1914	Freddie Roach	Brown Sugar
		Next Time You See Me
1915	Hank Mobley	The Turnaround Part 1
		The Turnaround Part 2
1916	Donald Byrd	Brother Isaac
		I've Longed and Searched for My Mother
1917	Stanley Turrentine	River's Invitation Part 1
		River's Invitation Part 2
1918	Lee Morgan	The Rumproller Part 1
		The Rumproller Part 2
1919	Grant Green	Corcovada
		I Want to Hold Your Hand
1920	Big John Patton	Fat Judy Part 1
		Fat Judy Part 2
1921	Blue Mitchell	Fungii Mama Part 1
		Fungii Mama Part 2
1922	Kenny Dorham	Mamacita Part 1
		Mamacita Part 2
1923	Horace Silver	Cape Verdean Blues
		Pretty Eyes
1924	Horace Silver/ J. J. Johnson	African Queen Part 1
		African Queen Part 2
1925	Jimmy Smith	I Cover the Waterfront
		I Can't Give You Anything But Love
1926	Big John Patton	Amanda
		Ain't That Peculiar

Appendixes

Label #	Artist	Record Title
1927	Jimmy Smith	Bucket
		Sassy Mae
1928	Three Sounds	It Was a Very Good Year
		The Frown
1929	Stanley Turrentine	And Satisfy
		Walk on By
1930	Lee Morgan	Cornbread Part 1
		Cornbread Part 2
1931	Duke Pearson	Ready Rudy
		Sweet Honey Bee
1932	Horace Silver	Jody Grind Part 1
		Jody Grind Part 2
1933	Stanley Turrentine	Feeling Good
		What Could I Do Without You
1934	Lou Donaldson	Alligator Boogaloo
		Reverend Moses
1935	Three Sounds	Makin' Bread Again
		Still I'm Sad
1936	Stanley Turrentine	Love Is Blue
		Spooky
1937	Lou Donaldson	Peepin'
		The Humpback
1938	Hank Mobley	Goin' Out of My Head
		Reach Out I'll Be There
1939	Horace Silver	Psychedelic Sally
		Serenade to a Soul Sister
1940	Stanley Turrentine	Look of Love
		This Guy's in Love with You
1941	Lou Donaldson	Love Power
		Midnight Creeper
1942	Three Sounds	Elegant Soul
		Harper Valley P.T.A.
1943	Lou Donaldson	Say It Loud
		Snake Bone
1944	Blue Mitchell	Collision in Black
		Swahili Suite
1945	Lonnie Smith	Think
		Son of Ice Bag
1946	Horace Silver	Take a Little Love
		Down and Out
1947	Lee Morgan	Hey Chico
		Sweet Honey Bee
1948	Stanley Turrentine	Always Something There
		When I Look into Your Eyes
1949	Lou Donaldson	Hot Dog
		Who's Making Love
1950	Three Sounds	Sittin' Duck
		Sugar Hill
1951	Lee Morgan	Midnight Cowboy
		Popi
1952	Eddie Gale	Black Rhythm Happening
		Ghetto Summertime

Appendix 11

Label #	Artist	Record Title
1953	Brother Jack McDuff	Down Home Style
		Theme from Electric Surfboard
1954	Blue Mitchell	H.N.I.C. Part 1
		H.N.I.C. Part 2
1955	Lonnie Smith	Soul Talk Part 1
		Soul Talk Part 2
1956	Lou Donaldson	Everything I Do Gohn Be Funky
		Minor Bash
1957	Brother Jack McDuff	The Vibrator
		Oblighetto
1958	Brother Jack McDuff	Hunk-O-Funk
		Mystic John
1959	Candido	Jump Back
		Soul Limbo
1960	Grant Green	Ain't It Funky Now Part 1
		Ain't It Funky Now Part 2
1961	Reuben Wilson	Orange Peel
		Knock on Wood
1962	Thad Jones	Ahunk Ahunk
		Us
1963	Horace Silver	The Show Has Begun
		There's Much to Be Done
1964	Horace Silver	The Show Has Begun
		There's Much to Be Done
1965	Grant Green	Sookie, Sookie
		Time to Remember
1966	Bobby Hutcherson	Ummh Part 1
		Ummh Part 2
1967	Richard "Groove" Holmes	Don't Mess with Me
		Theme from "Love Story"
1968	Jimmy McGriff	Black Pearl
		Groove Alley
1969	Grant Green	Does Anybody Really Know What Time It Is?
		Never Can Say Goodbye
1970	Lou Donaldson	Caterpillar
		Make It with You
1971	Bobbi Humphrey	Spanish Harlem
		Sad Bag
1972	Grant Green	The Battle Part 1
		The Battle Part 2
1973	Donald Byrd	The Emperor Part 1
		The Emperor Part 2
1974	Bobbi Humphrey	Ain't No Sunshine
		Sad Bag
1975	Horace Silver	Acid, Pot or Pills
		I've Had a Little Talk
1976	Bobby Hutcherson	Rain Every Thursday
		When You're Near
1977	Ronnie Foster	Summer Song
		Chunky
1978	Horace Silver	Cause and Effect
		Horn of Life

Label #	Artist	Record Title
1979	Joe Williams	Baby Bridges
1980	Bobbi Humphrey	Is This All Lonely Town, Lonely Street
1981	Marlena Shaw	Somewhere You Must Believe
1982	Gene Harris	Emily Listen Here
1983	Grant Green	Afro Party Father's Lament

1970

510002	Stanley Jordan/ Manhattan	Lady in My Life New Love

Liberty (reissues)

Label #	Artist	Record Title
54500	Julie London	Cry Me a River Come on-a My House
54501	Patience & Prudence	Tonight You Belong to Me Gonna Get Along Without You Now
54502	Eddie Cochran	Sittin' in the Balcony Hallelujah, I Love Her So
54503	Eddie Cochran	Summertime Blues Teenage Heaven
54504	Eddie Cochran	C'mon Everybody Somethin' Else
54505	Billy Ward/Dominoes	Stardust Deep Purple
54506	Margie Rayburn	I'm Available Freight Train
54507	Martin Denny	Quiet Village Enchanted Sea
54508	Johnny Burnette	Dreamin' Little Boy Sad
54509	Johnny Burnette	You're Sixteen Big Big World
54510	Bobby Vee	Devil or Angel Rubber Ball
54511	Bobby Vee	Stayin' In More Than I Can Say
54512	Gene McDaniels	A Hundred Pounds of Clay Tower of Strength
54513	Eddie Heywood	Canadian Sunset Like Young
54514	Jody Reynolds Olympics	Endless Sleep Western Movies
54515	The Fleetwoods	Come Softly to Me Mr. Blue
54516	The Fleetwoods	Runaround Confidential

Appendix 11

Label #	Artist	Record Title
54517	The Fleetwoods	Tragedy / The Great Imposter
54518	The Ventures	Walk — Don't Run / Ram-Bunk-Shush
54519	The Ventures	Perfidia / Blue Moon
54520	David Seville	Witch Doctor / The Bird on My Head
54521	The Chipmunks	Ragtime Cowboy Joe / Alvin's Orchestra
54522	Bob Wills / Tommy Duncan	San Antonio Rose / Heart to Heart Talk
54523	Bobby Vee	Take Good Care of My Baby / Please Don't Ask About Barbara
54524	Bobby Vee	Run to Him / Sharing You
54525	Buddy Knox	Lovey Dovey / Ling Ting Tong
54526	Timi Yuro	Hurt / What's the Matter Baby
54527	Gene McDaniels	Chip Chip / Point of No Return
54528	Dick & Deedee	The Mountain's High / Tell Me
54529	Troy Shondell	This Time / Tears from an Angel
54530	Si Zentner	Up a Lazy River / Autumn Leaves
54531	The Marketts	Surfer's Stomp / Balboa Blue
54532	Walter Brennan	Old Rivers / Mama Sang a Song
54533	Matt Monro	My Kind of Girl / Portrait of My Love
54534	Jan & Dean	Surf City / Honolulu Lulu
54535	Timi Yuro	Make the World Go Away / Insult to Injury
54536	Bobby Vee	The Night Has a Thousand Eyes / Charms
54537	Matt Monro	Softly as I Leave You / Charade
54538	Si Zentner	Tenderly / Blue Moon
54539	Julie London	Hey There / Misty
54540	Julie London	Where Are You / Sentimental Journey
54541	Vic Dana	More / Call Me Irresponsible
54542	The Ventures	Telstar / Out of Limits

Appendixes

Label #	Artist	Record Title
54543	The Rivingtons	Papa-Oom-Mow-Mow
		Mama-Oom-Mow-Mow
54544	Jan & Dean	Drag City
		Dead Man's Curve
54545	Jan & Dean	Sidewalk Surfin'
		Anaheim, Azusa & Cucamonga Sewing Circle, Book Review and Timing Assoc.
54546	Jan & Dean	The New Girl in School
		The Little Old Lady from Pasadena
54547	Vic Dana	Shangri-La
		Red Roses for a Blue Lady
54548	Gary Lewis/Playboys	This Diamond Ring
		Count Me In
54549	Jan & Dean	You Really Know How to Hurt a Guy
		It's as Easy as 1-2-3
54550	Gary Lewis/Playboys	Save Your Heart for Me
		Everybody Loves a Clown
54551	T-Bones	No Matter What Shape (Your Stomach's In)
		Let's Go Get Stoned
54552	Gary Lewis/Playboys	She's Just My Style
		Sure Gonna Miss Her
54553	Gary Lewis/Playboys	Green Grass
		My Heart's Symphony
54554		
54555		
54556	Julie London	Days of Wine and Roses
		King of the Road
54557	The Ventures	Secret Agent Man
		Wipe Out
54558		
54559	Bobby Vee	Come Back When You Grow Up
		Beautiful People
54560	Johnny Mann Singers	Up-Up and Away
		A Man and a Woman
54561	Vikki Carr	It Must Be Him
		Can't Take My Eyes Off You
54562		
54563		
54564	Garry Miles	Look for a Star
		Blue Velvet
54565	Jerry Wallace	Primrose Lane
		This One's on the House
54566		
54567		
54568	Gary Lewis/Playboys	Sealed with a Kiss
		Rhythm of the Rain
54569		
54570	Tommy Garrett	The Mexican Shuffle
		Maria Elena
54571		
54572	Canned Heat	On the Road Again
		Going up the Country
54573		

Label #	Artist	Record Title
54574	Matt Monro	Walk Away
		Softly as I Leave You
54575	Cher	You Better Sit Down Kids
		Sunny
54576		
54577	Jackie DeShannon	Put a Little Love in Your Heart
		Love Will Find a Way
54578	Classics	Traces
		Everyday with You Girl
54579	Classics	Spooky
		Stormy
54580	Vikki Carr	With Pen in Hand
		San Francisco
54581	Vikki Carr	For Once in My Life
		Raindrops Keep Falling on My Head
54582	Vikki Carr	The Lesson
		Your Heart Is Free Just Like the Wind

Imperial (reissues)

Label #	Artist	Record Title
001	Fats Domino	Fat Man
		Goin' Home
002	Fats Domino	Ain't It a Shame
		Going to the River
003	Fats Domino	Blue Monday
		I'm in Love Again
004	Fats Domino	I'm Walkin'
		Blueberry Hill
005	Fats Domino	Whole Lotta Loving
		Bo Weevil
006	Fats Domino	Walking to New Orleans
		Please Don't Leave Me
007	Fats Domino	Whole Lotta Loving
		Bo Weevil
008	Rick Nelson	Be Bop Baby
		Stood Up
009	Rick Nelson	Poor Little Fool
		Lonesome Town
010	Rick Nelson	Travelin' Man
		My Bucket's Got a Hole in It
011	Slim Whitman	Rose Marie
		Secret Love
012	Slim Whitman	Indian Love Call
		China Doll
013	Shirley & Lee	Let the Good Times Roll
		Feel So Good
014	Thurston Harris	Little Bitty Pretty One
		Over & Over
015	Gene & Eunice	Ko Ko Mo
		This Is My Story
016	Five Keys	The Glory of Love
		My Saddest Hour
017	Almos Milburn	Bewildered
		Chicken Shack Boogie

Label #	Artist	Record Title
018	Charles Brown	Black Night
		Drifting Blues
019	Ernie Freeman	Raunchy
		Jivin' Around Part 2
020	Rick Nelson	A Wonder Like You
		Hello, Mary Lou
021	Lloyd Glenn	Chica-Boo
		Old Time Shuffle
022	Chris Kenner	Sick and Tired
023	Peppermint Harris	I Got Loaded
	Fats Domino	Valley of Tears
		Let the Four Winds Blow
024	Fats Domino	Country Boy
		My Blue Heaven
025	Fats Domino	Jambalaya
		You Always Hurt the One You Love
026	Fats Domino	One Night
		Isle of Capri
027	Fats Domino	Your Cheatin' Heart
		Three Nights a Week
028	Fats Domino	Rosemary
		I Want to Walk You Home
029	Rick Nelson	Teenage Idol
		It's Up to You
030	Rick Nelson	Young Emotions
		That's All
031	Rick Nelson	It's Late
		Never Be Anyone Else but You
032	Rick Nelson	Believe What You Say
		Young World
033	April Stevens	That Warm Afternoon
		Teach Me Tiger
034	Jesse Hill	Ooh Poo Pah Doo Part 1
		Ooh Poo Pah Doo Part 2
035	Aaron Neville	How Many Times
		Over You
036	Sandy Nelson	Teen Beat
		Let There Be Drums
037	Irma Thomas	It's Raining
		Ruler of My Heart
038	Irma Thomas	Girl Needs Boy
		It's Too Soon to Know
039	Ernie K-Doe	Mother in Law
		I Cried My Last Tear
040	Ernie K-Doe	Lipstick Traces
		Fortune Teller
041	Showmen	It Will Stand
		Country Fool
042	Jimmy McCracklin	I Did Wrong
		Just Gotta Know
043	Johnny Rivers	Memphis
		Cupid

Appendix 11

Label #	Artist	Record Title
044	Jimmy McCracklin	Beaulah
		Every Night
045	Mel Carter	Hold Me, Thrill Me, Kiss Me
		(All of a Sudden) My Heart Sings
046	Irma Thomas	Take a Look
		Wish Someone Would Care
047	Billy J. Kramer/Dakotas	Little Children
		Bad to Me
048	Jackie DeShannon	What the World Needs Now Is Love
		A Lifetime of Loneliness
049	Johnny Rivers	Maybelline
		Mountain of Love
050	Hollies	I'm Alive
		Look Through Any Window
051	Slim Whitman	Twelfth of Never
		Reminiscing
052	Jimmy McCracklin	Think
		My Answer
053	Georgie Fame	In the Meantime
		Yeh, Yeh
054	Cher	All I Really Want to Do
		Dream Baby
055	Johnny Rivers	Midnight Special
		Seventh Son
056	The Players	He'll Be Back
057		
058		
059	Johnny Rivers	Secret Agent Man
		Under Your Spell Again
060	Johnny Rivers	Where Have All the Flowers Gone
		By the Time I Get to Phoenix
061	Johnny Rivers	
062	Hollies	Stop Stop Stop
		I Won't Let Go
063	Hollies	Bus Stop
		Just One Look
064	Cher	Bang Bang
		Alfie
065	Johnny Rivers	Poor Side of Town
		(I Washed My Hands in) Muddy Water
066	O'Jays	Lonely Drifter
		Stand in for Love
067	Johnny Rivers	Baby I Need Your Lovin'
		The Tracks of My Tears
068	Hollies	On a Carousel
		Pay You Back with Interest
069		
070	Showmen	39-21-46
		Swish Fish
54024	Fats Domino	My Blue Heaven
		Country
54031	Rick Nelson	Never Be Anyone Else but You
		It's Late

APPENDIX 12

Liberty LP and EP Discography

An LP and EP discography is presented for the Liberty label. It is divided into sections: 45 EPs, LPs, the Premier series, Classical series, Stereo series, and Jazz series. Thanks to Bob Lucieer for providing the bulk of the information in this appendix. Note that albums were not always numbered in correct chronological order, and that some numbers were doubtless never used.

Liberty Discography

Regular issue 45 Extended Plays:

LSX-1001	Cry Me a River by Julie London
LSX-1002	I'm Available by Margie Rayburn
LSX-1003	The Witch Doctor by David Seville
LSX-1004	Dreamin' by Johnny Burnette
LSX-1005	Look for a Star by Garry Miles & the Statues
LSX-1006	Devil or Angel by Bobby Vee
LSX-1007	Let's All Sing with the Chipmunks by David Seville & the Chipmunks
LSX-1008	Sing Again with the Chipmunks by David Seville & the Chipmunks
LSX-1009	
LSX-1010	Rubber Ball by Bobby Vee
LSX-1011	Johnny Burnette's Hits
LSX-1012	
LSX-1013	Bobby Vee (Take Good Care of My Baby & Run to Him)
LSX-1014	A Hundred Pounds of Clay by Gene McDaniels
LSX-1015	The Chipmunk Songbook by David Seville & the Chipmunks
LSX-1016	Christmas with the Chipmunks by David Seville & the Chipmunks

Liberty Album Discography

LRP-3XXX	Retail issue monaural copy
LRP-7XXX	Retail issue stereo copy
LRP-3001	Mucho Cha Cha Cha by Don Swan & Orchestra
LRP-3002	Bobby Troup and Trio
LRP-3003	Rare, But Well Done by Jimmy Ronles
LRP-3004	John Duffy at the Organ
LRP-3005	Nightfall by Harry Sukman
LRP-3006	Julie Is Her Name by Julie London
LST-7027	

Appendix 12

LRP-3007	V.I.P. by Conley Graves Trio
LRP-3008	Alexander the Great by Tommy Alexander
LRP-3009	Spectra Sonic Sounds by Leo Ornaud & Orchestra
LRP-3010	Ti Amo by Carl Coccomo
LRP-3011	Songs for a Lazy Afternoon by Rod McKuen
LRP-3012	Lonely Girl by Julie London
LST-7029	
LRP-3013	
LRP-3014	Our New Nellie by Nellie Lutcher
LRP-3015	Fabulous by Dom Frontiere Octet
LRP-3016	Powerhouse by Bobby Hammack Quartet
LRP-3017	The Best Things in Life Are Free — Original Soundtrack
LRP-3018	Sidewalks of Paris by Rud Wharton
LRP-3019	Carnival in Capri by Harold Spina
LRP-3020	
LRP-3021	Night by the Johnny Mann Singers
LRP-3022	Jazz for Jean-Agers by Claude Gordon & Orchestra
LRP-3023	Rock 'n' Roll Beach Party by Nino Tempo
LRP-3024	My Foolish Heart by Donna Fuller
LRP-3025	Affair by Abbey Lincoln
LRP-3026	Do-Re-Mi by Bobby Troup
LRP-3027	Pearls of Love by the Players
LRP-3028	Miss Calypso by Maya Angelou
LRP-3029	Just Rollin' with Johnny Olenn
LRP-3030	Will You Remember by the London Festival Symphony Orchestra
LRP-3031	
LRP-3032	
LRP-3033	My Fair Lady by the London Festival Symphony Orchestra
LRP-3034	Exotica by Martin Denny
LST-7034	
LRP-3035	
LRP-3036	Drango Original Soundtrack
LRP-3037	Solid! South Pacific by Bobby Hammack
LST-700	
LRP-3038	Hi Fi Shades of Gray by Jerry Gray
LST-7002	
LRP-3039	From This Moment On by the 4 Grads
LRP-3040	The Dazzling Sound of Keith Williams & Orchestra
LRP-3041	Just Meg and Me by Meg Myles
LRP-3042	Music for the Girl You Love by Pete King
LST-7003	
LRP-3043	About the Blues by Julie London
LST-7012	
LRP-3044	Sitting' on Top of the World by the Jones Boys
LRP-3045	Double or Nothing by Howard Rumsey
LST-7014	
LRP-3046	Let's All Sing by Jerry Collona
LRP-3047	Warm Winds by Hollywood Saxophone Quartet
LRP-3048	Hot Rod Rumble — Original Soundtrack
LRP-3049	Driftwood and Dreams by Henry Mancini
LRP-3050	M M M Myrna by Myrna Fox
LRP-3051	
LRP-3052	Happy Pierre in Hi-Fi
LRP-3053	Carousel Music in Hi-Fi by John Duffy

Appendixes

LRP-3054	Remember Waikiki by Ray Kinney
LRP-3055	Sleepy Lagoon by Si Zentner
LRP-3056	Sea of Glass by Billy Ward
LRP-3057	Dixie Small Fry in Hi-Fi by Bill Hollingsworth Orchestra
LST-7010	
LRP-3058	Roaring Twenties in Hi-Fi by Lionel Newman
LRP-3059	Our Gracie by Gracie Fields
LRP-3060	Make Love to Me by Julie London
LST-7060	
LRP-3061	Singin' to My Baby by Eddie Cochran
LRP-3062	Enchantment by Russ Garcia & Orchestra
LRP-3063	Essence of Romance by the Spencer-Hagen Orchestra
LST-7015	
LRP-3064	Drummin' the Blues by Max Roach & Stan Levey
LRP-3065	Hi-Fi Music for Children by Russ Garcia
LRP-3066	Sidewalks of Rome by Rud Wharton
LRP-3067	
LRP-3068	All This and Cha Cha Too by Don Swan
LRP-3069	Alone with You by Irv Orton
LST-7016	
LRP-3070	Out of the Mist by Tommy Hendrix
LRP-3071	Jazz Variations by Calvin Jackson
LRP-3072	Jazz Hall of Fame by Barney Bigard
LRP-3073	The Music of David Seville
LRP-3074	Warm & Easy by Jeff Chandler
LRP-3075	Birds of a Feather by Muzzy Marcellino
LRP-3076	The Explosive Lincoln Chase
LRP-3077	Exotica Vol. 2 by Martin Denny
LST-7006	
LRP-3078	Here's to My Lady by Bobby Troup
LRP-3079	Ain't We Got Fun by the 4 Grads
LST-7009	
LRP-3080	Sax Appeal by the Hollywood Sax Quartet
LRP-3081	Forbidden Island by Martin Denny
LST-7001	
LRP-3082	Keyboard Magic by Ami Aloni
LRP-3083	Yours Forever by Billy Ward & the Dominoes
LRP-3084	Fantastica by Russ Garcia
LST-7005	
LRP-3085	Polka Festival by Bruno Zielinski
LST-7026	
LRP-3086	The Torch Is Burning by Franklin MacCormack
LRP-3087	Primitiva by Martin Denny
LST-7023	
LRP-3088	Marimbita by Leo Arnaud
LRP-3089	Palladium by Jerry Gray & Orchestra
LST-7013	
LRP-3090	Swingin' Hi-Fi by Al Anthony & His Organ
LST-7021	
LRP-3091	
LRP-3092	Witch Doctor by David Seville
LRP-3093	Latin Fever by Jack Costanzo
LST-7020	
LRP-3094	
LRP-3095	

Appendix 12

LRP-3096	Julie by Julie London
LST-7004	
LRP-3097	
LRP-3098	
LRP-3099	
LRP-3100	Julie Is Her Name Vol. 2 by Julie London
LST-7100	
LRP-3101	Sophisticated Savage by Augie Colon
LST-7101	
LRP-3102	Hypnotique by Martin Denny
LST-7102	
LRP-3103	Sing to Me of Love by Vicki Benet
LST-7103	
LRP-3104	Exotic Dreams by Ethel Azama
LST-7104	
LRP-3105	London by Night by Julie London
LST-7105	
LRP-3106	Hula-La by Chick Floyd
LST-7106	
LRP-3107	12th Street Rag by Jad Paul
LST-7107	
LRP-3108	Inferno by John Buzon Trio
LST-7108	
LRP-3109	Bongo Fever by Jack Costanzo
LST-7109	
LRP-3110	Sondi by Sondi Sodsai
LST-7110	
LRP-3111	Afro-Desia by Martin Denny
LST-7111	
LRP-3112	Guitars by Al Viola
LST-7112	
LRP-3113	Pagan Love Song by Billy Ward & the Dominoes
LST-7113	
LRP-3114	Hot Cha Cha by Don Swan & His Orchestra
LST-7114	
LRP-3115	Half-Time by Russ Garcia
LST-7115	
LRP-3116	Exotica Vol. 3 by Martin Denny
LST-7116	
LRP-3117	R.S.V.P. by the Invitations
LST-7117	
LRP-3118	Have Harp—Can't Travel by Stanley-Johnson Orchestra
LST-7118	
LRP-3119	Swing Me an Old Song by Julie London
LST-7119	
LRP-3120	Tiger Rag by Jad Paul
LST-7120	
LRP-3121	Versitile by Henry Mancini
LST-7121	
LRP-3122	Quiet Village by Martin Denny
LST-7122	
LRP-3123	Latino by Don Swan Orchestra
LST-7123	
LRP-3124	Cha Cha on the Rocks by the John Buzon Trio
LST-7124	

LRP-3125 LST-7125	Bud & Travis
LRP-3126 LST-7126	Margie by Margie Rayburn
LRP-3127 LST-7127	Guitars Vol. 2 by Al Viola
LRP-3128 LST-7128	Way Out, Far! by the Lewis Sisters
LRP-3129 LST-7129	Little Grass Shack by Chick Floyd & Orchestra
LRP-3130 LST-7130	Your Number Please by Julie London
LRP-3131 (no stereo issue)	Cruising Down the River by Bobby Beers
LRP-3132 LST-7132	Let's All Sing with the Chipmunks by David Seville & the Chipmunks
LRP-3133 LST-7133	Thinking Man's Band by Si Zentner & Orchestra
LRP-3134 LST-7134	Alma Mater by Johnny Mann Singers
LRP-3135 LST-7135	Command Performance by Harry Sukman
LRP-3136 LST-7136	Ken Alford's Dixicats at Waikiki
LRP-3137 LST-7137	Afro-Can-Can by Jack Costanzo
LRP-3138 LST-7139	Spotlight on Bud & Travis
LRP-3139 LST-7139	Suddenly It's Swing by Si Zentner & Orchestra
LRP-3140 LST-7140	Omnibus by Spike Jones
LRP-3141 LST-7141	The Enchanted Sea by Martin Denny
LRP-3142 LST-7142	Cool Heat by Ethel Azama
LRP-3143 LST-7143	Black Coral by Rene Paulo Trio
LRP-3144 LST-7144	If You Want to Get to Heaven, Shout! by Gogi Grant
LRP-3145 LST-7145	The Invitations
LRP-3146 LST-7146	In Times Like These by Gene McDaniels
LRP-3147 LST-7147	Dos Flamencos by Jamie Grfo & Nino Marvino
LRP-3148 LST-7148	Chant of the Jungle by Augie Colón
LRP-3149 LST-7149	Roar Along with the Swingin' '20's by Johnny Mann Singers
LRP-3150 LST-7150	Fantastic Percussion by Felix Slatkin
LRP-3151 LST-7151	The Franz Liszt Story by Harry Sukman

Appendix 12

LRP-3152	Julie at Home by Julie London
LST-7152	
LRP-3153	Rebel by Jad Paul
LST-7153	
LRP-3154	60 Years of Music America Hates by Spike Jones
LST-7154	
LRP-3155	Imagination by Al Viola
LST-7155	
LRP-3156	Swing Along with the Singin' '30's by Johnny Mann Singers
LST-7156	
LRP-3157	Fantastic Brass Marches the Blues by Felix Slatkin
LST-7157	
LRP-3158	Exotic Sounds of the Silver Screen by Martin Denny
LST-7158	
LRP-3159	Sing Again with the Chipmunks by David Seville & the Chipmunks
LST-7159	
LRP-3160	
LRP-3161	Latino Vol. 2 by Don Swan
LST-7161	
LRP-3162	
LRP-3163	Exotic Sounds Visit Broadway by Martin Denny
LST-7163	
LRP-3164	Around Midnight by Julie London
LST-7164	
LRP-3165	Bobby Vee Sings Your Favorites
LST-7165	
LRP-3166	The Swingin' Eye by Si Zentner & Orchestra
LST-7166	
LRP-3167	
LRP-3168	Exotic Percussion by Martin Denny
LST-7168	
LRP-3169	
LRP-3170	Around the World with the Chipmunks by David Seville & the Chipmunks
LST-7170	
LRP-3171	Send for Me by Julie London
LST-7171	
LRP-3172	Summertime Blues by Eddie Cochran
(No stereo issue)	
LRP-3173	Together Again by Tommy Duncan & Bob Wills
LST-7173	
LRP-3174	
LRP-3175	Sometimes I'm Happy, Sometimes I'm Blue by Gene McDaniels
LST-7175	
LRP-3176	Laughs for Losers by Dave Barry
(No stereo issue)	
LRP-3177	Lean—Play Bongos by Jack Costanza
(No stereo issue)	
LRP-3178	The Original Hits by Various Artists
(No stereo issue)	
LRP-3179	Dreamin' by Johnny Burnette
LST-7179	
LRP-3180	Original Hits Vol. 2 by Various Artists
(No stereo issue)	

Appendixes

LRP-3181 LST-7181	Bobby Vee
LRP-3182 LST-7182	A Living Legend by Bob Wills & Tommy Duncan
LRP-3183 LST-7183	Johnny Burnette
LRP-3184	
LRP-3185 LST-7185	Rides, Rapes & Rescues by Hangnails Hennessey & W. Brubeck
LRP-3186 LST-3186	Bobby Vee with Strings & Things
LRP-3187 (No stereo issue)	Original Hits — Past & Present by Various Artists
LRP-3188	
LRP-3189	
LRP-3190 LST-7190	Johnny Burnette Sings
LRP-3191 LST-7191	100 Pounds of Clay by Gene McDaniels
LRP-3192 LST-7192	Whatever Julie Wants by Julie London
LRP-3193 LST-7193	Dynamic Hands by Remo Biondi
LRP-3194 LST-7194	Mr. Words & Music by Bob Wills & Tommy Duncan
LRP-3195 LST-7195	Naked City by Jack Costanzo
LRP-3196	
LRP-3197 LST-3197	Big Band Plays Big Hits by Si Zentner & Orchestra
LRP-3198 LST-7198	Ballads of the King Vol. 1 by Johnny Mann Singers
LRP-3199 LST-7199	The First Country Collection of Warren Smith
LRP-3200 (No stereo issue)	Original Hits Vol. 4 by Various Artists
LRP-3201 LST-7201	Drumsville by Earl Palmer
LRP-3202	
LRP-3203 LST-7203	Sophisticated Lady by Julie London
LRP-3204 LST-7204	Gene McDaniels Sings Movie Memories
LRP-3205 LST-7205	Bobby Vee Sings the Hits of the Rockin' '50's
LRP-3206 LST-7206	Johnny Burnette's Hits & Other Favorites
LRP-3207 LST-7207	Romantica by Martin Denny
LRP-3208 LST-7208	Hurt by Timi Yuro
LRP-3209 LST-7209	The Alvin Show by David Seville & the Chipmunks
LRP-3210 LST-7210	Eddie Haywood Plays the Greatest

Appendix 12

LRP-3211	Take Good Care of My Baby by Bobby Vee
LST-7211	
LRP-3212	Soul by Timi Yuro
LST-7212	
LRP-3213	
LRP-3214	Blue Grass Gentleman
LST-7214	
LRP-3215	Tower of Strength by Gene McDaniels
LST-7215	
LRP-3216	Up a Lazy River by Si Zentner
LST-7216	
LRP-3217	Ballads of the King Vol. 2 by Johnny Mann Singers
LST-7217	
LRP-3218	The Liberty Square Dance Club—with calls
(No stereo issue)	
LRP-3219	The Liberty Square Dance Club—without calls
(No stereo issue)	
LRP-3220	Never Forgotten by Eddie Cochran
(No stereo issue)	
LRP-3221	Johnny Ray
LST-7221	
LRP-3222	Bud & Travis in Concert Vol. 2
LST-7222	
LRP-3223	Fabulous Favorites of Our Time by Various Artists
LST-7223	
LRP-3224	Martin Denny in Person
LST-7224	
LRP-3225	Twistin' the Country Classics by the Raiders
LST-7225	
LRP-3226	Surfin' Scene by the Marketts
LST-7226	
LRP-3227	The Percolator Twist and Other Twist Hits by Earl Palmer
LST-7227	
LRP-3228	Bobby Vee Meets the Crickets
LST-7228	
LRP-3229	The Chipmunk Songbook by David Seville & the Chipmunks
LST-7229	
LRP-3230	The Carter Family Album
LST-7230	
LRP-3231	Love Letters by Julie London
LST-7231	
LRP-3232	A Bobby Vee Recording Session
LST-7232	
LRP-3233	Old Rivers by Walter Brennan
LST-7233	
LRP-3234	Let Me Call You Sweetheart by Timi Yuro
LST-7234	
LRP-3235	Original Hits Vol. 5 by Various Artists
(No stereo issue)	
LRP-3236	Tell Me by Dick & Deedee
LST-7236	
LRP-3237	A Taste of Honey by Martin Denny
LST-7237	
LRP-3238	

LRP-3239 / LST-7239	And Then I Wrote by Willie Nelson
LRP-3240 / LST-7240	Matt Monro
LRP-3241 / LST-7241	The President by Walter Brennan
LRP-3242	
LRP-3243	
LRP-3244 / LST-7244	A World of Miracles by Walter Brennan
LRP-3245 / LST-7245	Bobby Vee's Golden Greats
LRP-3246	
LRP-3247 / LST-7247	The Stripper by Si Zentner & Orchestra
LRP-3248 / LST-7248	Jan & Dean's Golden Greats Vol. 1
LRP-3249 / LST-7249	Love on the Rocks by Julie London
LRP-3250 / LST-7250	Eddie Heywood's Golden Encores
LRP-3251 / LST-7251	Golden Hits by Buddy Knox
LRP-3252 / LST-7252	Golden Favorites of Broadway by Frank Parker
LRP-3253 / LST-7253	Golden Folk Song Hits by the Johnny Mann Singers
LRP-3254 / LST-7254	Sing a Little Something by Sholom Socunda
LRP-3255 / LST-7255	Roses Are Red by Johnny Burnette
LRP-7256 / LST-7256	Christmas with the Chipmunks Vol. 1 by David Seville & the Chipmunks
LRP-3257 / LST-7257	"Twas the Night Before Christmas" — Back Home by Walter Brennan
LRP-3258 / LST-7258	Hit After Hit by Gene McDaniels
LRP-3259	
LRP-3260 (No stereo issue)	Original Hits Vol. 6 by Various Artists
LRP-3261	The Alligator and Other Poems by Henry Gibson
LRP-3262	
LRP-3263 / LST-7263	What's a Matter Baby? by Timi Yuro
LRP-3264 / LST-7264	Ernie Freeman's Soulfull Sound of Country Classics
LRP-3265	
LRP-3266 / LST-7266	Mama Sang a Song by Walter Brennan
LRP-3267 / LST-7267	Merry Christmas from Bobby Vee
LRP-3268	

LRP-3269 LST-7269	Folk Songs for the Rich by the Sundowners
LRP-3270	
LRP-3271	
LRP-3272 LST-7272	Something Old, Something New, Something Blue, Something Else by the Crickets
LRP-3273 LST-7273	Desafinado by Si Zentner & Orchestra
LRP-3274 (No stereo issue)	Original Hits Vol. 7 by Various Artists
LRP-3275 LST-7275	Spanish Lace by Gene McDaniels
LRP-3276 LST-7276	The Incredible Nancy Ames
LRP-3277 LST-7277	Another Taste of Honey by Martin Denny
LRP-3278 LST-7278	Latin in a Satin Mood by Julie London
LRP-3279 LST-7279	Manhattan Beat by Eddie Heywood
LRP-3280 LST-7280	Swingin' with the Starr by Kay Starr
LRP-3281 LST-7281	Organ Holiday by Johnny Duffy
LRP-3282 LST-7282	Doin' the Bird by the Rivingtons
LRP-3283 LST-7283	Limbo Dance Party by Ernie Freeman
LRP-3284 LST-7284	Waltz in Jazz Time by Si Zentner & Orchestra
LRP-3285 LST-7285	The Night Has a Thousand Eyes by Bobby Vee
LRP-3286 LST-7286	The Best of Timi Yuro
LRP-3287 LST-3287	Our Winter Love by Felix Slatkin
LRP-3288 (No stereo issue)	Original Hits Vol. 8 by Various Artists
LRP-3289 LST-7289	Bobby Vee Meets the Ventures
LRP-3290 LST-7290	Rhythm Plus Blues by Si Zentner & Orchestra
LRP-3291 LST-7291	Julie's Golden Greats by Julie London
LRP-3292	
LRP-3293 LST-7293	Bossa Nova with Strings by Bill Perkins
LRP-3294 LST-7294	Jan & Dean Take Linda Surfin'
LRP-3295 LST-7295	Naturally by Bud & Travis
LRP-3296 LST-7296	Golden Folk Song Hits Vol. 2 by Johnny Mann Singers
LRP-3297	

LRP-3298 / LST-7298	Today's Hits in Jazz by Dave Pell
LRP-3299 / LST-7299	A Portrait of Nancy by Nancy Ames
LRP-3300 / LST-7300	End of the World by Julie London
LRP-3301 / LST-7301	Folk Songs from the Country by Danny Dill
LRP-3302 / LST-7302	Relax by Nick Noble
LRP-3303 / LST-7303	Bob Wills Plays and Sings
LRP-3304 / LST-7304	Tex Williams in Las Vegas
LRP-3305 (No stereo issue)	Original Country Hits Vol. 1 by Various Artists
LRP-3306 / LST-7306	Golden Movie Greats by Various Artists
LRP-3307 / LST-7307	The Versatile Martin Denny
LRP-3308 / LST-7308	Here's Willie Nelson
LRP-3309 / LST-7309	Great Songs—Great Movies by Kay Stevens
LRP-3310	
LRP-3311 / LST-7311	The Wonderful World of Gene McDaniels
LRP-3312 / LST-7312	UNRELEASED ALBUM—The Wonderful World of Bobby Vee
LRP-3313 / LST-7313	Canadian Sunset Bossa Nova by Eddie Heywood
LRP-3314 / LST-7314	Surf City by Jan & Dean
LRP-3315	
LRP-3316 / LST-7316	Where Have All the Flowers Gone by George Mitchell Choir
LRP-3317 / LST-7317	The Wonderful World of Walter Brennan
LRP-3318 / LST-7318	Color Her Great by Vikki Carr
LRP-3319 / LST-7319	Make the World Go Away by Timi Yuro
LRP-3320 / LST-7320	Jackie DeShannon
LRP-3321 / LST-7321	Jazz Voices in Video by Dave Pell
LRP-3322	
LRP-3323	
LRP-3324 / LST-7324	The Wonderful World of Julie London
LRP-3325 (No stereo issue)	Original Hits Vol. 9 by Various Artists
LRP-3326 / LST-7326	More by Si Zentner

LRP-3327	Encore by Leon Bibb
LST-7327	
LRP-3328	A Taste of Hits by Martin Denny
LST-7328	
LRP-3329	I Never Will Marry by Nancy Ames
LST-7329	
LRP-3330	The Bob Harter Songbook
LST-7330	
LRP-3331	Comin' Home Baby by Ernie Freeman Combo
LST-7331	
LRP-3332	Hootenanny for Orchestra by Walter Raim
LST-7332	
LRP-3333	
LRP-3334	Christmas with the Chipmunks Vol. 2 by David Seville & the Chipmunks
LST-7334	
LRP-3335	Mario Solal Trio in Concert
LST-7335	
LRP-3336	I Remember Buddy Holly by Bobby Vee
LST-7336	
LRP-3337	
LRP-3338	Washington Square by Spike Jones
LST-7338	
LRP-3339	Drag City by Jan & Dean
LST-7339	
LRP-3340	The First Twelve Sides by The Just IV
LST-7340	
LRP-3341	Perspective on Bud & Travis
LST-7341	
LRP-3342	You Don't Have to Be a Baby to Cry by Julie London
LST-7342	
LRP-3343	Kay Stevens in Concert
LST-7343	
LRP-3344	
LRP-3345	Original Country Hits Vol. 2 by Various Artists
(No stereo issue)	
LRP-3346	Boss Drag by the T-Bones
LST-7346	
LRP-3347	12 String Guitar by Walter Raim
LST-7347	
LRP-3348	Motorcycles U.S.A. by the Hornets
LST-7348	
LRP-3349	The New Band of Spike Jones
LST-7349	
LRP-3350	Si Zentner Plays Big Band Hits
LST-7350	
LRP-3351	California Sun by the Crickets
LST-7351	
LRP-3352	Bobby Vee Sings the New Sound from England
LST-7352	
LRP-3353	From Russia with Love by Si Zentner
LST-7353	
LRP-3354	Discovery by Vikki Carr
LST-7354	

Appendixes

LRP-3355 / LST-7355	Golden Folk Song Hits by the Johnny Mann Singers
LRP-3356 / LST-7356	From Hollywood with Love by Matt Monro
LRP-3357 / LST-7357	5 String Banjo Greats by Various Artists
LRP-3358 / LST-7358	Cherries & Plums by Leon Bibb
LRP-3359	
LRP-3360 / LST-7360	In Memoriam by Joe Carson
LRP-3361 / LST-7362	Dead Man's Curve/New Girl in School by Jan & Dean
LRP-3362 / LST-7362	Sounds of the Big Irons — Actual Competition
LRP-3363 / LST-7363	Boss Drag at the Beach by the T-Bones
LRP-3364 / LST-7364	Big Drag Boats USA by the Hornets
LRP-3365 / LST-7365	Liverpool, Dragsters, Cycles & Surfin' by the Eliminators
LRP-3366 / LST-7366	Shut Downs & Hill Climbs by Various Artists
LRP-3367 / LST-7367	Mustang by the Zip Codes
LRP-3368 / LST-7368	Ride the Wild Surf by Jan & Dean
LRP-3369 / LST-7369	This Is the Girl That Is by Nancy Ames
LRP-3370 / LST-7370	My Man by Spike Jones
LRP-3371 / LST-7371	Hello Galahads by the Galahads
LRP-3372 / LST-7372	Gunfight at the OK Corral by Walter Brennan
LRP-3373	
LRP-3374 / LST-7374	Burkes' Law Original TV Soundtrack
LRP-3375 / LST-7375	In Person by Julie London
LRP-3376 / LST-7376	Fantastic Strings by Felix Slatkin & Orchestra
LRP-3377 / LST-7377	The Little Old Lady from Pasadena by Jan & Dean
LRP-3378 / LST-7378	Latin Village by Martin Denny
LRP-3379 / LST-7379	I'm Old Fashioned by Inga Swenson
LRP-3380 / LST-7380	Here and Now by Bob Florence
LRP-3381 (No stereo issue)	Original Rhythm & Blues Hits by Various Artists
LRP-3382 (No stereo issue)	Original Country Hits by Various Artists

Appendix 12

LRP-3383 LST-7383	Discovery Vol. 2 by Vikki Carr
LRP-3384 LST-7384	The Standells in Person at P.J.s
LRP-3385 LST-7385	30 Big Hits of the 60's by Bobby Vee
LRP-3386 LST-7386	Bud & Travis in Person at the Cellar Door—Washington D.C.
LRP-3387 LST-7387	Invisible Tears by the Johnny Mann Singers
LRP-3388 LST-7388	The Chipmunks Sing the Beatles' Hits by David Seville & the Chipmunks
LRP-3389 LST-7389	The Johnny Burnette Story
LRP-3390 LST-7390	Breaking It Up on the Beatles Tour by Jackie DeShannon
LRP-3391 LST-7391	The Ballad Sound of the Johnny Mann Singers
LRP-3392 LST-7392	Our Fair Lady by Julie London
LRP-3393 LST-7393	Bobby Vee Live! On Tour
LRP-3394 LST-7394	Hawaii Tattoo by Martin Denny
LRP-3395 LST-7395	The Roy Orbison Songbook by the Sunset Strings
LRP-3396 (No stereo issue)	Mr. President, Speeches of President Lyndon B. Johnson
LRP-3397 LST-7397	In Full Swing by Si Zentner & His Orchestra
LRP-3398 LST-7398	The Bud & Travis Latin Album
LRP-3399 LST-7399	Songs of Our Time by Elio Gallo
LRP-3400 LST-7400	Let It Be Me by Nancy Ames
LRP-3401 LST-7401	Hank Williams Hits by Spike Jones
LRP-3402 LST-7402	Walk Away by Matt Monro
LRP-3403 LST-7403	Command Performance by Jan & Dean
LRP-3404 LST-7404	Doin' the Jerk by the T-Bones
LRP-3405 LST-7405	The Chipmunks Sing with Children by David Seville & the Chipmunks
LRP-3406 LST-7406	Somewhere by P. J. Proby
LRP-3407 LST-7407	The Big Beats Live!
LRP-3408 LST-7408	This Diamond Ring by Gary Lewis & the Playboys

LRP-3409 LST-7409	Spanish Village by Martin Denny
LRP-3410 LST-7410	Live at the Ice House — The Pair Ex
LRP-3411 LST-7411	If I Loved You by the Johnny Mann Singers
LRP-3412 LST-7412	Genghis Khan Original Soundtrack
LRP-3413 LST-7413	Synanon Original Soundtrack by Neal Hefti
LRP-3414 LST-7414	Jan & Dean's Pop Symphony No. 1
LRP-3415 LST-7415	20 Golden Hawaiian Hits by Martin Denny
LRP-3416 LST-7416	Feeling Good by Julie London
LRP-3417 LST-7417	Jan & Dean's Golden Hits Vol. 2
LRP-3418 LST-7418	No. 1 Hits — Original Hits Vol. 11 by Various Artists
LRP-3419 LST-7419	A Session with Gary Lewis & the Playboys
LRP-3420 LST-7420	Anatomy of Love by Vikki Carr
LRP-3421 LST-7421	P. J. Proby
LRP-3422 LST-7422	Roses & Rainbows by the Johnny Mann Singers
LRP-3423 LST-7423	All My Loving by Matt Monro
LRP-3424 LST-7424	Chipmunks a Go-Go by David Seville & the Chipmunks
LRP-3425 LST-7425	Red Skelton Conducts
LRP-3426 LST-7426	Everything's Coming Up Broadway by Tommy Steele
LRP-3427 LST-7427	The Best of Si Zentner
LRP-3428 LST-7428	Everybody Loves a Clown by Gary Lewis & the Playboys
LRP-3429 LST-7429	Her Majesty's Royal Marines
LRP-3430 LST-7430	C'mon Let's Live a Little Original Soundtrack
LRP-3431 LST-7431	Folk & Roll by Jan & Dean
LRP-3432 LST-7432	Road Runner by the Gants
LRP-3433 LST-7433	Amen by the First Baptist Church Choir
LRP-3434 LST-7434	All Through the Night by Julie London
LRP-3435 LST-7435	She's Just My Style by Gary Lewis & the Playboys

Appendix 12

LRP-3436 LST-7436	I'll Remember You by the Johnny Mann Singers
LRP-3437 LST-7437	Yesterday by Matt Monro
LRP-3438 LST-7438	Martin Denny
LRP-3439 LST-7439	No Matter What Shape by the T-Bones
LRP-3440 LST-7440	The Pair Extraordinaire
LRP-3441 LST-7441	Filet of Soul by Jan & Dean
LRP-3442 LST-7442	Tears by Ken Dodd
LRP-3443 LST-7443	Her Majesty's Royal Marines Vol. 2
LRP-3444 LST-7444	Jan & Dean Meet Batman
LRP-3445 LST-7445	Hawaii a Go-Go by Martin Denny
LRP-3446 LST-7446	Sippin' 'n' Chippin' by the T-Bones
LRP-3447 LST-7447	Daydream by the Johnny Mann Singers
LRP-3448 LST-7448	30 Big Hits of the 60's Vol. 2 by Bobby Vee
LRP-3449 LST-7449	These Bones Are Made for Walkin' by Trombones Unlimited
LRP-3450 LRP-3451 LST-7451	The Mixed Up World of Ross Bagdasarian (David Seville)
LRP-3452 LST-7452	Hits Again! by Gary Lewis & the Playboys
LRP-3453 LST-7453	This Is My Bag by Del Shannon
LRP-3454 LST-7454	Ruben Rodriguez & the Guadalajara Kings
LRP-3455 LST-7455	Gants Galore by the Gants
LRP-3456 LST-7456	The Way of Today by Vikki Carr
LRP-3457 LST-7457	The Best of Si Zentner Vol. 2
LRP-3458 LST-7458	Popsicle by Jan & Dean
LRP-3459 LST-7459	The Best of Matt Monro
LRP-3460 LST-7460	Golden Hits Vol. 3 by Jan & Dean
LRP-3461 LST-7461	In-citement by the Pair Extraordinaire
LRP-3462 LRP-3463 LST-7463	That Old Time Religion by the Amen Choir

LRP-3464 LST-7464	Bobby Vee's Golden Greats Vol. 2
LRP-3465 LST-7465	Exotica Today by Martin Denny
LRP-3466	
LRP-3467 LST-7467	Golden Greats by Martin Denny
LRP-3468 LST-7468	Golden Greats by Gary Lewis & the Playboys
LRP-3469	
LRP-3470 LST-7470	His Newest Songs by Gilbert Becaud
LRP-3471 LST-7471	Everyone's Gone to the Moon by the T-Bones
LRP-3472 LST-7472	You're Gonna Hear from Me by Trombones Unlimited
LRP-3473 LST-7473	Gants Again by the Gants
LRP-3474 LST-7474	Maxted Makes It! by Billy Maxted & Manhattan Jazz Band
LRP-3475 LST-7475	The Deep Six
LRP-3476 LST-7476	Countryside by the Johnny Mann Singers
LRP-3477 LST-7477	Music from the Heart by Red Skelton
LRP-3478 LST-7478	For the Night People by Julie London
LRP-3479 LST-7479	Total Commitment by Del Shannon
LRP-3480 LST-7480	Look at Me Girl by Bobby Lee
LRP-3481 LST-7481	Swingin' Country by Si Zentner & Orchestra
LRP-3482 LST-7482	Bunch-a-Banjos by Freddy Morgan
LRP-3483 LST-7483	A Perfect Blend by the Johnny Mann Singers & the Si Zentner Orchestra
LRP-3484	
LRP-3485 LST-7485	Keys to Your Mind by Mike Melvoin
LRP-3486	
LRP-3487 LST-7487	Paint Me a Picture by Gary Lewis & the Playboys
LRP-3488 LST-7488	Hawaii by Martin Denny
LRP-3489 LST-7489	Too Much Tequila by Ruben Rodriguez & the Guadalajara Kings
LRP-3490 LST-7490	A Man and a Woman by the Johnny Mann Singers
LRP-3491 LST-7491	Film Music—Italian Style

Appendix 12

LRP-3492	Satin Doll by Billy Maxted
LST-7492	
LRP-3493	Nice Girls Don't Stay for Breakfast by Julie London
LST-7493	
LRP-3494	Big Boss Bones by Trombones Unlimited
LST-7494	
LRP-3495	Mon Amour by Gilbert Becaud
LST-7495	
LRP-3496	Bunch-a-Banjos on Broadway
LST-7496	
LRP-3497	Enigma by P. J. Proby
LST-7497	
LRP-3498	Warning Shot Original Soundtrack by Si Zentner
LST-7498	
LRP-3499	
LRP-3500	Original Golden Greats by Various Artists
LST-7500	
LRP-3501	The Nitty Gritty Dirt Band
LST-7501	
LRP-3502	Golden Greats by Gene McDaniels
LST-7502	
LRP-3503	Between the Two by Mike Melvoin
LST-7503	
LRP-3504	It's a Wonderful World by the Pair Extraordinaire
LST-7504	
LRP-3505	This Is My Country by the Johnny Mann Singers
LST-7505	
LRP-3506	Intimate Excitement by Vikki Carr
LST-7506	
LRP-3507	The Spooky Sound of Mike Sharpe
LST-7507	
LRP-3508	Bright and Beautiful by Nelson Riddle
LST-7508	
LRP-3509	
LRP-3510	
LRP-3511	
LRP-3512	Are We On? by Tim Conway
LST-7512	
LRP-3513	Exotica Classica by Martin Denny
LST-7513	
LRP-3514	With Body & Soul by Julie London
LST-7514	
LRP-3515	Phenomenon by P. J. Proby
LST-7515	
LRP-3516	Ricochet by the Nitty Gritty Dirt Band
LST-7516	
LRP-3517	Both Sides of the Globe by the Royal Marines
LST-7517	
LRP-3518	The Sharpest Sax by Mike Sharpe
LST-7518	
LRP-3519	New Directions by Gary Lewis & the Playboys
LST-7519	
LRP-3520	
LRP-3521	

LRP-3522 / LST-7522	We Wish You a Merry Christmas by the Johnny Mann Singers
LRP-3523 / LST-7523	We Can Fly by the Johnny Mann Singers
LRP-3524 / LST-7524	Listen! by Gary Lewis
LRP-3525	
LRP-3526 / LST-7526	Canned Heat
LRP-3527 / LST-7527	Holiday for Trombones by Trombones Unlimited
LRP-3528 / LST-7528	Presenting Toni Scotti
LRP-3529	
LRP-3530 / LST-7530	By My Love by Mel Carter
LRP-3531 / LST-7531	Right Here! Right Now! by Si Zentner & Orchestra
LRP-3532 / LST-7532	The Riddle of Today by Nelson Riddle
LRP-3533 / LST-7533	It Must Be Him by Vikki Carr
LRP-3534 / LST-7534	Come Back When You Grow Up Girl by Bobby Vee
LRP-3535 / LST-7535	Don't Look Back by the Johnny Mann Singers
LRP-3536 / LST-7536	The Hour Glass
LRP-3537 / LST-7537	Something Beyond by Rod McKuen & Orchestra
LRP-3538 / LST-7538	World Famous — Barney Peters

Following the release of LRP-3538, Liberty Records discontinued issuing both Mono and Stereo stock copies. However, the company continued to distribute Mono promotional copies through 1968. The labels used for these promotional copies were the standard black stock label. Also, there was no mention on the Mono label identifying it as a promotional release.

LST-7539	The Further Adventures of Charles Westover by Del Shannon
LST-7540	Rare Junk by the Nitty Gritty Dirt Band
LST-7541	Boogie with Canned Heat
LST-7542	A Today Kind of Thing by the Four Freshmen
LST-7543	More Original Golden Greats by Various Artists
LST-7544	Starring Toni Scotti
LST-7545	This One's on the House by Jerry Wallace
LST-7546	Easy Does It by Julie London
LST-7547	An Open Letter by Victor Lunberg
LST-7548	Vikki! by Vikki Carr
LST-7549	One of Those Songs by Trombones Unlimited
LST-7550	A Taste of India by Martin Denny
LST-7551	
LST-7552	Bull! by Tim Conway
LST-7553	Love Is Blue by the Johnny Mann Singers
LST-7554	Just Today by Bobby Vee
LST-7555	Power of Love by the Hour Glass

Appendix 12

LST-7556	
LST-7557	
LST-7558	T.I.M.E.
LST-7559	Love Sounds by Mort Garson
LST-7560	A Day in the Life of Bonnie & Clyde by Mel Torme
LST-7561	What's Wrong with My World? by P. J. Proby
LST-7562	Sensational by Mario Said
LST-7563	Tomorrow Is Today by the Four Freshmen
LST-7564	Another Time, Another World by Jerry Wallace
LST-7565	Don't Break My Pretty Balloon by Vikki Carr
LST-7566	Sixpenny Millionaire by Tommy Steele
LST-7567	Tomorrows Standard by Marble Arch Orchestra
LST-7568	Gary Lewis Now! by Gary Lewis & the Playboys
LST-7569	Original Golden Country Greats Vol. 1 by Various Artists
LST-7570	Original Golden Country Greats Vol. 2 by Various Artists
LST-7571	Original Golden Country Greats Vol. 3 by Various Artists
LST-7572	Original Golden Blues Greats Vol. 1 by Various Artists
LST-7573	Original Golden Greats Vol. 3 by Various Artists
LST-7574	Original Golden Greats Vol. 4 by Various Artists
LST-7575	Original Golden Greats Vol. 5 by Various Artists
LST-7576	Original Golden Greats Vol. 6 by Various Artists
LST-7577	Original Golden Greats Vol. 7 by Various Artists
LST-7578	Original Golden Greats Vol. 8 by Various Artists
LST-7579	Original Golden Greats Vol. 9 by Various Artists
LST-7580	Toad Hall
LST-7581	Heads Up by the Heads
LST-7582	My Nova Scotia Home by Barney Peters
LST-7583	
LST-7584	
LST-7585	Exotic Love by Martin Denny
LST-7586	Soul Party by Paul Nero
LST-7587	This Guy's in Love with You by the Johnny Mann Singers
LST-7588	
LST-7589	More Golden Greats by Gary Lewis & the Playboys
LST-7590	In a Class by Themselves by the Four Freshmen
LST-7591	Grazing in the Grass by Trombones Unlimited
LST-7592	Do What You Gotta Do by Bobby Vee
LST-7593	By Henry Gibson
LST-7594	Something Bad on My Mind by Timi Yuro
LST-7595	
LST-7596	Do It, Do It by Skiles & Henderson
LST-7597	Sweet Child of Sunshine by Jerry Wallace
LST-7598	
LST-7599	
LST-7600	Butterfly Lake by Paul Masse
LST-7601	Everybody's Talking by Mario Said
LST-7602	Come Heal with Me by Sammy Shore
LST-7603	Birthday Party by the Idle Race
LST-7604	For Once in My Life by Vikki Carr
LST-7605	Smooth Ball by T.I.M.E.
LST-7606	Close Cover Before Playing by Gary Lewis & the Playboys
LST-7607	
LST-7608	
LST-7609	Yummy, Yummy, Yummy by Julie London
LST-7610	

LST-7611   Alive by the Nitty Gritty Dirt Band
LST-7612   Gates, Grills & Railings by Bobby Vee
LST-7613   Patterns by Kiki Dee
LST-7614
LST-7615   Mystic Light by Mike Sharpe
LST-7616
LST-7617   Bittersweet by Jerry Wallace
LST-7618   Hallelujah by Canned Heat
LST-7619   Original Golden Greats Vol. 10 by Various Artists
LST-7620   Goodnight My Love by the Johnny Mann Singers
LST-7621   Exotic Mood by Martin Denny
LST-7622
LST-7623   Hayride/Rhythm of the Rain by Gary Lewis & the Playboys
LST-7624
LST-7625   Underground Gold by Various Artists
LST-7626
LST-7627
LST-7628   Motels and Stations by Paul Masse
LST-7629   Golden Mann by the Johnny Mann Singers
LST-7630   Different Strokes by the Four Freshmen
LST-7631   Mah-Na, Mah-Na by the Dave Pell Singers
LST-7632
LST-7633   I'm on the Right Road Now by Gary Lewis
LST-7634
LST-7635
LST-7636   The Humblebums
LST-7637   Come Together by Ike & Tina Turner
LST-7638   Sea Shanties by the High Tide
LST-7639   Food, Clothing & Sex by John Buck Wilkin
LST-7640   Sugarloaf
LST-7641
LST-7642   Uncle Charlie & His Dog Teddy by the Nitty Gritty Dirt Band
LST-7643   Fantasy
LST-7644   Thank Christ for the Bomb by the Ground Hogs
LST-7645   The Womack Live by Bobby Womack
LST-7646   Kentucky Express
LST-7647   Keep on Keepin' On by the Care Package
LST-7648
LST-7649
LST-7650   Workin' Together by Ike & Tina Turner
LST-7651
LST-7652
LST-7653
LST-7654
LST-7655
LST-7656   Open the Door by the Humblebums

The Premier Series

LMM-13000 = Mono Release
LSS-14000 = Stereo Release
LMM-13001   Paradise Found by the Fantastic Strings of Felix Slatkin
LSS-14001
LMM-13002   Portraits in Bronze by Bessie Griffin and the Gospel Pearls
LSS-14002

Appendix 12 747

LMM-13003	The Magic Beat by the Unique Sound of Richard Marino & Orchestra
LSS-14003	
LMM-13004	The Magnificent XII by the Fantastic Strings of Felix Slatkin
LSS-14004	
LMM-13005	50 Guitars Go South of the Border by 50 Guitars of Tommy Garrett
LSS-14005	
LMM-13006	
LSS-14006	
LMM-13007	
LSS-14007	
LMM-13008	Street Scene by Felix Slatkin
LSS-14008	
LMM-13009	
LSS-14009	
LMM-13010	
LSS-14010	
LMM-13011	Many Slendored Themes by Felix Slatkin
LSS-14011	
LMM-13012	
LSS-14012	
LMM-13013	Seasons Greetings by the Fantastic Strings of Felix Slatkin
LSS-14013	
LMM-13014	
LSS-14014	
LMM-13015	
LSS-14015	
LMM-13016	50 Guitars Go South of the Border Vol. 2 by 50 Guitars of Tommy Garrett
LSS-14016	
LMM-13017	Great Bands with Great Voices by the Johnny Mann Singers
LSS-14017	The Si Zentner Orchestra
LMM-13018	Evergreens of Broadway by 25 Pianos of Tommy Garrett
LSS-14018	
LMM-13019	Inspired Themes from the Inspired Films by the Fantastic Strings of Felix Slatkin
LSS-14019	
LMM-13020	
LSS-13020	
LMM-13021	
LSS-14021	
LMM-13022	50 Guitars Visit Hawaii by 50 Guitars of Tommy Garrett
LSS-14022	
LMM-13023	
LSS-14023	
LMM-13024	Hoedown by the Fantastic Strings of Felix Slatkin
LSS-14024	
LMM-13025	50 Guitars Go Country by 50 Guitars of Tommy Garrett
LSS-14025	
LMM-13026	
LSS-14026	
LMM-13027	Ballad of New Orleans by the Fantastic Strings of Felix Slatkin
LSS-14027	
LMM-13028	50 Guitars Go Italiano by 50 Guitars of Tommy Garrett
LSS-14028	

LMM-13029 LSS-14029	50 Velvet Brass
LMM-13030 LSS-14030	Maria Elena by 50 Guitars of Tommy Garrett
LMM-13031 LSS-14031	Bordertown Bandido by 50 Guitars of Tommy Garrett
LMM-13032 LSS-14032	Espana by 50 Guitars of Tommy Garrett
LMM-13033 LSS-14033	Return to Paradise by 50 Guitars of Tommy Garrett
LMM-13034 LSS-14034	
LMM-13035 LSS-14035	Love Songs from South of the Border by 50 Guitars of Tommy Garrett
LMM-13036 LSS-14036	Viva Mexico! by 50 Guitars of Tommy Garrett
LMM-13037 LSS-14037	The 50 Guitars in Love by 50 Guitars of Tommy Garrett
LMM-13038 LSS-14038	In a Brazilian Mood by 50 Guitars of Tommy Garrett
LMM-13039 LSS-14039	More 50 Guitars in Love by 50 Guitars of Tommy Garrett
LMM-13040 LSS-14040	Six Flags of Texas by 50 Guitars of Tommy Garrett
LMM-13041 LSS-14041	Our Love Affair by 50 Guitars of Tommy Garrett
LMM-13042 LSS-14042	El Hombre by 50 Guitars of Tommy Garrett
LMM-13043 LSS-14043	
LMM-13044 LSS-14044	The Sound of Love by 50 Guitars of Tommy Garrett
LMM-13045 LSS-14045	The Best of the 50 Guitars of Tommy Garrett

Classical Album Series

SWL-15001	The Comedians (KABALEVSKY)
SWL-15002	Symphony No. 25 in G Minor (MOZART)
SWL-15003	Symphony No. 5 in C Minor (BEETHOVEN)
SWL-15004	
SWL-15005	Concerto No. 1 in B Flat Minor for Piano & Orch. (TCHAIKOVSKY)

Stereo Only Releases (circa 1960–1961)

LST-100	Liberty Proudly Presents Stereo by Various Artists
LST-101	This Is Stereo by Various Artists
LST-7008	Mr. Accordian by Dom Frontiere
LST-7018	A Swinger's Holiday by Vic Schoen & His Orchestra
LST-7025	Terror Tales by "The Old Sea Hag"

Jazz Series

The following albums were released only as Mono pressings circa 1956.

LJH-6001	Jazz in Hollywood
LJH-6002	
LJH-6003	

Appendix 12

LJH-6004
LJH-6005 Hollywood Saxophone Quartet
LJH-6006 Jazz Mad by Steve White
LJH-6007
LJH-6008 Smorgasbord by Bobby Enevoldsen
LJH-6009
LJH-6010
LJH-6011 The Nash Brothers
LJH-6012 Red Norvo in Hi-Fi: Vibe-Rations
LJH-6013 Buddy Childers Quartet

APPENDIX 13

Liberty Family 45 Sleeves and Labels

The appearance of Liberty 45 record sleeves and 45 labels is depicted in five groupings.

(1) The Liberty 45 sleeve as it appeared over the years. The first three are from the fifties, and the "Big Hits" version listed Liberty artists on the back. (All other sleeves in this appendix are always the same on the front and back.) The first two are red and black; the rest are blue and black.

The next two are the most common sixties sleeves and are blue. The last sleeve is from the eighties, when EMI resurrected the label briefly.

(2) The evolution of the Dolton sleeves shows how the dolphins, which were basically irrelevant after the name was changed to Dolton in 1959, were phased out over time.

(3) The standard Imperial sleeve used before and after Liberty bought Imperial.

(4) The Liberty and Dolton sleeves as they appeared in the mid-sixties, when they were coordinated in style. The Liberty label was red and black; the Dolton label was blue and black.

(5) In the later sixties, all the Liberty family 45 labels were coordinated for the first time. Note that each is black with a strip of color on the left with the label's logo in the colored section.

Appendix 13 751

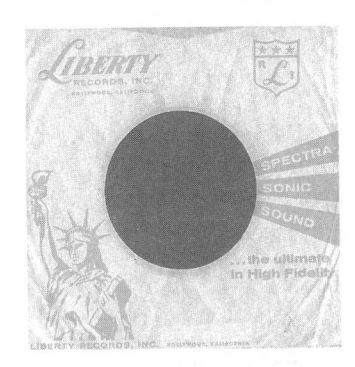

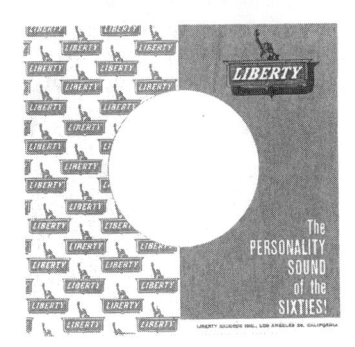

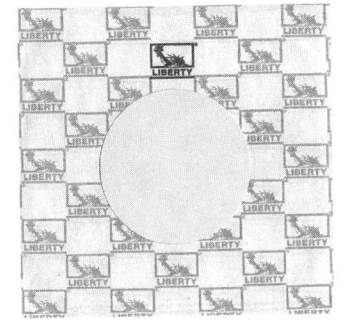

DOL-TON RECORDS INC.
LOS ANGELES 28 CALIFORNIA

A DIVISION OF LIBERTY RECORDS INC.

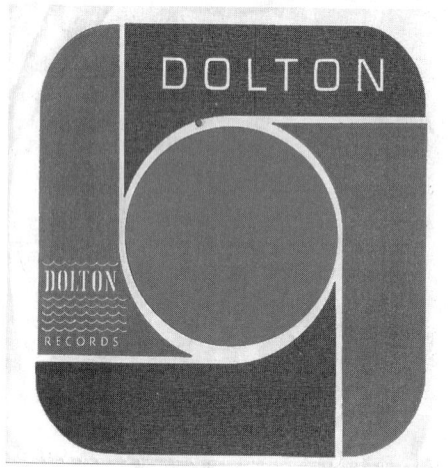

DOLTON

DOLTON
RECORDS

DOLTON
RECORDS
A PRODUCT OF LIBERTY RECORDS, INCORPORATED

Write for free illustrated Liberty/Dolton
catalog: Dept. 14, Liberty Records, 6920
Sunset Blvd., Los Angeles, Calif. 90028

Appendix 13 753

LIBERTY

DOLTON
RECORDS

Appendix 13

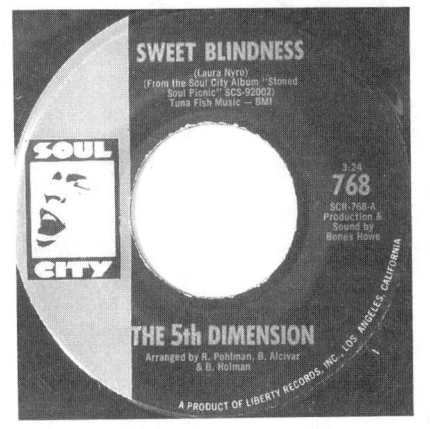

Index

Numbers in **boldface** refer to pages with an illustration.

A

A&M 23, 276, 349, 352, 388, 391, 392, 401, 500, 502, 518
"About My Baby" 141, 276, 353
About the Blues 17
"Across the Alley from the Alamo" 304
Adderly, Cannonball 301
Adler, Lou 52, 104, 137, 148, 165, 206, 212, 234, 242, 290, 348-350, **350**, 352, 356, 357, 360, 369, 370, 382, 393, 504, 508, 536, 545
"Again" 10
"Ain't That a Shame" 127
Akens, Jewel 287
Alfi and Harry 19, 20, 22, 528
"All I Have to Do Is Dream" 58
"All I Really Want to Do" 256, 396
All My Loving **200**
All Summer Long 483
"All the Way" 128
All This and Cha Cha Cha, Too 49
All-Time Smash Hits 96
Alley Cats 5
"Alley Oop" 44, 77, 283
Alligator 306
Allison, Jerry 131, 133-136, 170, 172-175, 177, 178, 359, 360, 374, 428, 431, 532
Allison, Joe 144, 358, 393, 394
Allman, Greg 527
Allman Brothers 393
Allsup, Tommy 133, 134, 144, 169, 170, 358-362, 427, 515
Almost There 71
Aloha **501**
"Along Comes Mary" 315
Alpert, Herb 23, 148, 276, 349, 352
Altfeld, Don 218, 471
Altman, Al 344-347, 403, 404
Alton and Jimmy 4
The Alvin Show 129

"Alvin Twist" 181, 221
"Alvin's Harmonica" 48, 52, 53, 69, 221
American Bandstand 3, 202, 228, 397
Ames, Nancy 171, 172, 207, 238, 311, 526, 527
Amherst Records 253, 534
Amy Records 57, 169, 271, 273
Anatieko, Dick 145
"& Come 11" 296
And Then I Wrote 148, 433
"Angel of Romance" 471
Angels 97, 193, 281, 318, 428
Animals 47, 415
Anita and th' So-and-Sos 99
Anka, Paul 28, 415, 416, 437
"Anonymous Phone Call" 439, 440
"Another Day, Another Heartache" 299, 325
"Answer Me, My Love" 212
"Anyway You Want Me" 153
"A-Ooga" 370
"Apache" 127
"Aquarius/Let the Sun Shine In" 213, 243, 299, 333
Ardells 48
"Are My Ears on Straight" 76
Are You Ready for This? **459**, 460
Argo Records 141, 317
Ariel Records 332
"Arkansas Pt. 1" 256
Arlen Records 6
"Armen's Theme" 19, 20, 44, 45, 47, 164, 220, 365
"Around Midnight" 50
Around the World with the Chipmunks 57
Art-Tone Records 251
Arwin Records 6, 36, 37, 164, 165, 250, 472
"As If I Didn't Have Enough on My Mind" 10

Index

ASA Music Company 341
ASCAP 152, 347
"Asia Minor" 77, 149
Association 3, 9, 194, 204, 205, 220, 221, 315, 372, 384, 409, 481, 541, 544
Atkins, Chet 442, 443
Atlanta Rhythm Section 370
Atlantic Records 24, 60, 149, 253, 291, 394, 464, 523, 534
Aura Records 300, **301**, 310
Autry, Gene 37, 137, 144, 344
Avalon, Frankie 49, 350, 415, 416
Avnet 68, 101, 163, 167, 169, 197, 198, 358, 384, 386, 516-518, 546
Avons 471
Axton, Dave 408

B

"Baby Elephant Walk" 157, 183
"Baby, I Need Your Lovin'" 237, 243, 320, **321**
"Baby Talk" 12, 137, 139, 165, 172, 206, 470, 472, 474, 483, 496, 507
"Bach 'n' Roll" 149
Bacharach, Burt 252, 439, 466
"Back on the Street Again" 320
Back to the Beach 534
"Bad to Me" 200
Bagdasarian, Ross 19, 20, 22, 37, 41, 44, 45, 48, **49**, 52, 104, 127, 140, 187, 197, 220, 221, 277, 318, 365, 409, 528; *see also* Seville, David
"Bailey's Gone Eefin" 48
"Ballad of the Alamo" 52
Ballads of the King 127, 247
The Band 19, 20, 63, 70, 78, 121, 126, 148, 225, 227, 228, 313, 327, 361, 419, 464, 498, 508, 536
"Band of Gold" 267
"Bang Bang" 256, 267, 320
"Barbara Ann" 165-167, 232, 273, 372, 496, 497, 509
Barbarians 232
Barber, Bob 407, 408
Bare, Bobby 178
Barker, Warner 376
Barons 194, 207, 471
"Barracuda" 49, 75, 76
Barsky, Ed **309**
"Bashful Bob" 432
"Batman" 206, 272, 273, 280, 423, 471, 498, 499, 506
"Battle of New Orleans" 359

Battle of the Bands 221, 495
BBC 209, 210, 390
"Be True to Yourself" 164, 166, 440
Beach Boys 5, 104, 120, 167, 170, 172, 187, 217, 232, 238, 241, 245, 273, 349, 352, 372, 413, 435, 446, 470, 483, 486, 495-497, 499, 500, 508, 509
Beat Club 311
"The Beat Goes On" 317
The Beatle Myth 268, 415
Beatles 5, 103, 105, 144, 147, 170, 172, 173, 175, 177, 194, 199-205, **203**, 208-210, 213, 217, 221, 224, 227, 233, 236, 238, 246, 250, 255, 268, 269, 280, 298, 317, 391, 401, 408, 433-435, 442, 458, 461, 462, 472, 489, 490, 522, 535, 542
The Beatles 1961 434
"Beautiful People" 326
Beck, Jeff 148
Becoming Colette 534
Beddell, Lou 12
Bee, Molly 192, 527
"Before and After" 71, 77, 218
"Before I Loved You" 524
"Behind the Door" 256, 267
Behind the Hits 153
Bel Air Bandits 370, 500
Bell Records 121, 213, 220, 243, 251, 299, 333, 343, 372, 458, 496, 536, 540
Ben, Vicki 76
Benay, Ben 139
Beneke, Tex 166
Bennett, Al 29, 41, 43, 44, 46, 51, 53, 68, 76, 78, 87, 88, 90, 95, 99, 101, 103, 108, 122, 123, 125, 144, 153, 154, 160, 161, 163, 167, 169, 174, 175, 181, 185, 188, 197, 198, 202, 204, 206, 213, 220, 252, 254, 255, 259, 271, 272, 282, 288, 289, 298, 303, 308, 310, 311, 326, 337, 341-345, 354, 355, 358, 359, 378-382, 384-386, 389, 391, 392, 399-401, 405, 406, 410-412, **419**, 457, 458, 502, 503, 515-519, 523-525, 545
Bennett, Max 368
Bennett, Tony 81, 178
BerLee Records 273
Berry, Jan 137, 165, 208, 217, 239, 240, 277, **350**, 351, 393, 471, **501**, 502-505, **503, 534**
Berry, William 165
"Beside a Bridge" 152
Best, Pete 472
Best of Bandstand 69, 248
Best of Canned Heat 328

Best of the Blues 191, 284
The Best of the Fleetwoods 248, 539
Best of Timi Yuro 108, 171, 191, 261
The Best of Willie Nelson 519
Bethlehem Records 13, 17
"Bewitched" 261
"The Bible Tells Me So" 192
Big Band Plays the Big Hits 127
Big Beats Live 247
"Big, Big World" 88, 127
Big Bopper 57, 134, 415
Big Dee Erwin 329
"Big Girls Don't Cry" 165
"Big Hunk of Love" 153
"Big Hurt" 273, 366
Big Top Records 140, 254, 273, 319, 409, 470
Bill Bodaford and the Rockets 471
Billboard 11, 55, 70, 74, 75, 80, 166, 183, 186, 191, 194, 196, 213, 232, 267, 268, 273, 280, 287, 305, 317, 324, 326, 331, 354, 376, 394, 397, 398, 408, 461, 464, 492, 498
Billy Joe and the Checkmates 93
"Birdland" 141, 262
"The Birds and the Bees" 287
"The Bird's the Word" 140, 141
Birth of the Beat 194
Black, Jay (David) 524
Blaine, Hal 91, 104, 135, 147, 206, 222, 226, 240-243, **242**, 245-247, 360, 428, 497, 508
"Blame It on the Bossa Nova" 6, 77, 238
"Bless You" 524
Blisters 193
Blocker, Don 40, 108, 169, 252, 303, 308, 313, 378-386, 388, 394, **419**, 515, 516
Blore, Chuck 144
Blossoms 91, 150, 151, 158, 159, 232, 245, 356, 357, 509, 533
Blue Cheer 28
Blue Horizon 95, 182
"Blue Moon" 107, 165, 166
"Blue Suede Shoes" 4, 20, 129
Blue Things 17, 531
"Blue Velvet" 81, 278
"Blueberry Hill" 127, 283
Bluer than Blue 359
"Blues, Go Away" 111, 185
BMI 123, 152, 347
Bob B. Soxx and the Blue Jeans 5, 150, 154, 532
Bob Wills and the Texas Playboys 358
Bob Wills Sings and Plays 172, 191

Bobby Fuller 4 237, 527
"Bobby Tomorrow" 439
Bobby Vee Meets the Crickets 132, 133, 175, 358, 430-432
Bobby Vee Meets the Ventures 132, 408, 448, **448**
Bobby Vee Recording Session **428**
Bobby Vee Sings Hits of the Rockin' '50s 128
Bobby Vee Sings Your Favorites 80, 264, **432**
Bobby Vee's Golden Greats 161, **162**, 432
Bobby Vee's Hits 131, 264
Bobrow, Norm 61
Bock, Dick 368, 389
Bogart, Humphrey 376
Bogle, Bob 95, 359, 442-455, 536
"Bolo" 529
Bonanza 383, 384
Bongo Fever 76
"Bonjour Tristesse" 44
"Bonnie" 75, 471
"Bonnie and Clyde" 250
"Boogie Woogie" 107, 334
"Book of Love" 430, 471
Booker T. and the MG's 149
Boone, Pat 36, 209
"Born to Be Wild" 354
Boss City 397
Boss Drag at the Beach 208
Botkin, Perry, Jr. 207
"Boys Do Make Passes at Girls Who Wear Glasses" 237
Bradley, Owen 344
Bratel, Jack 315, 355, 399
Bread 124, 146, 193
"Breakaway" 210, 211
Brennan, Walter 78, 131, 142, 144, 145, 157, 164, 171, 192, 207, 344, 393, 358, 526, 534
"Brighton Hill" 254, 334
"Bring A Little Sunshine" 247
"Bristol Stomp" 187
Britz, Chuck 246, 368, 370
Bronson, Fred 213
Brooklyn Bridge 524
Brooks, Garth 520
Brooks, Mel 298
Brown, Charles 191
Brown, James 232, 490
Brown, Les 127, 369
Brown, Les, Jr. 527
Brown, Lou 225, 258
Brubeck, Dave 261

Bruce, Edwin 4
"Bubble Bath" 292
Buddah Records 315, 331
Buddy Childers Quartet 292
The Buddy Holly Story 178, 415, 532
"Buddy's Song" 172
A Bunch of Banjos on Broadway 402
Buried Treasure 185, 219, 523, 537
Burke's Law 331
Burlison, Paul 81
Burnette, Dorsey 12, 81, 138, 170, 332, 381, 526, 527, 531
Burnette, Johnny 71, 76, 77, 81-84, **82**, 87, 88, 90-93, 98, 102-105, 116, 129, 131, 132, 134, 149, 164, 188, 212, 224, 236, 238, 243, 245, 259, 264, 271, 287, 288, 294, 307, 308, 315, 332, 350, 360, 367, 381, 383, 388, 389, 391, 394, 408, 420, 425, 448, 457, 470, 523, 524, 526, 531
Burnette Brothers 25, 194
"Bus Stop" 215, 267
"Buy for Me the Rain" 313
"By the Time I Get to Phoenix/I Say a Little Prayer" 329
Bye Bye Birdie 88
"Bye Bye Love" 418
Byrds 6, 166, 233, 372, 396

C

C&C Distributors 59, 94, 182, 379
Caddy Records 285
Cadets 97
Caesar and Cleo 256
Cale, J. J. 237, 527
"California Soul" 299, 333
"California Sun" 6, 175, 277
Camelot Records 528
Cameo 27, 104, 141
"Candy Apple Red" 75
"Candy Man" 437
Canned Heat 311, 326-328, 331, 336, 392, 393, 402, 523, 526, 536
"Can't Buy Me Love" 208
Capehart, Jerry 26, 30, 31, 86, 287, 363, 516, 532
Capitol 5, 6, 10, 11, 14, 15, 18, 23, 26, 45, 50, 59, 81, 89, 125, 126, 130, 140, 141, 148, 163, 167, 172, 202-204, 217, 248, 253, 270, 271, 289, 311, 327, 391, 394, 405, 407, 409, 365, 368, 377, 464, 483, 498, 499, 509, 519, 520, 523, 531, 532, 534, 536, 537, 546

Capps, Al 258
"Captain from Castille" 10
"Cara Mia" 522
"Caravan" 292
Carpenter, Richard 493
Carpenters 71, 112, 187, 479
"Carpet Man" 299, 326
Carr, Vikki 131, 141, 150-153; 155-157, 238, 260, 302, 311, 313, 314, **314**, 326, 332, 344, 381, 383, 389, 400, 402, 405, 526, 540
"Carrie Ann" 215
"Carrie-Ane" 321
Carson, Joe 170, 209, 358, 362
Carson, Johnny 314, 324
Carter, Mel 255, 267, 268, 289, 540
The Carter Family Album 172
Cascades 172, 311, 332, 527
Casey, Al 527
Cash, Johnny 3, 4, 144, 430
Cashbox 11, 75, 155, 305, 397
"Casino Royale" 276
Cason, Buzz 80, 88, 89, 174, 175, 278
"Catch the Wind" 148
Chad and Jeremy 415
Chaffin, Ernie 4
Challenge Records 137, 138, 164, 165, 250, 283, 304, 333, 349, 365, 423, 546, 502
Champs 37, 137, 283, 365
"Change of Heart" 333
"Changin' My Mind" 253
"Chant of the Jungle" 53
Chanteys 219, 446, 447
"Chantilly Lace" 57, 415
Chapell Story 345
"Charms" 91, 164, 429
Chase, Lincoln 527
Chattahoochie Records 327
Checker, Chubby 107, 141, 262, 268, 435
Checker Records 251, 394
Cher 141, 222, 245, 255, 256, **257**, 267, 290, 291, 316, 320, 364, 366, 392, 393, 396, 508, 522, 523, 526, 541
Cherilyn 248, 256, 541
"Cherish" 315, 539
"Cherished Memories" 29, 30, 143
Chess Records 394
"Chi-Hua-Hua" 91
Chiffons 193, 254
"Chip Chip" 137, 339, 344
"The Chipmunk Song" 30, 48-51, 87, 365
The Chipmunk Songbook 171
Chipmunks 43, 46-51, **47**, 52, 53, 57,

78, 92, 99, 128, 129, 157, 171, 181, 188, 220, 221, 237, 238, 243, 264, 277, 292, 318, 384, 405, 425, 526, 528
Chipmunks Sing the Beatles 238
Christian, Roger 217, 277, 508
Christie, Lou 305, 306, 428, 430, 529
"Christmas Is You" 523, 539, 540, 547
Christmas with the Chipmunks 157, 171
Christopher, Gretchen 61, **62**, 63, 67, 70, 71, 111, **114, 115**, 125, 146, 160, 161, 178, 184-186, 218, 248, 281, 355, 537, **538**, 539
Chudd, Lew 23
"Cincinnati Fireball" 425
"Cinnamint Shuffle" 275
Circus of Horrors 89
"City of Angels" 97
Clairemonts 471
Clanton, Jimmy 80, 116, 416, 452, 454
Clark, Buddy 166
Clark, Dee 127, 326, 527
Clark, Dick 51, 69, **82**, 108, 202, 228, 248, 319, 447, 451, 499, 527, 539
Clark, Petula **289**
Classics 262
Classics IV 313, 320, 326, 333, 334, 392, 523, 540, 547
Claude Thornhill Orchestra 166
"Clementine" 507
Clifford, Mike 76, 524, 527
"Climb Every Mountain" 537
Cline, Patsy 81, 148, 166
Clinton, Larry 34, 166
Clooney, Rosemary 20
"Close to Cathy" 76, 524
"Close Your Eyes" 193, 292
"Closer to Heaven" 193
Clovers 80, 329, 437
Clyde, Red 17, 368
C'mon Everybody **529**
"C'mon Everybody" 31, 51
C'mon, Let's Live a Little 424, **424**
Cochran, Eddie 23, 25-34, **27**, 40, 43, 45, 51, 52, 58, 65, 78, 81-84, **85**, 86, 88, 91, 97, 99, 108, 118, 128, 129, 134, 145, 166, 191, 212, 224, 259, 287, 302, 307, 360, 363, 392-394, 409, 411, 413, 425, 470, 516, 522, 523, 525-528, **529**, 532, 547
Cochran, Hank 84, 393, 394, 527
Cochran Brothers 84
Cocker, Joe 392
Coed Records 6
Cole, Nat King 17, 35, 430
Coleman, Bud 159

Collie, Shirley 150
Collins, Larry 532
Colon, August 53
Columbia Records 4, 20, 305, 354, 540
"Come Along with Me" 207
"Come and Stay with Me" 147, 251, 466
"Come Back When You Grow Up" 317, 318, 326, 335, 427
Come Back When You Grow Up **317**, 318
"Come on Down" 248, 253
"Come on Down to My Boat" 315
"Come Shake Hands with a Fool" 212
"Come Softly to Me" 12, 97, 111, 120, 125, 186, **249**, 283, 286, 343, 379, 539, 544
The Comedians 293
Command Performance 50, 245, 488, 498
Command Performance — Live in Person 238
Companion Records 3
"Congratulations" 26, 160, 212
"Conquest" 11
"Continental Walk" 107, **107**
Cooke, Sam 80, 148, 212, 249, 255
Cornerstone Records 335
Cornerstone Song Publishing Company 341
Cosby, Bill 376
Costa, Don 106
Costanzo, Jack 75, 76
"Count Me In" 224, 226, 243, 257, 269
Covay, Don 107
cover record 425, 438
cover version 12, 36, 37, 69, 70, 76, 93, 107, 130, 137, 151, 166, 183, 184, 199, 332
Cowen, Bobbie 396
Crawford, Cliff 144, 173, 344
Crawford, Johnny 471, 508
Cream 68, 84, 193, 276, 406, 545
Creedence Clearwater Revival 401
Crests 524
Crew, Bob 169
Crew Cuts 58, 128
Crickets 57, 91, 104, **129**, 130, 131-136, **132**, 164, 170, 172-175, 177, 178, 193, 209, 217, 237, 358, 359, 415, 418, 427, 428, 430-433, 508, 526, 532
"Crimson and Clover" 116
Critters 166
Crown Records 7, 285
"The Cruel Surf" 170, 200
Crusader Records 207, 272
"Cry Me a River" 14, 15, 17, 29, 43, 72, 111, 185, 191, 264, 303
"Crystal Chandelier" 247
Crystalette Records 181

Crystals 5, 151, 155, 245, 249, 313, 389, 392, 356, 357, 508
"Cupid" 212
Curb, Mike 318
Curtis, Ken 527
Curtis, Sonny 91, 170, 173, 353
Curtis, Tony 144, 344
"Customary Thing" 212
"Cut Across, Shorty" 29, 134
Cymbal, Johnny 171, 172

D

"Daddy" 17
Dain, Bud 85, 86, 145, 147, 243, 251, 278, 282, 333, 347, 354, 388-390, **389**, 392-395, 401, 409–411, 517, 545
Dakotas 170, 200, 213, 217, 232, 249, 291, 415, 526, 540
Dale, Dick 446
Dana, Vic 101, 111-113, **115**, 157, 160, 182-184, 187, 191, 193, 198, 207, 219, 243, 247, 260, 262, 267, 281, 286, 301, 303, 332, 334, 342, 354, 359, 391, 400, 526, 539, 544
"Dance from Bonjour Tristesse" 44
"Dance with Me Henry" 36, 438
"(Dance with the) Surfin' Band" 104
"Dance with the Teacher" 304
"Danger" 91, 112, 183, 184
Daniels, Billy 207, 527
Danny and Gwen 131, 142, 152, 314, 526
Dark, Johnny 409
"Dark Moon" 75
Darin, Bobby 77, 127
Darren, James 238, 420
Dave Clark Five 199, 415
Dave Dee, Dozy, Beaky, Mick, and Tich 328, **329**
David, Hal 252, 439, 466
Davis, Billy, Jr. 324, 540
Davis, Danny 527
Davis, Sammy, Jr. 112, 207, 437
Davis, Skeeter 20, 127, 150, 170, 182
Davis Sisters 182
Dawn 238, 524, 532
Day, Doris 38, 39, 104
"Dead Man's Curve" 178, 181, 205, 206, 232, 239, 243, 269, 278, 280, **351**, 374, 390, 393, 470, 471, 474, 476-478, 488, 490, 505, 507
Dead Man's Curve 207, 208, 243, **478**, 479, 481, 492

Deadman's Curve (soundtrack album) **500**, 519, 523
Deadman's Curve (movie) 278, 279, 499, 523
Dean, Jimmy 77, 144
Death, Glory, and Retribution 224, **224**, 524
Decca Records 6, 8, 9, 11, 23, 24, 30, 34, 59, 99, 125, 145-148, 166, 172, 188, 189, 195, 196, 204, 212, 235, 236, 311, 337, 346, 358, 394, 541
"Dede Dinah" 416
"Dedicated to the Songs I Love" 193
Dee, Jacki 145
Dee, Johnny 26
Dee, Kiki 527
Dee, Tommy, with Carol Kay and the Teen-Aires 134
Deene, Carole 210
Deep in a Dream 111, 185
"Deep Purple" 34, 39, 81, 193
Deep Six 237, 315
De-Fenders 296
Delcardos 196
Delegates 300
"Delta Dawn" 532
Demon Records 303, 304, **304**
Demonstration Record: January 1962 Album Release 307
Denny, Martin 49, 52-55, **54**, 57, 60, 84, 96, 102, 110, 129, 149, 156, 169, 172, 188, 191, 207, 238, 243, 261, 277, 292, 293, 322, 331, 383, 405, 526, 528
Derby Records 243, 251, 252, 254, 255, 259, 260
DeShannon, Jackie 29, 30, 86, 89, 111, 123, 129, 131, 145-148, 156, 164, 166, 191, 210, 213, 217, 243, 251, 252, **252**, 255, 260, 267, 277, 302, 322, 327, 333, 334, 341, 343-345, 347, 353, 356, **389**, 392, 394, 403, 410-412, 413, 423, **424**, 430, 457, 458, **459**, 460, 461, 463, 465, 466, 467, 522, 526, 534, 547
Desilu 344
"Detroit City" 178
"Devil or Angel" 80, 81, 84, 88, 329, 388, 437, 438
Dey, Tracey 20, 169, 526, 527, 534
"Diamond Head" 247
Diamonds 36, 430
"Diana" 416
Dick and DeeDee 101, 117-124, **118**, 141, 181, 197, 213, 243, 245, 358, 390, 403, 404, 408, 419, 502, 526, 540, 541
"Dick Tracy" 237, 532

Diddley, Bo 236
Dietrich, Marlene 527
Dig! 118, 119
Dig Records 285
Dimension Records 3, 179, 213, 243, 299, 310, 311, 313, 323-326, 332, 333, 348, 353, 371, 372, 374, 454, 540, 541
Dion 6, 186, 254, 272, 415, 524
"Dirty Water" 238
DISCoveries 12
Disneyland 223, 225, 227, 437, 449
Dixon, Floyd 191
"Do the Bird" 141
"Do What You Gotta Do" 438, **439**
"Do You Know How Christmas Trees Are Grown" 254
"Do You Wanna Dance" 128, 283
"Do You Want to Know a Secret" 201, 238, 343
Doctor Ross 4
Dodd, Jimmy 323
Dodd, Ken 237
"Doin' the Flake" 257, **290**
"Doin' the Jerk" 237
Dolphin Records 58, **59**, 64-68, 73-75, 113, 188, 248, 286
Dolton Records 52, 58, 59, 65-69, **66**, 71, 73-76, 78, 93–98, 102, 107, 109-111, 113, 114, 117, 124, 127, 128, 132, 133, 145, 146, 157, 160, 164, 181, 182, 183, 187, 188, 191-194, 198, 215, 218-220, 225, 243, 247-251, 253, 260-262, 267, 268, 272, 281, 283, 284, 286, 287, 301, 303, 305, 308, 310, 312, 318, 326, 332, 334, 336, 340-343, 348, 379, 391, 413, 442-444, 448, 450, 454, 470, 522-524, 528, 529, 534, 537, 543, 544
Domino, Fats 28, 36, 65, 104, 127, 164, 189-191, 196, 209, 283, 286, 288, 289, 345, 442, 522, 532, 541
Don Swan and His Orchestra 12, 99
"Donna, Leave My Guy Alone" 237
"Don't Ask Me to Be Friends" 369
"Don't Be Concerned" 296
"Don't Break My Pretty Balloon" **314**
"Don't Ever Change" 172, 174, 175, 217
"Don't Just Stand There" 524
"Don't Pull Your Love" 207
"Don't You Know" 71, 258
Dootone Records 285
Dore Records 12, 58, 68-70, 137, 138, 164, 165, 360, 365
Dorman, Harold 212
Dorsey, Tommy 34
Dot Records 23, 24, 40, 43, 59, 60, 68, 75, 87, 89, 142, 157, 181, 183, 184, 219, 291, 359, 365, 366, 378, 379, 384, 394, 545
Dovells 107, 187
"Down at Lulu's" 331
"Drag City" (song and or album) 170, 178, 179, **179**, 181, 191, 205, 206, 208, 243, 244, 272, 278, 370, 373, 382, 470, 474, 476, 477, **480**, 481, 490, 491, 493, 496, 506
Dragnet 13
Dream Babies 141, **542**
"Dream Baby" 141, 256
"Dream Lover" 127
"Dreamin'" 83, 88, 134, 371, 388, 391, 425, 524
Drifters 127
"Drive-in Show" 45
"The Drummer Plays for Me" 104, 245
Drums a Go-Go 246
"Drums Are My Beat" 194
drums! drums! a go go 104
Drumsville! 127
Duel with the Witch Doctor 44
Duke, Patty 524
"Dum Dum" 64, 145, 147, 251, 379
Dunhill Records 104, 207, 234, 246, 316, 348-350, 360, 372, 536, 545
"Dutchman's Gold" 142
Dylan, Bob 6, 148, 458

E

Eastman, Linda 166
Eastwood, Clint 424
"Easy as 1, 2, 3" 507
Easy Listening 188, 255
Echoes 75, 94, 160
Eddy, Duane 140, 356, 471
Edwards, Nokie 442, 443
"Eefananny" 48
"Eefin' Alvin" 48
"Effervescent Blue" 253
"Eleanor" 105
"Eleanor Rigby" 105
Ellington, Duke 261
Ellis, Barbara 63, **114**, **115**, 186, 537
ELO 482, 519
"Elusive Butterfly" 25, 243, 268, 296, 297, 345
Emergency 13, 124
EMI 23, 28, 133, 141, 163, 188, 202, 204, 213, 223, 311, 337, 373, 433, 483, 519-521, 523, 524, 546

Emory, Ralph 126
"The End of the World" 127, 150, 170, 182, 191
"Endless Sleep" 304
Endless Summer 296, 496
Enrico Records 6
Epic Records 48, 321
"The Epic Ride of John H. Glenn" 144
Epps, Jack 532
Epstein, Brian 202, 391
Era Records 6, 11, 12, 43, 44, 68, 81, 87, 135, 137, 138, 142, 144, 170, 172, 189, 194, 206, 217, 218, 256, 285, 287, 314, 327, 331, 365, 369, 376, 402, 411, 466, 470, 495, 516, 526
Ernie K-Doe 283, 526
"Eternity" 332, 527
Evans, Paul 212, 249
"Eve of Destruction" 490, 495
Everett, Betty 357
Everly, Phil 91, 123, 145, 190, 259
Everly Brothers 58, 91, 110, 114, 127, 145, 146, 174, 238, 348, 353, 369, 430
Every Father's Teenage Son 315
Every Mother's Son 315
"Every Night, Every Day" 251
Every Which Way but Loose 424
"Everybody Knew" 306
"Everybody Loves a Clown" **223**, 224, 226, 228, 229, 243, 269, 339
"Everyday" 80, 212, 333, 431
Everyone's Gone to the Moon (and Other Trips) 237
Excelsior Records 500
Exotic Percussion 57
Exotica 54, 55, 292, 331, 341
Exotica Classica 322
Exotica Publishing Company 341
Exotica II 54
Exotica III 54
Exotica Today 322

F

Fabares, Shelley 357
Fabian 350, 416, 486, 537
Fabulous Ventures 191
"Faded Love" 166, 251, 253
Faith, Adam 57, 79
Faithfull, Marianne 147, 466
Fame, Georgie 250, 267, 277, 291, 526, 540
Fantastic Baggies 217, 257, 258, 267, 495, 507, 523, 526, 545

Fantastica 54
Fantasy Records 401, 532
Farmer Jules 193
"The Fat Man" 13, 190
Federal Records 34
Feel Like Makin' Love 202
Feeling Good 17
Fencemen 149, 150
Fendermen 283
Ferrante and Teicher 77, 303
"Fiddle Around" 272, 278, 280, 492
Fifield, Jim 521
15 Number One Hits 172, 283, **283**
15th Anniversary Album 260
Fifth Dimension 179, 213, 243, 299, **300**, 310, 311, 313, 324-325, **324**, 332, 333, 348, 371, 372, 374, 540, 541
Filet of Soul 280, 488-491, 498
Filip, Gertie 533
"Fire in the Sky" 313
"Fire of Love" 304
The First Country Collection of Warren Smith 127
Fisher, Toni 273, 366
Five Keys 91
Five Pearls 286
Five Satins 63, 113, 438
Five Stairsteps 141
Five Whispers 75, 157, 160
Flack, Roberta 202
Flair Records 285
Fleetwoods 12, 52, 59, 61, **62**, 63-65, 67, 69-75, **72**, 89, 93, 94, 96, 97, 111-113, **112**, **114**, 120, 124, 125, 127, 128, 146, 147, 149, 157, 160, 161, 164, 178, 181, 184-187, **187**, 192, 218, 219, 248, **249**, 272, 281, 283, 286, 303, 308, 336, 343, 379, 390, 391, 358, 359, 420, 423, 442-444, 452, 522-524, 526, 528, 537-539, **538**
Fleetwoods' Greatest Hits 187
"Flight of the Batmobile" 273
Florence, Bob 383
Flower Drum Song 61
"Flying Saucer 1 & 2" 283
"Fog Cutter" 74
Folk 'n' Roll 233, 490, 495
Folk Songs for the Rich 157
Fontana, Wayne 415
"A Fool Never Learns" 238
"For Granted" 34, 423, 464
"For Lovin' Me" 281
For You **459**
Ford, Ernie 144
"Forever" 98, 305, **305**

"Fortune Teller" 297, 319
Four Cal-Quettes 193
"442 Glenwood Avenue" 193
Fowley, Kim 140, 327
Francis, Connie 528
"Frankenstein" 332
Frankie Lymon and the Teenagers 165
Franklin, Aretha 464
Frantics 52, 74, 75, 93, 160, 529
Freedom Records 81, 83, 87, 135, 220, 244, 286-288, **287**, 291, 346
Freeman, Bobby 128, 283
Freeman, Ernie 76, 77, 78, 90, 92, 93, 104, 134, 144, 152, 157, 159, 188, 192, 193, 238, 282, 286, 360, 385, 528, 542
"Freeway Flyer" 232
"From a Window" 200, **200**
"From All Over the World" 229, 232, **489**
"From Me to You" 175, 202, 204, 217, 433
Frost Brothers 354
"Frosty (the Snowman)" 139, 206, 507
Fuhrman, Mel 400
Funicello, Annette 147, 323
"The Funniest Thing" 334
"Funny How Time Slips Away" 519
Furmanek, Ron 524

G

Galore, Mamie 329
"Gamble on Love" 37
Gants 236, 277, 526
Gants Again 236
Gants Galore 236
Garrett, Snuff 23, 25, 29, 33, 43, 48, 53, 57, 65, 68, 71, 73, 75, 76, 79-81, 84, 86-92, 99, 103, 104, 106-109, 116-118, 131-135, **136**, 137, 138, 141, 144, 149–157, 161, 172, 174, 175, 178, 188, 189, 194, 199, 202, 204, 223, 225-228, **226, 229**, 237, 238, 245, 247, 256, 257-260, 267, 271, 273, 282, 284, 293, 294, 303, 308, 315, 320, 331, 333, 341, 345, 350, 354, 356, 358, 363, 369, 370, 372, 374, 378, 380-382, 388, 393, 411, 418, 421, **422**, 424, 425, 437, 438, 449, 457, 492, 504, 505, 508, 517, 528, 532, 542, **544**, 546
Gary Lewis and the Playboys 202, 222, **223**, 224, 225, 228, 245, 256, 268, 271, 277, 290, 336, 372, 393, 508, 523-525
"(Gary, Please Don't Sell) My Diamond Ring" 223, 237

"Gas Money" 497
Gates, David 146, 356
Gaudio, Bob 169
Gaye, Marvin 232, 356
Gayle, Crystal 519
Geld and Udell 258
Gems of Jazz 285
Gerry and the Pacemakers 232, 415
Gershwin, George 14, 323
Gershwin, Ira 323
"Get Away" 250, 267
Getz, Stan 256
Gibbs, Georgia 36, 438
Gibson, Henry 157
Gibson, Jill 206, 217, 507, 508
Gilberto, Astrud 256
Ginsburg, Arnie (of Jan & Arnie) 137, 165, 471, 472, **472**
Ginsburg, Arnie "Woo Woo" (deejay) 404, 472
"The Girl Can't Help It" 27, 30
"Girl Talk" 17
"The Girl Upstairs" 11
"The Girl with the Horn Rimmed Glasses" 237
"The Girls' Song" 299
Gladiolas 36
Glasser, Dick 131, 149, 150, 157, 193, 198, 218, 248, 340, 341, 343, 344, 354, 359, 360, 391, 432, 461
Glasser, Ted 354
Glenn Records 145
"Gloria" 236
"Go Away Little Girl" 6, 77
"Go, Jimmy, Go" 452
"Go Where You Wanna Go" 299, 371, 325
"God Bless the Child" 146
"God, Country, and My Baby" 88, 105, 383
Goffin, Gerry 103
"Going Up the Country" 327
Gold, Dave 363
Gold Crest Records 115
Gold Star Recording Studio 51, 83, 153, 155, 363-368
Golden Folk Hits 172
Golden Hits 90, 96, 138, 165, 170, 171, 191, 239, 280, 283, 526
Gone Records 68, 145
"Gonna Get Along Without Ya Now" **21**
"Good Groove" 296
"Good Luck Charm" 153
"Good Vibrations" 177
"Goodbye to Love" 121

Goode, Jack 147, 356
Goodlettsville Five 48
"Goodnight, My Love" 184-186, 218
Gordon, Claude 39
Gorme, Eydie 6, 238
Gorshin, Frank 527
"Gotta Get to Your House" 20
"Gotta Take That One Last Ride" 486, 493
"Gotta Travel On" 108, 192
"Graduation's Here" 71-73, 160, 184, 186
Grant, Gogie 12, 138, 527
Gray, Dobie 317
"The Great Imposter, (He's)" 111
"Great Pretender" 45
"Green Grass" 268
"Green Onions" 149, 447
Grey, Zane 13
Grier, Roosevelt 527
"Groovy Summertime" 320
"Growing Pains" 318
Guaranteed Records 249
"Guiro" 50
Guitar, Bonnie 64, 71, 75, 182, 534
"Guitar Twist" 359
Gusto Records 500
Guyden Records 48
"The Gypsy Cried" 305

H

Hagen, Spencer 292
Hair 333
Haley, Bill 58, 65, 71, 104, 294, 435
"Half a Man" 148, 393
Half Time 49, 55
"Hallelujah, I Love Her So" 259
Hamilton, Chico 298
Hamilton, Roy 268, 368
Hamilton, Joe Frank, and Reynolds 207
Hammerstein II, Oscar 323
Hancock, Herbie 301
"Hands Off" 12
"Hang on Sloopy" 317
Hank Ballard and the Midnighters 438
"A Hank of Hair and a Banana Peel" 273
"Hanky Panky" 116
"Happy" 320
"Happy Together" 372
"A Hard Day's Night" 317
A Hard Day's Night 522
"Hard to Find" 75, 228
Hardtimes 296, 297, 313, 319
Harris, Mike 207
Harris, Peppermint 191

Harris, Thurston 196
Harrison, Wilbert 178
Hatari 157
Hawaii 322
"Hawaii 5-0" 332, 442, 452
Hawaii 5-0 444
"Hawaiian Wedding Song" 60
Hawks 189
Haymes, Dick 170
"He Ain't Heavy, He's My Brother" 216
Hear the Beatles Tell All 246
"Heart and Soul" 137, 165, 166, 206, 349, 502, 506
"Heart in Hand" 146, 147
"Heartaches" 166
"Heartbeat" 360
"Heartbreak Hotel" 45, 50
Heider, Wally 246, 369
Height, Ronnie 12, 68, 70, 89
Heilicher, Amos 57, 88
"Hello Dolly" 402
"Hello, Mary Lou" 150, 213
"Hello Walls" 126, 130, 148, 237, 519
Henry, Clarence ("Frogman") 141
Hensley, Tom 140
"Here I Go Again" 216
"Here We Go Again" 289
Here's to My Lady 17
Here's Willie Nelson 148, 172, 191
Herman, Woody 369
"He's a Rebel" 5, 141, 150-153, **151**, 155-157, 313, 344, 356, 357, 389
"He's Got the Whole World in His Hands" 217, 253
"He's Old Enough to Know Better" 172, 173
"He's So Fine" 193, 254
"Hey, Baby" 155
"Hey, Big Brain" 49
"Hey Joe" 256, 320
"Hey Little One" 12, 81
"Heya" 316
Heywood, Eddie 527
Hi-Fi in Focus 442
Hi-Fi's 324
Hicklin, Ron 225, 227, 245
Highlights 97, 159, 502
Hill, Benny 332
Hill, Jessie 238, 336
Hill, Wendy 223, 237
"Hippy Hippy Shake" 214, **215**
"His Latest Flame" 109, 437
Hit After Hit 170, 255, 315, 403
"Hit the Road Jack" 96
"Hitchhike Back to Georgia" 91

Hits and Other Favorites 129, 523
Hits of the Rockin' '50s 128, 172
Hobaica, Richard 140
Hodges, Gary 75
"Hold Me, Thrill Me, Kiss Me" 255
Holden, Ron 74
Holiday, Jimmy 296
Hollies 189, 199, 204, 213-217, **216**, 224, 249, 260, 267, 289, 291, 321, **322**, 401, 526, 540, 547
The Hollies Greatest Hits 217
Holly, Buddy 4, 28, 30, 49, 57, 58, 80, 81, 88, 104, 105, 130, 131-135, 172, 173, 178, 190, 202, 207, 212, 217, 237, 358, 360, 361, 415, 418, 427, 430-432, 435, 438, 466, 508, 532
"Holly Go Softly" 335
Hollywood Argyles 44, 50
"Home on the Range" 52
"Homework" 147
Honeycombs 415
Honeys 20
"Honky Tonk" 127, 448
"Honolulu Lulu" 170, 178, **180**, 181, 470, 490
Hooker, John Lee 348
"Hootenanny" 48
Hopkins, Lightnin' 191
"Hoppy, Gene, and Me" 542
Horton, Johnny 77, 359
Hot Cha Cha 49
"Houdini" 142
"How Many Nights" 150
"How Many Tears" 109, 188
"How Wrong I Was" 145
Howard Ramsey and the Lighthouse All Stars 292
Howe, Bones 108, 145, 155, 179, 213, 217, 246, 256, 279, 333, 367, 368, 370, 372, 374, 508, 541
"Hula Love" 89
Hullabaloo 397
"Hundred Pounds of Clay" 103, 144, 202, 204, 268, 382; *see also* "100 Lbs. of Clay"
Hunter, Johnny 237
"Hurt" 108, 261, 266, 390
Hurt!!! 108
"Hurt So Bad" 254, 334
Hyland, Brian 207, 257, 258, 326
Hypnotique 54

I

"I Apologize" 108, 261

"I Can Make It with You" 253, 267
"I Can't Let Go" 215, 267
"I Can't Say Goodbye to You" 131, **353**
"I Care So Much" 125
"I Cried" 87, 193
"I Didn't Want to Have to Do It" 253
"I Don't Know Why (But I Do)" 141
"I Fought the Law" 91, 237
"I Found a Girl" 206, 232, 470, 504, 506, 507
"I Get Around" 490, 496
"I Got a Bongo" 75
"I Got You Babe" 256, 290
"I Had Too Much to Dream Last Night" 315
"I Have Faith" 145
"I Just Called to Say Hello" 300
"I Just Want to Stay Here and Love You" 6
"I Keep Wanting You" 253
"I Knew from the Start" 471
"I Left My Heart in San Francisco" 178, 182
"I Love an Angel" 74, 528
"I Love How You Love Me" 71
"I Love Paris in the Springtime" 292
"I Love You Drops" 281
"I Miss You" 471
"I Miss Your Kissing" 58
"I Put the Bomp" 165
I Remember Buddy Holly 172, **173**
"I Remember You" 276, 277
"I Saw Her Again" 545
"I Think I'm Gonna Kill Myself" 90, 91
"I Want Someone" 117-119
"I Want to Hold Your Hand" 175
"I Want to Kiss Ringo Goodbye" 207
"I Want to Take You Higher" 334
"I Was Checkin' Out, She Was Checkin' In" 107
"I Was the One" 33, 67, 153, 400
"I Washed My Hands in Muddy Water" 267
"I Wish I Could Find a Boy" 129
"I Wonder, I Wonder, I Wonder" 305
"I Won't Turn You Down" 129
"I'd Like You for Christmas" 15
Ierardi, John 402, 403
"If I Had a Hammer" 87, 92
"If I Want Long Enough" 150
"If the Things in My Room Could Talk" 237
"If You Can't Rock Me" 195
"If You Were" 37, 63, 398, 427
Ike and Tina Turner 5, 334, 336
"I'll Be Loving You Forever" 325
"I'll Be on My Way" 200
"I'll Get By" 170

"I'll Keep You Satisfied" 200
"I'll Walk the Rest of the Way" 152
"I'm a Man" 416
"I'm Afraid to Say I Love You" 76
"I'm Available" 37-39, 72, 97, 264, 365
"I'm Feelin' Better" 173
"I'm Happy Just to Dance with You" **203**
"I'm Henry the VIII, I Am" 237
"I'm in Love Again" 195
"I'm Not a Bad Guy" 172, 174
"I'm on the Outside Looking In" 106
"I'm Slippin' In" 189
"I'm Sorry" 80, 437
"I'm Stickin' with You" 114, 520
"I'm Walkin'" 127, 541
"Image of a Girl" 315
"Imagination" 537
Imperial Records 23, 24, 60, 66, 81, 89, 93, 104, 109, 141, 150, 188-191, 193-196, 200, 210-218, 225, 240, 242, 243, 245, 249-251, 253, 255, 256, 257, 260, 267, 268, 277, 281, 282-286, 288-291, 301, 303, 310, 311, 315, 319-321, 326, 328, 329, 332-334, 345, 347-349, 354, 358, 364, 369, 371, 372, 377, 382, 383, 386-388, 393, 394, 396, 401, 405, 442, 458, 464, 466, 470, 520, 522-524, 526, 532, 536, 541
In a Mellow Mood 160
"In a Turkish Town" 165
In Concert 295, 313, 418, 497
"The In-Crowd" 317
In Person at P. J.'s 238
"In the Hall of the Mountain King" 237
"In the Meantime" 17, 44, 100, 250, 386, 516
"In the Still of the Night" 113, 438
"In the Wee Small Hours of the Morning" 128
"In Time" 12
"In Times Like These" 102, 103
Incredible Nancy Ames 171
Infinity Records 383
Ingmann, Jorgen 127
"Inna-Gadda-Da-Vida" 490
"Into the Mystic" 334
Isley Brothers 208
"It Ain't That Way" 189
"It Doesn't Matter Any More" 28, 130, 427
"It Might as Well Rain Until September" 3
"It Might Have Been" 57, 58
"It Must Be Him" 313, 314, 401, 403
"It Was I" 217, **218**
"It Will Stand" 212, 394
"It's a Lonely Town Without You" 192

"It's as Easy as 1, 2, 3" **217**
"It's in His Kiss" 141
"It's Late" 81, 104, 132
"It's My Party" 135, 357
"It's Now or Never" 153
"It's So Nice" 254, 334
"I've Been Loving You Too Long" 334
"I've Cried My Last Tear" 251
"I've Got a Lot of Things to Do" 88

J

J&D Record 278
Jackie DeShannon **459**
Jackson, Michael 367
Jackson, Wanda 49
Jagger, Mick 255
"Jailhouse Rock" 26
"Jam Up and Jelly Tight" 331
"Jambalaya" 240
James, Fanita 150, 246, 356
James, Harry 127, 166, 170
James, Tommy 116
"James, Hold the Ladder Steady" 210
Jan & Arnie 137, 139, 471, 472, **472**
Jan & Dean 12, 28, 36, 50, 78, 81, 128, 131, 137-140, **138**, 141, 142, 148, 164-167, 170-172, **171**, 178, **179**, **180**, 191, 194, 199, 205-208, **205**, 212, 213, 215, 217, 218, 222, 225, 229, **230**, **231**, 232-234, **233**, **234**, 236, 238, 239-246, **239**, 241, **244**, 250, 256, 257, **265**, 266, 267, 269, 272, 273, **274**, **275**, 276-278, **279**, 280, 281, 283, 298, 299, 302, 315, 328, 336, 349–352, 356, 360, 369, 370, 372, 373, 375-377, 382, 390, 393, 394, 403, 411, 412, 413, 422, 423, 430, 438, 442, 446, 449, 452, 470-472, **473**, **475**, **476**, **478**, **479**, **480**, **482**, **484**, **485**, 486, 488, **489**, 490, 491, 493-497, **494**, 499, **500**, 501, 502, 504-509, **506**, **508**, 519, 522-526, 533, 545, 547
Jan & Dean Anthology Album **482**
Jan & Dean Studio Out Takes 507
Jan & Dean Take Linda Surfin' 171, **171**
Jan & Dean's Golden Hits 138, 165, 239
Jan & Dean's Pop Symphony No. 1 239
"Japanese Sandman" 237
Jay and the Americans 522, 524, 525
Jaynettes 6
Jazz Americana 298
Jazz Crusaders 296, 299
Jazz for Jean-agers 39
Jazz in Hollywood 292

Jazz Voices in Video 332
"Jennie Lee" 36, 37, 137, 139, 140, 165, 470-472, 492, 505, 522
Jimmy Rowles Trio 12
"Jingling Jeans" 89
"Jo-Ann" 531
"Joe the Grinder" 188, 189
"Joey Baby" 99, 305
John Duffy at the Mighty Columbia Square Wurlitzer 12
"Johnny Angel" 357
The Johnny Burnette Story 238
Joiner, Arkansas, Junior High School Band 78, 385
"The Joker Is Wild" 273
Jones, Brian 122
Jones, Joe 175, 277
Jones, Spike 37, 49, 172, 207, 238, 402, 527
Jones, Tom 247, 356
Joplin, Janis 392
Jordanairs 81
JRS Records 520
Jubilee Records 34
Julie at Home 49
Julie Is Her Name 15, **16**, 264
Jungle Girl 13
Junior Misses 471
"Just a Dream" 80, 116, 416, 452
"Just a Little Too Much" 83, 104, **189**
"Just Got to Know" 251
"Just One Look" 215, 216, 321
"Just Say I Love Him" 261
"Just Walkin' in the Rain" 210
Justice, Bill 93, 193, 283, 284

K

Kabalevsky 293
KABC 87
Kalin Twins 146, 249
Kama Sutra Records 335
"Kansas City" 178, 202, 448
"Kansas City/Hey Hey Hey" 202
Kapp Records 171, 201, 320
"Karma Chameleon" 89
KDOT 471
Keep, Cathy 299
Keep, Ted 292, 363
"Keeping My Fingers Crossed" 150
Kelly, Buzzie **531**
Kelly, Julie 299
"The Kelly Place" 142
Kennedy, Jerry 48

Kennedy, President John 100, 410
Kentucky Colonels 296
Kerr, Anita 99, 305
Kessell, Barney 51
KEWI 408
KFGO 417
KFWB 64, 140, 144, 297, 390
"Kickapoo Joy Juice" 49, 141
"Kicks" 285
"Kickstand" 281
Kim, Ken 298, 375-377
King, Ben E. 475
King, Carole 3, 109, 128, 131, 174, 254, 352, 353, 369, 382, 437, 524
The King and I 296
King of Kings 129
Kingsmen 224, 238, 248, 383
Kinks 415
Kirschner, Don 155
"The Kiss" 403, 404
"Kiss Me Baby" 81, 287
Kittyhawk Graphics 509
KJAN 471
Knight, Sonny 300
"Knock Three Times" 524
Knox, Buddy 71, 76, 77, 89-93, **90**, 98, 103, 114, 134, 170, 174, 224, 250, 254, 259, 271, 283, 284, 361, 515, 526, 531
Kokomo 77, 149
Kool Gold 541
KOWH 382, 390
Kramer, Billy J. 200, **201**, 204, 213, 217, 232, 249, 289, 291, 296, 297, 415, 486, 526, 540
KRLA 30, 390, 391, 409, 412, 458
K-Tel Records 452, 483, 499, 500, 529, 531-536, 540
K-TOP 407-409

L

"La Bamba" 57, 248, 415
La Bamba 175, 532
"Laddie-O" 76
Ladies and Gentlemen: The Fabulous Stains 545
Lama Records 117
Lane, Frankie 237
Lapuma, Tommy 383, 391, 400, 401
Laramie 13
LaRue, Florence 324
"The Last One to Know" 93
"The Last Song (I'm Ever Gonna Sing)" 170

"Laugh at Me" 256
Laurel Canyon 253, 458, **459**
Laurie Records 193, 254
Lavinger, Allan 44, 53, 406
Lawrence, Jack 166
Lawrence, Steve 6, 77, 89
Leaves 320
Led Zeppelin 147
Lee, Brenda 80, 89, 145–147, 166, 240, 251, 344, 394, 437, 460
Lee, Diana 49
Lee, Vik E. 192
"The Legend of Zanadu" 329
Legendary Masked Surfers 475, 499
Legendary Masters 28, 285, 481, 488, 520, 522, 524
LeGrand Records 32
Lennon, John 200, 217, 244
"Let Her Dance" 237
"Let There Be Drums" 194
"Let There Be Drums '66" 212
Let's All Sing Along with the Chipmunks 48
"Let's Call It a Day Girl" 332
"Let's Get Together" 471
"Let's Have a Party" 81
"Let's Turkey Trot" 356
"Letter from Betty" 164, 166, 440
"Letter to an Angel" 452
"Letter to Dad" 315
Lettermen 49, 113, 527
Levine, Hank 157, 183
Levinson, Bob 301, 397
Levy, Jack 140
Lewis, Sir Edward 23, 337
Lewis, Gary 156, 202, 222-229, **226, 229, 270,** 270-272, 277, 290, **316,** 326, 332, 336, 372, 374, 381, 393, 400, 437, 442, 508, 523-526, 529, 535, 536, 547
Lewis, Jerry 223, 225, 227, 228, 270, 400
Lewis, Jerry Lee 4, 96, 430
Lewis, Mel 368
Lewis, Patti **226**
Lewis, Ramsey 317
Liberty Annual Report to Stockholders 266, **310**
Liberty Belle **426**
Liberty First Annual Stockholders Report 308
Liberty Proudly Presents Stereo 292
Liberty Record **309**
Liberty Songs, Inc. 341
"A Lifetime of Loneliness" 253
Light, J. J. 316

"Light My Fire" 490
"Lightning Strikes" 305
"Like a Rolling Stone" 256
"Like a Summer Rain" 493
Lind, Bob 243, 267, 268, 296, 297, 345, 389, 526, 536
"Linda" 166, 170, 171, 178, 206, 242, 497, 505, 506, 524
"Ling Ting Tong" 91
Linick, Hal 59, 308
"The Lion Sleeps Tonight" 78, 240
"Lipstick Traces" 251
Little Anthony 334
"Little Boy Sad" 88, 105, 134, 236
"Little Darlin'" 36
"Little Deuce Coupe" 496, 498
"Little Did I Know" 306
Little Dippers 98, 305
"Little Eefin' Annie" 48
Little Eva 3, 353
"Little Girl Blue" 14
"Little Hollywood Girl" 172, 174
"Little Miss Go-Go" 257-258
"Little Old Lady (from Pasadena)" 205, 243, 277, 303, 470, 481, 505, 507
"Little Orphan Annie" 49
Little Richard 27, 104, 129, 202, 209, 390, 428, 474
"Little Sister" 109, 134, 437
"A Little Star Came Down" 76
Little Stevie Wonder 31
Little Willie John 474
"Little Yellow Roses" 253
Live on Tour 238
Liverpool, Dragsters, Cycles, and Surfing 208
Livingston, Allen 203
Loch, Sigfried 220
"Locomotion" 3, 353
London, Julie 13-18, **16,** 20, 22, 23-26, 29, 33, 39, 41, 43, 49, 53, 55, 65, 72, 76, 84, 96, 99, 110, 111, 127, 170, 171, 185, 188, 191, 193, 197, 207, 238, 261, 264, 277, 292, 293, 308, 322, 331, 339, 393, 400, 413, 425, 466, 526, 528
London, Laurie 217
"Lonely" 29, 30
"Lonely Bull" 148, 159, 261, 276, 349
"Lonely Drifter" 251
"Lonely Girl" 17, 39, 89
"Lonely Teardrops" 34
"Lonesome Town" 447
"Long Tall Sally" 129, 418
"Look Through Any Window" 215
"Look to Your Soul" 326

Lopez, Trini 20, 87, 92
Lory, Dick 130, 149, 150, 192, 343
"Loser" **316**
"Lost Dreams" 93
Loudermilk, John D. 26, 32, 118, 124
"Louie, Louie" 238, 248
Love, Darlene 5, 150-152, 158, 246, 276, 356, 508, 533
Love, Mike 483, 496, 500, **502**
"Love Alone" 160
Love Generation 313, 320, 322, 526
"Love Is All We Need" 193, 219, 267, 268
"L-O-V-E Love" 50
"Love Kept A-Rollin'" 81, 83
"Love Me Now" 193
"Love Me Tender" 58, 72, 127, 170
"The Love of a Boy" 137, 261
"Love Will Find a Way" 254, 333
"Love You So" 74
Lovers 471
"Lovers by Night" 160
"A Lover's Question" 34
"Love's Made a Fool of You" 237, 360
"Lovey Dovey" 89-91, 98, 361
Lowe, Geoff 237
Lucas, Matt 4
Lugee and the Lions 305
Luke, Robin 418
"Lullaby of the Leaves" 107, 443
Lundberg, Victor 314
Luniverse Records 6, 283

M

McCall, Bill 409
McCartney, Paul 166, 200, 217, 532
McCoo, Marilyn 324, 540
"The McCoy" 95
McCoy, Van 218, 527
McCoys 317
McCracklin, Jimmy 191, 222, 251, 256, 296, 311, 536
McCurn, George 148
McDaniels, Gene 71, 101-104, **102**, 108, 127, 131, **136**, 137, 164, 167, 170, 188, 191, 199, 202, 204, 224, 243, 259, 260, 264, 268, 271, 273, 286, 288, 301, 307, 308, 335, 336, 344, 352, 360, 369, 381, 382, 390, 403, 419, 448, 522, 532, 545
McGuire Sisters 184
McIntyre, Mark 19, 20, 41, 365
McKuen, Rod 39, 331, 527
McLemore, Lamont 324
McPhatter, Clyde 34, 91

"Made to Love" 189
Madonna 303, 367
Maestro, Johnny 524
Magic Lamp Records 500
"Mah-Na-Mah-Na" 332
Maharishi Mahesh Yogi 298
"Maid of Honor" 37
"Mairzy Doats" 50
Majors 6, 59, 196, 409, 436
"Make Love to Me" 17
"Make the World Go Away" 164, 166, 171, 192
"Malibu Wipeout" 208
"Mama-Oom-Mow-Mow" 141, 192
"Mama Sang a Song" 142
Mamas and Papas 104, 206, 228, 320, 348, 360, 370-372, 504, 545
Mame 402
Manfred Mann 415
Manhattan 178, 354, 520
Mann, Barry 165, 352
Mann, Gloria 128
Mann, Johnny 15, 28, 39, 49, 91, 92, 104, 106, 127, 137, 142, 149, 172, 207, 243, 247, 260, 273, 275, 277, 310, 322, 324, 429, 526
Mann, Shelley 368
Marcy Jo 305, 306
Marketts 131, 139, **139**, 140, 187, 243, 370, 526, 534
Martin, Dean 96, 105, 183, 225, 240, 428, 430
Martin, George 103, 170, 200
Martin, Steve 313, 393
"Masked Grandma" 277
Matadors 206, 505, 507
Mauldin, Joe B. 133, 134, 174, 532
May, Billy 10, 11
"Maybe Just Today" 326
"Maybelline" 212, **214**
"Me and the Bear" **287**
Meet the Beatles 202
"Melancholy Baby" 166
Melcher, Terry 372
Memories Are Made of Hits 96
"Memories Are Made of This" 96
"Memphis" 81, 149, 212, 381, 393
Mendel, Lee 203, 226, 232, 236, 247, 255, 268, 310, 311, 316, 326, 328, 335, 355, 397, 401, 402, 518
Mercer, Johnny 204, 207
Mercury Records 6, 36, 60, 108, 192, 193, 293, 534
Mermaids 327, 527
Merry Christmas from Bobby Vee 157

Metric Music 30, 198, 341, 343-347, 360, 354, 403, 410, 457, 518, 520
"Mexican Shuffle" 275
Meyers, Sherry Lee 145
MGM Records 4, 6, 11, 60, 237, 305, 315, 334, 336
"Michelle" 206, 297, 390, 541
"Midnight" 157, 333
"Midnight Special" 212, 249, 499
"Midnight Sun" 157
Mike and Dean 500, **502**
Miles, Garry 88, 89, 103, 117, 278
The Miles Chart Display of Popular Music 498
"Milk Cow Blues" 129
Miller, Glenn 96, 166, 207
Miller, Roger 353
Miller, Terry 50
Miller Sisters 4
"A Million and One" 183, 281
Mills, Garry 89
Mills Brothers 262
Miniature Men 157, 160, 183
Minit Records 188, 211, 212, 256, 282-284, 295, 296, 334, 394, 523, 526, 536
"Mr. Blue" 64, 71, **72**, 73, 113, 124, 125, 127, 184, 524, 544
"Mr. Bojangles" 313
"Mr. Custer" 44, 77
"Mr. Lucky" 55
Mr. President, Speeches of President Lyndon 247
"Mr. Sandman" 218
Misty and the Do-Drops 212
Mitchell, Guy 209, 260
Modern Records 8, 187, 285, 361
Modugno, Domenico 240
Mogull, Artie 519, 520
"Money Honey" 26
Monotones 430, 471
Monro, Matt **200**
"Montage from How Sweet It Is" 320
Moonglows 471
"More" 183, 262
"More Than I Can Say" 108, 188, 264
Moss, Jerry 23, 391, 392, 518
Most, Abe 51
"Mother-in-Law" 283, 295
"Motherless Child" 17
"Mountain of Love" 212, 243
"The Mountain's High" 117-119, 121, 345, 390, 403, 541
"Move It, Baby" 218

"Move Out Little Mustang" 206, 217, **218**, 507
"Movie Magazines" 193
"Movin' and Groovin'" 471
MTV 3, 78, 332, 464
Muchello, Tony 206
Mucho Cha Cha Cha 12, 49, 99
"Muddy River" 333
"Mule Skinner Blues" 283
Mulligan, Gerry 296
Mullins, Suzanne 125, 126, **126**
Mumford, Gene 35
"Mumph" 315
Music City Records 285, 378
Musicnote Records 262
Musicor Records 92, 104
Mustang 208
Mustang Records 91, 237
Mutual Distributors 345, 402, 403
"My Boyfriend's Back" 193, 428
"My Girl/Hey Girl" 326
"My Heart Reminds Me" 315
"My Heart's Symphony" 268, 269
My Years at General Motors 282
"Mystery Train" 105

N

NASA's 25th Anniversary Album 452
Nashville Teens 28, 415
"National City" 78, 79, 385, 386
"National Emblem" 78
"Needle in a Haystack" 356
"Needles and Pins" 166, 251, 253, 343, 344, 353, 356, 461, 463
Nelson, Ozzie 254
Nelson, Ricky 76, 81, 82, 104, 132, 150, 164, 189, 190, 193, 194, 195, 196, 212, 213, 228, 249, 256, 288, 290, 301, 318, 348, 369, 415, 442, 447, 522, 523, 525, 526, 529, 541, **543**
Nelson, Sandy 52, 54, 55, 81, 194, **195**, 196, 212, 256, 260, 277, 289, 301, 322, 354, 471, 502, 526, 541
Nelson, Willie 78, 108, 126, 127, 130, 131, 148, **149**, 172, 191, 358, 387, 393, 394, 519, 526, 527, 532
Neptune Records 251, 536
"Never Love a Robin" 164
"Never Never" 471
"Never Thought I Could" 273
Never to Be Forgotten 129
Neville, Aaron 296, 539
Nevins 154, 349, 350, 352, 369

New Day 277
"New Girl in School" 205, 207, 477-479, **479**, 481, 492, 500
New Girl in School **478**
New Image 322, 458, **459**, 464
"New Orleans Medley" 127
New Sound from England 209, 433, **434**
Newhart, Bob 376
Newman, Lionel 10-13, 23, 24, 49, 336, 527
Newman, Randy 91, 160, 341, 345
Nice Girls Don't Stay for Breakfast 17, 323, **323**
"The Night Has a Thousand Eyes" 137, 164, 191, **192**, 256, 433, 440
"Niki Hokey" 236
"1963" **431**, 432, 439
"The Ninth Wave" 192
Nitty Gritty Dirt Band 298, 299, 311, 313, 314, 331, 393, 402, 526, 536
Nitzsche, Jack 248, 365, 461, 508
No Matter What Shape 243, 246, 248, 275, 447
"No Matter What Shape Your Stomach's In" 236
No Wonder I Sing 150
"Nobody's Home to Go Home To" 253
Noel, Nick 89
"Non l'ete per armati" 218
"Norman" 210
Norvo, Red 51
"A Not So Merry Christmas" 157
"Not Just Tomorrow, But Always" 524
"Nothing Like a Sunny Day" 430

O

Ode Records 329, 500, 502
O'Dell, Kenny 326
"Oh, Boy" 38, 69, 137, 164, 212, 253, 439, 505
"Oh, Lord, Let It Be" 160
"Oh, Pretty Woman" 4, 247
O'Jays 194, 210, 222, 251, 267, 296, 536
O'Keefe, Johnny 157, 343, 382, 383, 386, 402
"Old Enough to Love" 195
"Old Rivers" 142, 144, 393, 344
Oldham, Andrew 122
Olympics 303, 304
"On a Beautiful Day" 320
"On a Carousel" 215, 321, **322**
On Stage **380**
On Stage and in Space 191

"On the Road Again" 327, 328
"100 Lbs. of Clay" 127; *see also* "Hundred Pounds of Clay"
"One Last Kiss" 79, 88, 388, 438
"One Night" 8, 9, 127, 145, 211, 433
"One Woman" 333
O'Neill, Jimmy 29, 30, 146, 254, 390, 391, 407, 409, **410**, 411, 412, 458
"Only the Lonely" 4, 247
"Ooby Dooby" 4
"Ooh Poo Pah Doo" 238, 336
"Open the Door" 336
"Opus Twist" 359
Orbison, Roy 3-5, 104, 105, 212, 247, 427
Original Country Hits 172, 284
Original Golden Greats 284
Original Golden Hits, Vol. 3 **284**
The Original Hits 96, 102, 172, 209, 245, 283, 284, 522, 531
The Original Hits Past and Present 96
Original Sound Records 70, 194
Orlando, Tony 524
Otis, Clyde 108, 293
Otis and Carla 91
"Our Day Will Come" 256
"Out of Limits" 140, 243, 370
"Outer Limits" 140, 246, 370
"Outside My Window" 71, 93
"Over and Over" 373, 382, 423, 474, 493
"Over Here" 49, 84, 85
"Own True Self" 386

P

Pacific Jazz Records 282, 284, 296-299, 310, 368
Page, Jimmy 147
Page, Patti 39, 360
Paine, Gordon 174, 532
"Paint Me a Picture" 268
Palmer, Earl 360, 428, 508
Pandoras 276
"Papa-Oom-Mow-Mow" 140, 141, 192, 412
"Paper Cup" 299, 325
Paris Sisters 71
Parkway Records 104, 107, 170, 262
"Party Doll" 89, **90**, 114, 254, 283, 284
Patience and Prudence 19, 20, **21**, 22, 24, 33, 41, 49, 58, 76, 102, 193, 308, 365, 524, 526, 528
Paxton, Gary 527
"Pay You Back with Interest" 321
"Peggy Sue" 132, 133, 415, 418, 435, 466

Pell, Dave 207, 267, 299, 311, 332, 368, 370, 491
Pello, Gene 140
Percy Faith Orchestra 71, 77
Perdarvis, Tracy 4
"Perfidia" 96, 98, 448
Perkins, Carl 3, 4, 27, 129, 202, 209, 430
Perkins, Joe 48
Perspective on Bud and Travis 172
Pete Kelly's Blues 15
Peter and Gordon 166, 199, 415, 496
Peter, Paul, and Mary 77, 458
Peters, Barney 331
Peterson, Earl 4, 104, 127, 135, 206, 240, 243
Peterson, Paul 420
Peterson, Ray 120, 184, 497
Petty, Norman 30, 31, 361
Petty, Tom 536
Phil. Int. Records 251
Philles Records 4-6, 32, 103, 150, 153, 256, 334, 449, 532
Phillips, Phil 58
Philo Records 286
"Pigmy" 300, **301**
"Pink Pedal Pushers" 4
"Pipeline" 219, 446, 447
Pitney, Gene 92, 104, 149, 150, 152, 153, 213
Pittman, Bill 140
Pixies Three 193
Platters 45
Play Country Guitar with Jimmy Bryant 248
Play Guitar with Chet Atkins 248
Play Guitar with the Ventures 248
Playmates 63, 531
Playthings 527
"Please Don't Ask About Barbara" 131, 134, 149, 352, **353**, 360, 427
"Please Don't Ever Change" 172
"Please Please Me" 175, 202, 217
"Pocketful of Rainbows" 117
Pohlman, Ray 241
"Point of No Return" 103, 137, 335, 493
"Pointed Toe Shoes" 4
"Pony Time" 107, 268
"Poor Little Fool" 82, 146, 190, 191, 213, 255
"Poor Little Girl" 111
"Poor Little Puppet" 165
"Poor Side of Town" 213, 243, 267
"Pop Goes the Weasel" 48
Pops in Japan 442

"Popsicle" 81, 178, 206, 272, 278, 280, **280**, 281, 299, 491, 492, 507
"Popsicles and Icicles" 327
Porter, Cole 261
A Portrait of Nancy — Folk Songs by Nancy Ames 172
Post Records 189
Powers, Jet 235
"The Preacher and the Bear" 87
Presenting the Crickets 175
Presley, Elvis 3-5, 24, 26, 27, 45, 49, 58, 72, 81, 85, 89, 92, 104, 105, 109, 127-129, 134, 145, 148, 153, 170, 181, 190, 212, 228, 235, 236, 247, 255, 264, 265, 272, 356, 364, 368, 386, 408, 427, 430, 435, 437, 461, 532
Preston, Billy 146
Price, Lloyd 58, 249
Prima, Buddy 315
Primitiva 54, 55
"Primrose Lane" 333
"The Prince" 145, 148, 253
Proby, P. J. 166, 222, 235, **235**, 236, 260, 302, 536
"Proud Mary" 336
"Psychotic Reaction" 449
"Punish Her" 131
"Purple People Eater" 44
"Put a Little Love in Your Heart" 253, 333
"Put Your Hand in the Hand" 335
Putnum, Bill 106, 368, 369

Q

"Queen of My Heart" 165
Quickly, Tommy 527
"Quiet Village" 53-55, **54**, 60, 149, 383

R

R&B 60, 78, 80, 83, 106, 107, 114, 140, 141, 167, 189, 193, 194, 285, 286, 300, 304, 310, 324, 326, 368, 383, 394, 397, 464, 526
Rafferty, Jerry 519
"Rag Doll" 170
Rag Dolls 170
"Ragtime Cowboy Joe" 48
Raik's Progress 315
"Raindrops" 127, 326, **327**
"Raining in My Heart" 58, 130, 427, 430
"Rainy Day" 93, 493
Ralke, Don 117-119
Rally-Packs 217

"Ram-Bunk-Shush" 107
"Raunchy" 93, 193, 282-284
Rawls, Lou 67
Ray, Alder 141
Ray, Johnny 210
Rayburn, Margie 23, 37-39, 43, 57, 58, 72, 76, 78, 80, 97, 107, 264, 365, 526, 528
Rays 28
RCA Records 3-6, 23, 39, 42, 49, 50, 55, 59, 99, 104, 105, 114, 117, 125, 127, 150, 159, 163, 170, 182, 245, 264, 265, 272, 305, 311, 346, 394, 408, 409, 359, 365, 366, 368, 369, 427, 443, 532
Ready, Steady, Go 147, 390
Rear Window 528
Record World 397
"Red Roses for a Blue Lady" 113, 191, 198, 243, 247, 342
"Red Wine" 318, 354
Redding, Otis 535
Reddy, Helen 532
Reese, Della 71, 315
Reiner, Carl 298
Reisdorff, Bob 58-60, 64-71, 73-75, 93, 111, 113, 124, 125, 133, 149, 157, 158-161, 181, 182, 183, 185, 186, 191, 193, 197, 198, 220, 236, 248, 286, 312, 315, 341, 348, 359, 379, 391, 443, 448, 449, 534, 537, 543-545
"Remember Mary" 336
"Remember the Rain" 268
"Reminiscing" 360
Reprise Records 28, 31, 92, 204, 312, 523, 531, 532, 542
"Restless Surfer" 206, 506
Revercomb, Kenny 169
Reynolds, Burt 424, 528
Reynolds, Debbie 71
Reynolds, Jody 304
Rhodes, Slim 4
Rhythm and Blues, the End of an Era 285, **285**
"Rhythm of the Rain" 172, 332
Richard, Cliff 209
Richards, Keith 122
Richardson, Rudi 4
Ricky Sings Again **543**
Riddle, Nelson 10, 11, 148
"Ride the Wild Surf" 205, 206, 208, 266, 470, 507
Ride the Wild Surf 142, 205-208, 266, 470, 476, **476,** 486, 506
"Right Relations" 326
Righteous Brothers 5, 364, 490, 508, 509
Riley, Billy 4

"Ringo" 383
Ringo 88, 461
Rip Chords 6, 208, 277, 470
Ripple Records 349
"Rising Sun" 237, 315
Ritter, Tex 344
"River Deep, Mountain High" 5
Rivers, Johnny 199, 212-214, **214**, 217, 242, 243, 249, 256, 260, 267, 273, 277, 281, 289, 290, 299, 302, 310, 311, 320, **321**, 322, 324-326, 333, 334, 348, 350, 370-372, 382, 392, 393, 522, 526, 540
Rivingtons 131, 140-142, 144, 145, 164, 192, 193, 243, 245, 360, 394, 411, 526, 534
"Road Runner" 236
Robbee Records 305, 306, **306**
Robbins, Marty 77, 260
"Robin, the Boy Wonder" 273
Robinson, Smokey 520
"Rock and Roll Music" 202
Rock and Roll Trio 81, 332
Rock 'n' Beach Party 39
"Rockin' Pneumonia and the Boogie Woogie Flu" 334
Rockin' with the King 336
Rocky 519
Roe, Tommy 104, 331, 415
Rogers, Kenny 519, 520
Rogers, Richard 323
Rogers, Roy 542
Rogers, Shorty 368
Rogers and Hart 261
Rollers 65, 91, 102, 104, 107, 222, 268, 272, 278, 526
Rolling Stones 122, 147, 211, 255, 442, 479, 486
Romero, Chan 214
Ronettes 5, 245, 508
"Ronnie" 305, 306, **306**
Ronny and the Daytonas 81, 470
Rooney, Mickey, Jr. 527
"Roses Are Red" 134, 249
Ross, Adam 140
Ross, Diana 460
Ross, Stan 83, 363-367
Roulette Records 89-91, 93, 96, 114, 250, 253, 254, 284, 305, 520, 531
"Route 66" 13, 17, 261
Routers 246, 370
Rowles, Jimmy 51
Ro-Zan Records 528
"Rubber Ball" 88, 92, 98, 104, 134, 150, 152, 153, 188, 264, 339, 419, 429, 431, 438

Ruben Rodriguez and His Guadalajara Kings 275
Ruby and the Romantics 256
Ruff Records 531
"Run to Him" 109, 110, 188, 352, 524
"Runaround" 93
"Runaround Sue" 254
"Runaway" 254, 257, 273, 535, 536
"Running Scared" 4
"Running Strong" 277
Russ Garcia Orchestra 54
Russell, Leon 146, 175, 223, 225, **226**, 237, 241, 245, 256, 257, 258, 271, 273, 356, 360, 393, 425
Rydell, Bobby 104, 207, 240, 415

S

"Sad Movies" 210
"Sailor Boy" 182
St. John, Dick 117, 122, 125, 181, 254, 355, 502, 540, 541; *see also* Dick and DeeDee
Sam the Sham and the Pharoahs 336
Sand Records 145
"Sandra, My Love" 76
Sands, Tommy 527
Sandy Nelson Plays **195**
Santamaria, Mongo 250
Sar Records 6
Sardo, Frankie 415
"Satisfaction" 479, 504
Save for a Rainy Day 493
"Save the Last Dance for Me" 127
"Save Your Heart for Me" 224, 243, 257, 258, 524
SBK Records 520
Schlesinger, Al 161
"Schlock Rod" 206, 493, 506
"School Days" 186, 278, 280, 370, 492
Schroeder, Aaron 151, 152, 156
Scott, Freddie 326
Scotti, Tony 329
Scrivner, Wayne 118, 119
"Sea of Love" 58, 536
Seafair Records 529
Searchers 166, 199, 201, 204, 205, 210, 224, 251, 344, 460-462, 526, 535
"Secret Agent Man" 217, 267, 281
Secret of My Success 532
Sedaka, Neil 138, 415, 437
Seeger, Pete 233
SESAC 347

A Session with Gary Lewis and the Playboys 256
77 Sunset Strip 50
Seville, David 19, 20, 22, 44, 45, 47, **48**, 49, 51, 53, 78, 99, 128, 164, 220, 237, 238, 264, 283, 293, 308, 318, 413, 526, 528, 547; *see also* Bagdasarian, Ross
"The Sewer Rat Love Chant" 315
Shadows 57, 417-419, **417**, 427, 433
"Shake, Rattle, and Roll" 368
"The Shaky Bird pts 1 & 2" 193
"Shangri-La" 219
Shank, Bud 292, 296-298, 376, 390
Shankar, Ravi 296
Shannon, Del 207, 228, 254, 257, 267, 273, **276**, 277, 322, 326, 526, 527, 535, 536
"Sharing You" 131, 202, 204
Sharp, Dee Dee 141, 353
Sharp Tones 189
Sharpe, Mike 313, 320
Shaw, Artie 34
"She Cried" 522, 524
"She Loves You" 175, 202, 204, 433
"She Was Mine" 273
"She'd Rather Be with Me" 495
Sheeley, Sharon 23, 28, 29, 31, 32, 81, 83, 84, 86, 88, 111, 117, 122, 145, 147, 148, 160, 161, 190, 210, 253, 254, 259, 341, 343-345, 353, 355, 363, 409, 515, 528, 532
Sheen, Bobby 150, 154, 508
Shelter Records 237
Shelyne, Carole 237
Sheridan, Bobby 4
Sherman, Garry 142
"Sherry" 145, 165, 169, 170
"She's Dancing, Dancing" 502
"She's Got Love" 354
"She's Just My Style" 224, 243, 258
"She's My Baby" 157
"She's Still Talkin' Baby Talk" 139
Shindig 29, 30, 122, 146, 147, 227, 235, 356, 390, 397, 407, 409
Shirelles 127, 182, 193, 435, 537
Shirley and Lee 196, 525
Shondell, Troy 115, 116, **116**, 224, 367, 390, 420, 526, 532
"Shoop Shoop Song" 141, 357
Shore, Dinah 127, 499
"Short Fat Fanny" 97
"Shortnin' Bread" 193
"Should I Cry" 253
"Show Me" 273
Showmen 212, 394

Showtime Records 285
Shut Downs and Hill Climbs 208, **208**, 285
"Sidewalk Surfin'" **205**, 206, 239, 266, 373, 470, 475, 481, 484, 488, 490, 499, 505, 507
Sigler, Bunny 91, 127
Signet Records 273, 366
"Silent Night" 157
"Silhouettes" 28
Sill, Lester 4, 153
Silvers, Ed 125, 142, 345, 517, 537, 543
Simon-Jackson, Inc. 341
Sims, Zoot 296
Sinatra, Frank 127, 128, 204, 247, 369, 428, 430, 486, 528, 535, 542
"Since Gary Went in the Navy" 305
"Since I Fell for You" 189
"Sincerely" 471
Sing Again with the Chipmunks 50
"Sing Sang a Song" 502
"Singin' the Blues" 209
Singin' '30s 49
Singin' to My Baby 40
"Single and Searchin'" 50
"Sittin' and Chirpin'" 236
"Sittin' in the Balcony" 26-29, 31, 99, 109, 118
"16 Candles" 524
60 Years of Music America Hates Best 50
"Ska Light, Ska Bright" 219, **219**
Skaff, Bob 57, 68, 140, 153, 225, 252, 307, 342, 354, 382, 383, 391, 516
Skip and Flip 217
Slades 527
Slatkin, Felix 78, 93, 129, 171, 198, 207, 294, 295, 308, 526
"Sleep" 474
Sloan, P. F. 217, 234, 372
Sloman, Mike 204
"Slow Motion" 142
"Smile" 108, 261
Smile 496
"A Smile and a Ribbon" 20
Smith, Dallas 267, 326
Smith, James Marcus 149, 235, 536
Smith, Johnny 442, 443, 446
Smith, Ray 4
Smith, Warren 127, 358, 527
Smokey Joe 4
Smokey Robinson and the Miracles 232
"Smoochin'" 39
"Sneaky Alligator" 306
"So Much Love" 530
"Society Girl" 170

"Soda Pop" 84, 471
"Soldier Boy" 182
Solid Gold Hits 285
Soma Records 57, 283, 418, 436
"Somebody Touched Me" 90
"Someday" 131, 193, 432
"Something Else" 30
Something Old, Something New, Something Blue, Something Else 172
"Somewhere" 236
"Song Through Perception" 327
"The Song's Been Sung" 240
Songs for a Lazy Afternoon 39
Sophisticated Lady 127, 261, **263**
Soul City Records 213, 243, 299, 310, 311, 318, 323-326, 333, 348, 372, 382, 470, 540
"Soul Train" 326
Sound-Stage Records 48
Sounds, Incorporated 237
"Sounds of Silence" 71, 439
Sounds of the Big Drags 208
"Spanish Lace" 137
Spanky and Our Gang 320
Spector, Phil 4, 5, 12, 31, 32, 39, 100, 103, 105, 108, 110, 116, 142, 150-156, 245, 256, 357, 364, 365, 371, 373, 383, 389, 392, 423, 508, 509, 532
Sperling, Mary 117, 502, 540; *see also* Dick and DeeDee
Spiders 189, 285
Spinners 149
Spivak, Charlie 166
"Spookie, Spookie, Lend Me Your Comb" 50
"Spooky" 313, 320
A Spoonful of Jazz 296, 297
Spotlight on Bud and Travis 49
Springfield, Dusty 146
Stafford, Terry 207
"Stagger Lee" 249
Standells **240**, 301
"Stardust" 34, 35, 58
Starr, Kay 39, 315
Statues 80, 81, 88, 278
"Stayin' In" 108, 109, 118, 188, 264
Steel, Don 366, 367
Steele, Tommy 209, 260, 526
"A Stench in Time" 273
Stevens, April 39, 193, 196
Stevens, Cat 148, 392
Stevens, Dodie 181-182
Stewart, Mike 335, 402, 406, 519, 523
Stick Shifts 470
"Sting Ray" 246, 278, 279, 370

"Stoned Soul Picnic" 299, 326
Stoneman Family 296
"Stop, Stop, Stop" 215, **216**
Stores, Todd 381, 382, 390
"Stormy" 236, 320, 326
"Stormy Weather" 63, 236
"The Story of Rock 'n' Roll" 495
"Straight Flush" 74
"Stranded in the Jungle" 97, 438
Strange, Billy 159, 245, 508, 527
"Stranger in Paradise" 292
Stray Cats 28
"Street Scene" 10
Streisand, Barbra 147, 391, 392
Stuart, Buddy Lee 58
"Stuck on You" 153
Studio Five 113, 308
"Submarine Races" 142, 152, 206, 314, 506
"Suddenly There's a Valley" 12
"Sugar and Spice" 201
Sugar Pie and Pee Wee 471
Sukman, Harry 12, 50
Sullivan, Ed 3, 4, 69, 78, 89, 120, 135, 225-228
"Summer Means Fun" 499
"Summer Rain" 320, 326, 493
"Summertime Blues" 28, 30, 31, 51, 84, 86, 97, 128, 405, 532
Sun Records 3-5, 105, 430
"Sunday Kind of Love" 139, 165, 166
Sunset Records 301, 302
Sunshine Company 310, 313, **319**, 320, 326, 526
Supergroup **450**
"Superman Lover" 170
Supremes 232, 334, 377, 486, 540
"Sure Gonna Miss Her" 243, 268
"Sure Is Lonesome Downtown" 192
"Surf City" 166, 167, 170, 178, 206, 232, 269, 370, 372, 373, 393, 394, 470, 476, 481, 493, 498, 501, 504, 505, 507
Surf City and Other Swingin' Cities 178
Surfaris 248, 446, 470
"Surfer Dan" 495
"Surfers' Stomp" 140
"Surfin'" 141, 167, 172, 187, 496
"Surfin' Bird" 141
"Surfin' Safari" 167, 172, 496
"Surfin' USA" 167
Surfing Beach Party 501
The Surfing Scene 187
"Susie Darlin'" 418
"Suspicion" 207

Suzanne *see* Mullins, Suzanne
"Suzie Baby" 57, 79, 88, 93, 199, 418, 422, 427, 436-438
Suzuki, Pat 61, 62
"Swahili Serenade" 318
Sweden Heaven and Hell 332
"Sweet Baby Doll" 287
"Sweet Blindness" 299, **300**, 326
"Sweet Dreams" 81
Sweet Marie 336
"Sweeter Than You" 83
"Sweetie Pie" 29, 30, 88
"The Swingin' Eye" 127
"Swingin' Gates" 149
Swinging Blue Jeans 199, 214, **215**, 217, 249, 415, 526, 539
"Swinging on a Star" 329
"Symphony for Soul" 322

T

"Take a Look" 290
"Take Five" 261
"Take Good Care of Her" 134
"Take Good Care of My Baby" 109, 128, 129, 131, 134, 170, 174, 188, 202, 209, 283, 318, 352, 390, 403, 433, 434, 436, 437
"Take My Hand" 343
"Talk That Talk" 299
"Tall Cool One" 193
"Tall Oak Tree" 12, 81, 138, 170
"Tallahassee Lassie" 178, 260
TAMI Show 229, 232, 238, 356, 486, **487**, 501
"Tammy" 71
"A Taste of Honey" 53, 172, 261, 383
Taylor, Mel 95, 442
Taylor, Tut 296
Taylor, Vernon 4
T-Bones 207, 208, 22, 236, 243, 246, 248, 275, 311, 316, 447, 526, 536
"Te-Ta-Te-Ta-Ta" 295
"Teach Me" 89, 193, 253, 423
"Teach Me, Tiger" 193
"A Tear" 103
"Tear Drops" 471
"Tears (for Souvenirs)" 237
"Tears from an Angel" 116, 117
"Tears on My Pillow" 106
Teddybears 12, 58, 72, 277, 365
Tedesco, Tommy 139, 155, 227, 240, 241, 508

"Teen Beat" 194, 471
"Teen Beat '65" 212, 256
Teen Queens 471
"Teenage Cleopatra" 169
"Teenage Heaven" 28, 52, 88
Teenage Nightclub 409
Teenage Triangle 420
"Tell 'Em I'm Surfin'" 217, 523
"Tell Her No" 52
"Tell Me" 117, 181, 524
Tell Me the Mountain's High 118, 119
"Tell Tale" 99
Telstar/Lonely Bull 159, 442
"Telstar—The Lonely Bull" **263**
Tempo, Nino 39, 193, 196, 508
"Tempo de Blues" 296
"Temptation (Make Me Go Home)" 333
Temptations 326
"Tennessee" 138-140, 144, 165, 492, 504, 505
10th Anniversary Album 442
"Tequila" 37, 137, 283, 365
Tequila & Cream 276
Terror Tales by "The Old Sea Hag" 292
Tex Williams in Las Vegas 172, 191
"That Old Black Magic" 207
"That'll Be the Day" 30, 131, 415, 432, 532
"That's All" 195, 317, 318, 530
"That's All There Is to That" 318
"That's Rock and Roll" 212
"Their Hearts Were Full of Spring" 17
"[The Theme from] Silver City" 107
"Theme from the Sundowners" 129
"Theme from the Wild Angels" 281, 318
"There's No Other (Like My Baby)" 150
"These Are Not My People" 194
"(They Call My Baby) La Bamba" 175
"They Remind Me of You" **189**
"They Tell Me It's Summer" 160
30 Big Hits of the '60s **128**, 238, 267, 326, 430
"This Diamond Ring" 156, 223-226, 227, 228, 257, 271, 374, 400, 437, 524, 542
This Is Stereo 292
This Is the Blues 284
"This Time" 115, 116, **116**
Thomas, Irma 199, 210-212, **211**, 217, 249, 290, 311, 536
Thompson, Johnny 137
Thompson, Sue 210
Three Chuckles 93
Three Friends 193
"Three Window Coupe" 208, 373
"Tijuana Taxi" 276
"Tijuana Wedding" 228

"'Til I Kissed You" 127
"Till Then" 262
"Time for You" 237
"The Time Has Come" 148
"Time Is on My Side" 211, **211**, 217
"Time Stands Still" 228, 229
"Time to Take Off" 329
Time to Take Off **329**
"Tina (I Held You in My Arms)" 535
Tiny Tim 237
Tipton, George 245, 273, 508
"To Be Free" 458
To Be Free **459**
"To Know Him Is to Love Him" 12, 58, 72, 277, 365
"Tobacco Road" 28
"Today's Teardrops" 196
Tokens 78, 240
"Tomorrow's Teardrops" 349
"Tongue in Cheek" 334, 336
"Tonight Show" 49, 314, 324
"Tonight You Belong to Me" 20, 41, 365, 524
"Too Old to Cry" 75
Top Gun 532
The Torch Is Burning 55
Torme, Mel 166, 527
Torrence, Dean 137, 165, 217, 272, 298, 299, 320, 327, 403, 376, 438, 449, 471, **502**, 507, 509, 522, **533**
"Tossin' & Turnin'" 283
Total Eclipse 322
"Totally Wild" 502
"Touch Me" 393
"Tower of Strength" 103, 202, 344, 345, 390
Tower Records 238
"Town Without Pity" 92
Townsend, Ed 527
Townson, Ron 324
"Traces" 251, 320, 333
"Tracks of My Tears" 243, 320
"Tragedy" 71, 111, 113, 184, 186, 304, 390, 417, 470, 545
Transamerica 198, 220, 337, 484, 485, 517-520, 523
Trashmen 141
"Travelin' Man" 190, 213
"Travelin' Mood" 471
Travis Music 518
Traynor, Jay 524
"Trouble" **66**, 146
"Trouble with Harry" 19, 45
Troup, Bobby 11-17, 43, 99, 24, 31, 261, 293, 294, 323, 527, 528, 545

Troxel, Gary 75, 111, **114**, 160, 185, 186, 219, 272, 281, 286, 305, 423, 515, 537
"Truly Julie's Blues" 268
"T-Shirt" 532
TSOP Records 251
Tucker, Tanya 532
Tuff Records 6
"Turn Around, Look at Me" 31
"Turn! Turn! Turn!" 233
Turner, Scottie 394
Turner, Tina 5, 121, 147, 334, 336, 526, 542
Turner and Hooch 532
Turtles 372, 495
"'Twas the Night Before Christmas Back Home" 157
"Twenty Flight Rock" 27, 129
20 Golden Hawaiian Hits 261, **263**
20 Hits the Beatles 434
"Twist and Shout" 208
Twist with the Ventures 187
"2 Degrees East, 3 Degrees West" 296
Two Girls and a Guy 73, 94, 248
"2,000 Pound Bee" 137, 160

U

Ullman, Tracey 210
Umiliani, Piero 332
"Unchained But Unforgotten" 126
"Unchained Melody" 74, 118, 184, 368
"Under My Thumb" 273
"Under Your Spell Again" 249
"Unexpectedly" 11, 44, 56, 76
United Artists Records 76, 141, 188, 220, 282, 291, 298, 299, 302, 313, 322, 334, 336, 337, 347, 354, 401, 402, 406, 475, 482, 483, 484, 485, 488, 493, 499, 500, 517-520, 522-524, 530
United Records 106, 519
United Western Studios 368
University Records 98, 99, 304, 305, **305**, 349, 471
"Up, Up and Away" 299, 323
Uptown 289, **289**

V

Valens, Ritchie 57, 128, 134, 165, 175, 207, 248, 415, 532
Valentine, Penny 207
Valery, Dana 335
Valiant Records 315, 332

Vanilla Ice 451, 520
Vee, Bobby 3, 20, 52, 56-58, **56**, 71, 79-81, 84, 88, 89, 92, 93, 98, 102-104, 108-110, 118, 127, 128–130, 131-134, 136, 137, 139, 140, 142, **143**, 149, 150, 152, 155, 157, **158**, 160-161, **162**, 164, 166, 170, 172, **173**, 174, 175, 183, 188, 191, **192**, 193, 194, 199, 202, 204, 209, 212, 213, 222-225, 228, 236, 238, 243, 245, 254, 256, 259, **262**, 264, 266, 267, 271, 273, 277, 283, 294, 308, 310, 311, 315, 317, **317**, 318, 322, 326, 329, 332, 345, 350, 352, 353, **353**, 358-361, 367, 374, 376, 377, 381, 384, 385, 388, 390, 403, 405, 408, 409, 411, 413, 415, **416**, **417**, 418- 425, **419**, **422**, **424**, 427-440, **428**, **429**, **431**, **432**, **434**, **436**, **439**, 448, 449, 452, 454, 457, 463, 515, 522-526, 529, 530, **530**, **531**, 532, 535, 547
"Vegetables" 493, 496, 522
Velvettes 356
Ventura Entertainment Group 520
Ventures 75, 77, 78, 94-96, **94**, 98, 107, 110, 111, 132, 133, 137, 158, 159, 160, 181, 182, 187, 191, 192, 194, 198, 219, 220, 243, 245, 247, 248, 260, 261, 277, 281, 283, 286, 296, 301, 303, 308, 311, 318, 332, 334, 336, 342, **342**, 359, 379, 380, **380**, 383, 387, 388, 391, 400, 408, 413, 420, 442-445, **445**, 447, 448, **448**, **450**, **451**, 452, **453**, 454, 455, 523, 526, 528, 536
The Ventures Play Telstar/The Lonely Bull 261
"Venus" 416
Verne, Larry 44, 77
Versatiles 325, 371
Versatones 444, 445
Verve Records 189, 194, 262, 536
The Very Best of Jan & Dean 302
Vic Dana Town and Country 187
Victor Feldman Quartet 383
Vincent, Gene 26, 84, **85**
Vinton, Bobby 129, 134, 249, 345, 415
VIP Records 356
Vita Records 285
Vogues 31
"Volare" 240

W

Wade, Adam 134
Wadsworth, Terry 160
Wagner, Robert 527

Wailers 193, 383
Wain, Bea 34, 166
"Waitin' in School" 104
"The Walk" 251, 387
"Walk Away" 199
"Walk, Don't Run" 94–96, 219, 220, 233, 236, 248, 332, 342, 379, 391, 442, 443, 445, 446, 448, 449
Walk, Don't Run 283, 450, **451**
Walk, Don't Run Vol. 2 **342**
"Walk Like a Man" 172
"Walk Right Back" 91
"Walk with Him" 145
Walker, T-Bone 191, 390
"Walkin' with the Blues" 50
"The Walking Birds of Carnaby" 318
"Walking with My Angel" 109
wall of sound 5, 32, 105, 152
Wallace, Jerry 333, 527
Wallack, Glenn 204
Warner, Alan 81, 141, 142, 188, 202, 209, 213, 220, 523-525, 530
Warner, Sandy 54, 55
Warner Brothers Records 33, 34, 91, 118, 121, 122, 124, 125, 140, 181, 272, 289, 293, 303, 369, 370, 375, 376, 391, 392, 401, 523, 534, 546
Waronker, Lenny 25, 33, 91, 192, 293, 294, 360, 391, 401, 546
Warren, Fran 166
Waters, Bob 385, 386
"The Way You Look Tonight" 113
Wayne, John 145, 158, 344, 348, 527
"Wayward Wind" 12
"We Go Together" 165
"We Never Knew" 207
"We Put the Bomp" 165
Webb, Jack 13, 14, 15
Webb, Jimmy 372
"Wedding Bell Blues" 213, 243, 299, 333, 372
Weed, Gene 64, 391
"Weekend" 29, 30
Weems, Ted 166
"The Weight" 253, 327, 464
"Well . . . all Right" 132, 134
"We're on Our Way" 299
"Werewolf" 74
Wes, Buddy, and Monk Montgomery 296
West Side Story 236
"Western Movies" 303, 304, **304**
Western Recorders 14, 271, 368
"We've Only Just Begun" 71
"What Is 1 and 1" 50
"What Is This" 70, 253

"What Makes Little Girls Cry" 141
"What the World Needs Now Is Love" 251-253, 465
Whatever Julie Wants 127
"What'll I Do" 418
"What's New, Pussycat" 247
"When" 146, 249
"When a Boy Falls in Love" 255
"When It's Over" 206
"When You Walk in the Room" 166, 251, 253, 343, 344, 461, 463
"When You're in Love" 132
"Where Have All the Flowers Gone" 249
"Where the Action Is" 319, 397
"Where Will the Words Come From" 268
Whipped Cream (& Other Delights) 276
"White Christmas" 47, 48, 157
White Whale Records 233, 372
Whitman, Slim 189, 193, 256, 260, 277, 289, 302, 322, 358, 523, 526
The Who 28
"Who Do You Love" 530
Who Sang What in Rock and Roll 209
"Why Did You Rob Us, Tank" 315
WIGS 385
Wild Things 277
"Will You Love Me Tomorrow" 127, 253, 460, 524, 537
Williams, Andy 60, 61, 238
Williams, Larry 97
Wilson, Brian 167, 177, 181, 206, 217, 232, 393, 480, 496, 505-508
Wilson, Don 95, 182, 442, 443
Wilson, Jackie 34
Wilson, Josie 182, 379
Wilson, Rocky 141
Wilson Phillips 520
Winding, Kai 183, 262
"Windows and Doors" 253
"Windy" 315, 372
Winter, Edgar 332
Winter, Johnny 332, 392
Winwood, Steve 327
"Wish Someone Would Care" 210, 217
"The Wishing Doll" 253, 321
"Witch Doctor" 43-47, **45**, 48-51, 87, 128, 188, 220, 264, 283, 293, 365, 384, 526
"Witchcraft" 49
"With Pen in Hand" 332
WKY 409
"Wolverton Mountain" 359
Womack, Bobby 527
The Wonderful World of Julie London 171

"Wonderland by Night" 127
Wood, L. G. 202
Wood, Randy 23, 40, 68, 89, 291, 365, 366, 378, 384, 394
Woodward, Dotty 297
Woodward, Woody 297, 375
Wooley, Sheb 44
Words and Music by Bobby Troup 17
"Workin' on a Groovy Thing" 299, 333
World Famous 331
World Pacific Records 243, 251, 268, 282, 296-298, 310, 319, 389, 405, 526, 534, 536
"The Worst That Could Happen" 524
WPIX 386
The Wrecking Crew 241-245, 247, 508
Wright, Ruby 134
WTAE 409
WTAM 386
Wynn, Keenan 498

Y

"Yankee Doodle" 48
Yardbirds 147, 148
"Yeh-Yeh!" 250
"Yeh, Yeh" **250**
Yellow Balloon **465**
"Yellow Balloon" 493
"Yes, I'm Lonesome Tonight" 181
"Yesterday" 20, 105, 164, 199
"Yesterday and You" 20, 164
Yost, Dennis 320, 540
"You Always Hurt the One You Love" 141
"You Are My Destiny" 416
"You Better Sit Down, Kids" 256
"You Can Have Her" 268
"You Can't Do That" 238
"You Don't Have to Be a Baby to Cry" 170

"You Don't Have to Be a Star" 540
"You Don't Love Me" 326
"You Keep Me Hangin' On/Hurt So Bad" 254, 334
"You May Never Know" 126
"You Really Know How to Hurt a Guy" 206, 232, 243, 266, 470, 495, 506
"You Send Me" 80, 252
"You Upset Me" 49
"You Won't Forget Me" 191, 253, 423, 458, **459**
Young, Faron 126, 130, 148
"Young at Heart" 128
Young Cougars 245
"Your Daughter's Hand" 148
"Your Heart Has Changed Its Mind" 138
"You're Mine" 37
"You're 16" 83, 84, 88, 134
"You're the One" 212, 538
"You're the Reason God Made Oklahoma" 532
Yuro, Timi 89, 101, 107, 108, **109**, 131, 137, 164, 166, 171, 191, 192, 213, 243, 261, 293, 301, 307, 336, 360, 390, 420, 523, 526, 532
"You've Got What It Takes" 522

Z

"Zabadak" 204, 329
Zappa, Frank 91
Zentner, Si 71, 73, 78, 127, 164, 171, 238, 261, 294, 322, 324
"Zip-a-Dee-Do-Dah" 150
Zip Codes 208
Zombies 52, 415
Zucker, Si 59, 65, 67
Zulu Spear 521